LUTHER
IN MID-CAREER

LUTHER
IN MID-CAREER 1521-1530

Heinrich Bornkamm

Edited and with a Foreword by
KARIN BORNKAMM

Translated by
E. THEODORE BACHMANN

FORTRESS PRESS   PHILADELPHIA

Translated by E. Theodore Bachmann from the German *Martin Luther in der Mittes seines Leben* by Heinrich Bornkamm, edited by Karin Bornkamm (Göttingen: Vandenhoeck & Ruprecht, 1979).

This translation was made possible in part by a grant from InterNationes Foundation, Bonn, Federal Republic of Germany.

Biblical quotations, unless otherwise noted, are from the Revised Standard Version of the Bible, copyrighted 1946, 1952, ©1971, 1973 by the Division of Christian Education of the National Council of the Churches of Christ in the U.S.A. and are used by permission.

Library of Congress Cataloging in Publication Data

Bornkamm, Heinrich, 1901–
Luther in mid-career, 1521–1530.

Translation of: Martin Luther in der Mitte seines Lebens. 1979.
Bibliography: p.
Includes index.
1. Luther, Martin, 1483–1546. 2. Reformation—Biography. I. Title.
BR326.6.B6713 1983   284.1′092′4 [B]   82–48591
ISBN 0-8006-0692-2

9753K82   Printed in the United States of America   1–692

Contents

CONTENTS

Translator's Preface

On January 21, 1977, Heinrich Bornkamm died at the age of seventy-five. His death marked the end of a productive scholarly career. As explained in the Foreword, the unfinished manuscript of this his final volume was edited by his daughter, Professor Karin Bornkamm of Bielefeld—herself an expert historian—assisted by others close to her father's research. Published by Vandenhoeck & Ruprecht in Göttingen in 1979, the volume immediately attracted wide attention because it filled a need in the field of Luther biography, and therefore it commended itself for translation into English.

Heinrich Bornkamm's narrative flows as an astonishingly instructive account, alive with issues and rich in detail, as it opens to our examination ten demanding years in the life of Martin Luther. The beginning and the ending of the account are set in the solitude of two hilltop castles—the Wartburg (1521) and the Coburg (1530)—where Luther's confinement under benevolent custody, by its very contrast, vivifies his otherwise crowded career.

Between the ages of thirty-seven and forty-six—in "the middle years of his life," as the German title reminds the reader—we find Luther wrestling with consequences springing from the position on the evangel he had bravely reaffirmed at the Diet of Worms. These consequences, virtually all of a practical nature, demanded that he make practical application of the gospel to ongoing life in church and society. Between his translation of the New Testament (1521) and his completion of the two catechisms (1529) runs an array of accomplishments—some brilliant, some flawed, all produced under pressure—which were to set the course in large parts of the church catholic for years to come.

Seldom has the formative moment in evangelically oriented Christianity been set forth with such clear regard for the substance of the message and the essential response to that message as Bornkamm has done here. Other studies have concentrated on Luther's theology; many have probed specific aspects of his life and times. Yet Bornkamm's work stands alone—in its sustained treatment of a spiritual legacy being fashioned amid the conflicting forces of a tumultuous era.

Bornkamm's extensive use of Luther's writings assumes that his readers have access to the Weimar Edition (WA)—a set of which in white vellum dominated his study. The present volume has the advantage of reference to the now completed 55-volume American edition of *Luther's Works* (*LW*). Quotations from this edition are verbatim, except in a few cases where Bornkamm's own translation from Latin into German conveys a slightly different meaning, or, as in quoting from Luther's lectures, Bornkamm has made use of the other of two alternative stenographic versions. Bornkamm's more than 2,500 footnotes have counterparts in English in nearly 1,000 instances, thus facilitating further Luther study in this language.

The immense erudition undergirding this book reflects the state of the art and science of Reformation research in many of the subjects treated. Yet the rapid pace of research in this field during the past couple of decades—including the time when the author was drawing upon his own gathered materials—has deposited new findings and challenged older views of which Bornkamm could not here make use. Some cognoscenti (e.g., B. Lohse) have noted a somewhat "dated" treatment of such a perennially debated issue as Luther and the Peasants' War. Time inevitably overtakes the historian.

As for the translation itself, I have endeavored to avoid a slavish literalism and to give the author facility of narration and felicity of expression of which Bornkamm was a master in German, while adhering to the rule of rendering the substance and meaning unchanged.

Happily, for the background of the present work, there is Heinrich Boehmer's *Road to Reformation* (Philadelphia: Fortress [Muhlenberg], Press, 1946), which is the translation by John W. Doberstein and Theodore G. Tappert of the longtime standard *Der junge Luther*. Bornkamm held this pioneer work in high esteem and, as his daughter reminds us, not only brought it out in successive editions (the sixth in 1968) but also regarded his own last book to be a continuation of Boehmer's volume—from the Wartburg event onward.

Unfinished, alas, remains the task of rounding out the story of Luther's career during its closing sixteen years. Granted, this part of the story has been told in English in part by Roland H. Bainton's *Here I Stand* (Nashville: Abingdon Press, 1950), Ernest G. Schwiebert's *Luther and His Times* (St. Louis: Concordia, 1950), and earlier in J. Mackinnon's *Luther and the Reformation* (whose four volumes appeared between 1925 and 1930). A few other works could also be mentioned. Yet even in German, as Tübingen's Reformation scholar Heiko Oberman deplores, it may be some time before the standard set here by Bornkamm for Luther's mid-career will be attained for the rest of the Reformer's years.

The 500th anniversary of Luther's birth—during which this translation of Bornkamm appears as a special mark of recognition in the English-speaking world—may help to stir a new appreciation of biography in general and of Luther's in particular. Scholars may well be spurred onward to complete the coverage so boldly attempted by this Heidelberg professor, whose own career is worthy of note.

Heinrich Bornkamm was born on June 26, 1901, in the village of Wuitz, some 30 miles southwest of Leipzig, and later resided in Görlitz, now on the Polish border of East Germany. He was the son of a Lutheran pastor and early became acquainted with the regional Luther lore. Bornkamm's theological education and specialization in church history as well as historical theology prepared him for a teaching career which took him successively to Tübingen (1925), to a professorship in Giessen (1927), and on to Leipzig (1935). During the Nazi era and its ideological struggles he sided with the Confessing Church, maintaining his scholarly pursuits during World War II to the extent that conditions permitted.

Called to Heidelberg University in 1948, Bornkamm was among those who gave that university's theological faculty an outstanding position in the resurgence of interest in the heritage of the Reformation and its relevance for modern times. As president for nearly thirty years of the *Evangelischer Bund*, a society formed in the 1880s to solidify Protestant positions against Roman Catholic inroads, Bornkamm turned it around and made the *Bund* an instrument of ecumenical research and a contributor to Christian unity. A longtime chairman of the Society for Reformation Research, a significant part of whose membership is currently in North America, his scholarship was recognized internationally. With his brother, Günther Bornkamm, noted professor of New Testament at Heidelberg, the two together represented a flowering of scholarship that transcends adversity and fills many with a sense of gratitude.

High among the people grateful to him are those who worked most closely under his direction, notably his doctoral candidates. These are now active worldwide. From Australia one of them (Maurice Schild) shared his experience with me in this way:

> With his talent for listening and stimulating further reflection, Bornkamm worked extremely well with groups in which some theological and historical knowledge could be presupposed. He created a circle of *Dozenten* and *Doktoranten* in church history, calling them the Centuriatoren (a reminder of early Lutheran achievers in historiography). Here, in an informal and yet quietly disciplined atmosphere, individuals presented the results of their studies for discussion and debate. "The master's" own contributions did not predominate but served to set tone and standard. Here his clear gifts of sum-

mation and of adding unexpected accents or perspectives really stood out. Here he would share his experiences in university life; past and contemporary scholars were remembered. I think, for example, of his portrayal of [his great teacher in Berlin] Karl Holl or Karl Müller; his evaluation of the work and methods of Joseph Lortz, his gentle skepticism as to what could come out of Rome at the time of the beginning of Vatican II, and so on.

In its own way a translation carries this thoughtful process forward, as Luther might agree, for the sake of Christ and his church.

E. THEODORE BACHMANN

Princeton Junction, N.J.
March 1983

Foreword

For decades Heinrich Bornkamm, my father, nurtured the plan of a Martin Luther biography. It was to be a chronological continuity of Heinrich Boehmer's presentation *Der junge Luther*,[1] of which he had published a new [fourth] edition [in 1951]. The initial work on this present book, then, lies far in the past. Among his other publications in the field of Reformation history, my father produced several monographs closely connected with his own projected Luther biography: "Erasmus und Luther" (1958),[2] "Luther als Schriftsteller" (1964),[3] "Luther und sein Vater" (1969)[4], and "Luther und sein Landesherr Friedrich der Weise" (1973).[5] Besides, there is his article "Luther, Martin (1483–1546): I. Leben und Schriften,"[6] later expanded into the essay "Martin Luther: Chronik seines Lebens."[7] And already in 1956 he lectured at the first International Luther Research Congress in Aarhus, [Denmark], on "Problems in Luther Biography."[8]

In the discussion of a meaningful periodization of a Luther biography, he had at that time focused on the year of the Nuremberg Truce (1532), as the "decisive turning point in the life of Luther, since the actual Reformation had begun with his return from the Wartburg." "Luther's entire subsequent activity stands on the basis of this truce."[9] The time span of this present volume was projected accordingly. Although in his later years my father was frequently preoccupied by other duties and had to cope with a diminishing of physical strength, he struggled to complete this book. He managed, however, with a curtailment of the plan, to bring the narrative

1. [H. Boehmer, *Road to Reformation: Martin Luther to the Year 1521*, trans. from the 3d German ed., 1938, by J. W. Doberstein and T. G. Tappert (Philadelphia: Fortress [Muhlenberg] Press, 1946).]

2. *LuJ* 1958, 1–20; reprinted in H. Bornkamm, *Das Jahrhundert der Reformation: Gestalten und Kräfte*, 2d ed. (Göttingen, 1966), 36–55.

3. "Sitzungsberichte der Heidelberger Akademie der Wissenschaften" (Heidelberg, 1965), reprinted in H. Bornkamm, *Luther: Gestalt und Wirkungen*, SVRG 188 (Gütersloh, 1975), 39–64.

4. *ZThK* 66 (1969): 38–61; reprinted in Bornkamm, *Luther*, 11–32.

5. *ARG* 64 (1973): 79–85; reprinted in Bornkamm, *Luther*, 33–38.

6. *RGG*³ 4 (1960): 480–95.

7. In Bornkamm, *Jahrhundert der Reformation*, 11–36.

8. In *Lutherforschung heute*, Referate und Berichte des 1. Internationalen Lutherforschungskongresses, Aarhus, August 18–23, 1956 (Berlin, 1958), 15–23.

9. Ibid., 19.

only to 1530, the year of the imperial diet at Augsburg. On his desk lay a little card with these hand-copied words by Luther: "It just won't get done. I see clearly, the years are closing in."[10] In the last chapter the manuscript breaks off.

In addition to the conclusion, the intended introduction is missing. It would have given an account of the scope and method of the book as well as prepared the reader for Chapter 1, which begins immediately at the Wartburg. As a substitute the following main points made in the lecture entitled "Problems in Luther Biography," mentioned above, may serve as commentary on the planning and execution of the volume before us.

First, the need for a new scholarly biography of Luther is established.

In our occupation with Luther's theology we run the risk of losing Luther the person. So many are the pens busily probing his theological thought in its details; so few today are exploring his life and personality. This is an understandable reaction to the period of historicism and against depicting Luther as a heroic man of genius. It was necessary that the objective interest in his theology and his ecclesiastical, intellectual, and political effectiveness should crowd out the interest in his person. Yet properly understood, it is precisely the real-life Luther that excludes every bit of hero worship and sentimentality from our contemplation of his life. Theological and biographical endeavors concerning him are therefore not mutually exclusive but complementary. And Luther research is ailing when one or the other of the two tasks is neglected.

The extent to which this [ailing] is true becomes evident from the fact that the only scholarly biography in Germany which embraces Luther's life inclusively and in context is still the one by Julius Köstlin, published in Gustav Kawerau's revised edition in 1903. . . . Our knowledge of Luther's life thus rests on a work . . . that in its fundamental conception took shape long before the beginning [1883] of the Weimar edition of Luther's works. [Not only is a confrontation with the Roman Catholic Luther research (Denifle, Grisar) missing], but also a half century of new findings and, most of all, intensive theological work lie between us and that biography. I would not disparage the value of numerous shorter or more popular presentations, partial biographies, or research monographs. . . . Yet they neither intend nor are able to overcome the deficiency under which Luther research has labored for a long time and which, as a task, grows increasingly difficult amid the ever-advancing accumulation and specialization of the literature.

This condition has serious consequences. When the theological and biographical presentations diverge, as they do today, both sides suffer. Our biographical knowledge remains positivistic, anecdotal, heroizing, devotional, sentimental. It should not surprise us that outside the field of theology and of Lutheranism completely inadequate and sometimes absurd impressions of Luther's image are spread abroad, especially when we ourselves simply repeat the same anecdotes instead of being able to offer—particularly to the

10. WA Br 5:316, 16–17. [Luther's letter to Melanchthon, May 12, 1530.]

scholarly research—an inclusive historical narrative of Luther's mind and labors capable of gripping also the modern educated reader. And our theological Luther research today, with its often purely systematic and abstract method, pursued frequently without any regard at all for stages of development and historical situations in which Luther worked, creates the impression that in treating his message we are dealing with a theology which is thought through but not with something experienced. Yet even the greatest respect for the accomplishments of Luther's mind are no substitute for the exact knowledge about how this theology grew out of ever new and historically demonstrable need as well as out of a certitude achieved through hard struggle. And finally, if precisely this view of a tempted and tested Luther prevents us from using him for idealistic or national hero worship, then we would indeed remind ourselves that such temptation and testing teach us to notice not only the word but also the example. Thus the fruits available to us from a pursuit of Luther's theology can be fully harvested only with a good and objective knowledge of his life and with a proper understanding of his person.

Having commented on the problem of a biographical treatment of the young Luther, Bornkamm presents methodological directions for the presentation of the subsequent decades of his career.

This treatment will have to be careful not to present a miniaturized history of the Reformation. Although quite naturally Luther's life, thought, and activity cannot be described without keeping sight of the broad history of the empire, the church, the territories, the other spiritual movements of the time, the focus of the presentation must remain on Luther and Wittenberg. In relation to this focal point everything else must find its perspective and place. Only by means of such concentration on the actual biographical task can an account of Luther's life render the service expected of it within the framework of Reformation history as a whole. By this same standard a Luther biography is not to be limited to an account of his theological development, and certainly not simply to a treatment of his writings. However useful the reliable account of Luther's works are, such as that offered us by the Köstlin-Kawerau biography, his literary work must be treated as part of his life story and to that end be integrated into it as well as handled with much less rigidity than otherwise. The most important rule, as it turns out, is that the presentation is to fit the man's actual career as snugly as possible. Of course there will have to be points of special emphasis; Luther's relation to humanism, illustrated by his contacts with Hutten and Erasmus, could be the occasion for viewing the larger context. We are surfeited with attempts to systematize Luther. A biography must energetically seek to counterbalance this fact and to give visibility to the theological material—which it must utilize fully—as an inseparable component of this life story at its respective stages. How a true-to-life presentation would have to differentiate itself from attempts made hitherto is readily shown, for instance, in the Köstlin-Kawerau description of Luther's confinement in the Wartburg."[11]

11. *Lutherforschung heute*, 15–16, 18–19.

Because my father left the work unfinished and was unable to apply the finishing touches even to the chapters already completed, it became my responsibility to ready the manuscript for publication. In the process it was not possible to take into account certain references to his anticipated inclusion of additional material, particularly further literature. In going over the text, I have confined myself to the adjustment of minor oversights, including the literal rendition of citations in German from Luther and various contemporaries. For citation the principle holds according to which my father treated his edition of Luther's prefaces to the Bible:[12] The Luther text, "in light of the original spelling and speech, was adapted so as to cause today's reader a minimum of linguistic difficulties, while permitting Luther's language to ring through as perceivably as possible."[13] The annotations were another matter, however, requiring a thorough technical reworking. All Luther texts are cited exclusively according to the Weimar edition (WA). The exceptions are *De servo arbitrio* (see Chapter 16), which for practical reasons is cited according to the Bonn edition of Luther's works (*BoA*) by O. Clemen, and the prefaces to the books of the Bible, which are readily available in my father's edition mentioned above. There has been virtually no attempt on my part to supplement bibliographic references with more recent titles, largely because the function of such listings is to refer to use made of such works in the text of the book itself and not to provide a complete bibliography on the subject being treated. A separate list gives the titles of frequently used sources and secondary works.

At this point I want to acknowledge the help of Christa Schönrich, who not only typed the entire manuscript while my father was still living but also contributed decisively toward the publication of the book by independently double-checking, coordinating, and, in given instances, completing the bibliographical references as well as by compiling the bibliographical listings. Likewise, she collaborated in the proofreading. Without her tireless and dedicated partnership this volume could hardly have appeared as soon as it did. Likewise my thanks go to two former assistants of my father who, while he was living, checked the references: Rainer Vinke for Chapters 1, 3–6, 8, 9, 11, 12, 15–18, and Christian Homrichhausen for Chapters 2, 7, 10, 13, 14, 19–24. I have utilized their corrections, while I once again checked the citations from Luther and

---

12. *Martin Luthers Vorreden zur Bibel*, ed. H. Bornkamm (Hamburg, 1967). [Cf. *LW* 35:235–51, 357–62.]

13. Ibid., 29. [An analogous policy has been followed by the translators of *Luther's Works*. Wherever available, the English version of *Luther's Works* (*LW*) has been used in the following translation of the book.]

Müntzer. In addition, I want to extend my sincere thanks to Eckhard Kruse, who rendered significant help in collaborating in the proofreading as well as in preparing the indexes, and to Bernd Moeller, who made available to this undertaking the help of his assistant. To the Society for Reformation History I owe thanks for financial assistance, notably for generously assuming part of the cost of the staff work; and to the United Lutheran Church in Germany, whose publication grant subsidized the publication of this volume in Germany.

The dedication of this book expresses the thanks of my father to his wife, Lieselotte née Mass, for the support, patience, and encouragement that she and others gave him.

KARIN BORNKAMM

Bielefeld
Christmas 1978

Abbreviations

AAAbo.H	*Acta Academiae Aboensis. Ser. A. Humaniora*
ADB	*Allgemeine Deutsche Biographie.* Edited by the Historische Commission bei der Königl. Akademie der Wissenschaften. 55 vols. Leipzig, 1875–1912.
AGP	Arbeiten zur Geschichte des Pietismus
AGTL	Arbeiten zur Geschichte und Theologie des Luthertums
AHKBAW	Abhandlungen der historischen Klasse der Königl. bayerischen Akademie der Wissenschaften. Munich.
AÖG	Archiv für österreichische Geschichte
ARG	*Archiv für Reformationsgeschichte*
Aug (L)	*Augustiniana* (Louvain)
BBGW	*Basler Beiträge zur Geschichtswissenschaft*
BC	*The Book of Concord: The Confessions of the Evangelical Lutheran Church.* Translated and edited by Theodore G. Tappert. Philadelphia: Fortress Press, 1959.
BDK	Bibel und deutsche Kultur
BGDS (T)	*Beiträge zur Geschichte der deutschen Sprache und Literatur* (Tübingen)
BGLRK	Beiträge zur Geschichte und Lehre der reformierten Kirchen
BHTh	Beiträge zur historischen Theologie
BKS	Die Bekenntnisschriften der evangelisch-lutherischen Kirche. 7th ed. Göttingen, 1976.
BoA	*Luthers Werke in Auswahl.* Edited by O. Clemen. Bonn, 1912ff.
BÖT	Beiträge zur ökumenischen Theologie
BPfK	Blätter für pfälzische Kirchengeschichte
BSHPF	Bulletin de la société de l'histoire du protestantisme français
BSKG	*Beiträge zur sächsischen Kirchengeschichte*
BThKG	*Beiträge zur thüringischen Kirchengeschichte*
BWKG	*Blätter für württembergische Kirchengeschichte*
CC	*Corpus Catholicorum*
CR	*Corpus Reformatorum*
CS	*Corpus Schwenckfeldianorum*
DTh	*Deutsche Theologie. Monatsschrift für die deutsche evangelische Kirche*

DVLG	*Deutsche Vierteljahrsschrift für Literaturwissenschaft und Geistesgeschichte*
EAS	*Erasmus von Rotterdam: Ausgewählte Schriften.* Edited by W. Welzig. Darmstadt, 1969.
EStL	*Evangelisches Staatslexikon.* Edited by H. Kunst and S. Grundmann. Berlin, 1966.
FBTK	*Freimüthige Blätter über Theologie und Kirchenthum*
FGLP	Forschungen zur Geschichte und Lehre des Protestantismus
FKDG	Forschungen zur Kirchen- und Dogmengeschichte
FKGG	Forschungen zur Kirchen- und Geistesgeschichte
GGA	*Göttingische gelehrte Anzeigen*
GUA	*Göteborgs universitets årsskrift*
HarzZ	*Harz-Zeitschrift*
HdJb	*Heidelberger Jahrbücher*
HV	*Historische Vierteljahrsschrift*
HZ	*Historische Zeitschrift*
JBrKG	*Jahrbuch für brandenburgische Kirchengeschichte*
JLH	*Jahrbuch für Liturgik und Hymnologie*
JNS	*Jahrbuch für Nationalökonomie und Statistik*
KiKonf	Kirche und Konfession
KJV	King James Version of the Bible
(K) MRG	Köhler, W. *Das Marburger Religionsgespräch 1529: Versuch einer Rekonstruktion.* SVRG 148. Leipzig, 1929.
KuD	*Kerygma und Dogma*
LCC	Library of Christian Classics
LThK	*Lexikon für Theologie und Kirche.* Edited by Michael Buchberger et al. 10 vols. 2d ed. Freiburg, 1957–65.
LuJ	*Luther-Jahrbuch*
LW	American Edition of *Luther's Works.* Philadelphia: Fortress Press; and St. Louis: Concordia, 1955–
MBW	*Melanchthons Briefwechsel: Kritische und kommentierte Gesamtausgabe.* Edited by H. Scheible, Vol. 1: Regesten 1–1169 (1514–1530). Stuttgart, 1977.
MGKK	Monatsschrift für Gottesdienst und kirchliche Kunst
MGP	*Monumenta Germaniae paedagogica*
(M) MRG	May, G. *Das Marburger Religionsgespräch 1529.* TKTG 13. Gütersloh, 1970.
MPL	*Patrologia Latina.* Edited by J. P. Migne. 217 vols. and 4 reg. vols. Paris, 1878–90.
MSA	*Melanchthons Werke in Auswahl.* Edited by R. Stupperich. Gütersloh, 1951ff.
NASG	*Neues Archiv für sächsische Geschichte und Altertumskunde*

NEB	New English Bible
NKZ	*Neue kirchliche Zeitschrift*
ODW	*Ostdeutsche Wissenschaft*
QFIAB	Quellen und Forschungen aus italienischen Archiven und Bibliotheken
QFRG	Quellen und Forschungen zur Reformationsgeschichte
QGP	Quellenschriften zur Geschichte des Protestantismus
QGT	Quellen zur Geschichte der Täufer
QODKG	Quellenhefte zur ostdeutschen und osteuropäischen Kirchengeschichte
RE³	*Realencyklopädie für protestantische Theologie und Kirche.* Edited by A. Hauck. 24 vols. 3d ed. Leipzig, 1896–1913.
RGG³	*Die Religion in Geschichte und Gegenwart.* Edited by K. Galling. 5 vols. 3d ed. Tübingen, 1957–65.
RGST	Reformationsgeschichtliche Studien und Texte
RKW	*Repertorium für Kunstwissenschaft*
RQ	*Römische Quartalsschrift für christliche Altertumskunde*
RSGG	Recht und Staat in Geschichte und Gegenwart
RSV	Revised Standard Version
RTA	*Deutsche Reichstagsakten: Jüngere Reihe.* Edited by the Hist. Kommission bei der Bayerischen Akademie der Wissenschaften. Gotha, 1893ff.; 2d ed., Göttingen, 1962ff.
SBAW.PPH	Sitzungsberichte der bayerischen Akademic der Wissenschaften—Philosophisch-philologisch-historische Klasse
SDG	*Sowjetsystem und Demokratische Gesellschaft: Eine vergleichende Enzyklopädie.* Edited by C. D. Kernig. 6 vols. Freiburg, Basel, and Wien, 1966–72.
SHAW.PH	*Sitzungsberichte der Heidelberger Akademie der Wissenschaften—Philosophisch-historische Klasse*
SKGNS	Studien zur Kirchengeschichte Niedersachsens
SMGV	Schriftenreihe des mennonitischen Geschichtsvereins
Suppl. Mel.	*Supplementa Melanchthoniana.* Edited by Melanchthon Kommission des VRT. Leipzig, 1910ff.; reprint, Frankfurt am Main, 1968.
SVRG	Schriften des Vereins für Reformationsgeschichte
ThA	Theologische Arbeiten
ThLZ	*Theologische Literaturzeitung*
ThStKr	*Theologische Studien und Kritiken*
ThZ	*Theologische Zeitschrift*
TKTG	Texte zur Kirchen- und Theologiegeschichte
TThZ	*Trierer theologische Zeitschrift*
VHKHW	*Veröffentlichungen der historischen Kommission für Hessen und Waldeck*

VLG	*Veröffentlichungen der Luthergesellschaft*
WA	*D. Martin Luthers Werke.* Kritische Gesamtausgabe. Weimar, 1883–
WA Br	*D. Martin Luthers Werke.* Briefwechsel. Weimar, 1930–
WA DB	*D. Martin Luthers Werke.* Deutsche Bibel. Weimar, 1906–61.
WA TR	*D. Martin Luthers Werke.* Tischreden. Weimar, 1912–21.
ZHTh	*Zeitschrift für historische Theologie*
ZHVG	*Zeitschrift des Harz-Vereins für Geschichte und Altertumskunde*
ZKG	*Zeitschrift für Kirchengeschichte*
ZThK	*Zeitschrift für Theologie und Kirche*
ZVKGS	Zeitschrift des Vereins für Kirchengeschichte der Provinz Sachsen

LUTHER
IN MID-CAREER

1

At the Wartburg

On that Saturday—it was May 4, 1521—about an hour before midnight, the gates of the castle closed behind Martin Luther. Hans von Berlepsch, warden of the Wartburg, showed the newcomer to his rooms. To the sequestered Luther the sudden calm was baffling. At first it felt good, for he was weary from the long day's circuitous route on horseback. Soon enough, however, he found the solitude oppressive. The remembered rhythms of the Wittenberg years were part of his life. And now this. Reluctantly he accepted the leisure and pondered his situation.[1]

Luther's benevolent guardian had lodged him in the apartment reserved for knights adjacent to the warden's own quarters in the outer castle. Confined to a living room and a small adjoining bedroom on the north side, he was remote from prying eyes. As his tonsure disappeared, the smooth-shaven monk became the curly-headed, dark-bearded Junker Jörg—a knight. During the early part of his "captivity" the only ones to see him were the warden and the two pages, lads of noble stock, who brought him food and drink. The others in the castle were kept away. Each night the narrow stairway to his rooms, rising from the hallway of the warden's quarters, was raised on its chain and locked. This was more than monastic solitude. In this place he was alone with his thoughts, yet not completely so. He had two books—the Hebrew Bible and the Greek New Testament—rescued from among his things in the wagon at the moment of ambush near Altenstein. Besides, there was the beauty of spring. A glorious landscape spread out beneath Luther's lofty windows.[2] The view was westward, away from Eisenach where he had spent part of his youth, over the rounded hills and hollows of the Thuringian forest. On a clear day he could see the distant Hessian ridges and Mount Meissner. The whole scene was alive with the fresh greenery of May. The springtime thrilled his heart and helped momentarily, at least, to chase away the nagging

1. For the early period at the Wartburg, see Luther's letters of May 1521, WA Br 2:330ff.; also WA TR 6, no. 6816, 209, 14ff. H. Nebe, "Die Lutherstube auf der Wartburg," VLG 11 (1929): 33ff. [LW 48, no. 75, 310ff.]

2. Goethe described this view from the Wartburg in glowing terms in his letter to Charlotte von Stein, September 13–16, 1777. He also recalled his great predecessor: "I am living in Luther's Patmos and am faring as well as he did" (September 28, 1777, to Kestner).

thoughts that burdened him.[3] As Luther mused, he felt himself "in the realm of the birds" and "in the domain of the air," where "the birds make melody from their perches, praising God day and night for all they were worth."

Nevertheless, Martin Luther missed being with people. Even the good conversations with his host, the warden, were no substitute for human companionship. He tried writing to his friends, but tore up his first attempts, doubting that the letters would ever be delivered. Yet after only eight days a letter arrived from George Spalatin. Posted in Worms, this was the first communication Luther had from the outside world. He had longed for such contacts to begin. Other letters followed, and the messengers of the elector Frederick the Wise enabled Luther to keep in touch with his friends in Wittenberg. His own letters allow us to follow the ups and downs of his moods. He was without any anxiety about his own person or future. A week after his capture he wrote to Philipp Melanchthon that he had consented only with reluctance to an imposed exile.[4] He feared others might think him a deserter, while actually he would rather have jumped into the fray and tangled bare-fisted with his raging opponents. Other cares also tormented Luther. "Sitting here all day, I picture to myself the state of the church. God, what a horrible picture of his wrath is that detestable kingdom of the Roman Antichrist! I abhor the hardness [of my heart], that I am not completely melted to tears." Forced to the sidelines now, he recalls, "You will be silent and the Lord will fight for you." Even though he himself should perish, the gospel will not lose anything.[5]

Luther bore exclusion from the field of battle "with great peace of heart." He reminded himself and others that "I was never engaged in the exposition of the Word by my own volition." As God had called him, so God could suspend him. To Spalatin he confided, "I know that any teacher who pushes himself into teaching is not called by God. So far I have always shied away from the office of teaching. No one need expect anything different from me on this point. I shall always flee it. Had I been eager [to teach in public], I never would have consented to go into this solitude."[6] Teaching or not, he trusted in God's guidance now as always, and that gave him comfort. Therefore he could not believe it when Melanchthon com-

3. *WA Br* 2:333 / 44; 355 / 16; 349 / 101. [*LW* 48:212–17.]

4. See this letter, with commentary by H. Rückert, *BoA* 6:28ff. [*LW* 48:215–17.]

5. *WA Br* 2:332 / 10ff.; 333 / 32–33. [*LW* 48:215, 217, 213, 232.]

6. *WA Br* 2:368 / 8ff. [*LW* 48:232, to Melanchthon, May 26, 1521; *LW* 48:274, to Spalatin, July 31.]

plained that he and his colleagues were straying like sheep without a shepherd. "Don't talk that way," Luther warned, "lest God be angered and we be found guilty of ingratitude" for the Word and its goodly supply of ministers in Wittenberg. His own inactivity, meanwhile, became oppressive. Spiritual burdens vied with physical complaints. Stubborn digestive disturbances—constipation, mostly—had bothered him in Worms and refused to leave him. Small wonder, for the Wartburg's well-meaning warden kept lavishing food on him and the lack of exercise threatened his health. In self-disgust, brought on by his first ten days of confinement, he remonstrated to Spalatin, "Lazy and full I sit here all day long."[7]

Even so, Luther's mind was alive with plans. Eagerly he would lay hands on those manuscripts lying unfinished in Wittenberg. He begged that they be sent posthaste. The items included galleys of the Magnificat as well as some materials on Psalm 22 which he needed in order to complete a [second] series of lectures on the Psalms—his *Operationes in Psalmos*. He also requested his Latin postil, which he planned to extend beyond the sermons for Advent that had already been printed. Up to this point his reading was limited to the Bible in the two original languages. He set to work on an exposition of Psalm 68, which contained the Introit for Pentecost (May 19 that year) and also the versicles for mass on Ascension Day. He had his friends in mind as he steeped himself in this exulting song of God's triumph over his enemies. Completing it on May 26, he dispatched this little exercise to Melanchthon forthwith. This work had done something for him. The floodgates of his mind had opened and his pent-up passion for work surged ahead.

Auricular confession—that widely debated issue—headed Luther's writing agenda. His consuming concern beckoned in the title: "On Confession: Whether the Pope Has the Power to Require It."[8] In reply, Spalatin surprised Luther with a copy of the small book, *Paradoxon*, subtitled "Confession, and How It Ought Not to Be Burdensome to Christians."[9] Recently published in Augsburg and Basel, it was the work of John

---

7. WA BR 2:337 / 32. [*LW* 48:234, 225.]

8. [The dedication was to Franz von Sickingen, a leader among the knights of the empire, and conveyed the author's greeting as of June 1, "from my Patmos." The way this swiftly written treatise emerged says something about how Luther worked. Only in mid-May, while writing to Spalatin of his plans, he had announced, "I shall write a German tract on the freedom of auricular confession." WA 8:140ff.; *LW* 48:246–47, 225.]

9. [Paradoxon: Quod non sit onerosa christianis confessio.] 64 Bll. 4°. Appeared in Augsburg [*sic*; Basel, says *RE*[3] 14:290 / 14. Also *Allgemeine deutsche Biographie*, "Oekolampadius"], April 20, 1521. Contents described in E. Staehelin, *Das theologische Lebenswerk Johannes Oekolampads*, QFRG 21 (Leipzig, 1939), 121ff., 154, 155, 156. [*Paradoxon*, trans. by Oe. and published in German, August 1521.]

Oecolampadius—priest, humanist, and a man to Luther's liking. Temporarily a member of the monastic community of St. Bridget in Altomünster, near Augsburg, Oecolampadius had here produced a treatise in learned Latin that soon created a sensation.[10] His sketch of the historical background of confession was followed by arguments against the scholastics. In *The Paradox*, aptly so named, the author sought to do two things: show that the Catholic sacrament of penance, once freed from its excessive demands, and especially from that of confessing every sin, is open to an evangelical interpretation; and give the faithful a good conscience in return for their confessing and thus satisfying traditional requirements. In this sense confession should not be burdensome to Christians.

Luther would agree, but he also felt there was more to be said. He himself had earlier produced pamphlets of protest against the Roman manipulation of conscience while at the same time coming out positively on the value of confession and absolution. Seeing that his earlier efforts had been to no avail, he now felt bound to take up the issue again. And with good reason. While he himself had been spirited away, his opponents imagined they had won the day. As Spalatin reported, they were about to bend the rules of confession as an excuse to search through his papers. This was enough. It spurred Luther on to write with renewed fearlessness and clarity. "One must wield God's Word like a bared blade and let it powerfully cut down all opponents and errors."[11] By dedicating this treatise to the noted knight Franz von Sickingen, Luther added weight to this assault on what was actually the centerpiece of Catholic piety and the care of souls. His aim was to liberate the conscience of believers from submission to the man-made ecclesiastical requirements surrounding confession. The Word of God, he insisted, "intends to exercise either all authority or none at all."[12]

With a seasoning of humor, Luther deftly plucked and examined the proof texts said to support auricular confession. A choice text from the Old Testament was Prov. 27:23 ("Know well the condition of your flocks, and give attention to your herds"). The sophists, he noted, have here performed a remarkable exegesis, for they seem to be unaware—even by

10. [John Oecolampadius (Johannes Hausschein), 1482–1531, in 1522 returned to Basel and led the already active reform movement in that city. *Paradoxon* was published first in Augsburg, soon thereafter in Basel; *RE*[3] 14:290 / 14 (see above, n. 9). See also G. Rupp, *Patterns of Reformation* (Philadelphia: Fortress Press, 1969), 17; on the career of Oecolampadius, see 3–46.]

11. *WA* 8:142 / 33ff.

12. *WA* 8:143 / 35.

their own teaching—that there is no such thing as confession in the Old Covenant but that it is a sacrament of the New Covenant. Another proof, this one from the New Testament, is James 5:16 ("Therefore confess your sins to one another"). *Alterutrum* [one another, in the Vulgate] makes a strange father confessor indeed; he can hardly be pleasing to the papists. Luther objects to man-made rules on the grounds that they offer only an illusory peace of conscience when followed and create a falsely uneasy conscience when neglected. For anyone desiring to go to confession he had this counsel: Go whenever you feel the need of it but, as a sign of being freed, try to avoid doing so around the prescribed time at Easter. Anyone at all serious about his sins should not be above making a heartfelt confession to a fellow Christian, be that person ordained or lay. Conversely, "anyone who makes confession to God by himself alone can hardly experience the intended confidence and security,"[13] for the word of God's grace, when spoken by another, is more powerful than any absolution mediated by one's own heart.

Luther claimed that historically, too, auricular confession [had trivialized sin and thereby] destroyed the parish discipline of the ancient church which had required the public confession of major (mortal) sins. Although he never found a suitable form to accomplish it, Luther tried throughout his career to revive the order of penance as practiced by the ancient church. Thereby he determined precisely the nature of his objection to the Roman care of souls as regulated by canon law.[14] Unlike Oecolampadius, he had no desire to make this practice tolerable; he wanted to abolish it altogether. He regarded forced confession as a terrible error, but when made from the heart, confession was a precious comfort. He would "praise confession most highly, but he would force no one to make it."[15] On this issue, which had ignited the great struggle in the church only three and a half years earlier, his thoughts were now formed. The way to a new beginning was open.

Most of the books Luther had requested soon arrived from Wittenberg, and he resumed his interrupted writings. First came Psalm 22, for which he promptly finished the exegesis of the final third and kept his theological comments to a minimum. With this he concluded his [second] series on the Psalms, the big *Operationes in Psalmos* at which he had labored over the past three years. The linguistic demands had been burdensome

13. WA 8:178 / 23ff.
14. [The Fourth Lateran Council (1215), the canon on requiring confession.]
15. WA 8:169 / 25–26.

and difficult to master alongside his many other duties in Wittenberg. Yet now, with more time, the Wartburg was not the best place for it either, with only the Hebrew text but no other helps. The steady struggle with Rome was at last forcing him to hang his harp "on the willows of this Babylon." His one consolation, he thought, was that in Wittenberg John Bugenhagen's current exposition on the Psalms offered a substitute superior to his own efforts.[16] Besides Luther's brilliant commentary on Galatians, which he himself had seen through the press in 1519, this work on the Psalms was his only other major scholarly exposition, and it remained a fragment. Under the pressure of other duties all his later commentaries had to be assembled from notes that were edited by others.

Next came the Magnificat. Luther plunged into this task with pure joy. He had already completed a good one-third of it before journeying to the imperial diet at Worms.[17] The much-beloved hymn in praise of the "tender Mother of God" once again spoke to his heart even as it had during those weeks of weighty expectation prior to Worms. This hymn meant so much to him because of its testimony to the free grace of God. [The heavenly Father] shows regard not for merit but for the "low estate of his handmaid." Then, said Luther, if one understands Mary correctly—as the greatest of all human examples refuting a righteousness based on deeds—"We ought to call on her, that for her sake God may grant and do what we request." One must simply remember that "she does nothing, God does all."[18] In his commentary on the God who deposes the mighty from their seats and raises those of low degree—comments that make this treatise an important source for his concept of history—the breath of Luther's own recent history-making hours can be felt. If ever, he could now stand erect on the mighty promises of this biblical hymn. "You must not only think and speak of a low estate but actually come to be in a low estate and be caught up in it, without any human aid, so that God alone may do the work."[19] "He has put down the mighty from their thrones, and exalted those of low degree." Thus does Mary sing the praise of the Lord of history (Luke 1:52).[20] He [God] deals in two ways: on the one hand,

16. WA 5:7. [Bugenhagen (1485–1558) arrived in Wittenberg in April 1521. He soon began to teach there, lecturing on the Psalms and serving as pastor of the main church in town.]

17. On the production of this publication, see the explanation to Luther's letter of March 31, 1521, to Duke John Frederick of Saxony, the elector's brother, to whom this work was dedicated (WA Br 2:295, n. 8). According to this, the statement in WA 7:539, n. 1, is to be corrected. [LW 21:299–358.]

18. WA 7:575 / 1; 574 / 35. [LW 21:328–29.]

19. WA 7:594 / 1ff. [LW 21:348.]

20. WA 7:589 / 13ff. [LW 21:343.]

through his creatures—so that everyone can see where there is might and where there is weakness, and one imagines that God helps the strongest. On the other hand, through history—where God operates with instruments we cannot see, that is, "through his arm." The stage for this is set in secret. God permits the wicked "to become great and to exalt themselves mightily. He withdraws his power from them and lets them puff themselves up in their own power alone, for where man's strength begins, God's strength ends. When their bubble is full-blown, and everyone supposes them to have won and overcome, and they themselves feel smug in their own achievement, then God pricks the bubble, and it is all over."[21] This does not mean that God does away with power for all time or that he breaks up the thrones of sovereigns. However, "he casts the mighty from their seats. [Mary] does not say he leaves those of low degree in their low degree but that he exalts them, for while the world stands, authority, rule, power, and thrones must remain." History consists of an unending shift of power, ever precipitated by the abuses of those momentarily powerful. In contrast to this there is still another opposite component of God's activity in history. God does not destroy "reason, wisdom, and right, for if the world is to go on, these things must remain."[22]

At another place in the Magnificat, Luther adds "a correct instruction in the law" as being complementary to the theology of history. He warned against a merely stubborn insistence on being in the right, as, for example, being against the "pope and his herd," on whose side "there is no hearing or giving way, it profits nothing to speak, to counsel, beg, or threaten."[23] It is necessary to distinguish between "confessing" (speaking out) and exacting one's rights. To demand one's rights is always legitimate, but one should not seek to exact them at the cost of doing greater harm.[24] Princes and governments especially should heed this when for the sake of a cause, however just, they "fill the world with bloodshed and misery."[25] This bears also on their responsibility to protect their subjects. Therefore

---

21. WA 7:585 / 23ff., 33ff.; 586, 21ff. [LW 21:340.] On the connection of these and other passages of the Magnificat which deal with Luther's concept of history as a whole, see H. Bornkamm, ["God and History"], *Luthers geistige Welt,* 4th ed. (Gütersloh, 1960), 199ff. [*Luther's World of Thought* (St. Louis: Concordia, 1958), 204ff.]. [LW 21:340.]

22. WA 7:590 / 3ff. [LW 21:344.]

23. WA 7:580 / 20–21; 581 / 10; 580 / 7ff. [LW 21:334.]

24. WA 7:582 / 19ff. [LW 21:336 / 26.]

25. WA 7:582 / 30ff. [LW 21:336.]

let them not impetuously smash a bowl to grab a spoon."[26] The model for combining "reason, wisdom, and right" is David who, as Luther said, "often looked the other way when he was unable to punish without bringing (greater) harm on others."[27] In the exposition of this incomparable poetic passage, Luther created a literary masterpiece of his own, while at the same time setting a course for the further development of his concepts of history, law, and government.

Luther's heart was set on writing his postil, and only reluctantly did he interrupt working on it in order to discharge a duty imposed on him from the outside. This duty concerned a disputation with the Louvain theological faculty which, though unauthorized, had joined the Cologne theologians in issuing and in February 1520 making public a condemnation of Luther's writings, thus bringing the conflict into the open. Virtually by return mail, in March, Luther countered with a sharp and scornful reply. The tone of his attackers had angered him; he found their method frivolous and calculated to incite heresy. "Who can imagine that the Holy Scriptures are still of any account when one is supposed to believe professors who spin their arguments without even referring to Scripture?" This arrogant tyranny, exercised in the name of the teaching church, made Luther all the more sure that the Antichrist had already taken over or was about to do so.[28] In Louvain itself, where Erasmus was residing, the theological faculty suspected him of being a friend of Luther and therefore kept him under constant attack. Disciples of Erasmus retaliated with an ironical sniper fire that finally moved one of the faculty members, James Latomus, to enter the arena with an extensive polemical work. Even the title of his tract showed that Luther's charges had been taken seriously: the Scriptures and the church fathers were amply cited.[29]

---

26. WA 7:583 / 18–19. [LW 21:337. The equivalent used in the English translation is "leap from the frying pan into the fire." This does not quite convey the willfulness Luther here implies.] The German proverb "Grab a spoon, smash a bowl" is found also in Luther's later handwritten collection of German proverbs: WA 51:655 (no. 276) and 661 (no. 477), "Löffel aufheben, Schüssel zertreten." For Luther's picture of David, see H. Bornkamm, *Luther und das Alte Testament* (Tübingen, 1948), 9ff., 12.

27. WA 7:583 / 25–26. [*LW* 21:337.]

28. WA 6:181 / 34ff. [*LW* 32:135.]

29. *Articulum doctrinae Fratris Martini Luther: per theologos Lovanienses damnatorum Ratio / ex sacris literis et veteribus tractatoribus per Jacobum Latomum sacrae theologiae professorem.* Cf. WA 8:36ff.; also P. Kalkoff, *Die Anfänge der Gegenreformation in den Niederlanden,* pt. 1, SVRG 79 (Halle, 1903): 68ff. By the same author, "Die Vermittlungspolitik des Erasmus und sein Anteil an den Flugschriften der ersten Reformationszeit," *ARG* 1 (1903–4): 1ff. P. Kalkoff "Erasmus von Rotterdam und seine Schüler Wilhelm Nesen und Nicolaus von Herzogenbusch im Kampfe mit den Löwener Theologen," in *Huldreich Zwingli sämtliche Werke* (Berlin, 1911), 7:402ff. [Jacobus Latomus (Jacques Masson), 1475–1544. See also LW 48:229, n. 3. Cf. "Against Latomus," LW 32:(135) 137–260.]

Immediately on receipt of Latomus's writing (Melanchthon had sent it to him from Wittenberg), Luther knew he would have to reply. Although this rambling and poorly written book annoyed him, Luther recognized that its arguments could not be sidestepped. These arguments touched the core of his theology: sin, grace, and the nature of man. Amid recurring feelings of aversion against his opponent, Luther concentrated on his reply and produced a most significant tract of his own.[30]

To be sure, this refutation did not take the place of a book on justification which Luther had often planned but never written. However, together with his lectures on Romans and Galatians as well as his disputations of the 1530s, this work against Latomus makes the most important presentation of his teaching on justification. Yet even here he did not tackle the whole range of issues he would necessarily have included in a book on the subject. Actually this effort against Latomus is the first major indication of how Luther was unfortunately to be handicapped throughout his career in all but his nonexegetical writings; they hardly ever became books as he would have preferred, but remained polemical tracts or responsory treatises, following lines determined by the opponent. In Luther's writings the debate thus hinged most often on biblical sources and proofs, accompanied by frequent digressions. These were most likely to be inserted when associated passages of Scripture came swiftly to his mind or when scholastic logic intruded and he sought to gain the upper hand by using the opponent's own weapons. For readers now as then, a further difficulty is that Luther's basic thinking was not always easy to untangle from his (exegetical) elaborations. Yet there was compensation for this in the almost inexhaustible wealth of formulations in which his writings abound. He did not hit on these formulations simply by spinning out his own thoughts, but he developed them in the rough-and-tumble of debate, where he was ever on the alert for new ways to down his opponent. Besides, he borrowed freely from the rich imagery of the biblical texts, for whose defense and utilization he was struggling.

The debate with Latomus turned on several specific questions. For his part, Luther operated with certain presuppositions based on convictions shaped by personal struggle during his formative years up to 1519. He held that only the grace of God offered in Jesus Christ is able to redeem us from our guilt, that our deeds are in no way the ground for, but ever only the fruit of, our justification, just as catholic theology had always done. So

---

30. *Rationis Latomianae por incendiariis Lovaniensis scholae sophistis redditae Lutheriana confutatio* (1521) (Luther's Refutation of Latomus's Argument on Behalf of the Incendiary Sophists of the University of Louvain, WA 8:36ff.) [LW 32:(133) 137–260.]

then, in man himself there is nothing good; sin lurks in every good work, so that even the saints are sinners. To Latomus this appeared to run counter to Scripture and the tradition of the church fathers. But Luther yielded not one bit.[31] Although he might come into conflict with the church fathers, and, here and there, perhaps even with Augustine—granted that his terminology was not always clear—Luther had Paul on his side. The human being is in fact, so long as we live, fully permeated with sin. Even of those who are justified—declared righteous—by God, it is not permissible to speak of sin simply as a flaw or as imperfection or to tone it down in some other way. Sin is like yeast that permeates the entire dough. No one, not even with the best of good works, can do without the grace of God. Catholic teaching to the contrary, sin is not removed by God either in baptism or at some later time when he responds to our penitent pleas and forgives our sins ever anew. Sin, Luther contends, is not eradicated but remains present and must be overcome ever afresh by God's help, for God intends, according to Luther, "that day by day we be drawn more deeply into Christ, that we do not stay put in what we have received but become transformed in Christ."[32] A Christian, he emphasized, can be utterly confident that all his sins are forgiven and must nevertheless continue to fight hard for victory over sin.

To the end of his life—Luther had been saying this ever since his lectures on Romans (1515–16)—the Christian is at one and the same time a righteous person [justified] and a sinner. This is not as though one could distinguish between these two conditions by some probing or instant testing. The Christian is and remains inseparably one person. Seen from the side of sin, the only side from which we can see ourselves, a person is all sinner. Seen from the side of grace, as we believe God sees us, a person is entirely justified. Luther pressed the point: "Whoever is under wrath is wholly under the whole of wrath and whoever is under grace is wholly under the whole of grace, for wrath and grace have to do with the [whole] person."[33] Man's only hope of salvation lies in the mercy of God and not in any kind of human progress or performance. With this image of man, portrayed in his lectures on Galatians in 1519,[34] and certain that man re-

31. Below, pp. 183ff.
32. WA 8:111 / 33ff. [LW 32:235,34ff.]
33. WA 8:106 / 38–39 [–107 / 2]. [LW 32:228 / 20ff.]
34. WA Br 2:585–86. Below, p. 195. Also the essay by H. Bornkamm, "Äusserer und innerer Mensch bei Luther und den Spiritualisten," in *Imago Dei* (Giessen, 1932), 85ff.; reprinted in H. Bornkamm, *Luther: Gestalt und Wirkungen*, SVRG 188 (Gütersloh, 1975), 187ff.

ceives his personality from God, a personality that then embraces this inner schism, Luther created for his thinking a basis that proved to be of far-reaching significance. From this position he [and his successors] could expose various other positions as untenable: that of the scholastics, attempting to separate the grace-full from the sin-full in man; and later that of the Anabaptists, endeavoring to separate the old man from the new man, the once-born from the twice-born. Luther's teaching on the unity of human nature is his strongest contribution to the modern quest for a more profound understanding of the human image. This remains true even where certain characterizations that he fought have reappeared, as, for example, in some forms of the anthropology of German idealism which may retain Anabaptist-Pietist features. Do "two souls, alas, dwell within my breast"? Not so, contends Luther. It is but a single soul, torn between heaven and earth, spirit and flesh. Taking his cue from Augustine, Luther seized on Paul's deeply moving account in Romans 7 and affirmed the indivisible "I," the human being. With an exposition of this chapter, Luther concluded his tract against Latomus and was thankful to return to more peaceful tasks.[35]

In the early weeks of his banishment the works flowed impetuously from Luther's hand. "I am both very idle and very busy here; I am studying Hebrew and Greek and writing without interruption," he told Spalatin in a covering letter of June 10, explaining a package of manuscripts ready for publication.[36] This was ten days before he finished the confutation against Latomus. The bounds of his captivity were relaxing a bit. In the company of his two pages, he was allowed to roam the woods and pick strawberries. Occasionally he would ride horseback, while a servant rode at his side.[37] In any case, those responsible for Luther were anxiously on the lookout lest anyone spot his identity. His little party once stopped at the nearby Reinhardsbrunn cloister, but someone recognized him, causing him and his companions to take off in haste. In many situations Luther had to be wary. If he so much as carried a little book, as he sometimes did, or showed interest in some printed matter, he was likely to attract attention. Literary interests on the part of a knight—and Luther

35. WA 8:116 / 25–125 / 17; 128 / 1ff. The interpretation of Rom. 7 has been debated since the time of the early church. Cf. G. Bonwetsch, "Römer 7:14 in der alten Kirche und in Luthers Vorlesungen über den Römerbrief," NKZ 30 (1919): 135ff. Also P. Althaus, *Paulus und Luther über den Menschen*, 2d ed. (Gütersloh, 1951), 21ff. [LW 32:242–60.] [See P. Althaus, *The Theology of Martin Luther* (Philadelphia: Fortress Press, 1972).]

36. WA Br 2:354 / 22ff. [LW 48:255.]

37. WA TR 5, no. 5353, 82; no. 5375d, 103 / 29ff. J. Mathesius, *Ausgewählte Werke*, ed. G. Loesche (Prague, 1906), 3:74ff.

was garbed as one—easily raised suspicion. Others had to remind Luther to act his part.

Despite such outings Luther found confinement oppressive. His initial literary spurt petered out. At least it had helped to clear his thoughts on two decisive issues: that of confession, which formed the centerpiece of Catholic pastoral care, and that of the doctrine of justification. To friends in Wittenberg he composed a comforting short exposition of Psalm 37, saying, "By the grace of God I am as bold and defiant as ever. At the moment I have overcome a little ailment. It has done me no harm. But if it bites me, that would serve me right."[38] Soon his "little ailment" bit him hard, as his troubles dealt him a severe blow. During July he fell into a deep depression fed by loneliness and enforced idleness. For eight days he was in no condition to eat or to pray.[39] The fat and lazy life, as he called it, took its revenge also with sensuous torments. He wrote about it freely to Melanchthon, not hiding references to the temptation of sexual drives. His "little ailment," meanwhile, had worsened to such a degree that (writing on July 13) he resolved to travel to Erfurt and seek medical help. Fortunately Spalatin had sent him some pills, which brought relief temporarily but no lasting cure. Only in the autumn did Luther feel fit again.

Had the plague not broken out in Erfurt in midsummer and prevented him from going there, his stay at the Wartburg might have ended early, for it was in Erfurt that he eagerly hoped to resume teaching publicly. Besides, he reasoned, on that territory, controlled by [the cardinal archbishop of Mainz, one of the empire's seven electors], he would not be a burden to his own elector. Much as he had come to cherish Wittenberg, he was eager to find some open door (in Erfurt, Cologne, or elsewhere) to teach the Word. Every bit of good news from Wittenberg brought him a peculiar kind of joy, for it seemed to assure him that he was not really needed there. Repeatedly he encouraged Melanchthon to rejoice over the wealth of talented colleagues at hand and to make vigorous use of his own considerable gifts. In early September, Luther urged the Wittenberg friends to provide Melanchthon with a preaching position [in addition to his teaching post].[40]

Reflecting on his depression—in July and again several times in later months—Luther was sure he knew the cause of this physical and spiritual

38. WA 8:240 / 4ff.

39. See Luther's letters of July. [LW 48:256–57. To Melanchthon, July 13, 1521. The constipation must have caused a lesion of the anus (n. 8) as well as hemorrhoids; 48:268, 276.]

40. [LW 48:258, 262, to Melanchthon, July 13, 1521; LW 48:269, to Spalatin, July 15, 1521; LW 48:274, again, July 31.]

buffeting. Who else but Satan would contrive to destroy an instrument of God from without and within? And thus his inner struggles were compressed into experiences of an apparition of the devil, an aspect of his life on the Wartburg about which, on the strength of his "table talk," students would later circulate gruesome tales.[41] Basically these were harmless apparitions. The lofty Wartburg was exposed to the full force of the winds, and poltergeist noises might well sound like the devil throwing nuts at the ceiling from the chest on the table, or like kegs being rolled down the stairs. One night Luther even came upon a strange black dog in his bed. As in everything else Luther told about the devil's deeds and wiles, there is here hidden a fantastic reality. Luther's was a fantasy rich in imagery and knowledgeable concerning the reality of the great Enemy confronting him in a thousand disguises at every turn. To be sure, the tale of Luther hurling the inkpot at the devil is a later invention. When first told (1591), the action was even reversed and had the devil himself heaving the inkpot at Luther.[42] The ink spot became a standard feature later on, added to the walls of one after another of the houses occupied by Luther. Its presence on the Wartburg was first attested by an illustration in the Merian's *Topografie* of 1650. In any event, this tale helped to reassure the devout, who themselves have known despair, that Luther's hair-raising experiences were authentic to him.

Despite his periodic ailing and agonizing, Luther kept his sense of humor. His retort to an old opponent, Jerome Emser (1478–1527), is a case in point.[43] The two men had exchanged broadsides over the past couple of years. With sophisticated mockery Luther had poked fun at the old "mountain goat" [a *steinbok*, the mascot on Emser's coat of arms]. From Emser this drew a sharp rebuttal entitled "Quadruplica" [against the "Bull" in Wittenberg]. Challenged, Luther at first felt like asking one of his friends to respond, but changed his mind and did it himself. In a few pages he turned out one of his most agile polemics. It bore the mocking

41. WA TR 3, no. 2885, 50 / 22ff.; no. 3814, 634 / 8ff. WA TR 5, no. 5358b, 87 / 5ff. WA TR 6, no. 6816, 209 / 14ff. [LW 54, no. 3814, 280.]

42. J. Luther, *Legenden um Luther* (Berlin and Leipzig, 1933). Cf. the appendix to H. Boehmer, *Der junge Luther*, ed. H. Bornkamm, 6th ed. (Stuttgart, 1971), 353–54. [This appendix is not in the English translation of H. Boehmer, *Road to Reformation: Martin Luther to the Year 1521*, trans T. G. Tappert and J. W. Doberstein (Philadelphia: Fortress [Muhlenberg] Press, 1946).] See the references to the devil in R. H. Bainton, *Here I Stand* (Nashville: Abingdon Press, 1950), esp. 193–95.

43. [Emser, chaplain at the court of Duke George in Dresden, was a humanist when Luther first heard him lecture in Erfurt in 1504. He became chaplain to Duke George in 1509. Trained in the law as well as in theology, he became one of Luther's most bitter opponents. *Evangelisches Kirchenlexikon*, 3:420.]

and misleading title "Dr. Luther's Retraction of the Error Forced on Him by the Most Highly Learned Priest of God, Sir Jerome Emser, Vicar of Meissen."[44] Luther mingled wit and irony as he repeated his reasons for opposing Emser's attempt to limit the statement of 1 Pet. 2:9 ("You are . . . a royal priesthood") to ordained clerics. Next, feigning defeat under the cutting arguments of his opponent ("He is striking at me [and his blade goes] one ell deep into the hard rock"[45]), Luther went through the motions of a retraction. In order to dispose of his opponent completely, he then turned serious and offered a correct interpretation of the disputed text. To his great glee, the "goat" promptly fell in the trap. In his rejoinder, Emser took Luther's "recantation" at face value. Luther never followed up his successful prank, and he turned a deaf ear to his persistent accuser.

Toward other opponents, like the University of Paris faculty, Luther's mood was dead earnest and matched the gravity of the encounter. This one concerned the Leipzig disputation of 1519. Duke George's formal request of the theological faculty in Paris in two years' time brought the verdict, published on April 15, 1521.[46] His friends had hoped that the Parisians would side with Luther, although he himself had never dared hope as much. He was right. The Paris document, a compilation with commentary, seized on 104 sentences taken from Luther's writings, especially from his treatise *The Babylonian Captivity of the Church* (1520),[47] and declared them heretical. The faculty assailed Luther with strong language, the kind reserved customarily for heretics under the church's condemnation. Luther's work was seen as the resurgence of that brood of vipers and lackeys of the devil whose poison had plagued the church from of old. This godless arrogance, fumed the Parisians, was not worthy of refutation on grounds of reason but deserved for its author not only the ban but also imprisonment and ordeal by fire. The Paris verdict had been awaited with intense anticipation in many quarters, among Catholics and humanists, as well as reformers. For his part, Melanchthon attached such high importance to it that, upon receipt of a copy, he at once composed a

---

44. ["Quadruplica auff Luthers Jungst gethane antwurt, sein reformation belangend." See E. L. Enders, ed., "Luther und Emser," in *D. Martin Luthers Briefwechsel* (Frankfurt am Main, 1884ff.), 2:130–83. On the "Quadruplica," *LW* 39:227. For the writings of Luther against Emser, see *LW* 39:(107) 111–35; (139) 143–224; and for the text of this pamphlet, the last in the sequence, see *LW* 39:(227) 229–39.]

45. *WA* 8:250 / 7–8. [*LW* 39:232, 22.]

46. [Eck and Luther had agreed to entrust the decision concerning the victor at the Leipzig disputation to the universities of Erfurt and Paris. *LW* 48:258, n. 3.]

47. [*LW* 36:3–126.]

rebuttal. The verdict and Melanchthon's refutation of it reached Luther by different routes almost at the same time in mid-July. To his relief he was spared the necessity of making a reply himself, a task for which he had little relish, especially since he regarded the Paris performance as clumsy. Giving it a lower rating, he proceeded to recast it, and Melanchthon's refutation of it, into German. Indeed, it would not have been the real Luther had he simply gone along with Melanchthon's "gentler style, smoothing things over with a carpenter's plane." Instead, he seized the opportunity "to handle those crude blocks with a peasant's axe, giving them the woodsman's treatment, lest they not feel anything." To him this was a moment of reckoning with the most famous of theological faculties. It was more than a scuffle with an average opponent to whom he would simply reply in kind. Indeed, Luther saw the verdict from Paris as a sign of promise. The historic hour had come. As Luther sized up developments, God himself was providing Satan with such wretched helpers so that the Word might break through victoriously. "How that spirit of evil must tremble when he sees such a great light rising that he is powerless to put it out. The more he tries, the brighter it grows. . . . I hope that Judgment Day is at the door."[48]

Invigorated by this kind of conflict, Luther resumed work on his postil during the second half of August and progressed with it more rapidly than before. Then came a brief change of scene when for two days (August 12 and 13) restless Junker Jörg, for the first time in his life, took part in a hunt. He came away with mixed feelings over this "bittersweet sport of heroes." Colorful as the sight might be, it nevertheless pained his compassionate heart. One incident seemed to depict his own situation. When a small rabbit found refuge in the sleeve of his cloak, the pursuing hounds sniffed it out and bit it to death. He applied the lesson. "Thus the pope and Satan rage to destroy even the souls that have been saved and care nothing about my efforts."[49] An experience like this one intensified Luther's sense of loneliness in the society of knights and made him yearn for friends with whom he was at home—all the more so since he was now troubled by a question he felt obliged to discuss with others because he could not handle it alone: the question of monastic vows.

An age-old problem in the church was the celibacy of priests. Over the centuries it had undergone a basic transformation, from something practiced voluntarily to something required by canon law. The Council of

48. *WA* 8:292 / 12ff.; 294 / 10ff.
49. To Spalatin, August 15, 1521, *WA* Br 2:380 / 56ff. [*LW* 48:295.]

Nicaea, recognizing that some individuals had opted for celibacy, ruled out priestly marriage after ordination. Centuries later, the weight of reforms introduced especially by the Cluniac and Gregorian made celibacy a requirement for anyone entering the priesthood. Celibacy was being debated vehemently, transgressed a thousandfold, attacked by earnest reformers, and mocked by countless satirists, making it high on the agenda of nearly all movements seeking to renew the church. Luther himself took up the issue. Initially he raised it briefly in February 1520 in the course of his Latin refutation of the decree against him by the bishop of Meissen. He then treated it more fully in German in his soon-to-be famous address *To the Christian Nobility of the German Nation*.[50] He had already contested the church's right to force celibacy on the priesthood inasmuch as the New Testament testimony recognizes marriage as accepted and beyond reproach for those in ministerial office (1 Tim. 3:2; Titus 1:6). Therefore he himself was advising future clergy not to take the vow of celibacy and urged those currently living in concubinage to change it into an honorable and openly respected marriage. Even so, he was astonished when one of his circle of friends (Bartholomäus Bernhardi, dean of the Kemberg district) became the first to marry. Writing to Melanchthon, Luther commented with an undertone of gentle scoffing when the news reached him at the Wartburg in May, "May the Lord guide him, and blend delights into his bitter herbs (Exod. 12:8): This will be done even without my prayers."[51] The next time it happened (November 1), Luther sent his best wishes to Nicholas Gerbel, the Strassburg humanist. Compared with the monstrosities he noticed going on among the celibates, Luther considered matrimony "to be a paradise, even if it has to endure greatest poverty."[52] The thought of himself marrying was still far from his mind. "They will not push a wife on me!" he wrote to Spalatin on August 6 [when commenting on Andreas Karlstadt's recent tract on celibacy]. In December he reaffirmed his position, [assuring the vicar-general of his order, Wenceslaus Link,] "I shall remain in this cowl and manner of life, if the world does not change."[53]

Luther would have had no difficulty defending Bernhardi and others for their step into matrimony. They had good grounds, yet were summoned

50. "Ad schedulam inhibitionis sub nomine episcopi Misnensis editam," WA 6:147 / 27ff. *An den christlichen Adel deutscher Nation*, WA 6:440ff. [*LW* 44:175ff.]

51. WA Br 2:347 / 31–32. [*LW* 48:231.]

52. WA Br 2:397 / 51ff. [*LW* 48:322.] (With Enders I read line 57 "arbiter.")

53. WA Br 2:377 / 4–5; 415 / 25–26. [*LW* 48:290, 359. To Link, December 18, 1521; Link and others were alarmed over the recent exodus of friars from the community in Wittenberg.]

to appear before an ecclesiastical court. In Wittenberg the situation was already further along. There the mood was one of readiness to permit not only priests but also monks and nuns to marry. Luther was shocked. Earlier, in *To the Christian Nobility,* he had made a sharp distinction between the requirements of celibacy as imposed on priests and the vows of chastity as assumed voluntarily by monks [and nuns]. He concluded, "If they have taken this burden on themselves, then let them also carry it."[54] Luther's own reluctance to cross this frontier into freedom intensified when he received some theses and an explanatory statement drawn up in Wittenberg by Andreas Karlstadt. This restless character had sailed into the center of the controversy over vows and seemed eager to dominate it. Luther noticed at once that Karlstadt was twisting Scripture to bolster his arguments. For example, Karlstadt cited 1 Tim. 5:9ff. to prove that there should be none but married priests. Worse yet, he was giving poor advice, urging people to dare a lesser sin instead of a greater one: better to break the vow of celibacy than fall into prostitution and fornication.[55] What sort of advice was this for those seeking certainty of conscience? Luther reasoned that so long as a monk's vow of chastity was an obligation assumed voluntarily, the breaking of that vow is a sin, and there was no ready promise of liberation from it. The priest's vow of celibacy, he reasoned, is another matter, for it was a regulation imposed on the priest from without; to reject that kind of vow gave Luther no qualms. Nevertheless, the thought burdened him that so many men and women once having assumed the vow of chastity were now miserable under it. He would gladly have shown them the way out [but he was not sure what to do]. To Melanchthon he confided, "If Christ were here, I do not doubt that he would dissolve these chains and annul all vows."[56]

The longer and the more impassioned these letters from his Patmos, the closer he came to a solution. The circumstances at the Wartburg [as well as the pressure of the issue at hand] made it hardly bearable for him to be alone any longer. Involvement in this kind of literary monologue made him plot a secret meeting with chosen friends. The same letter in which he broached his scheme to Melanchthon (September 9) was also the one where he hit on a way to untie the difficult knot that was holding together the diverse strands of this complex subject. To be sure, he did not proceed from the premise that chastity as such is an impossibility.

54. *WA* 6:441 / 23–24. *WA Br* 2:370 / 2ff. [*LW* 44:175.]
55. *WA Br* 2:371 / 35ff.; 373 / 5ff. [*LW* 48:293, 279, 284.]
56. [August 3, 1521.] *WA Br* 2:375 / 58ff. [*LW* 48:279, 286.]

Were that the case, the same argument could be used, humanly speaking, for the impossibility of keeping any of God's commandments. The answer lay not on rational or practical grounds; rather, the whole issue was lodged on the "rock of conscience." Luther had already said, "We seek the scriptural basis and the testimony of God's will."[57] He thus prodded his friends to "concentrate on the root, that is, the law of the vow, and not on the fruit, or the consequences of the vow."[58] Why had he, Luther, and the other friars made their vows? They had done so to please God. The use of ascetic means to enhance their own righteousness now seemed a denial of the very gospel of God's justifying grace. The vow itself seemed a sacrilege in the presence of God. Let the vow be cast off or, if taken anew, let it be done with evangelical freedom, for Luther well knew that a person is also free to bind himself, provided that such binding is not seen as a service to God, as viewed by monasticism.

In order then to help his Wittenbergers to a little more clarity, Luther sent them for disputation a list of 139 theses which he attached to the same letter to Melanchthon. A few days later he sent an additional 141 theses. In broad categories Luther drew together the main aspects of the problem of celibacy: as seen from a Pauline understanding of law and gospel, in comparable ascetic movements outside Christendom, and in relation to the other monastic vows of poverty and obedience. Yet Luther was not concerned with celibacy by itself. As little as this issue was driving him out of the monastic life, so little was he ready to isolate it as a problem when advising others. The issue at stake was much larger: whether to live within the world or apart from it. His line of thought was determined by the highest norm governing an understanding of commitment: "We can and dare do nothing against God, but everything for God." God forces no one to forsake the cloistered life. Rather, "according to Paul, the law is not law when you keep it of your own accord, so the vow is not a vow when you keep it freely."[59] He clarified the decisive point and drew a persuasive conclusion only after prolonged personal struggle. The result impressed his friends powerfully. The letter with the accompanying theses reached Melanchthon just as he and his daily table companions were at the noon meal. One of them was John Bugenhagen, a man of mature years who had arrived in Wittenberg a half year earlier in order to resume the study of theology after having given up his post in Treptow-on-the-Rega as canon

57. WA Br 2:371 / 39ff. [LW 48:279. To Melanchthon, August 1, 1521.]
58. WA Br 2:383 / 44–45. [LW 48:299. To Melanchthon, September 9, 1521.]
59. WA 8:326 / 7; 331 / 23–24.

and school director. Reading the theses carefully several times, and then pondering them, he exclaimed, "This will transform public life. Any teaching prior to these theses could not have done so." To which Melanchthon added, "This is the real beginning of the freeing of the monks."[60]

The voice of the man in banishment, silenced for a while, was again being heard and heeded even beyond Wittenberg. Already in June his vigorous protest against the papal Antichrist (the reply to Ambrosius Catharinus, the Dominican, which Luther had completed just before his journey to Worms) had appeared all over Germany and beyond its borders as well. From Brussels, for example, Jerome Aleander (serving the Roman curia and responsible for carrying out the Edict of Worms against Luther) sent a copy to the papal vice-chancellor, Julius de Medici, in Florence.[61] Luther's writings from the Wartburg would have followed this one in rapid succession had not the workload of the printers in Wittenberg become so heavy. Impatiently Luther waited for the galley proofs and began to scold his own printer, Grunenberg, for sloppy work. At last, in September and October his publications began to appear. In various quarters expectations had been running high. The mere notice that a tract of Luther's on confession had gone to press was enough to prompt the Franciscans in Weimar, as early as August 15—and on authorization of their general chapter—to solicit Elector Frederick's backing for a projected assault on Luther. While these negotiations were in progress, they assured Duke John of Saxony, the elector's brother—holding court in Weimar at that time—that their intentions were on the right track. They argued, was not the command of Jesus to the ten lepers a validation of auricular confession when he commanded them, "Go and show yourselves to the priests" (Luke 17:14)? Lest there be any misunderstanding on his own part, Duke John made use of a stopover in Eisenach in order to request of Luther an exposition of this Lukan passage. Quite by coincidence the duke there stumbled on the whereabouts of Luther, whose incognito status had been strictly maintained. Communication between the duke and the illustrious captive had to be mediated through the warden of the Wartburg.[62] Luther responded readily, although it required him to rearrange his work on the postil, skipping from the Epiphany season to the fourteenth Sunday after Trinity. Besides, by so doing he counted on providing "his dear Germans with a

60. WA 8:317.
61. WA 7:700.
62. CR 1:449. Suppl. Mel. 6 / 1 (1926): 154. MSA 7 / 1:129ff. MBW 160. WA Br 2:391 / 5. G. Mentz, Johann Friedrich der Grossmütige 1503–1554 (Jena, 1903), 1:33, assumes that the duke saw Luther, but this is uncertain. [See LW 48:313.]

foretaste from the middle of the barrel of his postil. "[63] The silly and forced allegorizing in the customary expositions of this passage induced Luther to make sport of his attackers and flush out their claims like game chased in a hunt. He then came with his own exposition, psychologically and spiritually so rich that this particular sermon became a model of combined polemical and religious power. As requested, Spalatin had one of the secretaries at the elector's court prepare a fair copy for the duke and then sent the manuscript off to the printer's. Spalatin also sent with it Luther's dedication, dated September 17, which named Hugold von Einsiedel, Hans von Dolzig, and Bernhard von Hirschfeld—the evangelically minded councillors at the elector's court—who in this subtle way became linked to the outlaw.

A life in hiding now seemed but another way of making Luther a power to be reckoned with. His writings proved it. An incident suddenly brought him out, as it were, fully armed. The opponent was Albrecht of Mainz, cardinal archbishop and a man ever in need of money. Once again he had hired John Tetzel to sell indulgences and replenish his low supply of cash. The faithful were urged to view an exhibit of precious relics from the outstanding collection in the Stiftskirche, the endowed church in Albrecht's city of Halle. For the devout this was a rare chance to earn an enormous indulgence.[64] Already in 1520 Albrecht had published an elaborate catalog. Prefaced by a splendid engraving of the cardinal himself by Albrecht Dürer, the catalog told the pilgrims about the treasures they would see. From a pinch of soil out of which Adam had been created to a pair of breeches of Saint Thomas à Becket of Canterbury, the devout viewer was promised a wide choice of relics. The selection was astonishing: manna, branches from the burning bush that confronted Moses, some vials of the Virgin Mary's milk, two jugs and a quantity of the miraculous wine from the wedding in Cana, bones and other remains of each of the apostles (of Peter alone, forty-three pieces), the finger Thomas placed in the pierced side of Jesus, the finger of John the Baptist which pointed to Jesus as the Lamb of God, a thumb of Saint Ann the grandmother of Jesus, nine thorns from Christ's crown, among them one "which separated itself from others in the presence and testimony of many people," and even the "true Holy Body of Christ which he offered in death to his heavenly Father"—transubstantiated flesh of Christ. This exhibit surpassed any-

63. WA 8:337. [LW 48:312ff.]
64. A. Wolters, Der Abgott zu Halle, 1521–1542 (Bonn, 1877). G. von Térey, Cardinal Albrecht von Brandenburg und das Heiligtumsbuch von 1520 (Strasbourg, 1892).

thing to be seen elsewhere. According to the "sacred catalog" no less than 8,933 items were listed, including forty-two entire bodies of saints. Together they offered an aggregate indulgence of unimaginable magnitude: a release from 39,245,120 years and 220 days in purgatory, besides an additional 6,540,000 quadragenes (or "forties," being indulgences merited by a forty-day practice of penance). This brazen renewal of the old evil stirred up violent resentment among the general public. Adding fuel to this mood was the imprisonment of several married clergy on Albrecht's orders. While the cardinal archbishop himself appears to have lived beyond reproach, he was known to have permitted others to live in concubinage— for a handsome fee.

Luther anonymously vented his indignation in a satirical pamphlet against the newest indulgence traffic. The pamphlet appeared on St. Martin's Day (November 11) and threw down the gauntlet to the members of the Stiftskirche chapter, challenging them, "Despise my demand, and I'll begin a game for which you'll find Halle too small."[65] Who knows whether the frivolous yet fearful cardinal sensed the lion's claw in this challenge, or whether he was apprehensive lest Luther himself speak up. At any rate, Albrecht made a precautionary move. In haste he dispatched two trusted conciliators to Wittenberg in order to forestall any threatening storm. This one was Albrecht's cathedral chaplain and chancellor, humanist Wolfgang Capito (1472–1541), who at the moment was still making up his mind whether to continue in the cardinal's service or to follow his own inclination and embrace reform. The second was Albrecht's personal physician, Heinrich Stromer von Auerbach, a man whom Luther had come to respect ever since their friendly meeting in Leipzig, at the time of the debate with John Eck, when Auerbach had invited Luther to dine with him. On September 30, in Melanchthon's house, after much beating around the bush, the two conciliators divulged their assignment: Would Melanchthon kindly exert a moderating influence on Luther's vehemence? They wrapped their request in neat examples and precedents drawn from antiquity, reasoning that Luther stood a better chance of achieving his aims by exercising caution than by other means. Melanchthon reported to Spalatin in detail, saying that he had given the overture a friendly but firm rejection. He was aware how people would be judging this latest indulgence flareup. Some would regard Luther as evil, others would think him foolish. Melanchthon himself was satisfied that Luther was approaching the issue with wisdom and a clean conscience and that he was called of

65. *Suppl.Mel*.6 / 1:164–65.

God for the task at hand. No single individual, Melanchthon reasoned, could be carrying so many people with him were he not propelled by the Spirit of God. Besides, Luther had so far not abused anyone, except some sophists—those scholastics who were the arch-opponents of all humanists. And even if Luther were to broaden his attack, the times evidently required the most severe remedies. As Melanchthon assessed the situation, no one besides Luther was teaching the gospel; indeed, no one in a thousand years had been setting forth the gospel with such blessed results. Critics, he contended, should permit Luther to continue under the guidance of the Spirit and not themselves oppose the will of God. The issue is not to be judged by human standards, for the gospel is preached as an offense to the godless and as a call to the sheep of Israel to turn back. Having noted in the request of the two emissaries from Halle that their lord, the cardinal archbishop of Mainz, would not himself proceed against the movement of reform, Melanchthon remained skeptical. He knew that Albrecht had already published the Edict of Worms, a copy of which he just happened to have at hand. An extended theological conversation at table and on a long walk helped Melanchthon and Capito come closer to agreement, however, the Wittenberger realizing that Capito was caught in an embarrassing bind and was actually better suited for quiet study than for devious diplomacy.[66] The two emissaries had better luck the following day when they visited the elector's court, where they were promised energetic steps to influence Luther. Indeed, to Duke John's court at Weimar, Albrecht sent his personal physician, Dr. Stromer. His mission found support from Simon Pistoris, the envoy of Duke George of Saxony, who happened to be there.

Luckily Luther seemed unaware of the cardinal's scheming. For a man like Albrecht, serving then as chief chancellor of the empire, these lamentable moves to secure mercy from the outlawed Reformer and his friends verged on the comic. Lucky too that Capito, having failed to persuade Melanchthon, never mailed the letter in which he had mingled sage advice and brash threats.[67] Even without an opportunity to see the notorious catalog of indulgences, Luther became amply wrought up by reports coming to him about Albrecht's desperate venture. As he declared to Spalatin on October 7, he would not allow himself to be restrained from proceeding privately or publicly against the "idolatrous man from Mainz." Again in full health, Luther went indefatigably to work and, by November 1,

66. *CR* 1:462ff. *Suppl. Mel.* 6 / 1:164. *MSA* 7 / 1:143ff. *MBW* 175.
67. *WA Br* 2:393. [*LW* 48:316–17.]

finished his sharp polemic *Against the Idol at Halle*. Before he could send the manuscript off, however, a letter from Spalatin arrived containing the elector's prohibition against Luther's writing anything against Albrecht of Mainz. This so angered Luther that at first he decided not to reply at all. Then, on November 11, he mailed the manuscript to Spalatin. The accompanying letter was beautifully aboil with wrath:

> I would rather lose you, the sovereign himself, and the whole world [than be quiet]. If I have resisted [the] creator, the pope, why should I yield to his creature? Your idea about not disturbing the public peace is fine, but will you allow the eternal peace of God to be disturbed by the wicked and sacrilegious actions of that son of perdition? Not so, Spalatin! Not so, Elector![68]

Luther dared Spalatin to prevent the publication of this manuscript. Nevertheless Spalatin published it, because he was bound to the elector's orders.

During the same October weeks Luther took up a still more significant work, this time on the mass. Since July he recognized that alongside the vow of celibacy loomed the mass. As such it was the second big issue in Wittenberg among the proponents of church renewal. It had come up superficially in some theses Karlstadt had prepared for a baccalaureate disputation on July 19. Among the theses was this one: Whoever receives only the bread at Holy Communion commits a sin. It is therefore better not to partake at all than to be communed in one kind only.[69] Writing to Melanchthon on August 1, Luther immediately rejected this exaggerated demand of Karlstadt's. Instead he argued that Christ had instituted the Lord's Supper under both kinds—bread and wine—and that the currently customary form [as practiced in the mass], is nowhere in Scripture declared a sin. Whoever contrary to his own wishes receives only the bread and not the cup commits no sin. In any case, Luther claimed that had he been allowed to return directly from Worms to Wittenberg he would have preferred to restore the Supper to the manner as instituted by Christ. At the same time, Luther announced that he would forever abstain from celebrating private masses (that is, any mass not for the congregation but for a private purpose, such as a secret mass read for the dead and which, as a rule, involved no communing of members of the congregation). He saw such masses as sacrifices pure and simple, and these comprised the host of daily masses (as said in churches and chapels). Luther's comments, born of

68. WA Br 2:402 / 6ff. [*LW* 48:326. Also the Excursus, 344–50, and its comment (349) regarding the text in WA 10²:105ff.]

69. H. Barge, *Andreas Bodenstein von Karlstadt* (Leipzig, 1905), 1:290–91.

intense conviction, put the emphasis where it belonged in the first place: on the transformation of the divine gift of grace, present in the Supper, into a great sacrifice of reconciliation.

Although Luther had thereby rejected the exaggerated conclusions of Karlstadt, he nevertheless phrased his letter in a way that gave direction to the ongoing discussion in Wittenberg about the issues of the cup and of the sacrifice. The Wittenbergers thus felt themselves cleared to take further steps. At any rate, there could be no more doubt about the basic question. Already in 1519, and with growing clarity, Luther had attacked the prevailing doctrine and practice of the mass. His treatise on the *Babylonian Captivity of the Church* had been directed especially toward freeing the Supper from its own kind of captivity, that is, from the denial of the cup to the laity. So far Luther had avoided the subject of changes in the order of divine worship, such as had emerged from his criticism of the mass as sacrifice. For the time being he had been content merely to encourage a proper usage of existing forms.

It was not surprising, however, that Luther's friends in Wittenberg readily fell in line when Gabriel Zwilling, one of Luther's colleagues in the local Augustinian cloister, delivered a series of stormy sermons demanding the abolition of the mass in its traditional form. On Michaelmas, Sunday, September 29, Melanchthon and his students for the first time received Communion in both kinds in the Town Church. Melanchthon himself did not miss a single one of Zwilling's sermons. The little one-eyed Augustinian drew a large part of Wittenberg, especially its students, into his following. His sermons, gathering strength, increased in an impassioned crescendo from one Sunday to the next. But what made them remarkable was the consistency with which they applied the essentials of Luther's thought, for Zwilling was concerned about the mass as such and not simply about its form. The mass is not a sacrifice, but rather the pledge and token of our salvation and thus derives its meaning from the fact that bread and wine as signs of grace are actually received by the congregation. Private masses and a mere veneration of the elements amount to no more than idolatry and must therefore be abolished. The visible effect of this bold zeal is reflected in the letter of a student from Silesia who, on October 8, wrote home: "God has raised up a second prophet among us, a monk of the same order [as Luther], who is proclaiming the gospel so purely and honestly that everyone is calling him the second Martin." This student expressed a deep concern that his parents still imagined they were serving God by adoring the elements. And even Melanchthon, on the very next day, appealed to Luther's old friend in

Nuremberg, Wenceslaus Link (vicar-general of the German Augustinian congregation) not to oppose but if possible to approve the movement now under way that aimed to change the mass back into the Supper of the assembled congregation.

In Melanchthon's eyes, private masses were now mere theatrics.[70] He and his students (and probably some of the townspeople as well) would from now on at times celebrate the Supper in its New Testament simplicity: The words of institution, hitherto read silently by the priest and inaudible to the assembled congregation, were now spoken audibly and probably in German, giving content and meaning to what Christ had instituted. Bread and wine were both distributed. Others, however, could not help but follow these developments with mounting anxiety. Conrad Helt, prior of the Augustinian cloister, was forced by his fellow monks to make a difficult choice: to relax the obligation of all to say mass daily (instead of allowing only two or three of the brothers to celebrate, while permitting the rest to commune in both kinds), or to abolish the mass entirely. Helt decided for what seemed to him the lesser of two evils, and suspended the celebration of mass pending a decision by the elector and by the superiors of his order. Long before this, however, Gregory Brück, the electoral chancellor, reported on October 8 to his sovereign, then in Lochau, informing him of an incident threatening worse things to come. When, a couple of days earlier, mendicants from St. Anthony's cloister in Lichtenberg, near Prettin, had come to town on one of their customarily audacious begging tours, students mocked them by pelting them with clods and stones. Such reaction was not surprising, for the mendicancy of the monks was particularly unpopular among students, most of whom were themselves forced to live frugally.[71] The elector lost no time. Forthwith he ordered the university and the chapter of his Castle Church to prepare for him an opinion on the issue of the mass. Meanwhile, his chancellor, Brück, underestimated the seriousness of the situation and jested that the restless Wittenberg monks would soon feel the pinch in kitchen and cellar if they refused to conduct mass.

Public discussion went on and reached its high point in a disputation on October 17. Two students have left us vivid reports. Karlstadt, officiating as dean of the theological faculty, had again prepared a long list of the-

---

70. Sebastian Helmann to John Hess, October 8, 1521; printed in N. Müller, *Die Wittenberger Bewegung 1521 und 1522*, 2d ed. (Leipzig, 1911), 16–17. On Melanchthon, ibid., 22–23. *Suppl. Mel.* 6 / 1:163–64. *MSA* 7 / 1:141ff. *MBW* 173.

71. The following is based on Müller, *Wittenberger Bewegung*, 19ff.

ses.[72] In some way they reflected Luther's position. Yet their main emphasis once again was on the manner in which the laity should be given the cup. Besides, Karlstadt continued to waver on the issue of private or secret masses. The latter, he thought, could even be a means of encouraging the desired goal of Communion under both kinds by any laity present, and that with a minimum of change. Yet he failed to recognize that a secret mass and a private Communion have little in common besides the name. He simply got himself into a bind over the question raised by the Augustinians. The result was a remarkable exchange of roles, brought on, to be sure, by the tensions raised in the course of the disputation. A Karlstadt otherwise so zealous for reform had suddenly become a Karlstadt opposed to abolishing the mass. Moreover, from his lectern he promised to pay a guilder to anyone able to provide sound argument from Scripture in favor of the abolition of the mass. Recognizing the gravity of the case, he argued that it would not be right to act hastily or without the approval of the town council. Melanchthon was not about to accept such temporizing. He had the Augustinians on his side as he argued: If Paul abolished circumcision, then one also had the right to alter the mass. Enough has been preached in Wittenberg, in this latter-day Capernaum. The time for action had come, he asserted. The Augustinians had done well to suspend the mass in their own cloister church. Besides, what business is that of the town council? Let him who has laid his hand to the plow not look back.

In the following days the disputation, as well as the evening discussions led by a committee comprising members from the Castle Church chapter, helped to straighten out the differences between the two leaders, Karlstadt and Melanchthon. The requested opinion, presented to the elector on October 20, showed the committee siding with the Augustinians on all the decisive points. It requested urgently that "abuses of the mass be removed soon and promptly from the lands and principalities of Your Electoral Grace."[73] On one point only did the committee side with Karlstadt, and that was in his wish—for the sake of the weak—to retain a while longer the individual communions of the priests, meaning the private mass in form but not in substance. On the main questions, though, the committee rejected the notion of the mass as a sacrifice and a good

72. Albert Burer to Beatus Rhenanus, October 19, 1521, and Felix Ulscenius to Wolfgang Fabricius Capito, October 23, 1521. Printed in Müller, *Wittenberger Bewegung*, 33–34, 47–48. Barge, *Karlstadt*, 1:316ff., 484ff. K. Müller, *Luther und Karlstadt: Stücke aus ihrem gegenseitigen Verhältnis untersucht* (Tübingen, 1907), 10ff. Also K. Müller, *Kirche, Gemeinde und Obrigkeit nach Luther* (Tübingen, 1910), 87ff.

73. Müller, *Wittenberger Bewegung*, 35. *CR* 1:469. *MBW* 174.

work and came out decisively in favor of giving the cup to the laity. There was but one dissenting opinion, that of the professor of theology, John Dölsch—often called Dr. Feldkirch, the name of his home town. He had signed the formal opinion of the committee, but he had also drawn up his own dissenting opinion in order to dissociate himself from the Augustinians and to put in a word defending broadly the notion of the mass as a sacrifice and also the reading of masses for the departed. The devout elector was visibly moved by this powerful appeal to conscience on the part of his university's leading minds. Yet characteristically he could not bring himself to move quickly. In his rescript of October 25 he cautioned against any hasty change in the mass, a form of worship so many centuries old. Besides, he recalled how the large numbers of endowed masses provided substantial revenue for the support of the churches and cloisters of his territory. He therefore urged that dissension be avoided. His anxieties returned and intensified when, on October 30, Conrad Helt, as prior of the Wittenberg Augustianians, sent the elector a complaint about their behavior. The sore point was All Saints, the Castle Church. Most of its canons—opposing their dean, Justus Jonas (1493–1555), a proponent of reform—complained bitterly to the elector against the suspension of masses in the Augustinian cloister. Some of the chapter members also complained about the sharp utterances of Zwilling and his attack on the monastic life as a whole. On November 12, Prior Helt reported that thirteen of his monks had quit the monastery and the cowl. In Wittenberg, moreover, two issues burned as one: the mass and the monastic vow. All Saints Church was divided and the Augustinian cloister was in dissolution.

When Luther got wind of these developments in Wittenberg he was deeply moved. In the abolition of the mass and the abandonment of the cloister there ripened the first visible fruits of his long conflict with the Roman church and its forms of life—a conflict, now public, he had first experienced in his own heart. He wondered, however, whether the brethren in Wittenberg would be able to sustain what they had begun. "It is indeed a remarkably great undertaking to resist such a long-established custom and the opinion of all men, to suffer patiently their accusation, judgment, and condemnation, and to stand immovable in the face of such a storm of winds and waves." Recollections of his own tormented conscience returned. "How often did my heart hang in suspense, punish me, and reproach me with its single strongest argument: Are you the only wise man? Can it be that all others are in error and have erred for so long a time? What if you are mistaken and lead so many people into error who might all be eternally damned?" This was surely not simply a contest of human wills. This was an issue of accountability before God, of a conscience at peace in the hour of death. "For such consciences must be treated with faith and trust, so that we not only look on the judgment of the whole world as straw and chaff, but also in death may be adept in fighting against the devil and all his might, even against the judgment of God." Would his fellow Augustinians in Wittenberg be able to hold out against the storms that as yet were only beginning? So far Luther had borne virtually all by himself this entire burden of conscience. Bearing it also for others was an experience that revealed one thing needful above all others. He confessed: "Christ with his clear, unmistakable Word steadied and confirmed me, so that my heart no longer quails, but resists the arguments of the papists, as a rocky shore resists the waves, and laughs at their threats and blasts."[74]

It is characteristic of Luther that in dealing with Catholicism at two points—the mass and monasticism—so decisive for its very life, his two pivotal writings convey not a polemical intention but a pastoral intention. Therefore, his treatise *The Misuse of the Mass* was written with the intention of providing his brethren in the Wittenberg cloister with solid ground for transforming the mass into the supper of the congregation. His approach was therefore comprehensive. In a manner similar to the witty polemic against Emser, Luther began by disclosing the unbiblical character of the Catholic priesthood and episcopal office. To him it was clear that the New Testament speaks neither of clergy nor of a monarchical episcopate covering a larger ecclesiastical territory. As he saw it, the New Testament instead speaks of various local churches and of a number of bishops, that is, of elders charged with overseeing the congregation's affairs. Proceeding from the basis of this critique of the Roman concept of the church, Luther launched his attack on the mass. He is not interested chiefly in striking at the absurdity of the assumptions or at the ahistorical character of the ceremonies surrounding the mass. Rather, he intends to deal with its very essence, according to which the sacrament as Christ instituted it has been changed into its opposite: from God's promise into a human work; from Christ's testament and witness (which we may receive) into a sacrifice (which we present) to God. Now every sacrifice presupposes a

74. [Luther's Latin text, *De abroganda missa privata M. Lutheri sententia*, 1521.] WA 8:411–12. Bornkamm cites Luther's own German translation from the Latin original, *Vom Missbrauch der Messen*, 1521. WA 8:482–563, *loc. cit.*, 482 / 20ff., 32ff.; 483 / 12ff. [See *The Misuse of the Mass*, the English translation from Luther's German text in *LW* (36:133–230) 36:133, 134.]

god who must be appeased. Yet the Lord's Supper itself proclaims a reconciled and gracious God. Every sacrifice, moreover, is clouded by the uncertainty about whether it is acceptable to God. This, Luther claims, is what makes the mass so extremely dangerous for souls. We cannot offer God his own will and testament. We can only accept it in gratitude and faith. For God's gift of grace is the forgiveness of sin, and indeed we can accept it only for ourselves and not for somebody else, certainly not in a private mass for the dead. In that connection, the alleged appearances of deceased people posed a problem. Many a legend about the saints told of certain departed souls returning and begging that their full redemption be assisted by masses for the dead. Luther called this sort of thing devil's mischief. Yet he took it seriously in order that this medieval—and often also modern?—superstition be removed and replaced with a genuine religious perception. "Try this," he wrote his Augustinian brothers. "Show your true faith, and you will see that these same ghosts will desist at once from their mischief and foolishness."[75] This perversion of the gospel in the mass made Luther burn. His mood of anger reached uncommon heat as he took the papacy to task. All ten commandments, he charged, have been twisted into their opposite by the papacy. Yet Luther's practical proposals appear strangely cautious as he played for time. Even if the surest thing were to give up the mass entirely, he said, and to return to the testament of Christ as instituted by him, the time is not ripe for such a general transformation. Let the existing forms remain a while longer, especially for the sake of those among his Augustinian brethren in Wittenberg who do not yet fully grasp the new situation. If individual priests celebrate or commune not with an eye to the stipend paid by the faithful nor to the priestly office but solely with a heart hungering for forgiveness, so let it be. Besides, in the case of private masses, let the bread be distributed. For his Wittenberg—to which it was given "to see the pure and primal face of the gospel"—Luther, however, could only wish that the mass be given up completely.[76] What Luther was writing during that second half of November—initially in Latin and then rendering it immediately into German—was intended to make a twofold impact on the movement in Wittenberg. It should bring clarity and strength to those whose personal conviction rejected the mass, and bring moderation and caution to those who would coerce a reform of worship.

"I have decided to attack monastic vows," Luther informed Spalatin on November 11. This was the other of the two burning issues on which he

75. WA 8:455 / 10–11; 535, 7ff.
76. WA 8:475 / 9ff.; 476 / 18–19; 561 / 7ff.; 562 / 27–28.

was working almost simultaneously, and his announced intention was in the letter accompanying the completed Latin manuscript, *De Abroganda Missa*. The subject had occupied him ever since his exchange of letters with Melanchthon and his theses on monastic vows. Already then, probably in mid-September, he had once again taken up the subject in his treatment of the gospel for the festival of the Epiphany, which he really loaded with attacks on the medieval church and its popular piety. Consequently this sermon became the longest in the postil.[77] Then, in the letter of November 1 to the humanist Nicholas Gerbel in Strassburg, Luther not only gave a quick rundown on his literary accomplishments thus far at the Wartburg, but also confided that between himself and Melanchthon a scheme was under way. "For Philipp and I have a powerful conspiracy concerning the vows of monks and priests. They have to be abolished and made void."[78] Presently, however, there were reaching him vague rumors that more Augustinian brethren in Wittenberg were abandoning the cowl. He was "afraid that they might have done this with a conscience not sufficiently sure." This fear "has wrested out of me this little book."[79] Completed in about ten days, the 120-page treatise shows no trace of hastiness. What he set down so rapidly was simply the result of a protracted coming to terms with his own youth as well as a painstakingly balanced attempt to point out to other struggling people a reliable way to freedom.

The book was intensely personal. Its long letter of dedication was addressed to his father and attached to the completed manuscript on November 21. This letter must be reckoned among the great historical documents on the confrontation between fathers and sons. Luther's memory of his entrance into the cloister was bound up with the most painful breach in his life, acting contrary to his father's hopes for him. Indeed, for a long time his father had withheld consent, giving it later only with greatest reluctance. So the memory of it all continued to burn within him unquenchably. As Luther celebrated his first mass his father still entertained doubts about the events two years previously. Had his son really heard the voice of God speaking in the storm? His father had reproached him for violating the obedience a child owes his parent. Belatedly now (1521) Luther confessed to his father, "You suddenly retorted with a reply so fitting and so much to the point that I have hardly ever in all my life heard any man say anything that struck me so forcibly and stayed with me

77. WA 10¹ 1:555–728. [*LW* 48:328; 52:268 (sermon).]

78. WA Br 2:397 / 47–48. [*LW* 48:321. *The Judgment of Martin Luther on Monastic Vows, 1521, LW* 44:251–400.]

79. To Spalatin, November 22, 1521. WA Br 2:404 / 6ff. [*LW* 48:337, esp. n. 4.]

so long." After a lapse of sixteen years, the hour had come for Luther to confess to his father how hard of hearing he had been and to admit with humble pride how much good the merciful God in heaven had nevertheless allowed to spring from his own errors and sins. "Would you not rather have lost a hundred sons than not to have seen this good? I think that from my childhood Satan must have foreseen something in me [which is the cause] of what he must now suffer. He has therefore raged against me with incredible cunning to destroy or hinder me, so that I have often wondered whether I was the only man in the world he was seeking." Luther can no longer recognize his father's authority over him, although paternal concern would even now like to see the son quit the monastic life and marry. There is another who has taken precedence over his father. "He who has taken me out of the monastery has an authority over me that is greater than yours." "He is himself (as they say) my immediate bishop, abbot, prior, lord, father, and teacher; I know no other. Thus I hope that he has taken from you one son in order that he may begin to help the sons of many others through me."[80]

Luther now sensed that his suffering in the cloister, his agonizing to be liberated from his vows, had a vicarious aspect. This probably accounts for his great care in structuring this treatise and undergirding its basis. He later called it the "best fortified" of all his books.[81] In treating the cardinal points at issue, Luther followed the general line his correspondence and theses had taken in September [see above, pp. 29–30]: Monastic vows are contrary to the faith on which alone our relationship to God can stand. It is and remains God's power "to be the wind that blows over the grasslike vows and their bloom—he lets the grass dry up and the blossoms fade."[82] But Luther pursued his theme according to a well-developed design. Vows are contrary to the Word of God, which knows nothing of the Catholic distinction between commandments and mere counsels for a life of higher perfection, namely, the monastic vows. These vows run counter to Christian liberty according to which there can be vows freely taken yet revocable and not legally binding. These vows break God's commandments, especially that of love, because they remove from a monk the pos-

80. WA 8:574 / 5ff.; 575 / 23ff., 35; 576 / 16ff. On the events of 1505 and 1507, see Boehmer, Der junge Luther, 41–42, 46. [Eng. trans., Road to Reformation, 33–35, 40–43. LW 48:332, 333, 335. LW 44:251–400. The Judgment of Martin Luther on Monastic Vows, 1521.]

81. WA 8:569 (munitissimus). On the authority of his father over him, see Bornkamm, "Luther und sein Vater," ZThK 66 (1969): 38ff. Reprinted in Bornkamm, Luther, 11ff. [LW 44:245ff.]

82. WA 8:595 / 1–2. [LW 44:279–80.]

sibility of fulfilling his duties of love toward his parents or his fellow human beings. Yet love is the judge of all our deeds. "Therefore we can keep our vows, but we are not obliged to do so inasmuch as love is our sole obligation."[83] These vows are meaningless in the light of reason; promises that are untenable lose their power. This applies to the person for whom celibacy has become too great a burden, especially since chastity, required of all people by God, can be practiced better in the married estate. So then, Luther perceives how a direct conflict can arise between the chastity required by God and the celibacy vowed by man. "If one keeps the commandment but is unable to keep the vow, then vows must go so that commandments remain."[84] At the moment, Luther had no desire to make this breaking of vows a general rule. Whoever would and can keep his vows, let him do so, just as he himself was doing it—"I am still a monk and yet not a monk."[85] The main thing is that the liberty of Christ is maintained: "A vow of celibacy is made for the sake of man, not man for the sake of a vow of celibacy. Therefore, the Son of man is also Lord of the vow and of celibacy."[86] Luther himself enlarges on the issue of celibacy mainly for the sake of others. For himself celibacy is only part of a larger problem. At thirty-eight years of age, he could well have considered starting a family of his own, but for him such personal use of freedom still lay a few years ahead. The thing that bore down on him most heavily in monasticism was something else. "In my life as monk I experienced nothing more painful than the cruelty and frivolity of having denied love. And no one was ever able to convince me, so that I could quite believe it, that this monastic obedience which raves so shamefully against love is right and permitted"[87]—wherefore his wish that by dedicating this treatise to him a son might heal the old wound in his father's heart. He desired above all to render a service of love which he knew was due. In fact, Luther's treatise made public a great piece of confessional counsel. Its intent was to comfort and strengthen the conscience and not simply to launch a public debate. It pointed also toward the agonizing hour of death and the summons to appear before the judgment seat of Christ, that ultimate moment "when no matter how bitterly they may have fought us people must let go of us." Therefore he closed with the wise advice that anyone intending to quit the cloister should first examine his conscience thoroughly. Let no one feel

83. *WA* 8:664 / 30. [*LW* 44:395.]
84. *WA* 8:632 / 29. [*LW* 44:341.]
85. *WA* 8:575 / 28–29. [*LW* 48:335.]
86. *WA* 8:665 / 10ff.
87. *WA* 8:625 / 20ff. [*LW* 44:330.]

guilty later for having taken it as though "lured by the novelty of it all or as doing it out of a contempt or hatred of people."[88]

In these same November days—while writing on monastic vows—Luther also brought the first part of his postil to a preliminary conclusion. It was his most inclusive production so far, and he had taken it up periodically as a change of pace during his enforced confinement. From the beginning it had been on his Wartburg agenda,[89] but work on it awaited the arrival from Wittenberg of his Latin postil for Advent.[90] Originally he had intended to translate the already completed Latin portion into German. While waiting, he set to work in early June on an exposition of the Christmas pericopes. By mid-September he had apparently reached those for Epiphany. From time to time he kept sending completed portions to Wittenberg. By mid-October some parts had even been turned over to the printer, an action which greatly annoyed Luther, for he had left express instructions not to use the printer Grunenberg, who had badly bungled his manuscript on confession. Various urgent matters preoccupied Luther, so that only on November 19 could he write the dedicatory preface to Count Albert of Mansfeld. It went under a covering letter to Spalatin on November 22 with the request to hold it until the postil was completed. Luther evidently had in mind making a single German book of the translated Latin Advent postil and the recently completed Christmas postil. The Wittenberg friends, however, having received the Christmas materials, brought these out as a separate book. This was followed by a second one containing the Advent pericopes on which Luther continued to work from late November until the end of February. This accounts for the odd inversion that the Christmas postil came out in early March and the Advent postil followed about six weeks later.

It is regrettable that Luther's church postil—intended to cover the entire church year—ended here. Overloaded by many duties, he had to leave it to others to take down and edit his preached sermons. He hardly overstated the case when, in 1527, he called the Wartburg postil his best book.[91] This verdict holds despite the fact that still later he reproached himself for having been too wordy.[92] True enough, yet the wordiness con-

---

88. WA 8:668 / 35ff.; 669 / 5ff.

89. Above, p. 3.

90. Latin Postille (Advent pericope), WA 7:463–537. [See LW 52.]

91. WA 23:278 / 13. ["Dass diese Worte Christi, 'Das is mein leib' noch fest stehen" (1527).]

92. WA TR 1, no. 965, 488 / 24ff. To Gerbel, November 27, 1535, WA Br 7:329 / 3ff., esp. 323 / 14ff.

tributes a certain charm. When read alongside his Wartburg writings, the postil shows—as does none of the other writings—that it became an unnamed friend to him, one in whom he could confide those matters that moved him in his "wilderness." So the postil became the recipient of his heart's spiritual riches. To be sure, he seldom made reference to any of his day-to-day experiences or struggles. Yet the postil contains an incomparable reflection of his thoughts and observations on nearly all theological questions, even to the discovery of America or vivid comments on the chicken yard.[93] In none of his books is the whole Luther so engagingly present as in that portion of his postil which he did entirely on his own. In contrast to most of his other works where haste is evident, the postil radiates an atmosphere of composure and enjoyment. His exposition of the texts seemed to proceed in the way he sought it for the Christmas gospel: Let the gospel play on the heart as the sun plays on a placid pond. "So if you wish to be illumined and warmed and to see God's mercy and wondrous deeds, so that your heart is filled with fire and light and becomes reverent and joyous, then go where you may be still and impress the picture deep into your heart. There you will find no end of wondrous deeds."[94] Already at the end of his Christmas postil Luther was justified in hoping that "in these twelve epistles and gospels the Christian life may have been so fully depicted that more than enough has been said to the Christian about what is necessary for salvation."[95] Thereby he hinted at the real purpose of his postil. It was not to be a collection of model sermons. It contained no sermons actually preached, but rather expositions that (like homilies in the ancient church) followed the thread of a text. They were in the main intended for private reading, whether to stimulate the preacher or to edify the faithful. By this device, Luther rerouted the aim of the medieval monastic postil in a grander direction. And yet his expositions in the postil were simply a means to a higher end:

> Would to God that my exposition and that of all doctors might perish and each Christian himself make the Scriptures and God's pure word his norm. You can tell by my verbosity how immeasurably more powerful God's words are in comparison to any human word, how no single man is able to fathom sufficiently any one word of God and expound it with many words. It is an infinite word and must be contemplated and grasped with a quiet mind. . . . And so, my dear Christians, get to it, and let my exposition and that of all the doctors

93. Cf. W. Köhler, in *WA* 10[1] 1:vii–viii. [See also R. Bainton, *The Martin Luther Christmas Book* (Philadelphia, 1948), 10ff., 35ff.]

94. *WA* 10[1] 1:62 / 11ff. [*LW* 52:8–9.]

95. *WA* 10[1] 1:728 / 6ff. [*LW* 52:286.]

be no more than a scaffold, an aid for the construction of the true building, so that we may ourselves grasp and taste the pure and simple word of God and abide in it.[96]

Presently there came a pause, and restlessness seized him. On November 25 he had finished a German translation of his treatise on the mass (*The Misuse of the Mass*) [above, p. 23]. He may have felt the fatigue that comes at the end of much writing. The program he had set for himself after entering the Wartburg was done, and so too the tasks meanwhile thrust on him from the outside. He had treated decisive issues of church practice: confession, the mass, celibacy, monastic vows, and on these he had formed conclusions and expressed them. In the tract against Latomus he had treated anew and in detail the basic questions on the doctrine of justification. Even so, he could not claim that his half year from May to November had been one of his most creative periods. Nearly everything he had written had grown out of perceptions developed and expounded earlier. Nevertheless, this quiet half year had been a time to clarify and give orderly expression to his thoughts. What next? Winter was in the air. He must have a change of pace. In early November he protested that his loneliness proved he was not cut out to be a hermit. He felt as though he were fighting a thousand devils. They " 'amuse' me, as one says, but in a disturbing way."[97] Rumors about Wittenberg, the exact nature of which we do not know, reached him and contributed to his sudden decision to go there secretly in order to get a picture of the situation.[98]

The mood in which Luther left the Wartburg is shown by his proud and pugnacious letter of December 1 (the day before his departure) to Albrecht, cardinal archbishop of Mainz. Despite his two earlier but futile warnings (October 31, 1517, and February 4, 1520), Luther applied the evangelical counsel (Matt. 18:15ff.) and tried a third time to admonish Albrecht. With good reason, Luther was furious, for Albrecht was once again plying the indulgence trade in Halle [above, pp. 20–21] and, in fact, erecting an idol that operates with villainy and deceit. He warned Albrecht to mark well what had been happening to the pope. To him God had already shown "what a horrible fire was kindled by ignoring this little spark." The pope's situation is daily growing worse, Luther warned, "so that one may see the hand of God at work."

96. WA 10¹ 1:728 / 9ff. [*LW* 52:286. Sermons for the Festival of the Epiphany, conclusion.]
97. To Gerbel and Spalatin, November 1, 1521, WA Br 2:397 / 17; 399 / 9. [*LW* 48:319, 324, 28, n. 10.]
98. To Spalatin, January 17, 1522, WA Br 2:444 / 2–3. [*LW* 48:380.]

Let no one doubt that this God still lives, that he knows how to handle a cardinal of Mainz, even if four emperors should support him. . . . Your Electoral Grace should not at all think that Luther is dead. He will so gladly and joyfully rely on the God who has humbled the pope and who will start a game with the cardinal of Mainz such as few people imagine. . . . Therefore be it finally made known in writing to Your Electoral Grace: If the idol [i.e., the indulgence traffic] is not taken down, my duty toward divine doctrine and Christian salvation is a necessary, urgent, and unavoidable reason to attack publicly Your Electoral Grace, as I did the pope. Then I shall have to oppose such a venture without restraint, and shall have to blame all the previous abomination of Tetzel on the [arch]bishop of Mainz, and show all the world the difference between a bishop and a wolf. Your Electoral Grace may decide how to react and what to do.

In somewhat milder tone Luther begged Albrecht "to leave in peace those priests who have married to avoid unchastity," otherwise there would be an outcry "demanding that it is up to the bishops to tear first the beams out of their own eyes [Matt. 7:5] and that justice would have the bishops first do away with their harlots[99] before daring to separate devout wives from their husbands." Luther knew what a sore point in Albrecht's life he was touching. Finally, he demanded a reply from the cardinal within two weeks, otherwise he would release for publication his little book *Against the Idol at Halle*. Nor would he allow anyone to prevent him, even "should this letter be intercepted by Your Electoral Grace's councillors." "Councillors should be faithful, and a bishop should run his court so that whatever is intended for him actually gets through." In his latest indulgence protest—blasting the idol at Halle—Luther used this letter to circumvent the hesitations of his own elector's court in Saxony. Alone, therefore, he endeavored to make his point, laying the matter directly into his opponent's hand, even awaiting a response before he would proceed against him publicly.[100]

With this ultimatum in his pocket, Luther left the Wartburg secretly on horseback on December 2. The following day he took his noon meal in Leipzig at the tavern of Hans Wagner "on the Brühl," who was later interrogated by the authorities on order of Duke George.[101] Wittenberg supplied him with the fellowship he had been missing so intensely as he met with friends at Melanchthon's, whose lodgings were in Nicholas von

99. [On Albrecht's harlots, see WA 30²:338, n. 3.]

100. WA Br 2:406 / 25; 407 / 42–43, 51ff.; 408 / 91–92, 108–9. [LW 42:340, 341, 342, 343.]

101. F. Gess, *Akten und Briefe zur Kirchenpolitik Herzog Georgs von Sachsen* (Leipzig, 1905ff.), 1:273.

Amsdorf's house. He was especially delighted when they failed to recognize the bearded gentleman with curly head in knight's attire. Nor did the artist Lucas Cranach see through the disguise when called in to do a portrait of the strange knight. Thanks to Cranach's familiar painting, and to the woodcut made from it, we can vividly visualize the Luther of the Wartburg episode. In Wittenberg, Luther avoided his Augustinian cloister for fear of being recognized.[102] Only "one drop of wormwood oil" spoiled the joy of these days. He discovered that the manuscripts he had sent to Spalatin for forwarding had not arrived in Wittenberg. These included his three recent tracts: *On Monastic Vows, The Misuse of the Mass*, and *Against the Idol at Halle*.[103] Had they been intercepted? Had Spalatin held them back? Luther immediately sent Spalatin a distraught inquiry, intimidating him with the threat of himself getting into an angry mood and of waging a still more violent attack on those burning issues. Spalatin yielded and sent at least the first two manuscripts. He still held back one, *Against the Idol*, even securing Luther's consent for this. Luther then, the more strongly, demanded that the letter of December 1 be forwarded to Cardinal Albrecht.[104]

What Luther saw in Wittenberg on the condition of the reform movement pleased him. He had come with some anxiety. On the way he had picked up various tales about unbridled action on the part of some who said they sided with him. Therefore he determined that immediately on returning to his "wilderness" he would write a public exhortation against insurrection and disturbances.[105] At the moment, however, what he found in Wittenberg gave him little cause for anxiety. To be sure, issues had become more sharply drawn, yet he could hardly find fault with the fact that during his absence most of the masses had been discontinued and that worship services—with sermon and the Lord's Supper—had replaced them. Nor did he mind that still more friars had been leaving the cloister. The ardent Zwilling was among them. On November 30, Zwilling had discarded the cowl and left town, bent on preaching the gospel somewhere else.[106] The days of Luther's visit also saw some disturbing developments. Early on December 3 some students and burghers prevented the priests from entering the Town Church and reading mass. When some

102. To Link, December 18, 1521, WA Br 2:415 / 29–30.

103. To Spalatin, around December 5, 1521, WA Br 2:409–10. [*LW* 48:350–53.]

104. To Spalatin, around December 14, 1521, WA Br 2:412 / 1ff. [*LW* 48:353.]

105. To Spalatin, around December 5, 1521, WA Br 2:410 / 19ff. [*LW* 48:351–52.]

106. Ulscenius to Capito, November 30, 1521, printed in Müller, *Wittenberger Bewegung*, 71–72.

priests managed to get into the church on that dark winter morning and began to chant the Magnificat (the Office of Mary), they were pelted with stones. The next day a poster, originating with the students, appeared on the cloister of the barefoot friars, and a student group was on hand to mock the fathers. There were fears abroad that the cloister would even be stormed some night. We cannot tell how much Luther may have known of what was going on. It is worth bearing in mind that, like police reports generally, anxious accounts from the town council to the elector[107] were probably painting an excessively gloomy picture. At any rate, Luther could not have been kept completely in the dark, nor would he have approved of these current tactics any more than he approved of the earlier assaults by students on the mendicants from the neighboring Order of St. Anthony. Though he disliked such youthful pranks, he wondered, "Who can hold everyone in check everywhere and at all times? . . . It will not destroy the gospel if a few of our people sin against propriety."[108] During his brief December stay Luther probably perceived the movement among the students in terms of what the Swiss student Felix Ulscenius wrote to his friend Wolfgang Capito on November 30: "Today in the hearts of the Wittenbergers the love for God and one's fellowmen is burning most intensely, so that they would gladly be ready to endure everything for the sake of Christ's truth."[109] But Luther would soon have to admit that he should have taken these first signs of boisterous disturbances more seriously. For the moment, however, as far as we can tell, his one unpleasant impression of Wittenberg remained the sad tales of how the friars were leaving their cloister.[110]

After six days Luther was on his way back to the Wartburg, feeling reasonably reassured. On December 10 he again dropped in at the same Leipzig tavern for his noon meal. Late on December 11 he rode his horse into the Wartburg. His heart was lighter than it had been seven months earlier, yet conversations on the way had convinced him of the immediate necessity of opposing some of the undesirable consequences of the movement, precisely because his visit in Wittenberg had given him "a convincing impression" that the Reformation cause was not to be stopped. Besides, he set Easter as a deadline for his stay in the Wartburg. Meanwhile he was returning to his "wilderness" with a great new task. The friends in

107. Ibid., 73ff.

108. Ulscenius to Spalatin, November 11, 1521, WA Br 2:402 / 24ff. [LW 48:327.]

109. Müller, *Wittenberger Bewegung*, 72.

110. To John Lang and to Wenceslaus Link, December 18, 1521, WA Br 2:413 / 3; 415 / 16–17. [LW 48:356, 358.]

Wittenberg had urged him strongly to translate the New Testament into German.[111] As he pondered this task, as well as the completion of his postil and other lesser duties, he knew that in the early months of 1522 he would have more than enough to do.

Zealously he set to work. The trip to Wittenberg had refreshed him greatly. He had an unheard-of confidence now that reform would triumph. For that reason—and not on grounds of anxiety—he at once composed a popular appeal to restraint. His pamphlet *A Sincere Admonition to All Christians to Guard Against Insurrection and Rebellion* hit the mark. It came from his pen in about two days' time. Bright images and apt formulations flowed in profusion from these pages. Whoever has the notion that the authorities may be dillydallying or even opposing reform, and that therefore this is a time for direct and violent action to dismantle the papal church, such a person—Luther argued—has not yet caught on that God himself has begun to carry out his judgment on this church.

> O Lord God, no such mild punishment awaits them. An inexpressible severity and limitless wrath has already begun to break on them. Heaven has turned to iron, the earth to brass. No prayers can save them now. Human hands will no longer have a chance to manage affairs when God in his judgment now sends an advance messenger of the Last Day.

Therefore Luther does not really take the danger of insurrection seriously, but he "must nevertheless instruct men's hearts a little." Whoever practices violence does the devil's work, for the devil delights in nothing so much as bringing the gospel into ill repute—"when one of ours is not all spirit and angel." "The devil has become fatigued; he must let up when God wants him to because he perpetrates such lame and loose and lazy attacks." At the same time Luther voiced categorically his deep and lifelong revulsion against every kind of revolution.

> There is no reason for insurrection, and generally it does more harm to the innocent than to the guilty. . . . I am and always will be on the side of those against whom insurrection is directed, no matter how unjust their cause; I am opposed to those who rise in insurrection, no matter how just their cause, because there can be no insurrection without hurting the innocent and shedding their blood.

Should one be surprised when a few years later during the Peasants' War Luther maintained the same position he announced here? The gospel

111. According to the letters to Lang and Link, December 18, 1521, above, WA Br 2:413. [*LW* 48:356, 359.]

is permitted to fight only with the Word as its weapon, yet this is the mightiest weapon of all. "See what I have done. Have I not, with the mouth alone, without a single stroke of the sword, done more harm to the pope, bishops, priests, and monks than all the emperors, kings, and princes with all their power ever did before?" Yet Luther has not achieved this by himself. "A far different Man is the driving power. The papists do not see Him but lay the blame on us," for the time is coming (as Dan. 8:25 has foretold) when the enemy shall be broken "by no human hand."[112] In conclusion, Luther directed two requests to those who would side with him. First, that they "call themselves Christians, not Lutherans. What is Luther? After all, the teaching is not mine. Neither was I crucified for anyone." The second request was "If you want to handle the gospel in a Christian way, you must take into account the people to whom you are speaking." "With wolves you cannot be too severe; with weak sheep you cannot be too gentle."[113] These few powerful pages set forth Luther's stand against revolution and his drive for organic reformation by means of the gospel. Such a reformation, as he saw it, would bring about not a lesser transformation but a transformation greater than violence could ever achieve. To this the spiritual or blessed insurrection "we should commit our mouths." This is what Christians can and should do. "Just see what has been accomplished in a single year, during which we have been preaching and writing this truth. See how the papists' camouflage clothing has shrunk in length and breadth. . . . What will be the result if the mouth of Christ continues to thresh by his Spirit for another two years?" It is not presumptuous to look for Christ's mouth among men. "I for my part am certain that my word is not mine but the word of Christ. My mouth, therefore, must also be the mouth of him whose word it speaks."[114]

In his mind Luther could justify the greatest of upheavals, provided it were brought about solely by the preaching of the Word. His thinking was not conservative. The great nineteenth-century historian Leopold von Ranke either misunderstood Luther or told only half the truth when he praised Luther as one of the greatest conservatives who ever lived.[115] Nevertheless, Luther condemned every violent insurrection. Over the

112. *WA* 8:677 / 14ff.; 679 / 22ff.; 681 / 37; 680 / 18ff., 32ff.; 683 / 8ff., 24; 677 / 22; 683 / 12. [*LW* 45:57–74 (full text). Citation from 59, 61, 62–63, 66, 67. "Is the driving power" = literally, "makes the wheel go around" (*LW* 45:68, n. 28).]

113. *WA* 8:685 / 5ff.; 687 / 13–14. [*LW* 45:70, 73.]

114. *WA* 8:683 / 13ff., 31; 684 / 9ff.

115. L. von Ranke, *Deutsche Geschichte im Zeitalter der Reformation*, 2d ed. (Meersburg and Leipzig, 1933), 4:4.

centuries his followers have been entrusted with the warning not to anticipate the judgments of God by taking recourse to revolution or violence. It
is not possible to separate Luther's immovable stand against revolution
from its religious foundation. As in classical antiquity, so also later on the
more rational western European way of thinking—whether Catholic or
Calvinist—raised the issue whether or not a people had the right to rise
up against an unjust government, and also looked for some justification of
tyrannicide as well as of revolution. For Luther such questions had been
answered even before they could be raised. God's action at a given time
was to Luther an inscrutable but also an undoubted reality. For Luther, to
wait for God's hour was no passive resignation—as one has too often
thought it to be—but a clear recognition that great decisions are not to be
spoiled by halfway measures. Nothing appeared more certain to him than
that God, in his own time and far beyond all human standards, creates the
turning points in history. To do battle for God's truth with the weapon of
the Word—and to oppose any clearly recognized injustice of the authorities—ultimately to risking one's own life, was to Luther the only
promising kind of revolution. And backing it up was the consent and
might of God himself.[116]

No sooner had Luther dispatched the *Admonition* to Spalatin—with the
request that the manuscript be published at the earliest opportunity—
than he seized on a pair of projects. The one was to resume his work on
the postil, interrupted by his trip to Wittenberg; the other was to translate
the New Testament. Anger had a way of raising Luther's productivity. His
threatening letter to Spalatin from Wittenberg (December 5, above) indicates as much. Now, crossing into the new year, a copy of the notorious
papal bull *In coena domini* reached him at the Wartburg. Here was an old
story with a new twist. Annually, since the thirteenth century, on Maundy
Thursday the pope published his condemnation of a number of noteworthy crimes, including all sorts of moral and spiritual heresies. It tended to
be a pretentious and largely ineffectual declamation. In 1521 this bull
cited Luther and his followers for the first time, charging them with offenses against property rights as well as against the rights of the ecclesiastical state, the church, the clergy, and other insignificant matters. In
Luther's estimation, such offenses—legal infractions though they might
be in Roman eyes—should not be called sins, and he had said as much in
his address *To the Christian Nobility of the German Nation*.[117] For cen-

116. *WA* 8:682 / 12–33. [*LW* 45:66.]
117. *WA* 6:432 / 2ff. [*LW* 44:192ff.]

turies, before as well as after Luther's time, this bull had occasioned end-less friction between the apostolic seat and political governments. Luther therefore decided to translate the 1521 bull into German, making it a New Year's gift to the pope and letting it serve to document the papal lust for power and money. Translating *In coena domini* freely, Luther dubbed it "Bull of the Supper-Devouring Most Holy Lord, the Pope." In the language of the times he added coarse and outraged glosses. He claimed that this particular bull was drafted in scullery Latin and done on a night of drunkenness, "when the tongue was strutting on stilts and reason was sailing around with its sails half-reefed." While writing, Luther was struck by a sense of irony. Unsparingly he sketched the blatant contradiction between the worldly power of the pope and the way of Christ, who had nowhere to lay his head and who had advised his followers to surrender cloak as well as coat (Matt. 5:40). What, if anything, has this papacy to do with the discipleship of the apostles? Luther sneered, "Hail, Peter, King of Sicily and Fisherman of Bethsaida!"[118] To Wilhelm Dilthey, Luther's wild humor in this script expressed "the feeling of power that grips a fearless man."[119]

Luther's fearlessness toward the mighty was spurred on from another quarter. In mid-January 1522 he actually received a reply to the ultimatum he had addressed to Cardinal Albrecht. Outwardly Luther's triumph could hardly have appeared more complete. In a miserable letter dated December 21, 1521 (its writer had not dared to dictate to a secretary) the hard-pressed elector of Mainz addressed Luther as "Dear Sir and Doctor," assuring him that the matter causing offense had long since been removed. As for himself, Albrecht promised to deport himself "as befits a devout, spiritual, and Christian prince." He saw himself as a poor, sinful man. "I realize fully that without the grace of God there is nothing good in me and that my shit stinks as much as the next fellow's, if not more so. This is something I have not wanted to hide in responding to your well-intentioned letter, for I am more than willing to show you grace and goodness for the sake of Christ. Brotherly and Christian punishment I can indeed endure."[120] Was this honest remorse or clumsy hypocrisy? Luther's at-

118. *WA* 8:693 / 8–9; 704 / 1ff.; 700 / 6.

119. Wilhelm Dilthey (1833–1911), German historian, *Gesammelte Schriften*, 6th ed. (Stuttgart, 1960), 2:54.

120. *WA Br* 2:421. See also Wolfgang Fabricius Capito's letter to Melanchthon, December 21, 1521. *Suppl. Mel.* 6 / 1:174–75. *MBW* 190. [Capito, one of the archbishop's officials, seeking reconciliation between Luther and Albrecht, was suspected of hypocrisy by Luther, whose long letter of reply to Capito, January 17, 1522, is in *LW* 48:372–79.]

tempt to find the answer was not made easier by an accompanying letter to him from Wolfgang Capito. This official on Cardinal Albrecht's staff went to some lengths to claim that by the exercise of Erasmus-like caution he had been having some success in bringing his sovereign to a better understanding of the aims and purpose of church reform. Besides, such an incident as the resumption of the indulgence traffic at Halle [above, p. 20] should be regarded simply as a regrettable lapse. "Why should I not be honest with you?" wrote Capito to Luther. "I have acted adroitly yet devoutly and have employed human effort in the interest of the faith." He entreated Luther to go easy and not to spoil good beginnings by being too harsh and courting disaster.[121] Even an inkling of human nature could have told Capito that Luther hated nothing more than such halfway measures in spiritual matters. But Capito met his match. Luther replied on January 17 with a letter that was friendly but very earnest. He set Capito's well-intentioned art of diplomacy over against Christian faith and love. In the first place and at all costs, Luther insisted, the truth must be told. Then love could indeed show its concern for the weak brother. But love without truth leads to hypocrisy. For Luther the view backstage took away any joy over Albrecht's conversion. He therefore preferred not to answer the cardinal's letter but requested Melanchthon to do him a favor: to take good care of that manuscript of Luther's *Against the Idol at Halle* and hold it in readiness for some future eventuality. It really was not necessary for Luther to shoot this second arrow.[122] The first arrow, his letter of December 1, to the cardinal had sufficed to put an end to the insane venture at Halle. Two decades later, however, the indulgence ghost roamed again. That was in 1542, when Albrecht was relocating the treasury of relics from Halle to Mainz and once again used indulgences in order to reduce his indebtedness. At that time Luther engaged the cardinal in a lively game through the "New Journal of the Rhine, Anno 1542," but this time his mood rang with the liberating laughter of a winner. Now he no longer had to view the indulgence game as posing a serious threat to souls.

Luther was impatient to get on with the Bible translation, the most demanding assignment he had brought back from Wittenberg. Circumstances dictated that he begin with the New Testament. He was alone, and the slim number of philological helps available at the Wartburg precluded any thought of translating the entire Bible, or (as he would have

---

121. Capito to Luther, December 20–21, 1521, WA Br 2:416ff.; 417 / 31.

122. Luther made use of this manuscript later in 1522 as the basis of his tract *Against the Falsely So-Called Spiritual Estate of the Pope and the Bishops*, WA 10²:93ff.

preferred) of beginning with the Old Testament. If there were some chance of slipping back to Wittenberg and remaining secreted there, then—he mused—he could consult with colleagues and benefit from their counsel. Even so, as he now made the best of his situation, he gave his friends in Wittenberg something to think about, writing "it would be a worthy translation for Christians to read, for I hope we will give a better translation to our Germans than the Latins have."[123] Love for his people moved Luther to undertake this monumental task. This sentiment animated the writings he had already composed at the Wartburg, and to his friend Nicholas Gerbel he summed up his desire, "I am born for my Germans. Them I also want to serve."[124] More specifically, Luther's entire reforming career now pointed logically to his translating the Bible into the language of the people. Besides, it was only through the Bible that he himself had become what he was. It was through the Bible that he had learned how to escape the confinement of scholastic theology, and it was in the Bible that he had rediscovered the heart of the gospel. The Bible was his sole companion during his hours of loneliness, the one weapon in his struggle against a thousand-year-old system. If he dared to believe that hitherto he had won his literary and verbal battles, then this victory was thanks to the Bible. The urging of the Wittenbergers that he undertake a complete translation was like unlocking the last door, but what he was now about to undertake was a consistent continuation of his very own work. By translating the Scriptures he would not only be giving his people access to the source from which he himself was drawing, he would also be justifying on a grand scale the direction in which he had so far been moving. Henceforth, everyone could and should be judging for himself and thus be exercising the foremost duty and chief right of the priesthood of all believers. This general priesthood Luther had rediscovered in the Bible as the very basis of the nature of the church itself.

Even though at first Luther would be translating only the New Testament, this was by no means an easy task. By training he was not a humanist but had been reared on scholastic theology. His main contacts had been not with the newly revived language studies going on around him but with the Latin of the Vulgate Bible and of the ecclesiastical establishment. The latter remained for him lifelong a more normal means of thought and expression than the Greek. Even so, he had been making

123. To Amsdorf, January 13, 1521, WA Br 2:423 / 48ff., esp. 53ff. To Melanchthon, January 13, 1521, WA Br 2:427 / 128. MBW 205. [LW 48:363, 372.]

124. WA Br 2:397 / 34. [November 1, 1521. LW 48:320.]

significant progress in Greek under the expert tutelage of Melanchthon, yet he never attained the full mastery of it as did his humanistic friends. The difficulties peculiar to the Greek of the New Testament would have been beyond him had his limited selection of books at the Wartburg not included two essential helps. The first was his Vulgate Bible. He was well aware of its deficiencies but was accustomed to using it and knew large parts of it by heart as a result of his years of avid biblical study. The second and far more important work was the Latin translation that Erasmus supplied, complete with detailed notes, for his edition of the Greek New Testament.[125] Luther had learned his way around in this product of the latest scholarship. Its second edition (1519) was probably the one on his desk in the Wartburg as he launched into the German translation. This was an improvement over the first few months of his confinement when he apparently had only the Erasmus text (Gerbel's reprint) without the new Latin translation and annotations by Erasmus. Luther was grateful to Gerbel for dedicating and sending him this New Testament text which to him was like a wife, bearing him many sons and being "still fertile and highly pregnant." In short, the fresh Latin translation and annotations by Erasmus had stimulated Luther's thinking and also made possible a number of his treatises.[126] If one follows Luther's translation sentence by sentence, say, of Romans, then one can recognize how he repeatedly makes use of his two Latin helps. In some of his sentences it is the Vulgate, whose expressions or constructions are embedded in memory and set the tone of the translation. In others he is indebted to Erasmus, especially for clarifying explanations and important references. Luther makes use of all this with freedom that is slave to no system and that corresponds to the lively and ever-changing individual decisions that translating requires. With racing speed he completed the entire New Testament in the amazing time of eleven weeks. In the process he did not always make use of Erasmus's critical comments, but sometimes retained interpretations growing out of the Vulgate. A more careful use of Erasmus would have pointed out such mistakes, but in the great majority of cases Luther made grateful and careful use of Erasmus's notes and paraphrases. Now and

125. See the note in WA DB 6 and 7, as well as H. Dibbelt, "Hatte Luthers Verdeutschung des Neuen Testaments den griechischen Text zur Grundlage?" ARG 38 (1941): 300ff.

126. November 1, 1521, WA Br 2:397 / 41ff. [LW 48:321. To Nicholas Gerbel, Strassburg, a man trained in law as well as theology, a friend of Erasmus, and active in the still new printing trade. See R. H. Bainton, *Erasmus of Christendom* (New York: Scribner's, 1969), 133–147, and his Luther biography, *Here I Stand*, 125–26.]

then, but not always happily, he went his own way, running counter to his proven mentor and against the Vulgate while following the Greek text.

Although he could readily check the exact wording of the original Greek text with the old and new Latin versions, he was forced on his own ingenuity to develop the German New Testament. Even if he had then had at hand one of the medieval German translations of the Bible, he would hardly have made use of it. They were based entirely on the Vulgate, a text that Luther had to improve on at countless points. In fact, those earlier translations were on the whole too clumsy and too tightly bound to the Latin to be of much help to him. However highly one might rate some of these earlier attempts, they were dated performances and—as opposed to refinements in the use of languages emerging in the early sixteenth century—they represented a contrast too great to make an impact on Luther's translation. In spite of many attempts, it has not been proven that during his time at the Wartburg Luther made use of one of the late medieval German Bibles, such as that printed by Günther Zainer in Augsburg in 1475.[127] Of course, he had become acquainted earlier with these older German versions. The ample quotations from them in German sermons, religious books, and other writings explain the fact that through his own recollection certain aspects of the older version found their way into his own version. Yet it is worth noting that such harmonies lead back not to any single earlier printed edition but to the various medieval versions as a group; in other words, Luther made use of a then traditional German church language and not of some single literary source.

The Wartburg New Testament shows how much Luther was growing beyond his own earlier literary performances. It may therefore seem unjust to compare his translation with its medieval predecessors, for his language soars like an eagle and arouses amazement. Indeed, this was not the first time he had translated Bible passages into German. His German tracts, sermons, and expositions abound with passages he had done himself. It is therefore astonishing how Luther rose above his earlier performances—including even the biblical exposition in his Christmas postil—and created a new and unified style for the entire New Testament. Where his

---

127. Cf. H. Bornkamm, "Die Vorlagen zu Luthers Übersetzung des Neuen Testaments," in his *Luther*, 65ff.; and G. Bruchmann, "Luther als Bibelverdeutscher in seinen Wartburgpostillen," *LuJ* 17 (1935): 111ff., as well as his "Luthers Bibelverdeutschung auf der Wartburg in ihrem Verhältnis zu den mittelalterlichen Übersetzungen," *LuJ* 18 (1936): 47ff. Cf. also *Verdeutschung der Evangelien und sonstiger Teile des Neuen Testaments von den ersten Anfängen bis Luther: Beiträge zu ihrer Geschichte*, ed. H. Vollmer, BDK 5 (Potsdam, 1935), 21ff. [Michael Reu, *Luther's German Bible* (Columbus, Ohio: Lutheran Book Concern, 1934). *LW* 35: (177–80), 181–202, n. 129 below.]

earlier attempts often retained the colorings of earlier—especially Latin—linguistic usage, his work on the New Testament resulted in a language thoroughly German in all respects. His narration is in the imperfect tense, not the perfect. His placement of the predicate—aside from well-pondered exceptions—is at the end of a sentence. He separates nouns into shorter sentences. Compare, for example, his style in the Wartburg postil (P) with his new style in the New Testament (NT). Matt. 12:34, "Out of the abundance of the heart the mouth speaks" (P) becomes "What fills the heart overflows the mouth" (NT). Or, Rom. 8:7, "The wisdom of the flesh is God's enemy" (P), becomes "The wisdom of the flesh is hostile to God" (NT). Whenever possible Luther dropped foreign (Latin) words and let the German take over.[128] This reveals a deliberate and methodical procedure. Years later he described it in his little treatise *On Translating: An Open Letter*.[129] The essential element in his performance is something born of the unconscious depths of his poetic heart. He had a facility with language that could adapt itself to every task, whether to the tenderness of the nativity story or to the dread of the Apocalypse. He operated not according to set rules from without but according to precepts guiding him from within. The uncanny marksmanship with which he hit the hidden intention of the text came not only from conscious reflection but much more from a supersensible clairvoyance. This is the hallowed story. He hears and sees it as something alive in the present. He conveys its tone so that the reader grasps it as a living, spoken word. Through sentence structure and punctuation he turns the Bible into a book to be heard and not simply read. With greatest sensitivity he allows the poetic pieces to emerge and responds to them with the poetic means of the German language with rhymes and rhythms. So it happened that many verses in the Luther Bible virtually sang themselves and only then disclosed their secrets when Bach—would that Luther could have experienced him!—caught the music hidden in them. Even so, more than a poet's genius is here at work. This new creation of the biblical word—incomparable among translations anywhere—could succeed because Luther not only found his way into the text with consummate skill but especially because over countless hours the story had permeated his own life. He read the Holy Scriptures "as though they were written yesterday"[130] and as though

---

128. W. Delle, "Luthers Septemberbibel und seine deutschen Zitate aus dem Neuen Testament bis 1522," *LuJ* 6 (1922): 66ff. [Matt. 12:34 (P) German original: "Wes das Herz voll ist, des geht der Mund über"; see *LW* 22:12; cf. *LW* 35:190. Romans 8:7 (P), "Die Weisheit des fleisches ist gottes feind"; cf. *LW* 25:350 for the equivalent in his lectures on Romans.]

129. [*LW* 35:175–202.]

130. *WA* 12:444 / 19–20.

God were comforting and admonishing him through them. Indeed, it was this astonishing fundamental perception in his theology—that God speaks and that God reveals the depths of his being by means of his Word—that freed Luther to develop his use of language. His achievement sprang not simply from poetic intuition; it was the human word being born from the Word of God. During those quiet months of winter at the Wartburg, it was not something he begat but something born in him.

It could hardly have been otherwise. His translating sprang purely and simply out of the understanding of the gospel which had been given to him. Like a buoyant overtone the comforting message of the undeserved grace of God reverberates through his text. He does everything possible to preserve that text in its purity and to protect it from misinterpretations. For example, out of his own experience he translates the term "righteousness of God" (so easily subject to double meaning) as "the righteousness valid in God's presence." Luther clearly carves out the Pauline meaning by means of a doubly added "alone": "So that he (God) alone is righteous" (Rom. 3:26) and "that a man is justified without the additive of works of the law [since 1527: without the works of the law], by faith alone" (Rom. 3:28). Instead of "by works," Luther says more pointedly "from the merit of works" (Rom. 9:12, 32; 11:16). His intention is to allow the evangelical message to come through undistorted. This is evident in his careful rendering of one and the same word in strictly observed derivations. The word is *gerecht* (righteous, just). When applied to a human being he allows it to stand only where it speaks unmistakably of righteousness as a gift of grace. Otherwise he substitutes *fromm* (devout, pious), a word which for Luther conveys the full content of the gospel. Then there is his treatment of the common Greek word group *sozein, soteria* (to save, salvation). His handling of it at the Wartburg was subject to later refinement. On the one side he placed expressions connoting external action: saving, helping, sustaining; and on the other, internal action: to save, to be saved, salvation.[131] For the main word, *soteria*, Luther developed a still further and profound distinction: *Heil* (God's great redemptive act of saving humanity) and *Seligkeit* (the blessedness of being saved, which works on the heart in this life and in eternity).[132] All this Luther drew from a single root word. Again he deliberately avoided the term "church" wherever it occurred and used "congregation" in its place. He thereby sought to prevent every projection of the false Roman Catholic ecclesial idea on to the primitive Christian era.

131. *[Selig machen, selig werden, Seligkeit.]*
132. E. Hirsch, *Luthers deutsche Bibel* (Munich, 1928), 56ff.

Luther's Bible translation gave the evangelical movement an inexhaustible source for its proclamation and provided the German people with an
everflowing well for nourishing its new language. By so doing, Luther
participated in the development of High German. He himself did not
initiate this language, but he contributed greatly to its advance and spread
across the southern as well as northern parts of Germany. Indeed, since
the beginning of the sixteenth century High German had been gaining
ground against the regional and local dialects that made for disunity. Prov-
identially also this greatest shaper of the German language was able to
exert influence in the area where for some time a common German language was in the making: in the settlement of eastern Germany. In those
regions newcomers from lower Germany, the Netherlands, the Frankish
areas of the Rhine and Main valleys, and Bavaria were mingling their
linguistic legacies. The unity already developed among settlements in the
region of the Main River found expression in a common language,
Meissen German. Moreover, the expanding political and economic power
of the dual state of the Wettin dynasty[133] was more important for Germany
culturally than the more powerful but geographically more peripheral
Hapsburg territories. From these lands of Wettin [mainly in Saxony,
Thuringia, yet not confined there] this unifying language spread out to
most of the remaining German peoples. Luther recognized this phenomenon, explaining, "I speak the language of the Saxon chancery, which all
the German princes are now using." He was likewise aware that this language was so new that its rise—as a conscious effort to create a unified
language—could be fairly set during the reigns of Emperor Maximillian I
(1459–1519), of Hapsburg, and Elector Frederick the Wise (1463–1525), of
Saxony.[134] As Luther made use of this new language—it came naturally to
him—he could count on being intelligible to most Germans. Besides, no
one else was as effective as Luther in opening the gates of the future to
what was being called High German. "The new German language provides the Reformation with a powerful thrust extending across the territories."[135] The language of Luther's Bible, and of the Reformation preaching

133. [Name of the town on the Saale River, near Halle, where this dynasty arose in the
tenth century. In 1425 the head of the house of Wettin was made elector of Saxony. The most
significant subdivision of Wettin occurred in 1485 when the dynasty was divided and named
for Frederick's two sons, Ernest and Albert. Elector Frederick and his family were of the
Ernestine line, become evangelical; Duke George, of the Albertine line, remained Roman
Catholic.]

134. WA TR 2, no. 2758a and b, 639 / 7ff.

135. T. Frings, "Grundlegung einer Geschichte der deutschen Sprache," *Zeitschrift für
deutsche Geisteswissenschaft* 1 (1938–39): 209.

nourished by it, was universal not only in that it spanned the broadest linguistic latitude but also in that it spoke the language of the entire people, from the studies of the learned to the huts of the common folk, and thanks to its unprecedented spread through print it reached all levels of society. What raw material, in terms of words and pronunciation, Luther received from German settlements to the east, he returned, for he made this language capable of the mightiest achievement in the history of the German tongue. Only by means of a union of substance and spirit was the new German given a character it never would lose. It was from Luther's Bible that the German people learned to speak the language they were to have in common.

2

Unrest in Wittenberg and Zwickau
Luther's Return

While Luther was working on his translation of the New Testament, disturbing reports kept coming from outside. He had returned to his Patmos from Wittenberg with reassuring impressions, and the next developments he heard about were not disquieting. Yet even in those days while he was secretly in Wittenberg, a request to the university from Elector Frederick for an opinion on the question of the mass began to split the academic community into two camps.[1] Arguments and counterarguments based on biblical, traditional, or historical grounds began to compete for the decision of Frederick the Wise. In the one camp were the reform group under Karlstadt and Melanchthon, fired by a sense of mission bordering on that of the "enthusiasts" and contending that the smallest group is the most likely to represent the truth.[2] In the other camp were the [Castle Church] chapter members, bent on upholding things traditional. Instead of one opinion, the elector received a sheaf of opinions, which made him conclude that the time was not yet ripe. So he forbade any changes in the mass, although he permitted further writing, preaching, and debate on the issue, provided this were done in a reasonable and Christian manner.[3]

But Karlstadt was not the type to be bridled. On Christmas Day 1521 he celebrated mass in his own way in the Castle Church. He wore no priestly vestments. The words of consecration, offered in German, departed from the traditional Latin liturgy. Besides, he handed each communicant the bread and the chalice.[4] While none of this may have departed from what Luther had in mind (the elimination of the notion of sacrifice from the mass), for those present on this occasion the change in outward form nev-

1. Instruction of the Elector of October 25, 1521, printed in N. Müller, *Die Wittenberger Bewegung 1521 und 1522*, 2d ed. (Leipzig, 1911), no. 20, Bericht der Universität, December 12, 1521, with the votes of the members of the senate and of the Stift Church chapter, nos. 42–45, 48–51, 55. Report of the Elector's Council, Dr. Christian Beyer, December 13, 1521; ibid., no. 47.

2. Müller, *Wittenberger Bewegung*, no. 43.

3. Instruction, December 19, 1521, in ibid., no. 56.

4. In ibid., nos. 57–58, 61, 68. H. Barge, *Andreas Bodenstein von Karlstadt* (Leipzig, 1905), 1:358ff. K. Müller, *Luther and Karlstadt* (Tübingen, 1907), 43ff.

ertheless stirred up a commotion. Some took it as a sign of freedom, others as an act of sacrilege. Suddenly the town was plunged into a dangerous mood. During the Christmas midnight mass, mobs created disturbances in all the churches. Still more upsetting was the coming of three men from Zwickau who showed up on December 27 at Melanchthon's place. Two weavers, Nicholas Storch and Thomas Drechsel, were joined by Melanchthon's former student, Marcus Thomae, whom Melanchthon remembered well. To him they boasted of having had personal revelations, but when they expressed doubts about infant baptism, Melanchthon was in a quandary. Still, that same day he wrote an excited letter to the elector, urging that Luther was now the only one who could help. Frederick the Wise responded quickly and had Melanchthon as well as Amsdorf visit him in Prettin on New Year's Day 1522. The elector warned them against becoming involved with the restless characters from Zwickau, not even to argue with them, and he rejected the thought of Luther's returning to Wittenberg at that time.[5]

Sparks had hereby blown to Wittenberg from a fire that had already done plenty of damage in Zwickau. Zwickau lay in a region where Waldensian congregations had infiltrated secretly until the late fifteenth century and where the population was open to Hussite influences from Bohemia; it had thus been more susceptible than most other places to a long succession of new religious thought.[6] The city itself was famous for its textile industry, and for more than a half-century its leading families had enjoyed phenomenal prosperity from the surprisingly rich silver mines in the Schneeberg mountains. The burghers of Zwickau had developed a sense of independence as well as a taste for education of quality, and their town panorama had acquired a new profile. The local Latin school drew students from near and far and was complemented in 1519 by a Greek school, the first of its kind in Germany. In this well-cultivated ground Luther's thoughts on the renewal of the church quickly took root. As early as 1518 the Franciscan Frederick Myconius had begun there to preach the gospel in a new spirit, so that Zwickau—the most brilliant and educationally receptive city of Electoral Saxony—became the model among the German

5. Melanchthon's letters to the elector and Spalatin, and Spalatin's record of the discussion in Prettin, in Müller, *Wittenberger Bewegung*, nos. 59, 60, 64. (*CR* 1:513–14, 533ff.) *MSA* 7 / 1 (1971): 158ff. *MBW* 192.

6. See P. Wappler, *Thomas Müntzer in Zwickau und die Zwickauer Propheten*, SVRG 182 (Gütersloh, 1966). H. Boehmer, "Die Waldenser in Zwickau und Umgegend," *NASG* 36 (1915): 1ff.

cities by its rapid reception of the Reformation. But behind those forces which aimed the first blows against the old church, the clergy, the monks, the indulgence traffic, and more besides, there lurked a second and more radical wave.

The one who set it rolling was Thomas Müntzer (1488–1525), who had come to Zwickau in May 1520 as the new preacher at St. Mary's Church. He was one of the earliest and most impassioned followers of Luther, whom he honored as his spiritual father. This sentiment was shown by the way he signed a letter to Luther: "The one whom you have begotten through the gospel."[7] Since 1506 he had studied the liberal arts (artes) in Leipzig and for several years thereafter was active as a collaborationist [ecclesiastical assistantship] in Aschersleben and in Halle. There it was that he first displayed the gift of attracting a personal following. In Halle he led a group pledged to oppose Archbishop Ernst (1513), confessing as much to the authorities when imprisoned in 1525 in Frankenhausen.[8] He continued his studies in 1512 in the University of Frankfurt-on-the-Oder, a young institution, founded only in 1506. This school—a competitor to Wittenberg, only four years its senior—endeavored to make a name for itself in humanistic studies.[9] In this setting Müntzer was neither influenced by nor alienated from the scholasticism Konrad Wimpina taught in a practical polemical rather than philosophical vein. Müntzer was no theological thinker but a curious mixture of an avid reader hungry for knowledge, a hothead full of vivid experiences, and a passionate agitator. So far as we can make out from his writings and from his extensive book lists,

7. WABr 2, no. 141, 97–98. *Thomas Müntzer, Schriften und Briefe: Kritische Gesamtausgabe*, ed. G. Franz, QFRG 33 (Gütersloh, 1968), no. 14, 361. This form of address, incidentally, makes it unlikely that Müntzer was born as early as 1468, or fifteen years before Luther, as G. Franz assumes (*RGG*[3] 4 [1960]: 1183), in connection with H. Goebke, "Neue Forschungen über Thomas Müntzer bis zum Jahre 1520," *HarzZ* 9 (1957): 1ff., esp. 3, n. 5. H. Boehmer, *Studien zu Thomas Müntzer* (Leipzig, 1922), 12, surmises December 20 or 21, 1488 or 1489, as Müntzer's birth date. Research by other scholars has come up with similar conclusions; see A. Zumkeller, "Thomas Müntzer—Augustiner?" *Aug (L)* 9 (1959): 380ff., esp. n. 3. Also E. Iserloh, "Zur Gestalt und Biographie Thomas Müntzer," *TThZ* 71 (1962): 248ff. T. Nipperdey, "Theologie und Revolution bei Thomas Müntzer," *ARG* 54 (1953): 146, n. 11. E. W. Gritsch, "*Reformer Without a Church: The Life and Thought of Thomas Muentzer, 1488(?)–1525* (Philadelphia: Fortress Press, 1967), 1–2. H. J. Goertz, *Innere und äussere Ordnung in der Theologie Thomas Müntzers* (Leiden, 1967), 20, n. 1. S. Bräuer, "Zu Müntzers Geburtsjahr," *LuJ* 36 (1969): 80ff. (bringing new material). The definitive biography is that of W. Elliger, *Thomas Müntzer: Leben und Werk* (Göttingen, 1975).

8. Elliger, *Müntzer*, 548–49. I see no reason to doubt this reference, and agree with O. Schiff, "Thomas Müntzer als Prediger in Halle," *ARG* 23 (1926): 292–93. Apparently Müntzer was working in Halle a decade later. Artes equal the liberal arts, introductory university studies, *RE*[3] 20 (1908): 304–5; also *LThK* 1 (1957): 909–10.

9. Again, Elliger, *Müntzer*, 18ff., 32ff., 39ff., on Müntzer's early activity and his study career, especially in Frankfurt-on-the Oder and Frose.

Müntzer's reading included neither the scholastics, the exegetes, nor Aristotle, but rather the mystics, the authors of classical antiquity, the new humanists, and the pamphleteers of reform. With much erudition and little clarity or even an absorbing set of issues, Müntzer left the university in 1516, a Master of Arts and restlessly in search of a livelihood that would enable him to pursue his inclinations. For a time (between 1516 and 1518) he worked as dean of the convent at Frose near Aschersleben. He may have gone from there to Braunschweig, where a clash of opinions sent him packing again.[10]

Around New Year's Day 1519 we come across Müntzer in Leipzig, jobless yet earning his keep as helper at a book printer's. Here Müntzer's first connection with Wittenberg shows up. The esteemed goldsmith and book publisher Christian Döring,[11] a friend of Luther's, had prevailed on Dean Bernhardi in Kemberg, near Wittenberg, to take on Müntzer as a chaplain. This may also have been the time when Nicholas Hausmann, who became one of his successors in Zwickau, heard Müntzer preach in Wittenberg.[12] But Müntzer apparently did not accept the Kemberg offer. Instead he responded to the request of a friend, Franz Günther in Jüterbog[13] (a student of Luther's) to take his place, for Günther had become embroiled in conflict with the Franciscans, who then complained about him to the bishop of Brandenburg.

During the Easter season of 1519 Müntzer's sermons indicate that he himself was joining the conflict and waging it with the same severity as Günther. In the process some of his demands or theses for church reform became clear: The pope must convene a council for every five years; should he fail to do so, the bishops could convene one even without him. The pope, at any rate, is head of the church only as long as the bishops put up with him. Only a council, not the pope, has the right of canonization, as, for example, canonizing a Bonaventure or a Thomas Aquinas—men who, according to Müntzer, had converted no one, not even a heretic. Besides, men of their type operated on the premises of reason, and "all these are of the devil." The prime responsibility of bishops is to conduct

10. According to the report of Bernhard Dappe (see below, p. 55, n. 14), Müntzer, *Schriften*, 561ff.

11. See below, p. 85.

12. Letter of Hausmann, September 7, 1521, to the Elector Frederick and Duke John, printed in P. Kirn, *Friedrich der Weise: Seine Kirchenpolitik vor und nach Luthers Hervortreters im Jahre 1517* (Leipzig and Berlin, 1926), 183ff.

13. For Günther's academic disputation on September 23, 1517, Luther had drawn up his significant theses, *Contra scholasticam theologiam; WA* 1:224–28. For more on Günther, see Müller, *Wittenberger Bewegung*, 376ff.; also Elliger, *Müntzer*, 49ff.

visitations and education in the faith. Let them not become involved in a whole range of activities, from disciplinary proceedings (an exercise as elusive as chasing bats) to excommunication, which Müntzer called "letters from the devil." Bishops, he fumed, used to be set in office as fathers, but now they are self-seeking tyrants. For four hundred years the gospel had been kept under the table, and now anyone seeking its reactivation must risk his neck.[14]

All this sounded Lutheran; indeed, much of it was super-Lutheran. Luther himself had not as yet raised such sweeping demands concerning the pope, a council, or bishops. A year earlier, however, the rector of St. Martin's School in Braunschweig, himself a former student of Müntzer's, had turned to Luther with several questions on the indulgence problem and various other current issues.[15] This was, after all, the world in which Müntzer lived and with which he took issue in his characteristic way. For him to do so required no personal meeting with Luther. Such a meeting may have occurred on the fringe of the Leipzig disputation (1519), if not earlier. That Müntzer ever studied in Wittenberg is out of the question. Yet Luther undoubtedly had long kept an eye on this younger and polemical partisan. It was probably through John Eck's publication of the Franciscan complaints that the Jüterbog conflict became generally known. This may have prompted Luther to introduce himself to Müntzer and Günther in an open letter of May 15, 1519, to the Franciscan convent in Jüterbog. Luther wrote that he had no knowledge of what specifically "Müntzer had been preaching during the preceding month, but if Müntzer was in general attacking the church authorities, he was not only within his rights but acting on the example of Christ. Indeed, Luther contended, it would have been a different matter had Müntzer named names in his attack.[16] Müntzer, meanwhile, had found another position that from time to time was more to his liking. He had become chaplain to a convent at Beuditz near Weissenfels, where he had modest lodgings and plenty of time for study. But the fact that he could not obtain many of the

14. See the report on Müntzer's sermons in the letters of complaint by the Jüterbog Franciscan Bernhard Dappe to the episcopal vicar Jakob Gropper and Bishop Scultetus of Brandenburg of May 4 and 5, 1519. The text is in Müntzer, *Schriften*, 561ff. See also M. Bensing and W. Trilitzsch, "Bernhard Dappens Articuli . . . contra Lutheranos." On the dispute of the Jüterbog Franciscans with Müntzer, see *Jahrbuch für Regional Geschichte*, 2 (1967): 113ff. In this controversy Luther sided moderately with Müntzer. See Elliger, *Müntzer*, 49ff.

15. 1518? (According to the content this date is more likely than that proposed by Boehmer: prior to the end of June 1517.) Müntzer, *Schriften*, no. 2, 347–48.

16. WA Br 1:392 / 107ff.

books he needed was "in the Lord Jesus a bitter cross." "I am researching not for myself but for the Lord Jesus. As he wills, so he will send me wherever he chooses. In the meantime I am satisfied with my lot."[17] The nuns were also satisfied with him. He knew how to humor them, as revealed by a jolly letter that one of the nuns wrote him after he had taken up work at his next assignment in Zwickau.[18]

It was therefore not surprising that Luther commended this extraordinarily accomplished and vivacious man to the prestigious post of pastor of St. Mary's Church in Zwickau. He was John Sylvius Egranus (John Wildenauer of Eger), a friend of Erasmus as well as of Luther.[19] Müntzer seemed just the right man for that lively and exciting city, but Luther would soon be bitterly disappointed. Müntzer at once resumed his wild sermons against the Franciscans and eventually attacked his colleague Egranus also.[20] As a result the city of Zwickau was torn into two parties, with old social cleavages colliding. The happy discovery of silver in the Schneeberg had had its sorry side.[21] In contrast to the newly rich owners and operators of the silver mines, many an old patrician family of cloth-makers had become impoverished. The rising quantity of silver had lowered the real value of money; prices rose and left the buying power of wages behind. A growing proletariat of weavers resulted, impoverishing masters and apprentices. Already in 1516 they had become the driving power in the uprising against the city council.

Some of that old Waldensian spirit was still around, demanding apostolic poverty on the part of the church and clergy. In fact, many of the protesters were anticlerical, seeing the true church as requiring a leadership not of priests but of spiritually awakened laity. The case of Nicholas Storch was revealing. He was an intelligent man, uncommonly well read in Holy Scripture and a master cloth-maker of an old but now impoverished family. He had brought some of his sectarian ideas from Bohemia and further developed them with visions and revelations he claimed to have received directly from God. Storch aroused Müntzer. In

17. Müntzer, *Schriften*, no. 7, 353 / 7ff. These letters carry the same numerical designation in the edition of Franz [QFRG 33 (Gütersloh, 1968)] as in *Thomas Müntzer: Briefwechsel*, ed. H. Boehmer and P. Kirn (Leipzig and Berlin, 1931).

18. Müntzer, *Schriften*, no. 11, 356.

19. The friendship with Luther dates from the time of the Leipzig disputation. See Egranus looking back on his association with Luther, May 18, 1522 (draft), WA Br 2:345–46, no. 2. See also Müntzer's self-defense to Hausmann of June 15, 1521, printed in Müntzer, *Schriften*, no. 25, 371ff.

20. Elliger, *Müntzer*, 128.

21. K. Blaschke, *Sachsen im Zeitalter der Reformation*, SVRG 185 (1970): 39ff.

the lean and goggle-eyed Storch, who could cast an extraordinary spell, Müntzer found a person who seemed to corroborate what he had read in the late medieval German mystics (John Tauler, Henry Suso, and others) about the tempted and calmed heart's experience of God. Müntzer's sermons publicly praised Storch as one truly trained in the Spirit. He also encouraged Storch to conduct secret meetings in order to teach others the steps of mystical immersion: amazement, disengagement, contemplation, endurance, and so on, down to "the very righteousness of God."[22] Rumor presently exaggerated news about Storch into a sect and had him sending out twelve apostles and seventy-two disciples, just like the Waldensians long ago.

Müntzer's passionate sermons finally ignited this explosive tinder. On Second Christmas Day 1520, a pastor whom Müntzer had vehemently attacked from the pulpit was almost killed by the mob.[23] Despite the city council's warnings, Müntzer became increasingly aggressive, until on Shrove Tuesday 1521 his opponents smashed the windows of his house. The city council's efforts at moderation were futile; so also were interventions by letter from the Wittenbergers, who had been alarmed by reports from Zwickau that Müntzer was "bent on murder and bloodshed."[24] A renewed encounter at Easter, and a devastating attack with disgraceful diatribes, finally brought matters to a head. On April 16 the city council expelled Müntzer. When his followers rallied to his support, some fifty-six weavers' apprentices were jailed. Overcome by fear at what he had caused—yet not for the last time in his life—Müntzer fled from town that same night. Five days later, Egranus himself resigned and preached his farewell sermon. For some time he had sought a way to escape from this witches' cauldron and had applied for service elsewhere. Only the faithful ministry of Nicholas Hausmann, Egranus's successor and a close friend of Luther, could make a new beginning, but it still entailed a stern struggle against the adherents of Storch and Müntzer, the latter continuing from a distance to intervene with inflammatory letters.

Finally, in December 1521, Duke John—prodded by his watchful cousin Duke George—asserted his authority over the leading city in his territory[25] and had the religious situation in Zwickau investigated. Storch

22. John Agricola to Reusch, 1525, in A. Brecher, "Neue Beiträge zum Briefwechsel der Reformatoren und ihnen nahestehender Männer," *ZHTh* 42 (1872): 405.

23. Elliger, *Müntzer*, 111.

24. John Agricola to Müntzer, February / March 1521. In Müntzer, *Schriften*, no. 15, 362. A letter from Luther to Müntzer was lost, but see that of July 9, 1523, in WA Br 3:104 / 4–5; and Müntzer, *Schriften*, no. 40, 389 / 19.

25. Kirn, *Friedrich der Weise*, 3, n. 4.

preferred not to appear before the council and decided instead to leave town. To the accompaniment of a song, "Steal Away, Lest Evil Strike You Down," Storch was joined by his adherents, Drechsel and Thomae (whose other name, "Stübner," derived from the bathhouse [*Badstube*] run by his father). Thomae had recently been with Müntzer to Prague. Now that things had fallen apart in Zwickau, the three mission-conscious prophets—Storch, Drechsel, and Thomae—were looking for a new field of activity in and around Wittenberg.

For most Wittenbergers the year 1522 began with eager expectations and hopes and for the old believers—opposed to reform—with considerable anxiety. Judging from the response the burghers had given his action, Karlstadt felt he had a mandate to undertake further reforms. On New Year's Day about one thousand people received Holy Communion in both kinds. Between Christmas and Epiphany virtually all the townspeople had communed. Preaching attracted such crowds that the time seemed to have come for weekday services as well, which would feature biblical exposition.[26] The example of Wittenberg was followed elsewhere. In many towns and villages of this district of Electoral Saxony, the laity came to mass in growing numbers, receiving the wine as well as the bread. This occurred especially in Eilenburg, where Gabriel Zwilling (Luther's erstwhile fellow Augustinian and Karlstadt's kindred spirit) had been preaching such strong sermons since Christmas that the people were moved to throw stones through the windows of the local parsonage. On New Year's Day, Zwilling was in Wittenberg preaching in the Castle Church and conducting a new form of worship in which the leading local officials of Electoral Saxony participated. Later, when Zwilling was again in Wittenberg—and much against his will—a gang of ruffians stormed the pastor's house and went on a rampage. Only after hand-to-hand encounter were they subdued and clapped into jail.[27] In the various locations the new forms of worship differed from each other considerably, yet they all had one intention in common: to release the faithful from their magical timidity to touch the eucharistic elements and from the requirement of prior confession and

26. Müller, *Wittenberger Bewegung*, no. 68. Justus Jonas writing to John Lang, January 8, 1522, ibid., no. 69.

27. J. K. Seidemann, *Erläuterungen zur Reformationsgeschichte durch bisher unbekannte Urkunden* (Dresden, 1844), 35ff. "Georg Helts Briefwechsel," ed. O. Clemen, *ARG* supp. vol. 2 (Leipzig, 1907), 10–11. Müller, *Wittenberger Bewegung*, no. 73. Barge, *Karlstadt*, 1:363. Müller, *Luther und Karlstadt*, 47. K. Pallas, "Der Reformationsversuch des Gabriel Didymus in Eilenburg und seine Folgen, 1522–1525," *ARG* 9 (1911–12): 347ff.; 10 (1913): 51ff.

its attendant works of satisfaction. The fruit of receiving the Lord's Supper was seen as "exercising a new life in faith and love, and day by day to grow more fully with that life." These are the words of an unknown country pastor to whom we are indebted for his admirable report of these weeks.[28]

Karlstadt's rapid success went to his head. He became convinced that he had become the leader of a widespread movement. And so he married, inviting the university community, the town council, and numerous distinguished guests to the event on January 19, 1522. He had spent a small fortune to provide delicacies from Leipzig; he even sent a formal invitation to the elector of Saxony, but omitted the little postscript requesting his personal appearance.[29] Karlstadt's marriage had found joyous approval also from Luther[30] and encouraged others to follow suit. Justus Jonas, dean of the Stift, and even John Dölsch (also known as Dr. Feldkirch, from the name of his birthplace), a member of the Catholic faction in the chapter, joined the procession into matrimony.[31]

No less a sensation was caused about that same time when the Augustinian cloister, from which a third of the friars had already left during the previous November, began to undertake revolutionary reforms. The convention of the German Augustinian congregation [including representation of an impressive number of cloisters] met in Wittenberg during Epiphany 1522 and determined to give every friar the choice either to leave the order or to remain in the cloister and assume new duties. In place of the mendicant journeys to raise funds, the saying of votive masses, and the immoderate number of liturgical duties, those friars staying on would henceforth concentrate on preaching, physical work, and service among the ill and the poor.[32] These decisions were published, and throughout Germany they served as the signal for many friars to quit the order. Only a few days later, however, probably under the influence of Zwilling, a much more radical spirit exploded: The paintings in the church and the consecrated oil were burned and all the side altars were

28. Müller, *Wittenberger Bewegung*, no. 68, 151.

29. Ibid., 159. The invitations of January 5 and 6, 1522, ibid., nos. 65 and 66. On this see K. Schottenloher, "Erfurter und Wartburger Berichte aus den Frühjahren der Reformation nach Tegernseer Überlieferungen," in *Festschrift für Hans von Schubert*, ed. O. Scheel, *ARG*, supp. vol. 5 (Leipzig, 1929), 88. Karlstadt's purchases cost him 50 florins. His well-endowed position brought him an annual income of 129 florins, as well as contributions in kind. See the list of 1514 in Barge, *Karlstadt*, 1:44.

30. Letter to Amsdorf, January 13, 1522. WA Br 1:423 / 45. [*LW* 48:363: "Karlstadt's wedding makes me very happy."]

31. Müller, *Wittenberger Bewegung*, no. 101, 210. E. Fischer, "Zu den Wittenberger Unruhen," *ZKG* 23 (1902): 615ff.

32. Müller, *Wittenberger Bewegung*, no. 67, 70.

removed. Here for the first time one of Karlstadt's most recently expressed demands had been put in action.[33]

As for the Zwickau prophets, the two weavers had left Wittenberg as unexpectedly as they had come, but the people who had heard them kept on telling one another about their dreams. Only the third Zwickau man, Thomae (Stübner) remained in Wittenberg and engaged in prophesying. Soon, he claimed, the Turks would be coming and kill all the priests, including those who had married. And, he went on, after a revolution in five or seven years the devout people would still be alive and one faith and one baptism would be supreme. Melanchthon had good-naturedly taken Thomae into his own house and defended him against the mockery of the students. But Melanchthon himself must have laughed when, one day at table, Thomae awoke from a brief nap and announced that now he was John Chrysostom—with the sad face of one in purgatory.[34] Storch, meanwhile, was traveling hither and yon across Germany. He was a fantastic agitator, skilled in capturing people's attention with ever more amazing tales about himself. One of them told that the angel Gabriel had appeared to him and promised that Storch would sit on Gabriel's throne. Beneath these flights of fantasy, Storch sowed the seeds of revolution which in a few years would bear harvest in the Peasants' War. In the early stages of that war, Storch's tracks disappear.

The situation was getting out of hand. Every pastor was managing his parish as he pleased. Each day brought new surprises. And the Wittenberg town council at least realized that merely to forbid was not the answer and that only a forward step could restore order. Having been advised by a university committee, the council issued its "Praiseworthy Order of the Princely Town of Wittenberg on January 25, 1522." Since late 1521 the town had its "pouch order," which had been drawn up under Luther's influence and which not only regulated the care of the poor in Wittenberg but eventually influenced similar policies adopted in many other places.[35] Now, however, for the first time a reform-minded town gave itself an inclusive order for church and society. This order had a

33. Ibid., no. 72, 102. Barge, *Karlstadt*, 1:386.

34. Report in Müller, *Wittenberger Bewegung*, no. 160. Camerarius, "De Philippi Melanchthonis ortu totius vitae, curriculo et morte narratio (1566)," 50–51. On the role of Melanchthon during the unrest in Wittenberg, see W. Maurer, *Der junge Melanchthon zwischen Humanismus und Reformation* (Göttingen, 1969), 2:200ff.

35. Barge, *Karlstadt*, 2:559–60. For determining the date and significance, see Müller, *Luther und Karlstadt*, 202ff. O. Winckelmann, "Über die älteste Armenordnung der Reformationszeit (1522–1525)," *HV* 17 (1914): 202, 396ff.

threefold aim. The first aim was to combat poverty. The entire churchly and charitable income, as already provided on a smaller scale by the recent "pouch order," was now funneled into a common chest. This was designed to help people with a variety of needs: the destitute, schoolchildren, students, priests deprived of their sources of income. The common chest was also to provide loans for artisans and those indebted through no fault of their own. Henceforth begging was banned in the town. Whoever refused to work was expelled from town. The mendicancy of monks was no longer tolerated. The second aim was to combat immorality. Prostitutes were to be banished and the keepers of brothels heavily punished. The third aim was to provide the Town Church with a new order of worship. Karlstadt's Christmas mass was the model, the rule being the "evangelical meal"—with Communion in both kinds and the reaching of the laity for both the bread and the wine permitted. This order was Karlstadt's triumph, even if it was accomplished largely with the help of Luther's ideas, for the social and regulatory measures stemmed almost wholly from Luther's writings, notably his *To the Christian Nobility* and his tract on usury. Likewise, the new understanding of worship drew heavily on Luther's teaching and writings. The actual liturgical form was Karlstadt's, and especially the iconoclastic attack reflected his mind-set. He set forth his position in a special tract in which he radically reaffirmed the Old Testament prohibition against images and hammered home to the Wittenbergers ancient prophets' warnings of divine judgment on all who worshiped idols. Even Melanchthon had zealously promoted the new town order so as to keep the mounting chaos in check.[36]

At any rate these dikes were no longer able to confine the current of change. Karlstadt's and Zwilling's wild sermons surged beyond the existing order. They reminded the congregations of their right to manage their own affairs wherever "the authorities were negligent," and they turned the orderly removal of pictures into an act of God's judgment. So it happened that a number of pictures in churches were destroyed by meddling hands. Of course the town council acted immediately and punished any culprits it could catch.[37] But with the sudden outburst of passions, no matter how swift the intervention, something happened for the first time

36. See "Die Wittenberger and Leisniger Kastenordnung, 1522, 1523," ed. H. Lietzmann, *Kleine Texte* 21 (Bonn, 1907). Müller, *Luther und Karlstadt,* nos. 74, 75, 93. On a text differing from the printed version, the hand of Stephan Roth, see O. Clemen, "Miscellen zur Reformationsgeschichte," *ThStKr* 70 / 4 (1897): 820–21. A. Karlstadt, *Von Abtuhung der Bilder und das keyn Bedtler unther den Christen seyn sollen,* 1522, ed. H. Lietzmann, *Kleine Texte* 74 (1911).

37. Müller, *Wittenberger Bewegung,* nos. 74, 84, 89.

that in the succeeding decades was to find terrible imitation. Reports of these developments—the ever-widening breach in the keeping of the regulation on fasting, and the renewed controversy among the preachers concerning confession—alarmed the government. The personal efforts of Hugold von Einsiedel, the evangelically inclined councillor of the elector, to make Karlstadt and Zwilling more moderate, proved fruitless. He therefore ordered all those involved to appear at Eilenburg on February 13 and to give an accounting. Thereafter von Einsiedel reported to the elector, whose decision on February 17 revealed his perplexity.[38] He could ascertain only "with a troubled mind" that his command not to introduce a new order of worship had been disobeyed. Little as he had formerly considered himself competent as a layman to comment on the mass, on the Zwickau prophet, or on iconoclasm,[39] he now dared to intervene with a specific instruction. He simply required that in no case should it even be hinted that he had consented to the order.

The decision of the elector helped not in the slightest to create clarity in Wittenberg. Things boiled on. One especially painful consequence of this confusion was that some of the student body abandoned Wittenberg.[40] Until recently many of the students had supported themselves in part by begging, but mendicancy was now forbidden, and many came to regard it as no longer worthy. Indeed, all reforms reflected the determination that people earn their living by working with their hands. And finally, many asked, what need is there for higher education? If everything depends on the simple proclamation of the gospel, what need is there any longer for the scholastic exercise of thought? A simple Christian illuminated by God had a better grasp of what is needed than an ever so learned theologian— especially, it was claimed, when one could draw on special revelations directly from God, like the Zwickau prophets. Karlstadt and Zwilling asked simple people, to their own astonishment, what they understood certain Bible verses to mean.[41] In any case, there seemed to be no longer any ground for humanistic studies. It happened that, right in the midst of one of Karlstadt's lectures, a student would decide "to bid farewell to the

38. Ibid., nos. 76–99.

39. Ibid., pp. 52, 141, 191.

40. Felix Ulscenius to Capito, January 24, 1522, in Müller, *Wittenberger Bewegung*, 173. Instruction of the Elector to Officer John Oswald in Eisenach, around February 26, 1522, WA Br 2:450/23. Fröschel, in O. Clemen, *Beiträge zur Reformationsgeschichte aus Büchern und Handschriften der Zwickauer Ratsschulbibliothek* (Berlin, 1902), 2:26–27.

41. The report of Sebastian Fröschel in *Das Buch der Reformation, geschrieben von Mitlebenden,* ed. K. Kaulfus-Diesch (Leipzig, 1917), 289. Similarly in Clemen, *Beiträge zur Reformationsgeschichte,* 2:26–27.

muses."[42] No wonder rumor spread that even Melanchthon and the Hebraist Aurogallus were planning to leave Wittenberg. Melanchthon was full of anxiety lest the light of the gospel, which had so recently begun to shine, again be taken from the people.[43] To Melanchthon and the more levelheaded elements of the university, as well as the town council itself, there now remained but one way out of chaos: to call Luther back to Wittenberg.[44]

Luther had been following events in Wittenberg attentively and at first with quiet confidence. He could hardly take issue with the premise on which Karlstadt had reformed the mass, for that premise was like his own, and as yet he apparently had no details on how the changes were carried out. Besides, the Zwickau prophets had made no impression on him at all. How could a man like Melanchthon, of so much spirit and education, be induced by such prophets to doubt? So Luther consoled Melanchthon in a long letter of January 13, 1522, giving him a recipe: He should inquire of the prophets what kind of distress of conscience they had experienced. Agonizing, "the sign of the Son of man [the cross] . . . is the only touchstone of Christians and a certain differentiator between the spirits." No other alleged revelations count. And that the Zwickauers raised the question of infant baptism did not surprise Luther. "I have always expected Satan to touch this sore, but he did not want to do it through the papists. It is among us and among our followers that he is stirring up this grievous schism," Luther forewarned. "But Christ will quickly trample him under our feet." On this matter of infant baptism he was not the least bit uncertain, although he knew that some questions would arise which were not to be answered from the Scriptures with complete finality. So he held fast to the marvelous unity of the church in the practice of infant baptism. Thus far no heretic had denied it. Besides, the Old Testament example of circumcision supported it.[45] As Luther pondered the thought of returning to Wittenberg soon, it was not prodded by the Zwickauers—whom he in no

42. Philip Eberbach, according to a report of Erasmus Alberus. Barge, *Karlstadt*, 1:422, n. 233.

43. See n. 40, above, the letter of Ulscenius; and Melanchthon's letter to Spalatin, *CR* 1:547 (not of February 6, 1522, but around November 20, 1522; *MSA* 7 / 1:180ff. *MBW* 247).

44. Luther to the Elector, March 7, 1522, WA Br 2:460 / 22. [*LW* 48:394ff.] Melanchthon to Michael Hummelberg, March 12, 1522, *CR* 1:566. *MSA* 7 / 1:171–72. *MBW* 220. For the travel costs of the Wittenberg treasury: E. L. Enders, ed., *D. Martin Luthers Briefwechsel* (Frankfurt am Main, 1884ff.), 3:298, n. 1. WA Br 2:462 / 4. On overcoming the crisis in Wittenberg: Maurer, *Melanchthon*, 2:200ff.

45. WA Br 2:424ff., esp. 427 / 117ff. [*LW* 48:366ff., 371–72.]

case wished to see punished by police methods—but was made urgent by his difficulties with the Bible translation and the need to consult on it with friends.[46] Only when he learned of the tumult in Eilenburg did Luther earnestly plan to return to Wittenberg.[47] With these developments the good name of the "Martinians," as Luther's followers were then generally known, was dishonored.[48] Apparently he learned that the fire there had been extinguished rapidly, and no doubt also that in Wittenberg they were drawing up a new and comprehensive order. But then, when the town's cry for help suddenly reached him and he was made aware of the indecision and distress of the elector himself, he decided quickly to return home. He sent the elector notice of his coming, filling the letter with confident reassurance and, as he often did, mingling expressions of faith and humor. He congratulated his lord, long a collector of relics: "Grace and joy from God the Father on the acquisition of a new relic! . . . God has now . . . sent Your Grace without cost or effort a whole cross, together with nails, spears, and scourges. . . . Your Grace should not be terrified by it; stretch out your arms confidently and let the nails go deep. Be glad and thankful." Let him now be wise and undaunted, and let him not pass judgment on the basis of reason or outward appearances, for as Luther well knew these are "tricks of Satan."[49]

Elector Frederick was actually deeply troubled not only by what was happening in his own country but also, during a period paralleling the unrest in Wittenberg, by the mounting political pressures from without. His cousin Duke George [in Ducal Saxony] kept warning and threatening him relentlessly about the consequences he could expect for giving priority to the Hussite heresy—to which Frederick replied wisely, not only defending his policy of restraint but also reminding George of the bloody consequences from which the battles in Bohemia had sprung when force was used to resolve a disputed issue such as offering the chalice to the laity in the Lord's Supper.[50] Duke George's anger, however, had flared up afresh because of the events in Eilenburg. On January 22, 1522, came an explosive diplomatic encounter in Nuremberg, at the seat of the imperial

46. WA Br 2:423 / 51ff.; 427 / 127ff. [LW 48:372.]

47. To Spalatin, January 17, 1522, WA Br 2:444 / 5ff. [LW 48:380ff.]

48. Clemen, ed., "Helts Briefwechsel" (see n. 27 above), 11. Further reports on Eilenburg in E. Wülcker and H. Virck, Des Kursächsischen Rathes Hans von der Planitz Berichte aus dem Reichsregiment in Nürnberg 1521–1523 (Leipzig, 1899), 67–68. F. Gess, Akten und Briefe zur Kirchenpolitik Herzog Georgs von Sachsen (Leipzig, 1905ff.), vol. 1, nos. 284, 293.

49. Around February 24, 1522, WA Br 2:448 / 7ff., 449 / 17. [LW 48:387.]

50. Gess, Akten, vol. 1, nos. 259, 274, 276, 282.

government, between the ambassadors of Duke George and Elector Frederick. Despite the objections of Frederick's envoy, Hans von der Planitz, Duke George's man was able to get the government to issue a sharp mandate against any changes in the mass and against any exodus from the cloisters; furthermore, the territorial princes were ordered to intervene and punish the criminals.[51] Frederick the Wise did not allow himself to be intimidated even by those threats. Then George came back at him with still another urgent letter: In the face of those defected friars and schismatic priests, he was not to show himself a doubter but was to show himself a faithful and obedient elector of the Holy [Roman] Empire and [son] of the Christian church. Frederick replied that he wished to hear nothing "that is of no business for Your Honor to write." Likewise when the [Saxon] bishop of Meissen and Merseburg requested the aid of his temporal arm to intervene, Frederick refused.[52]

The ducal allegation "doubter" was on target, as Frederick revealed further ambivalence. Indirectly he acknowledged Luther's letter, giving instructions to his top official in Eisenach and taking into account Luther's announced intention to leave the Wartburg.[53] Dealing with certain broad allusions made earlier by Luther, citing illustrations while gently correcting him, Frederick then candidly admitted his own perplexity with regard to the Wittenberg developments. Besides, he did not wish to oppose God's word and will. The Wittenbergers, however, were themselves not in agreement, and among them "no one knows who is the cook or who the keeper of the wine cellar." For his part, Frederick said he was not afraid to suffer. "If this be a genuine cross and chastisement from God, then His Electoral Grace would not be dismayed." God would then also provide him with the needed help. Let Luther write to him what to do or refrain from doing in this dilemma. Indeed, the fact that Luther intended to see him filled him with deep concern. Let him in no case—at least not for a

51. Wülcker and Virck, *Berichte Planitz*, 59–60, 67–68. Gess, *Akten*, vol. 1, no. 288.

52. Letter of George, February 1, 1522, Gess, *Akten*, vol. 1, no. 293, 262 / 23. Letter of Frederick the Wise, March 9, 1522, ibid., nos. 314, 286 / 3. Reply of George, March 21, 1522, ibid., no. 321. Exchanges of correspondence with the bishop of Meissen, in K. Pallas, "Briefe und Akten zur Visitationsreise des Bischofs Johann VII, von Meissen im Kurfürstentum Sachsen 1522," *ARG* 5 (1907–8): 217ff.; and of the bishop of Merseburg, in K. E. Förstemann, *Neues Urkundenbuch zur Geschichte der evangelischen Kirchen-Reformation* (Hamburg, 1842), 1:89. Also in Clemen, *Beiträge zur Reformationsgeschichte*, 2:4ff.

53. Instruction to John Oswald (around February 26, 1522), *WA Br* 2:449–53, esp. 451 / 35 and 88ff., 72. See also the interpretation of Müller, *Luther und Karlstadt*, 95ff. In the disputed interpretation of the closing sentence (*WA Br* 2:452 / 110), I disagree with Müller and agree with Kawerau and von Bezold.

while—do so. What if the emperor should find out and then demand that Luther be turned over to the imperial authorities? Then, as elector, he could hardly protect Luther any longer. More than a gracious hearing, said the elector, he had never been able to provide for Luther. Should he, as elector, refuse to hand over Luther, it would be hard to say how Saxony would fare in the future. Besides, it would be one of the worst kinds of injustice if something happened to Luther, because—again as elector—he did not consider Luther as having been refuted. Perhaps, so he went on, the announced spring meeting of the imperial diet would bring a big change. In any case, he requested Luther to send him some advice. Well might the elector also have borne in mind the new pope, Hadrian VI [1522–23]. But finally—so Frederick closed this virtual soliloquy—that God's will and work remain unhindered, he left everything up to Luther's "understanding, for he is experienced in these high matters."

Luther received the elector's answer on the eve of his intended departure, March 1, from the Wartburg. The conscientious indecision and confidence-inspiring character of his prince's letter did not confuse Luther, but made him all the more resolute. Now, so he reasoned, he would have to assume responsibility alone. He acted the way he would later on and to a much greater extent during the Peasants' War. The buoyant confidence with which he traveled back home has been caught for us by two Swiss students who at that moment were also en route to Wittenberg. They ran into Luther (still Junker Jörg) in the Black Bear Tavern in Jena. Luther was carrying on a lively conversation, full of allusions, with two merchants as well as with the students. He quietly paid for the students' evening meal and asked them to convey his greeting to their Swiss countryman in Wittenberg, Jerome Schurff, in the cryptic message "He who should be coming, greets you." Later Luther enjoyed their surprise when they came on him in the company of Schurff.[54]

Luther was able to write his elector only on March 5, from Borna, where he was staying at the home of his escort Michael von der Strassen, a good friend of the evangelical cause. Borna was a strategic stop, near Leipzig and just before having to cross the border and ride across the "enemy" territory of Duke George. Luther's letter to Frederick, one of the most glorious he ever wrote, was a worthy response to the elector's own straightforward confessing of his dilemma. Luther's confidence and Frederick's humility were complementary. Luther overlooked the mildly

54. J. Kessler, "Sabbata, mit kleinen Schriften und Briefen," published by the Historischer Verein des Kantons St. Gallen (St. Gall, 1902), 76ff.

chiding tone Frederick had used in replying to his earlier letter and dwelt instead on the trust he had in the elector. "Your Electoral Grace knows my heart better than to suppose that I would sneer at Your Electoral Grace's well-known wisdom." To which Luther added the warm confession, "I have a thoroughly unconditioned love and affection for Your Electoral Grace above all other sovereigns and rulers." He further admitted that what he had written previously stemmed from anxiety over the elector's burdens caused by the nasty events in Wittenberg—which in the eyes of God and the world are irresponsible but which remain oppressive to him personally as well as detrimental to the gospel. By comparison all previous struggles are as nothing. "This pains me profoundly." In light of human experience let the elector realize that while Luther was not at that moment obeying him he was nevertheless acting "on higher than human reconaissance." This was the recurring theme in Luther's letter. When seen from the heights on which the actual battle was being waged, the cares and hesitations of the elector appear groundless. Therefore Luther spoke frankly about duty and protection.

> I have written this so Your Electoral Grace might know that I am going to Wittenberg under a far higher protection than the elector's. I have no intention of asking Your Electoral Grace for protection. Indeed, I think I shall protect Your Electoral Grace more than you are able to protect me. And if I thought that Your Electoral Grace could and would protect me, I should not go. The sword ought not and cannot help a matter of this kind. God alone must do it—and without the solicitude and cooperation of men. Consequently, he who believes the most can protect the most.

So Luther absolved his prince from any responsibility should he be captured or put to death. Were the emperor determined to get him, let the elector offer no resistance. No harm should befall the elector or his realm because of Luther. Above all, Luther reminded the elector that behind the people engaged in all these human events there were the hidden players of the great drama: "My Lord Christ," whom Duke George takes "to be a man of straw," and the devil, who is also different from the duke, "who knows me rather well, and I have some knowledge of him too." But this drama is visible only to the eyes of faith. "If Your Electoral Grace believed, you would see the glory of God. But because you do not believe, you have not yet seen."[55]

On March 6, 1522, Luther returned to Wittenberg. His first duty was to write the elector a new letter. Not that the elector would have had to take

---

55. Luther to Elector Frederick, March 5, 1522, WA Br 2:453–57, esp. 454/18, 19ff., 32–33, 12–13; 455/75–456/82; 455/66; 456/122; 457/123ff. [LW 48:389–93.]

exception to his letter from Borna, but it was not the kind that Frederick wished to circulate publicly. Through Schurff he sent Luther a gracious greeting along with an urgent request for a letter which, if need be, could be politically useful. Luther succeeded only after several drafts, and Spalatin helped him put it in a way to satisfy the elector. At issue—and this did not disturb Luther—was the need to omit any mention of his being urged in writing to return to Wittenberg and simply to state his own reasons for returning to Wittenberg. He was also ready to refer to the emperor, in the language of the day, as his "Most Gracious Lord"—even though all the world knew that he was Luther's grim enemy. However, a little laughable hypocrisy was more bearable than beating the cautious elector over the head. The new letter was at once delivered in Nuremberg and circulated through the government offices. The letter even persuaded Duke George that his cousin was innocent in the matter of Luther's return.[56]

---

56. Correspondence between the elector, Schurff, Luther, and Spalatin, March 7–13, 1522, WA Br 2:457–73. Wülcker and Virck, *Berichte Planitz*, 107ff. Gess, *Akten*, 1:303. [*LW* 48:393–98.]

3

Order Restored
Bible Translation Published

On Invocavit Sunday, March 9, 1522 (three days after his return to Wittenberg) Luther was back in the pulpit of the Town Church for the first time in a long while. His first words fell on the congregation like those of a judge pronouncing sentence: "The summons of death comes to us all, and no one can die for another. Everyone must fight his own battle with death by himself, alone. We can shout into another's ear, but everyone must himself be prepared for the time of death, for I will not be with you then, nor you with me."[1] So saying, he summoned the Wittenbergers out of their frenzy and back into the personal sense of accountability which faith requires. Unlike his usual practice, and at least for this first sermon, he had put it all in writing[2]—a good sign of how seriously he regarded this moment in time. But presently he departed from his prepared text and struck a more conciliatory tone, a change seen by comparing the stenographic and subsequently printed version of the sermon (published a year later) with his original manuscript.

Luther went easy on Karlstadt and Zwilling, a tactic that intensified his reproach, which returned like a refrain and included everyone else: You have forgotten what love is, when it exercised patience with the weak and the slow. The Wittenbergers are well informed in matters of faith, and this is praiseworthy. However, "a faith without love is not enough—rather it is not faith at all, but a counterfeit faith, just as a face seen in a mirror is not a real face but merely the reflection of one."[3] Faith and love relate to each other as do "must" and "free."[4] Toward the end of his first sermon, Luther thus struck the theme recurring in the seven sermons on the following successive days. Faith, a right understanding, and the proclamation of the gospel are "musts" and permit no restriction. But love allows others to exercise freedom in matters of practice, such as observing or not observ-

---

1. *WA* 10³:1–2. [*LW* 51:70.]
2. *WA* 10³:lviiff.
3. *WA* 10³:4 / 10ff. [*LW* 51:71.]
4. *WA* 10³:11 / 4–5. [*LW* 51:74.]

ing the rule of fasting, serving or not serving the Lord's Supper in both kinds, or taking or not taking the bread in one's own hand. Love forbids us to turn practices like these into laws others must obey. That would amount to meddling in God's handiwork, for God, so far as concerns the efficacy of the preached gospel, has taken that function from us and reserved it for himself. "I can get no further than people's ears; their hearts I cannot reach. . . . We have the *jus verbi* [right to speak] but not the *executio* [power to accomplish]."5 The "loveless liberty" with which the Wittenbergers have discarded the old and introduced the new can lead only to further coercion. This perversion of his work, down to its very foundations, is what disturbed Luther profoundly. If the people would not desist from this course of action, there would be no need for an emperor to chase him from Wittenberg. Without being expelled he would leave them and then have to tell them, "No enemy, no matter how much grief he may have caused me, has so turned the heat on me as you have right here."6

If coercion is to be avoided in essentials—the preaching of the gospel and the purification of the mass are undoubtedly essentials—then how much more is it to be avoided in those matters which are not "musts" and in which God himself allows the exercise of freedom? Are images to be discarded from the churches? To be sure, images have been greatly misused, and yet God has given us the choice to use them or not. This is what Luther declared, in sharp contradiction to Karlstadt's claim that God has forbidden images as strictly as he has forbidden murder, theft, and divorce.7 The emperors of the eastern Roman Empire, who in the eighth century forbade the veneration of images, and the popes who have encouraged veneration, have made the same mistake. "They wished to make a 'must' out of that which is free. This God cannot tolerate."8 Indeed, images put us into a quandary in two ways. In spite of the prohibition against making an image of God, there are images in the Bible: the bronze serpent of Moses (Num. 21:9) or the two "cherubim" on opposite ends of the "mercy seat."9 Of course these cherubim were not to be worshiped, for God alone is to be worshiped. How then is one to prove to our opponents that they have been worshiping images? They will of course deny it ("even though it is true"). "Then I cannot press them any further, but must put

5. WA 10³:15 / 5ff. [*LW* 51:76.]
6. WA 10³:42 / 9ff. WA 10²:56 / 8ff. Luther had already written to the elector in this vein on March 5; WA Br 2:454 / 28ff. [*LW* 48:392.]
7. A. Karlstadt, *Von Abtuhung der Bilder* (see above, p. 61, n. 36), 22, 9–10.
8. WA 10³:26 / 11–12. [*LW* 51:82.]
9. Exod. 25:18ff. [Also Exod. 37:7. *LW* 51:82.]

my flute back in my pocket."[10] The Wittenbergers, Luther insists, should have begun their struggle against images from another angle: not from that of reproach and then of inability to prove that veneration has actually been taking place, but from that of reality, from the fact that no one can deny that images and costly works of art have been donated to church buildings in the mistaken notion of rendering God a service thereby.

Luther used the same key to unlock the otherwise so puzzling problem of monastic vows.[11] Thereby he recognized once and for all the cancerous effect of pious works undertaken to serve the church. Moreover, images as such are not to be discarded out of hand. "They are neither good nor bad, and we are free to have them or not."[12] Only our own abuses of them make images our enemies. In that case do we also want to abolish women and wine and gold and silver, which have brought about the downfall of so many? In that case, we would finally have to put ourselves to death, "for none of us has a more destructive enemy than our own heart."[13] This is Luther's position on the place of images within the scheme of Christian worship, a problem troublesome to the church during its entire history. Luther himself does not favor images. In his opinion the church would be better off without them. To Count Ludwig zu Stolberg he confided, "It's true. I'd rather see the images removed from the churches—not for fear that they would be venerated (though I suspect that the saints are held in higher esteem than the Bible) but for fear that images build up a false sense of trust and that people come to believe that by maintaining images they render God some sort of service." But this, according to Luther, does not mean that images should be thrown out; rather, there should be preaching that educates people against the misuses of images. "Since people's hearts are still clinging to images without being aware of the danger, one cannot simply discard the images without at the same time tearing the people's hearts." Basically it is Luther's pastoral concern that makes him at once opposed to and protective of images in the churches. This twofold concern in no way removed Luther's fundamental desire that all crafted things receive their due, for to him it was also conceivable that a person could indeed have a proper appreciation of images [paintings, stained-glass windows, statues] in the church.[14] In keeping his distance from an

10. WA 10³:28 / 13–14. [LW 51:83.]
11. See above, pp. 29ff.
12. WA 10³:35 / 8–9. [LW 51:86.]
13. WA 10³:34 / 1–2. [LW 51:85.]
14. WA 10³:26 / 6–7. Letter to Count zu Stolberg, April 25, 1522, WA Br 2:514 / 20ff. WA 10³:35 / 10ff.

inflexible position, as held by each of the opposing sides, he left himself room to remain objective as well as to cultivate his own joy in art. In a later conflict with Karlstadt over the image issue, Luther allowed this sense of appreciation to find fuller expression.[15]

With this same combination of love and freedom Luther approached the other issues that were stirring up the Wittenbergers and found them fairly ready to resolve their differences. Is it permitted to receive the Host with one's own hands? There was a time when Luther rebuked the clergy sharply in his sermons for monopolizing the right of handling the Host and claiming thereby to honor the sacrament. Now he passed equally sharp judgment on some of his Wittenbergers who had come to feel themselves good Christians because they claimed the right to handle the Host as they communed and wanted to force everyone else to do the same.[16] Yet a participation in the Lord's Supper under both kinds—much as it pleased Luther that some of them had resumed this biblical practice—was not the kind of thing they should legislate into general usage.[17] For the sake of the weak they should be just as little inclined to break the regulations on fasting as a testimony to their evangelical liberty, and least of all should they be ready to do away with private confession.[18] In no case is such abolition to be coerced by church legislation. Indeed, private confession, when practiced freely and in response to deep desire, is the kind of thing he would not give up even for all the treasures in the world. "For I

---

15. On the renewed discussion of the problem of images, see *Against the Heavenly Prophets in Matters of Images and Sacraments*, 1924–25 [*LW* 40:79–223]. Cf. below, p. 169. Also, on the whole subject—with the illuminating portrayal of the contrast between Luther and the viewpoint of the Reformed—see Hans von Campenhausen's essay "Die Bilderfrage in der Reformation," in his *Tradition und Leben: Kräfte der Kirchengeschichte: Aufsätze und Vorträge* (Tübingen, 1960), 360ff., esp. 385ff. A noteworthy treatment of the subject, which weighs the dangers encountered by the religious and aesthetic value of images, is in Franz von Sickingen's pamphlet addressed to Dieter von Handschuhsheim in the summer of 1522: To burn the pictures is folly. The question is whether such an act would promote or impede the way to salvation. If images are not misused in an idolatrous manner, and if instead the steadfast life and the firm faith in Christ on the part of the saints were contemplated, "then they would be fruitful for us and should be tolerated." However, in most cases it will be only a matter of seeing the "pretty features," in which case "the disposition and the true inward contemplation in prayer concerning the right, high, and ascending way to God falls short." For that reason, pictures of the saints were better placed in the rooms where people live than in the churches. E. Kück, *Schriftstellernde Adlige der Reformationszeit*, vol. 1: *Sickingen und Lantschad, Schulprogramm* (Rostock, 1899), cf. 18; cf. below, pp. 92 ff. This treatment approximates that of Martin Bucer, for whom images must be seen in balanced perspective (cf. his letter to Zwingli, April 19, 1524 [Zwingli, *Sämtliche Werke* 8:170ff.], which nonetheless has its own mystical tone).

16. WA 10³:43 / 7ff.; 46 / 9ff. [*LW* 51:89, 91.]

17. WA 10³:45 / 10ff. [*LW* 51:90.]

18. WA 10³:36 / 10ff.; 58 / 23ff. [*LW* 51:86, 97.]

know what comfort and strength private confession has given me. Nobody really knows its importance who has not struggled often and hard with the devil. I for one would have been strangled by the devil long ago were it not that the practice of confession had sustained me."[19]

As Luther wound up this series of eight sermons, he reminded the Wittenbergers once again of one whom they had not taken into account: the devil, who had led them into the folly of trying to bear witness to their being Christian by grasping the Host with their hands at Communion, by eating eggs and meat on days designated for fasting, and so on, instead of letting their witnessing be done in faith and love.[20] Because the devil cannot effectively attack the gospel in broad daylight and head-on, he prefers to make flank attacks. He would have rubbed his hands with delight if Luther had instigated widespread bloodshed in Germany, for if one can get something started by means of rumor, then sooner or later the whole business collapses of itself.[21] With their foolish arguments concerning images, the Wittenbergers have shown how little they know the devil. It is as though they had taken chalk instead of coal to make him black. And now, in face of his cunning dialectics, they no longer know which end is up.[22] By singling out the devil as the arch-opponent, Luther could go easy on his co-workers in the presence of the congregation. The commanding quality his sermons radiated did not spring from rhetorical skill or simply from the fact that he was the first "whom God had called to this work."[23] Rather, it grew out of the fact that he knew the wiles of the demonic enemy. "For I have eaten a clump of salt or two with him. I know him well, and he knows me well too."[24]

These sermons convey a distillation of the results of Luther's writings at the Wartburg. Without months of preparation in seclusion he could hardly have given such straightforward and compelling answers to the questions that had plunged the Wittenbergers into conflict. This set of sermons also contains Luther's principle for carrying out reform: Undertake no renewal unless the gospel is thoroughly preached and recognizable in it.[25] Luther questioned the justification of hardly any of the reforms undertaken by the Wittenbergers. He contended only that the time was not yet ripe to carry them out.

19. WA 10³:61 / 15ff. [LW 51:98.]
20. WA 10³:lx, 64ff.
21. WA 10³:9 / 2ff.; 19 / 3ff. [LW 51:73, 78.]
22. WA 10³:36 / 5–6. [LW 51:86.]
23. WA 10³:8 / 5ff. [LW 51:73.]
24. WA 10³:64 / 14–15. [LW 51:100.]
25. WA 10³:45 / 3–4. [LW 51:90.]

The spare stenographic copies of these sermons delivered during the octave of Invocavit [the first full week in Lent] give us some idea why it was possible for Luther, at one bold stroke, to recapture the heart of the townspeople and quash the mischief of the Wittenberg zealots. It was not only that the old-timers were thankful for a restoration of order: Jerome Schurff, for example, who only recently had been complaining bitterly over the local mischief, now wrote the elector "that great joy and exultation among the learned and the uneducated has sprung from Dr. Martin's return and from his sermons. By his mediating divine help he is putting us misled and angry people back on the way of truth by daily showing us where we went wrong and by using irrefutable arguments to get us out of the mess into which the interloping preachers got us."[26] An even stronger proof of the powerful effect of Luther on the people is the testimony of students, some of which has been preserved in letters. They breathe a youthful exuberance while bearing the same rhetorical style that Martin Bucer had used a little earlier when describing Luther's participation in the Heidelberg disputation to his friend Beatus Rhenanus.[27] Take the case of Albert Burer describing to Rhenanus what had been going on in Wittenberg: "Luther has come to restore order and to straighten out what Karlstadt and Gabriel (Zwilling) had messed up with their violent sermons. They had not shown the slightest consideration toward the weak. Martinus, however, like Paul, knows how to feed them with milk, until they have matured. . . . Judged by his face, Luther is a kind man and appears mild and good-natured. His voice is pleasant and sonorous, and one must marvel at his winsome gift of speech. What he says, teaches, and does is quite pious, even though his godless opponents claim the opposite. Whoever has heard him once—unless he is a stone—would gladly hear him again and again, for he drives home his points, like nails, into the minds of his hearers."[28] An even more personal note comes from the calm testimony of the young patrician from Nuremberg, Jerome Baumgartner, who must have been not far removed from Karlstadt's machinations. To a friend he wrote,

You will probably be eager to know what moved Luther to come back to us— nothing else but that we acted so thoughtlessly and impulsively, without realizing the scandal we were creating. All week long Luther did nothing but set up what had been knocked down and took us all severely to task. In short, we

26. March 9 and 15, 1522, WA Br 2:463ff.; 472 / 11ff.
27. WA 9:161ff.
28. March 27, 1522, WA 10³:liii. *Briefwechsel des Beatus Rhenanus*, ed. A. Horawitz and K. Hartfelder (Leipzig, 1886), 303–4.

had behaved terribly, so that we gave offense to the whole world. But God is faithful, and he was not about to leave us in error any longer.[29]

The Wittenberg congregation was not alone in readily readapting its ways to Luther's confident leadership. Those who had been leading the movement for renewal during Luther's absence now gave him a free hand. Melanchthon was glad to be relieved of the burden to act in Luther's place and promptly subordinated himself to his more famous friend. Zwilling realized at last what he had been doing and fell in line with Luther's thinking.[30] Only Karlstadt was resentful. Three years Luther's senior, it was difficult for him now to stand aside. In fact, he felt that Luther's decisions amounted to standing still in a half-finished task. So he had to put up with a number of reprimands. No longer was he allowed to preach in the Town Church, whose pulpit he had frequently filled without any official authorization; his ministerial functions were limited to the Castle Church of All Saints. And when he undertook to publish a report justifying his course of action on the issues raised during the past months—a report which, despite all his protestations to the contrary, was directed against Luther's procedure—the rector of the university intervened and stopped the press. Luther had not instigated this intervention, but he had requested Karlstadt not to fan the flames of controversy again. But if Karlstadt should insist, Luther warned that despite his own reluctance to do so he would brave an open scandal and take his opponent "by the horns." Then, to prevent the printer's suffering a financial loss, Luther at once supplied him with a manuscript of his own. For his part, it seems that Karlstadt refrained from sending a second tract to press, this one dealing with saints and images.[31] For these humiliations Karlstadt could blame only his own thoughtlessness and his suppressed but continually felt need for recognition. He was a poor loser in a regrettable cause. The old relationship between him and Luther was not restored, even though

29. To Hector Poemer, March 18, 1522, printed in H. Bornkamm, "Briefe der Reformationszeit aus dem Besitz Johann Valentin Andreäs," ARG 34 (1937); 148–49; later testimonies in WA 10³:lii ff. For a compilation by students of the main thoughts in these sermons of Luther, see O. Clemen, Beiträge zur Reformationsgeschichte aus Büchern und Handschriften der Zwickauer Ratsschulbibliothek (Berlin, 1902), 1:30–31.

30. Jerome Schurff to the Elector, March 15, 1522, WA Br 2:472 / 20–21. Luther to Link, March 19, 1522, WA Br 2:478 / 6. Luther to the Elector, May 8, 1522, WA Br 2:521 / 36ff.

31. For the university commission's excerpts from Karlstadt's tract, see H. Barge, Andreas Bodenstein von Karlstadt (Leipzig, 1905), 2:562. The correct interpretation is that of K. Müller, Luther und Karlstadt (Tübingen, 1907), 124ff. Letters: Luther to Spalatin, April 21 and 24, 1522, WA Br 2:509 / 12ff.; 511 / 12–13; Melanchthon to Spalatin, May 6, 1522, CR 1:570. Suppl. Mel. 6 / 1:187. MBW 227. Barge, Karlstadt, 1:453ff.

Luther continued to accord him friendly treatment.[32] All the more gratifying, therefore, was the fact that another relationship, which had hitherto been a handicap for Luther, was righted just at this time. It was the one with Wolfgang Capito, whom Luther had given a difficult time just two months earlier. Capito had traveled from Halle to find out how Luther was coping with the situation in Wittenberg. After hearing two of Luther's sermons, Capito was so impressed that a reconciliation ensued. Soon thereafter Capito resigned from the service of Cardinal Albrecht and moved to Strassburg as a preacher of the gospel.[33]

The Zwickau prophets were another story. The claims with which they had originally come on stage guaranteed some sort of ritual dance before the matter was settled. Lucky for them that they happened to be away from Wittenberg during the octave of Luther's sermons; he surely would not have spared them. But in early April, Marcus Thomae (Stübner) was back, bringing with him a convert, Magister Cellarius (Borrhaus). The two of them looked up Luther and tried to convince him of their own prophetic powers. In the course of this conversation Luther's subsequent image of the preachers of fanaticism took shape, its outlines remaining etched indelibly in his mind. The clever Thomae was out to prove to Luther syllogistically that there is no such thing as original sin: For Adam, the just, there is (according to 1 Tim. 1:9) no law and thus no sin. Thomae went on to explain the "talent" he had received, meaning thereby the mystical stage he had attained. Luther, he went on, was now standing in the first stage of mobility, but had a good chance of reaching the first stage of steadfastness in which he, Thomae, now found himself. When Luther appeared little impressed and asked for some sign to prove the presence of a prophetic spirit in him, Thomae said impudently that Luther might guess his thoughts—meaning that, according to Thomae, Luther was still pondering whether his own teachings might be true. Luther was so taken by surprise that only on the second visit, the next day, did he let Thomae have it. Two texts from Scripture had come to mind, as Luther—quoting the prophet Zechariah—told Thomae, "The Lord rebuke you, O Satan!" (Zech. 3:2, which, according to Jude 9, leaves judgment to God). If possible, Cellarius made a still more dismal impression on Luther. He began by flattering Luther, calling him more than an apostle. When Luther declined this designation, his caller went to the other extreme and relieved

32. To Speratus, May 16, 1522, WA Br 2:531 / 31. To Christopher Hofmann(?), late May 1522(?), ibid., 510 / 11ff.

33. See above, pp. 42–43. WA Br 2:435ff.

himself of a torrent of filthy scolding so that Luther could not get a word in edgewise. In short, Luther's impression was vivid: "I have spoken with the devil incarnate." He dismissed these two fickle spirits with the scorn worthy of an Old Testament prophet: I forbid your god to perform any miracles contrary to the will of my God.[34] Thereupon Thomae and Cellarius left town, their role in Wittenberg spent. Nor did things change when the two other members of the Zwickau triumvirate came to see Luther unexpectedly: Drechsel, the most clumsy of the three, and Nicholas Storch, the so-called "prince of the prophets" who raised the issue of infant baptism. Instinctively Luther perceived the flippant spirit of a wind-bag who hardly took his own thoughts seriously.[35]

This assault of the devil, as Luther called it, was repulsed, but what it had revealed was indeed worth pondering. It showed Luther how easily people could be misled and how quickly even his friends could waver in the matter of testing the spirits. More sobering still was that Luther was made to recognize the danger that the gospel itself was being misunderstood as a license to give up "something no longer required of you."[36] Alongside the lovelessness of this turn of events, nothing angered Luther more than the popular notion of the signs of a truly Christian faith: the eating of meat and eggs, taking the Host in one's hands, and receiving the cup in Communion. By way of contrast and caution it now became to Luther an equally important sign of Christian liberty and Christian love to hold off from any more reforms for the time being, even though those thus far undertaken were in themselves fully justifiable. It is no small proof of Luther's power over the hearts of the people in Wittenberg that he succeeded in gaining their support for his position and in shaking off the unauthorized agitators of reform. In doing so he regained such support as he had earlier enjoyed during the years of his initial breakthrough.

These March weeks proved decisive for the future course of the Reformation. Insofar as Luther was able to prune its wild offshoots, he retained for the ecclesial tree the powers of quiet growth. By doing so he introduced an unusual feature into his work of renewal, one that remained characteristic of it. The strength of other reformers, notably Zwingli and

34. To Spalatin, April 12, 1522, WA Br 2:493 / 17ff. WA TR 1, no. 362, 153, WA TR 2, no. 2060, 307 / 9ff. WA TR 3, no. 2837a and b, 13ff.

35. Drechsel, in WA TR 2, no. 2060, 307 / 17. WA TR 3, no. 2837a, 14 / 11; no. 2837b, 15 / 18. WA TR 5, no. 5568, 249 / 2. On Storch, Luther to Spalatin, September 4, 1522, WA Br 2:597 / 25ff. [LW 54, no. 5568, 455.]

36. See Jakob Burckhardt, "Historische Fragmente aus dem Nachlass," in his collected works, Gesamtausgabe, 7:314. Cited in H. Bornkamm, Luther im Spiegel der deutschen Geistesgeschichte, 2d ed. (Göttingen, 1970), 91.

Calvin, lay in the consistency with which they carried out their aims. Luther's work, on the contrary, was marked by repeated interruptions and the retarding force of questioning: Is the time ripe? Are the motives pure? Luther's considerations concerning the reform of church order were in the future to be twofold. One consideration was the matter of timing, the other was the role of the people. How can one find the right moment to introduce change? And how, in spite of the question being often raised but never really answered, should the people participate? Should one gather the more mature members of the parish as a kind of advance team for a subsequently general restructuring?

For the time being, Luther devised a moratorium for Wittenberg. In the Town Church, Sunday masses continued as formerly. Easter Communion in 1522 was celebrated according to traditional usage: without the cup, in Latin, and with the usual vestments and ritual. Only the canon of the mass was unobtrusively cleansed of anything that might suggest the notion of sacrifice. But for those who desired it, there was also a special celebration of the Lord's Supper in which the communicants received both the bread and the wine.[37] This arrangement took care of things for one year. After all, according to prevailing custom and in the absence of any emergency, no one anticipated a massive Communion turnout until the following Easter. In the meantime, preaching on the proper meaning and form of the sacrament would be having its desired effect. Private masses dropped away of their own weight. None of the clergy said them anymore, nor did parishioners request them anymore. As a result, services that used to be held in the churches on weekdays were discontinued. Only once, later on during Lent (between the Sundays Oculi and Laetare), did Luther present a week-long series of sermons as he had done earlier during the octave of Invocavit, and this time he treated the Ten Commandments. Later he may have preached on other parts of the catechism.[38]

The importance of these events in Wittenberg is clear. Luther's decisions had to become the example for the entire Reformation movement. Therefore he was intent on keeping the results in a generally usable form. He did this with the treatise *Receiving Both Kinds in the Sacrament*.[39] While he had cast his sermons on this subject in a pastoral vein for the

---

37. Luther to Nicholas Hausmann, March 26, 1522, WA Br 2:438 / 21ff. In both kinds, WA 10²:29ff.

38. WA 10³:xxxviii.

39. WA 10²:11–41. [LW 36:(231) 237–67.]

benefit of his Wittenbergers, he now distilled the essence of those sermons in the form of guidelines for all pastors and congregations facing the same issues. Above all, he admonished that they should stay on the "right track," not let the devil push them too far to the right or to the left. "Formerly the devil made us too papistic, and now he wants to make us too evangelical."[40] External church practices are neither good works nor sin, so they allow freedom. Then why does one not change them? To this Luther raises the counterquestion: "Where are the people who are qualified to begin and carry the changes out?"[41] He wonders, for a moment, whether it might not be best for the people to abstain from the sacrament temporarily while the gospel is preached to them and they have an opportunity to gain a proper understanding of the sacrament. After all, Luther insists, everything depends a thousand times more on the words of Christ in the sacrament than on the enjoyment of it. But again he must ask, "Where do we get such preachers?"[42] The people are accustomed to coming to the sacrament; for the sake of those who cannot bring themselves to give up the old ways it will be necessary [for a while longer] to commune them in the manner to which they are accustomed. Even priests who may still be saying private masses ("off in a corner") should not be stopped in their tracks; rather, let sermons be preached against such abuses. In time one can skip this or that mass and interpose a service of worship with Communion in both kinds. This is the counsel of patient and deliberate procedure. Luther allows for only one exception: on the debated issue of the marriage of priests. Here he gives the priests a clear answer. A priest is permitted to marry when he feels that he cannot get along without a wife. Luther's basic motif—consideration of the conscience—makes its point also on the opposite side, for the congregation is summoned to exercise love and should not take offense at priests that do marry.[43]

Disturbances or not, Luther would in any case have returned to Wittenberg after Easter 1522. The Bible translation was his big unfinished task. He had mastered its beginnings amid the storms at the Wartburg and now he was anxious to get on with it. To do so, however, required the resource materials in Wittenberg as well as the counsel of friends who knew the

40. WA 10²:12 / 1–2. [LW 36:237.]
41. WA 10²:24 / 13–14. [LW 36:249.]
42. WA 10²:27 / 3ff., 26; 29 / 18ff.; 30 / 5ff.; 32 / 3ff. [LW 36:252, 251, 254, 257.]
43. WA 10²:35–36. [LW 36:260.]

subject. His preoccupations with settling the local tumults, and the added duties that were thrust on him, only intensified his desire to get at the job. Now at last the help of friends, especially of Melanchthon, was available. First they carefully went over Luther's translation of the New Testament. For problems that baffled them, they sought advice elsewhere. Through Spalatin, Luther was able to borrow precious stones from the elector's treasury in order to provide a more accurate rendering of the heavenly Jerusalem's ornamentation (Rev. 21). Melanchthon dug up information on the approximate current valuation of coins mentioned in the Bible, and with delight he worked his way into the "enigmatic field" of ancient numismatics. From an antique dealer in Leipzig he ordered a Roman map of Judea which would accompany the published text, but unfortunately no such map could be found. Difficult passages and terms were submitted to their friend Spalatin, himself a learned scholar.[44] To him a delighted Luther on May 10 sent a copy of the first page of the German New Testament as a taste of more to come. On July 26 he reported that the halfway point had been reached, yet he sighed over the slow pace of production even though three presses were daily printing an impressive quantity. On September 20, 1522, the book was finished.[45]

Not only had Luther gone over his translation thoroughly before publication, he had also provided a number of supplements, the most important of which were his prefaces to the New Testament books. In providing them he followed the precedent of the Vulgate Bible and at the same time differentiated from it an evangelical understanding of the New Testament Scriptures. His preface to the New Testament as a whole preceded the four Gospels, and each of the other books, beginning with The Acts of the Apostles, received its own preface. Later Luther did the same thing for

44. Luther to Spalatin, March 30, 1522, WA Br 2:490 / 8ff. (Cf. also May 10 and 15, 1522, WA Br 2:524 / 6ff.; 527 / 19ff.) Melanchthon to Spalatin, March 30, 1522, CR 1:567. *Suppl. Mel*. 6 / 1:185. *MSA* 7 / 1:172ff. *MBW* 224. To George Sturz, May 5, 1522, CR 1:571–72. *Suppl. Mel*. 6 / 1:186. *MBW* 226. To Spalatin, May 6, 1522, CR 1:570. *Suppl. Mel*. 6 / 1:187. *MBW* 227; September 1522, CR 1:574–75. *Suppl. Mel*. 6 / 1:195. *MSA* 7 / 1:177ff. *MBW* 237. To Cruciger, November 1522, CR 1:583. This should probably be placed with Otto Albrecht (WA DB 6:xlv), because of its suggestion, near that of February 25 (CR 1:563), that is, in March 1522 and not in September, *Suppl. Mel*. 6 / 1:194, or November, *CR. MSA* 7 / 1:169–70. *MBW* 219. [*LW* 49:3ff. Among various works in English, see M. Reu, *Luther's German Bible* (Columbus, Ohio: Lutheran Book Concern, 1934), 146–84.]

45. WA Br2:524 / 5ff.; 580 / 19ff. To Schwarzenberg, September 21, 1522, WA Br 2:601 / 32. Extended information on the history of Luther's Bible translation is in the introductions to the edition of the German Bible, WA DB, 12 vols. (1954–61). On the whole subject, see W. Walther, *Luthers Deutsche Bibel* (Berlin, 1917), and the introduction by H. Volz to the new edition, *Martin Luther: Die ganze Heilige Schrift Deutsch, Wittenberg 1545* (Munich, 1972), 33ff. [*LW* 29:15.]

the books of the Old Testament and of the Apocrypha prior to the publication of the entire translated Bible (1534). These prefaces provide the most informative and lively introduction to his understanding of the Scriptures.[46] Luther intended that his introductory words provide the reader with the key to seeing the New Testament in its wholeness as well as its diversity. There is but one gospel, and it is this that unifies the New Testament even as it is the law that gives unity to the Old Testament. The gospel itself is not a book but "a good story and report sounded forth into all the world by the apostles, telling of a true David who strove with sin, death, and the devil and overcame them." This living, orally transmitted message is in itself a "New Testament." Just as a dying person makes a will, so Christ has made it his will that the gospel be spread throughout the world. Indeed, both he and the apostles offer also "law and precept," but they do it quite differently from the Old Testament, not in the form of stern commands but in the form of friendly encouragement, such as "Blessed are . . . ," "I exhort," "I entreat," "I beg." According to the contents of this message the various New Testament writings derive their different characteristics. Those that offer this proclamation of the benefits of Christ in strongest and purest terms are the "kernel and marrow" of the New Testament: John's Gospel and the First Epistle of John, the epistles of Paul and the First Epistle of Peter. In a separate section on "the true and noblest books of the New Testament," Luther states reasons for assigning priority, for these are "the books that show you Christ and teach you all that is necessary and salvatory for you to know."[47] Because John's Gospel writes very little about the works and miracles of Christ, but very much about his message, it is "the one, fine, true, and chief gospel."[48] Like the letters of Paul and Peter, it "far surpasses the other three Gospels." When measured by these standards, "James's epistle is really an epistle of straw, . . . for it has nothing of the nature of the gospel about it."[49] Luther's noted judgment on James thus holds only in comparison to those New

---

46. Cf. the introduction by H. Bornkamm in *Martin Luthers Vorreden zur Bibel*, ed. H. Bornkamm (Hamburg 1967), 7ff. An extended examination in comparison to prefaces in the tradition of the early and medieval period is in M. E. Schild, *Abendländische Bibelvorreden bis zur Lutherbibel*, QFRG 39 (Gütersloh, 1970). "Vorrede zum Neuen Testament," in WA DB 6:3ff. *Luthers Vorreden zur Bibel*, 135–39, on the following. WA DB 6:4 / 4ff., 13; 8 / 12–13, 20ff.; 8 / 23; 10 / 12. [*LW* 35:357–411.]

47. WA DB 6:10 / 7ff., 31–32. Bornkamm, ed., *Luthers Bibelvorreden*, 140–41. This last section on assigning priorities, differing as it does from the scheme of the preface as a whole, was subsequently omitted by Luther with the first publication of the complete German Bible (1534). [*LW* 35:357–62, esp. 361, 362, 358, n. 5.]

48. WA DB 6:10 / 25–26. Bornkamm, ed., *Luthers Bibelvorreden*, 140. [*LW* 35:362.]

49. WA DB 6:10 / 33–34. Bornkamm, ed. *Luthers Bibelvorreden*, 141. [*LW* 35:362.]

Testament writings which he regards as central, and he clarifies his position in the preface to the Epistle of James. In fact, he praises this letter because "it sets up no doctrines of men but vigorously promulgates the law of God" and contains "many good sayings" besides.[50] Yet Luther does not regard this letter as "the writing of an apostle," for it does not once mention the suffering, resurrection, or spirit of Christ. Unlike the authentic apostolic writings it does not "inculcate [treibe] Christ" or preach him, but speaks only of a general faith in God. Luther's doubts about the authorship of James sprang from a comment by Jerome included in the Vulgate as well as from the suspicion expressed by Erasmus in his annotations to the Greek New Testament (1516). Luther then adds his own historical reason: James quotes (4:5 and 5:20) from Galatians (4:5) and from 1 Peter (4:8). Therefore, as commonly assumed, this could not have been a writing of the apostle James the son of Zebedee, who had been martyred at an earlier time.[51] This epistle, Luther contends, may be from a disciple of one of the apostles who wished to guard against the misunderstanding that faith without works is enough but who was not equal to the task he had set himself, for "he tries to accomplish by harping on the law what the apostles accomplish by stimulating people to love." New Testament research has long ago corroborated Luther's position.

The same thing holds with regard to Luther's contention that the Epistle to the Hebrews—down to its doctrine of repentance, "a masterfully and profoundly learned" epistle—is not Paul's work. Nor can the Epistle of Jude or the Revelation of John claim apostolic authorship. Luther also observed the differences between the visionary Johannine Apocalypse and Old Testament prophecy and, on the basis of comparison with 4 Esdras [as included in the Vulgate Apocrypha], he properly classes it with the late Jewish apocalyptic literature. Luther was also aware that the place of the Book of Revelation in the New Testament canon was long disputed by the ancient church. In short, "My spirit cannot accommodate itself to this book. . . . Christ is neither taught in it nor known in it. . . . Therefore I stick to the books which present Christ to me clearly and purely." In the year 1530 Luther replaced this preface with another. There, without giving up his doubt as to its Johannine authorship, he set forth his own inter-

50. WA DB 7:384 / 5–6; 386 / 19. Bornkamm, ed., *Luthers Bibelvorreden*, 177. [*LW* 35:395, 397.]

51. Taken from Jerome, *De viris illustribus* 1, into the Vulgate. *MPL* 23:639. F. Stummer, *Einführung in die lateinische Bibel* (Paderborn, 1928), 260–61. Schild, *Abendländische Bibelvorreden*, 62. Erasmus, *Annotationes*, cited in J. Leipoldt, *Geschichte des neutestamentlichen Kanons* (Leipzig, 1908), 2:19–20, n. 1. Luther: WA DB 7:386 / 10ff. Bornkamm, ed., *Luthers Bibelvorreden*, 177. [*LW* 35:396, 397.]

pretation and application of this book over which so many have puzzled.[52] By means of these free and bold prefaces accompanying his translation of the New Testament, Luther not only gave the reader freedom but also provided the cradle for a critical study of the Scriptures, a task that became one of the distinguishing marks of Protestantism—for the meaning of "critical" is to make the gospel the standard of measurement and not simply to make use of general historical or rational criteria of authenticity or probability. Thereby he meant in spiritual (not temporal) terms that the proclamation of Christ has priority over the reporting of his deeds. In the course of subsequent investigation this understanding of Luther's has proven itself an insight of highest significance. The reports of the [synoptic] Gospels hardly make sense without a prior proclamation of Christ. Since Luther's time, however, the objective as well as the historical problem has become more complicated. If it still sufficed in his time to accord the apostolic letters and the Fourth Gospel a leading position over the synoptic Gospels, it has since that time—and entirely in line with Luther's thinking—become an essential task to look for the gospel within the Gospels and, when necessary, to place it critically over against the Fourth Gospel and the apostolic letters. Luther's principle of turning the Christ proclamation into the [prime] inner criterion of the Scriptures signified a revolution. Without discarding it, he ended the formal sameness of the canonical Scriptures. He gave drastic notice of how seriously he meant this by placing the Epistle to the Hebrews and the Epistle of James near the end of the New Testament, just ahead of the Epistle of Jude and the Revelation of John. He located these four books at the end of the table of contents and did not number them as he had the others, thus denoting them as writings of secondary importance. He adhered to this practice as long as he lived.

In all but one of the prefaces, Luther introduced the reader to the variations of the gospel in the respective books of the New Testament, providing a brief and lively notice of the contents. The one exception was his preface to Romans. Its contents and significance called for fuller treatment. Luther completed this preface last, and it was inserted as a special folio just before the entire New Testament came off the press.[53] He followed a style like that employed by Erasmus in his edition of the Greek

52. WA DB 7:344 / 20; 386 / 22ff.; 404 / 6–7, 25–26, 29–30. Preface of 1530, WA DB 7:406ff. Bornkamm, ed., *Luthers Bibelvorreden,* 176, 179, 179–80. Preface of 1530, WA DB 7:180–90. [*LW* 35:397, 399. Preface of 1530, *LW* 35:399–411.]

53. Luther's letters to Spalatin shortly before September 20, 1522, WA Br 2:598–99. [*LW* 49:14–16.]

New Testament and Melanchthon in his learned *Loci Communes* (1521) in that he first explained the basic Pauline concepts, magnificently clustered around the concept of the Spirit: The law of God intends a spiritual fulfillment, that is, from the bottom of one's heart, and so to do the works of the law and to fulfill the law are two different matters. Sin is lack of the Holy Spirit; its opposite is faith. Luther described the immense life of faith in immortal words:

> Faith is a divine work in us which changes us and makes us to be born anew of God.... Faith is a living, daring confidence in God's grace, so sure and certain that the believer would stake his life on it a thousand times. This knowledge of and confidence in God's grace makes men glad and bold and happy in dealing with God and with all creatures. And this is the work which the Holy Spirit performs in faith. Because of it, without compulsion, a person is ready and glad to do good to everyone, to serve everyone, to suffer everything out of love and praise to God who has shown him this grace. Thus it is impossible to separate works from faith, quite as impossible as to separate heat and light from fire.[54]

Following this explanation of concepts there comes a precise analysis of the epistle chapter by chapter. This preface is a short summary of Luther's theology and, as prefaces to Romans go, it stands in a class by itself. As long as it was retained in the published Bibles it proved a boon to many a reader. It had its most memorable effect some two hundred years later in England. In 1738 the reading of this preface led to the conversion of John Wesley and thereby became the impulse for a renewal of Christianity in England that extended far beyond the bounds of Methodism.[55]

In addition to the prefaces, Luther provided his published translation with a wealth of marginal notes, definitions of words, and historical data, along with polemical references to the Roman interpretation and occasional theological expositions. Since no single printer in Wittenberg had the capital sufficient to launch an undertaking this ambitious, it became the venture of a partnership. The printer, Michael Lotther, Jr., supplemented the text with decorative initials. Lucas Cranach, Sr., prepared twenty-one full-page woodcuts. The two men designated as publishers were Cranach (by vocation an apothecary as well as painter and artist) and

---

54. WA DB 7:10 / 6ff. Bornkamm, ed., *Luthers Bibelvorreden*, 148. [*LW* 35:367, 370–71.]

55. *The Journal of the Rev. John Wesley, A.M.*, ed. N. Curnock, 2d ed. (London, 1938), 1:475–76. M. Schmidt, "Die Bedeutung Luthers für John Wesleys Bekehrung," *LuJ* 20 (1938): 125ff., 138–39. Also, M. Schmidt, *John Wesley* (Zurich and Frankfurt, 1953), 1:232–33. For the widespread effect of this preface in German pietism, see M. Schmidt's essay "Luthers Vorrede zum Römerbrief im Pietismus" in his *Wiedergeburt und neuer Mensch*, "Gesammelte Studien zur Geschichte des Pietismus," AGP 2 (Witten, 1959), 299ff.

Christian Döring. The latter was a man of many facets: a goldsmith by vocation, an innkeeper, owner of a transport business, a publisher and book dealer, and (to use Luther's designation of him) a *homo theologissimus,* a man quite well conversant in theology.[56] All indications are that Luther intended to make the Bible a book to be used in the home. In this he succeeded beyond expectation, despite the high price of at least a half guilder.[57] The first edition of three thousand copies was quickly sold out. Already by December, Luther had to bring out a second edition, slightly improved in details.

Even before the New Testament was completely printed Luther was at work on the first part of the Old Testament and finished the Pentateuch in mid-December.[58] Early in 1523 it went to press, and by the end of the year this sequence of the five books of Moses had gone through three editions. The first edition had appeared by mid-year [not only in Wittenberg but also] in two separate printings in Augsburg. For the process of checking out his translation, Luther found Melanchthon and Aurogallus, the Wittenberg Hebraist, knowledgeable helpers. Ever since the time he had lectured on the Psalms (1513–16) Luther had been intent on going beyond the Vulgate and seeking the meaning of the original Hebrew text. His own linguistic abilities would not have been sufficient of themselves. Aside from Jewish scholars, there were only a few humanists in Germany—above all, Reuchlin—who were at home in Hebrew. But there were resource books that brought the original Hebrew text along with a Latin translation and explanations. Foremost among these was the literal translation of the Psalms by Jerome. Luther was familiar with it from the *Psalterium Quincuplex*—a compilation of five translations—produced by the French humanist Lefèvre d'Etaples (Faber Stapulensis, 1450–1536). He also made use of Reuchlin's *De rudimentis linguae Hebraicae* (1506), an introduction to the Hebrew language with lexical and grammatical information, a work he may already have purchased during his student days

56. *WA DB* 6:xlv. H. Volz, *Hundert Jahre Wittenberger Bibeldruck 1522-1626* (Göttingen, 1954), 15ff. On the pictures, A. Schramm, *Die Illustration der Lutherbibel* (Leipzig, 1923), and P. Schmidt, *Die Illustration der Lutherbibel, 1522–1700* (Basel, 1962). On Döring, *WA DB* 8:xlviii, n. 11. N. Müller, *Die Wittenberger Bewegung,* 2d ed. (Leipzig, 1911), 126ff. Luther's comment on Döring is in *WA Br* 1:96 / 22. [*LW* 49:15. Luther to Spalatin, September 20, 1522. Cf. *LW* 48:42, n. 8.]

57. The estimates vary between one-half, one, and one and a half florins. *WA DB* 6:xliii. Also *WA DB* 6:xlvi, n. 1, and Volz, *Bibeldruck,* 19. The price of one-half florin was per copy as it came off the press, without the illuminated capitals. G. Buchwald, "Lutherana, Notizen aus Rechnungsbüchern des Thüringischen Staatsarchivs zu Weimar," *ARG* 25 (1928): 26.

58. Luther to Link, December 19, 1522, *WA Br* 2:633 / 48. [*LW* 49:25.]

in Erfurt.[59] With aids like these, and also with other translations, he sought to establish what the Hebrew text said and meant, without entirely bypassing the Vulgate, which was based on a Greek translation of the Old Testament Hebrew.[60]

Just as Luther had provided the German New Testament with prefaces covering the whole and its parts, so he now prefaced the Pentateuch with an introduction to the Old Testament as a whole. This concise preface was based on the relation between the Old Covenant and the New and is his most important introduction to the Scriptures as such. He endeavors to see the Scriptures as a whole, not by spiritualizing the Old Testament or dissolving it in allegorical meanings, the way Origen, Jerome, and others had done. Instead, according to Luther, the Old Testament must be understood in its historical reality, and as this reality becomes visible in retrospect from the New Testament. The eschatological expectation that runs through the Old Testament has found its goal in Christ. The character of law, which marks the Old Testament throughout, is really recognized in its essence and in the coherence of all its pronouncements for the first time from the gospel of Christ. In him the salvific quality of the law is abolished and its juridical quality reaffirmed. Precisely in its unordered diversity, which does not separate temporal and spiritual commandments, it is authentically law. This confusion corresponds to the character of human life itself and to God's manifold way of dealing with it. In Luther's words, "God governs all the laws mixed together, like the stars in the heavens and the flowers in the fields, in such a way that at every hour a man must be ready for anything and do whatever the situation requires."[61] Nevertheless, all laws that God has given man possess an inner coherence: "faith toward God and love toward one's neighbor, for all God's laws come to that."[62] When understood so deeply, the law requires not only a person's deeds but also his heart. "Accordingly, whoever does not keep this

59. Inferred from Luther's letter to John Lang, May 29, 1522, a friend who had helped him with his study of Hebrew; WA Br 2:547 / 2ff. Lang made Luther a gift of Wolfgang Faber's *Institutiuncula in Hebraicam Linguam* (Basel, 1516); WA 9:115.

60. A detailed assessment of Luther's knowledge of Hebrew during his earlier years (to 1516) is in S. Raeder, "Das Hebraische bei Luther untersucht bis zum Ende der ersten Psalmenvorlesung," BHTh 31 (Tübingen, 1961). See also K. A. Meissinger, *Luthers Exegese in der Frühzeit* (Leipzig, 1911), 55ff. And O. Scheel, *Martin Luther: Vom Katholizismus zur Reformation*, 3d and 4th eds. (Tübingen, 1930), 2:413ff. [Reu, *Luther's German Bible*, 75–145, provides helpful information on Luther as a translator; pp. 185–232 survey his work on the Old Testament in German.]

61. WA DB 8:18 / 31–20 / 5. Bornkamm, ed., *Luthers Bibelvorreden*, 37. [*LW* 35:239–41; the quotation, 241.]

62. WA DB 8:14 / 34. Bornkamm, ed., *Luthers Bibelvorreden*, 34. [*LW* 35:238–39.]

good law, or keeps it unwillingly, cannot be righteous or good in his heart."[63] And Christ has come not only to inculcate the law anew but also to make it a concern of the heart. "Through the grace of Christ," as Luther contends, "the heart has now become good, loving the law and satisfying it. The office of Moses can no longer rebuke the heart and make it to be sin for not having kept the commandments and for being guilty of death, as it did prior to grace, before Christ came."[64]

His ardor undiminished from the time he had begun to translate the Old Testament while the New Testament was being printed, Luther hurried from the Pentateuch and plunged into the historical books (from Joshua through Esther). Already on December 3, 1523, he could report to his friend Nicholas Hausmann in Zwickau that he had completed the translation of this second part. Although this part was to be off the press before Christmas, it did not appear until February 1524. By that time, he wrote, he had taken up the poetic books (Job, Psalms, Proverbs, Ecclesiastes, Song of Solomon, the Prophets), which he called "the biggest and the most difficult."[65] He was right about that. The intricate work required a cut into his other duties if the entire translation project was not to be too long delayed and from the practical angle the publisher thereby penalized. By the autumn of 1524 only a portion of this third part appeared in print, and the prophets had to be postponed.[66] Luther then combined his work on them with his lectures on the prophets. In May 1524, after his teaching had been interrupted for three years, he commenced his lecturing with the prophet Hosea.[67] But the workload of these years rose like a tide—the bitter debates with the fanatical "Enthusiasts," the peasants, Erasmus—so that he could accomplish little more than a seriatim publication of individual prophets, each translation being supplied with the usual preface. When his life once again became more settled, his ardor for translating returned. At last, in 1532, the complete edition of the prophets appeared. Two years later the entire German Bible came off the press.

63. WA DB 8:24 / 15–16. Bornkamm, ed., *Luthers Bibelvorreden*, 40. [*LW* 35:244.]

64. WA DB 8:24 / 25ff. Beginning with the 1536 edition of the complete Bible, Luther expressed himself more cautiously: "For through Christ sin is forgiven, God is reconciled, and the heart has begun to feel kindly toward the law. The office of Moses ..."; WA DB 8:25 / 25. Bornkamm, ed., *Luthers Bibelvorreden*, 41. [*LW* 35:244, esp. n. 17.]

65. WA Br 3:199 / 11–12.

66. WA DB 10²:xv.

67. WA DB 11²:ix, n. 2. He had concluded his lectures on March 29, 1521, just before his journey to Worms. Even now he was hesitant to resume lecturing because the Bible translation had his primary consideration. To the Elector Frederick he wrote on March 23, 1524. WA Br 3:258, 10. Luther felt he had been adequately replaced by Melanchthon's lectures on the Bible; which was quite the opposite to Melanchthon's opinion, for he himself did not feel that he could in any way measure up to the task that had been given him. W. Maurer, *Der junge Melanchthon*, 2:421–22. [*LW* 49:74–76.]

4

The Spread of the
Evangelical Movement

For Luther a fortunate year was unfolding. [It was 1522, and] peace had
been restored in Wittenberg. "Here there is nothing but love and friendship," he wrote Spalatin.[1] Whatever his congregation may still have owed
him in terms of understanding the heart of his message was amply com-
pensated by the news coming from all sides about the advance of the
gospel's proclamation. In Wittenberg, Luther completed a piece he had
probably begun while still at the Wartburg[2] in which, deeply moved, he
expressed his joy that the knight Hartmut von Kronberg had in two separate writings confessed his adherence to the gospel movement. The knight
had attracted Luther's attention when in May 1521, after the Edict of
Worms had been promulgated, he renounced a stipend he had been receiving annually from the emperor.[3] Now things had changed. Through
the perverse behavior of his Wittenbergers, Luther felt he had been hit
hard by the Enemy so that "the smoke is smarting my eyes."[4] Besides,
persecutors like Duke George of Saxony were a real threat to the gospel,
so it was comforting for Luther to be able to look to a man like Kronberg
and see how "a person handles the tender truth and treasures it."[5] A
frustrated longing for fellowship thus found fulfillment from afar, for it was
part of the nature of faith that it must be able to speak, "until wherever
possible we are all kneaded together into one loaf."[6]

Luther opened his heart to this friend whom he had not met personally.
He was greatly concerned over the future of Germany, a land that he saw
as persecuting and killing the messengers of God. But he was also full of
stubborn confidence in the "almighty resurrection of Christ," which put

1. May 10, 1522, WA Br 2:524 / 13.
2. WA 10²:53ff.
3. To Melanchthon, May 12, 1521, WA Br 2:333 / 29–30. MBW 139. [LW 48:216. The
stipend amounted to 200 guilders per year.]
4. WA 10²:56 / 8ff.
5. WA 10²:53 / 27.
6. WA 10²:54 / 16ff.

all enemies to shame.[7] Kronberg replied at once and gave Luther the kind of pastoral encouragement he seldom received. Kronberg agreed with Luther's concern over the German people, but he also reminded Luther of certain great reassurances: of the Word of truth which God had revealed to the German nation more than to others; of the printer's art, "first invented on German soil," which permits the Word to be spread "in good, clear German" through Luther's translation; of the heavenly Teacher, the Holy Spirit, promised to everyone who prays for His presence.[8] Luther took courage from this as well as from Kronberg's subsequent letters, noting that "the Word of God is making considerable progress among us in various places."[9]

From all possible quarters similar reports were coming in. A number of cities invited Luther to visit them immediately. He responded, and immediately after Easter (April 20) he began a journey that for him, an outlaw, was not without danger because much of it led through the territory of his enemy Duke George. At least once he rode on horse at night, wearing civilian attire and accompanied by a bodyguard.[10] Between April 27 and May 6 he preached eleven times, including the towns of Borna, Altenburg, Zwickau, Eilenburg, and Torgau, mainly on the issue of faith and good works in order to dispel the gossip that he had little regard for such matters. And in Zwickau he also preached on infant baptism.[11] There, in the place where Müntzer and the "Enthusiasts" had upset so much by their agitation, the whole town turned out. The large St. Mary's Church could not hold the crowd, so Luther had to speak again from the town hall in the marketplace and yet a third time at the castle. In Altenburg the town council asked Luther to name someone to fill a vacant pulpit in the local church. Luther obliged by suggesting Gabriel Zwilling, who had repented of the unrest he had helped stir up in Wittenberg. This was a generous but hardly diplomatic proposal inasmuch as the filling of this post had become a heated jurisdictional dispute, to which we shall return in another connection. When the elector was called on for his decision, his vivid recollection of Zwilling's behavior in Eilenburg and Wittenberg made him withhold approval.[12] The people in Eilenburg and Erfurt were

7. WA 10²:55 / 19ff.

8. April 14, 1522, WA Br 2:500 / 104ff.

9. August 14, 1522, WA Br 2:588 / 14–15.

10. May 3, 1522. R. Hofmann, "Bilder aus einer sächsischen Stadt im Reformationszeitalter," NASG 15 (1904): 56.

11. WA 10³:86ff. WA Br 2:516, n. 1.

12. Correspondence between the town council, Luther, and the Elector, around April 15 and 17 and May 6, 8, and 22, as well as Luther's letter to Zwilling, May 27, 1522; WA Br 2:502ff. Cf. above, p. 58.

also making requests for preachers or asking for advice. Farther away, in Silesia, Duke Karl von Münsterberg, a grandson of the Utraquist Bohemian King George of Podiebrad, requested Luther to send him something in writing on the scriptural basis for administering the Lord's Supper in both kinds. Besides, Münsterberg had already made John Hess [1490–1547], a friend of Luther and Melanchthon, his chaplain at the court in Oels.[13] Other authors were sending Luther copies of their tracts. Paul Speratus, ousted from Würzburg and then from Vienna but now serving in the town of Iglau in Moravia sent him an admirable booklet on monastic vows (a sermon he had preached in Vienna's Cathedral of St. Stephen). And the knight Silvester von Schaumberg, a friend of Luther over the past two years, sent him his tract on the creed. Over developments like these Luther exulted: "The very stones are beginning to cry out when the apostles are being muzzled."[14] And again, after the royal Polish general secretary Louis Dietz (Decius) of Cracow, an Alsatian skilled in many things, had paid him a visit, Luther rejoiced, "Everywhere people are thirsting for the gospel. From all sides they are begging us for preachers."[15]

When a prince of the empire for the first time approached him with a request for a preacher, Luther was happy indeed. The man was Count George von Wertheim, an optimal example, as Luther described him to Spalatin. The count had been a member of the small committee of the imperial diet at Worms before which Luther appeared on April 24, 1521. The impression that Luther made on the count on that occasion had won him over. How well he had understood Luther presently became evident in an initial experiment. To Wertheim, Luther commended Jacob Strauss, a former Dominican monk who some months earlier had been matriculated at the University in Wittenberg. He was a refugee from Hall [Hallein (?), not far from Salzburg, in the Austrian Tirol] where he had been preaching evangelical sermons with great success. In a recent pamphlet he acknowledged himself a kindred spirit of the Wittenbergers. However, no sooner was Strauss in Wertheim than he showed colors more akin to those of Karlstadt than of Luther, for he was the type who relied mainly on orders from the prince to bring about rapid changes in ecclesial

13. The duke's letter, of around March 20, 1522, is probably identical to that delivered on June 29, 1522; WA Br 2:569ff. Luther and Melanchthon to Hess, March 25, 1522, WA Br 2:482. CR 1:566–67. MBW 222.

14. To Spalatin, May 15, 1522, WA Br 2:527 / 50ff. Schaumberg's first letter to Luther was on June 11, 1520; WA Br 2:121–22.

15. To Spalatin, July 26, 1522, WA Br 2:580 / 5–6.

practices. The count, on the contrary, was looking for an understanding preacher of the gospel, the kind who would allow the Word to take its course among the people. After two short months Strauss was dismissed by Wertheim. Luther felt that this act of Wertheim's was fully justified, for he had in the meantime experienced similar embarrassments: "D. Strauss has a head of his own and is now doing the same thing in Eisenach, as he pleases, and leaves it to us to talk and write about it."

The successor to Strauss, also sent to Wertheim by Luther, was Franz Kolb, a former Carthusian monk who had become a distinguished preacher in Nuremberg. With Kolb in mind, Luther once again expressed his understanding of reformation: "That he first of all inculcate the Word thoroughly, before changing anything, in order to see whether faith and love have begun to grow among the people."[16] But even Kolb did not long continue on the course—the middle way of moderation—Luther was pursuing in his reforms in the field of worship. In a letter full of respect for his count and for Luther, Kolb on August 27, 1524, earnestly and humbly requested a published guideline on the question of ceremonies, to the effect that nothing be added to the simple words of Christ. At the same time he admitted to having espoused Zwingli's position on the Lord's Supper. All this gave Luther the feeling that Kolb, like Karlstadt (he put them in the same group), was lost as a partner. Early in 1525 Wertheim released Kolb, who later found a place suited to his disposition as he became a leader in the Reformation in the Swiss city of Bern.[17]

The Word was visibly gaining ground. A report from Kronberg in August 1522 substantiated this fact in a way that must have delighted Luther. The report was a pamphlet written by the knight Franz von Sickingen,

16. Luther to Spalatin, September 4, 1522, WA Br 2:597 / 31ff. On Count George of Wertheim in Worms, WA 7:843 / 13. Luther later lamented Wertheim's death (1530), WA TR 1:44. On Strauss, see Barge, *Jakob Strauss: Ein Kämpfer für das Evangelium in Tirol, Thüringen und Süddeutschland*, SVRG 162 (Leipzig, 1937): 31ff. J. Rogge, *Der Beitrag des Predigers Jakob Strauss zur frühen Reformationsgeschichte* (Berlin, 1957), 21ff., 31ff. Luther to Count George, June 17, 1523, WA Br 3:88–89.

17. L. Eissenlöffel, "Franz Kolb, ein Reformator Wertheims, Nürnbergs, und Berns: Sein Leben und Wirken" (diss., Erlangen, 1893), 21ff. On Kolb as preacher in Nuremberg, see the report of Planitz to Elector Frederick, January 2, 1523, printed in E. Wülcker and H. Virck, *Des Kursächsischen Rathes Hans von der Planitz Berichte aus dem Reichsregiment in Nürnberg, 1521–1523* (Leipzig, 1899), 304, 32. Kolb to Luther, August 27, 1524, WA Br 3:329ff. H. Waldenmaier,· *Die Entstehung der evangelischen Gottesdienstordnungen Süddeutschlands im Zeitalter der Reformation*, SVRG 125–26 (Leipzig, 1916), 41. W. Köhler, *Zwingli und Luther*, QFRG 7, ed. E. Kohlmeyer and H. Bornkamm (Gütersloh, 1953), 1:178–79. When Luther finally in 1526 came out with an order of worship of his own in the "German Mass," Count George of Wertheim and his new preacher soon adopted it. F. Kobe, *Die erste lutherische Kirchenordnung in der Grafschaft Wertheim: Aus der Zeit von 1526–1530* (Lahr, 1933), 14.

who endeavored to persuade a relative of his, Deiter von Hand-schuhsheim, that the Roman doctrine of the Lord's Supper and sacrifice of the mass, monasticism, and the veneration of the saints do not conform to the mind of Christ. As Kronberg reported, in the castle Ebernburg they were now daily including in the mass a reading in German of the gospel, the epistle, and then a portion of the prophets. The enthusiasm of von Sickingen crescendoed with the cry "For a long time, indeed for a decade, the Spirit of God and of righteousness has been dwelling in this house of Franz—of this I am certain."[18] Luther had long been aware of von Sick-ingen's good will. Several times during the year 1520 he had offered Luther sanctuary in his castle and had extended the invitation through his fellow knight Ulrich von Hutten. Luther was in no hurry to thank Sick-ingen for the offer because he had not been thinking seriously of accepting it. But the very thought of having so powerful a protector on his side heartened him in his distress. Nevertheless, he kept such human as-surances in proper perspective. "Remember," he had told Spalatin on July 17, 1520, "it is for the sake of the Word that we must suffer. For even though Silvester Schaumberg and Franz von Sickingen may make me se-cure against fearing men, the assault of demons is still impending. The final assault will then have come when I have become a burden to myself."[19]

18. August 14, 1522, WA Br 2:587 / 7ff. The pamphlet is in E. Kück, *Schriftstellernde Adlige* (see above, p. 72, n. 15), 11ff. It is doubtful that Sickingen himself wrote this pam-phlet, for it is cleverly composed and supplied with a large number of pointed Scripture passages. It apparently gathers together the substance of theological conversations held in Ebernburg, on which Johann Schwebel reported in the foreword of June 30, 1522, to Knight George Lutrummer in Pforzheim: "I wish that Your Honor (the appellation of a knight) could have been with me to hear this evangelical Christian conversation, such as is going on stead-ily among us" (p. 11). Schwebel probably also secured the original written copy. H. Ulmann, *Franz von Sickingen* (Leipzig, 1872), 174–75. P. Kalkoff, *Ulrich von Hutten und die Reforma-tion: Eine kritische Geschichte seiner wichtigsten Lebenszeit und der Entscheidungsjahre der Reformation (1517–1523)*, QFRG 4 (Leipzig, 1920), 144, n. 4. In this discussion Luther's moderate stand on the matter of images must have been found agreeable. The cautious reforms of worship at the Ebernburg were carried out by the then chaplain of the castle, Oecolampadius. See E. Staehelin, *Das theologische Lebenswerk Johannes Oekolampads*, QFRG 21 (Leipzig, 1939), 163ff.

19. "Novissimus erit, cum mihi gravis ero" (a play on Job 7:20 ["Why have I become a burden to thee?]), WA Br 2:145 / 40ff. Cf. also Luther's letter to Link, July 20, 1520, WA Br 2:146 / 8ff.; and to John Voigt, August 3, 1520, WA Br 2:162 / 10ff. Silvester von Schaumberg, on hearing the rumor that Luther was being threatened and might have to flee to Bohemia, notified him that he had the protection of a hundred nobles in Franconia [today, northern Bavaria]; June 11, 1520, WA Br 2:121–22. Already in December 1519 Luther had learned that Sickingen was acting as John Reuchlin's protector (WA Br 1:572, n. 2); the same in more detail by Bucer, WA Br 1:616 / 79ff. One gets an idea of how lively the correspondence was during the first half of the year 1520 when reviewing extant evidence on Sickingen's proffered help to Luther; see Hutten to Melanchthon, January 20 and February 28, CR 1:131–32; 147–48; MBW 72, 74. Also Crotus Rubeanus to Luther, WA Br 2:91 / 150ff. Again, Luther to Hutten, about April 30 (now lost), WA Br 2:94 / 30; 98 / 5–6. Still another, Luther to Sick-ingen and Hutten (also lost), but cf. WA Br 2:111 / 4. And Hutten to Luther, June 4, WA Br 2:117 / 36–37. And Luther to Sickingen, June 30 (lost), cf. WA Br 2:131 / 15.

Sickingen's favor was valuable to Luther, the more so because this powerful and feared knight of the realm had persisted in waging warfare by feud with considerable success despite the ban on it since 1495 by virtue of the act declaring a public peace. For a year he had also been in the service of the young Emperor Charles V, having played an important part in the troop demonstration before the city of Frankfurt am Main at the time of the imperial election (June 28, 1519).[20] When Luther in his "Appeal" in late August 1520 sought the emperor's ear as well as his protection, he turned at the same time also to Sickingen, who gave him friendly assurance of "help and favor."[21] The first time he might have availed himself of this offer, Luther turned it down. For their own part, Hutten and Sickingen allowed themselves to be intimidated by Armstorff, the imperial chamberlain, and Glapion, the emperor's father confessor, who warned them of the dangers awaiting Luther at Worms and thereby lured them into holding a secret conversation in the safety of Ebernburg. Had the stratagem succeeded, it would have cost Luther the last days of his free escort. In Oppenheim on the Rhine it was Bucer who mediated the invitation, but Luther declined it almost intuitively (or, as he said later, "out of pure simplicity").[22]

In hours of conversation with Glapion, Sickingen demonstrated his excellent knowledge of Luther's German writings (he did not know Latin) and showed himself an ardent follower of the Reformer insofar as he would usher in the greatly needed renewal of the church. Should Luther, however, be convicted of heresy in matters of faith, he (Sickingen) would be the first to pitch Luther's writings into the fire.[23] The high degree to which he was considered Luther's protector is revealed by the rumor spread after the Reichstag in Worms that he had sequestered the Re-

20. Ulmann, *Franz von Sickingen*, 157ff., 161ff. K. Brandi, *The Emperor Charles V: The Growth and Destiny of a Man and of a World Empire* (New York: Knopf, 1939; trans. from the German, 3d ed., 1937), 105.

21. Luther sent his letters to the emperor and to Sickingen on to Spalatin, August 31, 1520, for transmittal; WA Br 2:179 / 8–9 (cf. WA Br 2:174). Sickingen answered on November 3, 1520, WA Br 2:208. [*LW* 48:175–79, introduction to and text of Luther's letter to Charles V.]

22. WA TR 3, no. 3357b, 285 / 13. Cf. also WA TR 4, no. 5107, 667 / 5; WA TR 5, no. 5342b, 69 / 4ff., and no. 5375b, 101 / 10ff. A similar futile attempt to settle the matter secretly was undertaken by Glapion already in February 1521 through Elector Frederick's chancellor, Brück. K. E. Förstermann, *Neues Urkundenbuch zur Geschichte der evangelischen Kirchen-Reformation* (Hamburg, 1942), 1:48ff., 52ff.

23. Aleander (April 15, 1521, according to Glapion's report) in *Die Depeschen des Nuntius Aleander vom Wormser Reichstage 1521*, trans. P. Kalkoff, 2d rev. and enl. ed. (Halle, 1897), 158. For a critique, H. Delekat, "Ulrich von Huttens Charakter und Bedeutung im Lichte seiner inneren Entwicklung," *LuJ* 5 (1923): 81. Ulmann, *Franz von Sickingen*, 178ff.

former in one of his castles near the French border.[24] Luther did not forget Sickingen's readiness to help him, and during the year of his banishment on the Wartburg he dedicated to Sickingen the tract *On Confession*, writing, "I am herewith sending it to Your Honor to show my good will and gratitude for the many encouragements and offers you have given to my unworthy person."[25] A year later, when he received Kronberg's letter, Luther could read it as a sign that during the interval the evangelical seed had been sown and was coming up on the territory of his protector. However, Sickingen's only a few months later taking a political course contrary to his admonition to Christians "to avoid insurrection and rebellion" was an action that proved deeply repugnant to Luther but was, at that moment, unforeseen.[26]

Other knights were likewise turning to the evangelical faith, among them Hans Landschad zu Neckarsteinach, "the gallant Kerlin," as he was called for his exploits during the war against the Turks and for his administrative services in the electoral palatinate. His commitment to reformation in the church ran deeper than that of Sickingen. Crippled from war injuries, Landschad had time to read and ponder the religious issues of the era. Since 1518 he had been attentive to Luther, and after reading Luther's *To the Christian Nobility* he wrote with urgency to Elector Frederick the Wise. In his letter of October 25, 1520, Landschad declared that God "without doubt through the activity of the Holy Spirit is performing a remarkable work on the princely territory of Your Electoral Grace through a single person" and is uncovering the countless flaws in the church. Let the elector now intercede in all earnestness with the emperor and with the estates in the imperial diet toward achieving improvement. Landschad had thoroughly studied the Bible and all the writings of Luther available to him. "Although I am not a scholar, I would not hesitate to respond to the learned theologians and doctors on the basis of Luther's teaching, insofar as I have come to know it," he added. Its essence—the teaching of the cross and of redemption—had gained Landschad's wholehearted acceptance. It was this doctrine, and not the critique of conditions in the church, that won him to Luther's side. In a decisive and warmhearted "missive" in 1522 he admonished Elector Louis of the Palatinate

24. As reported by Duke John of Saxony, who was not privy to the Wartburg plan, to his brother on May 30, 1521, from the Coburg. Ulmann, *Franz von Sickingen*, 182, n. 2 (from the Weimar archives). The reassuring verbal information given by the elector on May 31, in Förstemann, *Neues Urkundenbuch*, 19.

25. "Written on my Patmos. June 1, 1521," WA 8:139 / 23ff. [*LW* 48:246, 247.]

26. See below, pp. 305–6.

to adopt Luther's teaching for himself and his land. If this pamphlet ever reached Luther—and this we do not know—he could feel that Landschad understood him as few others did.[27]

Luther found sympathy and interest among the princes and lords on various grounds. Foremost among them was his own territorial lord, Count Albrecht of Mansfeld, at whose court Luther's struggle had been followed with marked attentiveness ever since the controversy over the Ninety-five Theses. Immediately after the Diet at Worms, Albrecht had requested a report on its outcome, and Luther was able to get it off to him on May 3 from Eisenach, just before his abduction to the Wartburg. Since the count was among those being made uneasy because of Luther's being decried as "a disgrace and dishonor to Your Grace's realm, that is, a poor, despised, fully evangelical 'Cinderella,' " he dedicated his postil to Albrecht as a mark of gratitude.[28]

Other supporters included Duke Barnim of Pomerania, a former student of Luther's at Wittenberg and later rector of the university. Barnim was among those who had accompanied Luther to the Leipzig debate against Eck in 1519. Soon after the bull of excommunication was issued in 1521, Barnim sent Luther a letter assuring his continued support.[29] On the dispute over images, Count Ludwig zu Stolberg requested instruction, and the counts of Schwarzenberg were looking for advice in a highly complex question involving church law, one that would keep Luther busy for some time to come: what to do when a monastery into whose holdings a local church had earlier been incorporated prevents the congregation from calling an evangelical pastor.[30] Duke Karl von Münsterberg in Silesia, a grandson of the Hussite King George of Podiebrad,[31] whose family had been cursed by the pope to the fourth generation, expressed his thanks to Luther for his teaching on the proper reception of the Lord's

27. G. Berbig, "Ein Brief des Ritters Hans Landschad zu Steinach an Kurfürst Friedrich den Weisen, 1520," ARG 2 (1904–5); 394–95. Short excerpts from Landschad's pamphlet are in Kück, *Schriftstellernde Adlige,* 23ff. G. Blochwitz, "Die antirömischen deutschen Flugschriften der frühen Reformationszeit (bis 1522) in ihrer religiös-sittlichen Eigenart," ARG 27 (1930): 163–64, 176–77, 253. This work deserves to be reprinted. G. A. Benrath, "Zwei Flugschriften des Reichsritters Hans Landschad von Steinach von 1522 und 1524," BPfK 40 (1973): 257–87.

28. WA Br 2:319ff. WA 10^1:11ff.; 6 / 15–16. [LW 52:6.]

29. October 20, 1520, WA Br 2:203–4. Duke Barnim had permitted Luther to preach during the disputation against John Eck in Leipzig; WA Br 1:423 / 125ff.

30. Luther to Stolberg, April 25, 1522, WA Br 2:513–14. To John Henry von Schwarzenberg, December 12, 1522, WA Br 2:626–27. On the question of incorporation, see below, pp. 121ff.

31. See below, p. 105.

Supper in both kinds and requested still further writings on the subject—
"to comfort our conscience, to moderate the blight now lying over the
house of Münsterberg, and to protect our princely dignity and that of our
heirs"—with the understanding that nothing of this particular request be
made public.

John Hess, Münsterberg's chaplain, fit into this pattern of political caution. He was a hesitant man, and despite his visits in Wittenberg and close
ties with Luther and Melanchthon, he still required a great deal of moral
support, according to his count.[32] Hess was one of the circle of humanists
around the bishop of Breslau, John Thurzo, a man whom Luther respected highly and whom, upon learning of his death, he called "the best
of the bishops of this age." Shortly before Thurzo's death Luther had sent
him a respectful and warm letter of comfort in his illness. Through one of
the many Silesians then studying in Wittenberg, or with whom he corresponded, Luther would also have learned that in Liegnitz, under Duke
Frederick II, a robust center of evangelical faith had gotten off to an early
start. The inspiring head was the ducal councillor, Caspar Schwenkfeld,
who not only won the duke for the evangelical side but also kept on prodding Hess to drop his mood of reserve and to come over [from Münster-
berg] to the court of this "patron of evangelical doctrine."[33]

While independent nobles and knights were opening the door to evangelical preaching, the same thing was happening—at first quietly and
then more openly—in a growing number of cities and towns in and beyond Electoral Saxony. Often it was Luther's fellow friars in the Augustinian order who started things on their own and who found a ready response
especially among those of humanistic education. The classic example was
Nuremberg, where the Augustinian monastery rapidly became the center
of an awakened spiritual life. It had begun there in the winter of 1515–16
with a series of sermons by John Staupitz [the order's vicar-general in
Germany], who then, in 1517, installed Wenceslaus Link as prior. Link

32. The duke's letter of around March 20, 1522, is probably identical with that delivered
on June 29; WA Br 2:569ff. Later, under his impressions of the Peasants' War, the duke's
loyalties reverted to the Roman church. Luther to Hess, March 25, 1522, WA Br 2:482.
Melanchthon to Hess, April 27, 1520, and March 25, 1522, CR 1:156ff.; 566–67. MBW
84:222.

33. Luther to Thurzo, July 30, 1520, WA Br 2:152–53. Regarding Thurzo's death, Novem-
ber 13, 1520, WA Br 2:214/31–32. Melanchthon to Thurzo, August 1, 1520, CR 1:209–10.
MBW 103. D. Erdmann, Luther und seine Beziehungen zu Schlesien, insbesondere zu
Breslau, SVRG 19 (Halle, 1887). Schwenkfeld to Hess, June 13, 1522, CS 1:36,10ff. W. Knörr-
lich, "Kaspar von Schwenkfeld und die Reformation in Schlesien" (Ph.D. dissertation,
Bonn, 1957).

was an outstanding preacher and by virtue of his years of partnership in the Wittenberg faculty was a confidant of Luther. With a sure hand he led the *"sodalitas Staupiciana,"* the Staupitz club that the monastery had attracted, in the direction of his great friend. "The patricians, the majority of the burghers, and all the intellectuals are on the side of Sir Martin," wrote Christopher Schuerl to Melanchthon on April 1, 1520. Continuity was retained even though later in that same year Link was called as Staupitz's successor and left Nuremberg, but he returned to the city five years later. Without much ado the city council began in 1522 to place likeminded evangelical pastors in the most important parishes. Andrew Osiander was called to St. Lorenz Church. Dominicus Schluepner, an excellent Silesian who had studied in Wittenberg during the stormy spell, 1519–20, became preacher in the Church of St. Sebaldus. Thomas Venatorius, the learned Reuchlin scholar, was placed in the Spital Church. Nor was that all. Already in 1520 and 1521 two of Luther's former students in Wittenberg, Hector Poemer and George Besler, were elected by the city council to serve as deans, respectively, of the Churches of St. Lorenz and St. Sebaldus, offices of less importance than preaching but of much influence otherwise. Not until 1525, however, did the city itself adopt a new order of worship and church constitution, thereby declaring itself on the side of the Reformation. Yet well before that event the city councilmen and the theologians were on sufficiently solid ground, and the wealthy city itself—to which countless princes and nobles were financially indebted—was independent enough, so that during the years 1522–24, when Nuremberg was host to the imperial diets of the empire and to the papal legates, it could openly demonstrate its evangelical character. Its leading politician, Lazarus Spengler (secretary of the city council), was heartily devoted to Luther; he well deserved that association. Because of his speech in defense of Luther at Worms in 1520, his name was included in the bull of excommunication.[34]

To the Nurembergers, Luther was initially a "second sun"[35] shining alongside the trusted star of Staupitz. The way had been prepared for him

34. H. von Schubert, *Lazarus Spengler und die Reformation in Nürnberg,* ed. H. Holborn, QFRG 17 (Leipzig, 1934), 141–42, 147ff., 189ff., 331ff., 379ff. Further material in G. Ebeling, "Die reformatorische Bewegung am Ort der Reichsregierung in den Jahren 1522 bis 1524" (Habil. diss., Tübingen, 1946). The Staupitz club is described to Luther by Schuerl on November 3, 1517, and to Staupitz on January 7, 1518, and includes the most important names; WA Br 1:116 / 10ff. "Christoph Schuerls Briefbuch, ein Beitrag zur Geschichte der Reformation und ihrer Zeit," ed. F. L. Freiherr von Soden and I. K. F. Knaake (Potsdam, 1872), 2:42–43. On the diets of the empire (*Reichstage*), see below, pp. 296ff.

35. Schubert, *Lazarus Spengler,* 149.

by the several years of preaching that had been going on in Nuremberg and that had progressively clarified the biblical verities of salvation. Luther's incisive critique attracted fellow Augustinians in various places. The members of the order in Wittenberg had set the example, especially the vehement Gabriel Zwilling, preacher in Eilenburg and later in Torgau. Consider Luther's native Eisleben, where his friend Caspar Güttel was most troubled over the way the poor were burdened by any number of senseless church practices and by the issue of whether monks have a right to quit the cloister. Small wonder that for the time Güttel still saw Erasmus as the "far-famed and cherished man," the great example, and that he wished to be known not as a "Martinian" but simply as a Christian. However, he soon became one of Luther's most loyal followers.[36]

Luther was much concerned over the direction that the large episcopal sees of Erfurt and Magdeburg might take, where the evangelical movement was having an uphill fight against the opposition of Cardinal Albrecht. In Erfurt it was Luther's friend John Lang caught in the bind between the hotspur radicals and the traditionalists. While still at the Wartburg, Luther had condemned sharply the excesses of students against the older clergy; soon the prophetic word would be fulfilled: *Erfordia Praga* (Erfurt a second Prague). Thereby Satan is simply playing the students into the hands of their enemies.[37] After what he had learned from the struggle in Wittenberg against the radicals, Luther was doubly concerned to see calm restored in Erfurt between the people attacked from without and torn from within. For this purpose he chose to deal with the veneration of saints, a question which at that time was addressed to him from various quarters. To be sure, Luther was himself well experienced in this subject. In retrospect he could really not tell when he had ceased calling on the saints. For anyone who has honestly prayed to Christ and God the Father, the change one day simply happens by itself.[38] To the Erfurters he therefore addressed an *Epistle or Instruction on the Saints*. He called it one of those superfluous questions by means of which the

---

36. On his two writings on church reform (1522), see G. Kawerau, "Caspar Güttel: Ein Lebensbild aus Luthers Freundeskreis," ZHVG 14 (1881): 32ff., 39ff. He remained in Eisleben from the time of the dissolution of the Augustinian cloister in 1523 until his death in 1542. For a few months in 1523 he helped to restore order in Zwickau after the disturbances caused by Müntzer and the "prophets."

37. To Spalatin, May 14, 1521, WA Br 2:337 / 14ff. Erfurt was probably called Prague because of the strong accession of German teachers and students who had left Prague in protest in 1409. WA Br 2:340, n. 11. [LW 48:223–24.]

38. To John Lang, May 29, 1522, WA Br 2:548 / 21–22. To Adam Kraft, July 28, WA Br 2:582 / 12ff.

devil tries to divert people from essentials. Should the weak still be praying to the saints, even though their trust is now fixed on Christ alone, then their prayers stand a chance of reaching him. And then this [kind of diversionary practice] will of itself find an end, "because one of these days we simply must lay off the saints and ourselves so that we know no one but Christ alone and everything else drops away." If one simply sticks with it, to "inculcate Christ," the devil will soon "become tired of pestering."[39] While in Erfurt the evangelically minded could count on support from the city council, it was another matter in Magdeburg. There the mayors of the city themselves demanded that Archbishop Albrecht intervene. In September 1521 Albrecht expelled Andreas Kaugsdorff, chief preacher of the cathedral and a man so highly regarded by Luther that "there is hardly another like him in the entire territory of the cardinal."[40] Only some time later was there an evangelical spokesman again at work in Magdeburg, Melchior Mirisch, an Augustinian from the Netherlands, formerly prior in Ghent. Luther was not especially pleased, for he had by no means agreed with the position taken by Mirisch during the time of persecution in the Netherlands. In the new situation at Magdeburg, however, Luther soon became satisfied with him.[41]

Next to Wittenberg a second strong center of Lutheran thought had developed, remarkably in the Low Countries. For a long time the cloisters in this region of the Observant Augustinian Hermits comprised a congregation (since 1437) regarded as German. Within the order, it was under its own vicar. There Staupitz's predecessor as vicar was Andreas Proles, the extraordinarily vigorous and successful reform-minded leader in the order, who had drawn many convents, including those of Enkhuizen and Haarlem, into the strict observance of the houses under the administration of his vicarage. His followers were dubbed "Vicarians." In 1493 the Haarlem cloister had been founded by a group of Observant Augustinians from Saxony. The new cloister in Antwerp which joined the congregation in 1513 had been a special responsibility of Staupitz during

39. *Epistel oder Unterricht von den Heiligen an die Kirche zu Erfurt* (Epistle or Instruction on the Saints, to the Church in Erfurt), July 10, 1522, WA 10²:164ff., esp. 166 / 31ff., 35, 10. Cf. the letter to Speratus, June 13, 1522, WA Br 2:561 / 67ff.

40. To Capito, January 17, 1522, WA Br 2:433 / 109ff. [LW 48:378. Alternate spelling: Andrew Kauxdorff.]

41. To Mirisch, WA Br 1:304, n. 3; WA Br 2:181, n. 9. Luther to Link, January 16, 1523, WA Br 3:17 / 8–9.

its period of formation.[42] So it happened that many Augustinians from the Netherlands came to study at Wittenberg, the university of the order's vicar, and early in Luther's career the first ones were returning to their places as his enthusiastic followers. In Antwerp their championing of the poor and their preaching against the disgraceful financial schemes of indulgences soon made enemies as well as friends for the little monastery. Among the friends was Erasmus, who in 1519 wrote to Luther, "In Antwerp there is a prior in the [Augustinian] cloister, a genuine Christian with nothing false about him, who glows with love for you; a former student of yours, as he boasts. He is virtually the only one who preaches Christ. Nearly all the others simply prattle and think of profit." And Albrecht Dürer, while residing in Antwerp in 1520–21, was especially pleased to associate with the Augustinians. He esteemed the prior, Jacob Propst, so highly that he painted a portrait of him and made him a gift of it on leaving the city. Propst had studied in Wittenberg in 1505–9 and returned again in 1520–21 to earn his theological degree. His having been a student of Luther's, as Erasmus noted, was thus based on the readings and tales of the friars in the cloister. In Wittenberg a cordial friendship developed between Luther and the "fat little Fleming," as Luther greeted him from the Wartburg. Then there was Henry von Zütphen, prior in Dortrecht, who like Propst in 1520 resumed his studies in Wittenberg and earned his theological degree.[43]

This band of Augustinians in the Low Countries paid dearly for following Luther, being the first to be seized by the Inquisition. The papal legate Jerome Aleander and the Hapsburg regent Margaret of Austria [1480–1530] were determined to carry out the Edict of Worms rigorously and to nip heresy in the bud. In December 1521, only a few months after his return from Wittenberg, Propst was taken to Brussels. Subjected to painful interrogation, he was gradually worn down. On February 9, 1522, he recanted publicly. Luther was pained deeply by this news. All the greater was his joy over the report that Propst had repudiated his forced recantation, but with his joy came the fear that his friend might be ar-

42. T. Kolde, *Die deutsche Augustiner-Congregation und Johann Staupitz* (Gotha, 1879), 82ff., 147–48, 260ff. The term "Vicariani" for the Observants can be traced back to 1474; ibid., 111, n. 2.

43. Erasmus to Luther, May 30, 1519, WA Br 1:413 / 50ff. O. Clemen, "Das Antwerpener Augustiner-Kloster bei Beginn der Reformation (1513–1523)," *Monatshefte der Comenius-Gessellschaft* 10 (1901): 306ff. P. Kalkoff, "Zur Lebensgeschichte Albrecht Dürers," RKW 20 (1897): 449ff. "Flemmichen," May 26, 1521, WA Br 2:349 / 96. [LW 48:233, Luther to Melanchthon, May 26, 1521.] Propst's theses for the licentiate, July 12, 1521, in O. Clemen, *Beiträge zur Reformationsgeschichte* (see above, p. 62, n. 40), 1:34ff. J. F. Iken, *Heinrich von Zütphen*, SVRG 12 (Halle, 1886), 6ff., 12ff.

rested again. For weeks Luther remained in suspense, for several reports rumored that Propst had been burned at the stake. Then, as by a miracle of God, Propst was able to escape and make his way to Wittenberg. Luther reported the exciting news to Spalatin on August 11, 1522.[44]

Henry von Zütphen picked up where Propst had been forced out and in the summer of 1522 preached in Antwerp in the same spirit and with great fearlessness. His bold attack on the latest papal indulgence traffic offended much of the populace, and he soon found himself in the hands of the Inquisition. Under the pretext of a requested sick call, he was lured into a trap on Michaelmas, September 29. But even before he could be transported to Brussels that night an incensed crowd set him free. Like Propst, Henry took flight. Escaping to Bremen [a center of trade and a free city of the empire], he had remarkably rapid success in winning the city council and the burghers for the Reformation over the opposition of the archbishop. Like Boniface centuries earlier, however, Henry was restless after this success and sought a new mission field, and there, like his ancient predecessor, he too met a martyr's death. At Meldorf, in the ruggedly independent Dithmarsch region [northeast of Hamburg], a mob of enraged peasants burned him at the stake on December 10, 1524. Meanwhile, in January 1523 the radical Augustinian cloister was leveled. Among the arrested friars there were two—Henry Vos and John van den Eschen—who remained steadfast to the end. On July 1, 1523, in the marketplace of Brussels, they too were martyred by fire. Such martyrdom, endured by others for a cause he himself had launched, shook Luther profoundly.[45]

Among the more than one hundred Augustinians whom Staupitz had drawn to the University of Wittenberg during his term as vicar of the order (1520), a rich crop had come out on Luther's side.[46] Even then oth-

44. Propst's own report of his twofold imprisonment appeared in 1522 in Wittenberg. Clemen, *Beiträge zur Reformationsgeschichte*, 1:37ff. Kalkoff, *Die Anfänge der Gegenreformation*, pt. 2 (see above, p. 8, n. 29), 62ff. Luther to Spalatin, August 11, 1522, WA Br 2:586 / 5ff. Luther did not hesitate to let his friends everywhere know about his anxiety over Propst: to Spalatin, April 12, WA Br 2:493 / 16–17; June 5, WA Br 2:555 / 11ff.; to Lang, June 11, WA Br 2:559 / 7–8; June 26, WA Br 2:565 / 21–22; to Staupitz, June 27, WA Br 2:567 / 30ff.; to Hausmann, June 30, WA Br 2:572 / 9ff. [*LW* 49:12. Luther to Staupitz, June 27, feared that Propst faced certain death for having repudiated his recantation.]

45. Sources for the imprisonment of Henry von Zütphen are in Clemen, "Antwerpener Augustiner-Kloster," 311, n. 4, and Kalkoff, *Anfänge der Gegenreformation*, pt. 2, 77ff. Iken, *Heinrich von Zütphen*, 32ff., 74ff.

46. W. Friedensburg, *Geschichte der Universität Wittenberg* (Magdeburg, 1926), 2:48. [Cf. E. G. Schwiebert, *Luther and His Times: The Reformation from a New Perspective* (St. Louis: Concordia, 1950), 604ff., on student enrollment, attendance from various parts of Germany, and so on.]

ers studying at Wittenberg would be carrying the same message to West-phalia: John Westermann to Lippstadt, and Gottschalk Gropp to Herford, where the convent of the Brethren of the Common Life would also be won. In Osnabrück the Augustinian Gerhard Hecker had been preaching in Luther's vein since 1521, and so also were the friars of the cloister in Wesel. Likewise in Alsfeld (Upper Hesse) and its cloister, Tilemann Schnabel, director provincial of the Augustinian province of Thuringia-Saxony, came over to Luther's side. Landgrave Philip of Hesse, as late as 1523 [before he had made up his mind about the Reformation] forbade Schnabel to preach. From Leisnig, where Luther had found him a tempo-rary position, Philip recalled Schnabel with honors and made him one of his most important helpers.

[Geography was a factor.] To be sure, the influence Luther had thus far radiated on the Augustinian order had been confined mainly to middle and northern Germany. With the exception of Nuremberg, the South German cloisters—locked in the deadly tensions that permeated the order—all remained in the Roman camp for the time being. With the exception of Würzburg, however, the next few decades saw them all capit-ulate to the Reformation movement. As for people, it was Michael Stiefel, an outsider to the South German Augustinians, in whom Luther found his most unusual spokesman. Residing in Esslingen, this clever and eccentric Swabian was inspired by the Revelation of John and its invitation to apoc-alyptical mathematics. Schnabel was convinced that the angel bearing the eternal gospel (Rev. 14:6ff.) had appeared to Luther. Beginning in 1522 he therefore undertook to compose a didactic poem in a masterful vernacular German, whose thirty-three stanzas carried brief explanations of Luther's teaching. Unfortunately, when word got around, Schnabel was forced to flee Esslingen. Temporarily he found asylum with Hartmut von Kron-berg, until the castle fell to enemies. From there he escaped to Witten-berg, where his personal friendship with Luther really began, proving itself durable despite many ups and downs.[47]

In larger contexts, and in contrast to the evangelical movement burst-ing into flame here and there, Luther's contacts led him to that older

---

47. "Von der christförmigen, rechtgegründeten leer Doctoris Martini Lutheri," Flugschriften aus den ersten Jahren der Reformation," ed. O. Clemen (Halle, 1909), 3:263ff. Very likely without realizing it, Stiefel took up an old Joachite [for Joachim, father of Mary the mother of Jesus(?)] tradition and made a new one: the pericope later became the Epistle for Reformation Day. Likewise, Stiefel's suggestive comparison (ibid., 282) of Luther and Elias (from Rev. 11:3ff.) is of humanistic origin. H. Volz, Die Lutherpredigten des Johannes Mathesius: Kritische Untersuchungen zur Geschichtsschreibung im Zeitalter der Reforma-tion, QFRG 12 (Leipzig, 1930), 63ff.

endeavor to reform the church, to the Hussites, for whom he had long felt kinship. Cautious though he had initially been to avoid even the mention of their name (it was associated with their outrageous crusades), he was moved by the initial writings of John Huss which he had received from Bohemia. To Spalatin, Luther had confided early in 1520, "Without knowing it, we are all Hussites."[48] Now for the first time men from both branches of the Hussite movement, which had grown out of the conflict with Rome, sought out Luther. The Bohemian Brethren, the smaller of the two branches and the one he preferred, got their deputation to Luther first. The fellowship of these quiet people was one of the purest and, in any case, the most durable of the various medieval attempts to make discipleship of the poor, gentle, and suffering Christ a way of life for the individual as well as for the congregation. They had dissociated themselves from the secularized papal church as well as from the degenerated Hussite majority, among whom Waldensian ideas had distorted their founder's original intention. Since 1467 this smaller offshoot, cleansed by inner crises and steadfast amid severe persecution, had maintained itself in the territories of Bohemia and Moravia. Its still active Unity of Brethren (Unitas Fratrum)—to focus for a moment on the eighteenth century—was the context from which, under Count Zinzendorf, the Moravian church came forth and gained worldwide significance.

Luther was skeptical toward this separatist church, in the distance and forbidden in any case by the law of the land. He knew its adherents only under the then heretical name "Picards,"[49] and he had little reliable information about them. For a long time Luther had thought of them as representing an exemplary life as well as a stubborn heresy. This impression was strengthened in 1520 when he concluded from one of their writings that they did not believe in the presence of the body and blood of Christ in the Lord's Supper.[50] Now, however, he received some reasonably reassuring information on the subject from his friend Paul Speratus in Moravia, and especially from two Brethren priests who visited him in Wittenberg in

---

48. Mid-February 1520. WA Br 2:42 / 24. [LW 48:153.]

49. Derived from Picardy, northern France, from which refugees fleeing the Inquisition in 1418 had found haven in Bohemia. In the main they were rejected by the "Bohemian Brethren." LThK 8 (1963): 503–4. For a survey of Luther's attitude toward the "Bohemian Brethren," see W. Köhler, Luther und die Kirchengeschichte nach seinen Schriften (Erlangen, 1900), 1:168ff.; J. T. Müller, Geschichte der Böhmischen Brüder (Herrnhut, 1922), 1:400ff.; E. Peschke, Die Theologie der Böhmischen Brüder in ihrer Frühzeit, FKGG 5 (Stuttgart, 1935), 1:333–34; K. Bittner, "Erasmus, Luther und die böhmischen Brüder," in Rastlos Schaffen: Festschrift F. Lammert (Stuttgart, 1954), 107ff.

50. WA 6:80 / 25ff.

May 1522.[51] Presumably the two were John Horn and Michael Weisse, the later great poet of the Bohemian Brethren whose choice hymns are still sung in Protestant churches. The Brethren were eager for Luther's favorable judgment of them, for within four weeks they sent a second deputation, probably the same two representatives, to stay with him "in order to ask him about their faith." Through these messengers Speratus sent Luther additional questions on the Lord's Supper drawn up by a priest whom Speratus had won for Luther's side. On the whole, Luther found the teachings of the Brethren correct, even though at times they were expressed obscurely. The main issue giving Luther second thoughts was that the Brethren did not see infant baptism as a direct imputing of the fruit of faith and that they required people joining their Unity of Brethren to be rebaptized. Besides, their teaching on faith and works left him in doubt. These open questions would keep him busy for some time. Despite the many ties linking him to the Brethren, it was a resigned Luther who concluded, "Nowhere at all in the world is the pure gospel to be found."[52]

Differences like these, however, were minor when compared to the worries the Hussite territorial church in Bohemia gave Luther. These Utraquists [with their insistence on Communion in both kinds] were a many-layered creation. As heirs of John Huss, they retained the demand for Communion in both kinds, the abolition of church property, and separation from Rome. These three criteria made them allies of Luther. In other matters they were more conservative. They left untouched whatever Roman practices or positions did not contradict their basic demands. As a result, the question of reunion with Rome remained alive. An external mark of this was the practice, since the death in 1471 of the Hussite king George of Podiebrad, for good Catholic kings of the Jagiello dynasty (Vladislav II and Louis II) to wear the crown of Bohemia, while an internal mark was the continuing presence of Rome-minded clergy among the Hussites who strove for reunion. By way of contrast, there was also evidence that in some quarters of this Utraquist church an antisacramentarian idea persisted secretly and much in the manner espoused earlier by the radical and outwardly overthrown Taborite branch of the Hussite movement.

Luther now acquainted himself with some of these matters as he studied Hussite doctrinal articles sent him by Speratus, in which he saw,

51. To Speratus, May 16, 1522. WA Br 2:531 / 11ff.

52. To Speratus, June 13, 1522, WA Br 2:560 / 12ff. To Spalatin, July 4, 1522, WA Br 2:573 / 11ff., 17.

first, that chapter 6 of the Gospel of John was used to support a symbolical interpretation of [Christ's presence in] the Lord's Supper.[53] Luther noted his indignation only briefly at this point, not realizing what struggles were yet to swirl around this chapter in the great conflict with the Swiss over the Lord's Supper. At the moment Luther was more alarmed by the visit of a priest representing the Utraquists and explaining their reunion plans. He therefore took an unusual step and on July 15, 1522, wrote directly to the Bohemian estates [the territorial diet] then assembled in Prague. He chose to introduce himself as one who had been more attacked for the sake of their country than they themselves. How often was he accused of being a "born Bohemian" or of "intending to flee to Bohemia"! How gladly he would visit them sometime, but at home he would not dare to risk looking like a deserter. Yet he hoped that through the gospel Bohemia and Germany would soon be of one mind and name. He urged the estates to be patient, for not everything can be made new at once. For this purpose one requires good evangelists who will lead people to the one Christ. Never can their own divisions be overcome by annexation to the papal church which itself is torn by dissension. He pleaded with them earnestly to resist, lest the sacrament in both kinds and, by implication, the innocently shed blood of their own John Huss and Jerome of Prague, as well as their teachings, stand condemned among them. "In any case, I myself, along with our own, will acknowledge John Huss even if—may God forbid!—all Bohemia should deny him. Huss will be ours—(as members of the Roman church) we had once put him to death—if you abandon him whom you once defended."[54] To strengthen this writing of his, which was not intended for print, Luther on that same day wrote a letter to Count Sebastian Schlick, a large landowner in northern Bohemia, which included the dedication to Schlick of a little book he had just completed against England's King Henry VIII.[55] In it Luther repeated his warning and his promotional appeal to make common cause, doing so publicly and more acidly. We do not know how the Bohemian estates received Luther's appeal. In any case, it did not go unheard in the Utraquist church, as the coming years were to reveal.

Refreshing as the overall impression of the evangelical movement might be as its forces were advancing near at hand and far away, Luther was not

---

53. To Speratus, May 16, 1522, WA Br 2:531 / 26ff.

54. WA 10²:173 / 1–174 / 13. ["Schreiben an die böhmischen Landstände."]

55. [*Contra Henricum Regem Angliae*, July 15, 1522. Luther's reply in German to King Henry's book against Luther, including the dedication to Sebastian Schlick. WA 10²: 180–222.]

unaware of the shadows gathering over it. His neighbor Duke George saw to that, for George had warned his cousin Elector Frederick of the dangers of this movement soon after the return of the outlaw to Wittenberg. "Though he may act as sweet as can be, yet from behind he strikes in any direction with the tail of a scorpion."[56] George admittedly was watching Luther's every step and utterance and repeatedly alerted the imperial government authorities in Nuremberg to this effect.[57] Wherever there was evidence of a Lutheran movement in his own country, George immediately took measures to oppose it. Thanks to his efficient secret service, he had a copy at once of Luther's letter to the Bohemian estates in Prague.[58] These mainly preventive measures in Ducal Saxony, on the one hand, and the outright persecutions [under the Inquisition] in the Netherlands, on the other, were the two major points of leverage for the rapidly rising political struggle against the Lutheran movement. How this struggle was waged and whether it achieved success depended on the possibilities open to the empire and the emperor during the coming years.

56. March 21, 1522. Gess, *Akten*, 1:295.

57. For the spring and summer 1522, cf. Gess, *Akten*, 1:315ff., 325–26, 327–28, 335–36, 343–44. WA 10²:502ff.

58. WA 10²:169.

5

The Issues of Marriage,
Government, the Congregation,
Worship, School

Tasks carried over from the Wartburg days as well as the jumbled situation in Wittenberg kept Luther amply occupied until the autumn of 1522. On top of that came such extra duties as rebutting an attack by England's King Henry VIII[1] and the acceptance of preaching assignments. Disputes over the reform of worship and of congregational order had abated temporarily while the interim arrangements he had made for Wittenberg remained in effect. But the lull could not last. One after another major issues in public life and church life confronted Luther, demanding to be resolved.

Marriage and the laws pertaining to it headed the agenda. In marriage more than in any other field, questions of law were at the same time questions of conscience. For some time this had been troubling Luther's sense of pastoral responsibility. Yet he was well aware of the mountain of legal difficulties he would be tackling now that the canonical laws on marriage had been circumvented and nothing equivalent in civil law had been fashioned. Earlier (1520), in his *To the Christian Nobility of the German Nation,* and especially in *The Babylonian Captivity of the Church,* it had already been necessary for him to touch on this issue.[2] But now that a flood of emergencies required a more thorough clarification, Luther endeavored to clarify the matter in his *The Estate of Marriage,* which appeared in the autumn of 1522. Here too he saw the issue as a liberation from captivity, first from a whole range of impediments imposed by canon law. With recourse to Mosaic and Roman law, he lessened the number of forbidden degrees of affinity and gave validity only to the cases of blood relationship citied in the Bible.[3] He did so surely not only on grounds of

1. *Contra Henricum Regem Angliae* (1522), WA 10²:175ff.
2. WA 6:446 / 27ff.; 468 / 8ff.; 550ff. [*LW* 36:92–106. In dealing with the seven sacraments, Luther inevitably had to comment on the sacrament of marriage. He refers briefly to this subject in addressing the nobility, *LW* 44:183–84.]
3. WA 10²:275ff. Lev. 18:7ff.; 20:17ff.; Deut. 27:22–24. [*LW* 45:23ff.]

biblical commandment but also because the line of reasoning therein set forth struck him as sensible and convincing. What outraged him especially, however, was the readiness of the church to grant dispensation from virtually any of its self-imposed impediments in return for a fee. Actually, then, there are really no impediments to marriage at all. Just as little is spiritual kinship an impediment, being a prohibition introduced by the church itself in connection with sponsors at baptism and confirmation. In those days this prohibition was applied much more broadly than today and required special dispensation. Furthermore, the prohibition against marrying an unbeliever struck Luther as being in direct contradiction to early Christian practice which permitted marriage to a pagan and saw in this a special task for the Christian (1 Cor. 7:13; 1 Pet. 3:1). This view nullifies the often misquoted word of Luther's that "marriage is an outward, bodily thing, like any other worldly undertaking" one can do with pagans.[4] What he said was not intended to degrade marriage but to give it the honor of a proper and godly estate in the world that God created.

For a long time Luther had recognized that it was a faulty exegesis of Eph. 5:32 to give marriage a sacramental basis; in that verse the word "sacrament" occurs (the Vulgate translation for the Greek word, *mysterion*), meaning the mystery of union between Christ and his congregation, which is like that of marriage.[5] Marriage is not to be derived from this simile, but the other way around: Marriage is a primal given factor in the divine creation, which in Ephesians is employed as a simile or image. Besides, it is not simply a commandment God has given man. It is more than that. It is a "divine work," an "order" into which God has placed the forcible power of nature and the full blessing of his creative grace. Luther would therefore liberate marriage from its imprisonment in an inferior status. Even though sin clings to the married life, the estate of matrimony is nevertheless a work of God which "amid and despite sin retains all the attributes that he has implanted and blessed in it."[6] For this reason spiritual vows have no validity over against [understanding of God's] order. It is no disgrace to recognize a vow one cannot keep and should not have made in the first place. "Here I advise you: If you want to make a wise vow, then vow not to bite off your own nose. That's a vow you can keep."[7]

4. WA 10²:283 / 8. In the same connection with 1 Cor. 7:13, see WA 12:120 / 20. [*LW* 45:25.]

5. *The Babylonian Captivity of the Church* (1520), WA 6:551 / 6ff. Also, *Contra Henricum Regem Angliae* (1522), WA 10²:221 / 10ff.; 259 / 3. [*LW* 36:93, 94.]

6. WA 10²:276 / 9ff.; 304 / 6ff. [*LW* 45:18.]

7. WA 10²:284 / 22ff. [*LW* 45:27.]

There will, of course, always be exceptions where someone will voluntarily and without the legalistic pressures of the vow of celibacy make a vow in order to facilitate serving God. Luther speaks most respectfully of such a voluntary vow, since it refers to the single estate of Christ and Paul. By doing so, Luther reverses the moral gradation of estates hitherto prevailing: Celibacy derives its value not from aceticism but from service. "The Word of God and preaching make the chaste estate better than the married. . . . By itself, however, the single estate is much less." Finally, Luther also seeks a way through the question of divorce. He approves of it in cases of impotence, adultery, or persistent refusal of marital duty. He also justifies divorce when a marriage has become completely ruined, the one condition being that neither party marry again. He adds, however, that "it would be a really blessed cross and a genuine way to heaven" for a Christian to tolerate an evil spouse.[8]

Considering the vacuum created by the withdrawal from the canonical marriage laws, one must admire Luther for his attempt to give marriage a new legal basis and distinguishing character. His attempt rests ultimately on one fundamental thought: Marriage is under the protection and promise of God and therefore is released from all man-made limitations, excessive hindrances, and ecclesial vows. Even though it is never without sin, marriage has a cogent natural life sprung not from unbridled drives but from the creative will of God who perpetuates humanity by means of it. There are limits beyond which marriage loses its meaning and may be dissolved. Conversely, people may not deprive others from participating in this natural law of God, or even exclude themselves from it by some legal self-imposition, the one exception being voluntary surrender to special service. Luther's teaching on marriage, with its rejection of celibacy and monastic vows, signified no capitulation to the irresistible sinfulness of human nature, as some have misinterpreted him. Rather, it is part of his teaching on creation which declares that nature—despite the sin that lays hold of it—recognizes that marriage is willed and given by God. In the process of nature God's hidden order is embedded, and the only people who may break through it are those whom God has called to undertake particularly wondrous works.[9] Though he offered this treatment on the estate of marriage with some hesitation, Luther was sure that this was not the end of it and that difficult questions on marriage would still be giving him and others much to do.[10] Nevertheless, the foundation for a new

8. WA 10²:279 / 15ff.; 302 / 5ff., 13ff.; 287ff.; 291 / 5ff. [LW 45:21, 38, 30, 34.]
9. WA 10²:279 / 20–21. [LW 45:21.]
10. WA 10²:275 / 1ff. [LW 45:17.]

111

understanding and legal basis of marriage had been laid. Luther's later pronouncements on the subject contained nothing essentially new but treated mainly the objections raised by his opponents. The latter relied mainly on their interpretation of Paul's statements on marriage. In a thorough exposition of 1 Cor. 7 in July 1523, Luther strikingly showed the contrast between the opinion of the apostle and the Catholic teaching on the virtues of virginity. But then Luther also took the liberty of putting his own praise of the married estate on the lips of the apostle, an ascription not quite attuned to the basic ascetic and eschatological tone of that seventh chapter.[11]

No sooner had Luther completed his treatise on marriage, the subject that had led him into the field of jurisprudence, than he tackled a much more extensive task, a presentation on the nature of civil government.[12] However strictly stored within the bounds of his spiritual tasks, Luther was by nature passionately political. His *To the Christian Nobility of the German Nation* is proof of this as he addressed the various representatives of governmental authority. Besides, the writing of this tract had for the first time forced him to ponder in detail the intersecting boundaries between the realms of church and state. Two occasions now prompted Luther to develop the plan of a fundamental treatise. The outstanding jurist of the empire was Count John Henry von Schwarzenberg, an adviser to the bishop of Bamberg. Schwarzenberg's widely known work on capital punishment, the *Lex Bambergensis* (1507), had served as the model for the imperial code of criminal law. Recently he had sent Luther a manuscript on various matters of faith. In response, Luther declared himself in full agreement except on one point: "I disagree with Your Grace entirely when you make the point that the use of the sword by temporal authorities can be made to agree with the gospel. So I intend to publish a little book on this subject especially."[13] We would give a great deal today if a copy of Schwarzenberg's "mighty book" were still available, especially because it is the first documentation of his inclination toward the Reforma-

11. WA 12:88ff. [*LW* 28:9ff.]

12. The following section is taken almost verbatim from H. Bornkamm, *Luthers Lehre von den zwei Reichen im Zusammenhang seiner Theologie* (Gütersloh, 1958), 7–14. Cf. also H. Bornkamm, *Luther: Gestalt und Wirkungen*, SVRG 188 (Gütersloh, 1975), "Der Christ und die zwei Reiche," 255ff.

13. Luther to Schwarzenberg, September 21, 1522, WA Br 2:600/29ff. On Schwarzenberg's *ingens liber* to Spalatin, ca. December 12, 1522, WA Br 2:630/8ff. This concerned more than "a little book" or "Schriftchen" (W. Scheel, *Johann Freiherr zu Schwarzenberg* [Berlin, 1905], 330).

tion, and also because Luther's own position was shaped somewhat in taking issue with it.

The second occasion was completely different. Here Luther encountered the problem of the state when his translation of the New Testament was forbidden in Ducal Saxony and other territories and all copies of it were ordered confiscated by the authorities.[14] On what grounds did the authorities have the right to do this? By asking this basic question about the nature of civil or governmental powers, a parallel question was also raised about the limits of those powers. These two cases [Schwarzenberg and Ducal Saxony] led Luther to develop his thoughts on them in sermons preached in Weimar on October 24 and 25 before beginning to write on the subject toward the end of December. In March 1523 he published his treatise *On Temporal Authority: To What Extent It Should Be Obeyed*. The two occasions giving rise to the writings of this treatise are readily discernible in the title as well as in the contents. The dual question is treated in the first two parts, and the style—given Luther's tendency to digress—is uncommonly severe. The third part is a guide for the Christian prince, where Luther follows a precedent set by Augustine's *City of God*.[15]

All three parts of this treatise are encompassed by a fundamental distinction of the "two kingdoms" Luther perceived as operative within humanity. The best way to comprehend this widely misunderstood term is to recall the burning issues under which the evangelicals were oppressed in Catholic territories. Luther here turns against a twofold misunderstanding of civil powers. Instead of the bishops governing people with the Word of God, they have become involved in governing "castles, cities, lands, and tenants." And instead of the temporal lords governing their lands properly and not exploiting them, these lords are eager to exercise "spiritual governance over the souls of people," to prescribe the papal faith and to eradicate the Lutheran heresy by force.[16] Between the realm of faith, which requires freedom, and the realm of function, which requires external order, there are boundaries just as real as the territorial boundary between Leipzig and Wittenberg. For Christians, however, it is necessary

14. F. Gess, *Akten und Briefe zur Kirchenpolitik Herzog Georgs von Sachsen* (Leipzig, 1905ff.), vol. 1, no. 400. WA 11:267 / 14ff.; 483.

15. W. Berges, *Die Fürstenspiegel des hohen und späten Mittelalters* (Stuttgart, 1938; reprinted 1962, *Monumenta Germaniae Historica* 2). The two sermons of Luther: WA 10³:371–85. [*Temporal Authority* . . . LW 45:(77), 81–129. For the text of two of the six Weimar sermons, LW 51:(103), 104–17.]

16. WA 11:265 / 7ff., 11, 19. [LW 45:110.]

to discover these boundaries ever afresh by means of decisions freely made. In matters pertaining to themselves and their own interests, let Christians refrain from insisting on their own rights and on coercion. In such situations the commandment of Jesus obtains: to do good and to endure injustice. On the other hand, where it is a matter concerning the neighbor or the community, Christians are obliged to combat injustice with all proper means.[17] If the world contained only true Christians, there would be no need for laws or legal administration. True Christians are so "natured" in spirit that they know better what they are supposed to do than any laws could tell them; they require laws as little as an apple tree requires instruction to bear apples and not thorns. However, "the world and the mass of people are and remain unchristian, even though all may be baptized and called Christian." True Christians are few and far between. In order that evil not triumph, law and order are necessary. In their own lives Christians must thus "satisfy" both kingdoms: You "endure injustice like a regular Christian in matters pertaining to your own affairs . . . and you tolerate no injustice toward your neighbor."[18] This holds particularly for Christians in public office. In sharp contrast to the Zwickau enthusiasts and, later on, to the Anabaptists, Luther urges Christians to make themselves available for this role and to accept a duty more fitting for them than for anyone else on earth—for this concern for justice is also a service to God in the same way as matrimony, farming, or a trade; indeed, it is even more essential than these because it is the most difficult service of all, one without which the world would go to pieces.[19]

When he speaks of two "kingdoms," Luther does not confine himself to the paired realms of church and state, or of proclamation and the rule of law, but he includes as well the two contexts of relationships in which the Christian lives. On the one hand, it is the Christians' own existence, their personal relations with fellow human beings, their own standing up for the gospel, which involve application of the boundless commandment to forgive, to endure, to sacrifice. On the other hand, there is the common life with other people in which justice [the law] must set the necessary firm boundaries against evil, and there Christians must help so that no one suffers injustice or becomes victimized by others. These two contexts have corresponding means available to them. Or, as Luther put it, the two

17. WA 11:259 / 7ff.; 260 / 17ff. [LW 45:103.]
18. WA 11:249 / 24–254 / 26; 250 / 19; 251 / 36–37; 255 / 12ff. [LW 45:88–96, 89, 91, 96.]
19. WA 11:254 / 27ff.; 258 / 1ff. [LW 45:95, 100.]

"kingdoms" contain two modes of governance: the nonviolent Word and the law-enforcing powers of the government. The government bears the sword on the basis of powers granted by God, its right to do so being based on the power to punish transgressors at home and to protect against enemies from abroad. Both these governments are under God. Unhappily, more recent research has played these two "kingdoms" and governments against each other. Luther had a meaningful but not abstract way of differentiating between them, for they belong inseparably together. So Luther must always make a double pronouncement: For Christians there are always two clearly separated conditions of life, yet these conditions are not rigid compartments into which their lives are divided. Christians cannot exist simply in one or the other. They live in them only when, by means of the one or the other "regime," they do the will of God, who holds the world together. This requires of the Christian an ever new and conscientious making of decisions for which there is but one norm: What is here the appropriate form of love, to endure injustice or to exact justice?

In a world torn by sin, the two kingdoms in which Christians find themselves are separated by a pronounced boundary that is not to be weakened lest chaos engulf everything. Yet in both these realms the same single and loving will of God is at work, even though it may employ various means. Thereby the two forms of service are inseparably joined. Luther enumerates all kinds of contrasts between the two realms—kingdom of God, kingdom of the world; realm of the gospel, realm of the Law; realm of the believing, realm of the unbelieving; realm of the spiritual, realm of the worldly; realm for self, realm for others; domain of the Word, domain of the sword; and so on. Yet as he says, it is never a matter of kingdom of love, kingdom without love. Love encompasses both. It is possible to say the same thing of both kingdoms. Concerning the enforced order of law [justice] one can say, "One's behavior is determined by love and one puts up with no injustice toward one's fellow man." And concerning the personal life of true Christians you can say, "They do wrong to no one; they love everyone, and they are ready and willing to put up with injustice."[20] Because love encompasses both these orders of God and because God carries out his order of justice also through non-Christians, love is for Luther a consistent and universally "natural" commandment and not simply one for Christians. Whoever shuns the word of Christ can nevertheless be apprehended by this "natural law." "For nature teaches me, as love itself does, that I should do as I would like to have done toward me."

20. WA 11:255 / 19–20; 250 / 3–4. [LW 45:96,98.]

There is no better guide to the making of legal decisions than that "love and natural law ever keep hovering above them."[21] Love and natural law, which address people through their reason, are the two clamps that hold the world together, and when pondering them according to the will of God, the two are but one.

Insofar as the law of reason, according to God's determining of it, is secretly also the law of love, all temporal justice *[Recht]* also enjoys a motive of freedom. Freedom is not only the controlling factor in the realm of spiritual relations, it is likewise indispensable in the domain of law. Written laws *[Gesetz]* do not suffice. "Reason remains the supreme law and master of all that is just." Alongside the rigidity of the letter, reason is spiritual and alive. This reveals its origin in the hands of God the Creator, while all written law is changeable human achievement. "A really sound judgment can be rendered not from books but from a free understanding, as though there were no book. . . . But such free understanding is provided by love and natural law, in which reason abounds."[22]

Luther expressed his opinion on the life of a Christian amid the temporal order not simply in theory but also developed in his portrayal of the Christian prince, which comprises the third part of this treatise. For a comprehension of his teaching, this part is as helpful as a grasp of the historical situation out of which the treatise arose. The office of governing requires a degree of wisdom and untrammeled power of decision that could drive one to despair. How should Luther presume to offer counsel to a prince? "While my knowledge of jurisprudence does not qualify me to prescribe to a prince, I shall simply desire to instruct his heart."[23] He proceeds to do so with a mixture of Christian counsels and sensible experiences that correspond to the unity of God's two kingdoms. His counsel for the prince is fourfold. He goes into detail but offers this summary: "First, toward God there must be true confidence and earnest prayer; second, toward his subjects there must be love and Christian service; third, with respect to his counselors and officials he must maintain an untrammeled reason and unfettered judgment; fourth, with respect to evildoers he must manifest a restrained severity and firmness." Punish too little rather than too much, and in no case punish so much that it results in greater injustice. Luther also touches briefly on the issue of war, a question he treated more fully later. He exhorted the princes to peacefulness, and

21. *WA* 11:279 / 19ff. [*LW* 45:128.]
22. *WA* 11:272 / 6ff., 16–17; 279 / 30ff. [*LW* 45:118, 128.]
23. *WA* 11:273 / 2–3. *WA* 10³3:380 / 10ff. [*LW* 45:119.]

their Christian subjects to be loyal followers in a necessary war, or in the case of an apparently unjust war to refuse obedience.[24]

This treatise of Luther's contains the sum total of his political ethics. Basically he did not alter it later on. By writing this treatise Luther had achieved more than a clarification of some pressing issues from which conclusions could readily be drawn. The evangelicals are not supposed to deliver New Testaments in Catholic territories, because in that case the rulers of those evangelicals would be going beyond the boundaries of their own "kingdom." "Not a single page, not a letter, should they surrender, on pain of losing their salvation." But the evangelicals should not retaliate if these Testaments are forcibly taken from their homes.[25] Moreover, against the Enthusiasts—who were misleading Christians into a complete renunciation of the political world—Luther had also made it clear why and how Christians are to render service in public office.

This treatise signifies much more, however. It brought about a fundamental separation of temporal and spiritual powers, which in medieval practice had added political governance to bishops and spiritual duties to princes [in the exercise of their respective functions]. Luther saw through this spiritual-temporal unit of medieval times and found it full of contradictions, for this unity embraced an unavoidable rivalry that could be kept under control only as long as the primacy of spiritual law was honored. How rapidly this tension could get out of hand had been amply demonstrated in conflicts great and small over the past centuries. Luther thus developed a counterformulation that gave a separate identity to the church and to the state, setting them the task, as independent partners, of working out their relationship to each other. While many problems remained and new ones arose to occupy Luther and his church, it was this separation of the two kingdoms that always provided a point of orientation. This was especially useful inasmuch as Luther had from the outset embedded the question of the relationship of the church to the world in that of the Christian and the world. Whatever he had to say about this issue was resolved in terms of the central problem of Christian ethics, which exerts ever new pressures on Christendom: the reconciling of life's realities, on the one hand, with the radicalness of Jesus' precepts in the Sermon on the Mount, on the other. Although Luther would later give detailed attention to this question and to the medieval response to it (a matter to which we shall return), the outcome of his thinking is already

24. WA 11:278 / 19ff.; 276 / 27ff. [LW 45:126, 125.]
25. WA 11:267 / 14ff. [LW 45:112.]

present here. Luther takes away nothing from the unconditional precepts of the Sermon on the Mount, nor does he limit the Sermon's applicability to certain estates, like monasticism, or to given times, like the final stage of human history. Instead, he clears the ground on which alone these precepts are meaningful and have binding validity for every Christian. Luther associates the commandment of Jesus with the Creator's continuing preservation of the world. The doctrine of the two kingdoms is thus nothing other than a description of the situation of Christians in the world; and the corresponding treatment concerning the two divine kingdoms is the instruction according to which Christians can in faith make ever fresh decisions about their actions. To be sure, the ideas used by Luther, derived in a transformed way from the Augustinian doctrine of the two realms, in his day facilitated an understanding [of the human situation]; today those ideas are more likely to complicate such understanding. Everything therefore depends on our comprehending that we are dealing here not with a world split into two rigidly separated domains but with the same world seen from two different vantage points. "For me—for others." Between these two points Christians have to make up their minds with alertness and ever anew.

This basic book on Luther's political ethic grew out of his theology and is founded on the faith in God's unchangeable relation to the world. This relationship—despite the abyss that sin has interposed—experiences no change in will or aim, only in means. Love's free order, which God had shared with the human family and which again is shimmering through in the common life of true Christians, has been turned by sin into an order of law and coercion. These two orders, which the young Luther recognized gladly, differentiate themselves as God's "alien" and his "proper" work. Just as God's mode of judgment is a form of the mercy by which he seeks us, so the office of governance is at the same time both a terror to the wicked and a proof of God's protective love. This love is universal; it is valid for the whole world, not only for the Christian world. Luther inevitably held also that the human awareness of such love is universal. One can therefore expect reason to give its affirming yes to the mutual duties of love and helpfulness. Reason itself is not simply a calculating intelligence that sees advantages in reciprocal relationships. The threefold combination of love, reason, and natural law leads to an insight—however slightly preserved—into the law of life with which God has endowed his creation. However one may wish to interpret this basic agreement of reason and love, it belongs in any case to Luther's frequently reaffirmed fundamental convictions. The deeply hidden unity in God's dealings, by means of which he preserves his world through the two "kingdoms," corresponds to a hidden unity in the hearing of believers, on the one hand, and of non-believers, on the other, for God makes use of the unbelieving as well as the believing in his work of providence. The ability to hear, and especially to do—in response to hearing—varies greatly. Christians and non-Christians are thus joined in the same responsibility, from which no one is exempt. But because Christians are illuminated and renewed by the Holy Spirit, and because their experience of grace enables them to understand that God's severity is actually his love, they above all others are called to service in the temporal realm and are not permitted to evade it. Luther's political ethic for Christians thus contains a general ethic in basic outline, for the temporal order is a possession to be preserved by common concern. Because Christians have received more, Luther gives Christians the higher responsibility for temporal order.

Luther's treatment of the problem of governance—which medieval presuppositions had bound up so closely with the matter of religion—was bound to attract widespread public attention. Evidence of this lies in the large number of printings through which *Temporal Authority* rapidly passed: ten High German printings and one Low German printing within the year of publication (1523). Soon there followed a Dutch and a Latin translation. The political significance of this treatise was underscored by Luther's dedication of it to Duke John, Elector Frederick's brother. Let this act be understood as a sign of agreement.

Luther's understanding of governance was still to be tested in exemplary situations. The ecclesial and political domains were more easily separated in theory than intertwined in practice. This was especially true in those many places where the inherited order in the local church had already been dissolved and only the political (temporal) government remained as the unaltered partner. Where to begin? How to provide the church with a new structural base? Problems that Luther had tackled in addressing the German nobility [1520] were coming alive again. To borrow [patterns of action] from the temporal government was unavoidable. Yet if one failed to pay close attention, this sort of thing would lead to developments having all the appearances of a denial of Luther's teaching on the two kingdoms. The distinguishing feature and good fortune of the hour was that the question of new structures for the church was being brought to Luther's attention by all kinds of local congregations and not simply by his own prince, the elector, or by some other territorial ruler. Luther welcomed such diversity, for it corresponded with his understanding of the church. In other words, the new was growing of its own accord instead of having to be organized from the top down.

In Wittenberg the forms remained which Luther had fashioned after his return from the Wartburg. Even so, by the autumn of 1522 it had become the practice in the Town Church to offer the Lord's Supper in both kinds. Besides, in the celebration of mass each Sunday only those who had a desire for the sacrament communed.[26] Even as the time for the big Communion turnout was approaching in Easter 1523, the outward form of the Lord's Supper was no longer a problem. Luther, however, pondered the pastoral side of the problem, asking himself whether it was right simply to administer the sacrament to all who came to the altar. His earnest sermon on Maundy Thursday (April 2, 1523) impressed it on his hearers that whoever is not ready for an honest renewal of the heart might as well not commune. At the same time, he announced that the coming year would see him develop an inquiry enabling prospective communicants to make use of a short prepared statement, by means of which they could indicate a right understanding of the sacrament as well as express their faith in it.[27] When he said he would most like to see those of right faith gather in one place—though evangelical preaching admittedly had not yet been in progress long enough—Luther seemed ready for a first step in a new direction. When the *Order of Mass and Communion* appeared toward the end of 1523, Luther proposed that those desiring to commune should sit in the choir stalls.[28]

With these wishes and simple regulations Luther kept the pastor and the individual communicant in mind. The pastor required an opportunity to ascertain the earnest intentions of the participants. For most people reception of Communion once a year would suffice, for the prudent perhaps once in a lifetime or not at all. For those with whom the pastor was unacquainted, or of whom he had a poor impression, this arrangement was important, yet it was not the occasion to subject such people to painful interrogation. Above all, Luther's intention was to stimulate the individual to do his own rigorous self-examination. Belief in the objective presence of Christ in the sacrament is not enough. Instead, one must receive the sacrament as a firm assurance of the forgiveness of one's own sin. At the same time, those who receive the sacrament should be aware

26. Report of Sebastian Fröschel, *Fortgesetzte Sammlung von alten und neuen theologischen Sachen* (1731), 689ff. See also K. Müller, *Kirche, Gemeinde, und Obrigkeit nach Luther* (Tübingen, 1910), 33–34.

27. WA 12:476ff., esp. 477 / 17ff. (i); 479, 14ff. (i); and 484 / 4ff. (ii).

28. WA 12:485, 4–5 (ii); 215 / 20ff. [*LW* 53:32.]

that in doing so in plain sight of the congregation they publicly attest to this evangelical faith.[29] Luther was here at pains, like Calvin later in Geneva, to keep the Lord's Supper free from unworthy guests, and to do so—aside from the outright sins everyone knew about—on the grounds not of passing ethical judgment but of awakening a conscious faith. His intention was to transform the custom of communing into an act of personal confession. He would be quite content if the number of communicants were to decline. Unlike Zwingli and Calvin, Luther would never have thought of urging attendance at Communion, for communing, in contrast to hearing a sermon, is a matter of the inwardly committed Christians. And even though he still often pondered the thought, Luther could never bring himself to band those particular Christians together as pietists did later. Instead, his main concern was to cultivate a free group of convinced believers within the undivided congregation.

As a preacher of the gospel and as one charged by the town council, which had called him back to Wittenberg, Luther knew that he was authorized to undertake these innovations. The same was true elsewhere as well. His preaching mission after Easter 1522 was at the express invitation of the town councils of Altenburg and Zwickau.[30] Still others had sent letters of invitation to Luther. In any case, was he not hereby leaving it to the temporal authorities to decide on ecclesiastical affairs? Not so, contended Luther. He was leaving the decisions to the local congregation. For him, the town council was the mouthpiece for the congregation. After all, it had no other spokesman. Whenever a town council asked for a preacher of the gospel, Luther saw the town as a Christian congregation making the request through its council.[31]

For Luther and his times this was not yet a day of separate political and ecclesial structures. The congregation alone has the right to order its ways of worship and its life, as well as to call suitable preachers. This naturally given right of the congregation takes precedence over all contrary rights, indeed, shows them up as unjust. This was becoming clear to Luther as new preachers were being called to all kinds of places, for it was then that one of the worst developments in church law during the late Middle Ages confronted him: the incorporation of countless pastorates and preaching posts into the jurisdiction of some cloister, institute, or university.[32] This

---

29. WA 12:481 / 10ff.; 215 / 18–216 / 30. [LW 53:32–34.]

30. Altenburg: ca. April 15, 1522, WA Br 2:502–3. Zwickau: R. Hofmann, "Bilder aus einer sächsischen Stadt im Reformationszeitalter," NASG 15 (1904): 56.

31. Cf. the example of Leisnig, below, p. 122.

32. For example, Orlamünde was incorporated in the All Saints Castle Church Foundation in Wittenberg. See below, pp. 143–44.

arrangement of incorporation provided even distantly located institutions with a source of income from the benefices, to which they reserved the right of appointing the incumbents.

Luther first encountered this problem in Altenburg, where the town's entire complement of churches and chapels, as well as the most important cloister—the convent of Our Lady on the Hill (the Hill Cloister)—had come as gifts through Emperor Frederick II in the year 1214. A conflict now broke out over a certain preaching benefice established there in the fifteenth century. Its endowments were administered by the town council as trustee. Upon request of the evangelically inclined townspeople, however, the council arrogated to itself also the right to name the incumbent and promptly requested the protection of the elector against any action by the cloister.[33] Luther assisted the council and himself wrote several letters on the councilmen's behalf to the elector. In so doing, he shifted the question from the level of formal, historic rights to that of the fundamental right of a congregation to hear the gospel proclaimed. Luther sees the congregation as the corporate expression of the priesthood of all believers. Not only the town council of Altenburg, as a temporal government, but also "all Christians . . . together and severally" have been charged to guard against false prophets and to call authentic preachers. Inasmuch as the council took up the matter, it was discharging its duty as a part and an organ of the congregation.[34]

The same need for justice, as in Altenburg, was presented to Luther a little later by the small town of Leisnig on the Mulde River in Freiberg. By the freshness of its initiative this case can claim credit for having moved Luther to produce his basic writings on the new structures of the congregation. The situation in Leisnig was that one of the town's vicarages had been incorporated among the assets of the neighboring Cistercian cloister. Upon thorough consultation with Luther, who responded to the appeal of

33. Exchange of letters after mid-April 1522, WA Br 2:502ff. The papers were published by J. Löbe, "Mitteilungen über den Anfang und Fortgang der Reformation in Altenburg," *Mitteilungen der Geschichts- und Altertumsforschende Gesellschaft des Osterlandes* 6 (1863): 1ff. References in Müller, *Kirche, Gemeinde, und Obrigkeit*, 103ff. Further treatment in P. Kirn, *Friedrich der Weise: Sein Kirchenpolitik vor und nach Luthers Hervortreten in Jahre 1517* (Leipzig and Berlin, 1926), 114–15. Luther's draft of the request of the Altenburg council carried to the elector, April 28, 1522, WA Br 2:507–8; 507 / 22–23.

34. Similarly and in the same year, Luther cautioned Count John Henry von Schwarzenberg to interrogate in the presence of "several knowledgeable people" the Dominicans in Leutenberg, whose sermons to him seemed unevangelical. "If it turns out publicly to be as they are accused, then Your Grace has the power and the right—indeed the duty—to take away their positions and to fill them with devout and educated men who will teach the people properly, for it is not unjust—indeed, it is the highest form of justice—to chase the wolf out of the sheep stall." December 12, 1522, WA Br 2:626 / 12ff.

the town council by spending an entire week in Leisnig during the autumn of 1522, the congregation decided to elect an evangelically minded pastor. The townspeople were acting on the basis of a 1,500-year-old right given by Christ to every Christian congregation, a right preceding all earthly and historical rights.[35] It so happened, however, that in the Leisnig case the filling of the office was inextricably bound to the use of the church property and of other ecclesiastical foundations. Consequently a comprehensive order was worked out and brought to Luther by two emissaries in January 1523 with the request that he himself confirm in writing a congregation's right to elect a pastor, and that he also provide them with some guidelines for worship.[36] This prompted him in April 1523 to write simultaneously on the three unanswered questions of congregational composition: church property, clergy appointments, and ways of worship.[37]

Luther approached the broad issue of the disposition of church property and endowments by making a "common example" of the constitution drawn up for Leisnig. His general preface went far beyond this particular situation.[38] He was concerned lest the collapse of ecclesial organization tempt many people to recoup the vast wealth amassed in the churches. And since Luther was held responsible for the exodus from the cloisters and religious establishments as well as for the changed attitude of the clergy, he was not about to let it be charged that he kept silent or spoke up too late. He had no power to give orders, but could only advise. His only weapons were to call by name the enemies with whom he had to deal—the "greedy potbellies" and the "Satanic prince of this world"—and to point as a warning to the example of Bohemia, where a general looting of church property had broken out.

Luther's chief advice was to take whatever cloister properties or ecclesial endowments had become free and to place them in a "common chest" for assisting the poor or granting them loans. In this way, at least, the will of the donor—that something be done to honor God—would be respected. But first it would be necessary to carry out several special obligations. Let the cloisters admit no new applicants, but provide well for those

---

35. G. Kawerau, "Zur Leisniger Kastenordnung," *NASG* 3 (1882): 81ff.; an excerpt from this is in *WA* 12:3–4. For a correction of the *WA* version, cf. P. Mehlhose, "Das Schloss Leisnig in der Zeit 1437 bis 1546," *Mitteilungen des Geschichts- und Altertumsvereins zu Leisnig* 17 (1932): 28 (*WA* Br 3:22, n. 2).

36. *WA* Br 3:21–22.

37. *WA* Br 3:59.

38. *WA* 12:11–15; 11 / 21–22. [*LW* 45:169ff. The full title and text, *Ordinance of a Common Chest, Preface, LW* 45:(161), 169–94.]

who wish to remain. Let those who leave the cloister receive a grant in order to take up another occupation, assuming that monastic life had taught them no useful one. In cases where the family of a donor has run into hard times, let a portion of the donated capital be restored to them. As for the disposition of the cloisters themselves, let those of the mendicant orders in the towns be turned into good schools for boys and girls or be put to some other use by the community. It was not only the local but also the general possessions of the church as a whole that called for reordering, however. Consider the bishops and abbots, who were "temporal lords under a spiritual name." Luther offered them the alternative either to go completely temporal or to surrender their properties, turning them over to impoverished former owners or to the common chest. In that connection, the endowments that had been loaned out at interest posed a different problem. A few years earlier (1519), in his *Sermon on Usury,* Luther had sharply attacked the money-lending interests, which, he was now shocked to learn, "had devoured the whole world in a few short years." This was particularly offensive in the case of church endowments, inasmuch as God is the enemy of "sacrifices derived from robbery" (cf. Isa. 61:8, "I hate robbery and wrong"). Besides, in the case of long-term loans, the amount of the initial capital is repaid several times. Indeed, Luther promised himself that his new guidelines would result in a general curbing of usury as hitherto practiced and justified in connection with church property. Other results that he hoped would follow from his proposals included an end to begging as well as to the ban and the interdict, practices that involved the exclusion of specific places or countries from the sacraments and that mostly involved churches and cloisters.[39]

Luther was disposed not to turn his advice into an inclusive regulation but rather to stimulate basic thinking on the subject. He well knew that some things simply cannot be caught in rules and regulations but must be decided ever anew on a basis of Christian love. The order for the common chest at Leisnig could serve as an example for the realization of these thoughts and also as a means of spelling out what he had not developed in the preface. This connecting of theory and practice is most characteristic of Luther's way of proceeding. The test cases would gather up experiences. In fact, Leisnig was a model example. A community operating through its town government, yet doing so as a Christian congregation, that is, as a duly constituted congregational assembly whose geographic

---

39. For the numerous cases of the ban and the interdict in Electoral Saxony, as drawn from official records, see Kirn, *Friedrich der Weise,* 53ff., 198–99.

bounds included not only the town itself but also eleven villages and three privately owned pieces of real estate. "Honorable gentlemen" (the landed property owners), the town council, and the masters of the free trades— "upon request of each and every inhabitant in the town and villages embracing our ecclesial congregation"—had issued and signed the order.[40]

The Leisnig order had its spiritual and temporal sides. The spiritual right to elect a pastor—which the Leisnig order assigned to the congregation—corresponded to the spiritual obligation faithfully to hear the Word as well as to maintain discipline and moral standards in the homes; in emergencies, the congregational and the governing authorities could be summoned for help. The latter was a late medieval practice, and no further details were included in the order. But the administration of the common chest—such as that started in Wittenberg in 1521–22[41]—was spelled out in detail. Income and expenditures for the ministry and for the sexton's quarters and duties, as well as for aid to the needy and for the schooling of boys and girls, were to be accounted for precisely. Ten overseers were assigned responsibility for contents of the chest, a strong box with four locks. Each Sunday they were to consult on expenditures, and they were to keep a record of the finances in three sets of books. Three times a year they were to give an accounting to the entire congregation.

This Leisnig order had been worked out with the meticulous love of a craftsman, yet it was more easily put down on paper than carried out in practice. The town council balked. It refused to relinquish to the overseers its trusteeship over income from endowments and wills. From the outset, therefore, the income of the common chest was much less than anticipated. Soon the pastors fell into dire need, and the conflict was appealed to Elector Frederick. In spite of repeated pleas from Luther, the elector could not make up his mind to approve the order for a common chest.[42] Had he done so, he would have turned down the claims of Abbot von Buch, which were based on the earlier policies of incorporation and, by implication, would have denied his own policy of delay in church affairs. In 1524 Frederick proposed mediation, but when this failed he let the matter lie. Not until 1529, after the visitation [of Saxony's congregations], did Elector John [1525–32] formally approve the order for the common chest. For Luther this whole affair became doubly painful when he

40. WA 12:30 / 20ff. [LW 45:194.]

41. See above, pp. 60–61.

42. Luther to the Elector, August 11 and 19, 1523. To Spalatin, November 24, 1524. WA Br 3:124–25; 128–29; 390–91. On the negotiations of the elector with Abbot von Buch, cf. Kirn, *Friedrich der Weise*, 116–17, and the supporting documents, 189ff. [LW 49:45–47.]

saw how the initially hopeful beginnings were being frustrated by the many internal and external difficulties that impeded a new constitution for the congregations.

At the same time as the publication of this community chest order, Luther filled the two requests of the Leisnig parish. First was an exposition of the right to elect a pastor. Many congregations had begun to claim that right—and Luther brought out a short treatise entitled *That a Christian Assembly or Congregation Has the Right and Power to Judge All Teaching and to Call, Appoint, and Dismiss Teachers, Established and Proven by Scripture,* in which Luther reviewed the primitive Christian conviction that congregations have the right and duty to distinguish between true prophets and false prophets. Words of Christ (Matt. 7:15, 24:4; John 6:45, 10:4ff., 27) and of the apostles (1 Thess. 5:21; Rom. 16:17ff.; 1 Cor. 10:14–15; Col. 28; and indeed even the appeals of Paul to the wavering Galatians [chaps. 3–5]) gave Luther the confidence that the congregation, as in apostolic times, would be equipped with the needed gifts. "That is why all teachers and their teaching should and must be subject to the judgment of the listeners." This then is how a congregation operates "which is in possession of the gospel." It does so out of "divine right" and for the sake of the salvation of souls when on its own it calls a preacher and thus withdraws from the presumed governance of bishops and cloisters into which the pastoral charges had been incorporated.[43] Of course, such self-help on the part of a congregation arises from an emergency, and it does not cause Luther to lose sight of the possibility of the church as a whole being renewed. The normal procedure would be for "upright bishops" to install preachers already elected or approved by a congregation.[44] Yet the opposite is also possible—that the authentic Christian congregation comprises only a small minority of the members. Even then it could and would be obliged to exercise its right for itself. For the sign, like a military flag, by which one recognizes a Christian congregation is the preaching of the pure gospel. Luther's favorite promise overarches such preaching: "So shall the word which comes from my mouth prevail; it shall not return to me fruitless" (Isa. 55:11, NEB). Where the gospel sounds forth, it always gathers those who believe.[45]

This deeply charismatic groundswell in Luther's thought on the church is not to be denied. He was not blind to the fact that his mode of thought

43. WA 11:410 / 19; 411 / 13ff. WA 12:187 / 29ff. [*LW* 39:307, 308–9.]
44. WA 11:414 / 1ff., 30ff. [*LW* 39:312.]
45. WA 11:408 / 5ff. [*LW* 39:305.]

risked difficulties; his experiences in Wittenberg had made that clear. Nevertheless, he had a twofold reason for espousing this primitive Christian understanding of the congregation. For the short term, he used it to blast the armor of hierarchical church law so that congregations might regain their sense of responsibility. For the long haul, he chose it as a means of maintaining the congregations' power to make decisions in matters of faith over against an otherwise easy relapse into the rigidities of order and tradition.

A few months later Luther again had the opportunity to make a public statement on the establishment of evangelical congregations. In the summer of 1523, Master Gallus Cahera, a pastor of the Utraquist church in Bohemia, was spending some time in Wittenberg. Aware of Luther's previous letter to the Bohemian territorial estates,[46] Cahera urged him to make contact once again with the Hussite church, since Luther's earlier contact affairs there had taken a good turn. Counseled by Cahera, Luther composed a detailed treatise, *De instituendis ministris ecclesiae*, which was published in November 1523. In two respects this statement differed from Luther's earlier treatment of the congregational issue. First, the Bohemian situation was different. This was not a case of a united, evangelically minded congregation approaching him. Instead, the approach was being made by a small minority of the Utraquist church, although it was the side, Cahera claimed, on which the city council of Prague stood. Second, because he had to communicate in Latin, Luther was able to use more precise terms in setting forth his concepts. In German it would have been impossible, but in Latin he was able to develop an entire point of view by differentiating between *sacerdos* (priest) and *presbyterus* (presbyter/elder). In the Roman church these two terms were being used interchangeably. His thesis was *Sacerdotem non esse quod presbyterum vel ministrum, illum nasce, hunc fieri*—"Priest is something other than presbyter or servant; the former is born, the latter is become."[47] Christ is born, the priest of the new covenant, and with him the Christians, his brethren, who are one body with him and are flesh of his flesh (1 Cor. 10:16–17; Gal. 3:27–28; Eph. 5:30). From Christ they have all received the same tasks: to spread the gospel, to baptize, to forgive or retain sin, to judge teaching, and to engage in intercessory prayer. They also have something else in common, which the Roman priests have reserved for themselves: to sacrifice and to consecrate, that is, to distribute the Lord's

46. *WA* 12:178 / 9ff.
47. Ibid.

Supper, for the New Covenant knows no other sacrifice than to offer ourselves the way Christ did (Rom. 12:1; 1 Pet. 2:5). "For if the greater things—Word and Baptism—are entrusted to all [believers], then one will be justified in saying that the lesser thing (namely, consecrating [the bread and the wine]) cannot be denied them.[48]

Luther thus saw nothing in the administration of the Lord's Supper which could signify that certain Christians have precedence over others. To him the sacrament itself is part of the proclamation of the gospel, a responsibility given to all believers. Taken together, all these aspects [of proclamation and administration] are part of the *ius commune* [the common right] of Christians. Yet because it is the common right of all, no one may claim to exercise it on his own authority, but only when called to do so by the congregation or the church. In this manner the priesthood of all believers is distinguished from those publicly commissioned: the servants (ministers), deacons, bishops, administrators (dispensers of assigned tasks), presbyters (because of their age), or whatever they are called.[49]

Luther's advice to the Bohemians was self-evident. They should simply cease what they had been doing: under false pretenses sneaking ordination through bishops in Italy. Instead, let the Prague city council assemble those Christians ready for church renewal so that they can elect preachers and commend them to the entire congregation as true shepherds. When this shall have taken place in a number of congregations, then let the territorial estates (parliament) debate the issue and decide whether this procedure should be followed throughout Bohemia, without any kind of compulsion. The issue, after all, will not be settled by sheer numbers. Even among six or ten Christians, caught by the gospel, the church of God is present. Then, if a number of bishops select someone to act as their visitor [chief inspector], perhaps Bohemia will again become a "rightful and evangelical archbishopric," which for over a hundred years has stood vacant.[50]

The hopes Luther pinned on his proposals were in for bitter disappointment. At first everything seemed set to move forward as desired. On February 2, 1524, at an assembly of the Utraquist estates, Cahera was actually elected administrator of the archbishopric of Prague, but his subsequent attempt to abolish clerical celibacy aroused the resistance of old-timers in the Utraquist ranks who clung to the idea of a special order of clergy.

48. WA 12:185 / 16ff.; 183 / 12ff.; 182 / 35–36.
49. WA 12:189 / 17ff.; 190 / 11ff.
50. WA 12:193 / 22; 194 / 20; 170 / 12ff. [LW 40:40–44; 9–10.]

When the vainglorious Cahera next sought to confirm his position by negotiating with Rome, a coup d'état toppled the government in Prague and landed the Lutheran-minded town councilmen in jail. For a while Cahera, impervious now to further influence from Luther, managed to weave his way between the contending parties, but his day came and he was banished from Bohemia. He wound up his career as an innkeeper in the Franconian city of Ansbach. Contrary to Luther's hopes, Utraquism did not grow rapidly into a reformation movement, but became frustrated by prolonged inner conflicts. In the course of these events, the young Utraquists who stood close to Luther won lasting control, but they did so in the chilly atmosphere of a nascent counterreformation. For Luther this was disheartening. He had trusted Cahera without reservation and had agreed completely with his proposals for Bohemia.[51]

Yet the lasting fruit of these dashed hopes is the treatise Luther had written under their inspiration. By means of this exercise he opened up the seam through which long ago the early Catholic church had joined the gospel to the sacral priesthood of antiquity and the Old Testament. By restoring its New Testament meaning to the priesthood (1 Pet. 2:5, 9; Rev. 1:6, 5, 10), he abolished the notion that a special class is required in order to perform certain functions. He thereby cleansed Christendom of an element quite alien to the message of Jesus. In the applied linguistic usage of the New Testament which makes all believers priests (an application he came upon after the Leipzig disputation in 1519) Luther now discovered a spiritual, evangelical constitutional concept for the proper church of Christ, namely, the common responsibility of all believers. This concept was flexible enough that at one place it could achieve a complete breakthrough while in another it could initiate a modest beginning. Besides, the way Luther had thus far developed this concept, it was still free from any infiltration on the part of temporal government.

According to principles Luther had been upholding for some time and had now set forth in his writings of 1523, evangelical preachers were being called to a number of places—and it was all being done without either consulting with the elector or formally abolishing the existing laws.[52] Understandably, Wittenberg proved the easiest place to transfer the electoral

---

51. Luther's letter of consolation to the imprisoned chancellor of the city of Prague, the knight Burian Sobek von Kornitz, October 27, 1524; and his letter to Cahera, November 13, 1524. *WA Br* 3:363–64; 370–71.

52. Those cases occurring simultaneously with the events in Altenburg and Leisnig (namely, Wittenberg, Eilenburg, Belgern, Erfurt, Lautenberg, Orlamünde, Kemberg) were not all of the same legal states. See Müller, *Kirche, Gemeinde, und Obrigkeit*. 113ff. Material newer than that in Müller has been brought out by Kirn, *Friedrich der Weise*, 115–16.

franchise to the congregation. There the All Saints Foundation, in which the Town Church was incorporated, could offer only weak resistance against a united front of the town council, the university, and the congregation. With the Town Church pulpit vacant after the death of its pastor in 1523, the foundation's chapter dallied, extending a call to several unlikely candidates in order to gain time. Even Luther was approached, but he was not about to add anything more to his professional duties. When the chapter defaulted in proposing a candidate during its final extension of time, the town council lost patience. Backed by the representatives of the university and the parish, the council elected John Bugenhagen, currently teaching at the university. Luther knew how he should treat his hesitating friend. Even before Bugenhagen had said yes, Luther announced him from the Town Church pulpit as the new pastor of the Wittenberg congregation. Luther thus gained the best man available for a congregation that would serve as model for innumerable other places.[53]

This contest over filling the Wittenberg pastorate was also an episode in the feud between Luther and the canons of All Saints over the continued use of the old mass. For years this richly endowed foundation had disgusted Luther. Ample stipends for masses from the illustrious dynastic house of Wettin undergirded All Saints financially. Its rich collection of relics and the influential indulgence traffic of its Castle Church made Luther brand it "Bethhaven" (the house of idolatrous worship; Hos. 4:15; 10:5; Amos 5:5).[54] He had not even succeeded in having the indulgence traffic entirely eliminated. That traffic had flared up again in 1520, and three years later the relics were still being exhibited on request. Not only the canons but also the elector himself bore the blame for this state of affairs. [There is a story behind this.] The All Saints Foundation had always been the elector's heavy favorite.[55] By resisting the challenge to submit it to total reform or to dissolve it altogether, he tacitly admitted to something in addition to his proven method of neutrality.

The issue over All Saints touched the deep feeling of kinship with his house of Wettin. Luther's two-year struggle against the continued existence of this foundation—the only place in Wittenberg where the old-style mass was still being said—was actually a struggle against his ter-

53. On Bugenhagen, see below, pp. 270ff.

54. To Spalatin, November 22, 1521, WA Br 2:405 / 14. [LW 48:338. Details in E. G. Schwiebert, *Luther and His Times: The Reformation from a New Perspective* (St. Louis: Concordia, 1950), 259–60.]

55. Kirn, *Friedrich der Weise*, 166ff., and the text cited there.

ritorial lord. At first all Luther's attempts to change matters failed. His representations to Spalatin were fruitless, as the notorious unchastity of the canons continued.[56] And his hopes that a new dean, with opinions akin to his own, would head the chapter were not realized. Among the evangelical canons, neither Justus Jonas nor Karlstadt was qualified for the position. Nicholas von Amsdorf, though actually elected, turned down the deanship on grounds of conscience, for the office would force him to conduct votive masses and masses for the dead as well as to authorize them. This, he declared, would be impossible for him to do, "even if doing so could earn him a princedom."[57] Luther's attempts were similarly in vain when he tried to admonish the chapter with letters (March 1 and July 11, 1523) and finally, in a public warning from the pulpit (August 2), to discontinue the masses. The men of the foundation always appealed to the elector, who in turn refused to allow any changes in the traditional practice, even when, thanks to the withdrawal of several canons, the reform-committed evangelicals had become the majority and when these, with Luther's agreement, had presented the elector with proposed compromises on August 23 and September 29. At that time Frederick even forced the resignation of three newly elected canons who, though promising to obey the statutes, declined to read mass any longer. For a year and a half Luther was stalled by All Saints and resigned to things having to take their course.

Then in November 1524, pent-up resentment exploded. Contrary to the promise of the dean of the chapter, Communion in one kind (*sub una specie*) was resumed, and this a full two years after the practice had ended in the inclusive Wittenberg congregation. On November 17, Luther presented the foundation with an ultimatum to abolish the mass. When still nothing happened, and in spite of attempted appeasement by the elector—to whom the three traditionalists among the canons had appealed—Luther censured the All Saints situation from the pulpit for the second

56. Luther to Spalatin, December 22(?), 1522; January 2 and 14, 1523; WA Br 2:635 / 11. WA Br 3:2 / 16ff.; 16 / 5ff.

57. Amsdorf to the Elector, March 16 / 17, 1523, ARG 1:609ff. The material on Luther's debate with the foundation is in the papers of N. Müller and has been published by K. Pallas, "Urkunden, das Allerheiligenstift zu Wittenberg betreffend, 1522–1526," ARG 12 (1915): 1ff., 81ff. See also N. Müller, *Die Wittenberger Bewegung 1521 und 1522*, 2d ed. (Leipzig, 1911), 238ff. See WA 18:8ff., and comments in WA Br 3. To the basic issues of the mass there was added the mass production of masses, to which the canons were obligated. Spalatin calculated this production at 1,242 sung and 7,856 said masses per year. Pallas, "Urkunden," 26, n. 2.

time.[58] Whereas a year earlier Luther had earnestly admonished the canons and summoned the congregation to intercessory prayer on their behalf, before possibly having to deny them the common name of Christian, he now switched completely and treated them as obstinate blasphemers. As evidence in support of these charges he produced a passionate and discerning critique of the canon of the mass. In the offertory prayers, said Luther, man presumes to ask God's favor because of the proffered gift— the sacrificed Christ. "How could one more shamefully disgrace Christ? He himself must beg for me, and I must beg for him?" According to prevailing law, which had Luther's approval, open blasphemy required the intervention of the government. Therefore Luther admonished the council and heads of government in Wittenberg to bring the evildoers to trial and, if necessary, to banish them.[59] Thereupon the town council, the university rector, and the pastor of the Town Church went to the three [traditionalist] canons and demanded the discontinuance of masses, or all fellowship with them would be broken off and no further food supplies would be delivered to them. Even the elector, to whom the three appealed, this time did not come to their rescue. Instead he now agreed to take under advisement the request of the director of the boy's choir to be released from participation in the mass, which he, as director, had come to recognize as godless.[60]

The three canons gave up. On December 24, 1524, a new order of worship was introduced also in the Castle Church, the last of the Wittenberg churches to fall into line. No more masses were to be sung or said in it, because the indispensable prerequisite—the approval of the congregation—was missing. Canons desiring to commune should henceforth do so in the brotherly fellowship of the Town Church. If in connection with a princely visit the Lord's Supper be desired as part of worship in the Castle Church, then Luther or the town pastor (Bugenhagen) or another preacher should be the celebrant. Henceforth the daily worship under auspices of the foundation should consist simply of readings from Scrip-

58. Luther's letter to the All Saints Foundation, March 1, July 11, August 19, 1523; November 17, 1524. WA Br 3:34–35; 111ff.; 129ff.; 375ff. His sermons of August 2, 1523; November 27, 1524, WA 12:645ff., WA 15:758ff. The sermon of July 12, 1523 (contrary to WA 12:620, 645; WA 18:8) has nothing to do with the All Saints issue. The proposals of the chapter of August 23 and September 29, 1523, are printed in Pallas, "Urkunden," 24–25, 35–36. (On this see CR 1:628ff., WA Br 3:134.) The statement of the elector and the councilmen, of August 7, 1523, in WA 3:121ff.; of October 4, 1523, CR 1:640ff.; of May 1524, CR 1:661ff. Also Pallas, "Urkunden," 93ff.

59. WA 15:769 / 3; 774 / 9, 21ff.

60. December 24, 1524. Pallas, "Urkunden," 110–11.

ture, exposition, preaching (on Sundays, by the provost, Justus Jonas), and hymns. For the latter, exact instructions or suggestions were provided (e.g., the singing of German chorales from the Wittenberg hymnal of 1524). The traffic in masses, hitherto the cause of offense, having been terminated, the foundation gained the character of an evangelical resident community with appropriate forms of daily worship.[61]

Viewed from today, this long struggle and its discordant ending makes one wish it could have been avoided. Yet this does not release us from the task of acquainting ourselves with Luther's motives and principles. As he reminded the elector, Luther had waged this struggle for a year and a half with the Word only, using personal and public admonition in the manner corresponding to the primitive Christian procedure on repentance (Matt. 18:15–17), without, however, taking the final step and banning the offenders. Likewise, Luther's earlier urgent request to Spalatin—that the elector please put an end to private masses by himself ceasing to support them—was a personal appeal to conscience such as he directed toward all Christians that they endow no more masses. Similarly, Luther appealed to the conscience of the canons of All Saints Foundation when admonishing them to decide personally to end private masses and not evade this duty by asking the elector's opinion.[62]

Only at the end, when the unexpected reversion to administering the sacrament in one kind set off two years of accumulated tension, did Luther change his tone. Then he not only announced the third step in ecclesial discipline, according to which the congregation is supposed to exclude the recalcitrants from its midst, but also reminded the town council of its duty to prevent public blasphemy. Were these steps not taken, Luther feared that the wrath of God would not spare the city but increase considerably; for some time he had felt that the meager fruits of the Word were causing divine wrath.[63] Here for the first time Luther was acting on the basis of conviction expressed earlier, that even in a sacrilege which is simply tolerated, to say nothing of being perpetrated, God lays down his

61. The order of worship was drawn up by Bugenhagen and Jonas with Luther's assistance (according to notations by the hand of Jonas on the original order deposited in the Weimar archive); printed in E. Sehling, *Die Evangelischen Kirchenordnungen des XVI. Jahrhunderts* (Leipzig, 1902ff.), 1:698ff. Pallas, "Urkunden," 11ff. L. Fendt, *Der Lutherische Gottesdienst des 16. Jahrhunderts* (Munich, 1923), 193–94.

62. To Spalatin, January 2, 1523, WA Br 3:2 / 20. To the canons, July 11, 1523; November 17, 1524, WA Br 3:112 / 26ff.; 376, 21. Sermon of August 2, 1523, WA 12:649 / 19ff.

63. To the canons, July 11, 1523; to Spalatin, October 12, 1523; WA Br 3:112 / 15ff.; 169 / 17ff. Sermon of August 2, 1523, WA 12:649 / 16ff.; 650 / 10ff. Sermons of November 27, 1524, WA Br 15:774 / 6ff., 25ff. *Vom Greuel der Stillmesse* (1525), WA 18:23 / 2ff.; 36 / 26ff.

challenge which would have to avenge itself on the town or on the nation. This objective linking of community guilt and divine punishment derived from a medieval understanding of blasphemy is rooted in biblical thought, notably in the pronouncements of the prophets on the effects of idolatrous cults on the land of Israel. When Luther finally demanded that the authorities take steps against such idolatry, he was only reminding them—according to his understanding—of their very own temporal obligation to protect their nation from calamity. Reluctant though he was to reach this decision, once he had taken it he defended it resolutely in his treatise *On the Abomination of the Secret Mass* (early 1525). In this treatise he publicly repeated his critique of the canon of the mass on the basis of his sermon of November 27, 1524.[64]

In another brief work, *Concerning the Order of Public Worship,* Luther provided the impetus for the shaping of the liturgy. In contrast to working out his ideas on the structuring of the congregation, which involved a multitude of concrete questions and required laying down a lasting foundation, his approach to worship was more direct. Here his intention was simply to abolish certain abuses and to follow but a single principle in all forms of worship: "That the Christian congregation henceforth ought never to assemble for worship without the Word of God being preached and prayed, even if only briefly."[65] On weekdays two services will suffice: one in the early morning, the other in the early evening. The reading and exposition of Scripture is central to both—at matins, the Old Testament; at vespers, the New Testament. The duration of these services should at most be one hour, "for one must not overload souls or weary them, as was the case until now in monasteries and convents, where they burdened themselves like mules."[66] The chants of Sunday mass and vespers, even the readings from the legends of the saints and the cross, the source of superstitious signing of the cross, "can be shelved . . . until they have been purged, for there is a horrible lot of filth in them."[67] "This is the sum of the matter: Let everything be done so that the Word may have free course instead of prattling and rattling that has been the rule up to now."[68] As yet Luther did nothing further about the main traditional form of worship, the

---

64. *WA* 18:22–36. [*LW* 36:(309) 311–28.]
65. *WA* 12:35 / 20–21. [*LW* 53:(9) 11–14.]
66. *WA* 12:36 / 15ff. [*LW* 53:12.]
67. *WA* 12:37 / 10ff. [*LW* 53:14.]
68. *WA* 12:37 / 27ff. ["Loren and Dohnen" =] Plärren und Lärmen, the sound effects characterizing much medieval worship. [*LW* 53:13.]

mass. He simply limited it to Sundays, while matins and vespers replaced the mass on weekdays. The main thing is the Word, not the mass, Luther insisted. If anyone should desire the sacrament during the week, however, let mass be held as inclination and time dictate, for in this matter one cannot make hard-and-fast rules.[69]

Toward the end of that same year, 1523, Luther once again set forth his reservations concerning the traditional mass and outlined his version of how this worship service should be understood and celebrated. His friend Nicholas Hausmann—in Zwickau amid the confusion created earlier by Müntzer and Storch—had repeatedly importuned Luther to send him advice on the reform of worship. The result was Luther's noted *Formula missae et communionis*, in which he describes how the congregation in Wittenberg employs a revised version of the Latin mass in its worship. He also shows plainly in what respects the Roman mass has been changed or left unchanged. First, his emphasis is on the unchanged:

> I have used neither authority nor pressure, nor did I make any innovations, for I have been hesitant and fearful, partly because of the weak in faith, who cannot suddenly exchange an old and accustomed order of worship for a new and unusual one, and more so because of the fickle and fastidious spirits who rush in like unclean swine without faith or reason and who delight only in novelty and tire of it as quickly when it has worn off.

Such people are a nuisance at most times, but "in spiritual matters they are absolutely unbearable. Nevertheless, at the risk of bursting with anger, I must bear with them, unless I want to let the gospel itself be denied to the people."[70] Luther thus had to be circumspect toward both sides— toward the old believers and toward radicals like Karlstadt. Both cases involved a misunderstanding of the gospel. The old believers equated the gospel with the long-familiar forms of worship, the others with the new forms. In this respect the worship service as such was no problem to Luther. In its basic form he found it sound. "We cannot deny that the mass, that is, the communion of bread and wine, is a rite divinely instituted by Christ himself."[71] In the course of time many readings and chants have been added, and against these one cannot object. The early purity of the mass was lost only when it was turned into a sacrifice, and this happened in the canon of the mass, which then became the main part

---

69. WA 12:37 / 6ff. [LW 53:13.]

70. WA 12:205 / 12–206 / 2 [LW 53:19. Text: *The Order of Mass and Communion for the Church at Wittenberg* (1523), pp. 19–40.]

71. WA 12:206 / 17ff. [LW 53:20.]

of the Roman mass. Through the ostensible presentation of gifts for all sorts of purposes, the mass became a monopoly of the priests, who enriched themselves from it. "Who can ever name the causes for which the mass was made a sacrifice?" And what craft has not benefited from the mass for all the external embellishments and priestly vestments added to its celebration?[72] The mass is not understood correctly as a sacrifice, but "we do accept it as a sacrament, a testament, the blessing (as in Latin), the thanksgiving (eucharist, as in Greek), the table of the Lord, the Lord's Supper, the Lord's memorial." The mass is not to be abolished or changed, but to be celebrated properly.[73]

The language of the Wittenberg mass, which Luther then described in detail, was still Latin. The people were familiar with its liturgical structure, so all the more importance attaches to the sermon. Like a voice crying in the wilderness, calling the unbelievers to faith, the sermon should preferably precede the introit of the mass, the meal of the believing Christians. Yet Luther prefers to make nothing binding. Freedom is to be vouchsafed for the future. Indeed, Luther himself felt free to change his opinions, as, for example, he relocated the sermon to the middle of the service, following the creed.[74] Even the possibility of a mass entirely in German was at this time still only a wish—"may Christ grant it." At that time the selections in the pericope [the Scripture lessons and other components in the propers for each Sunday and festival] would also have to be examined.[75] Meanwhile the tone of Luther's approach to the ways of worship remained clear: "We must be careful not to turn freedom into law."[76]

During these years, Luther kept running into self-confident prophets of the intellect on all kinds of contending issues: the understanding of revelation and faith, the sacraments and images, the congregation, and the structure of the state. Of necessity he still had to grapple with one of the presuppositions of this pervasive array of contrasts: the fundamentally differing evaluation of learning and education. The problem arose in practical and urgent terms. Because the "Enthusiasts" had so badly misin-

72. WA 12:206 / 23–208 / 4. [LW 53:22.]

73. WA 12:208 / 15ff. [LW 53:22.]

74. WA 12:211 / 5ff. According to Sebastian Fröschel, who visited Wittenberg repeatedly after November 1523, Luther began his preaching at that point (1524–25) and then included this location for the sermon in his "German Mass" (Deutsche Messe) of 1525. Fröschel, Fortgesetzte Sammlung, 691. On the "German Mass," see below, pp. 474ff.

75. WA 12:210 / 2ff. [LW 53:24.]

76. WA 12:214 / 14. [LW 53:30.]

terpreted the reformation movement, the schools had suffered severely. With his own eyes, Luther could see how it was happening in Wittenberg,[77] while others reported what was happening elsewhere. He was especially pained by the decline of his old University of Erfurt, where the anti-intellectual slogans of radical preachers had taken a heavy toll.

Luther's friend of student days Eobanus Hessus, the leader of the Erfurt humanists and adherent of the reformation movement, dedicated a long elegy to him, *Ecclesiae afflictae epistola ad Lutherum* [A Letter to Luther from the Afflicted Church]. The prison from which the grieving church writes (hence also the designation "captive" for this poem) is described entirely in terms of the corruptions of the Roman church. But the liberation from these corruptions, which is already evident in several places, has led to licentiousness, rebellion, and a contempt for education. In return for his elegy, which he had sent to Wittenberg as a manuscript, Eobanus requested letters from his friends there which would aid him in combating the dangerous currents. In fact, Eobanus feared that the new theology would make the Germans more barbarous than ever. Luther tried to calm his fears, writing:

> I am convinced that without a knowledge of the sciences [*Wissenschaften*] true theology cannot endure, just as until now the collapse and depressed condition of scholarship has done the same thing to theology. Indeed, I see that the wonderful revelation of the Word of God would never have happened had the way not been prepared, as with forerunners, for a resurrection and flowering of languages and scholarships.

Eobanus at once published this letter of Luther's with two from Melanchthon, and several others as well, accompanying them by some of his own poems, under the title *De non contemnendis studius humanioribus futuro theologo necessariis* (1523). Therewith he let the complaints of the humanists be Luther's encouragement. For their part, the friends in Wittenberg saw to it that Eobanus's elegy was published, turning it over to the student Johannes Setzer, who took it with him to Alsace. There, in Hagenau, he opened his own and later famous printing establishment, with the Eobanus manuscript as his first publication.[78]

---

77. On the condition of the schools in Wittenberg during the disorders of 1521–22, Sebastian Fröschel reports in *Das Buch der Reformation, geschrieben von Mitlebenden*, ed. K. Kaulfuss-Diesch (Leipzig, 1917), 288ff. The late recording of these recollections does not make them a literary invention; cf. H. Barge, *Andreas Bodenstein von Karlstadt* (Leipzig, 1905), 1:421–22, n. 232.

78. C. Krause, *Helius Eobanus Hessus: Sein Leben und seine Werke* (Gotha, 1879; reprinted, 1963), 1:352ff. Luther, March 29, 1523, WA Br 3:49–50, 50 / 21ff. Melanchthon, CR 1: 573, 613. Also *Suppl. Mel.* 6 / 1:189–90, 216. MBW 233, 273.

These developments persuaded Luther to write a clarifying follow-up to the proposals on education he had made earlier in his *To the Christian Nobility of the German Nation* (1520).[79] Early in 1524 he issued his *To the Councilmen of All Cities in Germany That They Establish and Maintain Christian Schools*.[80] This treatise was far more than a program for the schools. As sometimes happens in occasional writings—when motives of a great life work emerge enforced, enriched, and simplified by the demand for application—this little booklet is a brief summary of the thoughts that moved Luther during these years. The rediscovery of the gospel and the regained knowledge of the biblical languages together mark the "golden years" of God's gracious visitation that has now begun. Despite his manifold cares, Luther's happy feeling shines through as he sees further signs of this new beginning in the many learned "young associates and other men adorned with languages and the arts" who are now available to proclaim the gospel and to teach the young people.[81] A time of grace like this one had never yet occurred in Germany. Hence Luther's rallying appeal not to let it slip by:

> O my beloved Germans, buy while the market is at your door, gather in the harvest while there is sunshine and fair weather, make use of God's grace and Word while it is there! For you should know that God's Word and grace is like a soaking shower which does not return where it has once been. It has been with the Jews, but when it's gone it's gone, and now they have nothing. Paul brought it to the Greeks, but again when it's gone it's gone, and now they have the Turk. Rome and the Latins also had it, but when it's gone it's gone, and now they have the pope. And you Germans need not think that you will have it forever, for ingratitude and contempt will not make it stay. Therefore, seize it and hold it fast, whoever can, for lazy hands are bound to have a lean year.[82]

In light of this extraordinary hour, Luther saw the nature of his own mission. God had now "prescribed" him for the whole of Germany. Luther's word was Christ's word, and whoever ignored it despised not Luther but Christ. This was not self-praise, no more so for Luther than for the Old Testament prophets. He could honestly say, "I am not seeking my own advantage, but the welfare and salvation of all Germany."[83] The gos-

---

79. WA 6:439 / 37ff.; 461 / 11ff. [*LW* 44:193, 206–7.]

80. Cf. O. Scheel, "Luther und die Schule seiner Zeit," *LuJ* 7 (1925): 141ff. F. Falk, "Luthers Schrift an die Ratsherren der deutschen Städte und ihre geschichtliche Wirkung auf die deutsche Schule," *LuJ* 19 (1937): 55ff. I. Asheim, *Glaube und Erziehung bei Luther* (Heidelberg, 1961), 66ff. [*LW* 45:(330–46) 347–78.]

81. WA 15:31 / 8ff. [*LW* 45:351.]

82. WA 15:32 / 4ff. [*LW* 45:352–53.]

83. WA 15:27 / 25ff.; 53/8. [*LW* 45:348, 377–78.]

pel and the languages belong together inseparably. Only when one ponders God's revelation through Word and Scripture does one grasp the purpose of languages. Then even such an event as the expulsion of the Greeks by the Turks—Luther must have had in mind men like Bessarion [1395(?)-1472, the humanist scholar and proponent of the Renaissance]— appears as an act of divine providence; they, as expellees, should spread the knowledge of Greek "and provide an incentive for the study of other languages as well."[84] Luther meant, first of all, the "sacred languages," which God used as the media to communicate his word. Yet the translation of the Bible into whatever other languages hallows these as well. Even more, Luther sees the connection between the knowledge of foreign languages and the mastery of one's own. If we neglect foreign languages, "the time will come when we shall be unable either to speak or write correct Latin or German."[85]

The study of languages makes theology a science. In stronger terms than before, Luther is emphatic toward the "Enthusiasts" and the simple-minded, among whom he included the Bohemian Brethren,[86] reminding them that the Reformation is not simply a pious awakening but a scholarly movement. He distinguishes between ordinary preaching and teaching, for which translations supply what is necessary, and the exposition of Scripture, the prophetic character of it in the primitive Christian sense. Such exposition keeps the message of the gospel pure and guards the church from error. Wherefore "there must always be such prophets in the Christian church who can dig into Scripture, expound it, and carry on disputations. A saintly life and right doctrine are not enough." To God's gift of the new knowledge of languages the rediscovery of the gospel is indebted.

Luther went on, "Now that the languages have been revived, they are bringing with them so bright a light and accomplishing such great things that the whole world is amazed and has to acknowledge that we have the gospel just about as pure and undefiled as the apostles had it." Part of the grateful pride which this hour of grace awakens is that the superiority of the contemporary scholars over the church fathers [in the expounding of Scripture] can virtually be grabbed with both hands. How often they— Hilary, Jerome, Augustine, even St. Bernard, whom Luther ranks above the rest—have not gone off the track because of their insufficient knowl-

84. WA 15:37 / 11ff. [LW 45:359.]

85. WA 15:37 / 17ff.; 38 / 12ff. [LW 45:359, 360.]

86. WA 15:42 / 15ff.; 43 / 7ff. Concerning the veneration of the sacrament (1523), see WA 11:455 / 27ff. [LW 45:365, n. 36.]

edge of language! Herein Luther has a sharper eye than Erasmus. Despite all their efforts, these [fathers in the faith] gathered up only a few crumbs of the gospel, "while we with half the labor—yes, almost without any labor at all—can acquire a whole loaf! Oh how their efforts put our indolence to shame!" Not enthusiasm but grammar leads to a sound understanding. "Say what you will about the Spirit. I too have been in the Spirit and have also seen the Spirit." Yet Luther admitted that he would not have achieved clarity and "would surely never have flushed a covey if the languages had not helped me and given me a sure and certain knowledge of Scripture."[87] Because God's Word is not simply something captured in the head, the mind, or the emotions, but is language as well, Luther could readily account for the uprising of those who rage against languages. Behind them, like behind so much else, is the great Enemy. "The devil knew what was cooking and perceived that if the languages were revived a hole would be knocked in his domain which he could not easily stop up again." He well knew that only a command of languages conveys the conviction that can be shared by others. "The devil does not respect my spirit as highly as he does my speech and pen when they deal with Scripture, for my spirit takes from him nothing but myself alone, but Holy Scripture and the languages leave him little room on earth and wreak havoc in his kingdom." This invisible dimension injected the earnestness into Luther's appeal. "And let us be sure of this: We will not long preserve the gospel without the languages. The languages are the sheath in which this sword of the Spirit (Eph. 6:17) is contained."[88]

Alongside this combining of theology and linguistics in the context of revelation, what drove Luther to write this passionate treatise in the first place was his concern for a proper education of the young. As elsewhere, when dealing with temporal issues, Luther here drew illustrations from nature, from the care animals show for their young, and from the grand example of the pagan Greeks and Romans, in order to lay the responsibility for education on the hearts of the parents. And if parents in their greed and princes in their pleasure-bent stupidity failed to respond to this challenge, then the cities and towns had here their first opportunity.[89] After all, the towns themselves will reap the greatest benefits from having an educated youth. Beside the languages there should be instruction in history, that incomparable mirror which helps us be "witty and wise about

---

87. WA 15:40 / 14ff.; 39 / 4ff.; 40 / 27ff.; 41 / 22ff.; 42 / 17ff. [LW 45:363, 361, 363, 364, 365–66.]

88. WA 15:38 / 26; 36 / 26ff.; 43 / 3ff.; 38 / 7ff. [LW 45:358, 366, 360.]

89. WA 15:32 / 27ff.; 35 / 1ff.; 28 / 17ff.; 44 / 33ff. [LW 45:353 (367, 370), 356, 348, 368.]

what to seek and what to avoid in this outward life." If Luther had children of his own he would "have them study not only languages and history, but also singing and music together with the whole of mathematics." For boys and girls generally he proposed one or two hours of schooling each day, so that they would also have time to learn a trade and to help at home. However, "the exceptional pupils, who give promise of becoming skilled teachers, preachers, or holders of other ecclesiastical positions," should be allowed to continue in school longer.[90]

These proposals make Luther the father of neither the primary school nor the secondary school. This differentiation of types of schools was not yet applicable. Preparatory schools for the university were already an old institution. The new thing was Luther's proposal that schooling for higher education should grow out of a broadly based public education, which he later demanded be made compulsory.[91] In doing so, he always kept a twofold aim for the Christian schools in view: They are necessary for the life of the mind and the salvation of the soul, and—more conventionally— they are important to the "temporal regime," as Luther called the urban social order. Indeed, even if there were no such thing as a soul and we would need no schools for the sake of the sacred Scriptures, "this one consideration alone would be sufficient to justify the establishment everywhere of the very best schools for both boys and girls, namely, that in order to maintain its temporal estate outwardly the world must have good and capable men and women, men able to rule well over land and people, women able to manage the household and train children and servants aright." This is something the town councilmen should be able to understand better than the princes and lords in the countryside, who are preoccupied with "sleigh-riding, drinking, and parading about in costumes. They are burdened with the high and important functions of the cellar, kitchen, and bedroom."[92] To sum up, Luther was demanding nothing less than the most inclusive basis then imaginable of school and education for future mothers as well as for future men of the spiritual or temporal estates.

Scholarship and instruction require books. Luther therefore proposed that libraries or book repositories be set up in the larger towns and cities. A good selection of books, he wrote, should include "the Holy Scriptures in Latin, Greek, Hebrew, and German and any other language in which

90. WA 15:45 / 12ff.; 46 / 13ff.; 47 / 1ff. / 13ff. [LW 45:369, 271.]

91. "A Sermon on Keeping Children in School" (1530), WA 30²:586 / 7ff. [LW 46:(209) 213–58.]

92. WA 15:44 / 24ff. [LW 45:368.]

they might be found. Next, the best commentaries. . . . Then books that would be helpful in learning the languages, such as the poets and orators, regardless of whether they were pagan or Christian, Greek or Latin. . . . Finally, there would be books of law and medicine." But foremost would be chronicles and histories "in whatever languages they are to be had, for they are a wonderful help in understanding and guiding the course of events, and especially for observing the marvelous works of God." What profoundly troubled Luther throughout was the arrested development and poor reputation of his people; about whom there would also be much good to report, if only there were historical accounts. Yet there was no one to write them down, and no one to preserve the books had they been written. Alas, therefore, "we must be content to have the rest of the world refer to us as German beasts who know only how to fight, gorge, and guzzle."[93]

93. WA 15:49 / 10ff.; 52 / 1ff., 11ff. [LW 45:376, 377.]

6

Opponents from Within:
Karlstadt and Müntzer

After the Wittenberg radicals had been overcome and the Zwickau prophets warded off, it looked for the moment as though the disturbers of the peace had vanished from the earth. Karlstadt had submitted, but he was full of resentment. He continued to lecture, and until 1523 he remained dean of the theological faculty. Yet it was not simply the broken relationship with Luther and with his former friends which made him look for a change; it was also economic factors. Karlstadt's task at the university was dependent on income drawn from his position as archdeacon of the All Saints Foundation. For the most part this income came from stipends from masses and offerings from people attending masses for the dead and other endowed services of the chapter. Even though he himself had long since ceased saying secret masses, he nevertheless—like Amsdorf and Jonas, the two other reform-minded members of the foundation—could not do without the offerings of those attending them. Not until 1523 do we see how the conscience first of one and then of the others became burdened, and they gave up this passive participation in the masses.[1]

In Karlstadt's case, this entailed the loss of one-fourth of his income, but a way out lay open to him in Orlamünde, a parish on the upper Saale River which was incorporated in the archdiaconate of All Saints in Wittenberg. As ranking clergyman at All Saints, he was entitled to the Orlamünde income as long as he did not have to pay a resident vicar.[2] It so

1. Amsdorf to the Elector, March 16, 1523, CR 1:610. Karlstadt, to Duke John, ca. May 26, 1523. See E. Hase, "Karlstadt in Orlamünde," *Mitteilungen der Geschichts- und Altertumforschenden, Gellschaft des Osterlandes* 4 (1858): 91. Jonas to the Elector, August 24, 1523, CR 1:637. On Karlstadt's income, see H. Barge, *Andreas Bodenstein von Karlstadt* (Leipzig, 1905), 1:44.

2. Documentation in Hase, "Karlstadt," 85ff.; esp. also K. Müller, *Luther und Karlstadt: Stücke aus ihrem gegenseitigen Verhältnis untersucht* (Tübingen, 1907), 137ff. (according to which details in the accounts in WA 18:90ff. and WA Br 3:255 should be corrected). The publication of the settlement by Duke John of the conflict between Karlstadt and his vicar, Glitzsch, of April 9 and October 14, 1522, has clarified the disputed legal basis of the Orlamünde issue. See J. Trefftz, "Karlstadt und Glitzsch," ARG 7 (1910): 348ff. This material has not been used in W. Kohler's valuable report on the controversy between Barge and K. Muller, "Bericht über die Literatur zu Karlstadt," published in connection with H. Barge's biography in GGA 174 (1912): 505ff. Even so the agreement (under Duke John) cannot presuppose Karlstadt's taking over the Orlamünde vicarate. It was first intended for another vicar. For Luther's account of these developments, see his treatise *Against the Heavenly Prophets* (1525), WA 18:85ff. [LW 40:111ff.]

happened that the incumbent vicar still owed Karlstadt a considerable sum of money, which he was unable to repay out of his income from the parish. Already in April 1522, in an agreement with Duke John, he was ready to give up the position while still being obligated to make certain payments to Karlstadt.

In the course of these negotiations, which dragged on until May 1523, Karlstadt hit on the idea to take over the parish himself for a while, so that he could make up for the lost offerings at All Saints and be assured of income from the Orlamünde parish, a sum not sufficient to support two persons. The Orlamünde town council, no doubt prompted by Karlstadt, was pleased with this proposal. The town would gain a double benefit: The strain on congregational finances would be reduced, and the town would have the services of a famous scholar as pastor instead of some obscure vicar. The town council also requested [Duke John] that during his incumbency Karlstadt be released from the obligation to contribute part of his Orlamünde income to All Saints Foundation in Wittenberg. This, however, was the sore point. The blanket that the Orlamünders and Karlstadt were cozily pulling around themselves suddenly was too short on the other side. After all, some of the income Karlstadt drew from the incorporated Orlamünde parish also paid for part of his professorship at the university. When Duke John asked his brother, the elector, to make a decision on the Orlamünde council's request, the answer was no.[3] The income belonged to All Saints. The elector would have nothing against Karlstadt's leaving the university, since he seemed to be traveling around the country most of the time anyway. Elector Frederick would allow Karlstadt to take the position in Orlamünde only as convener; the payments to the All Saints Foundation would have to continue. Likewise, the university was not about to give in to a scheme allowing one of its professors—and the income designated for the professorship—to take time off. They still remembered how in 1515–16 Karlstadt had engineered a trip to Rome, absenting himself on no other authority but his own.[4]

This time, as then, the university stepped in. After lengthy negotiations in the spring of 1524, Karlstadt was granted a leave, and a time was set for his return. On April 4, Karlstadt appeared before the university and solemnly pledged readiness to resume his activities in Wittenberg under

3. Letter of the Orlamünders of May 26, 1523, in Hase, "Karlstadt," 88ff., no. 4 (cited in *WA* 18:97, n. 2). Duke John to the Elector, June 2, 1523, in Hase, "Karlstadt," 92, no. 6. The elector's reply: ibid., 93, no. 7 (no date).

4. Documents in J. J. Müller, *Entdecktes Staatscabinet, zweyte Eroffnung* (Jena, 1714), 315ff. More in K. Müller, *Luther und Karlstadt*, 223ff.; Barge, *Karlstadt*, 1:49ff.

certain conditions. Melanchthon, then rector of the university and friendly toward Karlstadt, felt relieved; and yet, as he wrote to Spalatin, he still had his doubts.[5] Karlstadt returned again to Orlamünde. But there a final break was in the making. The town council formally elected him pastor, claiming to apply Luther's principle,[6] yet wrongly so, for Luther had never declared it permissible to dismiss a pastor from a position to be filled not only by a parish but by a patron. The elector therefore turned down the requests of May 26, 1524, from Karlstadt and the Orlamünde council.

Karlstadt had no choice but to give up the planned arrangement.[7] Worse yet, in wake of the run-in with the university he could not come back to Wittenberg. After some hesitation he paid a brief visit in Wittenberg during August 1524 and at that time surrendered his post as archdeacon at All Saints. The rest of his income, accumulated during these proceedings, unhappily was not sufficient to cover the debts he had incurred some time earlier in the university. Indeed, as his lavish wedding had shown, he enjoyed the appearance of a big spender. The university named a new vicar for Orlamünde.[8]

If for the moment this Karlstadt conflict was simply a disciplinary action that involved him not directly but only as a member of the theological faculty, then Luther was soon to learn that the intemperate spirit he had succeeded in silencing in Wittenberg was being revived in Orlamünde [nearly one hundred miles to the south]. Word was reaching Luther from there that the Old Testament legalism with which Karlstadt had waged his war on images had returned with such gusto that Luther mockingly said the Orlamünders would probably have themselves circumcised and go completely Hebrew.[9]

It disturbed Luther that a press had been set up in Jena for Karlstadt's own use, allowing a man disposed to teach where he was not called, while remaining silent where he was called to teach. Thus Luther demanded that Karlstadt's writings be subject to the mandate of 1523, as enacted by the Nuremberg diet of the empire, and—like the Wittenbergers them-

5. April 4 and 6, 1524, CR 1:651, 762. The second of these letters (as Müller, *Luther und Karlstadt*, 152, n. 1, has shown) is mistakenly included in the year 1525 in CR 1:762 (not noted in O. Clemen, *Suppl. Mel.* 6 / 1:298). MBW 316, 318.

6. To Duke John, May 3, 1524, Hase, "Karlstadt," no. 9: 97–98; quotation from WA 18:97, n. 1. The council and Karlstadt to the Duke, May 22, 1524, Hase, "Karlstadt," no. 15, 16:103ff.

7. Luther to the electoral prince, John Frederick, June 18, 1524, WA Br 3:307 / 66ff.

8. Hase, "Karlstadt," no. 21:112.

9. To Brück, January 13, 1524, WA Br 3:231 / 20.

selves—be under a censor appointed by the elector.[10] In rapid succession Karlstadt published five tracts in Jena, justifying the reforms he had meanwhile undertaken in Orlamünde. The initial tract, *Why Has Andreas Karlstadt Kept Silence so Long?* (December 1523, dated Orlamünde), provides insight into his complex personality as none of his other writings does. He has given up, as he says, his teaching and writing and steeped himself in "lay activity," because he did not feel called of God and had received no command from Christ. Besides, he felt he lacked the internal testimony of gifts which "genuine shepherds and reapers" require in order to proclaim God's Word powerfully and bravely, and so to uproot and break down, gathering the scattered, restoring the broken, healing the sick, "and doing a thousand things like that, yet being unable to do any of them. Since I do not find these fruits in me, I had better . . . wait a while longer, until I should be remarkably inspired and raised up by the Spirit."[11] The reference to a "legitimate and not fraudulent calling," according to the subtitle, indicates that the thrust of the tract is against Luther's reference to legitimation and responsibility as expressed through an orderly call to an office [in this case ministry] which [as a corroborated calling] is alone able to lend courage and certainty over against the trials and temptations he knew so well. But Karlstadt was waiting not for an officially mediated call but for some sign of the Spirit. This position of his had grown out of a conviction held by Müntzer that God cannot have grown dumb and that a congregation possesses not only preachers called by the Spirit but also elects "spiritual" people. "Therefore, only those people should elect, call, and install whom the Spirit of God leads and who have the Spirit of Christ, the supreme shepherd."[12] From this time of hesitation, he concluded, "To remain inward is always far less dangerous than venturing forth" should there suddenly be a catastrophe. "However that may be, I see counsel. God's will should be done, and I want to obey him."[13] Karlstadt is willing to endure the punishment, scorn, and ridicule for his deficiencies, just as Christ himself suffered. Such experiences will make him "Christ-formed" in his following Christ. "So then, I trust that my risky venturing forth will [in spirit] be virtually as though I remained inward." Karlstadt does not intend to bury his talent, but rather to follow

10. To Brück, January 14, 1524, WA Br 3:233 / 15ff.

11. *Karlstadts Schriften aus den Jahren, 1523–1525*, Neudrucke deutscher Literaturwerke des 16. und 17. Jahrhunderts 325, compiled and edited by E. Hertzsch (Halle, 1956), part 1, 3 / 9; 8 / 10ff.; 9 / 8–26.

12. Ibid., 8 / 16; 13 / 8ff.

13. Ibid., 16 / 29, 36.

the commandment of God who has made everyone a priest. "We must slay our [own] thoughts and worrisome fears . . . or put them behind us and accomplish God's will." "For this reason I venture forth in God's name, trusting in him."[14]

In Karlstadt there appears to have been a mounting tension between a Müntzerlike doctrine of the Spirit and of election, on the one hand, and a strangely applied theology of the imitation of Christ, on the other. An "unauthorized" venturing forth without waiting for the Spirit—described in three-fourths of the tract as arrogance before God—is suddenly turned around in the last part of the treatise into a command of God, and not to obey this command [with or without human authorization] would be sin. This attests to Karlstadt's desire for some higher authorization then inherently present in the service he had taken over. Here, in this treatise, is a mixture of uncertainty as well as commitment to a purpose, a mixture that had already caused so much confusion and, over a longer period, had made him an unhappy man.[15]

In the mysticism of these writings of Karlstadt, Luther sensed the spirit of the Zwickau prophets, especially of Nicholas Storch. It is reported that in 1523 and early 1524 Storch was pursuing his interests in Thuringia. Luther's surmise that this was a case of deeply intertwined sectarian religiosity was substantiated. The extent to which it had developed was shockingly evidenced when the firebrand of this movement, Thomas Müntzer, let himself be heard again. Following Müntzer's flight from Zwickau in April 1521, he had remained for a time in Bohemia and in the Vogtland district south of Zwickau. Accompanied by Marcus Thomae (Stübner),[16] he moved to Prague, where Müntzer hoped to find an open door for worldwide missionary activity in the pattern of Paul. To a friend he wrote, "If possible, I would like to be all things to all people until they recognize the Crucified in the likeness of their own renunciation. . . . I am traveling the entire world for the sake of the Word."[17] In Prague both

14. Ibid., 17 / 2ff., 8–9, 18ff., 35ff.; 18 / 24ff.; 19 / 30–31.

15. At this point, according to the handwritten notes of the author [Bornkamm], a listing of Karlstadt's four other Jena tracts should follow, as well as a notation of their content. In WA Br 3:233, n. 4, O. Clemen lists the following four: *Ursache, dass Andreas Karlstadt eine Zeit still geschwiegen* (see above [n. 11]); *Von dem Priestertum und Opfer Christi; Ob Gott ein Ursach sei des teuflischen Falles; Von dem Sabbat und geboten Feiertagen; Verstandes des Wortes Pauli: Ich begehre ein Verbannter zu sein von Christo* [Rom. 9:3], according to Barge, *Karlstadt*, 2:100–101. [Cf. G. Rupp, *Patterns of Reformation* (Philadelphia: Fortress Press, 1969), 121–22, 123–30, 142–43.]

16. See above, p. 58.

17. To Michael Gans, June 15, 1921, in *Thomas Müntzer, Schriften und Briefe: Kritische Gesamtausgabe*, ed. G. Franz, QFRG 33 (Gütersloh, 1968), no. 24, 371 / 7 / 11–12.

Müntzer and Thomae were welcomed with open arms by the Utraquist Hussites. Invitations to preach and to lead discussions followed.[18] In Hussite eyes, long seeking contact with Wittenberg, they rated as emissaries of Luther. Müntzer's former followers understood him in those terms too and provided him with news about Luther and developments at home.[19]

Müntzer himself, however, without at this time breaking with Luther, considered himself the pioneer of a new and exclusively true proclamation of the gospel. He pulled his thoughts together in a manifesto that (probably not just by chance) bore the familiar All Saints date of Luther's Ninety-five Theses and was itself perhaps intended for posting in some public place.[20] There, for the first time and in briefest compass, the original shape of Müntzer's theology becomes comprehensible. The decisive thesis—the one he never gave up—is this: "One who is among the elect must have the Holy Spirit" ("even sevenfold," as Isa. 11:1–2 adds). Only the "Spirit of the fear of God," "trained in useful hours of agonizing," makes a Christian. Faith in the Scriptures, which the priests have "stolen" from the Bible, does make a Christian. The priests act as if God had become dumb and as if his word had vanished in the air, yet then it would not be the eternal word.[21] With threats and promises he bolstered this sole content of his message: "God will perform wonders with his elect, especially with those in this country." For those who turned him a deaf ear he had this warning: "If you don't fall in line God will leave it to the Turks to destroy you during the coming year."[22] As for his own prophetic mission, Müntzer claimed legitimacy by stating that ever since his youth he had tried harder than anyone else he knew to acquire the "holy, unconquerable Christian faith."[23] Besides, he stakes his own soul's salvation on his

18. Cf. E. Gritsch, *Reformer Without a Church: The Life and Thought of Thomas Muentzer* (Philadelphia: Fortress Press, 1967), 52ff., who utilized the documentary material in V. Husa, *Thomáš Müntzer a Čechy* (Prague, 1957). [For a different perspective on Müntzer, see G. H. Williams, *The Radical Reformation* (Philadelphia: Westminster Press, 1962), 44–58.]

19. Hans Pelt to Müntzer, June 25, 1521, in *Müntzer Schriften*, no. 26, 373ff.; and September 6, 1521, ibid., no. 28, 377.

20. According to the original in Müntzer's own hand, Müntzer, *Schriften*, 491ff. Like the Latin text, also in Müntzer's hand (see below, p. 149, n.25), it was written on a very large page. O. Clemen, "Das Prager Manifest Thomas Müntzer," *ARG* 30 (1933): 74, justifiably doubts that these two texts were intended for public posting. At most these texts might have been so intended, yet they disappeared in Müntzer's own mailbag, which was taken as booty after the battle of Frankenhausen by mercenaries of Duke George. This cache has preserved a remarkable collection of literary and other remains of his life. (See below, pp. 382–83.)

21. Müntzer, *Schriften*, 491 / 10ff.; 492 / 29ff.; 493 / 22ff.

22. Ibid., 494 / 16–17, 21ff.

23. Ibid., 491 / 3ff.

proclamation "Should I fail in this art which I prize so highly, then I'm ready to be a child of temporal and eternal death. I can make no higher pledge."[24] That was the heart of the matter. Yet Müntzer must soon have learned that with this simple dialectic of spirit versus letter he could arouse no great response.

In a few weeks he had reworked his text and given it a propagandistic slant. He aimed at two classes of readers: in German, and in Czech translation, for the mass of people; in Latin for the intellectuals.[25] The German text, as rewritten, now contained a hail of crude expletives aimed at the "padres anointed with pitch," "sanctimonious monks," "donkey-drivel doctors," and the "Neronian, holy, most wooden pope and chamber pot in Rome." These "money-grabbing rascals" have reproached the "poor, poor, poor little people"; like crusts of bread to the dogs, they have tossed them Bible texts, the meaning of which they themselves have never experienced.[26] The oft-repeated word "poor" has a double meaning: These are the spiritually betrayed as well as those exploited by their betrayers. Almost like a cartoon, Müntzer's self-awareness acquired overdrawn features.

> Wow, how ripe are those rotten apples! Wow, how brittle the elect have become! The time for harvest is here! So God himself has hired me for his harvest. I have sharpened my sickle, for my thoughts are passionately for the truth, and my lips, skin, hands, hair, soul, body, and life curse the unbelievers.[27]

Adopting a completely different tone, he addressed the intellectuals in elegant Latin. No hail of coarse expletives for them, no propaganda pitch for the poor. Even the Turkish danger was transformed into a promise; the encounter would bring Bohemia a measure of fame as great as the shame and hatred the nation had hitherto experienced at the hands of Rome. Müntzer's conclusion in the Latin text was also a different one. While in the German version he had warned that unless the people heeded him the Antichrist would get them, in the Latin his tone was conciliatory, expressing the hope that God would again set up his revived church. He warned,

---

24. Ibid., 494 / 27ff.

25. Ibid., 495–505; Latin, 505–11. A comparison of the two texts is in A. Lohmann, *Zur geistigen Entwicklung Thomas Müntzers* (Leipzig and Berlin, 1931), 19ff. Unfortunately, the Czech text is missing in the edition of Franz, but it is supplied in incomplete form in a Dresden manuscript first printed in *Thomas Müntzer: Briefwechsel*, ed. H. Boehmer and P. Kira (Leipzig and Berlin, 1931), 150ff.

26. Müntzer, *Schriften*, 495 / 12–13; 496 / 10; 502 / 29–30; 500 / 13–14.

27. Ibid., 504 / 17ff.

"Let the church worship not a dumb God but a God who is alive and speaks. For no god is more despicable in pagan eyes than one who is alive but of whose presence Christians feel nothing."[28] Müntzer's efforts to win followers in various cultures by adapting himself to their language and ways of thinking were without success. Perhaps it was the wild talk in his German-Czech manifesto that led to his expulsion from Bohemia toward the end of 1521.

Müntzer went back to his native Electoral Saxony. His attempt to pick up influence from the older, Hussite reform movement as leverage for a renewal of Christendom had collapsed. Once back in the territory of the Reformation, he picked up with a band of loyal followers. Even the Wittenberg theologians were singled out for conversion to the truth of his teaching. In this case too the same ideas came into play as those he had expounded earlier in Prague. This is evident from his two letters, one to Melanchthon (March 27, 1522), the other to Luther over a year later (July 9, 1523). Although his tone was respectful, Müntzer did not hesitate to take sharp issue and to criticize Melanchthon and Luther for some fundamental deficiencies in their theology. He charged that they worshiped a "dumb God," one who they believe no longer speaks to his elect. "Beloved, make the effort to prophesy, otherwise your theology isn't worth a red cent. Bear in mind that your God is near and not somewhere far away. Really believe that he is more willing to speak than you are to listen." To prophesy—that means to make room for the living voice of God, perhaps even in faces and in dreams, the way Müntzer defended the whole business in his letter to Luther. And the meaning of this? To live conformed to the Crucified, to live without lust, to regard marriage simply as the way of procreating an elect generation and to see the sign of the end of time. "The bowl of the third angel—I fear it and know it is so—has already been poured into the springs of water and has turned them into streaming blood" (Rev. 16:4). There is no more time to spare the weak. "Our precious Martinus does not know what he is doing when he tries to avoid offending the little ones, who are about as 'little' as those aged a hundred and yet accursed (Isa. 65:20, one of Müntzer's countless allusions to unexpected Bible passages). . . . Dear brothers, quit your dawdling. It is time! No more fiddling around. Summer is at the door!"[29]

28. Ibid., 510–11 / 3ff.

29. To Melanchthon, March 27, 1522, *Supp. Mel.* 6 / 1:182ff. *MBW* 223, Müntzer, *Schriften*, no. 31, 380 / 6, 16ff.; 381 / 4ff., 20ff. To Luther, July 9, 1523, ibid., no. 40, 389ff. *WA* Br 3:104ff. "Mahren"—to dawdle—in the vernacular of Saxony, Silesia, and elsewhere.

This is how the self-styled "messenger of Christ" addressed the Wittenbergers: still in a friendly mood, still trying to win them over. Even so, Müntzer was already making it clear that if they failed to follow his admonitions he would have to reckon them among the godless. Luther and Melanchthon, wrote Müntzer to another, "have the opinion that they are armed with God's grace, a reality about which they know as much as a goose knows about the Milky Way."[30] With this kind of talk it was a foregone conclusion that Müntzer was moving close to Karlstadt, the head of the Wittenberg opposition. For the time being Karlstadt could offer him no other help—in the "Misery of My Exile," as Müntzer dated his letters—than to offer him shelter and peasant employment on his little farm in Wörlitz.[31] Even though Müntzer did not take him up on the offer, and although this connection between the two men did not last long, there remained nevertheless, as Müntzer wrote, "our thing" (res nostra) about which they kept in conversation through a trusted messenger. "I speak with you as though with my self," he wrote Karlstadt.[32] Their common cause was not simply their opposition to the Wittenbergers but also their preaching of mystical experience. For Karlstadt, meanwhile, had quickly appropriated some of Müntzer's thoughts, just as he had done earlier with thoughts of Luther and of the German mystics. He assured Müntzer that in his time at Wittenberg he too had spoken more about faces and dreams than any other professor.[33]

Even the little that Luther had heard or read of Müntzer (he could not have known the classic Prague document on Müntzer's sense of mission) and the things he remembered of the Zwickau prophets as well as the writings of Karlstadt made him aware that he was here having to deal with a uniformly contrary spirit. Luther was broadly correct, even though today we can separate the several features from one another more plainly. Yet here one flame had been lit by another, and all of them finally were derived from the flaming enthusiasm of Nicholas Storch, giving the impression of a common phenomenon and function. This was an ecstatic brand of mysticism, relying on revelation through visions and dreams. Even when these were known only from hearsay, as was undoubtedly the

30. To an unknown, July 14, 1522, Müntzer, *Schriften,* no. 35, 385 / 3ff.

31. Karlstadt to Müntzer, December 21, 1522, Müntzer, *Schriften,* no. 37, 386–87. Müntzer to unknown adherents in Halle, March 19, 1523, ibid., no. 38, 388 / 13.

32. July 29, 1523, Müntzer, *Schriften,* no. 43, 393 / 7–8, 14.

33. Karlstadt to Müntzer, December 21, 1522, Müntzer, *Schriften,* no. 37, 387 / 15. One year later, in his *Why Has Andreas Karlstadt Kept Silence So Long?* (see above, pp. 146ff.), he sounded different, claiming that the Spirit spoke to the apostles (Acts 13:1ff.) not in their sleep or in dreams but "inwardly." *Karlstadts Schriften,* pt. 1, 12 / 37ff.

case with Karlstadt and for years also with Müntzer, they were widely quoted.[34] Such mysticism demanded of the authentic believer a deep experience of inward self-effacement, and the conviction of being crucified with Christ became the mark of election. To gather the elect, to separate them from the world by means of a rigorous application of the divine law, and to permeate the members with the spirit of this ascetic enthusiasm— this was the sum of their common endeavor. Luther, to the contrary, had deliberately avoided the temptation to separate the true Christian from the masses. So the sectarians, impatient with Luther, kept up an attack on his protectiveness toward the weak and on the slowness, even the piecemeal character, of the Wittenberg reformation. The preaching of the sectarians, so full of apocalyptic threats, warned that there was no time to lose.

Luther was now forced to recognize that it was precisely those among his former opponents whom he had taken least seriously—the ecstatic men of Zwickau—who were proving to be the toughest survivors. A new battle was at his door. Karlstadt had given him the first skirmish, but now it was Müntzer who first brushed his sword. "Satan is setting up a sect among us at yet another place, and this sect supports neither the papists nor us. Its members boast that they are being moved by pure spirit, without the testimony of Holy Scripture," Luther wrote on May 6, 1524. Two months later he charged that they would resort to arms in order to advance their cause.[35] He was referring to the formation of a congregation of the elect and eventually of a sworn alliance based in Allstedt, a little town on the Kyffhauser [Creek] in Electoral Saxony where Müntzer had been occupying a preaching post since Easter 1523.

During his two-year period of wandering, Müntzer's zeal had been dammed up. Now he was bent on making public his image of the true congregation of Christ. Quickly, and long before Luther, he fashioned a completely German order of worship. This was no mean feat, considering the binding weight of tradition, and we shall come upon this aspect of Müntzer's activity later, when dealing with Luther's liturgical reforms.[36] Müntzer took a long running start for justifying this innovation, beginning with the Christianization of the Germans "six hundred years ago." At that time, according to Müntzer's oft-quoted saying of Hegesippus, the church had long since ceased being a virgin (which she had been until the end of

34. Müntzer to Luther, July 9, 1523, WA Br 3:105 / 50ff. Müntzer, *Schriften*, no. 40, 389ff.

35. Luther to Gerbel, May 6, 1524, WA Br 3:284 / 10ff. To Briessmann, July 4, 1524, WA Br 3:315 / 12ff.

36. See below, pp. 467ff.

the postapostolic age) and had become an adulteress.[37] The "pious, good-hearted fathers who converted our country" and who had to use Latin instead of our then still unformed German language certainly contributed a substantial improvement. Since then, however, human intelligence strives for ever greater improvements. "Should God remain so powerless as to be unable to raise his own work higher still?" Indeed, God is even now doing that very thing through him, Müntzer, in a German way, so that the poor people need no longer go forth from worship uninstructed but truly edified.[38] This confidence in an inner progress of humankind, plus his information on the apocalyptic nature of the hour, combined to create an unusually strong sense of history.

The new way of worship and Müntzer's thunderous preaching attracted crowds even from afar, so much so that Count Ernest of Mansfeld, citing a mandate of the Nuremberg diet, forbade his subjects to leave their local church and attend in Allstedt. On September 13, 1523, from the pulpit Müntzer shot back that if the count will not himself come to Allstedt and allow his heresy to be exposed, then he would have to be declared a knave, a Turk, and a heathen. The count tried in vain to have the town council arrest Müntzer. The count's ensuing correspondence over this issue came to Luther's attention and gave him his initial shock over the turn of events in Allstedt. Müntzer had sent the count a threatening letter: "Don't move, or the old coat will tear. You just dare to stop me, and I'll treat you a hundred thousand times worse than Luther treated the pope."[39]

Müntzer and the count both appealed at once to the elector, Müntzer in a letter of booming self-confidence: "Since almighty God has made me the ranking preacher [in Allstedt], I am going about blowing the moving and versatile trumpets, so that they resound with the ardor of God's knowledge, that no person on this earth be spared who resists the word of God." Zeal for the poor, that part of Christendom worthy of mercy, is eating him, he says. And as always with prophets, the mockery of the godless has now landed on him. By means of an unrestrained preaching of the pure word, however, he has—like Jeremiah (1:18)—made himself into an "iron wall of the needy." To them his name "is the sweet aroma of life, but to the profligate it is an offensive abomination signaling a rapidly approaching

37. Fragments from Hegesippus in Eusebius, *Ecclesiatical History* 4.22.4ff. Also cited in Müntzer's, "Auslegung . . . Daniels," Müntzer, *Schriften*, 243 / 22ff.

38. E. Sehling, *Die evangelischen Kirchenordnungen des XVI. Jahunderts* (Leipzig 1902ff.), 1:497–98. Müntzer, *Schriften*, 161–162.

39. September 22, 1523, Müntzer, *Schriften*, no. 44, 394 / 30ff.

destruction" (2 Cor. 2:15–16). He appealed to the elector for protection and for the first time sounded his eschatological warning: If the princes fail to stand up for the gospel, "the sword will be taken from them and given to the raging people for the destruction of the godless."[40] He signed his letter to Count Ernest "A destroyer of unbelievers," while to Elector Frederick he began signing himself "A servant of God." Müntzer's appeal was quite the opposite of Luther's, who had renounced his claim to the elector's protection.

It was rapidly becoming apparent that here a second phase of the Reformation was in the making, the phase of armed intervention by the evangelical princes. At this point Müntzer admonished the elector "to be bold here too," in the confidence that God has always stood by him. "The lucky beginning which you appear to have made with Luther you will conclude with Müntzer."[41] In return, Elector Frederick did what he had always done in such situations when deluged with questions of conscience from many sides during these years; he limited himself to a mild admonition and let the matter take its course.

Only a half-year later the fruits of his hesitation became evident. The throngs of outsiders pressing to hear Müntzer's sermons increased steadily, with miners from Mansfeld in the lead. On Sundays, according to one report, there were some two thousand strangers in Allstedt.[42] Meanwhile, Müntzer was becoming more confident of nearing his goal, a congregation of the elect, so he began by founding a secret society made up of the promised ones who vowed "to stand by the gospel and to give not one penny more to monks and nuns, helping instead to destroy and expel them.[43]

The first fiery warning of worse things to come was the destruction of a chapel in Mallerbach, at the gates of Allstedt. There on March 24, 1524,

40. Müntzer to the Elector, October 4, 1523. Müntzer, *Schriften,* no. 45, 395 / 8ff., 23, 15ff.; 396 / 28–29. On *Clavis scientiae,* cf. Luke 11:52. Count Ernest of Mansfeld to the count's representative and the Allstedt Council, September 21; to the Elector, September 24; the Elector to Count Ernest, September 28; to the count's representative and council in Allstedt, September 28 and October 11, 1523, all in K. E. Förstemann, *Neues Urkundenbuch zur Geschichte der evangelischen Kirchen-Reformation* (Hamburg, 1842), 1:228ff. For background, C. Hinrichs, *Luther und Müntzer: Ihre Auseinandersetzung über Obrigkeit und Widerstandsrecht* (Berlin, 1952), 5ff.

41. Hinrichs, *Luther und Müntzer,* 10.

42. Report of the count's representative Schultheiss and the council to the Elector, April 11, 1524. W. Fuchs, ed., *Akten zur Geschichte des Bauernkrieg in Mitteldeutschland,* 2 vols. (Leipzig, 1923, 1934; Jena 1942; reprinted Aalen, 1964), 2:30 (hereafter cited as *Akten Bauernkrieg*).

43. "Zur Geschichte des Bauernkriegs in Thüringischen und Mansfeldischen," *Neue Mitteilungen aus dem Gebiet historischantiquarischer Forschung* 12 (1869): 215.

the attack centered on an alleged miracle-working picture of the Virgin. This drew bitter protest from the nearby nunnery, which owned the chapel. Duke John, regent of the territory, led an investigation in the face of which excited excuses from Müntzer and the town council followed. Luther learned quickly of these disturbing developments. Surely it was through Spalatin [in the elector's chancellery] that Luther was apprised of the correspondence developing between the contesting parties, and especially of a letter from the Allstedt council to the duke in early June 1524, which Duke John dutifully shared with his brother the elector. Müntzer's hand is readily recognizable. How could such "good-hearted, pious people" sit in jail simply for having put an end to the "devil at Mallerbach," who has so long been venerated out of ignorance? This sort of treatment is as intolerable as being subservient to the Turks. Let the duke remember that it is written "You shall not join hands with a wicked man" (in this case with the idolatrous monks and nuns) "to be a malicious witness (Exod. 23:1)." Let him also remember that he has been given the sword just as much for the punishment of evildoers as for the protection of the pious (Rom. 13:4). And again this subtle threat: They are ready to offer the elector the obedience due him, unless his grace "should decide to obey men more than God, which we would in no way surmise of his and your grace."[44]

Encouraged by the favorable stand of the town council [as shown in its letter to Duke John], Müntzer went full-speed ahead. With his colleague Simon Haferitz, whom he had won over completely to a radical mysticism, he preached incendiary sermons and incited the people against the prince's house. In those same days he succeeded in getting the entire citizenry of Allstedt divided into military units. The point was that, if necessary, outside interference in Allstedt's affairs was to be repulsed by force of arms. So Müntzer transformed his association into an organization of over five hundred members. Of these, about three hundred were outsiders. No longer were these men kept hidden in a dry moat outside the city wall; they were now lodged in the cellar of the town hall and duly registered. Aptly for a book-fancier like Müntzer, the association was patterned after a literary example in a pamphlet by Eberlin von Günzburg.[45]

44. Müntzer, *Schriften*, no. 50, 405 / 20ff.; 406 / 1ff.; 405 / 25ff., 30ff.

45. Sermon by Haferitz, January 6, 1524, in O. Clemen, *Beiträge zur Reformationsgeschichte aus Büchern und Handschriften der Zwickauer Ratsschulbibliothek* (Berlin, 1902), 14ff. On the Pentecost sermons of Müntzer and Haferitz, see "Zur Geschichte des Bauernkriegs," 155. On Müntzer's association, ibid., 159, 165, 185, 215. Hinrichs, *Luther und Müntzer*, 11ff., 21–22.

As for Luther, he had been following the unrest in Allstedt for some time with mounting alarm, and through Spalatin, he repeatedly urged the elector to intervene.[46] With more of Müntzer's writings at hand, Luther was able to round out his impression of the man. Early in 1524 two tracts by Müntzer appeared in rapid succession. They did not yet say anything about establishing the kingdom of God by force, but they did lay down a barrage against the Wittenberg reformers' kind of preaching. No names were named, and many statements remained veiled, but the message was clear enough. The tract was in a mystical vein, playing on Luther's thought in order to use it to attack him: that it is difficult to attain faith, that the struggle for it must pass through agonizing and despair, and that it will emerge only after the natural light in man has first been extinguished. What Luther had described as God's way of dealing with man, Müntzer turned into a method of preaching and pastoral care. Thus, in preaching and counseling it is necessary first and foremost to shock and cause distress and not to comfort; to kill and not to make alive; to lead into the highest degree of ignorance and astonishment, and not into faith. Where Luther was concerned about assisting the disturbed person, whose need he knew at first hand like none other, and where he endeavored always to help that person to a solid footing, there Müntzer had nothing but ridicule for him, counting Luther among "our mad, debauching pigs, which are horrified by the windstorm, the raging billows, and by all the waters of wisdom." Luther is only a hireling (John 10:27) preacher: "Believe, believe! Hold on tight, tightly with a strong, strong faith." This is nothing but preaching a honey-sweet Christ—not the bitter one, but only half a Christ, not the whole one, for no one can believe in the whole Christ except he has first become like him.[47]

The second of Müntzer's two tracts was a sharp attack on infant baptism. Entitled *Protestation or Summons of Thomas Müntzer*, this tract charged that the practice of infant baptism, though nowhere commanded in Scripture, is a proclamation of the honey-sweet Christ and an evasion of the necessity first to place a human being into the painful condition of "expectation." A person must first learn "to endure the Word." In this stage there can be no comfort, and it must seem to last an eternity, "so that a person imagines he has no faith at all." Such a person feels only "a meager desire for the right kind of faith," a desire that is hardly perceptible. "Here God is tormenting me with my conscience, with unbelief, despair,

46. WA 18:85, 19ff.
47. Müntzer, *Schriften*, 218ff.; 220 / 31; 220 / 6–7; 222 / 17–18, 21ff.

and blasphemy of him." Of what help is it then when those learned in the Scripture say, "Yes, dear fellow, you shouldn't really worry about such exalted matters. Simply have faith and get rid of those ideas. It's all a futile fantasy. Go out among people and be happy, and forget your cares." According to Müntzer, this distortion of the true message of Christ puts us on the same level with all other religions which, after all, require some sort of faith. Now because we do not intend to put up with "tender herbs," we flee to the saints the way the pagans flee to their idols. Virtually like the Muslims, we do not think the Crucified One is real. The Roman church granted indulgences and absolution. Shall we then become guilty of the same things by practicing infant baptism and granting forgiveness without conditions? This would simply be giving an old house a fresh coat of whitewash.[48]

Both the content of these tracts and the reports from Allstedt must have agitated Luther profoundly. Here someone who knew about experiences of the soul was touching on most secret and dangerous things. Luther must have been outraged at how in this manner the disturbed person was thrust back into and imprisoned in despair. Likewise, the person who was not disturbed was required to become so as a spiritual exercise without being shown even a trace of light and comfort. To Luther, Müntzer's method was nihilistic; its only aim was destruction, and it had nothing to say about salvation. Moreover, Müntzer's method destroyed everything that Luther's experience of need had enabled him to test out on himself and others, namely, the acceptance expressed in baptism of God's unshakable grace—instead of turning over a person to the uncertainty of "active expectation"—is a fresh, simple encouragement to faith and extends beyond all scruples. Müntzer's caricature of Luther was nearly on target, for Luther indeed had high regard for a pastoral counselor's warm and strong consolation. Yet with Müntzer's method of induced suffering the preaching of the kingdom of God which was to be brought in by force was inextricably bound. The sufferings individuals are to expect in this conflict are the agony of the cross through which we, as followers of Christ, must pass. The great struggle, which Müntzer forecast, has a universal eschatological meaning, and at the same time it offered the possibility of individual perfection for the elect. Müntzer, however, betrayed his teaching by a claim none could exceed. He demanded he be given a hearing in the presence of representatives of all nations and all religions, and not without adequate witnesses.[49] This meant that he was rejecting

48. Ibid., 225ff.; 228 / 9–10; 234 / 23; 237 / 21ff.; 238 / 15ff.; 232 / 14; 234 / 22.
49. Ibid., 240 / 1, 18.

publicly the proposal, probably Luther's to the elector, that he be tried by the Wittenberg faculty.

In the face of all that had been happening and put in print, Luther could no longer keep silent. The destruction of the chapel shrine and the formation of an armed association gave him the feeling that rebellion was at the door. Müntzer's letter to the princes, with its hidden threats, simply highlighted the impending danger. So Luther lashed out while the princes were still hesitating and the anxious elector was still finding only appeasing words.[50] In July 1524 Luther wrote an open *Letter to the Princes of Saxony Concerning the Rebellious Spirit,* in which he distinguished two sides of Müntzer's behavior, that of violence and that of precept. Only the side of violence concerns the princes, and to this subject Luther devoted almost the entire letter. Satan can here be seen at work in a new way and has shown his hoofprint all too plainly—meaning that one is not to leave it up to the Word but that it is time to resist the authorities with fists, with the sacking of cloisters, and with the destruction of images. Luther demanded that the princes respond preventively by rigorous prohibitions. If the Allstedters wished to defend themselves and show their true colors, let them do so in a public trial, before whomever they chose, "before us or the papists." With angry mockery Luther sketched out the contradiction that, on the one hand, Müntzer withdraws from all perseverance and, on the other, takes refuge under the elector's protection, and from the safety of his nest sounds forth fearless words as though he were "filled three times over with the Holy Spirit." And in return, what has he done? He enjoys the freedom others have achieved for him. Then comes one of those rare moments when Luther lapses into a Pauline-style "foolish boasting" (2 Cor. 11). He reminds others that in Leipzig, Augsburg, and Worms he stood up to his enemies alone and weak, "even though I had never heard of a heavenly voice or of God's talents and works or of the Allstedt spirit."[51]

Luther's letter to the princes of Saxony is noteworthy not because he admonished them to suppress violence but much more because he drew boundaries for them to observe. They do not have to defend themselves against Müntzer's teaching.

50. Elector Frederick to the council and parish of Allstedt, June 27, 1524, "Zur Geschichte des Bauernkreigs," 167ff.

51. *WA* 15:210ff.; 215 / 23–24; 213 / 28–29; 214 / 19ff., 26–27. *Pfund* [= pound, talent] (according to Luke 19:11ff.; cf. also *WA* 15:211 / 28) is a term in the mysticism of Storch which Luther had picked up from Thomae (*WA TR* 3, no. 2837b, 15 / 13); the term is also used occasionally by Müntzer. [The full text, plus introduction, *LW* 40: (47–48) 49–59; specific references thus far to pp. 49, 54, 52, 53.]

Let them preach as confidently and boldly as they are able and against whomever they wish. . . . There must be sects, and the Word of God must be under arms and fight. . . . Let the spirits collide and fight it out. If meanwhile some are led astray, let it be; such is war. Where there is battle and bloodshed, some must fall and some are wounded. Whoever fights honorably will be crowned.[52]

These words signify an epoch in the age of tolerance. Here Luther has freed himself from a medieval way of thinking, which saw the misleading of souls as the greatest crime. If counterfeiters are punished with the death penalty, how much more should heretics be punished with the death penalty, how much more should heretics be punished who rob people of their faith and thereby of their eternal life, as Thomas Aquinas had argued?[53] By the same argument, John Calvin justified the burning of Michael Servetus. Luther, to the contrary, put aside the very idea of the murdering of souls. The combat of spirits must be free. Therefore souls must risk the struggle. So he carries his separation of the spiritual and temporal realms to the point of tolerating false doctrine openly taught. If he later substantially reduced the area open to such combat, it was because he observed its political dangers with mounting anxiety. Basically, for him the differentiation that matters is "that in this matter we act only according to the Word of God, as is fitting for Christians. Only thus can we eliminate the causes of sedition."[54] This alone is the concern of government.

When this warning call of Luther's was published, he found himself in a situation of rising tension. The loyal and somewhat uncertain Duke John, under pressure from all sides for a decision, determined to form his own judgment of Müntzer, and July 13, 1524, was the day. On the duke's invitation—and in the presence also of the electoral prince John Frederick, the chancellor, Gregory Brück, and a number of other officials gathered in the Allstedt castle—Müntzer preached. He used this incomparable opportunity to unfold his apocalyptic hopes. With an unerring instinct for the dramatic, he chose the second chapter of Daniel as his text. It contained everything he required for this hour: the king, Nebuchadnezzer, excited by a dream; the wise men, conversant in sacred scriptures yet unable to interpret the dream; and the elect prophet, enabled by God's illumination to interpret the dream in terms of four successive kingdoms.

52. WA 15:218 / 19ff. [LW 40:57.]
53. In *Summa Theologica* 2, 2. 11, art. 3.
54. WA 15:221 / 2ff. [LW 40:59.]

With a grandiose personal assessment, Müntzer saw history repeating itself in the contemporary situation. In the abject failure of the well-stocked stable of theologians at the princely court, he found perfect ammunition to attack the godless, namely, the day's "untested" keepers of the Scriptures, who are ignorant of God's revelation and who know nothing of the "pure art of God," but who are glad "to devour juicy morsels at the court," [notably] "Brother Fattened-Hog and Brother Soft-Life." These epithets were here applied by Müntzer for the first time to Luther and Melanchthon, though he did not name them specifically. To Müntzer, this chapter of Daniel made it sufficiently clear "that God reveals his divine secrets" to his dear friends through recognized faces or through his word conveyed orally. Müntzer claimed to find the same testimony in a large number of authors whom he cited. If Peter had been unfamiliar with the faces, how then could he have experienced his liberation from prison by the angel (Acts 12) as a reality?[55] No one, claimed Müntzer, perceives that sort of thing through the "babbling" of those learned in the Scriptures, "even though one may have gorged himself on a hundred thousand Bibles." The elect must be one secluded from all things worldly and from all "momentary fascination." They must become "fools within" so as to be able in "lofty astonishment" (left unspelled for the moment by Müntzer) to be "overshadowed" by the power of the divine Word. Only with such elect people can God bring about the great "transformation of the world" as promised by the prophet. "For if Christendom were not to become apostolic . . . , why preach?" The Spirit of God is now revealing it to many that a "first-rate, unbeatable, future-oriented reformation" is needed.[56] Moreover, the princes of Saxony are being called on to bring it about. Now if a pagan king was attentive to the spirit of truth, how false it is (considering Luther's differentiation between the two realms) to say that "the princes are pagans with respect to the way they discharge their office; they are not supposed to do more than maintain unity among the citizens." "Therefore, my precious rulers of Saxony, step up boldly onto the cornerstone (Christ)"; "you must dare to do it for the sake of the gospel." As themselves elect they will indeed "have to endure a heavy cross and much distress," yet this simply means that God is chastening his favorite children. They are not supposed to fall for the talk about sparing the weak out of love. Christ has ordered otherwise: "As for these enemies of mine . . . bring them here and slay them before me" (Luke 19:27). Nor did Müntzer

55. Müntzer, *Schriften*, 248 / 7; 245 / 11; 248 / 27; 254 / 12–13; 247 / 16ff.; 255 / 8–9.
56. Ibid., 247 / 14; 251 / 19; 252 / 4; 250 / 19; 251 / 19–20; 253 / 20; 255 / 16ff.

abolish the Old Testament commandment to destroy the altars and burn the images of idols (Deut. 7:5–6). Should the princes not step in and act, then God will take their idle sword from them.[57] There is ample reason why the princes need a "new Daniel," who interprets what has been revealed to them and preaches courage to them like the ancient priest before the battle (Deut. 20:2). As in the days of Nebuchadnezzar, the princes of Saxony should now install this new Daniel so that he may make good and just judgments, "for the godless have no right to live except as the elect are willing to grant it to them."[58] Müntzer's own shadow thus came on stage. Who else could be this Daniel?

That was the program of the second Reformation. Full of hope, Müntzer invited the princes to join the association of the elect. However, he also hinted broadly about to whom else he would turn: "the poor lay folk and the peasants." These are the ones who see the stone rolling irresistibly toward [the clay feet of the great statue] (Dan. 2:34) "much more clearly than you [the princes] do." Indeed, the stone is already so great that any hostile neighbors, should they decide to attack for the sake of the gospel, would be expelled by their own people. There was certainly some truth to this. Müntzer thus determined to apply the match to the powder keg. The greatest hindrance, however, was Luther, whom he now regarded with a veritable eschatological hatred. "In the last days," according to Müntzer, "the lovers of pleasure will take on an appearance of graciousness (when, like Luther, in face of the Wittenberg unrest they preach the forgotten love of Christ) but will deny their power, for there is nothing on earth that cuts a better figure or wears a better mask than contrived (false) graciousness."[59] In Müntzer this was a theologically sublimated hatred sprung from a disappointed discipleship; to call it disappointed love would be too strong for one who was unable to love. The likes of Müntzer's hatred of Luther, in style and substance, recurred only once again, in Friedrich Nietzsche.[60]

Müntzer's sermon to the princes and Luther's open letter to them—the program of the violent reformation and the summons to the defense against violence—were on a collision course. The impact came at the end of July 1524. Not suspecting Luther's intervention, Müntzer was still full

57. Ibid., 257 / 29ff.; 256 / 29ff.; 259 / 28–29, 22; 258 / 14–15; 260 / 16.

58. Ibid., 261 / 18–19; 257 / 19; 262 / 32ff.

59. Ibid., 256 / 21; 262, 23ff.

60. On Nietzsche's position on Luther, see H. Bornkamm, *Luther im Spiegel der deutschen Geistesgeschichte*, 2d ed. (Göttingen, 1970), 92–94, 305–14.

of high hopes and ambitious plans. To Duke John he renewed his offer to stand trial before the whole world, but not before the Wittenberg faculty alone. "In the process I want to get the Romans, the Turks, and the heathen," he vowed.[61] In haste he breathlessly brought his sermon to the printer, and seeing his adherents, expelled from neighboring Catholic lands, flooding as refugees into Allstedt, he saw himself forced to more drastic measures. In this highly volatile situation Müntzer dashed off letter after letter. He raised his adherents' spirits, claiming "that more than thirty plans and alliances of the elect have been made. In all lands the game is catching on. In short, we must suffer; we are in for it." To the imprisoned he pictured the martyrs. To the persecutors he threatened that if they would not desist, "then I will no longer hold back the people who want to molest you. You must choose between one of two things: You must accept the gospel, or you must confess yourselves heathen."[62]

Feverishly Müntzer awaited the decision of the territorial lords. Would they, or would they not, join his band of the elect? He therefore importuned Hans Zeiss, the warden of Allstedt's electoral castle, to apply pressure on the lords. He supplied Zeiss with the clearer version of the covenant idea as set forth in his sermon of July 24.[63] Again he had chosen an impressive Old Testament text, the renewal of the covenant between God and his people under King Josiah through the acceptance of the Book of the Law discovered in the Temple and through the radical removal of all idolatry (2 Kings 22, 23). So let the lords too transform their duties and oaths "into a faithful covenant of the divine will," so that the people may take courage and the covenant escape its persecution. It is not intended to cease paying taxes to the government. At the same time, however, Müntzer again warns the lords against any inaction on their part. They would then make their people timid and would themselves become more despised than their Roman Catholic counterparts. "It is an enormous impudence to take comfort in the old usage of [public] offices (Luther's treatise *On Temporal Authority* shows here!) after the whole world has changed so mightily."[64]

61. July 13, 1524, Müntzer, *Schriften*, no. 52, 407 / 23.

62. The warden, Hans Zeiss, sent the princes' sermon to Spalatin on July 20, 1524; Fuchs, ed., *Akten Bauernkrieg* 2:941. Müntzer's letters to his persecuted followers in Sangerhausen and to the town council there, ca. July 15, 1524, Müntzer, *Schriften*, nos. 53–55, 408ff.; 408 / 21ff.; 410 / 24ff.

63. Letter of July 22 and 25, 1524, Müntzer, *Schriften*, nos. 57–59, 416ff. The sermon of July 24 has been lost. A report on it, Zeiss to Duke John, is in "Zur Geschichte des Bauernkriegs" (see above, p. 154, n. 43), 179ff.

64. To Zeiss, July 25, 1524, Müntzer, *Schriften*, no. 59, 422, 15 / 1ff.

This explosive state of affairs at last opened the eyes of Duke John. Luther's open letter to the princes of Saxony, published during these days, helped to do so, as well as the expostulations of the duke's son, John Frederick, the elector apparent. The young prince had been keeping a sharp eye on the turn of events in Allstedt and had found Luther supportive over against his father's condoning ways.[65] Müntzer, for his part, was bitterly disappointed with Warden Zeiss and three members of the Allstedt council, because he had been summoned to Weimar, to be interrogated there on August 1, 1524. An eye witness reported that he came out of that hearing as white as a sheet.[66] Even though he was still at liberty, his high hopes had come crashing down, for he had been constrained to await the decision of the elector and to remain passive. Nor did it help that while in Weimar the three Allstedters were interrogated separately and revealed Müntzer's secret plans. However, Müntzer persuaded them to repeat the request that the elector guarantee him the right of publication and support for his oft-repeated request for an international hearing. For his part, Müntzer provided the elector with a theological basis for this request. Writing on August 3, Müntzer said that although he did not agree with Luther he nevertheless shared the belief "that is the same in the hearts of all the elect the world over." Even a born Turk could have such faith.[67] Müntzer, however, could not help but see that he had lost the game in Allstedt and that he could carry on elsewhere only with the power of his pen and the spoken word. Just as he had three years earlier in Zwickau, when things got too hot for him there, Müntzer quit. Late in the night of August 7–8 he climbed over the Allstedt wall. His secret association and his congregation felt humiliated and left in the lurch.[68]

Electoral Saxony was glad to be rid of this agitator, at least for the time being, and especially since Duke George (who had recently been protest-

65. Luther to the Electoral Prince, June 18, and the Electoral Prince to Luther, June 24, 1524, WA Br 3:306ff.; 309–10; 307 / 66ff.; 310 / 44ff.; 311.

66. Ein nützlicher Dialogus oder Gesprächsbüchlein zwischen einem Müntzerishen Schwärmer und einem evangelischen frommen Bauern (1525), WA 15:230, n. 1. Citation found in Hinrichs, Luther und Müntzer, 77–78. Protokoll of the interrogation in "Zur Geschichte des Bauernkreigs," 182. [Cf. Williams, The Radical Reformation, 57, a convenient summary of this incendiary situation. Also Gritsch, Reformer Without a Church, passim.]

67. Letter of the Allstedters to the Elector, August 3, 1524. Printed in "Zur Geschichte des Bauernkriegs," 186ff. Müntzer to the Elector, August 3, in Müntzer, Schriften, no. 64, 430ff.; 430 / 29.

68. Zeiss to the Elector, August 25, 1524, in "Zur Geschichte des Bauernkriegs," 202–3. [Cf. Williams, The Radical Reformation, 57, who shows how Müntzer's colleague Haferitz had stirred up the people and how Müntzer, returning from Weimar, was faced with a virtually impossible situation.]

ing Müntzer's presence) could be given a reassuring reply.[69] Luther, however, was quite certain that the "spirit of Allstedt" had anything but expired. When he learned that, only eight days after fleeing Allstedt, Müntzer had shown up [farther west] in the imperial city of Mühlhausen and was beginning to attract a following there, he got off a letter on August 21, warning the town council.[70] He was writing from Weimar while commencing a visitation of parishes in eastern Thuringia. This region, under Duke John's governance, was an area his son had invited Luther to visit.[71] For some time the rulers [the duke and the elector] had had problems on their hands in this territory, mainly over Orlamünde and the effects Karlstadt's sermons and reforms were having on the many congregations in the Saale River valley. Luther's main concern was not over Karlstadt as a person but over the "spirit of Allstedt," meaning the spirit of violence which was a threat to order everywhere. Without doubt the waves of unrest churned in Allstedt had run to Orlamünde and merged themselves with Karlstadt's own influence. Besides, Müntzer had old ties to Orlamünde, and he was remembered in this region from his Zwickau period. Luther himself presumed that Nicholas Storch, the leader of the Zwickau prophets, had found refuge in Orlamünde.[72]

Karlstadt himself, still in Orlamünde despite his resignation and dismissal, thought it a good idea to anticipate Luther by means of an invitation. He moved the town council to send Luther a message that did two things. It recalled the Reformer's blunt protest (Luther had called them heretics for their removal of idolatrous images) and it requested the Reformer to come over so that the entire matter could be discussed amicably.[73] The letter was delivered to Luther in Jena, where he was visiting. Karlstadt traveled there to meet him, hearing him preach on August 22. Although Luther's sermon did not mention him by name, Karlstadt felt implicated when Luther blamed not only the boisterous spirit of Allstedt but also the elimination of baptism and the Lord's Supper for the prevailing iconoclasm. Karlstadt therefore requested Luther for an opportunity to talk things over. Luther agreed. The two men met in the Black Bear

69. October 7, 1524, F. Gess, *Akten und Briefe zur Kirchenpolitik Herzog Georgs von Sachsen* (Leipzig, 1905ff.), 1:754ff.

70. *WA* 15:238ff. P. Kirn, *Friedrich der Weise und die Kirche* (Leipzig and Berlin, 1926), 3.

71. Letter of the Electoral Prince to Luther, June 24, 1524, *WA* Br 3:309–10; 310 / 44ff.

72. Müntzer to Karlstadt, July 29, 1523, Müntzer, *Schriften*, no. 19, 366–67. On Storch, see above, pp. 56–57.

73. August 16, 1524, *WA* 15:343; delivered to Luther August 22 or 23.

Tavern, the same place where Luther had spoofed the two Swiss students thirty months earlier,[74] only this time Luther received Karlstadt in the presence of a large company.

One of Karlstadt's followers has left us a lively account of the conversation. Luther was friendly. He did not attack Karlstadt, and if he felt offended, he probably was. The central issue came out clearly enough: Is there but one spirit at work here, or must one distinguish two? "The murderous spirit in Allstedt, on the one side, and the spirit of iconoclasm and violation of the sacraments, on the other?"[75] More than he had expected, Karlstadt found Luther ready to differentiate him from Müntzer's revolutionary schemes. Luther had simply been describing Karlstadt as sympathic toward the satanic sect in Allstedt,[76] but after the publication in Wittenberg, in early August, of the warning letter *The Writing from Orlamünde to Those in Allstedt on How to Fight as a Christian*,[77] Luther was satisfied that Karlstadt was not committed to violence in promoting his cause.[78] Yet the spirit that Luther attacked was something more subtle, and implied much more than outright agitation for revolt. Luther's objection was the mixing of objective legitimacy (as in the case of the Old Testament ban on images) and subjective inspiration. He was convinced that the essence of this entire prophetic exercise was confusing the lawful and the unpredictable and would lead inevitably to a dissolution of one tie after another until finally all ties or legitimate obligations would be dissolved. In this sense Luther held his ground, charging Karlstadt, "You are nevertheless on the side of the new prophets." Karlstadt himself seemed to substantiate this to a degree, admitting, "Where they are right, they have the truth on their side; where they are wrong, the devil stands by them."[79]

In spite of everything, Luther soon gave the conversation a relaxing turn with his good humor. When Karlstadt claimed that Luther had gone back on his earlier teaching, Luther retorted, "My dear doctor, if you really know that to be the case, then write it out freely and boldly so that it comes to light."[80] A little later, Luther repeated the challenge, adding that

74. See above, p. 66.

75. *WA* 15:334ff.; 336 / 17ff.

76. To Johann Briessmann, July 4, 1524, *WA Br* 3:315 / 15.

77. A friendly but decidedly warning letter from Karlstadt to Müntzer, July 19, 1524, had preceded the matter; Müntzer, *Schriften*, no. 56, 415.

78. *WA* 15:336 / 14ff.; 395 / 22ff.

79. *WA* 15:339 / 27–28.

80. *WA* 15:336/30ff.

he would give Karlstadt a guilder. He reached into his pocket and tossed the bewildered Karlstadt a gold piece, adding that he should not be sparing in his criticism. "The more boldly you attack me, the dearer you will be to me." Karlstadt took the coin, showed it to those sitting around them, and bent it a bit in order to identify it as Luther's promised permission to write out his charges.[81]

The skirmishing in Jena gave a seemingly chivalrous introduction to an anticipated literary combat. But two days later, August 24, an unedifying scene took place in Orlamünde when Luther turned up there unexpectedly and asked to see the town council. What was he up to? Either he had not reflected sufficiently on what he would do or, angered by the crude letter of the Orlamünde town council handed him in Jena, he simply overturned his prior arrangements. At any rate, he hit on the unfortunate idea of making the council's letter a subject of discussion on the spot. Luther's appearance was too sudden. Most of the councilmen had to be summoned from their work in the fields. He declined their spontaneous invitation that he stay awhile and preach for them. Instead he was gruff with them, first because in the letter they had designated Karlstadt as their pastor, which was no longer the case since the recent decision of the elector's court. Besides, Karlstadt himself was present, and when he began to speak Luther demanded that he leave the room. In this tense atmosphere Luther himself raised the decisive question: "Where in Scripture can you prove that images should be abolished?" When the obvious answer came back, naming the prohibition of graven images in the Decalogue, Luther tried to clarify the difference between Christian images and idolatrous images, between possessing images and venerating them. "How can a crucifix on the wall harm me when I do not venerate it?" But Luther asked in vain. At that moment not only Karlstadt's legalistic interpretation of Scripture but also his mystical theology was aired in Luther's presence by the farmers of Orlamünde. In effect, they said, If the soul is to be emancipated from all legitimate creatures, how much more is it then handicapped "when it allows itself, bedecked and entwined, to be entertained by forbidden images"? A councilman, citing Jesus, claimed that like a bride for her bridegroom the soul must come forth naked and divested of all creatureliness. When asked for the scriptural reference, he gave up. For Luther this alleged proof for the abolition of images was too much. He sank into a chair and hid his face in his hands. When another councilman agreed that Luther was probably among the damned, the Reformer finally

81. WA 15:340 / 4ff. Cf. Barge, *Karlstadt*, 2:129–28 and n. 93.

broke off this hopeless exchange and, under a volley of abuses, took to the road. [82]

For Luther that day in Orlamünde was a bad one. But even if he had remained calm he could not have changed the minds of the peasants, who for more than a year had imbibed the unfermented arguments and the spirit of distrust toward Wittenberg which Karlstadt kept pouring out for them. After a valid settlement of the issue had failed, Duke John decided on September 18, 1524, to expel Karlstadt, and not only from the region of the upper Saale valley (as Luther had proposed) but from the entire electoral territory. At the same time, however, Karlstadt was assured that the duke would not hinder him from publishing against Luther. [83] Nearly three months passed before Luther learned where the banished Karlstadt had gone. In mid-December a messenger delivered him a letter from the preachers in Strassburg. They reported on the violent agitation Karlstadt had stirred up in their city during his brief stay in early October. [84] They requested Luther to clarify the grounds of controversy between himself and Karlstadt, enclosing with their letter five short tracts that Karlstadt had just published in Basel, the city to which he meanwhile had moved. Luther had long been waiting to see what would come of his guilder-backed challenge to Karlstadt in Jena. His immediate response was to send a hasty acknowledgment to the Strassburg pastors. Undoubtedly this kind of confusion being sown by Karlstadt was worrying him. The tracts were being read eagerly by the Strassburgers, and even the pastors thought that some of Karlstadt's arguments could be defended.

While the messenger from Strassburg waited a few days in Wittenberg, Luther had his own reply printed. It was addressed to the entire

82. WA 15:339 / 27–28; 341ff.; 345 / 22–23, 28–29; 346 / 5ff.; 347 / 8ff. *Against the Heavenly Prophets* . . . , WA 18:83–84. [*LW* 40:100–101.] *Letter to the Christians in Strassburg,* WA 15:25ff. It is amusing to learn first-hand from one of the Orlamünders about a mystical parable that Karlstadt once read in a work by John Staupitz (the pamphlet *Libellus de Executione Aeternae Praedestinationis* [1517]) and apparently used in sermons. (Cf. Scheurl's German translation of this *Libellus* in Knaake, *Johannes von Staupitzens sämtliche Werke* [Potsdam, 1867], 1:161.) The work of Staupitz was decisive in Karlstadt's switch from Thomas Aquinas to Augustine; cf. E. Kähler, *Karlstadt und Augustin* (Halle, 1952), 4ff. D. C. Steinmetz, *Misericordia Dei: The Theology of Johannes von Staupitz in Its Late Medieval Setting* (Leiden, 1968), 163, 171ff.

83. Luther's conversation with Prince John Frederick, in late August 1524. Cf. Luther's letters to Spalatin of September 13, and to the prince, September 22; WA Br 3:346 / 21ff.; 353. His instruction for Wolfgang Stein, early September, WA Br 3:343; and his report of the case in *Against the Heavenly Prophets* . . . WA 18:86 / 7ff.; 99 / 10ff. The order for expulsion, in draft, is in Hase, "Karlstadt," no. 29, in the original (with the permission to write added) in Karlstadt's tract *Ursachen, derhalben Andres Carolstatt . . . vertreiben.* See Müller, *Luther und Karlstadt,* 174ff. WA 15:328ff.

84. Letter of November 23, 1524, WA Br 3:381ff.

Strassburg congregation.[85] Cast in the vein of a New Testament epistle, Luther's reply indicated at once that he intended to rise above all things personal and petty. He urged the Strassburgers, "Ask your evangelists, my dear sirs and brothers, to turn you away from Luther and Karlstadt and direct you always to Christ." He reminded them that in dealing with disputed issues there is but one valid position from which they should judge: Does that which someone is teaching make us Christians, or does it not?[86] There they have a standard for distinguishing the important from the unimportant; the superficial from the truly evangelical. So much for questions concerning the mass and images. On the problem of the sacrament, Luther included only a brief word in his open letter, yet that word should establish trust between himself and the Strassburgers: He shared their doubts.

> I confess that if Dr. Karlstadt, or anyone else, could have convinced me five years ago that only bread and wine were in the sacrament he would have done me a great service. At that time I suffered such severe conflicts and inner strife and torment that I gladly would have been delivered from them. I realize that at this point I could have given the papacy the biggest blow. . . . But I am captive and cannot free myself. The text is too powerfully present and will not allow itself to be torn from its meaning by mere verbiage. Even if someone during these days might try more persuasively to prove that only bread and wine are present, it would not be necessary that he attack me in bitter spirit, which I unfortunately am inclined to do, if I assess the nature of the Old Adam in me correctly. But the way Dr. Karlstadt carries on this question affects me so little that my position is only fortified the more by him.[87]

Yet in spite of this certainty, Luther still was not proof against the wiles of temptation. He realized that it would be the devil's delight to separate people from the simple essentials of faith. In that case it is even better to pluck the thorn from despair by abstaining from the Lord's Supper. "Yes, even if you don't receive the sacrament, you can yet be saved through the Word and faith."[88]

While Luther's open letter to the Strassburgers was an intentionally pastoral word, it cleared the way for his full-scale debate with Karlstadt,

---

85. *Letter to the Christians in Strassburg in Opposition to the Fanatic Spirit* (1524), WA 15:391–97. [WA 40:(61), 65–71.] This little tract was posted in Wittenberg on the same day, or one following, along with a letter dated December 17 to Katharina Zell, wife of the Strassburg preacher Matthew Zell (WA Br 3:405–6). [*LW* 49:94–96.]

86. WA 15:396 / 16–17; 394 / 4–5. [*LW* 40:70, 67.]

87. WA 15:394 / 12ff.; 396 / 12–13. [*LW* 40:68.]

88. WA 15:396 / 12–13. [*LW* 40:70.]

for which he presently stated his position in a resounding monograph, *Against the Heavenly Prophets in the Matter of Images and Sacraments*. Published in two parts, the first came out in December 1524, the second in January 1525. Luther is pained that he must now face an opponent sprung from his own camp. "As God and our dear Lord Jesus Christ govern, there has been a change in the weather. I had almost relaxed and thought the matter was finished, but now it suddenly breaks out anew. . . . Doctor Andreas Karlstadt has deserted us, and on top of that he has become our worst enemy." The war against Satan has entered a new phase. Unable to suppress the gospel by force, Satan is now bent on doing so by an insidious interpretation of the Holy Scriptures.[89] Luther is bitterly disappointed with Karlstadt in a personal way. Years earlier someone had wagered that Karlstadt would not long adhere to his own teaching. "Karlstadt is an unstable person and has never stuck to one thing. I didn't want to believe it then, but now I see it with my own eyes!"[90]

This is an authentic polemical document, born in the heat of conflict and reporting in detail on Karlstadt's behavior in Orlamünde and on Luther's visit there. It refutes Karlstadt's charges against the princes of Saxony as well as against Luther. It attacks Karlstadt's weak sides, his ridiculous laying aside of the title of doctor and his playing up to the laity,[91] as well as his unclear gossipy style. Despite its polemics, this book amounts to one of the most important differentiations in intellectual history which Luther produced. Luther's debate turns not on a sequence of separate points but on the issue as a whole: on the true renewal of the church. False reformers tackle only external matters; none of them is concerned with faith and a good conscience before God.[92] In other words, the clash is over law and freedom.

Examples of this accompany the questions Luther treats in part one, "Images and the Outward Forms of the Mass." He is not satisfied simply to repeat his earlier thesis: That the use—certainly not the veneration—of images lies in the realm of freedom. The more eagerly then, Luther seeks to crack open the concept of law as such, so as to bring out the hidden kernel of freedom in every sensible law. Here the digging for his lectures[93] in the Old Testament book of the law, as well as the application of his

89. *WA* 18:62 / 1ff. [*LW* 40:79.]

90. *WA* 18:115 / 22ff. [*LW* 40:133.]

91. Since March 1523 Karlstadt described himself on the title page of his publications as a "new layman." *WA* 18:100, n. 6.

92. *WA* 18:63 / 9–10. [*LW* 40:80.]

93. See below, pp. 241ff.

seemingly quite different concept on the problem of governmental authority,[94] stand him in good stead. It is always the same simple distinctions that call for attention. Consider the Old Testament prohibition of images. It is not applicable on two grounds. First (and here Luther's historical intuition is sounder than his exegesis), because the prohibition concerns not the mere making of images but the idolatry that accompanies it; in short this prohibition presupposes an entirely different religious and historical situation. Second, this particular part of the Mosaic code is not binding on the Christian.[95] All external questions are dated. For Christians the dread of idolatrous worship is as much a thing of the past as that of pagan temples or of meat offered to idols (1 Cor. 8). These external idols are no longer a temptation to the Christian. The ceremonial parts of the Mosaic law are simply historical, Jewish precepts, the *Sachsenspiegel* [the Jewish equivalent of the old Saxon code of law] as Luther aptly expressed it. As Christians we are obliged only by those requirements of the law which apply to everyone and are valid for all times, for example, "To honor parents, not to murder, not to commit adultery, to serve God, and so on." Luther calls these "natural" because they embrace an undeniable inner evidence, without which such commandments would convince no one. "Were it not naturally written in the heart, one would have to teach and preach the law for a long time before it became a concern of the conscience." Our hearts are so blinded by the devil "that they do not always feel this law. Therefore one must preach the law and impress it on the minds of the people until God assists and enlightens them, so that they feel in their hearts what the Word says."

Just as he outlined the conduct of the Christian in the context of a general political ethic, so Luther regarded the authentic commandments of God as universal, as rooted in the condition of man as creature, and thus forever binding. Whatever has been added from the Mosaic law served its purpose at times when faith in God and also the common life were threatened by certain forces, but now this law is "free, null, and void."[96] The same thing pertains also to the ceremonial part of the otherwise general law of God so pointedly formulated in the Decalogue, when it prohibits images and demands sabbath observance. To have images and pictures is not only permissible but also highly desirable, and indeed pictures of all sorts that delight us with created things such as frogs and snails, but fore-

---

94. See above, pp. 112ff.
95. WA 18:69 / 1ff.; 75 / 11ff. [*LW* 40:86, 92.]
96. WA 18:80 / 35ff.; 81 / 7ff. [*LW* 40:98, n. 20; 97.]

most with biblical scenes. "Would to God that I could persuade the rich and mighty that they would permit the whole Bible to be painted on houses, on the inside and outside, so that all can see it. That would be a Christian work." Such pictures are a sermon for the eyes, and besides, without trying, we are always seeing pictures. "When I hear of Christ, an image of a man hanging on a cross takes form in my heart, just as the reflection of my face naturally appears in the water when I look into it. If it is not sin but good to have the image of Christ in my heart, why should it be sin to have it in my eyes?"[97] So it is that again and again Luther bases his argument on the "natural." Whatever is natural in a good sense cannot really be forbidden. Of course, images in the churches are a temptation to some people, but Luther did not endorse an orderly removal of them. Indeed, he had not raised a finger to approve such action. For him all that mattered was to remove faith in images from the hearts of people.[98]

The same freedom applied to the upheaval created by Karlstadt over the bread and wine at the Lord's Supper. Luther pointed out that both the pope and Karlstadt are misleading the people in the same legalistic manner: the pope, by demanding the elevation of the host; Karlstadt, by forbidding it. "Here Christ is driven away by both parties. One pushes him out the front door, the other drives him out the back; one errs on the left, the other on the right, and neither remains on the path of true freedom." Although Luther had intended to do away with the elevation of the Host, he now decided not to do so—"to defy for a while the fanatic spirit."[99] Only in 1542, after Karlstadt's death, was the practice of elevating the Host discontinued in Wittenberg. This was a noteworthy sign of freedom directed against liturgical as well as antiliturgical legalism.

Part two of Luther's polemic against the "heavenly prophets" deals with issues over doctrines of the Lord's Supper. Karlstadt's absurd exegesis of the words of institution had given Luther an easy point of attack. Karlstadt claimed that the phrase "This is my body" (*touto esti to soma mou*) could not be contextually part of the preceding one ("take and eat") because, as he insisted, the two phrases are separated by a period and a capital letter. Besides, the neuter *touto* could not modify the masculine *artos* (bread). Christ, according to Karlstadt, was thus initiating a new idea and intended *touto* (this is my body) to refer to himself [and not to the bread]. These

97. WA 18:83 / 3ff.; 9ff. [LW 40:99–100.]
98. WA 18:68 / 4ff., 17ff.; 72 / 30ff. [LW 40:88, 92.]
99. WA 18:111 / 13ff., 29ff.; 116 / 1ff. [LW 40:129, 133.]

notions were spun out by Karlstadt in the form of a popular dialogue in which he was repeatedly applauded by one of the participants. Luther seized on this fanciful performance, especially on "dear Tuto," with his own superior linguistic knowledge and held it under the magnifying glass of his scorn.[100]

Luther did not stop there. He knew all too well the misgivings about the Lord's Supper to let the case rest simply on arguments of grammar. At issue was the fact that in the sacrament the body and blood of Christ are actually given. And more powerfully than any grammarian, the words of institution themselves in the Gospels and in Paul (1 Cor. 11:24–25) say so, as well as the Pauline commentary: "'The cup of blessing which we bless, is it not a participation in the blood of Christ? The bread which we break, is it not a participation in the body of Christ?' (1 Cor. 10:16). This verse has been the life-giving medicine of my heart in my trials concerning this sacrament."[101] At issue is an unworthy eating and drinking, not an unworthy remembrance (1 Cor. 11:27ff.).[102] What gives Luther certainty is not a cheap victory over Karlstadt but the observation that the words of the text stand firm and mutually reinforce each other. If one is not ready to take them as they are, one is tempted to twist them with allegorical subtleties, as Karlstadt did with his strange grammatical attempts. But where does allegory—this spiritual juggling act—land you? Fantasizing produces no meaningful assertions: "I might make out of the legendary Dietrich of Bern, Christ; out of the giant with whom he fought, the devil; out of the dwarf, humility; out of his prisons, the death of Christ."[103]

The conflict with Karlstadt gave a marked impetus to Luther's understanding of the Scriptures as well as to his teaching on the sacraments. He became sharper than before in recognizing the bottomlessness of allegorical exegesis so that in the future he became more bent than ever on avoiding it. Besides, in his clarified understanding of the Scriptures he found the unshakable foundation of his concept of the Lord's Supper. As he wrote to the Strassburgers, "The text is too powerfully present and will not allow itself to be torn from its meaning by mere verbiage."[104]

Although from now on he defends his realistic understanding of the sacrament with full certainty, unassailed by any doubt, Luther does not

100. WA 18:144 / 3–159 / 7. [LW 40:198–214.]

101. WA 18:164 / 31ff.; 166 / 34–35. [LW 40:175, 177.]

102. WA 18:172 / 24ff. [LW 40:182.]

103. WA 18:180 / 8; 178 / 8ff. Cf. also the letters of Gattenhofen to Hochmeister Albrecht, February 9, 1524. WA Br 3:419, n. 5. [LW 40:188. Dietrich of Bern, legendary name for Theodoric the Great (A.D. 454–526).]

104. See above, pp. 167–68. [LW 40:68.]

for a moment overstep the boundary he drew for the material elements in the sacrament. Not the enjoyment of the sacramental elements but faith in the Word accompanying the elements vouchsafes the forgiveness of sins. "Whoever has a bad conscience from his sins should go to the sacrament and obtain comfort, not because of the bread and wine, not because of the body and blood of Christ, but because of the Word which in the sacrament offers, presents, and gives the body and blood of Christ, given and shed for me." Indeed, even if Karlstadt's claim were right and there were only bread and wine in the Lord's Supper, "as long as the words, 'Take, eat, this is my body given for you,' etc., are there, there is forgiveness of sins." The Lord's Supper would then be not otherwise than baptism, where only ordinary water is present. "But since the Word of God, which forgives sin, is connected with it, we readily say with Paul that baptism is a bath of regeneration and renewal. Everything depends on the Word." Faith in the Word is essential on the part of each individual. The Word imparts the readily available forgiveness. "For while the act (Jesus' death on the cross) has taken place, as long as I have not appropriated it, it is as if it had not taken place for me."[105]

Luther could hardly have expressed himself more clearly as to where salvation lies in the sacrament than in relinquishing hypothetically the booty he had wrested from Karlstadt and in thus looking equally at two so different sacraments as the Lord's Supper and baptism: as though in one there were "only bread and wine," and in the other "only water." Of course, Luther had not wrestled for the booty only to give it up again. Yet by airing this consideration he let go to get a better grip on the main point: Everything depends on the affirming Word, and on trusting in it. In the same breath in which Luther pronounces his full sacramental realism with renewed conviction, he also confesses with equal decisiveness to the personal reception of salvation hidden in the sacrament. For Luther there is no such thing as a self-sufficient (*opus operatum*) efficacy of the sacrament; its only efficacy is by faith in the word of forgiveness. From this position Luther kept his distance from two opposite sides: from the symbolism as represented by Karlstadt and later Zwingli, and from the Roman Catholic thinking about the sacrament.

The two parts of *Against the Heavenly Prophets* are held together by infrequent references to what comprises the common denominator of the various currents of Karlstadt's thought—his spiritual mysticism. For

105. WA 18:204 / 5ff., 15ff.; 205 / 18–19 [LW 40:214, 215.]

the most part Luther contents himself with mockingly adducing a number of graphic terms typical of mysticism, such as refinement, astonishment, examination, boredom, the seven stages of sprinkling, and so on. What is more, he sees in this mysticism the common root of Müntzer's mode of thinking as well as Karlstadt's. The hostility toward images, the puritanical attitude toward worship, the legalistic and ascetic life-style, and the symbolical rationalization of teaching on the sacraments have all sprung from this root. These are human attempts to spiritualize people's relations to God, attempts that necessarily accentuate external signs, while before God all things external are beside the point and only the inward contents count. And this inwardness we cannot achieve on our own; God must grant it. However, it comes to us from him, from without, and we are enabled to receive it only by faith. By contrast, the heavenly prophets turn God's human dealings upside down. "What God has ordered to be of an inward faith and spirit they turn into a human work. Again, what God has ordered to be external word and signs and works they turn into an inward spirit."[106] Luther likes to point out that this reversal of the external and internal is not simply a willful tampering with an order God has set for his dealings with people, but also a termination of these dealings as such. God alone can take the initiative. We cannot move him to do so by our own mystical meditation. God himself must open our inner life, doing so from without by means of his Word which lays hold of us. Whatever therefore matters is not the visible signs of the spirituality we have already achieved but our faith which responds to God with a whole heart.

At these deep levels of opposition Luther was concerned no longer about the argument with Karlstadt but with someone else: "Dr. Karlstadt does not matter that much to me. I keep my eye not on him but on the one who has possessed him and speaks through him."[107] This awareness of the unseen opponent enables Luther to remove the conflict completely from the person of Karlstadt.

At Mühlhausen, meanwhile, Thomas Müntzer's latest activities were amply demonstrating an affinity to Karlstadt's Old Testament legalism and its attendant iconoclasm, all of which were linked to designs for a violent revolution. Besides, in Mühlhausen Müntzer found some things about which he had dreamed already accomplished. Like a forerunner, Heinrich Pfeiffer, a native of Mühlhausen and a former monk, had brought about an

106. WA 18:139 / 3ff.; 171 / 32ff.; 175 / 9–10. [LW 40:148ff., 181ff., 185.]
107. WA 18:139 / 9–10. [LW 40:149.]

upheaval there even before Müntzer commenced his own activities in not too distant Allstedt. It turned out that Müntzer and Pfeiffer were kindred spirits. Pfeiffer's role as agitator surfaced on a Sunday afternoon in February 1523. As the procession around St. Mary's Church ended with the customary enjoyment of the newly brewed beer, Pfeiffer in civilian attire mounted the high stone by the church entrance from which the beer hawker had just praised his product. Pfeiffer began, "Listen to me. I want to tell you about another kind of beer." After enlarging on the gospel for the day, he wound up with an intemperate attack on the clergy and the monks. The next day, in response to a summons, Pfeiffer appeared before the city council with so large a following that the councilmen detained him only briefly and allowed him to continue preaching. On April 1, he gave evidence of consolidating his forces. From the pulpit he challenged the congregation, shouting, "Whoever is ready to side with the gospel raise a finger!" Everyone responded. The men fetched their weapons. In the church square they elected eight spokesmen to present the people's case to the council. It was hardly surprising that Pfeiffer drew such a response. Mühlhausen at that time was an imperial city with twice as many inhabitants as Dresden and Leipzig, but its most flourishing times were already past. Some 45 percent of its inhabitants owned no property and thus had no influence on the city government.[108] But things began to change. After several riots against clergy and the cloisters (the houses and churches of the well-propertied Teutonic Knights) certain modest reforms were introduced. The agreement with the city council on July 3, 1523, included a representative principle: Eight men, two from each of the city's four quarters, were permitted to participate in the city government. The free preaching of the gospel was also vouchsafed. Saxony's Duke George, however, as lord protector of Mühlhausen, in August pressed the city government to expel Pfeiffer and another of the preachers. Yet Pfeiffer was permitted to return by December. Meanwhile, Saxony's good-natured Duke John, having difficulty in forming a clear judgment on Müntzer, now interceded also for Pfeiffer.[109]

108. G. Franz, *Der deutsche Bauernkrieg*, 4th ed. (Darmstadt, 1956), 249–50. Fuchs, ed., *Akten Bauernkrieg*, 2:xxv.

109. Fuchs, ed., *Akten Bauernkrieg*, vol. 2, no. 1087 (February 1, 1523, first appearance of Pfeiffer); no. 1092, 3 (agreement, early July); no. 1099 (banishment); no. 1101, n.2 (November 10, intercession). A background account of these developments is in the *Chronik der Stadt Mühlhausen in Thüringen*, ed. R. Jordan (Mühlhausen, 1900), 1:166ff. Excerpts are in O. H. Brandt, *Thomas Müntzer: Sein Leben und seine Schriften* (Jena, 1933), 85ff. (includes the *Rezess* [agreement] of July 3, pp. 88ff.). See also G. Franz, ed., *Akten Bauernkrieg*, vol. 1/2, *Rezess* no. 161. Literature listed in K. Schlottenloher, *Bibliographie des deutschen Geschichte im Zeitalter der Glaubensspaltung, 1517–1585* (Leipzig, 1933ff.), 2:604–5; 5:359. Also O. Merx, *Thomas Müntzer und Heinrich Pfeiffer, 1523–1525*, pt. 1 (Göttingen, 1889). J. Zimmermann, *Thomas Müntzer* (Berlin, 1925), 123ff. W. Elliger, *Thomas Müntzer: Leben und Werk* (Göttingen, 1975), 45ff. [See also Gritsch, *Reformer Without a Church*, and G. Rupp, *Patterns of Reformation*, pt. 3, chap. 16, pp. 221ff.]

During the Christmas season 1523–24 and the following months, scenes in Mühlhausen unfolded much like those two years earlier in Wittenberg and Eilenburg. Meanwhile Pfeiffer had learned from Karlstadt to recognize conflict against images as the most important divine commandment of the hour. Indeed, it was the hour—as Pfeiffer let Müntzer tell him—when the kingdom of God was at the door. In August 1524, Pfeiffer joyfully welcomed Müntzer to Mühlhausen. On September 19 a small incident triggered an explosion. Images (pictures and statues) as well as altar vessels were either destroyed or stolen. The citizenry was split, but no one dared stop the well-organized followers of Müntzer and Pfeiffer. The presidium of mayors and part of the city council fled. The longed-for moment to raise up God's congregation in Mühlhausen seemed to have come. Yet for Müntzer this was just the prelude to greater things. Therefore his immediate concern that these developments—including the installation of a new city council, which had been decided upon—be not misinterpreted outside Mühlhausen. His manifesto to the congregation, dated September 22, advised that all mischief of which the former city council was guilty be published and made known to the world. Then, he reasoned, everywhere people will say, "See how much patience these pious people have practiced for too long," and people will apply Deut. 4:5ff. to the residents of Mühlhausen: "Surely this great nation is a wise and understanding people. For what great nation is there . . . a people ready to venture with God." The refugee councilmen would then find it impossible to be accepted in any other city. "For the common man, praise God, is open to the truth almost everywhere." The linen-weavers guild threw its support to Müntzer and added a statement of its own to the two fugitive mayors. In it the weavers demanded, in an amendment to the manifesto, a new city council according to the command of God and the Holy Scriptures.[110] This propaganda campaign was launched with an eleven-article statement that provided for the installation of the new council and expressed Müntzer's principle of separating the evil and the good—those outside and those within—lest the community become all one mixed loaf, for the guilty are not simultaneously to sit as judges. The new council was to be installed without delay and to begin at once to receive its pay, lest its members fall into temptation and extort other people. The members of the old city council were warned that the evidence of all their mischief over the past twenty years was being collected and would be made public.

110. Müntzer, *Schriften*, no. 70:448 / 12ff., 23. Fuchs, ed., *Akten Bauernkrieg*, vol. 2, no. 1129.

Besides, if the ousted council should try to hinder the new one, the latter would take appropriate countermeasures. Even more than the individual proposals the spirit of Müntzer was conveyed by the adventurous quotations from Scripture as well as the tone of the document as a whole.

> For it is our common opinion and decision that all our work and business be carried out according to God's commandment and righteousness. . . . Far rather would we have God as our friend and men as our enemies than to have men our friends and God our enemy, for it is a fearful thing to fall into the hands of the living God.[111]

The eleven articles ran into stiff resistance among the peasants dwelling in the agricultural lands attached to the imperial city. The peasants' immediate reaction was to withhold their pledges of loyalty to the new council. Here it was—actually within a half-year of the full-blown Peasants' War—that the revolutionary procedure of the guilds still appeared to rural folk as an "unchristian insubordination."[112] That sort of reaction restored the ousted council's courage, and the council ordered the two agitating preachers out of the city. Pfeiffer—who apparently did not share Müntzer's faith in the power of the printed word and who had high hopes for Mühlhausen rather than for the world at large—made one last try, during a fire on September 26, to take the city by surprise. But he failed. The old council was on the alert and received swift support from a two-hundred-man contingent of peasants. Müntzer himself, as in Zwickau and Allstedt, took flight for a third time. He had indeed roused the townsfolk to the verge of rioting, but he lacked the final measure of boldness to carry out the plot.

Off Pfeiffer and Müntzer went to Nuremberg, where Müntzer showed how little he was cut out to be a revolutionary. While waiting for his polemical tracts to be published, he was urged by many to preach. Either Müntzer did not have the nerve to preach, or he was convinced that he should not. In any case, the Nuremberg city council was much relieved: "When the gentlemen learned of this decision, their ears began to ring, for why not be fond of good days?" Had Müntzer been so minded, he could have agitated and led the councilmen on a merry chase. Instead he pursued his literary battle, boasting, "With my words I shall make all my opponents so cowardly that they cannot deny it." His confidence in vic-

---

111. Fuchs, ed., *Akten Bauernkrieg*, vol. 2, no. 1128–29 (p. 47, n. 1, misses the meaning of art. 1). G. Franz, ed., *Akten Bauernkrieg*, vol. 1/2, no. 165; 492/9–10; 494/3ff. [Heb. 10:31.]

112. Merx, *Müntzer und Pfeiffer*, 83.

tory was boundless: "Where formerly I scolded them with arms, I shall now thunder over them with God from heaven."[113]

Müntzer went heavy on the thunder. The first of his Nuremberg tracts, *The False Faith Expressly Unmasked,* bore a motto from Jeremiah: "I have set you this day over nations and over kingdoms, to pluck up and break down, to destroy and to overthrow, to build and to plant. . . . I make you this day . . . an iron pillar . . . against . . . kings [and] princes [and] priests" (Jer. 1:10, 18). Müntzer had written two drafts of this tract while still in Allstedt. The milder version he had turned in at the time of his hearing in Weimar on August 1, 1524. The more extreme version he had given to his disciple Hans Hut, later an outstanding Anabaptist leader, to have it published in Nuremberg. This version was the beginning of his big program: An exposition of the Gospel of Luke, by means of which he intended "outrageously to unmask the poisonous damage that had penetrated so deeply."[114] The leading characters, Zechariah and Mary, in the first chapter (which he did not get beyond) became exemplary for his theme: "How unfaith is exposed among all the elect." They "have been shocked in the fear of God until faith, like a mustard seed, overcomes unfaith."[115] Only the elect have their experience of anxious unfaith. It is denied to the godless preacher of faith and "stealers of Scripture."[116] A new John the Baptist must come, "a preacher full of grace, who will have experienced faith everywhere through his own unfaith, for he must know how to understand an arch-unbeliever." The identity of this coming preacher, who "through a tested life . . . must have known the cross from his youth," was not left in doubt by the tone of his tract.[117]

If this "express unmasking" brought no new ideas but only a more blaring tone to Müntzer's debate with Luther, the next tract surpassed it in several ways. Müntzer no doubt had composed it in Mühlhausen and was now having it printed in Nuremberg. The sneering title, *A Highly Justified Apology Against the Spiritless, Soft-living Lump of Flesh at Wittenberg,* portrayed the opponent with desirable clarity. The dedication (to "The most illustrious, firstborn Prince and almighty Lord Jesus Christ,

---

113. To Christopher Meinhard, November / December 1524, Müntzer, *Schriften,* 450 / 14ff.; 449 / 17–18. G. Baring, "Hans Denk und Thomas Müntzer in Nürnberg, 1524," *ARG* 51 (1959): 154, dated after mid-December, but mid-November is also a possibility.

114. Müntzer, *Schriften,* 269 / 20ff.

115. Ibid., 271–72; 271 / 29ff.; 272 / 12ff.

116. Ibid., 303 / 11; 305 / 5; 307 / 26; 312 / 9; 314 / 11; 315 / 16.

117. Ibid., 296 / 31ff.; 309 / 1–2; cf. 300 / 16; 307 / 5ff., 17ff.; 308 / 23ff.

the gracious King of all kings, the brave Duke of all the faithful, my most gracious Lord") was a parody of Luther's letter to the princes of Saxony. What came forth from Müntzer was more than unbridled hatred, and its torrent seethed with venomous vituperation. As an antithesis to Luther's writing, the doctrinal contrasts between the two stood out more plainly than ever. Müntzer concentrated pointedly on the question of the law. In no way has Christ abrogated the law. The Wittenbergers may claim that he did, but Christ actually expounded and deepened the law. We should deal not according to its face but according to the spirit of the law. The authentic preacher is thus obliged to preach on the "seriousness of the law." It is then that the Holy Spirit himself, through his word, exposes the unfaith and the sin in human hearts. Whoever preaches only the gospel, "the most precious treasure of Christ's graciousness," "disgraces the Father along with the earnestness of the law," for God by his will alone leads to the goal through the terror of conscience. In the law which punishes there is at the same time also grace. "The graciousness of God ... is not dislodged through the suffering inflicted by the law, for it is a suffering that the elect do not choose to avoid." Whatever appears as God's wrath "arises out of the distorted fear which human beings have of God, for they are shocked by the immediacy of suffering and do not look beyond. If they did, they would see how, by means of his chastising, God leads the way through all torment to his eternity."[118]

While Müntzer left Nuremberg and headed south, Pfeiffer managed to reenter Mühlhausen by December 1524 and to stir up his followers to commit acts of violence. Early in the new year a bout of plundering and image-smashing caused the local cloisters to dispatch an excited protest direct to the imperial authorities in Esslingen. As the sense of alarm became general, the rulers of the countryside surrounding Mühlhausen, the dukes of Saxony, and Landgrave Philip of Hesse were named imperial commissioners and given the mandate—well in advance of any peasant uprising—that would make any intervention on their part legitimate.[119] By the end of February, Müntzer himself showed up in Mühlhausen again. Without delay he got a preaching position in the Church of Our Lady [St. Mary's] and lodging in the former headquarters of his enemies, that is, in the commander's quarters of the Teutonic Knights, who had meanwhile been expelled from the city.

118. Ibid., 322 / 11ff.; 328 / 10; 331 / 9–10; 330 / 8ff.
119. Fuchs, ed., *Akten Bauernkrieg*, vol. 2, nos. 1147, 1150, 1151, 1154, 1155, 1157, 1180. Brandt, *Thomas Müntzer*, 92ff. Franz, ed., *Akten Bauernkrieg*, vol. 1 / 2, no. 166.

Müntzer brought with him the first impressions of the Peasants' War. [The conflict had broken out in southwestern Germany.] In the Klettgau region, specifically in Griessen (southwest of the city of Schaffhausen on the Rhine), Müntzer had been active as a preacher for about two months. To the uprising there already in progress he added fuel to the fire with his article "How to Govern as the Basis of the Gospel." This issue loomed large in his conversations at that time with Oecolampadius in Basel. Müntzer's ideas also left traces in Waldshut, near Basel, where the Anabaptist leader Balthasar Hubmaier was active. However, Müntzer was neither a mentor nor a leader of the insurrection, and he apparently represented no basically new departures from the earlier ideas. Nevertheless, he tried to connect the uprising on the Upper Rhine with that in Mühlhausen. With his flair for propaganda, he tried to impress the Klettgau people with developments in Mühlhausen, where some of them were ready to go if paid, for Müntzer had shown them how much bigger the cannonballs in Mühlhausen were than those in Klettgau.[120]

At any rate, what Müntzer himself had experienced on the Upper Rhine gave wings to his designs. He returned to Mühlhausen convinced that the hour had come for a breakthrough. By mid-March the old city council, which until then had offered tough resistance, was ousted by a town meeting held in Müntzer's church, and a new council was installed. This council comprised the elect, had dictatorial powers, and was self-perpetuating. The clever city magistrate, seeking to remain in office, claimed loftily, "He has put down the mighty from their thrones and exalted those of low degree. What a wonderful God is he!"[121] Now Müntzer had an important imperial city and its environs as a stage for applying on a grand scale the plans he had spun in Allstedt. He was in a position to resurrect his former secret society and to brace himself with a respectable military force in anticipation of the coming showdown. Luther had his own word for it, warning, "In Mühlhausen Müntzer is king and emperor, not just the teacher."[122] In fact, Müntzer had reached the point where,

---

120. Müntzer's own data, presented during the hearing of May 16, 1525, after his arrest. Müntzer, *Schriften*, 544ff., 549. See Oecolampadius's letter to Pirkheimer, September 21, 1525, and February 1527, as printed in E. Staehelin, *Briefe und Akten zum Leben Oekolampads*, QFRG 19 (Leipzig, 1934), 1:389ff.; 2:21–22. O. Schiff, "Thomas Müntzer und die Bauernbewegung am Oberrhein," *HZ* 110 (1913): 67ff. To the reports in H. Bullinger's work, *Der Widertoufferen Ursprung* ... (1560), cf. H. Fast, *Heinrich Bullinger und die Täufer*, SMGV 7 (Weierhof, 1959), 99–100. On the departure from Mühlhausen, see Merx, *Müntzer und Pfeiffer*, 103ff. [Rupp, *Patterns of Reformation*, 231–35.]

121. Brandt, *Thomas Müntzer*, 97–98.

122. To Amsdorf, April 1525, *WA* Br 3:472 / 7.

now with Pfeiffer, he was able to apply what he had long been teaching and turn it into political action.

[This part of the story resumes with Luther and the Peasants' War (below, Chapter 14). Many of the issues were confronting Luther during these years. As varied as the continuing polemics with Roman Catholic theologians, the nurture of the Christian life amid the new-found freedom in the gospel, the evangelical exposition of Scripture from pulpit and lectern, the ordering of common concerns in Wittenberg, the interventions of imperial politics, the turn of events in Prussia and eastern Germany, the encounter with Erasmus over the will—these and other matters demanded Luther's attention while the social and spiritual ferment led by Müntzer and others was coming to a head. Reformation in the early 1520s disclosed its many-sided character in a collection of challenges, not the least of which was in the realm of accepted Roman theology confronting the evangelical advance, an encounter to which we turn next.]

7

Justification and Hermeneutics: The Disputation with Latomus

In the search for a concise presentation embracing the essence of Luther's theology in the early 1520s, there is nothing comparable to his response to the Louvain theologian James Latomus. We have already noted in broad outline how the necessity of a reply was high on his Wartburg agenda.[1] Now we need to trace the effects of this exercise on the development of Luther's thought. Nowhere else, whether earlier or later (and at most in the concise form of disputation theses), has Luther had to grapple with the central themes of traditional theology in such concentrated form. His other controversial writings dealt mainly with limited theological questions, important in their own right, to be sure, or with the fundamentals and manifestations of church life. Besides, he was to an ever-increasing extent being forced to cope with opponents who were not yet on his horizon during the years of his breakthrough, including revolutionaries of a spiritualist stamp, among them, humanists, Zwinglians, and others. Even in the matter of interpreting the Scriptures, opportunity for debate with the scholastic viewpoints was confined to specific textual references, without providing any inclusive context.

An exception arose with the condemnation pronounced on Luther by the Louvain faculty (1520), and its elaboration against specific sentences in Luther's writings by [their spokesman] Latomus.[2] Latomus's attack singled out basic theses and contexts in Luther's earlier writings, all of which had to do with justification. Luther's response was initially in the form of extended exegesis, not in abstract dogmatic statements. At issue was not the immanent conclusiveness of a system but a demonstration of the truth as drawn from the biblical message. Yet it is precisely here, in *Anti-*

---

1. *Rationis Latomianae confutatio* (1521), WA 8:43ff. See above, pp. 8ff. [*LW* 32:133ff. This *LW* translation from the Latin original at times varies from Bornkamm's German translation from the same source. In most cases the *LW* translation is followed here.]

2. *Articulorum doctrinae Fratris Martini Lutheri per theologos lovanienses damnatorum ratio* (Antwerp, 1521).

latomus, as Melanchthon called this treatise,[3] that the two decisive impulses which with Luther brought about a revolution in theology are contained: a new understanding of justification as the all-inclusive theme of the Christian faith, on the one hand, and a new understanding of the Bible as the comprehensive corroboration of justification, on the other.

As with many a dispute, Latomus had attacked Luther's position on justification not in terms of its substance but in terms of its consequences. According to Luther's statements on sin—as Latomus understood him—God requires the impossible from man. Then even every good work is tainted and the saints themselves are sinners. Latomus did not deny that in every person after baptism a weakness or inclination to sin remains, a punishment of sorts for previous sin, and for the sin generally that pervades humanity as a curse, just as evil begets evil. Yet this, Latomus maintained, is not sin in the true sense of the word, "for he in whom evil desire and its appetites are present commits sin only when he consents to engage in a forbidden act."[4] Luther admitted that his controversy with Latomus could look like a battle of words inasmuch as for both of them an evil residue remains after baptism and deserves condemnation whether called sin or punishment.[5] This differentiation, however, is not thereby seen as a matter of indifference, especially when one is made aware of the dimension within which theological discourse necessarily takes place. "Thus we [pretend] to know [so much] about the fearful and eternal Majesty. We dispute about him as if we were arguing about an ordinary man." Yet why, on the contrary, do the saints tremble before his divine judgment and perish as if they do not know Christ as their protector? "The greatness of the refuge indicates well enough how great is the sin."[6] "No man can ever discover or comprehend his wickedness, since it is infinite and eternal. On the other hand, you will then discover that the work of God accom-

3. On the strong influence of this writing on Melanchthon's *Loci,* cf. W. Maurer, *Der junge Melanchthon zwischen Humanismus und Reformation,* vol. 2: *Der Theologe* (Göttingen, 1969), passim. He lists (pp. 377ff.) the changes Melanchthon made in his own manuscript after reading Luther's treatise against Latomus.

4. From the work by Latomus, cited by E. Iserloh, "Gratia und Donum: Rechtfertigung und Heiligung nach Luthers Schrift, 'Wider den Löwener Theologen Latomus'" (1521), in *Studien zur Geschichte und Theologie der Reformation: Festschrift E. Bizer* (Neukirchen-Vluyn, 1969), 145. For more on the position of Latomus according to his writings, see *Ratio* (1521) (above, p. 8, n. 29) and his *Responsio ad Lutherum* (1525), in R. Hermann, "Zur Kontroverse zwischen Luther und Latomus," in *Luther und Melanchthon,* Papers from the Zweiten internationalen Lutherforscherkongresses, Münster, 1960, ed. V. Vajta (Göttingen, 1961), 104ff.

5. *WA* 8:112 / 16ff. [*LW* 32:236.]

6. *WA* 8:115 / 21–22, 17–18. [*LW* 32:241, 240.]

plished for you in Christ is boundless in that he has foreordained such powerful grace for you in Christ."[7] Sin in its full power versus the glory of that grace freeing us from sin appear as two sides of the same coin.

All human attempts to treat sin and punishment as mere evil, like a boil or a fever, contradict the sense of the divine commandments. Natural suffering and privation lie outside the realm of our will and guilt. "Commandments have to do with sins and the things that make us subject to punishment."[8] Indeed, Luther doubts whether the customary use of language, which regards sin as specific deeds, corresponds with the biblical meaning. "To me [Scripture] seems almost always to refer to the radical ferment that bears fruit in evil deeds and words."[9] One cannot add up a man's sin according to deeds done or errors committed; sin is an inclusive term. This is the Pauline concept: to be a slave to sin (Rom. 6:17; 7:25). "Servitude is not the name of a work but the name of a state that includes all the strivings of the entire life."[10] But this also applies to the person of whom Paul says, "In spirit I serve the law of God." "The righteous serve God absolutely, for that has to do with the person." On the contrary, whoever—even on the basis of help received through grace—claims to be partly free from sin or regards certain deeds as substantially good is a hypocrite, and "hypocrites serve him only with the flesh, because they do so only with works, not with faith from the heart." Two things Luther does not deny. One is that deeds of nonbelievers can be useful, for they themselves are "useful creatures of God" through whom he can do good. The other is that the justified can sin again; indeed, "the sins of the righteous are truly evil and harmful."[11] The decisive criterion for standing in the presence of God is whether people know themselves to be completely dependent on divine forgiveness, or whether, in part, they charge their sin to the account of natural weakness. Latomus, thus judging the residue of postbaptismal sin in Christians, even in saints, "sets aside forgiving mercy and claims that according to nature sin is no longer present."[12] Faith in the holy God is indivisible and will not have itself combined with a remnant of self-righteousness.

Likewise, the salvation God offers the believer in Christ is indivisible. No part of human life is exempt from the need for forgiveness, yet forgive-

---

7. *WA* 8:115 / 4–5. [*LW* 32:240.]
8. *WA* 8:96 / 39ff. [*LW* 32:214.]
9. *WA* 8:104 / 4ff. [*LW* 32:224.]
10. *WA* 8:125 / 38. [*LW* 32:256.]
11. *WA* 8:124 / 35; 125 / 40ff. [*LW* 32:254, 256.]
12. *WA* 8:93 / 15–16. [*LW* 32:209.]

ness itself embraces the entire human being and in a new sense makes him a person in the presence of God. "What, then, are we sinners? No, rather we are justified, but we are justified by grace. Righteousness is situated not in those qualitative forms but in the mercy of God."[13] Here Luther is operating on two sides. On the one, toward Latomus, he emphasized that in baptized people, even at their best, sin hangs on, but "because they have faith and live under the sway of mercy, the sin is already forgiven and is constantly being put to death in them." The miracle of divine forgiveness lies in that "God looks on you as though you were without sin. All you must do is continue to put to death what he has already condemned and virtually vanquished. On the other side, Luther defines two terms. Mercy means that God draws a person into putting sin to death, and faith means that a person desires to be thus drawn. Therefore, forgiveness and repentance are inseparable parts of Christ's proclamation. They are the same event under a twofold point of view. "Repent, for the kingdom of heaven is at hand"—this is not a description of a human and divine action, but it describes an inseparable dealing of God both upon and within a person. Upon a person: thereby that he is placed under God's lordship, "as is accomplished by forgiving grace." Within a person: thereby that he changes his way of life, "as is done by faith in purging away sin."[14]   Luther's *Antilatomus* describes this twofold event by distinguishing between the grace and the gift of God. "Grace" means a change in a person's situation toward God, so that grace really reaches the person from without, from God's point of view. Grace is God's favor as expressed toward the sinner. "Gift" means the change in a person as accomplished by grace, the inward event in faith and in the attendant overcoming of sin which faith brings about.[15] It is that which the gospel calls "righteous-

13. "In formis illis qualitatum"; cf. the following in WA 8:92 / 38–93 / 12. [LW 32:208.] On this subject, R. Hermann, *Luthers These "Gerecht und Sünder zugleich": Eine systematische Studie* (Gütersloh, 1930; reprint, Darmstadt and Gütersloh, 1960), 49ff., 78ff. Also W. Joest, *Gesetz und Freiheit: Das Problem des tertius usus legis bei Luther und die neutestamentliche Paranaise* (Göttingen, 1951), 82ff.

14. WA 8:109 / 11–22. [LW 32:231–32. Alternate.]

15. Luther also employs this differentiation later in the catalog of concepts as he explains them in his preface to Romans in the German translation of the New Testament. (See above, p. 83.) [WA DB 7:10 / 6ff. LW 35:366ff.] This passage provides a good commentary on Luther's elaborations in his work against Latomus. "Between grace and gift there is a difference. Grace actually means God's favor, or the good will that in himself he bears toward us, by which he is disposed to give us in Christ and to pour into us the Holy Spirit with his gifts. [This is clear from chapter 5, where Paul speaks of "the grace and gift in Christ," etc.] The gift and the spirit increase in us every day, but they are not yet perfect since there remain in us the evil desires and sins that war against the Spirit. . . . Nevertheless grace does so much that we are accounted completely righteous before God, for this grace is not divided or parceled out, as are other gifts, but takes us completely into favor for the sake of Christ our Intercessor and Mediator. And because of this, the gifts are begun in us." WA DB 7:8 / 10–22. *Martin Luthers Vorreden zur Bibel*, ed. H. Bornkamm (Hamburg, 1967), 147.

ness." It is not only the relationship to God that has been changed by his favor, but also the renewal [in us] which the work of the Holy Spirit has brought about through faith.

> The gospel preaches and teaches two things, namely, the righteousness and the grace of God. Through righteousness the gospel heals the corrupted nature, that righteousness which is God's gift, namely, faith in Christ. . . . And this righteousness which constitutes the opposite to sin is understood in Scripture as the deepest root, whose fruit is good works. . . . Grace I take to mean in the strict sense—the way it must be understood—as God's favor, not as an attribute of the soul, as our more recent theologians have taught. This grace finally brings about authentically the peace of heart whereby people, healed from their corruption, feel that they have a gracious God.

Luther sharpens the contrast still more. "Faith is the gift and the inward good set over against the sin which it drives out. . . . God's grace, however, is the outward good, the favor of God and the opposite of his wrath." Thus God is at work in a person: by his grace against wrath, by his gift (i.e., faith) against sin.[16] Luther's picture language brings out his distinctions most clearly. He speaks of the "cloud of grace" under which our doings are pure before God and of the "righteousness" born of faith as the root of good fruits in us, which God grants us in his mercy, or as the "leaven" which works against the leaven of evil in us.[17] In terms of the good, as a concept, and as something capable of being experienced, as Luther is suggesting here, the measure of grace exceeds that of the gift, for on grace alone depends the "peace of heart," people's assurance that, through faith in Christ, God receives them as they are. On this subject he would learn nothing by reflecting on his own righteousness of faith, even if

16. WA 8:105 / 36–106 / 28. [LW 32:226–28.] "Grace" and "gift" are taken from Rom. 5:15–17 without any further exegesis by Luther, which he had done in his lectures on Romans (WA 56:318 / 12ff. WA 57:173 / 23–174 / 10) [LW 25:305–6. Luther, *Lectures on Romans*, LCC 15, 174–75.] Luther sees correctly that Paul treats the two apparently distinct concepts as actually identical in meaning. He employs them here simply as memorable distinctions for the two sides of the divine dealing with man. His understanding of the renewing power of the gift (i.e., of righteousness) was readily applicable, on sound biblical grounds, also to grace, "for, as the Scriptures say, the grace of God renews, transforms, and from day to day makes us over into new people. Speaking earnestly, the matter at issue is not that relationships are dissolved (*respectus*, between the God who punishes and the sinner), but the content and life itself is transformed" (*Assertio Omnium Articulorum* [1520], WA 7:109 / 17ff.). It is better not to try to systematize prematurely this kind of a didactic usage of biblical terms on Luther's part. His position may be determined by the scope of whatever the situation, in this case, against Latomus, to exclude every notion of grace as a quality of the human soul. Luther utilizes the distinction not only in his preface to Romans (WA DB 7:8 / 10ff.) [LW 25:305ff.], but also presupposes it for his hearers later on. So, e.g., his exposition of Psalm 51 (1532), WA 40²:421 / 3ff. [LW 12:376–77], as cited in Hermann, *Luthers These*, 85, n. 3, which, however, only mentions the time of printing (1538); WA 40²:421 / 18ff.

17. WA 8:69 / 5; 106 / 5, 21; 107 / 22; 104 / 6. [LW 32:175, 227, 229, 224.]

he would recognize God's working in it.[18] This is the boundary line separating Luther's understanding of the gospel not only from every sort of moralism but also from any spiritualized faith in the inner man, or from a puritanical or pietistic search for fruits of the Spirit intended to foster a certainty of forgiveness.[19] Such people are looking in the wrong place for something that can be experienced. And that something is the gracious Word of God alone, not the transformation of a person's own inner life.

Luther did not often set forth the basics of his teaching on justification so simply and clearly. Most of the time he favored a fully formed description of what took place inwardly between God and man, rather than a dogmatic analysis. But this time his scholastic opponent forced him to be precise in order to make his objection clear: that grace is in no way a quality of the soul, but rather God's favorable disposition toward man; that faith in Christ alone unites us with God. Here grace and gift are joined together. "A gift through the grace of that one man is what Paul (Rom. 5:17) calls faith in Christ (whom he often also calls a gift), which is given to us in the grace of Christ, because he alone was well-pleasing and accepted by God among all people, and he had a gracious and merciful God, so that he earned this gift and this grace for us." So grace and gift have their origin in the Christ-event, yet comprise two inseparable phases of the divine action. "By grace all is forgiven, but not everything has as yet been healed by the gift."[20] This does not mean that a person's relationship to God is torn into two parts. Rather, as seen from God's standpoint, man is always a whole person, entirely under grace or disgrace. "He whom God receives in grace, he receives completely, and he whom he favors, he favors completely."[21] Whenever the relationship to God is involved, Luther does not think in the categories of philosophical or psychological concepts of the person. Instead his thought is from the vantage point of God, or from that of faith, which is the same as a human perspective. "Wrath and grace have to do with person."[22] This believing one is thus able to know that he is

---

18. WA 8:106 / 15ff. Iserloh's contradiction, *Gratia und Donum*, 148, n. 13, does not apply to Hermann, *Luthers These*, 84. He maintains correctly that between grace and gift there is no precedence in time of value and thus no difference of an objective quality. Rather, Luther speaks of a possession *(Gut)*, i.e., something that can be experienced, such as "peace of heart." [*LW* 32:227.]

19. Cf. Luther's contrasting of "outward" and "inward" in H. Bornkamm, "Äusserer und innerer Mensch bei Luther und den Spiritualisten," in *Imago Dei* (Geissen, 1932), reprinted in H. Bornkamm, *Luther: Gestalt und Wirkungen*, SVRG 188 (Gütersloh, 1975).

20. WA 8:106 / 25ff.; 107 / 21. [*LW* 32:227–28. The translation above is based on Bornkamm's German translation of the Latin.]

21. WA 8:107 / 2–3. [*LW* 32:228.]

22. WA 8:107 / 1. Cf. also above, p. 10. [*LW* 32:228.]

accepted by God as an entire person, including his sin. Luther develops these differentiations most rigorously in order to safeguard a person from the deadly danger of relying on certain good deeds or of offering his deficiencies as an excuse. "So certain are we of the pure truth of the Word that we ought to die for it, but who would dare to die for his own good works even if they are wholly without fault?"[23]

The extent to which Luther is bent on making this focal point of his teaching on justification and faith understandable becomes evident from the fact that he supports his thesis by means of two quite distinct auxiliary operations. The attack by Latomus has put him to it. The one operation is hermeneutical; the other—surprisingly—is philosophical. Luther contended that every good work is a sin, and in support of this contention and its consequences he drew on Isa. 64:6: "We have all become like one who is unclean, and all our righteous deeds are like a polluted garment." Latomus had explained this passage by means of a grammatical tropism, a figure of speech suggesting the exchangeability of the whole and the part, claiming that in this text not each and every but only some righteousness is meant.[24] Luther calls this sheer arbitrariness. He is well aware that this figurative way of speaking occurs frequently in Scripture,[25] yet its interpretation is bound to firm hermeneutical rules: either the literal meaning must produce nonsense, or the context must dutifully require the conveyed interpretation.[26] In this particular passage from Isaiah, however, the general obligation of the pronouncement is expressly stated by "we all" and "all our righteous deeds." Nor can Luther agree with Latomus that the applicability of this passage is limited to the Jews of that day, for the history of human beings in the presence of God—its spirit "in each one in his time and in his temptation"—is universal. "Times change. So do things, bodies, and temptations. Yet the same spirit remains, the same [need for] food and drink among all and everywhere."[27]

As little as in this case a text may be robbed of its clarity by the substitution of figurative language, so little dare other biblical texts be deprived of

23. WA 8:81 / 18ff. [LW 32:192.]

24. On the application of the *synecdoche* in this writing by Latomus, see G. Krause, *Studien zu Luthers Auslegung der Kleine Propheten* (Tübingen, 1962), 206ff. The issue here turns on the *totum pro arte*, not on the *pars pro toto*, which Luther employed in the controversy over the Lord's Supper (cf. below, p. 512, n. 49). On the use of ancient grammar and rhetoric in the Reformation era, cf. H. Rückert, "Das Eindringen der Tropus-lehre in die schweizerische Lehre vom Abendmahl," *ARG* 37 (1940): 199ff.; reprinted in H. Rückert, *Vorträge und Aufsätze zur historischen Theologie* (Tübingen, 1972), 146ff.

25. WA 8:65 / 18ff.; 66 / 14ff. [LW 32:170, 171.]

26. WA 8:64 / 10–11; 71 / 32ff. [LW 32:168, 179.]

27. WA 8:69 / 22, 24ff. [LW 32:176.]

their clear meaning by differentiations. Latomus had tried to do so with the concept of sin; in Holy Scripture it means the cause or the activity of sin or the punishment for it or the sacrifice for it or guilt. Against this Luther set the rigorous definition "Sin is nothing other than what is contrary to God's law." Only according to this standard is the word to be understood throughout the Bible. [28] Luther saw the differentiations of Latomus as equivocations and ambiguities, as hypostatizing a single concept into various independent meanings and thereby destroying its unconditional characters. [29] He distinguished such equivocations from the genuinely figurative language with which, to his delight, the Bible was more richly endowed than any other book. Such figurative expressions all have the effect of giving a new image to words of one and the same meaning. For the "memory and understanding this is a marvelous help, and for the heart a sweet enjoyment." "I don't know why, but this figurative language has such extraordinary power. It penetrates so movingly into the heart that everyone quite naturally finds pleasure in hearing as well as speaking pictorially." [30] By this Luther means not simply picturization in the narrower sense but also the entire catalog of figures of speech which places an infinitely varied mode of expression at the service of language. Since his schooldays Luther was familiar with the introduction to this subject as supplied by the rhetoricians of classical antiquity, and the words of Quintilian rang in his ear: "Quam quidem gratiam et celectationem adferunt figurae" (What grace and delight figures provide)! [31]

Through Luther the incomparable power of figurative language receives a peculiarly penetrating application to Christology. This power pulsates through the metaphors with which the Bible expresses the relation between Christ and the sinner: He was made to be sin for us, was sacrificed, condemned, cast out, so that nothing at all distinguished him from sinners, only that he paid not for his own guilt but for that of all human beings. As in all metaphors, sameness and difference are combined, like-

28. WA 8:82 / 19ff.

29. WA 8:84 / 14ff. [LW 32:196.]

30. WA 8:84 / 24ff.; 83 / 31ff. The word "figure" is the main concept for a whole row of rhetorical forms of decorative language, to which, among others, metaphors (pictures) belong. R. Frick (see above, p. 9, n. 30) regularly translates it as "picture language" (bildliche Rede) and thereby narrows the more ample headroom intended by Luther. For an excellent presentation of the figure concept, see Krause, Kleine Propheten, 181ff. [LW 32:196.]

31. Luther's first acquaintance with the use of figures in rhetoric came in the liberal arts curriculum, the trivium (grammar, rhetoric, logic) in the teaching manual, the Doctrinale, Alexander de villa Dei. Cf. O. Scheel, Martin Luther Vom Katholizismus zur Reformation, 3d and 4th eds. (Tübingen, 1930), 1:44ff.; 118–9; 157ff. Quintilian 2.13.9, cited by Krause, Kleine Propheten, 182.

ness is not identity. Just as with pictures employed by language, a "transfer" [trope], according to the law of resemblance, takes place, yet with a difference. "In this transfer [trope] there is a metaphor not only in the words but also in the actuality, for our sins have truly been taken from us and have been laid on him, so that everyone who believes in him really has no more sins, for they have been transferred to Christ."[32] The reality of this event reveals itself in that Christ, though himself without sin, felt and bore the consequences of sin as well as the anguish of death and hell. On this reality Luther lays the greatest emphasis. To him the usual theological talk about Christ being "sentenced as guilty" and "charged with punishment" is mere whimsy. "For Christ felt that attribution and was similar to one to whom sin is attributed, yet is without guilt. . . . What, then, is an attribution that one does not feel?" Christ thus experienced the same thing as the worst of sinners who is condemned to death and hell. "Certainly this kind of reality "is a thing to be experienced rather than to be discussed and grasped in words."[33] Once again this discloses the qualities of likeness and uniqueness in the imagery of language. "Just as figurative language is sweeter and more effective than the simple and ordinary use of words, so also real sin is burdensome and intolerable to us, while transferred and metaphorical sin is wholesome and brings us supreme joy."[34]

This short train of thought, in itself unusual in Luther's theology, is not part of a speculative Christology but belongs in its entirety in the context of his defense against Latomus. Luther's intention is to set forth the unabridged reality of sin, in terms of the linguistic clarity of the concept as well as of the reality of the transference of sin. To make this actual transference (of sin) unmistakable, he makes metaphorical use of the metaphor. With the power of pictorial imagery that moves the heart, Luther discloses the depths of the actual suffering of Christ and of the redemption which Christ's act brings to the believing sinner; moreover, this very knowledge of redemption reaches down into our human feelings.[35] The front toward which Luther directs his attack is the actuarial Christology [disposed to reckoning up sins] which does not know what it is saying about the attribution of sin to Christ or the transferring of sin to him. Luther's reflection on the uses of metaphor impresses the reality of the event [Christ's redemptive act] on the believer, for the pictorial language

32. WA 8:87 / 6ff. [LW 32:200.]
33. WA 8:87 / 37–88 / 3. [LW 32:201.]
34. WA 8:87 / 10ff. (sin transposed to Christ). [LW 32:200.]
35. See n. 33, above.

is always an expression of that act. Luther does not intend his own descriptions to create any distinction between the biblical use of imagery and a naturally picturesque speech; instead, he would rather place such speech at the service of christological pronouncements. Thereby, however, he seeks not to derive from Christology the clarity of figurative discourse but to make it serve a christological end. After all, picturesque speech is embedded in language itself, and Luther is ever concerned about what is happening to language. His aim is to retain the minor unity and clarity of language, also that of the Bible, particularly as over against a medieval style of exegesis with its allegorizing and equivocal interpretations—all done in a spirit of profiteering arbitrariness. This is the profit Luther has drawn from classical rhetoric for the benefit of hermeneutics.[36]

Alongside the hermeneutical consideration there was also a philosophical argument that Luther employed in order to attain the same goal, to prove the reality of sin down to the "residual sin" in the justified believer. And this is what lay at the root of Luther's conflict with Latomus and the scholastics.[37] When his scholastic opponents appraise this residual sin

36. Exceptionally well formulated in Krause, *Kleine Propheten*, 191, n. 35: "The new thing about Luther is really that he mobilizes the classical art of rhetoric—built on [that key concept] perspicuity—by combining it with his own great sense of language as such, and then campaigns against the prevailing allegorical and dogmatic beclouding of Scripture." Luther's concentrated exposition has repeatedly attracted the interest of researchers. I cannot agree completely with any of them. In a stimulating essay, "Gedanken Luthers zur Frage der 'Entmythologisierung,'" in *Festschrift R. Bultmann* (Stuttgart, 1949), 208ff., and reprinted in his *Wort und Gestalt: Gesammelte Aufsätze* (Witten-Ruhr, 1956), 165ff., F. K. Schumann has treated the "figural," and also the "mythological," as a more highly structured instrument of language, to be distinguished fundamentally from "the pictorial language of other realms of being (aside from poetry, perchance) (pp. 172, 174). Schumann found in the "inactuality" of speech its existential "actuality," as measured by the intended content. Being able, at this point, to go into Schumann's built-in shades of meaning, I find justified the criticism that K. Löwith makes of Schumann in his essay "Die Sprache als Vermittler von Mensch und Welt," in *Das Problem der Sprache in Theologie und Kirche*, Lectures at Deutschen Evangelischen Theologentag, May 1958, Berlin, edited by W. Schneemelcher (Berlin, 1959), 52; reprinted in *Festschrift W. Szilase* (Munich, 1960), 157ff.; and also Krause, *Kleine Propheten*, 191, n. 35, and 193, n. 43. Luther himself made use of the figural possibilities of language, using it as a means of clarification, and did not simply claim "a secret correspondence between the essential character of what is intended in the kerygma and the inactual, figural, as well as often mythological language of Scripture" (Schumann, "Gedanken Luthers," 172). Had he done so, Luther would have deprived himself of the means whereby he intended to convince Latomus. In other respects, I could not say with Krause, *Kleine Propheten*, 195, that the clarity of figural speech ought to be "christologically grounded." Still less could I agree with Löwith, "Sprache als Vermittler," 52, that "language as such . . . had for Luther no decisive significance for an understanding of the world and of human beings," and that he [Löwith] would refrain "from going deeper into the essentials of subject and language." Actually, without noticing or expressing the difference, Löwith proceeds from a skeptical concept of the "multiple meanings of the metaphorical in language" (p. 54), while Luther, quite to the contrary, proceeds from the connection between the intended subject—be this a concept or an event—and the metaphor applied to it. Claiming that in Luther's thinking there is a "dogmatic short-circuit," Löwith pushes aside this problem in the logic of language and elaborates no further.

37. WA 8:89 / 10–11 [*LW* 32:203.]

simply as weakness or imperfection, Luther contends that they have not exhausted the categories of Aristotle but have limited themselves to the category of substance only. Luther here again differentiates himself from them. He understands substance—expressly not according to Aristotle but once again according to Quintilian—as the being or essence of a subject, that is, not simply as matter, which may be quantitatively more or less (e.g., a man or a fly or also sin).[38] In the rest of their work all other categories are missing: "What it (sin) is according to the terms quantity, quality, relation, action, and passion (suffering) they know next to nothing."[39] Only with titles like these can sin be described, not only definitively but also in its living qualities; also in its evil activity, always worse than what people would have it be; in its ever-contrasting relationship to grace and to the wrath of God; and in its suffering, a category they miss altogether. For the scholastics, sin does not suffer under the law, which indicts them; indeed, their kind of sin does not even feel itself implicated by the law.[40]

Strange as an application of this table of categories from classical antiquity to theological pronouncements may appear to us today, for Luther this was a convenient instrument to vivify for his opponents—who after all were trained in the same Aristotelian-scholastic tradition—the reality and power of sin. Luther was not arguing on the basis of a connection in principle between theology and philosophy, but he was making use of logical and fundamental possibilities in order to illuminate purely theological problems.[41] He can apply it equally well, with adaptations, to show how,

38. WA 8:88 / 9ff., 15. For a definition of substance as essence of the subject (synonymous with *res*) in the *Institutio Quintilian*, cf. U. Knoche, in Frick (see above, p. 9, n. 30), 174–75. [*LW* 32:201–2.]

39. WA 8:98 / 3ff. [*LW* 32:216. Alternate translation.]

40. WA 8:88 / 3ff. [*LW* 32:201.]

41. The passage from Luther's lectures on Romans—at first glance very similar to the section treated above— "Be transformed by the renewal of your mind" (12:2) makes use of Aristotelian categories corresponding to its exegetical requirements, namely, to explain the concepts that teach of the unending process of the Christian's inner renewal through repentance. For Aristotle every "new being" is also again "in truth not-being," and so it goes "from him again into another (being)." "This Aristotle philosophizes over things and does it well, but they [the scholastics] do not understand him that well" (WA 56:441 / 24–442 / 14). Therefore a person is "always sinner, always penitent, always righteous" (WA 56:442 / 17; see below, p. 195, n. 49). For an understanding of that section, see Hermann, *Luthers These*, 245–46. W. Joest, *Ontologie bei der Person bei Luther* (Göttingen, 1967), 325ff. For an understanding of grace (in contrast to gift) Luther employs later on also the category of relatedness "of which the logicians say that it possesses a minimum of being [essence] and a maximum of power *(minimae entitatis et maximae virtutis esse)*, which is not to be confused with the category of quality, in the scholastics' manner of fantasizing." *Exposition of Psalm 51* (1538 printing), WA 40²:421 / 20ff. [*LW* 376–77], cited in Hermann, *Luthers These*, 85, n. 3. Likewise, but more fully, this is spelled out in the theses for academic promotion of July 3, 1545; in the process Luther also draws on the Ockhamists' interpretation. WA 39²:340 / 1ff.; also WA 39²:363 / 1ff.; 383 / 9ff., 27ff. Cf. also WA TR 1, no. 11, 5 / 12ff.; no. 855, 418 / 37ff.; no. 1057, 533 / 5ff.

through Christ and baptism, sin is rendered powerless. Meanwhile, the category of suffering under sin pertains in full measure to believing Christians; in them the substance, the essence, of sin remains unchanged. Yet the power of sin (expressed in the categories of quality, quantity, and activity) has been broken by grace. Evil lust remains the same "before and after grace."[42] "We still must die, and labor under sin. But Christ has set us free from the law of sin and death; that is, from the rule and tyranny of sin and death. Sin is still around, but it has no more authority because it has lost its tyranny. Death, likewise, is still ahead for us, but it cannot harm us, because it has lost its sting."[43] Therefore faith has the symbol of baptism as its testimony. "In baptism all your sins are forgiven, forgiven entirely, but as yet not completely destroyed." Faith in forgiveness embraces the endeavors no longer to submit to sin as well as the certitude of sin's ultimate destruction. Taken in this sense, Luther can say, "Those who work at it [who submit to sin no longer] are doing a good work. Look, this is my own kind of faith, for this is the Catholic faith."[44] "Good works"—not for the sake of their quality, but for the sake of trusting in the grace and power of God. "Not thanks to your running, but thanks to God's mercy, your works are good."[45] "Catholic" means to be in agreement with the old biblical doctrine of the church, yet in opposition to the scholastic teaching, according to which Luther was condemned by the faculties of Cologne and Louvain and attacked by their champion Latomus.

In short, Luther defines this process—demonstrated in the categories of philosophy—as "ruling" and "overruled" sin, a process in which the turning point is the work of Christ and the goal lies in an eschatological direction. Sin remains sin, even in the person who believes in justification. "In no way at all does sin differentiate itself from itself." Now, however, God "treats it differently from before." Treated is more than judged, for it means (as in Christ[46]) tangible reality. Before we became aware of grace God deals with sin "as something existing, so that we recognized it and it crushed us." But when we have learned to hold fast to grace alone, then God deals with sin in a way "that it does not exist and is thrown out." God receives us not halfway but completely, "as person," yet not for the sake of our own works but for the sake of the "gift" working in us to drive

42. WA 8:91 / 35ff. [LW 32:207.]
43. WA 8:92 / 5ff.; 107 / 26ff. [LW 32:207.]
44. WA 8:96 / 6ff. [LW 32:213.]
45. WA 8:96 / 1–2. [LW 32:213.]
46. See above, pp. 190ff.

out sin.[47] The gift, as we have seen,[48] is the "righteousness" which through faith embodies us in Christ, which spoils it for us to remain sinners, and which awakens a new human being in us.

Luther's entire thought process, its theological content as well as its flanking hermeneutical and philosophical thrusts, serves to establish, among his pronouncements on justification, his pregnant and incomparable thesis: The Christian is ever a "righteous person and a sinner at the same time" *(simul justus et peccator)*. From time to time, ever since his lectures on Romans, Luther made use either of this concise formula or of the idea it expressed, doing so not only in exegetical writings but also in his immediate arguments with ecclesial dogma.[49] For him this formula was not simply an abstract pattern that had been opened up; instead it comprised a precise formulation of the ambivalence in the Pauline description of the justified sinner. So, commenting on Rom. 4:7, he summarized, "They are unknowingly righteous and knowingly unrighteous; they are sinners in fact but righteous in hope." "Wonderful and sweet is the mercy of God, who at the same time considers us both as sinners and as nonsinners. Sin remains, and at the same time it does not remain." "Sinner and righteous at once; sinner according to the actual condition *(re vera)*, yet righteous in the sight and promise of God, that he makes us free from sin until he has made us completely whole."[50]

---

47. WA 8:107 / 26ff. To say that sin does not exist does not mean that it has no right to exist, according to Frick (see above, p. 9, n. 30), 106. But it does mean that it no longer exists in God's presence and that people, aware of sin's being disarmed, know that it can be overcome. [*LW* 32:229.]

48. Above, pp. 186–87.

49. From the extensive literature on this subject, besides the already noted work of Hermann, *Luthers These*, I mention only the more recent studies: W. Joest, "Paulus und das Lutherische Simul justus et peccator," *KuD* 1 (1955): 269ff. Idem, *Ontologie*, 265ff., which includes references to earlier works. R. Köster's *Luthers These "Gerecht und Sünder zugleich";* see the work by the same name by R. Hermann in *Catholica* 18 (1964): 48ff., 193ff.; ibid. 19 (1965): 136ff., 210ff. This essay is a comprehending dialogue with its evangelical counterpart and has cleared up many Catholic doubts over Luther's doctrine of justification. Agreeing, and leading the way further into the broader field of justification, is O. H. Pesch, *Theologie der Rechtfertigung bei Martin Luther and Thomas von Aquin* (Mainz, 1967), 109ff., 527, 827, 954, etc. Also Iserloh, "Gratia und Donum," who pursues his work under the question "whether differences are so great and divisive" and whether only nuances are at issue—the way it would always be between schools of theological thought, "inasmuch as the one truth cannot be adequately captured" ("Gratia und Donum," 142, n. 5). As gratifying as such disposition may be, it must nevertheless be asked whether this heuristic viewpoint is sufficient to keep an eye on the problematic subject. In his analysis and evaluation, Iserloh inadvertently makes use of that very language, common in scholastic thought in isolating and grading questions, from which Luther dissociated himself. The meaning of the Lutheran *simul* and *totus* is thus shortchanged.

50. *Lectures on Romans* (1515–16), WA 56:269 / 30; 270 / 9ff.; 272 / 17ff. [*LW* 25:258.]

This theme returns in Paul's description of inner conflict (Rom. 7:7ff.): "I am at the same time both sinner and righteous, for I do evil and I hate the evil I do." "See how one and the same person serves both the law of God and the law of sin, is righteous and commits sin."[51] Righteous and sinner at the same time—who will resolve this contradiction? . . . When you regard faith, then the law is fulfilled, sin is destroyed, and no law remains, yet when you regard the flesh, in which there is no good thing, then you must designate even those who in the Spirit are righteous through faith."[52]

Even the few sentences we can here cite from Luther's earlier statements reveal the double aspect of the moment's perceptible reality in which sin and believed righteousness coexist and in which eschatological hope in the promised fulfillment is disclosed. Out of this anthropologically determined situation of the Christian, based on Pauline premises, Luther had drawn the consequences. These were his arguments in the great debate over the Roman teaching on repentance and justification, and they were the issues on which his conflict with Latomus turned. Even the deeds of the righteous are never without sin, and there is thus no such thing as a substantially good work. "If on those terms (according to the previously cited passsage, Rom. 7:22–23) every person is at once sinner and righteous, what conclusion can be clearer than that a deed is partly good and partly evil?" Christ said that the fruit can be no better than the tree. "If this substantiation, this authority, is not convincing, then I don't know what can convince you."[53] *Simul* is a concept denoting time.[54] It is the existential "at the same time," not a placing together of different components or a designation of human development in various layers. As do the Pauline expressions from which Luther proceeds, *simul* pertains only to the believing Christian, not to the person for whom the question

51. WA 56:70 / 9–10; 347 / 2ff. [*LW* 25:62, 336.]

52. *Lectures on Galatians* (1519), WA 2:497 / 18–19, 22ff. (includes a more detailed substantiation).

53. *Assertio omnium articulorum M. Lutheri per bullam Leonis X, novissimam damnatorum* (1520), WA 7:137 / 18ff., 24. Cf. the reference already in *Resolutiones Lutherianae super propositionibus suis Lipsiae disputatis* (1519), Luther's writing against which Latomus levels his main attack, WA 2:408 / 30ff.

54. The significance of this time element in Luther's theology is treated by E. Schott, "'Zugleich': Mensch und Zeit in Luthers Rechtfertigungslehre," in *450 Jahre lutherische Reformation 1517–1967: Festschrift F. Lau* (Göttingen, 1967), 333ff. An attempt to expand *simul* into an inclusive principle of Lutheran theology is shown in the subtitle of the study by K. O. Nilsson, *Das Miteinander vom Göttlichen und Menschlichen in Luthers Theologie*, FKDG 17 (Göttingen, 1966). This, however, deprives the concept—the word *simul*—of its specificity. The Latomus debate thus plays only a slight role in Nilsson's expansive work. Cf. H. Beintker's review, "Kjell Ove Nilsson, Simul," *LuJ* 35 (1968): 100ff.

whether he is right with God does not exist. Opposite *zugleich* (at the same time) Luther places *irgendwann einmal* (*aliquando*), some time or other. Latomus would agree that even the righteous person sins at some time or other.[55] Human life, however, does not consist of such changeable "sometime" moments. Rather, a human being is universally the active subject, to whom sin adheres as a characteristic of life that cannot be shaken off.[56] "Righteous and sinner alike" is thus not simply a matter of relations, although being declared sinner and righteous occurs under God's judgment and thus expresses man's relation to God. There is something more, and this pertains to the powers: to sin, which is real enough to feel, and to God's help, the gift, the leaven, out of which faith grows. God in us takes up the battle against sin, so that we are enabled to work at its annihilation.[57] The term "at the same time" unites everything: on the one hand, the old life, the lostness, which a person cannot get rid of by himself, and on the other, the new life, the redemption, of which he has been assured in forgiveness and which has been set in motion by faith.

No more than Paul in Rom. 7 does Luther here, in his treatment,[58] account psychologically for man's dividedness as such. Rather, Luther ponders this dividedness in which the believing Christian lives—ill and yet certain of health, thanks to the assurance of the divine physician. Just as there is no talk here about man as such, so also there is none about God as such. Instead, everything turns on him who became man for us and who is armed with God's mercy and full power. According to Luther, when one sees it this way, the issue is simple; only its entanglement in the philosophy of scholasticism has made it so complicated. "The gospels are not so difficult that children are not ready to hear them. . . . How then did Christ himself teach?"[59] With that Luther again turned angrily away from the teaching of scholasticism. The din the scholastics make is "the death of the soul." "They got themselves sick over me," he said. Although Luther hardly lacked understanding, he spared no effort to understand. His backward glance over fifteen years of experience roused the passion with which he braved the attack from the scholastic establishment and to which he replied fully in the same field of ideas.

55. WA 8:76 / 18ff.; 77 / 3ff. [*LW* 32:185–86.]
56. WA 8:77 / 8ff. [*LW* 32:186.]
57. See above, p. 195, n. 47.
58. WA 8:99 / 126. [*LW* 32:217–56.]
59. WA 8:127 / 3ff. [*LW* 32:258.]

8

Preaching for the Renewal of Piety

The years since Luther's return from the Wartburg included a more quiet, almost invisible task: the nurture of his congregation. His other activities were far more visible, including a new order for the Wittenberg situation, debates with opponents right and left, treatises dealing with current issues, and more. As for his congregation, he knew how necessary it had been to remove them from an inherited world of piety. Everything now depended not simply on accounting for what he had done but also on replacing it with something new. He assumed this responsibility with great solicitude. In just one year, 1523, along with the daily round of lectures, writing, correspondence, Bible translation, and so forth, he preached 137 sermons. Most of these were on the pericopes of the day, but many were also devoted to individual books of the Bible (2 Peter, Jude, Genesis), as well as to parts of the catechism.[1] This profusion, and the inexhaustible riches opened by the ever-changing sermon texts, offers a ready occasion for drawing up a balance for the constructive years 1522–24. This enables us to win a firm perspective from which to examine Luther's preaching both in retrospect and in anticipation.

What Luther proclaimed in these hundreds of sermons did not stay within the walls of the Town Church or, occasionally, the Castle Church.[2] Since 1521 printers in Augsburg, Erfurt, Nuremberg, Strassburg, Basel, and elsewhere were competing for the manuscripts of copyists who took down Luther's sermons. Singly in pamphlets, or collectively in books (up to twenty-seven in one book), the sermons poured forth. Some books were reprinted up to a dozen times. Luther himself was not pleased with this and therefore repeatedly begged and warned the printers to desist from

---

This chapter appeared previously in H. Bornkamm, *Luther: Gestalt und Wirkungen*, SVRG 188 (Gütersloh, 1975), 212–37.

1. WA 11:1. During 1522, the first two months of which Luther was at the Wartburg, he preached 117 sermons, proportionately the same amount of preaching activity; WA 10³:xl. On consecutive sermonic expositions of biblical books, as well as on the lectures of these years, see below, Chapter 9.

2. For instance, February 24 and 25, 1523, in connection with the visit of Duke Bogislav of Pomerania. G. Buchwald, "Zu Luthers Predigten in der Schlosskirche zu Wittenberg," *ARG* 25 (1928): 71. WA 11:33ff. WA 12:427ff.

this unbridled use of the press. He even hoped that once the people had the Holy Scriptures in their entirety [he was still translating the Old Testament] there would be no need for his own books. He encouraged people to "drink more from the spring itself than from the little streams that have led you to the source."[3] Happily, however, Luther could not put a stop to the turn of events. Deficient though these elaborated transcripts often were, they nevertheless conveyed Luther's ideas better than anything else, as uncounted quantities of pamphlets gushed from Wittenberg and found their way especially into southern Germany. This printed flood did not yet provide a complete overview of Luther's homiletical activity during these years. That began to happen with the appearance of a far more inclusive treasure of transcripts from the swift and clever pen of George Rörer, Luther's amanuensis.[4] Beginning at Christmas 1522 he took down Luther's sermons and lectures in his own shorthand and ably captured their trend of thought.

There is no way to assess what Luther presented to his hearers during these years of new developments, 1522–24, in terms of helping them come to feel at home with the Bible. All those things of prominence in medieval preaching—the game of allegorical exposition, the miraculous legends of the saints, the extolling of aids to devotion such as the rosary or other prayer forms, as well as the moralizing—were dropped. He preached precisely and penetratingly on the text, not on a dogmatic theme suggested by the text. To be sure, he did not simply expound or illustrate the text but led his hearers on to the enduring truths, valid then as well as earlier, in and behind each word of Scripture. Only rarely did he touch on current events that had nothing directly to do with the text, such as the imperial mandate of 1523 or the conflict with the chapter members of the Castle Church.[5]

Allegory virtually disappeared from his sermons, and if used at all (with expressed reservations) it was only on matters of immediate applicability, such as the transition from the bodily aspect to the spiritual aspect of Christ's passion.[6] For example, concerning Luke 1:39ff., any attempt to show that Mary means the church, Elizabeth the synogogue, and their meeting the concord of the Old and New Testaments in Christ is only for

---

3. WA 10³:176 / 12–13. WA 11:150 / 26.

4. Of the 137 sermons of the year 1523, 47 were supplied by Rörer. For the others, Rörer provided a host of corrections as well as the means of dating them more precisely.

5. WA 11:126 / 34ff. WA 12:645ff. On the mandate, see below p. 301.

6. WA 15:515 / 13ff.

those who "wish to go on speculating," the sophists.[7] Therefore allegorization would be more likely to show up in his lectures. Nor is it pure allegorization when he uses the name Herod (in German, the "Giant"; in Saxon, the "Guy," one of the "great devourers of people," like Dietrich of Bern) to illustrate the brutalities of the law,[8] for this is the kind of play on words that the etymology of the name itself invites. This is for Luther fully as irreproachable a reference as the grammar itself, which is his favorite exegetical weapon.[9] He also enjoys the figurative use of a biblical event— such as Christ passing through closed doors then and, through his word, coming into our heart now—without breaking or altering anything in our natural being. "For when God's Word comes, it does not injure the conscience, nor does it alter the heart and senses."[10]

Moreover, Luther expounds on the parables of Jesus for his congregation according to a method that has become generally accepted only in modern times. Earlier he had thought it necessary to follow a "stiff" (point by point) interpretation of the parables, but in the 1520s he realized that only the "main meaning" matters.[11] Wherever necessary, he breaks down mythical notions. The bosom of Abraham, into which poor Lazarus was received, means the Word of God, in which the fathers of the old covenant, who also hoped in the coming Christ, are safe; hell is the bad conscience; the chasm is despair; the conversation between the rich man and Lazarus is the thoughts coursing through the conscience. About the temporal duration of the rich man's suffering there is nothing we can say. The whole story is an example for us.[12]

Luther treats specific textual difficulties with great care. Why, for instance, was there a practice so repulsive to us as circumcision? Luther's extended response is that our sin is lodged in our nature, and the sign of God's creation [circumcision] was applied there where our evil lust comes from. "We must indeed put on another skin if we would become godly."[13] The humiliation of Christ in Phil. 2 refers not to the birth of Christ but to his life: He became sick with the sick, poor with the poor.[14] On John 14:23 ("If a man loves me, he will keep my word, and my Father will love him"),

7. WA 11:144 / 5ff. WA 12:617 / 3ff.

8. WA 15:413 / 5ff.

9. Cf. H. Bornkamm, *Luther und des Alte Testament* (Tübingen, 1948), 99–100.

10. WA 12:518 / 19ff.

11. WA 15:423 / 32ff.

12. WA 10³:191 / 10ff.

13. WA 12:401ff.; 403 / 24–25.

14. WA 12:469 / 17ff.

Luther asks himself whether this is not the first responsive act required of a person (the same question as asked by the nominalist doctrine of justification). Luther distinguishes perceptively between sensing something and commencing something and points out the paradox of all religious life: how only in our own ignited heart can we sense whether God's Spirit has taken hold of us, and in our own love of God that God loves us. And yet it is God who must take the first step.[15] Luther's expository precision in individual passages, coupled with his power to transport his hearers into the position of biblical characters and his suggestive application of biblical experiences to his hearers, was quite extraordinary.

The content of Luther's preaching was as many-sided as it was simple, many-sided through the impulses from the texts and through what lay on his heart, simple through the keynote that permeated everything. "Trust God, help your neighbor, this is what the whole gospel teaches."[16] Faith and love are the one ever-freshly varied theme of his sermons.[17] This theme dominates the new meaning he would impart to the piety of the Christian and determines Luther's polemics against the old meaning. He provides a few basic instructions on how to understand faith properly. This understanding of faith is actually the new thing, actually "his" theme. "Unless you yourself by God's grace and mercy fashion a faith of your own, you will not be saved."[18] To have faith is not simply to believe in facts, even in the facts of salvation, but to believe in what they mean. To believe in the resurrection means not simply to recognize the fact that it happened but to believe "that Christ took our sin and the sin of the whole world on himself"; this is the "content of the resurrection."[19] Luther liked to explain this matter to the congregation by distinguishing between "believing in God" and "believing God."[20] Even the devils know about the existence of God (James 2:19). But to believe God means "affectionate confidence and complete trust in God's grace."[21] At the same time this means to ponder God not in his naked [abstract] majesty but in the way he offers himself to us, "clothed in flesh." Luther finds the Latin and Greek

15. WA 12:574 / 22ff., 27.

16. WA 10³:361 / 13–14.

17. Cf., e.g., WA 12:632ff. WA 11:10 / 7 (*Fides accipit, caritas operatur*). WA 11:47 / 33; 15:435 / 1–2.

18. WA 10³:306 / 25ff.

19. WA 10³:137 / 2ff.; 138 / 2ff. WA 15:517 / 16ff.

20. Luther did not always make use of the familiar distinction in Peter Lombard's *Sentences* 3, dist. 23:4. Cf. Luther's exposition of Rom. 3:22, WA 56:252 / 3ff. [*LW* 25:242–43.]

21. WA 11:49 / 5ff.

usages helpful to impress "believing in God" on the congregation.[22] Therefore "believing in Christ" and "believing in God" are the same thing. Only through the love for Christ do we ascend to the love for the Father and learn to call him "loving Father."[23] Luther describes this faith relationship to Christ with complete inwardness and still enjoys using the language of mysticism, especially the beautiful picture of the wedding. "You alone will I have," says the true bride, neither the ring nor other gifts matter. Whoever cannot say to God without doubting, "You are mine, that person is not yet a Christian."[24] The believing ones are those who "allow themselves to live into Christ; they have everything he has";[25] they are "one loaf" with him and also with their neighbor.[26]

Faith, then (as in Luther's preface to Romans[27]), is something "most highly perceptible." "Where Christians are, there God sees to it that they perceive one another's faith."[28] Yet this is also why in times of temptation they feel one another's weaknesses. Even at those times God's hand is in the situation, "that he might humble us so that we see what weak creatures we are."[29] When Luther spoke about the intense struggles of faith, he realized that only few could follow him. As long as he was dealing with temptations, such as unchastity "wherein the devil inflames the veins and body," blowing on us as a bellows on hot coals, everyone understood him.[30] Yet there are worse struggles: death, suffering, and, above all, "when the conscience countermands"; "when our conscience feels that it has lost Christ," "when the conscience says, 'God does not want you;' " when it seems as if "God is not at home"; when one doubts whether one belongs to those whose prayers God is willing to hear (Matt. 21:22) or to the lost sheep whom Christ came to rescue (Matt. 15:24).[31] "It takes strength of spirit to withstand such drubbings, and there are not many people whom God treats this way. Yet we must prepare ourselves so that should it happen we will not then despair."[32] This answers the ques-

22. *WA* 11:51 / 20ff., 52 / 16ff.
23. *WA* 10³:158 / 27ff.; 159 / 9.
24. *WA* 10³:417 / 19ff., 419 / 2–3.
25. *WA* 12:435 / 10–11.
26. *WA* 10³:145 / 11. *WA* 12:583 / 16–17; 485 / 2; 486 / 8; 488 / 9. *WA* 14:125 / 3.
27. See above, p. 84. *WA DB* 7:10 / 16ff. [*LW* 35:370–71.]
28. *WA* 11:49 / 16ff.
29. *WA* 12:511 / 18ff.
30. *WA* 11:24 / 1ff.
31. *WA* 11:25 / 19. *WA* 12:411 / 12–13; 412 / 31–32. *WA* 11:50 / 10; 44 / 7–8.
32. *WA* 12:411 / 19ff. *WA* 11:44 / 2, 9.

tion that overcomes the reader of such dead-earnest descriptions: What use can it be to a congregation to hear of such extraordinary experiences? Did Luther know of anyone near his pulpit who had had such an experience or might soon be having one? Quite apart from his own experience, he had learned to know people who thought they were possessed by the devil.[33] For their benefit these examples were in the Bible. It was up to him to preach about them. And finally, the advice he could offer on the basis of the gospel was always the same: Look to Christ! Let the tempted person look to the tempted Christ who recognized the tempter. That is already half the victory, for Christ overcame the tempter.[34] And let the person who is agonizing look to the "weak Christ, who hangs there on the cross and dies." This is the supreme wisdom, "which, alas, is known to few people on earth."[35] And at the same time, listen to his "naked Word"! No one can understand it "who has not been miserable in his conscience."[36] The Christian may hold fast to the promise Luther cherished so much: "My word shall not return to me empty, but it shall accomplish that which I purpose" (Isa. 55:11).[37]

At this point there comes a remarkable reversal of the relation between "feeling" and "believing," as Luther applies psychological insight. Whether you feel yourself in heaven or hell, accepted or rejected, that is not what matters. Rather, close your eyes and cling to the Word. Even if you feel only your own inner coldness, you nevertheless feel—and this is a hopeful sign. "You are already prepared [for more] when you feel ready to be helped and when your need presses you to come (to the sacrament)."[38] Then Luther offers a few practical pointers from his own experience: Go to a devout person and confess your failure to that person; read a portion of Scripture and speak with others about it. "The best thing is when two or three earnestly speak with each other about it. Let the living voice be heard. Then assurance comes through much stronger, and the devil must clear out."[39] Luther prized the living voice of neighborly conversation as well as confession, the latter being not obligatory but born spontaneously from the soul's need.[40] Here the feeling of faith resumes its rightful place,

---

33. *WA* 11:44 / 18–19.
34. *WA* 11:24 / 13ff.
35. *WA* 12:511 / 15–16, 510 / 14–15.
36. *WA* 11:43 / 11–12; 42 / 24–25.
37. *WA* 12:500 / 33ff.
38. *WA* 12:500 / 16ff.
39. *WA* 12:499 / 32ff.; 501 / 12ff.; 505 / 10ff.
40. On confession, see *WA* 12:516 / 33ff.; 522 / 26ff. *WA* 15:481–89, and above, pp. 3–5. [*LW* 35:9ff., esp. 14.]

having been dissolved from a form of self-respect not orientated entirely in God's Word. Faith is something alive and growing. "When we come out of it (through this time of stress) we have gained experience and become more sure of our faith." The entire Bible is filled with "examples of an increasing faith," wherever new experiences have followed a successful passing of the first test.[41]

God strengthens faith not only through special signs but also through the numerous miracles of daily life, which we simply take for granted: that persons can procreate, that the world is full of light, that there are growing things everywhere. These are indications enough to the "supreme article of faith": "to believe that God is my Father."[42] But because we do not see what is before our eyes, God lets it be proclaimed to us so we cannot miss it, penetratingly and in unison. The gospel has no other tone than this, for it is not a book but purely a living voice, "a glad shout, a good sermon of Christ," "a proclamation in person . . . which ought to be proclaimed before all creatures, so that all who have ears may hear" the Word that passes through closed doors.[43] Luther never wearies of impressing this fact on the people. Already in 1522 he is ready to claim: "Your love now knows, I trust, what the gospel is."[44] In this definition lies the whole secret of that which for Luther is the Word of God, faith, and church. The gospel is not a codified sacred code, as in the Old Testament law and in the Roman church, not the tradition of a profession like that of the rabbis or clergy, not a single document or collection of documents. Instead, the gospel is an ever-freshly raised cry that has but a single content: Christ. And it brings about but a single context in the church across the centuries: that of proclaiming, hearing, and believing. Because it is live news about a specific event, it does not contradict itself. To the objection that "the gospel and scripture are dark and obscure" and therefore it is best to rely on the exposition of the church fathers, Luther calmly replies: How much more contradictory are interpretations of the fathers themselves! And where we stumble as to obscurities in the Scriptures, a closer look reveals that they are their own light and thus interpret themselves.[45] One simply has to retain a clear eye for what the gospel is, and then one will learn to make the proper distinctions.

41. *WA* 10³:426 / 18ff., 427 / 28–29. *WA* 11:50 / 26–27.
42. *WA* 11:50 / 19ff., 27–28.
43. *WA* 10³:400 / 4. *WA* 11:42 / 8. *WA* 12:556 / 9ff.; 518 / 19ff.
44. *WA* 10³:400 / 3.
45. *WA* 10³:263 / 6ff.; 238 / 10–11. *WA* 15:434 / 8–9.

Do the Scriptures not contain law as well as gospel? Luther does not evade this question. To begin with, he is not satisfied simply "to take coarse people who have no feel for the gospel and therefore to preach the law to them until they cave in and recognize their weaknesses; when this is done, the gospel can begin."[46] Instead, he repeatedly takes the time during these years to give his congregation a sermon series on the Ten Commandments.[47] Yet he preaches in such a manner that in connection with each commandment the sum total of the law becomes evident: "You should be friendly, open, and gracious in your disposition, work, and deeds." When the Jews reply, "That's not in the Scriptures," and when the pedantic theologians say, "Ah, that's not what God meant, for who could keep such a commandment? He did not command it, but only suggested it to those who would be perfect," Luther has an answer. He refers to the living law, on which believing as well as the word depend: "That's what Christ did. Do likewise, and you'll be a Christian."[48] The law, as Luther sees it, always has a twofold sense—an outward and an inward sense—which he elucidates in connection with each of the commandments. The outward sense can be kept readily: worship no idols, do not murder or steal, and so on. But the inward, true sense is the purity of heart toward which every commandment, from a new side, leads the way.[49] Unlike that of the Old Covenant, the law is not simply the order of life for a God-fearing people but is to the highest degree something personal; it is truly spiritual, and its aim is perfection. To understand it spiritually, therefore, means also to realize "that one cannot fulfill a single letter of the law."[50] We would all be lost if we thought our salvation depended on this kind of fulfillment. The law becomes the mirror of our true being which cannot shake off sin, and it permits us to become attentive to the word of grace that our self-righteous moral zeal does not hear. By this "spiritual" understanding of the law Luther means the Holy Spirit. Where no written command and no pedagogical precept does any good, the Spirit "writes with flaming letters in our heart and makes us alive." "Such a person is above all law, for the Holy Spirit is a better teacher than all books. That kind of person understands the Scriptures better than any-

46. WA 12:529 / 23ff.
47. The years 1516, 1517, 1519, 1522, 1523.
48. WA 12:624 / 8ff., 625 / 10ff. WA 11:148 / 20ff., 36ff.
49. Cf. the sermons on the Decalogue (1523) in Rörer's transcript, WA 11:30ff. [LW 51:137–93, on the full catechism (1528).]
50. WA 11:31 / 23; 48 / 19.

one can tell him, and does of himself what God wills, so that the law need make no demands of him."[51]

Were these not illusions? And is it not understandable that the "prophets of the Spirit" and the "Enthusiasts" misunderstood Luther also at this point? Everything unconditional has been misunderstood in the history of faith as well as of thought, and Luther had no way of avoiding this dilemma. Yet his thinking was too down-to-earth to be illusory. The first sermon in which he made this double understanding of the law clear to his hearers ends with Rörer's postscript "*Internus intellectus* concerns few people,"[52] and even these few always live between joyfulness in the Spirit and alarm over their sin. "It must always be mixed, so that one feels both, the Holy Spirit as well as our sin and imperfection."[53] One does not cancel the other. As much as Luther warned against "boasting too defiantly or boldly of having the Holy Spirit,"[54] he also impressed it on his hearers' hearts that the right kind of faith must do good, "just as a living person cannot withdraw but must rouse himself, eat, and drink, and have something to do."[55] Everything depends on getting the point that faith is not simply insight but life as well. True faith in Christ "produces joy in the heart, so that without coercion or pressure I take hold of my own accord and gladly do what I should, saying, Because of what my Lord has done for me, I will do what he wills."[56] An overrating of deeds corresponds to an underrating of faith. Because one usually equates faith with agreeing to the teaching of the church—everything else already belongs to other concepts: love, virtue of all kinds—the notion takes hold that "faith is not enough, there must be something more and greater."[57] So one gets into zealousness, keeping score, bragging, and frightening oneself. The decision, however, is made at a much deeper level, not in the realm of these visible performances but in the invisible root system of the individual. I must know "that it depends not on my deeds but on my entire person."[58] God judges a person not according to separate actions, which can be isolated, counted, and weighed, "but according to the depths of his con-

51. *WA* 12:570 / 5ff.; 572 / 14ff.
52. *WA* 11:33 / 13.
53. *WA* 12:573 / 26–27.
54. *WA* 12:573 / 10–11.
55. *WA* 12:559 / 21ff.
56. *WA* 12:515 / 20ff., 547 / 22–23.
57. *WA* 10³:285 / 11.
58. *WA* 12:516 / 18–19.

science."[59] Therefore it is faith that gets the message not to expect to be saved by anything achieved by the self but to entrust everything to God. This includes the cleansing of the believer's past through the forgiveness of his sin, and the acceptance of his future as the renewal of his being. The mistake of the old piety was not that it required the Christian to do good but that one nursed the notion that doing good was an atoning cancellation of sin. This was the basis on which the entire ecclesial system of "good works" was built, and the effectiveness of such works was presumed to reach even into purgatory. Yet none of our deeds is pure enough to atone for sin.[60] Good works have a completely different meaning. Luther endeavored to impress this on his congregation in the same impassioned way that he tried to eradicate the wrong understanding of works. Since works are the spontaneous fruit of the Spirit, they are outward "signs and seals" of faith.[61] They are valid not for "the relation between God and man, but for the relations among people."[62] In the presence of God, only faith is of any account, not deeds."[63] But among his fellow human beings a Christian must and is able to prove himself through his deeds. Indeed, not only among people, but also toward himself. Luther is surprisingly and emphatically intent on making the meaning of works clear to his hearers, "for where no works ensue, a person cannot know whether he genuinely believes; indeed, he is sure that his faith is a dream and not something real."[64] To forgive from the heart helps a person to have confidence in the forgiveness of his own sin.[65]

To forestall misunderstandings, Luther speaks of a twofold "justification": an inward one, in God's presence through faith, and an outward one. "Outwardly and publicly in the presence of people and toward himself he becomes justified through his deeds; that is, he becomes known and thereby assured that he is inwardly upright, believing, and devout."[66] This formulation—it sounds dangerous to the ear trained in the later disputes over justification—is something other than the doctrine of a "double righteousness" with which efforts have been made temporarily to find a

59. WA 12:543 / 37.
60. WA 12:545 / 35ff. WA 11:92 / 19ff.; 94 / 25ff.
61. WA 10³:225 / 35ff.
62. WA 12:646 / 34–35.
63. WA 11:158 / 2.
64. WA 10³:287 / 20–21.
65. WA 10³:226 / 2ff.
66. WA 10³:287 / 27ff. WA 11:157 / 13ff. (WA 12:646 / 16ff.)

compromise between Roman Catholic and Reformation teaching.[67] What is here intended is no manner of separating justification into a divine and human part or of making it into steps of a process. Actually, Luther was saying that these are two distinct aspects which, like the observers of justification—God and man—are absolutely separated from each other. Luther did not have to be told that good appearances can deceive or that one can found one's confidence in salvation on the experience of one's own being forgiving and loving. What Luther meant is not the famed practical syllogism, the inference from the effect to the cause—from the deeds to the state of faith, in the strict sense.[68] In any case, Luther is attracted to the idea. It should give people encouragement and confidence when they notice that they are succeeding in keeping up with God's commandments or are now and then enabled to follow Christ's example. And they can take it as a sign of worthily receiving the sacrament when they can love their neighbors, even their enemies, from the heart, while all this could grant them no certainty if—without this experience—they were to receive the sacrament ever so reverently a hundred times in one day.[69]

Luther could offer his hearers no certainty when assailed by temptation—only God's unbreakable word can do that—but he did assure them that they could trust in the power of God. The believers' deeds become for them a part of the gospel. They show them that they have a "chest full of guilders," their faith, which is of no use to them when they know nothing about it;[70] indeed, one should add, the chest is not at hand if they do not share the contents. Luther's repeated endeavors concerning the issue of faith and works are collectively but a single attempt to open the eyes of his hearers to this treasure. As a treasure it eludes those who think they could force it loose for themselves with levers and screws, regulations, and thoughts of merit; it is there, and nothing more, when one lets the treasure flow. The proper relation of faith and works is that place where, for man's standing in the presence of God, there is all to win or all to lose.

67. The attempt was undertaken by Catholic reform theologians, notably by John Gropper and Gaspar Contarini. It was the basis for the Formula of Union in the *Regensburger Buch,* as produced by the negotiation on religion in Regensburg (Ratisbon) in 1541. It was discussed at the Council of Trent and rejected.

68. M. Schneckenburger, *Vergleichende Darstellungen des lutherischen and reformierten Lehrbegriffs* (Stuttgart, 1855), 1:265ff. O. Ritschl, *Dogmengeschichte des Protestantismus,* Vol. 3: *Die reformierte Theologie des 16. und 17. Jahrhunderts in ihrer Entstehung und Entwicklung* (Göttingen, 1926), 207ff., 298–99.

69. *WA* 15:500 / 7ff., 34ff.

70. *WA* 10³:226 / 9–10.

Therefore Luther treats the subject so tirelessly. He is not about to talk a congregation brought up to do good works out of doing works; instead, he intends to show them the true meaning of works. The one to whom all really good deeds are offered is not God but one's neighbor. The criterion of the good is whether it is of any use to the neighbor. According to this standard God will pass judgment. "On the last day he will ask you whether you have done any deeds not for the sake of yourself being justified by them but for the sake of your neighbor's being served."[71] So there is a judgment based on works. In reality, however, it is a judgment according to faith, one that dispenses with every trace of self-justification. And that judgment frees believers, by means of all the good they can do, to think not of their own salvation but only of the neighbor.

These elementary insights into the essence of grace, faith, and the good determined Luther's overall critique of the traditional piety. His criticism questioned not so much its outward degeneration as its inward perversion of meaning, evident in the most important and commonly used devotional practices. Even there his intention was not to destroy but, so far as possible, to guide devotional life back into a proper understanding of its meaning. This applies also to the veneration of saints, a practice to which he had become unaccustomed but which continued to dominate the prayer life of the people.[72] Luther's critique of this practice was not born of skepticism. Surely the saints are living. How could we doubt that what we call "life" is a single grand mystery? A child in a cradle, a person asleep, indeed, all of us awake—we are alive without knowing the secret of life. "Therefore as God deals with us here on earth, in this confined prison that is hardly half of life, and where we don't fathom how we live, how much more free will his dealings be in heaven where everything is far and wide and life is what it should be." Yet we do not know more than that the deceased faithful, and even the Mother of God, are alive; "but how they are doing, this inquiry we leave in the dear God's keeping."[73] Like some curious fantasy, moreover, the superstitious belief in the miraculous workings and blessings ascribed to specific saints is something Luther intends to ward off. This popular practice—as he already assessed it in 1518 in his sermons on the Ten Commandments—falls under the First Command-

71. WA 11:94 / 27ff. Cf. A. Peters, *Glaube und Werk: Luthers Rechtfertigungslehre im Lichte der Heiligen Schrift,* AGTL 8 (Hamburg, 1962), esp. 83ff.: "Our deeds as God's deeds to us in the law, and in us through the gospel."

72. L. Pinomaa, "Luthers Weg zur Verwerfung des Heiligendienstes," *LuJ* 29 (1962): 35ff. (Cf. Pinomaa's expanded treatment in his *Die Heiligen bei Luther* [Helsinki, 1977]—K.B.)

73. WA 10³:269 / 1ff., 17ff.

ment's prohibition of idolatry and magic.[74] Just as little as on their miraculous powers should we look on the moral superiority of the saints, be their lives even as rigorous as John the Baptist's: "Let us see what they taught." This depends on their word and their faith; this is the "holy of holies" and is no different than with Christ himself, "for Christ did the greatest work with his teaching, and his miracles are not contrary to his teaching."[75] Someone truly a saint becomes so not by deeds but as one who trusts, a "preaching saint," as Luther called John the Baptist, for inviting us to Christ.[76] Luther is not ready to deny the intercession of the saints. Yet the prayers of one believer do not avail more than those of another. "The prayer of the humblest lad or lass on earth count as much as that of St. Peter or the angel Gabriel in heaven, and for no other reason than that they all have the same Christ." It is, then, no sin to beseech the saints, but it is advisable to turn to Christ alone.[77] When we place our trust in him alone we honor the saints at the same time. To be sure, Luther adds, if that would indeed be our practice, then the cult of the saints would vanish.[78] Similarly, it would be a better idea to switch the intercessory prayer for the dead to intercession for the living, for whom we owe concern.[79] Above all, the money that the faithful have been taught to lavish on prayers to the departed saints should be given to the poor and defenseless. This is what God has commanded, not endowments for dead saints.[80]

While the cult of the saints left him relatively cool, Luther was aroused to impassioned protest by the abuses surrounding the honoring of the Virgin Mary. Here his heart was involved, for it is in Mary that a biblical character whom he cherished as much as anyone was idolatrously distorted by ecclesiastical devotion. Were she among us on earth today, Luther thought, she herself would weep tears of blood over what went on. The humble, trusting maid and loving mother has been transformed into a queen and elevated above all the choirs of angels. Again and again Luther objects to the "Salve regina, mater misericordiae, vita, dulcedo . . . ," sung to her everywhere. "Who will answer for it that she should be our

74. WA 11:36 / 2ff.; 137 / 23ff. "Decem praecepta Wittenbergensi praedicata populo," WA 1:398ff.
75. WA 10³:205 / 5, 8ff. WA 15:416 / 25–26.
76. WA 12:604 / 41. WA 11:139 / 3.
77. WA 10³:204 / 5ff., 20.
78. WA 11:137 / 32ff.
79. WA 11:61 / 24ff.
80. WA 10³:407 / 29ff., 318 / 15ff.

life, our compassion, our sweetness, she who herself was content to be a humble vessel?"[81] God alone, who has raised her so high, is to be praised, not she herself. Not a thread remains for Mary herself. This is precisely what comforts us, that God has taken her, a nobody, and filled her with his grace. As he has done it for her, so we are encouraged to hope it for ourselves. The great talents ascribed to her could only frighten us.[82] Luther therefore takes pains to return all that is said about her to the biblical standard. Certainly, she was a virgin, and God intended it so. Yet that is not of great account; everything turns on the fact that her son becomes our Lord.[83] She was without sin, yet not of herself but like all the rest of us by the grace that does not ascribe sin. Luther sees the story of the twelve-year-old Jesus as an example of sin in Mary; she has lost God's son and therefore, after having been so highly favored, she must have endured hellish fear and despair, for our benefit. This is how grace deals with us. It removes despair from the sinner and places it on the saint, making the saint insecure. In this way we are placed on a common footing. In God's presence there is no difference between Mary the mother and Mary Magdalene the prostitute.[84]

The human portrait of Mary remains, and Luther sketches it for his congregation with the few lines the Bible offers.[85] Yet in doing so he does not intend to close the door on Mary as intercessor, for as such she is in no way different from the duty we all have to intercede for one another. One must be able to say to one's neighbor, "Your prayer is as important to me as hers."[86] In this respect we are her brothers and sisters, even though she received the incomparable honor of becoming the mother of the Lord. This implies no spiritual difference. She has need of the same faith in the gospel and the same redemption. Christ alone is the Mediator; there is no such thing as an auxiliary mediating role for Mary. Because of its misuse in the devotion to Mary, Luther would like to see the "Hail Mary" discontinued, although he did not object to the words. Only those standing firmly in the faith are able to say the "Hail Mary" without risk.[87] However, the picture of Mary has been so terribly distorted by her devotees that it would be better to get rid of it altogether.[88] Indeed, the very Luther who

81. WA 10³:321 / 7ff.
82. WA 11:142 / 36ff. WA 12:613 / 9ff.
83. WA 15:411 / 21ff.; 477 / 5–6; 480 / 32ff.
84. WA 15:416 / 4ff.
85. WA 11:60 / 35–36.
86. WA 10³:322 / 6ff.
87. WA 15:480 / 33ff. WA 11:60 / 3–61 / 32.
88. WA 11:61 / 26.

expressed his love for the Mother of the Lord so poetically in his exposition of the Magnificat (1521), and who never ceased in this affection, on one occasion sighed deeply, It were better if we had never known anything about her "than that we have so dishonored her."[89]

The worst feature of the veneration of the saints and Mary remained for Luther the cult of relics and the promotion of pilgrimages. Here his skepticism shakes things loose. Who knows whether the bones of the Three Kings in Cologne were not actually the bones of three peasants? At any rate, they were not kings who visited the Holy Child, or Herod would have received them quite differently; they were priests or wise men.[90] The legend of the eleven thousand virgins seemed to Luther "pretty close to a lie."[91] The unsupported fable that the apostle James is buried in Compostella in Spain is dismissed with sarcasm. Perhaps a dog or a horse lies buried there, where at great expense throngs of people go on pilgrimage instead of doing genuinely good works. Other fables locate James in Toulouse.[92] Luther is especially angered over the "atrocious game" in Trier, where, first in 1512 and again much more brilliantly, they exhibited the alleged seamless robe of Christ.[93] To him, this sort of thing, along with the veneration of the presumed recovery of Christ's cross, is a trick of the devil, because it lures the people off the true way of taking up their cross and induces them to perpetrate "abuse and folly" and to will costly endowments and undertake pilgrimages and gorgeous festivals while they let the poor go on starving. There are so many fragments of the holy cross all over the world that one could build a house with them; something like seven skulls of St. Barbara receive homage.[94] Compared to the space they occupied in popular piety, Luther's mockery in his sermons over these phenomena plays only a minor role. His main concern is that the two fundamental precepts of the Christian life—faith and love—are transgressed [by this exploitation of popular religiosity]. Instead of the finding and elevation of the cross in festivals, every believer "should find and take up his own cross" as Christ commanded.[95] Above all, however, Luther

---

89. WA 11:142 / 13–14. On the Magnificat, see above, pp. 6–7. On the enduring attitude of Luther toward Mary, and on his position on the festivals of Mary, cf. H. Düfel, *Luthers Stellung zur Marienverehrung* (Göttingen, 1968); H. D. Preuss, *Maria bei Luther*, SVRG 172 (Gütersloh, 1954): W. Delius, "Luther und die Marienverehrung," *ThLZ* 79 (1954): 409ff.

90. WA 15:409 / 2ff.

91. WA 10³:352 / 22ff.

92. WA 10³:235 / 8ff.

93. WA 10³:369 / 23ff. Cf. later, WA 30²:297 / 3ff. WA 30³:315 / 33–34.

94. WA 10³:332 / 8ff.; 333 / 9ff.

95. WA 10³:335 / 21ff.

finds pilgrimages a perversion of Christ's will. "Before one gives a poor man 30 guilders, one has rather run to and fro, spending 40 to 100 of them."[96] The impoverished person is the living shrine "to which God's word directs us, and not to the bones of the saints adorned with gold." One object Luther was particularly impatient to see removed was a big favorite among many pilgrims: the crucifixes that sweat blood. If this deception were to cease, the way of faith would be more readily learned.[97]

While these flagrancies of popular piety irritated him, and he plausibly rebuked their outward and superstitious strains, Luther turned most of his attention to the underlying motives. Here his mockery turned to impassioned earnestness. Although everyone was praying and much was being said and written about prayer, Christians were being poorly prepared to pray. They were taught the words but not the meaning, and they were advised to multiply and count their prayers. "There is quite a difference between saying and praying the Lord's Prayer. . . . You can say twenty Lord's Prayers per hour without praying a single syllable." Praying, Luther pointed out, is a "spiritual matter."[98] In two of his sermons on the Lord's Prayer (1523) he provided some instruction whose power still pulsates through Rörer's transcript. With the opening words of the Lord's Prayer, "I preach to myself and reflect: You are speaking with the Father, whom you cannot see, who is in heaven; he can help you." With each petition one must visualize the need out of which one speaks. Nothing keeps the heart so constant in prayer as need. "So, then, if you would keep on praying, consider the need of your neighbor,"[99] of your fellow human beings. Luther applies this advice to all seven petitions, so that the trials of the individual are bound up in the kingdom of God. The lively visualized need is then answered ever anew by the promise received in the Father's name and in the preached word. Luther's advice not only pertains to the words but also deals penetratingly with the feelings that bear on faith. Medieval piety was flooded with motifs from Christ's passion, ranging from its popular patterns to its mystical depths. Luther sensed the unusual risk of such motifs misleading people into feelings of sympathy [for Jesus], which missed the point of passion. Only the tear-jerking "pulpit-pounders" take this route. "Christ does not want your tears," said Luther, "and his passion was endured for your joy." Let people

96. WA 10³:235 / 14ff.
97. WA 10³:334 / 23–24; 335 / 17ff.
98. WA 11:55 / 16ff., 25ff.
99. WA 11:56 / 2–3, 20–21, 30ff.

hear the word of Christ, "Look, this is what you would have had to suffer. I've taken everything on my shoulders." This trusting reception of fruit of Christ's passion is the right kind of meditation, not simply the pious contemplation of its unfolding event. From such meditating in faith there arises love for God and discipleship of the Crucified One.[100]

And where does this discipleship lead? Whatever Luther had to say about faith and love as content of a true Christian life, and whatever he set as a criterion over against all forms of devotion, always pointed in the same direction: to a deepening of Christian individuality, to a deliberate appropriation of the message of grace, and to a personal sense of responsibility for one's neighbors. Given these impulses, the picture of the congregation—the visibly emerging image of the church—had to be transformed. With tireless concern Luther the preacher lays it on the hearts of his hearers that they themselves are responsible for the congregation; they are to learn to stand in the front ranks and no longer behind the protecting phalanx of clergy, which had been deciding the questions of doctrine as well as of conscience. Just as Wittenberg is a community of citizens, so it is also a communion of saints, as the creed calls the church. In place of the much misused word "church," Luther preferred to speak of [the people of God as] *Christenheit*, Christendom. This kind of designation is not easily perverted into juridical or hierarchical notions, as happened with "church." *Christenheit* conveys the sense of communion of saints, that is, of the communion of faithful Christians *(communio fidelium)* throughout the world.[101]

This call of Luther's to self-reliance had its outward and inward aspects. Where a person has hindered Christians, as a responsible person, to judge for himself and to differentiate where the gospel is preached and where the voice of the true Shepherd is heard, and where not, one has "taken the sword [of the Spirit] from them." This right to judge must be regained not by violence but by the Word alone.[102] Yet a right that has been lost for about a thousand years points to a condition within and becomes a serious admonition to the Christian himself. Just as he had done in his first sermon on returning from the Wartburg, Luther continued to impress on his hearers that in the face of death they could not count on popes or councils or even on angels, but they themselves would have to know whom they have believed. "It's worth your neck! It's worth your life!

100. WA 15:509 / 26ff.; 510 / 1ff.; 511 / 29ff.; 512 / 13–14.
101. WA 11:53 / 13ff., 24.
102. WA 10³:174 / 6ff.

215

Therefore God must tell it to your heart: This is the Word of God—otherwise it is uncertain. So, then, you yourself must be certain, even if there is not another soul around." In this responsibility for himself and for the community, the being of the "spiritual man" (1 Cor. 2:15), the Christian, finds realization. In the spiritual realm there is a standard of measurement different from that in the temporal. In the latter, an older person is more intelligent than a younger, and an educated person wiser than a lay person. "But in spiritual matters a child or a servant or a woman or a lay person possesses the grace of God as readily as an elder, be he a pope or a doctor."[103] Therefore lay people, for once, may preach, when the bishops keep silent.[104] To be sure, this is only an emergency measure and not intended to be permanent. An outcome of the general priesthood of the Word is that it comprises the basis for an ordained ministry. It is precisely because all Christians have been called to bear witness that this ordained ministry needs to be controlled by the congregation. Otherwise, like women in the marketplace, everyone would talk and no one would listen.[105]

Two things are part of the office of every Christian. One is intercession, which really makes us disciples of Christ in his priestly dealing before God and puts us on the same footing not only with the clergy but also with Mary and all the saints. Rightly understood, such intercession must always be for a strengthening of "the own faith" of others, and not simply a substitute for their faith—as it is with the prayers of monks and nuns, as an offering compensating for the faith and praise lacking in others.[106] The other—also part of each Christian's office—is that of hearing confession. Luther is well aware of the special responsibility of the preacher to hear confession, and he treasures it, but that does not rule out that a believing Christian, on request, can hear another person's confession and pronounce forgiveness. Whoever has a heartfelt need for forgiveness should be able to receive it from a fellow Christian, "as though Christ himself were your father confessor." This is no different from hearing it from an ordained pastor: "Take these words as though God had spoken them from heaven."[107]

Luther's summonses to his sermon audience were not revolutionary in the sense of a transformation of conditions in the church. They were revo-

103. WA 10³:262 / 8ff.; 263 / 18ff.
104. WA 12:463 / 36.
105. WA 10³:396 / 3ff.; 397 / 17–18. Cf. above pp. 127–28.
106. WA 10³:306 / 4–310 / 30.
107. WA 10³:395 / 22ff. WA 12:493 / 3; 522 / 27ff.; 524 / 1ff.

lutionary in only one sense, that of summoning the Christian to his spiritual responsibility. In outward appearances he let the scene remain as open as ever. When one grasped the significance of faith as central to all that went on in the church, its appearance had to change only a little. For bishops in the evangelical sense, for pastors as servants of the Word, for the purged mass as for genuine confession, there was room for change. Just as little as Luther was reluctant to adopt rigid new forms of worship, so he was in no hurry to introduce new offices. Nor could he make up his mind to revive the early Christian diaconate. Gladly he would have tried it, but he feared that the original office of loving service had become devaluated into a lecture service. Besides, he claimed not to have the people suitable for the office and therefore did not trust himself to make a beginning.[108] This is the kind of hesitancy that frequently showed up with him, and in this case in connection with an undisputed office. He thus showed he did not place very high value on the educational work of offices and structures; he was content with too little rather than too much organization.

Just as with their spiritual estate, Luther encouraged Christians to come to grips with their temporal estate, for it is there that faith must pass its real tests, especially in marriage and family life with all its toils and care, its responsibilities of couples caring for one another and for their children. "If faith is really to be tested, then everything must be insecure." Therefore Luther urged that marriage, hitherto regarded as in the temporal sphere, be with far more logic called a spiritual estate.[109] Preaching on the wedding at Cana (1524), he drove home to his hearers that God has blessed marriage with his Word, work, and cross; that he has given us the married estate as a place of training in fidelity, faith, and love; and that he has "salted it well with work, otherwise maggots would spoil it."[110]

Going beyond this most personal estate, Luther endeavored repeatedly to prepare Christians for their place in the world. Here his concept of the two kingdoms was applicable, as he set forth in two sermons in Weimar, out of which grew his treatise *On Temporal Authority*.[111] In other sermons, both before and after 1528, he spelled out other aspects of the subject. But he was especially intent on Christians being ready and able

---

108. WA 12:693 / 33ff.
109. WA 11:145 / 7ff. WA 12:618 / 13ff.
110. WA 15:417ff.; 419 / 33–34.
111. See above, pp. 113ff.

217

to participate in judicial office, for as he explained, only Christians were in a position to judge fairly, doing so impartially in the knowledge of God, who is no respecter of persons.[112] To be sure, the norm for necessary legal decisions is not biblical but worldly and requires wisdom as well as fairness. In a sermon Luther drove home the point, illustrating it from a favorite emblem: the crossed swords on the coat of arms of Electoral Saxony. The hilt of the sword on the white field is to remind one of the friendliness and mercy from which all justice should be derived. The sword point in the black field represents the earnestness and severity with which justice must be applied when necessary. That the swords cross and mutually restrain each other points to the fact "that a judge be intelligent and wise, and that he see where to moderate and temper the severity of the law, and recognize when one law cancels another."[113]

If Luther was to nurture his hearers in a new understanding of community and of the responsibility of Christians in its civic as well as spiritual aspects, he would have to tear them away from the concept of the church in which they had hitherto believed. His preaching on this subject was marked not so much by sharp polemics, although these were not lacking, as by a broad exegetical foundation. On this basis he employed his texts as standards for examining the various sides of the popular notion of the church. Let the Bible enable the congregation to judge for itself. The pope was the chief target of Luther's acrimony, for the pope was the figure symbolizing the complete perversion of the church; in him was concentrated the hopeless confusion of the church's primary spiritual task with all sorts of temporal, judicial, and political powers. The realm, or kingdom, of Christ is only spiritual, for it is a lordship over human hearts through the Word and through suffering. In the hour of his arrest, Jesus sent his disciples away, and he forbade Peter to defend his master by the sword: "I must face danger standing alone." Yet the pope summons the temporal arm: "Christ and his deputy—how do you rhyme that?"[114] If only the pope would be content simply to be a temporal ruler, but he is determined to rule over the conscience of people by coercive law and to require deeds of devotion which have nothing to do with God's Word. "This is where the kingdom of Christ ends. Whoever sits in the papal chair is the Antichrist."[115] For the Antichrist is no enemy from without but a perver-

112. WA 11:47 / 15ff.
113. WA 10³:254ff.; 255 / 9ff.
114. WA 15:512 / 29ff.; 513 / 10; 514 / 18.
115. WA 11:73 / 21ff. WA 12:334 / 20ff. WA 15:452 / 17ff.; 361 / 27ff.; 392 / 8ff.

sion of Christ from within the church itself. With grim irony Luther also assails the intermingling of spiritual and temporal powers among the bishops. What, after all, still distinguishes them from the princes and lords of the land? The princes wear hats and plumes, the bishops wear miters and tonsures.[116]

What could such a critique of its contemporary representatives do but produce a different panorama of the church's history? Not only in his writings but also from the pulpit, when the text was appropriate, Luther destroyed the notion that from its beginning the church was one and without error. Never was there a time in the church when one could rely on the authority of particular individuals. Even the age of the apostles abounded in heresies, and on occasion some of the apostles themselves erred gravely, as in the case of the Jewish Christians in Jerusalem (Acts 15:5ff.) or Peter and Barnabas in Antioch (Gal. 2:11ff.).[117] Peter especially is a case in point as to the true foundation of the church. It is not the word or faith of a person; Peter failed badly enough, and Christ had to send him away as a tempter. "Rock" (Matt. 16:18) is Peter's designation only insofar as he himself stands on Christ, the Rock, and by faith becomes part of that Rock, just the way all of us can become equals with Peter through the recognition of Christ. He was no second rock, alongside Christ and against which the powers would not be able to triumph. The power of the keys is therefore not Peter's alone; it is the power of the believing church which stands on Christ the Rock.[118] Peter, however, in recognizing and confessing the uniqueness of the Son of God became first in the line of faithful who repeated this confession after him. He himself is therefore a witness against any sort of reliance on the authority of a particular person. The truth alone, which he believes and shares, is authority. Peter is therefore not the head of the church but the firstborn and model of all preachers. The pope and the bishops are like Peter only insofar as they preach the pure Word of God.[119]

Luther found this portrait of the apostle, derived from the gospel texts, substantiated in the First Letter of Peter. To his Wittenbergers Luther preached a long sermon series on this letter in 1523, expounding it during the Sunday afternoon and weekday services.[120] This letter, "one of the

116. *WA* 11:152 / 25ff.
117. *WA* 12:467 / 9ff.; 417 / 3ff.
118. *WA* 10³:208–16.
119. *WA* 11:146 / 14ff. *WA* 12:619 / 12ff.
120. *WA* 12:249–399. [*LW* 30:3–145.]

noblest in the New Testament,"[121] supplied him the essentials for a proper understanding of the congregation and of the spiritual office (ordained ministry): the true holiness of the church alone through the Spirit (1 Pet. 1:2); the gospel as message of the Lord dying and rising for us (1:3ff.); the apostolate as the preaching of this gospel, "whoever does not preach is no apostle"; the spiritual priesthood of all believing Christians (2:5ff.), replacing the external priesthood of the Old Covenant; the spiritual house of Christ's congregation, instead of the temple and its ceremonies.[122] This ecclesiological picture made it seem to Luther that through Peter himself all that the church had over the centuries been making of itself was refuted. Popes and councils have no rights of their own, but only those derived from the Word of God and from faith; the pope is not to coerce Christians by laws but must govern in the power of the Spirit; the bishop's office is not an honor but a function, bound only to God's Word, not to lord it over others but to tend the flock, and to be committed to an exemplary faith and life (5:3–4).[123] The fact that this First Letter of Peter emphasizes specifically the requirement of obedience to temporal authority leads Luther to review his picture of the church from the opposite side. This lies in the distinction between the two kingdoms of God, on which the understanding of Christ's spiritual kingdom depends; again, in the contrast between [the people of the New Covenant and] the Old Covenant, wherein God leads his visibly separated people with an external set of laws as well as with an internal set (the commandment to love God and one's neighbor). The external have attained their end in Christ, "however, whatever pertains to the spiritual realm has not been abolished, but remains forever."[124]

In the light of this broad foundation, embracing the Old and New Testaments, the appeal to councils and the church fathers made no impression on Luther. For him there was but one true tradition in the church of Christ: the proclamation of the gospel, and faith. Human traditions growing out of anything but this core are nullified in advance by virtue of the promised "Spirit of truth," which is to bear witness to Christ (John 15:26).[125] Indeed, the Spirit "will lead you into all the truth" (16:13).

121. WA 12:260 / 22–23. Besides this, see the two prefaces to Luther's translation of the Petrine letters in the New Testament, above, pp. 80ff. [LW 30:4; cf. LW 35:390–92.]

122. WA 12:262 / 15ff.; 265ff; 268 / 20–21; 306ff.; 316ff.; 386ff. [LW 30:6, 9, 13, 51, 62, 130.]

123. WA 12:278 / 15ff.; 331 / 31ff.; 390 / 3ff.; 379 / 30ff.; 391 / 8ff. [LW 30:22, 77, 135, 125, 136.]

124. WA 12:334ff.; 275 / 35ff. [LW 30:79, 20.]

125. WA 11:108 / 17–18. WA 12:576 / 14–15.

Yet widespread exegesis then current committed the outright folly of applying this work of the Spirit to councils and popes with their many decrees on ecclesiastical law, "spiritual" estates, ceremonies, rules on fasting, and so on. If this kind of thing was supposed to emanate from the Holy Spirit, the apostles themselves never even came near the truth.[126] Even if some of the apostles erred, God let it be so in order that we might learn not to trust in people but in God's Word alone. How then does the church claim inerrancy for councils and popes?[127]

Luther enlivens his sermons from time to time with examples of errors made by famous church fathers. There was the case of Augustine, for instance, and his understanding of the Second Commandment (or at least an interpretation ascribed to Augustine, which Luther himself had earlier shared), when Luke 14:23 "compel people to come in") was applied as justifying coercive measures against heretics. There was the case of Thomas Aquinas and his high esteem for the natural man's perception of God, or his distinction between commandments and counsels, which items the popes subsequently declared binding.[128] There was also still another, the rule of Francis of Assisi, which did not catch on to the fact that wisdom in the presence of God commences not with ascetic deeds but with the perception of the hidden revelation of Christ.[129] And there was also the widespread exegesis of the parable of the sower and the application of the variety of soils (Luke 8:5ff.) to marital continence, widowhood, and virginity.[130] "Let me tell you this, so that you'll know it: The fathers often erred; this too is part of God's providence, so that we stick to the gospel and do not believe everything people say, even if they be the saintliest."[131]

Even though the claim that the fathers of the church could not err was disproved by the New Testament and of itself shown absurd, a deeper question gnawed at Luther. How could he in conscience, as a single individual, take on himself the responsibility for steps leading to a split in the church? This was his real agony. Repeatedly he confessed it openly to his hearers. He did not defend himself by blaming others, those who had caused the corruption of the church and its teaching. Even a recognition of the fact that throughout history there have been divisions in the church

126. WA 12:550–51.
127. WA 12:415 / 7ff.; 418 / 3ff.
128. WA 12:414 / 21ff. WA 11:149 / 2ff. WA 12:625 / 5ff.
129. WA 11:29 / 28ff.
130. WA 11:19 / 6ff.
131. WA 11:19 / 25–26.

did not ease his burden even halfway, for this time the question was direct and personal; it came at him from within: "Do you consider yourself alone to be intelligent? Think of the many saints and learned men." "You fool, who are you to pass judgment on all those councils and decrees of the bishops and oppose them all alone?" "Had you sided with the pope, things would not have gone this way."[132] Luther had to draw on every resource of faith to turn back these objections, to refute their scriptural arguments from Scripture itself, to stand like Christ against the tempter and to say to the opponents, "Gentlemen, I will gladly be your fool, but I will trust in my Christ."[133] Under such circumstances the solitary individual must then inquire of the Word of God, and then he may be confident that God will judge the whole matter according to his Word.[134]

There was for Luther still another, a tangible comfort amid the trial. Paradoxically it was the unrest itself with which he was being reproached. It was a sign that the Word of God was at work. Luther interpreted it to his congregation in terms of the parable of Christ and the devil: "When a strong man, fully armed, guards his house, his goods are in peace; but when one stronger than he assails him . . ." (Luke 11:21–22). This is exactly what Christendom has experienced. For a long time there was no need for the devil to draw his sword. "So long as the canon law was preached, things remained calm. Here a prince endowed a university, there a cloister. The nuns were called brides of Christ, the monks were called lords. Why? Because the devil was sitting secure. . . . When someone stronger comes along, however, calm vanishes, and the devil goes mad with rage." So far, despite minor conflicts, people agreed on the main points. They believed in the pope and in their own good works. "But when Christ said, Your works are of no account . . . , then the devil got hopping" and activated his master heretics. Yet monks, of all people the ones he believed the most dependable, now began to preach against him. "Therefore thank God that you live in these times. The surest sign of the true gospel is the devil's raging."[135] Even such reassurance gave no leave to take matters in stride, especially not when in the very practice of proclamation the scene disclosed "disunity and disorder" aplenty. And the word goes round, "Though we may have the gospel, we have few Christians among us, and those who have learned better are not united among themselves." This is

132. WA 11:110 / 7; 154 / 36ff. WA 12:467 / 33.
133. WA 15:451 / 26ff.; 452 / 16. WA 11:155 / 1–2.
134. WA 12:418 / 5–6. WA 11:110 / 8–9.
135. WA 15:460 / 12–461 / 8. WA 12:466 / 20ff.; 467 / 15ff.

also what they told Christ.[136] Besides, what the congregation has already experienced it will experience still more in the future: "When the gospel is spread among the people, many frivolous spirits will lay hold of it, this one or that one, picking up whatever is appealing." In that case, the only safeguard is for each person to remain faithful to the Word and not to relax, "working and striving that they may all be of one mind."[137]

One had better not be misled by the principle that external practices in the church can vary. That is not the point. What matters is that the marks for the forgiveness of sin are there: the Word, baptism, the Lord's Supper, confession, and absolution. "Where these outward signs are present, never doubt that most certainly Father, Son, and Holy Spirit are there, as well as the forgiveness of sins." In plain terms Luther was instructing his congregation in the true unity of the church. As it was when he confronted John Eck at Leipzig, so now [four years later, while preaching on the creed] he cited the Eastern church as an example. It has the same gospel and the same marks of the church as we. Between us we can be as different as man and woman if only we are one in faith in the forgiveness and in the use of the marks through which God would forgive our sins: the Word and sacraments.[138]

Indeed, everything depends on a proper understanding of these signs. They possess no dignity or power in themselves which they then convey to the recipient, nor do they possess an intrinsic symbolic meaning of their own. They are merely external acts, yet God uses them to convey his grace. Just as little is it an indication of worthiness when people avail themselves of these acts. The worst temptation of the believing Christians is to delay reception of the sacrament until they feel worthy. To the contrary, "People should joyfully make use of the Word and sacrament when they feel lacking in faith." There is only one proper preparation: Hear and read God's Word again and again. Otherwise the fact is: "Without all my getting ready or priming, God's Word comes to me."[139] Luther has two sides of the story in mind. He chides the timidity which for sheer scruples of conscience make some people distrustful of communing, and he also opposes the methods of mystical contemplation whereby some people try to become certain of an inner revelation, as in the case of a Müntzer, a Karlstadt, or the fanatics of Zwickau. To the timid, Luther preaches confi-

136. WA 12:466 / 20–467 / 8; 507 / 28–29.

137. WA 12:466 / 5ff.; 467 / 36ff.

138. WA 11:54 / 4ff. [The sermon, in Latin, is on the Apostles' Creed, the "Symbolum," and is part of his series on the catechism.]

139. WA 12:498 / 29ff.; 497 / 2–3. WA 11:84 / 30ff.; 82 / 16ff.

dence, to the others, humility. He shudders when he thinks of the self-confidence of the sectarian enthusiasts, charging: "We have prophets who go to and fro in the land and teach the people all too brashly and defiantly and address the supreme Majesty as they would a cobbler's apprentice."[140] It is precisely the heart that feels cold and empty that is ready to receive help, if it so desires, and believes in the promise of God, that his Word will not return to him void (Isa. 55:11). No one should put communing off until he feels "all aflame with faith." It is better to trust that the Word intends to ignite the hearer as fire does wood.[141]

Luther explains the proper understanding of Word and sacrament in the three transactions which, besides preaching and instruction, comprise the worship life of the believing. Baptism is only an outward sign, like Noah's rainbow; and circumcision is only a seal or crest by which one recognizes one's master. Even an unbaptized person can believe,[142] and yet baptism is not to be regarded lightly or frivolously omitted. In contrast to the various signs which God gave to the fathers in the Old Covenant and which have disappeared, baptism is the sign that remains until Judgment Day. It is a sign given not to a single people, such as circumcision, but to the whole of humanity. It signifies what everyone has need of: the dying of the old man in us and birth of the new. Therefore baptism removes our old name, which is *Omnis homo mendax* (Ps. 116:11) ["All men are liars," KJV]. God recognizes us from now on not by our name but gives us Christians the new one, the name of Christ: "We are called by thy name" (Jer. 14:9).[143]

Likewise, with the Lord's Supper the outward sign is of no help by itself. Often Luther drives home this point by a favorite play on the Latin: *edere est credere*. "Eating and drinking in the Lord's Supper is nothing other than believing."[144] Only in faith does the Christ who appeared in flesh and blood and who is proclaimed in the gospel become our possession. This is no different from my neighbor "eating" me when I serve him with all that is my own.[145] At this point there is something to be borne in mind later, as part of a tension difficult to resolve: this repeated emphasis on the "spiritual food" in the Lord's Supper,[146] which through the Word is

140. WA 12:499 / 15–16. WA 11:83 / 20–21.
141. WA 12:500 / 15ff., 33ff.; 496 / 14. WA 15:437 / 12–13.
142. WA 10³:141 / 30ff.; 142 / 18ff. [Ascension Day sermon, May 29, 1522.]
143. WA 12:405 / 24ff.; 406 / 14ff., 28ff.
144. WA 12:582 / 10–11. WA 11:126 / 1ff. WA 15:471 / 4.
145. WA 15:503 / 6, 26ff.
146. WA 15:471 / 10; 465 / 15ff.

handed to the believer and stands in sharp contrast to the impassioned defense Luther later made, in the controversy over the Supper, for "bodily eating." And yet in his sermons of these years (1522–24) Luther said nothing he did not uphold later on. The genuine enjoyment of the sacrament was for him always a spiritual one, that is, the interplay of the Word and faith. Christ offers himself to us in no other way. Only the people Luther confronted were different. At this point in time—when faced with traditional Roman thinking about the sacrament, in which the Wittenberg congregation was raised—there was an absolute need for a spiritual appropriation of the meaning. Later, when facing the proponents of a symbolical meaning, he upheld the inseparable correlation of Christ and the signs by which he indicates his presence.

Although Luther at this particular time hardly had occasion to begin the debate on this second front, the first weapons for this coming encounter were already at hand. Proof of this was not only the debate with Karlstadt (which was going on during these years, as we have seen earlier, in Luther's treatise *Against the Heavenly Prophets*[147]) but also his oft-repeated objection against applying John 6:55ff. to the sacrament of the altar, an application prevalent among the church fathers.[148] What Christ says there about himself as the living bread and about the eating of his flesh and blood has to do exclusively with the Word and faith. By contesting the Roman sacramental interpretation of this Johannine passage, he precluded any later use of it by his opponents through his realistic concept of the Supper's elements. Like on a revolving stage the exegesis of John 6 kept on changing the scene: from the gospel for the Feast of Corpus Christi (vv. 55–59) the discussion moved on to the star witness passage of the Zwinglians (v. 63: "It is the spirit that gives life, the flesh is of no avail"). From the outset of these exegetical debates Luther had cleared the ground on both sides of this ambivalent passage. This Johannine passage permits itself to be interpreted neither one way nor the other.[149] In

---

147. See above, pp. 169ff.

148. *De captivitate Babylonica ecclesiae praeludium* (1520), WA 6:502 / 7ff. [LW 36:15, *Preface to the Babylonian Captivity of the Church*.] Opposed (without mentioning Luther) Zwingli, "Ad Matthaeum Alberum de coena domini epistola (1524)," *Sämtliche Werke* 3 (1914): 336 / 19ff. See also W. Köhler, *Zwingli und Luther: Ihr Streit über das Abendmahl nach seinen politischen und religiösen Beziehurgen*, vol. 2, QFRG 7, ed. E. Kohlmeyer and H. Bornkamm (Gütersloh, 1953), 1:74, 305–6. WA 11:125 / 18ff. WA 12:581 / 15ff. WA 15:465 / 15ff.

149. Cf. R. Bultmann, *Das Evangelium des Johannes*, 11th ed. (Göttingen, 1950), 214–15, 321, 340ff. G. Bornkamm, "Die eucharistische Rede im Johannes-Evangelium," in *Geschichte und Glaube I, Gesammelte Aufsätze* (Munich, 1968), 3:60ff. For a further treatment of the Lord's Supper controversy, see below, pp. 508ff.

the process, Luther dropped Corpus Christi from the church year calendar. In 1522 he had told his congregation that he had "never been as hostile to any festival as to Corpus Christi and to the Immaculate Conception." A year later he preached for the last time on Corpus Christi. This was his strongest testimony for the contention that faith in the real presence of Christ, taken by itself, is of no avail, because everything depends on receiving that presence in the Spirit.[150]

In a similar vein Luther directed the attention of his congregation from considering confession as an event to appropriating it as a part of life. In contrast to baptism and the Lord's Supper, confession has no outward sign. Therefore, as early as his treatise on the *Babylonian Captivity of the Church* (1520), in which he reviewed critically the seven sacraments of the Roman church, Luther no longer counted confession a sacrament.[151] In place of the sign come the words that, when treated impartially, can make people miss the point. Neither the confessing of the confessor nor the word of the priest works forgiveness; faith is the one and only effective agent. To be sure, God has entrusted the absolving word to his servants. Therefore Christians should hold fast to the absolution and not to their own acts of confessing. "After all, God is not watching to see how well you have confessed, but he keeps track of his Word and on how you believe in it."[152] The father confessor cannot create faith. He can plant and water only; he cannot give the increase (1 Cor. 3:5). Those who confess must know that they are invited to have faith and that unfaith toward God's goodness is the greatest of blasphemies.[153] Luther thus nurtures his congregation in a twofold way. He releases his hearers from anxiety over the sufficiency of their confession. What matters is not its completeness or the use of the usual categories in the catalog of sins in the confessional manuals. All depends on the heart, that it be relieved of that which depresses it most.[154] Correspondingly, Luther points Christians to that place where they are asked point blank what is at stake. And they will reply, The issue is faith, not the performance of a sacrament.

A review of Luther's preaching during these years of restructuring (1522–24) underscores the wealth of theological impulses which the Wittenberg congregation received from him. In his sermons more than in his

---

150. *WA* 12:581 / 31–32. *WA* 11:125–26. Feast of the Immaculate Conception of Mary, December 9.

151. *WA* 6:572 / 15ff. [*LW* 36:124.]

152. *WA* 15:489 / 25–26. *WA* 12:516 / 32ff. *WA* 11:91 / 31ff.

153. *WA* 12:523 / 31ff. *WA* 11:97 / 17ff.

154. *WA* 15:489 / 2, 12ff.

writings the *viva vox* of the gospel rang forth. And the cumulative content of his preaching conveyed a remarkable unity. Whether he treated faith and works, the calling of the laity in the church, the office of priest or bishop, the nature of prayer and the sacraments, the law, or the married estate—whatever the subject—he was ever at pains to make one thing clear: what is a life of faith, what is truly of the Spirit. He declared his hearers free from human regulations in the church, free from the burden of works which had saddled them. Yet at the same time, he bound them to the responsibility for their own faith, to the spreading of the Word, and to concern for fellow human beings. All these things together comprised a life in the Holy Spirit that Christ wants to see in his own. Thereby the auspices for Christian living are fundamentally changed from what they hitherto had been. Whereas they had formerly stood under rules and regulations, Christians are now free, and they bear those responsibilities themselves which they had formerly left to the priest and the organized church. In the process the church was pruned of its pseudo-spirituality and legalism down to the truly spiritual: the Word of God and the sacraments—when these, as signs, are grasped for their meaning. Luther was well aware what such rethinking implied for his congregation. Simple though it was, there remained plenty of resistance in the people's hearts, for what person is not inclined to desire freedom in the wrong place and to be bound at the wrong place? He knew that the preaching of grace could make the insolent more insolent still. In the transcript of one of Luther's sermons, Rörer had the sentence, missing in the printed version, "I am concerned lest we also contribute to the fact that by our preaching they are becoming worse."[155] How great is the temptation for a person to brag about the gifts received in Christ; instead, he should always remember, "God grant that I am not among the first who shall be last" (Matt. 19:30). "I don't care about the pope or the devil, but these are the passages that depress me."[156] Yet the presence of dangers is no excuse for silencing the truth. Part of the war that God's Word wages against the devil, Luther wrote, is that "some will fall and get hurt."[157] Nor would it be a way out to conceal the evangelical freedom that stems from the gospel, for the preaching of the law, much more so than the gospel, leads to security and arrogance toward God and neighbor. Only the gospel can confront the dangers of abuse, thanks to the twofold thrust of its message. "It can frighten the saints and comfort the humble."[158]

155. WA 12:573 / 31ff. WA 11:113 / 5–6.
156. WA 15:425 / 23ff.
157. WA 15:219 / 3.
158. WA 15:424 / 6.

9

Exposition of Scripture in Pulpit and Classroom

Luther's *Operationes in Psalmos*[1] marked the point where he had closed the sequence of major lectures during his first Wittenberg period. Most of the lectures were on New Testament epistles of central significance—Romans, Galatians, Hebrews. Even the one set of lectures devoted to the Old Testament, a twofold exposition of the Psalms, often bore a New Testament character thanks to the prophetic-christological method Luther employed. Two of his lecture series, those on Galatians and Psalms, were sufficiently inclusive to produce commentaries of basic importance for Luther's hermeneutics.

Returning in March from his exile on the Wartburg, Luther had been absent from Wittenberg almost exactly one year. An array of other immediate concerns prevented him from resuming his normal university duties. The restructuring of the chaotic Wittenberg congregation, the various journeys this task required, and his literary responsibilities, especially the preparations for publishing [his translation of the] New Testament, preoccupied Luther. The fact that he had able colleagues eased his situation at times. For example, Melanchthon's exegetical lectures had enjoyed a strong student following since 1519. Other colleagues could also be counted on, among them Karlstadt, John Dölsch, Justus Jonas, and John Bugenhagen.[2]

At any rate, Luther resumed a practice that the trip to Worms had interrupted: the exposition in sermons of selected books of the Bible. His intention was twofold as he combined a homiletical-devotional approach with a popular-hermeneutical goal. Besides, as if to make up for his absence, he offered two series of sermons simultaneously, one from the Old

---

1. See above, p. 5.

2. Cf. P. F. Barton, "Die exegetische Arbeit des jungen Melanchthon 1518 / 19 bis 1528 / 29," *ARG* 54 (1963): 52ff. W. Maurer, *Der junge Melanchthon zwischen Humanismus und Reformation* (Göttingen, 1969), 2:103ff. On the exegetical lectures in Wittenberg during these years, see the reference to Spalatin in J. B. Mencken, *Scriptores rerum Germanicarum praecipue Saxonicarum* (Leipzig, 1728), 617. Also Friedensburg, *Geschichte der Universität Wittenberg* (Magdeburg, 1926), 1:166–67.

Testament (Genesis), the other from the New (Matthew).[3] Both themes [the homiletical and the hermeneutical] return with this fresh resumption of his preaching, if not simultaneously then at least sequentially, and are repetitive at times in order to make their interconnection plain. Meanwhile the demands of a hermeneutic for the laity [that the people should grasp the meaning of the Scriptures] had become an even more pressing responsibility. This emphasis appeared in short segments in the prefaces to his translation of the New Testament books and simply required deepening by means of a thorough exegetical exposition. In the course of his series of sermons over the next few years, Luther was fond of treating the interrelationship of the two Testaments. The difference between his exegesis in the pulpit and that at the lectern was one of degree but not of kind. Later Melanchthon could readily draw on the transcripts of Luther's Genesis sermons for his own *Comments on Several Obscure Chapters in Genesis* (1523).[4]

Luther led off with a sequence of presentations on 1 Peter (ca. May to December 1522).[5] In point of time it runs parallel to the printing of the New Testament and his prefaces. Two things here are of fundamental importance: First, there is but one proper subject of correct Christian teaching, namely, the gospel, the way the great apostles preached [taught] it.

[They] are the best evangelists. Therefore Paul's epistles are gospel to a greater degree than the writings of Matthew, Mark, and Luke, for the latter do little more than relate the history of the deeds and miracles of Christ. But no one stresses the grace we have through Christ as powerfully as Paul does, especially in his Epistle to the Romans. Now since greater value attaches to the words of Christ than to his works and deeds (and if we had to dispense with one or the other, it would be better for us to do without the deeds and the history than to be without the words and the doctrine), those books that mainly treat Christ's teaching and words should in all conscience be esteemed most highly, for even if Christ's miracles were nonexistent, or if we knew nothing about them, His words would be enough for us. Without them we could not have life. Accordingly, this [First] Epistle of Peter is also one of the noblest books in the New Testament.[6]

3. On the sermons of 1519–21, cf. *WA* 9:314ff. On the burden of these sermon series as well as his preaching on the pericope to his fellow Augustinians, cf. *WA* 9:322–23 and *WA* Br 2:274, n. 5 of the collected places in his correspondence.

4. *In obscuriora aliquot capita Geneseos annotationes, CR* 13:761ff. Cf. H. Sick, *Melanchthon als Ausleger des Alten Testaments* (Tübingen, 1959), 29. For more detail, see Maurer, *Der junge Melanchthon,* 2:115–14, 526–27.

5. The dating of this performance in 1523 in *WA* 12:249–50 is corrected in *WA* 14:2 by Georg Buchwald. The printer's manuscript is correctly dated 1523. [*LW* 30:ix.]

6. *WA* 12:260 / 10ff., 22–24. [*LW* 30:4.]

The canon for Christ's teaching is then not only his message as recorded in the Gospels but also the word of the risen Lord, which he speaks through the mouth of his true apostles. It is recognizable as proclamation of the resurrection, which is more than pure history or miracle. Beyond doubt, the message is the message only because of the gift it brings the sinner. "For He ascended into heaven to bestow his Spirit on us, to give us a new birth, and to give us the courage to come to the Father and say, 'See, I come before you and pray, not in reliance on my petition, but my Lord Christ represents me and is my intercessor.'" The writings of the true apostles are recognizable from this gospel of the risen Lord. "This enables one to observe that the Epistle of James is no truly apostolic epistle, for it does not contain a single word about these things."[7] Thereby Luther once again made clear to his congregation, as he had in his preface, why the Epistle of James is "straw" and unfruitful—not because it lacks spirit but because it is silent on the central fact of faith.[8]

The second basic hermeneutical problem is raised by the relation of the Old and New Testaments. In his sermonic treatment of 1 Peter, Luther presented a masterful little lesson which he could hardly have given his students more concisely.[9] Again the cardinal point where the two Testaments are joined and divided is the gospel. The Old contains the gospel prophetically, the New in actuality. "The books of Moses and the prophets are also gospel, since they proclaimed and described in advance what the apostles preached or wrote later about Christ." Strictly speaking, only the Old Testament is "Scripture," while the New "should not really be written but should be expressed with the living voice [which resounds and is heard throughout the world]." The real theme of the Old Testament is the law, as set down in the books of Moses. The gospel stands only on the distant horizon as God's response to humankind's foundering on the law to which the historical books of the Old Testament give ample testimony.[10]

So, then, the Old Testament, on the one hand, is "the foundation of our faith" because it points toward our salvation from the law through Christ. On the other hand, the Old is "abolished and discarded." Luther clarifies this on two counts. First, "the former pointed to Christ, while the New

7. WA 12:268 / 11ff., 23ff. [LW 30:12.]

8. Preface to the Epistle of James (1522). "Which ones are the genuine and noblest books of the New Testament." WA DB 6:10 / 33. WA DB 7:384 / 19ff. Martin Luthers Vorreden zur Bibel, ed. H. Bornkamm (Hamburg, 1967), 177. [LW 35:396–97.]

9. WA 12:274 / 33–277 / 13. [LW 30:19–22.]

10. WA 12:275 / 5ff. [LW 30:19.]

Testament now gives us what was promised and prefigured in the Old."[11] Furthermore, "in the Old Testament, God carried on a twofold government: external and internal. . . . This explains why he gave them so many kinds of laws mingled together." One kind might be temporal, such as the bill of divorce; another might be spiritual, like "You shall love your neighbor as yourself." "Now, however, God reigns only spiritually in us through Christ. He executes the temporal and external rule through the civil government." The only thing remaining unchanged is that which applies to "spiritual government" and which the law of Moses also contained: the love toward God and one's neighbor, "Thus all that is not external in the Old Testament still stands."[12]

In this little presentation on 1 Peter, Luther voices the fundamental historical insight that God meets the Israelites as deity of the people and that he consolidates his elect by means of their own law and secures them against other peoples. Ever since Christ there is, then, no longer a temporal law of God, only the universal divine law of love. The law has become temporal, at least by God's charge and in responsibility before him. Likewise all cultic requirements are abolished, even though the Old Covenant was full of them. "Everything is the same in Christ, to whom all was directed."[13] Given a law with such a goal, Luther nevertheless discerned some spiritual implications in it. Certain otherwise superseded legal or cultic prescriptions bore analogies. For example, as the right of divorce is based on grounds of adultery, so God has the right to reject the Jews who refuse to believe in Christ. Or again, as the old Levitical law allows the widow to conceive a son by the brother of her deceased husband (Deut. 25:5ff.), so we, for the sake of the deceased Christ, are commanded to "make souls pregnant and fruitful through the gospel."[14] Those were the days when Luther still liked to ferret out the hidden meaning in such defunct rights and rituals. It was difficult for him to ignore this still-blooming medieval art of allegory. In time, however, he succeeded, and concentrated on the verities of faith. On the one hand, the prophetic-christological interpretation, which he shared with the tradition of the church back to New Testament times, was for him the indispensable bridge to the Old Testament. On the other hand, this same bridge led him

11. WA 12:274 / 35; 277 / 11; 275 / 24ff. [LW 30:19, 21, 20.]
12. WA 12:275 / 35–276 / 14, 35. [LW 30:20–21.]
13. WA 12:275 / 31ff. [LW 30:20.]
14. WA 12:276 / 24ff. [LW 30:21.] The same allegory of Deut. 25:5ff. is in Luther's treatment of Deuteronomy (1525), WA 14:719 / 37ff. [LW 9:248.]

to the depths of contrast between law and gospel and the differentiation between the Old and New Covenants.[15]

It is the message of the apostle himself, not only the hermeneutical interplay between 1 Peter and the Old Testament, that holds Luther's interest. [As we saw above], Luther's interest in Peter[16] grew as he came to see him increasingly as the decisive figure in his confrontation with the papacy. In fact, Luther proceeded to confront the Roman myths about Peter with a whole set of sobering statements. Not only had the apostle Peter denied the person of Christ, he had, even more important, perverted the intention of Christ; he was guilty of the latter when at Antioch he refused to eat with the Gentiles. In this way he surrendered the liberty of the gospel in favor of the limitations of the law. Paul was therefore right in taking Peter severely to task (Gal. 2:11ff.). Given this manner of performance, there can be no talk of giving Peter precedence over the other apostles, and certainly not of carrying it over to the later popes. The New Testament accounts permit nothing of the kind.[17] Over against this misplacement of Peter in Roman tradition, Luther rehabilitated the apostle by soundly expounding his epistle and according Peter the recognition due a teacher of the gospel. The very things Luther charged Rome with denying he found substantiated in Peter: everyone's right to search the Scriptures independently as the sole source of the Spirit of Christ, as well as the right and the duty freely to assume responsibility for it (1 Pet. 1:11, 3:15); the spiritual priesthood of all Christians (2:5, 9); the ecclesial office as a shepherding function and not a domineering practice (5:1ff.).[18] In Peter's mind the image of bishop is the opposite of the papal portrait as it has become in the course of history. The popes demand obedience without any basis in Scripture. They keep Christians in line under external laws instead of under the admonishing Word of God, to which popes themselves are bound and required to give spiritual leadership.[19] They turn their office into a soft life. "They lounge around on cushions and act

15. On Luther's use of allegory, cf. G. Ebeling, *Evangelische Evangelienauslegung: Eine Untersuchung zu Luthers Hermeneutik* (Munich, 1942; reprint, Darmstadt, 1962), 49ff., 160ff.; and H. Bornkamm, *Luther und das Alte Testament* (Tübingen, 1948), 76ff. [*Luther and the Old Testament* (1969), 87ff.] On the relation between the two Covenants and Testaments, see Bornkamm, *Luther und das Alte Testament*, 69ff.

16. See above, pp. 219–20.

17. Cf. F. Rickers, "Das Petrusbild Luthers: Ein Beitrag zu seiner Auseinandersetzung mit dem Papsttum" (theology diss., Heidelberg 1967).

18. WA 12:277 / 31ff.; 360 / 1ff.; 306 / 25ff.; 316 / 20ff.; 386 / 15ff. [*LW* 30:22, 102, 55–56, 62, 133–37.]

19. WA 12:278 / 15ff.; 331 / 31ff.; 379 / 30ff. [*LW* 30:22, 76, 125.]

like landed gentry, laying burdens on us such as they themselves would never touch."[20] Commenting on the verse "not as domineering over those in your charge but being examples to the flock," Luther summarizes it thus: "With a single word Peter has overturned and condemned all government as the pope now runs it." "From this you can roundly conclude and clearly prove that the pope with his bishops is an Antichrist or counter-Christ, because he simply carries out nothing of what Peter here requires."[21]

Luther knew this was an enormous indictment. At first it was only a dark surmise that he had simply "whispered into the ear" of his friend Spalatin.[22] On reading Ulrich von Hutten's newly published edition of Lorenzo Valla, which proved the *Donation of Constantine* a forgery, Luther could "hardly doubt any longer that the pope is the Antichrist." The papal bull threatening Luther with excommunication made him completely certain of it.[23] After his own prolonged hesitation, Luther took all the greater pains to impress on his hearers that they too would have to be ready with the evidence, like that which he had meanwhile rounded out broadly during his recent theological polemics.[24] The point was this: "You should be able not only to rebuke the pope as an Antichrist but to prove it as well."[25] The apostle Peter's image of the true shepherd of the church gave Luther some welcome intuitions.

In the meantime, he had not completely dropped the idea (it had long calmed his uncertainty over the issue of obedience) that according to Rom. 13 the pope is also one of the powers-that-be. Now he applied the idea in order to distinguish sharply between the temporal function and the spiritual function of the pope. When, for example, the pope acts as a temporal sovereign and gives orders concerning clothing or fasting, he is to be obeyed, but when he does this on spiritual grounds, making his orders seem like a command of God, simply reply, "Your grace, sir, I shall

20. WA 12:391 / 25–26. [*LW* 30:137. Translation updated.]

21. WA 12:391 / 13ff., 33ff.; 361 / 30. [*LW* 30:135, 107.]

22. Letter to Link, December 18, 1518, WA Br 1:270 / 11ff. To Spalatin, March 13, 1519, WA Br 1:359 / 29–30; "I'll whisper it in your ear. I don't know whether the pope is the Antichrist himself or his apostle." [*LW* 48:114.]

23. To Spalatin, February 24, 1520, WA Br 2:48 / 20ff. To the same, October 11, 1520, WA Br 2:195 / 22–23. Cf. E. Bizer, *Luther und der Papst* (Munich, 1958), 35. H.-G. Leder, *Ausgleich mit dem Papst?* (Stuttgart, 1969), 60ff. E. Mühlhaupt, "Vergängliches und Unvergängliches an Luthers Pabstkritik," *LuJ* 26 (1959): 70ff.

24. *Responsio ad librum . . . Ambrosii Catharini*, WA 7:722 / 20–778. Luther here links Dan. 8:23ff. with 2 Thess. 2, and with various passages from Revelation.

25. WA 12:392 / 14ff.

not do it."[26] Here too[27] the profane character of temporal law is set off clearly from things spiritual. Therefore Luther does not miss his chance to let 1 Pet. 2:13–17 draw the distinction between the two realms. He did so often at that time, notably in his treatise *On Temporal Authority.*[28] Let Christians willingly do their duty in the political realm "for the Lord's sake," and not for the sake of any compensation. So the political realm remains a temporal one in which both believer and unbeliever stand shoulder to shoulder. "The secular rule has nothing to do with the office of Christ; it is an external matter, as are all other offices and estates. And just as these are outside the pale of Christ's office, so that a non-Christian can administer them as well as a Christian, so it is not the office of the secular sword[29] to make people either Christians or non-Christians."[30] By way of contrast, the Christian church must "be led and governed only in the Spirit." The popes, however, keep the church itself—not only the states run by the church—under their own control by means of external laws and punishment.[31] The counterpart to this is that the church demands the immunity of the clergy from the jurisdiction of the civil courts and uses the threat of excommunication against the temporal authorities in order to have its way.[32] In either case, they transgress the basic divine order of the world and fail to differentiate between the two realms.

Compared to the rich results drawn from 1 Peter, those from 2 Peter and Jude were less rewarding for the congregation. Luther's sermons covered these letters during January and February 1523. Nevertheless, he employs the strongly expectant character of 2 Peter in order to bring out clearly the function of good works in the Christian life. Such works do not make a person "devout and pleasant" in the sight of God, for that depends on faith, but good works are the fruits of faith and are therefore to be taken seriously. Besides, with reference to a thought raised by 2 Pet. 1:10,[33] good works of this kind liberate the Christian from the great question of

26. WA 12:334 / 15–335 / 28; 334 / 28. [LW 30:80.]

27. See above, pp. 231ff.

28. Further, on pp. 113ff.

29. *Des weltlichen Schwerts,* Luther's expression for juridical powers as such.

30. WA 12:328 / 27ff.; 331 / 6ff. [LW 30:74, 76.]

31. WA 12:332 / 1; 331 / 31ff. [LW 30:77.]

32. Exposition of 2 Peter, WA 14:53 / 8–9, 30ff. [LW 30:183.]

33. See passages in A. Peters, *Glaube und Werk: Luthers Rechtfertigungslehre im Lichte der Heiligen Schrift,* AGTL 8 (Hamburg, 1962), 106, n. 1. No attention is paid to election in Peter's treatment. In the disputation of June 15, 1537, Luther stresses that although works are testimonies of faith they have nothing to do with justification; WA 39¹:293 / 28ff. Checking out this idea and its source, P. Althaus, *Die christliche Wahrheit,* 3d ed. (Gütersloh, 1952), 644ff., pursues the matter beyond Luther.

election under which so many are suffering. One comes to God not by groveling over works but by following the way that proceeds from faith. "This is the route to the kingdom of heaven." Neither dreaming about it nor getting ideas about faith will admit you. "It must be a living, well-practiced, and propelled faith."[34] In the presence of the congregation Luther discusses the authenticity of these letters. For instance, the genuineness of Petrine authorship could be questioned by mildly criticizing 2 Peter (3:16) in light of the difficulty of the Pauline letters and the somewhat dubious eschatology (3:19) which "falls a little below the apostolic spirit." Yet Luther draws a different conclusion: Because the apostle is dealing not with faith but with love, "he condescends in a way typical of love."[35] The letter of Jude, to the contrary, cannot be ascribed to the apostle Jude (Thaddeus), for it is lifted almost verbatim from 2 Peter.[36] Luther has no qualms about telling his congregation that even 1 Pet. 4:6 must be reckoned a corrupted text.[37]

Consideration of these lesser New Testament letters presently yields to a far more significant Old Testament subject: the Book of Genesis. As with no other book of the Bible, Luther expounded on it three times (1519–21, 1523–24, 1535–45).[38] It is easy to see what attracted Luther to Genesis. For one thing, the creation story and the Promised Land motif provided the countertheme to the gospel and the fulfillment in it of all promises in Christ. For another, the art of the narrator of this primal account, so incomparable in manner, stimulated Luther's own narrative powers and expository fantasy. The one side, the hermeneutical goal, comes out in Luther's very first sermon, "in order that every Christian might see how Scripture agrees in all its parts, and how all examples and stories—indeed the entire Scripture—are so directed that one recognizes Christ."[39] In this case, however, we must bear in mind a decisive presupposition. We are

34. WA 14:23 / 27ff. [LW 30:158–59.]

35. WA 14:73 / 22ff. [LW 30:198. Alternate.]

36. WA 14:75 / 12ff. He says as much in the foreword to his translation, WA DB 7:386, 22ff. Had Luther known that modern scholarship has reversed this judgment, he would certainly have given free play to his doubts about 2 Peter. [LW 30:203.]

37. WA 12:375 / 25ff.

38. I leave it an open question whether Luther lectured on Genesis already in the summer of 1518, as Hans von Schubert claimed. On Luther's lecture sequence, see SHAW.PH 9 (1920): 4, 9; and P. Meinhold, Die Genesisvorlesung Luthers und ihre Herausgeber (Veit Dietrich, Michael Roting, Hieronymus Besold) (Stuttgart, 1936), 141ff. If this 1518 version were from the copy in possession of Poliander, we would have no documentation for the sermons of 1519–21, for which there are several attestations (WA 9:321–27).

39. This citation is from the printed first sermon of 1523 (WA 12:438 / 8ff.), not the later copies (WA 14:97ff.)

not permitted to comment simply according to the letter or to the ways of reason, or simply to spin ideas "from the sound of the words." This is a demanding task indeed. The Jews were wise to deny the reading of Scripture to those under thirty years of age. A proper understanding comes only "when the Holy Spirit teaches us what cannot be caught by human thought, and when God grants a right understanding and an experience in the heart." And since a right understanding is God's gift, a person can become open to it in that he expounds it "simply" according to the "effect, as Moses intended it."[40] Luther's differentiation has nothing in common with the exegetical methods of the ancient church. Actually, he is here formulating what he later called the double clarity of Scripture (the outer and inner), which he applied in his debate with Erasmus.[41]

In Luther's case, the connection between the doctrine of creation and Christology finds beautiful expression in that alongside the pronouncement on Christ as the central concept of Scripture he places one of his most inclusive formulations of faith in God's creation.

> Without a doubt this is the loftiest article of faith in which we declare, "I believe in God the Father, almighty, maker of heaven and earth." And whoever honestly believes this has already been helped and has been brought back to that relationship from which Adam had fallen away. But there are few who have come so far that they believe completely that it is God who creates and sustains all things. Such people must be those to whom everything else had died, good and evil, death and life, hell and heaven, and who can from the heart confess that they are unable to achieve anything by their own powers.[42]

The word of creation and the word of grace converge here, as by means of them God seeks to set man aright again. The gently mystical tones serve Luther as a linguistic channel for expressing the tremendous significance of this message.

From this insight Luther's burning interest in the Genesis narrative takes its rise, for it combines experience of the world as well as of faith. He sketches and expounds it in a wealth of ways that elude condensation at this point.[43] Only then does this insight unfold fully when it moves from

---

40. WA 12:439 / 1–26.

41. See *De servo arbitrio*, below, pp. 426, 435–36.

42. WA 24:18 / 26ff. I am citing from the version of the Genesis sermon which Cruciger prepared for printing in 1527. This is the best summation of the available copies. On this matter, see P. Althaus, "Der Schöpfungsgedanke bei Luther," *SHAW.PH* 7 (1959): 8–9. [Cf. *LW* 1–8 bringing the 1535–45 lectures on Genesis, in WA 42–44.]

43. Luther does so in even greater detail in the Genesis lectures of 1535–45 (WA 42–44), in which he includes his earlier expositions. [See above, n. 42.]

the creation and the family of Adam into the expanding account of the fathers. Here the tale is told of "both kinds of people," children of God and children of men,[44] devout fathers as well as would-be invaders of heaven, like the builders of the tower of Babel, or the great rulers who like heirs of Nimrod "rule the world by force." Yet even Nimrod stood in the service of a world order under God, "making civil authority indispensable and keeping it so."[45] Conversely, the revered fathers sometimes appear as great sinners. Luther alerted his hearers to recognize what a misreading of the gospel it is when people draw a distinction between those old-timers and our own. To do so is "to insult God's grace and to trust too little in Christ, as one seeks to put the separation of heaven and earth between us and them." "They have fallen just as low as we, and we have been as exalted as they."[46] "Jacob, Isaac—those are our brothers even though they were more gifted than we. Yet the cost of our redemption has been the same."[47]

Without covering up their sin, Luther treats the great patriarchs deferentially, seeking ways of excusing them. Thus Abraham's notorious lie in Egypt, when to save his life he claimed his wife was his sister, seemed to Luther proof of Abraham's faith. Had not God promised to make Abraham the father of a great people? So the end seemed to justify the means.[48] The patriarchs are human beings like ourselves also in that they suffered pain as, for instance, Jacob and his son Joseph. "In this way God demonstrates that he does not reject nature but permits it to remain in the saints," doing so in contrast to many foolish saints (especially those monastic fathers in the desert) "who were bent on breaking or extinguishing all natural desires."[49] God makes it difficult in this life, especially for his true saints. So, for example, Jacob: first a scullion, serving twenty years, then wrestling with an angel, and finally experiencing the greatest of grief with his children. "These are the authentic golden legends. In them God teaches us how he cooks and fries his saints and how he toys with them as if everything he had promised them was fake. . . . Nevertheless, the saint must hold fast to the word of promise and leave it to God to fulfill his promise as he wills."[50] In their sinfulness and suffering the patriarchs became exam-

44. WA 24:229 / 6ff.
45. WA 24:221 / 29; 222 / 9ff.
46. WA 24:484 / 28ff.; 485 / 18–19.
47. According to the copy, WA 14:373 / 1–2.
48. WA 24:226 / 14ff. WA 24:259 / 36ff. Cf., on this whole subject, Bornkamm, *Luther und das Alte Testament*, 16ff. [*Luther and the Old Testament*, 22–24.]
49. WA 24:614 / 11ff., 35ff.
50. WA 24:613 / 11ff., 26ff. WA 14:466 / 15; 467 / 1ff.

ples of true faith, pointing beyond their own probing situation to the faithfulness God revealed in the sending of Christ. They instructed their household and servants accordingly, so that an entire Old Testament church history runs through this patriarchal narration.[51]

In this coexistence of faith and unfaith in primal history, Luther clarifies still another point, namely, how faith and unfaith differ and what consequences flow therefrom. This has to do with a complete difference in our consciousness (*conscientia*) in which a totally other God meets us.

> For I have often said: As your conscience is toward God, so is he. If you regard him gracious, then gracious he is. If you fear him as you fear a terrifying judge, then he is that too, for he judges you according to your conscience. In whatever way the conscience changes toward God, so also the language of Scripture changes, which speaks of him as one feels the presence of God.[52]

Conscience is for Luther not simply a moral court but also an expression of the relationship to God, in faith or unfaith, in which the unchangeable God meets us in a fundamentally different manner. So, for example, Ludwig Feuerbach made use of this kind of Luther statement to support his own theory that man is ever creating God in his own image.[53] This, however, is the opposite of what Luther meant: not illusion, but a real relationship, which finds expression in faith or unfaith. Luther makes his point in the tower of Babel story, the consequences of which he uses to illustrate the difference between faith and unfaith. He sees the confusion of tongues not simply as a linguistic event but also as an expression of the common loss of God. Human beings felt God's disfavor. "The way they now feel, so it was indeed. . . . The heart despaired and error prevailed. Therefore they could not remain together, for the purpose of unity in language is to enable people to remain together on friendly terms."[54]

Two quite different methodological guidelines are significant for Luther's exposition of Genesis in the narrower, technical sense. On the one hand, he emphasizes that the text must be taken literally, the way it stands. Not only did he make this point repeatedly in his lectures, but he

---

51. For an overview, see Bornkamm, *Luther und das Alte Testament*, 176ff. [*Luther and the Old Testament*, 207ff.]

52. WA 24:231 / 14ff. Formulated in Latin in the copy of Luther's sermon made by Stephan Roth, the original is worth repeating: "Si sentis deum, habes eum, et ita habes, ut sentis. Sicut conscientiae sensu dei mutantur, ita mutat se scriptura de deo loquens. . . . Ita sentio in corde et conscientia diversum deum, quem tamen scimus in se immutabilem. Sicut ego deo sum, ita ille mihi. In quo natura fidei et infidelitatis notata est." WA 14:213 / 34ff.

53. Cf. H. Bornkamm, *Luther im Spiegel der deutschen Geistesgeschichte*, 2d ed. (Göttingen, 1970), 89ff.

54. WA 24:231 / 25ff.

also illustrated it in response to inquiries from Spalatin. God has really created the world in six differentiated days. The serpent was indeed a serpent that the devil was using as a tool. "One is not warranted to alter the words of Moses arbitrarily," but where the wording remains untouched, it allows rational clarification. When Rebecca inquires of the Lord concerning the two infants in her womb (Gen. 25:22–23), this can signify (as Jewish exegetes agree) that she sought counsel from the 500-year-old Sem [Shem] or one of the other patriarchs of that time. So too the words of God to Cain are to be thought of not as spoken by God's voice but through a priest who was responsible for the offering of sacrifices, namely, Cain's father, Adam. Under Moses this duty was later conferred on the prophets and priests. They were therefore called gods (Elohim, Exod. 22:27), for they gave God's word as their reply. "In the new covenant every Christian is someone like that."[55]

On the other hand, the unity of the history of faith (embracing the Old Testament and the New) prompts Luther to illustrate his exegesis with allegory. Compared to the medieval recourse to allegory as well as to his own usage of it earlier, Luther had become much more restrained,[56] except in his sermons on Genesis. Even here allegory is not Luther's actual or only method for making Scripture come alive, but he relishes the use of it as a means of coaxing forth its secrets, for these do not simply lie on the surface, since the Old Testament speaks only indirectly of Christ and of faith [in him]. For Luther there are the traditional allegories: the flood, denoting baptism; the ark, the church; Joseph [in Egypt], a Christ-type; and so on. Yet he also allegorizes along his own central lines of thought. For instance, when Adam and Eve discover their nakedness and make aprons of leaves, this is much like many Christians who, "having lost faith and seeing themselves stuck in sins resort to self-help, covering and beautifying themselves with works they have thought up."[57] Or, again, Luther allegorizes on the words of the deceived elderly Isaac, "The voice is Jacob's voice, but the hands are the hands of Esau" (Gen. 27:22). His vivid play of thoughts is strange to us, but was by no means estranging according to exegetical rules inherited by people of the sixteenth century. Only the scope Luther gives it is new. The voice signifies the gospel; the hands

55. To Spalatin, January 22, 1525, WA Br 3:426 / 7ff. More on this in the Genesis sermons, WA 14:128 / 12ff., 36ff.; 325 / 6ff., 26ff.; 164 / 4ff., 15ff.

56. Bornkamm, *Luther und das Alte Testament*, 76ff., 211. On Luther's diminished use of allegory in gospel exegesis in the 1520s, see the evidence offered by Ebeling, *Evangelienauslegung* (see n. 15, above), 49ff. [*Luther and the Old Testament*, 87ff., 249–50.]

57. WA 24:91 / 21ff.

signify works. Hands have to do what is obvious to all. "Christians do everything that others do too; only the voice must be different. . . . Let there be no preaching of law to the conscience, no placing of gospel in the hands."[58] Thus Luther cautions those who would rely on their own good works, as well as those who despise them. "We desire to do no works since we are committed through faith. What works would we do? Not so, but let the voice be Jacob's and the hands be Esau's; bring the old Adam into line and hold fast to grace."[59] At that time [1520s] Luther still liked to use these allegorical interpretations as a means of applying gospel-content to Old Testament texts. Gradually, however, he cut back on such devices and eventually dropped them entirely.[60] His experience with Müntzer and Karlstadt made it clear to him that the "spiritual interpretation" carries the danger of a spiritualizing dissolution of the texts themselves, a danger he found present also in Origen and Jerome and their follower Erasmus.[61]

Nevertheless, Luther gave allegory one more intensive application, doing so in his lectures on Deuteronomy, where he treated the problem of law in the Old Testament. From February 1523 and into the year 1524, he conducted a private course in the Augustinian cloister, which included opportunity for discussion. The participants included some of the friars in his order as well as several others. Two transcripts of the proceedings remain. One of them was Bugenhagen's, who soon thereafter made thorough use of them in his own lectures. The turmoil of the mid-1520s delayed Luther's further work on the subject, so that only later than intended did he rework these lectures into book form. As planned, he dedicated this work to Bishop George von Polentz in that part of Prussia under the order of Teutonic Knights. For this purpose Luther made his own Latin translation of Deuteronomy, and Wittenberg printer Hans Lufft initiated its publication in 1524. But it took Luther another year to complete his commentary (*Annotationes*).[62] Understandably, the many-sided character of Deuteronomy excited Luther. Here was a composite of historical narrative, a code of law, the song of Moses, and the account of Moses' death. Luther called it "a compend of Moses and a summation of the entire law and wisdom of the people of Israel" which when seen from

---

58. WA 24:481 / 22ff., 31ff.

59. According to Stephan Roth's version, WA 14:369 / 31ff. Cf. WA 24:481 / 11ff.; 482 / 9ff.

60. In his extensive Genesis lectures (1535–45) there is more of this. Cf. the exegesis of this passage (Gen. 27:22) in WA 43:516ff. [*LW* 5:127ff.]

61. Ebeling, *Evangelienauslegung*, 314ff., 324ff.

62. WA 14:489–96; 497 / 7; 745ff. On the dedication to Polentz, see Luther's letter to Johann Briessmann, July 4, 1524, WA Br 3:316 / 53ff. [*LW* 9:4–311.]

the perspective of a Christian "is an ultra-rich unfolding of the Decalogue." The inward realm of conscience, the political order, and the outward ceremonies are here "regulated most wisely and justly."[63] From the wealth of Luther's comments on these themes, consider the following three.

1. Secular law is a subject not for books but for judges. Before there were laws, God had appointed judges and endowed them with reasonableness as the balancing norm. "Judges are the living laws or the soul of the law."[64] This places the highest demands on a judge. "He must subdue all feelings of fear, love, favor, sympathy, greed, ambition, reputation, life, or death, and be a simple lover of simple truth and just judgment."[65] This implies that the judge knows his office is conferred on him by God and is given its order by common legal forms. In other words, there is no such thing as popular justice without [an accompanying] form or office.[66]

2. In its history and its incomparable law, Israel's superiority over the Gentile nations becomes manifest. Seen externally, historical events look alike everywhere, yet among the Gentiles history deals with the great and small aspects of human activity. In Israel's history, on the contrary, only the Word of God is worthy of honor, "according to whose guidance and sign everything takes place."[67] God has chosen the Jewish people without any consideration of its merits; indeed, he has done so despite its frequently demonstrated unfaith. If Moses' address to the people (Deut. 9)—in which he cannot express himself severely enough against their faithlessness—is strong medicine against the plague of self-righteousness among God's people, the Jews, then how much more must it be so for us "Gentiles and sinners"?[68] Seen politically, the election of Israel therefore has only a limited goal: the overthrow of the Canaanites, whose land God had promised Israel, not the overthrow of any other people.[69]

3. Deuteronomy sharpened Luther's inquiry concerning law and gospel, largely on the grounds of his admiration for the unsurpassed wisdom of the law of Moses as it ranged from the Decalogue to the law of taxation by the levy of a tithe. Luther saw the merit of tithing in its dependence on production and gladly would have seen it introduced in Germany.[70] For

63. WA 14:545 / 17–27. [LW 9:14.]
64. WA 14:554 / 38ff. [LW 9:20.]
65. WA 14:667 / 1ff., where he cites 2 Chron. 19:6–7. [LW 9:163.]
66. WA 14:665 / 11ff. [LW 9:161.]
67. WA 14:566 / 37ff.; 567 / 23. [LW 9:33.]
68. WA 14:634 / 30ff.; 636 / 24ff. [LW 9:102, 105.]
69. WA 14:625 / 26–27. [LW 9:83.]
70. WA 14:652 / 15ff. [LW 9:138.]

him the distinction between the two Testaments lies not in any claim that the New Testament proclaims a better, profounder, or more humane law than the Old.

> What could one add to the Decalogue (not to mention other [aspects of the Old Testament])? What nobler precepts could be taught than to believe in God with one's whole heart, to trust, love, and fear him and not to tempt him. Besides, what can be esteemed more righteous and more holy than what Moses has set forth concerning the worship of God, government, or love of neighbor?[71]

The distinction between the two Testaments lies instead in the different human situation to which the law (the same in the New [as in the Old]) applies. In the Old Testament, the law convicts and destroys sinners; in the New it drives them into the arms of the gracious God, by whom alone they are enabled to fulfill the law. To be sure, there are commandments also in the New Testament, "yet only for the sake of the remnants of the old [human] nature, to mortify what has not yet conformed; from the latter [remnants] the Spirit is free, being content with faith alone." The gospel therefore addresses the new human being who knows that the impediments toward God have been abolished. And so, at the same time, the gospel instructs as to "whence you receive the power to fulfill the law."[72] This, which we call the new covenant and which comes into being through faith and the Spirit, is the primal covenant between God and humankind. "The New Testament is that which was promised most anciently, before the beginning of the world and of time . . . yet was first fulfilled in Christ." By way of contrast, the old covenant, sealed by God with the people of Israel, embraces only a limited part of history: the promise of the land. "The Old Testament was promised under Moses and fulfilled under Joshua." The preservation of this fulfillment depends on whether the laws and the justice proclaimed by Moses are kept.[73] God's two covenantal offers not only follow one on the other but also, at a decisive point, are interrelated. The law of Moses is not simply the folk law of the Israelites, "the Jewish Saxon-mirror,"[74] historically conditioned and geographically limited like the law of any other people. Rather, it contains a kernel of universal validity, a "natural" law that anyone in his own conscience can

---

71. WA 14:675 / 30ff. [LW 9:176.]

72. WA 14:677 / 23–678 / 9. [LW 9:179.]

73. WA 14:602 / 34ff. [LW 9:63.]

74. See Luther's *Against the Heavenly Prophets* (1525), WA 18:81 / 10ff. WA 16:378 / 11. Also Luther's and Melanchthon's formulated opinion on this question from the year 1524, WA Br 12:62ff., including the cited Bible passages. MBW 388, 389. [LW 40:98, n. 20.]

recognize. Already in 1519, in his commentary on Galatians, Luther had drafted a superb definition of this law:

There is a law that extends throughout all times, is known to all people, written in all hearts, and that from beginning to end leaves no one an excuse. Among the Jews, to be sure, cultic laws were added just as distinctive laws were added among other peoples. But these additions were not binding on the entire world; only this was binding: that the Spirit addresses all hearts unceasingly.[75]

The Decalogue comprises the incomparable summary of this law, even though it contains Jewish ceremonial law (such as the prohibition of images, Sabbath observance) which does not concern other peoples. However, the law of the heart—and this comprises its universality—is bound up in God's primal covenant with humankind, a covenant made not only to demand but also to help. Therefore, preceding the "thou shalt" of all the commandments stand the words "I am the Lord, thy God," God's own promise to humankind which comes before all his demands. The First Commandment embodies both at once. In the beautiful passage Deut. 10:12ff. (where the social commandments are derived from God's unmerited kindnesses toward his people and his love for widows, orphans, and strangers), Luther first hears the comfort that the First Commandment vouchsafes the oppressed, and then the threat of judgment on those who do not follow God's example.

This is what it means to expound on the First Commandment. This is Moses' own commentary. This is how he teaches us to understand what God is, and what it means to have a God, and what it means to keep the First Commandment. What a resource these words alone have been to the prophets! From them the prophets have drawn everything that, on the one hand, justifies their complaints in behalf of the weak, the nobodies, the poor, the sinners, the widows, the orphans, the sentenced, the condemned, the wretched, and that, on the other hand, calls forth their thunderings of the wrath and vengeance of God toward the rich, the tyrants, the mighty, the judges, the violent, the hardhearted, and the proud. All this flows out of the mighty ocean of the First Commandment and returns to it again. No more effectual or completely comforting voice was ever, or will ever be, heard than this, nor any more stern and severe one than this proclamation of the First Commandment: I am the Lord, your God.[76]

In his own way, Luther here establishes a connection between Deuteronomy and Israelite prophecy. While today's research assumes a rela-

75. WA 2:580 / 18ff.
76. WA 14:640 / 23ff. [LW 9:112.]

tive contemporaneity between that book and the later prophets, Luther sees a much greater time span between them historically. This is precisely what arouses his zest for discovery. What he noticed seems to agree with the observations of his own era which saw in Homer "the father of all poets, the fountain—indeed the ocean—of all learning, wisdom, and elo-quence." Luther continues, "Since in this age everything begins to be restored, as if that day of the restoration of all things (Acts 3:21) were near, I got the idea to see if Moses could be restored and I might return the brooklet to the fountain." In his foreword to Bishop von Polentz, where the above citation occurs, Luther confesses his delight in this sort of hu-manistic exercise which has shown him how the later prophets "read, learned, and taught Moses and had him in their hands day and night."[77]

The impact of this powerful linkage of Moses, the prophets, and the gospel induced Luther once again, and in a manner he never matched later, to illustrate his interpretation of each chapter allegorically. To be sure, he was emphatic that the literal sense alone is reliable and that the allegorical is risky and often subject to misuse, depending on the mood of the expositor. Nevertheless, Luther is moved to employ this secondary method to draw still more out of such texts which speak of the veil over the face of Moses and which induce Paul (2 Cor. 3:13) to find an analogy of faith between Deuteronomy and the other major books of the Bible.[78] All Luther's allegorizations are thus conformed strictly to the analogy of faith. Here are a few examples: That Moses did not make it over the Jordan means that the law does not lead into the kingdom of God. Crossing the Jordan was reserved for Joshua, whose name and experience point to Christ (Deut. 3).[79] Cloven-hoofed and cud-chewing animals which Moses names as suitable for food (Deut. 14:6) point toward the proper distinction between law and gospel and to the heartfelt meditation on the Word of God.[80] The ban on cutting down fruit trees during a siege (Deut. 20:19) denotes that teachings "supported by true pronouncements of Scripture should not be denied, for there never was any heresy which did not also utter some truth."[81] The ban against planting a vineyard with a variety of

77. WA 14:499 / 16ff. This is the only passage in which Luther makes more than a passing reference to Homer. Cf. WA TR 5, no. 5834, 376 / 9ff.: Videte Virgilium, Homerum, Liuium: When things became difficult, they ran to the churches. "Et nos christiani ita stertimus in dubitatione in illo certissimo cultu." See also WA DB 3:272 / 3–5. [LW 9:6.]

78. WA 14:560 / 13–561 / 36. [LW 9:25–26.]

79. WA 14:579 / 34ff. [LW 9:43.]

80. WA 14:649 / 16ff.; 650 / 20ff. (according to 2 Tim. 2:15; in WA this passage is er-roneously made 2 Tim. 4:2). [LW 9:134, 135.]

81. WA 14:694 / 28ff. [LW 9:206.]

vines and against plowing with an ox and a donkey yoked together (Deut. 22:9–10) implies that we are not to inculcate faith and works simultaneously. Luther's allegorizations are christological or bear on grace and law. Other forms of allegorization he rejects as trifling. Then there is the case of the female prisoner of war and the requirement that she may be married only when she has received a new set of clothes and been permitted to use her month of mourning to take farewell of her parents (Deut. 21:10ff.). Jerome applied this requirement to the classical art of eloquence which the Christian writer may espouse with some modification. Luther applied this requirement to the synagogue. Its beauty, according to Paul (Rom. 9:4–5), is in the gifts granted it: laying aside the prisoner's garb means liberation from imprisonment in the law; paring the nails means liberation from self-righteousness that lacerates the conscience; mourning time means insight into the depths of congenital sin which no law can abolish. "And so she may marry, that is, she should receive the word of God and in faith become the bride of Christ."[82] These examples show that allegories are not based on the worthiness of ideas which emerges in the process of reinterpretation. "Allegorical meaning, as we have said, is most safely applied to matters of faith."[83] To this extent, then, allegorization is still an integrating element in Luther's hermeneutic; although in time his use of it diminished, he never quite gave it up.[84]

Luther's exposition of Deuteronomy must be counted among his most significant lectures, even though it contained a far smaller offering of theological themes than his lectures on the Psalms, the prophets, or the New Testament texts. During the years 1523–24, in the wake of the Wittenberg disorders and at a time when the future course of the Reformation was being determined, the Deuteronomy lectures enabled him and his students to focus attention on the main Old Testament text for clarifying the relation between law and gospel. As a result, the formulation of this relationship acquired a wealth of biblical associations and clarity, while providing him with arguments for two debates in which he was engaged. One debate was with Karlstadt and Müntzer, men who made no clear distinction between law and gospel[85] and whose programs, measured by the

82. WA 14:698 / 9ff. Jerome, Epistle 21.13. 5–6, 9. On this see Hagendahl, "Latin Fathers and the Classics," GUA 64 / 2 (1958): 109. [LW 9:214.]

83. WA 14:698 / 10–11; 649 / 27–28. [LW 9:214, 134.]

84. Bornkamm, Luther und das Alte Testament, 79ff., brings further examples from the Deuteronomy lectures. [Bornkamm, Luther and the Old Testament, 93ff.] Several additional examples are in H. Gerdes, Luthers Streit mit den Schwärmern um das rechte Verständnis des Gesetzes Mose (Göttingen, 1955), 116ff.

85. See n. 84, above, on the book by Gerdes.

imposing structure of Old Testament law, inevitably appeared to Luther as outright bungling. The other was with conservatives with whom the basis and limits of Christian action in the realm of jurisprudence and government had to be thought through afresh, especially in light of medieval practices that confused relations between the church and civil authority. [We shall return to these debates.]

On the matter of lectures again, the sequence on the minor prophets ran from May 1524 to early 1526.[86] Luther had just begun on them in 1521 when his teaching was interrupted [by the Worms and Wartburg events]. [In contrast to Deuteronomy] the minor prophets confronted Luther with a completely different and especially difficult task. On the basis of short texts, he had successively to identify with a dozen authors their personality, their thought, their style, and he had to become clear on the matter of prophecy in its twofold character: its actual meaning for its time and its anticipation of Christ and the gospel. The task fascinated him intensely, as shown by the fact that in rapid succession he published extensive German expositions of three of these prophets: Jonah (1526), Habakkuk (1526), and Zechariah (1527). They were begun as lectures but were greatly expanded for publication.[87] These published commentaries are useful only in a limited way for ascertaining the text of the lectures themselves, which were taken down by students, but they are of fundamental importance for capturing Luther's understanding of the prophets, for this is something he had initially worked out for himself in these lectures.[88] From this standpoint we are justified in basing our observations on the three later, more broadly developed, and freshly thought through commentaries. They set forth three different sides of the prophetic element.

The Jonah presentation is one of Luther's masterpieces as an author. On the basis of its narration, which distinguishes this book from the other prophetic texts, Luther could depict the suffering of the prophet in terms

86. WA 13:xxxiii. The opening date, given as March 1524, is correctly deferred to the beginning of the semester in early May. WA DB 11²:ix, n. 2. On the subject as a whole, see the painstaking and rewarding research on Luther's hermeneutic by G. Krause, *Studien zur Luthers Auslegung der kleinen Propheten* (Tübingen, 1962). [For the English translation of the minor prophets, see *LW* 18, 19, 20.]

87. WA 19:169–251 (Jonah), 337–435 (Habakkuk). WA 23:477–664 (Zechariah). See further in Bornkamm, *Luther und das Alte Testament*, 26ff. [*Luther and the Old Testament*, 31ff.] [*LW* 18:ix–xii, introduction to minor prophets. *LW* 19:(ix–xi), Jonah, lectures from the Latin text, 3–31; German commentary, 35–104. Habakkuk, lectures from the Latin text, 107–48; German commentary, 151–237. *LW* 20: (Zechariah, lectures from the Latin text, 6–152; German commentary, 158–347).]

88. As for the question of sources, cf. the introduction to the lecture volume (WA 13) and to the volumes bringing three German commentaries (WA 19 and WA 23). Also Krause, *Kleinen Propheten*, 1ff. [*LW*, see above, n. 87.]

of the struggle between temptation and faith. Jonah, the man in flight, suddenly realizes that the storm at sea is God's way of catching up with him. He learns from this the "tender virtue of sin" what it means to be ashamed and to hide, until he admits to the ship's company that he is a Hebrew, that he is ready to take the sins of his travel companions on himself and to offer himself as a sacrifice. In dread of death in the belly of the great fish, he experiences hell during what must have been "the longest days and nights that anyone under the sun has ever endured." "For everyone wherever he may be carries his own hell with him, so long as he feels the final anguish of death and God's anger."[89] Jonah's prayer nevertheless sustains him in the confidence of God's mercy, "for even hell would not be hell or would not remain hell, if its occupants could cry out or pray to God."[90] Even though God rescues him, Jonah lapses into the same sin, although now not as a mere man but as a prophet. He argues with God because he is as yet unready to deliver the sermon of judgment which God has assigned to him, for he would still spare the Gentile city. So God toys with him, teaching him a lesson through his own anger over the withered plant that had shaded him. So the sulking prophet "must allow himself to be vanquished and to return home shamed and humbled, but with great awe and with increased understanding."[91] It is fully the story of the prophet that Luther here interprets, and fully the story of all people who, with sin and dread of death, faith and prayer, despair, grumbling, and confusion experience God.

Alongside this very human portrait of a prophet is that of the prophetic "office," which Luther finds portrayed magnificently in Habakkuk. In contrast to Jonah, the assignment of Habakkuk is not so much that of passing judgment[92] (which is by no means excluded) as it is of ministering comfort.[93] It was Habakkuk's task to give Judah advance warning of the

89. WA 19:211 / 1; 219 / 12ff.; 225 / 28ff. Here Luther concedes his doubts about the traditional representations of hell: "I am not yet completely sure what hell may be in terms of the last judgment." Only after that will it come to a separation of the condemned. WA 19:225 / 12–13, 34ff. [LW 19:74, 75.]

90. WA 19:222 / 16–17. [LW 19:71.]

91. WA 19:242 / 15; 243 / 30ff. Cf. the fine analysis of the Jonah book in G. von Rad, *Theologie des Alten Testaments* (Munich, 1960), 2:302ff. [*Old Testament Theology* (New York: Harper & Row, 1960), 289–92.] [LW 19:95, 96.]

92. WA 19:363 / 11ff.

93. WA 19:353 / 22. The following section, WA 19:353 / 23–354 / 24, served later as Luther's preface to his translation of the prophets (1532) and was later included in the complete edition of the German Bible. WA DB 11²:298–301. [LW 19:155–56.] WA 19:352 / 27ff.; 387 / 10ff.

catastrophe awaiting it at the hands of Babylon,[94] and at the same time to keep the faith alive that the promised Messiah would come and establish his kingdom in Jerusalem.[95] This requires in Habakkuk a "fighting faith over against the luck of the Babylonians" and makes him "contend against and combat the unbelief of his people to whom he is preaching. He must both comfort them and strengthen them."[96] It is God's assignment alone that draws the utmost out of this agonizing prophet: "When he enters on his office and is expected to console and preserve an entire nation engaged in the same struggle, this entails toil, misery, and trouble."[97] In the severe test to which this office subjects the prophet ("even though faith remains firm, it nevertheless cracks a bit")[98] everything depends on the prophet "to stand firmly on his word, to cling to it strongly, neither yielding nor swerving because of misfortunes, unbelief, murmuring, and blasphemies among the people. For if he who is to administer the Word and dispense comfort yields and swerves, all goes to pieces, the banner lies in the dust, and the watchman is dead. But if he stands his ground at least a few will adhere to him and look to him."[99] A watchman of this sort deserves to be called an "Encourager," one who, as Luther interprets the name Habakkuk, comforts others and "takes them in his arms."[100] Nowhere has Luther portrayed more vividly than here, in treating the figure and name of this prophet, the intertwined character of two different functions: that of combating and that of comforting. A dual proclamation of this kind is not based merely on an allegorical agreement with the New Testament events.[101] Actually Luther interpreted the prophetic office as a direct

94. Contrary to tradition, which dated Habakkuk in the era of Daniel (Krause, *Kleine Propheten*, 136), Luther regarded Habakkuk as one of the older contemporaries of Jeremiah (WA 19:354 / 11, 16). In this respect Luther is in general agreement with today's research. [*LW* 19:155.]

95. *WA* 19:388 / 31ff. [*LW* 19:191.]

96. *WA* 19:386 / 5ff. [*LW* 19:189.]

97. *WA* 19:380 / 21ff. [*LW* 19:182.]

98. *WA* 19:378 / 4. [*LW* 19:179.]

99. *WA* 19:388 / 16ff. [*LW* 19:191.]

100. *WA* 19:354 / 18ff. [*LW* 19:156. The word "caress" in the English translation seems to fall short of Luther's intention.] Luther follows the explanation given in the *Interpretationes Nominum Hebraicorum*, which is based on Jerome's work by the same name and which was appended to many editions of the Vulgate. *WA* DB 11²:301, n. 2. K. A. Meissinger, *Luthers Exegese in der Frühzeit* (Leipzig, 1911), 71. Habakkuk may have been derived from a plant or a type of fruit tree. *RGG*³ 3 (1959): 3.

101. Apart, e.g., from allegories of geographical names, which Luther applies only when it lies close to the prophetic context. The picture language of the prophets is another matter, and Luther interprets this according to its natural sense. Krause, *Kleine Propheten*, 165–66, 197ff. Bornkamm, *Luther und das Alte Testament*, 78ff. [*Luther and the Old Testament*, 91ff.]

promise of Christ, seeing in that promise the ultimate goal toward which was directed the prophets' faith in the way God was leading Israel through the realities of history.

This content of the prophetic message Luther discerned most generously in the Book of Zechariah. In the two main tasks entrusted to all prophets—to hold the people in check in order to prepare for the coming kingdom of the Messiah, and to prophesy concerning this kingdom as well as to extol it—Zechariah "is a model, and in my opinion the outstanding one."[102] However, Luther did not understand this prophecy as a format open to random meanings read into it allegorically. Only then does the content [of Zechariah] point to Christ when it bears witness to the truth of the gospel, to justification by faith in him that came into the world. This pertains, for example, to the prophetic promise concerning "my servant the Branch" (Zech. 3:8). Even his [Hebrew] name, Zemach (Branch), points to the "marvelous growth" of Christ's cause despite the cross and persecution, a matter that can be appropriated only by faith. "Simply give attention to the Word and cling to it. If you do not hold to the Word, you will not be able to stand against the offense that the kingdom of Christ brings with it."[103] This understanding of the prophetic anticipations of Christ makes Luther assume a critical stance toward traditional christological interpretations. Chapter 8 focuses quite naturally on the return of Israel from its captivity and on the rebuilding of Jerusalem. It induces Luther to paint a glowing picture of peace and of a wholesome life of the people. There he specifically rejects the conventional and surely well-intended interpretation of this chapter as foreshadowing the coming of all peoples to Christ and his apostles.[104] He did so in the German commentary of 1527, even though he had still employed the conventional interpretation in his lectures of 1525–26.[105] He likewise rejected the interpretations of Zech. 4:7 and 11:15ff. used customarily in support of tradition, and of chapters 12 and 14 as denoting the Antichrist and Judgment Day. Luther read the account there given of the fall and plundering of Jerusalem as referring not to the end of time but to the city's destruction by the Romans and the scattering of its inhabitants. The times of persecu-

---

102. WA 23:501 / 17ff.; 502 / 15–16. Luther later uses similar words in the preface to his translation of Zechariah (1532): he is "truly one of the most comforting of the prophets." There he interprets the several chapters as specifically prophesying Christ and his story. WA DB 11²:328 / 5ff. [LW 35:330ff.]

103. WA 23:552 / 1ff., 37ff. For Luther's understanding of the Christ-prophecies, see the clarifying statement in Krause, Kleine Propheten, 361ff., 372ff. [LW 20:216.]

104. WA 23:598 / 14ff.; 599 / 23ff.; 607 / 31ff. [LW 20:270, 271, 280.]

105. Krause, Kleine Propheten, 367.

tion to which the prophet points are still times of struggle and therefore times for preaching and faith. Only "when evening comes will there be light" (Zech. 14:7). "The evening, however, is the end of the world, when faith shall cease and the eternal light shall be revealed."[106]

However frequently he employs traditional exegesis, which moves beyond temporal history and seeks fulfillment in a future salvific history, Luther nevertheless takes pains to let all signs pointing to Christ and his kingdom be formed exclusively by the gospel and faith and to avoid any loose prefiguring of the story of Christ and the church. Repeatedly one can observe in Luther his progressive abandonment of a formal christological exegesis and his rising concentration on the scope of the gospel in the prophetic texts; the place for such observation lies between his lectures and his three German commentaries or several sermons preached during this period.[107]

---

106. WA 23:655 / 9ff.; 656 / 1ff.; 657 / 22–23; 658 / 4ff. Krause, *Kleine Propheten*, 327–28. [*LW* 20:337, 338, 339, 340.] "At evening time there shall be light" (Zech. 14:7).

107. Further examples in Krause, *Kleine Propheten*, 367ff.

10

Everyday Life in Wittenberg

On his return from the Wartburg, Luther resumed living in the Augustinian Eremite cloister. Having shed the attire of a gentleman, he was back in
his black cowl. This garb of the order gave its name to the "Black Cloister," one of the buildings erected in connection with the founding of the
university. At first it consisted simply of a dwelling built in the plain style
of the mendicant orders, comprised of individual cells for about forty
monks, a refectory, and a dormitory.[1] Frederick Myconius, who later became superintendent in Gotha, in 1541 wrote the first history of the Reformation with local color. He has left us a vivid picture of the place where it
all began.

> In Wittenberg the Augustinian cloister, where Dr. Martinus is still living, was
> at first little more than a dormitory. Subsequently it was extended. The foun-
> dations for the church were laid but were no higher than ground level. In the
> midst of these foundations stood a small whitewashed wooden chapel. It was a
> rickety structure, propped up on all sides. As I recall seeing it, the dimen-
> sions were about thirty shoes and twenty shoes broad. In it was a small, dirty
> balcony, with standing room for twenty people at most. On the south wall was
> a pulpit made of old unplaned boards; it stood about one and a half ells above
> the earthen floor. In short, it had every appearance of the artist's version of
> the stable in Bethlehem wherein Christ was born. Like a similar one in
> Prague, where John Huss had preached, this little chapel was called
> Bethlehem.

With devout feeling Myconius observes that in this woebegone Wittenberg chapel, God "in these latter days has let his clear and holy gospel,
and the dear infant Jesus, be born anew." Here Luther preached his first
sermons against indulgences.[2] Indeed, he loved this little chapel and was

---

1. On the history of the cloister, see *Germania Sacra* 1.3.2, ed. F. Bünger and G. Wentz
(Berlin, 1941), 440ff., 457–58. G. Krüger, "Wie sah die Stadt Wittenberg zu Luthers
Lebzeiten aus?" *Luther* 15 (1933): 29–30.

2. Frederick Myconius, *Geschichte der Reformation*, ed. O. Clemen, Voigtländers
Quellenbücher 68 (Leipzig, 1915), 22ff. For a description of the present-day condition, see O.
Thulin, *Die Lutherstadt Wittenberg und Torgau* (Berlin, 1932), 29ff. A general description of
the town in the sixteenth century is in O. Scheel, *Martin Luther: Vom Katholizismus zur
Reformation*, 3d and 4th eds. (Tübingen, 1930), 2:314ff. This is based on the then highly

later grieved to see it torn down.[3]

Luther soon began to feel the progressive pinch of poverty in this local Bethlehem. His disputations over monastic life were bound to become evident in his own cloister. Resignations rapidly reduced the number of friars.[4] Although this change reflected his own position, he was nevertheless unhappy at times over the alleged reasons for it. For instance, his friend John Lang had resigned from the Erfurt cloister and given sixteen reasons for doing so, foremost among which was the complaint against the unhealthy living quarters that seemed to endanger life itself. To him Luther wrote on March 28, 1522, "I am fully convinced that your resignation from the cloister was not without good reasons, although I would have been more pleased had you been above it."[5] In other words, not reasons but *the* one reason—the rejection of a merit-oriented basis of monasticism—was decisive for Luther, and he had put it bluntly in his treatise on monastic vows.[6] However, he had no reason to doubt the decision of the closest companion he had had in these years. Luther simply deplored that such a variety of reasons could easily cast doubt on the objectivity of the

---

modern guidebook in which the dialogue of Andreas Meinhard persuades Fux Reinhard [René the Fox?] to attend the new university (*Dialogus illustrate ac augustissime urbis Albiorenae, vulgo Vittenberg dicte situm, amenitatem ac illustrationem docens, tirocinia nobilium artium jacientibus editus*, 1508). See also W. Friedensburg, *Geschichte Universität Wittenberg* (Magdeburg, 1926), 44. Among the sermons against indulgences which Luther is said to have preached in the cloister chapel, Myconius mentions the one entitled "Indulgence and Grace" (WA 1:243–46) and "The Freedom to Preach on Papal Indulgence and Grace" (WA 1:383–93). Apparently neither of these sermons was actually preached (WA 1:239), but they are among the literary remains of the indulgence controversy in the year 1518, being responses to Tetzel's pamphlets. Cf. T. Kolde, *Martin Luther: Eine Biographie* (Gotha, 1884), 1:375–76. T. Brieger, "Kritische Erörterungen zur neuen Luther Ausgabe," *ZKG* 11/1 (1889): 112ff. J. Köstlin, *Martin Luther: Sein Leben und seine Schriften*, 5th ed., ed. G. Kawerau (Berlin, 1903), 1:169, 187. *BoA* 1:10–11. H. Volz, *Martin Luthers Thesenanschlag und dessen Vorgeschichte* (Weimar, 1959), 138–39.

    3. According to *Germania Sacra* 1.3.2, p. 458, the little chapel was torn down to make way for the fortification of Wittenberg, at this point for an embankment and moat and a double brick wall. The information on this activity (G. von Hirschfeld, "Die Beziehungen Luthers und seiner Gemahlin, Katharina von Bora, zur Familie von Hirschfeld," *BSKG* 2 [1883]: 200ff.) does not mention the destruction of the chapel but speaks only of the transformation of the Franciscan church into a storehouse and of the accompanying destruction of the gravestones and epitaphs of the Saxon electoral princes buried there, 1273–1435. According to WA TR 5, no. 5349, 77, n. 13, the little Augustinian chapel was no longer standing in 1540. On the composition of this group of Table Talk items (WA TR 5, nos. 5342–54), compiled by an unknown copyist, see E. Kroker, WA TR 5:5xiff., and Volz, *Die Lutherpredigten des Johannes Mathesius*, QFRG 12 (Leipzig, 1930), 117.

    4. From more than thirty (end of 1521) to five or six (February 1522), then a temporary slight increase, and again a further decline. *Germania Sacra* 1.3.2, pp. 451–52.

    5. WA Br 2:488 / 3ff. On Lang, *Germania Sacra* 1.3.2, pp. 482–83.

    6. [*De Votis Monasticis* (1521), WA 8:573–669. *The Judgment of Martin on Monastic Vows* (1521), LW 44:(243) 251–400.]

resignations. Therein lay the reason for postponing his own decision. For the cloisters, resignations brought no economic relief but an added burden. The resignees had the right to demand a return of at least part of the property they had donated on entering. As an act of fairness, Luther himself strongly supported this right.[7] A poorly endowed cloister like this one at Wittenberg[8] had a difficult time indeed coming up with the compensation for its resignees. The income from the begging tours of the friars (the "terminees") fell away. In fact, Karlstadt's constitution for the town of Wittenberg, drafted on January 24, 1522, forbade mendicancy. The Augustinians themselves wrote to the elector that in light of the "limited fare . . . and the drudgery" by which the townspeople live, "it is difficult and a burden on their own conscience" to go about begging. Luther estimated that his cloister was losing 300 guilders per year.[9] The requests for financial assistance which Spalatin kept forwarding to the elector were becoming ever more urgent. The renters on the cloister's lands were not paying, while the electoral administrator showed no concern and was instead harassing the cloister with persistent demands. Luther reminded Spalatin, "The prior is broke and won't be able to get any money. The begging sack has a hole, and it's a big one. . . . If I had not had to squander so much money on ex-monks and ex-nuns, I could well have rendered the prior a service."[10]

At last the number of resident friars dwindled to two besides Luther. They were the prior, Eberhard Brisger, and the steward, Bruno.[11] Brisger confided in Luther about the miserable circumstances, and Luther did not want to oblige him to his post any longer, "because his conscience was forcing him to change his way of life." Luther himself was at the end of his rope, especially over "the daily woes of trying to collect the rent." He saw no other solution than to return the cloister to its founder, the elector

---

7. Letter to Wenceslaus Link, vicar-general of the German Augustinians in Altenburg, January 7, 1523, WA Br 3:11 / 1ff.

8. On the property and income of the cloister, see *Germania Sacra* 1.3.2, pp. 453ff.

9. See above, pp. 123–25, on the Wittenberg and Leisnig order for a common chest. [Cf. *LW* 45:(159) 169–94.] E. Sehling, *Die evangelischen Kirchenordnungen des XVI Jahrhunderts* (Leipzig, 1902ff.), 1:697. "Unterricht der Augustiner von dem abgetanen Bettel sampt des Klosters Einkommen," in N. Müller, *Die Wittenberger Bewegung 1521 und 1522*, 2d ed. (Leipzig, 1911), 218–19. Luther to Spalatin, May 10, 1522, WA Br 2:524 / 12–13.

10. To Spalatin, May 27, 1523, WA Br 3:73 / 8ff., for the reference to the electoral administrator; also, WA Br 3:58 / 3–4; 196 / 1ff. Two nobles who refused to pay the land rent are named in letters of April 10 and October 16, 1523; WA Br 3:58, 173. Luther himself was at the end of his resources after tiding over the nuns fleeing the convent in Nimbschen (see below, pp. 258ff.), April 10, 1523; WA Br 3:55 / 27ff.

11. *Germania Sacra* 1.3.2, p. 452. On Brisger, ibid., pp. 493–94.

himself. As he had notified Spalatin earlier, if the prior quits, he himself would remain in the cloister no longer. In order to avoid being left empty-handed, Luther requested that either Brisger or he be granted a piece of the adjacent land that belonged to the cloister. Luther's request grew out of the prior's own situation; under the current circumstances he was in no way able to return to his wealthy paternal inheritance in the archdiocese of Trier.[12] The elector indeed took over the cloister and, going beyond Luther's request, gave him and Brisger the right to continued residence in it. This grant was formally renewed by Frederick's successors, the electors John (1532) and John Frederick (1536). In 1564 the university bought back the cloister building from Luther's heirs.[13]

Luther's own financial plight, coming to light in his ultimate request to the elector, resulted from his receiving no salary at all for his academic teaching. His "professorship in Bible," which he had held since 1512, was counted as the Augustinian cloister's compensatory payment to the elector in return for his own expenses in founding the cloister. Luther's pay had thus far consisted in free lodging in the cloister. His only cash was the modest sum of "9 old *Schock*" [8 guilders], which he had been receiving since 1514 for his services as preacher in the Town Church.[14] But this was

12. To Elector Frederick (probably mid-November 1523), *WA* Br 3:196 / 8ff. Also H. Volz, *WA* Br 14:xix. First consideration of the plan and hint at leaving Wittenberg in Luther's letter to Spalatin, October 16, 1523, *WA* Br 3:173 / 12ff., and April 10, 1523, *WA* Br 3:58 / 4. Through Spalatin, Luther renewed his request to the elector on February 1, 1524 (*WA* Br 3:241 / 10ff.) and reported on July 31, 1525 (*WA* Br 3:549 / 4ff.) to Link on the completion of the transaction.

13. *Germania Sacra* 1.3.2, p. 452. J. K. Seidemann, "Luthers Grundbesitz, " *ZHTh* 30 (1860): 475ff. E. Kroker, *Katharina von Bora, Luthers Frau: Ein Lebens- und Charakterbild* (Leipzig, 1906; 7th ed., Berlin, 1974), 83 (the year given is to be changed for 1523). Brisger, along with Bruno the steward, in 1525 received the requested piece of land in perpetuity. On it he built a "shack" [*bude*] and after becoming pastor in Altenburg let it be managed by the pastor of Dobien, near Wittenberg. Luther acquired the "shack" in 1541. *Germania Sacra* 1.3.2, p. 459. *WA* Br 9:576ff. *Bude* means a small wooden house without building rights, such as housed the poor population. Cf. E. Eschenhagen, "Wittenberger Studien: Beiträge zur Sozial- und Wirtschaftsgeschichte der Stadt Wittenberg in der Reformationszeit," *LuJ* 9 (1927): 31.

14. The obligation of the cloister to provide one full professor (ordinarius) for the professorship in Bible and one reader (lector) in moral philosophy in the faculty of arts (Luther's first appointment in Wittenberg [1508]; Scheel, *Martin Luther,* 2:360) is contained in a deed of November 11, 1504. W. Friedensburg, *Urkundenbuch der Universität Wittenberg* (Magdeburg, 1926), 1:13. *Germania Sacra* 1.3.2, p. 445.

As for Luther's salary, see Volz, *WA* Br 12:423ff. The declaration "9 *alte Schock*," *WA* Br 3:55 / 28 and *WA* TR 4, no. 5151, 685 / 24. One "*alter Schock*" = 20 *Groschen* (pennies) in Meissen [Saxony] currency; 21 *Groschen* = 1 guilder, *WA* Br 13:55–57, n. 14, and *WA* Br 13:46–84 / 43ff. Luther's cash income was 8 guilders. By comparison, in 1521 the two professors in medicine (Wild and Augustin Schurff) and the Hebraist Aurogallus each received 50 guilders. Melanchthon in 1518 received an initial salary of 60 guilders, and after 1520 some 100 guilders. Friedensburg, *Urkundenbuch,* 1:116–17, 133, 142–43. H. Volz, *MSA* 7 / 1 (1971): 37–38, n. 13; 179, n. 7.

far from enough to fill the gaps in the cloister's income or to cover the costs of helping those people who turned to him in emergencies.

His cowl advertised his poverty. "I have worn my habit until it could hardly be mended any more." Jerome Schurff is said to have offered him money several times to buy a new cassock. Presumably it was Schurff who got the elector to send Luther a piece of the finest cloth. As Luther learned, the elector is said to have joked, "What if [Luther] had them make him a Spanish cloak?"[15] Luther had this costly cloth tailored into a burgher's coat. Many people, especially his father, urged him to shed the monastic garb. With the exception of an occasional change of clothing at home,[16] Luther could not yet bring himself to take the final step. "Some day even I shall lay aside the cowl, but until now I have continued to wear it in order to spare the weak and to spite the pope," he wrote to a friend.[17] Not until October 9, 1524, did he preach for the first time without his cowl. On October 16 he wore it again for the morning service, but for the last time; at the afternoon service he appeared without it.

Spalatin, who kept track of these details, has also revealed the motive behind Luther's final decision. In a letter to Spalatin, on September 6, Erasmus had singled out Luther as an example of one who, contrary to many others, was not championing the gospel for economic gain. Others were abandoning the cowl, marrying, and even acquiring impressive property, whereupon they proceeded to write in defense of the gospel while keeping their identity anonymous or signing with a pseudonym. "In this respect," wrote Erasmus, "I must praise Luther. He signs his name to his writings and teaches liberties of which he does not avail himself, even though they be generally permitted."[18] Luther took his praise, which surely did not remain hidden from him, in a double sense. Admittedly he was depriving the evangelical movement of credibility when he subjected it to the charge "If what he teaches were true, then he himself would also do it." Later, in looking back on this difficult situation, he said,

15. A garment in the Spanish style that was becoming popular under Charles V. Luther's comments, WA TR 4, no. 4414, 303 / 17ff. Cf. WA TR 4, no. 5034, 624. WA TR 5, no. 6430, 657. [LW 54:338.]

16. John Dantiscus, the later bishop of Ermland, who became an opponent of the Reformation, came on Luther without the cowl in the summer of 1523. See F. Hipler, Nikolaus Kopernikus und Martin Luther: Nach ermländischen Archivalien (Braunsberg, 1868), 73.

17. May 25, 1524, WA Br 3:299 / 23ff.

18. Opus epistolarum Des. Erasmi Roterdami, ed. P. S. Allen et al. (Oxford, 1906ff.), 5:551 / 12–13. Erasmus von Rotterdam, Briefe, ed. W. Köhler (Leipzig, 1938), 334. Spalatin in J. B. Mencken, Scriptores rerum Germanicarum praecipue Saxonicarum (Leipzig, 1728), 2:637, cited in WA Br 3:301, n. 6.

Had I not myself laid aside the cowl, eaten meat, and taken a wife, the papists would have mocked, saying my teaching is not true, because I act differently from what I teach. So I couldn't get rid of that awful garment without offending one side or the other. The whole business turned sour. I did it not because of my conscience but for the sake of others to whom I desired to be of service.[19]

Thus the original pastoral motive, based on consideration for the weak, was now supplanted by another that the ongoing conflict had made more urgent, namely, witnessing to the truth of his venture and proving his solidarity with those who had joined him.

The extent to which this tie was obliging Luther had already become evident more than a year earlier and virtually on his doorstep. "Yesterday I received nine nuns from their captivity in the Nimbschen convent, among them the two Zeschaus and a Staupitz," he wrote on April 8, 1523, to his friend Link in Altenburg.[20] These three, Veronica and Margaret Zeschau and Magdalene von Staupitz, the sister of Luther's former vicar-general and fatherly friend, as well as three others, all of the Electoral Saxon nobility, were now safe from prosecution in the land of Frederick the Wise. It was a different matter for the other three, who were originally from the other Saxony of Duke George. These were Margaret and Ave von Schönfeld and Katharina von Bora. Besides, their parents were deceased and their much younger brothers lived near poverty on a small estate in Zulsdorf.[21] Luther himself had set the stage for the plot to smuggle them out and liberate them. They had turned to him for help after their families had denied their request to fetch them out of the cloister. After all, where else could they live so cheaply for the rest of their lives? Nor was it initially clear to their families at home that this kind of life could one day become an issue of conscience.

Luckily Luther located a reliable man, a friend who was ready to risk a secret abduction, an act that carried the death penalty. He was Leonhard Koppe of Torgau, a member of the town council and a businessman; incidentally, he was also a relative of Nicholas von Amsdorf. Koppe regularly

19. March 18, 1539, WA TR 4, no. 4414, 303 / 26–27; 304 / 1ff. [LW 54:337, 338. Rendering Bornkamm's text results in a slightly different reading of Luther's comments than in the LW version.]

20. WA Br 3:53 / 7–8.

21. Data on the nuns in Kroker, Katharina von Bora, 45ff.; A. Thoma, Katharina von Bora: Geschichtliches Lebensbild (Berlin, 1900), 1ff.; and WA Br 3:56–57. [For a biographical sketch of Katharina, see R. H. Bainton, Women of the Reformation in Germany and Italy (Minneapolis: Augsburg, 1971), 23–44.]

delivered fish and beer in barrels, as well as other goods, to the cloister of the Cistercian sisters in Nimbschen, near the town of Grimma, so it hardly attracted attention when, on Easter Eve, April 4, 1523, he drove his delivery wagon up to the cloister and then, after nightfall, began his return trip. The refugees spent the Easter holidays in Torgau and arrived in Wittenberg on April 7. A witty student, Wolfgang Schiefer, of the Austrian nobility and an ardent follower of Luther and Melanchthon, sized up the situation. Writing on May 4 to Beatus Rhenanus, he quipped: "Several days ago a wagon arrived here with a load of vestal virgins, as they are now called. They would like to marry as much as to stay alive. May God provide them with husbands so that in the course of time they won't run into greater need!"[22]

The nuns, having entrusted themselves to Luther's protection, now received it to the extent of his meager resources. The people in Wittenberg were not about to lend a hand. In a recent emergency Luther had found them unwilling to lend him any help at all. From past experience he often spoke of the Wittenbergers as his "Capernites," who behaved much like the ungrateful inhabitants of Capernaum (Matt. 11:23). Therefore on April 10 Luther sent an urgent appeal to Spalatin, asking him in his own name to solicit contributions from the well-to-do at the elector's court so that the nuns could be tided over at least another week or two while other arrangements for them were being worked out. Luther added that his own income made it impossible to care for them single-handedly.[23]

Luther had the right instinct for this matter. He immediately published a pamphlet, giving a report of what had taken place, believing that com-

22. *Briefwechsel des Beatus Rhenanus*, ed. A. Horawitz and K. Hartfelder (Leipzig, 1886), 319. Vestals were set apart early in childhood for a thirty-year unmarried period of service. Schiefer was later the tutor of the sons of Ferdinand I [of Hapsburg]. In 1539, however, he was dismissed on suspicion of holding Lutheran ideas. He returned to Wittenberg. On November 7, 1539, Luther recommended him to Elector John Frederick as tutor for his sons: "He is at present one of my daily table guests and is a very fine man. He is still unmarried and will perhaps remain so" (WA Br 8:588). On the "wagonload of nuns," which Koppe drove from Nimbschen to Wittenberg, Amsdorf also had something to say, as told by Abraham Scultetus and edited by E. Kroker in his account of Luther's courtship: "Luthers Werbung um Katharina von Bora: Eine Untersuchung über die Quellen einer alten Überlieferung," in *Lutherstudien zur 4. Jahrhundertfeier der Reformation* (Weimar, 1917), 142. Although Kroker there (145) surmised that Schiefer's account was based on a second and otherwise unknown transportation of nuns from the cloister in Sornzig (Kreis Oschatz, cf. *Handbuch der historischen Stätten Deutschlands*, vol. 8: *Sachsen*, ed. W. Schlesinger [Stuttgart, 1965], 335), he himself apparently let it drop. In the second edition (1925) of his *Katharina von Bora*, Kroker repeated unchanged his original reference to the nuns of Nimbschen (reprinted, O. Clemen's 1939 new edition [Berlin, 1952, 1974], 44).

23. WA Br 3:55 / 18ff. Through Spalatin, on April 22, Luther assured the elector (for whom the whole business was a delicate political matter) that he would exercise strict discretion in distributing any anticipated grant from the elector. On Luther's own income, see above, pp. 256–57.

plete frankness would forestall nasty gossip.[24] Luther not only admitted his own part as instigator, but also named Leonhard Koppe as the smuggling agent, even though this guaranteed the cloister's wrath. He also gave the names of the nine nuns, which would make it impossible for the families to proceed individually against them.[25] Thereby this sensational coup became a flaming protest against the bitter injustice that had been uncovered by it: the humiliating and forcible depositing of young girls in cloisters, the coerced worship of God, and the involuntary renunciation of the natural task of the woman. Once again Luther stressed that ascetic vows must be secondary to the God-created estate of matrimony. "Who forces me or who calls me that I should live unmarried?"[26] Yet he did not use the occasion for an attack on monastic life but concluded: "May God Almighty graciously enlighten all friends of those who live endangered and unwillingly in cloisters, that they faithfully help them to get out. But those who know what they are about and who find profitable ways of utilizing the conventual life, let them stay there, in God's name."[27]

In the following weeks, with the help of their families, most of the nuns found at least temporary places. Only the three from Ducal Saxony had to remain in Wittenberg. Katharina von Bora was received into the home of Lucas Cranach, the painter and apothecary, as well as friend of Luther's. He owned a large new house on the marketplace.[28] From there on Katharina moved in Luther's closer circle of friends, and as a member of the reputable house of Cranach she became an active Wittenberger. In October 1523 the exiled Danish king Christian II, staying at the Cranachs',[29] honored Katharina, then an assisting daughter of the house, with the gift of a gold ring. She also won friends among the students. They

24. *Ursach und Antwort, dass Jungfrauen Klöster göttlich verlassen mögen* (1523), WA 11:394–400.

25. WA 11:394 / 27ff.; 400 / 18ff. The pamphlet is dedicated to Koppe.

26. WA 11:399 / 29.

27. WA 11:400 / 22ff.

28. According to Kroker, *Katharina von Bora*, 49ff., Katharina was taken in by the master and later burgomaster Philipp Reichenbach. Yet his assumption rests solely on an opinion of the Wittenberg theological faculty on Luther's marriage and was rendered only in 1630 (*Consilia Theologica Witebergensia* [Frankfurt, 1664], 4:17ff.). No relation of any kind between Luther and his wife and the Reichenbach family can be ascertained either then [1523] or later. On the contrary, Cranach and his wife took part in the Luther wedding (see below, p. 408), and Cranach became a sponsor to Luther's firstborn. Therefore the assumption that the Cranach residence was Katharina's place of refuge is correct. See Thoma, *Katharina von Bora*, 280; and H. Boehmer, "Luthers Ehe," *LuJ* 7 (1925): 42–43. On the possessions of Cranach, who in these years had risen to become one of Wittenberg's wealthiest citizens, see Eschenhagen, "Wittenberger Studien," 23–24, 99–100.

29. See below, p. 287.

nicknamed her "Catherine of Siena," not because she suggested the ascetic severity of that great mystic but because of her fearless bearing and her straightforward speech, which were other attributes of Siena's Catherine.[30]

The Nimbschen example set a pattern. Three more nuns of this cloister were taken out by their relatives. Sixteen quit the Augustinian nunnery in Widerstedt, near Mansfeld, in June 1523. Among them was Ottilie von Gersen, later the wife of Thomas Müntzer. For the time being they enjoyed the protection of the electoral administrator in Allstedt and of the evangelically inclined Count Albrecht of Mansfeld.[31] Much as Luther hailed the liberation of nuns from their involuntary cloister service, he retained a sober judgment of these events, for he knew, especially from the experience of monks, that their motives for resigning were often dubious.

> I see many of our monks quitting on no other grounds than they entered, that is, for the sake of their belly and fleshly liberty. Through them Satan will raise a big stink against the good odor of our word. But what shall we do? They are a lazy lot, looking out for themselves. Better let them do so without the cowl than sinning as they go on wearing it.[32]

Their exodus at least cleansed the church of some of the corruptions against which Luther had often complained. He was especially concerned that many were bent on marrying at once although they were entirely inexperienced in worldly responsibilities. The many refugees from the cloisters who came to Wittenberg took not only what little money he had but also an endless amount of time.[33]

Luther's association with the ex-cloister people, who had quit their orders because of his word, forced him to go beyond the bounds of personal aid and to confront them once more publicly with the central question behind their decision. According to the church's view, these refugees from the convent, as well as the already married priests, had broken the holiest of vows—and were guilty; besides, in the church's opinion, they had acted on the basest of motives. To defend this matter publicly Luther required more than his 1521 treatise on monastic vows. For one thing, what he had

30. Over against Thoma, *Katharina von Bora*, 39, and Kroker, *Katharina von Bora*, 55.

31. T. Kolde, *Briefe und Aktenstücke zur Geschichte Luthers* (Gotha, 1883), 442–43. W. Elliger, *Thomas Müntzer: Leben und Werk* (Göttingen, 1975), 374ff. (on his marriage). WA Br 3:100 / 9ff.

32. To John Lang, March 28, 1522, WA Br 2:488 / 21ff.

33. To Spalatin, July 11, 1523, WA Br 3:109 / 12ff. To Oecolampadius, June 20, 1523, WA Br 3:97 / 35ff. [*LW* 49:45.]

at that time directed inwardly to the monastic community, and had set forth in Latin argumentation, he would now have to repeat in terms more generally comprehensible. Besides, the whole issue of vows had broadened into a confrontation between the "spiritual estate" and the married estate. It was now a matter not simply of defending the right of vows [taken voluntarily] but also of upholding the divine dignity of marriage, over against the demotion it had endured in the church.

The vow issue had recently (1522) again been thoroughly treated in a polemical writing appearing in Rome. Its author, John Faber (Johannes Fabri), was vicar of the bishop of Constance. In 1523 Duke George had it reprinted in Leipzig, and Luther first saw it during the Easter season, when the nuns were being resettled.[34] Despite the preface, which cited many passages from Paul admonishing peace, Faber's attack was directed at Luther. Yet Luther was little inclined to respond to this compiler of endless testimonies from church tradition in support of papal power. In Luther's opinion the decision was not to be made on papal ground. "The whole of Faber is nothing but fathers, fathers, fathers, councils, councils, councils." With such a string of human citations a man could neither defend nor attack the pope; he could only show that he had read many books, and Luther did not begrudge him such praise. "I shall wait for other opponents."[35] One point, however, agitated Luther in this situation: Faber had defended the right of the popes to promote celibacy even apart from a biblical basis. In the process he had marshaled many ancient quotations—insulting and cynical as these were toward women—to serve him as weapons.[36] Luther therefore prodded Justus Jonas to confront Faber, at least on this burning issue. For a recent bridegroom like Jonas this looked like just the right subject for an initial opus.[37]

In any case, Luther considered the issue of marriage and celibacy important enough to tackle it once again himself, but this time not from

34. *Johannes Fabri Constantiensis in spiritualibus vicarii opus adversus nova quaedam et a christiana religione prorsus aliena dogmata Martini Lutheri*, WA 12:81. The Leipzig reprint is mentioned by Luther in his letter to Elector Frederick on May 29, 1523, WA Br 3:77 / 84ff. [*LW* 49:41–42.] A new addition (at the expense of the publisher, Johannes Romberch) appeared under the martial title *Malleus Ioannis Fabri . . . in haeresim Lutheranam* (Köln, 1524), *CC* 23–26.

35. Foreword to Justus Jonas, *Adversum Iohannem Fabrum*, WA 12:85 / 21ff.; 87 / 1–2. [See M. Lehmann, *Justus Jonas, Loyal Reformer* (Minneapolis: Augsburg, 1963), 92–95.]

36. *Malleus Tract*. 4, text 18, *CC* 23 / 24, 262ff. For this inclusive work the unusually long section is aimed at thesis 18 in Luther's small treatise *Warum des Papstes und seiner Jünger Bücher von D. Martin Luther verbrannt sind*, WA 7:172,6ff.

37. WA 12:85 / 3ff., 14ff. Jonas originally had his doctorate in jurisprudence, but in October 1521 he also received a doctorate in theology. He had been married since February 1522.

the sterile ground of ecclesial tradition but from the most difficult point: Paul's pronouncements on marriage and the single life in 1 Cor. 7. Here lay the most important biblical testimony on which the champions of celibacy since Jerome had relied. Because Luther made it a purely exegetical presentation, several of his finest and most important thoughts on marriage are here more veiled than revealed.[38] Much like today's exegetes, Luther read these sayings of Paul in light of the history of salvation, yet in exactly opposite terms. Today one here interprets Paul as awaiting the imminent End, making marriage inadvisable and unnecessary.[39] Luther, however, saw chapter 7 in terms of his hermeneutical common denominator, that is, as part of Paul's argument with Mosaic law. "Moses commanded that every person be married." To be unmarried was branded as a fruitless estate, on eschatological grounds, even though with a different goal in mind. "Everything happened this way because Christ was promised from Abraham's seed. Because no one knew from which person he might come, all Jews were to marry in honor of this seed and submit until [the Messiah] came."[40] Thus, according to Luther, if under Moses the accent fell on marriage as a duty, then under Paul (in the changed situation of salvific history) the accent falls on freedom to remain unmarried.

With the situation changed again in his day, in which marriage was forbidden to certain estates, Luther saw his task as that of proclaiming freedom to marry as well as freedom to remain unmarried. His treatise is thus balanced in both directions. He was not yet ready to surrender the inherited order of values. "Wherever one compares marriage and virginity, virginity is a nobler gift than marriage. Nevertheless, marriage is as much God's gift as virginity (according to Paul). A man, also, is nobler than a woman. Yet in God's eyes, all things are equal which among themselves would be unequal."[41] Yet Luther's attack was intended in the first instance not as a balanced presentation of the married and the unmarried estates

38. *Das siebente Kapitel S. Pauli zu den Corinthern* appeared ca. August 1523; WA 12:92–142. He dedicated the commentary to the Saxon hereditary marshal Hans von Löser in the Castle Pretzsch, with whom he had had a conversation on the marriage question. Luther intended this treatise as a "Christian epithalamium," a bridal song, to encourage Löser to marry.

39. G. Bornkamm, *Paulus* (Stuttgart, Berlin, Cologne, 1969), 212ff. J. Weiss, *Der erste Korintherbrief* (Göttingen, 1910), 169ff. H. Lietzmann, "An die Korinther 1 / 2," in *Handbuch zum Neuen Testament* 9, 5th ed., ed. W. G. Kümmel (Tübingen, 1969) on this passage [chap. 7]. [LW 28: (Commentary on 1 Cor. 7) 5–56.]

40. WA 12:97 / 14ff. [LW 28:9ff.]

41. WA 12:97 104 / 24ff. Here Luther's use of *edler* (nobler) means more useful (with virginity as an exception, the man because of his gifts). [LW 28:16. LW prefers to translate *Jungfrauschaft* as chastity, but Luther means virginity, or he would have used *Keuschheit*.]

but as an objection against engrafting these two ways of life into the church's value system. The Roman church has turned the unmarried estate, actually open to anyone, into an ecclesial institution appearing to be especially high in God's favor. Celibacy is thus rated as the spiritual estate, marriage as the secular estate. "It should be the reverse. Marriage should be called the proper religious order, which it really is, and the other orders be called the real secular orders, which is what they really are,"[42] for that estate is spiritual in which faith must defend itself. This is not what life is like in a cloister, where the work of others and the generosity of strangers provide the necessities. Married life is altogether different; for the rest of your days you wrestle with the question of providing for a wife and children. "So the married estate is by nature such that it teaches out of God's hand and grace and forces one to . . . faith." And as it leads to faith, so it leads also to works, for marriage also means diligent work.[43] Luther thus distinguished between the falsely called "Christian" estate of celibacy, which he rejected, and the "chaste," unmarried but self-supporting estate which he, following Paul, prized highly.[44] But the latter only then accords with God's intention when one has not been forced into it or when one does not have to engage in relentless personal struggle to keep it up, a struggle to which the "mad teachers" of the church attached merits.[45] Matrimony is not the higher way of living, but it is the natural way of living and is the target of the sexuality God has implanted in human beings. Luther had many a frank and serious word to say about sexuality, yet without any legalistic prescriptions. "A Christian person will probably know how to behave in this matter, employing moderation."[46] Luther's commentary on 1 Cor. 7 is no marriage manual in the conventional sense but an attempt to enable Paul, precisely in this difficult chapter, to bring freedom to bear on this subject. Hitherto the apostle had been cited as a proponent of the legal basis of celibate vows, and his authority was even used to justify the delivery of young people into the cloister.

The more Luther became isolated in the cloister, the more the town seemed to him to fill with friends.[47] Foremost and youngest among them was Philipp Melanchthon. At the age of twenty-one, in 1518, Melanch-

42. WA 12:105 / 21ff. [LW 28:17.]
43. WA 12:106 / 9ff., 24ff.; 107 / 21ff.; 108 / 9ff. [LW 28: 18, 19, 20.]
44. WA 12:108 / 34ff. [LW 28:21.]
45. WA 12:116 / 7ff. [LW 28:28.]
46. WA 12:101 / 27–28.
47. See the sensitive but unfortunately obscure essay by H. Volz, "Luther und sein Freundeskreis," *Tübinger Forschungen* 42 / 45 (1968–69): 6ff.

thon commenced his professorship in Greek at Wittenberg University. Within a short time an exuberant friendship developed between the two men, the only highly gifted people on the university faculty. Each accorded the other the palm of genius and quality.[48] Melanchthon was awed by the spiritual and theological power of his older friend. Luther, in turn, marveled at the learning of the young Melanchthon and at his impetuous openness to his older friend's rapidly advancing theological insights. For example, the manner in which Melanchthon defended the theses set for his baccalaureate examination in theology (some of them probably set by Luther himself) prompted this enthusiastic note to Staupitz: "He defended them in such a way that he seemed to us all a veritable wonder. Please Christ, he will surpass many Martins and will be a mighty foe of the devil and of the scholastic theology."[49] A little earlier Melanchthon had told John Lang, "I cherish the works of Martin, his theology (*pias literas*), and the man himself. Humanly speaking, I cherish him most deeply and have taken him completely to heart."[50] Luther was well aware of their difference in temperament, yet he saw this as providential. To Lang's complaint over the intense tone of his *To the Christian Nobility*, Luther replied, "Perhaps I am the forerunner of Philipp, for whom, like the example of Elias, I am in spirit and power preparing the way, and am thus to destroy Israel and the house of Ahab."[51] And when he sat handi-

48. Cf. G. Mix, "Luther und Melanchthon in ihrer gegenseitigen Beurteilung," *ThStKr* 74 (1901): 458ff. For Melanchthon's development and his relationship to the theology of Luther in the mid-1520s, the now basic study is that of W. Maurer, *Der junge Melanchthon zwischen Humanismus und Reformation* (Göttingen, 1969), 2:68ff., which extends the circle of Melanchthon's friends to the humanist side.

49. October 3, 1519, WA Br 1:514 / 34ff. The first eleven of the baccalaureate theses probably originated not with Melanchthon but with Luther, according to the research of O. Ritschl, *Dogmengeschichte des Protestantismus* (Göttingen, 1926), 2:239, n. 2. Also O. Ritschl, "Die Entwicklung der Rechtfertigungslehre Melanchthons bis zum Jahre 1527," *ThStKr* 85 (1911–12): 518ff. Likewise, Maurer, *Der junge Melanchthon*, 2:102–3. Luther is here characterizing not the content of the examination as miraculous (ibid., 102) but the manner in which Melanchthon defended the theses; this manner was *miraculum*. [Cf. C. L. Manschreck, *Melanchthon: The Quiet Reformer* (Nashville, 1958), 51–52, 54, to date the best available on Melanchthon in English, although now somewhat overtaken by more recent research.]

50. *CR* 1:106. *MSA* 7 / 1:76–77, 35ff. *MBW* 62.

51. August 18, 1520, WA Br 2:167 / 7ff., according to Luke 1:17. On this see Maurer, *Der junge Melanchthon*, 2:156. H. Volz, *Die Lutherpredigten Mathesius*, QFRG 12 (Leipzig, 1930), 63ff. H. Grabs, "Luthers Beinamen in der reformationsfreundlichen Literatur 1517–1525" (theology diss., Halle, 1922). The Elias designation for Luther was first discussed among the South German Swiss humanists. Cf. Zasius to Zwingli, November 13, 1519; Zwingli to Oswald Myconius, January 4, 1520, in *Huldreich Zwingli sämtliche Werke*, ed. E. Egli, G. Finster, et al. (Berlin, 1905ff.), 7 (1911): 222 / 11; 250 / 11. Its origin with Erasmus is uncertain. Elias was a name used also by the Swiss adherents of Luther in differentiating themselves from the Anabaptists of Zurich. Cf. the unpublished letter of Erhard Hegenwald to Conrad Grebel and his brethren in the faith, January 1, 1525, for which information I thank Heinhold Fast.

capped in his Wartburg detention, Luther confessed as much to Melanchthon: "Even though I perish, the gospel will not be the loser, for you
already surpass me; and, as Elisha after Elijah, you will follow with redoubled spirit the one with whom the Lord Jesus has graciously made you
a partner."[52] Melanchthon no doubt read that with an uneasy heart, for he
felt himself entirely the younger man and the learner in theology.

Significant fruits were quickly appearing from this rapidly growing
friendship. In the years 1519–21 Melanchthon willingly assumed the task
of taking down Luther's sermons on Genesis as well as on the pericopes
for the Sundays and festivals on which Luther preached in the Town
Church, the Castle Church, and the cloister church.[53] We can hardly
overestimate the value of this exercise for Melanchthon's theological development.[54] This writing procedure, receptive and correspondingly productive, led him to the spiritual core of Luther's theology, and by simultaneously translating into Latin he was forced to appropriate Luther's
thought in his own way. So, for instance, in a short exposition of the first
six chapters of Genesis, published in 1523, Melanchthon had transformed
Luther's sermons into a running commentary, complete with his older
colleague's teaching on sin and grace.[55]

Yet Melanchthon's reception of Luther's thought can be perceived far
beyond such a common exegetical theme. Alongside one or another of the
sermon transcripts, Melanchthon apparently also had access to Luther's
lecture notes, at any rate the lectures on Romans and Hebrews.[56] He
made use of them partly for his own lectures on Romans and Corinthians
and partly for his initial attempts to give the new Wittenberg theology a
systematic format. This was of decisive importance. Luther himself lacked
the gift of being able to present his theology in an inclusive academic
pattern, but Melanchthon was surprisingly swift in perceiving the neces-

52. May 26, 1521, *WA Br* 2:348 / 48ff., according to 2 Kings 2:9–10.

53. On these sermons, see above, pp. 236ff.

54. Maurer, *Der junge Melanchthon*, 2:114.

55. *CR* 13:761–91. For his dependence on Luther, see H. Sick, *Melanchthon als Ausleger des Alten Testaments* (Tübingen, 1959), 7ff., 29ff., as well as Maurer, *Der junge Melanchthon*, 2:116ff.

56. W. Maurer, "Zur Komposition der Loci Melanchthons von 1521: Ein Beitrag zur Frage Melanchthon und Luther," *LuJ* 25 (1958): 159ff., was the first to show Melanchthon's use of Luther's lectures on Hebrews in his composition of the *Loci Communes*. The bearing of Luther's lectues on Romans on other aspects of Melanchthon's work has been demonstrated by E. Bizer, *Theologie der Verheissung* (Neukirchen-Vluyn, 1964), 133ff., 215ff., while R. Schäfer, "Zur Prädestinationslehre beim jungen Melanchthon," *ZThK* 63 (1966): 353ff., has found exact connections in Luther for Melanchthon's commentary on Romans (lectures of 1520, published as *Annotationes in Epistolas Pauli ad Romanos et Corinthios* [1522]).

sity of responding to the classical dogmatic traditions, as exemplified by John of Damascus and Peter Lombard,[57] and of providing a clear outline of the new theology as it grew out of biblical exegesis. We still have drafts showing us the content and form that eventually comprised the widely admired *Loci Communes* of 1521. The substance came from the formulations Melanchthon had drawn from Luther's sermons, lectures, and other writings. The form and the conceptualization, set forth in the *Loci*, show how Melanchthon—following the great humanists of his era, such as Agricola and Erasmus—readily appropriated the structures of Ciceronian rhetoric.[58] Employing the form, he provided the substance by creating major concepts based on a historico-biblical foundation and ready to serve in advancing biblical exegesis and creating a systematized theology.

What Luther had poured out to Melanchthon in loose profusion he now received back in packaged form in such a way as to make his teaching usable to the full in the education of a new academic generation. Luther was delighted with the *Loci*, which was but one among other works to which he inspired his young colleague. Later on, Luther praised the *Loci* to Erasmus as "an invincible book which, I am convinced, deserves not only immortality but also canonization by the church." Even though he wanted hereby to irritate Erasmus, it was an honestly intended word.[59] Luther even began a translation of the *Loci* from Latin, but it remained unfinished.[60] The book served Luther in still another way. It helped to deflect the wrath of the opponents from Luther and, momentarily at least, let Melanchthon take the brunt of their attack. Cochlaeus, influenced by a first reading of the *Loci*, denounced the book as "a new Koran that will have a more damaging effect than Luther's book on the Babylonian Captivity . . . because you (Melanchthon), compared to him, have a more pleasing style and a more learned spirit, as well as a greater cleverness and caution with which to cite Scripture for the purpose of deception."[61]

57. Introduction to the *Loci Communes* (1521), *MSA* 2 / 1 (1952): 5. [Cf. also W. Pauck's introduction to the *Loci Communes Theologici*, as well as his translation of the text, in *Melanchthon and Bucer*, ed. W. Pauck, LCC 19 (Philadelphia, 1969), 3–17, 18–152.

58. Cf. W. Maurer, "Melanchthons Loci Communes von 1521 als wissenschaftliche Programmschrift," *LuJ* 27 (1960): 1ff. This contains Maurer's rebuttal to P. Joachimsen, "Loci Communes: Eine Untersuchung zur Geistesgeschichte des Humanismus und der Reformation," *LuJ* 8 (1926): 27ff. For details on the *Loci*, see Maurer, *Der junge Melanchthon*, 2:139ff., 230ff. [Cf. LCC 19:9–18.]

59. *WA* 18:601 / 4ff.

60. To Amsdorf, October 27, 1524, *WA* Br 3:361 / 3ff. Also Maurer, *Der junge Melanchthon*, 2:147–46, 531. There and in *CR* 21:78–79 are further references to the impact of the *Loci* on contemporaries. [Cf. LCC 19:16–17.]

61. *CR* 21:78–79; this writing of Cochlaeus appeared first in 1531. In Germany, *Die Loci Communes Philipp Melanchthons in ihrer Urgestalt, nach G. L. Plitt*, ed. T. Kolde (Erlangen and Leipzig, 1890; 4th ed., 1925), 55.

In Melanchthon, Luther gained an invaluable colleague in the eyes of the humanists and the scholastic theologians. Most important, perhaps, was the fact that with his *Loci* Melanchthon presented a subtle but, for one who knew the situation, unmistakable differentiation from Erasmus. Substantively this became notably evident in Melanchthon's rejection of free will, a passage with which he opened the *Loci*. And methodologically he rejected the allegorical exegesis of Origen and the other church fathers whom Erasmus had so strongly recommended in his *Ratio seu methodus compendio perveniendi ad veram theologiam* (in several editions, 1518–20). In some respects, Melanchthon's *Loci* would have to be seen as a refutation of this work by Erasmus. The profound differences between the two authors were apparent not only to Erasmus but also to a wider circle of humanists.[62] A few years later Erasmus reminded Melanchthon of their differing positions, doing so in the covering letter for his newly published *De libero arbitrio* (1524). Melanchthon's commitment to Luther's theology was all the more effective because shortly before this Erasmus had sent out letters rejecting Luther's position.[63] Erasmus had even gone so far as to elicit the help of Justus Jonas, then newly come to Wittenberg, to woo Melanchthon away from Luther and restore him to the tasks of pure scholarship.[64] The issue affected also the Wittenberg students. One of them, Albert Burer, the young aide to Beatus Rhenanus, expressed lingering amazement in his first report to his master from the scene. The judgment of the Paris faculty against Luther had just come out, and Burer commented: "The higher they esteem Erasmus [in Paris], the lower he is esteemed here. Some consider him a mere flatterer, but in my opinion only because he tackles everything more moderately than Martinus does. Here they think Erasmus has not yet attained the spirit that Luther possesses." Some, moreover, hold Erasmus for more of an adherent of Plato than of Christ; others say he is a Pelagian. Here Origen and Jerome do not rate as highly as Augustine.[65]

62. Cf. W. Maurer, "Melanchthons Anteil am Streit zwischen Luther und Erasmus," in his *Der junge Melanchthon*, 2:264ff. Erasmus, September 6, 1524, to Melanchthon, *Opus epistolarum Des. Erasmi Roterodami*, ed. P. S. Allen et al. (Oxford, 1906ff.), 5; no. 1496; and Erasmus, *De libero arbitrio Diatribe sive Collatio*, ed. J. von Walter, QGP (Leipzig, 1910; 2d ed., 1935), 64 / 1ff. See also Luther, *De servo arbitrio*, WA 18:740 / 32ff. [Cf. *LW* 33:8–10.]

63. Especially in the copies and the letter to Ludwig Ber in Basel, May 14, 1524, and published soon thereafter; see *Opus epistolarum*, ed. Allen, 4:493–94. On the copies and printing of the letter, see *Suppl. Mel.* 6 / 1:155.

64. Letter of May 10, 1521, *Opus epistolarum*, ed. Allen, 4: no. 1202.

65. June 30, 1521, *Briefwechsel des Beatus Rhenanus*, ed. A. Horawitz and K. Hartfelder (Leipzig, 1886), 280–81. Among other things, thanks to this letter, we gain a vivid account of Wittenberg University life.

Upon this rapidly—indeed, too rapidly—blossoming theological fellow-ship between two so dissimilar friends as Luther and Melanchthon, there soon fell the first frost. Melanchthon admittedly was outclassed and by no means as yet sure enough of the common cause to assume top responsibil-ity, as happened when Luther was confined to the Wartburg and pre-cipitous events broke out in Wittenberg.[66] Halfheartedly he went along with Karlstadt's reforms, holding back where he could. But when the "Zwickau prophets" looked him up he became completely helpless. To their rejection of infant baptism, or their enlistment of the Holy Spirit, he had nothing to say. Distraught, he wrote the elector on December 27, 1521, seeking advice and had to be content with Frederick's reply that "as a layman and inexperienced in the Holy Scriptures" he would not know how to proceed against people who style themselves as apostolic and pro-phetic. From the Wartburg, Luther wrote that he could not understand Philipp's timidity; after all, "you far excel me in spirit and learning." De-spite these two pointed admonitions to self-confidence, Melanchthon re-mained uncertain.[67] He was saved when at last he had his wish and Luther returned. After this failure, who would blame Melanchthon for desiring to withdraw from the theological field? But Luther would hear nothing of it and sought instead to maintain Melanchthon's association in theology, es-pecially by encouraging him to continue his biblical lectures. But Philipp seemed equally determined to resist, especially Luther's attempts be-tween 1522 and 1524 to draw him from the faculty of arts into the faculty of theology. Melanchthon never considered himself a full-blown theologian and thought of his lectures in this field as only a temporary help rendered when Luther was overburdened or, as during the Wartburg interval, ab-sent from Wittenberg. Besides, he regarded his instruction in Greek as an indispensable contribution to theology, particularly since humanistic studies were still as much neglected as during the era of scholasticism.[68] Only in 1526 was he again ready to engage in a modest theological activity, as he saw it. This, however, did not make him a member of the theological

66. See above, pp. 52, 62.

67. N. Müller, *Die Wittenberger Bewegung 1521 und 1522*, 2d ed. (Leipzig, 1911), 29–30. On this, see Spalatin's note on the correspondence and the negotiations with the electoral councillor Hugold von Einsiedel on January 1, 1522, ibid., 137ff. *MBW* 201ff. Excerpts from this in *MSA* 7 / 1:158ff. Luther to Melanchthon, January 13, 1522, WA Br 2:424 / 9–10. *MBW* 205. For his advice, see above, p. 63. [*LW* 48:365–66.]

68. Cf. esp. Melanchthon's letters to Spalatin, end of September and end of November 1522, in *MSA* 7 / 1:179ff., 182–83, 185–86 (with some corrections pertaining to *CR*). Details in Maurer, *Der junge Melanchthon*, 2:419ff. Maurer's use of the term "career crisis" *(Berufskrise)* is not exactly fortunate. Melanchthon never was confused about his actual calling; on relevant personal grounds he simply refused to give it up or to curtail it unduly.

faculty. It was slow in coming, but Melanchthon regained his confidence in the theological field by accepting specific assignments. One was pedagogical, when he helped to prepare the Saxon visitation instructions (1528). Another was ecclesial, when he drafted the great confessional documents (1530–31) in which he had to sum up the teachings of his church. Still another was outright theological, when he reworked his *Loci* into an inclusive system (an exercise, completed in 1535) that combined the elements to which he was committed: humanism and Reformation faith.

Back in 1521–22 Melanchthon had been not only too young but also too weak and religiously inexperienced to have stood firmly under that baptism of fire.[69] As a result, the relation between Luther and Melanchthon returned to that of personal friendship, in lieu of what Luther had hoped would be a comradeship in arms. The inevitable tension between two such dissimilar personalities was easier for Luther to bear than for Melanchthon; the one was by nature more robust and richly endowed, and bore the tension with greater composure than the other, who was more delicate and sensitive. Melanchthon lamented his loneliness not only to trusted friends, like Joachim Camerarius, but also to visitors. Humanists and traditionalists in the Roman camp took note.[70] Unembarrassed, Luther accepted what his friend Philipp had to offer and treated him according to the image of what he wished him to be rather than according to what he actually was. The disappointment lingering from the period of unrest in Wittenberg did nothing to diminish the full affirmation Luther had always accorded Melanchthon. "In him I see no one other than myself, his learning and the purity of his life excepted, for in these matters he shames me and excels me," Luther wrote to a friend in 1523.[71]

The like-mindedness and active support Luther found missing in Melanchthon was provided for him by John Bugenhagen.[72] Luther met

69. Maurer, *Der junge Melanchthon*, 2:203ff., 216, 223ff., 435ff., has interpreted Melanchthon's failure as the beginning of his return to biblical humanism. That surely is true. But it is also true that his earlier impetuous devotion to Luther is an expression of his weakness, his need to have someone to lean on, and his lack of formative religious experiences.

70. To Camerarius, October 31, 1524, *CR* 1:683. *MSA* 7 / 1:218. *MBW* 351. On the basis of personal impressions, John Dantiscus made this judgment in his report of August 8, 1523, to the bishop of Posen (see below, p. 291). No doubt the same was expressed by Jost Ludwig Dietz, who on July 26, 1522, visited Wittenberg; in a letter to Dantiscus from Naples on November 10, 1523, which presumably was a reply to Dantiscus. Dietz wrote: "Oh how gladly would I pull this man [Melanchthon] out of this tragedy, if only I had the power to do so!" *WA* Br 2:581, n. 1. Comments of Hipler, *Nikolaus Kopernikus* (see n. 16, above).

71. To Theobald Billikan, September 17, 1523, *WA* Br 3:154 / 14–15.

72. *Dr. Johannes Bugenhagens Briefwechsel*, ed. O. Vogt (Stettin, 1888). An old or newer inclusive edition of Bugenhagen's writings does not exist, neither is there a modern biogra-

Bugenhagen at the right moment, just when he had returned from the Wartburg and was standing in need of a reliable co-worker ready to help restore order in Wittenberg. Bugenhagen, born June 24, 1485, in Wollin, Pomerania, was two years Luther's junior. With dogged persistence he had pursued the way to Luther. In Greifswald he had put in two years (1502–4) studying the arts and humanities. The influence of Erasmus had directed him to the church fathers and the Bible. Since 1504 he had been lecturing on these subjects as rector of the town school just outside Trep-tow on the Rega River. The pastoral counseling growing out of his work rapidly attracted a growing number of adherents, including lay people, and made him seek ordination in 1509. The fact that he had not studied theology prior to ordination was not unusual in the late Middle Ages.

Presently came Bugenhagen's first scholarly assignment, indirectly from Electoral Saxony. Frederick the Wise had ordered his chancellor Spalatin to write an inclusive history of Saxony. To expedite that effort pertinent records and books were requested from friendly neighboring princes. Frederick had thus turned also to Duke Bogislav of Pomerania. The latter responded promptly, not only satisfying Frederick's request but also initiating a search for sources of Pomeranian history. The man as-signed this dual task in the summer of 1517 was John Bugenhagen. Travel-ing the country from east to west, he found few sources pertaining to Saxony, but many on his own country. So he decided to write a history of Pomerania. No one had hitherto undertaken anything like it, and despite frequent dead ends Bugenhagen persisted with dogged determination. To be sure, his *Pomerania* was no loosely narrated history but a well-ordered compilation from older chronicles and other sources. Despite obvious pride of country and efforts to praise the achievements of the princely house, he claimed that nowhere did he set forth anything contrary to his conscience. "What a disgrace it would have been for me, if I, a priest of Christ, had written against my conviction simply to flatter my prince!"[73]

---

phy. The best is that by H. Hering, "Doktor Pomeranus Johannes Bugenhagen," *RE*[3] 3 (1897): 525ff. *Johann Bugenhagen: Beiträge zu seinem 400. Geburtstag*, ed. W. Rautenberg (Berlin, 1958), with valuable essays and a bibliography exceeding that of Schottenloher, by H.-G. Leder, supplements K. Schottenloher, *Bibliographie der deutschen Geschichte im Zeitalter der Glaubensspaltung 1517–1585* (Leipzig, 1933ff.), 7 (1966): 26–27. E. Wolf, "Johannes Bugenhagen: Gemeinde und Amt," in his *Peregrinatio: Studien zur refor-matorischen Theologie und zum Kirchenproblem* (Munich, 1954), 1:257ff.

73. "Pomerania durch Johannem Bugenhagen Pomeranum mit eigener Handt be-schreven," the title page. *Johannes Bugenhagens Pomerania*, ed. O. Heinemann, Quellen zur Pomerschen Geschichte 4 (Stettin, 1900), 4.

We do not know when John Bugenhagen first came on Luther's writings. In any case, when Bugenhagen first leafed through the *Babylonian Captivity of the Church,* he regarded its author as the worst heretic who ever lived. A more careful reading, however, changed his mind completely. He declared to his brethren, "The whole world is blind as can be, but this is the one man who sees the truth." Traces of this treatise as well as references to Luther's commentary on the Lord's Prayer and the Ten Commandments show up in Bugenhagen's open letter to his Treptow students, but he was not yet ready to come out openly as a partisan of this controversial man. Decades later he commented again on an early perception that reminded him of an important turning point in Luther's life. In their Table Talk in the winter of 1542–43, Luther recalled how luminous a sentence of Paul had suddenly become for him. "The just shall live by faith" (Rom. 1:17, KJV) in the Pauline understanding of *justitia Dei* referred not to an attribute of God but to a righteousness given the believer by God. Bugenhagen added from his own experience: "My change, too, began when I was reading about the love of God. I found that it was to be understood passively as the love with which we are loved by God. Before that I always understood divine love in the active voice."[74] A letter from Luther to Bugenhagen, accompanying a gift copy of the tract on Christian liberty, neatly sums up what Bugenhagen received from Luther. From the letter Bugenhagen entered these lines into his copy:

> To Dr. Johannes Bugenhagen: You have written me asking that I give you some instruction for living. The true Christian needs no moral precepts, for the Spirit of faith leads him to everything that God wills and that brotherly love requires. Therefore read this little book. Not everyone believes the gospel, for faith is what one feels in the heart.

Instead of the requested instruction, Bugenhagen received a hint about the source from which a genuinely Christian life flows. This persuaded him.[75]

We possess only splinters of information on John Bugenhagen's early years, yet these indicate the kind of wood from which he was carved. His personality was manly and forthright, interested not in scholastic brood-

---

74. WA TR 5, no. 5518, 210 / 17ff. Also E. Kähler, "Bugenhagen und Luther," in *Johann Bugenhagen: Beiträge,* ed. Rautenberg, 110–11.

75. "D. Joanni Bugenhagen. Scripsisti ut modum vivendi tibi scriberem. Vere Christianus non indiget preceptis morum. Fidei enim spiritus ducit eum ad omnia que deus vult et fraterna exigit charitas. Hec itaque lege. Non omnes credunt evangelio. Fides sentitur in corde." Reprinted from Bugenhagen's handwriting by Kähler, "Bugenhagen und Luther," 113. See also the "Bucheintragungen Luthers," *WA* 48:289.

ing but in the clarity of the human relation to God and in the application of faith to life. From the beginning of their relationship one can understand what Luther must have gained from this friend and helper. At age thirty-six, Bugenhagen nevertheless resolutely gave up his work in Pomerania in order to study theology at the best available source. In late April 1521 he matriculated in Wittenberg. Besides his studies he also lectured privately on the Psalms to a small group of fellow Pomeranians, thus continuing the academic activity begun in Belbuck. Soon the rapid increase of his auditors made him change his lectures from a private offering to an official offering. Because he was not yet a regular faculty member, he had to depend on student fees for his support; official lectures were free. This irked the students because they did not want to miss his lectures [neither did their own poverty make them eager to pay voluntarily]. Besides, there was the risk that he might be called to Erfurt. Luther therefore pressured Spalatin to persuade the elector to remedy the situation. Luther's proposal was that Bugenhagen be paid out of the income of All Saints Foundation, which thus far "was being wasted on the sophists (scholastics), for according to Melanchthon, Bugenhagen, "is here and in all the world the number-two professor of theology."[76]

When these efforts brought no results, Luther resorted to self-help. It happened that in the autumn of 1523 the pastor of the Town Church died. The right of placement lay with the chapter of All Saints, which proposed two names: Nicholas von Amsdorf, Wittenberg professor and one of the chapter canons; and Wenceslaus Link, currently pastor in Altenburg and former vicar-general of the Augustinians. Both men were friends of Luther, and they both declined the nomination. When the chapter delayed making a third nomination, the town council and representatives of the parish acted on their own and elected Bugenhagen. He too could not readily make up his mind, feeling that the office was beyond him. The salary, moreover, was for an unmarried man, and Bugenhagen had just married the previous year. Besides, much of the income from All Saints was also to cover other expenses: two chaplains, one servant, one maid, and one horse, for use on pastoral visitations outside town. On top of that a sizable sum went to the All Saints Foundation as well as to the heirs of the deceased pastor. Luther solved the problem with a *fait accompli*. From the pulpit he announced Bugenhagen's election by the town council and stated the man's qualifications for the office. He thus brushed aside the nominating role of All Saints, a role that stemmed from the incorpora-

76. September 1520(?), January 2, 1523. *WA* Br 2:598 / 7ff. *WA* Br 3:2 / 35ff.

tion he had already been opposing.[77] Besides, this served as an example of the direct election of a pastor instead of his placement through the All Saints chapter. Later this procedure was cited as a precedent in the Wittenberg church order [constitution] of 1533 ("which began with Mr. John Bugenhagen").[78] At the same time, by this direct action Luther dispelled Bugenhagen's hesitation. His justified financial second thoughts were apparently cleared up as well. His activity in the university and compensation for his extracurricular duties improved his situation. For the rest of his life he remained faithful to his pastorate in the Town Church, declining many tempting calls from other princes or cities.

In this position Bugenhagen also became Luther's father confessor, being to him like a second Staupitz. What Luther prized in both these counselors, and what he often mentioned with great gratitude, was the gift of hearty encouragement, at times enlivened with a shot of good humor. Typical was Luther's oft repeated story of his conversation under the pear tree in the Wittenberg cloister garden, when he was fighting the doctorate that would later underlie his teaching and preaching ministry. "Mr. Staupitz," he protested, "this is killing me, and I won't even survive it three months." To which came the calm reply, "For God's sake, our Lord God has big business, and he needs smart people up there too."[79] Bugenhagen once put Luther on the right track in an hour of despair, saying: "God must surely be asking himself, What can I still make of this man? I have given him so many excellent gifts, and now he questions my grace. For me (Luther added) this was a great comfort, like the voice of an angel ringing in my heart. And I'm sure he didn't even know what he had said or how well he had said it." He was reminded of a word by his father confessor in the cloister (a man unknown to us) who told Luther, "You are a fool. God is not incensed against you, but you are incensed against God."[80] Sometimes the masterful comforter, Staupitz, was at his wit's end: "I don't understand you." "Even this," Luther added later, "was real consolation."[81] And sometimes Staupitz took the dubious tack and,

77. Cf. the events in Leisnig and Altenburg, above, pp. 122–26. On this and other cases, see K. Müller, *Kirche, Gemeinde, und Obrigkeit nach Luther* (Tübingen, 1910), 103ff.

78. E. Sehling, *Die evangelischen Kirchenordnungen des XVI. Jahrhunderts* (Leipzig, 1902ff.), 1:700. Hering, "Bugenhagen," 20–21. Müller, *Kirche, Gemeinde, und Obrigkeit*, 113. Friedensburg, *Geschichte der Universität Wittenberg*, 170–71.

79. WA TR 3, no. 3143, 188 / 16ff. Cf WA TR 1, no. 885, 442 / 9ff. WA TR 4, no. 3924, 13 / 30ff. WA TR 5, no. 5371, 98 / 21ff.; no. 6422, 654 / 34ff.

80. WA TR 1, no. 122, 47 / 21ff. Also H. Mülbe, "Bugenhagen im Urteil Luthers," *Wartburg* 34 (1935): 198ff., and to the second statement, Kähler, "Bugenhagen und Luther," 119ff. [*LW* 54, no. 122, 15.]

81. WA TR 1, no. 518, 240 / 12ff.; no. 122, 50 / 27ff. WA TR 2, no. 1288, 26 / 5–6. [*LW* 54, no. 518, 94; no. 122, 18; no. 1288, 133.]

according to the confessional's catalog of sins, minimized Luther's self-reproach, calling it "mimicry and doll-baby sins" in contrast to "honest-to-goodness sins" such as murder, blasphemy, and divorce.

Bugenhagen could not go so far. If need be, as in counseling, he resorted to sharp reproof, "You are not to despise my consolation; I know it is the Word of God given to me from heaven." "There it dawns on one," said Luther, "what it means: 'Thy Word has brought me to life'" (Ps. 119:50).[82] He found this confirmed repeatedly, saying, "The Holy Spirit speaks through people to people without any kind of revelation. Pomeranus (Bugenhagen) has often consoled me with unexpected words, and I find them comforting to this day. This is how the Holy Spirit speaks with us quite unexpectedly."[83] Bugenhagen would not have had access to the substance of consolation [encouragement] had he not himself known something of soul-testing and despair. He and Luther could meet on common ground in their love for the Bible's great book of consolation, the Psalter. It is hardly a coincidence that both men devoted their first exegetical efforts to the Psalms, yet only Bugenhagen reached the goal of completing (1524) an inclusive commentary. Luther provided a foreword, saying that among those who have published, Pomeranus deserved to be called the best of all commentators on the Psalms. Luther no longer lamented his inability to complete his own commentary, which he had begun during the years of unrest in Wittenberg: "I must decrease, he must grow." Let readers no longer await Luther's own commentary but share his joy over Bugenhagen's work.[84] The theme of this commentary is actually the problem of spiritual agonizing and its conquest. Bugenhagen expressed it again a little later in words that could have been Luther's:

> Such agonizing [testing of the soul] the Psalter describes often, in different ways and with different words. And at the same time you read there how God thereby liberates his own, the very ones who, so long as they suffer, can see nothing else but that they have apparently been forsaken by God; and God plagues them often, intensely, and for long periods of time. This is how you come to have examples in the psalms of saints, and of God's word of promise— in order that you might have firm consolation or be refreshed and be made hopeful even in the midst of your agonizing; after all, you are not the only one

82. WA TR 2, no. 2268b, 389 / 14ff. This reminder of Bugenhagen appears in the correspondence from Aurifaber to Enders and is in Luther's letter to Wenceslaus Link, July 14, 1528, pushed in with two other pieces (cf. WA Br 4:495), and thus it appears also in the fine translation of R. Buchwald, *Luthers Briefe: Auswahl* (Stuttgart, 1956), 187–88. [Cf. English, Ps. 119:49 "thy word . . . in which thou hast made me hope."]

83. WA TR 2, no. 1352, 66 / 24ff.

84. WA 15:8 / 16ff.

who endures this. There are also saints like Abraham, David, and others who have endured the same kind of burdens and even greater ones. Be comforted that you have the same promises of God.[85]

Bugenhagen was modest enough not to permit his pastoral care of Luther to give him a false estimation of himself. He always regarded himself as being under the two great men of Wittenberg. Typically he wrote Spalatin on November 27, 1522: "You elevate me to the office of prophet, while I simply play the role of a preacher who sets forth the Scriptures. You know that these are two different offices. Prophets are people who preach like Martin and teach like Philipp. Somewhere further behind I set forth what I find the two prophets saying."[86] The interrelationship of the three Wittenberg reformers could not remain so neatly balanced. With regard to his own humanistic background, Bugenhagen actually stood closer to Melanchthon. Indeed, soon after resettling in Wittenberg, Melanchthon dedicated his text edition of the letter to the Romans with this humanistically styled testimony to Christ, "the primal image of life," plus a strong rejection of scholasticism.[87] Yet the overshadowing figure of Luther soon shifted the balance. Whatever their differences, their common emergence out of a monastic piety, with its abiding inwardness and hazards, the determination of both men to follow new ways for the sake of Christ and of the people entrusted to them, and their fearlessness and their humor—all these things made Luther and Bugenhagen spiritual brothers. Foregoing the temptation to search out his own way, Bugenhagen faithfully followed Luther's trail. As a result, his many practical services did not convey his own brand of reformation theology. For Melanchthon the combined power of the two others must have felt oppressive at times. Frequently he complained of the "crude Pomeranian" in the same critical tone he had characterized Luther. Nevertheless, such criticism did not seriously undermine the trio's relationship.

Besides Melanchthon and Bugenhagen, who had come to Luther from elsewhere, other and older significant friends gradually formed the second rank of his co-workers. As partners on the way, who had long been

---

85. To Joachim von Anhalt, December 27, 1535, *Bugenhagens Briefwechsel*, ed. Vogt, no. 57; according to Kähler, "Bugenhagen und Luther," 118. Bugenhagen himself was no poet, which is evident when one compares his work with Luther's spiritually so much akin 1528 preface to the Psalter. *WA DB* 10¹:98ff. *Martin Luthers Vorreden zur Bibel*, ed. H. Bornkamm, (Hamburg, 1967), 15 / 51ff.

86. *Bugenhagens Briefwechsel*, ed. Vogt, no. 5, cited by Maurer, *Der junge Melanchthon*, 2:581, n. 11.

87. *CR* 1:521–2. Also *Suppl. Mel.* 6 / 1:178. *MBW* 142. Maurer, *Der junge Melanchthon*, 2:72.

familiar with the Wittenberg scene and in part had engaged in the local struggles, they remained inseparable from Luther. Chief among them was Nicholas von Amsdorf. Born less than a month after Luther (December 3, 1483), he came from Torgau, the son of a Saxon noble family and a nephew of Staupitz.[88] As one of its first students, Amsdorf had experienced the history of the University of Wittenberg from the time of its founding in 1502 and had earned its degrees up to that of licentiate in theology [permitting him to teach], but not the doctorate. He lectured mainly in philosophy and, in an assisting capacity, in theology, yet he was not counted a member of the theological faculty. The philosophy department of the faculty of arts was divided into Scotist and Thomist lectureships. The main lectures for both came mornings at six, Karlstadt giving the Thomist lectures, Amsdorf the Scotist lectures.[89] Amsdorf's scholastic training had enhanced his gift of disputation, while his abilities as an administrator made him a canon of the All Saints Foundation (1508) and frequently rector of the university as well. Unable to extricate himself from scholastic thought, he owed it to Luther, who unexpectedly showed him the new way. This led him to study Augustine, an undertaking to which Luther's challenge proved irresistible. One day, as Amsdorf himself told it, Luther sent him a complete set of Augustine's works.[90]

Thereafter Amsdorf remained a resolute adherent of Luther. His absoluteness and polemical acuteness made him the first Lutheran church father of strictest observance. To be sure, this became apparent only later in the various controversies in which Luther's cause required defense from within as well as from without. During the earlier Wittenberg era he was completely eclipsed by Luther and made no theological contributions of his own. He kept himself out of the local uprising of 1521–22 [while Luther was at the Wartburg]. In critical situations, however, he rendered Luther supportive service, as during the Leipzig disputation [Eck] in 1519 and at the Diet of Worms [the emperor] in 1521, to both of which events he accompanied Luther. Amsdorf's departure from Wittenberg in 1524 struck Luther as a personal loss for the rest of his life. Amsdorf left to assume the difficult task of superintendent in Magdeburg. Then in 1542

88. A modern biography of Amsdorf is lacking, and likewise an edition of his works and correspondence, except from the partial collection and partial biography (to 1542) by H. Stille, "Nikolaus von Amsdorf" (philosophy diss., Leipzig, 1937). References include RE[3] 1 (1896): 464. RGG[3] 1 (1957): 334. Schottenloher, *Bibliographie* 1 (1933): 19; 7 (1966): 10.

89. Friedensburg, *Geschichte Universität Wittenberg*, 66, 100, 109. See also his *Urkundenbuch der Universität Wittenberg* (Magdeburg, 1926), 15, for a listing of the teachers in 1507.

90. Amsdorf to Spalatin, January 17, 1518; reprinted in *ThStKr* 51 (1878): 698–99.

he accepted the still more trying role of bishop of Naumburg-Zeitz [also in the province of Saxony]. Yet the old friendship was carried on, by sometimes extensive correspondence, until Luther's death.

If Amsdorf's scholastic education predisposed him to subsequently championing a sterile sort of reformation doctrine, then something similar happened in the case of Justus Jonas,[91] whose initial training was in law. He was ten years younger than Luther and, closer to Melanchthon, he brought a modern, humanistic flair into the circle of Wittenberg friends. Born in Nordhausen in 1493, Jonas's studies took him initially to Erfurt, where he gained admission into the noted circle of humanists under Canon Mutianus Rufus of Gotha. Then came three years (1511–14) in Wittenberg, whither he had followed his highly rated professor of law, Henning Goede. Returning to Erfurt, Jonas earned his doctorate in law and was immediately made a professor. His second period in Erfurt found him becoming more deeply rooted in the humanism of a religious turn as represented by Erasmus. In this vein he also lectured in Bible. Through friends, and especially from reports on the [Luther-Eck] disputation in Leipzig, Jonas kept close to developments in Wittenberg as well. Upon the early death of Goede (1521), he readily accepted the Wittenberg professorship in canon law as well as the deanship of All Saints Foundation.

The intellectual currents of the times seemed to converge remarkably in the person of Jonas. His former teacher Mutianus (actually the first choice to succeed Goede), in declining the Wittenberg call, recommended Jonas most cordially to Frederick the Wise. There is not another man in Germany, he declared, who is at once so much at home in jurisprudence as well as in theology; he is an outstanding preacher and teacher, well known to Staupitz and beloved by Luther.[92] In fact, Luther had sent him such an enthusiastic greeting in April 1519 through John Lang that one must infer a friendly relationship between Luther and Jonas from the latter's period in Wittenberg.[93] Jonas reciprocated, and the succeeding years strengthened the bond of friendship. When Luther was heading for Worms, Jonas rode out from Weimar to meet him. Then, after

91. Here too a full biography is lacking in German. A more recent, short biography is by W. Delius, *Lehre und Leben, Justus Jonas* (Berlin, 1952). See also G. Kawerau, *Der Briefwechsel des Justus Jonas*, 2 vols. (Halle, 1884–85). [In English there is the short biography by M. Lehmann, *Justus Jonas, Loyal Reformer* (Minneapolis: Augsburg, 1963), originally a doctoral dissertation for Princeton Theological Seminary.]

92. *Der Briefwechsel des Conradus Mutianus*, comp. and ed. K. Gillert, Geschichtsquellen der Provinz Sachsen und angrenzender Gebiete 18 / 1 (Halle, 1890), n. 603. Delius, *Justus Jonas*, 27.

93. April 13, 1519, WA Br 1:370 / 95–96.

the brilliant reception accorded Luther by the University of Erfurt, Jonas accompanied him to the diet. In Worms Jonas had no official function;[94] he simply attended Luther as a friend. Indeed, he was often to be found in Luther's company. When Cochlaeus looked up Luther privately in Worms after the diet had finished with him, the two lawyers (Justus Jonas and Jerome Schurff), standing outside the closed door, eavesdropped on the conversation.[95] Cochlaeus himself recalled an impromptu and lengthy conversation with Jonas in the street. He carried this vivid impression of him: "Undoubtedly a splendid young man, elegant bearing, slender stature, in no way uncultivated. What a shame if he were to be sucked into Hussite and Taborite errors with all their barbarous lack of culture and irreligion." So that was the notion Cochlaeus had of the dangers of Lutheran teaching. Jonas defended Luther with an array of citations from Paul and also warned Cochlaeus not to write against Luther, lest "at least forty learned people push their pens against me."[96]

In this widely recognized man, Wittenberg had won a prize and Luther gained a close friend. In Wittenberg, Justus Jonas soon had his wish and moved from the faculty of law to that of theology. Having earned his doctorate in theology, he never became a significant theologian but was a highly esteemed preacher and pastoral counselor, as well as a perspicacious church administrator. More significant than his own writings were his translations of works by great friends (among others, Melanchthon's *Loci Communes* and the *Apology to the Augsburg Confession*, and Luther's *De servo arbitrio*). His humanistic and juridical education gave him a distinctive position in the Wittenberg circle. He remained part of it until 1541, when he was called to be superintendent in Halle. There, in the city where Albrecht, cardinal archbishop of Mainz, had his residence, he carried out the Reformation with energy and skill.

In addition to these four important friends and co-workers of Luther there was another group, with an occasionally rapid turnover. In it

94. Jonas was not a councillor from Electoral Saxony, as listed in the index of *Der Reichstag zu Worms 1521: Reichspolitik und Luthersache*, ed. F. Reuter (Worms, 1971), 524; instead he was still professor in Erfurt. It was in Worms that Jonas received the call to Wittenberg.

95. J. Kessler, "Sabbata, mit kleinen Schriften und Briefen," published by the Historischer Verein des Kantons St. Gallen (St. Gall, 1902), 74 / 19ff.

96. "Colloquim Cochlaei cum Luthero Vormatiae olim habitatum, 1540," *D. Martin Luthers Briefwechsel*, ed. E. L. Enders (Frankfurt am Main, 1884ff.), 3:187. Delius, *Justus Jonas*, 28–29.

Luther's old friend, lawyer Jerome Schurff, deserves a special place.[97] This son of a patrician family in St. Gall [Switzerland] was two years older than Luther. From its founding in 1502 and for the next forty-five years, he was the very embodiment of continuity at the University of Wittenberg. Beginning his own career with the study of Scotist philosophy in the faculty of arts, he moved on to canon law. Receptive early to humanism, he subsequently became a close friend of Melanchthon, who years later confessed that he loved Schurff like a father and that he was grateful to God for giving him Schurff not only as a scholarly mentor but also as a lifelong guide.[98] Likewise, Schurff was open to Luther's new understanding of the gospel. At the Diet of Worms (1521) he served publicly as Luther's legal counsel.[99] During the ensuing period of unrest in Wittenberg he sought to curb the radical plans of Karlstadt and Zwilling by working through the university committee. He remained equally loyal to Luther and Melanchthon. Later, however, he upheld his own position on canon law over against Luther's attempts to get away from it. In this matter he had on his side Melanchthon, whose historically oriented thinking agreed with his own.

Successors to the generation of founders began to appear. They were young people of various types and backgrounds. From Eisleben, Luther's birthplace, came John Agricola (born about 1492 [as John Schneider]), who had already been a teacher. On learning he was a compatriot, Luther exclaimed to Agricola, "Ah, now we're in business." Luther engaged him to help in various ways; at the Leipzig disputation with Eck (1519), Agricola served as Luther's secretary.[100] He began as a glowing admirer of Luther. Already in 1518, and not completely to Luther's liking, he had copied Luther's sermons on the Lord's Prayer, made small additions of his

97. The actual family name was Schürpf, also Schurpf, which in those times often became Schurff or Schurffius. Cf. W. Schaich-Klose, "D. Hieronymus Schürpf: Der Wittenberger Reformationsjurist aus St. Gallen 1481–1554," in 107. Neujahrsblatt, ed. Historischer Verein des Kantons St. Gallen (1967), 1ff. Friedensburg, Geschichte Universität Wittenberg, 57–58, 200–201. Also Maurer, Der junge Melanchthon, 2:74.

98. From a speech, De legum fontibus et causis (1550?), CR 11:17. He also gave the memorial address for Schurff in 1554. CR 12:86ff. (not 11:817ff., as mistakenly noted in Maurer, Der junge Melanchthon, 2:74, n. 12).

99. In Der Reichstag zu Worms, ed. Reuter, Schurff is identified now as theologian (281), now as councillor from Electoral Saxony (530).

100. J. Rogge, Johann Agricolas Lutherverständnis, ThA 14 (East Berlin, 1960), 14, according to E. Thiele, "Denkwürdigkeiten aus dem Leben des Johann Agricola von Eisleben," ThStKr 80 (1907): 253. The widespread assumption (e.g., H. Boehmer, Der junge Luther, ed. H. Bornkamm, 6th ed. [Stuttgart, 1971], 156, 372) that Agricola witnessed Luther's posting of the Ninety-five Theses, has been refuted by Volz, Martin Luthers Thesenanschlag (see above, p. 254, n. 2), 103–4, n. 150.

own, and published them.[101] For the time being, Agricola stayed put on the first academic rung; he was promoted to bachelor of theology on September 15, 1519, at the same time as Melanchthon. The following year, again almost at the same time as Melanchthon, he married. For a while he took up the study of medicine, which promised greater income. Typical of the spirit at Wittenberg University, a young lawyer from Electoral Saxony, Caspar von Teutleben, pricked Agricola's conscience. In light of the great lack of preachers, he urged Agricola to study theology and not to block the Holy Spirit. Later Agricola confessed, "This word stuck in my heart." But already on the day after Teutleben's urging, Agricola went to Luther, who gave him strong encouragement. From the pulpit Luther announced that on the following day Magister Eisleben, as he usually called Agricola, would preach the sermon. Luther did so without having first asked Agricola. This was similar to his announcement concerning Bugenhagen's election. Luther imagined that he could overcome Agricola's lingering indecision.[102] Both men would likely have been happier later if Agricola had not made the switch back to theology. Not long before his death he confessed, "Oh, if only I had become a physician, the way I had started out."[103]

As it was, Agricola got into years of heated disputes first with Melanchthon, then with Luther, in which he charged them both with a deficient reformation theology. Presumptuously, he reproached Luther for an excessive appreciation of the law over against the gospel. Could he outdo Luther? Quite apart from factual differences, the controversy revealed on Agricola's side a mixture of exaggerated uncertainty and need for recognition, and on Luther's side (indeed, rather belatedly) an excessive rejection born of disappointed affection.

Yet this gets us ahead of the story. Until the mid-1520s Agricola still rated as Luther's squire. In an effusive letter in the spring of 1525 he praised Luther for his rediscovery of justification by grace alone, from which good works come forth as fruits, and for his being "the good bur-

101. With a somewhat irritated foreword, Luther then published his own version of the sermons, WA 2:74, 80. Meanwhile, five editions of Agricola's version appeared in 1518–19. See J. Benzing, *Lutherbibliographie: Verzeichnis der gedruckten Schriften Martin Luthers bis zu dessen Tod* (Baden-Baden, 1966).

102. Rogge, *Agricolas Lutherverständnis*, 16. Thiele, "Denkwürdigkeiten," 255. Concerning Bugenhagen, see above, pp. 270–76. According to Friedensburg, *Geschichte Universität Wittenberg*, 201, Teutleben was a private tutor in law. He lectured on canon law, for which the university no longer had a regular professor (*ordinarius*) and in 1528 was officially named to that post. Friedensburg, *Urkundenbuch*, 149.

103. Rogge, *Agricolas Lutherverständnis*, 17, on the source of information (*Apophthegmata*), there on 301.

gher who for the sake of a fatherland oppressed by Roman tyrants" had taken on himself ever so great perils. "He has broken the power of the Antichrist, foiled the perfidy of princes, and restored the liberty of Germany." Agricola found nothing of the sort in Karlstadt, about whom the addressee of this letter had inquired. Instead he saw both Karlstadt and Müntzer as muddleheaded, betrayed by their characteristic vocabulary, beclouded by words like "bewonderment," "refinement," "studification," "boredom," and other mystical terms they employed. Agricola was still riding the crest of an infatuation that identified himself in the great example of Luther, until his feelings later backlashed into hatred.[104]

Wittenberg University's reputation was attracting students from near and far, especially to its theological and humanistic teachers. "The students are taking over the whole town. Here it's easier to catch a lot of lice than a landlord," wrote Albert Burer, a student from Switzerland.[105] Wittenberg's power to attract was substantiated by one of the teachers, Francis Lambert, from southern France.[106] Lambert, born about 1487, came from Avignon. Having there entered the Franciscan cloister of Strict Observants, his zeal and extraordinary homiletical gifts soon led to his being named preacher apostolic. Writings of Luther had penetrated even that strict cloister; they were among the heretical writings marked for burning. His order sent him on an extended preaching mission that in 1522 brought him to Basel. Lambert went on to Zurich, where he joined in a disputation against Zwingli and defended the veneration of saints. Returning to Basel, Lambert decided to proceed to Wittenberg and track the new reform movement to its source. For security he traveled under an assumed name. Aleady in Eisenach this born activist tried to stage a disputation. His posted list of 139 theses directed its thrust more against the sacraments and life-styles than against the basic teachings of the church. To his dismay not an opponent showed up.

By the time Lambert reached Luther in Wittenberg, he was no longer an inquirer but a confessed companion in reform. "I consider myself

104. Although not signed, this letter is properly attributed to Agricola and printed by A. Brecher, "Neue Beiträge zum Briefwechsel der Reformatoren und ihnen nahestehender Männer," *ZHTh* 42 (1872): 399ff., 405. Also Rogge, *Agricolas Lutherverständnis*, 32ff. [The words *Verwunderung, Entgrobung, Studierung,* and *Langeweile* in part, at least, resist exact equivalents in modern German or English.]

105. To Beatus Rhenanus, June 30. 1521, in *Briefwechsel des Beatus Rhenanus*, ed. Horawitz and Hartfelder (see above, p. 259, n. 22), 281. Burer estimated the number at 6,500. This was of course much too high. See Friedensburg, *Geschichte Universitäts Wittenberg*, 148, n. 1. Yet it was worth noting that Burer made such a high estimate.

106. For the following data, see G. Müller, *Franz Lambert von Avignon und die Reformation in Hessen*, VHKHW 24 / 4 (Marburg, 1958), 1ff.

called by the Lord to visit Martinus, so that brother with brother can together build a mighty fortress."[107] Having received advance reports from Eisenach, Luther anticipated Lambert with certain reservations. Nevertheless, Luther asked the elector for travel money for Lambert, whom he at least wanted to meet. When Lambert arrived and introduced himself under his real name, he completely authenticated himself by letters of introduction as well as by testimonials from Wittenberg students. Luther was pleased with him and provided for his lodging, even though this soon became quite a burden, considering Luther's scant income. Besides, the anticipated grant from the elector was slow in coming, which made Lambert uncomfortable too. Moreover, Luther did not esteem Lambert as highly as Lambert esteemed himself. "He won't stay here long, I reckon, for he will find his equal here, or even one superior to him. But we must show hospitality to the banished."[108] Good attendance enlivened Lambert's lectures on the prophet Hosea and the Gospel of Luke, prompting him to have them printed immediately. A facile writer, he also translated some of Luther's writings into French.[109] Although his circumstances were hardly improved, he nevertheless soon married a simple local girl. Later, full of pride, he announced, "I was the first to roll away this stone [of celibacy] from France."[110] In any case, Lambert liked to think of himself as number one. He dreamed of becoming the reformer of France, so he considered relocating to Strassburg in order to be closer to his home country. Luther tried in vain to argue him out of it, deeming Lambert unsuited to the task. "For the sake of peace," Luther finally wrote his friend Gerbel in Strassburg, "people like this should rather come from you to us, than from us to you. . . . You see what I must put up with. Through me such people go exploring and burdening my friends."[111] Only intellectually did Luther meet him again.

In Strassburg, Lambert made himself disliked by his tactlessness and excessive zeal. Lucky for him that in 1526 Philip of Hesse called him to Marburg, where he impressed Philip as a diligent and learned man and as one still free from entanglement in the then rapidly forming evangelical

107. Letter, Lambert to Elector Frederick, January 20, 1523. Herminjard, *Correspondance des Reformateurs dans les pays de langue française* (Geneva, 1866), 1:113. Müller, *Lambert von Avignon*, 15.

108. To Spalatin, January 22, 1523, WA Br 3:19 / 17ff. I. Höss, *Georg Spalatin 1484–1545: Ein Leben in der Zeit des Humanismus und der Reformation* (Weimar, 1956), 230.

109. WA Br 3:200–201.

110. WA Br 3:100, n. 2. Herminjard, *Correspondance*, 1:143. Müller, *Lambert von Avignon*, 16.

111. December 4, 1523, WA Br 3:200 / 3ff.

groups. In Hesse, Lambert found the kind of stage he had dreamed of. At his suggestion, Landgrave Philip called a conference in October 1526, the so-called "Homberg Synod." There this Frenchman played the decisive role. He read the opening address. Theses that he proposed were discussed. The concluding paper, on the reformation of the churches in Hesse, was essentially of Lambert's drafting.[112] But more important than the papers was the breakthrough that occurred at this time. Philip visibly led his land into the camp of the Reformation. The constitutional draft contained not only Reformation and biblical elements but also medieval and legalistic features. At any rate, it was not a hierarchical legalism but one based on the congregation and the pastors. It included strict discipline and called for the abolition of images. At the university, just then founded, nothing was to be taught that would impede the kingdom of God, while civil law was made subject to correction by the Word of God.[113] When the landgrave asked Luther's opinion, he urgently advised against introducing "such a stack of laws with such high-sounding words." It were better first to place qualified people in the schools and congregations and then to build up regulations one after another.[114] There is no way of telling whether Luther knew that his former "problem child," Lambert, was back of it all. But Luther's comment at least implied it. Philip became convinced that Luther was right. He delayed introducing the Reformation and followed the more deliberative model of Electoral Saxony. Meanwhile, with all his pressuring and gossiping, which won him little favor, Lambert found that he had played his hand in church politics. Switching back to teaching, he remained a professor at Marburg until his early death in 1530. Within the secure bounds of this office he felt satisfied and performed at his best.

The inner circle of co-workers around Luther during these years bears scrutiny. At close range it reveals not only characteristic differences but also some noteworthy difficulties. Alongside faithful partners and reliable helpers like Bugenhagen, Amsdorf, and Jonas stood the timid and sensitive Melanchthon, who worried him. There were also those who, like Agricola and Lambert, tried to climb up on him in order to advance, as they imagined, their own more consistent notions of reform. Or, take a Karl-

---

112. W. Maurer, "Franz Lambert von Avignon und das Verfassungsideal der Reformatio ecclesiarum Hassiae von 1526," *ZKG* 48 (1929): 208ff. Müller, *Lambert von Avignon*, 33ff. Text of the *Reformatio* is in E. Sehling, *Die evangelischen Kirchenordnungen des XVI. Jahrhunderts* (1956), 8:43ff.

113. Sehling, *Kirchenordnungen*, 8:63.

114. January 7, 1527, WA Br 4:157–58.

stadt or a Müntzer—the one a former companion-in-arms, the other a former student who still in 1522–23 revered Luther and Melanchthon,[115] yet both of them had now broken with Luther completely. Thoroughly independent of him, they now regarded themselves as the true renewers of the church. Except for these two, Luther possessed unchallenged authority over and above the acknowledged differences. Respect for him is revealed in the salutations gracing the letters sent back and forth. Luther could affectionately address "My Spalatin, My Philippe, My Nicholai (or Amsdorfi)." In return, there was no such intimate vocative as "My Luthere." His superiority was forthrightly recognized: "Reverend Doctor in the Lord" or "Most Cherished Father" or (even as Müntzer still wrote in 1523), "Among others, Sincerest Father."[116]

Besides students and scholars who tried to be near Luther, usually for a longer period and if possible to work with him, there was the growing number of visitors to Wittenberg who wanted to meet Luther or convey some sort of request. Besides, there were a number of the princely families who wished to hear Luther preach.[117]

Among the first to visit were members and relatives of the elector's household. The elector, Frederick the Wise, in some respects a shy man, consistently put off meeting with Luther. Although united in a common destiny, each holding the other in high esteem, the two men never once spoke a word to each other. The only time they saw each other was at the diet in Worms.[118] By contrast, Frederick's sister, Duchess Margaret of Braunschweig-Lüneburg, heard Luther preach twice during her visit to Wittenberg in June 1524. She too was a timid woman, made so, according to Luther, by her upbringing in a convent. Despite the urging of her brothers, she never could bring herself to a clear religious decision. However, her meeting Luther may have helped her, a year later, to espouse his concept of faith. Her son Ernst, who heard Luther preach in September

115. Letter to Melanchthon, March 27, 1522; to Luther, July 9, 1523. *Thomas Müntzer, Schriften und Briefe: Kritische Gesamtausgabe*, ed. G. Franz, QFRG 33 (Gütersloh, 1968), 379ff.; 389ff. WA Br 3:104ff.

116. ["Mi Spalatin, mi Philippe, mi Nicolai (or Amsdorfi)" employ the shorter Latin dative for *mihi* (to me) = "my." Or, conversely, again the Latin salutation in addressing Luther, *"Reverende domine doctor"* or *"Carissime pater"* or *"Sincerissime inter ceteros pater."*] Volz, "Luther und sein Freundeskreis" (see n. 47, above), 8. Müntzer, *Schriften*, 389.

117. More information in G. Buchwald, *Luther-Kalendarium*, SVRG 147 (Leipzig, 1929). On his sermons, G. Buchwald, "Luthers Predigten in der Schlosskirche zu Wittenberg," *ARG* 25 (1928): 71ff.

118. H. Bornkamm, "Luther und sein Landesherr Friedrich der Weise (1463–1525)," *ARG* 64 (1973): 79ff. Reprinted in H. Bornkamm, *Luther: Gestalt und Wirkungen*, SVRG 188 (Gütersloh, 1975), 33ff.

1524, was ahead of her in this respect. He had been educated in Wittenberg by Spalatin and later carried out the Reformation in his lands and was one of the signers of the Augsburg Confession.[119] From the court of Wettin, Luther's faithful adherents Duke John, the brother and successor of Frederick the Wise, as well as his son John Frederick, came several times to hear him.[120] Another early visitor in Wittenberg was Duke Bogislav of Pomerania, who used the occasion of his trip to Worms for a stopover in Wittenberg in February 1521 in order to hear Luther. He did the same while en route to the diet in Nuremberg in February 1523, as well as on returning from it in May.[121] Also, in late February 1525, Duke Henry of Mecklenburg, then already called "the Peace-loving," was among his hearers. For some years he continued to retain traditional Roman worship while at the same time permitting evangelical preaching. Only in 1533, a decade later, did he publicly profess adherence to the new teaching.[122] The Castle Church of All Saints was the usual place of worship for the princely visitors.[123] The intention was not to separate them from the local congregation, for the service was open to parishioners, but it was rather an indication of the political situation in Electoral Saxony: such worthies were to be welcomed on official premises when hearing Luther.

Besides territorial princes, others visited Wittenberg during these years. Two may be singled out. The one was Albert of Hohenzollern, grand master of the order of the Teutonic Knights. Already in June 1523 he had sent word to Luther requesting his counsel in a proposed reorganization of the order. He showed up in person on November 29 and received from Luther the decisive impulse to convert the order's lands into a secular state.[124] Albert had come from Denmark, where he had just at-

---

119. The sermons of June 8 and 9 and September 14, 1524, WA 15:622ff., 633ff., 683ff. Luther wrote about the duchess to the preacher Gottschalk Crusins in Celle, October 30, 1524, WA Br 3:366 / 7ff. Duke Ernst attended Luther's sermons often, e.g., in company with Christian II on April 17, 1526 (see n. 133, below), as well as in February and May 1527. Buchwald, "Luthers Predigten," 74, 76. Melanchthon later wrote an academic address that was presented in Wittenberg only in 1557, long after the duke's death (in 1546, shortly before Luther died); CR 12:230ff. On Duke Ernst, see A. Wrede, *Ernst der Bekenner, Herzog von Braunschweig und Lüneburg,* SVRG 25 (Halle, 1888).

120. Buchwald, "Luthers Predigten," 72–73. January 26 / 28, February 11 / 12(21?), March(?) 13 / 14, 1525. WA 17¹:32ff., 37–38, 52ff.

121. Buchwald, "Luthers Predigten," 71. Letter to Spalatin, February 3, 1521, WA Br 2:260. Sermon, February 25, 1523, WA 11:33 / 15. WA 12:427ff. Sermon, May 3, 1523, WA 11:104 / 22. WA 12:540ff.

122. November 19, 1525, sermon, WA 17¹:469 / 7. Buchwald, "Luthers Predigten," 74. H. Schnell, *Heinrich V, der Friedfertige, Herzog von Mecklenburg, 1503–52,* SVRG 72 (Halle, 1902).

123. Buckwald, "Luthers Predigten," 71ff.

124. Further details below, pp. 322ff.

tempted, unsuccessfully and in the face of internal strife, to restore Denmark's King Christian II to his throne.[125]

The other visitor was King Christian himself. A fugitive from his own country for a good half-year and in search of allies, he too had been in Wittenberg several times during recent weeks. Christian II heard Luther preach on October 6, 1523, in Schweinitz, where he was put up as a guest of the elector. Coming to Wittenberg on October 10, he was welcomed in the house of Lucas Cranach.[126] Luther himself composed a letter of request on behalf of Christian II and sent it to the elector on November 6; the letter itself is in Luther's own hand.[127] On March 8, 1524, the Danish king again attended church in Wittenberg, this time with a large entourage, including his queen, Duke Franz of Braunschweig-Wolfenbüttel, the bishop of Minden, and a Danish bishop.[128]

Luther retained the picture of Christian II in vivid memory. To be sure, the king was able to return to Denmark briefly in 1531–32, but he thereafter remained a royal prisoner until his death in 1539. Christian II was for Luther the living example of the line in the Magnificat: "He has put down the mighty from their thrones" (Luke 1:52), or, as Luther liked to say, "God keeps an eye on kings the way children keep their eye on a card game. As long as they play, they hold the cards in their hands; after that they toss them into a corner, under the bench, or in a box. That's how God deals with the potentates. As long as they govern well, he counts them important; but if they overdo it, he drops them and lets them lie, like the king of Denmark."[129] Justus Jonas told how he saw the queen, a sister of Emperor Charles V, sobbing audibly on leaving Wittenberg for Denmark.[130] Later Luther probably did not get to see the full extent of Christian II's indebtedness with which he had been "making it." The king's struggle for power did not make him choosy in religious foreign currency. Christian had perpetrated the Stockholm "bloodbath" in 1521 as a judgment on heretics. It led to the Vasa rebellion and cost him Sweden. Fighting the nobles and bishops in his own country, he lost Denmark in 1523. Then, encouraged by his trip to Wittenberg, he counted himself a Lutheran. Again, to win the support of his brother-in-law the emperor,

125. G. Ritter, *Die Neugestaltung Europas im 16. Jahrhundert* (Berlin, 1950), 152ff.

126. See above, p. 260.

127. WA Br 3:186ff. (see n. 1 on the above-mentioned sequence of dates in 1523).

128. Luther's sermon of March 8, 1524, WA 15:466ff.

129. WA TR 2, no. 1810, 222 / 4ff.; no. 1762, 209 / 1ff. WA TR 3, no. 3470b, 340 / 3ff. WA TR 5, no. 6137, 507 / 27ff.

130. WA TR 3, no. 3470b, 340 / 8–9.

Christian II reopened the bridge to the Roman church. During his brief return period he put Denmark once again on the evangelical map.

In any case, whether or not he had all the facts, Luther had a conflicting impression of Christian II. He was early aware that the Danish king had come on to his side and was opposed to the papal bull banning Luther. The king had also issued orders forbidding the University of Copenhagen to engage in polemics against Luther.[131] Concerned for church reform, Christian II had called two young Wittenberg theologians to Denmark. When these proved disappointing, he tried to enlist the services of either Luther or Karlstadt. Since Luther was unavailable after the Diet of Worms in 1521, he called Karlstadt. The latter accepted, but after only one month he was back in Wittenberg, presumably because Christian, as a brother-in-law of the emperor, was using political tactics and therefore curbed Karlstadt's anticipated freedom.[132] Luther learned to know Christian as a man attracted to his sermons. Yet a few years later, in January 1526, when the king sent news of his queen's death, Luther was moved by the accompanying explanatory letter. Resisting all attempts at a deathbed conversion, she had clung to a firm confession of her faith and received the Lord's Supper according to evangelical usage. In a wonderful way, Luther wrote Spalatin, the poor widower relies alone on Christ. Perhaps, wrote the king to Luther, God wants a king and queen in heaven as wild game, "and indeed the king, of whom in human terms this would be expected least."[133] Christian was probably thinking mostly of his own undisciplined life, which, as he would later admit, damaged his career and contributed to his fall.[134] Within a few months he showed up again, hearing Luther preach in the Castle Church on April 3 and 17, 1526.[135] The destiny of the Danish king, for whom a promising beginning turned into a visible judgment of God, was the sole piece of European history that touched Luther in Wittenberg directly.

By contrast, Luther had a fleeting contact with Savoy. Anémond de Coct, a knight studying in Wittenberg in the spring of 1523, was his connection. Like many others who came from afar, he described the gains of his journey forthrightly:

131. Luther to Spalatin, March 7, 1521, WA Br 2:283 / 15ff.

132. H. Barge, *Andreas Bodenstein von Karlstadt* (Leipzig, 1905), 1:255ff.

133. Christian to Luther, January 28, 1526, WA Br 4:23ff. Luther, March 27, to Spalatin, WA Br 4:41 / 8ff. Corrections in the text: WA Br 13:82. Christian attended Luther's sermons on April 3 and again (with Duke Ernst of Lüneburg) on April 17, 1526. Buchwald, "Luthers Predigten," 74, 76. [*LW* 49:143–44.]

134. WA TR 4, no. 4343 (February 1539).

135. WA 20:209 / 6, 16. Rörer's stenocopy of the sermons, WA 20:348ff., 371ff.

I came from France to Germany for no other reason than to become acquainted with those very people of whose reputation I had already learned. So I found out how purely and authentically they had brought Christ to light after he had been obscured for so many years. I did not venture forth in vain, for aside from seeing and hearing them [the Reformers] and enjoying their friendship, I have managed to be helpful to others. First I went to Luther. After mutual confidence was established, I talked with him about the situation in Christendom. [136]

In writing, he also praised Duke Charles III of Savoy, about whom Luther had heard favorably.

Upon his departure from Wittenberg on September 8, 1523 (he was accompanying Schurff to Basel), Luther gave Anémond a letter to his duke in which he summed up the main points of evangelical teaching. Justification *sola fide*, not by works—with masterful condensation Luther defined how faith is made active in love. From this vantage point Luther attacked the entire Roman system sharply: the arrogant jurisdiction over souls by popes and priests whose only office is that of proclamation; the merit-oriented monasticism; the truncating of the Eucharist by withholding the cup from the laity, and the corruption of the mass from an offering of the Word into a work of sacrifice. Luther also touched on the office of government, entrusted as it is to Christians not to tyrannize souls but as an essential service to ward off evil and to preserve peace. [137] The most important perceptions Luther had set forth in his writings of 1520 up to his treatise on civil government in 1523 can be seen in this frankly confessional letter. Luther, however, like de Coct, hoped for too much when he expressed to the duke the wish that the live spark in the house of Savoy would one day ignite all of France, so that the house might with justification bear the name of "the most Christian kingdom." [138] Charles III, like Christian of Denmark, was a brother-in-law of the emperor and had to remain on good terms with him. But Charles was a political loser. In his bitter struggle over the possession of Geneva he was ambivalent, now serving the bishops, now fighting them. He had even installed an illegitimate and immoral offspring of his house as bishop, hoping thereby to get control of Geneva. [139] It is not surprising that Luther's appeal to him fell on

136. Anémond's foreword to the publication of the above-named letter of Luther, n. 2, WA Br 3:148.

137. WA Br 3:150–53.

138. WA Br 3:153, 135ff.

139. F. W. Kampschulte, *Johann Calvin: Seine Kirch und sein Staat in Genf* (Leipzig, 1869), 1:32ff.

deaf ears. The letter was delivered, but into a context quite different from that described to him. The Genevan canon Philibert of Lucinges wrote to Erasmus on January 20, 1524:

> The duke follows little of what Luther has written. Luther, for instance, admonished that the duke, by means of his good works, should lead his own people to the true faith and through evangelical teaching keep them free from hypocrisy and duplicity, which are here in full flower. I count Germany lucky that it has been freed from so many errors and so much delusion and to a great extent has been led back to an apostolic life. May the gracious and sublime Christ cause this France of ours to receive a spark of this true light![140]

This was the same kind of spirit in which de Coct had been dealing. The only success from this well-intentioned effort was the publication of Luther's letter. De Coct published it, adding his own foreword on January 24, 1524, and including a work by Zwingli. In it Zwingli was challenging the preacher in Grenoble, Pierre de Sebéville, to put on the armor of Christ and "to proclaim in trumpet tones the gospel of Christ, even if young and old do not want to hear it." One year later, in February 1525, Sebéville was burned at the stake; his crime: breaking the law against preaching.[141]

De Coct, a nobleman, was a thoroughly attractive man. "Learned and devout and wonderfully aflame for the gospel, for the sake of which he has come here from France" was how Luther recorded his first impressions of him.[142] With friends in Switzerland as well as in France, he hoped to advance the Reformation. Even Conrad Grebel, son of a Zurich priest, sought de Coct's support for arousing interest in his own struggle against infant baptism, the abolition of which Grebel considered the most powerful weapon against the papacy. De Coct, however, turned him down in no uncertain terms, sensing that Grebel was trying to sow discord between him and Zwingli.[143] This friendship with the Swiss, affected by early skirmishes in the controversy over the Lord's Supper, brought about a turning point in de Coct's relations with Luther. Joining Oecolampadius and Pel-

140. Allen, ed. *Opus Erasmi* (see above, p. 257, n. 18), 5:388 / 28ff. WA Br 3:148.

141. Letter of Zwingli, in *Zwinglis sämtliche Werke* (see above, p. 265, n. 51), 8:142ff. There, and in *WA* Br 3:72, n. 1, the information on de Coct has been collected, mainly according to Herminjard, *Correspondance*, 301ff. Cf. also N. Weiss, "Études historiques: Les débutes de la reforme en France, d'après quelques documents inédits," *BSHPF* 70 (1921): 197ff.

142. To Spalatin, May 22(?), 1523, *WA* Br 3:71 / 3–4.

143. *Quellen zur Geschichte der Täufer in der Schweiz*, ed. L. von Muralt and W. Schmid (Zurich, 1952), 1:122–23, 72. H. S. Bender, *Conrad Grebel, 1498–1526* (Goshen, Ind., 1950), 141–42.

likan in a statement from Basel, published in late 1524 or early 1525, and voicing agreement with Karlstadt's teaching, de Coct added his own threat. If Luther did not change his mind, de Coct warned, he would write against him. Luther took this as a painful blow, exclaiming to Spalatin, "There you see the bewitching powers of Satan!"[144] No literary feud ensued. De Coct died in March 1525.

Added to these personal encounters were Luther's contacts with the early developments of the Reformation movement in the German territories and their rulers, as well as with the Dutch Augustinians and the Bohemian Brethren.[145] In short, many strands of the movement were converging in Wittenberg during the early years following Luther's return from the Wartburg. Nor was there any lack of curiosity seekers. One of these was John Dantiscus, the ambassador of the Polish king at the court of Charles V. En route to Poland after three years in Spain, Dantiscus could not pass up the opportunity to meet Luther. He described the situation in which he found the Reformer and recorded his impressions of him. The observations of this versatile diplomat, gifted with the ironic style of a humanist poet laureate, provide us with the liveliest picture we possess of the scene in Luther's house. His official report to the chancellor of the kingdom of Poland, then also bishop of Posen, carried this appended description:

> Over Cologne I reached Leipzig safely, yet not without danger on account of the many highway robbers who ply their business everywhere. When I learned that his most serene highness, the duke of Saxony, Sir George, had departed for Nuremberg, it may have been my excessive curiosity that would not let me pass Luther by, seeing that Wittenberg lay so near. Yet I could not get there without difficulty. The rivers were so swollen (especially the Elbe, which flows by Wittenberg) that in the lowlands virtually all the sown fields were flooded. On my way the farmers filled my ears with insults and reproaches against Luther and his accomplices. Because most people had been eating meat during Lent, they argued, God was now devastating the entire country. So I left my horses at the riverbank and crossed over to Wittenberg in a boat.
>
> And now I'd like to be given plenty of time, otherwise I cannot write about everything that's going on there. In Wittenberg I came on several young men very learned in Hebrew, Greek, and Latin—above all, Philipp Melanchthon, who is regarded foremost for his thorough knowledge of the Scripture and of doctrine. He is a young man of twenty-six. During my stay of three days Melanchthon was most winsome and hearty toward me. Through his media-

144. January 13, 1525, WA Br 3:422 / 9ff.
145. On this subject, see above, pp. 100ff., 104ff.

tion I was able, as follows, to explain to Luther the reason for my visit. Whoever sees Rome without the pope, or Wittenberg without Luther, so they say, has really seen nothing. Therefore I expressed the wish to see Luther and to speak with him. And to prove that I bear no ill will, I simply affirm that I have no other request than to offer him my greeting and farewell. Incidentally, not every chance visitor has ready access to him, yet he received me without any trouble.

So it was that after supper Melanchthon brought me over to Luther, who had invited several brothers of his order. They all wore white cowls of the prescribed cut.[146] From this they appeared as friars, although with their hair grown out you would take them for peasants. Luther stood up, extended his hand somewhat self-consciously, and asked me to be seated. There we sat, and for almost four hours we talked into the night about all kinds of things. I found this man intelligent, learned, and eloquent. Yet, aside from some verbal attacks, disdainful and biting comments against the pope, the emperor, and several princes, he revealed nothing new.

Luther's face is like his books; his eyes are piercing and twinkle almost uncannily, the way one sometimes sees in a person possessed. The king of Denmark has a similar look, and I can hardly believe otherwise than that both men were born under the same constellation. Luther's manner of speaking is passionate, loaded with banter and taunts. In attire he would be difficult to distinguish from a courtier, yet when he leaves the house (he lives in a former cloister) they say he dons the habit of his order.

So while we were sitting with him we not only conversed but in good humor we drank wine and beer, as is customary here. In every way Luther seems to be a "good guy," as the people say. The holiness of his life-style, for which he has often been praised among us, bears nothing that distinguishes him from the rest of us. But it is easy to spot his pride and arrogance; his scolding, contradicting, and mocking is apparently unbridled. How he is otherwise becomes apparent from his books. They say he is very well read and writes much. At present he is translating the books of Moses from Hebrew into Latin,[147] an exercise for which he enlists Melanchthon's aid a great deal. This chap I like best of all among Germany's learned men. By no means does he agree with Luther in everything.[148]

This is how Luther looked in the critical eyes of an interested opponent. His manner of meeting this sort of diplomat with a jolly challenge comes out most vividly in the account. This meeting had a late sequel. After

146. This was the domestic attire of the Augustinian Eremites. In public they wore black cowls. *LThK* 1 (1957): 1084.

147. Cf. *WA* 14:494–95.

148. The Latin text of this letter with its later title, *Iudicium meum de Lutero 1523*, was published by F. Hipler, *Nikolaus Kopernikus* (see above, p. 257, n. 16). I have followed the translation in *Das Buch der Reformation, geschrieben von Mitlebenden*, ed. K. Kaulfuss-Diesch (Leipzig, 1917), 305ff., adding improvements from the original Latin and from Hipler's translation. For Dantiscus's estimate of Melanchthon, see n. 70, above, p. 270.

Luther's death, Duke Albrecht of Prussia sent Dantiscus the reports he had received as well as a copy of Melanchthon's memorial address. Dantiscus, meanwhile, had become bishop of East Prussia and good neighborly relations obtained between the two. Albrecht's covering note suggested that a Christian prelate like Dantiscus would probably be cheered in this testimony of divine grace and Christian dying. Dantiscus replied on April 7, 1546, that he had pleasant memories of the visit with Luther and the other Wittenbergers, by whom he had been received in a most friendly and honorable way. He went on to express the wish that Luther, besides other teaching, had also bequeathed love and unity in the resistance against the Turks and other enemies of Christendom. To that end may God, "regardless of our disunity and manifold misdeeds, help us, and may he vouchsafe to each one who confesses Jesus Christ as Savior and Redeemer in that final hour—as I pray also for your Serene Highness—a Christian end and eternal blessedness. Amen."[149]

149. This exchange is in Hipler, *Nikolaus Kopernikus*.

11

Reformation and Imperial Politics

Luther was spared the dangers threatening him in the wake of the emperor's ban because Elector Frederick continued as his protector and did nothing to prevent his return to Wittenberg. Even so, it is astonishing that the reformation movement survived the year without a leader and despite the attempts to radicalize it. The situation could have been catastrophic. The gratifying outcome was due not entirely to Charles V, Luther's major opponent, having withdrawn from the German scene, for he had accounts to settle with his great rival, Francis I, in the struggle to dominate Europe. Credit for the Reformation's survival must also go to an internal development [in representative government] that in the most crucial of times opened new doors. "It is a magnificent coincidence that just at the moment when the most powerful national movement (the Reformation) arose, it was paralleled by the emergence of that very form of government, through the estates, which had been the goal of so much prolonged and manifold striving."[1] In the autumn of 1521 the imperial Council of Regency was at last set up in Nuremberg. Initially granted in 1500 as a concession by Emperor Maximilian, it collapsed from weakness two years later. Yet the election of Charles V was made conditional on his promise to reinstitute this governmental body. During the emperor's absence, governmental authority lay with the Council of Regency. The mere fact that it existed offered fresh possibilities for deliberation on the religious problem. At the same time, the innate weakness of this imperial agency prevented any overestimation of its actions. So the issue of prosecuting the reformation movement—its rights and its opportunities—could be discussed in the council almost as openly as if there had been no Edict of Worms at all, and Luther's adherents in the council could defend him as though he were neither despised nor banned. Besides, not only did this governing body include the electors and other imperial estates, but the six newly formed imperial districts were also represented. Here, in short, the tensions within the empire were realistically reflected. Inevitably this precluded one-sided decisions.

1. L. von Ranke, *Deutsche Geschichte im Zeitalter der Reformation*, 2d ed. (Meersburg and Leipzig, 1933), 2:19.

Political struggle over the Reformation, seemingly settled at Worms, thus stood at a new and, indeed, legal beginning, the more so since many doubted the legality of the Edict of Worms.[2] In the process, opinions about Luther changed. Prior to Worms [1521] it had been difficult to defend Luther against the charge that more than anyone else he was inciting general unrest. But now, after the taming of the stormy Wittenbergers— when neither the town, the university, nor the elector was pressed to the brink—Luther had proven himself the only one able to hold the movement on course. On his own inner authority, empowered by no ecclesiastical position, he had become a political influence. Frederick the Wise's intelligent and outgoing representative in the imperial governing body, Hans von der Planitz, operated smartly with Luther's newly acquired reputation, easing him out of the caricature that no longer fit him. So Planitz was able to fend off the dangerous attacks of Saxony's Duke George, whose warnings about Luther were always linked to memories of Hussite times. Planitz, to the contrary, maintained that without Luther things would get much worse, that insurrection would be inevitable. And the fear of insurrection was breathing down the necks of most of the estates. Planitz reported, "Only the bishops do not believe in the Peasant Alliance or that there will be insurrection. I promise you . . . they will learn about it soon enough."[3] Later [when insurrection came], the bishops were the prime targets of peasant fury.

Luther's cause had gained an unexpectedly strong position politically through the good offices of two men in particular: Planitz, with whom Luther had been on close terms since the time of the Leipzig disputation (1519), and the elector, who in the summer of 1522 took his turn presiding over the Council of Regency. The coming sessions of the imperial diet were to feel the effects. They took place in the same town hall, and in terms of personnel were closely interlocked. Whatever the diet had by way of agenda was discussed in advance by the Council of Regency. This became fatefully significant very soon. In the winter of 1522–23 the second imperial diet received a demand from the new pope—a demand based on newer and sounder arguments—that the Edict of Worms be

2. H. von Schubert, *Lazarus Spengler und die Reformation in Nürnberg*, ed. H. Holborn, QFRG 17 (Leipzig, 1934), 322–23.

3. E. Wülcker and H. Virck, *Des Kursächsischen Rathes Hans von der Planitz Berichte aus dem Reichsregiment in Nürnberg, 1521–1523* (Leipzig, 1899), 323 / 12ff. These reports provide a gripping picture of the proceedings of the imperial governing body [*Reichsregiment*] and of the diet [*Reichstag*]. Also, with particular regard for the Reformation in Nuremberg, see von Schubert, *Lazarus Spengler*, 312ff. [Also H. J. Grimm, *Lazarus Spengler: A Lay Leader of the Reformation* (Columbus, Ohio, 1978), 58ff.]

carried out. The previous January (1522), Hadrian VI, a Dutchman, had succeeded to the papal throne. He was a man of theological learning and ascetic discipline. For years he had been tutor, then adviser, and finally viceroy in Spain for Charles V while the latter was in Germany during 1520–21. Every aspect of Hadrian's life-style was the opposite of his predecessor's, Leo X, and a silent protest against the accepted life of the curia. He was convinced that the Lutheran reformation was not undeserved, but had come as judgment on a degenerate church. Were anyone to check its advance, then only an honest admission of this sort as well as genuine efforts to renew the church could take the wind out of the sails of this movement. Hadrian had no other way to demand that the empire put a stop to the illegal reform. With this program he sent his like-minded nuncio, Chieregati, to the imperial diet. Yet neither the pope nor his nuncio seemed to have a clear idea of the situation in Germany. In fact, the pope believed that if he confessed guilt and promised reform he could achieve his intention to intensify the suppression of the Lutheran movement. This strategy had worked for him when he was grand inquisitor in Spain. In Germany, however, his approach shocked more than only the Lutherans in the imperial estates, for the pope was challenging them (should other measures fail) to prepare an end for this "new Mohammed" like that suffered by John Huss and Jerome of Prague. A similar spirit marked the numerous instructions forwarded to Chieregati from Rome in late November 1522, replete with flattery for the well-intentioned, like Archduke Ferdinand, and with warnings for the willful or the wavering. Moreover, Chieregati waited until January 3, 1523, before divulging the part of his instruction which contained the papal admission of the sins of the church.[4] The opposite sequence would have been the more sensible for Germany. In actuality, the curia's custom of leading with threats took away much of the effectiveness of the pope's subsequently shared confession, a loss completed by Chieregati's folly when, on the heels of explaining the papal position, he demanded in Nuremberg that the estates carry out the Edict of Worms. In that connection the four most important Lutheran-minded preachers and the prior of the Augustinian cloister were to be imprisoned.[5]

Because most of the pro-papal members of the imperial estates shied away from such aggravation, those friendly to Luther on the committee of

4. The most important documents in these negotiations appeared in print in 1523. RTA 3:391–92. Later, in 1537, the evangelical members of the imperial estates cited these documents when stating their position on the issue of a council. In 1538 Luther published them again; WA 50:352ff.

5. Von Schubert, *Lazarus Spengler*, 378ff. [Cf. Grimm, *Lazarus Spengler*, 61–62.]

the diet found it not too difficult to push through a polite rejection of the nuncio's demands. It could be argued that the persecution of a popular movement—arising, as it had, solely on account of abuses in the church—would create the impression that corruptions would be defended and "evangelical truth" suppressed. The outcome would surely be revolution and civil war. There could be no other way than the one commendably urged by the pope himself, that is, authentic reforms. Besides, this way also recognized the grievances presented by the temporal members of the diet, when as early as 1521 the cities had opposed a stricter enforcement of the Edict of Worms.[6] Best of all would be, within a year, to convene a "free Christian council" in some German city where clergy and laity might enjoy unfettered consultation on matters pertaining to God's honor, the salvation of souls, and Christendom. In the meantime, Luther and his adherents should be constrained from writing, and preachers should preach nothing that might incite unrest or aberration.

> Let them preach solely the holy gospel as expounded in the trustworthy writings of the four doctors, namely, Jerome, Augustine, Gregory, and Ambrose; so let them preach and teach pending further declaration and recognition by the future council, and let them avoid debatable subjects that are not only unintelligible to the common man but also unnecessary for him to know about and which await the decision of the proposed council.[7]

These formulations, closely approaching a reformation position, were the work not of Planitz (he was not a member of the parliamentary committee) but of three other Luther-oriented men: Hans von Schwarzenberg and Dr. Zoch, representing Cardinal Albrecht of Mainz, as well as Sebastian von Rotenhan, for the bishop of Würzburg. Foremost of the three was Schwarzenberg, a powerful figure, widely esteemed as the author of the Bamberg laws on capital punishment of 1507, the forerunner of Charles V's criminal code of 1532. His own deep brand of piety, early expressed in his writings on religion, had led him to Luther's side. Toward the end of 1524, in a daring venture that carried the death penalty, Schwarzenberg liberated his daughter from a convent in Bamberg, where she was the prioress. His report of this to Luther drew hearty felicitations from the Reformer.[8]

6. Von Schubert, *Lazarus Spengler*, 384–85. RTA 3:493. Wülcker and Virck, *Berichte Planitz*, 322ff.

7. RTA 3:421 / 19ff., 24ff.; 424 / 23ff., 426 / 4ff.

8. W. Scheel, *Johann Freiherr zu Schwarzenberg* (Berlin, 1905). E. Wolf, *Grosse Rechtsdenker der deutschen Geistesgeschichte* (Tübingen, 1951), 97ff. Luther's letter of December 21, 1524, WA Br 3:407. Planitz praised the superb cooperation with him, as mentioned in K. Hofmann, "Die Konzilsfrage auf den deutschen Reichstagen von 1521 bis 1524" (theology diss., Heidelberg, 1932), 50ff.

However, not even these clever councillors were able to prevent certain changes (to which Luther later called attention[9]) in the diet's final reply to the nuncio's demand. But the tone and meaning of the response remained unchanged; in effect the Edict of Worms was declared impracticable.[10]

Luther felt little of these political negotiations concerning him and his movement. What we have of his correspondence on this subject reveals no trace of anxiety over or interest in what was going on in Nuremberg. Eventually Luther would learn what happened in the imperial Council of Regency. For him political opposition was first of all embodied in one person: Duke George of Saxony. The more the duke threatened, the greater Luther's enthusiasm for retaliating. In a letter to his friend Hartmut von Kronberg (1522), not intended for publication, Luther set the power of the risen Christ in drastic contrast to that "water bubble, George of Saxony," who sought to devour Christ "as a wolf would devour a gnat; he even fancies that he has already bitten no small scratch into the left spur."[11] Without Luther's knowledge, Kronberg had published Luther's letter along with his own reply. Before the end of 1522 three printings had already appeared. The incensed duke formally asked Luther on December 30, 1522, as in the challenge to a duel, if he was ready to confess having written the offending letter. On January 3, 1523, the duke had his answer. Luther would take back nothing; he only reaffirmed his scorn. "Desist from raving and raging against God and his Christ instead of placing service to me first! Ungracious Prince and Lord!" rang the salutation. "Martinus Luther by God's grace evangelist in Wittenberg," ran the princely signature. A dozen times in that short letter the customary title "Your Princely Grace" was twisted into "Your Princely Disgrace." The duke's question as to whether Luther be ready to confess received a sarcastic reply: What he may have written remains to him a matter of indifference. Take it whatever way you please, "standing, lying down, sitting, or running." He sticks to the substance of what he has written. To prove it, he repeated the words that had so much insulted the duke: "I'll not be scared to death by any water bubble." More than George, he claimed the right to complain of "injuries to the soul, to honor, and to good reputation." Luther claimed to be not the duke's enemy and as al-

9. See below, pp. 302–3.

10. RTA 3:438 / 12ff.

11. WA 10²:55 / 22ff. O. Clemen, WA Br 2:484–85, correctly counters WA 10²:45 that Luther's original letter, as well as the first printing of it in Strassburg, contained the duke's name. Geographic propinquity made it seem wiser to substitute N for the name when the letter was reprinted in Wittenberg.

ways continued to pray for him, if only he would cease blaspheming and slandering the Christian truth.[12] Outright wrath over the oppression of evangelicals in the duchy of Saxony as well as enjoyment in showing the duke his fearlessness had guided Luther's pen. Besides, Luther was sure that with all his complaining the duke was making himself ridiculous. Indeed, George gained nothing from his immediate remonstrances either to the elector or to the imperial Council of Regency. The elector gave him an imperturbable reply, assuming that since George "had been endowed by God with particular grace and understanding" and because he had good counselors to advise him, he would no doubt know how to help himself.[13] In the Council of Regency, meanwhile, the nature of the theme remained unchanged: "Whenever Luther or something pertaining to him came up for discussion there was fire in every alley." Every time the action was the same. The duke was referred to the elector, in whom, without a doubt, he would find "the loyal sympathy of a cousin."[14]

Even when Count Albrecht of Mansfeld endeavored to mediate and to elicit an apology from Luther (he had spoken with him in Wittenberg on February 24, 1523) there was the standard reply: Luther had expressed himself to Kronberg in that particular way because the duke was suppressing his teachings and writings; indeed, Luther would be ready to show the duke all respect "if His Princely Grace would allow the gospel to reach out and work unhindered."[15] Naturally, the duke could not accept the count's report as rendering satisfaction. To the duke's renewed demand that he publicly humble himself and take back his defamation, Luther no longer made reply.

The proceedings of the imperial diet itself left Luther unruffled. He reacted only to matters of direct personal concern to him, and then did so swiftly and sharply. Among the many propaganda instructions which Chieregati was receiving from Rome was one addressed to the town coun-

12. WA Br 3:4–5.

13. January 21, 1523, F. Gess, *Akten und Briefe zur Kirchenpolitik Herzog Georgs von Sachsen* (Leipzig, 1905ff.), 1:444 / 12ff. George persisted with the elector but always received an evasive reply. Cf. ibid, 451–52, 454–55, 455–56, 459, 460, 462, 478. When George challenged the elector to proceed against Luther because of the latter's treatise *On Temporal Authority* (March 21, ibid., 486ff.), Frederick rejected the demand outright (March 24, ibid., 488–89). On April 8, George finally realized that legal proceedings against Luther were futile, but he continued to resent being called a "water bubble" (ibid., 492 / 13–14).

14. Planitz to the Elector, February 28, 1523, Wülcker and Virck, *Berichte Planitz*, 381 / 7ff. Cf., in addition, ibid., 374 / 19ff.; 379 / 17ff.; 396 / 3ff. For Planitz it was "a difficult task" to prevent direct intervention by the council; ibid., 401 / 35. Communication of the Council of Regency to Duke George, February 28, 1523, in Gess, *Akten*, 1:473 / 23.

15. WA Br 3:7 / 47–48.

cil of Bamberg, a place where a strong evangelical movement was clashing head-on with a new and energetic bishop. Probably through Schwarzenberg a copy of the German version of the papal instructions reached Luther in February 1523. In it he encountered a form of polemics whose vulgar manner he had experienced countless times, but the fact that it here came from the chief shepherd of the church made him furious. Its gist was that Luther had separated himself from the common body of Christian doctrine and from the church fathers, that he has cast doubt on everything hitherto accepted as customary, and that he has not hesitated "to lay another foundation in place of that already laid . . . , just as though he alone were endowed by the Holy Spirit and as though he was recognizing evangelical truth only now at the end of the world."[16] Luther had this instruction printed, adding his sarcastic comments as well as a conclusion. In it he vehemently tore apart the lazy argument by which the pope had made light of the matter at issue.

> Isn't it a sin and a shame that the pope, who would be master over all Christians, can find nothing better to say than: This Luther wants to be the only intelligent one, and should we, with so many forebears, be the ones who have erred? What sort of complaints are these—effeminate, childish, sophomoric? A pope should be able to cite Scripture and to say boldly: Look here, this is God's Word and this is how Luther has spoken against it. But, alas, he is silent on this, and says instead: Thus and so Luther has spoken against long usage, against custom, against the teachers of the church. As if our faith was founded in matters of ancient usage and custom and the word of teachers. The name of our God is not "Custom" but "Truth," and our faith relies not on custom but on the truth which is God himself.[17]

The imperial diet's action of February 9, 1523, must have surprised Luther. "Astonishingly free and gratifying" was his initial reaction.[18] Why not? After all, he was well aware that even in a friendly Nuremberg there had to be those who saw themselves forced to reaffirm the ban imposed at Worms on his writings.[19] Now that the decision had been made to air the religious issue thoroughly, he could justifiably feel "that according to this

16. *Ein päpstlich Breve dem Rat zu Bamberg gesandt wider den Luther,* WA 11:344 / 5ff. Printed ca. mid-March 1523, in German only. Soon thereafter a Latin translation of the letters of Chieregati and of the pope (but not of Luther's conclusion) appeared in print, decked out with sarcastic comments on the style and content. This was the work of a young humanist (either Wilhelm Nesen or Joachim Camerarius); WA 11:337–38.

17. WA 11:355 / 16ff.

18. "Decreta . . . mire libera et placentia," to Spalatin, March 8, 1523, WA Br 3:41 / 11. Reichstagsabschied, RTA 3:736ff., esp. 745ff.

19. January 7, 1523, to Link, WA Br 3:11 / 21. See also n. 14, above.

mandate I, Martinus Luther, should reasonably be under papal and imperial ban and restraint until the future council."[20] But he soon also spotted certain traps concealed in the decree. He therefore thought it wise to give notice—first to his elector and then publicly—that he was not about to let himself be bound by them. In early May, Frederick had received not only the general regulations as passed by the Council of Regency on the religious issue but also a special communication. In it the elector was asked to make sure that, until the future council, Luther and his followers would not publish anything.[21] Frederick sent Luther both items through Jerome Schurff. As he had done after Luther's return from the Wartburg, the elector requested an immediate reply through his messenger, so as to be able to assure the Council of Regency that he had carried out their instructions.[22] Candidly and cleverly Luther tossed back the ball. First, in a letter of May 29, he recapitulated in some detail the wording of the Council of Regency's communication to the elector, except that he could not bring himself to write "Your Holiness" and everytime it occurred substituted "the pope." Luther reassured the elector that it had never been his intention to slander any of the diet's members, be they prominent or obscure. Whatever he had written "harshly and earnestly" against one or another was not without some reason, but certainly without malice and for the sake of God's Word alone. But he also called attention to the limits of his own good will on the matter of keeping silent. How could he do so when John Faber and Jerome Emser had just come out with books attacking him. One would surely not forbid him, in a given situation, to defend himself against such attacks "more to protect the divine evangelical truth than my own innocence." In passing, Luther reassured Frederick initially that he had appeared on the scene without the elector's advice or knowledge and that only in the previous year had he returned to Wittenberg from the Wartburg at his "own risk," and that his outspoken writings had admittedly often earned the elector's displeasure. Luther wrote his reply in a way that the elector, should he so wish, could send it on to the Council of Regency. Luther therefore set down the conditions, as well as the exceptions, under which he would consent not to publish until the future

20. *Wider die Verkehrer und Fälscher kaiserlichs Mandats* (1523) [*Against the Perverters and Falsifiers of the Emperor's Mandate*], WA 12:67 / 13–14.

21. "Mandat des Reichsregiments," March 6, 1523, RTA 3:447ff. Communication to Elector Frederick, some time after April 16 (backdated to March 10; cf. Wülcker and Virck, *Berichte Planitz,* 426 / 30).

22. The elector's letter to Planitz, June 20, 1523, on the calculated application of Luther's reply, in Wülcker and Virck, *Berichte Planitz,* 469 / 13ff.

council. He was emphatic in his willingness to go along with the main demand of the Council of Regency, namely, that no one publish or teach anything "that might cause disturbance, disobedience, disunity, and rebellion in the Holy Roman Empire or that might lead Christians into error." After all, he himself had often written harshly against such things.[23]

Following this diplomatic correspondence, Luther soon felt himself moved to take a stand publicly on the action of the imperial diet. Pleased though he might be about its general direction, its ambiguity did not escape him. And that was to prove decisive. Let the gospel be preached "according to the exposition of the Scriptures as approved and accepted by the holy Christian church."[24] The intention of this formula becomes apparent when one compares it with the original version of the diet's committee: "according to the accepted writings and exposition of the four teachers."[25] Between these two versions lay the fundamental question as to the norm: Is it the church in its entire history up to the present; or is it the ancient church, close to the time of origins and not yet corrupted by centuries of distortion? Without knowledge of the change, Luther was thinking like Schwarzenberg and the committee and was surmising correctly: If the Roman church is meant, as it exists today, then why convene a council? Were that the case, then a far more comprehensive judgment would have been made than the most hostile of councils could have pronounced.[26] This kind of interpretation could only be an ill-willed misinterpretation, and Luther was bent on dispelling it without delay. In July 1523 he published the short tract *Against the Perverters and Falsifiers of the Emperor's Mandate*. First he expressed his "high gratitude" to the Council of Regency for the mandate God has entrusted to them and stated that he would honestly be ready to conform to it.[27] Next he clarified the term "Christian church." It is to be understood as a historical and normative reality, not simply as the contemporary hierarchical institution. He gladly voiced approval of the task assigned to the bishops: to appoint people conversant in Holy Scripture to monitor sermons and to instruct the

---

23. WA Br 3:74ff., esp. 76 / 62ff. The warning against rebellion in the diet's action and in the Council of Regency's mandate (RTA 3:747 / 15ff.; 450 / 4ff.) was shunted off to the papal legate in the council's communication to the elector. See Wülcker and Virck, *Berichte Planitz*, 390 / 17ff. This warning would have sounded strange in the ears of Frederick the Wise and Luther. [LW 49:36–42, esp. 40.]

24. RTA 3:747 / 18–19

25. WA 12:63, n. 1.

26. WA 12:64 / 2ff.

27. WA 12:62 / 4ff.

erring. There is but one problem: "This article lacks nothing, except that no one will observe it. Why? Because it is much too good." Where is one suddenly to find so many people who understand the Scriptures, after scholasticism has for centuries miseducated the theologians? As for consenting to publish nothing until the future council, he exempted his translation and exposition of the Bible.[28] There was one point in the decision of the imperial diet that earnestly troubled him, however. Priests who had married and people who had left the cloisters were declared not to be under the protection of civil government but, according to canon law, to be subject to the loss of their privileges and benefices.[29] He was ready to recognize even this point, severe though it was, provided the other articles were also carried out. But on this issue the pastoral need, which he knew so well, got the better of him. "God in heaven help us. Will we ever learn that impossible vows are no vows at all and cannot be kept?" "I wager that those who are now my bitterest enemies—if they but knew what I hear daily from all quarters—would tomorrow help me storm the cloisters." The major questions gave Luther no grounds to request changes, but this "human article," with its impossible demands on nature, made him speak up. Not for self "but for the miserable crowd I beseech you, my dearest Lord, that you would graciously hear: We would ask for nothing unfair."[30] Toward the end of this treatise Luther became so worked up and repeatedly fell into such crude language that a man like Hans von der Planitz, on reading it in Nuremberg, was little pleased. Things he wished had been left unsaid now had to be washed out, and, he sighed, he would not mind if "Doctor Martinus would unburden himself somewhere else for a while."[31] Thoughts about an alternative place for Luther had occurred to Planitz before. Already early in the year the uncertainty of the whole situation had prompted him to express his thoughts to the elector; even Christ and Paul often had to flee from their enemies.[32] Luther, however, got wind of this and immediately nipped it in the bud. He informed Spalatin on January 12, 1523, "Don't get the notion that I'll crawl back into some corner, however much the dragon and his gang may rave."[33]

28. WA 12:63 / 11ff.; 64 / 31ff.; 65 / 7ff.; 24ff.

29. RTA 3:748 / 22ff.

30. WA 12:66 / 16ff., 32ff.; 67 / 18ff.

31. Planitz, July 16, 1523, Wülcker and Virck, *Berichte Planitz*, 491 / 20ff.

32. Planitz, January 2, 1523, ibid., 305 / 15ff.

33. WA Br 3:15 / 9–10. Behemoth (i.e., Leviathan), Job 40:25ff. For Luther this was an eschatological figure, as he and Melanchthon at that time were explaining in a commentary, WA 11:378 / 9, 40ff. (on Job 41:7).

In Nuremberg, meanwhile, the clouds had gathered again. Duke George was at it, warning that any siding with Luther on the part of his prince could cost Frederick the electorship; in fact, Planitz had already in January been threatened with the same thing by his dangerous opponent, Elector Joachim I of Brandenburg.[34] Worse yet, rumor had it that in the environs of the elector of Trier (specifically, in Ebernburg castle) letters had been found in which Luther was advising Franz von Sickingen, the leading knight, to attack the archbishop. Planitz at once wrote to his lord, Frederick, advising that if any of this were true it would pay to get Luther away from Wittenberg and Electoral Saxony for a while—better to act in time than to have the elector hand over Luther.[35] The elector did nothing, but Planitz grew increasingly apprehensive about Luther the closer the next imperial diet came.[36]

Meanwhile, the main points of tension in imperial politics at the moment were not in the Luther affair at all. In the short time since its formation, the Council of Regency had energetically grasped the reins of running the empire. With courage and foresight it had taken up the significant tasks entrusted to it, but it had also made enemies of all parties whose wishes it was not fulfilling, a dilemma awaiting even the ablest of administratively competent commissions operating without real political power. By the autumn of 1523 nearly all the estates had turned against the regency. The strongest objections came from the imperial cities against the newly adopted act imposing duties and granting monopolies. The measure was intended to bring unity to the empire's economy as well as to combat usury and the high cost of borrowing money. If it worked it would also provide the Council of Regency with a durable financial base. The cities, however, sent their own delegation to Spain and in August 1523 secured the emperor's full support. What else was Charles to do, seeing himself dependent on the financial assistance of the big commercial houses? Nor could he but welcome any curbing of the Council of Regency.[37]

---

34. Report on the conversation with Joachim I, January 19, 1523, Wülcker and Virck, *Berichte Planitz*, 329–30. Conversation with Duke George, July 15, ibid., 489 / 25ff.; 493 / 31ff. (on July 22).

35. July 27, 1523, ibid., 502 / 7ff.; 503 / 3ff. Already in November 1522 the archbishop of Trier had spread this charge against Luther in his letter to the papal nuncio. Planitz sent a copy forthwith to Elector Frederick. Ibid., 249 / 12ff.

36. Ibid., 523 / 8ff.; 524 / 20ff.; 533 / 12ff.; 564 / 15–16.

37. Von Ranke, *Deutsche Geschichte* (see above, p. 295, n. 1), 2:94ff. F. von Bezold, *Geschichte der deutschen Reformation* (Berlin, 1890), 423ff. K. Brandi, *The Emperor Charles V: The Growth and Destiny of a Man and of a World Empire* (New York: Knopf, 1939), 187.

Similarly, a growing number of electors and princes were irritated by the regency and turning away from it. Their number included not only the likes of Duke George, but especially the group bearing the brunt of the military adventures of Franz von Sickingen. Fortunately none of these matters had any direct connection with the Luther question, even though the archbishop of Trier persisted in trying to implicate the Wittenberg reformer. To be sure, Luther had earlier struck up friendly relations with Sickingen, but these were completely unpolitical and at a time when the latter was a confidant of Charles V. Yet Sickingen, full of vainglorious plans, disappointedly abandoned the emperor. Staking his fortune on support from the unity movement among the knights of the empire, he took up arms. Luther was horrified and feared the worst. He therefore saw Sickingen's death as divine judgment. That God is just, and a remarkable judge. Melanchthon, too, had branded Sickingen's attack as an "atrocious raid," deeply distressing to Luther and bound to bring the knights into disrepute.[38] The Council of Regency itself was dragged into a nasty situation by this feud. Unable to keep the peace and hold the rebellious knights in check, the council now tried to restrain the victors (the Palatinate, Trier, and Hesse) in their retaliation as they attacked and robbed a number of Frankish nobles for allegedly being in league with Sickingen.[39] The council was caught, unable to bypass the complaints of injured parties. The problem was clear enough, but also delicate. Only with difficulty could the council make up its mind, so that Planitz lamented, "What a marvel this is. Jurisprudence is as much in need of a reformation as theology received it through Luther."[40] To impose sentence on the aggressors, the powerful princes, was out of the question, so developments took an opposite turn, and inevitably so. In the spring of 1523 the unloved and

38. Luther to Link, December 19, 1522: *Res pessima futura est*, WA Br 2:632 / 23–24. The remark concerns the war in the Palatinate (since November 1522), about which Luther must have heard most readily inasmuch as at that time Sickengen had dismissed Bucer, Hutten, and Oecolampadius from his service. P. Kalkoff, *Huttens Vagantenzeit und Untergang* (Weimar, 1925), 318. E. Staehelin, *Das theologische Lebenswerk Johannes Oekolampads*, QFRG 21 (Leipzig, 1939), 169. One cannot determine whether Luther knew anything of the feud in Trier or of the outlawing of Sickingen (October 10). Luther on Sickingen's death, ca. May 22, 1523, WA Br 3:71 / 6–7 (based on Ps. 7:12). On Luther's earlier relation to Sickingen, see above, pp. 90–95. Melanchthon, January 1, 1523, to Johannes Hess, CR 1:598, and to Joachim Camerarius, CR 1:597. *MBW* 256. *MSA* 7 / 1:183. *MBW* 255.

39. See the introduction to Wülcker and Virck, *Berichte Planitz*, cxliv ff., grievances of the Frankish nobles, January 30, 1523. RTA 3:727ff. On the public echo of the council's confrontation, see K. Schottenloher, *Flugschriften zur Ritterschaftsbewegung des Jahres 1523*, RGST 53 (Münster, 1929).

40. May 31, 1523, Wülcker and Virck, *Berichte Planitz*, 450 / 4–5; cf. further on, 457 / 27ff.; 496 / 20ff.; 497 / 16ff.; 563 / 10ff.

powerless Council of Regency was dissolved. What Nuremberg thus lost presently reappeared in Esslingen, this time on Austrian territory. Half the expenses of the change were charged to the emperor, whose pockets were empty anyway. Members of the council were, above all, educated and alert advisers to princes. Their thinking was modern, and with remarkable nerve they had performed as on a tightrope for which no constitutional or financial supporting net had been provided. Blame the estates. With virtually the same unanimity shown four years earlier, when demanding that Charles allow its creation, the estates now went about dismantling the council as an institution. The attempt, under their own power, to set up the beginnings of an imperial central governing authority as a counterpart to the emperor had miscarried. Nor had the emperor derived full use of the council. More than ever, the politics of the empire would be dominated for centuries by the most varied territorial alliances of convenience. Among them the emperor or the House of Hapsburg, depending on the situation, could find allies or powerful opponents. At the moment the Swabian Alliance was the most important bloc. Formed in 1488, that alliance had never missed a chance to show its contempt for the regency arrangement.

Surprisingly, the fiasco of the Council of Regency had no decisive influence on the policy it had initiated toward the Reformation. Its span of activity, though short, had been enough to provide a breather after the Edict of Worms. But it now became evident that the Reformation was indebted not only to the skill of those councillors friendly to Luther but also to the visibility these men had gained in the process. With friends like this, a movement hitherto intended and led as purely religious now became a political reality as well. It so happened that, at the second imperial diet of Nuremberg, apprehensiveness lest the Reformation cause a general revolution became the dominant theme. To this theme both sides applied their most powerful leverage. In his brief to the estates of November 22, 1522, Pope Hadrian declared:

> Are you not aware, princes and people of Germany, that this is only a prelude to the crimes Luther and his followers have in mind? Can you not plainly see that the Lutherans have been championing evangelical truth only as a subterfuge for what is now unmasked as the theft of your possessions? Or do you imagine that these sons of malice still intend something other than in the name of freedom to abolish all obedience and to introduce the option that anyone may do as he pleases? . . . This lamentable disaster is aimed at your property and possessions, at your homes, women, and children, at rights and rules, and at the churches, if you do not oppose it in time.[41]

41. RTA 3:402 / 11ff., 27ff.

An exactly opposite view was set forth by Planitz in a lengthy conversation with the legate Chieregati: Without the knowledge or approval of the elector Luther had left the Wartburg and gone back to Wittenberg. Yet without doubt "extensive disorder would have broken out there, had not Luther returned at the right time." Should he once again be expelled, then they would say, "It has not been possible to overcome Luther with the truth of Scripture, so now one must use force, because he has preached the gospel and told the truth. No one else is behind this but the clergy, and they have misled us before." Any use of force "would arouse a considerable and widespread rebellion in the empire, which would not easily be put down. Much of it would involve the clergy, and all present plans against the Turks and others would be overturned." Planitz therefore advised the convening of a free and irenic discussion of learned men from all Christian lands to meet with Luther and his followers at some appropriate place. Thereafter a general council could deal with issues on which agreement had not yet been reached. In this way "a new and good reformation of all Christendom could be launched."[42] The imperial diet gave the legate the same kind of answer: Any enforcement of the Edict of Worms, as demanded by the pope, "would meet with nothing but violent rebellion and civil wars."[43]

This warning expressed a widespread feeling.[44] The political situation corresponding to it remained unchanged during the second imperial diet gathered in Nuremberg from January to April 1524, but the circumstances had changed. Pope Hadrian VI's death on September 14, 1523, had come much too early for practical results to emerge from his assessment of the dismal church situation. He had been unable to advance his plan to call an inclusive council for the renewal of the church. The time for this would have been determined by the conclusion of the European war then engaging Charles V and his French rival, Francis I.[45] Once again a Medici was pope, as Clement VII, a nephew of Leo X, succeeded the devout Hadrian. In place of a reform-minded churchman the new incumbent was

42. Detailed report, in German, of the conversation presumably conducted in Italian (Planitz had studied for three years in Bologna; cf. Wülcker and Virck, *Berichte Planitz,* xxix), December 11, 1522, ibid., 270ff., esp. 273 / 26ff.; 274 / 12ff.; 275 / 23ff.

43. "Unde indubie nihil aliud quam gravissimi tumultus populares intestinaque bella speranda essent," February 5, 1523, RTA 3:438 / 16–17. An equivalent draft by the committees of the Council for Regency, January 15 and 19–23, 1523, RTA 3:421 / 17ff.; cf. also RTA 3:432 / 13ff.

44. Further examples in Hofmann, "Konzilsfrage" (see n. 8, above), 38ff.

45. Notice of this in Baronius-Raynald, *Annales Ecclesiastici,* 20 (1693), on the year 1523, n. 115, p. 395; quoted in Hofmann, "Konzilsfrage," 65.

a worldly-wise politician. Foremost on his mind was the grandeur of the papal states and of his own house. His legate, Cardinal Campeggio, was as much like Clement in outlook as Chieregati had been like Hadrian. His brusque manner quickly made him many enemies in German public life as well as in the imperial diet, even though the situation he faced was more favorable to the curia than during the previous year. The clerical estates and ecclesiastical princes were in the majority in both Nuremberg diets; those estates leaning toward Luther were few indeed.[46] Besides, the influence of the Council of Regency had vanished. In light of frequent membership changes, at this diet the tone among the representatives was set by the dukes of Bavaria. It was a case of "the clergy courting the Bavarians, and the Bavarians the clergy," wrote Planitz. As usual, he found colorful language for his summary.[47] Even so, the diet stuck to its chosen line. The steadying influence came from the cities and a few of the other estates. They brought up the decision of the previous diet and pointed out emphatically that "the common man everywhere is eager for the Word of God and the holy gospel." Were coercion attempted to enforce the Edict of Worms (as demanded by the papal legate and the Roman Catholic majority among the princes) the consequences would unquestionably cause "much rebellion, disobedience, murder, bloodshed, and indeed a complete destruction . . . [because] without borrowing trouble the air everywhere appears dangerous, tense, and anxious. Even the common man would be saddled with many more unbearable burdens and taxes."[48]

The outcome was a twofold or, more precisely, a threefold action. The demand of the 1523 diet was repeated, that is, to call a "free general council" in "an appropriate city in the German nation" to deal with the Luther issue and "other matters of common concern in Christendom." By way of preparation, a "general assembly of the German nation" should be held in Speyer on St. Martin's Day in November of that year, 1524, so as to "sort out the good from the bad" in the new teaching and to consider the grievances for which redress was being sought. In addition, the estates and their subjects were reminded emphatically to be obedient to the Edict of Worms. There had been no mention of it in the diet's action in 1523. Even now, however, the accent on obedience was weakened by the added clause

46. Hoffman "Konzilsfrage," 35ff.

47. Wülcker and Virck, *Berichte Planitz*, 616 / 11.

48. "Protest der Städte," April 6, 1524, RTA 4:507 / 26ff. The cities also stand aloof from the customary language of the majority: new teaching, "wie man der Namen geben will." RTA 4:507 / 12–13. Also RTA 4:517 / 28.

"so far as possible for them."[49] Frederick the Wise, having left the diet in disappointment on February 26, had his deputy, Philipp von Feilitzsch, present his protest against the majority decision. Similar negation came from the counts and the cities. Despite strong pressures on them from the majority, they refused to add their seal, for they believed that enforcement of the edict would lead to disorders.[50]

Modern knowledge of the historical sources and contexts is prerequisite if we are to recognize the origin of the contradictory political aims as gathered up in the diet's latest action [*Reichstagsabschied*]. The contradictions were embodied in the careful wording of the action: free discussion in a council, on the one hand; enforcement of the ban pronounced in the Edict of Worms, on the other. To complicate matters, between these two alternatives an intermediate arrangement was now proposed. The composition and competence of this arrangement were still unclear. The initially used term, "national council," was dropped at the objection of the papal legate. Behind this apparently hovered the idea of some connection between the diet and a meeting of many theologians and laymen.[51] The proposal for a "synod of the German nation" came not from the Lutheran side but from the Bavarian side. The intention was practical: in place of a council in the indeterminate future, to create an opportunity where the new teaching (confined as it was to Germany) "could be taken in hand and brought onto a good Christian course."[52] Planitz himself had already earlier developed the idea of such a free conference, but as we have seen it would be in a larger format representing "all Christian kingdoms and lands."[53] Actually, given the opportunity for open discussion with access to the public, the reform-minded could see possibilities diametrically opposite to those intended by the Bavarians. In any case, for the time being the proposed plan excluded any enforcement of the Edict of Worms.

And Luther? From his vantage point he judged the diet's resolution as completely illogical. There is no point in blaming him too much for this; he was not privy to the political ingredients of the compromise, and at any rate he was basing his judgment not on political results but on essential

49. RTA 4:603 / 26.

50. "Protest Kursachsens," April 11, 1524, RTA 4:570–71, 577–78. Report of the imperial speaker, Hannart, on negotiations with the counts and cities, to Regent Margaret, April 20, 1524, RTA 4:776 / 29ff.; 778 / 14ff.

51. Hofmann, "Konzilsfrage," 76ff. RTA 4:827, regarding 470. The cities had called the planned gathering a "Christian hearing" [or trial]. RTA 4:508 / 20–21.

52. Cf. Hofmann, "Konzilsfrage," 71–72. RTA 4:434 / 13ff.

53. In conversation with the legate Chieregati. See above, p. 297. Wülcker and Virck, *Berichte Planitz*, 274 / 32.

results. "Hereby I am both damned and deferred for later judgment, and the Germans are supposed to regard me as one already condemned and persecutable, as well as to go on waiting until I am condemned." Thus Luther tore apart the two incongruous components, the edict and the national assembly, doing so in a vehement pamphlet and publishing it with a commentary as well as a short preface and conclusion.[54] If theirs was political wisdom, then Luther despaired of the intelligence of responsible princes. That the emperor, "this poor mortal bag of worms who cannot be sure of his life for a single moment," should pretend to be "the prime protector of the Christian faith" ("what does God do meanwhile?"[55]) seemed to Luther like still another sign of the delusions under which God had humbled Germany's princes. "This is the reward they have earned for persecuting the Word of God. Therefore they run into one another and are being punished with a rampant case of blindness. God deliver us from them and by his grace give us other regents. Amen."[56]

Luther's outcry sprang from no thought of arousing resistance or rebellion against the imperial estates responsible for the resolution. Fools or not, they remained the authorities whom God alone could call off. Luther had in no way intervened in the political game played at the diet; even in the main demand for a council, made in Nuremberg by the friends of reform, there was no such intervention. For years Luther had taken this position and publicized it. "I'm not worried about the diet. I know who Satan is." These words to Spalatin on February 1, 1524, are echoed in his letter of May 2: "I hear that in Nuremberg they are hatching monstrous threats."[57] When rumors reached him that the Edict of Worms was being republished, "so that the Lutheran sect be completely extinguished," and that fear was abroad in many cities, Luther contended calmly, "Neverthe-

54. *Zwei kaiserliche uneinige und widerwärtige Gebote den Luther betreffend,* August 1524, WA 15:254 / 18ff. Luther's poor impression was intensified by the fact that he did not have a copy of the diet's resolution itself but had the Mansfeld copy of the mandate released in the emperor's name, in which Archduke Ferdinand conveyed the decisions on the Luther issue to the estates, including therewith a new edition of the Edict of Worms. See RTA 4:571; RTA 4:615ff., for the Hessian copy. In the mandate [in contrast to the resolution] the emphasis was different because of transpositions, omissions (the part on the preaching of God's Word; Resolution, RTA 4:605 / 8ff.; see above, p. 302), and the repeated emphasis on the Edict of Worms. WA 15:275 / 21ff. Besides, there was the description of the prevalence of Lutheran teaching and its consequences in an addition to the mandate; WA 15:273 / 19–20.

55. WA 15:278 / 1ff.; 258 / 13.

56. WA15:278 / 18ff.

57. WA Br 3:241 / 5–6; 283 / 18–19. Apparently the first indication that Campeggio's aims, a failure in Nuremberg, were now to be attained by a political alliance of the Roman Catholic estates (Regensburg Union, June 24, 1524). [H. J. Grimm, *The Reformation Era* (New York: Macmillan, 1954), 201.]

less, Christ lives, and we shall conquer and triumph."[58] As for the political possibilities of the planned national assembly in Speyer, Luther had as yet no overview. Later, however, in retrospect, beyond the catastrophe of the Peasants' War, he would assess that planned assembly in a transfiguring light. "You doubtless still well remember how," he wrote in 1530 to the clergy assembled at the Diet of Augsburg, "the Diet at Speyer was summoned with such glorious, consoling hope that the whole world looked to it with great eagerness and heartily expected good to come of it."[59] But now [in the summer of 1524], his reactions were still characteristically personal. First, he heard only the challenge thrown down by the renewal of the Edict of Worms and replied in the most defiant language he ever used:

> Now then, my dear princes and lords, you are very much in a hurry to put this poor lone individual to death, and when that's done, you will have won. . . . If Luther's life counts so much in God's sight, how is it that when he's not living none of you would be sure of his life or power and that his death would be the misfortune of you all? You don't play jokes on God. Go to it, then. Strangle and burn. As God wills, I'll not budge. Here I am.

Deeper than defiance, a most profound concern made him speak like that.

> I beg you for God's sake, look at things through God's eyes and tackle the matter differently. Disaster is truly at hand. God's wrath is kindled, and you won't escape him when you act like this. What are you after, dear sirs? God is too smart for you, and he'll make fools of you soon enough. A line from his rhyme runs like this: *Deposuit potentes de sede*. This means you, dear sirs, right now, when you ignore it.[60]

What Luther here said to the princes was the opposite of what he wrote the peasants a year later. It was completely nonpolitical—and for that reason political to the highest degree. He did the one thing he could do: He was demonstrating, without intending or realizing it, that he was a power, and he was doing it solely by means of the tenacity with which he answered every threat, authenticating ever more strongly his fearlessness

---

58. To Johann Briessmann, July 4, 1524, WA Br 3:315 / 18ff.; to n. 7 this comment: The rumor was probably started by the fact that a new copy of the text of the edict was sent out by Ferdinand along with the mandate. This reached the estates between mid-June and mid-July; RTA 4:571, 791, n. 1. On the proclamation of the edict there was considerable correspondence between the cities; RTA 4:271, 272, 274. There was no need for Luther to have awaited a first hearing from the electoral court, where the mandates of the diet arrived on July 18; RTA 4:793.

59. WA 30²:274 / 1ff. Concerning this communication, see below, pp. 669ff. [LW 34:12.]

60. WA 15:254 / 26ff.; 255 / 16ff., 28–30 (Luke 1:52, "He has put down the mighty from their thrones.")

and his trust in God's guidance. How could his elector, despite the sighs of frustration he often caused him, reprimand him for this? Luther was a weapon that Frederick's opponents could not knock from his hand.

As for the emperor, he promptly voided the diet's ingeniously balanced decision. In a communication to the estates, he forbade the planned national assembly. At the same time, he declared himself ready to approach the pope on the matter of calling a council. Above all, however, he emphasized the need for strict enforcement of the Edict of Worms against the "inhuman and unchristian Luther," for he regarded Luther as a man determined "with his accursed sweet venom to poison as many as possible and to ruin them in body and soul, and by exercising his malicious cunning to exalt himself and overawe the people." Like his tutor, Hadrian, the recent pope, Charles V saw Luther as a follower of "that infamous great seducer Mohammed, who with his sect and error has alone inflicted more harm and injury on Christendom than all other nations and peoples in all the world combined have been able to do."[61] During the next few years, however, came war instead of a council, and because this involved armed conflict even between pope and emperor [the "sack of Rome," 1525], Charles V was prevented from forcing compliance with the Edict of Worms. Once again and unexpectedly the Reformation enjoyed a moment of reprieve. Indeed, hope for a peaceful settlement of the Luther issue was soon dashed. Yet the very idea of an irenic outcome had caught hold. People on both sides were convinced of the need to prepare thoroughly for the great public debate. The evangelical side, particularly, would have to beware, lest it stumble into the role of disturber of the peace. As early as July 1524 the advisers of Duke John of Saxony recommended that he convene a meeting of the learned in the universities of Wittenberg and Erfurt and that they take counsel together, "so that Your Electoral and Princely Grace would not be found lacking in anything, should the coming diet in Speyer beget a follow-up."[62] Similarly several "old believers" [those on the Roman side] requested considered opinions from informed sources or convened informally to take counsel.[63] The emperor's veto

61. From the copy of the document for Elector Frederick, received in Lochau on September 30, 1524. K. E. Förstemann, *Neues Urkundenbuch zur Geschichte der evangelischen Kirchen-Reformation* (Hamburg, 1842), 1:204ff. On Hadrian VI ("Mohammed"), see above, p. 297.

62. RTA 4:795 / 25ff.

63. Hofmann, "Konzilsfrage," 95. E. Brasse, "Die Geschichte des Speirer Nationalkonzils vom Jahre 1524" (theology diss., Halle, 1890), mentions opinions prepared by the universities of Vienna, Freiburg, and Heidelberg. These, however, have not been preserved (H. von Schubert, *Die Anfänge der evangelischen Bekenntnisbildung bis 1529 / 30*, SVRG [Leipzig, 1928], 13–14) and may not even have been replaced [in the Halle library].

caused zeal to cool quickly. In one of the territories, however, work had already progressed so far that it could not be stopped in the lands of the margrave of Ansbach-Kulmbach and in the neighboring city of Nuremberg. There the energy of Margrave Casimir [1515–27] was contagious. On the religious question he was at the time still undecided, the more so because he was seeking a legal regulation at the imperial level on the religious issue. Within a short time, his Lutheran secretary, Jörg Vogler, as well as pro-Reformation friends in Nuremberg (foremost among them Lazarus Spengler, secretary of the city council) had gathered some twenty opinions, several prepared by Roman Catholics. The evangelical opinions are the enduring fruit of the aspirations for a national assembly. Equally important, they constitute the first detailed confessional statements of doctrine on the Lutheran side. The gathering of these opinions created a tradition of solid theological preparation for great actions of the Reformation, among them the introduction of the Reformation in Nuremberg, the visitation of the territorial churches, the Diet of Augsburg, and so on. These elaborations (by 1530 they totaled eighty) by rural and urban Franconian pastors testify how early and how powerfully Luther's teaching had taken root, doing so alongside influences exerted by Zwingli and the distinctive character of Osiander's theology in Nuremberg.[64] Although a product of imperial politics, these confessions found only local application, for it was only with the return of Charles in 1530 that an empire-wide approach to the religious question was possible. But by then the schism had grown deeper.

After the Nuremberg diet of 1524 imperial business rolled on—and not unfavorably for the Reformation. After all, the majority of the estates could not bring themselves to fight it with the sharp weapons of the edict. For the empire itself, however, the times were growing ominous. The emperor's prohibition bitterly disappointed most of the estates and the newly reconstituted Council of Regency as well. Its members were almost exclusively on the Roman side, and Archduke Ferdinand warned them to "stay away from the devilish and heretical teachings of Luther" and neither discuss them nor read anything about them.[65] The regents had antici-

64. *Die Fränkischen Bekenntnisse: Eine Vorstufe der Augsburgischen Konfession*, ed. W. F. Schmidt and K. Schornbaum (Munich, 1930); includes a dedicatory theological monograph. On this, see von Schubert, *Bekenntnisbildung*.

65. Hofmann, "Konzilsfrage," 104ff. Among the imperial estates, Elector Ludwig of the Palatinate was especially outspoken in a letter to the emperor on October 15, 1524. W. Friedensburg, *Der Reichstag zu Speier 1526 im Zusammenhang der politischen und kirchlichen Entwicklung Deutschlands im Reformationszeitalter* (Berlin, 1887), 8. On the Council of Regency, see the first report by Planitz to the elector from Esslingen, July 5, 1524, Wülcker and Virck, *Berichte Planitz*, 634 / 10ff.

pated the national assembly as the one means of preventing either outright rebellion or at least an insidious further spread of the Reformation. The worries of the emperor and the curia were evident; an extraordinary council for Germany would have a difficult time setting aright what had already gone wrong. Instead of pressing for a general council as quickly as possible, the established powers came forward with nothing better than the stern but sterile threatenings of the Edict of Worms. An otherwise politically oriented pope failed to see that the larger opportunity was slipping away. Even in Germany the choice fell to political expediency. Concern for a council or for church reform as such went into eclipse as Campeggio, the papal legate, pushed for the formation of the Regensburg Union [Ratisbon] (June 27 to July 7, 1524). In it Austria, Bavaria, and a dozen South German bishops allied themselves for the purpose of enforcing the Edict of Worms and for mutual assistance in case of rebellion. The union's modest and almost entirely financial and disciplinary reform program was limited to the grievances of the imperial estates. The program did not respond to issues raised by the Reformation, and such reforms as it advocated were quickly shot down by the refractoriness of the bishops. But the union made history: For the first time the empire was split by a special alliance on confessional grounds. A year later the evangelical side responded with its own League of Dessau. In northern Germany the league allied the electors of Brandenburg and of Mainz, Duke George of Saxony [sic], and the dukes of Braunschweig-Wolfenbüttel.[66] Did the emperor's veto of a German national assembly contribute to the outbreak of the Peasants' War? This is more easily claimed than proven.[67] At least the warning that this might happen had been sounded often enough, and after the domestic war was over, the estates of the empire were not slow to remind the emperor of their earlier warnings.[68] In retrospect, Luther too saw how interrelated these developments were. [With bitterness he reminded the clergy at Augsburg in 1530,] "There your counsel was full of wisdom and succeeded in getting that diet called off ungraciously, insultingly, and shamefully. Then quickly thereafter came the whip, namely,

66. More on this below, pp. 609ff.

67. G. Franz, *Der deutsche Bauernkreig*, 4th ed. (Darmstadt, 1956), 91. H. Baumgarten, *Geschichte Karls V* (Stuttgart, 1888), 2:393ff. H. von Schubert, *Revolution und Reformation im 16. Jahrhundert* (Tübingen, 1927), 25. Also, *Der Reichstag von Augsburg im Zusammenhang der Reformationsgeschichte*, SVRG 150 (Leipzig, 1930), 13. More careful is von Ranke, *Deutsche Geschichte*, 2:136, 140ff.

68. *Instruktion für die Gesandtschaft an den Kaiser nach dem ersten Speyrer Reichstag, August 1526*, printed in Friedensburg, *Reichstag zu Speier*, 560. Hofmann, "Konzilsfrage," 106.

Müntzer with revolt, and gave you a blow from which you still have not recovered and from which we unfortunately have suffered even greater damage."[69]

69. *Vermahnung an die Geistlichen* (1530), WA 30²:274 / 5ff. [*Exhortation to All Clergy Assembled at Augsburg, LW* 34:12.]

12

Reformation and the Formation of Prussia

Of the evangelical movement's early gains outside Electoral Saxony, none busied or pleased Luther more than those in East Prussia, the distant land of the Teutonic Knights. Next to the course of events in his native Electoral Saxony, that in East Prussia involved him very closely indeed. This was not another case of former Wittenberg students making the connection. While that tie was missing entirely, he was nevertheless able to send a couple of good and capable friends as preachers. East Prussia, especially, offered two points of contact not available elsewhere for a restructuring of political as well as ecclesial relationships. One was the necessity of recasting a state structure in which the traditional ecclesial-temporal relationship had become untenable. The other was the possibility for an authentic reformation from above, inasmuch as the two bishops in the territory had both joined the Lutheran movement. The uniqueness of this historic hour gave Luther direct or indirect influence, through his writings, far beyond ecclesiastical developments as such and into the main course of German history.[1]

Luther became involved unexpectedly. A messenger, Master Johann Oeden, brought Luther a highly confidential document in late June 1523. Dated June 14, it was from Albert of Brandenburg, grand master of the Teutonic Knights, whom Oeden served as privy counselor. Immediately on having read it, Luther was to burn it and to keep silent about it "to his dying day." Albert's confidence in Luther was evident in the salutation, "Dear Sir and Doctor, and in Christ beloved Brother!" The grand master had left it to his messenger, Oeden, to divulge "how we are learning that our order requires a reform 'in head and members,' and we intend to seek it by God's help. May God in heaven grant his grace thereto." Luther was requested "to amend" the accompanying statutes and regulations of the order. The grand master would then follow Luther's advice and undertake

1. Original introduction in the fine account by W. Hubatsch, *Geschichte der evangelischen Kirche Ostpreussens*, vol. 1: *Darstellung mit Literatur;* vol. 2: *Bilder ostpreussischer Kirchen;* vol. 3: *Dokumente* (Göttingen, 1968).

the reform, "so that it might be accomplished to God's glory and without creating resistance or rebellion." Besides, Master Oeden was to ask Luther how the grand master should deal with his territorial clergy, from bishops to parish priests, in order to enlist them in an honorable Christian undertaking and exercise.[2] Surprised as he might well have been by this overture, Luther had already for some time formed a good opinion of the grand master. He might still confuse the name, but to his friend Link he confided that he had been edified by Albert's recent retort to the papal legate, Chieregati [in Nuremberg], when he reportedly said "that he would willingly assist the church, but that condemning open truth and burning books is not a way to do it; they also say that he does not think badly of the gospel."[3] The relationship now developing had long antecedents.

The Teutonic Knights were a remnant of the great Christian militia of the crusades and the embodiment of the German nobility's ideal of service to the church and to public peace. During the fifteenth century the order regained its sense of purpose as well as found a new home base in its conquest of the then still pagan Prussians.[4] In the image of its own organization the order had created in East Prussia the first centralized German administrative state. It was a cross between a state in the empire and a component of the international church. Its distinctive and proud existence was based on its own performance and on assistance from its considerable possessions in the empire. The order experienced its bright political and intellectual flowering in the fifteenth century, before its subsequent irreversible decline set in. Now the antiquated military tactics of the Knights proved no match against the superior military power of the Poles and Lithuanians, who at Marienburg in 1410 had administered a decisive defeat. At the same time, a crisis in agricultural life ruined its German possessions and the circles from which the order drew its recruits. At first this occasioned an influx into the order from the lesser nobility, and in 1453 it commended itself to Emperor Frederick III as "the refuge of the German nobility."[5] At the same time, however, this led to stormy rivalries among

2. WA Br 3:86 / 3, 14; 87 / 17, 25ff. [Cf. LW 45:133–39 for background information.]

3. December 19, 1522, WA Br 2:633 / 31ff. Luther called Albert by his predecessor's name, Frederick (below, p. 319). [LW 49:22–24.]

4. For what follows, an overview and bibliography is in the writings of E. Maschke, [1] "Ritterorden," in RGG³ 5 (1961): 1121ff.; [2] "Die inneren Wandlungen des deutschen Ritterordens," in Geschichte und Gegenwartsbewusstsein: Historische Betrachtungen und Untersuchungen, Festschrift für H. Rothfels (Göttingen, 1963), 249ff.; [3] "Der Ordensstaat Preussen in seinen deutschen und europäischen Beziehungen," in ODW 8 (Munich, 1961), 187ff.

5. Cited in Maschke, "Innere Wandlungen," 272.

groups of compatriots who depended on the order for their sustenance. Above all, there was sharp opposition between the impoverished but still elitist Knights, on the one side, and the nobility and burghers, on the other. These tensions burst into a thirteen-year-long insurrection in which the nobles and burghers, with the help of the Poles, imposed on the Knights the Second Peace of Thorn (1466). This confined the order to the marginal eastern parts of Prussia and required the grand master to render the Polish king his oath of fealty as well as military support, though he was not forced to recognize the king formally as his overlord. The order, however, largely ignored the peace, although at times the Polish demands were inescapable. In its efforts to shake off these fetters, the order sought help no longer from the powerless empire but from certain German territorial states.

This was the first sign of a new age. With Frederick of Saxony the change began. He was in the Albertine line of the Wettin family and a brother of the later Duke George of Saxony. In 1498 he became the order's grand master, the first prince of the empire called to such a post.[6] Having studied in Italy, Frederick fostered modest beginnings of humanism and courtly splendor in the Königsberg castle, the residence of the grand master since the order's loss of Marienburg. The landed gentry found a welcome here, even though they were still denied membership in the order. Moreover, separation between the order and its administration widened as lay people became more and more prominent in the latter, a change made noticeable also by the secular attire now worn by the laity. The lands of the order were thus being transformed into a modern state, complete with representatives (estates) and officials. The sagacious grand master's lively game of diplomacy enabled him to refuse further recognition of the Peace of 1466 without renewed Polish intervention, for Poland was being threatened at its back by Russia. When the situation became too dangerous, the grand master switched tactics, and in 1507 he moved his residential seat to Rochlitz in Saxony. There Frederick bided his time amid an uneasy balance of power; on the one hand, the empire and Hungary; on the other, Poland—and the calculated passivity of the Roman curia, on whose decision the Poles waited. Things remained this way until Frederick's death in 1510.

Again in 1511 the order elected a prince of the empire as its grand master. This time it was twenty-year-old Albert of Brandenburg-Ansbach, ap-

---

6. K. Forstreuter, *Vom Ordensstaat zum Fürstentum: Geistige und politische Wandlungen im Deutschordensstaate Preussen unter den Hochmeistern Friedrich und Albrecht 1498–1525* (Kitzingen, 1951). W. Hubatsch, "Die inneren Voraussetzungen der Säkularisation des deutschen Ordensstaates in Preussen," *ARG* 43 (1952): 145ff.

parently a most fitting choice. On his father's side he was a Hohenzollern, a house that wielded significant influence in the empire. On his mother's side he had Polish ties, his maternal grandfather being Poland's King Casimir IV.[7] Appearances were misleading, however. When princes of the empire, especially the elector of Brandenburg, saw war threatening, they refused to take sides against Poland. For them Poland was a more welcome neighbor than the grand duchy of Moscow. Emperor Maximilian I, initially a supporter of the Russians, had encouraged the Teutonic Knights to resist the Poles, but now he favored the acceptance of a Polish offer of settlement between the Jagiello and the Hapsburg dynasties. The terms assured the Hapsburgs rights of succession in Hungary and Bohemia and thus strengthened the Austrian position against the Turks. In the ensuing Peace of Vienna, in 1515, King Sigismund guaranteed that the emperor would not support the Teutonic Knights against Poland. Since his accession in 1519, Maximilian's grandson, Charles V, had continued this political line.

Thus the young grand master, Albert, finding himself isolated, nevertheless saw his situation as anything but lost. He had campaigned with Emperor Maximilian and had always wished for an opportunity to fight the Turks. Animated and fearless, he prepared for a confrontation with Poland. His aim was to recover the order's lost territories and to regain its independence. His adviser, the daring but dangerous Dietrich von Schönberg, had but recently entered the grand master's service. Even so, a close friendship was developing between the two of them.[8] Never at a loss for plans, the highly gifted and confident Schönberg could formulate them with brilliance, verbally or in writing. Himself a nobleman from Meissen [Saxony], he was determined to guide Albert's political designs out into the open. Alliances with Russia and several of the imperial states were to secure his position east and west, and a large armed force recruited in Germany was to support the weak troops of the grand master. Alas, while Schönberg's plans progressed only slowly, Albert was growing anxious. The Poles, meanwhile, had become suspicious and challenged Albert. He was soon in dire straits, especially because he had already dissipated his forces in smaller ventures. Ill-advised though his acts were, he nevertheless proved himself resolute under trial. At last, in April 1521, he managed to wrest a temperate four-year armistice from this bad situation. The terms

7. W. Hubatsch, *Albrecht von Brandenburg-Ansbach: Deutschordens-Hochmeister und Herzog in Preussen, 1490–1568* (Heidelberg, 1960), 26ff.

8. Forstreuter, *Ordensstaat*, 60ff.

included a settlement of all disputed issues by a court of arbitration composed of foremost princes of the empire and of the church. Schönberg, meanwhile, continued to promote his flamboyant plans for an anti-Hapsburg scheme of alliance. After the armistice, his trips to Moscow led to other journeys. Yet in Denmark, England, Scotland, and France he met scant success. Participating with the French in the battle of Pavia [against the emperor's forces] on February 24, 1525, he was on the losing side and lost his life, a fitting end for a man of his tireless but unpromising political activity.

With the name Schönberg the first mention of Luther came up in the circle of Albert's associates. At a secret meeting in Lochstedt in September 1521, Albert assigned Schönberg the task of inquiring of Elector Frederick the Wise about the possibility of having Luther examine the Rule of the Teutonic Knights. It is not clear whether Schönberg, with his knowledge of Saxony, actually did make the proposal, but it may be assumed that he did.[9] Indeed, he himself had seen Luther in Worms, but then, as well as to the time of death, Schönberg clung to the side of the old believers. Shortly after Worms he visited Wittenberg, but missed Luther. On grounds of caution he avoided forwarding the rule of the order whether through the mediation of the elector or otherwise.[10]

During these years Grand Master Albert had given Schönberg a free hand, but politically he had to find his own way. Virtually bereft of outside help, and with time running out on the four-year armistice, Albert redoubled his efforts to secure support from the empire, opportunely so at the second Nuremberg diet (1522–23).[11] As an active participant, he sat on no less than six committees, among them the important one on "how to respond to the pope on the Luther issue." Ironically, he was representing his high Catholic Hohenzollern relatives, among them Cardinal Albrecht of Mainz (1523) and Elector Joachim I of Brandenburg (1524). His urgent appeal to the imperial estates in mid-February 1523 (to secure Poland's participation in the court of arbitration and in the peace negotiations or, in case of another war, to grant imperial assistance to the Teutonic Knights) fell on receptive ears. His would-be supporters were as diverse as the

9. On his slip there was simply this reminder: "Nota churfurst Sachssen, reformacionem libri per doctorem Luther." In E. Joachim, "Des Hochmeisters Albrecht von Preussen erster Versuch einer Annäherung an Luther," ZKG 12 (1891): 119. Forstreuter, Ordensstaat, 75.

10. According to letters of January 16 and February 12, 1522, Schönberg indeed spoke with the elector but did not send the book to Wittenberg for Luther to read because he heard "that Martin was having much trouble in that place," an allusion to the Wittenberg unrest. Joachim, "Albert von Preussen," 121.

11. Hubatsch, Albrecht, 104ff.

Council of Regency, the emperor's viceroy, King Ferdinand, the curia, and the Franconian imperial knights—the latter already partly evangelical. But things never moved beyond the stage of talk and print. In view of the emperor's unclear political situation within and beyond the empire, no one in Poland took the sounds emanating from Nuremberg seriously. For Albert, the grand master, the diet's importance lay finally not in using it as a political stage but in experiencing it as a place of personal decision, for it so happened that the perceptive prince was deeply moved by the impassioned preaching of Andreas Osiander, in Nuremberg's Church of St. Lawrence. Much later Albert assured him, "You alone are the instrument through which I came to a godly, right, and true understanding."[12] So it was with Albert's other associations while in Nuremberg. He mingled with the evangelically oriented local patricians, especially Lazarus Spengler, as well as with Electoral Saxony's councillors and, even more so, with Franconia's. Men like Schwarzenberg and Vogler, among others, contributed to his planned approach to Luther. After an initially fruitless attempt (no doubt in April 1523), developments at last had reached the point where, as mentioned at the outset, we find Master Oeden.[13]

The results of the connection with Luther were determined by three partly antecedent assumptions: (1) The territory of the Teutonic order had over a long period been detaching itself from its original constitution and was developing the features of a modern state. (2) The territory faced a virtually hopeless situation with no prospect of outside help but with the need to make a decision before 1525. (3) Grand Master Albert had personally found support in the gospel during these difficult years and had quietly joined the reform movement led by Luther. At first Luther was aware only of Albert's personal change, yet this carried implications for his office as grand master as well as for the future of his order. As these aspects

---

12. Letter to Osiander, April 30, 1540. J. Voigt, *Briefwechsel der berühmtesten Gelehrten des Zeitalters der Reformation mit Herzog Albrecht von Preussen: Beiträge zur Gelehrten-, Kirchen- und politischen Geschichte des 16. Jahrhunderts, aus Originalbriefen dieser Zeit* (Königsberg, 1841), 479. Cited by P. Tschackert, *Herzog Albrecht von Preussen als reformatorische Persönlichkeit*, SVRG 45 (Halle, 1894), 14. Albrecht called Osiander to Königsberg in 1549. A survey of unpublished religious notes of Albrecht from a later period is in E. Roth, "Neues Material zur Reformationsgeschichte," *ThLZ* 75 (1950): 763ff. Additional literature in *RGG*³ 1 (1957): 219, and K. Schottenloher, *Bibliographie der deutschen Geschichte im Zeitalter der Glaubensspaltung, 1517–1585* (Leipzig, 1933ff.), 7 (1966), nos. 61768ff.

13. The consignment mentioned by Hubatsch, *Albrecht*, 118, from Bastian Staartz, in Nuremberg, to Luther, followed not in 1523 but in 1524 (as becomes apparent in ibid., 317, n. 25; later the reference is correct in Hubatsch, *Geschichte*, 1:13). A journey with Melanchthon to Magdeburg is first mentioned for June 1524.

were all interwined, they pressed for a broad settlement. We do not know Luther's reply to Albert's modest initial request that he improve on the rule, or statutes, of the order. But in late November 1523 the grand master himself visited Wittenberg and opened the way for a more inclusive discussion of the order's problem. Albert's situation had recently worsened. A costly effort of his to help restore Denmark's refugee king, Christian II, to the throne had miscarried. Of course, he had hoped thereby to gain a future ally. It was on his return from Denmark that Albert, in frustration, came to Luther on the first Sunday in Advent, November 29.[14] Later, on July 4, 1524, Luther summed up this meeting in a letter to a friend.

> The first time I spoke with Prince Albert, the grand master, he asked my opinion of his order's rule. I advised him to drop this foolish and confused rule and instead to marry and to give Prussia the political format of either a principality or a duchy. From Philipp Melanchthon he received the same reaction and advice. At that time Albert simply smiled and said nothing. Meanwhile, I see that this advice pleased him and that he desires to carry it out as soon as possible.[15]

Surely the idea was not new to Albert. But it was important for him to hear it straight from Luther, who in the course of that long-sought discussion brushed aside any mere patching of the rule.

For his part, Albert's concern extended beyond the affairs of his order and the issues of territory. The larger problem, that of the church, was on his mind. The questions he left for Luther to answer indicate as much. For instance, how is the papacy founded on Peter? What is the power of the pope, of the bishops, or of councils of the church? As for church regulations on fasting, holy days, and other externals, to what extent are they binding? Likewise, in the case of adultery how valid are papal dissolutions of marriage or, otherwise also, the impediments to marriage as papally claimed yet not forbidden by divine law? Luther's response, conveyed in a

---

14. Cf. WA Br 3:207 and the letter to the pastor in Königsberg, Briessmann, of July 4, 1524; WA Br 3:315 / 22ff. The surmise that Albert had already been in Wittenberg once before, on November 14, 1523, and had spoken with Luther (WA Br 3:195) is ruled out by the expense record of the grand master's stay in Berlin, October 24–November 26. See *Urkundenbuch zur Reformationsgeschichte des Herzogtums Preussen*, ed. P. Tschackert (Leipzig, 1890; reprint, Osnabrück, 1965), 2:15, n. 1. The November 14 date (a recorded delivery of oats in Wittenberg) implies preparation for the visit of an entourage. See G. Buchwald, "*Lutherana*. Notizen aus Rechnungsbüchern des Thüringischen Staatsarchivs zu Weimar," *ARG* 25 (1928): 27–28. The first conversation, as mentioned to Briessmann, does not imply an earlier one. WA Br 3:195, no. 686, but that of November 29, 1523; this is in contrast to the second one of May 12, 1524, about which our only evidence is a reference in the grand master's itinerary. Tschackert, ed., *Urkundenbuch*, 2:15.

15. To Johann Briessmann, WA Br 3:315 / 22ff. Cf. also n. 44, below, p. 331.

brief Latin composition, was guided by the comprehensive maxim "In the church, the pope and all servants of the Word have but one thing to promote: the 'mysteries of God' (1 Cor. 4:1), the Word of life, the doctrine of faith, and they are not to promote their own opinions or anything contrary to the Word of God." Whatever exceeds this Word or is contrary to it is not permitted. Luther sent his reply (probably in January 1524) through Spalatin, who like the grand master was at the diet in Nuremberg. Albert was so pleased with this utterly precise reply to issues at the center of the current ecclesiastical and political debate that he ordered a German translation. Within the year it had appeared in eight almost exclusively South German printings.[16]

More important, however, was the simultaneous and decisive step that Luther took publicly on the issue of the order. His *Exhortation to the Knights of the Teutonic Order That They Lay Aside False Chastity and Assume the True Chastity of Wedlock* appeared in Wittenberg still before the end of 1523 and, in the customary practice, was quickly reprinted elsewhere.[17] As might be expected, Luther here applied his critique of monastic vows to the situation of the Knights' order. As a mongrel organization, it at least raised the question how to "reconcile" the temporal and the spiritual.[18] Small wonder that in this semi-military existence, replete with motives of adventure or physical maintenance, the traditional monastic vows were far more jeopardized than in the more shielded cloister life. Nor was it helpful when a Duke George, to whom the grand master had

16. Latin and German abbreviated text (*Concerning the Marriage Question*), WA Br 3:207ff. Printings in J. Benzing, *Lutherbibliographie: Verzeichnis der gedruckten Schriften Martin Luthers bis zu dessen Tod* (Baden-Baden, 1911), nos. 2010–17. [Cf. *LW* 45:135–39.]

17. WA 12:229ff. Older research, based on the Jena edition, dated the publication as of March 28, 1523. It is unlikely that Luther would have gone ahead on his own and intervened so sharply in the affairs of the order. But Kawerau (WA 12:229–30), taking into account the printing practices of that day, has shown convincingly that this work could have been published only in late 1523, after the grand master's visit. (The original printing is dated 1523. Cf. Benzing, *Lutherbibliographie*, no. 1716, and the always rapidly following reprints of 1524.) In his reworking of Köstlin's *Lutherbiographie*, 621–22, Kawerau has made a pertinent presentation. Also, the date first given by Tschackert in his *Urkundenbuch* (1890, see n. 14, above), is corrected in his monograph *Herzog Albrecht von Preussen* (1894; n. 12, above), 98–99, in which he follows *WA*. Likewise T. Kolde, *Martin Luther: Eine Biographie* (Gotha, 1884), 573. A sure indication of when Luther's exhortation initially appeared is that the always well-informed Duke George of Saxony first received it on January 4, 1524; F. Gess, *Akten und Briefe zur Kirchenpolitik Herzog Georgs von Sachsen* (Leipzig, 1905ff.), 1: nos. 594, 599–600. Unfortunately his use of old editions of Luther's works and letters causes the wrong date to appear in the two works by Hubatsch (*Albrecht*, 118ff., and *Geschichte*, 1:11). (See also n. 28, below.) [Cf. *LW* 45:138–39.]

18. WA 12:232 / 13. [*LW* 45:141–42.]

unburdened himself on the problem of chastity, suggested that the men need not necessarily adhere to the rules of the order.[19]

At the same time, however, Luther saw an easier escape from this dilemma when dealing with an order of Knights than with a cloister community. He wrote:

> Your order has the advantage of being provided with the temporal necessities of life. Its wealth can be parceled out among the Knights; they could become landholders or officeholders or take up some other useful calling. You are not faced with the wretched poverty that keeps many a mendicant friar and other monk in the monastery for the sake of his belly.[20]

Even though this was more true of the Teutonic order's commanderies in Germany than of the poor circumstances in East Prussia, Luther nevertheless saw the possibility that in time there would develop "a true and duly constituted knighthood, free from hypocrisy and a false name and acceptable in the sight of God and of the world."[21] In God's sight—in Luther's eyes, over against all human viewpoints, that was the decisive point. Therefore he did not hesitate to be emphatic with the members of the order, holding up their real sin and their disobedience against God's Word: "'It is not good that the man should be alone; I will make him a helper' (Gen. 2:18). Unless, of course, God himself by a miracle should make an exception of me. We should stand in fear and terror of this Word, which has the support of all angels and creatures from the beginning of the world."[22] God is blasphemed by the coercion which the church has exercised against this law of creation. Besides, "fornication or unchastity is certainly a great sin, but it is a minor fault when compared with blasphemy."[23] Let this be the standard by which men of the order measure their dutiful obedience, and not church regulations. And against the objection (stated in terms of church law) that it takes a council to revoke the decision of a previous council,[24] Luther contended that the thing at issue

19. Forstreuter, *Ordensstaat*, 66, and Albert's personally written note on Duke George's comments [namely, that the requirements, if important at all, should be followed by those in the order as well as by those in cloisters. Members are not warranted to do wrong in secrecy].

20. *WA* 12:232 / 25ff. [*LW* 45:142.]

21. *WA* 12:232 / 31ff. [*LW* 45: 142.]

22. *WA* 12:235 / 25ff. [*LW* 45:145, 146.]

23. *WA* 12:237 / 12–13. [*LW* 45:148.]

24. So, e.g., John Faber in his polemic against Luther (1522), to which Justus Jonas in August 1523 wrote a rebuttal, with a preface by Luther. *WA* 12:81ff. [Cf. *LW* 45:147.]

concerns a human destiny. Now "suppose the councils should delay, and I should have to die before they could make up their minds. What would become of my soul, meanwhile, since it is not supposed to know what to believe but to await the decision of councils, when I need faith here on earth?"[25] Let the Knights therefore not be like Lot's wife and look around to see what others are doing. Instead, "if you feel your nature and know that God wishes you to be married, you ought to go right ahead, even though you should have to be the first and the only one to marry, and regardless of what all men, friend and foe, have to say about it."[26]

Luther's penetrating counseling of the consciences of the men of the order certainly did not run counter to the intention of its grand master. It is a safe bet, even if we cannot prove it, that this subject was discussed during Albert's visit in Wittenberg; none other than Duke George surmised it and immediately reported it to Albert's brother Casimir.[27] The grand master knew the sore point of celibacy only too well as it affected his order. Although Luther's proposal aimed at a dissolution of the order's hitherto governing rule, it also advocated a closer bond with the land on the part of the order's members. Were this to happen, it would reduce the threat of men quitting the order and, correspondingly, would strengthen Albert's position.[28]

Luther's advice to the men of the order landed in a reform movement already under way in Prussia.[29] As we focus again on June 1523 and Master Oeden's conveying the grand master's request for assistance in renewing the East Prussian priesthood, Luther recommended that Dr. Johann Briessmann be called. Luther rated Briessmann highly. Born in Cottbus in 1488, Briessmann joined the Franciscans, studied in Wittenberg, and received his doctorate in 1522. Following the Leipzig disputation in 1519, he found himself drawn increasingly to Luther's side.[30] Earlier in 1523

25. *WA* 12:236 / 32ff. [*LW* 45:148.]

26. *WA* 12:243 / 7ff. [*LW* 45:156.]

27. January 2, 1524, Tschackert, ed., *Urkundenbuch*, 2:45. Gess, *Akten*, 1:599.

28. The different estimate of this tract and the presumably different reaction of Albert, in Hubatsch, *Albrecht*, 120–21, arises essentially from the question of chronology (see n. 17, above).

29. Basic for what follows is Tschackert, *Urkundenbuch*, vols. 1 and 2.

30. "For about twelve years I was tied up in scholastic disputes and was very much opposed to the gospel. At last my gracious God, who is rich in mercy, pulled me out of the stew of sophistry in which I had nearly drowned and led me on." Thus Briessmann reported in his tract *Unterricht und Ermahnung . . . an die Christlich gemeyn zu Cottbus* (1523) [Instruction and Admonition . . . to the Christian Congregation in Cottbus] printed in *ZHTh* 20 (1850): 502ff. He there provides a fine brief summation of the Reformation thought he had preached in Cottbus the previous year. R. Stupperich, "Johann Briessmanns reformatorische Anfänge," *JBrKG* 34 (1939): 3ff. C. F. D. Erdmann, "Briessmann," *RE*³ 3: 398–405.

Luther had left it to Briessmann to refute a published attack by Schatzgeyer on Luther's book concerning monastic vows. Indeed, Luther could not have sent a better man to Königsberg. Briessmann was discreet, thoroughly educated in theology, and a trusted friend. Presently his sermon in the cathedral on September 27, 1523, struck the keynote of the Reformation in Prussia. Immediately he addressed himself to the most pressing task at hand: to provide the clergy with a concise, communicable outline of the gospel from the standpoint of the Reformation. Already in October he published 110 theses under the title *Flosculi de homine interiore et exteriore, fide et operibus* [Selected Blooms on Man's Interior and Exterior Life, on Faith and Works].[31] He let no one be mistaken as to the two fronts he opposed: the Erasmian anthropology and the Catholic doctrine of grace, with the concepts of ministry and church included for debate.

In theme and language, Briessmann's treatment reflects a monastic perception of the theological realm and thus binds him more intensively to Luther than was the case with Melanchthon's *Loci*. With Briessmann, Luther's style, especially that in his tract on Christian liberty and commentary on Galatians, shines through again and again. Luther's example and his own native freshness of experience enabled Briessmann to compose masterful formulations. He knew that in God's apparently unattainable commandments our own despair takes its rise. Thesis 24, for example, declares, "This despair is not the least important element in Christianity. But trusting in our own powers is just that, for the very doing of what is just within our power is the main article of a hypocritical perversity." With the armor and shield of faith we can banish despair. Faith decides our eternal destiny. Thesis 35, in its clipped Latinity, recites "*Sicut sola fides justificat, ita sola infidelitas damnat* [Just as faith alone justifies, so also unfaith alone condemns]." But genuine faith, as Thesis 28 says, "at once breaks out in good works and does not leave us idle; indeed, it enables us to do any and all things freely, without any law, and joyfully, without any commandment, so that our light may shine among men." Faith, when properly understood, unites us with Christ "in happy wedlock," wherein all Christians stand equal. Therefore, as Thesis 67 goes on, it has been the greatest misfortune in the history of the church to separate the "spiritual" and the "temporal" from each other. Whoever has done this "we declare him guilty of extinguishing faith, grace, and Chris-

31. The *Flosculi* (Selection of Blooms) has been reprinted recently in the collection of documents published by R. Stupperich, *Die Reformation im Ordensland Preussen, 1523–24*, QODKG 6 (Ulm, 1966), 36ff. The accompanying translation required correction, however.

tian liberty and of destroying the whole of Christianity." Briessmann's Thesis 98 affirms realistically that the radicality of the split in human nature, the absoluteness of faith in the Word of redemption, and the impulse to love are inseparably bound up with one another. Moreover, "from Christ we have received the name 'Christian' not simply to represent ourselves nominally so but in order that we really are as a Christ to our neighbor, in that we endeavor to live like Christ." Thesis 108 concludes, "We are called Christians not only because of the absent Christ but also because of the indwelling Christ."

The most important testimony on the influence exercised by Briessmann is that of his bishop, George von Polentz.[32] Born into an old line of Meissen [Saxony] nobility, Polentz had studied law in Italy, had served Pope Julius II and Emperor Maximilian in political office, and finally joined the Teutonic order. Upon the proposal of Grand Master Albert, who had gladly made use of his administrative talent, Polentz was elected bishop of Samland, yet not until his still missing ordinations [as deacon and priest] were hastily acquired in 1519. Three years later, when Albert had to be absent in Germany, he named Polentz his regent. For three years, beginning in 1522, Polentz governed a land devastated by war and hounded by poverty, while at the same time widespread unrest contributed to a creeping dissolution of the Teutonic order. No wonder such circumstances enabled him to perform his spiritual duties only seldom. All the greater, then, was the attention his Christmas sermon attracted when he peached in the cathedral in Königsberg in 1523.[33]

Passionately Polentz owned up to the new understanding of the gospel, setting the inclusive and joyful message of the angels over against the current conditions and religion business of the church. He spelled it out, asking, What have a complicated scholastic theology and Aristotelian philosophy, the casuistry of church law, the vows and the rivalries of monastic orders, votive masses and masses for the dead, indulgences, rosaries, pilgrimages, rules of fasting, veneration of saints and meritorious works— what have all these human contrivances to do with the message of the birth of Christ our Savior? "You must believe that he was born for you—I say, *for you*." In order that people might more readily grasp the meaning of the gospel, Polentz announced that henceforth baptism would be performed in German and that, because he himself was overloaded with

32. P. Tschackert, "Georg von Polentz, Bischof von Samland," *Kirchengeschichtliche Studien: H. Reuter zum 70. Geburtstag* (Leipzig, 1888), 145ff. Hubatsch, *Geschichte*, 1:23ff.

33. Printed in Stupperich, *Reformation*, 14ff., and Hubatsch, *Geschichte*, 3:1ff.

work, he was appointing Briessmann as cathedral preacher. In the torrent of complaint against the inherited church enterprise, Polentz nevertheless injected a personal tone of earnestness and warmth. He blamed himself also for the current state of the church and acknowledged the weighty burden of his office, seeing that he had now been installed as an "overseer of souls" in his diocese. "Therefore, with divine help I willingly assume the task of holding forth on the subject of God's Word and the gospel, even though it may cost me my life and living, possessions and honor, and all I have."[34]

Proceeding from his Christmas sermon, a January 28, 1524, mandate from Polentz to his Samland pastors spelled out the first steps toward church reform. He began with the points most obvious to the congregations: Baptisms henceforth would be in German. After all, what can come forth from the sacrament without the Word or faith? He also pointed out the necessity of recognizing the Lithuanian, Prussian, and Sarmatian languages, "so that these people too may not be lacking in Christian instruction." To the preachers he recommended Luther's Bible translation as an aid to understanding the Scriptures. He further endorsed a number of Luther's writings: *The Freedom of a Christian Man, A Treatise on Good Works,* his *Postil* [book of sermons], *The Magnificat,* his exposition of the Psalms, and others.[35] As a liturgical aid, Polentz published a Königsberg edition of Luther's baptismal booklet.[36] In a sequence of sermons on the festival days of the church year, Polentz repeatedly demonstrated his talent for telling the truth of the gospel with pointed simplicity; his style was gripping, at times brightened with a flash of humor. Attacks on him were not long in coming, but these made him the more resolute. The sharpest and crudest blow came on January 20, 1524, from a fellow bishop, Moritz Ferber of Ermland, who attacked not Polentz as much as the invading plague of Luther's teaching.[37] From this time forward, the two parts of East Prussia went progressively separate ways, so enduring was the impact of the opposing stand taken by the two bishops. Luther gave these developments his characteristic interpretation. For him the content and tone of the two dissimilar episcopal mandates embodied effectively the

34. Stupperich, *Reformation,* 17. Hubatsch, 3:6.

35. Stupperich, *Reformation,* 108ff.

36. WA 12:41. Benzing, *Lutherbibliographie,* no. 1638. [*LW* 53:95–103. *The Order of Baptism* (1523).]

37. The usual assumption—that Polentz's mandate to his pastors was to refute Ferber's attack—is difficult to believe. The mandate arises quite naturally from the Christmas sermon and its single theme, baptism. There is not even one syllable in Polentz's mandate that refers to the hail of reproaches from the bishop of Ermland.

fruits of the old and the new spirit, and he elaborated on this turn of events in a pamphlet.[38]

Luther well knew that something extraordinary was afoot in East Prussia. For the first time a bishop in office had espoused the new teaching, and a movement had begun. It had not been kindled by externals like the indulgence issue, but was being fed by the source of the gospel. Also, the later sermons and homilies by Polentz, which Briessmann published in 1524, testify to a rich experiencing of the Reformation's central themes: "A Sermon . . . on the Struggles of Faith and Hope" (on the woman of Canaan, Matt. 15:21ff.), "A Sermon on Three Kinds of Confession," "Some Comforting Verses for the Fearful and Fainthearted" (or "Weak Consciences," the latter title used in later editions).[39] Luther never doubted that here was a place full of promise, and he accordingly lent a hand as much as possible—and all the more so when a second preacher, Johannes Amandus, recommended by Luther to the grand master, turned out to be an egocentric demagogue. As Luther reflected later, Amandus had something of Karlstadt's temperament and some of his aggressive legalism. There was more to it than what the chamberlain Christoph von Gattenhofen reported to the grand master, that the councilmen and church fathers, attacked by Amandus, "would like to get rid of him and maybe accept another who had been preaching about Dietrich of Bern." No, Amandus had already gone as far as to incite the people to violence, and at Easter 1524 he got them to storm the cloisters.[40]

News of the tumults made Luther apprehensive. From what he himself was experiencing at that moment in the struggles with his own "prophets and sects" (Karlstadt and Müntzer) he surely knew how quickly a situation could become radicalized. But he breathed easier when Briessmann sent him reassuring news. Besides, Luther happily had been able to provide an outstanding co-worker whom the grand master had called to Königsberg. He was Dr. Paul Speratus, "a worthy man who has suffered much."[41] Only recently Speratus had completed an odyssey of several years in Wittenberg. In 1521, while serving as cathedral canon in Würzburg, he took up Luther's line of thought, married, and was forced to

38. *Duae episcopales bullae . . . super doctrina Lutherana et Romana* (1524), WA 15:146–54.

39. Stupperich, *Reformation*, 54–55.

40. Tschackert, *Urkundenbuch*, 1:48–49, 83–84, 95ff. Material assembled by O. Clemen, WA Br 3:317, 419. The letter from Gattenhofen, February 9, 1524, is in Tschackert, *Urkundenbuch*, 2: no. 183. Luther's assessment is in WA Br 3:418 / 10.

41. July 4, 1524. WA Br 3:315 / 9ff.

surrender his office. Then in Salzburg and again in Vienna he was ousted after only brief periods as a preacher. A call to Ofen, Hungary, fell through. Even in Iglau, Moravia, where he was remarkably effective, Speratus was tried for heresy and condemned to the stake, a fiery death which he escaped thanks to the intervention of some influential followers.[42]

The grand master had met Speratus in Luther's house in November 1523, yet it was only after a return to his Iglau congregation became impossible that Albert could authorize Bishop Polentz to call Speratus to Königsberg as castle chaplain. At the same time, Albert used the opportunity to reemphasize that the clergy in his territory are to preach "nothing but the gospel" and to avoid anything beyond that which could arouse "insurrection and resentment."[43] Given this situation, Luther pressed that his proposal, so approvingly received by Albert, be carried out. He regarded a territory governed by an order as anachronistic, "a hermaphrodite, neither monk nor layman." Let it be changed into a temporal principality. He also urged the grand master himself to get married. As for Luther, he assured Briessmann that he would keep his ears open to petitions from the people, especially from the upper levels, which should carefully stimulate the preacher.[44] In Königsberg, meanwhile, Polentz energetically cleared the stage. Amandus, again charged with intrigue, was run out of town. His explusion was fortunate in light of imminent developments. In the peasant revolt in Prussia in 1525, the only significant one in eastern Germany and one intensified by postwar conditions, Amandus would surely have played the part of a Prussian Thomas Müntzer.[45]

In the meantime the reform movement was spreading rapidly, especially when the newly elected bishop of Pomerania (based in Riesenburg) joined it. Bishop Erhard von Queiss, like Polentz, had been a lawyer and a diplomat, but unlike Polentz he was not much in theology. On January 1, 1525, he gave his diocese a formal constitution, but its focus was limited to ceremonial and legal matters. He abolished much: Except for baptism and the Lord's Supper, the other five sacraments were dropped; so also were excommunication, mandatory confession and fasting, pilgrimages, proces-

---

42. P. Tschackert, *Paul Speratus von Rötlen, evangelischer Bischof von Pomeranien in Marienwerder*, SVRG 33 (Halle, 1891). K. Schottenloher, *Bibliographie der deutschen Geschichte im Zeitalter der Glaubensspaltung, 1517–1585* (Leipzig, 1933ff.), 2: nos. 20373–96; 7: no. 58288.

43. July 13, 1524, Tschackert, *Urkundenbuch*, 2: no. 230.

44. WA Br 3:315 / 27–316 / 47. Continuation of n. 15, above, p. 323, at the place cited.

45. Tschackert, *Urkundenbuch*, 1:98. On the peasant revolt in Prussia, see G. Franz, *Der deutsche Bauernkrieg*, 4th ed. (Darmstadt, 1956), 276ff.

sions, daily mass and masses for the dead, and many customs, as well as
church-imposed impediments to marriage and celibacy for priests and
cloister folk. With so much abolished, mention of the Reformation faith—
in the context of church law—occurred in only this one anathema: "If
anyone should think himself capable, on his own, to make satisfaction for
his sin and to save himself without the merit of Christ, let him be anathema—anathematized be that person!"[46] Though the changes were only
ceremonial, they made Pomesia too a diocese of an evangelical type, a
change achieved before the Teutonic order's territory went secular. Unlike
Polentz, Queiss ran his diocese himself, and in 1527 he allowed it to become a new duchy. However, he continued as bishop until his early death
in 1529.[47]

Despite the continuing presence of many old believers, Prussia had
become an evangelical country in spiritual as well as formal ways. The
political decision in this direction had become unavoidable for the grand
master. The 1521 armistice with Poland expired. Neither the emperor nor
the empire nor any of the imperial princes had been able to promise him
help. Charles V simply warned him not to let things lapse into war. Plans
of a court of arbitration, which Albert had pursued for years, were proving
impracticable. In this hopeless situation there was, indeed, more at stake
than the existence of an order's territory. Once it fell (which was inevitable
without help) Livonia [to the north, on the Baltic] could no longer be
defended against the Russians. In June 1524 the grand master explained
his plight to the emperor's viceroy, Archduke Ferdinand. With emphasis,
and with reference also to the archduke's own situation, the grand master
summarized the dilemma one more time: the German nation, "in any
case, would soon have a young Turk lodged at its side."[48] Yet this was
precisely one reason that the empire was powerless to help. For Albert,
finally, it became a matter of taking the advice of shrewd friends (like that
of John von Schwarzenberg and Bishop Erhard von Queiss, whom he had
come to know well in the Council of Regency) and then of awaiting the
terms Poland would present him in due course. Finally, in Cracow, on
Palm Sunday, April 9, 1525, a peace treaty was signed. Behind it lay

46. *Themata Episcopi Risenburgensis*. Full text published for the first time in Tschackert,
Urkundenbuch, 2: no. 300. Also in Stupperich, *Reformation*, 111, citation no. 21.

47. Hubatsch, *Geschichte*, 1: 26ff.; literature cited there, 486. The diocesan deed of transmittal to Duke Albert, October 23, 1527, ibid., 3:10–11.

48. E. Joachim, *Die Politik des letzten Hochmeisters in Preussen Albrecht von Brandenburg*, vol. 3, Publikationen aus den K. Preussischen Staatsarchiven 61 (Leipzig, 1895), no.
180. Hubatsch, *Albrecht*, 127.

lengthy negotiations in which Grand Master Albert's Silesian relatives (his brother, Margrave George in Jägerdorf, and his brother-in-law, Duke Frederick of Liegnitz) had played a mediating role. Some dormant issues revived. The old provision in the Peace of Thorn (1466), requiring the Teutonic order's grand master by a personal oath of fealty to recognize His Highness the King of Poland, was now expanded into a feudal relationship of dependency.[49] Although he had resisted this kind of hereditary homage as long as possible, Albert went through the full ceremony on the day following the signing of the treaty. It was a bitter pill, but he had at least retained a limited independence for Prussia under his family, inclusive of the descendants of his three brothers—the latter provision having been added at the last moment. Easter came, the armistice expired, and any countermeasures against a far superior Poland were thereafter unthinkable.[50] At least he was confident that the nobles and burghers of his country would agree with him. So far they had urged him in this direction. Likewise the country folk. The peasants had had their fill of those gentlemen of the castles—members of the order—who came mostly for only a brief period and upon departing took with them whatever goods they had amassed. "If these lands were made hereditary, then things would remain here and the country could be improved and developed."[51]

It did not require the Reformation to find this solution, but under the circumstances this was the only way out. Nevertheless, church reform compounded the complexity of events. Luther's advice aimed entirely at the secularization of the Teutonic order's territory. He advocated it on two grounds: to abolish an unwholesome, unevangelical mongrel organization and to give the land a settled governance and an upper class. The issue of feudal dependence on Poland lay outside Luther's horizon. For Albert, however, his own determined turning toward the reforming evangel, as well as the rapid spread of the Reformation in his country, presented in some ways a rising political danger: the imposition of excommunication and outlawry, should it come, would make him turn to Poland for protection. Yet at the moment these were minor worries. Indeed, imperial action against him was even less likely than the repeatedly sought imperial

49. G. Rhode, *Kleine Geschichte Polens* (Darmstadt, 1965), 156, 192. Hubatsch, *Albrecht*, 125ff.

50. In a letter from Cracow on April 11, 1525, to Archduke Ferdinand, Albert thus justified the step he had taken, pointing out that what they had discussed in June 1524 had now inevitably occurred. Joachim, *Politik*, 3: no. 232.

51. Tschackert, *Urkundenbuch*, 1:109, n. 1, from a letter of the collector of revenues, Rentmeister Breuer, December 18, 1524. Also, ibid., 2: nos. 283, 293.

help had been. At this decisive turn in Prussia's history, however, it was far more important that Albert became not only politically but also spiritually committed to the gospel, a fact uniting him closer to his country than ever before. Alongside the painful capitulation of full sovereignty there was now also a new beginning worthy of his most intense application. On May 9, 1525, he returned to Prussia as duke. Paul Speratus welcomed him home in the name of the people. At once Albert tackled his new options, and among other things quickly overcame the minor opposition lurking within the order.

On the broader scene, the act of homage by the territorial assembly brought two major changes: the oath of allegiance of the estates and their commitment to the treaty with Poland, and the surrender by Bishop Polentz of temporal power in his diocese and its transfer to the new duke. The first step was thus taken to end the very old episcopal system of territorial governance. This was a reformationlike act of recognition: "That for him, a prelate and bishop obligated to preach and proclaim the Word of God, it is not fitting to rule over lands and people or to possess castles, land and towns." For Polentz this was an impressive act of assistance for his prince, now deeply in debt because of war and other burdens. Far rather than his own little diocese, Polentz would like to have offered Duke Albert one like Mainz, Trier, or Cologne.[52] As for the parishes, Albert's first mandate, published July 6, 1525, called on the clergy to preach the plain and pure gospel and the congregations to support the clergy and to live like Christians.[53] To the next territorial assembly Duke Albert even invited Luther, counting on his help to draw up a new constitution for the church. Unfortunately, the peasant unrest kept Luther away. Albert himself was required urgently in Silesia and had to postpone the assembly. During his absence a peasant revolt broke out also in Prussia. The peasants were not against their duke but against the nobles and the very severe Polentz, who was functioning as Albert's deputy. But the revolt collapsed quickly on the return of the duke and his imposing company of horsemen.[54]

Meanwhile, Luther had sent Albert a detailed sketch for an order of worship.[55] That sketch has not been preserved, but it probably became basic to the "Articles on Ceremonies and Other Church Orders," pub-

---

52. Ibid., 2: no. 356.
53. Ibid., 1:118–19; 2: no. 371.
54. Hubatsch, *Albrecht*, 144ff. Franz, *Bauernkrieg*, 276ff.
55. According to his letter to Briessmann (after August 15, 1525?), WA Br 3:555 / 4–5.

lished by the two bishops on action by the December assembly.[56] The order for the mass was essentially that of Luther's *Formula Missae et Communis* (1523). This was supplemented with beautiful liturgical forms and suggestions for other worship services. During Holy Communion, for example, Luther's hymns from his little hymnal of 1524 should be sung, including "Jesus Christ our blessed Savior" and "May God be praised henceforth and blest."[57] The connection with the evangelically purified mass as well as his own additions breathe Luther's spirit. The same is true of the language question: All parts carrying the actual proclamation are to be intelligible, while Latin is retained in the chanted portions, largely on educational grounds. The two languages are interdependent. Indeed, they should both be promoted "wherever Latin schools get more fully under way." Besides, consideration for the many non-Germans living in the country requires "that some portions remain in Latin, so that they can now also understand their part in our singing and reading." And when the non-Germans flock in from the country to the towns for the high festivals in order to receive the sacrament, then interpreters should be provided for them so that they may know what is being said. Conversely, let the interpreters find out from these people "what they are seeking and what they believe."[58]

Luther was greatly encouraged by this unexpectedly rapid breakthrough. The advance of the Reformation in Prussia was fortunate, particularly in view of the many troubles burdening Luther during these two years. In gloomy contrast to the Prussian scene were the martyrdoms to which it had come in other regions. Luther captured the stark contrast of joy and sorrow in the introduction to his commentary on Deuteronomy, which he dedicated to Bishop George von Polentz. In it he recalled those who had recently paid with their lives: the two Brussels martyrs, Henry Vos and John van den Eschen, in the year 1523, as well as the Bremen

56. According to the only available copy of the printed edition, in Stupperich, *Reformation*, 118ff. Also in E. Sehling, *Die evangelischen Kirchenordnungen des XVI. Jahrhunderts* (Leipzig, 1902ff.), 4 (1911): 30ff.

57. Stupperich, *Reformation*, 123. Sehling, *Kirchenordnungen*, 4:33. [The two hymns, widely used in Europe to this day, in the original are "Jesus Christus unser Heiland" and "Gott sei gelobet und gebenedeiet." Luther based the first of these two on a hymn by John Huss. The second is likewise an adaptation of a fifteenth-century Latin hymn. The English version of the first is by an unknown translator; of the second, by Richard Massie (1800–1887). Both hymns appear in *Laudamus*, hymnal of the Lutheran World Federation, 4th ed. (1970), in three languages; nos. 11 and 18. Cf. *LW* 53:250ff.; 252ff.]

58. Stupperich, *Reformation*, 119, 124. Sehling, *Kirchenordnungen*, 4:31, 33.

preacher Henry von Zütphen, whose grizzly end he had made public in his letter of condolence to the congregation in Bremen.[59]

As for the Prussian scene, Luther perceived in it a double measure of God's grace. For one thing, Polentz had not simply accepted the gospel for himself but had made it the substance of his episcopal office as well; for another, God had placed at Luther's side a prince to whom it had been given "to devise noble things" (Isa. 32:8). Now, under the care of these two men the gospel is coursing freely through the land and bearing fruit—in Prussia, of all places, which until recently possessed only a darkened and tainted version of the gospel.[60] "See these marvels: To Prussia the gospel runs in full course and under full sail where nobody called it or sought it, but in Germany, north and south, where it came and entered of itself, it is blasphemed, rejected, and chased away with all frenzy and madness." Here God acts the way he did toward Israel, "All day long I have held out my hands to a disobedient and contrary people" (Rom. 10:21; Isa. 65:2).[61] Luther could hardly have expressed more beautifully what the transition in the old land of the Teutonic order meant to him in this historic hour, for it was there in the Baltic coastland that a current development was showing forth something of the ancient mystery of [biblical] Israel.

59. WA 14:497 / 20ff.; 498 / 15ff. (February or April 1525, WA Br 3:448–49.) On Henry von Zütphen's martyrdom, see above, p. 102. On Luther's hymn composed for the Brussels martyrs, see below, pp. 461–62. [LW 9:4, 5.]

60. WA 14:498–99. [LW 9:5.]

61. WA 14:499 / 2ff. [LW 9:6.]

13

The Attack of Erasmus

In Luther's day intellectual life and public debate generated forces that drew him progressively into their field, acquainting him ever more perceptibly with influences emanating from one who, in the eyes of the younger generation, dominated that field: Desiderius Erasmus.[1] About fifteen years older than Luther, Erasmus was one of Europe's famous men.[2] He had published a rapid succession of works, stimulating in content and brilliant in style. A man on the move, his periods of residence in the Netherlands, England, and Italy had made him a star among Europe's scholars. Already in 1515 he began publishing his collected letters,[3] when from the distant and only recently founded University of Wittenberg the name of an unknown monk-theologian popped up and incredibly soon was on everyone's lips. From then on neither man could remain indifferent to the other. Their courses were not parallel but converging.

Already in 1503 Erasmus's *Enchiridion* or *Dagger of the Christian Soldier* promptly ranked him among the religious reformers. Its wider popularity, however, was deferred until 1518, when penance, indulgence, and related issues become subjects of public debate there was demand for a second edition. Far more significantly, Erasmus's edition of the Greek New Testament (published in 1516 and improved in 1518) gave the new theological movement its most important tool. His annotations and essays on method accompanied the sacred text or came out in later supplements. In effect this made Erasmus an energetic partner in the discussion over a

---

1. [The best discussion of this subject in English, according to E. G. Rupp (*Luther and Erasmus*, LCC 17 [Philadelphia: Westminster, 1969], p. 10), is H. J. McSorley, *Luther: Right or Wrong? An Ecumenical-Theological Study of Luther's Major Work, "The Bondage of the Will"* (New York: Newman; Minneapolis: Augsburg, 1969). Cf. Bornkamm's critical estimate, below, p. 419, n. 13.]

2. The exact birth year of Erasmus remains debatable. Newer research favors 1469, although E.-W. Kohls has again supported the 1466 date, while R. R. Post maintains the later date. See E.-W. Kohls, "Das Geburtsjahr des Erasmus," *ThZ* 22 (1966): 96ff., 347ff. Also, R. R. Post, "Nochmals Erasmus' Geburtsjahr," ibid., 319ff.

3. J. Huizinga, *Erasmus* (New York, 1924; London, 1952); German trans. W. Kaegi, 4th ed. (Basel, 1951), 110. [*Erasmi Epistolae*, ed. Mr. & Mrs. P. S. Allen, 12 vols. (Oxford, 1906–58). *Epistolae: The Epistles of Erasmus*, selection trans. and ed. F. M. Nichols, 3 vols. (London, 1901–8). For biography, R. H. Bainton, *Erasmus of Christendom* (New York: Scribner's, 1969).]

new understanding of the Bible and in the countless problems of specific exegesis. There was no dodging the question of destiny: How would Erasmus and Luther relate to each other? That question hung on, hounding Luther at every stage of his open struggle after 1518 and forcing Erasmus himself to take a stand. At first it escaped public notice, but soon this question became integral to a widespread struggle.

As one might have foreseen then, even these two intellectual giants would either join forces or turn against each other. Their natures were too contrasting for them to become allies. See Erasmus, busy with his own interests, devoted to letters and style and studies, scholarly monk and man of the world all in one, fascinated and frightened by the business of politics, a man aroused by the faults of church and society, yet one who fought them with well-intentioned moralistic admonitions and needling irony. In the other corner, see Luther, a man of passion and word power, daunted by no radical truth or intimidating opposition, a monk who had exchanged the cloistered cell and bookish study for open conflict, a man responding to the challenge that required the church as well as the individual to make decisions in matters of faith.

Luther had early detected differences between himself and Erasmus. In October 1516 he had requested his friend Spalatin to point out most respectfully to the famous scholar that his understanding of Old Testament law was flawed and that this was the result of his favoring Jerome at the expense of Augustine.[4] Six months later, writing to a friend, Luther bared his opinion of Erasmus in a way that accurately anticipated the nature of their future relationship, saying, "My joy in Erasmus is diminishing daily. . . . With him the human counts more than the divine. . . . One judges things differently when trusting the capacities of man than when knowing nothing else but grace."[5] Not only his theology but also Erasmus's way of criticizing the church made Luther unhappy. He missed a tone of seriousness and of heartfelt injury in that critique. Not long after his own struggle for the church renewal had begun, Luther came on a satirical "dialogue" on Pope Julius II circulating under the name of Erasmus. Luther found this anything but the work of a kindred spirit in a common cause. Erasmus, he confided to Spalatin, "is so amusing, elegant, and witty (that is, so Erasmian) that he makes you laugh and banter about the very faults and misery of the church of Christ that should in-

4. October 19, 1516, WA Br 1:70–71. The differing viewpoints of the two men are treated in more detail in H. Bornkamm, "Erasmus und Luther," in the book by the same author, *Das Jahrhundert der Reformation: Gestalten und Kräfte*, 2d ed. (Göttingen, 1966), 36ff.

5. March 1, 1517, to John Lang, WA Br 1:90 / 15–16, 19–20, 25–26. [CF. *LW* 48:40.]

stead make every Christian lament before God with deep sighing."[6] Melanchthon and other friends kept insisting that the two men should come closer together, but it took Luther a while before bringing himself to write to Erasmus at all. He then did so in the humanist style of the day—an encomium with scatterings of verbal incense. At the same time he tested Erasmus's sense of humor on matters of faith—a sense that really was lacking—as he observed: Judging from the multitude of his friends, God must indeed be gracious to him. Dated March 28, 1519, this letter, paralleling similar expressions from Melanchthon, was part of an effort to forestall a conflict between Erasmus and the Wittenbergers.[7]

Erasmus was equally concerned about preserving good relations, yet it was a tricky situation, requiring him to defend himself on all sides against charges of siding with Luther. Nevertheless, he found common ground in the conflict against corruption in the church and therefore, while critical of Luther's acerbity, he defended Luther's intentions, even against high princes of the church. At that time he had no intention of breaking with Luther. His reply, on May 30, to Luther's letter was reserved but not unfriendly; he wanted to remain neutral so that he might continue to be useful to the flowering sciences. He urged moderation. This was how Christ won the world and how Paul abolished the Jewish law—interpreting it allegorically.[8] The contrast was clear. Where Luther saw the deep difference opening up between the law and the gospel as ways of salvation, Erasmus imagined it possible to bridge the gap by means of a clever exegetical rule allowing the wording to remain untouched but to transpose it—as insight and learning afford—into a higher spiritual truth.

For his part, Luther would gladly have seen Erasmus keep out of the conflict. Seeing no chance for the two to reach agreement, he repeatedly

6. November 1517, WA Br 1:118 / 5ff. Cf. the differently accented but basically felt similar judgment in Luther's letter to Schuerl on February 20, 1519; WA Br 1:346 / 7ff. The authenticity of this dialogue is challenged by C. Stange, *Erasmus und Julius II: Eine Legende* (Berlin, 1937). But K. Schätti, "Erasmus von Rotterdam und die Römische Kurie," *BBGW* 48 (1954): 37ff., has again made it probable that Erasmus was indeed the author, inasmuch as the "dialogue" agrees with what he said also on other occasions. Convincing arguments against Stange and references to later utilization of the "dialogue" in Lutheran polemics appear in R. H. Bainton, "Erasmus and Luther and the Dialogue Julius Exclusus," in *450 Jahre lutherische Reformation, 1517–1967: Festschrift F. Lau* (Göttingen, 1967), 17ff.

7. March 28, 1519, WA Br 1:362 / 7ff. W. Maurer, "Melanchthons Anteil am Streit zwischen Luther und Erasmus," in his *Der junge Melanchthon zwischen Humanismus und Reformation* (Göttingen, 1969), 160–61.

8. May 30, 1519, WA Br 1:413 / 34ff. Details on the letters of Erasmus and the Luther issue in WA 18:552ff. In our context the letters of Luther take precedence. On the antecedent history of this confrontation, see K. Zickendraht, *Der Streit zwischen Erasmus und Luther über die Willensfreiheit* (Leipzig, 1909), 1ff. Huizinga, *Erasmus*, 157ff.

spoke with Melanchthon, wondering "how near or how far" Erasmus might be from their own position. So Luther hung on, rejecting flatly the suspicion expressed by a humanist in Nuremberg (it was then November 1520) that Luther "disliked or was averse to" Erasmus. "Please God, Erasmus and I intend to remain together."[9] Luther took no offense that Erasmus, meanwhile, had requested an avoidance of his name, and the names of his friends, in the Reformer's writings, so as not to bring them under suspicion.[10] At the same time Erasmus still stepped in to protect Luther, writing to Elector Frederick the Wise and also publicly demanding that the one now banned not be delivered over to Rome but be given a trial under nonpartisan judges in Germany.[11] The ban, however, aroused Luther's will to fight, so that Erasmus eventually despaired of a peaceful solution to the conflict. Directly following the Diet of Worms, Erasmus remarked bitterly: Luther may now be in security, but this gives his enemies a chance to rage all the more against everyone they suspect on his side; Stephen was stoned but once, yet here in Louvain he is getting it hot and heavy in sermons and discussions. How hard he [Erasmus] had been working for peace! "But then the burning of the decretals, the 'Captivitas Babylonica' and the all-too-bold assertions have, as it seems, made the evil incurable."[12]

When it became clear that the Edict of Worms was unable to eradicate the Lutheran movement, which instead was growing ever more dangerous and radical, Erasmus came under the heaviest pressure yet to do something in a literary way so as to dissociate himself from it and not to appear

9. November 17, 1520, to Spengler, WA Br 2:217 / 13–14, 18–19. [LW 48:185.]

10. Erasmus to Luther, August 1, 1520, WA Br 2:157 / 66ff. Probably the reply to a lost letter of Luther's to Erasmus which (like the letter of April 30, 1520, WA Br 2:93ff.) he had given to Ergramus. Luther's answer is likewise lost yet is attested in the letter to Spengler (n. 7, above).

11. *Erasmi opuscula*, a supplement to the *Opera omnia* (ed. J. Clericus [Leiden, 1703ff.; reprint, Hildesheim, 1961–62]), ed. W. K. Ferguson (Haag, 1933), 329ff., 352ff. The axiomata for the elector, Luther, *Samtliche Werke* (Erlangen, 1826ff.), 5:241–42, appear in German in K. A. Meissinger, *Erasmus von Rotterdam*, 2d ed. (Berlin, 1948), 267–68. Luther was aware of these efforts. He knew of Erasmus's letter of April 14, 1519, to Frederick the Wise, because it appeared in print (*Opus Epistolarum Des. Erasmi Roterodami*, ed. P. S. Allen et al. [Oxford, 1906ff.], 3: no. 939), and with many contemporaries regarded the proposal for an anonymous council as coming from Erasmus. (Erasmus may at least have had something to do with it. Cf. P. Kalkoff, "Die Vermittlungstheologie des Erasmus und sein Anteil an den Flugschriften der ersten Reformationszeit," ARG 1 [1903–4], 1ff. Opus Epistolarum Erasmi, 4: no. 1149. Meissinger, *Erasmus*, 392ff.)

12. To Ludwig Ber in Basel, May 14, 1521, *Opus Epistolarum Erasmi*, 4:494 / 10ff., 24ff. Luther learned about the letter soon thereafter in the Wartburg from a Leipzig pamphlet. It made him charge that Erasmus "is concerned not for the cross but for peace." To Spalatin, September 9, 1521, WA Br 2:387 / 3ff. Concerning the *Assertio*, see n. 42, below. [LW 48:306.]

as an accomplice in it. An initial step was to leave Louvain. He had lived there nearly four years, and moving away removed some immediate pressures. His chief antagonists were the local clergy and especially the Dominicans, who dominated the university's faculty of theology.

The friends of reform kept an anxious eye on the gathering storm but continued by correspondence and conversation to reassure one another that there were no grounds for worry. Yet no one who knew him would have dared to appeal to Erasmus the way Dürer had done earlier. In May 1521, on learning of Luther's capture, Albrecht Dürer confided in his diary,

> O God, if Luther is dead, who will henceforth offer us the holy gospel? . . . O Erasmus of Roderdame, where are you hiding? . . . Listen, you knight of Christ, ride forth alongside the Lord Christ, defend the truth, attain the martyr's crown! As it is, you are a little old man, and I have heard that you give yourself only another two years to do anything effectively. Invest these two in the gospel and in the true Christian faith. Let yourself be heard, and the gates of hell—the Roman chair—will not, as Christ has promised, prevail against you.[13]

People in Basel were at that time happy to report to Wittenberg that Erasmus had come out with a notably balanced response—"cautious and timid in all directions"—so as not to offend any party and to calm the troubled. Melanchthon quickly passed the word along, giving it his own joyous exaggeration while assuring Spalatin that nothing had less basis than the rumor many numbskulls have been spreading, as though Erasmus had anything against Luther.[14] Yet a mere three months later Glarean had to tell Zwingli, "I fear that a duel between Luther and Erasmus is building up," and it will harm scholarship immeasurably. Zwingli at once mobilized friends who were "secretly with Luther . . . and secretly with Erasmus" to work for peace.[15] For his part, Erasmus had by no means as yet decided to fight. Instead, on March 30, 1522, he poured out his heart to his fellow humanist Willibald Pirkheimer in Nuremberg, lamenting, "My life is nearing its end." Indeed, the Christian cause is in trouble. Some are seeking to make their fortune, others to save what they have,

---

13. *Albrecht Dürers schriftlicher Nachlass, auf Grund der Originalschriften und theilweise neu entdeckter alter Abschriften*, ed. K. Lange and F. Fuhse (Halle, 1893), 164–65.

14. Konrad Pellican to Melanchthon, November 30, 1521, *Suppl. Mel.* 6 / 1:17–72. *MBW* 182. Melanchthon to Spalatin, mid-December 1521, *CR* 1:448. (Date based on *Suppl. Mel.* 6 / 1:173.) *MBW* 191 (December 26 / 27).

15. Glarean to Zwingli, March 4, 1522, *Huldreich Zwinglis sämtliche Werke*, ed. E. Egli, G. Finster, et al. (Berlin, 1905ff.), 7 (1911): 494–95. Zwingli to Beatus Rhenanus, March 25, 1522, ibid., 496ff.

and for those who simply lie still a dangerous fire could suddenly break out. "The ill will of certain people has so swamped me in hate that anything I try is in vain." Some theologians supposed that the study of antiquity, awakened by Erasmus, was undermining their authority. "Yet Luther gave them a weapon with which they could kill me. At the same time, however, I have always kept my distance from this Luther business, with the single exception that I cautioned him emphatically to write differently, if he sought success." And then came Aleander, the papal nuncio and his own embittered foe, destroying everything for him [Erasmus] with hatred and lies. "The Lutherans threaten me openly with their abusive writings, and the emperor is as good as convinced that I am the source and head of the whole Luther tumult. So I run into greatest danger on both sides, while having made them both indebted to me." Vividly this letter revealed the acid context in which Erasmus now saw Luther, and Luther was getting into it more deeply, not intentionally but because of his radicality. Courage had left Erasmus: "I had intended to write something, not against Luther but for concord. But I now see both parties so in heat that it is better to remain silent." And still, a few lines further on, a theme occurs to him that he will choose for the confrontation: the freedom of the will. Apparently, it had angered him that several theologians had objected to his paraphrasing of Romans 9 claiming that he had given the human will too great a significance.[16]

Rather than take on Luther, Erasmus was eager to escape from his unhappy dilemma between two fronts. Escape finally seemed to lie in dissociating himself completely from Luther's ideas. In the spring of 1522—so he reported in a long letter describing his life and literary work[17]—he was toying with the idea of writing three dialogues in which he could treat a number of the issues standing between himself and Luther and then letting one of the partners in conversation decide. It would be such an irenic book that he was afraid the opposing party would become more furious over it than Luther, "if only he had a little of the disposition which many people praise in him. Happy I am indeed if he has it, but I wish he had it not." Those goading him to write would hardly have been satisfied with this kind of effort. The goaders whom he mentioned included the papal nuncio Carraciolo, accredited to the emperor; the papal legate

16. *Opus Epistolarum Erasmi*, 5: no. 1268. To Glapion, the emperor's father confessor, Erasmus's literary reflections sounded somewhat more militant (ca. April 21, 1522, ibid., 5: no. 1275, 48 / 17ff.).

17. To Johann Botzheim, cathedral canon in Constance, April 1523, and published by Erasmus. Ibid., 1:34–35.

Aleander; the emperor himself, whose father confessor conveyed the proddings; Duke George of Saxony; and others as well. He was in no mood to write, unable to put down more than a few pages of his vague plan.[18] Yet the longer he delayed, the more intense the pressure.

Erasmus found it difficult to drop the idea of taking a stand openly, especially because letters continued to bring him evidence of what Luther was up to. And always there was the accompanying assurance that Luther had no intention of attacking him, although among friends Luther was saying bluntly how little regard he had for Erasmus's theology. In those days, letters among the learned—open letters, really—were a form of press release. Publishers grabbed them up unscrupulously, with no intention of asking the writer's permission. They were copied by hand or printed and quickly reached those interested in literary controversy. Often such letters also fell into hands for whom they were not intended. So Erasmus came on a letter of Luther's, sent on May 28, 1522, to someone in Leipzig unknown to Erasmus (and still unknown to us). In it Luther said, "Erasmus is not to be feared in this question (of pre-destination, about which he understands nothing), or on just about any [other] question concerning the Christian faith. The truth is mightier than prudence, the Spirit more powerful than genius, and faith greater than learning." Luther admittedly will not challenge Erasmus to combat, yet if Erasmus should wish to try his luck, than "a stammerer like me will confidently stand up to the eloquent Erasmus and will not be awed by his authority, his name, or his fame."[19] We can hardly blame Erasmus for detecting "much bitterness"[20] in this letter, for Luther was feeling exuberant after having overcome the machinations of Satan in Wittenberg. A year later he learned of another of Luther's letters, this one to Oecolampadius on June 20, 1523, whose lectures on Isaiah apparently did not please Erasmus:

> What Erasmus knows about judging spiritual questions, or what he pretends to know, is borne out amply in his writings, from the first to the latest. I am not insensitive to his assorted barbs, but while outwardly he acts as though he is not my foe, I do the same, as though I did not understand his cunning—although I catch on better than he realizes. He has delivered in the field to which he was called; he has introduced us to the languages and steered us away from the godless studies (of scholasticism). Perhaps, like Moses, he will

18. Ibid., 1:35 / 11ff.

19. *WA Br* 1:544 / 11ff.; 545 / 25–26. Erasmus probably came upon this letter a good deal later (cf. his letter to Spalatin, March 11, 1523).

20. *Opus Epistolarum Erasmi*, 5:251–22, esp. citations 35–36. In the summer of 1523, Capito published this letter in Strassburg.

die in the plains of Moab (Deut. 34:5), for he is unlikely to advance to the higher studies (which cultivate the fear of God). . . . He has done enough in exposing the evil. (So far as I can see) he is unable to show us the good and to lead us into the promised land.

Oecolampadius [Luther adds] should not let criticism of Erasmus intimidate him. Rather, let him rejoice over the criticism, for Erasmus "is a man unable or unwilling to have a right judgment in these matters, as almost the whole world is beginning to perceive."[21] When Erasmus saw this letter, he wrote angrily to Zwingli: Luther claims, "I am not much to be trusted in matters concerning the Spirit. I don't know what that should mean." "I'd like to learn from you, learned Zwingli, what kind of spirit that is."[22]

Tension toward Luther mounted as it fed on another literary affair which annoyed Erasmus greatly. This time it was Ulrich von Hutten who, in June 1523, fired a violent polemic at him. Erasmus retaliated in kind. This shrill dissonance lowered the curtain on a friendship begun initially with high hopes. To be sure, from the outset they had somewhat misjudged each other, a misunderstanding covered up by an enthusiastic feeling of belonging together in the fellowship of the Muse, on which their heart was set. At first, in 1515, in a new edition of his book *Nemo*, Hutten recognized Erasmus as an ally in the struggle against the scholastic boneheads. Like "a German knight" approaching a prince, so Hutten, in a letter, offered Erasmus his services. For years he remained attached to Erasmus in an "almost boyish love" (Werner Kaegi), even after differences of opinion began to emerge.[23] And Erasmus, flattered by the homage of a talented nobleman—twenty years his junior and "a unique delight of the Muses"—had already in 1516 erected an astonishing monument to him: "How could Attica evoke more wit and elegance than this man possesses? Is not his language sheer beauty and pure charm?"[24] Three years later, in 1519, came an equally impressive tribute when Erasmus cast his skillfully crafted biographical sketch of Thomas More, his closest friend, in the form

21. WA Br 3:96 / 14ff., 24–25; 97 / 27ff. [Cf. LW 49:44. The translation above is based on Bornkamm's. The original letter is in Latin.]

22. *Opus Epistolarum Erasmi*, 5:329 / 54ff.; 330 / 88–89. *Zwinglis sämtliche Werke*, 8 (1914): 116 / 6–7; 118 / 2–3.

23. Foreword to *Nemo*, Ulrich von Hutten, *Opera quae reperiri potuerunt omnia*, ed. E. Böcking (Leipzig, 1859; reprint, Osnabrück, 1963), 1:183. Letter to Erasmus, October 24, 1515, ibid., 102. On this whole subject, W. Kaegi, "Hutten und Erasmus," *HV* 22 (1924 / 25): 200ff., 461ff.; cf. here 204ff., 215.

24. Annotation to 1 Thess. 2, in "Novum instrumentum omne" (1516), p. 555, in Böcking, Hutten, *Opera*, 1:103. Kaegi, "Hutten und Erasmus," 209.

of a letter to Hutten.[25] Then, however, the shadow of a greater figure—that of Luther—fell between them. Hutten accepted Luther with such enthusiasm that he could only imagine Erasmus with the same qualities. Impulsively, still in 1519, Hutten made public a letter entrusted to him from Erasmus to Albrecht of Mainz, which contained a warning that Luther might be tried for heresy. If this was not meddling in something of no direct concern to him, it at least got Hutten in trouble with the cardinal.[26] As for the Erasmus-Hutten relationship, dissonance became evident in 1520, when for the first time in four years Hutten visited Erasmus secretly in Louvain. There, June 20–21, Hutten sketched his plans for a war on the clergy. His "Pfaffenkrieg" was to add political clout to his hitherto literary polemic. In disbelief, Erasmus at first would not take these plans seriously, and Hutten put up with his master's attitude. Their relationship remained intact. Then two years later, to Hutten's dismay, the bottom dropped out.

In late November 1522, Hutten arrived in Basel a broken man. His big war had shriveled into a couple of plunderings. Ill and no longer fit to fight, he (like Bucer and Oecolampadius) had been forced to abandon Sickingen's threatened territory. A few days later he found refuge in Basel, where he came on Erasmus who, escaped from opponents in Louvain, had already in 1521 settled in Basel. Eagerly Hutten tried to see his old friend, but Erasmus anticipated him and asked him to forego a visit.[27] A tale-bearer may have made things worse, but the rejection could hardly make him feel anything but helpless and embittered. For his part, Erasmus gave so many reasons for not wanting to see Hutten (as he explained painstakingly to various correspondents) that he too must have felt bad about the matter. Who would take seriously Erasmus's excuses? Hutten could not endure the cold where Erasmus was lodging; Erasmus could not stand the oven heat; he feared contagion; he feared that Hutten's visit

---

25. Hutten, *Opera*, 1:278ff. *Opus Epistolarum Erasmi*, 4: no. 999, 12ff. Kaegi, "Hutten und Erasmus," 218–19. Text and translation of this letter [into German] in K. Büchner, *Die Freundschaft zwischen Hutten und Erasmus* (Munich, 1948), 28ff.

26. Date of the letter, October 19, 1519, according to Allen, ed., *Opus Epistolarum Erasmi*, 4: no. 1033 (there 96ff., from the letter and the account of Erasmus on the event in his *Spongia* [1523]) [The Sponge]; November 1, 1519, according to Böcking, Hutten, *Opera*, 1:315. In January 1520 the letter to Luther became public. Luther read it with relish and recognized in it the fine hand of Erasmus artfully veiling his statements: "He is quite concerned about me in this letter (perhaps it will be published sometime) and protects me quite nobly, yet in his usual skillful way, which is to defend me strongly while seeming not to defend me at all." January 26, 1520, to John Lang. WA Br 1:619 / 14ff. [*LW* 48:150.]

27. Kaegi does a thorough examination of this situation in his "Hutten und Erasmus," 461ff.

might compromise Erasmus in the eyes of his spiritual patrons and of the emperor. The latter was surely the only real reason, and yet it too simply echoed Erasmus's dread of further unrest. Having eluded to some extent the pressures of the Luther opponents, Erasmus was not about to be drawn into the wake of the Luther friends, among whom Hutten had proved the most impetuous. A man of Erasmus's temperament could not have told Hutten to his face that he desired either to salvage what was left of their friendship or to make a clean break of it. Others did it for him. In mid-January 1523 the Basel city council, taking offense at Hutten's inflammatory speeches, expelled him. Confused and hurt, Hutten left Basel and found refuge in Mühlhausen.

Erasmus, meanwhile, believed it necessary to do one thing more for his own reputation. He wrote an open letter addressed to Marcus Laurinus, dean in Brügge, and dated February 1, 1523, intended for immediate publication. In it he told in detail of his most recent years, yet backed away from the concerns of Luther, who had justifiably called attention to many a corruption. To prove the esteem he enjoyed on the opposing side, Erasmus listed all the letters of homage and all the promises with which Rome had tried to lure him.[28] Besides, it hardly occurred to him that this well-planned tactic would drive Hutten to extremes. Not the letter's untrue story of the aborted visit so much as the detested impartiality of a learned man—and the implied betrayal, so it seemed, of a once common cause—triggered the "challenge" *(Expostulatio)*[29] that Hutten published in Strassburg in June of that same year.

Erasmus struck back at once. His rebuttal, *The Sponge (Spongia)*, appeared at the beginning of September. Writing it hurriedly in July, Erasmus chose the title to convey his intention to wash off the mudslings of Hutten. Ironically, *The Sponge* came out just a few days after Hutten's death in Ufenau, too late for Erasmus to take stock of what was really going on. The best he could do was add a foreword to the quickly following second edition. Its thrust was that had he but known he would have answered Hutten differently or not at all.[30] That would have been better. By retaliating, Erasmus admittedly had hurt himself more than Hutten.

---

28. *Opus Epistolarum Erasmi*, 5: no. 1342, 203ff. Hutten, *Opera*, 2:158ff.

29. Hutten, *Opera*, 2:180ff. The announcement of the "dialogues" in the writing to Botzheim (see above, n. 15) strengthened the suspicion that Erasmus now intended to proceed against Luther.

30. The *Spongia* in Hutten, *Opera*, 2:262ff., is better presented than in the Leiden edition of *Werke des Erasmus* (reprinted 1962), 10:1631ff. The second edition foreword, in Hutten, *Opera*, 2:263. Also *Opus Epistolarum Erasmi*, 5. no. 1389, 335ff. A lively survey of the two polemical writings is that of D. F. Strauss, *Ulrich von Hutten*, 2d ed. (Bonn and Leipzig, 1871; later ed. O. Clemen, Leipzig, 1914; K. M. Schiller, Leipzig, 1930), 2d book, chap. 10. For the dedication, Kaegi, "Hutten und Erasmus," 479ff.

Both writings are the melancholy fruit of love soured into hate. Indeed, Hutten's *Expostulatio* aimed to tell everything that he had been prevented from telling his friend in Basel. It was hardly a tract but more an *omnium-gatherum* of a conversation never held. He dredged up petty recollections of endured insults. He reproached Erasmus painfully for failing to remain true to his promising beginnings, implored him finally to come over to the side of the truth, and predicted pointedly that his half-measures would also cost him the respect of his opponents; indeed, they would never forget what his critique had inflicted on them.[31] Hutten's tract was not only damaging to Erasmus, but also hurt him deeply. In the welter of exaggerations and distortions lay at least some irrefutable moral truths which Hutten threw up to Erasmus, doing so with characteristic timidity, vanity, and fawning as he operated artfully along the boundary of truth and falsehood.

Erasmus reacted accordingly. While Hutten had stood up for a cause, Erasmus was in the more difficult position of defending an attitude, plunging ever deeper into the mire of personal polemics. What else could *The Sponge* then be but a naturally subjective chronicle of all the gossip accumulating around him for years. And yet it was easy for Erasmus to brush aside the phantasmal image of himself with which Hutten had confronted him. As a matter of fact, he had never stood on Luther's side; it was therefore unfair to charge him with having changed his mind. Nor had he changed his ways, as Hutten claimed. To the issues stirred up by the church and the empire, Erasmus made only his standard appeal to moderation; he contributed nothing and gave the impression, unwillingly, of helplessness and deficient inner conviction. He thus allowed opponents to prescribe the weapons, and repaid them in the same polemical coin, here and there adding icy mockery, which Hutten, in all his verbal extravagance, never employed. Hutten perhaps possessed nothing more for which he need fear; therefore he is so brave [snapped Erasmus].[32] The extent to which he forgot himself becomes plain in two other things he did after writing *The Sponge*. For one, he warned the Zurich city council against Hutten, calling him a dangerous agitator, for the Zurichers had given Hutten asylum in neighboring Ufenau. For another, he dedicated *The Sponge* to Zwingli, of all people, seeking thereby to forestall any rebuttal from Hutten.[33]

31. *Expostulatio*, paras. 218–19. Hutten, *Opera*, 2:234.

32. *Spongia*, para. 237. Hutten, *Opera*, 2:300.

33. To the Zurich council, August 10, 1523, *Opus Epistolarum Erasmi*, 5: no. 1379, 311. To Zwingli, *Zwinglis sämtliche Werke*, 8 (1914): 119–20.

Although Hutten's sudden death removed that worry, Erasmus did not let the matter rest. Turning to Strassburg, he wrote two letters to the city council, lodging complaints against Hans Schott, the printer, for having published Hutten's *Expostulatio*. Then, when he learned that one of the councilmen, Kaspar Hedio, had opposed any punishment, he wrote Hedio that he too loved the gospel but that it was having a gruesome effect on him. If Schott, Erasmus wrote Hedio, had a wife and children, let him go begging. Were he ashamed to do so, then let him prostitute his wife; that at least is not forbidden by law, but the publication of libelous works carries the death penalty.[34]

This miserable literary feud had a twofold significance for Erasmus's relationship to the Reformation. Two of his writings had plainly, and more publicly than hitherto, moved him away from Luther and in part had rendered some flatly critical judgments against the movement. In the process, Erasmus had degraded himself, a state against which he could hardly expect to remain immune. It all indicated that a realistic confrontation with Luther would gradually become unavoidable. The Hutten affair thus raised a swarm of rumors, which Erasmus eyed anxiously.[35] In Wittenberg, meanwhile, Hutten's polemic *Expostulatio* had made a miserable impression,[36] to be outdone only by Erasmus's own *Sponge*.

Soon Erasmus received a copy of the hearty letter Luther sent on October 1, 1523, to Konrad Pellikan in Basel. For some time Pellikan had associated with other kindred spirits to prevent the outbreak of a quarrel between Erasmus and Luther. Luther wrote, "I wish Hutten had not challenged, and still less that Erasmus had wiped him off. If it's what it means to sponge off, then I ask you, what does it mean to insult or to offend? . . . If Erasmus writes this way for himself, then one could wish that he would write something against himself." Doing this sort of thing had damaged him so much that Luther was really sorry for him. Returning to his main objection, Luther put it bluntly, "I have always been waiting for him to come to the point (to the question of faith). On moral issues it is

---

34. To the council, March 13 and August 23, 1524. *Opus Epistolarum Erasmi*, 5: no. 1429, 416–17; no. 1477, 511ff. To Hedio, June(?), August(?) 1524, ibid., no. 1459, 7ff.,37ff. Erasmus complains to Melanchthon about Hedio, September 6, 1524, ibid., no. 1496, 544ff.; 546 / 70ff. *MBW* 341.

35. A number of passages in letters, in *WA* Br 3:37, gathered there in n. 5.

36. Cf. the sharp criticism of Melanchthon of July 3 (on "hearsay"); August 23 and 24, *CR* 1:616, 625–27; *MBW* 279, 284, 288; September 8 to Oecolampadius, *Suppl. Mel.* 6 / 1:225–26; *MBW* 292—all of these before knowledge of the counterpublication of Erasmus. Melanchthon saw at once that Hutten's attack would worsen the relations between Erasmus and the Wittenbergers.

always easy to make fine speeches." Besides, since Luther has just seen—
he had earlier only suspected it—"how far that man is removed from an
understanding of Christian truth," he now cared little what Erasmus
might say about him. "When I am praised, I feel sadness and fear, but
when I am slandered and insulted, I feel joy. If this sounds strange to
Erasmus, I am not surprised. May he come to know Christ and kiss
human wisdom good-bye. May God illuminate and make a new man out of
Erasmus." Words of such unshakable steadfastness, and easily read, were
bound to irritate Erasmus. Nor were they easier to take because Luther
expressed displeasure that some of his earlier letters had been made public, letters in which he had assured Erasmus that his feelings for him were
not unfriendly, that he felt only sorry for him.[37]

This game of indiscretions had at least some value. On November 21,
Erasmus sent John Faber, the vicar-general in Constance, a copy of
Luther's letter with the notation "These are the preludes to war." The
original he sent in February 1524 to Campeggio, the papal legate, seeking
to prove thereby that he had nothing to do with the Luther affair.[38] He did
the same thing again when after long hesitation Luther decided to clarify
the tense situation and to approach Erasmus directly. This time Erasmus
sent the original of Luther's letter (April 1524) along with two earlier letters to Poland's King Sigismund I, using as courier Jerome Laski, brother
of the later Reformed theologian John Laski.[39] Everything Luther put into
this letter he had written earlier to others. But here, candidly and to his
face, he struck an impressively engaging tone: Luther had nothing against
Erasmus because of his aloofness and manifold needling, and never had he
asked Erasmus to come over to his side. "Indeed, we have endured your
weakness and respected the 'measure of God's gift within you,'" the
"glorious and incomparable gift" that has brought the scholarship to
bloom and made possible a clean-cut study of the Bible. Hutten and, most
of all, he, Erasmus, would better have kept quiet. Yet Luther himself was
aware how difficult it is in that kind of conflict to practice moderation.
Luther voiced his genuine regret that Erasmus had become the target of
so many hateful attackers, he himself having already dissuaded many from
doing so, and that he himself had let satirical snipes lie unanswered. "But
what shall I do now? The affair is highly exasperating for both sides."
Luther would be glad if Erasmus and his opponents would spare each

37. WA Br 3:160 / 7ff., 11–12, 16–17, 25–26, 32ff. [LW 49:79.]
38. Opus Epistolarum Erasmi, 5: no. 1397, 345–46; no. 1415, 331ff.; cf. esp. 333 / 39.
39. WA Br 3:268. [LW 49:76–81.]

other. Luther's favorable sentiments toward Erasmus made him "wish that disposition which is worthy of your fame."

> If the Lord defers giving this to you, then I ask you, if you can do nothing else, in the meantime to be only a spectator to our tragedy. Only do not give comfort to my enemies and join their ranks against us. Above all, do not publish booklets against me, as I shall publish nothing against you. . . . There has been enough snarling; now we must see to it that we "do not devour each other" (Gal. 5:15). [40]

Unfortunately, Luther's efforts to prevent this dangerous skirmishing of the lesser spirits from setting off a war between the two major powers came too late. Indeed, it hastened the outbreak. As a peace effort Luther's approach was most undiplomatic. Despite all its friendly trimmings it insincerely veiled what Luther really thought about him, and this had an injurious effect on Erasmus. What else could he do in return but give Luther's messenger a cool reply to relay to Wittenberg. The messenger, Joachim Camerarius, was a pleasant young fellow to whom Erasmus took a liking. From Basel, on May 8, 1524, Erasmus wrote that he could not concede that Luther was more genuinely concerned than he for the purity of the gospel.

> Some of the things of yours I have been reading make me earnestly fear that Satan has deluded you with his subtleties; again, other things of yours grip me so that I only wish these worries of mine were unfounded. I would not like to represent anything of which I was not convinced, much less anything I do not yet understand.

Erasmus, continuing, admitted that as yet he had written nothing against Luther, even though that would have won him great applause from the princes. However, he hinted, his own restraint could change.

> Since you are prepared to give everyone an accounting of your faith, why do you take it amiss when someone, in order to learn, would dispute with you? Maybe an Erasmus, writing *against* you, will serve the gospel better than certain boneheads now writing *for* you. For their sakes, how can one be a mere spectator to this kind of tragedy (may its outcome by no means be tragic!)? People of their ilk drive me to the other side, even when the princes do not do it!

Erasmus concludes with what he had taken hardest: that Luther has placed him and Hutten and Hutten's defenders on the same level. "To think that you mention these people and me in the same breath! I count

---

40. WA Br 3:270 / 11ff.; 271 / 43, 59ff., 65. [LW 49:78, 79–80.]

them not human beings but furies, and I haven't the least intention to recognize them as my kind!" Then Erasmus ended dryly, "The Lord Jesus direct your spirit to decisions worthy of his gospel!"[41]

Oecolampadius, in Basel, was present when Erasmus read Luther's letter with impassive face. The Basel reformer's incorrigible optimism concluded, also from his reply, that Erasmus would probably not write against Luther, at least not without further pondering, for Erasmus had assured him a second time (when replying to Luther) that he could do his book "on free will" in three days.[42] In any case, a major confrontation was impending and was not to be stopped. Actually, it was already in progress, fired by indiscretions to which Erasmus himself was party. The latest Luther-Erasmus exchange was quickly circulated in copies, much to the annoyance of Camerarius, who swore his own innocence in the matter. Besides, the letters of November 1523 were appearing in print even now, in the summer of 1524, along with a booklet by Albers against *The Sponge* of Erasmus.[43]

Everything finally drove Erasmus to complete his treatise against Luther. Long he had pondered it, often he admitted it confidentially, and still more often he denied it. In place of the three dialogues, as initially projected, he now felt that the time had passed to treat marginal issues, that it was now time to zero in on one pivotal theme: the question of the freedom of the will. Luther had caused a shock as well as a sensation when, in the Heidelberg disputation of 1518, he had defended the thesis [14]: "Free will, after the fall, has power to do good only in a passive capacity, but it can always do evil in an active capacity." Later he again defended this thesis, protesting the papal bull of condemnation (1520).[44] The subject touched many nerves. England's King Henry VIII, as part of his own controversy with Luther, corresponded with Duke George of Saxony in 1523. The letters were immediately made public, revealing Henry's indignation and, according to George, showing up all the evils in Luther's teaching as being rooted in his determinism.[45] Here Luther's Roman Catholic opponents saw the most dire consequences of his theology. "He

41. WA Br 3:285 / 5ff., 22ff.; 286 / 50ff., 55ff. [Cf *LW* 33:7ff.]

42. Oecolampadius to Luther, May 9 and 15, 1524, WA Br 3:287 / 8ff.; 294 / 17ff.

43. WA Br 3:158–59.

44. *Liberum arbitrium post peccatum res est de solo titulo,* WA 1:354 / 5. *Assertio omnium articulorum M. Lutheri per bullam Leonis X. novissimam damnatorum* (1520), WA 7:142ff.

45. F. Gess, *Akten und Briefe zur Kirchenpolitik Herzog Georgs von Sachsen* (Leipzig, 1905ff.), 1:504ff., 499, n. 1.

makes God the author of all evil . . . so that no one is in any condition to do anything good, even if he wished to do so," wrote Cuthbert Tunstall, bishop of London, to Erasmus on June 5, 1523. Tunstall was trying to spur Erasmus on to attack Luther.[46] Such outside prodding proved to be superfluous, so far as Erasmus's selection of a theme was concerned. He had long been convinced that alongside the grace and goodness of God a certain measure of freedom of the will must be assumed if human beings are to be brought up morally. Likewise, he had often lamented that because of his effort to steer between the Scylla of trusting in good works and the Charybdis of moral nihilism,[47] followers of Luther had charged him with Pelagianism. "In their lectures the Lutherans tear me down as a Pelagian because I make too much allowance for free will. Don't they cavort with me nicely?"[48]

At the same time, Erasmus could hope that this theme would rally a front against the radicals. Perhaps it would also serve to draw the humanists in the following away from Luther's extreme position. Besides, no theme lay closer to Erasmus's heart; from no other could he expect greater approbation than from Luther's opponents—they were impatiently goading him to write—and finally, he could count on this theme more than on any other to attract the attention of those as yet undecided. He could not have made a better choice. He sent a first draft, in February 1524, to his theological adviser Ludwig Ber, in Basel, and another copy to King Henry VIII. Yet in late July he still acted as though he were being forced into print because his work was already being so much discussed.[49] As September began, he was sending the first copies in all directions—some to Wittenberg, but only to Melanchthon, with a wordy covering letter. In it he assured Melanchthon of his sympathy, complained over some dozen mutual acquaintances, and declared that he had written this book only for

---

46. *Opus Epistolarum Erasmi*, 5: no. 1367, 290ff., esp. 291 / 16ff.

47. To Marcus Laurinus, February 1, 1523, ibid., 5: no. 1342, 203ff., esp. 226, 952ff., 959ff. The cause was his paraphrase of Rom. 9, mentioned above, p. 342. See, in addition, ibid., 926ff.

48. To Pirkheimer, February 12, 1522, *Opus Epistolarum Erasmi*, 5: no. 1259, 16 / 12. Cf. also to Peter Barbirius, August 13, 1521, ibid., 4: no. 1225, 562, 282; and to Glapion, ca. April 21, 1522, ibid., 5: no. 1275, 48 / 27. While requiring correction in various details, the extensive background survey of the dispute by A. Freitag in *WA* 18:551–96 errs particularly in two points: (1) that the theme of free will was "urged on Erasmus from the outside" (577) and (2) that he "attacked Luther entirely against his own will" (579).

49. To Ber, *Opus Epistolarum Erasmi*, 5: no. 1419, 399–400. To Henry VIII, ibid., no. 1430, 417–18. To Pirkheimer, July 21, 1524, ibid., no. 1466, 496 / 58. To Peter Barbirius, ca. July 26, 1524, ibid., no. 1470, 506 / 46.

the sake of his many enemies—although naturally what he said was his own opinion.[50]

Melanchthon was relieved that the attack was not worse. In fact, he was almost happy that someone had for once come to grips with this central problem of Christianity. So he replied to Erasmus in his characteristically balanced manner. He sided with Luther, yet he reassured Erasmus, saying that his book had been received calmly in Wittenberg and that Luther was able to take it, and promised to reply to it with the same moderation.[51]

Luther's own calmness, to be sure, was something special. After years of going to and fro, he had no immediate appetite to start reading this book, and when he did so he was so repelled by it that by the end of October he had read only a few pages.[52] Other things kept getting in the way. Besides, to the crowded daily round came added tasks of urgency, such as that other front, the confrontation with the "heavenly prophets," and the still greater anxieties over the peasant unrest. So this work of Erasmus lay unanswered for over a year.*

[Continued below, Chapter 16.]

50. Covering letter, ibid., 5: no. 1481ff., 525ff. Zickendraht, *Streit* (see n. 8, above, p. 339), 50. To Melanchthon, September 6, 1524, *Opus Epistolarum Erasmi*, 5: no. 1496, esp. 549–50. *CR* 1:667ff., esp. 671–72. *MBW* 341. Five other short covering letters, written on the same day, have been preserved. On the critique of this letter and for what Erasmus wrote about Melanchthon's *Loci*, cf. Maurer, "Melanchthons Anteil am Streit zwischen Luther und Erasmus," in his *Der junge Melanchthon*, 137–38.

51. September 30, 1524, *Opus Epistolarum Erasmi*, 5: no. 1500, 553ff. *CR* 1:674ff. *MSA* 7/1:204–9. *MBW* 344. Earlier, Melanchthon to Spalatin, end of August 1524. *CR* 1:673. *MBW* 338. Maurer, "Melanchthons Anteil am Streit zwischen Luther und Erasmus," 141ff. Erasmus hurriedly passed on the news of the calm reception in Wittenberg; *Opus Epistolarum Erasmi*, 5: no. 1526, 603, 230; no. 1528, 607/44; no. 1529, 610/25; no. 1531, 611/1.

52. *WA Br* 3:368/29.

14

The Peasants' War

During these years the differentiation between gospel and politics—between the spiritual realm and the temporal realm—had become the second great theme with which Luther wrestled. Second only to the theme of faith and justification, it would soon be subjected to a test quite different from the physically harmless literary war. In fact, before its basic reformation-oriented principles could appear, it would be undergoing a test of fire of unforeseen magnitude. For years the peasants had staged demonstrations, which after 1524 they enlarged into confrontations to demand their rights. A glowing hope animated them. Demands made earlier by their fathers now seemed mightily enforced by the gospel. Thus their grounds appeared irrefutable and likely at last to secure victory.[1] For Luther the peasant revolt was not merely a short-term event, like many another, but a life-and-death challenge to the Reformation itself.

The injection of religious ideas into the already intertwined economic and judicial demands of the peasants was nothing new. Ever since organized peasant revolts began—the big revolts in Flanders in 1323 and in northern France in 1356 stand out—their target was the nobility, the landlords, and the church. Indeed, it was the church that upheld the existing social system. The rich possessions of its cloisters, bishoprics, and parishes were themselves an imposing part of the system. Small wonder that forays prior to the big revolt in Germany often carried an anticlerical thrust. Already the English rebellion in 1381 bore John Wyclif's motto, *Lex Dei*. The law of God was seen as requiring the poverty of the church and its priests. No doubt through John Huss, attracted by Wyclif's motto,[2]

---

1. G. Franz, *Der deutsche Bauernkreig*, 4th ed. (Darmstadt, 1956). Also G. Franz, ed., *Akten zur Geschichte des Bauernkrieges zur Mitteldeutschland*, vol. 1/2 (Leipzig, 1934; reprint, Aalen, 1964). W. Stolze, *Bauernkrieg und Reformation*, SVRG 141 (Leipzig, 1926). H. von Schubert, *Revolution und Reformation im 16. Jahrhundert* (Tübingen, 1927). I. Schmidt, "Das göttliche Recht und seine Bedeutung im deutschen Bauernkrieg" (philosophy diss., Jena, 1939). A. Waas, "Die grosse Wendung im deutschen Bauernkrieg," *HZ* 158 (1938): 457ff.; 159 (1939): 22ff. Also A. Waas, *Die Bauern im Kampf um Gerechtigkeit 1300 bis 1525* (Munich, 1964), offers a wealth of background material. See also *Bauernkriegs-Studien*, ed. B. Moeller, SVRG 189 (Gütersloh, 1975).

2. J. Loserth, *Huss und Wyclif: Zur Genesis der hussischen Lehre*, 2d ed. (Munich and Berlin, 1925), 75. On Wyclif, see M. Schmidt, "John Wyclifs Kirchenbegriff," in *Gedenkschrift für Werner Elert* (Berlin, 1955), 72ff. [See *Advocates of Reform: From Wyclif to Erasmus*, ed. M. Spinka, LCC 14 (Philadelphia: Westminster, 1953); on Wyclif, 21–31; on Huss, 187–95.]

and the Hussite movement, appealing to the divine justice seen as present in the gospel created literature critical of society. Of course, the medieval mind never thought otherwise than that all authentic justice was founded in the divine law and in the order of creation. Any improvement of justice could therefore be nothing other than a re-formation of the original natural and divine law.[3] When applied to stubborn violations of justice, however, such convictions required a powerful revolutionary push. Above all, this religious element provided the basis of the peasantry's demands, of the people who felt themselves oppressed increasingly by a chronic and incalculable diminution of their rights. Already during the protracted revolt of 1513–17, under the sign of the shoe (a symbol older than Wyclif's motto),[4] successive waves of revolt had rolled over upper southwestern Germany.

For a long time rural folk had simply appealed to ancient law and, bound to antiquated codes, had waged their unequal struggle against numerous and confining innovations as well as against an alien Roman law. But in the sixteenth century the tide began to turn as the hitherto most inclusive and best organized peasant movement, the Bundschuh, came on stage. Since about 1450 the movement had been gathering force in Switzerland, Alsace, and the Upper Rhine valley. Its leading idea, "divine justice," consolidated the peasants' demands. The prime target was their own serfdom. Medieval law books had already branded serfdom as an injustice, as something contrary to God's intention for human beings, and as a condition of then recent developments.[5] The great reform document, drafted at the time of the Council of Basel by a secular priest pleading for the empire and the church, bore the title "Emperor Sigismund's Reformation" and gave voice to peasantry's protest. "Therefore everyone knows," ran the statement, "that he who claims his fellow Christian as property is no Christian. He is against Christ and nullifies all God's commandments. God has freed all Christians and released them from all bonds."[6] It was bitter irony that, according to the document, the sharpest criticism of serfdom came from a Turk [a Muslim]. He pointed out the contradiction

3. L. Graf zu Dohna, *Reformatio Sigismundi: Beiträge zum Verständnis einer Reformationsschrift des fünfzehnten Jahrhunderts* (Göttingen, 1960), 109ff.

4. A peasant's laced shoe, contrasted with the knight's riding boot.

5. H. Grundmann, "Freiheit als religiöses, politisches, und persönliches Postulat im Mittelalter," *HZ* 183 (1957): 49ff.

6. *Die Reformation Kaiser Sigmunds*, ed. K. Beer (Stuttgart, 1933), 119, 15–16, 39. The oft-repeated assertion that the Bundschuh program was dependent directly on the "Reformation Sigismundi" is doubtful (Dohna, *Reformatio*, 197ff.), but the spread of its ideas through a large number of pamphlets and handwritten papers is well attested.

between the salvation claimed through Christ and the rights valid among his own people. "We are freer than you," he boasted. "We act more justly than you in all things."[7] The redress of other grievances could likewise be derived from divine justice, such as freedom to utilize the forest, to hunt and fish, to marry [without securing the lord's consent], to inherit without restriction, to pay off debts through interest. The peasants appealed to old legal codes and to divine justice. The two categories were not contradictory in substance but stood side by side in separate territories as successive waves of revolt swept across upper Germany during 1513–17. The revolt surged from the eastern Alps to Switzerland, from Franconia to Alsace. The future belonged to the Bundschuh, the party then still a minority, seeking a dynamic solution in terms of divine justice. For a time the movement still bore features of the traditional faith. So, for example, in 1476 a vision of Mary, seen by a certain Hans Böheim, the piper of Niklashausen in Taubertal, authenticated the sermon in which he challenged the people to revolt. Popular belief in the great indulgence, offered through the pilgrimage Böheim had organized, on the one hand, and hatred of the clergy, on the other, were the two contrasting forces through which this popular leader worked on the crowd.[8] "Lord, uphold thy divine justice!" banners reminded the rebels in the diocese of Speyer and in Breisgau (1513). And there were paintings, like the one depicting a *Bundschuh* at its center, above it a cross; on either side of it were Mary and John the disciple, and kneeling below, a peasant. The banner depicted in whose name one fought. Besides, the imperial crown and the papal tiara showed from whom help was expected.[9] The religious tension underlying the movement was caught in the couplet of the conspirators in Bruhrain (lands under Speyer around Bruchsal): "God greet you, partner! What's going on? For all the clerics we'll hardly make it."[10] A certain priest in Lehen, near Freiburg, was more pointed as he coached fellow conspirators: "It's a godly concern to put justice first, for God wills it, and in the Scriptures they've found that justice must come first."[11] Then there

---

7. Beer, ed., *Reformation*, 23 / 9ff. Also Grundmann, "Freiheit," 50–51.

8. Franz, *Der deutsche Bauernkreig*, 48ff. See also Franz, ed., *Akten Bauernkrieg*, 1 / 2:62ff.

9. Franz, *Der deutsche Bauernkrieg*, 72. R. M. Radbruch, *Der deutsche Bauernstand zwischen Mittelalter und Neuzeit* (Munich, 1941), 70.

10. Franz, ed., *Akten Bauernkrieg*, 1 / 2:73.

11. A. Rosenkranz, *Der Bundschuh, die Erhebung des südwestdeutschen Bauernstandes in den Jahren 1499–1517*, vol. 1: *Darstellung* (Heidelberg, 1927), 188, 303. W. Andreas, *Der Bundschuh: Die Bauernverschwörungen am Oberrhein* (Köln, 1936; 2d ed., 1953), 29, 42ff. Franz, *Der deutsche Bauernkrieg*, 66ff., 70ff. (see also his map 1).

was the case of the unidentified revolutionary on the Upper Rhine whose widely read and gloomy lamentation described the misery of the peasant class and the manifold injustice of the times. He saw but one remaining way out: an apocalyptic hope in a mighty uprising and the installation of a simple, pious peasant as the new "Emperor Frederick," who would reign a thousand years.[12]

Such dreams of individuals had limited effect until linked to a faith greatly strengthened by a biblically spelled-out divine justice. And this took place through the movement of renewal within the church that was appealing to the Scriptures as the standard of all theological pronouncements and ecclesiastical action. Seven years after the Bundschuh party's failure, new waves of unrest arose in 1524. In short order all demands were coordinated under the universal law of divine justice. The demands now included the right of congregations to elect their own pastors—who would preach the true Word of God and who would be supported by the hitherto customary tithe. This demand had a precedent in Wyclif's struggle to cleanse the church, although the calling of pastors and the refusal to tithe had no direct connection with the peasant revolution. In the uprising of 1478 in Kärnten [Austria] the local election of priests had already been on the program for a future peasant state.[13] It now became a demand under which the peasants united visibly for a sweeping church reform. The dynamic biblicism of the Zurich reformation fell like a firebrand, igniting the hearths of unrest in the southernmost Black Forest. Zwingli's disciple Balthasar Hubmaier of Waldshut (a powerful preacher as well as a quick decision-maker and activist) led off. As canon in Regensburg's cathedral, he had earlier launched an uprising against the Jews and also rallied a huge pilgrimage to a place called "Lovely Mary." From 1523 he was preaching on the evangelical side. Even so, it was plain hyperbole when a contemporary clerical chronist called him the "initiator and prime mover of the entire peasant war."[14] Yet Hubmaier was undoubtedly a compelling character. The peasants of the region, busily organizing in 1524, were attracted

12. H. Haupt, "Ein Oberrheinischer Revolutionär aus dem Zeitalter Maximilians I: Mitteilungen aus einer kirchlich-politischen Reformschrift des ersten Decenniums des 16. Jahrhunderts," in *Westdeutsche Zeitschrift für Geschichte und Kunst* 8 (1893): 77ff. O. Eckstein, "Der oberrheinische Revolutionär" (philosophy diss., Leipzig, 1939). Franz, *Der deutsche Bauernkreig*, 68–69.

13. Schmidt, "John Wyclifs Kirchenbegriffe," 81–82, 94. Franz, *Der deutsche Bauernkrieg*, 81.

14. F. J. Mone, "Chronik des Andreas Lettsch, von 1519–1531," in *Quellensammlung der badischen Landesgeschichte 2* (Karlsruhe, 1854), 46, cited in Franz, ed., *Akten Bauernkrieg*, 1 / 2:85ff.

to Hubmaier. He had proven his leadership by liberating Waldshut, with Zurich's help, from Austrian control. The difficult struggle had also extorted the right to evangelical preaching. As everyone knew, Hubmaier was now advising and encouraging the peasants.[15] Soon the names of a half-dozen other preachers joined that of Hubmaier on the list of the leaders or advisers heading the several rebellions.[16]

In one territory after another the "Christian Union" emerged as a firm federation. Everyone was pressured to join; the reluctant were threatened with the ban (exclusion from the rights of church life) or with expulsion from the territory. Peasant convictions ran deeply. They not only itemized specific grievances, which they compiled in detail, but also advocated an absolute standard of justice applicable to all and to which they themselves conformed. This divine justice [or fundamental law] could for them be nothing other than the gospel. What else would they call it after the preaching of God's Word had made its breakthrough in so many places. Thus their primary demand was that the Word be proclaimed freely and purely and that it be recognized as the norm for the settlement of all disputed questions. In Alsace the slogan ran "Support the Gospel and Justice," and the peasants in the region lettered their banners "Jesus Christ" or VDMIE (*Verbum domini manet in eternum* [The Word of the Lord abides forever]). This expressed the basic motivation of all the rebellions that in February 1525 began to surge across southern Germany.[17] Appeals to the gospel at times overarched specific demands. "The holy gospel: Let what it turned over, be turned over, and what it raises up, be raised up," proclaimed the Rothenburg peasants on March 25, 1525. Six weeks later, Florian Geyer, addressing the Rothenburg town council, set forth the aims of the Franconian peasants, which included the above exhortation.[18] Opponents were quick to associate the peasants' appeal and

15. J. Loserth, "Die Stadt Waldshut und die vorderoesterreichische Regierung in den Jahren 1523–1526: Ein Beitrag zur Geschichte des Bauernkrieges und der Reformation in Vorderoesterreich," *AÖG* 77 (1891): 1ff. Again Loserth, "Balthasar Hubmaier," *Mennonitisches Lexikon* 2 (1937): 355–56. W. Stolze, *Bauernkrieg und Reformation*, SVRG 141 (Leipzig, 1926), 62ff. W. Stolze, "Die Stühlinger Erhebung des Jahres 1524 und ihre Gründe," *HZ* 139 (1929): 295ff. Franz, *Der deutsche Bauernkrieg*, 103ff. T. Bergsten, *Balthasar Hubmaier: Seine Stellung zu Reformation und Täufertum, 1521–1528* (Kassel, 1961), 146ff., 192ff., 223ff.

16. At first in Forchheim near Nuremberg, in the territory of Bamberg, Otto Brunfels in Neuenburg (Breisgau), Schappeler in Memmingen, Teuschlein in Rothenburg, Denner and Hollenpack in Taubertal, Eisenhut in Kraichgau, and others unnamed. Cf. also von Schubert, *Revolution und Reformation*, 28, n. 56.

17. Franz, *Der deutsche Bauernkrieg*, 144. Franz, ed., *Akten Bauernkrieg*, 1/2: consult its index under "Evangelium."

18. Franz, *Der deutsche Bauernkrieg*, 182. Franz, ed., *Akten Bauernkrieg*, 1/2:367/4ff.

the key words of the Reformation; they essentially blamed that movement for fomenting revolt in the first place. "How Luther greases the Bundschuh and lures the simple people" read the heading over a woodcut in Thomas Murner's satire "The Great Lutheran Fool," which suggested how this activity of Luther's was contributing to an impending armed conflict.[19]

Events were happening simultaneously. While the idea of the gospel as the criterion of godly righteousness gathered up the older slogans and appeals to justice, the rising revolt formulated its program in the *Twelve Articles*. These appeared in late February 1525, the product of the southern Swabian peasantry in the region of Memmingen. The *Twelve Articles* did not rule out supplemental articles addressed to local grievances, but they soon caught on as the confessional document of the entire uprising. The articles owe their fame as much to moderation as to wide publication. In moderate tones the grievances and desires of the peasants were summed up biblically. Cleverly and resourcefully the articles were circulated among the masses. As an agreed proclamation of the peasants, they swiftly broke into print and within three months had run through twenty-five printings.[20] The keynote ringing through all twelve articles is struck in Article 1: "First, we humbly ask and request" that the local congregation have the power to elect its pastor and to depose him should he conduct himself improperly. He "shall preach the holy gospel to us clearly and purely. He is to add no teaching or commandment of men to the gospel." As Scripture clearly says, "we can come to God only through true faith." Virtually all the other articles appeal to God and his Word. The peasants are willing to pay their tithe of grain, "but it must be done in a proper way," for the modest support of the pastor and for distribution to the poor and needy. Anything that remains shall be kept in reserve, so that if a war tax be required "no general tax may be laid on the poor." The "small tithe," which is levied on cattle, "we will not pay at all, for God the Lord created cattle for the free use of men" (art. 2). As for the prevailing status of serfdom, this is seen as a contradiction, "for Christ has redeemed and bought us all with the precious shedding of his blood." "Therefore it agrees with Scripture that we be free and will to be so. Not that we intend

19. Depicted in Waas, *Die Bauern im Kampf um Gerechtigkeit* (see n. 1, above), 73.

20. Franz, ed., *Akten Bauernkrieg*, 1/2:174ff. "Urkunden zur Geschichte des Bauernkrieges und der Wiedertäfer," ed. H. Boehmer, *Kleine Texte* 50/51 (Bonn, 1910; reprint, Berlin, 1933). Facsimile in Waas, *Die Bauren im Kampf um Gerechtigkeit*, 97ff. G. Franz, "Die Entstehung der 'Zwölf Artikel' der deutschen Bauernschaft," *ARG* 36 (1939): 193ff. (lists the older literature). Also Franz, *Der deutsche Bauernkrieg*, 123ff.

to be entirely free, for God does not teach us that we should desire no rulers." Indeed, in following the commandments, the peasants would be humble toward everyone. "We willingly obey our chosen and appointed rulers (whom God has placed over us) in all Christian and appropriate matters" (art. 3). The prohibition on hunting and fishing, as imposed on the poor, is "not according to the Word of God," for God the Lord has given man "authority over all animals" (art. 4). Congregations arbitrarily barred from cutting wood should have these rights restored. Over any forests not honestly purchased, "a brotherly and Christian agreement should be reached" (art. 5). The same holds for meadows and common fields that have been taken from a congregation (art. 10). Because the amount of free labor required by the lords has rapidly been increasing and demands an excessive number of days, such labor should be limited. "We ask that we be dealt with as graciously as were our forefathers, who provided these services according to the Word of God" (art. 6). Excessive rents on many of the holdings should be reset at a reasonable rate, "for the laborer deserves his wages" (Luke 10:7) (art. 8). The death tax (where the lord expropriates a peasant's inheritance) should be abolished. For such a tax is "contrary to God and to honor" (art. 11). The appeal to God's Word indeed obligated the peasants—they honestly felt it to be so—to place themselves under him. They concluded by promising: "If one or more of the articles here set forth is not in agreement with the Word of God . . . we shall withdraw such an article." Conversely, "if additional articles are found to be properly based on Scripture and more offenses against God and our neighbor be revealed thereby, [they will be added to these articles]" (art. 12). The biblical tone of the *Twelve Articles* was accentuated by numerous Scripture citations in the margin. Yet these passages applied for the most part only allegorically. The dangerous question of what this Christian manner of speaking really meant in the minds of thousands of peasants, rallying to fight for their rights, was treated courageously and aptly in an introduction by a manifestly different hand. Those who now scoff, saying, "These are the fruits of the new gospel!" are themselves "counter-Christians," because they have withdrawn themselves from the gospel of peace, patience, and unity to which the peasants are appealing. How can one charge the peasants with insurrection when they desire to live according to this gospel? And who will meddle in God's judgment and resist his majesty? Is he who freed Israel from Pharaoh's hand not able today to rescue his own? "Yes, he will deliver them! And quickly!" This remarkable combination of demands—utter earnestness, biblical proofs, Christian responsiveness, and eschatological hope—placed the *Twelve Ar-*

361

ticles foremost among the various peasant programs. They were the joint product of two men of Memmingen: Sebastian Lotzer, a journeyman furrier, and Christoph Schappeler, the local pastor and an adherent of Zwingli. Lotzer had emerged as a lay preacher and most probably was author of the *Twelve Articles* as such. Schappeler presumably wrote the introduction and supplied most of the citations from Scripture.[21]

We must allow the tone of these articles as a whole to work their crescendo on us if we would grasp two things in particular: first, their suggestive power, which speedily enveloped an entire peasant movement; second, the unavoidable question they asked of Luther. In it he was confronted by the medieval mix of gospel and temporal politics yet in a manner far different from the cold canon law of the church. To have faced a church styling itself as the *civitas Dei terrena* (the city of God on earth) with claims to rule, riches, and military might all drawn from the Bible was one thing. But now Luther faced something else. Before him loomed a whole scenario of medieval sectarian movements—Waldensians, Wyclifites, Hussites—revived and recast by the social reshuffling of the times and by the preaching sprung from the Reformation. Permeating it all was the primal thought of the church as poor and of the people as sovereign, having rights of immediate access to Holy Scripture, to the source of the law of Christ—the divine justice—that shapes all relationships.

As for the peasants' demands for a renewal of the church, Luther largely agreed. Yet to him the entire approach must have appeared ominously reversed, threatening to rob the gospel of its newly recovered fundamental meaning and to press it into the service of a temporal program, be it ever so righteous and justifiable. This problem was one not simply for theological disputation but also for practical decision on a new front. Effects emanating from it were visibly signaling its might. The *Twelve Articles,* indeed no mere pamphlet, was the program of a movement that in a few weeks' time had gripped all of southern Germany. No pitched battles or bloody deeds as yet, but armed mobs, insubordinations, and plunderings foreshadowed things to come. Even if the peasants themselves had not asked for it, Luther could not have remained silent. His stand would oppose a political use of the gospel, as events were making this direction visible. Meanwhile, the peasants had listed Luther, along with some twenty other preachers of reform, as one from whom they sought an exposition on divine justice, and expressed their readiness to submit to it.

21. M. Brecht, "Der theologische Hintergrund der Zwölf Artikel der Bauernschaft in Schwaben von 1525: Christoph Schappelers und Sebastian Lotzers Beitrag zum Bauernkrieg," *ZKG* 85 (1974): 30ff. [Text of the *Twelve Articles* in *LW* 46:8–16.]

But [south of Ulm] the Memmingen town council thwarted this approach.[22] Whether Luther ever saw this list, we do not know, but he was sent not only the *Twelve Articles* but also another pamphlet in which the peasants proposed that he, along with Melanchthon or Bugenhagen, serve as a court of arbitration.[23]

Luther's reply and his subsequent tracts on the Peasants' War require patient analysis, if for no other reason than that a modern observer does not find it easy to recapture the presuppositions of those writings. The stand Luther took did not bear directly on the social conflict which the historian is to describe. Besides, it is difficult to see how Luther would have been in a position to pass an overall or realistic judgment on this event. Nor would he have been able to make an adequate assessment of the peasants' economic situation; even the amassed sources available to research today have left discussions without an agreed interpretation.[24] Nor could Luther perceive the extent of social transition then in progress: the peasantry's lagging behind the rise of the cities, and the older society's worsening legal situation compared to the growing rights of the territorial states and to the changes in jurisdiction. Beside these came the endless and more immediately aggravating causes of general unrest. For his part, Luther had to depend on isolated impressions or symptoms. Certainly these shocked him, yet they fell short of being a threat to the general peace which was now at the door. His disposition toward the peasants was friendly but realistic. He breathed neither the haughty mockery of the humanists nor the romantic glorification of the peasants, and the latter mood had been spreading since the end of the fifteenth century.[25] Luther's own heritage linked him to the peasantry, and he understood its weaknesses. To be sure, he called himself a son of the soil: "My great-

22. "Bundesordnung der drei oberschwäbischen Haufen vom 7. März 1525," printed in Böhmer, ed., "Urkunden," 24.

23. Franz, *Der deutsche Bauernkrieg*, 130. Franz, ed., *Akten Bauernkrieg*, 1 / 2:149–50. C. A. Cornelius, *Studien zur Geschichte des Bauernkrieges* AHKBAW 9 (Munich, 1866), 163–64. WA 18:280.

24. Waas, "Die grosse Wendung," 22ff. F. Lütge, "Luthers Eingreifen in den Bauernkrieg in seinen sozialgeschichtlichen Voraussetzungen und Auswirkungen," *JNS* 158 (1943): 375ff. Cf. the short survey of the different Western as well as Marxist modes of historiography, by T. Nipperdey and P. Melcher, "Bauernkrieg," *SDG* 1 (1966): 611ff.

25. F. von Bezold, "Die 'armen Leute' und die deutsche Literatur des späteren Mittelalters," *HZ* 41 (1879), reprinted in Bezold's *Aus Mittelalter und Renaissance* (Munich and Berlin, 1917), 49ff. K. Uhrig, "Der Bauer in der Publizistik der Reformation bis zum Ausgang des Bauernkrieges," *ARG* 33 (1936): 70ff., 165ff., esp. 77ff., 95ff. P. Böckmann, "Der gemeine Mann in den Flugschriften der Reformation," *DVLG* 22 (1944): 186ff. F. Martini, "Das Bauerntum im deutschen Schrifttum von den Anfängen bis zum 16. Jahrhundert," *DVLG* 27 (1953). Andreas, *Der Bundschuh*, 433ff. Radbruch, *Der deutsche Bauernstand*.

grandfather, grandfather, and father were real peasants." But that oft-quoted comment came years later. Besides, it was no outburst of pride, but an objection against the astrologists who were baffled at how this kind of ancestry could account for the strange course Martin's life had taken.[26] Luther held the rural estate in high regard, especially in contrast to the uncanny money-mad business of the cities. Peasants, after all, repre-sented the earliest form of work instituted by God himself at the dawn of human history. And when Luther liked to recognize peasants and shep-herds, instead of clergy and scholars, as the type to whom God had en-trusted his revelation, he praised them not really because of their piety but because of God's mercy, which favors the poor, the wretched, and those tested by suffering. To him the unrest of the peasants was no nov-elty, but for a long time he let it lie on the edge of his horizon. When, for example, he addressed the Christian nobility (1520), his proposals for re-form did not even mention the peasants. He put in a good word for the virtues of farming, yet this was only to underscore the pitfalls of business and usury.[27] In a letter from the Wartburg, Luther's quip to Melanchthon that "Germany has very many *Karstenhansen*" [grubbers, or stooped wielders of the hoe], intended no disparagement, for those were the days when this designation for peasants was being popularized in literature. Luther meant it to convey reassurance: Should the pope proceed with force, he will be wrecked by the resistance of the people.[28] But as soon as he sensed that the hard-pressed "grubbers" could spontaneously stage a revolt against the bishops, clergy, and monks, he promptly came out with his *Sincere Admonition to All Christians to Guard Against Insurrection and Rebellion*. He drew the line in no uncertain terms between the gospel and the use of force. He himself did not yet believe the danger to be as serious or as imminent as it actually was.[29] Neither in his correspondence nor in his sermons during the next few years does he reflect anything of

26. WA TR 5:558 / 13–14; 255 / 10.

27. WA 6:466 / 40ff. [*LW* 44:214.]

28. May 26, 1521, WA Br 2:348 / 65. *Karsthans*, in the German-Frankish language area, denotes the peasant who works with a hoe [or mattock, actually a "grubber"]. Cf. A. E. Berger, *Die Sturmtruppen der Reformation: Ausgewählte Flugschriften der Jahre 1520–25*, Deutsche Literatur, Reihe Reformation 2 (Leipzig, 1931), 48–50. Böckmann, "Der gemeine Mann in den Flugschriften," 194ff. The concept is carried in the impressive title of a pam-phlet, in early 1521, for Luther and against Thomas Murner, which was written not by Vadian but possibly by the Freiburg physician and lay preacher Hans Murer (Maurer), WA Br 2:351, n. 35. W. Näf, *Vadian und seine Stadt St. Gallen* (St. Gall, 1957), 2:121, n. 224. In the summer of 1521 there appeared, likely from Bucer's pen, "Neu Karsthans." *Martin Bucers Deutsche Schriften*, ed. R. Stupperich (Gütersloh, 1960), 1:385ff., 406ff. [*LW* 44:233–34.]

29. WA 8:676 / 10ff., 22ff.; 679 / 9ff., 35ff. See above, pp. 38–39. [LW 45:51–74.]

the unrest among the peasants, even though he tangled amply with Karlstadt, Müntzer, and other "Enthusiasts." He had not yet made the connection between these two developments. Only on receipt of the *Twelve Articles*, probably early in April 1525, and very soon after the initial alarms coming from events in southern Germany, did Luther perceive the extent of the movement and the connection between its demands and its theology.

The events now set in motion had dimensions which, in Luther's perception, went far beyond any social confrontation.[30] From the outset, his *Admonition to Peace: A Reply to the Twelve Articles of the Peasants in Swabia* set a position to which he adhered steadfastly. It contains the gist of his later utterances, although his pronounced earnestness here is still balanced when compared to his subsequent writings so charged with emotion—all of which sprang from his grief over a boundless calamity and from his anger over the peasants' proceedings. Luther began to write his *Admonition* while en route in Eisleben, in the garden of Johann Duhren, a councilman in Mansfeld. There, on April 19–20, he was discussing the opening of a secondary school.[31] As he wrote, he was still under the impression that he could expect a hearing, for the peasants had declared their readiness, at the end of the *Twelve Articles*, to desist from any demonstrably unjust demands. However, as we have also seen, they reserved the right to add such other articles on grievances that are an offense "against God and a hardship on the neighbor."[32]

In replying, Luther cited three reasons: (1) If this rebellion were to get the upper hand, "both kingdoms would be destroyed and there would be neither temporal government nor Word of God."[33] (2) "Germany will be laid waste, and if this bloodshed once starts, it will not stop until everything is destroyed. It is easy to start a fight, but we cannot stop the fighting whenever we want to."[34] (3) Both sides are risking their soul's salvation, the lords because of their tyranny and hardheartedness, the peasants because of their recourse to violence.[35] Luther's reasoning is based not on

30. P. Althaus, "Luthers Haltung im Bauernkrieg," *LuJ* 7 (1925): 1ff. Also printed in P. Althaus, *Evangelium und Leben* (Gütersloh, 1927), 144ff., and separately later (Darmstadt, 1953). M. Greschat, "Luthers Haltung im Bauernkrieg," *ARG* 56 (1965): 31ff.

31. *WA* 18:281. Cf. *WA Br* 3:474 / 6–7. Luther's much-corrected manuscript has been preserved and the final version is printed along with the original, *WA* 18:291ff. [*LW* 46:(3–)8–43.]

32. See above, p. 361.

33. *WA* 18:292 / 16–17. [*LW* 46:18.]

34. *WA* 18:332 / 3ff. Cf. 292 / 17–18; 297 / 13–14; 329 / 8–9. [*LW* 46:42, 18, 22, 40–41.]

35. *WA* 18:329 / 2ff.; 331 / 6ff.; 333 / 11ff. [*LW* 46:40, 42, 43.]

political grounds but on human and pastoral grounds. He is eager to ward off injustice and impending calamity and to protect the life of the innocent; these are always the ones who suffer most in a rebellion, as he had warned three years earlier in his *Sincere Admonition*.[36] What he wrote now was simply an application of basic principles he had set forth earlier.

Luther therefore appeals to the conscience on both sides, yet with characteristic differentiation. The lords sin by misusing their rights. "As temporal rulers you do nothing but cheat and rob the people so that you may lead a life of luxury and extravagance. The poor common folk can bear it no longer." Besides, "what good would it do a peasant if his field bore as many guilders as stalks of wheat if the rulers only taxed him all the more and then wasted it as though it were chaff to increase their luxury, and squandered his money on their own clothes, food, drink, and buildings?"[37] Let the lords note well, for the sake of their temporal and eternal good, that in this peasant rebellion it is actually God's wrath rising up against them. "It is not the peasants, dear lords, who are resisting you. It is God himself, visiting your raging on you."[38] Because of God's wrath let the lords not be obstinate but "deal reasonably with the peasants."[39] Luther sees the signs of the times in the sky and on the earth, substantiating his anxiety, for these signs include the false prophets and the riotous mobs of peasants, and they are meant for the lords to read.[40] Therefore let the lords feel themselves anything but secure: "The sword is already at your throats." "God wills to defeat you, and you will be defeated."[41]

For their part, the peasants sin by proceeding unlawfully.[42] Their demands may be just, but their rebellion is all wrong. Therefore every form of law is arrayed against them, natural law as well as "Christian" law, to say

---

36. *WA* 8:680 / 18ff. [*LW* 45:62–63.]

37. *WA* 18:293 / 15ff.; 299 / 7ff. [*LW* 46:19, 23, edited.]

38. *WA* 18:295 / 4ff. [*LW* 46:20.]

39. *WA* 18:297 / 10. [*LW* 46:21.]

40. *WA* 18:293 / 4ff.; 294 / 7ff.; 334 / 5ff. [*LW* 46:18, 19, 43.] Only three weeks earlier Spalatin had sent Luther a pamphlet illustrating a phenomenon (miracle) in the sky showing a sun and two satellite suns. Luther and Melanchthon interpreted one of the satellites as the setting sun of France's Francis I, who had been defeated near Pavia on February 24. The other satellite presumably depicted Emperor Charles V. *WA Br* 3:464 / 4ff. In the winter Luther and Melanchthon had on several nights seen a rainbow over Lochau which Luther interpreted later, even as he interpreted two miscarriages in Wittenberg, as signs of the death of Frederick the Wise on May 5. Letter to John Rühel, May 23, 1525, *WA Br* 3:508 / 28ff. Astrological prophecies then current (Franz, *Der deutsche Bauernkrieg*, 92) were certainly not meant by Luther. [As for Luther's own thoughts at the time, see his letter to Rühel of May 4, 1525, *LW* 49:106–12.]

41. *WA* 18:293 / 17; 295 / 4. [*LW* 46:19, 20.]

42. *WA* 18:306 / 6ff. [*LW* 46:27.]

nothing of which one is applicable. Their guilt is not like that of the lords—a flagrant abuse of rights—but their guilt lies in an uncanny depth into which they do not care to look. Therefore Luther goes to greater lengths than with the lords so as to open their eyes for what he means. First, he must remove the claimed legal entitlement underlying their appeals. Neither divine law nor natural law allows one to be judge of one's own case.[43] He calls on the peasants themselves to bear witness to where things would likely be heading if in their own crowd every one undertook "to function as his own judge and avenger."[44] Even the heathen know that there must be law, rulers, and order in the world. "Would to God that the majority of us were good, pious heathen who kept the natural law."[45] Now the peasants outdo the lords in that they would take away the best thing the lords have, namely, their authority.[46] For example, on their own authority the peasants refuse to pay the tithe. While they may not be aware of having attacked natural law, they have done something far worse; they have arrogated a "divine law" to themselves, and in no way can they justify this act on the basis of the gospel. The law of a "Christian association," as the peasants call themselves, does not consist in personal revenge and force of arms. "Suffering! Suffering! Cross! Cross! This and nothing else is the Christian law!"[47] Christ's teaching in the Sermon on the Mount (Matt. 5:39ff.) and his words to Peter, who drew the sword (Matt. 26:52), as well as Paul's admonition against taking revenge (Rom. 12:19 and 1 Cor. 11:20) and against Christians dragging their disputes into court (1 Cor. 6:1ff.), prove the Christian position. Therefore, Luther is angered outright that the preface to the *Twelve Articles* was composed by a preacher of lies and studded with Bible references, with passages unrelated to the peasants' demands and sometimes having quite the opposite meaning.[48]

Having made his charge, Luther now attacked his real opponents: not the peasants but their betrayers, the "false prophets," those who summoned the peasants to violence in the name of Christ and of Christian liberty. His polemic is against these betrayers and permeates the entire tract.[49] Here is the continuation of Luther's struggle against Thomas

43. *WA* 18:304 / 7–8; 307 / 5, 17–18. [*LW* 46:25, 27.]

44. *WA* 18:306 / 15ff. [*LW* 46:27.]

45. *WA* 18:310 / 17–18. [*LW* 46:29.]

46. *WA* 18:306 / 4. [*LW* 46:26.]

47. *WA* 18:301 / 14–15; 310 / 10–11. This is said not against the peasants in contrast to the lords but against their styling themselves a Christian movement. [*LW* 46:24, 28–29.]

48. *WA* 18:309ff.; 319 / 14ff. [*LW* 46:28–29, 30.]

49. *WA* 18:294 / 10ff.; 296 / 6ff.; 301 / 6; 308 / 1ff., 14; 310 / 4ff.; 316 / 16; 328 / 15ff. [*LW* 46: 19, 21, 28, 29, 33, 40.]

Müntzer, who turned to the peasants for support after having failed to challenge the princes to join in an eschatological battle against the Roman church. Müntzer, now in Mühlhausen, was rallying the rebellious, and the seed he had sown was springing up everywhere in the cries of the peasant crowds. These "prophets of murder" are teaching the peasants "in the name of the gospel to act against the gospel." Therefore, like the Antichrist pope, the false prophets belong to the signs of divine judgment. Here the warning of the Second Commandment applies: "God will not hold them guiltless (leave unpunished) those who take his name in vain."[50] Luther was not troubled by anxiety over his own undertaking—he frequently spoke of "my gospel"—yet he realized that the rebellious peasants could harm the Reformation more seriously than either pope or emperor had thus far been able to do. He committed the matter to God, "relying stubbornly at all times on his hand."[51] What plunged him into deep unrest was something else: conscience. Their rebellious misuse of God's name, thought Luther, could not give the peasants a good conscience; they might enjoy victory for a while, but they would be lost, body and soul, in eternity.[52] He saw them as squandering their only sure help, the help of God. If as Christians they would cling only to the example of Christ, "You would soon see God's miracle, that he would help you as he helped Christ." In Luther's words, this was no cheap comfort, for he did not conceal the possibility that their course could lead them through defeat and death. They could, however, keep a good conscience and the gospel.[53] Realistically, he no longer hoped to persuade them all. "That does not worry me. It is enough for me to save some of the good-hearted and upright men among you."[54] This was the one goal he could set for himself in this public act of pastoral care.

Luther's appeal to conscience on both the embattled sides led quite naturally to his proposal for a settling of the conflict. He advised them "to choose certain counts and lords from among the nobility and certain councilmen from the cities," asking them "to arbitrate and settle this dispute amicably." He was blunt: "You lords, stop being so stubborn! . . . Give these poor people room to live and air to breathe." Likewise, "You peasants, let yourselves be instructed and give up the excessive demands of some of your articles." He hoped that "in this way it may be possible to

50. WA 18:316 / 9–10; 294 / 10ff.; 302 / 1–2. [LW 46:32, 19, 24.]
51. WA 18:313 / 6ff., 11. [LW 46:31.]
52. WA 18:300 / 4ff. [LW 46:23.]
53. WA 18:312 / 10–11; 313 / 3ff. [LW 46:31.]
54. WA 18:301 / 8–9. [LW 46:24.]

reach a solution of this dispute through human laws and agreements, if not through Christian means."[55] For his part, Luther commented only on the three articles bearing directly on the basic premises of his tract. (1) The desire for the right of a congregation to elect its own pastor is legitimate. However, such congregational holdings belonging to the ruler may not be claimed. If the ruler does not make such holdings available, then the congregation must itself support the pastor, but if the ruler does not tolerate a given pastor locally chosen, then let the pastor flee to another town, "and let any flee who desire to do as Christ teaches."[56] (2) Retaining the tithe so as to support the pastor and the poor and to meet emergencies is "nothing but theft and highway robbery." This is the same as deposing the rulers altogether and acting like lords of the land and taking over the rulers' property.[57] (3) Christian liberty, as shown by the biblical stand on slavery, does not mean the abolition of serfdom, but is to be exercised in the context of serfdom as well as in any other form of imprisonment. Yet the peasants at this point misunderstand not only the gospel but also temporal order. "This [third] article would make all men equal." But this is impossible, for "a worldly kingdom cannot exist without an inequality of people," all of them part of a manifold diversity of vocations and positions.[58] The other nine articles—hunting, fishing, cutting wood, required labor, rents, taxes, fines, and so on—Luther regards as "matters for the lawyers to discuss," adding, "It is not fitting that I, an evangelist, should judge or make decisions in such matters."[59]

Different though Luther's arguments confronting the two sides may be, the substance of his appeal is one. He directs both sides to the same mentors, Holy Scripture and history. Scripture, as here employed, appears not in the robes of dogmatic authority but as the teacher of wisdom, that alert eyes can also discern in history. Experience, moreover, shows that the violent are finally destroyed by violence, that rebellion has never ended well but has always cost mutual destruction. History supports what

---

55. WA 18:333 / 19ff. [LW 46:43.]

56. WA 18:325 / 2ff. [LW 46:38.]

57. WA 18:325 / 18–19. [LW 46:38.]

58. WA 18:326 / 15ff., esp. 327 / 4. Waas, "Die Bauern im Kampf um Gerechtigkeit" (see n. 1, above), 205, on this issue cites a statement of Luther's taken not from the sources but from Ricarda Huch, Das Zeitalter der Glaubensspaltung (Berlin and Zurich, 1937), 215 (Siebenstern ed., 188). Waas admits that this citation pertains not to a common statement by Luther and Melanchthon during the Peasants' War but to something Melanchthon wrote to Heinrich von Einsiedel, July 13, 1549, CR 7:431ff., preceded by correspondence of Einsiedel with Spalatin and Luther in 1539.

59. WA 18:327 / 12ff. [LW 46:39.]

Scripture says: God is judge over the world; whoever takes the sword will die by the sword.[60] The embittered antagonists, lords and peasants, are in truth not separated but bound together in a common destiny. "In short, God hates both tyrants and rebels; therefore he sets them against each other, so that both parties perish shamefully and his wrath and judgment on the godless are fulfilled."[61]

This is the viewpoint from which to size up the event through Luther's eyes. We must look from the visible to the invisible—where lies not a lesser reality but the true reality. From that vantage point the question of justice gains its distinctive perspective. Luther's concept of law is oriented in a positive sense of justice. He is still far from conceding natural rights to the peasants which an emergency would allow them to extort by revolution. The halfway meeting that he urges on the lords is not a legal matter but a humanitarian matter. In this sense Luther can speak of the "human and natural right" of the peasant,[62] yet not in the sense of the personal rights of natural law. This recourse to absolute maxims (always a debatable tactic in emergency situations) is foreign to Luther's thought, for he constantly bears in mind the righteousness [justice] of God, a much more reliable and decisive power amid conflict. In its own time and manner this divine justice will act, often differently, to be sure, from our own thoughts and desires, yet always according to divine law. Luther had already commented to this effect on the Magnificat in 1521: "He has put down the mighty from their thrones, and exalted those of low degree" (Luke 1:52). The quest for humane justice (it alone moves us in today's social conflicts) does not find Luther indifferent, yet he finds it applied in an unsuspected manner when the Christian does not force the matter on his own but places it in God's hands. This does not prevent Luther from raising the subject. He reproaches the lords that among the *Twelve Articles* some are "so fair and just as to take away your reputation in the eyes of God and the world." He adds, "I would have formulated other articles against you," still better than these.[63] Whatever is sought must not be sought in the name of the gospel. Luther refuses to allow this mixing of the spiritual and the temporal even there where the peasants most readily counted on his support, namely, by their reproach that the gospel is being denied them. Certainly to try to correct the abuse by force is bitter injustice. Neverthe-

60. WA 18:329 / 13ff. [*LW* 46:40–41.]
61. WA 18:331 / 2ff. [*LW* 46:41.]
62. WA 18:328 / 6; 333 / 7–8. [*LW* 46:40.]
63. WA 18:298 / 3ff. [*LW* 46:22.]

less, "it is impossible to keep the gospel from anyone." A person, contends Luther, can leave these cities or places and follow the gospel to some other place where he has freedom to live according to it.[64] Under no circumstances is a withholding of the gospel by any temporal authority to be made an article in a program of insurrection. In the spiritual realm as well as the temporal realm, Luther differentiates soundly between reformation and revolution.

His *Admonition* completed, Luther soon learned that his proposal for arbitration was on the right track. There was still a chance to keep the peace. During the very days that Luther was writing his treatise the peasants in the regions of Lake Constance and Allgäu had signed a treaty with the commanding general of the Swabian League, the lord high steward of Waldenburg. The event occurred with surprising suddenness in Weingarten, Easter Monday, April 17, 1525.[65] The treaty had sprung from the anxieties of both sides, just as their armed forces were moving into battle. The peasants already had been disheartened by a severe defeat at Leipheim, near Ulm, on April 4. For the Swabian League, the commanding general was not sure that his forces could defeat the peasants as now augmented by forces from the lake region, so he played for time. In the treaty, as subsequently concluded, the peasants pledged to disband their mobs; to vacate the occupied castles, cloisters, and towns; to renounce rebellion; and to pay the usual taxes until equitably regulated. To ease the peasants' complaints a court of arbitration (comprising representatives of the cities) was to be convened, each side naming half the court's four or six members. In case of disagreement, the chairman would be determined by casting lots or by action of the Swabian League assembly. Archduke Ferdinand of Austria became the agreed chairman. Luther was glad to receive a printed copy of the treaty as authenticated and printed in Ravensburg on April 22. "This treaty between the praiseworthy league in Swabia and the peasants' association at Lake Constance and in the Allgäu I have received with great joy. It is a particular evidence of God's grace in these times made desolate and horrible by the devil through his gangsters and murderous prophets."[66] With these words Luther prefaced his own immediate reprint of the treaty. Perhaps the South German example would still bring the other peasants to their senses, even though they were mobilizing for

64. *WA* 18:322 / 16ff. [*LW* 46:36.]

65. Franz, *Der deutsche Bauernkrieg*, 133ff. Franz, ed., *Akten Bauernkrieg*, 1 / 2:211. Waas, "Die grosse Wendung," 479ff. (see n. 1, above). Waas, "Die Bauern im Kampf um Gerechtigkeit," 152ff., which includes a facsimile of the treaty at Weingarten, 192.

66. *WA* 18:336 / 2ff.

their rebellion. Once again he appealed to their conscience: through insurrection, plundering, and murder ("under the Christian name and appearance of the gospel") they were heaping enormous sin on themselves.

> Therefore, dear peasants, lay off, listen, and let it be told you: As for your souls, you are already condemned in God's sight; who knows how you will still fare in body and possessions. . . . God will not long put up with this sort of thing. Submit yourselves to peace and agreement; even if it be at some physical cost, let this sin and destruction to your soul cease, for nothing further is to be gained.[67]

Some additional treaties even then being concluded would have substantiated Luther's contention, yet news about them never reached him.[68] As the ray of hope that peace might still be possible faded, his disappointment grew all the deeper. The course of events rushed on. Rebellion broke out full force in middle Germany.

This region gave Luther a personal vantage point and shaped his judgment of the rebellion. Developments here had long been making him apprehensive—but not, to be sure, because the peasant uprising could here be particularly anticipated and its rise observed. To the contrary, developments here came only as an aftereffect of the South German insurrection. In April and May it ignited like fire in straw. What had long disturbed Luther was the internal prehistory of the event, its connection with the radical preaching of Müntzer, Pfeiffer, Karlstadt, and others. Here more than anywhere else Luther came to grips with the radical forces. Often enough he was reminded that the violent results of this radicalism were charged to the reformation he himself was leading. Among the "old believers" [i.e., the Roman side] the turbulence in Mühlhausen was instantly branded as "Martinian" or "Lutheran." Duke George of Saxony had strongly reproached Elector Frederick that all the disorder and unrest was traceable exclusively to Luther's teaching and that all the other agitators, seduced by him, simply added new errors.[69] So far Luther had been able to refute such charges as malicious distortions, but now the

---

67. WA 18:343 / 3, 14ff.

68. Waas, "Die grosse Wendung," 475ff.

69. W. Fuchs, ed., *Akten zur Geschichte des Bauernkriegs in Mitteldeutschland*, vol. 2 (Jena, 1942; reprint, Aalen, 1964), no. 1089a (May 16, 1523), no. 1107 (February 5, 1524), no. 1125 (mid-July 1524), no. 1127 (September 17, 1524), no. 1147 (January 11, 1525), no. 1604 (May 30, 1525). The same connection plays a part in the numerous hearings of prisoners after the Peasants' War. Duke George, August 8, 1524, printed in F. Gess, *Akten und Briefe zur Kirchenpolitik Herzog Georgs von Sachsen* (Leipzig, 1905ff.), 1: no. 708. George's councillors followed the same line of argument against the elector's Saxon councillors at the Naumburg diet (after November 25, 1525; Fuchs, ed., *Akten Bauernkrieg*, no. 1945).

sincere testimonies of the peasants seemed to implicate Luther increasingly. The peasants, unlike Müntzer and Karlstadt, were not at odds with Luther. One example among many was the "Evangelical Christian League," on the edge of the Thuringian forest, writing on April 26, 1525, to the town of Ilmenau:

> Faithful Christian Evangelicals, dear Brothers. Our greetings in Christ. You have heard that we have formed a brotherhood to advance the gospel, doing so on our honor and for the impoverished common good, and to act according to the content of the *Twelve Articles,* as drawn up by the Black Forest peasants and as favored and advanced by them. We intend to make the same demands and to give our support to [the cause of] justice.

They reserved the right to make additional demands. As they urged the Ilmenauers to join, they promised them "brotherly support of an evangelical sort, as befits faithful evangelicals."[70] The district magistrate of Ilmenau forwarded this communication to his lord, Count Wilhelm of Henneberg. A mere one week later there could be no thought of opposition. The count had to appear in the camp of the peasants near Meiningen and pledge his support of the *Twelve Articles of Christian Liberty* as well as of any additional articles of a demonstrably Christian basis; he was also forced to sign and promise to keep them. "[We] hereby declare and grant freely, and exempt everything that Almighty God has made free in and through Christ, his beloved Son, that we attest this in good will and believing heart, intending to prove our faith with appropriate deeds."[71] In countless documents this was the jargon that garbed the rapid flow of events during the next few weeks. Today the documents fill volumes of archival records. Luther received reports by the earful from all sides. He could not help but see that his efforts to inculcate a true understanding of Christian liberty had been in vain.

Only now, however, did the insurrection reveal its full extent. From south and west, from the dioceses in Franconia and the lands of the Fulda abbey [in Hesse], the storms surged into the regions of Thuringia and Saxony. Like the initial eruptions of the rebellion, they originated in ecclesial territories not as yet evangelical. Luther observed correctly, "The rebellion has come precisely from those parts that have rejected the gos-

---

70. Merx, ed., *Akten zur Geschichte des Bauernkriegs zur Mitteldeutschland,* vol. 1 / 1 (Leipzig, 1923; reprint, Aalen, 1964), no. 383.

71. Franz, ed., *Akten Bauernkrieg,* 1 / 2: no. 579. Still that same evening the count sent a sigh of relief to his wife: "Matters are now as they should be. God in heaven be praised." She should reassure the courtiers (no. 581). Similar declarations in Merx, ed., *Akten Bauernkrieg,* 1 / 1: no. 350. Fuchs, ed., *Akten Bauernkrieg,* 1 / 2: no. 1203.

pel most of all."[72] At first nothing seemed able to stop it. The Joblike news was bad. Towns and castles were capitulating, cloisters were being plundered, peasant mobs were massing. The *Twelve Articles* or similar articles were being adopted, often village by village.[73] Fraternization with the nobles was extorted by the rampant peasantry. All these things tumbled upon one another. The threatened princes were fully frustrated. Requests were rushed among them for military aid. Always the same reply: We have none to spare in this emergency. The crisis was heightened in that the peasant revolt now rolled in waves. From middle and northern Thuringia it was surging toward the much older radical reformation of Müntzer and his partners. The Müntzer movement had been undermining the land for years and accumulating power in Mühlhausen, its center. Here, then, the originally spiritualist-eschatological revolutionary movement finally joined the peasant revolt, and in doing so tried to take over its leadership.[74] At first Müntzer and Pfeiffer, his more adventurous colleague, had little luck; their first attempt against Langensalza, on April 25, 1525, failed. But the Mühlhausen people were a cohesive group and soon attracted more. Finding no resistance in the Eichsfeld region, they plundered it. Pfeiffer was not exaggerating when he boasted he would make the castles ready for storming by bombarding them with soft cheese.[75] Within a few days the revolutionary sparks ignited Müntzer's own former regions of revolt around Allstedt, Sangerhausen, and Mansfeld. From there they spread over the entire Harz region. If proof were needed, here again the uprising was more than a peasant matter. Towns became involved, especially those in ecclesial hands. But why? Wherever the Reformation had been suppressed, the townspeople now linked up with the peasants: Fulda, Erfurt, Merseburg, Halle, the church holdings in Quedlinburg and Halberstadt, also the imperial cities of Nordhausen and Goslar. In these cities the *Twelve Articles* or their equivalent were adopted and for the first time, though only temporarily, evangelical worship was introduced.[76]

72. *Wider den Ratschlag der Mainzischen Pfafferei* (1526) [*Against the Proposals of the Clergy in Mainz*], WA 19:279 / 15–16.

73. Characteristic are the grievance articles of twenty separate towns and villages in the Schwarzburg region (ca. April 25, 1525). Fuchs, ed., *Akten Bauernkreig*, 1 / 2: no. 1208, 110ff.

74. Franz, *Der deutsche Bauernkrieg*, 257ff. O. Merx, *Thomas Müntzer und Heinrich Pfeiffer, 1523–1525*, pt. 1 (Göttingen, 1889), 101ff. R. Bemmann, "Thomas Müntzer, Mühlhausen in Thüringen und der Bauernkrieg," in *Festschrift für G. Seeliger* (Leipzig, 1920), 167ff.

75. Franz, *Der deutsche Bauernkrieg*, 260.

76. Ibid., 239ff., 261ff. Sources indicated in Fuchs, ed., *Akten Bauernkrieg*, 1 / 2; see the index there.

For the moment no one knew what to do or what would happen next. For weeks letters had hurried between the princes and nobles in Luther's territory. The old elector, weakened by his final illness, once again practiced his characteristic humility. It had often helped him amid trying circumstances. If Luther's appearing, he reasoned, could be seen as God at work, then why not claim the same significance for the peasants' demands? Now no more than then was Frederick ready to intervene with force. His was a mood not of despair but of submission to the inscrutable will of God.

> Perhaps the poor people have been given a reason for such rebellion, especially by forbidding them the Word of God. In many ways the poor are being burdened by us temporal and spiritual rulers. May God turn his wrath away from us. If God wills it, then it will happen, and the common man will rule. Yet if this should not be his will, and he be against a revolt to his praise, things will change rapidly. Let us pray God to forgive our sin and implore him, and he will make things turn out according to his will and praise.[77]

At the same time Frederick hoped that the Swabian League would bring the peasants into line. These were his sentiments as sent in a letter of April 14 to Duke John, resident in Weimar and closer to the events than his ill brother. As gently as possible, John conveyed to Frederick one piece of bad news after another. On April 30 and May 1, John sent two field reports, of which only the first arrived before Frederick died. They contained substantially the same information Luther had gathered from personal observation as well as from numerous reports, detailing what was happening and what might be feared. Duke John estimated the peasant forces at 35,000 men, with the biggest forces concentrated around Schmalkalden (the following day, May 1, he reported the fall of that city). Other forces were besieging Ichtershausen and Stadtilm. Both these Henneberg area towns fell. The list of peasant successes seemed to grow endlessly: many castles destroyed or plundered by the mobs from Mühlhausen (among them the castle of Luther's good friend Hans von Berlepsch, warden of the Wartburg); many more destroyed or plundered in the valley of the Saale River (near Neustadt, Pössneck, Jena), and some of them still under siege; and the cloisters, many of them stormed and robbed (Reinhardsbrunn, Georgental, Bürgel, and others). In Mansfeld, too, insurrection broke out. Not a few nobles saw no way out but to

---

77. K. E. Förstemann, *Neues Urkundenbuch zur Geschichte der evangelischen Kirchen-Reformation* (Hamburg, 1842), 1:259. Excerpt in Fuchs, ed., *Akten Bauernkrieg*, 1/2: no. 1183.

join the insurrectionists, a step some of them quickly regretted. There was no use relying on the towns. Duke John's orders remained as good as ignored. "It's wild around here. Everyone is in shock. God grant us his divine grace. We probably had it coming to us. The dear Christ wants to reveal himself—that *he* is the Lord and not we poor sinners." How could Duke John know what next? He himself thanked God for having thus far spared him from involvement in the opinions of "clever and wise people." He saw no other way than to follow the oft-repeated advice of his brother the elector: Hear the peasants out and deal with them fairly.[78] Still, the day before his death, on May 4, Elector Frederick expressed the hope that the peasants would not proceed as viciously against him and his brother John as they had against so many others. So he proposed "that on their territory someone be enlisted who is known to the peasants, who has their trust and confidence, and who could negotiate with them; may God grant that these grievous and anxious matters on the territory be quieted down and the people be made satisfied."[79]

Did the dying elector have Luther in mind? We cannot say. The words sound that way, and even a few hours before he died he remembered Luther with "all the best."[80] Luther himself would have realized that it was too late for such an attempt. Over the past two weeks he had gained an overall picture of the situation. On April 20, in Eisleben, he had begun writing his *Admonition to Peace*. Then, traveling through northern and middle Thuringia, he had repeatedly preached before the aroused people. Unfortunately we have no complete record of his itinerary, but his stopovers we can be sure of were: Stolberg, in the Harz (April 21); Wallhausen, near Sangershausen (May 1); Nordhausen (May 2); Weimar (May 3); Seeburg, near Eisleben (May 4). There, on May 5, he learned of the elector's death and at once hurried back to Wittenberg, arriving home on the evening of May 6.[81] It is doubtful whether Luther's journey took him into the Saale valley, even though his time schedule would have permitted it and must have included a number of stops en route.[82] At any rate, the

78. Förstemann, *Neues Urkundenbuch*, 275ff. Much abbreviated in Fuchs, ed., *Akten Bauernkrieg*, 1 / 2: nos. 1242, 1258.

79. Förstemann, *Neues Urkundenbuch*, 280. Fuchs, ed., *Akten Bauernkrieg*, 1 / 2: no. 1304.

80. *Spalatins historischer Nachlass und Briefe,* ed. C. G. Neudecker and L. Preller, vol. 1: *Friedrichs des Weisen Leben und Zeitgeschichte* (Jena, 1851), 68. WA 17¹:xxxii.

81. To Spalatin, May 7, 1525, WA Br 3:487 / 7; see also 480.

82. WA 17¹:xxxi–xxxii. WA Br 3:479, n. 5. G. Buchwald, *Luther-Kalendarium*, SVRG 147 (Leipzig, 1929), 40. The report of Luther's trip into the Saale valley is in Seckendorf, *Commentarius de Lutheranismo* (1692; 2d ed., 1694), 2:3 / 3.

territory covered was sufficiently large to give him an inclusive impression. Wherever Luther went he found the peasants past the point of conversation. As in Orlamünde a year earlier, they appeared to him as a people possessed, only this time more dangerous and armed with swords. They threatened him too. "I was in the midst of them and in danger of my life," he often recollected later.[83] Hans Zeiss reported to the elector on May 1 about the uprising in northern Thuringia, the "campaign" of the Mühlhausen mob, and the cloister raids and then added, "Doctor Luther is in the Mansfeld region but cannot'ward off such rebellion and rushing together in the Mansfeld region."[84] The more Luther experienced the powerlessness of an individual amid this storm, the more important for him it was to observe the example of his native Count Mansfeld. Here, amid such chaos, a determined ruler could still accomplish something. He gave Albrecht of Mansfeld high praise for being "at that time the first to don his armor." In doing so, the count not only succeeded in preventing the miners from joining the peasants, but—while everyone else was hesitating or taking flight—he dared to be the first one to attack a peasant mob. "There [the restoration of order] won a thrust and a support when the laudable count intervened."[85] Given this situation, the only thing Luther could advise his hesitating territorial lord was not to negotiate. When passing through Weimar on May 3, where Duke John asked whether he should consent to the demands of the *Twelve Articles,* Luther advised: Not to a single one! Though the impression on him of the humility of two devout princes remained unforgettable, Luther now admonished the rulers to exercise their responsibility.[86] The solitariness in which he stood among the wavering and helpless made him all the more resolute. Therefore Luther warded off those who gave the contrary advice. "Honored dear Doctor and Relative," he wrote, while still en route on May 4 (or 5), to John Rühel, the Mansfeld town councilman and his steady source of information,

> . . . I urge you not to influence my gracious Lord, Count Albrecht, to be soft in this affair. Let His Grace continue as he has begun, even though the devil

83. *Wider den Ratschlag der Mainzischen Pfafferei* (1526), WA 19:278 / 23ff.; also WA 30³:279 / 13. On the charged atmosphere during his sermon in Nordhausen, cf. WA TR 5, no. 6429, 657 / 14ff.

84. Fuchs, ed., *Akten Bauernkreig,* 1 / 2: no. 1261.

85. WA 19:279 / 16ff. Franz, *Der deutsche Bauernkrieg,* 261. Meant is the attack on Osterhausen on May 5; WA Br 3:479.

86. WA TR 1, no. 166, 78 / 22ff. WA TR 2, no. 2071, 311 / 26ff.; no. 2505a and b, 496 / 12ff.; 497 / 1ff. WA TR 3, no. 3845, 655 / 29ff.

becomes angrier as a result and rages more through the demonic members of his body. For we have God's Word, which does not lie; it says in Rom. 13 [:4], "He does not bear the sword in vain, etc.," so there never can be any doubt that the count's office was decreed and ordained by God. Therefore, as long as life is in him, His Grace ought to use his sword for punishing the wicked. Should the sword be forcibly struck from His Grace's hand, we must endure this and leave it in God's hands; he first gave the sword and he may take it back by what means he wishes.[87]

Herewith Luther sounded the keynote of his subsequent treatises on the peasant problem. Commitment to the will of God does not free the prince from carrying out the duties of his office, but it should free him from all human anxiety over what might befall him in this exercise of duty.

The larger scene, as Luther learned on his return to Wittenberg, emerges clearly from a letter written on May 10 by Hans von der Planitz to Duke Albrecht of Prussia: the peasants of Mühlhausen, Erfurt, and Nordhausen and in the counties of Schwarzburg and Mansfeld "are in a state of massive rebellion against the clergy and the rulers; at the one place some 20,000 have converged; at the other, about 18,000; they are storming the cloisters and clerical dwellings, and in places have destroyed or burned the castles and barns of the nobles." The same thing is happening in adjacent lands managed by bailiffs [for the nobles]. Against these angry crowds Duke John, Duke George, and the archbishop of Magdeburg could marshal only a few hundred horsemen and could "put no foot soldiers in the field"; they did not dare to send their retainers in town and country against the peasants. "Nothing in this part of the country is faring well; faithlessness abounds."[88]

After all Luther had seen and heard, the worst was indeed to be expected and not one day more was to be lost. Therefore, in great haste, he again raised his voice, this time with utmost severity. He did not sacrifice his admonition to peace. In fact, he published it again, adding a short, sharp supplement, *Against the Robbing and Murdering Hordes of Other Peasants*.[89] In later reprints this treatise appeared separately, but its title indicates that its basic purpose was to supplement the foregoing *Admoni-*

---

87. WA Br 3:480 / 1ff. [*LW* 49:108–9.]

88. Published by A. Clos, "Zur näheren Bestimmung der Abfassungszeit von Luthers Schrift 'Wider die räuberischen und mörderischen Rotten der Bauern, 1525,'" *ARG* 33 (1936): 126ff., esp. 130.

89. Hans von der Planitz sent this latest addition, presumably just off the press, with the "Admonition," on May 10 in his letter to Duke Albrecht of Prussia. Later, John Rühel mentions it in his letter to Luther from Eisleben on May 26, WA Br 3:511 / 64ff. For an account of how this tract was published, see K. Aland, "Eine Anmerkung zu Luthers Haltung im Bauernkrieg," *ThLZ* 74 (1949): 299ff.

tion to Peace. Consequently it contains nothing that had not already been premised in the first treatise. Yet in Luther's eyes the situation had become much intensified. Under the influence of fanatical leaders the peasants were now resorting to violence, whereas in the *Twelve Articles* they had declared their willingness to heed other voices. With the exception of Count Mansfeld—presuming Luther was aware of the count's bold action at the time of his writing—the rulers had not gone into action; indeed, they were undecided as to what to do. Luther could only remind the peasants again of the "three kinds of terrible sins against God and man": the breach of faith and obedience; the act of insurrection, which has set the whole country aflame, caused incalculable bloodshed, and brought suffering to widows and orphans as a consequence; and the claim that their action is based on the gospel.[90] Having said this to the peasants, Luther now felt obliged to update his instructions to the temporal authorities, saying "how they may act with a clear conscience in this matter."[91] Presupposing his *Admonition to Peace* as a first stage [and seeing this had failed], he came with instruction for a second stage, in which Christian authorities should "proceed with fear." First they must "take the matter to God," recognizing his amply deserved wrath in this matter. Thereby chastened, let a ruler "humbly pray for help against the devil," for this is a combat not alone against flesh and blood but also "against the spiritual host of wickedness in the air [Eph. 6:12, 2:2], which must be attacked with prayer." Then, as for the peasants ("though they are not worthy of it"), let rulers go beyond duty and offer them "an opportunity to come to terms." "Finally, if that does not help, then swiftly take the sword."[92] In this extremely tense situation Luther aims to embolden the rulers in terms of what he sees as God's command. Should they fail to use the sword when the situation demands it, the rulers sin against their duty—just as the others sin who in revolt seize the sword and commit murder. Whoever dies in this kind of combat may be sure that he dies "while obeying the divine Word and commandment."[93] "These are strange times, when a prince can win heaven with bloodshed better than other men with prayer!"[94] This deliberately pointed sentence is not a relapse into the abolished notion of merit but intends, rather, to say that

90. *WA* 18:357 / 21; 358 / 19ff. [*LW* 46:49, 51.]
91. *WA* 18:359 / 17–18. [*LW* 46:52.]
92. *WA* 18:359 / 27ff. [*LW* 46:52.]
93. *WA* 18:360 / 1ff., 30. [*LW* 46:54.]
94. *WA* 18:361 / 4ff. [*LW* 46:54.]

God requires something different from those entrusted with the sword than from those not so entrusted.

Still another reason should move the authorities to exercise their office, as Luther is moved to write. The peasants whom Luther addresses in this tract are the "other" peasants in the title, those terrorizing a great many people, who then follow them only out of fear or revulsion. If the authorities had no other ground than this, it alone would be reason enough to rescue these misguided people from their captivity and free them for their soul's salvation. For the authorities thus discharging their duties [and for them alone in that combat of liberation] apply the frequently cited words:

> Therefore, dear lords, here is a place where you can release, rescue, help. Have mercy on these poor people! Let whoever can stab, strike, strangle. If you die in doing it, good for you! A more blessed death can never be yours, for you die while obeying the divine Word and commandment in Rom. 13 [:1, 2], and in loving service of your neighbor whom you are rescuing from the bonds of hell and the devil.[95]

Frightening words are these, reflecting equally the boundless emotion of which Luther was capable and the measureless concern that drove him. Yet these words have a right not to be misunderstood. They flaunt no "glorification of power for power's sake,"[96] but state precisely the grounds on which the authorities are obliged to take a united stand against the violence of the peasants. Luther himself knew that these were hard words. He ended his treatise admitting, "If anyone thinks this too harsh, let him remember that rebellion is intolerable and that the destruction of the world can be expected any hour."[97]

Luther could not know that by the time his treatise was distributed the outcome of the tragic drama was already clear. As furiously as the revolt had spread, its first encounter with stern opposition caused its collapse. The two men determining the destiny of Middle Germany's peasants were none other than Philip of Hesse and Thomas Müntzer. Landgrave Philip was alone among the princes to arm immediately. Thus he was able to wedge apart the peasant hordes converging on Hersfeld (April 28) and Fulda (May 3).[98] Encouraged by this success, he also saw that the leader-

95. WA 18:361 / 24ff. [LW 46:54–55.]

96. E. Troeltsch, *Die Soziallehren der christlichen Kirchen und Gruppen* (Tübingen, 1912), 32 (reprint, Aalen, 1965, in *Gesammelte Schriften*, vol. 1).

97. WA 18:361 / 33ff. [LW 46:55. Altered.]

98. Franz, ed., *Akten Bauernkrieg*, 1 / 2: no. 151, 462–63.

ship and weapons represented by even a modest force of knights and yeomen could turn back a very large crowd of insurgents. So he directed his forces against the most important peasant concentration, that around Mühlhausen. The masses gathered at Frankenhausen on the Kyffhäuser were imposing. In planning his campaign, Philip secured the participation of the considerably weaker forces of his father-in-law, Duke George of Saxony. On the other side, among the peasants, Müntzer was the unchallenged spiritual and political authority, even though lacking the military authority to give commands. From his pen flowed the progressively vehement letters intended to rally the masses and intimidate the opponents. As April ended, he sent a summons to his former parish in Allstedt—the most red-hot testimony to his ecstatic style and a classic among the documents of revolution: "Beware. Don't be so fainthearted or careless. Stop flattering the absurd dreamers, the godless scoundrels. Get going, and take up the battle of the Lord. . . . All the German, French, and Swiss lands are on the move. The Master is game; the scoundrels are going to get it." In Fulda, he reported, Holy Week saw four parish churches desecrated. Meanwhile, the peasant forces in Klettgau, Hegau, and the Black Forest were growing steadily; his only fear was that they might be tempted to sign deceptive treaties.

> Now then, go to it, go to it, go to it. Now is the time. The scoundrels are as despondent as dogs. . . . They'll fawningly request, whimper, beg like children. Have no pity. As God gave orders through Moses, Deut. 7,[99] he has revealed the same to us. . . . Go to it, go to it, while the fire is hot. Don't let your sword get cold or go lame. Hammer out your cling-clang on the anvils of Nimrod. Topple their tower to the ground. So long as they are around it is impossible for you to be rid of human fear. And so long as they rule over you, no one can tell you anything about God. Go, go, while you have daylight. God leads on before you. Follow, follow! The stories described in Matt. 24, Ezek. 34, Dan. 74 [sic], Esd. 16, and Rev. 6 all are explained in Rom. 13. [Signed, as he had been doing for the past two years], Thomas Müntzer, a servant of God against the godless.[100]

The hammering "Go" and the clang of the anvil, the threatening words from the Old Testament, the judgment scenes like the apocalyptic horse-

---

99. Deut. 7:1–5 (no fraternization with the subjected Canaanites, and a destruction of their holy places).

100. *Thomas Müntzer, Schriften und Briefe: Kritische Gesamtausgabe*, ed. G. Franz, QFRG 33 (Gütersloh, 1968), no. 75, 454 / 8ff., 20ff., 25ff.; 455 / 14ff. ibid., no. 168, 502ff. Luther reprinted this from a different copy, "Eine schreckliche Geschichte und ein Gericht Gottes über Thomas Müntzer" (see below, p. 386), WA 18:367ff. Here and there it departs from the original and is smoothed out. Dan. 74 is a mistake for Dan. 7 (judgment passed on the four world empires); cf. Müntzer, *Schriften*, no. 45, 397 / 1. Esd. 16 is probably mistaken for 10 (divorce from pagan wives).

men or the revelation received personally—all these flow into an eschato-logical composition of martial music. This agrees with Müntzer's own in-terpretation of Rom. 13. Indeed, already in October 1524 Müntzer had explained it to Elector Frederick this way: The sword of authority—which according to Paul (Rom. 13:3–4) the faithful need not fear—must be drawn by the ruler against the malicious (that is, against those refusing to hear God's prophet, Müntzer). If the princes fail to do so, "then the sword will be taken from them and given to the expectant people for the destruction of the godless."[101] The people of the elect are the bearers of God's sov-ereignty; this is the manner in which the thought of popular sovereignty emerges in Müntzer.[102] Cleverly he thereby had turned the Pauline ad-monition to obedience to the authorities into a password for insurrection, and from among the people a new sword-bearing authority would arise. The hour had come for what he had foretold.

Following his April 1525 letter to the people of Allstedt, Müntzer sent out at least ten more letters we know of during the first half of May, in which he gave written support to the assembling peasants.[103] Two, dated May 12, were ultimatums to the two counts of Mansfeld, Ernest and Albrecht, calling for their "conversion." He challenged the counts to ap-pear before the peasants encamped near Frankenhausen to apologize for their tyranny and to prove their Christian faith. To the Catholic Count Ernest he wrote:

> If you intend to keep out of it and not unburden yourself, then I shall cry out for all the world to hear that all brothers should confidently risk their blood as though fighting the Turks. . . . In short, by God's mighty power you have been handed over to destruction. . . . Simply to inform you that we have di-rect orders, I tell you: The eternal and living God has decreed that you be removed from your chair by power given us . . . , for God has said about you and your kind, . . . "Your [eagle's] nest will be torn down and destroyed" (Obad. 4, altered from RSV).

To the Lutheran Count Albrecht he declared:

> In your Lutheran gruel and Wittenbergian soup, have you not been able to find what Ezek. 37 prophesies? Besides, have you not been able to taste in

101. Dan. 7:18. October 4, 1523, Müntzer, *Schriften*, no. 45, 396 / 26ff. Likewise, the Allstedt council to Duke John, ca. June 7, 1524, ibid., no. 50, 405 / 25ff. C. Hinrichs, *Luther und Müntzer: Ihre Auseinandersetzung über Obrigkeit und Widerstandsrecht* (Berlin, 1952), 35.

102. Hinrichs, *Luther und Müntzer*, 36; there, 35–36, also on Müntzer's interpretation of Rom. 13.

103. Müntzer, *Schriften*, nos. 76 (only as information), 77, 79, 81–84, 88–89; 456ff.

your Martinian peasant shit how the same prophet goes on to say in chapter 39 that God makes all the birds under heaven devour the flesh of princes and all the dumb animals guzzle the blood of the big shots, as described in the secret revelation in [chapters] 18 and 19? Haven't you caught on that God values his people more than you tyrants?

Should he fail to appear before the assembled peasants, "we will pay no attention to your boring old faces, and we shall fight against you as against the arch-enemy of the Christian faith." Both letters were signed the same: "Thomas Müntzer with the sword of Gideon."[104]

In contrast to this threatening prophet's tone there was a more sober ring in the urgent calls for help then crossing to and fro, one from the town of Frankenhausen, another from Müntzer to the city of Erfurt. The Frankenhausers required aid "so that we can match the superior power of the princes, counts, and noble and ignoble people."[105] Müntzer needed support, writing,

> Strength and comfort to you in Christ Jesus, dearest ones. We have noticed your steadfast love and your joyful turning to the truth, and we want to add to your fresh courage, so that you remain behind in nothing—unless the Lutheran gruel-gorgers could have made you soft by their greasy compassion. . . . Help us [here] with all you can; with people, with canons, so that we may fulfill what God has ordained, Ezek. 34, where he says [paraphrased], "I will rescue you from them who oppress you with tyranny." . . . Have you joy in the truth? Then join us on the rounds, for we are about to begin, so that we can give it back to the blasphemers for what they have palmed off on poor Christendom. . . . [Signed:] Thomas Müntzer on behalf of the common Christendom.[106]

Two days later it was all over. Daily for the past several days Müntzer had preached before masses of people. Always he had referred to the rainbow as the sign of the covenant God had made with them, and that God had taken the power away from the rulers and given it to the people.[107]

---

104. Ibid., nos. 88, 89. Franz, ed., *Akten Bauernkrieg*, 1/2: nos. 180, 181. Reprinted by Luther, WA 18:369ff.

105. Franz, ed., *Akten Bauernkrieg*, 1/2: no. 182.

106. Müntzer, *Schriften*, nos. 91, 471/2ff., 15ff., 25ff.; 472/6.

107. In this case it was probably a halo around the sun, easily confused with a rainbow. Cf. the information of Prof. D. Wattenberg of the Archenhold Observatory in Treptow, in M. Bensing, *Thomas Müntzer und der Thüringer Aufstand 1525* (Berlin, 1966), 225, n. 53. Testimony of the eyewitness Hans Hut at his trial in Augsburg, November 26, 1527; Fuchs, ed., *Akten Bauernkrieg*, 2: no. 2102. Franz, ed., *Akten Bauernkrieg*, 1/2: no. 183. According to Hut, the peasants carried on their flags a rainbow as a symbol. "Presumably the appearance of a halo around the sun finally persuaded the doubters and the waverers, and it cannot be gainsaid that Thomas Müntzer himself was fully convinced that the sign in the sky was evidence of divine approbation" (Bensing, *Müntzer*, 226).

The next day, May 15, the princes challenged the peasants entrenched on a height north of the city to hand over "the false prophets," Müntzer and his hangers-on, and to surrender themselves. If they complied, they would be treated mercifully.[108] The peasants remained under Müntzer's spell. He declared that the bullets of the enemy would not harm them; he himself promised to catch them up with his sleeve. The first shot, which fell short, he greeted with a cry of triumph. But when the next ones were on target, everyone broke up in mad flight into the city. When the pursuing troops caught up with the fleeing peasants, a terrible bloodbath ensued. Müntzer hid himself in an attic room and pretended that he was a poor, ill man. It was his misfortune that he could never separate himself from papers; letters found on him gave him away. He was hauled before the princes for an initial hearing. Duke George of Saxony sat down with him on a bench and, inquiring about the four emissaries sent to the camp in Artern,[109] asked why he had ordered them beheaded—to which Müntzer replied, "Dear Brother, I tell you I didn't do it; divine justice did it." A heated dispute followed between Müntzer and Landgrave Philip of Hesse. To Müntzer's supporting text from the Old Testament, Philip retorted with citations from the New Testament, a copy of which he carried with him.[110] The following day Müntzer went on trial, part of it "painful," under torture. In the process he divulged not only data and names concerning the uprising but also, probably at a second trial, recanted his sermons against the rulers and his departure from the Roman doctrine on the sacraments. Finally, he received the Lord's Supper—the bread only.[111] In his letter of farewell to the congregation and town council

108. Text of the ultimatum in Müntzer, *Schriften*, no. 93, 473 / 1ff. Report of the Landgrave, May 16, 1525, to the Archbishop of Trier, in Fuchs, ed., *Akten Bauernkrieg*, 2: no. 1469. Franz, ed., *Akten Bauernkrieg*, 1 / 2: no. 184.

109. Actually, only three emissaries, these from Count Ernst of Mansfeld. Cf. the confession of Müntzer, May 16, 1525, in Franz, ed., *Akten Bauernkrieg*, 1 / 2: no. 190, 533, n. 182. Müntzer, *Schriften*, 547, n. 76.

110. Extensive report to Luther by John Rühel, Eisleben, May 26, based on testimony of eyewitnesses, WA Br 3:509ff.; 511 / 50–51. More on this in Fuchs, ed., *Akten Bauernkrieg*, 2: no. 1574, n. 3a; also WA 18:373 / 16ff. For additional reports and literature, see Franz, *Der deutsche Bauernkrieg*, 268, n. 33. On Müntzer's love of papers, cf. *Thomas Müntzer: Briefwechsel*, ed., H. Boehmer and P. Kirn (Leipzig and Berlin, 1931), vii; on the execution of the (probably three) emissaries of Count Ernst, see Müntzer, *Schriften*, 547, n. 76; also Bensing, *Müntzer*, 229ff.

111. Müntzer's confession of May 16, in Franz, ed., *Akten Bauernkrieg*, 1 / 2: no. 190. Müntzer, *Schriften*, 543ff. His confession was immediately circulated widely in print. Cf. O. Clemen, "Reformationsgeschichtliches aus dem Zwickauer Ratsarchiv," ARG 26 (1929): 188ff. His recantation of May 17, in Müntzer, *Schriften*, 550. Also, Rühel to Luther, May 21, 1525, WA Br 3:505 / 9ff. The authenticity of this "recantation" has been challenged; cf. Bensing, *Müntzer*, 230–31. Nevertheless, the recantation and Communion according to the

in Mühlhausen on May 17, Müntzer accepted his fate yet said not a word about his own guilt. Instead, he blamed them that the Frankenhausen revolt had ended in defeat. "Without a doubt things happened that way because everyone there was seeking his own good more than the justification of Christendom." "I have often warned you that the punishment of God as undertaken by the authorities cannot be avoided unless one recognizes the wrong. . . . Therefore, be friendly toward one another and do not embitter the authorities further, the way many have done through their self-seeking." Müntzer admonished them now, "Flee from the shedding of blood," a risk he himself had initially challenged them to take.[112] Rühel interpreted Müntzer's statement correctly; it was not, as some thought, a recantation, but rather a reaffirmation of what he had intended. Yet he "would blame the peasants alone for seeking too much of their own advantage and thus bringing defeat and punishment on themselves."[113] On May 27 Müntzer and fifty three others were executed. Among them was his associate, Heinrich Pfeiffer, who escaped for a while but had been picked up near Eisenach. At his trial he did not beat around the bush but admitted, "One can see what he has done, so there's no use lying." He then summed up concisely toward what goal he and Müntzer had been struggling: "After annihilating all rulers he intended to carry out a Christian reformation."[114]

A continuous flow of reports, especially from the councilmen in Mansfeld (notably John Rühel), kept Luther informed.[115] The tragedy only reaffirmed for him what he had always said about Müntzer. As late as the eve

---

Roman rite is not questioned; Rühel, well informed, reported it to Luther on May 21; *WA Br* 3:505 / 9ff. K. Müller (contrary to Clemen, *WA Br* 3:506, n. 6) understands the accompanying "writing" in Rühel's letter (*WA Br* 3:505 / 14) as a copy of a statement on Müntzer's behavior in prison; Luther's correspondence with the Mansfeld friends in May 1525, in *Aus Deutschlands kirchlicher Vergangenheit: Festschrift für T. Brieger* (Leipzig, 1912), 31ff., esp. 33–34. That is possible, yet more probable still is that this concerns the so-called "recantation" of May 17, which in part corresponds literally with Rühel's report to Luther. (Cf. H. Volz, *WA Br* 13:74 on this passage.) This is a supplementary short taking down of the most important statements Müntzer had made earlier, and with which he would firm up his later statements. This is more likely than the notion that we are here dealing with a forgery. Contrary to Clemen's contention, this "Recantation" has nothing to do with the quite different detailed "Confession" of May 16.

112. Müntzer, *Schriften*, 473 / 20ff.; 474 / 9–10.

113. *WA Br* 3:510 / 9, 10–11.

114. Fuchs, ed., *Akten Bauernkrieg*, 2: no. 1582. Franz, ed., *Akten Bauernkrieg*, 1 / 2: no. 192.

115. During May at least ten letters reached Luther from Mansfeld. K. Müller, "Luthers Briefwechsel mit den Mansfeldern," 32–33.

of his execution,[116] Müntzer published his final frenzied words to the people in Allstedt and to the counts in Mansfeld, including what he had heard about his exhortation before the battle: "Not that I delight in his or his adherents' misfortune, for what would such knowledge about him help me when I don't know what God still has in store for me?" He wanted the people now at last to recognize that God as a phantom on whose revelation Müntzer had relied. "Who, then, is the God who has written such promises for nearly a year through the mouth of Müntzer?" Now God is sitting in judgment over the whole world. He alone can still help. "This is the time not for preaching but for beseeching. Wrath is rampant. Prayer is our defense." Of the victorious rulers Müntzer asked two things: "that they in no case be overbearing, but fear God, before whom they are indeed punishable," and "that they be merciful to the prisoners and to those having surrendered, even as God is merciful and faithful and humbles himself toward everyone, so that the weather does not change and God still give victory to the peasants." The end, however, was not yet in sight. Masses of peasants were still on the alert in the fields. Only prayer and the fear of God on both sides could move God to suspend his judgment.[117]

The good word Luther put in for the peasants could not dispel the widespread impression made by his severe attack on them. His treatise, written amid an uncertain and threatening situation, appeared almost simultaneously with the news of the rulers' victory in Frankenhausen. The Romanist Cochlaeus, however, managed to see the whole matter upside down when, not long after, he made a general criticism of Luther's position during the Peasants' War by summing up the opinion widely held in the opposing camp. "Now that the poor, unhappy peasants have lost their chance, you [Luther] turn to the princes. Yet in the previous booklet, when there was good hope on the peasants' side, you wrote far differently."[118] Actually, Luther had sent out his shrill warning while all around him were still wavering—whether or not one could, or even might dare to, stem the flood. Yet after the unexpected victory of the princes, Luther's treatise took on a still more shocking tone. Words written to rally the rulers to decision and toughness in a necessary struggle now sounded like

116. On the dating (May 17–22) and for an understanding of the writing as well as the following correspondence, see K. Müller, *Kirche, Gemeinde, und Obrigkeit nach Luther* (Tübingen, 1910), 140ff.

117. "Eine schreckliche Geschichte und ein Gericht Gottes über Thomas Müntzer," WA 18:367ff.; 373 / 26ff., 18–19; 374 / 8–9, 11–12, 16ff.

118. Reprint of *Wider die . . . Rotten der Bauern* and of the *Sendbrief* [open letter], with critical comments by Cochlaeus (1525). Cf. WA 18:348; 376 / 25ff. [On the *Open Letter*, see LW 46:(59–61), 63–85.]

a justification of senseless murder, allowing the soldiers of the rulers license to wreak death among the innocent as well as the guilty.

Those friends of Luther who had experienced the rebellion at close range were the first to see the incongruity. Rühel, from Mansfeld, gave Luther grizzly details on the victors as well on those now bent on pleasing them. For example, some women of Frankenhausen, having just secured the release of their surviving husbands, were given the task of punishing two priests charged with having taken part in the revolt. There in the marketplace, wielding cudgels, these women kept on clubbing the priests "for probably another half-hour after they had died." The princes plundered and assessed the towns with heavy fines. "Here nothing counts but pillage and murder." Luther's forecast in his *Admonition to Peace* seemed perversely on target. As Rühel reported, "I'm apprehensive, completely so, for [your treatise] can be read as though you'd like to be a prophet to the lords, but as a result the land they leave to their descendants will be a desolate one."[119] Rühel, esteeming Luther highly, was eager to dispel the suspicion that he had connived in the horrid event. "To many of those favorable to you it appears strange that the go-ahead for tyrants to strangle without mercy should come from you," he wrote on May 26. Requesting clarification, he said to Luther, "In time it will be necessary to strike [such statements] and to have them refuted by you, for the innocent should remain uncondemned."[120] On a position he had attained only after painstaking probing of conscience, any contradiction made Luther (now as always) more determined. Least of all was he disturbed by the allegation of being a "toady to the sovereigns." Rühel's well-meant but foolish letter included the further note that in Leipzig gossip had Luther seeking Duke George's favor, now that Elector Frederick had died. Luther counted this alleged flattery as just another of many honorary titles Satan was giving him. "I'd need lots of leather if I should bridle every [critical] mouth. It's enough that my conscience is clear in God's sight. I'll leave it for him to judge my tongue and pen." Even so, the war was by no means at an end. Rühel himself had written Luther on May 21, "They say the peasants are still strong around Würzburg, and those in the Bamberg region are again on the move."[121] And to Amsdorf in Magdeburg (conveyor of the sobri-

119. May 21, 1525, WA Br 3:505 / 21ff., esp. 27–30, 35, 29ff. Franz, ed., *Akten Bauernkrieg*, 1 / 2: no. 188. "Ermahnung," WA 18:332 / 12ff. On the capture and punishment of Mühlhausen, see Franz, *Der deutsche Bauernkrieg*, 270. Also Franz, ed., *Akten Bauernkrieg*, 1 / 2: no. 193. [*LW* 46:41ff.]

120. WA Br 3:511 / 64ff., 72ff. Franz, ed., *Akten Bauernkrieg*, 1 / 2: no. 189.

121. Rühel to Luther, May 21 and 26, 1525, WA Br 3:506 / 53–54; 511 / 53–54, 67ff. Luther to Rühel, May 30, WA Br 3:515 / 10ff. Luther to Amsdorf, May 30, WA Br 3:517 / 2ff. [*LW* 49:113.]

quet "toady to the sovereigns") Luther himself reported June 12 on the cruelties of the peasants in Franconia, and on the June 21 on the terrible murdering perpetrated by the princes after defeating the peasants near Königshofen and recovering Würzburg and other towns.[122] Even after the Frankenhausen catastrophe the need of the hour remained the same: to preach obedience, for the salvation of the people and the peace of the country. But "they will not listen to the Word and are frivolous, so they must hear the rod and the gun, as serves them right. Intercede for them we should, so they'll obey, and where they don't, there's not much need for mercy; let the gunshots whiz among them lest they act a thousand times worse."[123]

Luther was most angered when preachers like those in Magdeburg or Zwickau still failed to see what was at stake. The peasants took sword in hand without authority from God; the consequences can be nothing but the devastation of the spiritual and temporal realms. The princes, however, act on God's authority, even though at times they overstep their bounds; in this way both kingdoms can be preserved. Whoever justifies the peasants is simply lying and blaspheming and intent on toppling God from his heavenly throne. If these preachers get bolder, they will do so not with God's consent but with his curse. Luther is thus ready to endure extreme isolation from the rest. "Perhaps the time will come when even I may say: 'You all will fall away because of me this night' " (Matt. 26:31).[124] Such words might ring with inhumanity and blasphemous presumption, yet they were just the opposite. One need simply try to comprehend the dimensions in which Luther beheld this terrible course of events. In the wake of the first big catastrophe [at Frankenhausen] humaneness, to Luther, meant more than ever to resist the peasants, in deed and word, and thus to spare them from anything worse; so much was clear. And to fear God meant to recognize God's judgment, regardless of through whom he exercised it in order to restore peace in the social order. Luther was not

122. WA Br 3:528 / 1ff.; 541 / 12ff. Further news from Luther about the course of the war: July 31, to Amsdorf; September 28, to Spalatin, after he had already on July 19 reported to John Hess in Breslau and after August 15(?) to Briessmann in Königsberg that the war was over. WA Br 3:544 / 7; 550 / 4ff.; 583 / 17ff.; 556 / 30ff. [LW 49:123–24.]

123. To Rühel, May 30, WA Br 3:515 / 23ff.

124. To Amsdorf, May 30, WA Br 3:517 / 16–17, 26ff.; 518 / 34ff. Concerning the Zwickau preachers, Hermann Mühlpfort, the burgomaster, wrote Stephan Roth on June 4, "Doctor Martin is losing ground heavily among the common folk as among the educated and uneducated. They judge his writings to be very unstable. That's also why I am most urgently writing to you, for the pastor (Hausmann) and the preachers are horrified over his booklets now circulating, for one seems to contradict the other." WA 18:376. Mühlpfort had requested Roth to supply Luther with information. [LW 49:113, 114.]

impervious to the human tragedy that all this involved. For that very reason he saw it necessary to make the peasants lay down their arms as soon as possible and in this way remove from the victors any cause for excesses.

During these weeks the unfathomable course of events was moving Luther deeply, but he stood firm. Others might dispute his convictions, but for them he had a sign more powerful than language. He married. Could any other act have turned his critics against him more vehemently than this? How he came to do it will be told later, but that it took place at this point in time is history. He did it not to provide for Katharina von Bora, or to create for himself the security of a home. He did it to show the devil and his enemies his good conscience. And he did it before God, perhaps soon, would call him home. On June 13 he and Katharina were married by John Bugenhagen. Two days later, as then customary, came the wedding feast. Among the guests were his friends, the three Mansfeld town councilmen. They had been the most apprehensive among his critics, for they were much concerned about the unrest created by his writings on the peasants. This was his reply:

> What cries of bloody murder, dear sirs, have I not caused by my little book against the peasants! In that moment all is forgotten that God has done in the world through me. Now nobles, priests, and peasants are against me and threaten me with death. Well then, because they are mad and foolish I will manage that before my own end I too shall be found in that estate created by God. Retaining nothing of my former papal life and as fully as possible, I shall make them still more mad and foolish, down to the final adieu. For I have a notion that sometime God will help me to his grace.[125]

Even Luther's first intimation to Rühel on May 4 (or 5), in the days of greatest uncertainty about the war situation, carried this tone: "If I can manage it, before I die I will still marry my Katie to spite the devil."[126]

Luther was so convinced of the necessity of what he had said that only with difficulty could he be moved to publish a justification. To be sure, in his Pentecost sermon of June 4 he again briefly explained his intention.[127] Would he really have to spell out again and again the plain truths involved here? Evidently the conversation with the Mansfeld friends at the wed-

125. To John Rühel, John Thür (Dürr, Duhren), and Kaspar Müller, WA Br 3:531 / 4ff.

126. WA Br 3:482 / 1–2. The same to Briessmann, after August 15(?), 1525, WA Br 3:555 / 13ff. [LW 49:111 (to Rühel), 123 (to Briessmann).]

127. WA 17¹:265 / 24–267 / 34. Stephan Roth, in Zwickau, made use of this sermon to calm his people. Soon thereafter Luther learned about their poor opinion of him (see above, p. 388, n. 124). His elaboration is not a copy of anything. It mixes up the noticeably disciplined train of thought in Rörer's copy and anticipates the Open Letter, WA 17¹: 267 / 34.

ding celebration on June 27 convinced him at last. To Caspar Müller, town chancellor in Mansfeld and the one who had sent him his reservations in writing, Luther dedicated the promised sequel. Entitled *An Open Letter on the Harsh Book Against the Peasants*, it appeared in mid-July 1525.[128] Luther had a difficult time writing on this subject again, because (as the friends had reminded him) his was not to be a change of opinion but a softening of tone. Yet he had always seen this kind of situation as particularly dangerous: compromise in tone and form could create the impression that he was giving in and surrendering something. He had usually proceeded the other way around; in his looking back on Worms, in his literary polemics (as against Henry VIII),[129] or later, in the Smalcald Articles, Luther chose the sharper tone. Now that he stood practically alone on this issue he became bolder. "Well then, if I weren't accustomed to being judged and condemned, this argument of friends could excite me, but nothing makes me prouder than when my work and teaching suffers reverses and is crucified."[130] Of course he felt it, being "the target of opposition" and a man against whom "everyone has to win his spurs." Incredible, too, was the reproach of his being unmerciful—"I, who have taught and written more about mercy than anyone else in a thousand years."[131] It was especially irksome that the complaints against his book missed the point completely. "Where have I ever taught that no mercy be shown?" All his sharp words had been trained only on the violent and deluded peasants, while for the misled and even the surrendered he had pleaded for mercy.[132] Basically, however, he shrugged off the criticism. "If it pleases God, I really don't care whether you like it or not."[133] Critics were suspect to Luther anyway, for they had been sympathetic toward the revolt. Why then did they not speak out for mercy when the peasants were plundering and murdering? At that moment the only subject was peasants' rights.[134] Luther saw this as a double standard, irresponsibly shifting the weight of events during those critical weeks.

128. *WA* 18:375ff. [*LW* 46:(57–), 63ff.]

129. The game that Satan had set up for him in Wittenberg in 1522 seemed to Luther like punishment, "because in Worms, when I did a good turn for some friends, and in order to appear less stubborn, I toned down my delivery and did not come out more harshly and sternly in my testimony against the tyrant—after that, how roundly the faithless pagans scolded me with their haughty answers." Letter to Hartmut von Kronberg (1522), *WA* 10²:56 / 17ff.

130. *WA* 18:384 / 21ff. [*LW* 46:63.]

131. *WA* 18:384 / 25; 387 / 18–19. [*LW* 45:63, 66.]

132. *WA* 18:388 / 35–36; 392 / 17ff.; 399 / 10ff. [*LW* 46:64, 73, 82.]

133. *WA* 18:386 / 19–20. [*LW* 46:66.]

134. *WA* 18:385 / 28ff.; 387 / 24ff.; 390 / 36ff. [*LW* 45:65, 67, 71.]

More important than further involvement in these arguments was his renewed challenge, made for the benefit of the wavering, to drive home brazenly the fundamentals that had determined his previous pronouncement: (1) The kingdom of God and the kingdom of the world are to be strictly differentiated, and not mixed together as the peasants and their spokesmen had done. The kingdom of God has nothing to do with the sword, although the insurgents claimed it did. Conversely, the temporal or worldly power employs the sword and punishment; its role is not to exercise mercy, as the critics would have it. They overlook the fact that the preservation of justice through the authorities is in itself "not the least of God's mercies," for it is "to protect the righteous and to maintain peace and safety. Beyond all doubt, these are precious works of mercy, love, and kindness."[135] Such a work of mercy is when one protects wife and child, possessions and property against violation and robbery, or when a servant rushes to the aid of his assaulted master whether he be Jew, Turk, or Christian.[136] (2) Rebellion is worse than any other evil deed, because it is "the flood of all vices," for it trespasses not only against a single member or against the property of society but also against the head itself, against the authorities and the order of law. Therefore everyone here has the duty to resist, yet not everyone, for example, has the right to kill a murderer. So it is absurd, Luther retorts, to charge him with instigating rebellion when he was actually pledging everyone to resist it.[137]

The *Open Letter* forced Luther reluctantly to continue the issues of the Peasants' War intellectually, and although the battle of words irked him he once more pondered the outcome. Had one followed his advice and taken stern measures from the outset, "and quickly knocked down a peasant or a hundred of them . . . and not allowed them to get the upper hand, many thousands would have been spared who now have had to die."[138] However, had the revolt not been stopped, it would have led to a general devastation and murdering and to a free-for-all struggle, even of peasants among themselves, as the rivalries between their respective groups already indicated. This, indeed, was the devil's aim: "He intended to lay all Germany to utter waste, because there was no other way by which he could suppress the gospel."[139] The insurgents themselves, in their rage, missed the

135. WA 18:389 / 14ff.; 390 / 21ff.; 392 / 4ff. [*LW* 46:69, 71, 73.]

136. WA 18:390 / 23ff.; 397 / 34ff.; 398 / 30ff. [*LW* 46:71, 80, 81.]

137. WA 18:397 / 20ff.; 398 / 18ff. The same was in his 1525 Pentecost sermon (see above, p. 389), WA 17¹:266 / 22ff. [*LW* 46:80, 81.]

138. WA 18:393 / 27ff. [*LW* 46:75.]

139. WA 18:397 / 9–10. [*LW* 46:79.]

opportunity for a peaceful settlement, such as the situations Luther knew of: the Weingarten treaty [Swabian League], the negotiations with the Bamberg peasants, and Margrave Casimir's offer in the Brandenburg-Ansbach lands.[140] Besides, why all this vehement complaining on behalf of those compelled to participate? Luther reminds the rulers emphatically that the release of these fellow travelers is a matter of pardoning but not of acquitting or excusing them. "Why do they let themselves be forced?" To threaten is not the same as to coerce. So then, to participate in a rebellion under duress requires brutal, bodily compulsion. If threats were all, these could be claimed as excuse for any kind of sin. "Who is lord of his own heart? Who can resist the devil and the flesh?" "Good God!" you say, "if only we had known that!" So Luther replies, "Ought not a Christian to know what can be known?"[141]

Finally, there is the outcome of the tragedy. The most telling objection against Luther's "harsh booklet" was that it could be, and was, misread. The victors, in their wantonness, felt strengthened by it, therefore nothing damaged Luther so much as his decision to limit his response: to defend what he had written, and to defer to some other time his accounting with the princes and lords. This damaging fact seems to have escaped him, for he was fully determined to yield not a single inch of the bitterly won ground to those who, in the moment of danger, neither knew what to say nor dared to say it. More fortunately, and yet in Luther's shadow, Philipp Melanchthon had responded early in June to a request from Elector Ludwig of the Palatinate for a memorandum on the *Twelve Articles*. Although his sharp judgment matched that of Luther, he showed essentially less grasp of the peasants' demands than Luther had done in his *Admonition*. Nevertheless, Melanchthon was able in the conclusion to address the conscience of the princes, urging on them moderation and readiness to forgive, citing examples from the Bible and classical antiquity.[142] Melanchthon, to be sure, was writing in a different situation: not amid the heat and caprice of conflict but in a clarified setting, in which he could write instructively to both sides, which was quite different from the imploring call of alarm Luther sent to the wavering rulers. Therefore Melanchthon's memorandum also lacks Luther's apprehensiveness about

140. WA 18:391 / 17ff. [LW 46:72.]

141. WA 18:394 / 35–34; 395 / 20–21, 32, 33–34. [LW 46:76, 77–78.]

142. "Ein Schrift Philippi Melanchthon wider die Artikel der Baurschaft," CR 20:641–62. MSA 1:190ff. Elector Ludwig to Melanchthon, May 18, 1525, CR 1:742–43. *Suppl. Mel.* 6 / 1:291. MBW 401. The memorandum ends before the letter to Camerarius of June 5 (not 7), CR 1:748; *Suppl. Mel.* 6 / 1:293; MBW 404.

the violation and further stability of the gospel, as well as the eschatological dimension depicting the devil's assault and the need to repulse it.

Granting that Luther's *Open Letter* lacked a compensating admonition to the princes, this was not (as he was accused) a sign of servility. Even a year earlier, in his tract against the Nuremberg diet's decision of 1524[143] and then in his *Admonition to Peace,* Luther had blasted the princes more severely than Melanchthon did now. How many may have caught the significance of his egalitarian gibe: "I shall attack the princes and lords, too, for in my office of teacher a prince is the same to me as a peasant."[144] In the few places where he mentioned them, Luther did not spare words in excoriating the princes, "these furious, raving, senseless tyrants, who even after the battle cannot get their fill of blood . . . the Scripture calls such people beasts."[145] Yet the rulers' abuses did not relieve Luther of the duty to protest once again against illegal actions of the peasants and to state his reasons for doing so. To censure the rulers and to warn the peasants were two different tasks.[146] The bloodthirsty victors needed now as earlier to hear Luther's warning about the inescapable wrath of God. "Soon they will reap what they are now sowing." Indeed, it would have been a shame if these nobles had been killed by the peasants. That would have been a mere slap on the wrist compared to what awaits them in hell.[147] It is pointless to say more to them. By his own reckoning Luther noted that there were three occasions when he did not speak to them all but to those rulers "who might wish to deal in a Christian or otherwise honest way." He intended to instruct their conscience, so that they would not only use the sword on occasions when God commands it, but also "after they have won, show grace not only toward those whom they considered innocent but toward the guilty as well."[148] At the end of the tragedy Luther repeats what he had feared during its entire unfolding:

> I had two fears. If the peasants became lords, the devil would become abbott. But if these tyrants became lords, the devil's mother would become an abbess. Therefore I wanted to do two things: quiet the peasants and instruct the pious lords. The peasants were unwilling to listen, and now they have their reward; the lords too will not hear, and they shall have their reward also.[149]

143. See above, pp. 303–4.
144. *WA* 18:393 / 22–23. [*LW* 46:75.]
145. *WA* 18:400 / 24–25, 36ff. [*LW* 46:84.]
146. See above, pp. 365ff.
147. *WA* 18:399 / 23; 401 / 9–10. [*LW* 46:82, 84.]
148. *WA* 18:400 / 15ff. [*LW* 46:83, 84.]
149. *WA* 18:401 / 3ff. [*LW* 46:84.]

Thus the three lines of what Luther has to tell the peasants, the lords, and the critics converge: "We are acting as we mad Germans always do: we know nothing about God, and we talk about these things as though there were no God."[150] If that were different, then everything else would be in order.

We all have grounds to lament the terrible harshness of Luther, in this concluding treatise as well. Yet we need to look again at the root from which it all grew. Luther felt himself virtually alone in a situation where Germany, the gospel, and the common daily life hung in the balance. Who better than Luther had the task to be first in declaring God's threatening word against the defiance of the divine commandments, the divine judgment, as well as the abuse of the gospel? The ingratitude with which the gospel had been received in Germany was now taking its revenge. As Luther saw it, "Many persecute it; few desire it; fewer accept it. And they who do so are so lax and lazy that they let the schools go to ruin and the congregations and pulpits fall apart. No one gives any thought to maintaining the gospel and training the people."[151] In his own burning fear of the punishment God would mete out because of the people's ingratitude, Luther had raised his voice fortissimo.

No doubt he judged the consequences of the rebellion correctly. Were the peasants defeated, they would face terrible misfortune and drag thousands of innocent others with them. Had they at first won, then incalculable chaos would have followed. The lack of peasant leadership showed itself in the relatively easy victories of the rulers' yeomanry against the impressively large but poorly armed and trained mobs.[152] Even though a few wiser heads developed plans of reforms in the wake of the early and undisciplined outbreaks of the rebellion,[153] there became visible no political power that could have subdued this mighty current. The constitutional void between the weak imperial structure, on the one hand, and the broad masses of peasants and townspeople, on the other, could not readily be filled. Medieval political structures provided only the framework of

150. WA 18:396 / 34–35. [LW 46:79.]

151. WA 18:395 / 36ff.; cf. 385 / 15ff. [LW 46:78.]

152. Franz, *Der deutsche Bauernkrieg,* 281ff. Waas, "Wendung" (see n. 1, above, p. 355), 49ff. The will to put down the revolt, without Luther knowing it, was embodied in the decision-makers on the side of the princes, especially in Philip of Hesse and the Bavarian chancellor Leonhard Eck, the political leader of the Swabian League. The decision to suppress the revolt had been made long before Luther wrote his harsh book against the peasants. Ibid., 38ff.

153. H. Angermeier, "Die Vorstellungen des gemeinen Mannes von Staat und Reich im Bauernkrieg," *Vierteljahrschrift für Sozial- und Wirtschaftsgeschichte* 53 (1966): 329ff.

territorial states. Yet the peasants' plans of reform were far-seeing, over-arched by the idea of a strong emperor. Not since the days of Charlemagne had there been anything like it. Now reform should be founded on the gospel as the source of law and social righteousness, on equality in society, on a direct economy of production not dependent on trade, and on the requisitioning of church properties for the common good. The features of this model drew inspiration from a romantically transfigured past. Yet in sharp contrast the territorial rulers were even then introducing the begin-nings of the modern administrative or bureaucratic state. Actually, in the peasant revolt the rulers had passed their second ordeal by fire. The first had been but two years earlier, when the territorial lords had put down the rebellion of the knights. But this time, against far greater numbers and without any kind of help from the empire, the lords discovered their power. In fact, these tests were decisive steps in a direction which two or three decades later enabled them to challenge the emperor himself and come out on top. For the coming centuries the territorial rulers and their states [the lords and their lands] stood there strengthened from top to bottom.

Luther pondered no such distant political contexts. Had he known of them, the dreams of the peasants would have been more to his liking. He was perceptive enough to see that the terrible uprising, whichever direc-tion it took, could only spell catastrophe. Having taken his stand, he also laid the future course of the gospel in Germany on the line. Had he done like Müntzer and other preachers and joined the revolt, or had he written pamphlets rallying support for it, then after the defeat of the peasants the Reformation would have collapsed. In Luther's judgment that was Satan's aim. Luther's use of the name Satan was no quaint recourse to mythology. Quite the opposite, it was his way of perceiving the cunning power of evil, active in thousands of ways to silence the voice of God in this world, doing so mainly in secret but also, as demonstrated but recently, in a concen-trated and overwhelming insurrection. The devil feels that Judgment Day is soon and that his time is short. So it happens that he "undertakes such an unheard-of act, as though saying to himself, 'This is the end, therefore it shall be the worst.' " Or is it the other way around, that God, "perhaps as a prelude to the last day, may will, through the devil, to destroy all rule and order and cast the world on a desolate heap, on which he can then build his kingdom?"[154] The devil's raging and God's wrath are to Luther two aspects of the same situation. However, let this drive people not to

154. *Against the Robbing* . . ., WA 18:358 / 25ff.; 360 / 34ff. [*LW* 46:51, 54.]

despondency but to take refuge in the one healing remedy, submission to God's word. When the gospel was at stake, Luther, like no one else, was personally challenged, "so that I almost think it is because of me that the devil is making such a mess of the world, in order that God might vex the world."[155]

Through it all, Luther had not forgotten the differentiation of the two kingdoms. Indeed, just because this dual concept required it, he responded as he did to the task thrust on him in this historic hour. No advocate of increased power for the princes, politically or personally, he came to know all too well the guilt of the rulers in the rise of the revolution. For that matter, he was much friendlier to the imperial office than to that of the princes. It was not contradictory but very meaningful when, for the benefit of the princes, Luther wrote in his characteristic way that insurrection was both a sign of divine wrath as well as a challenge, conveyed through the Reformer, to carry out the duties of their ruling office. Like it or not, Luther thus became involved in the toils of political action. Nor was that all. Quite differently from Zwingli or Calvin, Luther had become political without being a politician. In politics he reacted rather than acted, as his comments on imperial politics in the years 1523–24 attest.[156] Responding to practical situations of the hour, when he felt forced to intervene, he spoke in strong terms that included fundamental historical and political convictions, yet lacked larger political concepts applicable to the questions raised. So he now failed to size up fully the political role thrust on him by the events of the peasant revolt. Being suddenly himself a political factor, and quite against his will, he did not realize the importance of fulfilling his political role also toward the princes, as he had already done toward the peasants. Of course, his participation politically at this point would hardly have changed anything in the outcome of the crushed uprising, even as he had contributed little to the defeat of the peasants. The issue had been decided even before his alarm-like tract had sounded. Nor did he realize that the function of arbiter, or conciliator, for which some had proposed him had actually drawn him into the situation as a whole, and that what he had earlier said to both sides now needed to be said again. As far as Luther was concerned, he was not about to deal politically with the process of rehabilitation but to advise the consciences of insecure Christian rulers at a time of most intense need. So he saw his own most urgent task as once more to reaffirm the basis of his

155. To John Rühel, May 4 (5), 1525, WA Br 3:481 / 64ff. [LW 49:111.]
156. See above, pp. 303ff.

advice and to defend it against unjust critics. And he did so in the concluding portion of his *Open Letter*. It was risky business, and it led him into the danger zone of his own temperament. On the one hand, he could react with redoubled defiance, when attacked at a point where he knew himself to be in the right; and on the other hand, he could unleash unbounded wrath as a mark of his enormous steadfastness in a critical hour. Given a man of such stature, he could not have the one without the other. In such moments, however, he no longer perceived the kind of environment he was addressing. He failed to notice that in a heatedly debated question people remember the last word, seldom the whole argument. At the same time he courted the risk often present in a policy determined in part by theological presuppositions, when absolute standards are set which do not fully fit the situation and which prevent a reasonable compromise. Luther had every reason to reject the peasants' misuse of the gospel, but the norms he then emphasized—to endure injustice and to obey the given authorities while hoping for God's help—though valid for the individual Christian, were far from meeting the needs of an entire estate or class of people, needs which Luther himself recognized to a large extent. These needs should have been addressed by him once again, but they were not.

The price of writing under pressure and rushing into print is clearly evident in Luther's treatises on the peasants, for they lacked counterparts on elucidating norms. In his treatise *On Temporal Authority* (1523) he had provided such a counterpart. "You govern yourself according to love and tolerate no injustice toward your neighbor."[157] Yet this is something he postponed until a later time. For the moment Luther was preoccupied with the task of unraveling the hopeless skein of spirits. The tragic aspect of Luther's position lay not in his being too middle-class or too conservative to catch the yearnings of the oppressed. This had reached his ear in distorted form from the beginning of the unrest. The initial juridical and social desire of the peasant movement had been crowded out by the image of a Christian revolution. Given that fact, Luther could not keep silent. The ones basically to blame for this miscarriage were the clerical "enthusiasts," who showed up everywhere as the uprising got under way and who coached the peasants in the name of Christ. That is why Luther detested Thomas Müntzer so thoroughly, not personally but objectively, just as the Old Testament prophets hated the false prophets of salvation.

Luther's attitude during the Peasants' War comprised a mixture of motives and factors. With mounting passion and uncompromising nature (he

157. WA 11:255 / 19–20. See above, p. 115. [*LW* 45:96.]

became more rigid the longer he stood alone) two things were combined. One was his theological conviction that rejected a direct application of the gospel to political action; the other was his decidedly political verdict on what had happened. He saw calamity coming. And he found substantiated his long-held conviction that rebellion creates more injustice and misfortune than it abolishes and "generally harms the innocent more than the guilty."[158] To oppose insurrection is thus a command not only of the Bible but also of experience. The things Luther had seen and heard gave sharp contours to his own picture of the event, especially as he gained it in the Franconian-Thuringian lands. There were the reckless abandon of the peasants, the inflammatory sermons of certain preachers, and the bewilderment of his princes. In the process, Luther experienced an awesome example of how a confusion of temporal and spiritual power destroys a world. If ever, now is the time when the distinction of the two kingdoms must be "dyed in the wool and assimilated well,"[159] for these had become new themes to him since his return from the Wartburg. And now was perhaps the hour Satan has chosen and when the end of time might be expected. Yet none of these elements taken singly is sufficient to account for Luther's actions and speech, not even the eschatological dimension.[160] This dimension pressed out of him only that which he brought to it by way of perceptive reason and faith, for it was in the proper relationship of law and gospel that he had found the signpost for the Christian life and the worldly life—although it has often been said of him, almost excusingly, Luther upheld a simply "religious interest,"[161] so that understandably his eyes were closed to social reality. Yet this is not the way he would allow himself to be dragged out of the target range of criticism. Certainly his estimate of reason and history was part of his theology, but what is said in God's Word about the basic facts of historical life can be recognized later again in the great historic experiences, especially in situations of extreme decisiveness where the lines become simple and clear. This is the kind of awareness Luther brought to his statements on the peasant rebellion, and this is why he was so upset over anything that might blur this simplicity of things to even the slightest degree.

Even in later years he never surrendered any of the basic principles he championed in 1525. The terrible suffering caused by the war affected him

---

158. *Eine treue Vermahnung in allen Christen* (1522), WA 8:680 / 19–20. See above, p. 39. [*LW* 45:63.]

159. *Exposition of Psalm 101* (1534 / 35), WA 51:239 / 22–23. [*LW* 13:194.]

160. Correct but one-sided is M. Greschat, "Luthers Haltung im Bauernkrieg" (see n. 30, above).

161. Waas, "Wendung," 33.

profoundly. To Johann Briessmann in distant Königsberg he wrote, presumably in mid-August of that year: "The affair of the peasants has quieted down everywhere after almost one hundred thousand have been killed, so many children orphaned, and the rest so robbed of their livelihood that the appearance of Germany was never more miserable than now. So the rulers rage in ways completing the wickedness of the peasants."[162] And yet the truths extracted from beginning to end of this terrible event remained unchanged.[163] The Peasants' War in Luther's thought continued to haunt him as the horrible example of the consequences of wantonness on both sides, of cowardice in the face of danger, and of the disregard for God's commandments as well as of the final judgment. Peace, Luther felt, was still a long way off and was jeopardized by the evil passions aroused by the war. Looking back, in 1530, Luther reflected,

> You've got to believe it that today among the Germans there is not a single soul who would preserve law and order in the face of these lawless and robbing nobles or protect government from such faithless and thieving subjects. Robbery and stealing abound so that in my opinion our present peace hangs by a silk thread. In fact, peace lies solely in God's hands, above and beyond our will and despite the fuming and raving of all devils. If human wisdom and the power of men alone were governing Germany today, the country would lie in ruins tomorrow.[164]

---

162. *WA Br* 3:556 / 30ff. [*LW* 49:124–25.]

163. H. Dörries, "Luther nach dem Bauernkrieg," in *Ecclesia und Res Publica: Festschrift für K. D. Schmidt* (Göttingen, 1961), 113ff.

164. *Exposition of Psalm 118 (Confitemini), WA* 31¹:83 / 7ff. [*LW* 14:54.]

15

Marriage and Domestic Life

One after another, friends in the closer and wider circles around Luther were getting married. Former priests or monks, humanists, and others were taking the step.[1] Yet he who for years had publicly encouraged withdrawal from coerced celibacy seemed personally immovable. How far from his mind lay thoughts of his own marrying? There were reasons for putting it off. His work overloaded him. His poverty was so grinding that it made support of a family seem foolhardy. Besides, he had a lurking anxiety lest by marrying he throw his confrontation with the Roman church into a false light.

In short, Luther's career seemed marriage-proof. It was not that he disliked women. His feelings toward women he kept to himself. Only to Spalatin, a fellow bachelor and trusted friend, did he air the subject. In fact, both men dared each other to take the step, and both hesitated. Spalatin was too shy. When he thought of possibly giving up his service in the electoral court, he could not trust himself to give the elderly elector the real reason, for to marry seemed to Spalatin a contradiction of his duties as court chaplain. Luther explained that marriage would indeed be the only reason for Spalatin to resign his chaplaincy, so he kept on urging him to take the step.[2] Spalatin, for his part, challenged Luther to marry. People simply were expecting it of him. If proof were needed, Spalatin forwarded Luther a letter from one of his loyal adherents in Bavaria, Argula von Grumbach. She had often protested publicly and courageously against the persecution of the evangelicals—to which Luther responded on November 30, 1524,

> Tell her I am in God's hand as a creature whose heart God may change and rechange, kill and revive again at any moment. Nevertheless, the way I feel now and have felt thus far, I will not marry. It is not that I do not feel my flesh or sex, since I am neither wood nor stone, but my mind is far removed from

1. Melanchthon (August 18, 1520), Agricola about the same time (1520), Bartholomäus Bernhardi (1521), Karlstadt (January 19, 1522), Justus Jonas (February 10, 1522), Bugenhagen (October 13, 1522), Wenceslaus Link (April 15, 1523), Francis Lambert (July 13, 1523), Thomas Müntzer (1523).

2. Luther to Spalatin, November 30, 1524, WA Br 3:393 / 1ff. [LW 49:92–93.]

marriage since daily I expect the death and punishment due a heretic. There-fore I shall not limit God's work in me, nor shall I rely on my own heart. Yet I hope God does not let me live long.[3]

In this melancholy mood Luther was not ready to bind the destiny of a woman to his endangered life. Ironically, he used his own indecision to spur Spalatin's spirit. Then he elaborated with characteristic humor,

Incidentally, regarding what you write about my marrying, I do not want you to wonder why a famous lover like me does not marry. It is rather strange that I, who so often write about matrimony and get mixed up with women,[4] have not turned into a woman, to say nothing of not having married one. Yet if you want me to set an example, here you have the most powerful one, for I have had three wives simultaneously and loved them so much that I have lost two who are taking other husbands; the third I can hardly keep with my left arm, and she too will probably soon be snatched away from me. But you are a sluggish lover who does not dare become the husband of even one woman. Watch out that I, who have no thought of marriage at all, do not some day overtake you too eager suitors, just as God usually does those things least expected. I am saying this seriously to urge you to do what you are intending.[5]

Later generations, in the wake of confessional polemics, humorlessly took Luther's joking to be an admission of a lively love life.[6] Luther's whimsical remarks overlay an earnest undertone: He is thoroughly capable of empa-thy for women, but as yet he cannot make up his mind to marry. Who the two may have been who "escaped" him cannot be said for certain.[7] The third was no doubt Katharina von Bora.

3. WA Br 3:394 / 17ff. [LW 49:93.]

4. The escaped nuns; providing for them put Luther to considerable trouble. See above, pp. 258ff.

5. April 16, 1525, WA Br 3:474 / 13ff. Cf. also April 10, 1525, WA Br 3:470 / 6ff. Because there was at that moment much gossip about his own prospective marriage, Luther called himself a "famous lover." "Left arm" does not signify "a left-handed marriage" or a legally recognized concubinage, as O. Clemen says in n. 10 on the letter of April 16, and Rückert also claims, BoA 6:127. In the laws of marriage there is only the "left hand" (= of unequal social standing, or worse). A correct translation is that of H. Grisar, Von Luther (Freiburg, 1911), 1:442.

6. Examples: W. Walther, Für Luther wider Rom: Handbuch der Apologetik Luthers und die Reformation (Halle, 1906), 646ff. From another angle, Grisar, Von Luther, 1:441ff.

7. The one was probably Ave von Schönfeld, a former nun from Nimbschen [see above, p. 258]. Luther later said of her that if he had married fourteen years earlier he would have married Ave (this comment in his later Table Talk bears no date, but it must have referred back to 1523 or 1524). Instead, Ave became the wife of a medical student, Basilius Axt, who at that time ran Lucas Cranach's apothecary and later became personal physician to Duke Albert of Prussia. The other ex-nun was either one of the escapees or Ave Alemann, from an evangelically-minded family in Magdeburg. Luther later referred to her as his bride (WA Br 3:3 / 8), perhaps because Amsdorf, the head pastor in Magdeburg, had recommended her to Luther (this is supposition, not fact, as in WA Br 3:3, n. 5).

Yet she was just the one whom Luther had tried to match with Jerome Baumgartner, son of a patrician family in Nuremberg. He was born in 1498, she in 1499. He had studied in Wittenberg 1518–22 and had taken his meals at Melanchthon's. He had experienced the episode of unrest in Wittenberg. In a letter of March 18, 1522, he had reported to a Nuremberg friend, Hector Poemer, on the powerful impression Luther's Invocavit sermons had made on him[8]—after Luther's return from the Wartburg. Back in Wittenberg on business in the summer of 1523, Baumgartner became much attracted to Katharina. The interest was mutual and known among their friends, but the elder Baumgartners in Nuremberg apparently talked their son out of marrying a former nun. Despite his return to Nuremberg, Katharina hoped he would come back to Wittenberg. He did not, and she never heard from him again.[9] In October 1524, when Luther had some other matter to bring up with Baumgartner, he once again became spokesman for Katharina. "By the way," he wrote, "if you intend to hold on to your Kate von Bora, then you'd better hurry before she becomes engaged to someone else who is on the scene. She has not yet done injury to your love. I would be pleased with the one marriage as with the other."[10] The other suitor was the equally eligible Caspar Glatz. The preceding year he had earned the degree of doctor of theology, and at the ensuing doctoral feast Luther conveyed Glatz's thanks for the roast wild game provided by the elector. In the summer of 1524, Glatz served as rector of the university.[11] During his rectorship the confrontation took place between the university and All Saints Foundation, on the one side, and Karlstadt, on the other, over the latter's claim on the parish in Orlamünde. Karlstadt yielded on June 8, 1524, and in the autumn Glatz himself was placed in that parish.[12] Luther's encouragement of her marriage to Glatz put Katharina in an embarrassing dilemma. The young woman had a mind of her own about the proffered suitors, and she turned to Amsdorf for help. Shortly before his call to Magdeburg, she came to him "complaining that Doctor Martinus was trying every which way for

8. Quotation from the letter, above, pp. 74–75.

9. On this, E. Kroker, *Katharina von Bora, Luthers Frau: Ein Lebens- und Charakterbild* (Leipzig, 1906; 7th ed., Berlin, 1974), 58ff. *LuJ* 7 (1925): 59–60.

10. October 12, 1524, WA Br 3:358 / 7ff.

11. Glatz and a second doctoral candidate passed their examinations in August 1523. The doctoral feast took place in the autumn. WA Br 3:180. Glatz was rector from May 1 to October 18, 1524. See C. E. Förstemann, *Album academiae Vitebergensis* (Lipsiae, 1894), 121.

12. On Orlamünde, see above, pp. 143ff. W. Friedensburg, "Der Verzicht Karlstadts auf das Wittenberger Archidiakonat und die Pfarre in Orlamünde (1524 Juni)," *ARG* 11 (1914): 70–71.

her to consent to Doctor Glatz. Yet for him she had neither interest nor love. Rather (if it could so happen and be God's will) she would marry either Doctor Martinus or Domine Amsdorf."[13]

That was Katharina von Bora. She well knew that even as a penniless nun she had her price, and she did not hesitate to name it. If she did marry, it would be with someone worthy in her eyes; no one would talk her into marrying some inferior suitor. Her shrewd estimate of Glatz impressed Amsdorf, and he let Luther know it in no uncertain terms. "What in the devil are you up to that you try to persuade good Kate and force that old skinflint, Glatz, on her. She doesn't go for him and has neither love nor affection for him."[14] Two years later it was clear how well founded Kate's rejection and Amsdorf's verdict had been. Both the new rector as well as the university complained to the elector most vigorously about the dubious financial machinations of Glatz and his infinite capacity for neglecting his Orlamünde parish.[15] Meanwhile, Luther remained irked over Katharina's resistance to his well-intended efforts. "If she doesn't like this one, she will just have to wait a while for another!"[16] It is probably because of this episode that Luther sometimes said he did not love her and always regarded her as proud. "But God has willed that I should have compassion on the poor. And his grace has given me a happy marriage."[17] The situation put Luther in a bind: silence from Baumgartner in Nuremberg; confirmed bachelorhood from Amsdorf (he remained single to the end); and at the center a solitary, orphaned, and penniless erstwhile nun waiting to be placed. How could Luther any longer evade the marriage issue as it bore in on him? His humorous April 16 letter to Spalatin, quoted above,

13. According to a verbal account of Amsdorf, December 16, 1552, as told to the two Eisenach preachers, Joachim Stigelius and Bartholomäus Rosinus, and written down at Amsdorf's request. Published according to the Vienna Manuscript Vind. 11847 (in possession of Friedrich Widebrams), cited in E. Kroker, "Luthers Werbung um Katharina von Bora: Eine Untersuchung über die Quellen einer alten Überlieferung," in *Lutherstudien zur 4. Jahrhunderfeier der Reformation* (Weimar, 1917), 142–43. A reference to the manuscript and the story is already in WA TR 1:xxiv. This report eluded Boehmer, "Luthers Ehe," 59, 75, n. 20c. Boehmer had only the generally known and much shortened Latin summary by Abraham Scultetus, *Annalium Evangelii reconditi prima* (Heidelberg, 1618), 274, as taken from the German text. According to this account's express notation, the visit of Katharina to Amsdorf took place shortly before his departure for Magdeburg, and not on the occasion of Amsdorf's visit to Luther in March 1525. Boehmer, "Luthers Ehe," 60. WA Br 3:455, n. 3; 458, n. 1.

14. Kroker, "Luthers Werbung," 142.

15. The Rector, Masters, and Doctors of Wittenberg University to Elector John, October 16, 1526; printed in H. Barge, *Andreas Bodenstein von Karlstadt* (Leipzig, 1905), 2:572ff.

16. Kroker, "Luthers Werbung," 142.

17. WA TR 4, no. 4786, 503 / 20ff.

veiled the deeper fact that God was changing his mind for him.[18] The decisive push came in the course of the visit to his parents in Mansfeld, while traveling through a region ripe with peasant unrest and ready to explode.[19] Now, as earlier, his father urged him to marry; he was eager for heirs from his eldest son. "Because of my dear father's desire" was Luther's way of triggering his motivation. From now on she was "my Kate," and self-evidently so at the first mention of her among friends.[20]

To decide was one thing, to cope with a gloomy situation was quite another. Multiple concerns combined to keep Luther on the run: the alarming disclosures of his recent journey through lands seething with unrest, and the shock caused by the death of Elector Frederick on May 5 ("How bitter is death, not so much for the ones dying as for those who survive them,"[21] Luther wrote to Spalatin); Luther's anxiety about the university, long overdue for reform (on May 20 Luther sent the new elector, John, his opinion posthaste);[22] the Peasants' War advancing into Thuringia, its sudden collapse at Frankenhausen, and the death of Müntzer. On top of it all came his fourteen sermons between May 9 and June 6, besides much correspondence.[23]

Conspiring pressures from without and within finally turned a long-pondered plan into action. Death had touched life around Luther at so many points, would it not also snatch him? Not that he feared it. Quite the contrary. But he might suddenly run out of time and be unable personally to respond to the question of priestly marriage, a response long overdue. To his friend Amsdorf, close to these developments from their outset, Luther summed up his motives, including them in his June 21 invitation to the wedding feast. He wrote:

> Indeed, the rumor is true that I was suddenly married to Katharina. [I did this] to silence the evil tongues which are so used to complaining about me, for I still hope to live for a little while. In addition, I did not want to reject this unique opportunity to obey my father's wish for progeny, which he often expressed so urgently. At the same time, I also wanted to confirm what I have taught by practicing it, for I find so many timid people in spite of such great

18. See above, p. 402.

19. See above, pp. 376ff.

20. The father's request in the letters of invitation to the wedding, June 21, 1525, WA Br 3:531 / 14; 541 / 5–6. The "my Kate" letter to Rühel, May 4 (5?), 1525, WA Br 3:482 / 81. [LW 49:115–16, 117, 111.]

21. May 7, 1525, WA Br 3:487 / 5–6.

22. To Spalatin, WA Br 3:502 / 2. W. Friedensburg, *Geschichte der Universität Wittenberg* (Magdeburg, 1926ff.), 173ff.

23. Briefly compiled by Boehmer, "Luthers Ehe," 75, n. 31.

light from the gospel. God has willed and brought about this step, for I am neither amorous nor in heat, but I love my wife.[24]

He had already taken the first step; the formal ceremony had been conducted.

Repeatedly, during these days, Luther commented on how the suddenness of the event was accompanied by God's inspiration. To Wenceslaus Link, in Altenburg, he confided, "Suddenly, while I still had other thoughts, God in a wondrous way threw me into matrimony with Katharina von Bora, the nun."[25] Luther found this step a divine liberation, coming as it did after a long period of indecision and virtually in the midst of current cares that would otherwise have prevented him from acting. It remained for another close friend, lawyer Jerome Schurff, for whom canon law was second only to the Bible, to point out how necessary Luther's step really was. "When this monk marries," observed Schurff, "the whole world will laugh, and so will the devil, destroying all that he has devised."[26] There was also a time when Luther thought that the public testimony of his own marriage might encourage the high prelates of the church to follow suit. Someone had told Luther that Cardinal Albrecht, archbishop of Mainz, had wondered why Luther did not marry, seeing as he was urging everyone else to do so. This prompted his friend John Rühel, the Mansfeld councilman and also legal adviser to Albrecht, to challenge Luther: Why not send the cardinal a letter too, suggesting a "change of estate" from celibacy to matrimony?[27]

Luther responded with alacrity and wrote Albrecht a brief letter that soon escaped into print. He reminded the cardinal of the evil reputation of the clergy, seeing in the peasants' rebellion a form of divine punishment of the clerical estate. The cardinal should marry and transmute his diocese into a secular principality. Herein he could follow the example of another Albrecht [Albert], the grand master of Prussia, through whom "God brought about such changes as were neither hoped for nor believed possible ten years earlier." Luther then addressed the cardinal man-to-man, inquiring, "What will you answer when God will ask: I fashioned you as a man who should not be alone but should have a wife—where is your wife?"[28] The cardinal did not reply. What could he have said? His

24. WA Br 3:541 / 2ff. [LW 49:117.]

25. [June 20, 1525.] WA Br 3:537 / 9–10.

26. According to Amsdorf's report in Scultetus, *Annalium Evangelii reconditi prima*, 274. Boehmer, "Luthers Ehe," 65.

27. WA Br 3:505 / 44ff.

28. WA 18:408 / 4ff.; 409 / 1ff.; 410 / 5ff., 28ff.

dissolute life was generally known. Luther's challenge to Cardinal Albrecht sharpened the latter's counterquestion: Why do you yourself not marry? Luther gave his reply via Rühel: "Insofar as my marriage would be an invigoration for His Electoral Grace, I would be ready to trot on ahead of His Electoral Grace as an example, especially since in any case I am minded to let myself be found in the married estate before I die, for I regard this estate as fostered by God, even if it should go no further than an engaged Joseph's marriage."[29]

The thoughts of his possible death which recurred in Luther's comments during these crowded weeks linked him to this uncanny historic hour. There was the peasant revolt, a veritable devil's dance, with its incalculable consequences. There too was his latest, impassioned treatise against the peasants. What more did he need to feel himself doubly challenged, to prove that nothing of his "former papistic life" remained and to make his enemies even "more mad and foolish?"[30] The final prod, after so much indecision, came from Katharina von Bora herself. Luther had left no doubt that if he married at all she would be the one. Even so, this choice met with no general approval. Quite to the contrary, "If I had not married secretly, all my friends would have cried, 'Not this woman but somebody else!'" So thus did he reminisce seven years later.[31]

Evidently Katharina was not popular, at least not among the older generation, although for a time she got on well with the students. She was no beauty, and for some she was too proud and energetic. Luther knew her better; she deserved no such peevish reactions. Hence the swiftness and the secrecy suddenly concluding his own slowly maturing decision. Luther, the liberated temporizer, quite readily had advice for others: "After an engagement is announced, proceed as quickly as possible to the wedding." During these emotional days he told Spalatin about the case of a couple who could not make up their minds. His own experience was reflected in the account. "They pretended they must first make certain of their inner feelings. This is nonsense. No one can examine his heart in his hand. The devil has all kinds of powers and can sometimes even separate married couples." Then Luther armed Spalatin with a dozen proverbs and Bible texts which added up to this: "God's temporal benefits are indeed

29. To Rühel, June 3, 1525, WA Br 3:522 / 13ff. "Joseph's marriage" denotes not an ascetic marriage without intercourse but the then popular notion of the marriage of an old Joseph and a much younger Mary.

30. Luther's wedding invitation to the Mansfeld councilmen, June 15, 1525, WA Br 3:531 / 10–11.

31. WA TR 3, no. 3179a, b; 212 / 5–6, 11–12. [LW 54:191–92.]

temporal. They do not stand still but are running and ever on the move. Therefore one must take hold, whatever it may be, when and where possible, so as not to lose it."[32]

Three days after expressing this mood, Luther finally took the decisive step. In doing so he followed the Wittenberg customs yet speeded up the legal ceremony, "to stop those mouths" from further gossip.[33] For the evening of June 13 [a Tuesday] Luther invited five witnesses to his Black Cloister, where the official ceremony took place. The witnesses included: Justus Jonas, dean of the Castle Church; Johann Apel, professor of canon law, who was married to a former nun; and Lucas Cranach and his wife [Barbara], the couple who had until then provided Katharina's lodging and who now represented her as family. Then followed the "copulation" or performance of the marriage ceremony by John Bugenhagen and, according to custom, the bridal couple lay down briefly on the future marriage bed in the presence of the witnesses. The next morning [in the cloister] the same circle gathered again for breakfast.[34] The basic acts of marriage, the betrothal and the copulation, required public affirmation in church, while the commencement of housekeeping was symbolized by the wedding feast.

Because Luther was eager to have his parents and special friends from home, the feast was delayed a fortnight. For this June 27 event he invited not only Wittenbergers and three Mansfeld councilmen but also a number of guests from out of town: Spalatin, of course; Leonard Koppe, of Torgau (who had facilitated Katharina's escape from the cloister); Wenceslaus Link, in Altenburg; Hans von Dolzig, marshal at the elector's court (he was asked to supply the venison for the feast); and Amsdorf, of Magdeburg. The dinner party numbered fifteen people.[35] Because of delays, Luther had to make sure that the invited guests already knew about the marriage ceremony that had already taken place. In almost all his letters

32. To Spalatin, June 10, 1525, WA Br 3:525 / 6–29. [Cf. LW 54, no. 3179a, 191.]

33. To the Mansfeld councilmen, June 15, 1525, as part of their letter of invitation, WA Br 3:531 / 15. Also, WA Br 3:533 / 4ff. Likewise in WA TR 3, no. 3179a, b; 212 / 1–2, 7–8. Detailed account of the legal ceremony and of Luther's marriage, in Boehmer, "Luthers Ehe," 40ff. [Cf. LW 54: no. 3179a, 191.]

34. G. Kawerau, Der Briefwechsel des Justas Jonas (Berlin, 1952), 1:94.

35. According to Hans von der Planitz's report in a June 30 letter to Duke Albrecht of Prussia. The company enjoyed good beer. Excerpt published by A. Clos, "Abfassungszeit von Luthers Schrift, 'Wider die räuberischen . . . Rotten der Bauern" (see above, p. 378, n. 88), 129, n. 6. According to a June 21 letter, whose authenticity was questioned by O. Clemen, Luther had ordered "a barrel of Torgau beer" from Leonhard Koppe, WA Br 3:539 / 8ff. [LW 49:116, to Spalatin.] [Kroker says the Wittenberg town council gave a barrel of Einbeck beer; Katharina von Bora, 75.]

the same whimsical sentence shows up as he expresses amazement over what has happened to him. "By this marriage I have made myself so unworthy and despised that I hope the angels will laugh and the devils weep."[36] "You too know what happened to me when I got braided into my girl's pigtails. God likes to perform miracles, to mock and fool me and the world."[37] "Doubtless my adventurous rumor has reached you. I'm supposed to have become a husband. It's all so strange to me that I can hardly believe it. Yet the witnesses are so considerable that for the sake of their service and honor I've got to believe it."[38]

Luther's step evoked not only surprise but also displeasure among those near him. Schurff's[39] dry comment was topped by Melanchthon's pained feeling. On June 16 he wrote his trusted friend Camerarius that "without taking a single one of his friends into confidence" Luther married. To keep his sentiments from prying eyes, Melanchthon's letter was in Greek, so that even Camerarius hardly knew what to make of it. Finally he brought it out in modified form when in 1569 he published Melanchthon's letters to him. Centuries later the surprise was all the greater when in 1876 the original text was recovered and published in full.[40] Melanchthon's letter reveals more about himself than about Luther during these June days. He claims to discern distress and confusion in Luther over the changed life situation. And he suspects that even Camerarius is astonished "that in these unhappy times, in which good people are suffering so much, this man lacks compassion and rather, as it seems, revels and compromises his good reputation, precisely at a time when Germany stands in particular need of his spirit and authority." For this reason Melanchthon seeks to console Luther, not, however, as though he had as yet done anything reproachable or unjustified. Yet for one so much at a loss as Camerarius, Melanchthon has a simple explanation:

That man is thoroughly good-natured, and the nuns plied all their arts to draw him to their side. Perhaps this manifold association with the nuns has weakened and taken the fire out of his noble nature and greatness of soul. This is apparently how he tumbled into such an untimely change in his way of

36. To Spalatin, June 16, 1525, WA Br 3:533 / 8–9.

37. To Koppe, June 17, 1525, WA Br 3:534 / 6ff.

38. To Dolzig, June 21, 1525, WA Br 3:537 / 4ff. WA Br 12:66 / 4ff.

39. See above, p. 406.

40. The best rendition of the letter, revealing the alterations of Camerarius, is that of H. Volz in *MSA* 7 / 1:238ff. *MBW* 408. On the transmittal, H. Scheible, "Überlieferung und Editionen der Briefe Melanchthons," *HdJb* (1968): 139ff. Translation by Walther, *Für Luther wider Rom*, 660ff., and H. Boehmer, *Luther im Lichte der neueren Forschung*, 5th ed. (Leipzig, 1918), 174ff.

life. However, the gossip that he slept with her even before marriage is a plain lie. Now there's no use either to scold or to think evil of what has happened. I for one believe that by nature we are made for marriage. This way of life, to be sure, is humble yet also holy and more pleasing to God than celibacy.

Melanchthon concluded, saying that he had all along wished Luther to be made humble instead of exalted, for, according to Demosthenes, well-being awakens a poor disposition not only in the simple but also in the wise. "Besides, I hope that this way of life will make him more dignified and enable him to shed the jesting that we have so often criticized in him." Let Camerarius therefore bear the change with an even temper, for he has Luther's good reputation at heart, and according to the Scriptures marriage is an honorable estate. "Probably we are really forced into matrimony. In any case, it's most godless to condemn a doctrine because of a teacher's misstep."[41]

This pedantic letter, triggered by irritation over the secrecy of Luther's move, and designed to calm Camerarius concerning the suspicions against Katharina and the other nuns as well as concerning his own presumed criticism, makes it clearer than any other document why Luther withdrew himself from the Wittenbergers' gossip and the interventions of local friends. Between the lines of Melanchthon's letter there are also indications of the cool climate of his own marriage of 1520 to another Katharina, the daughter of Wittenberg's mayor, Hans Krapp. Katharina Melanchthon apparently had no liking for the renegade noble nun. Nor did Melanchthon himself appreciate his current isolation from Luther during this year supercharged by the Erasmus debate and other pressing questions.[42] Luther, of course, was not aware of Melanchthon's letter, yet he sensed an air of disapproval coming from him, and ironically so: Marriage was normally rated as a "devout and holy work of God," but in Luther it was seen as "godless and devilish."[43] In Luther's presence Melanchthon could not simply feign approval, but to Camerarius he could freely unburden his displeasure. In any case, he took part in Luther's wedding feast on June 27. Indeed, he had already on June 20 voluntarily supported Luther's rather hesitating letter to Wenceslaus Link with a little note of his own,

41. *MSA* 7 / 1:240ff.

42. G. Mix, "Luther und Melanchthon in ihrer gegenseitigen Beurteilung," *ThStKr* 74 (1901): 458ff. On Melanchthon's wife, see W. Maurer, *Der junge Melanchthon* (Göttingen, 1969), 2:100–101. Again W. Maurer, "Melanchthons Anteil am Streit zwischen Luther und Erasmus," in ibid., 144., G. Elliger, *Philipp Melanchthon* (Berlin, 1902), 217, 367.

43. Twice during these days Luther cites his marriage as an *opus dei*, a work of God. To Spalatin, June 16, and to Link, June 20, 1525, *WA Br* 3:533 / 10; 537 / 14.

charged with a humorous reference. "For the sake of our friendship I beg you to come, so that Dr. Jerome [Schurff] will get more material for disputation."[44] As the former vicar-general of the German Augustinian Congregation, Link—now married for two years—would indeed have been the right opponent for Schurff, the rigid canonist.

As for Katharina herself, an abundance of tasks faced her. Imagine a young housewife, age twenty-six, taking charge of a still unfinished cloister, meant originally for forty monks, which should now become a home. For this purpose the building seemed utterly ill-suited.[45] It required furnishing and endless improvements, having been long neglected. Luther's faithful servant, Wolfgang Seberger, was not the most diligent and had little sense of order or cleanliness.[46] For an entire year Luther's straw mattress had not been decently shaken out. "I was tired and worked hard all day. Then I just fell into bed and noticed nothing."[47] As for furniture and other household goods, Luther brought little and Katharina nothing. Wedding gifts from friends eased the situation, but goblets and other items of value were of little practical use, except as security when Luther posted bond for someone borrowing from the parish's common chest.[48] Kate was reluctant to sell such gifts. Luther was much more ready to do so, especially when it meant helping others. Then his motto was "Give and it will be given to you" (Luke 6:38). On such occasions he would tell his wife, "Dear Kate, when the money's gone, the goblets are next."[49] Most of those things, later said to have been wedding gifts, were not especially valuable.[50] Best of all was that the new elector, John, sent the couple a gift of 100 guilders and ordered that henceforth Luther be paid an annual salary of 200 guilders, the same amount Melanchthon had been receiv-

---

44. Luther to Link, June 20, 1525, WA Br 3:537 / 9ff. Melanchthon to Link, June 20, MSA 7 / 1:245. MBW 409. On Schurff, see above, p. 280, n. 97.

45. Details on Kate Luther's housekeeping in Kroker, *Katharina von Bora*, 81ff. (unfortunately no sources are cited). On the building and grounds, see above, p. 256, n. 13.

46. Not Sieberger, about whom see WA 38:290, WA Br 12:421, nn. 10–11. In his famous lamentation, Luther not only complained to the birds about his birdlike style of life (WA 38:290ff.) but also named his [Seberger's] laziness among his housefatherly cares. He would gladly pay God something for their alleviation: "So I was ready to pay our Lord God one hundred florins (guilders) if my Kate had more milk and my Wolf less inertia." WA TR 2, no. 1626, 155 / 14–15. Cf. also WA Br 9:168 / 32ff.

47. WA TR 4, no. 5117, 670 / 24.

48. At the beginning of 1527 he had placed one goblet for 50 guilders and one for 12 at the disposal of "Fat Hermann." To Brisger, February 1, 1527, WA Br 4:164 / 4ff.

49. WA TR 4, no. 5181, 701 / 2ff.

50. Kroker, *Katharina von Bora*, 73ff.

ing.[51] This wedding present and the few remaining items from the cloister's supplies (the rest had been stolen) did not last long. Indeed, much went to cover expenses Luther had incurred for tiding over erstwhile nuns and monks.[52]

Fortunately Luther got a wife who knew how to manage a household, provide food from the garden, and keep track of all income—insofar as Luther's impulsive generosity allowed. So, for example, without his knowledge, she quietly kept a wedding gift of 20 guilders from Cardinal Albrecht [of Mainz], which Luther had declined to accept but which had come indirectly through the cardinal's councillor, Rühel, in Mansfeld.[53] Years later, when Luther spoke of his "remarkable home economy," in which he consumed more than he received,[54] this pertained especially to the early years of his marriage. It was made possible only by gifts and by Kate's rapidly expanded agricultural enterprise. Luther did all his preaching and pastoral care without remuneration—also during periods when he substituted for Bugenhagen in the Wittenberg congregation. Nor would he accept honorariums for his publications, even though these profited the printers considerably.

In short, Luther's way with money kept his income from increasing. In his second year of marriage he even tried his hand at woodworking to earn some money. For that purpose he made a special request of his friend, Wenceslaus Link, preacher in Nuremberg as of 1525. Luther asked him not only to send an assortment of garden seeds for Kate, for which he enclosed one gold guilder, but also a lathe and accessories, because he and

51. WA Br 9:581 / 49–50. WA Br 12:423. Kroker, *Katharina von Bora*, 83, 89, conjectures that a salary of 100 guilders had been authorized even before the wedding, but he lists no source for this assertion. Luther's Table Talk, which contains most of these details, mentions nothing about an earlier salary. There is, of course, some probability that Frederick the Wise or John did not leave Luther entirely uncompensated for his lectures. That his professorship was presumably provided free of charge by the Black Cloister is to be inferred from the fact that (as with Jonas) on the personnel roster of October 13, 1525, Luther is listed as unpaid. Luther was now paid by the electoral administration; Jonas, as dean, by the All Saints Foundation. Jerome Schurff (160 guilders) and Christian Beyer (100 guilders) received additional pay as assessors of the superior court. W. Friedensburg, *Urkundenbuch der Universität Wittenberg* (Magdeburg, 1926), 142ff. By the same author, on financial matters, *Geschichte der Universität Wittenberg* (Magdeburg, 1926). Also H. Hausherr, "Die Finanzierung einer deutschen Universität: Wittenberg in den ersten Jahrzehnten seines Bestehens (1502–1547)," in *450 Jahre Martin-Luther-Universität Halle-Wittenberg* (Halle, 1952), 1:345ff. [Cf. E. G. Schwiebert, *Luther and His Times* (St. Louis: Concordia, 1950), 257–68.]

52. Cf. the review in Luther's so-called domestic account of 1542, WA Br 9:580–81.

53. WA TR 3, no. 3038b, 154 / 10ff. Whether the letter of April 20, 1526 (WA Br 4:57 / 1ff.) had anything to do with this matter is not certain, yet probable, considering the circumstances as described. Kroker, *Katharina von Bora*, 77, and also Boehmer, "Luthers Ehe," 67–68, assume it did.

54. WA TR 3, no. 2835a and b, 13.

his servant Wolfgang had taken up wood-turning. "Tools we have, but we need several more elegant ones in your Nuremberg style."[55] With thanks for the shipment, Luther asked whether Link had some new kind of instruments that "would be self-propelled when Wolfgang snores or just loafs." He also thanked Link for sending him a quadrant with platen and a wooden clock, adding, "I'm nearly perfect at telling time, especially when I must tell my drunken Saxons what time it is. They'd rather measure it by the jug than by the clock, and they don't let a mistake by the sun or the clock or the boss bother them."[56] Luther himself never became a master of the lathe, but he delighted in the garden and did not leave his Kate in the lurch. He let Link know that the melons, squash, and cucumbers were growing enormously. At year's end he requested seeds from Link again, but this time in as great a variety as possible, "for if I stay alive I'll become a gardener."[57] His workload and correspondence left little time for gardening [but even a little if it could be refreshing]. At any rate, he knew how to graft trees. Some years later he still expressed amazement over the wonders of this process, "It is one of God's miracles of creation that the entire tree is determined by the little twig and eyelet; how much simpler it would seem for the tree to determine the twig."[58] Let Kate and her helpers take the credit, it was still his garden and his joy; he could think of it as his very own. "I have planted a garden and built a well very successfully. Come, you shall be garlanded with lilies and roses," he wrote exuberantly to his old friend Spalatin. With jubilation he added that on June 7, 1526, Katharina bore his first child. "From the best woman and most beloved wife, a little son, Johannes Lutherulus. By the grace of God I have received him. By God's marvelous grace I have become a father."[59]

Yet even at that moment cares were multiplying. The little cloister garden was too small, and Kate's desire to enlarge it by purchasing a nearby plot had to be given up. Meanwhile the debts were mounting as the family grew. On December 10, 1527, a second child, Elizabeth, was born. Luther did not hesitate once again to send a note to Eberhard Brisger, his last companion of the old cloister days, requesting a loan of 8 guilders, for he himself had put up security for a debt of over 100 guilders. Luther, like Melanchthon, had often bailed out borrowers from the community chest.

55. January 1, 1527, WA Br 4:148 / 17ff. [LW 49:158.]

56. May 19, 1527, WA Br 4:203 / 1ff. He repeated his thanks on July 5, 1527, WA Br 4:220 / 4ff.

57. July 5 and December 29, 1527, WA Br 4:220 / 13ff.; 310 / 12ff.

58. WA TR 4, no. 4741; 462 / 5ff. *Billiger = einfacher, das Gegebene* [= simpler].

59. June 17, 1526, WA Br 4:89 / 4ff., 16ff.

Cranach and Christian Döring, keepers of the chest, felt Luther was too credulous and no longer let him risk his money for others.[60]

A hardly insignificant part of his workload consisted of the constant stream of visitors or regular boarders at his table. At the very outset of Kate's housekeeping an unexpected guest showed up whose whereabouts had to be kept secret. It was Karlstadt. On June 12, 1525, he had written Luther of his urgent desire to return to Electoral Saxony. He disclaimed any participation in the Peasants' War, having himself "hated it and been an enemy of it." He begged Luther to intercede with the elector for him and his family, and sent his wife in advance. Melanchthon, apprised of the situation, expected her on June 27.[61] As for Luther, even before his marriage he had taken in as many student boarders as possible. Now, with a woman in charge, the number of boarders jumped. In line with university town custom, Katharina asked a modest fee from her table guests to help defray her considerable expenses. As a recent university town, Wittenberg had as yet only a small number of lodging and eating places for students. It was thus expected that professors would take students into their homes and, on the side, also tutor them as needed. Melanchthon's example was noteworthy. From the outset of his teaching in Wittenberg (1518–19) his *schola privata* had become famous.[62] Yet as late as mid-winter 1524–25 there was only one other, and older, private school like it, that of mathematician Johannes Longicampianus, who came in a poor second in terms of his skills in pedagogy. This mathematics school had provided Melanchthon with the incentive to found his own school. His house really became a "home school," complete with a well-cast program.

Luther approached the matter differently. Alongside his students' often desperately needed material aid, he gave them what he could for their studies and other needs. Students counted themselves fortunate to be accepted in either Melanchthon's or Luther's house, where they were secure against the overcharging so prevalent among most other professors

60. To Brisger, February 1, 1527, WA Br 4:164–65. Here also the note on the pawned goblet. See n. 48, above. Cf. the note to Brisger, February 12, 1526, WA Br 4:31 / 4ff.

61. Contrary to Boehmer's assumption in "Luthers Ehe," 67, it is impossible that Karlstadt was given lodging by Luther already on the evening of this day, his wedding day. See Karlstadt's letter to Luther, June 12, 1525, WA Br 3:529–30. Melanchthon to Camerarius, June 27, CR 1:750–51 (date in *Suppl. Mel.* 6 / 1:295–96). MBW 410. Cf. also WA 18:433–34. According to WA TR 2, no. 2064, 308 / 28ff., Karlstadt remained secreted in Luther's house for over eight weeks.

62. L. Koch, *Melanchthons schola privata: Ein historischer Beitrag zum Ehrengedächtnis des Praeceptor Germaniae* (Gotha, 1859). Maurer, *Der junge Melanchthon,* 2:96ff.

who in this way tried to supplement their own income.[63] Melanchthon soon found out that under the circumstances an honest housefather at best broke even financially.[64] Luther's table always abounded in guests who could pay little or nothing. Some of them were older men ousted from their church positions, others were indigent erstwhile monks or nuns. Such table companionship, however, would later provide the housefather [and housemother] with an incomparable monument. In time, over a dozen young men habitually jotted down the essence of conversations at Luther's table. He permitted this practice with splendid candor, setting no limitations even when conversation turned to quote personal matters. The result was a unique collection of comments on Luther's life and on life in general. After appearing in various earlier editions, the Table Talk now comprises six volumes in the modern Weimar edition of Luther's works. Gathered from numerous manuscripts, these fragments of table conversation have now been arranged in comprehensive order.[65] Without these recorded bits we would be left in the dark about many events in and aspects of Luther's career. Yet who would reproach Kate for becoming at times impatient with the endless talk and note-taking while the food on the table got cold. The "Doctoress," as she was often called, earned the respect of everyone and was even feared by some. She had the lifelong gratitude of many; they did not forget her solicitous care. Later, wherever they became established, they remembered her with favors and gifts. It was, however, only in 1531 that this prandial record of the Luther household became a literary source, and it continued so for a dozen years. In fact, the earliest biography of Luther, the achievement of Johannes Mathesius, relied in large part on narratives that he himself, and others, heard and jotted down at Luther's hospitable table.[66]

63. Elector John Frederick, in 1538, set a maximum of 30 guilders per year. Friedensburg, *Urkundenbuch*, 208.

64. Cf. his letter to Spalatin, end of December 1524, beginning of 1525. *MSA* 7 / 1:224 / 24ff. *MBW* 366.

65. WA TR (1912–21). The deserving editor is Ernst Kroker. His frequently cited biography, *Katharina von Bora*, 166ff., has supplied us with an attractive account of the table companions. On the subject of the language and reliability of the Table Talk there is the important study of B. Stolt, *Die Sprachmischung in Luthers Tischreden: Studien zum Problem der Zweisprachigkeit*, Stockholmer Germanistische Forschungen 4 (Stockholm, 1964).

66. Kroker, *Katharina von Bora*, 175–76. H. Volz, *Die Lutherpredigten des Johannes Mathesius: Kritische Untersuchungen zur Geschichtsschreibung im Zeitalter der Reformation*, QFRG 12 (Leipzig, 1930), 6:114ff. [*LW* 54, Table Talk, ed. and trans. T. G. Tappert, (Philadelphia: Fortress Press, 1967). See also references to Katharina von Bora, who "understood Latin quite well," ibid., xxi. Tappert's introduction to this volume is illuminating; ibid., ix–xxvi.

16

The Conflict over Freedom
of the Will

[Continuation of Chapter 13.]

For over a year after launching his attack on Luther, Erasmus seemed in command of the field. [His diatribe on the *Freedom of the Will*—literally, freedom of choice (*arbitrium*)—found Luther, as we have seen, not only loathe to respond precipitously but also preoccupied by other urgent matters.] However, Luther's friends pitched in early, pledging him not to keep silent. The most penetrating initial appraisal of Erasmus's treatise came from the seven Strassburg preachers who, on November 23, 1524, sent Luther a letter relating the confusion it was creating in the Netherlands and in Cologne. While they themselves were indebted to Erasmus for rudiments of truth, they now declared excitedly,

> What is he up to? Does he not everywhere brush aside the authority of Scripture and prefer the calm of the Antichrist to the revolutionary character of the kingdom of Christ? . . . We therefore implore you for Christ's sake: Don't let yourself be appeased by flesh and blood![1] Give priority to what you once wrote Erasmus—for the sake of Christ one must be able to hate one's parents—and which men of letters are not likely to advise. For the Word belongs to Christ. Out with the trimmings of the Latin language; away with the awe of learning, which dims the praise of Christ. His Word saves us; the words of others lead us to ruin. . . . After all, you know how much the Lord has sought to lay on you, how many thousands hang on to your lips—being confident that this is the mouth of the Lord. And you also know full well that your service has induced the world to detest whatever is not founded openly in the pronouncement of Scripture.[2]

Luther discerned the fine hand of Capito in this humanist rhetoric. Let the Strassburgers unload their conflict; Luther remained cool. He had his own agenda, and heading it was the need to conclude his confrontation with Karlstadt, a task of which the Strassburgers were well aware, as they urged him with equal urgency to do something about Karlstadt too.[3]

1. Gal. 1:16.
2. *WA Br* 3:386 / 13ff.
3. *WA Br* 3:382 / 14ff.; 383 / 84ff.

Luther himself had completed his big book,[4] *Against the Heavenly Prophets,* in January 1525 and turned at once to the publication of his important lectures on Deuteronomy, a wearying task as it dragged on. "I am forced to finish Deuteronomy, so that the printers don't have to take a loss," he wrote Spalatin on February 11, 1525. Meanwhile, he put off Erasmus a little longer. He will "get his answer as soon as there's time for it." Similarly Luther reassured others.[5] It was April 4 before Melanchthon could calm down his friend Camerarius, who was so beset by problems that he could hardly wait for Luther's response to Erasmus. "I notice," wrote Melanchthon, "that the response has been begun and hope therefore that it will soon be finished. For with him (Luther) it is particularly true: *arche emisu pantos* (well begun, half done)."[6] Soon, however, the first waves of the peasant revolt reached Wittenberg and preoccupied the next months.[7] So Melanchthon's statement came true only about six months later. When Nicholas Hausmann came with a question, Luther replied on September 27, 1525, "Do meanwhile what you will. I'm fully absorbed refuting Erasmus."[8] The next day he wrote Spalatin, "I'm completely in orbit around Erasmus and the free will, and will take pains not to concede at any point where he has said something correctly; in fact, he has said hardly anything correctly. But you pray the Lord that he support me, so that my work may be to His praise. Amen."[9] Finally Luther was fired up. During the following weeks he pushed aside everything else. By mid-November his reply to Erasmus was probably completed, for it was off the press by the end of December. It was a book pulsating with excitement over events of the year 1525. It also breathed the air of being free again to address central issues in theology. The reader could sense this in the passion and forcefulness of Luther's formulations. Both parties in this match gave their utmost. Their respective polemics rate among the greatest documents of intellectual history. Only a common and penetrating analysis can do them justice.

Erasmus leads off with a light skirmishing. He reminds the reader briefly of the laborious treatment that has been expended from antiquity to Karlstadt, Eck, and above all Luther on that "tangled labyrinth," the

4. See above, pp. 169ff.

5. *WA* 14:490. On this, see above, p. 241. *WA Br* 3:439 / 10–11. See the survey of Luther's comments in letters, *WA* 18:581.

6. *CR* 1:734 (dated according to *Suppl. Mel.* 6 / 1:287). *MRW* 387. On Melanchthon's attitude at this time, see W. Maurer, *Melanchthon-Studien* (see above, p. 268, n. 62), 141ff.

7. See above, p. 373.

8. *WA Br* 3:582 / 4–5.

9. *WA Br* 3:583 / 14ff.

question of free will. Instead of taking up this subject—his actual opponent—immediately, he first gave a hearing to "certain people" who will
cry out, "The rivers run backward! Dare Erasmus attack Luther, like the
fly the elephant?"[10] His opening of this second front is a masterpiece of
dialectics. It enabled him to approach Luther with deference and friendliness, or even to assume "a certain favor toward him, as an investigator may
do toward an arraigned prisoner."[11] At the same time, however, this strategem enables Erasmus to unfold his talent for irony. Even his short "Preparatory Observations" pour forth generous helpings of it at a half-dozen
places concerning Luther's foolish adherents. He intensifies this effect of
ever-changing colors as he alternates between good-naturedness and
mockery, adding tones of sardonic wit and self-abasement from the reper-
tory of humanistic style. So, for instance, he calls himself undoubtedly as
ill-prepared as hardly another to enter combat, having "always preferred
to sport on the wider plains of the Muses rather than to brandish a sword
in a hand-to-hand fight." In a more serious vein he hints at the *Assertio
omnium articulorum* (1520), in which Luther, condemned by the pope yet
defending his own concept of the unfree will, claims to have so little liking
for hard-and-fast assertion that "I would really like to take refuge in the
opinion of the Skeptics, wherever this is allowed by the inviolable authority of the Holy Scriptures, and by the decrees of the church, to which I
everywhere submit my personal feelings, whether I pray what it prescribes or not."[12]

Thus Erasmus declares himself neither a skeptic in principle nor a blind
believer in authority. Instead, he sees skepticism and belief in authority as
two opposite possibilities open to anyone, according to his insight, who
would avoid making a decision on a problem difficult to decide.[13] He finds

10. *De libero arbitrio diatribe*, ed. J. von Walter, QCP (Leipzig, 1910; 2d ed., 1935). (Also
in the translation taken over from O. Schumacher, *Vom Freien Willen*, 2d ed. [Göttingen,
1956], I follow the chapter divisions and paging of von Walter's edition [hereafter cited as
Diatr.] *Diatr.* Ia 2, 2 / 3ff.) [The English translation used here is that of E. G. Rupp, *Luther
and Erasmus: Free Will and Salvation*, LCC 17 (Philadelphia: Westminster; London: SCM,
1959) (hereafter cited as *FW*, Rupp trans.). *FW*, Rupp trans., 36.]

11. *Diatr.* Ia 5:4 / 21–22. [*FW*, Rupp trans., 37.]

12. *Diatr.* Ia 4:3 / 11–20. [*FW*, Rupp trans., 37.]

13. H. J. McSorley's question, "Was Erasmus a skeptic interested in faith?" is to be answered in the negative. This question also misses the point of Luther's critique as well as that
of modern research, against whom McSorley then turns. His equating of Luther's image of
Erasmus and of Cochlaeus's image of Luther is doubly misleading; it compares two things
that defy comparison and it is a gross exaggeration. Cf. H. J. McSorley, *Luthers Lehre vom
freien Willen*, BOT 1 (Munich, 1967), 260ff., a book valuable for the history of dogma but
unsatisfying on the Erasmus-Luther controversy. [Cf. H. J. McSorley's *Luther: Right or
Wrong? An Ecumenical-Theological Study of Luther's Major Work, "The Bondage of the
Will"* (New York: Newman; Minneapolis: Augsburg, 1969), 278ff.; for judgment other than
Bornkamm, cf. ix–x.]

this mode of thinking preferable to that of those "certain others," who "twist whatever they read in the Scriptures into an assertion of an opinion they have embraced once for all. They are like young men who love a young girl so immoderately that they imagine they see their beloved wherever they turn; or, a much better example, like two combatants who in the heat of a quarrel turn whatever is at hand into a missile, whether it be a jug or a dish." He adds, "Who will learn anything fruitful from this discussion, beyond the fact that each leaves the encounter bespattered by the other's filth?"[14] If anybody ascribes his ironic disposition to a lack of intellect or knowledge, let him do so. And yet it may be permitted even to the less gifted to discuss with the more amply gifted, if for no other reason than to learn! "Luther attributes very little importance to scholarship, and most of all to the Spirit who is wont to instill into the more humble what he denies to the wise."[15] Here Erasmus applies concretely a precise and pertinent observation of one of the differences between himself and Luther.

Having brought his characters on stage and positioned them properly to each other, Erasmus proceeds like an experienced rhetorician and takes two preparatory steps into the issue at hand. Is a confrontation on free will, as Luther launched it with his *Assertio*, even justifiable? At least God is wise enough not to reveal all his secrets to us. Some questions are much like those of which Pomponius Mela tells about the cavern near Corycos. It draws the visitor to itself by its pleasing aspect. Then, as one goes deeper, a certain horror and majesty of the divine presence that inhabits the place make one draw back. This is how Erasmus understands the cry of Paul in Rom. 11:33, "O the depth of the riches and wisdom and knowledge of God!" Erasmus takes the apostle's hymn of praise—because God's revelation has disclosed to human thought the unfathomable mystery of his redemption of Israel—and turns it into a word of skepticism.[16] His warning to the all-too-curious rests on evidence of the sort that remains a secret to us, including such secrets as the hour of death, the day of judgment, the relation of the Persons in the Godhead, the two natures of Christ, the unforgiveable sin (Mark 3:29). All such things have nothing to do with what we must know unconditionally, namely, "the precepts for the good life." These are inscribed in our heart. The other things, the secrets, should remain in God's keeping and honored "in mystic silence." Nor is it

14. *Diatr.*, Ia 4:3 / 20–4 / 14, 11. [*FW*, Rupp trans., 37.]
15. *Diatr.*, Ia 6:4 / 27ff. [*FW*, Rupp trans., 37.]
16. *Diatr.*, Ia 7:5–6. [*FW*, Rupp trans., 38–39.]

always necessary to speak publicly about things one has recognized as true. Erasmus names a few drastic examples: that God is not less present in the hole of an insect than in heaven above, that there are three Gods (which to a certain extent could be correct dialectically), that (although he does not share this view) confession was not instituted by Jesus and would not dare to have been instituted by human beings. Indeed, there is in any case high usefulness in compulsory confession.[17] Or, from the realm of intellect: What if Wyclif and Luther were right in their teaching of the unfree will, and what if Augustine too were correct in making the point that God works both good and evil in us and that he therefore rewards or punishes his own works in us. What would be more useless than to spread abroad such paradoxes? What a window were thus opened for fire! Man is already so bad, fleshly minded, and inclined to unfaith and transgression "that there's no need to pour oil into the fire."[18] Paul differentiated wisely between what is permitted and what serves the neighbor, between the strong, who can take it, and the weak, who require consideration. "Holy Scripture has its own language, adapted to our understanding." Prudence dictates that certain problems be treated only among the learned or in theological schools instead of publicly, and better yet is it for people "not to waste their time and talent on labyrinths of this kind." Were this generally recognized, Erasmus would gladly forego either refuting or affirming the views of Luther.[19]

Next, before becoming more involved, Erasmus seeks to expose Luther's hopeless isolation from the church tradition in the questions under debate. He had already disclaimed earlier that he had no intention of burdening Luther thereby. Now, however, he must admit that this argument does not really apply to Luther, who recognizes only the Holy Scriptures as judge. Even so, what harm would it do the reader, precisely when caught between two opinions, to visualize the ranks of most learned church fathers whom Erasmus summons to pass in review.[20] Since the days of the apostles there have been but two authors who, like Luther now, have "totally taken away the power of freedom of choice, save only Manichaeus and John Wyclif," leaders of heresies known worldwide. Whom shall we accord more trust: "to the previous judgments of so many learned men, so many orthodox, so many saints, so many theologians old

17. *Diatr.*, Ia 9:7–9. [*FW*, Rupp trans., 39–41.]
18. *Diatr.*, Ia 10:9–10. [*FW*, Rupp trans., 41. Alt.]
19. *Diatr.*, Ia 11:10–11. [*FW*, Rupp trans., 41–42.]
20. *Diatr.*, Ib 1:11 / 22ff. Ib 2:12 / 6–13 / 6. [*FW*, Rupp trans., 42–43.]

421

and new, so many universities, councils, so many bishops and popes—or
the private judgments of this or that individual?" Without hesitation Erasmus throws the weight of these names onto his scales. It is not the Scriptures that are at stake, but the interpretation of Scripture. Who could
stand a chance in biblical interpretation against such a wealth of learned
Greek and Latin interpreters? "You will see," he concludes triumphantly,
"the caliber of the champions in the past that defrauds free choice!"[21]

Only after setting the stage like a prosecutor does Erasmus fleetingly
touch on the key issue: Luther's assertion that on this question the Holy
Scriptures are clear and therefore require no interpretation. Yet he mentions the issue only to leave it again with a short counterquestion: "If there
is no obscurity in Scripture, what was the need of the work of prophecy in
those days of the apostles?" "You (Luther) say 'this was the gift of the
Spirit.'" To whom, then, will God grant his Spirit today? Surely to those
in office, and not to any old private people! If it so happens that the Spirit
is granted to some unlearned person, then there must be evidence of it.[22]
With a rhetorical trick he turns the objections around which might be
raised against his phalanx of witnesses.

> I hear you say, "What has a multitude to do with the meaning of the Spirit?" I
> reply, "What have the handful?" You say, "What has the miter to do with the
> understanding of Holy Scripture?" I reply, "What has a sackcloth or a cowl?"
> . . . You say, "What has an assembled synod to do with the understanding of
> Scripture?" I reply, "What, then, of private conventicles of the few?"[23]

Finally Erasmus asks, "How can it be believed that for more than thirteen
hundred years the Spirit would have concealed the error in his church?"[24]
Regardless of what others may claim for themselves, Erasmus argues, "I
claim for myself neither learning nor holiness, nor do I trust in my own
spiritual experience. I shall merely put forward with simple diligence
those considerations that move my mind."[25]

Finally Erasmus arrives at his theme: the contemplation of free will
[freedom of choice] in Holy Scripture. At once he fixed on the problem:
Many biblical passages clearly support his contention, others seem to dismiss it. "Yet it is clear that Scripture cannot be in conflict with itself, since
the whole proceeds from the same Spirit." This thesis places Erasmus

21. *Diatr.*, Ib 2.3:13 / 6–14 / 25. [*FW*, Rupp trans., 42–43.]
22. *Diatr.*, Ib 4:14 / 29–15 / 13. [*FW*, Rupp trans., 44.]
23. *Diatr.*, Ib 5:16 / 5–14. [*FW*, Rupp trans., 45.]
24. *Diatr.* Ib 7:7 / 14ff. Ib 8:18 / 3ff. [*FW*, Rupp trans., 45, 46.]
25. *Diatr.*, Ib 9:18 / 7ff. [*FW*, Rupp trans., 46.]

completely with Luther, and this is the point of crossing where their respective attempts to resolve this dilemma go separate ways.

Then Erasmus proceeds to define precisely also his understanding of the issue under dispute: "By free will here we mean a power of the human will by which a man can apply himself to the things that lead to eternal salvation, or turn away from them."[26] He had prepared the ground for this definition by an earlier statement on what we learn from Scripture about free will thus understood:

> If we are on the path of true religion, let us go on swiftly to better things, forgetting the things that are behind; or if we are entangled in sins, let us strive with all our might and have recourse to the remedy of penitence, that by all means we may entreat the mercy of the Lord; . . . and what is evil in us, let us impute to ourselves, and what is good, let us ascribe wholly to divine benevolence, . . . for none ought to despair of the pardon of a God who is by nature most merciful. This, I say, was in my judgment sufficient for Christian godliness.

All other questions are irreverent inquisitiveness.[27]

No one could fault Erasmus for implying that the preface was almost more relevant to the main issue than the disputation itself.[28] Here, in fact, the main issues were already decided. For one, the rhetorical manner and the spurious arguments spoiled Luther's taste for Erasmus's book from the start. No wonder he often interrupted his reading of it as he put off the decision to respond. Yet Erasmus had already exposed so many of his own fundamental convictions that Luther felt challenged to produce an equivalent reply. This had the advantage of leading off with a treatment of fundamental principles before moving into the laborious exegetical debate over specific biblical texts. Luther was bound to pin down his opponent wherever the rhetoric of Erasmus often only hinted at opinions that called for full disclosure. The required thoroughness and the immediately joined debate let Luther's introduction take its style from the Erasmian.

In the prevailing humanistic manner Luther begins by complimenting his opponent, yet not without his own cutting sarcasm. He hands Erasmus the victor's palm for intellectual eloquence, but also says, "You have quite damped my spirit and eagerness and left me exhausted before I could strike a blow."[29] And why? Because Erasmus was offering nothing

26. *Diatr.*, Ib 10:19 / 4–10. He has begun to define the question earlier; *Diatr.* Ia 8:7 / 1ff. [*FW*, Rupp trans., 47. His earlier partial definition, 39, lines 23–25.]

27. *Diatr.*, Ia 8:6 / 10ff. [*FW*, Rupp trans., 39.]

28. *Diatr.*, Ia 11:11 / 19ff. [*FW*, Rupp trans., 42.]

29. *WA* 18:600 / 14ff. *BoA* 3:94 / 16ff. [*LW* 33:15–16.]

that others had not already said, and because he steered more cautiously than Odysseus between Scylla and Charybdis. "How, I ask you, is it possible to have any discussion or reach any understanding with such people, unless one is clever enough to catch Proteus?"[30] As he himself begins, Luther offers two judgments on the subject, one on himself: "Although I am unskilled in speech, I am not unskilled in knowledge." With Paul he ventures to claim knowledge for himself which he confidently denies Erasmus.[31] The other judgment is that Erasmus has already unwillingly borne testimony against himself on the subject under debate. "For you have made me far more sure of my own position by letting me see the case for free will put forward with all the energy of so distinguished and powerful a mind, but with no other effect than to make things worse than before. This is plain evidence that free will is a pure fiction."[32]

Luther then takes up Erasmus's premises point by point. The first and broadest premise pertains to the peculiar cleavage between skepticism and faith in the authority of Scripture, which Erasmus himself admitted.[33] One might expect that to a Luther such a premise must have offended his soul. Later, in his rebuttal, *Hyperaspistes* (Defender, 1526–27), Erasmus felt that on this point Luther had attacked him unfairly. He modified his position accordingly, thus making it necessary to measure the distance between him and Luther carefully. Three closely intertwined statements in Erasmus's prefatory observation shocked Luther. His dislike of "assertions" draws Luther's riposte "Take away assertions and you take away Christianity."[34] Next, in the same breath, Erasmus admits his leaning toward skepticism and his readiness to submit to the "inviolable authority of the divine writings and the decrees of the church"—to which Luther retorts, "What Christian would talk like that?" unless Erasmus is speaking about useless and indifferent matters in which everyone can exercise freedom.[35] The third "shocker" to Luther was Erasmus's declared readiness to submit to decisions of the church whether he grasped them or not. "How can a Christian believe what he does not grasp?" Naturally, "grasp" does not mean perfect knowledge and insight, but if the Christian "had grasped

---

30. WA 18:60 / 1, 34ff. *BoA* 3:95 / 9–10; 96 / 11ff. [*LW* 33:17.]

31. WA 18:601 / 15ff. *BoA* 3:95 / 26ff. [*LW* 33:16.]

32. WA 18:602 / 22ff. *BoA* 3:96 / 39ff. [*LW* 33:18.]

33. *Diatr.*, Ia 4:3 / 11–20. [*FW*, Rupp trans., 37.]

34. "Tolle assertiones et Christianismum tulisti." WA 18:603 / 28–29. *BoA* 3:98 / 14–15. [*LW* 33:21.]

35. WA 18:604 / 22–23. *BoA* 3:99 / 11–12. [*LW* 33:21.]

one thing, he would have grasped all—in God, I mean—since whoever does not grasp God never 'grasps' any part of his creation."[36]

So the appeal is for a resort that offers us neutrality. Even so Luther is ready to absolve the heart of Erasmus: "So long as you display it no further. See that you fear the Spirit of God, who tries the minds and hearts." Besides, "the Holy Spirit is no skeptic, and it is not doubts or mere opinions that he has written on our hearts, but assertions more sure and certain than life itself and all experience."[37] Luther does not intend to declare Erasmus an outright skeptic, but he means to disclose the bad light on his words and to refer him to the passage from Lucian which Erasmus is secretly fostering in himself: a hidden godlessness which allies itself with a mockery of those who faithfully bear witness. Surely Erasmus would not have recognized himself pictured thus, yet Luther intended to make Erasmus aware also of subconscious factors operating in him, showing him how his words "sound" and must influence others. Not the declared skepticism, but the protean diversity of his opponent tormented Luther. Therefore Luther's words absolve as well as accuse, express hope as well as sound shrill warning, "till Christ calls you too."[38] Perhaps, if this book should reach Erasmus at a happy hour, Luther may "win a very dear brother."[39]

Luther leads off attesting to the vital interest of faith in certitude—"for what is more miserable than uncertainty?"[40]—and then proceeds directly to the core of the cardinal problem, to that point from which Erasmus had derived the manifold uncertainty of faith, namely, the alleged unclarity of Scripture. At this point, therefore, a preliminary decision on the disputation theme was required. This forced Luther to unfold, in utmost brevity, the hermeneutical basis of his entire commentary on Scripture. First, he differentiates between God and the Scriptures. In God remain hidden many things that not even the Scriptures unlock. In Scripture itself there are numerous obscure passages,[41] yet these lie not in the realm of substance but in the realm of speech. Neither vocabulary nor grammar always

36. *WA* 18:605 / 8–14. *BoA* 3:100 / 1–9. [*LW* 33:23.]

37. Cf. above, n. 13. At most Luther speaks of Erasmus as having a *moderata sceptica theologia* (a moderately skeptical theology). *WA* 18:613 *(sic)* / 24 [actually 605 / 24ff.] [*LW* 33:24.]

38. *WA* 18:605 / 15–34. *BoA* 3:100 / 10–33. [*LW* 33:24.]

39. *WA* 18:602 / 21–22. *BoA* 3:96 / 38–40. [*LW* 33:18.]

40. "Quid enim incertitudine miserius?" *WA* 18:604 / 33. *BoA* 3:99 / 25. [*LW* 33:22.]

41. *WA* 18:606 / 10ff. *BoA* 3:101 / 5ff. [*LW* 33:25.]

suffices to express the secret of Scripture, yet this does not alter the fact that Scripture is clear, "for what still more sublime thing can remain hidden in the Scripture, now that the seals have been broken, the stone rolled from the door of the sepulcher (Matt. 27:66; 28:2), and the supreme mystery brought to light, than, namely, that Christ the Son of God has been made man, that God is three and one, that Christ has suffered for us and is to reign eternally?" This wraps up the whole content of Scripture. "Take Christ out of the Scriptures, and what will you find left in them?"[42] While the words in certain passages may not be clear, one cannot deny that the subject matter is amply attested. Would anyone claim there is no fountain in the marketplace because he cannot see it from his little alley?"[43]

From this kind of approach Luther derives his two hermeneutical rules: We can understand the substance of Scripture only when we constantly recall its bearing on Christ, from the broad area of the Trinity to his eternal lordship. We can understand the language of the Bible, where at first it seems obscure, only when comparing Scripture with itself, learning to compare the clearer passages with the more obscure. These guidelines on method presuppose a recognizability of the content of Holy Scripture. To be sure, according to Luther, we must be able to distinguish a twofold clarity in Scripture: an internal clarity, located in the understanding of the heart, which no one achieves on his own but only receives through the Holy Spirit; and an external clarity, which has been laid by God into the Word of Scripture and into the proclamation flowing from it, so that it contains nothing uncertain.[44] The effect of this double definition is disproportionate: here it is man, the subject of clarity; there it is Scripture. Later Luther adjusts this disparity when he speaks of the internal and external "judgment" of the Christian. The one is that through which the Spirit grants him certitude concerning the message of salvation as it pertains to himself; the other he is enabled to understand and transmit it appropriately. Controversy, like this one with Erasmus, can involve only the "external" judgment of Holy Scripture, as unlocked for us by Christ. It does not involve the awakening of faith, for example, through preaching or, we would say, biblical scholarship. On this "external" judgment, moreover, rests the possibility granted a congregation to "test the spirits."[45]

42. WA 18:606 / 16–29. BoA 3:101 / 13–29. [LW 33:25–26.]

43. WA 18:606 / 30–39. BoA 3:101 / 30–102 / 2. [LW 33:26.]

44. WA 18:609 / 14–14. BoA 3:103 / 9–22. [LW 33:28.]

45. WA 18:607 / 4; 653 / 13–31. BoA 102 / 6–7; 141 / 32–142 / 14. For a fuller grasp of these passages, cf. R. Hermann, Von der Klarheit der Heiligen Schrift (Berlin, 1958). F. Beisser, Claritas scripturae sacrae bei Martin Luther, FKDG (Göttingen, 1966). E. Wolf, "Über die 'Klarheit der Heiligen Schrift' nach Luthers 'De servo arbitrio,' ThLZ 92 (1967): 721ff. [LW 33:27, 90.]

Given the proper means, Luther has such confidence in this mode of interpreting Scripture that he challenges Erasmus, "See, then, whether you and all the Sophists can produce any simple mystery that is still abstruse in the Scriptures."[46]

With these bold conclusions drawn from his understanding of Scripture, Luther seizes on the decisive thesis of Erasmus: that it is "irreverent inquisitiveness to rush into those things which are hidden, not to say superfluous: whether God foreknows anything contingently; whether our will accomplishes anything in things pertaining to eternal salvation; whether what we do, be it of good or ill, we do by necessity or rather suffer to be done to us."[47] Before answering in his own words, Luther decides to clobber Erasmus with his own weapons.[48] On two counts Luther charges him with fumbling the essence of the very Christianity he would defend. First, if the Christian, as Erasmus contends, strives with all his might and has recourse to the remedy of penitence, that by all means he may entreat the mercy of the Lord without which no human will or endeavor is effective,[49] he nevertheless presupposes that the Christian knows something about his own powers and endeavors and something about the mercy and grace of God! How then can Erasmus call it inquisitive and in vain to ask about such matters? "It therefore behooves us to be very certain about the distinction between God's power and our own, God's work and our own, if we want to live a godly life." Actually Erasmus teaches quite plainly that free will is able to do something in the attainment of grace. "Thus that prudence of yours makes you veer about, determined not to commit yourself to either side. . . . You assert everything you deny, and deny everything you assert."[50] Again, it "is something fundamentally necessary and salutary for a Christian to know that God foreknows nothing contingently but that he foresees and proposes and does all things by his inimitable, eternal, and infallible will." How else could we believe in God's righteousness and mercy, his wisdom and goodness, if these were not eternal and unchanging?[51] "From this it follows irrefutably that everything we do, everything that happens, even if it seems to us to

46. WA 18:607 / 7ff. BoA 3:102 / 11ff. [LW 33:27.]
47. Diatr., Ia 8:6 / 22ff. Cited verbatim by Luther, WA 18:609 / 24ff. BoA 3:103 / 34ff. [FW, Rupp trans., 39. LW 33:29.]
48. WA 18:610 / 23; 615 / 17–18. BoA 3:104 / 22; 108 / 13–14. [LW 33:30, 37.]
49. Diatr., Ia 8, cited almost verbatim by Luther. Cf. above, p. 423. [FW, Rupp trans., 39.]
50. WA 18:611 / 1–24; 614 / 15ff. BoA 104 / 23–105 / 11; 107 / 1ff. [LW 33: 35, 33.]
51. WA 18:615 / 12ff. BoA 3:108 / 7ff. [LW 33:37.]

happen inevitably and contingently, happens in fact nonetheless necessarily and immutably, if you have regard to the will of God. For the will of God is effectual and cannot be hindered, since it is the power of the divine nature itself."[52] Indeed, this is not to say, as the sophists have needlessly sought to define it, that everything that happens is of itself necessary; this pertains to God alone. But it is necessary from the side of God, through his will and decision. In this sense "the proposition stands and remains invincible that all things happen by necessity."[53] Luther supports this sentence with a surprising reference.

Luther cites pagan poets and folk wisdom as his witnesses. "How often does Virgil (for one) remind us of Fate." And it is part of our common parlance to say, "God's will be done" and "God willing, we will do it." From this we can see "that the knowledge of God's predestination and foreknowledge remained with the common people no less than the awareness of his existence itself." Poets and proverbs, and the conscience of the individual as well, support Luther in what he finds Paul (Rom. 1:19ff.) saying about general revelation and the perception of God available to all people, only here Luther expands it from God's work in creation to his action in history. If Christians have permitted this perception to become darkened in their own heart, they are indeed the people whom Paul has described as "claiming to be wise, they become fools" (Rom. 1:22).[54] Then the entire gospel collapses. "For this is the one supreme consolation of Christians in all adversities, to know that God does not lie but does all things immutably, and that his will can be neither resisted nor changed nor hindered."[55] Not only faith but every other way of "honoring God" (worship), about which Luther speaks quite naturally, stands or falls with this kind of knowing.[56] If Erasmus calls such questing inquisitive and futile, then—from the viewpoint of whatever religion—he insinuates that Christians are godless and "that Christianity is a matter of no moment at all, but vain, foolish, and really irreverent."[57]

Luther was surely convinced that this precise examination of the Erasmian reproach supplied him with an especially effective argument against

52. WA 18:615 / 31ff. BoA 3:108 / 30ff. [LW 33:37–38.]

53. WA 18:616 / 13–617 / 19. BoA 3:109 / 10–36. The same kind of polemic against the scholastics already appears in Luther's lectures on Romans (on 8:28). WA 56:382 / 21ff. [LW 33: 39–40. On Romans, LW 25:371–72.]

54. WA 18:617 / 23–618 / 18. BoA 3:109 / 40–110 / 24. On "Fate," WA 18:718 / 18–19. BoA 3:213 / 39. [LW 33:41, 40.]

55. WA 18:619 / 16ff. BoA 3:111 / 8ff. [LW 33:43.]

56. WA 18:618 / 21–22. BoA 3:110 / 27–28. [LW 33:42.]

57. WA 18:620 / 6ff. BoA 3:111 / 26ff. [LW 33:43.]

the great humanist. Yet in the process Luther's own teaching on the un-free will [no free choice] came close to the fatalism and determinism of pagan antiquity. In his rebuttal, *Hyperaspistes,* Erasmus was quick to see this exchange of roles. "Now at last the poets are wise people, and more perceptive than even the philosophers!" There is, however, a difference between the poets speaking of Fate, and the theologians—Luther and Erasmus—probing "whether our will is capable of anything in matters of eternal salvation."[58] We shall return to this dilemma.[59]

The thesis of the Erasmian *Diatribe* and the antithesis of Luther's reply confronted each other with utmost severity. Of Erasmus's prefatory obser-vations, only the pedagogical-tactical ones remained to be debated, that is, those rejected by Erasmus as useless or even dangerous to any discus-sion of the will. Besides, Luther was not inclined to be an opportunist. Each man was here touching on a profound truth. Erasmus's idle talk might echo the scholastic obscurantist talking about God's presence even in the hole of a dung beetle. Yet this should not obscure the fact that the Son of God was born in the womb of the Virgin and lived in a human body—facts that could be bantered in dirty words—or, most horrifying of all, that he descended into hell.[60] Or, if Erasmus wished to avoid the battle over confession and penance or over abuses by the papal church, then he showed that his priority is not the truth but the calm of external peace. "Even we are not made of stone." Did Erasmus think he alone was moved by these tumults? Then he did not grasp "that it is the most un-varying fate of the Word of God to have the world in a state of tumult because of it."[61] Should not Christians recognize with fearless heart what even heathen writers testify, "that changes of things cannot take place without commotion or tumult, or indeed without bloodshed." Luther adds, "For myself, if I did not see these tumults I should say that the Word of God was not in the world."[62] At still another point, where Erasmus counsels prudence, it amounts to nothing, for he advises against admitting publicly that decisions of church councils could be wrong, lest the author-ity of the fathers suffer damage. "But in the meantime, Erasmus, what will souls do that are bound and (in their conscience) slain by that unjust

58. *WA* 18:618, n. 3 (excerpt from *Hyperaspistes* I). Erasmus, Opp. ed. *Clericus* X, 1275F. (In *WA* read *viri* instead of *viris*. The reproduction of the citation is not without flaws and unfortunately also omits the sources.) Cf. there, ibid., 1294E.

59. See below, pp. 447ff., 455ff.

60. *WA* 18:623 / 5ff., 14ff. *BoA* 3:113 / 38ff.; 114 / 8ff. [*LW* 33:47.]

61. *WA* 18:625 / 25–626 / 9. *BoA* 3:116 / 10–26. [*LW* 33:51–52.]

62. *WA* 18:626 / 27–32. *BoA* 3:117 / 8–15. [*LW* 33:52.]

statute?" How could he ever dare willfully to postpone the hour of the Word? "God has commanded that the gospel be preached to everyone, at all times and in all places."[63] Or, take the matter of tactics. Here too the ways of Erasmus and Luther run diametrically opposite. For Erasmus pedagogical caution, public peace, and the authority of the church set the direction. For Luther, a categorical order to preach the gospel and to be concerned for people shows the way, for a person has this life only, and in it he has a right to the truth.

A fear of evil consequences hounds Erasmus especially when grappling with the teaching of free choice. "Who will take pains to correct his life?" Luther hears Erasmus asking, and replies, "No one!" "Who will believe that he is loved by God?" "No one!"[64] Why then should anyone speak of these mysteries? Because only so does it dawn on us what the nature of grace is and what faith is. Not he who may still think he can do even the least thing about his salvation, but he who "has no doubt that everything depends on the will of God, has come close to grace and can be saved. Such a person completely despairs of himself and chooses nothing for himself, but waits on God to act." "It is thus for the sake of the elect that these things are published."[65] The other reason for speaking of these mysteries is the essence of faith itself. Luther is ever on the alert for the invisible.

> Hence, in order that there may be room for faith, it is necessary that everything which is believed be hidden. It cannot, however, be more deeply hidden than under an object, perception, or experience that is contrary to it. Thus when God makes alive he does it by killing, when he justifies he does it by making men guilty, when he exalts to heaven he does it by bringing down to hell. . . . Thus God hides his eternal goodness and mercy under eternal wrath, his righteousness under iniquity.[66]

Luther presses his roster of paradoxes to the limit. "This is the highest degree of faith, to believe him merciful when he saves so few and damns so many, and to believe him righteous when by his own will he makes us necessarily damnable, so that he seems, according to Erasmus, to delight in the torments of the wretched and to be worthy of hatred rather than of love." Herewith Luther returned Erasmus's challenging complaint against

63. WA 18:630 / 1ff.; 629 / 17ff. BoA 3:120 / 32ff., 21ff. [LW 33:57.]
64. WA 18:632 / 3ff. BoA 3:123 / 3ff. [LW 33:60, 61.]
65. WA 18:632 / 27ff., 36ff. BoA 3:123 / 33ff.; 124 / 6ff. [LW 33:62.]
66. WA 18:633 / 7ff. BoA 3:124 / 16ff. [LW 33:62.]

a statement of Augustine by throwing out a challenge of his own.[67] To emphasize his point, Luther repeats his basic argument: If these facts of the matter—this they are for him (in conjunction with Rom. 9:11ff.)[68]— could be comprehended by reason, then there would be no need of faith. Yet here "is room for the exercise of faith," noting that "when God kills, the faith of life is exercised in death."[69] Understood in these terms, the dogma of human unfreedom and of solely divine determination becomes "a door to righteousness, an entrance to heaven, and a way to God."[70] What more impassioned way could Luther have found than with these steeply ascending sentences to affirm that for him not some truth but the whole truth is at stake. Erasmus would have had to give up on himself had he here tried to follow Luther more than a fraction of the way. Later on, Erasmus conceded that such faith-testing situations may exist. Yet he held that Luther exaggerates, contending that God gives our senses and reason various kinds of evidence that we may indeed have confidence in his loving kindness.[71]

It is worth noting that here, as with the fatalistic faith of the heathen, Luther does not ridicule the helpfulness of reasonable experience, for it proves something other than what Erasmus considers reasonable. Where a person is really committed to something, there is no changing his will; resistance merely stiffens his will. "Ask experience how impossible it is to persuade people who have set their heart on anything." By contrast, if there is no commitment, things are left to run their course. Also, the picture of steadfast, saintly men shows that "when force is used to compel them to other things, they are all the more spurred on to will the good, just as fire is fanned into flames rather than extinguished by the wind."[72] With simple examples Luther clarifies the issue: not wishing but willing, not mere activity (which abounds among such people) but direction, not

67. WA 18:633 / 15ff. BoA 3:124 / 26ff. Diatr. Ia 10:11ff. It is not clear to which word of Augustine or pseudo-Augustine Erasmus refers. Cf. J. von Walter's note on this passage (above, p. 268, n. 62.) [LW 33:62–63.]

68. Here they are not drawn from the essence of faith, but this passage establishes the open discussion of these mysteries.

69. WA 18:633 / 19ff. BoA 3:124 / 31ff. Exercere here means an active application of faith rather than a quiet cultivation of it. [LW 33:63.]

70. WA 18:632 / 13–14. BoA 3:123 / 16. [LW 33:61.]

71. Hyperaspistes I. Erasmus, Opp. ed. Clericus X, 1286F, 1287A. WA 18:633, n. 2. [LW 33:30, n. 27, and 63, n. 69, provide excerpts of Erasmus's reply to Luther. In lieu of a ready English version of the entire document, the original Latin, plus German translation, is in EAS 4:197–675. See below, n. 175.]

72. WA 18:634 / 33–635 / 5. BoA 125 / 37–126 / 8. [LW 33:64–65.]

an awareness of spontaneity versus coercion but a deity experienced as freedom. The issue of freedom, as debated by Luther and Erasmus, concerns solely the innermost fulfillment of a human being, the charged core, the spirit. This means a power struggle between God and anti-God for human control. A person appears like a beast of burden, as the psalmist (Ps. 73:22) says: "I was stupid and ignorant, I was like a beast of burden toward thee" (Vulgate) [and RSV]. "If Satan rides it, it wills and goes where Satan wills; nor can it choose to run to either of the two riders or to seek him out, but the riders themselves contend for the possession and control of it."[73]

To take this much-discussed picture out of the context in which Luther placed it would be a mistake. The objection that this parable depersonalizes man misses the point. The beast of burden depicts man insofar as he is capable of letting himself be taken over by a conviction, including the aforementioned holy men driven by the Spirit of God. The only comparable feature according to which one can expound this parable or any other is that of defenselessness against superior spiritual power, whether this proceeds from an idea, from grace, or from evil. This picture had had a long history already by Luther's time, but only in half-completed form, where grace is the rider of the human will.[74] Luther simply added the second panel, without which it would not realistically be the image of the helplessness of anyone caught by the devil. There is no pushing the parable beyond this point. Luther himself does not pause to ponder how human desire may thus have become captive. Desire is not extinguished under such dominion but can become most intensely inflamed toward one side or the other. The battle is settled not in some heavenly prologue but in the human heart. Luther simply describes man's actual situation over against these superpowers, as these are attested by the Bible and by experience. However—and this is often misunderstood—Luther does not sur-

---

73. WA 18:635 / 17ff. BoA 3:126 / 23ff. [LW 33:65–66.] Luther here varies a picture that was familiar in his time from the work Hypomnesticon, mistakenly held to be by Augustine, in which Satan, cast as an evil shepherd, becomes the other rider. This competitive struggle over the helpless beast conveys decisive meaning for Luther. So far, however, no direct antecedents of this picture have been found, not even in Augustine (as A. Adam has tried) or Hugo Cardinalis (according to H. Vorster), whose commentary Luther used in his lectures on the Psalms (1513–15). A. Adam, "Die Herkunft des Lutherwortes von menschilchen Willen als Reittier Gottes," LuJ 29 (1962): 25ff. H. Vörster, Das Freiheitsverständnis bei Thomas von Aquin und Martin Luther, KiKonf 8 (Göttingen, 1965), 415ff.

74. On the history of this picture in scholasticism, cf. McSorley, Luthers Lehre vom freien Willen (see n. 13, above), 309ff. In time and context the nearest contemporary use of this imagery is that of K. Schatzgeyer, Scrutinium divinae scripturae pro conciliatione dissidentium dogmatum (1523), ix, CC 5:124 / 17ff.

render his powerlessness. On the contrary, his entire book is but a sustained summons, despite the deadly danger, not to rely on one's own willing and capabilities but to rely entirely on the power of God who seeks to take hold of a person. Faith in God's power is the context making man aware of his own unfreedom. Faith opens the portal to true freedom in the Spirit of God, that "royal freedom" identical with the captivity under it.[75]

It is evident that both Luther and Erasmus meant not a formal or simply psychological freedom but an effective possibility for man to turn either toward or away from grace. However, is it really effective? Luther takes Erasmus at his word in certain extreme statements in order to win him over to his own side: the power of free choice is very slight and of a kind that is entirely ineffective apart from the grace of God,[76] Erasmus conceded. "How different is an ineffective power *(vis inefficax)* from no power at all?"[77] Luther replies as he tries to approach Erasmus. Call this kind of free choice a mere "disposition" *(dispositive qualitas)* and a "passive aptitude" *(passiva aptitudo)*, then Luther could agree. Yet this kind of thing hardly rates the pompous designation of "free will." This power can be properly applied to God alone. To apply it to man is as ridiculous as the custom of princes and kings to adorn themselves with the titles of lands they have long since lost.[78] If there is reluctance to drop this term altogether, then a proper grasp of its meaning simply admits "that free choice is allowed to man only with respect to what is beneath him and not what is above him. That is to say, a man should know that with regard to his faculties and possessions he has the right to use, to do, or to leave undone, according to his own free choice, though even this is controlled by the free choice of God alone, who acts in whatever way he pleases."[79] Thus, in distinction to what Erasmus held, Luther gave not only his opinion of the unfree will but also his definition of free choice. The latter he called a passive "disposition" toward what is above man, an actual freedom toward what is beneath him, the outcome of which, however, remains not with him but with God alone.

Having cleared much ground around basic questions before getting to the central subject, Luther concluded the preliminaries by noting again

75. WA 18:635 / 14ff. *BoA* 3:126 / 19ff. [*LW* 33:65.]

76. *Diatr.*, IV 8:83 / 7ff. *Diatr.* IV 9; 83 / 21–22. *Diatr.* IV 11:84 / 18ff. WA 18:635 / 27ff. *BoA* 3:126 / 34ff. [LCC 17; *LW* 33:66.]

77. WA 18:636 / 10. *BoA* 3:127 / 9. [*LW* 33:67.]

78. WA 18:636 / 16ff., 27ff.; 637 / 7ff., 20ff. *BoA* 3:127 / 16ff., 29ff.; 128 / 2ff., 18ff. [*LW* 33:68, 69.]

79. WA 18:638 / 4ff. *BoA* 3:128 / 40ff. [*LW* 33:70.]

Erasmus's encircling maneuver. Let this show his opponent something of his own oppressive isolation in the very midst of the church's history: "So there remains only Luther, a private individual, a mere upstart." Luther feels that reference to this state of affairs will make an impression on Erasmus. He himself was more impressed by the course of events over the past decade than anyone else; indeed, he had been deeply disturbed by them. This admission indicates how long he had felt himself in contradiction to his church. Yet he "found it incredible that this Troy of ours" (the papal church) "could even be taken." And, God knows, he would still doubt it "but for the pressure of my conscience and the evidence of facts that compel me to a different view." *Conscientia et evidentia rerum,* again one of those revealing formulations for the forces that propelled him on the road to reformation. His heart is not of stone, and he dared to do what he saw "would bring down all the authority of those whom you (Erasmus) have listed, like the Flood on my head."[80]

What, however, do all these developments prove about free will? Erasmus had introduced three validating signs for them: manifestations of the Spirit, miracles, and sanctity. How he had ridiculed Luther's followers, gibing that as for performing miracles they couldn't even cure a lame horse[81]—to which Luther retorted by asking whether anyone in the Erasmian cloud of witnesses had ever performed a single miracle of his own free choice, and was it not much more by the power of God? Neither Erasmus nor his witnesses would wish to deny it, and some of them, like Augustine and Bernard, have affirmed it clearly enough.[82] And when some of them in the course of theological comments have spoken of free will, they have at the same time spoken against their own heart and against their own deeds which stem from God. The way things are, "men are to be measured by their feelings rather than their talk."[83] The words of those whom Erasmus cites as authorities are therefore no proof at all, for their deeds prove the contrary.

By now the tip of the Erasmian proof was actually pointing in still another direction. Erasmus did not merely try to impress by claiming that where stands a mighty majority there too the truth must lie. Instead, on his own, he wished to pronounce a far deeper and more penetrating postulate of faith: God would not have concealed an error in his church for so

80. WA 18:640 / 10–641 / 12. *BoA* 3:130 / 17–38. [*LW* 33:72–73.]

81. *Diatr.,* Ib 6:17 / 3–4. WA 18:641 / 20ff. *BoA* 3:131 / 8ff. [LCC 17:45] [*LW* 33:73.]

82. WA 18:641 / 31ff.; 644 / 4ff. *BoA* 3:131 / 22ff.; 133 / 32ff. [*LW* 33:74, 77.]

83. WA 18:644 / 15–16. *BoA* 3:134 / 4–5. [*LW* 33:77.]

many centuries.[84] Really not? Erasmus's claim causes Luther to spell out his understanding of the church and its history with concise brevity. Proof of this is already in the Old Testament, with its many apostate kings, priests, and false prophets. Nevertheless, in the time of Elijah there were the seven thousand who kept the faith; "they were the church which God preserved for himself among the common people" (1 Kings 19:18)[85] or the remnant of which Isaiah prophesied (Isa. 10:20ff.). In this regard the New Testament church is no different from the Old. All the disciples at some time denied their Lord. The Arians and the papacy have almost wholly misled the church. "The church of God is not as commonplace a thing, my dear Erasmus, as the phrase 'the church of God.' "[86] "Who knows but that the state of the church of God throughout the course of the world from the beginning has always been such that some have been called the people and the saints of God who are not so, while others, a remnant in their midst, really were the people or the saints but were never called so?" And yet "the church of God is the pillar and ground of truth" (see 1 Tim. 3:15).[87] Certainly, *abscondita est ecclesia, latent sancti*.[88] In no way does Luther evade the fact that when someone calls the visible ecclesial organization "church" he had better know what he is doing. This, however, is valid according to the "rule of love," which always thinks well of everyone and which calls anyone baptized a saint, for love would rather be deceived than to distrust. But this does not hold for the "rule of faith," whose business it is to seek the truth and whose nature it is not to let itself be deceived.[89] Having set limits beyond which he cannot retreat, and having shown cordial respect for the great names on Erasmus's listing, Luther faces again the decisive question: "What and whom are we to believe?"[90] Where is the truth?

Once again Luther has only one answer: In the Holy Scriptures, and specifically in what he had been calling "the external clarity of the Scriptures." This is the clarity openly demonstrable through the public ministry of the Word and its outward office, and readily conveying the meaning of Scripture. That this kind of clarity exists is Luther's *primum prin-*

---

84. WA 18:649 / 26ff. BoA 3:137 / 36ff. *Diatr.*, Ib 8:18 / 3ff. [*LW* 33:85; LCC 17:46.]

85. WA 18:650 / 11ff. BoA 3:138 / 19ff. [1 Kings 19:18.] [*LW* 33:85–86.]

86. WA 18:651 / 24ff. BoA 3:139 / 39ff. [*LW* 33:88.]

87. WA 18:650 / 27ff.; 650 / 1–2. BoA 3:138 / 38ff.; 138 / 6–7. [*LW* 33: 86, 85.]

88. "The church is hidden, the saints are unknown." WA 18:652 / 23. BoA 3:141 / 1–2. [*LW* 33:89.]

89. WA 18:651 / 34ff. BoA 3:140 / 12ff. [*LW* 33:88.]

90. WA 18:652 / 24. BoA 3:141 / 2. [*LW* 33:89.]

cipium, his first principle, and an axiom of Scripture itself, and he supports it with numerous passages from the Old and New Testaments.[91] Still it may be that Erasmus has no desire to doubt that in general the teachings of Holy Scripture are demonstrably clear; all he insists is that on the question of free will, and on a few similar issues, the Scriptures are obscure.[92] Luther comes back with a twofold answer. For one, he draws a conclusion from the essence of the Scriptures: Christ intends that his word be a bright light to Christians; thus everything that concerns them must be clear. If the problem of free will were obscure, then we would have to conclude that the problem concerns neither us nor the Scriptures, which would be absurd.[93] Luther builds up his argument with all kinds of examples in which true doctrine may not have convinced its opponents but made them stubbornly resistant, so that, against conscience, they have been possessed by the devil and have continued obdurately to advance their opinion.[94]

One must admit that this kind of proof is somewhat shaky. For a postulate drawn from Scripture, this one has no direct scriptural support. But Luther does not stop here. The other part of his twofold answer follows a different line of thought. With it he tries to trap his opponent in his own contradiction. Actually Erasmus had been wavering between affirming free will and denying that Scripture has a decisive word on the subject. Earlier Luther had already taunted him: "And why do you yourself, Erasmus, set out the nature of Christianity for us if the Scriptures are obscure to you?"[95] So Luther fires the other barrel of his argument: Those many witnesses, theological and saintly celebrities in his opponents' eyes, who, Erasmus claims, all taught free will, these must surely have found the Scriptures clear on this point! The tally? Not Luther, as his challenger had claimed, but Erasmus himself is now found standing alone. There he is, with his private opinion on the obscurity of Scripture, caught between two fronts: his serene supporters on the one, and Luther on the other. And both fronts, although with opposite effect, consider Scripture clear on this question.[96] Satisfied, Luther thus ends his prefatory remarks to

91. WA 18:653 / 13ff., 22–35. BoA 141 / 32ff.; 142 / 3–19. Cf. the list of scriptural proofs, WA 18:654 / 1–656 / 11. BoA 3:142 / 20–145 / 8. [LW 33:90–91; cf. the index to Scripture passages, 304–7.]

92. WA 18:656 / 12ff. BoA 3:145 / 9ff. [LW 33:94.]

93. WA 18:656 / 18–25. BoA 3:145 / 17–26. [LW 33:94–95.]

94. WA 18:656 / 40–659 / 33. BoA 3:146 / 4–149 / 10. [LW 33:95–100.]

95. WA 18:656 / 3–4. BoA 3:144 / 38–39. [LW 33:94.]

96. WA 18:659 / 36–660 / 33. BoA 3:149 / 14–150 / 14. [LW 33:100–102.]

the pending disputation, saying: "There can be no stronger proof than the personal confession and testimony of a defendant against himself."[97]

Luther had some ground for supposing that he had thereby virtually "put an end to this whole question about free will."[98] In their respective preliminaries both men had played all their essential cards. No matter how much more they unloaded in exegetical proofs and more precise definitions, the essential lines of their dispute had virtually run out. They had held back nothing. Behind Erasmus's rhetorical feints—he was always trying to maneuver Luther into a bad light by calling attention to the Reformer's unruly adherents and, by contrast, to strengthen his position behind a phalanx of fathers—there lay quite simple thoughts and deeply rooted convictions. Erasmus feared for the moral nurture and self-directed endeavors of man, lest some doctrine of unfree will place a tempting excuse in man's hand. So he conceived of God as the Great Pedagogue who wisely had locked up a number of mysteries. For us, as human beings, there is no use brooding over them or talking about them; all it takes is humbly to await their disclosure. These mysteries are quite heterogeneous and remain riddles, from the Trinity to the presence of God in an insect's hole, the Immaculate Conception of Mary, from the historic introduction of penance by Jesus to the hour of our death or the last judgment.[99] As Erasmus placed free will on the inventory of "superfluous questions,"[100] he took it out of the context of problems basic to Christian existence: grace, bondage in sin, human cooperation in salvation—all of them realities which to Luther were inseparable from the question of will. Erasmus, to the contrary, wavered between the insolubility of the question, on the one hand, and a forthright defense of free will, on the other. Whence came this strange ambivalence? Apparently from his pedagogical predilection. On the subject of the will his two considerations collided, the one veiling those divine mysteries considered nonessential for us, the other appealing to the free moral activity of man. The contradiction between his dim views of human nature[101] sprang from the dominance of the pedagogical element in his thinking versus his consistently confident estimate of biblical prophecy: "If we are in the path of true religion, let us go on swiftly to better things, forgetting the things that are behind, or if we are entangled in sins, let us strive with all our might to work our way

97. WA 18:661 / 23–24. BoA 3:151 / 1–2. [LW 33:102.]
98. WA 18:661 / 21–22. BoA 3:150 / 40. [LW 33:102.]
99. Diatr. Ia 7:5 / 17ff. Diatr., Ia 9:7 / 6ff. See above, pp. 420-21. [LCC 17:38, 39.]
100. Diatr. Ia 8:6 / 24–25. [LCC 17:39.]
101. See above, p. 421.

out."[102] On the basis of reason, Erasmus intended no more than to set forth a morally rewarding statement of the problem and thereby to regain as much as possible from hard-and-fast assertions. In the process, however, he had already to lay bare his most profound views of God and man, of the Bible and the church, of the meaning and limits of theological pronouncements.

Luther was thus forced to anticipate and to disclose the entire root system of his thought on the question of the will. If we take into account what the situation of literary controversy required in terms of defense and counterattack, of arguments and supporting texts, then Luther's reply yields a rapid succession of solid comments on cardinal questions of theology. Many of the most famous sentences in this book—indeed, in all his writings—are present in the introduction. Because he followed Erasmus move by move, Luther was prevented from setting forth his own train of thought. The result, however, enhanced the character of the discussion as the opponents met eye-to-eye. Everything between them was controversial, even to the deepest points they touched—honoring the majesty of God. Wherever reason failed to cope with the mysteries of Scripture, Erasmus saw it as a bid for silence, Luther as a bid for speech, qualifying it by saying, "God has willed [these mysteries] to be published, and we must not ask the reason for the divine will, but simply adore it."[103] Shunning the dark, Erasmus hankered for a brightness to God's ways that would make them understandable, as well as for a clear concept of man, of the sort who knows God's commandments and has confidence that with God's help he can follow them. Luther, to the contrary, contended that man is indeed lost if he does not know that God is present also in the dark, that God leads through dying to living, through agonizing to redemption. Therefore Luther relies entirely on faith and solid certitude, while Erasmus evades the dark and treats the hard questions with a shot of skepticism. He operates with the artificial light of authority, using it to get his bearings. Therefore he is reluctant to criticize the church, the fathers, or the councils too openly. Not so Luther. For him the church is hidden, just as God's dealing in history and with human beings is hidden. The church is hidden by what calls itself church; only by faith can one see it and belong to it. Precisely because reason views these hidden things as areas of darkness of which it cannot conceive unaided, Luther is too passionately confident that the only view we have of them is the Word of God in Holy Scripture—and this Word is clear.

102. *Diatr.*, Ia 8:6 / 11ff [LCC 17:39 (alt. to give Bornkamm's version).]
103. WA 18:632 / 22ff. *BoA* 3:123 / 28–30. [*LW* 33:61.]

Here again contacts and cleavages of the two disputants lie alongside each other. Erasmus, like Luther, had said that Scripture cannot contradict itself.[104] Yet, unlike Luther, whenever he came across anything seemingly obscure he put it aside, attempting, perhaps, to explain it by some anthropomorphic turn of phrase. Basically, he followed the majority opinion, as he judged it to be, treating the Scriptures similarly to the writings of the church fathers. This way was not for Luther. For him it was fundamentally important that scriptural statements on obscure, or dark, questions be clear, so that comments on a given passage could, according to hermeneutical rules, be derived from the Bible's common denominator, the gospel. To be sure, any ensuing clarification is the work of the Holy Spirit. It is he who makes the obscure truths of Scripture—those inaccessible to reasoned understanding—clear from "within" to both reader and hearer.

These diverse premises of scriptural understanding having been set up, the field was staked out where alone meaningful discussion by the two partners could take place. What was true of Scripture was, alas, not true of theology. Here the basic axioms were diametrically opposite, so that a direct conversation on them was out of the question. This was evident in the choice of terms for free will, the subject with which Luther remained until taking up the exegetical debate.[105] Luther found Erasmus entangled in a twofold contradiction: in contradiction to the concept of freedom and in contradiction to himself. According to Luther, freedom is an absolute concept. It will not have itself fenced in. To will, as such, and the action preceding from it, is understood as totally free.[106] The absoluteness of this freedom to will is by its own nature something attributable to God alone. A "certain measure of choice" in earthly decision-making can perhaps be attributed to man, yet not as applied to divine things,[107] for man could then do everything God can do and subsume God's freedom under his own.[108] From the very outset, this "definition of the name" [freedom] as well as Erasmus's "definition of the object" (free will) contradicted each other.[109] In the same way Erasmus actually undercuts the true meaning of freedom. Luther's concept of it as pure autonomy is meant in a philosophical sense. He thus employs the philosophical understanding of freedom

104. See above, p. 422.
105. WA 18:661 / 29ff. BoA 3:151 / 8ff. [LW 33:102ff.]
106. WA 18:662 / 40ff. BoA 3:152 / 22ff. [LW 33:104–5.]
107. WA 18:662 / 5ff.; 636 / 27ff. BoA 3:151 / 18ff.; 127 / 29ff. [LW 33:103, 68.]
108. WA 18:664 / 9ff.; 665 / 15–16. BoA 154 / 5ff.; 155 / 15ff. [LW 33:106–7, 109.]
109. WA 18:662 / 12ff. BoA 3:151 / 27ff. [LW 33:103.]

which he learned from his nominalist teachers, especially from Gabriel Biel. They strictly distinguish it from the theological problem of freedom which was narrowed down to the relation of sin and grace.[110] To Luther the philosophical concept of freedom was so important not because everyone—the people, as he said—hears what he wishes[111] in the word "freedom," but because this concept is applicable neither to man's relation to God nor to man's eternal salvation.

If Luther saw that this discrepancy of concepts put philosophical logic on his side, then the other contradiction—still more effective dialectically—forced even his opponent on to his own side. Erasmus had striven to achieve formulas of compromise and in the process had permitted himself to make far-reaching concessions. Now Luther nailed him down. Among three possible opposing positions, Erasmus had designated as alone probable the opinion held by those who say "they deny that man can will the good without peculiar grace, they deny that he can make a beginning, they deny that he can progress, they deny that he can reach his goal without the principal and perpetual aid of divine grace."[112] In another passage Luther is more blunt. "The will with which we choose or refuse was thus so far depraved that by its natural powers it could not amend its ways, but once its liberty had been lost it was compelled to serve that sin to which it had once and for all consented."[113] Nailing Erasmus to his own words, Luther wrote, "What an exquisitely free choice which has lost its liberty and is called by Erasmus himself a slave of sin!"[114] "Lost liberty, according to my grammar, is no liberty at all."[115] Here, as in other places, Erasmus's *Diatribe* testifies against itself. On the point that man has lost his liberty and is enslaved by sin, Luther is in full agreement with Erasmus. But then there is no such thing as a neutral will which can turn toward one side or the other; this is a mere "dialetical fiction" born of ignorance of the way things are.[116] Would Erasmus have it described? Then Luther offers this witty word, "You make free choice equally potent in both directions in that it is able by its own power, without grace, both to apply itself to the good and to turn away from the good.

110. L. Grane, *Contra Gabrielem* (Copenhagen, 1962), 114ff. Vörster, *Freiheitsverständnis* (see n. 73, above), 286ff.

111. *WA* 18:637 / 3ff. *BoA* 3:151 / 27ff.

112. *Diatr.*, IIa 12:30 / 24ff. [LCC 17:53.]

113. *Diatr.*, IIa 3:21 / 14ff. Cf. also *Diatr.*, IIa 4:22 / 14 and *Diatr.*, IIa 5:24 / 1. [LCC 17: 48–49. Cf. LCC 17:49.]

114. *WA* 18: 668 / 16–17. *BoA* 3:158 / 14–15. [*LW* 33:113.]

115. *WA* 18:670 / 36–37. *BoA* 3: 160 / 27–28. [*LW* 33:116.]

116. *WA* 670 / 1ff. *BoA* 3:159 / 25ff. [*LW* 33:115.]

You do not realize how much you attribute to it by this pronoun 'itself.' "[117] Even the Sophists [scholastics] knew how weak this presumably self-moving "I" really is. They learned it from Peter Lombard, as did Luther, and he found the "master of the *Sentences*" more tolerable on this point than the definition given by Erasmus.[118]

At long last the battle begins, and around the biblical entrenchments on both sides it runs through three successive phases. The tripartite development of Erasmus's *Diatribe* provides the battle plan: (1) Luther attacks the passages Erasmus has mobilized in support of free will; (2) Erasmus strikes back, and Luther defends his own supporting passages; (3) Luther attacks again, this time with his heaviest reserves under the two "high commanders," Paul and John the Evangelist "with a few of their battalions."[119] Luther likes to employ military imagery; so does Erasmus, but with a characteristic difference. Like Ignatius Loyola, Erasmus prefers the traditional picture of the Christian soldier summoned to manly discipline and promised eternal reward for his valor. Luther, however, thinks of battle as a parable of the great spiritual wars, be it God against the devil, the Bible against its adversaries, or Christendom against its opponents. Down to the very choice of picturesque speech, we can distinguish between the way of the law, on the one hand, and the way of faith, on the other.[120]

To pursue this verbal campaign in detail would be boring and pointless. In contrast to the lengthy preliminaries, in which the two contestants

117. WA 18:665 / 11ff. BoA 3:155 / 11ff. [LW 33:108–9.]

118. WA 18:665 / 6ff., 21ff. BoA 3:155 / 4ff., 22ff. [Cf. also WA 18:681 / 29ff. BoA 3:173 / 14ff. [LW 33:109, cf. 134.]

119. WA 18:756 / 24ff.; 757 / 9–10. BoA 3:256 / 10ff., 23–24. [LW 33:246, 247.]

120. On Erasmus, cf. his *Enchiridion militis christiani* (1503), or his references to reward in his catechism (*Explanatio symboli* [1533]). "Our high commander prepares a reward for his soldiers if they follow the example of their captain, fight conscientiously under his insignia, and prove themselves zealous to the death" (Erasmus, Opp. ed. *Clericus* X, 1140B, cited by K. Bornkamm, "Das Verständnis christlicher Unterweisung in den Katechismus von Erasmus und Luther," *ZThK* 65 [1968]: 209). Literature on the history of the solider-image in E.-W. Kohls, *Die Theologie des Erasmus* (Basel, 1966), 2:31, 87. For Luther (among countless applications): "When these two Gods are at war with one another (the true God and the god of this world), what can there be but tumult in the whole world?" *De servo arbitrio*, WA 18:626 / 23–24. BoA 3:117 / 4–5. [LW 33:52.] "It was a strange and dreadful strife when life and death contended" (from Luther's hymn, "Christ Jesus lay in death's strong bonds," "Christus lag in Todesbanden" [*D. Martin Luthers Briefwechsel*, ed. E. L. Enders (Frankfurt am Main, 1884ff.), no. 134, *Laudamus*, hymnal of the Lutheran World Federation, 4th ed. (1970), no. 65]). Commenting on Thomas Müntzer's movement: "There must needs be sects, and the Word of God must be in the field to do battle. Thus the evangelists are called a heavenly host, Ps. 68(:12–13), and Christ the "Lord of hosts" in the prophets. . . . So let the spirits strike and burst upon one another. If some of them meanwhile get waylaid, let it be. That's the way it is in real war. Wherever the skirmish or the battle, some must fall or be wounded. But whoever fights bravely will be crowned." WA 15:218 / 20. All these illustrations pertain to faith.

reflect themselves incomparably, the big battle breaks up into countless fights over individual Bible passages. It is easy to lose the panorama. Erasmus had marshaled over two hundred texts to support free will or to refute any anticipated counterattacks. Luther pursued him, text by text. In the process Erasmus often repeated himself, and Luther even more so, as with passion aglow and vocabulary boundless he threw himself into the fray. The outcome of it all, in terms of biblical commentary, is here best left aside. Neither party applied biblical exegesis in the modern sense of allowing for historical differentiation. Instead, each took the Bible as a uniform testimony to its respective positions. What thus concerns us are the efficacious main lines of the argument. Under these everything else is understood as a systematization according to given theological contexts. This procedure, however, creates the greatest risk of misunderstanding not only of the several problems treated but especially of the complex positions taken by Luther. Our prime attention therefore focuses on the dual strategy that Luther was forced to adopt by Erasmus's challenge. (1) He had to refute the postulating logic ("you can because you must") which Erasmus applied to numerous ethical and appellative Bible passages. (2) He had to disclose, as never before or ever again in such compact form, the depths of his concept of God and of man, being forced to do so in the face of the contradictions and foolishness Erasmus had claimed to find in Luther's comments on God and his dealing with the world and humanity.[121]

Admittedly serving up almost too much of a good thing, though it by no means exhausted the Bible, Erasmus adduced precepts and premises requiring our practice. Consider his exegetical comments to such passages as, for example, Paul's words "Let us then cast off the works of darkness" (Rom. 13:12) and "Put off the old nature with its practices" (Col. 3:9). They all end with the same refrain: "How are we commanded to cast off or put on anything if we can do nothing?"[122] Be they commands or threats, words about obedience or disobedience, even the Bible's examples and parables of God's gracious help in our efforts—all these are meaningless, contends Erasmus, unless we have at least a weak, even inadequate but yet effective and basically free, will.

---

121. These two aspects, taken together, comprise the inner logic of the schematic arrangement Erasmus had given the citations he had brought to the discussion: proofs of free will, apparent proofs against free will. In treating the first group he argued on the basis of their immanent logic; the other he refuted by showing the absurdity to which Luther's exegesis led.

122. *Diatr.*, IIb 5:44 / 19ff.; the proof texts are there, 19–46. [LCC 17:63.]

Let Erasmus present his logic ever so penetratingly, and Luther's stubborn response is that none of this jibes. To be sure, this has not yet become a case of philosophical versus theological thinking; the discussion remains tied to logic. The "ought," Luther asserts, proves nothing about the "can." Imperatives are not indicatives. Conditional sentences, as in many biblical promises—"If you will, you can keep the commandments" (Eccles. 15:14 [15]; "If you are willing and obedient, you shall eat the good of the land" (Isa. 1:19)—are not descriptions of a state of affairs.[123] All forms of "ought" call attention to what should be done, and by that standard our conduct does not measure up. "That is the reason God gives laws."[124] Perceiving is itself not power; it simply awakens an awareness of the law and of guilt.[125] Biblically, this is the richly blessed function of Moses over against Satan, who strikes people blind. Only from this kind of insight can people, after all, be led to Christ.[126] Erasmus misses the point of "ought" when he holds ridiculous the decreeing of laws that cannot be kept.[127] Likewise, he misses the point of difference between law and gospel when he tries to derive the capability from the command—you ought, therefore you can.[128] Luther's concern is for the highest and most inclusive understanding of "ought," that under which man's entire being has been placed: "You shall love the Lord your God with all your heart." Who would here talk about fulfillment of one's own power? Yet on this one law, as Christ said, "depend all the law and the prophets" (Matt. 22:40).[129] From no commandment, therefore, can we derive free will. Although Erasmus too meant the freedom to choose between good and evil, and not simply the choice among ordinary tasks, he admits that the moral imperatives span stages of varying difficulty and of corresponding grace-granted help. In each of these cases considerable free will must be assumed.

Given his line of argument, it was but natural for the New Testament promises of reward, indeed, the words of Christ himself, to play a signifi-

123. WA 18:672 / 32ff.; 676 / 2–3; 677 / 28; 678 / 9ff.; 679 / 38ff.; 681 / 26ff. BoA 3:162 / 37ff.; 166 / 31–32; 168 / 13; 169 / 11ff.; 171 / 11ff.; 173 / 11ff. [LW 33:120, 124–25, 127, 128, 134.]

124. WA 18:673 / 39ff. BoA 3:164 / 6ff. [LW 33:121.]

125. WA 18:677 / 12ff. BoA 3:168 / 10ff. [LW 33:127.]

126. WA 18:679 / 21ff., 33ff.; 687 / 37ff. BoA 3:170 / 34ff.; 171 / 5ff.; 180 / 22ff. [LW 33:130, 144.]

127. Diatr., IIa 14 / 16:33 / 2ff.; 35 / 24ff. WA 18:673 / 4ff.; 674 / 6ff.; 679 / 36–37. BoA 3:163 / 5ff.; 164 / 17ff.; 171 / 9–10. [LCC 17:54, 57. LW 33:120, 122, 130.]

128. WA 18:680 / 23ff. BoA 3:172 / 3ff. [LW 33:132.]

129. [Bornkamm text errs, citing Matt. 22:4.] WA 18:680 / 34ff.; 681 / 12–34. BoA 172 / 18ff.; 172 / 34—173 / 20. According to Luther's frequently expressed interpretation the commandment to love God is the one from which the other is derived: "Love your neighbor as yourself." [LW 33:133–34.]

cant role. "Rejoice and be glad, for your reward is great in heaven" (Matt. 5:12), or the parable of the workers in the vineyard (Matt. 20:1–16), to cite examples. Does not reward presuppose some sort of personally achieved performance? Luther took the long view in replying to this kind of question. It had come up so frequently from the onset of Christian history to the present that it prompted two provocative thoughts: (1) True, a yes or a no to the word of Jesus is a decision that lasts forever and brings inevitable consequences. Yet the decision's goal is not some performance for which reward is expected; instead, the target is faith in that grace which grants rewards not for something done but for something to become; as God has promised, "he gave (them) power to become children of God" (John 1:12). "Here a person (as they say) shows up passive; here he does nothing but become something through and through."[130] (2) Merit is thus out of the question. "How can they merit that which is already theirs and is prepared for them before they are born? . . . For the Kingdom is not being prepared, but has been prepared, while the sons of the Kingdom are being prepared, not preparing the Kingdom."[131] As words of law have their function in perception, so also do words of promise and of reward: the perception of grace, of salvation, and of the believer's belonging to God forever.

Shining through this debate are the contrasting concepts of God as held throughout by the two contestants. Freedom as a postulate of practical reason for Erasmus, as later for Kant, subsumes the postulates of a righteous God, comprehensible in his dealings and compensating in his rewards in the world beyond. This is not to turn Erasmus into an eighteenth-century rationalist. Concerning the will, he ever remained the philosophical theologian and in the medieval manner counted continually on the supportive help of prevenient grace. Despite these differentiated premises, however, like Kant he argued with a consistent logic to which (he presumed) God adheres. For Luther it was the other way around. God is not bound to our constraints of thought. As human beings we can perceive only the factuality of his dealings, not its logic. Luther is thus able to set down together, freely and without limit, such basic axioms of Christian existence as the wickedness of sinful man, the unconditional demands of the law, and the simply unmerited grace. Is Luther's a mere recital of unconnected biblical pronouncements? How does he connect the seemingly separating parts of (man's) picture of God?

130. WA 18:693 / 38ff.; 697 / 21ff., 27–28. BoA 3:186 / 36ff.; 191 / 7ff., 15–16. [LW 33:151, 157.]
131. WA 18:694 / 22ff. BoA 3:187 / 27ff. [LW 33:153.]

In God himself alone does he find the connections. Luther develops neither a theoretically resolved concept of God nor a Christian doctrine of God. Instead, he simply endeavors to repeat what he has found already recited in the Bible and—not to overlook it—in the secret knowledge of the human heart. The essence of the divine superiority over the world and humanity is caught in the word "majesty": *Deus in majestate et natura sua, deus absconditus in majesta* [God in his nature and majesty is God hidden in majesty]. What this means eludes definition. It can only note negatively what man is able to express "about God as he is not preached, not revealed, not offered, not worshiped," or, stated differently, "God himself" as distinct from "Word of God."[132] In his Word, God has made himself known comprehensibly so that we can make him known to others. These distinctions are to remind man of the boundaries set for him but not for God. "For (in doing so) he has not bound himself by his Word but has kept himself free over all things."[133] So also the faith founded on God's word must acquiesce and realize that "God does many things he does not disclose to us in this world."[134] Despite this assertion, Luther does not regard the Word of God as only partial truth, as though it should make us question whether Scripture gives us the complete God. Earlier Luther had used a simile to clarify this question nicely: Consider human speech and the song of the birds ("you know a bird by its song"); so the heart, with its full being, is in the Word. "So it is in God as well, his Word is like him; the Godhead is fully in the Word—and whoever has the Word has the full Godhead."[135] Luther does not take back any of this, nor does he contradict himself, for the Word itself made him aware of God's hidden-ness, which it does not reveal for us.[136] Indeed, it was the Word that gave

132. WA 18:685 / 3ff., 25ff. BoA 3:177 / 13ff., 40ff. [LW 33:139, 140.] Already in his hermeneutical premise (see above, pp. 426–27) Luther had made this distinction: "God and the Scripture of God are two things, no less than the Creator and the creature are two things. In God there are many things hidden, of which we are ignorant, no one doubts." WA 18:606 / 11ff. BoA 3:101 / 6ff. [LW 33:25.]

133. WA 18:686 / 23–24. BoA 3:177 / 38–39. [LW 33:140.] As the *tum* and the use of the perfect tense in the context show, the issue in the disputed case concerns God's historic action, in contrast to his continuous work ("He works life and death and all in everything"). Cf. R. Hermann, "Beobachtungen zu Luthers Lehre vom Deus Revelatus nach seiner Unterscheidung vom Deus Absconditus," in *Vom Herrengeheimnis der Wahrheit: Festschrift für H. Vogel* (Berlin and Stuttgart, 1962), 196ff.

134. WA 18:685 / 26–27. BoA 3:178 / 2–3. [LW 33:140.]

135. *Kirchenpostille* (1522), WA 10¹1:188 / 4ff.

136. Exod. 33:20ff. Rom. 9:14ff.; 11:33ff. In his letter of February 23, 1542, Luther cited the warning not to inquire into God's "secret counsels" (Job 15:8) and Prov. 25:27, "Whoever would explore the (divine) majesty will be fallen upon" (according to the Vulgate ["You have no need to worry over mysteries," Ecclus. 3:22, JB] familiar to him and differing from his own Bible translation); cf. Acts 1:7. WA Br 9:627 / 33–628 / 73.

him the concept of *Deus absconditus* (Isa. 45:15) ["Truly, thou art a God who hidest thyself"]. Why God hides himself and what lies beyond our limits of understanding remains his business. That also pertains to the question why God regards our will-to-evil as making us guilty when, alas, our will is not free.

> But why that majesty of his does not remove or change this defect of our will in all men, since it is not in man's power to do so, or why he imputes this defect to man, when man cannot help having it, we have no right to inquire, and though you may do a lot of inquiring, you will never find out. It is as Paul says in Rom. 11 (9:20), "Who are you to answer back to God?"[137]

Luther made an impassioned warning not to go beyond these limits, otherwise man will fall into an abyss of temptation and will break his neck. God is withdrawn from every attempt to get the better of him, be it by means of the moral logic of an Erasmus or the abstract Father-image of Christian tradition. Nor does Luther intend to suggest that the antitheses he employs would offer a scheme for comprehending God, not even in terms of opposites: *Deus absconditus* and *Deus revelatus* (or proclaimed), mentioned so often yet occurring only at this point in his treatise.[138] For Luther this is not a handy formulation for a divine dual polarity, for God is the same, whether he hides or reveals himself: hidden in majesty, revealed in the word *(absconditus in majestate et revelatus in verbo)* would be a better citation.[139] It is a matter not of two sides of God but of an event, of God's veiling himself in majesty or of his moving from that majesty into the Word. How should these two aspects of deity ever be separated from each other? Without the obscurity of majesty, revelation would

---

137. *WA* 18:686 / 8ff. *BoA* 3:178 / 19ff. [*LW* 33:140.]

138. *WA* 18:685 / 3ff. *BoA* 3:177 / 13ff. Cf. F. Kattenbusch, "Deus absconditus bei Luther," in *Festschrift for J. Kaftan* (Tübingen, 1920), 180, n. 12. W. von Loewenich, *Luthers Theologia crucis*, 5th ed., FGLP 2 / 2 (Munich, 1967), 45. Also outside *De servo arbitrio* this formula—about it only are we here concerned—seldom shows up in Luther's writings. Aside from a few places in the Heidelberg disputation (see above, p. 351, *WA* 1:362 / 9–10) and in the *Resolutiones* of 1518, the term shows up again only in Luther's Genesis lectures (1535–45); cf. von Loewenich, *Theologia crucis*, 38ff. The strongest supporting source is in the penetrating transcript of the Genesis lectures; these erroneously show up in *WA* under Table Talk (*WA TR* 5, no. 5658a, 293–96; also *WA* 48:363–64. Also H. Volz, "Wie Luther in der Genesisvorlesung sprach," *ThStKr* 100 [1928]: 167ff., bringing parallel texts of the original copy and the printed version).

139. *Absconditus* and *revelatus* are participles, not expressions of attributes. On earlier occasions (rare ones) Luther turned them around, i.e., christologically, employing them: *absconditus in passionibus* (hidden in the passion). *Probationes* to the Heidelberg Theses 20 and 21, *WA* 1:362 / 9, 23. *BoA* 5:388 / 19, 35. [*LW* 31:52, 53.] Luther had already noted five different modes of hiddenness, all of them counter to the language used in *De servo arbitrio*, in his earliest lectures on the Psalms, *WA* 3:124 / 29ff. *BoA* 5:94 / 14ff. [*LW* 10:118ff.] On this subject, see Kattenbusch, "Deus absconditus," 204, n. 29.

not be revelation. Therefore the word can never dismiss the majesty, and faith itself can only silently worship the unfathomableness of God.[140]

The second elementary word with which not only the Bible but also reason attests to God's deity is omnipotence.[141] This is the life in everything alive, no matter what it becomes. To live means to desire. "Man is as incapable of not desiring and seeking as of not existing, for he is a creature of God, though a vitiated one."[142] Luther differentiates: God creates and does not will evil, otherwise he would not be God; but he cannot withdraw life, else he would not be God either.[143] "It therefore remains for someone to ask why God does not cease from the very motion of omnipotence by which the will of the ungodly is moved to go on being evil. . . . The answer is that this is wanting God to cease to be God on account of the ungodly."[144] Therefore Luther ventures to make the most frightening of statements. God himself can harden a person's heart, just as he did Pharaoh's. Luther infers of God,

> Inwardly, I will move his evil will be my general motion so that he may proceed according to his own bent and on his own course of willing, nor will I cease to move it, nor can I do otherwise than move it; but outwardly I will confront him with a word and work with which that evil bent of his will clash, since he cannot do other than will evilly when I move him, evil as he is, by virtue of my omnipotence.[145]

What a sinister psychology, how evil necessarily intensifies itself on the good, yet an even more sinister theology if God is behind it all—only, Luther would reply, because God himself becomes sinister when we begin brooding over him. Nor does it help us when, be the grounds ever so good, we would simply not like to believe certain aspects of his being which "prevent him from being anything else." It is helpful only when we turn our gaze to the place where he has revealed himself and promised his help. Then also his incomprehensible dealings become testimonies to the power he directs toward us. "Don't be frightened at Pharaoh's hardness, for even that itself is my work and I have it in hand; I who am setting you free, I shall use it only to do many signs and declare my majesty to help

140. WA 18:690 / 1–2, 22; 712 / 25ff. BoA 3:182 / 28–29; 183 / 13–14; 207 / 33ff. [LW 33:146, 180.]

141. WA 18:709 / 11–12. BoA 3:203 / 41. [LW 33:175.]

142. WA 18:710 / 17–18. BoA 3:205 / 12–13. [LW 33:177.]

143. WA 18:708 / 31ff.; 710 / 31–711 / 10; 747 / 16ff. BoA 3:203 / 16; 205 / 29–206 / 9; 245 / 25ff. [LW 33:175, 178, 232.]

144. WA 18:712 / 20ff. BoA 3:207 / 27ff. [LW 33:180.]

145. WA 18:712 / 6ff. BoA 3:207 / 9ff. [LW 33:180.]

your faith."[146] Such sentences should not be crossed out. They are extreme examples of talking about God without suppressing anything about him. Luther avoids every foreshortening of his all-embracing power of life. Any diminishing of God would be akin to blasphemy in that it is hubris, human pride. Luther desires to lead people, in the midst of the uncanny, to the place of safety which God has disclosed for us in Christ.

Faith in free will is shattered in still a third aspect of God's being which not even our reasoned thought can deny: foreknowledge (*praescientia*), the foundation of his absolute truth. "If God foreknew that Judas would be a traitor, Judas necessarily became a traitor, and it was not in the power of Judas or any creature to do differently or to change his will . . . for it is an irrefutable and self-evident proposition that God does not lie and is not deceived."[147] Derived from this it follows that "God wills that which he foresees." This sentence of predestination was eventually conceded by Erasmus, to Luther's considerable reassurance. Erasmus called the sentence difficult and tried to get around it by modifying it: God can change his foreseeing intention, can make use of secondary causes, and there are examples that foreseeing need not be causal, as, for example, the forecasting of an eclipse of the sun. Luther pushed such considerations aside. "We are arguing about the foreknowledge of God, and unless you allow this to carry with it the necessary occurrence of the thing foreknown, you take away faith and the fear of God, make havoc of all the divine promises and threatenings, and thus deny his very divinity."[148] The concept "divinity" (deity) allows for a generally human notion. Actually, this is the heaviest weapon Luther trained on his wavering opponent. "The living and true God must be one who by his freedom imposes necessity on us, since obviously he would be a ridiculous God, or idol rather, if he foresaw the future uncertainly or could be proved mistaken by events, when even the heathen have given their gods an 'ineluctable fate.' "[149]

With this assertion Luther again summoned the idea of destiny as witness, yet no longer as earlier.[150] Fleeting references to heathen poets or proverbial phrases in popular parlance are not enough. Luther now

146. WA 18:714 / 9ff. BoA 3:209 / 23ff. [LW 33:183.]

147. WA 18:715 / 18ff. BoA 3:211 / 1ff. The imprecise word *versehen* [oversee] which Jordahn employs in his translation (Martin Luther, *Ausgewählte Werke*, ed. H. H. Borcher and G. Merz [Munich, 1951ff.], supp. vol. 1) most frequently, obscures the precise meaning of *praescire* [to foreknow]. [LW 33:185.]

148. WA 18:716 / 13ff. BoA 3:211 / 21ff. *Diatr.*, IIIa 6:49 / 24; 5:49 / 15ff.; 8:51 / 9ff. [LW 33:186. LCC 17:66ff., 66, 67.]

149. WA 18:718 / 15ff. BoA 3:213 / 35ff. [LW 33:189.]

150. See above, pp. 427–28.

turned more deeply and inclusively to biblical statements of faith. Even so, he permitted not the slightest doubt to remain that what he meant is the clear testimony to *ratio naturalis* [natural reason], saying, "Even Natural Reason herself, who is offended by this necessity and makes such efforts to get rid of it, is compelled to admit it by the force of her own judgment, even if there were no Scripture at all, for all men find these sentiments written on their hearts."[151] This is what reason has in common "with every other law which (according to Paul) is written in our hearts."[152] By analogy Luther extended the natural knowledge of creation (Rom. 1:18ff.) and the law of conscience (2:12ff.) to the omnipotent action of God in the history of the world and of individuals, providing the biblical testimony for that which reason knows but cannot contradict, no matter how much it may resist or take offense. The three elementary attributes of God—majesty, omnipotence, foreknowledge[153]—enabled Luther to draw conclusions that are no concession at all to the thinking of Erasmus; they are no mere defensive arguments but emerged from the core of his thought and experience. Their weightiness can be measured by the fact that Luther here added one of the strongest reminders of his struggle over predestination: "I myself was offended more than once, and brought to the very depth and abyss of despair, so that I wished I had never been created a man, before I realized how salutary despair was, and how near to grace."[154] Similarly, despite its resistance and the blindness of so many teachers over the centuries, reason can unquestionably lay hold of God's omnipotence and man's impotence.[155] Thus it can direct the would-be faithful to "God's truth and mercy," to the biblical pronouncements on "that active power by which God works all in all" and which he uses to carry out his promises.[156] The sense of these elemental pronouncements that Luther employed so powerfully is not only latent in them, but he also transcends them. Omnipotence aims to show that "salvation depends on the work of God alone"; foreknowledge aims at the "oversize light of se-

---

151. WA 18:719 / 20ff. *BoA* 3:214 / 41ff. [*LW* 33:190–91.] Again at the conclusion of this book Luther calls on the testimony of reason and the *natura magistra*. WA 18:784 / 21; 786 / 6. *BoA* 3:289 / 29; 291 / 27. [*LW* 33:290, 293.]

152. WA 18:719 / 33ff. *BoA* 3:215 / 14ff. [*LW* 33:191.]

153. Noted again in WA 18:719 / 22ff. *BoA* 3:215 / 1ff. [*LW* 33:191.]

154. WA 18:719 / 9ff. *BoA* 3:214 / 28ff. [*LW* 33:190.]

155. WA 18:722 / 15–14. *BoA* 3:218–45. [*LW* 33:195.]

156. WA 18:713 / 25ff.; 714 / 4ff.; 718 / 28ff. *BoA* 3:208 / 40ff.; 209 / 15ff.; 214 / 11ff. [*LW* 33:182, 183, 189.]

cure truth," at the insuperable and compelling sentence "God does not lie and is not deceived."[157]

Luther well knew that difficult problems and paradoxes slowed the way to these truths. Again and again he employs conceptual contrasts to make himself more readily understood. When he speaks of the will as unfree, he does not mean psychological compulsion but posits the necessity of a higher order that guides the will from above, no matter how spontaneously it may act. "What does it matter to me if free choice is not compelled but does what it does willingly? It is enough for me that you grant that it must necessarily do what it does willingly and that it cannot do anything else, if God has foreknown it."[158] It amounts to the same thing when Luther speaks of two sorts of necessity, "one of force with reference to the work, the other of infallibility with reference to the time." So, for example, it depends not on whether Judas willingly or unwillingly turned betrayer, but on whether it had to come to a betrayal at a time predetermined by God.[159] To this extent Luther can agree with Erasmus's sentence "Not all necessity excludes free will," for of course he means not "coercion of force" but "immutability" on God's part.[160] Certainly Luther has no intention of diagnosing man as psychologically without a will. What advantage would that be for the proclamation of the gospel? Instead, Luther desires to open man's eyes to the fact that his entire person, will and all, is bound, and to awaken him to faith in God's liberating power. Faith is a matter not of willing but of comprehending which sees through a person's own will—with its relentless striving against God—and awaits salvation from God's hand alone.

Irrefutable as are the elements of majesty, omnipotence, and omniscience in any meaningful concept of God, so also are they preliminary, when seen from the essence of faith. These elements suffice only to distinguish the Creator from his creation. "Cause and reason can be assigned for a creature's will, but not for the will of the Creator, unless you set up over him another creator."[161] Nothing could clarify more tellingly the absoluteness of the divine will than this sort of "retreat to infinity." These statements, which rational thinking cannot evade, form the coordinated

157. WA 18:634 / 16–17; 716 / 1, 9. BoA 3:125 / 16–17; 211 / 6–7, 16–17. [LW 33:64, 185.] Relates to Heb. 6:18.

158. WA 18:722 / 6ff. BoA 3:217 / 34ff. [LW 33:194.]

159. WA 18:720 / 35ff.; 722 / 9ff. BoA 3:216 / 22ff.; 217 / 37ff. [LW 33:193, 195.]

160. Diatr. IIIa 9:52 / 7–8. [LCC 17:68.] WA 18:720 / 28ff.; 747 / 21ff. BoA 3:216 / 14ff.; 245 / 31ff. [LW 33:192, 233.]

161. WA 18:712 / 37–38. BoA 3:208 / 7ff. [LW 33:181.]

system outside which there can be no talk about God or man. Nor can such statements be pruned from Luther's theology without damage to it as a whole. Yet they are not the last word about God. Taken by themselves, they would simply imply that the world is as nothing in God's sight. Actually they are like the law known to Jews and Gentiles which testifies that "the whole world is held accountable to God" (Rom. 3:19). Whatever faith has to say is entered on a new page, yet in the same history book of God's dealings with human beings and taken in the same sense. Just so little can it become a "new creature." Whatever holds about the sovereignty of God and the creatureliness of man, the same holds also for faith to express the power of grace.

Luther therefore opens the last part of his disputation against Erasmus with the "troops" of the New Testament, commanded by Paul and John.[162] The passages Luther sends into battle deal with salvation exclusively in Christ by grace (Rom. 3:21ff.; Rom. 4–7; John 1:16; 6:44, etc.) and with its necessary opposite: the exclusion of any kind of human cooperation and of every sort of personal righteousness (Rom. 1:16ff.; 3:9ff.; 8:3ff.; 10:20; John 1:5; 3:1ff.; 16:9, etc.).[163] At these points, in Luther's opinion, Paul hurls "veritable lightning bolts against free will."[164] Other passages (John 15:5; Rom. 7:14ff.; Gal. 5:16ff.) he likes to dub his "Achilles spears."[165] Luther derives the connection between absolute salvation and the absolute need of salvation from the results not of anthropology but of the gospel. But when the gospel is understood as the work of Christ, then in that moment Erasmus's anthropology is turned completely around.

In his contest against Luther, Erasmus employed the trichotomy common since antiquity and divided the human being into flesh, soul, and spirit. He called "spirit" the moral endeavor, or reason, or—with a stoic concept brought by Origen into Christian theology—the hegemonic or governing element in man. To be sure, he distinguished the human spirit from the divine Spirit, going so far as to say: "If anyone should wish to argue that the most excellent part of human nature is none other than flesh, that is, wicked desire, I would readily yield—if he proves his asser-

162. See above, p. 441. WA 18:756 / 24ff.; 757 / 9–10. BoA 3:256 / 10ff., 22ff. [LW 33:246–47.]

163. WA 18:768 / 10ff.; 771 / 34ff.; 772 / 36ff.; 777 / 21ff.; 781 / 29ff. BoA 3:269 / 37ff.; 274 / 5ff.; 275 / 17ff.; 281 / 6ff.; 286 / 13ff. [LW 33:264, 270, 272, 279, 284ff.] WA 18:757 / 10ff.; 760 / 17ff.; 763 / 5ff.; 774 / 19ff.; 775 / 19ff.; 776 / 7ff.; 778 / 17ff.; 782 / 12ff. BoA 3:256 / 24ff.; 260 / 16ff.; 263 / 24ff.; 277 / 10ff.; 278 / 22ff.; 279 / 19ff.; 282 / 9ff.; 287 / 1ff. [LW 33:247, 252, 256, 244, 276, 277, 280, 286.]

164. WA 18:767 / 25–26. BoA 3:269 / 4–5.

165. WA 18:748 / 10–11; 749 / 23; 783 / 3. BoA 3:246 / 25; 248 / 4; 287 / 40.

tion by the testimony of Holy Scripture!" John, however, put it differently: That which is born of the Spirit is spirit; and did he not call such people "children of God," yes, even "gods" (John 1:12; 10:34). Down almost to the counterproof Erasmus seemed bent on adhering to the authority of the fathers, "who say that there are certain seeds of virtue implanted in the minds of men by which they in some way seek after virtue, but mingled with grosser affections which incite them to other (opposite) things."[166] Luther's detailed response[167] found him reluctant to replace the classical anthropology with another one. In fact, he had often made unprejudiced use of it. Over a decade later, in his *Disputation Concerning Man* (1536), Luther still gave recognition to this trichotomy. There he calls reason (consciously avoiding the use of "spirit") "the highest in rank among all things and, in comparison with other things of this life, the best and something divine."[168] In any case, Luther contends that this threefold participating of the human being is only psychology, a description of the human composition. It provides no clue to the value of man in the sight of God. God sees man whole; sin cannot be localized. Therefore rebirth through the Holy Spirit is essential. Were it otherwise, then Christ would be "the redeemer not of the whole person but only of the least valuable part, the flesh," the instincts (or drives). Then Satan would be a weakling if it were this part only, and not the other parts also, that he could bring under his dominion.[169] Luther's line of argument thus proceeds from the question of salvation and not from the position of immanence. Yet this is exactly what Erasmus had intended, for his philosophical anthropology carried religious weight. Therefore he had insisted on bringing in counterproofs from Scripture (part two: passages that seem to oppose free choice), hoping thereby to disarm Luther and to show that, as he saw it,[170] Luther was right in refuting this as a misunderstanding: "One who has been born anew is no longer flesh except as regards the remnants of the flesh that was against the first fruits of the Spirit he has received."[171] Here the difference between Luther and Erasmus lay in their respective concepts of the spirit. Erasmus understood spirit as a given human compo-

---

166. *Diatr.*, IIIb 4:63 / 13–14; 64ff. [LCC 17:76–77.]

167. WA 18:739 / 23–745 / 19. BoA 3:236 / 35–243 / 16. [*LW* 33:220–29.]

168. WA 39¹:175 / 9–10. [*LW* 34:137.] Cf. H. Bornkamm, "Der Mensch," in *Luthers geistige Welt,* 4th ed. (Gütersloh, 1960), 84ff. On *De homine,* cf. G. Ebeling, Lutherstudien, vol. 2: *Disputatio de homine,* pt. 1 (Tübingen, 1977).—K.B.

169. WA 18:744 / 9ff., 17ff. BoA 3:241 / 39ff.; 242 / 8ff. [*LW* 33:227–28.]

170. *Diatr.* IIIb 4:64 / 10ff. [LCC 17:76.]

171. WA 18:745 / 5ff. BoA 3:242 / 39ff. [*LW* 33:229.]

nent, weakened, to be sure, by sin, yet not destroyed, and freshened by the divine Spirit. Luther, to the contrary, understood spirit as something new, a gift received from God by faith. In this central issue Erasmus was particularly vulnerable, inasmuch as this cleavage had for some time already penetrated the humanist ranks. So, for instance, the young Melanchthon, whom Erasmus had once hailed so hopefully, already in 1521 had completely incorporated Luther's concept of the "whole man" into his *Loci Communes*. To Melanchthon "flesh" was not simply a term denoting a part of the human being but also "a word for all the strivings of human nature"; likewise, he rigorously distinguished the Holy Spirit from all aspects of the human spirit. Erasmus, aware of what was happening, had also noticed these deviations from the axioms of humanism and, as Luther perceived, also attacked Melanchthon, without, however, mentioning his name. Directly or indirectly, it mattered not.[172] In any case, this is the point of deepest difference between Erasmus, on the one side, and Luther and his adherents, on the other. It was not simply a difference in perspectives, psychological or theological; it extended to the very foundation of man's relation to God.

According to Luther, history—we would say the history of religion—itself attests the fact that the Spirit begets the new, that Spirit is not evolution but an act of creation, and that grace is more than simply a stimulus and aid to our moral strivings. Luther challenged,

> Show me any one of the whole race of mortals, even if he is the holiest and most righteous of them all, to whom it has ever occurred that the way to righteousness and salvation is the way of faith in One who is both God and man, who for the sins of men both died and rose again and is seated at the right hand of the Father.[173]

Not to the Jews, striving so zealously to be righteous, but to the Gentiles "it has been given to hear and to know Christ, though previously they could not even think of him, much less seek him or prepare themselves for him by the power of free choice."[174] Although faith surely has many new and unprecedented things to say, Luther showed no hesitation in drawing

172. The passage in question, above p. 451, was "If anyone should wish to argue. . . ." *Diatr.* IIIb 4:64 / 1ff. [LCC 17:76.] Melanchthon, *Loci Communes* (1521), *MSA* 2 / 1:26 / 24–27 / 4. [LCC 19:38.] Luther WA 18:740 / 32ff. BoA 3:238 / 9ff. Later Erasmus did not publicly retract his little attack on Melanchthon, "And if so, what is dangerous about it?" *Hyperaspistes* II (1527), Opp. ed. *Clericus* X, 1458E. On Erasmus's critique of Melanchthon, cf. Maurer, "Melanchthons Anteil am Streit zwischen Luther und Erasmus," in Maurer's *Melanchthon-Studien* (see above, p. 268, n. 62), 137ff.

173. WA 18:758 / 37ff. BoA 3:258 / 24ff. [LW 33:250.]

174. WA 18:775 / 19ff. BoA 3:278 / 22ff. on Rom. 10:20; 9:30. [LW 33:276.]

on historical experience and "reason" to show that this is so. Everyone can see it for himself. Here he did not have in mind the question so often asked by humanists about the possible salvation of the heathen; Erasmus himself misunderstood that question, thinking that God might have given them credit for a general faith in deity.[175] Rather, Luther meant the historic fact that salvation came in a remarkable way precisely to those who had neither known nor done anything about it. This evident history, to be sure, corresponds with the hidden history of God known only to faith, that is, the history of the Old Testament prophets, who were misunderstood and often put to death. "For it is well known among Christians," Luther asserts, "that everything done by the prophets was done in the name of Christ who was to come, concerning whom it had been promised that he should be God incarnate. Hence whatever has been offered to men from the beginning of the world through the ministers of the word is rightly called the will of Christ."[176]

This image of man's faith and of the history of his redemption as determined in Christ alone is in a remarkable way supplied with insights—they appear repeatedly—by means of which Luther relates to the Word man's acquired rational thought about God and human history. At one moment he can depict God as "unattainable by human reason," and in the next he can exclaim, "Consult your own reason! Must she not be commanded and compelled to confess that she is foolish and rash in not allowing the judgment of God to be incomprehensible, when she admits that everything else divine is incomprehensible."[177] Luther is thereby not rationalizing faith. He is simply demanding that reason own up to what it already knows at its deepest: God is simply superior, the one for whom we prescribe no rules. This perception is not to be separated from trust in his gracious decision in Jesus Christ. Surely perception and trust together make a Christian. When Luther reaches the end of his book he can summarize the two in a universal sense under the concept of faith. Keeping his eye on the human condition, he built up his case:

> If we believe it to be true that God foreknows and predestines all things . . . , even reason would have to concede this . . . ; if we believe that Satan is the ruler of this world . . . ; if we believe that original sin has so ruined us that even in those who are led by the Spirit it causes a great deal of trouble . . . ; if the Jews, who pursued righteousness to the utmost of their powers, ran head-

175. *Hyperaspistes* II (1527), Erasmus, Opp. ed. *Clericus* X, 1488E. [See above, p. 431, n. 71, on the full text, Latin original and German translation, in EAS 4:197–675.]

176. WA 18:690 / 5ff. BoA 3:182 / 33ff. [*LW* 33:146.]

177. WA 18:784 / 12, 27ff. BoA 3:289 / 18, 37ff. [*LW* 33:290. Alternate.]

long into unrighteousness . . . ; if we believe that Christ has redeemed men by his blood, we are bound to confess that the whole man was lost.[178]

This drawing together of basic thoughts—natural, human, salvific, and christological—central to faith and aimed toward one goal, makes it possible to understand why Luther, with utmost emphasis, drew this conclusion:

> For my own part, I frankly confess that even if it were possible, I should not wish to have free choice (as defined) given to me . . ., since even if I lived and worked to eternity, my conscience would never be assured and certain. . . . But now, since God has taken my salvation out of my hands into his, making it depend on his choice and not mine . . ., I am assured and certain both that he is faithful and will not lie to me, and also that he is too great and powerful for any demons or any adversities to be able to break him or to snatch me from him.[179]

After a testimony like this—of which there are several toward the end of this book—we can also understand that not only was Luther pleading with Erasmus to allow himself to be taught by One better than he, but Luther was also showing him a most earnestly intended honor. "Unlike all the rest you alone have attacked the real issue . . . and have not wearied me with irrelevancies about the papacy, purgatory, indulgences, and such like trifles. . . . You and you alone have seen the question on which everything hinges and aimed the knife at the vital spot, for which I heartily thank you."[180]

Luther's thanks were forthright, and not less so than his anger—expressed at the outset and periodically repeated—over the fact that Erasmus had ventured to tackle a subject beyond his powers. He brought this out vividly by quoting Erasmus's concluding sentence, "I have completed my discourse; now let others pass judgment."[181] [Luther's mood was different as he concluded his book with this retort]:

> No one writes like that who has a thorough insight into the subject and rightly understands it. I for my part in this book *have not discoursed, but have asserted and do assert and do assert,* and I am willing to submit the matter to anyone's judgment, but advise everyone to yield assent. But may the Lord, whose cause this is, enlighten you and make you a vessel for honor and glory. Amen.[182]

178. *WA* 18:786 / 3ff. *BoA* 3:291 / 23ff. [*LW* 33:293.]
179. *WA* 18:783 / 17ff. *BoA* 3:288 / 16ff. [*LW* 33:288–89.]
180. *WA* 18:786 / 26ff. *BoA* 3:292 / 11ff. [*LW* 33:294.]
181. *Diatr.,* IV 17:92 / 8. [*LCC* 17:97.]
182. *WA* 18:787 / 10ff. *BoA* 3:293 / 3ff. [*LW* 33:295.]

Compared with these words of certitude, rising to a crescendo like those of an ancient prophet, Erasmus took it easier, and at the end of his less fortunate rejoinder, *Hyperaspistes* (1527), he commented that, unlike Luther, he expects neither a verdict nor obedience. Instead, "What has taken place between us I submit to the church and am prepared to correct anything that may have departed from the truth."[183]

This was something Luther could not do. For Luther the problem had been decided by Scripture, in agreement with the absolute and profoundly felt difference between Creator and creature. Alongside the clear testimony of the Bible, this felt difference is "itself a law." Paul had said as much when speaking of the Gentiles' hidden knowledge of God (Rom. 2:14; 1:19ff.). The elementary attributes of a broadly human representation of God (majesty, omnipotence, foreknowledge) which Luther employs constantly, and the complex of elements comprising salvation (grace, atonement, resurrection, faith), are not treated separately by Luther as though they were unassembled parts of a building. Rather, faith compels these "reasonable" insights to move in a new direction: toward Christ, who has come to rescue man, lost in his own unfree will. God—dwelling and hidden in terrifying mystery, and giving life to all the living, even to the evil ones—has disclosed himself in Christ. A person may, and indeed should, have faith in this Father of Jesus Christ also there where he cannot be comprehended. Now this gives the unalterable attributes of God a new meaning altogether. Majesty and love are a unity. "To say it with Luther, one must continuously allow these two concepts of God to permeate each other."[184] The same holds for God's omnipotence: This is the foundation of trust on which faith relies, that God has the power to deliver what he has promised in Christ. Likewise "foreknowledge"; this is the basis of God's truthfulness: his word cannot deceive. "Christian faith is entirely extinguished, the promises of God and the whole gospel are completely destroyed, if we teach and believe that it is not for us to know the necessary foreknowledge of God and the necessity of the things that are to come to pass."[185] This necessity to "integrate" is no arbitrary arithmetical exercise, for the concepts of reason are not discovered by man but implanted by God. They are expressions of God's "identity with himself."[186] Faith

183. Erasmus, Opp. ed. *Clericus* X, 1536F. EAS.

184. Kattenbusch, "Deus absconditus" (see n. 138, above), 207.

185. WA 18:619 / 16ff. *BoA* 3:111 / 8ff. [*LW* 33:43.] This is a continuation of the citation on p. 428, above, n. 55.

186. R. Hermann, "Luthers Theologie," in the author's *Gesammelte und nachgelassene Werke* (Göttingen, 1967), 1:147, n. 2.

therefore cannot dispense with these tools of reasoning. Indeed, whenever faith would really talk about God, it must embody them into itself. Faith thus embraces the wholeness of divine action: creation and redemption. This is God's way, ever giving breath to all life and placing himself in the midst of a lost world, giving new access to himself through the death and resurrection of Jesus Christ. Only at this point is God transparent to faith. However, in his providence worldwide he remains veiled, otherwise he would not be God. Now faith, according to Luther, lives with this tension, not only bearing it but also penetrating it, in hope alone. The decisive thing has already happened: The wall of separation—of guilt and estrangement—has been broken down. Yet perfection is still deferred, namely, the light of glory that will unveil the most puzzling of mysteries: why God crowns this unmeriting sinner and not that one. Then, ultimately, that which had seemed to us incomprehensibly unjust will appear in the light of day as most just. Luther does not make the slightest attempt to formulate a theodicy. [God's justice remains inscrutable]; we can only believe it. Not a stone can be pried out of the solid bridge between reason and eschatological certitude, for reason, created by God and set toward him, becomes guilty from its own knowledge, while the certitude oriented to the end confidently awaits the moment when incomprehensible mysteries will be resolved as we are given to see through God's own eyes. Luther has made it difficult enough for us to let the mysteries stand from here to eternity. Not for the sake of some seemingly higher quality of faith did Luther forego that which must be said alone by God about God, although this in itself would have comprised a comprehensible redemptive faith and an illuminating portrait of God.

It is not our task to undertake a critical examination of the views Luther set forth in his *De servo arbitrio*. His unheard-of passion, his critical daring in defending his theses, the abandon with which he strides along abysses of problems—all this leaves little doubt that this book drew ample criticism. Whether it struck him is indeed a quite different question. Here we have simply been at pains to sketch the ways traveled by this great debate. By means of at least a suggestive analysis of Luther's resources of thought, we have tried to recreate the mighty field of tension wherein his views unfolded some vivid sense of unity. Individual narrators and critics have brought their own manifold religious, theological, and philosophical presuppositions to the task, often despairing of it and more likely than not finding Luther's pronouncements like a bundle of truly splendid yet contradictory intentions. More relevant, however, is the fact that the consequences, far more often than the presuppositions and basic points of departure in the development of his thought, have attracted attention. Luther himself was far from developing an inclusive doctrine on questions of faith extending into the realm of the unthinkable. Instead, he opened up perspectives. To be sure, these were all of a type, containing stern truth and requiring a sure hand to keep them on course. Wherein, then, lay their unity? First of all, and formally, in the theme of the book; in the intention to demolish faith in free will. Luther not only confronts that faith with another, namely, a faith of biblical origin; he also does something else. He presents an insight: Free will [free choice] is a postulate, a fiction. Erasmus has overlooked, charges Luther, "that we ourselves are will and that we do not simply will this or that or do not will it." Erasmus, accordingly, forgets that what our human will lacks is "the freedom of a beginning."[187] This is the direction in which Luther aims his general as well as theological arguments. These come armed with the heaviest of weaponry, designated by the infelicitous term "doctrine of predestination" and even "double predestination." In Luther's usage, this is no independent doctrinal thought.[188] Nor is it simply the obverse side of a doctrine, because it is, instead, the mighty support of the actual and central pronouncement of faith: that God, in his sovereign freedom, elects. God does so without the slightest injection of human endeavor. And in electing, he offers his grace, so that we may believe it. Behind this offer stands God's complete power. He who is believing is saved. Believing is not willing but exalting; it is receiving in the purest sense and is therefore certitude.

187. Formulation of Hermann, "Luthers Theologie," 154–55.

188. Despite their differences two scholars here agree. M. Doerne, "Gottes Ehre am gebundenen Willen: Evangelische Grundlagen und theologische Spitzensätze in *De servo arbitrio*," in *LuJ* 20 (1938): 70ff., and Hermann, "Luthers Theologie," 166–67. Just as the double formula *deus absconditus* and *deus revelatus* appears at only one place in Luther's book (see n. 138, above), so also Hermann ("Luthers Theologie," 166, n. 17) finds but a single place where Luther speaks of a "double predestination," and not in a dogmatic (say, a Reformed) sense at any rate. Luther is bent on excluding every notion of merit, intending to apply this exclusion to his understanding of man as such. WA 18:725 / 2–3. BoA 3:221 / 7–8. [*LW* 33:199.]

17

Church Hymns and New
Worship Patterns

"We must be careful not to turn freedom into law."[1] This was Luther's
principle when he first began working on a renewal of traditional ways of
worship. He approached the task with utmost care, retaining Latin as the
liturgical language but introducing German for the proclamation of the
Word through the readings from Scripture and the sermon. He cautioned,
however, that a decision for the gospel [a basic change] was not to be
confused with a decision to introduce a new form of worship. He read
clear warnings in some earlier attempts at reform, notably the false em-
phases introduced by Karlstadt's changes in Wittenberg which forced the
people to commune in both kinds and to receive the bread in their hands.[2]
Luther therefore delayed introducing German as the exclusive language of
worship, although he had no objection to it in principle. He had said as
much already in 1520 when in *The Babylonian Captivity of the Church* he
drew a comparison: Given the elevation of the elements during the celebration of the mass as a communication through the eye, what equivalent
is there for the ear? "Why should it be permitted to celebrate mass in
Greek, Latin, and Hebrew and not also in German or some other language?"[3] Four years later he was more explicit: "I am happy the mass now
is held among the Germans in German. But for him (Karlstadt) to make a
necessity of this, as if it had to be so, is again too much." Luther was here
objecting to Karlstadt's claim: "It is a fact. The churches in our German
lands now have reading, preaching, and more besides—as Christ taught—
all of it in the German tongue. This is not only as it should be, but it is a
necessity as well."[4]

1. See above, p. 136. [Cf. *LW* 53:30.]
2. See above, pp. 51, 61.
3. WA 6:524 / 29ff. [*LW* 36:54.]
4. *Against the Heavenly Prophets* (1524), WA 18:123 / 5ff. [*LW* 40: 141.] The citation from
Karlstadt, *Wider die alte und neue papistische Messen* (1524) (Against the Old and New
Papistic Masses). Karlstadt here went beyond his own Wittenberg mass of 1521–22, which
had retained essentially the form of the Latin mass, simply omitting the canon. Only the
words of institution (according to linguistic usage in the narrower sense these alone could be
called "the mass") had been rendered into German by him. Cf. the report of Christian Beyer
of January 25, 1522, in N. Müller, *Die Wittenberger Bewegung, 1521 und 1522*, 2d ed.
(Leipzig, 1911), no. 75, p. 174.

The simplest and most natural means of promoting a fuller participation of the people, without altering the structure of the worship service, was to introduce congregational singing of hymns in German. As in preaching, Luther could here latch on to an older tradition. In his *Formula Missae* of 1523, he reminded the people of the laudable custom in the ancient church of complementing the celebration of the Lord's Supper with biblical and other texts. These additions included psalms, the Gloria, the Alleluia, the (Nicene) Creed as the confession of faith, the Sanctus, the Agnus Dei, and other items as well; initially these were only spoken, but later they were chanted.[5] He believed that some of these chants, now done by the choir, were sung by the entire congregation in ancient times. Thus he aimed to restore a custom that the church itself had destroyed. Yet at this point any solution would involve the question of language. He made his preference known: "I also wish we had as many songs as possible in German which the people could sing during mass, immediately after the gradual and also after the Sanctus and the Agnus Dei." Latin and German could be used on alternate weekdays or Sundays, "until the time comes when the whole mass is sung in the vernacular. But there are wanting among us, or not yet discovered, poets who could compose evangelical and spiritual songs, as Paul calls them (Col. 3:16), worthy to be used in the church of God." For the time being, certain medieval German Communion hymns (with omissions, of course) could be used, such as "Let God be blest, be praised, and thanked" or "Now let us pray the Holy Ghost" or also "A little Child so worthy praise." But the choice was limited, "for there are not many that catch an earnest style. I mention this to encourage any German poet to compose proper devotional hymns for us."[6]

This appeal was meant mainly for Luther's friends, but it included himself as well. A whole dimension of worship reform was in the making here, one with a good churchly tradition and one (unlike Karlstadt's demands concerning the Lord's Supper and the Bible) that would avoid being made

---

5. *WA* 12:206 / 15ff. [*LW* 53:20–21.]

6. *WA* 12:218 / 15ff. [*LW* 53:36–37] [These hymns, like many others by Luther himself, have appeared in various English translations (*LW* 53:173). "Let God be blest" (Gott sei gelobet und gebenediet) (*LW* 53:252–54) also appears as "May God be praised henceforth and blest forever," no. 18 in *Laudamus*, hymnal for the Lutheran World Federation, 4th ed. (1970). "Now let us pray the Holy Ghost" (Nun bitten wir den heilgen Geist) (*LW* 53:263–64) appears as "We now implore the Holy Ghost," no. 75 in *Laudamus*, and "To God the Holy Spirit let us pray," no. 317 in the *Lutheran Book of Worship* (Philadelphia: Board of Publication, Lutheran Church in America, 1978). M. K. Stulken, see also *Hymnal Companion* to the *Lutheran Book of Worship* (Philadelphia: Fortress Press, 1981), 373–74. "A little Child so worthy praise" (Ein Kindelein so löbelich) is not translated, but the German first line has here been given in English.]

an article of faith. Only recently Luther had discovered his own poetic gifts and put them to work. The burning of two fellow Augustinian monks, Henry Vos and John van den Eschen,[7] took place on July 1, 1523. They both had followed Luther's teaching and were burned at the stake in the marketplace in Brussels. Their deaths disturbed Luther profoundly and evoked from him two literary pieces. The one was a pamphlet in the manner of the times entitled *A Letter to the Christians in the Low Countries*. It went beyond being an impassioned protest against the murderous act of the Inquisition, for it also published the charges made against the men. Normally one would not have dared to flaunt custom and make the matter public. The "letter" was in part a hymn in prose:

> Praise and thanksgiving to the Father of all mercies, who at this time has again permitted us to behold his marvelous light, which until now has been hidden from us because of our sin, allowing us to be subject to the cruel powers of darkness, to err so blasphemously, and to serve the Antichrist. But now the time has returned when the voice of the turtle-dove is heard and the flowers bloom in our land (Song of Sol. 2:12).

Luther lauds the Netherlanders:

> For it has been given you before all the world not only to hear the gospel and to confess Christ but also to be the first who for Christ's sake now suffer shame and harm, fear and want, imprisonment and danger. And now, become strong and bearing fruit, you have affirmed and shed your own blood while among you two noble jewels of Christ, Henry and John, in Brussels cared little for their life in order that Christ and his Word might be praised.[8]

From this pamphlet, with its combination of praise and documentation (the questions asked by the prosecution), the poet in Luther[9] spontaneously burst forth:

> A new song here shall be begun—
> The Lord God help our singing!
> Of what our God himself hath done,
> Praise, honor to him bringing.
> At Brussels in the Netherlands
> By two boys, martyrs youthful,
> He showed the wonders of his hands,
> Whom he with favor truthful
> So richly had adorned.

7. This is the name given in a notice posted by the inquisitor present at the burning (*WA* 35:91, n. 4); Luther's version, Johannes Nesse; possibly Johannes von Essen (born in Essen) (*WA Br* 3:115 / 11; 116, n. 3).

8. *WA* 12:77 / 6ff.

9. *WA* 35:411ff. [*LW* 53:211–16.]

> The first right fitly John was named.
> So rich he in God's favor;[10]
> His brother, Henry—one unblamed,
> Whose salt lost not its savor . . .

With popular mockery the prosecution, the scholastics (sophists) of Louvain, are depicted:

> Oh! they sang sweet and they sang sour;
> Oh! they tried every double;
> The boys, they stood firm as a tower,
> And mocked the sophists' trouble.

There follows a detailed recital of the charges and the burning. In pondering this work, Johann Gottfried von Herder (1744–1803), schooled in the folk music of many lands, asked, "How many modern song writers (I say this not about content but style) could have composed stanzas like these?"[11] [Stanza 10 continues the tale:]

> Leave off their ashes never will;
> Into all lands they scatter;
> Stream,[12] hole, ditch, grave—
> nought keeps them still
> With shame the foe they spatter.
> Those whom in life with bloody hand
> He drove to silence triple,
> When dead, he them in every land,
> In tongues of every people,
> Must hear go gladly singing.

And when opponents slanderously claimed that in their last moments the two young men had recanted, Luther refuted this in the final stanza:

> Let them lie on for evermore—
> No refuge so is reared;[13]

10. Hebrew name: "God has been merciful."

11. J. G. von Herder, "Von deutscher Art und Kunst" (1773), *Sämtliche Werke*, ed. B. Suphan (Berlin, 1891), 5:202.

12. WA 35:415 / 3. This wording is in the later editions. The first printing, the "Erfurter Enchiridion" of 1524, begins the line with "Die." [The German text reads: "hie (Die) hilft kein Bach, Loch, Grub noch Grab."]

13. *Nutzen* (use). Cf. WA 35:92. [George MacDonald, the English translator, has paraphrased the German line: "Sie haben's kleinen Frommen." Taking this couplet as a whole: There's no use for liars to seek refuge behind the honest testimony of devout young lads.] [*LW* 53:409.]

462

> For us, we thank our God therefore,
> His word has reappeared.
> Even at the door is summer nigh,
> The winter now is ended,
> The tender flowers come out and spy;
> His hand when once extended
> Withdraws not till he's finished.

These dozen stanzas roll with epic breadth.[14] The sharply etched characters, the mingled shock and scorn, as well as the many angles of style unfold the model of the historic folk ballad. Luther not only had an ear for all this, but also must have surmised its effect.

Splendid though this first spontaneous poem of Luther's is, it hardly signified the kind of renewal in worship he had in mind. He was not equipped to face this larger task alone. After seeking the Wittenberger's advice, he turned directly to certain friends, doing so in line with the appeal he had included in the *Formula Missae* [his revamped Latin mass of 1523]. First he wrote to Spalatin, doing so at the end of 1523 and outlining what he had in mind: "(Our) plan is to follow the example of the prophets and the ancient fathers and to compose psalms for the people (in the) vernacular, that is, spiritual songs, so that the Word of God may be among the people also in their singing. Therefore we are searching everywhere for poets." Spalatin, a recognized master of the German language, was now being asked to help; indeed, a little earlier Luther had requested his aid in translating specific terms in the New Testament.[15] At the same time, he advised Spalatin characteristically,

> I would like you to avoid any new words or language used at court. In order to be understood by the people, only the simplest and the most common words should be used for singing; at the same time, however, the words should be pure and apt; further, the meaning should be clear and as close as possible to the psalm. You need a free hand here: maintain the meaning, but don't cling to the words; (rather), translate them with still other appropriate words. I myself do not have so great gifts that I can do what I would like to see done

14. There were but ten stanzas in the "Erfurter Enchiridion" of 1524 (see WA 35:338ff.). The *Wittenberger Sangbüchlein* of 1524 inserted two additional stanzas, now 9 and 10. Wilhelm Lucke (ibid., 93–94) surmises that in the Wittenberg edition Luther forgot to strike out the last two stanzas (11 and 12) or that he crossed them out so lightly that the printer failed to see it. This appears unlikely. Luther was enough of a poet to take some repetition in the bargain—"glaring contradiction" is putting it too strongly—as is shown in stanzas 9 and 11. Why should Luther have sacrificed the incomparable last stanza? It is indispensable if for no other reason than that the use of *wir* (we) ties the whole piece together.

15. Letter of March 30, 1522, WA Br 2:490 / 8ff. [*LW* 49:4.]

here. So I shall find out whether you are a Heman or an Asaph or a Jeduthun.[16]

The same request Luther made of the "richly gifted and highly cultured" electoral Saxon marshal Hans von Dolzig. Luther set forth proposals to him also: please, the seven penitential psalms—a copy of Luther's translation of them in the year 1517 is in Spalatin's possession— would Spalatin please adapt poetically the first (Psalm 6) or the seventh (Psalm 143), and Dolzig the second (Psalm 32). Luther himself had already done the sixth (Psalm 130) (De profundis, "Out of the depths"), and the fourth (Psalm 51) (Misereri mei, "God be merciful to me") is already assigned to someone else.[17] For Dolzig and Spalatin Luther included a sample sheet, either printed or handwritten.[18] Luther had no idea how soon these two friends would find time to oblige; at the moment both were in Nuremberg attending the imperial diet. Unhappily, they never obliged. Thus the first little hymnal, the so called *Acht liederbuch* (the Eight Hymn Book), though published in Nuremberg early in 1524 by the printer Jobst Gutknecht, contained only Wittenberg contributions. Four of the eight were by Luther: "Aus tiefer Not," "Ach, Gott, vom Himmel sieh darein," "Nun freut euch liebe Christen gmein," "Es spricht der Unweisen Mund" ("Out of the depths I cry to thee," "O Lord, look down from heaven," "Dear Christians, let us all rejoice," and "Although the mouth of fools doth say"). Paul Speratus (1484–1551), temporarily in Wittenberg, contributed three others: "Es ist das Heil uns kommen her" ("Salvation has drawn nigh to us"); "In Gott glaub ich" ("I believe in God"); "Hilf Gott, wie ist der Menschen Not" ("Oh help us Lord, our need is such"); while the author of the eighth ("In Jesu Namen")[19] remains unknown. As the title suggested, this little hymnal was to make Wittenberg a model. It offered several Christian songs, hymns of praise, and psalms, consonant with the Word of God and drawn from Holy Scripture

16. Heads of Levitical families of singers (2 Chron. 25, etc.) *Ego von habeo tantum gratiae . . .* , WA Br 3:220 / 1–13. [LW 49:69.]

17. WA Br 3:220 / 13ff. The numbering of the psalms is here given according to the Luther Bible. [LW 49:69.]

18. WA Br 3:220 / 7. [LW 49:69.]

19. WA 35:12ff. Besides the material in WA, see also the new and inclusive work, complete with sources, by G. Hahn, *Martin Luther, Die deutschen geistlichen Lieder, Neudruck deutscher Literaturwerke*, n.f. 20 (Tübingen, 1967). The debated question of meter in Luther's hymns is not treated here. See, therefore, the painstaking report by E. Sommer, "Die Metrik in Luthers Liedern," *JLH* 9 (1964): 29ff. [On these and other hymns by Luther, see LW 53. His four earliest hymns, 217–31, are in the MacDonald translation. Two of the four are in the *Lutheran Book of Worship*: "Out of the depths I cry to thee" (no. 295) and "Dear Christians, one and all rejoice" (no. 299).]

by a number of highly educated people, designed for singing in church in a manner already being done in Wittenberg. Although printed in Nuremberg and soon thereafter in Augsburg, this hymnal named Wittenberg 1524 as the place and year of publication.[20] Around the same time another Wittenberg hymn, "Fröhlich wollen wir Alleluja singen" (With joy let's sing our Alleluia), appeared, placed at the end of Speratus's German translation of Luther's *Formula Missae*.[21]

Also in the year 1524 the two Enchiridia collections raised the number of Luther's own hymns to eighteen, while new editions of the Wittenberg hymnal soon pushed his total to twenty-four.[22] It would be arbitrary to account for this springtime of song simply as a reaction to the hymns already inserted into the masses of Thomas Müntzer,[23] or even to interpret Luther's letter to Spalatin, quoted above, as a "battle plan."[24] The creation of hymns in the vernacular was far more a part of the reform of worship which Luther joyfully set in motion. The radical interventions into liturgical substance had caused him to hesitate. Now he was able to let the congregation itself respond by sharing in the proclamation of God's Word that had been moved into the center of worship.[25]

Meanwhile, however, the question of worship as such had in many places became an issue more immediate than the production of hymns.

20. Exact title and publication data in WA 35:336–37.

21. A second printing included also Luther's hymn "Es wollt uns Gott gnädig sein" (WA 12:202. Two copies of it bear the sales mark January 1524; WA 35:123). ["May God bestow on us his grace," no. 500 in *The Lutheran Hymnal* (St. Louis: Concordia, 1941)—or, in another, less used English version, "Would that the Lord would grant us grace"; LW 53:232–34.]

22. WA 35:5, 316.

23. See below, pp. 467ff.

24. W. Lucke in WA 35:75ff. wrongly claims (78) that when the All Saints Foundation was reformed in August 1523, Luther would have had "the best opportunity to stand up for the introduction of German hymns in worship." This was a case not of congregational worship but of the celebration of mass by the canons of the foundation. In that domain the power of decision lay with the cautious Elector Frederick the Wise, with whom Luther was then engaged in the far more important striving to reform the mass itself (cf. above, p. 51). The foundation did not receive an order of worship until the reign of Elector John; that order was drafted by Bugenhagen and Jonas on October 16, 1525 (E. Sehling, *Die evangelischen Kirchenordnungen des XVI. Jahrhunderts* [Leipzig, 1902ff.], 1:698ff.). Even there hymns in the vernacular play only a minor role, simply because the canons normally did not require them except in the case of special visitors (ibid., 698b, 699).

25. See above, p. 463, the citation from the letter to Spalatin. If Müntzer had been the issue, then Luther would not have kept the matter secret, for at that time he was engaged theologically and politically against Müntzer's activities in Allstedt. See I. Höss, *Georg Spalatin* (Weimar, 1956), 264ff. K. Burba, *Die Christologie in Luthers Liedern*, SVRG 175 (Gütersloh, 1956), has tried to show that Luther's attempts to ward off the "Enthusiasts" became the motivating force in his poetry. To be sure, Luther's hymns contain a Christology of features different from that of the Enthusiasts, yet neither specifically nor generally does this disclose a governing intention on Luther's part "to protect the congregation from the corrupting musical resources of the Enthusiasts" (ibid., 9; cf. 28–29, 30, 50, and elsewhere).

During the years 1523 to 1525 two types of congregational worship emerged.[26] One comprised the essentially cautious patterns of Luther's *Formula Missae;*[27] the other made the transition to a completely German form. The local situation in church and community usually determined which form it would be. So, for instance, in Nördlingen at a conspicuously early date (the year is 1522) the Carmelite cloister had introduced a mass entirely in German as prepared by Prior Kantz.[28] Meanwhile, Nördlingen's city church moved more slowly, introducing a revised Latin mass in 1525 and, following Luther, exercising caution toward the German on pedagogical grounds. Various principalities also shared Luther's reluctance. For example, there were the transitional arrangements in Count Schlick's town of Elbogen, where in 1523 the prescribed pattern was mass in Latin, sermon in German, and weekday and baptismal services in German.[29] Likewise, according to the constitution of July 6, 1525, of the duchy of Prussia, a good deal of Latin was retained in the mass, at least optionally, in ways Luther had in mind. This retention of Latin was out of consideration for many "non-Germans" (Wends, and others of Slavic birth) for whom a completely German service would have been even stranger than Latin.[30] In patrician Nuremberg changes in the worship were undertaken only in closest consultation with Luther. The city church [St. Lorenz] celebrated mass in Latin, using Luther's *Formula Missae* as a model.[31] But the city was large enough to provide for experimentation, allowing a German mass to be given a trial. The first venture by the Augustinian prior, Wolfgang Volprecht, during Holy Cross Week 1524 soon found acceptance. Thereafter the German mass became permanent in the forms introduced by Andreas Döber in 1525 in the local hospice.[32] The

26. J. Smend, *Die evangelischen deutschen Messen bis zu Luther's deutsche Messe* (Göttingen, 1896). L. Fendt, *Der lutherische Gottesdienst des 16. Jahrhunderts: Sein Werden und sein Wachsen* (Munich, 1923).

27. See above, pp. 135–36.

28. Sehling, *Kirchenordnungen*, 12:273ff., 285ff. Kantz's mass became the pattern for the 1524 "German Mass" in Worms, and via Worms it influenced a German mass in Strassburg that same year. Proof of this, plus valuable comments on this type of mass, is in P. Brunner, "Die Wormser Deutsche Messe," in *Kosmos und Ekklesia: Festschrift for W. Stählin* (Kassel, 1953), 106ff.

29. Fendt, *Lutherischer Gottesdienst*, 130ff.

30. See above, p. 329.

31. Sehling, *Kirchenordungen*, 11:46ff. Also H. von Schubert, "Die älteste evangelische Gottesdienstordnung in Nürnberg," *MGKK* 1 (1897): 276ff., 316ff., 349ff., 402ff. B. Klaus, "Die Nürnberger Deutsche Messe 1524," *JLH* 1 (1955): 8ff., 39ff. Smend, *Die evangelischen deutschen Messen*, 160ff. Fendt, *Lutherischer Gottesdienst*, 156ff.

32. Volprecht, Rogate to Ascension (at the time May 1–5), Klaus, "Nürnberger Deutsche Messe," 1ff., 36ff. Sehling, *Kirchenordnungen*, 11:18 / 39ff. Döber, ibid., 19–20, 51ff. Klaus, "Nürnberger Deutsche Messe," 40ff. Smend, *Die evangelischen deutschen Messen*, 162ff. Fendt, *Lutherischer Gottesdienst*, 160ff.

example of the Nuremberg parish churches was followed until 1524 in the not very distant Electoral Saxon city of Coburg.[33]

The first known congregational mass in German was that of Thomas Müntzer. Introduced at Easter 1523 in Allstedt, his mass appeared in print the following year. Müntzer surrounded himself with two other liturgical works published even earlier. One was the *Deutsches Kirchenamt* [German church office], which contained matins and vespers for the five major festivals of the church year. The other was his *Ordnung und Berechnung (Rechenschaft) des Deutschen Ampts zu Alstadt* [Regulation and account of the German (language) ministry in Allstedt], which explained and gave reasons for the composition of the mass.[34] The meaning of these books is evident from the title of the first of them. This "German Office of Ministry" prescribes raising the crafty lid under which the Light of the world was restrained but now shines forth once more with these songs of praise and divine psalms which are there edifying a growing Christendom according to God's unchangeable will for the destruction of all the pompous works of the godless. This statement reveals Müntzer's twofold intention: one, a removal of the liturgical form of the Roman mass and its foreign language, "because we in Allstedt are German people and not of Roman descent."[35] The other was a restoration of primitive worship. In radical, structural, and musical terms, Müntzer's mode of transition to the German makes him "of all Reformation liturgists the most conservative."[36] It turned out to be just the old mass dressed in a new language. Whatever challenge it directed to the Roman liturgy lay in the ornate printing of the two volumes and their makeup. Both volumes featured large musical notation and woodcut illustrations. In appearance Müntzer's product contrasted sharply with the modest masses of the South German reformers and of Luther.[37] Müntzer, of course, went beyond appearances, as he claimed that "with the sure counsel of the Holy Spirit I have translated the psalms more according to their sense than according to the words."[38] He disparaged the Latin as used in the mass ("where, like sor-

33. Sehling, *Kirchenordnungen*, 1:541ff. Fendt, *Lutherischer Gottesdienst*, 166ff.

34. *Thomas Müntzer, Schriften und Briefe: Kritische Gesamtausgabe*, ed. G. Franz, QFRG 33 (Gütersloh, 1968), 25ff. Fendt, *Lutherischer Gottesdienst*, 168ff. K. Schulz, "Thomas Müntzers liturgische Bestehungen," *ZKG* 47 (1928): 369ff. O. J. Mehl, "Thomas Müntzer als Liturgiker," *ThLZ* 76 (1951): 75ff. A painstaking comparison of Müntzer and Luther on this subject is in R. Hermann, "Thomas Müntzers 'Deutsch-evangelische Messe,'" *ZVKGS* 9 (1912): 57ff.

35. Müntzer, *Schriften*, 213 / 22–23.

36. E. Jammers, "Th. Müntzers deutsche evangelische Messen," *ARG* 31 (1934): 121.

37. Müntzer, *Schriften*, 207.

38. Ibid., 162 / 20–21.

cerers, they ascribe power to the words") and seasoned his own language with expressions characteristic of his spiritualistic mysticism, such as "refining," "elect," and "boredom."[39] In the process, Müntzer's translated text became estranged from the original.[40]

We cannot be sure that Luther knew about these texts of Müntzer.[41] At any rate, he had his opinion of the mystification of biblical language and had told Karlstadt, who likewise indulged in this exercise, so.[42] We likewise have a judgment of his that touched the core of the liturgical task. Luther wrote late in 1524:

> I would gladly have a German mass today. I am also occupied with it. But I would very much like it to have a true German character. To translate the Latin text and retain the Latin tone or notes has my sanction, though it doesn't sound polished or well done. Both the text and notes, accent, melody, and manner of rendering ought to grow out of the true mother tongue and its inflection, otherwise all of it becomes an imitation the way monkeys do it.[43]

Luther emphasizes that language and music are inseparable, therefore both must be "translated." Müntzer had boldly recast the words into his

39. "Elect" appears, e.g., constantly in the Te Deum, without any equivalent in the original text. Müntzer, *Schriften*, 111. *"Entgröben,"* ibid., 162 / 24. A drastic example is in W. Elliger, "Müntzers Übersetzung des 93. Psalms in 'Deutsch Kirchen Amt,' " in *So lange es heute heisst: Festschrift für R. Hermann* (Berlin, 1957), 56ff.

40. Müntzer's comments on the Sanctus are in this vein: A person "should and must know that God is in him, that he does not think about God as though He were a thousand miles away; rather, as heaven and earth are full of God and as the Father and the Son dwell in us constantly, so the Holy Spirit does nothing other than explain the Crucified to us [who listen] in contrite sorrow." Müntzer, *Schriften*, 210 / 32ff.

41. One would like to surmise this, but any direct reference to them is missing. In the Erfurt mass formulas, which Luther commended for adoption in 1525 (*WA* Br 3:591–92., October 28, 1525) and which were an almost unaltered reprinting of corresponding ones by Müntzer, Luther did not recognize the original model. This does not support the surmise that he was acquainted with Müntzer's liturgical works. He may have known about them from hearsay. Müntzer's own claim points in this direction: that Luther was driven by concern and envy over Müntzer's success in the environs of Allstedt to secure, though in vain, an electoral ban on the publication of Müntzer's *Office [Amt]*. "Hochverursachte Schutzrede" (1524), Müntzer, *Schriften*, 332 / 28ff. Cf. also the foreword, "Vorrede zur Deutsch-evangelischen Messe" (1525), ibid., 163 / 7ff. On Erfurt, see C. Martens, "Die Erfurter evangelische Messen 1525–1543," in *Mitteilungen des Vereins für deutsche Geschichts und Altertumskunde Erfurts*, 18 (1896): 91ff. On this, also Smend, *Die evangelischen deutschen Messen*, 118ff. Fendt, *Lutherischer Gottesdienst*, 168ff. Cf. also nn. 43, 53, below.

42. *Against the Heavenly Prophets* (1525), *WA* 18:101 / 8ff. [*WA* 40:118.]

43. *WA* 18:123 / 19ff. Luther is here spelling out a formative principle that poses certain problems in creating a mass in German (as he wrote Hausmann, November 17, 1524, *WA* Br 3:373 / 14–15 [*LW* 49:90]). He then goes on, in *Against the Heavenly Prophets*, saying, "Now since the enthusiast spirit presses that it must be so and will again burden the conscience with law, works, and sins, I will take my time and hurry less in this direction than before, only to spite the sin master and soul murderer, who presses works on us as if they were commanded by God, though they are not." [*LW* 40:141–42.] Had Luther here wished to attack Müntzer, he would have done so, because the polemic between them had long since become public and names were named, much as Luther mentions Karlstadt's name.

own theology, but he has taken over the music unchanged. Despite this difference, Müntzer and Luther were related in that both of them were authentic liturgiologists. Even though they worked by different methods and means, they intended that any renewal should retain the expressive elements of worship. Müntzer's masses, swiftly and vigorously developed as well as lucid though conflicting in principle, were a significant contribution. Yet they embodied no new conception such as would spring from the reformation movement itself. He could not extricate himself from the model and limitations of the Roman mass. As for Luther, the complexities of the task as well as the pressures from the Enthusiasts for a German service of worship, as if ordered by God, made Luther take his time instead of hurrying.[44]

What finally moved Luther to act was not Müntzer's head start[45] but developments in the general situation and proddings from a different direction. A second root of a purely vernacular worship service lay in Strassburg. On February 16, 1524, in the minster, an assistant, Theobald Schwarz, for the first time read mass in German.[46] None of the parts was sung. Basically this was purely a spoken Communion service. The sermon was at first reserved for a separate service preceding Communion. Later, with revisions during 1524–25, the sermon became part of the mass and tended to dominate it more and more.[47] At this stage the extensive experimentation in Strassburg soon became objectionable. Disturbed by the disunity of worship services in their city, and in others as well, the Strassburg ministers at last turned to Luther. Their long letter of November 23, 1524, expressed concern not only over public worship but also over a number of other matters, such as Karlstadt's writings on Holy Communion, infant baptism, and Erasmus's book on free will. With much candor they poured out their anxieties.[48] They wrote:

> For us it is no small offense to see that our disunity in worship is playing into the hands of the godless, giving them occasion to ridicule the teachings of Christ and to tear them apart. Although we have so far celebrated Holy Communion in the vernacular only twice, we have done it differently each time. . . . Our critics mock us, saying, "You celebrate the Lord's Supper dif-

44. WA 18:123 / 26ff.

45. This is an all too often repeated assertion by Smend, *Die evangelischen deutschen Messen*, 116.

46. Ibid., 123ff. F. Hubert, *Die Strassburger liturgischen Ordnungen im Zeitalter der Reformation* (Göttingen, 1900), esp. xviiiff. H. Waldmaier, *Die Entstehung der evangelischen Gottesdienstordnungen Suddeutschlands im Zeitalter der Reformation*, SVRG 125 / 6 (Leipzig, 1916), 64ff. Fendt, *Lutherischer Gottesdienst*, 138ff.

47. Waldmaier, *Evangelische Gottesdienstordnungen*, 67–68.

48. WA Br 3:381–87. [*LW* 49:94ff.]

ferently; differently from Nuremberg, differently from Nördlingen; we do it one way, our neighbors another." Understandably, many people see this as a sign of wavering and uncertainty.[49]

Imploringly they asked Luther's advice on this and other questions.[50]

We do not know whether Luther replied to his letter. In any case, he could hardly have written anything other than what he had said a little earlier (November 17, 1524) to Nicholas Hausmann in response to the same kind of plea: "I desire a German mass more than I can promise one. I am not qualified for this task, which requires both a talent in music and the gift of the Spirit. Meanwhile I charge each one to use his judgment until Christ gives us something different."[51] Hausmann's proposal to convene an evangelical council to settle ceremonial questions got a swift rejection from Luther.

If in these external matters one congregation does not voluntarily wish to follow another, why should it be compelled to do so by conciliar decrees, which are soon converted into laws and snares for souls? Of its own accord one congregation should therefore follow another, or else be allowed to enjoy its own customs; only the unity of the Spirit should be preserved in faith and in the Word, however great may be the diversity and variety with respect to the flesh and the elements of the word.[52]

But even though Luther now, and later too, clung to his principle of freedom in worship, the proliferation of inquiries as well as of experiments forced him to create a fully vernacular worship service for Wittenberg. Hausmann presented Luther with a bundle of masses to look over. The more he examined them, the more clearly he recognized their decisive failing: "I am absolutely not pleased to see Latin musical settings retained for German words."[53]

Amid all these attempts, the eyes of many continued to be on Wittenberg. In that connection and still in 1524, an expanded version of the

49. WA Br 3:384 / 108ff.
50. WA Br 3:387 / 225ff.
51. WA Br 3:373 / 13ff. Cf. Rom. 14:5. [LW 49:90.]
52. WA Br 3:375 / 23ff. [LW 49:91–92.]
53. March 26, 1525, WA Br 3:462 / 3ff. It is quite improbable that (as WA 19:47 and WA Br 3:463, nn. 2, 3 assume) Müntzer's Allstedt mass would have been in this bundle of masses. Hausmann, well acquainted with Müntzer's provocative activity in Zwickau, would hardly have included Müntzer's mass, with its abused texts (above, pp. 467–69), nor, even aside from the question of music, would he have considered that particular mass bearable (patior ita cantari; WA Br 3:462 / 2). Examples of German masses from the years 1524–25 are in WA 19:46ff. An individual solution was presented to Luther by Franz Kolb, pastor in Wertheim, in his letter of August 27, 1524, asking for Luther's corrections. WA Br 3:330 / 29ff.

German mass by Kantz (probably at the instigation of its users in Strassburg) was printed in Wittenberg and linked to Bugenhagen. In disgust, Bugenhagen vehemently denied having had anything to do with it. Certainly it was not put to use in Wittenberg. Like Luther, Bugenhagen declared: "It vexes me especially, and I find it pointedly evil, that they have made certain things a requirement which are not at all necessary." The Strassburgers apparently were giving no consideration to the weaker brethren, for "even before the gospel has been sufficiently preached they feel ready to act with full authority, even to the point of offending their brothers."[54] This again was testimony as to how freely the Wittenbergers were thinking. But this too had its limits. It really hit home when Luther received a report, in mid-June 1525, from the lay preacher, Melchior Hoffmann, detailing the controversies among the rapidly emerging congregations in Livonia [on the eastern Baltic]. This development emphatically confirmed the fears of the Strassburgers. Luther now was forced to recall the converse side of his concept of freedom as he had done earlier (1520) in his treatise on a Christian's freedom. Assisted by Bugenhagen and Hoffmann, Luther brought out a booklet for the Livonians under a similar title, *A Christian Exhortation to the Livonians Concerning Public Worship and Concord*.[55] The accent, when given by the standards of faith, no longer lay on the principle that the outward forms of worship are free. The accent fell on another constraint: "From the viewpoint of love you are not free to use this liberty, but bound to consider the edification of the common people." Therefore he can admonish them, "By faith be free in your own conscience toward God, but by love be bound to serve your neighbor's edification." He therefore added this convincing instruction: "Go to it, then. Hold mass, sing, and read uniformly, according to a common order—the same in one place as in another—because you see that the people want and need it and you wish to edify rather than confuse them."[56]

Only in the autumn of this memorable year, 1525—the year of the Peasants' War, his marriage, the change of electors, the work on *De servo arbitrio*—did Luther get around to his task, now sufficiently mellowed. Yet he still regarded that task as a burden alongside his other weighty

---

54. Appendix to *Ein Sendbrief widder den neuen Irrtumb bei dem Sakrament des Leibes and Bluts unseres Herrn Jesu Christi*, Wittenberg 1525. Reprinted in Smend, *Die evangelischen deutschen Messen*, 88, n. 2. About the Wittenberg printing of the Kantz mass, ibid., 39, n. 2, 72(B), 86ff., 152ff.

55. WA 18:415, 417ff. [LW 53:45–50.]

56. WA 18:419 / 77ff., 22ff.; 420 / 4ff. WA 19:47–48. [LW 53:47, 48.]

duties. Replying to the repeated importunings of his friend Hausmann, he wrote on September 27: "I am completely absorbed in refuting Erasmus. I know that the congregations must be reorganized and that unified forms of worship must be created, and I am already up to rolling aside this rock and will encourage the prince's help."[57] On October 11 the princely councillors, Hans von Dolzig and Hans von Gräfendorf, came to Luther empowered to negotiate "how singing and ceremonies should be conducted in the future in the Stiftkirche."[58] Luther sent a draft to Elector John and in return requested him to send his two choral directors, Konrad Rupff and Johann Walther, to Wittenberg to work out the musical setting of the mass. Three memorable weeks followed. Even forty years later Walther shared his vivid recollections of what it was like to work with Luther. He was astounded at how admirably Luther proposed and sang the notes to the intonations for the Epistles, Gospels, and words of institution. Luther, he asserted, had "composed most of the words and music of the German chants."

> How else account for the German Sanctus ("Isaiah in a vision did of old" [Jesaia dem Propheten das geschah]). There, as in other instances as well, he arranged all the notes to the text with the right accent and concent harmony in masterly fashion.[59] At that time I took the opportunity to ask His Reverence from whence he had these pieces and this knowledge, whereupon the dear man laughed at my simplicity. He told me, "The poet Virgil taught me this, for he is able so artistically to fit meter and words to the story which he narrates. All music should be so arranged that its notes are in harmony with the text."[60]

Surely it was not simply Luther's sharp observance of Virgil's coordinating of poetry and subject matter that made him such a good partner for the two music masters. Rather, the good fortune in this kind of partnership lay in the fact that Luther himself was not only a poet at heart but also musically highly gifted and well trained. Already during his schooldays in Mansfeld, Magdeburg, and Eisenach he had received thorough training in vocal music, the focus, quite naturally, being almost entirely on church

57. WA Br 3:582 / 5ff.

58. WA Br 3:588, n. 6. Citation from the detailed instruction of the elector on the secularization of All Saints Foundation. Friedensburg, *Urkundenbuch der Universität Wittenberg* (Magdeburg, 1926–27), 1:138ff. (140), sec. 3. [All Saints, the Castle Church, had been founded by Elector Frederick and was thus of territorial and not simply of local significance.]

59. ["Concent": a more melodious style of Gregorian chant. Paul Nettl, *Luther and Music* (Philadelphia: Fortress Press, 1948), 76, n. 7.]

60. Walther's reminiscences are printed in Michael Praetorius, *Syntagmatis Musici*, tomus primus (Wittenberg, 1614–15), 451ff. See also WA 19:49–50. [*LW* 53:55ff.]

music. The Erfurt cloister provided more of the same, with a strictly disciplined follow-through. Small mistakes in chanting had to be acknowledged at once by touching one hand to the floor and then striking the chest with the other. An important feature was that the Augustinians were oriented essentially to the Roman rite and not toward the liturgy of any particular order or diocese. Luther's favorites included early Gregorian traditions, and even late in life he sang the old sequences and hymns with his sons or friends.[61]

The order of worship set up for All Saints became the model for further developments in Wittenberg. On Sunday, October 22, 1525, the main service in the Town Church for the first time used the order of the German mass. George Rörer, deacon and faithful student of Luther's, was the liturgist. In the copy he made of Luther's sermon on that occasion, Rörer included an account of this noteworthy event: "Today, for the first time, I have sung a mass in German."[62] In his sermon, Luther again excused his delayed procedure, saying,

> You have often heard that no one should teach unless he knows it is God's Word. Likewise, one should not order or initiate something unless it pleases God. Nor should one tumble into something merely by strength of reason, because if it does not start on its own, then nothing will come of it. Therefore I too have put off until now with the German mass so as not to give the riotous spirits an excuse to jump in thoughtlessly, paying no heed to whether God would have it so. Yet now, since so many requests have come to me from many lands, in writing and in letters, and because the temporal authorities are likewise pushing me, I could not easily excuse or talk myself out of it, but must instead pay attention to this development and consider it to be the will of God.[63]

These words reveal once again Luther's understanding of the reformation process. The one thing commanded is to proclaim the Word of God. Everything else is legitimized by growing out of its proclamation. To this extent, at least, the many groping attempts to find new forms of worship and of congregational structure made sense when carried out unforced

---

61. Johann Walther also reported, among other things, that "the saintly man of God, Luther, . . . took great delight in the music of choral and counterpoint songs; with him I sang many a delightful hour and often saw how singing lifted this dear man's spirit, so much so that he really never tired of singing." Praetorius, *Syntagmatis Musici*, 451; cited by F. Gebhardt, "Die musikalischen Grundlagen zu Luthers Deutscher Messe," *LuJ* 10 (1928): 73. On Luther's education in music, ibid., 69ff. Also in O. Scheel, *Martin Luther: Vom Katholizismus zur Reformation*, 3d and 4th eds. (Tübingen, 1930), 1:40, 93–94, 256; 2:7 [*LW* 53:55, n. 7. Cf. Johann Walther's own report of the visit in Nettl, *Luther and Music*, 75–76.]

62. *WA* 17¹:444 "zu 12."

63. *WA* 17¹:459 / 18ff.

and, finally, also when done on the wish of the elector. These developments were like fruit from the seed of the Word, yet they were not the
seed itself. An advance training period was necessary lest the newly understood faith be thought to consist in new ways of worship only. An initial
period of freedom was thus necessary, so that the old and the new could
be used side by side. It is a well-established consensus that Luther was
the first in the proclamation of the Word and the last in the introduction of
a new service of worship. And this service he offered only as an example,
"for I do not propose that all Germany should uniformly follow our Wittenberg order." Even the Latin masses among the Romans were not identical in the cathedral chapters, cloisters, and congregations. Of course, it
would be gratifying if an entire principality, or a given city with its surrounding towns and villages, were to follow the same order.[64]

At Christmas 1525 the "German Mass" had its premiere in Wittenberg.
On New Year's Day 1526 that mass appeared in print in a larger published
version under the same title.[65] Unlike most masses in the vernacular, this
publication of the "German Mass" was not simply a liturgical agenda but
also an introduction into the subject of worship itself. Only then came the
liturgical formulation. This is a decisive difference. From the very start
this procedure placed the new image of divine worship in the context of an
inclusive nurture of the congregation and of the "young people" especially.[66] For their sakes, above all, the freedom of honoring God (here
emphatically given the first word) must be shaped into a recognizable
order. Urged from all sides for a vernacular order of worship, Luther thus
responded by giving an assignment not contained in other orders. He led
off: "First the German service requires a plain and simple, fair-and-square
catechism."[67] It all hinges on this one thing, that the children learn to
respond to questions like: What do you pray? (The Lord's Prayer) What do
you believe? (The Apostles' Creed), that they learn to grasp faith and love
as "the complete summary of Christian understanding," and that in these
two "little pouches" they keep the Bible verses "to repeat them at mealtime for the parents."[68] The worship of God, with the help of this memory
game, really begins at home. Besides, for the sake of educating the young
(boys especially), Luther is by no means ready to give up the Latin mass,
as adapted in the *Formula Missae*. Indeed, it if were possible and he had

64. WA 19:73 / 3ff. [*LW* 53:62.]
65. The date as given in WA 19:51 is in error. Cf. on this O. Clemen, *BoA* 3:294.
66. WA 19:73 / 17. [*LW* 53:62.]
67. WA 19:76 / 1ff. [*LW* 53:64.]
68. WA 19:77 / 23ff. [*LW* 53:66.]

the music, he would conduct mass not only in Latin and German but also in Greek and Hebrew. "I do not agree with those who cling to one language and despise all others."[69] As for the German service, spelled out in this book, Luther concludes, "It is best to plan the services in the interests of the young and for such of the unlearned as may happen to come."[70] For them one should conduct worship, not for those who want to see something or hear singing. As he was bent on expressing the meaning of all Christian action, Luther could hardly have made a stronger case than to place it in this inclusive pedagogical context. Whatever is thus undertaken in the context of home and school occurs also in the open "among the Turks or the heathen in a public square or out in a field"; "the gospel must be publicly preached (to such people) to move them to believe and become Christian."[71]

To prevent strikingly new forms from weakening the prime task of the mass, Luther made only the most necessary changes. Everything in the Roman mass that reminded of sacrifice, of the cult, of the saints, and of Mary was dropped; so was the silencing of the congregation in favor of the priest and the choir. The far greater participation of the congregation was outwardly the most noticeable change. In Müntzer's vernacular mass, the choir still changed the introit; now Luther has the people sing a psalm. Normally Psalm 34 was his pattern; sometimes a hymn would be substituted. Other pieces by the choir are also eliminated; between the Epistle lesson and the Gospel for the day, a hymn by the congregation replaced the gradual by the choir. A favorite of his became "To God the Holy Spirit let us pray" [Nun bitten wir den heiligen Geist]. The creed, following the Gospel, was replaced by Luther's hymned paraphrase "We all believe in one true God" [Wir glauben all an einen Gott]. In place of the Sanctus now came Luther's new hymn, "Isaiah in a vision did of old" [Jesaia dem Propheten das geschah]. The customary mass thus became an antiphony between the liturgist and the congregation. The bond between the two parties was strengthened in that the pastor faced the people for the reading of the lessons and oriented toward the altar only for the prayers. In fact, Luther wished to relocate the altar somewhat, as he explained: "In the true mass, however, of real Christians, the altar should not remain where it is, and the priest should always face the people as

69. WA 19:74 / 10–11. [LW 53:63.]
70. WA 19:112 / 2–3. [LW 53:89.]
71. WA 19:74 / 27ff. [LW 53:63.]

Christ doubtless did at the Last Supper. But let that await its own time."[72] The structural change, bearing on the character of the mass as proclamation and on the dialogue and common confessing and praising, emphasized the way liturgist and congregation belong together. This understanding penetrated more deeply than the outward forms Luther retained: vestments, candles, and (what Karlstadt had so vehemently opposed and Müntzer, to the contrary, retained[73]) the elevation of the elements in the Lord's Supper. Indeed, Luther found this act to be entirely consonant with the proclamation of the gospel:

> We have no intention of abolishing the elevation, but retain it because it goes well with the German Sanctus and signifies that Christ has commanded us to remember him. For just as the sacrament is bodily elevated, and yet Christ's body and blood are not seen in it, so he is also remembered and elevated by the word of the sermon and is confessed and adored in the reception of the sacrament. In each case he is apprehended by faith alone, for we cannot see how Christ gives his body and blood for us and even now daily shows and offers it before God to obtain grace for us.[74]

A transformation of the musical style followed inevitably Luther's recasting the Roman mass into the vernacular and his giving it a changed meaning.[75] Like so many others, Luther prized highly the "fine melodies and songs" of the Latin mass,[76] which he was eager to turn into musical language, the language of proclamation, prayer, and confessing. Because the congregation was to sing (chant) the texts, or was at least to understand them, he simplified the modes considerably; with later pieces he even returned to the musical key customary for the Introit. The Collect should be sung in unison, followed by the recitation of the Epistle in the same key. In contrast to the sustained unity of these components, he introduced lively new settings for the biblical pieces; some came in the Epistle, but still more came in the Gospel for the day. There he also made use of the then customary dramatic readings of the passion, differentiating the recitation tones of Christ, the evangelists, and others.[77] This same device

72. WA 19:80 / 28ff. [LW 53:69.] [The three hymns above, which paraphrased the Gradual, the Creed, and the Sanctus are in WA 19:263ff., 271ff., and 282ff. For their modern forms, see Lutheran Book of Worship, nos. 317, 374, 528.]

73. Ordnung und Berechnung (1523), Müntzer, Schriften, 212 / 21.

74. WA 19:99 / 17ff. [LW 53:82.]

75. On this, see the thorough inquiry of Gebhardt, "Die musikalischen Grundlagen zu Luthers Deutscher Messe."

76. WA 19:74 / 7. [LW 53:63.]

77. Gebhardt, "Die musikalischen Grundlagen zu Luthers Deutscher Messe," 148. Jammers, "Müntzers deutsche evangelische Messen," 128.

was especially effective in the words of institution, which Luther thus treated completely as a portion of the Gospel. He himself composed this setting, as Johann Walther later reminisced: "He wrote the notes over the text of the Epistles, the Gospels, and over the words of institution of the true body and blood of Christ. He sang them for me and wanted to hear my reaction."[78] Thus Luther's "German Mass" became lyrically as well as musically a powerful counterpart to the concord of congregational song and prayer, the whole of it governed by the manifold character of the divine Word.

As he had announced, the Latin mass was retained in Wittenberg along with the new German mass. "It shall not be affected in the form we have followed so far, but we shall continue to use it when or where we are pleased or prompted to do so."[79] A decade later it was still in use. Augsburg preacher Wolfgang Musculus, in Wittenberg in 1536 for the negotiations over the so-called Wittenberg Concord [between Lutherans and Reformed], attended the early service on [Sunday], May 28. Bucer preached. Having been oriented by Zwingli's view on worship, he noted—as he had done two weeks earlier in Eisenach—that every "papal" residue is still noticeable in the Wittenberg Town Church. Not only were the vestments for mass worn by the celebrating pastor, but there were also the Latin pieces chanted by the boys' choir or the priest (Introit, Confiteor, Kyrie, Gloria, Dominus vobiscum, Collect, Da pacem, Oratio de pace, Agnus Dei, Epistle, and Gospel). In addition there was the elevation of the elements for the Lord's Supper and the orientation toward the altar. The only German, aside from the sermon, were the words of institution and the Lord's Prayer, as chanted by the liturgist, as well as the prayer of thanksgiving and the Benediction. In German, the hymns sung by the congregation included "God the Father with us be," "In one true God we all believe," "Jesus Christ,"[80] and "Let God be blest" (all composed by Luther in 1524).[81] The solemnity of worship had been retained. In this case the service was conducted with young people who understood Latin in mind. The Sunday afternoon service (in German), on May 28, comple-

---

78. According to Praetorius, *Syntagmatis Musici,* cited in WA 19:50. Gebhardt, "Die musikalischen Grundlagen zu Luthers Deutscher Messe," 141ff., 147ff. [*LW* 53:55–56, 57, 58–60. Text in Nettl, *Luther and Music,* 75–76.]

79. WA 19:74 / 2–3. [*LW* 53:63.]

80. Very likely the Communion hymn "Jesus Christ our God and Savior / Turned away God's wrath for ever." [*LW* 53:249.]

81. [The hymns are in *LW* 53:268, 271, 252.]

mented that of the morning. Luther was the preacher, having recovered from a bout of dizziness which had forced him to leave the early service.[82]

As counterpoint to this archaic form and as companion to the "German Mass," Luther touched on a "third form of service which should be a truly evangelical order." He wrote, "Those who want to be Christians in earnest and who profess the gospel with hand and mouth should sign their names and meet alone in a house somewhere to pray, to read, to baptize, to receive the sacrament, and to do other Christian works." The advantages of this sort of nonpublic worship would be that those who do not lead Christian lives could be made known, reproved, corrected, or if necessary excommunicated according to the rule of Christ. Here, too, benevolent gifts could be solicited for the poor. This kind of service of worship would "be in no need of much and elaborate singing." Besides, "here one could set up a brief and neat order for baptism and the sacrament (Lord's Supper) and center everything on the Word, prayer, and love." Here too "one would need a good short catechism on the creed, the Ten Commandments, and the Our Father." Much as Luther warmed to his picture of an intimate house congregation and its celebration, he declined with equal determination to bring it to life, "for I have not yet the people for it, nor do I see many who press for it." However, "if I should be urged to do it and could not refuse with a good conscience, I would gladly . . . help as best I can." Until that time he is content to leave it to the two major forms—the Latin and German masses—to set the mode of worship. His main concern is a practical one. "If I should try to make it up out of my own need, it might turn into a sect, for we Germans are a rough, rude, and reckless people, with whom it is hard to do anything except in cases of dire need."[83] This shows Luther's caution even when expressing something close to his heart.

As with the introduction to the "German Mass" itself, Luther intended to take no premature step. It is the same feeling that things must be slowed down which marked his words against Karlstadt and Müntzer in their impatient overturning of parish life and congregational worship. These are the kind of people, in Luther's view, who begin church renewal

82. From the travel diary of Musculus, printed in T. Kolde, *Briefe und Aktenstücke zur Geschichte Luthers* (Gotha, 1883); Eisenach, 216ff.; Wittenberg, 218. Also Fendt, *Lutherischer Gottesdienst*, 192, 259–60. A. Boes, "Die reformatorischen Gottesdienste in der Wittenberger Pfarrkirche von 1523 an und die 'Ordnung der gesenge der Wittembergischen Kirchen' von 1543 / 44," *JLH* 4 (1958–59): 20.

83. WA 19:75 / 3–30. On the problematic side of the "special congregation" in Luther's thought, see M. Doerne, "Gottes Volk und Gottes Wort," *LuJ* 14 (1932): 89ff., and the references there to older studies on the subject. [*LW* 53:63–64.]

at the wrong end, from that of visible forms. His own "third form," unlike Müntzer's procedure, does not even consider the idea of a congregation of the elect. Luther's concern is only for the worship life of those "who earnestly would be Christian." He does not mean a second or real church in addition to the usual local congregation. The latter, according to Luther, will necessarily remain and be presupposed for the small groups. Instead of himself taking the initiative to form such house congregations, he would continue "to train the young and to call and attract others to faith, and—besides preaching—help to further such public service for the people, until Christians who earnestly love the Word find one another and join together."[84]

In sketching out his desires he is simply trying to encourage something to grow, a feeling no doubt shared by others too. And the grounds for his hesitation? These were not simply his worry over sectarianism—a case of "earnest" Christians regarding themselves as the elite or the only ones—but also his personal restraint in regarding himself as a real Christian. Near the beginning of his preface to the "German Mass" he put it this way: "We prepare such [worship] orders not for those who already are Christians, for they need none of them. We do not live (and work) for them. But these orders live for us who are not yet Christians so that they may make Christians out of us. Their aim is worship in the spirit."[85] Luther did not count himself among them, yet he was ready, whenever the impulse came, to help, which is one of the signs of how little he was inclined to bind others to himself. Not until the early stages of seventeenth-century German pietism, with its scattered attempts at church renewal—notably in the house meetings (collegia pietatis) stimulated by the writings of Philipp Jacob Spener—was Luther's idea translated into action. However, so far as can be determined today, Luther's "third form" of worship, as sketched in the preface to the "German Mass," played no direct part in the rise of the collegia. Actually, the much more evident decline of spiritual life in the established churches of that later period, as well as the widespread readiness of people to form societies for the most varied purposes, gave the decisive impulses.[86] In any case, the outcome of that seventeenth-century development added up to approximately the same gains and hazards that had prompted Luther to express the idea yet not to carry it out on his own.

84. WA 19:75 / 24ff. [LW 53:64.]

85. WA 19:73 / 10ff. [LW 53:62. Alternate.]

86. J. Wallmann, Philipp Jakob Spener und die Anfänge des Pietismus (Tübingen, 1970), 253ff.; see there (254, n. 2) also a reference to the dissertation of W. Bellardi, "Die Vorstufen der Collegia Pietatis" (theology diss., Breslau, 1931).

A derived benefit of Luther's "German Mass" was *The Order of Baptism Newly Revised*, which came out in that same year, 1526. As the title indicates, this was not simply the Roman baptismal ritual translated into German—Luther had done that already in 1523—but it was an alteration of the ritual itself, mainly through the removal of certain parts. In the earlier edition a desire "to spare the weak consciences" had kept Luther from making any marked changes, "lest they complain that I want to institute a new baptism and criticize those baptized in the past as though they had not been properly baptized."[87] This procedure, however, had earned him an earful of fault-finding from friends. He thus addressed himself chiefly to the symbolical acts (blowing, salt, saliva, oil) which the Roman baptismal form had added to the Word of God and the act of baptism.[88] Luther at first had retained them, although with some misgivings. But now he dropped them. The one thing he retained was the exorcism of the devil, yet without the customary long address to him.[89] For Luther such exorcism was a word of power uttered in the name of God, and he would not be denied the use of it.[90]

87. *WA* 12:48 / 17ff. [*LW* 53:103.]

88. Cf. *WA* 19:531, the collected reactions of Franz Kolb, pastor in Wertheim; the Strassburg pastors; and Nicholas Hausmann.

89. Cf. *WA* 12:44 / 8ff.; 45 / 11ff.; 47 / 21ff. *WA* 19:539 / 4ff. [*LW* 53:97, 99, 102.]

90. Luther once expressed the context of all this in an unusual way: "In no way do we deny that children must be baptized, nor do we claim that they receive baptism without faith. Rather, we have this to say about baptism, that children believe through the power of the Word—the Word through which they are exorcised—and through the faith of the church which brings them to be baptized, and through whose prayers which seek faith for them." *Adversus armatum virum Cokleum* (1523), *WA* 11:301 / 23ff.

18

Restructuring the Church

Luther's hesitation to introduce new ways of worship was prompted in part by an accompanying problem. Who was authorized to set in motion such a decisive change in church life? He did not feel so authorized. He had turned down the role of arbitrator which the Strassburgers had asked him to assume. Likewise he rejected Hausmann's idea of convening a council of reformation-minded churchmen to decide on matters of reform in worship.[1] So for the time being he confined himself to general and self-evident postulates: to abolish the sacrificial character of the mass, to avoid every kind of coercion, to spare the weak. Only an order from the elector gave him the decisive prod to introduce the new vernacular service in Wittenberg as a model that could be followed elsewhere.[2] Luther was not simply revealing a readiness to obey orders when he acknowledged the elector's authority in this field, for he rendered an exact accounting of what was happening. In a letter, Spalatin repeated the question Luther himself had raised, asking whether a territorial prince who abolishes certain forms of worship is not actually exceeding his temporal powers and exercising coercion in matters of faith. Luther replied: "Our princes do not exercise compulsion in matters of faith or of the gospel, but they combat external abomination. . . . After all, princes must prevent open crimes like perjury or notorious blasphemy, of whatever sort these might be. . . . We are here speaking of the public slander and blasphemy that insult God." Whatever is done in connection with abolishing the mass has its example in Christ's cleansing of the temple. In his day Christ himself punished temple violations with temporal means. In that situation, as Luther said later in a sermon on this text, Christ was acting "like Moses" in temporal governance.[3] In Luther's thought two trends converge, one from classical antiquity and one from his own time: (1) blasphemy against God is a public offense: it must be combated because, one must add, God

1. See above, p. 470.
2. See above, p. 473.
3. To Spalatin, November 11, 1525, WA Br 3:616 / 20–617 / 41. Sermon on the cleansing of the temple (1538), WA 46:726–37. Cf. H. Bornkamm, *Luthers Lehre von den zwei Reichen im Zusammenhang seiner Theologie*, 3d ed. (Gütersloh, 1969), 26.

will not allow the abuse of his name to go unpunished. The Roman mass, which has abolished the uniqueness [the once and for all character] of Christ's sacrifice and which continually reenacts the atonement, is itself blasphemy. Therefore, if the issue is properly understood the temporal rulers may, indeed must, abolish the [Roman] mass or alter it substantially, in order to ward off God's wrath from their lands. (2) Faith is free and is not to be coerced. Luther strongly opposed the hasty reforms of worship which Karlstadt and his friends had undertaken, simply because such rapid changes overtaxed the conscience of many.

Sooner or later Luther would have to act—but how to tell when the time was ripe for restructuring? He watched three successive signs for the moment when things would start of themselves:[4] (1) the complete or preponderant agreement of those who called for these questions, meaning the pastors of a given city or land, or beyond it; (2) the consent of the local congregation through its regular representative, the council; (3) the prince's affirmative participation, in the case of a territory, and his readiness to render practical help. The question whether the town councilmen, in this case, act in their capacity as civic officials or as representatives of the Christian congregation cannot be posed as alternatives. The councilmen comprised the community's only organ capable of acting in an unresolved situation. For years the magistrates had been assuming a growing number of ecclesiastical functions. So, for instance, in order to curb the system of granting church benefices, in which the Roman curia had become increasingly interested, the town councils had acquired the rights of patronage and clerical presentation and in that way had also won a limited right for the congregation to elect its own pastor. Other developments, likewise, had largely removed the boundary between things ecclesial and civil, so that a town council's duties came to include such matters as administering the numerous endowed masses for the dead or functioning as protector of the cloisters. Out of this had grown the councils' participation in cloister reform and property management, as well as the assumption of tasks formerly carried out by the cloisters themselves, including schools, relief of the poor, hospitals, and still other functions. The more duties the councils took over, the more rights they claimed, as well as income arising therefrom.[5] Prerequisite to these developments was the awareness of the town as a society set on a Christian foundation. This held not only for the

4. WA 17^1:459 / 21, cited above, p. 482.

5. A. Schulze, *Stadtgemeinde und Reformation*, RSGG 11 (Tübingen, 1918), 9ff. B. Moeller, *Reichsstadt und Reformation*, SVRG 69 (Gütersloh, 1962), 10ff. Both cite earlier sources and studies.

imperial cities (they had certain advantages) but also for towns within the territories, in which case town councilmen shared their rights with the territorial prince.

So it was nothing entirely new to turn to the town council for assistance in dealing with a live issue like that of devising a new church order. This had already been the case in Altenburg and Leisnig and became a precedent for other towns and cities.[6] The elector was not immediately drawn into the process. For the time being his best help was to assure the town councilmen of his protection while they exercised their rights.[7] In the long run, however, the princes sought to make church reform in their respective territories uniform. The radical slogans under which many a peasant mob had demanded an overturning of the ecclesiastical structures and conditions—the election of pastors by the local congregations, the abolition of church lands, the destruction of cloisters—made it necessary to draw up inclusive regulations. Given this situation, the territorial government naturally exercised the preponderant power as over against the towns on its lands. Territorial government alone was in a position to cope with the consequences of internal changes in the church situation. Academically, the territorial government alone could carry out the university reforms decisive for the church's future, whether through the calling of new professors or through changing the lecture catalog, such as offering biblical and humanistic lectures in place of the traditional scholastic ones or the struggle over canon law. The powers of the territorial ruler enabled him to create a changed ecclesial life, whether through his rights of patronage [appointment] or through churches directly under his governance, like All Saints [the Castle Church] in Wittenberg, which could serve as a model. Within the scope of his general right of oversight he could spur and sustain the town magistrates in matters of church renewal. He also had the duty as well as the right to combat crimes like blasphemy, which now included the Roman mass. A number of practical starting points thus already existed for a legitimate participation by the territorial government in the ordering of the church life even before the question was pondered thoroughly and undertaken on a large scale. Yet as the first examples in Altenburg and Leisnig had shown, the point of orientation was the local congregation. In this way the now advancing reforms differed from those in medieval times, for those had led to a territorial form of

6. See above, pp. 122ff.
7. K. Müller, *Kirche, Gemeinde, und Obrigkeit nach Luther* (Tübingen, 1910), 49ff.

church government in the first place.[8] The present efforts sprang from an older rivalry between the territorial ruler and the bishops and became acute in lands where the struggle was for tangible power: for influence over the cloisters, so important to the finances and culture of the land; for restricting the political rights of bishops, especially of their independent status in the empire; for participating in the filling of bishoprics and cathedral chapters; for the right to supervise the affairs of priests and monks; for limiting the jurisdiction of ecclesiastical courts; and so on. Rivalries like these had become largely a thing of the past and did not bear directly on the Reformation. The new congregations had taken themselves out of episcopal jurisdiction without benefit of legal sanction. And for that hybrid called "spiritual" territories, Luther had but one consistent solution: to turn them into temporal territories, the way Grand Master Albert of Prussia had done and the way Luther had advised Archbishop Albrecht of Mainz to do,[9] for these spiritual lords "are in truth temporal lords under an assumed name. Therefore one should make them temporal lords or distribute their possessions among the poor, [disinherited] heirs, friends, and the common chest."[10]

Unity and order within a given territory was the object. Movement toward this goal grew quite naturally out of the fact that regulations and rights had been developed in the local parish. The fluid as well as confused situation called for a next and more inclusive stage of church organization. A darker side was the personal appropriation of this new freedom. The earlier and unexpectedly violent confrontations between Luther's Wittenbergers and other new preachers (Karlstadt, Müntzer, Strauss) now turned the quest for unity and order into a matter of urgent necessity. The first to recognize this task was the young duke, John Frederick, the most active of Electoral Saxony's three princes and the one most loyally devoted

8. J. Hashagen, *Staat und Kirche vor der Reformation* (Essen, 1931). A. Werminghoff, *Verfassungsgeschichte der deutschen Kirche im Mittelalter*, 2d ed. (Leipzig, 1913), 87ff. On Saxony, R. Zieschang, "Die Anfänge eines landesherrlichen Kirchenregiments in Sachsen am Ausgange des Mittelalters," *BSKG* 23 (1909): 1ff. K. Pallas, "Die Entstehung des landesherrlichen Kirchenregiments in Kursachsen vor der Reformation," in *Neue Mitteilungen aus dem Gebiet historischer-antiquarischer Forschung* 24 (1910): 129ff. P. Kirn, *Friedrich der Weise und die Kirche* (Leipzig and Berlin, 1926). A. Loebeck, "Das Hochstift Meissen im Zeitalter der Reformation bis zum Tode Herzog Heinrichs 1541," *Mitteldeutsche Forschungen* 65 (1971): 20ff. For the succeeding epoch, K. Blaschke, "Wechselwirkungen zwischen der Reformation und dem Aufbau des Territorialstaates," *Der Staat* 9 (1970): 347ff.

9. See above, pp. 331ff., 406.

10. *Ordinance of a Common Chest* (1523), WA 12:14, 16ff. [*LW* 45:174.] On this see H.-W. Krumwiede, *Die Entstehung des landesherrlichen Kirchenregiments in Kursachsen und Braunschweig-Wolfenbüttel*, SKGNS 16 (Göttingen, 1967), 53ff.

to Luther. He it was who offered Luther a proposal for dealing with the disturbances:

> May God hear our complaint, but there are too many enthusiasts, and these are causing us plenty of trouble up here. But in my opinion there would be no better way of quieting things down than for you to take some time to travel from one town to another in this principality and to see for yourself (as Paul did)[11] what kinds of preachers are serving the faithful in the towns. I believe that among us here in Thuringia you could hardly do a more Christian task. Whichever preachers proved unsuited you could then remove with the help of the authorities.[12]

Luther had too high a regard for the function of visitation, as derived from the biblical office of bishop, to undertake such a thing alone and only under the authorization of his territorial prince. Already in his writing of 1523 to the Prague Senate, *De instituendis ministris ecclesiae* [How ministers of the church are to be installed], Luther had found the key for the making of an evangelical church. Yet he thought of this as being implied in the election of one or several from the circle of bishops who had themselves been elected by the congregations; that is, as a process arising from below—to which the council in Prague had given initial impulse but could not carry out on its own.[13] Although the electoral prince's one-time visitation was neither thought through nor workable, Luther did not immediately dismiss the idea.

Even an initial practical attempt had not turned out very convincingly. Around New Year 1525 in Altenstein castle, Duke John had assigned Jacob Strauss, the preacher in Eisenach [Thuringia], and ducal councilman Burkhard Hund of Wenkheim, to visit in the environs of Eisenach. After only a few days (probably between January 10 and 14), the ill-advised attempt was called off on orders from the duke; miserable wintry travel conditions were blamed. At least this first attempt provided experience. Unfortunately, Burkhard Hund had been prevented from going along. This left Jacob Strauss on his own, yet not alone. His energetic manner rubbed people the wrong way, so that the local nobility gave him a hard time.[14] Having enlisted Strauss for a second try, the duke, under the date

11. Acts 15:36.

12. June 24, 1524, WA Br 3:310 / 44ff.

13. See above, p. 126. WA 12:193 / 23–194 / 20.

14. Report by Strauss to Duke John, January 15, 1525, printed in R. Hermann, "Die Kirchevisitationen im Ernestinischen Thüringen vor 1528," *BThKG* 1 / 2 (1930): 167ff.; there too (170–71) the comments of Justus Menius (1532) and Georg Witzel (1534), who accompanied Strauss, on this visitation. On it, see J. Rogge, *Der Beitrag des Predigers Jakob Strauss zur frühen Reformationsgeschichte*, ThA 6 (Berlin, 1957), 86ff. Hermann (continuation in *BThKG* 3 [1933 / 35]: 1ff.), and supplementing it, R. Jauernig, "Die Einführung der Reformation in den preussischen Landen," ibid., 2 (1932 / 33): 68ff. These accounts provide a valuable survey of the sources and history of the visitations.

of March 17, 1525, provided his visitor with the necessary authorizations. These were addressed to a spectrum of officials, village headmen and preachers, informing them that Strauss had the duke's confidence and ordering them to render the visitor every needed assistance. In doing so, Duke John kept in mind the religious situation of the land. He wrote:

> While Almighty God has in these times let his divine Word and saving gospel shine forth again among men—so that by his godly grace that gospel is now being preached again in many places, being proclaimed and expounded to the people—it so happens[15] that a number of false preachers have slipped in among the sound ones; under guise of the divine Word they have introduced false doctrine and are inculcating it into the people.

This explains the religious motivation behind the intervention of the duke and the assignment he gave Strauss.[16] Not a word is set down here concerning the external, that is, churchly, situation. Luther could hardly be

15. Draft, printed in Hermann, "Kirchenvisitationen," 169. Undoubtedly we are to read *befunden* instead of *befreunden* (so Hermann, after him Krumwiede, "Die Entstehung des landesherrlichen Kirchenregiments," 79). Cf. *befinden* in the Instruction of 1527 (see n. 16, below).

16. Because of its importance in the prehistory of the church visitation, the [actual directive order of authorization]—not readily obtainable otherwise—is here appended to the piece already cited above: "As we acknowledge ourselves most highly obligated to honor Almighty God and to love our neighbor and foremost to foster well-being, peace, and unity among our subjects, and to pursue ways of advancing these aims as far as the grace of God permits, so we have engaged the honorable gentleman, our dear and devoted friend Dr. Jakob Strauss, preacher in Eisenach—one whom we regard suited as well as capable—and do hereby direct him, according to the Word of God, to visit our subjects, especially those in each place installed in the preaching office; so he is to visit, and upon inquiry, to make use of what he has learned and to gain insight—as is fitting and proper according to Holy Scripture; thereupon we desire from you and from all who are presently your subordinates that first you inform the preachers that Dr. Strauss is our authorized visitor in matters where he may apply the divine Word by warning or punishing, testing or reproving; hear him with good will and obediently, and follow his instruction, which he will base chiefly on the divine Word." (Hermann, "Kirchenvisitationen," 170.) Parts of the directive printed and examined, mainly under the viewpoint of the titles and authorization, also in Krumwiede, "Die Entstehung des landesherrlichen Kirchenregiments," 74ff. The "we" of the 1525 directive and the "we along with all our own" of the 1527 Visitation Instruction make it difficult to see any decisive difference between the two documents (ibid., 79). The scope of the sentences is different. In 1525 the princes emphasized their own legitimation of authority as higher [in church affairs] than that of those who resisted it, as Strauss reported. They are "most highly obligated" who now undertake the necessary measures to the glory of God (see above). In 1527 they [the princes] acknowledged themselves, "along with all our own," as obligated to praise God and to show themselves grateful for his grace. "Yet we learn from daily experience that some among us have not really taken this to heart or absorbed it into their minds." Therefore the rulers ordered the visitation (E. Sehling, *Die evangelischen Kirchenordnungen des XVI. Jahrhunderts* [Leipzig, 1902ff.], 1:142–43; continuation of the citation on p. 492, below). Their bond with "our own" the princes could well have expressed already in 1525, yet the targets of their directive at that time were the nobles and officials who resisted; in 1527 their target was the entire body of subjects with whom they, as princes, were bound by the same religious duty.

delighted that Strauss had been given such a weighty responsibility. Like Melanchthon, Luther had had his doubts about Strauss ever since the controversy over usury.[17] He bluntly told Spalatin, "I would wish that Dr. Strauss, who is looking around for a power base of his own, would be curbed by the princes. The man has no lack of enthusiasm, but he lacks a sense of place and time."[18]

A new visitation-oriented advance in the lands of Duke John was undertaken on May 2, 1525, by the energetic Nicholas Hausmann in Zwickau. The reason given was that since the bishops were not exercising their supervisory function "it was the duty of the duke, indeed of every territorial ruler, as foremost lord protector to ward off eternal destruction from the souls of his people." Let him screw up his courage and deal like the Roman emperor who, recognizing the importance of synods, convened them behind the backs of indolent popes. "Now Your Princely Grace sees that there is nothing more important than visitation." Countering the anticipated doubts of the duke, Luther pointed to the example of King Jehoshaphat, who sent out his ranking officials in order to instruct the people in the law of the Lord; or of Kasimir Margrave of Brandenburg-Ansbach, who convened his territorial diet to discuss the problem of "what is Christian and useful for maintaining both realms [the temporal and the spiritual] in a steady coexistence." Why, then, would he [the duke] not follow him, "inasmuch as the bright light of the divine Word has gone up like a morning star . . . in Your Princely Grace's town of Wittenberg as it once did over Bethlehem?" Besides, in Luther he had the best man for these tasks, and he surely would not fail.[19]

The exciting year 1525 at first sidetracked Hausmann's proposals, yet intensified the underlying anxieties. Although still fully occupied with his refutation of Erasmus, Luther finally presented them himself to the new Elector John. These, after all, were concrete matters that concerned a territorial ruler directly. Pending the anticipated gratifying outcome of university reform, Luther wrote the elector on October 31, 1525, reminding him that "there remain two matters that require the attention and

---

17. See above, p. 124.
18. To Spalatin, April 10, 1525, WA Br 3:470 / 12–13.
19. According to an oral account (autumn 1524) of a written report, May 2, 1525, which also describes the deficiencies of education in the schools. Printed in L. Preller, "Nicolaus Hausmann, der Reformator von Zwickau und Anhalt," *ZHTh* 22 (1852): 325ff. Excerpts in C. A. H. Burkhardt, *Geschichte der sächsischen Kirchen- und Schulvisitationen von 1524–1545* (Leipzig, 1879), 5ff. Also in Sehling, *Kirchenordnungen*, 1:34. The reference to Jehoshaphat is likely based on 2 Chron. 17:7ff. On the diet in Ansbach of September 1524, cf. Sehling, *Kirchenordnungen*, II:66.

action of Your Electoral Grace as the secular authority. The first is that everywhere the congregations are in very poor condition. No one contributes anything, no one pays for anything, endowments for mass[20] have been abolished." If the elector did not intervene, congregations [pastorates] and schools would soon be ruined. Yet there were enough monasteries, collegiate chapters, benefices, and endowments [whose income could be used for church support]. All the elector would have to do is issue an order that they be inspected, accounted for, and set in order. The second matter would be that the elector "should also have the [local] secular government inspected in order to find out how the city councils and all other district officials govern and deal with the commonweal."[21] Both matters derive from the territorial government's temporal guardianship of the law. Likewise, both matters are expressions of a Christian ruler's responsibility, founded naturally in the medieval ideal government. Luther indeed supported the elector's request for aid to the chaotic parishes by adding his own piece of pastoral admonition: may the elector permit himself to be used as God's instrument, also for the comforting of his own conscience, inasmuch as "it is God who asks and requires this action of you through the emergency situation itself."[22] Even so, this does not transform the elector's legitimation to act into a spiritual [ecclesial] action. His dealing remains temporal [secular], well within his range of responsibilities for the care of his subjects. At first, the elector was at a loss as to how he should respond to Luther's plea; though penetrating in appeal, it lacked concrete proposals concerning how this practical church problem could be tackled. Was the tone of the elector's reply on November 7 somewhat irritated? Luther himself would no doubt also see, wrote his territorial lord, that the destitute congregations and preachers could hardly be supported from the electoral treasury. The townspeople and rural dwellers would also have to do something for themselves in order to assure their spiritual care. So the elector asked Luther for suggestions. How to get something like this started? He assured Luther of his good will in the matter. To be sure, Luther's challenge to have the local "secular governments inspected" was in some respects already being done, although the effects of the peasant uprising and other duties had been hindering the elector from doing more.[23]

20. Endowments for masses for the dead.
21. WA Br 3:595 / 36ff., 56ff. [LW 49:135, 136.]
22. WA Br 3:595 / 48–49. [LW 49:135.]
23. WA Br 3:613–14. The elector had probably not misunderstood Luther's letter of October 31 (Krumwiede, "Die Entstehung des landesherrlichen Kirchenregiments," 65), but was raising the quite natural objection that he could not do it all himself—others too must help. Hence his request for more specific suggestions.

Luther was hereby pressured into developing his own ideas. Replying on November 30, he limited himself to questions of finance, which he naturally did not expect the electoral treasury to resolve. He wrote:

> Since Your Electoral Grace has graciously requested my judgment on how this matter should be handled, I submit my humble opinion: Your Electoral Grace should have all the congregations in the whole territory inspected. If one finds that the people wish to have evangelical preachers but the congregation's assets are not sufficient for their support, then Your Electoral Grace should command that his community provide a certain sum yearly, be it from the town hall or any other way, for if the people desire to have a pastor, it is Your Electoral Grace's duty to see to it that they also reward the laborer, as the gospel provides.[24]

For the purposes of this "inspection," Luther proposed that the elector divide his territory into four or five districts and send into each of them two men commissioned for the task, be they from the nobility or the district officialdom. Let them examine the economic situation of the congregations and order the payment from the annual taxes of whatever the preacher requires for his living. For this function one could also commission burghers from the town. In the process one should allow old or otherwise incapacitated preachers to receive their due, "for it would not be good to oust these men [from their offices] without any compensation, if they are not against the gospel." Others, who are [no longer] able to preach but who do not oppose the gospel, could at least be obliged, or permitted, to read the gospels along with the sermons in the postil. "Thus a true ministry of the gospel would be given to the people, whom the pastors ought to nourish."[25] This financial visitation thus touched on spiritual matters on two sides: that of the congregation thirsting for the gospel and that of the preachers and their further service. Regarding the latter, the congregational inspection would show whether or not to allow the present [older] preachers to continue in office or to employ them further in some limited service. From this viewpoint trial visitations on a small scale were conducted in the Borna and Tenneberg circuits. In these places at best only half the ministers qualified, while in most places the proportion was substantially fewer.[26] In the long run this kind of inspection would require visitors other than teams of nobles and officials. Above all—as Frederick Myconius (Mecum), pastor in Gotha and one of the visitors of

24. WA Br 3:628 / 5ff. Cf. Matt. 10:10, Luke 10:7. [LW 49:137–38.]

25. WA Br 3:628 / 14–29. [LW 49:138–39.]

26. Figures according to Krumwiede, "Die Entstehung des landesherrlichen Kirchenregiments," 67, based on Burkhardt, *Geschichte der sächsischen Kirchen- und Schulvisitationen,* 10–11, and Hermann, "Kirchenvisitationen," 183–84.

the Tenneberg circuit, pointed out—let no local official have the right to expel or install a pastor. This duty must be reserved for the ruler of the territory. Myconius also proposed that in the most important places "one pastor could be designated as supervisor, yet not as a superior lording it over the others, for they should all be equals, servants of one another, recognizing themselves as servants together." Besides, should he come on anything improper among the clergy, he would in a friendly way seek to set things aright; only in extreme cases would he report the matter to the authorities.[27] This was the impulse leading to the creation of the office of superintendent, with its dual function of visitation and pastoral care.

One year after his initial proposal of October 31, 1525, Luther presented a second proposal. Dated November 22, 1526, this one drew on the experiences of the first experiments and presented an expanded plan of visitation. His tone this time was more anxious and urgent. "First of all . . . the complaints of the pastors in nearly every place are beyond all bounds. . . . There is no more fear of God, or any discipline; since the pope's excommunication has been abolished, everyone does as he pleases." Luther's chief concern, therefore, was for the youth. "Where young people are neglected and remain untaught, the government is to blame and the land teems with wild and immoral people." With the ending of papal influence, the elector, "as supreme head," retained control of the monasteries and cathedral chapters in his hands. With such control now came "the duty and burden to put things in order." Luther therefore proposed that the number of visitors be doubled to four: two knowledgeable in questions of taxation and property, and two with good judgment in doctrine and people. The elector should order such congregations as are able to set up schools, preaching points, and congregations. As "supreme spokesman for the young and for all who require it," let the elector "hold them to it and make them do these things" just as people are made to participate in building the bridges and roads the country needs. The entire visitation was thus seen in light of the country's common good. "Nothing is now more important than to train the people who will come after us." This is the kind of service to God for which the monasteries were originally founded. Therefore it would be an injustice to tolerate a takeover of the monasteries by the nobles or simply to requisition them for the electoral treasury. Whatever is left over could be applied to the needs of the country and the welfare of the poor.[28] Luther hereby touched on the

27. According to his *Consilium*, which Myconius appended to the visitation report on the Tenneberg circuit. Sehling, *Kirchenordnungen*, 1:34–35.

28. *WA* Br 4:133 / 5–134 / 51.

elector's sense of duty. Four days later John gave his approval and asked Luther, with other professors, to nominate two visitors from among their own circle who would be good judges of doctrine as well as of people. The elector was now determined "to have our towns, hamlets, and villages visited—wherever necessity required." And he would not allow the venture to fail for lack of funds. [29] In the course of this correspondence Luther had explained broadly how he saw the elector's responsibility: He is protector against injustice and oppression as well as a father figure to the country's youth; he is executor of the wills of the country's founders as well as a Christian deputized by God for this office. Luther's estimate of the territorial ruler's function contains no specifically ecclesiastical function. In this broadly conceived framework the visitation gradually got under way.

At first the necessary preparations still had to be completed. The university responded at once to the elector's request and informed him already on December 6 that Jerome Schurff [professor of law] and Philipp Melanchthon were its elected nominees to serve on the visitation commission. That Melanchthon was preferred over the practical churchmen Bugenhagen, Jonas, and Pauli, all of whom had also received votes, is plausible not only because Luther recommended Master Philipp but also because of the nature of the assignment. For a visitation of local churches and schools, and for a representative of the university, not a better man could have been found. [30] On February 13, 1527, alongside the two Wittenberg professors, Elector John named his council members, Hans von der Planitz and Asmus von Haubitz, thus completing the four-man visitation team. Their "Instruction" was published on Trinity Sunday (June 16). In spirit and plan the Instruction is the fundamental document of the first comprehensive evangelical visitation. Introduced by a proclamation—like heralding it to an assembly of nobles, mayors, pastors, schoolmasters, and others—it was ready for presentation at one or more places, declaring: Almighty God has allowed his eternal and divine Word graciously to appear to the world "in these latter days." "Wherefore we, with all our people, are bound forever to laud and praise him with thanksgiving." Daily experience, however, shows "that among our people this is taken to heart but little, nor is there the disposition to do so." There are some who still do not make room for the gospel. Others, having accepted it, continue to

29. WA Br 4:137 / 16–17, 22–23.

30. This question is treated in Krumwiede, "Die Entstehung des landesherrlichen Kirchenregiments," 70, who brings the text of the university's statement, as deposited in the Weimar archives.

be ungrateful and unwilling to provide the necessary support for their preachers.[31] Arising out of this situation are the two main tasks of the visitors, which the Instruction spells out in detail: (1) The preachers must be examined as to whether they cling to the old "popishness," persist in errors of faith, are fit for office, and lead an acceptable style of life. (2) The preachers' necessary means of support must be found, whether from available chapter funds or, where these do not suffice, from a "considerable levy" on the parish members. Church income already requisitioned by the towns and villages should benefit the poor through the "common chest."[32] At the conclusion of numerous individual specifications, among them especially the installation of superintendents,[33] the visitors are empowered to deal directly where necessary and are required to present their report to the elector as soon as possible.[34] The field report, presented on August 13, 1527, is the indispensable companion piece to the Instruction and makes the latter too come alive, for the Instruction concerns not Romish but current deficiencies, notably "that almost everywhere only a part of the gospel is preached, the forgiveness of sins, and not also repentance, so that in their exercise of conscience people are worse and more indifferent than ever."[35] This is in Melanchthon's handwriting. For several years Melanchthon had given theological accent to the repentance with which the risen Lord had prefaced his preaching commission to the disciples (Luke 24:22), a repentance that is the fruit of the Holy Spirit.[36] Very likely the report itself stems from Melanchthon, including the penetrating admonition with which the visitors reminded the territorial ruler of his own responsibility.

> Wherefore our humble request is that Your Electoral Grace would favorably take to heart that it is a blessed and praiseworthy work to require intelligent and Christian preachers who shall honestly lead and direct the poor people to the way of salvation with their own teaching and good life—so that God's praise and man's salvation may be sought. . . . In this matter may Your Electoral Grace act favorably to the praise and honor of God and to the benefit of your neighbor, being ever filled with expectation in the rich promise of Christ our Lord.

31. Sehling, *Kirchenordnungen*, 1:35, 142ff. Cf. also citation to n. 16, above. [Text of the Instruction in English translation, M. Reu, *The Augsburg Confession* (Chicago, 1930), 3–23. Trans. by John C. Mattes. The Instruction (practical) differs from the Briefing (*Unterricht*) in theological matters.]

32. Sehling, *Kirchenordnungen*, 144ff.

33. Ibid., 146.

34. Ibid., 148.

35. *Suppl. Mel.* 6 / 1:369.

36. W. Maurer, *Der junge Melanchthon* (Göttingen, 1969), 2:491ff.

The candor with which also the two nobles, Planitz and Haubitz, signed[37] this appeal to the elector reveals impressively how they saw themselves acting in this matter not simply as officials but also as fellow Christians.[38]

Luther did not participate in the actual visitation, but the elector kept him informed and counted on his advice. Thus, on August 16, the elector sent him at once the report of the visitors as well as a larger treatment of the essential questions the visitation had raised. The only thing that has been preserved of the latter document is a list of thirty-five themes: questions of pastoral care and of doctrine, the pay of church and school personnel, the care of the poor, and an itemizing of public vices and crimes, down to the statement that "no one should imbibe new brew." The elector turned this catalog over to a central commission whose task it now was to develop a useful handbook on visitation. It first convened on September 25 and 26, 1527, in Torgau, in the presence of the visitors, as well as of Luther and Bugenhagen.[39] This business, however, had an unedifying side effect. On the basis of first impressions gained during the visitation from his conversation with parish pastors,[40] Melanchthon drew up a sequence of mainly theological articles that he regarded as particularly important in the warding off of erroneous inferences from Reformation teaching. They showed up in handwritten form among the papers the elector had forwarded to Luther for comment on August 16. The set of articles raised no objection from Luther, but it was different when Agricola, in Eisleben, read them. His friendship with Melanchthon was of

---

37. Schurff soon resigned his commission as visitor. Being a lawyer, he seems to have had little to do on this assignment. Besides, he was urgently required at the university, which had been relocated temporarily to Jena because of an outbreak of plague. W. Friedensburg, *Geschichte der Universität Wittenberg* (Magdeburg, 1926), 1:177–78.

38. The report, which Krumwiede in his analysis of the Instruction did not use ("Kirchenregiments," 71ff.), makes it clearer than other signs that in the entirely normal chancellery style of such regulations the visitation set in motion did not grow out of the concept of bureaucratic action. Krumwiede's finding, "that the elector, who with his subjects stands in the solidarity of service under the divine Word, yet in the same breath appears as the government over against his fellow Christians" (83), is valid according to the understanding of the visitors and also vice versa. In any case, it is a good idea not to overload this state of affairs with theological terms like "general priesthood" or to speak of the church as "an assembly at the end of time" (80, 90–91). There is too little basis for this in the sources.

39. *Suppl. Mel.* 6 / 1:388–89. *CR* 1:922 *(Suppl. Mel.* 6 / 1:404–5).

40. Especially important were the impressions received during the visitation in Weida. This is evident from the findings, which were set down in thirty-two articles. Sehling, *Kirchenordnungen*, 1:148–49. Excerpts from the documents assembled by Hermann, "Kirchenvisitationen," 18ff. (continuation). On this, also W. H. Neuser, *Die Abendmahlslehre Melanchthons in ihrer geschichtlichen Entwicklung (1519–1530)*, BGLRK 26 (Neukirchen-Vlynn, 1968), 267–68. Maurer, *Der junge Melanchthon*, 2:476–77. Both works cite earlier literature.

long standing but had cooled after his only half-voluntary departure from Wittenberg.[41] Melanchthon's shock over the "uneducated Lutherans"[42] he had found among the preachers made him state bluntly at the beginning of his articles:

> The parish pastors should follow Christ's example, for as Christ, in the last chapter of Luke (24:47), taught repentance and forgiveness of sin, so too the pastors must pass these [facts of life] on to the congregations. Today it is customary to speak only of faith, yet one cannot comprehend what faith is if repentance is not preached beforehand. They are pouring new wine into old wineskins if they preach faith without repentance, without teaching the fear of God or the law. Thereby they mislead the people into fleshly security. Such security is worse than all former errors under the pope.[43]

With this pedagogical bias Melanchthon had exposed his flank to attacks on his understanding of Reformation theology. Agricola immediately fired a salvo at Melanchthon's articles. This polemic exchange has not been preserved, although copies of it were soon in many hands, including those of the ever well-informed and rival court of Duke George.[44]

Luther found the controversy disagreeable. He asked Agricola to hold off until Melanchthon's return to Wittenberg, until the planned publication of the concluding "Instruction of the Visitation Commissioners" [or Briefing] and until the findings of the visitation could be discussed. It would be a pity if the work of visitation should be handicapped by premature debate.[45] Melanchthon remained calm and wrote also to Agricola, reminding him of their former friendship. He expressed no disagreement with Agricola's opinion that repentance stems from a love of righteousness, but again raised only a pedagogical question: Who (practically) understands that? Therefore one must first speak of the terrified conscience, which is something God calls forth, not man.[46] For the moment, Luther had put the controversy aside as a battle of words. Fear of punishment [attrition] and fear of God [contrition] can be distinguished in thought and

41. J. Rogge, *Johann Agricolas Lutherverständnis*, ThA 14 (East Berlin, 1960), 55ff., 98ff. On Agricola, see above, pp. 280ff.

42. To Caspar Aquila in Saalfeld, mid-November 1527. *CR* 4:960.

43. Articuli, de quibus egerunt visitatores in religione Saxoniae (not per visitatores, cf. K. Müller, *Kirche, Gemeinde, und Obrigkeit* [Tübingen, 1910], 63, n. 1). *CR* 26:9–10. [Cf. M. Reu, *The Augsburg Confession* (Chicago, 1930), 3ff., "Instruction of the Visitation Commissions" (1528).]

44. Cf. Melanchthon to Jonas, December 20, 1527. *CR* 1:915. *MSA* 7 / 2:38ff. *MBW* 634. Jonas to Luther, January 3, 1528, *WA Br* 4:323 / 44ff.

45. *WA Br* 4:241 / 24ff.

46. Ca. November 1527. *CR* 1:904ff. *Suppl. Mel.* 6 / 1:399. *MSA* 7 / 2:35ff. (end of October). *MBW* 615.

word, yet not in reality or experience. God will stand by his own, so that with the punishment they will also come to fear him. Teaching about the fear of God, then, is like teaching about the freedom of the spirit, about how the latter can lead to fleshly security while the former can lead to anxiety and despair. "Who would oppose something like this?" Luther thereby raised the controversy from the level of psychological inquiry as to priority—the level on which the two were disputing—to the climate of faith: "God will stand by his own."[47]

The tedious feud also reached the elector's ears. On September 26 and 27, Luther and Bugenhagen met with the visitors in Torgau and brought the consultation on the Articles of Visitation (the Briefing) to a conclusion. But already on September 30 the elector sent Luther a clean copy of the text as agreed upon at Torgau, requesting that he and Bugenhagen review it once more. The elector expressed anxiety over having heard that the papists were "frolicking" over the fact that the [Briefing] dealt with themes common among them, namely, the themes of repentance [penitence], confession, and so on. The elector advised that the articles therefore be supplied with explanations that made the proper differentiations. It was important at the outset to refute this vexatious twaddle.[48] Luther's reply to the elector was calm; he and Bugenhagen had altered little in the visitation order. They were satisfied because everyone could understand it. "If the annoyed opponents would like to cheer, as though we were crawling back, this is hardly worth playing up. Things will probably quiet down. Whoever would venture something godly must be ready to let the devil open his big mouth, heckling and lying against the venture, just as I have had to do until now."[49] The main thing these articles should prevent is that—as unfortunately has already happened—someone wants to prescribe what the parish pastors are to preach. One cannot regulate everything at once; just sow the seed and later remove the weeds. "For there is a great difference between these two things: setting up an order and maintaining an order. Ecclesiastes[50] teaches that one must do as much as one can and not give up on letting something else go whither it will and committing it all to God, for this is how things also happen in the temporal realm."[51] At a second conference in Torgau, November 26–29,

47. Luther to Melanchthon, October 27, 1527, WA Br 4:272 / 13ff. *MBW* 617.
48. WA Br 4:254–55.
49. October 12, 1527, WA Br 4:265 / 1ff.
50. Eccles. 11:6.
51. WA Br 4:265 / 17ff.

1527,[52] the controversy, which had already attracted wide attention, was put down with a firm hand by Luther. He permitted no reproaches against Melanchthon, even as he himself did not take sides against Agricola.

Luther now hoped that the visitation instruction, or Briefing, would soon appear in print.[53] However, the scrupulous elector turned to him again with still more requests and questions. Writing on January 3, 1528,[54] he asked Luther to supply the Briefing with a foreword. At the same time he reported objections against two sections originally not part of the Articles of Visitation but added by Luther himself: The first section was "On the sacrament of the Body and Blood of the Lord," in which Luther emphatically recommended a preaching of the doctrine of the real presence of Christ and of the reception of Communion in both kinds, yet not to demand this of preachers who may still have doubts on the subject. The people have for too long been held captive in Roman usage. "For this reason one must also leave the day its twelve hours and entrust matters to God's keeping." Luther's basic principle remained: "It is indeed unfriendly, even unchristian, to force such weak ones to commune in both kinds or to withhold it in one kind, for then they are made to sin, namely, when they receive it in both kinds against their conscience." This was once again Luther's protest against the legalism of Karlstadt and his adherents.[55] The elector would rather have left these considerations to the oral instruction of pastors during the visitation,[56] undoubtedly because he was not eager to see an already resolved problem needlessly revived to feed the triumphalism of the papists.

The second section concerned marital status. As a subject of visitation inquiry, marital status raised even greater misgivings in the elector's mind. Several entries by Spalatin on the subjects of divorce and the impediments of marriage among relatives and in-laws had been approved for inclusion in the visitation order. The elector was afraid that contradictions already existing between canon and imperial law would evoke resistance from the privileged estates and cause problems of inheritance for the chil-

52. Luther traveled back on November 30. G. Buchwald, "*Lutherana*, Notzen aus Rechnungsbüchern des Thüringischen Staatsarchivs zu Weimar," ARG 25 (1928): 85, n. 57; on Luther's travels, ibid., 5.

53. To Jonas, December 10, 1527, WA Br 4:295 / 25–26. To Hausmann, December 14 and 31, 1527, WA Br 4:300 / 19–20; 312 / 5.

54. WA Br 4:326–27. [LW 49:182.]

55. WA Br 4:330 / 27ff.; 328 / 25ff. I am quoting not from the initially printed individual drafts of Luther but from the scarcely altered form in which it was subsequently included in the "Instruction of the Visitation Commissioners," WA 26:214 / 10ff.; 215 / 18ff.

56. WA Br 4:326 / 19ff.

dren involved.[57] In this case Luther conceded the elector's point. Nevertheless, Spalatin's memorandum made many points that Luther could readily approve of;[58] significant too was his treatment of the important question of parental consent to the marriage of daughters, a passage quoting Luther directly[59] from an opinion of his written some time earlier. Luther left these matters to the elector's good judgment, because he was "the regular temporal authority and because marital matters are in part temporal and thus come under temporal law."[60] Thereupon the short section "On Marital Matters," which had been kept entirely pastoral in tone, was omitted from Spalatin's still-long list[61] for the "Instruction of the Visitation Commissioners." By contrast, and in a choice very significant for him, the elector retained the explication on the exercise of consideration for the weak.[62]

At last, in March 1528, when the Instruction was out, it was evident how much it had changed since the time of Melanchthon's Articles of Visitation of the previous August. The reworking of the contents and the two consultations in Torgau had not only increased its scope but also improved its quality. While Melanchthon, as one of the visitation commissioners, very likely had acted in a secretarial capacity, the contributions of the several participants cannot be determined exactly. Luther's contributions probably included the articles on repentance, confession, satisfaction, and consideration of the weak, items responding to the elector's questions.[63] The clever reformulation of the passages in Melanchthon's articles attacked by Agricola also come from Luther, who alone could have mediated in this matter. Nothing was taken away from Melanchthon's intention, but some of his more aggressive one-sidedness was toned down, bridging the controversy with a solomonic formula professing a "common faith" in God's Being, Command, and Judgment, better stated under the terms repentance, commandment, and law. Likewise, a "justifying faith" may be stated more specifically as "faith in Christ," who alone "makes us righteous and destroys sin, . . . which faith in commandments and repen-

---

57. *WA Br* 4:326 / 27ff.

58. *WA Br* 4:332ff.

59. *WA Br* 4:334 / 75–335 / 101 = *WA Br* 4:153 / 11–26.

60. *WA Br* 4:332 / 35ff.

61. *WA* 26:225 / 10–30.

62. It was already among the articles of Melanchthon's for the visitation in Weida (cf. n. 40, above; Sehling, *Kirchenordnungen*, 1:148), couched in blunt terms, in his Visitation Articles of August 1527 (CR 26:19); a brief basis was included, now with Luther's extended pastoral justification.

63. *WA* 26:217–22 / 214ff.

tance does not do."[64] One can see that both sides could feel their concerns understood and substantiated.

Luther's most significant contribution to the Instruction, or Briefing, was in any case the foreword Elector John had requested him to write. In it he gave meaning and reason for the task of visitation, recognizing that it had already begun and was now being carried forward on a broader basis. Such an exercise had distant antecedents. The prophets Samuel, Elijah, and Elisha journeyed among the faithful, "not for the sake of walking around" but for the sake of their preaching ministry. Likewise Christ and the apostles did the same. The bishops of the ancient church, as their name, *episcopos*, indicates, began as "supervisors or visitors," although later on bishops became temporal lords. The ancient organ of visitation, the "holy synod" that met variously across the land and was "such a noble and precious instrument," has long since been corrupted into a court, hearing financial cases and meting out punishment, while also degenerating into a court on matters of ritual. "Yet how one teaches, believes, loves, how one lives as a Christian, how one cares for the poor, comforts the weak, punishes the intractable, and whatever else belongs to such an office, has never been given attention."[65] These are the original and enduring themes of the visitation. What else was there to do, after the failure of the bishops, but to hold fast to the common ministry of love, that is, to hold to the elector, who himself is placed in this ministry and who alone is in a position to appoint visitors such as those of long ago. Luther circumscribed the electoral legitimation precisely: "That His Electoral Grace, in Christian love (to which temporal governance is not obligated) and for God's sake, would graciously appoint and support several capable people who would benefit the gospel and be of use and blessing to the wretched Christians in Your Electoral Grace's lands."[66] A second motivation joins the first: Should the visitors meet willful resistance, the elector's help must again be requested, "for even though it is not His Electoral Grace's task to teach and to govern in spiritual matters, he is nevertheless responsible, as temporal governor, for seeing to it that among his subjects neither dissension nor gangs nor insurrections occur." For such reasons the Emperor Constantine called the Council of Nicaea [A.D. 325], in order to

64. *WA* 202 / 32ff. Cf. Melanchthon's report to Jonas, December 20, 1527, on the Torgau consultation. *CR* 1:915–14. *MSA* 7 / 2:38ff. *MBW* 634. J. Rogge, *Johann Agricolas Lutherverständnis*, ThA 14 (East Berlin, 1960), 116–17. In the reformulation, moreover, Melanchthon's term "faith" is replaced by "forgiveness of sins." Cf. *CR* 29:9–10 with *WA* 26:202 / 8ff.

65. *WA* 26:196 / 21ff.

66. *WA* 26:197 / 25ff.

get rid of the dissension Arius had caused among the Christians of the empire and to hold fast to a "concord of doctrine and faith."[67] Luther thus distinguished between the ministry of love and the duty of governance. The one helps to revive the church's ancient task of visitation; the other helps to fend off opposition and disturbances that could plunge the land into discord. The two functions combine in the person of the elector, yet each does so in its own way. The service of love is personally rooted, as shown by the elector's membership in the Christian congregation, which hinders conflict within his land under his governing office. The "Instruction of the Visitation Commissioners" (the Briefing) is limited to spiritual themes, which here include also marriage questions and schools, but in the main it contains many doctrinal statements of a sort that recur later in the confessional documents [notably in the Augsburg Confession]. The Instruction treats none of the practical problems which, as we have seen, had already been regulated in the electoral order of June 16, 1527, such as an examination of church property, the payment of preachers, the levying of taxes for church maintenance, the care of the poor, and so on. It was not necessary to review all these matters, since the (1527) Instruction remained in force. That Instruction and the now completed Briefing thus comprise a unity and provide a common base to be taken into account by future visitations. In them secular officials would continue to participate as members of visitation teams.[68]

The letters Luther began writing in 1525 had indeed initiated the visitation and resulted in the Instruction and the Briefing, but they were not aimed at setting up a new church government. Before that could be done, whether under ecclesial or benevolent political auspices, there remained the task of ascertaining the facts and then, step by step, of introducing preliminary regulations designed to cover the most important matters and to prevent the easy return of dissension. In his foreword Luther declared expressly that the Briefing is not to set up a new system of church law or, as he put it, "a new kind of papal decretal." Rather, let the Briefing [and all its application implies] be understood as "a story of the present situation and a history, useful for what is to follow and helpful as a testimony or confession of our faith."[69] "Story" [*Historie*] means a legitimation of what is here undertaken in terms of the historical context known since Old

67. WA 26:200 / 28ff.

68. Survey of the multiplied temporal and ecclesial visitors for the entire Electoral Saxony since 1528, in Burkhardt, *Kirchen- und Schulvisitationen* (see n. 19, above), 28–29.

69. WA 26:200 / 10ff.

Testament times.[70] The future lies open, and the Visitation will usher it in afresh. It is Luther's hope that "all devout and peace-loving parish pastors," concerned as they must be for the gospel, will "offer their diligence to our sovereign and most gracious lord, so that they do not ungratefully and arrogantly despise our love and good intention, but willingly—without duress and motivated by love—submit to such a visitation and together with us live with it peacefully until God the Holy Spirit begin something better through them or us."[71] How things could look better, Luther does not say. It is possible that in line with his earlier proposals to the Bohemians he had in mind the election of ecclesial heads through the congregations and the parish pastors, yet hardly without cooperating with the territorial sovereign.[72] In any event, all this was still part of a future that Luther had not yet fully contemplated. The Visitation itself, he was confident, would give shape to basic assumptions.[73] To be sure, Luther's own disposition to persist in dealing with the needs of the hour made the way toward a more thorough restructuring of the church situation more difficult.

70. This is not identical with the "narration" the elector requested of Luther in his letter of January 3, 1528 (WA Br 4:326 / 9), and which Luther supplies for the prehistory of the Visitation in his backward glance. WA 26:197 / 12ff.

71. WA 26:197 / 12ff.

72. See above, p. 128.

73. Some of the difficulties in the lively discussion over the visitation's basic documents (a detailed survey of the research history is in Krumwiede, *Kirchenregiment* [see n. 10, above], 13ff.) arise from the fact that the preparatory character of the visitation has been viewed in various ways. With the Instruction of 1527, only that was undertaken which Luther defined more closely in his foreword to its companion piece, the Briefing of 1528, and which he sought to guard against being misunderstood. A contradiction between these two parts does not exist, according to Krumwiede (ibid., 109), yet it does exist according to Karl Holl ("Luther und das landesherrliche Kirchenregiment," in *Gesammelte Aufsätze zur Kirchengeschichte*, vol. 1: *Luther* [Tübingen, 1921], 373). Furthermore, the fact that Luther did not regard the visitors as adequate for the office of bishop (ibid., 108) cannot be described as "the decisive break in Luther's train of thought." Indeed, he derived the visitation as such from the episcopal office in the ancient church, and at times he even joked with his friends among the visitors, calling them "bishops" and "archbishops" (ibid., 376); yet at that time an episcopal office in the historic sense was not yet in sight.

19

Controversy over the Lord's Supper

Of the theological controversies engaging Luther during the mid-1520s, only one proved explosive in the life of the Reformation churches: the confrontation with Karlstadt on the issue of the Lord's Supper. As for Müntzer, his theological effect was consumed by agitation during the Peasants' War and, with his death, it ended early. Similarly, the Anabaptist movement reached Luther only later and was perceptibly weaker. By contrast, the expulsion of Karlstadt from Electoral Saxony brought him to the attention of other Reformation lands, especially in South Germany and Switzerland. His writings were widely circulated and gained him a number of adherents, some of whom were more noteworthy than he himself. Mingling elements of Bohemian and humanistic criticism of the Roman mass as traditionally conceived, the ideas of Karlstadt developed until they caused a profound breach in the Reformation movement. As a result Luther was put on the defensive, being accused that, at decisive points, he still represented the old faith and was denying the actually spiritual sense of the Lord's Supper. This charge requires us to look back to his early Reformation writings on the subject.

Luther's occupation with sacramental thought as a theme and with the several sacraments began with his German sermons in the year 1519. In his early lectures the sacrament of the altar played hardly any part, indicating that as yet no essential difference separated him from his church. On the question of Christ's real presence in the Supper, Luther neither then nor later differentiated himself in principle, but only in mode and result. Though he rejected transubstantiation as a mode, he appropriated the forgiveness of sin through faith alone as a result. Texts treated in his lectures gave him little occasion to deal expressly with questions on the sacraments; from his early teaching years there remain lecture notes but few sermons. It is significant that the analogy of Lord's Supper and covenant or testament, of a testator and his heirs—a thought so important to him later—first appears there where passages in Galatians and Hebrews bring up the subject.[1] Hebrews 9 impressed him above all, with its reveal-

---

1. On Gal. 3:15 and 17, WA 57, Gal. 24–25 (1515–16); on Heb. 7:22, 8:6, 10:9, 14–18, WA 57, Heb. 41, 193 / 44–45, 50–51, 207–13 (1517–18). [LW 26: (1535) 296ff., 299ff., LW 29:208–15 (9:14–18), etc.]

ing illustration of the blood of the covenant and the concept of a testament that cleanses the conscience. This caused Luther ever after to affirm the connection between the testamental words of Jesus (Matt. 26:28; Luke 22:10) and the forgiveness of sins. "It follows from this that the good, clean, composed, and joyful conscience is nothing other than faith in the forgiveness of sins; it can be founded only on the Word of God, which proclaims that the blood of Christ is shed for the forgiveness of sins."[2] And the result? "In the New Testament covenant it is not the sacrament but faith in the sacrament that justifies."[3]

In 1517–18 Luther's literary efforts also began to touch on a publicly oriented pastoral care. Before that time lectures had accounted for nearly all his writings. Now, amid the mounting excitement over the indulgence traffic, repentance became the theme. At first his engagement in the controversy was mainly at the academic level, with not much play on popular concerns. Only after the initial turmoil had somewhat subsided did he proceed in 1519 to present a planned sequence of sermons. These he preached before the town congregation, noting the prayer forms and life-styles of the church. In the process, he treated the sacraments of penance, baptism, and the Lord's Supper. Down-to-earth in character, these teaching sermons filled a felt need among the people. Soon they appeared in pamphlet form and were widely distributed.[4] These sermons, moreover, [like a trilogy] possessed a distinctive unity. At the suggestion of friends, Luther dedicated the printed version to the benevolent Duchess Margaret, widow of the duke of Braunschweig-Lüneburg. Like his other writings of this nature, these were shaped by experience in the field of pastoral concern. It moved him deeply to discover "that so many sad and anxious consciences show up—and I experience it myself—who neither recognize nor know how to make use of this holy sacrament so full of grace." People keep searching for reassurance by means of works instead of seeking peace through the sacrament of God's grace.[5] Likewise, the two Communion sermons of 1519 and 1520, part of this group, are neither doctrinal nor pedagogical but aim at a specific purpose. The *Sermon on the Blessed Sacrament of the Holy True Body of Christ, and of the Brotherhoods* unfolds the meaning of the mass, seeing it and the sacrament it conveys as a celebration of fellowship. Here is great comfort for the sinner and the tempted: With Christ and the other faithful he is "one loaf, one

2. WA 57:208 / 22ff.; cf. 1ff. [*LW* 29:210.]

3. WA 57:206 / 4–5. [*LW* 29:207.]

4. For these sermons see the reprint lists in J. Benzing, *Lutherbibliographie* (Baden-Baden, 1966).

5. *Sermon on the Sacrament of Penance* (1519), WA 2:713 / 20ff.

bread, one body, one drink, and it is all in common. Oh, that's a great sacrament *(mysterium)*, says Paul, that Christ and his church are one flesh and one body."[6]

When Luther in this way takes a person distressed by "a sin-stricken conscience" or terrified by death or by some burden on his heart, and when he seeks help "from the entire company of the spiritual body" in the celebration of the sacrament, he finds this an embracing comfort, a fellowship with Christ and all believing saints amid every sort of temptation, be it because of guilt, death, or misfortune.[7] The real presence of Christ's body and blood is here not the theme, for Luther can still at this stage confidently presuppose it in his readers. The theme—corresponding to the purpose of the sermon—is the proper use of this sacrament, that is, the renewal that Christ's sacrifice of love and the loving fellowship of the faithful should accomplish in each individual heart.[8] Up to that time all value was ascribed to believing and honoring Christ's bodily presence; only little thought was given to why Christ offered his life in the first place. "Therefore take heed. It is more needful that you discern the spiritual than the natural body of Christ; and faith in the spiritual body is more necessary than faith in the natural body. For the natural without the spiritual profits us nothing in this sacrament; a change must occur [in the communicant]—and be exercised through love."[9]

Luther nurtured this thought within the framework of the New Testament concept of the Lord's Supper, on the living fellowship with the Lord who is present and with his congregation. While the eschatological keynote is here not as dominant as it was in the primitive Christian melody, it is not absent. The sacrament thus has no merely symbolical significance, summoning the congregation to follow the Crucified One and to continue to practice the love of Christ. Rather, the real gift of love's fellowship roots in the presence of the crucified and risen Lord, offered and received in the elements. This gift, then, imparts the comfort of the forgiveness of sins,[10] a decisive accent that rings out as soon as Luther, in his second

6. WA 2:748 / 18ff. Cf. Eph. 5:32. [LW 35:58.]

7. *Sermon von dem hochwürdigen Sakrament des heiligen wahren Leichnams Christi und von den Bruderschaften* (1519), WA 2:745 / 1, 4–5. [LW 35:53.]

8. WA 2:752 / 17ff. [LW 35:63.]

9. WA 2:751 / 13ff. [LW 36:62.]

10. Most detail on this is in W. Joest, *Ontologie der Person bei Luther* (Göttingen, 1967), 399ff. There too the indispensable regard for the occasion and thus for the scope of Luther's several writings is carefully treated. Cf. also H. Grass, *Die Abendmahlslehre bei Luther und Calvin*, 2d ed. (Gütersloh, 1954), 17ff.; Luther's sentence cited in n. 6 has been misunderstood by Karl Barth, who interprets it in the sense of a symbolical [?] meaning. Accordingly, Luther at that time had already "said everything necessary—against himself, long before Zwingli came forward." K. Barth, "Ansatz und Absicht in Luthers Abendmahlslehre," in his *Die Theologie und die Kirche: Gesammelte Vorträge* (Munich, 1928), 2:26ff., esp. 57. Directly on this, A. Peters, *Realpräsenz: Luthers Zeugnis von Christi Gegenwart im Abendmahl* (Berlin, 1960), 51–52. More on the matter, Grass, *Abendmahlslehre*, 23–24.

sermon, explains the meaning not of the celebration but of the words of institution. He does so in terms long important to him: in terms of testament and inheritance. "What, then, is this testament, or what is bequeathed to us in it by Christ? Truly, a great, eternal, and unspeakable treasure, namely, the forgiveness of all sins."[11] By analyzing the instituting of the Lord's Supper, Luther comes up with the triad: Word, Faith, Spirit.[12] Here the Word only appears to take precedence over the elements in the Supper, for Christ's words are a pronouncement on these elements without which their meaning would be beyond us. He explains, "Now, as the testament is much more important than the sacrament, so the words are much more important than the signs. For the signs might well be lacking, if only one has the words; and thus without sacrament, yet not without testament, one might be saved."[13] Therewith Luther grasped the components of his conception of the Lord's Supper. How he developed them and what emphasis he gave to them figured prominently in the confrontations in which he presently was engaged because of them.

Toward the traditional Catholic side he sharpened his critique against the practice of withholding the cup from the laity and against the doctrine of transubstantiation. To begin, he had examined the entire sacramental system in his work of 1520, *The Babylonian Captivity of the Church*. At the same time he casually touched a nerve destined to become central in the confrontation with his non-Roman opponents: their interpretation that John 6 refers to the Lord's Supper. Besides, Roman theologians themselves regarded this chapter [on the feeding of the five thousand and Jesus as the bread of life] as proof that the whole Christ is distributed under only one of the elements, for Christ was here calling himself the living bread, not the living cup.[14] This caused Luther to present his own exegetical conviction that John 6 speaks of the sacrament "with not a single syllable," but rather that it refers to faith in Christ as the Word incarnate.[15] With the same argument, Luther had earlier refuted an attempt of the Bohemians to use this text in their argument with the Utraquists.[16]

11. *Ein Sermon von dem neuen Testament, das ist von der heiligen Messe* (1520), WA 6:358 / 14ff. [*LW* 36:85.]

12. "These words [of institution and forgiveness of sin] every Christian must have before him in the mass. He must hold fast to them as the chief part of the mass. . . . God must anticipate all [of man's] works and thoughts and make a promise clearly expressed in words, which man then takes and keeps in a good, firm faith. Then there follows the Holy Spirit, who is given to man for the sake of this same faith. WA 6:355 / 33ff.; 356 / 16ff. [*LW* 35:82, 83.]

13. WA 6:363 / 6ff. [*LW* 35:91.]

14. WA 6:499 / 18ff.; 500 / 1ff. [*LW* 36:14–15.]

15. WA 6:502 / 7ff., 26–27. [*LW* 36:19.]

16. *Verklärung etlicher Artikel in dem Sermon von dem heiligen Sakrament* (1950), WA 6:80 / 11ff. On the later significance of the John 6 controversy, see below, pp. 509–10, 534.

Still other questions came to Luther from Bohemia, and these went even deeper into the sacramental issue. His friend Paul Speratus, evangelical preacher in Iglau, Moravia, in 1522 sent Luther an article on the Lord's Supper by the Picards,[17] requesting his opinion of it. Like some other contemporaries, Luther mistook the Picards for the Bohemian Brethren. It happened that representatives of the Brethren were just then visiting Luther, and he quickly ascertained that they were being unjustly charged. He declared he had "not found that they regarded the bread in the sacrament of the altar as a mere sign of the body of Christ and the wine as only a sign of the blood of Christ, but that they believe the bread to be truly and really the body and the wine truly and really the blood of Christ, even though the same body and the same blood of Christ be there in other form than they are in heaven and different also from Christ among the spirits." If this was not said to him plainly enough, then at least it seemed to him "not much unlike the truth." Yet he censured certain other articles of the Utraquists for interpreting John 6 in terms of the Lord's Supper.[18] As Luther learned from them subsequently, the Bohemians rejected the adoration of Christ in the sacrament, and with this he found no fault. "To adore or implore Christ in the sacrament is a free choice. Neither he sins who does not adore, nor he who does." All that matters is whether this is done in faith and love. "Faith is satisfied to know that under the bread the body of Christ is present and under the wine is the blood of the living and reigning Christ. In this innocence faith perseveres and suspects all curious questioning."[19]

The term "plain meaning" became the key word of the subsequent controversy over the Lord's Supper. Against Speratus, Luther had taken the Bohemian Brethren under his protection, defending them against the suspicion of a symbolic interpretation of the Lord's Supper. One inquiry, which must have been disquieting, caused him to return again to the Bohemian teaching on the Lord's Supper. Margrave George of Brandenburg-Ansbach, loyally disposed toward Luther since the imperial diet at Worms in 1521, wrote him anxiously from Prague that he had been "approached by others, claiming that you are already teaching that it is not necessary to adore and revere the eucharistic elements in the sacrament." He therefore requested Luther's reply to this and other questions, "so that we may know what we are supposed to believe, for we are quite confused

17. Refugees from Picardy living in Moravia. See above, p. 104, n. 49. On Speratus, see above, pp. 330–31.
18. Letter to Speratus, May 16, 1522, WA Br 2:531 / 13ff.
19. Letter to Speratus, June 13, 1522, WA Br 2:560 / 31–32; 561 / 64ff.

in this matter and don't find our way out."[20] Luther produced his answer in a published treatise, *The Adoration of the Sacrament of the Holy Body of Christ* (April 1523) in the same free vein: Christ left no commandment to adore him by bowing or kneeling. One may do it or not do it; the one essential is to adore him in one's heart. "Every person can engage in this kind of worship wherever he may be or go or stay, even in the field or sick in bed or captive in prison, and not only in the churches or chapels, before the altar, or on his knees."[21] Luther objects to coercion, whichever side uses it. "The first group would like to compel people not to adore the sacrament, as if Christ were not there at all; and the other group would like to compel people to adore it, as if Christ's state of glory were in the sacrament as it is in heaven." There is no reason for mutual recriminations of heresy over such cultic postulates.[22]

More important than these ceremonial questions were several errors of a substantive kind. These Luther attacked with a short, sharp refutation preceding the announced theme of the tract. Here for the first time he turns against people "who frivolously and unsupported by Scripture twist the little word 'is' into 'signifies.' " Thus, "the bread signifies the body and the wine signifies the blood of Christ."[23] In making the charge, Luther alluded to ideas set forth by the Dutch humanist Honius (Hoen) in a tract on the Lord's Supper and subsequently taken up by Oecolampadius, Zwingli, and others. Like a spark, these ideas ignited the great controversy over the Lord's Supper that burned from the mid-1520s onward. Whether Luther had actually learned about these ideas from the Honius tract is not certain. In any case, their roots lay in the tradition of John Wyclif, and they continued effectively in radical Hussitism and in the *via moderna*, and the latter had stimulated Honius.[24] The Honius tract was

20. Letter of January 5, 1523, WA Br 3:9 / 49ff.
21. WA 11:455 / 18ff. [*LW* 36:292.]
22. WA 11:448 / 12ff.; cf. 3ff. [*LW* 36:295.]
23. WA 11:434 / 22ff., 7ff. [*LW* 36:279.]
24. Strictly speaking, the Honius tract is not a letter, a description given it by Zwingli when first he had it published in 1525 and gave it such a title. *Huldreich Zwinglis sämtliche Werke*, ed. E. Egli, G. Finster, et al., vol. 4 (Berlin, 1927), 505ff. Consequently, the disputed question as to the addressee is pointless. Years ago it was assumed that the addressee was Luther, which was declared doubtful by O. Clemen, WA 10²:315, n. 3. Köhler, *Zwingli und Luther* (Gütersloh, 1953), 1:155, surmises Erasmus. F. Blanke, in *Zwinglis sämtliche Werke*, 5 (1934): 907–8, again thinks it was Luther. It is worth noting that Luther, in his *Adoration*, attacks but two of the proofs adduced by Honius (WA 11:434 / 12ff.), while others (e.g., the mainly farcical reference to Matt. 24:23) Luther does not mention. Nor does Luther in his own treatise, or even later, mention the name of Honius. Köhler's surmise that Luther had learned about Honius's views only indirectly (155, n. 4) is thus not to be dropped. Examples of the figurative concept ["is" = "means"] in Wyclif are in R. Seeberg, *Lehrbuch der Dog-*

directed not against Luther, although this was long assumed, but against the traditional scholastic doctrine of the Lord's Supper. And it was not, as commonly surmised, brought to Wittenberg by Hinne Rode in 1521 at the request of Honius.[25] In any event, Luther's own treatise addressed to the Bohemians placed strong emphasis on the real presence, which for him was nothing new. He was only reconfirming what he had always presupposed as the self-evident basis, but one now under open attack.

The confrontation with Karlstadt, moreover, began at a time when Luther was already so certain of his position, which he had earlier been forced to think through, that this newest attack gave him no scruples. In his *Letter to the Christians in Strassburg Against the Enthusiasts*, in late December 1524, Luther replied to questions raised by the preachers there about his opinion of Karlstadt's teachings on the Lord's Supper. In it he dated his own struggle over the real presence as having occurred some five years earlier (1519). He now admitted that his doubts had since then been completely dispelled by means of his own study of the basic New Testament passages and also because of Karlstadt's own ridiculous commentary.[26] Nevertheless, as Karlstadt's teaching spread, it must have caused Luther much anxiety. His own former misgiving and enticement informed him that on the issue of the sacrament of the altar he would be able to strike the Roman church at its inmost core. The Strassburg preachers, in reporting the situation, had included five of Karlstadt's tracts on the Lord's Supper recently printed in Basel.[27] Criticism of the real presence was making headway in Switzerland, as Luther had learned several months prior to receiving the letter from Strassburg. His informant was Franz Kolb, originally of Wertheim near Würzburg, who had studied in

---

mengeschichte (reprint, Darmstadt, 1959), 3:792. [Eng. trans., *Textbook of the History of Doctrines*, trans. C. E. Hay (Philadelphia, 1903), 2:206.] Wyclif had begun on the side of the traditional real presence but later—in opposing transubstantiation—reinterpreted it into a presence of power and effectiveness in place of a presence in substance. Later, in his treatise *De eucharistia*, he gave up the presence completely. On the earlier teaching of Wyclif, see G. A. Benrath, *Wyclifs Bibelkommentar* (Berlin, 1966), 216–17, 268–69.

25. O. Clemen, in *WA* 10²:315, n. 3, has refuted this surmise, even though he himself had earlier believed it so. See his "Hinne Rode in Wittenberg, Basel, Zürich, und die frühesten Ausgaben Wesselscher Schriften," *ZKG* 18 (1898): 346ff. Cf. also the T. Kolde edition of J. G. Hoop-Scheffer, "Die Geschichte der Reformation in den Niederlanden" (Leipzig, 1886), *ThLZ* 13 (1888): 253. Also F. Loofs, *Leitfaden zum Studium der Dogmengeschichte*, 4th ed. (Halle, 1906), 802, n. 7. Nevertheless, Rode brought the Honius tract to Switzerland, presumably in 1524. Köhler, *Zwingli und Luther*, 1:62ff.

26. On this, see above, pp. 171ff. On January 13, 1525, Luther admitted to Spalatin that he "did not remain stuck to his error but was strongly tested by it." *WA* Br 3:422 / 18–19.

27. See above, p. 167.

Basel and was now pastor of a Swiss parish. Kolb wrote Luther on August 27, 1524, that he and Zwingli and Leo Jud had come to agree that the words of institution are to be taken significatively instead of indicatively, that is, as though Christ were saying "As bread is food that really nourishes the body, so also the reality of my passion or the word of faith in my death is food and life for the spirit and soul."[28] Plausibly, Luther made a connection between this claim and Karlstadt's.[29] The inference was correct, especially if one disregards some of Karlstadt's exegetical stunts. Even Oecolampadius, Zwingli's most important theological ally—indeed, he was the one who shaped the [German] Swiss teaching on the Lord's Supper—assured Zwingli, "On the question of the Eucharist, as far as I can see, he [Karlstadt] does not differ from our own position."[30] Soon thereafter Oecolampadius, Pellikan, and de Coct wrote quite openly to Wittenberg that they agreed with Karlstadt.[31]

The great confrontation resulting from these opposing views got off to a slow start. The awareness that decisive differences of faith were involved is evident from the cautious way the contenders felt one another out. At first came skirmishes on the sidelines. So, for instance, Zwingli made an initial move singling out Matthäus Alber, pastor in Reutlingen, south of Stuttgart, as his first candidate to enlighten. Zwingli did not know Alber personally, but he regarded him highly. He also had heard that this admirable man was just then burdened by weighty problems involving an understanding of the Lord's Supper. To Zwingli he appeared like a well-known Lutheran posted in an important South German city. In fact, he had made a name for himself by resisting Archduke Ferdinand of Hapsburg [the brother of Emperor Charles V] in the struggle for the Reformation in Reutlingen. Actually, Zwingli was aiming at Luther, not naming him but

28. WA Br 3:331 / 84ff. On Kolb, see above, p. 92.

29. On November 17 and December 2, 1524, Luther named Zwingli and Leo Jud partisans of Karlstadt. On January 13, 1525, he added the names of Oecolampadius, Pellican, and de Coct, apparently on the basis of a letter to Melanchthon of January 12, the previous day. E. Staehelin, *Briefe und Akten zum Leben Oekolampads* (Leipzig, 1934), 1:338. *Suppl. Mel.* 6 / 1:275–76. *MSA* 7 / 1:225ff. *CR* 2:11. *MBW* 370. WA Br 3:373 / 11ff.; 397 / 5ff.; 422 / 9ff. On de Coct, see above, pp. 289ff.

30. To Zwingli, November 21, 1524, *Zwinglis sämtliche Werke*, 8 (1914): 252 / 1–2. On the influence of Oecolampadius on Zwingli's teaching on the Lord's Supper, cf. H. Rückert, "Das Eindringen der Tropuslehre in die schweizerische Auffassung vom Abendmahl," *ARG* (1940): 199ff. Reprinted in H. Rückert, *Vorträge und Aufsätze zur historischen Theologie* (Tübingen, 1972), 146ff., esp. 160ff.

31. See above, pp. 290–91. Contrary to the doubt of Köhler about this communication from Basel (*Zwingli und Luther*, 1:181), Rückert agrees with Köhler and O. Clemen (WA Br 3:423, n. 7); see Rückert's "Tropus-lehre," in *Vorträge und Aufsätze*, 159, n. 49.

keeping his sights on him,[32] while addressing Alber on the basis of a rumor concerning a controversy over the Lord's Supper in which Alber was said to be involved.[33] Zwingli used the occasion to clarify his own conception of the Supper. He commented only cautiously on Karlstadt's most recent publication, taking a half-yes, half-no position. On the whole, he wrote, "I find Karlstadt's opinion not uncongenial, if I understand his booklet correctly. Yet the way he expresses himself does not match the demands of the subject." Meanwhile, it was said that Karlstadt had composed still another dialogue, much cruder than the others. Zwingli, however, had not yet read it, nor had he read anything else of Karlstadt's except the three aforementioned folio sheets.[34] In any case, Zwingli offered himself as an independent associate of the South German Karlstadt supporters, without thereby giving Luther and his partners cause to react. He still had hope of playing a compensating and conciliatory role. Yet this did not keep him from coming out with a massive verdict: "Until now we have been shooting wide of the target. Who the guilty one may be is hard to say in a letter that must be brief." He could only have meant Luther.[35]

Zwingli based his view on two proofs: (1) on John 6 (key verse 63: "It is the Spirit that gives life, the flesh is of no avail"); this then rules out the body and blood of Christ as gifts in the Lord's Supper. Now, as well as later, Zwingli can hardly get enough illustrations to express the meaning of this text: a well-fortified chain of outposts, a doorbolt, a shield, a bronze wall, an amulet, an unbreakable diamond.[36] Without saying so, he thereby contradicted the exegetical conviction of Luther, namely, that John 6 can in no way, positively or negatively, be applied to the Lord's Supper.[37] (2) The words of institution themselves, however, raise the cen-

---

32. "Ad Matthaeum Alberum de coena dominica epistola," *Zwinglis sämtliche Werke*, 3 (1914): 322ff. On his high regard for Alber: ibid., 335 / 6–7. On Alber himself: G. Bossert, "Alber, Matthäus," *RE* 1 (1896): 289–90. On the conflict in Reutlingen at that time, induced by the introduction of the German mass, see the mandate of Ferdinand of September 18, 1524, that the inhabitants of the duchy of Württemberg be ordered to avoid the city and especially its preacher. *Zwinglis sämtliche Werke*, 3 (1914): 352–53. Allusion to Luther, ibid., 330–31, 352 / 5, 335 / 11ff. Köhler, *Zwingli und Luther*, 1:74.

33. *Zwinglis sämtliche Werke*, 3:335 / 4.

34. Ibid., 336 / 3ff. In praise of Karlstadt and a cautious criticism of him, ibid., 343 / 6ff.

35. Ibid., 335 / 11–12. *"Peccati huius autor"* is aimed at Luther, according to Köhler, ibid., 330, and *Zwingli und Luther*, 1:74.

36. *Zwinglis sämtliche Werke*, 3:336ff. Citation in Köhler, *Zwingli und Luther*, 1:76, 88, 90, 96.

37. See above, p. 505. H. Gollwitzer, "Zur Auslegung von Joh. 6 bei Luther und Zwingli," in *In Memoriam: Ernst Lohmeyer*, ed. W. Schmauch (Stuttgart, 1951), 143ff.

tral question. For Zwingli the question is answered by means of the picture language in many Bible passages to which the Honius tract had led him. From Honius, Zwingli also drew his main illustrations: the seven fat cows "are" the seven fat years; the seed "is" the word of God; Jesus says "I 'am' the vine." "Is" can thus mean "signifies."[38] The two proofs can be seen as supporting each other. John 6 provides the substantive argument, the patent absurdity that excludes an expression of identity ("flesh avails nothing for faith"). This requires a transferred interpretation, which language readily allows. These two are the pillars on which the Zwinglian view of the Lord's Supper rests. Zwingli's letter to Alber, at first only in handwritten copies, was circulated a hundredfold. Apparently Zwingli did not yet wish to dig in on a front between Karlstadt and Luther, but this evasive tactic could not help but arouse curiosity and, among the Wittenbergers, anger. By March 1525, Zwingli had the letter printed for a still wider audience.[39]

Zwingli enlarged on the elementary proofs in the Alber letter step by step, adding three further arguments. First came his semantic explication of the word "sacrament." Having already made mention of it in his letter, he now drew on his more inclusive treatment of it in his commentary *De vera et falsa religione*, which he completed and published in March 1525.[40] According to [the pre-Christian Latin grammarian] Varro [116–27 B.C.], "sacrament" is a pledge or security laid on an altar, or (as in French and Italian) an oath, especially of loyalty to the flag. So the word, Zwingli claimed, has nothing to do with anything secret and holy or with a mystery—which for reasons unknown to Zwingli has been rendered as "sacrament" in the Latin Vulgate. A sacrament is thus to be understood as a solemn obligation (*initiatio aut oppigneratio*) or ceremony "through which a man of the church proves himself a disciple or soldier of Christ."[41] The second argument is historical in nature: a patristic proof from tradition which, in a sequence of citations up to Augustine, is supposed to show that the great ancient fathers conceived of the Lord's Supper as symbolic, departing thereby from the Roman concept of the mass as sacrifice.

---

38. *Zwinglis sämtliche Werke*, 3:345.

39. In a letter to Bugenhagen on October 23, 1525, Zwingli named "more than five hundred brethren" (alluding to the witnesses to the resurrection, 1 Cor. 15:6) as recipients of the handwritten copies. Cf. the figures given by Köhler in *Zwinglis sämtliche Werke*, 3:325 / 31–32.

40. Briefly mentioned: To Alber, *Zwinglis sämtliche Werke*, 3:348 / 21; *Commentarius*, ibid., 758–61.

41. Ibid., 758 / 15ff.; 759 / 5–6; 761 / 22ff.

Zwingli thus claimed he was not the first to break with Roman tradition.[42] In his letter to Alber, he had already shared several samples from Tertullian and Augustine.[43] He had no need to gather more references on his own because in the autumn of 1525 Oecolampadius summoned a still greater number of church fathers in support of his own and Zwingli's position.[44] In fact, Zwingli probably owes Oecolampadius also the third argument of his expanded repertoire, namely, an exact definition of his biblical interpretation of the words of institution in terms of trope, a concept developed by the rhetoricians of classical antiquity to denote the figurative use of language. The concept first appears in his tract of August 1525 *Subsidium sive coronis de eucharistia*.[45] In the trope concept, Zwingli found a scholarly term for his interpretation of the Lord's Supper that was applicable also to many other biblical passages.[46] This gave him an excuse to part company with Karlstadt and his "amply forced" exegesis, something over which Zwingli felt relieved, especially in view of Karlstadt's mounting popularity in Anabaptist groups.[47]

Meanwhile, Luther had fallen behind. In southwestern Germany and in German-speaking Switzerland the interpretation of the Lord's Supper in symbolical terms was spreading in many quarters and for various reasons. Luther's own position had been stated most recently in January 1525, when the second part of his *Against the Heavenly Prophets in the Matter of Images and Sacraments* was published, that part being devoted entirely to the question of the Lord's Supper. At the time of writing, Karlstadt was still his only opponent, and Luther's critique focused exclusively on allegory, a well-known exegetical method.[48] Luther himself

42. Ibid., 809–15; 816 / 1ff.

43. Ibid., 346–47. Tertullian *Adversus Marcionem* 1:14. Augustine *Enarrationes in Psalmis 3*. Cited in *Zwinglis sämtliche Werke*, 3:346–47. References to material in the church fathers and especially in Wyclif and the Waldensian writings were supplied to Zwingli by the young Bullinger. J. Staedtke, "Voraussetzungen der Schweizer Abendmahlslehre," *ThZ* 16 (1960): 19ff., esp. 20, 31–32.

44. Concerning *De genuina verborum Domini: "Hoc est corpus meum" iuxta vetutissimos autores expositione liber,* see G. Hoffmann, "Sententiae Patrum: Das patristische Argument in der Abendmahlskontroverse zwischen Oekolampad, Zwingli, Luther, und Melanchthon" (theology diss., Heidelberg, 1971), 5ff. Staehelin, *Lebenswerk Oekolampads,* 276ff. Köhler, *Zwingli und Luther,* 1:117ff. [On Oecolampadius's role, see also G. Rupp, *Patterns of Reformation* (Philadelphia: Fortress Press, 1969), 25ff.]

45. "Unterstützung oder Schlusschnörkel vom Abendmahl" (for Zwingli's *Commentarius), Zwinglis sämtliche Werke,* 4:440ff.; foreword dated August 17, 1525.

46. Ibid., 472ff.

47. Ibid.; 463 / 19–465 / 20; 466 / 14ff. H. Rückert, "Das Eindringen der Tropus-lehre in die schweizerische Lehre vom Abendmahl," *ARG* 37 (1940): 152ff. There, 160ff., on Oecolampadius as forerunner and supposed stimulator for the application of the trope teaching.

48. WA 18:178 / 8ff. [*LW* 40:188–89.]

made only incidental use of a grammatical aid called "synecdoche," the figure of speech that names a whole but means only a part.[49] The emphasis of his thought, however, lay in theological and pastoral arguments.[50] Thereupon, when the trope usage of the Swiss pushed the Lord's Supper controversy ever further into the field of language, Luther made synecdoche his chief linguistic weapon.[51]

Never short on words, Luther began speaking of the "Karlstadt-Zwinglian poison" as early as the summer of 1525, and for him it became a matter of deep anxiety. As a preventative, he sent out warnings as often as possible and as far away as Silesia and East Prussia.[52] However, the Peasants' War and the Erasmus controversy put him in such a bind that he could not well enter still another struggle. It was then that Bugenhagen stepped in for him and was soon going after Zwingli more vehemently than even Luther could approve.[53] Evidence of this was Bugenhagen's "Open Letter Against the New Error Concerning the Sacrament of the Body and Blood of Christ," which in mid-July he gave to Ambrosius Moibanus, who had just earned his degree at Wittenberg and was on his way to Breslau as the newly called pastor of St. Elizabeth's. This letter, requested by Moibanus in the first place, was soon circulating in print.[54] From many quarters Zwingli was challenged to reply. He did so vigorously, yet with poised composure. Rejecting the epithet "Karlstadtian," which he had been called, he took the occasion to declare his independence from Karlstadt.[55]

49. WA 18:187 / 14ff. [LW 40:198.] The synecdoche (understood by Luther as figure of speech: *totum pro parte et ediverso*. *Postil* 1521, WA 7:473 / 2) had even earlier won Luther's praise. In the controversy with Latomus, both parties had made use of it. According to Luther, synecdoche occurs repeatedly in the Scriptures, yet always as "a pleasant and necessary figure, a symbol of divine love and mercy." In this sense it is used often by the prophets. WA 8:65 / 17ff., 7ff.; 66 / 14ff. On Luther's use of synecdoche, see G. Krause, *Studien zu Luthers Auslegung der kleine Propheten* (Tübingen, 1962), 205ff., which also lists the earlier sources.

50. See above, pp. 172ff. On this subject, Grass, *Abendmahlslehre*, 33ff.

51. WA 26:322 / 31ff.; 444 / 1ff. H. Gollwitzer, *Coena Domini: Die altlutherische Abendmahlslehre in ihrer Auseinandersetzung mit dem Calvinismus, dargestellt an der lutherischen Frühorthodoxie* (Munich, 1937), 41ff.

52. To John Hess in Breslau, July 19, 1525; to Johann Briessmann in Königsberg, mid-August; WA Br 3:544 / 3ff.; 555 / 6–7 (where Luther speaks of "poison"). There is no mention of whether Zwingli's writings had already been circulating there. In both instances, Luther drops a word of regret and hope about Karlstadt, whom (just at that time) he was lodging for eight weeks under his own roof. Cf. above, p. 414.

53. T. Kolde, *Analecta Lutherana* (see above p. 261, n. 31), 74.

54. In rapid succession five German and six Latin printings were out. Entered with rejoinders by "Cunrat Ryss zu Ofen" (pseudonym) and by Zwingli himself, in G. Geisenhof, *Bibliotheca Bugenhagiana* (Leipzig, 1908), nos. 162–77.

55. *Ad Ioannis Bugenhagii Pomerani epistolam responsio Huldrychi Zwinglii*, including a detailed description of the controversy and a commentary on the text by G. Finsler in *Zwinglis sämtliche Werke*, 4:546ff. Köhler, *Zwingli und Luther*, 1:196–97, 283–84. A critique of Zwingli's self-portraiture is in ibid., 285–86. Rückert, "Tropus-lehre," 153–54.

The first round of this literary feud did the Wittenbergers little credit. They became acquainted at this time with still a third concept of the Lord's Supper which differed from Luther's. On the last day of 1525 Luther wrote to a supporter:

> The error concerning the sacrament has three sects, but they agree with one another. Zwingli fights Karlstadt with one set of arguments; Valentine, from Silesia, fights both of them, and everyone else, with another set. . . . This quarrel among the sects is a sign that their teachings are of Satan, for the Spirit of God is a spirit not of discord but of peace.[56]

A certain Krautwald, canon of the Castle Church in Liegnitz, supported his interpretation by claiming a special experience of the Spirit. He was one of the small circle of friends around the Silesian nobleman Caspar Schwenkfeld from Ossig, who had been won over by Luther's writings and had taken a leading part introducing the Reformation in the duchy of Liegnitz. Schwenkfeld himself was passionately moved by the theological issues of the times, while yet retaining an independent position. This he now did also in the Lord's Supper controversy. He had earlier sent Luther an account of his position in it. Then, on visiting Wittenberg on December 1, 1525, he handed Luther a letter from Krautwald, in which the canon described to Luther the revelations he had experienced.[57]

Psychologically this letter from Krautwald is a most interesting document, depicting how personal broodings became an inspiration. It went like this: A conversation on September 16, 1525, in Schwenkfeld's circle included a reading of Krautwald's manuscript, presumably the same text

56. To Michael Stiefel, December 31, 1525, WA Br 3:653 / 5ff.; cf. 1 Cor. 14:33. [LW 49:141.] More detailed is Luther's *Written Response to the Christians in Reutlingen* (1526), WA 19:120 / 25–122 / 15. Later Luther counted up to seven sects and "holy spirits." Cf. Schwenkfeld's open letter of 1527, in CS 2:452 / 16ff.; in detail in Luther's *Short Confession of the Holy Sacrament* (1544): "First of all, they were warned right at the outset by the Holy Spirit when they separated into seven spirits in their interpretations of the text, each one differing from the other at all times. . . . All these holy spirits, no matter how completely they disagree, nevertheless are in harmony about the sublime spiritual meaning that bread is bread, wine is wine." So Luther regarded all of them as Zwinglians at heart. WA 54:148 / 29ff.; 151 / 19ff. [LW 40:296, 298.] Cf. also WA Br 4:33 / 10; 42 / 35; 19 / 458ff. [LW 49:150, to Schwenkfeld, April 14, 1526.] Schwenkfeld from the outset counted two groups divided over the question whether the body of Christ is in the bread. CS 2:278 / 30; 446–47; 451–52. On this see E. Hirsch, "Schwenkfeld und Luther," *Lutherstudien* (Gütersloh, 1954), 2:35ff., esp. 44–45.

57. The Latin text of Krautwald's letter is in CS and is reprinted in WA Br 3:631–33. In CS there is also Schwenkfeld's published German translation, in his *Epistolar* (II, 1570). I have translated the original Latin text as in CS and WA. The editors of CS have commented on the date: September 15, 1525, becomes an important date in the history of the Middle Way; Schwenkfeld gladly used this term, sometimes also the Royal Way. Cf. S. Schultz, *Caspar Schwenkfeld von Ossig (1481–1561): Spiritual Interpreter of Christianity, Apostle of the Middle Way, Pioneer in Modern Religious Thought* (Norristown, Pa., 1946), 104ff.

he now sent Luther. The problem of the sacrament, according to Kraut-
wald, weighed on his heart "like an enormous rock." During the night this
question took him by surprise: "What if neither Martinus nor Zwingli has
understood the essence of the Eucharist truly and in the meaning of
Christ, and what if the authentic, true and pure meaning of the words of
Christ is an altogether different one, kept hidden from them and you
[Schwenkfeld]?" In vain Krautwald searched his books for advice, first in
Cyprian, which lay nearest at hand. Then at dawn, shortly after awakening, came a flash of illumination. The essential content of this revelation
was that the words of Jesus in John 6 must be the standard. Still, with a
frightened heart and tearful eyes Krautwald continued his reading, turning to those passages in the Gospels dealing directly with the Lord's Supper, "until at last my memory was transfixed before the sweetness of this
teaching and my exhausted spirit stood shaken before such teachers [as
Luther and Zwingli, presumably].[58] The inspired canon kept the experience to himself for ten days, reading in the New Testament and in the
canon law as well as the church fathers. Then he conversed eight days
with brothers close to him before setting down sixteen theses and supporting passages from the church fathers.[59] Unlike Zwingli's, the theses
did not converge on a single rhetorical trope (is = signifies) but utilized
yet another grammatical construction that Krautwald gave as a Hebraism:
the transposition of a subject and a demonstrative pronoun. Taking the
cup: "This is my blood" says "My blood is this," namely, the cup, one
draught and true wine, slaking the eternal thirst. Likewise, "This is my
body, which is given for you, thus is construed: My body, given for you, is
this, namely the bread. . . . The seed is the Word of God, construed as: the
Word of God is the seed."[60] Krautwald offers a succession of examples in
an attempt to avoid Zwingli's signification theory as well as the concept of a
real presence. As a result, he wound up with simply another form of
picturization.

> In me there arose a wonderful, penetrating, and mighty power, like light
> suddenly radiating from the darkness. It took me completely captive, be-
> stowed me with great wisdom, and led me to an understanding of the Euchar-
> ist. This power spread from my head throughout my whole being and illumi-
> nated for me as in a flash all the passages of Scripture bearing on the Euchar-
> ist. . . . Then it spoke to me in tender tones on still other matters.

58. *CS* 2:194 / 15; 196 / 10ff., 24; 198 / 11ff.; 200 / 20–21. *WA* Br 3:631 / 8–9, 16ff., 28, 37ff.;
632 / 65–66.

59. *CS* 2:200 / 30ff. *WA* Br 3:632 / 73ff. The theses, in *CS* 2:204–8. *WA* Br 3:633.

60. *CS* 2:206 / 9ff.; 204 / 16ff., 19ff. For the sake of clarification, only half the first sentence
is translated [into German, and here into English].

One can readily understand how this way of combining spiritual revelation and grammatical rules could impress a man like Schwenkfeld, sensitive yet lay-minded in his theology. Likewise, one can see why this made no impression on Luther. He listened to Schwenkfeld amicably on that December day in 1525, but soon withdrew and let Bugenhagen conclude the conversation.[61] Later in the day Luther assured him again that he had no desire to condemn him. Yet, said Luther, he must know whether Schwenkfeld could be sure of the authenticity of the revelation recounted by Krautwald. "This is a matter of faith, and I must first have it in my conscience and feel it." "It is not enough for me to have a good interpretation of it, for I must be sure, especially in such a major article of faith, that it is to be understood in this way and not in another."[62] Yet this is precisely what Schwenkfeld could not assure Luther. He too gave up relying with certainty on the revelation of Krautwald. From the year 1525 until his death in 1561, Schwenkfeld observed his own "truce," abstaining completely from the sacrament. His doubts as to the proper institution of the sacrament were matched by a mounting hesitation as to the worthiness of an individual or of a congregation to receive the Lord's Supper. Schwenkfeld's congregations followed his lead, and their example may well have exerted a continuing influence in England among spiritualists and Quakers especially.[63]

Luther took an unexpectedly long time to send Schwenkfeld and Krautwald his promised reply. This, after all, was a controversy born in his own camp, and it was difficult to take. So far his dealings had been with "vain, lazy devils" who were quarreling over profane and nonbiblical questions such as papacy, purgatory, "and similar foolishness." But now the struggle was becoming serious, for the devil himself was fishing questions out of

61. Only in 1540, in his fourth open letter to his uncle, Friedrich von Walden, did Schwenkfeld publish a full report of his conversations in Wittenberg. CS 2:240–82; concerning Luther, especially, CS 2:243–45, 276–82. Most of the account deals with Bugenhagen. It is difficult to prove whether this is an excerpt from Schwenkfeld's diary (CS 2:237). At any rate, the memory of conversations so meaningful to him leaves a reliable impression.

62. CS 2:276 / 17ff., 26; 277 / 8ff.

63. K. Ecke, Schwenkfeld, Luther, und der Gedanke einer apostolischen Reformation (Berlin, 1911), 235–36, 250. Toward the end of his life Schwenkfeld wrote in his Accounting: "Once having perceived a truth, we can no longer persist in some idolatrous folly or misuse, or presently avail ourselves of the sacrament, until the institution of Christ's Supper emerges from proper understanding and faith—as indeed we pray and hope it may. . . . Meanwhile, we busy ourselves . . . daily to celebrate the Supper with the Lord Christ, doing so in the spirit of faith" (ibid., 259). Cf. Hirsch, "Schwenkfeld und Luther," 51. G. Maron, Individualismus und Gemeinschaft bei Caspar von Schwenkfeld (Stuttgart, 1961), 89ff. Schultz, Schwenkfeld, 110ff., 407–8.

the Scriptures. "Schwenkfeld and his Krautwald have been saved up for this disaster. I lament it most profoundly."[64] Only on April 14, 1526, did Luther write separate but similar letters to each of the two men; his tone was not unfriendly but earnest. The focal point remained that the words of institution are not to be explained in terms of John 6.

> Of course you say that this is so, but you do not prove it. As a result, we cannot believe you and stake our souls on your word. It is therefore my courteous request that you renounce this obvious error and do not join those who now lead the world so miserably astray. If this should not happen, then God's will be done. Although I am heartily sorry, yet I am not responsible for your blood, or for the blood of all those whom you lead astray with your teaching. May God convert you. Amen.[65]

These were Luther's words to Schwenkfeld. The Lord's Supper controversy laid its stigma on the further growth of Schwenkfeld's theology. It contrasts with Luther's theology in at least these four points: facing Luther's biblical realism there was now a spiritual realism; opposite the body of the crucified Lord, the spiritually real heavenly flesh of Christ received by the believer in a spiritual enjoyment of communion; confronting the justification of the sinner, essentially a transforming rebirth; over against the incarnate humanity of Christ, the Son of God's hypercreaturely corporeality since birth, which draws us into its heavenly being.[66] Schwenkfeld's theology, aiming toward spiritualizing and deifying man, was the exact opposite of Luther's teaching on the incarnation and on God's entering into human history, as set forth in Christology and the doctrine of grace. On both sides attempts at persuasion proved in vain. Instead they left their mark subsequently on pietistic and idealistic modes of self-understanding.

In his state of alarm over the expanding Lord's Supper controversy, Luther discovered a ray of hope. Unexpectedly, allies showed up—the most important among them a group of Swabian theologians. Unrest had struck the duchy of Württemberg when the Swabians learned that their fellow countryman, Oecolampadius, now in Basel, had plans to oppose Luther's teaching on the Lord's Supper and to side with Karlstadt. Ingratiatingly, Oecolampadius had added a postscript to his latest publication, on the words of institution, and dedicated it to his Swabian fellow

---

64. To John Hess in Breslau, April 22, 1526, WA Br 4:61ff.
65. WA Br 4:52 / 9ff. [LW 49:150.]
66. See Hirsch, "Schwenkfeld und Luther," and H. E. Weber, *Reformation, Orthodoxie, und Rationalismus* (Gütersloh, 1937), 1 / 1:281ff.

clergymen. The book, in Latin and entitled *De genuina verborum Domini: 'Hoc est corpus meum' iuxta vetustissimos authores expositione liber,* brought the appeasing dedication to "Dilectis in Christo fratribus per Sueviam Christum annuntiatibus."[67] Instead of calming them, Oecolampadius's strategem alarmed them. The dedication actually revealed his opinion to Württemberg.

In late September and early October 1525 a group of theologians met with John Brenz in Schwäbisch-Hall and decided on a joint reply to Oecolampadius. Brenz was commissioned with the writing of it. On October 14 the fourteen participants again came to Hall and signed the copy destined for Oecolampadius. Not the signatories but the Augsburg printer, who published the reply without authorization, gave it the pompous title *Syngramma clarissimorum virorum, qui Halae Suevorum convenerunt, super verbis Coenae Dominicae, et pium et eruditum, ad Johannem Oecolampadion, Basileensem Ecclesiasten.*[68] The syngraph was written in short, strong, and clever strokes—a style bound to delight Luther. Brenz opens by noting the disunity of the opponents. Three sects they are: Karlstadt's, Zwingli's, and Oecolampadius's. Each party has its own notions of "this is my body"—the "Helen [of Troy] for whom we strive."[69] Then he brushes aside the charges of Oecolampadius that the Swabians are still following Peter Lombard and other scholastics[70] and comes quickly to the decisive point. "The Supper of the Lord has not only the bread as its sign but also the Word." The Word not only speaks, but it also gives. "The Word comforts the strugglers, raises the fallen, strengthens faith, and in short brings us all good things of God." Always, when Christ says something, he also gives what he says. "When he says: my body is given for you, my blood is shed for you, does he then not enclose body and blood in this Word?" Therein lies the energy of the Word. "Why should it not retain this energy when it accompanies the bread and the cup?" "There you see what a miracle is, namely, the miracle of the Word through which body and blood are distributed in bread and wine—not as

67. Staehelin, *Lebenswerk Oekolampads*, 282–83. Köhler, *Zwingli und Luther*, 1:117ff., 126.

68. Prehistory and text in John Brenz, *Frühschriften*, ed. M. Brecht, G. Schäfer, and F. Wolf (Tübingen, 1970), 1:222ff. Also M. Honecker, "Die Abendmahlslehre des Syngramma Suevicum," *BWKG* 65 (1965): 39ff. M. Brecht, *Die frühe Theologie des Johannes Brenz* (Tübingen, 1966), 73ff. Köhler, *Zwingli und Luther*, 1:127ff. Staehelin, *Lebenswerk Oekolampads*, 288ff. [The title translates "A syngraph of most famous men who convened in (the town of) Swabian Hall over the words of the Lord's Supper, and (addressed) to the pious and devout Johannes Oecolampadius, ecclesiastic in Basel.]

69. Brenz, *Frühschriften*, 1:236 / 1ff.

70. Ibid., 237 / 11ff.

bread and wine but, because they have the Word: This is body. This is blood."[71] Brenz puts Oecolampadius's detailed proofs from the church fathers in their proper place: "It were much more correct that we interpret the fathers through the Word of Christ than the Word of Christ through the fathers."[72] Brenz is as much at pains to exclude a crass materialism as he is to avoid a philosophical or trope-based denial of the reality given through the Word of Christ. The concern here is for an incomparable event whose meaning can be comprehended only through the accompanying Word of God or of Christ. "The body of Christ by itself is of no avail, but because of this, that he gave it for us and because he is the life of the world. Likewise the blood of Christ by itself is of no avail, but because it was shed for our cleansing it is of great benefit. And this is the only reason why we receive his body and his blood in the Supper." It is a receiving *sui generis*. "As faith does in its own way receive the Word that is heard with the ears, so also the body, taken in the bread, is received by faith."[73] Or, the way Brenz says in summary, "We do not ourselves from time to time take Christ from the right hand of the Father, but we receive with the heart's deepest thankfulness the gift of the body and blood, entrusted to the Word and preserved in it, and through the Word the bread is added."[74]

To be able to fathom Luther's joy over the document of the Swabian theologians, one must visualize the basic starting point of the *Syngramma* as well as the praise of God's gift in the sacrament, which is to understand the sacrament in terms of the accompanying and efficacious Word of God. On February 18, 1526, he wrote to John Agricola in Eisleben, "Against Oecolampadius and Zwingli some very learned Swabians have written admirably. Their book will be printed here also."[75] This happened immediately. Luther also planned a German translation of it, but Agricola pub-

---

71. Ibid., 240 / 22ff.; 242 / 6ff., 16ff., 25ff.

72. Ibid., 244 / 28ff.

73. Ibid., 272 / 14ff., 32ff.

74. Ibid., 278 / 5ff. Brecht, *Theologie Brenz*, 76–77, is critical, claiming that the *Syngramma*'s teaching on the Word "borders close to magic" and that Oecolampadius's rationalism is countered by a "problematic and massive concept of the Word." This critique does not affect Brenz, for it is based on a misunderstanding of the sentence "Ut quod vis verbum Dei miraculum est . . ." (*Dei* belongs to *verbum*, not to *miraculum*; see Brenz, *Frühschriften*, 1:241 / 16). What is at stake is that, to the sign as reality, the Word of God is added. The same thing is beautifully expressed in the greeting of peace with which the disciples are to convey the message of peace to each household. "Has he [Jesus] not enclosed peace itself in the salutation 'Peace be to this house'? To put it bluntly, did he not lock up peace, almost as something imprisoned in the word, for the apostles to offer the dwellers in the house?" (Brenz, *Frühschriften*, 1:241 / 32ff.)

75. WA Br 4:33 / 6ff.

lished one ahead of him so that a foreword from Luther sufficed. He would gladly have written an extended treatment of the sacrament question then and there, but he was pressed for time. The Swabians brought the opportunity to do so right to his doorstep, and he managed at least a brief acknowledgment, with a few powerful and readily understood arguments. As he had done in the case of the Schwenkfelders, he ridiculed the "sects" of the opponents, marveling that in a year they had grown five or six heads. Two of them already lay on the ground: "Karlstadt's '*tuto*'" and "Zwingli's '*significat*' is drooping its head and expiring rapidly." But he also highlighted sharply the two principal reasons for their error: "The one, that (the bodily presence of Christ) is something very awkward for reason. The other, that it is unnecessary for Christ's body and blood to be in the bread and wine. That is simply an absurdity and not a necessity."[76]

Writing to Spalatin on March 27, Luther not only praised the Swabians but added that Willibald Pirkheimer also had brought out a tract against Oecolampadius, "injecting more heart and zeal than I had expected from such an important man, for I had thought him too wrapped up in other matters."[77] Considered the prince of the Nuremberg humanists, this tract of Pirkheimer's created something of a sensation. Oecolampadius took it painfully, reproaching Pirkheimer, "You might well have treated a friend more nobly."[78] Actually, the two men had stood together in the early days of Oecolampadius's humanistic interests. On Pirkheimer's recommendation, Oecolampadius had been made cathedral preacher in Augsburg, and the two had remained in touch steadily. Yet, like his other friends, he had informed Pirkheimer of his own changed position on the Lord's Supper.[79] The learned Nuremberg patrician simply feared that Oecolampadius's treatment of this central question was an unwarranted break in the Christian tradition. He had seen it happen in the rise of spiritualist outsiders like Hans Denk, at one time recommended by Oecolampadius for the rectorship of Nuremberg's St. Sebald School. And again, the case of

76. WA 19:459 / 21; 460 / 6–7, 39ff.

77. WA Br 4:42 / 32ff. [LW 49:145–46.] *Bilibaldi Birckheimeri de vere Christi carne et vero eius sanguine ad Joannem Oecolampadium responsio*, WA Br 4:43, n. 13. See also P. Drews, *Willibald Pirkheimers Stellung zur Reformation: Ein Beitrag zur Beurteilung des Verhältnisses zwischen Humanismus und Reformation* (Leipzig, 1887), 94ff. According to Drews the tract appeared late in 1525, already bearing the date 1526 (likewise WA Br 4:43, n. 13); according to Staehelin, *Lebenswerk Oekolampads*, 301, in March 1526.

78. April 13, 1526, Staehelin, *Briefe und Akten Oekolampads*, 1:484. On the relationship of Oecolampadius to Pirkheimer, cf. Drews, *Pirkheimers Stellung*, 89ff. Also E. Staehelin, *Das theologische Lebenswerk Johannes Oekolampads*, QFRG 21 (Leipzig, 1939), 93 / 247ff., 301.

79. Staehelin, *Lebenswerk Oekolampads*, 273–74.

Thomas Müntzer had given him a bad scare. Pirkheimer therefore made a special study of the passages Oecolampadius had cited in support of his new teaching on the significative character of the Lord's Supper.[80] The controversy expanded into three attacks by Pirkheimer and two rebuttals by Oecolampadius. The former antagonists, Luther and Erasmus, both stood on Pirkheimer's side this time.[81] Among the Nuremberg preachers (Andreas Althamer) and in the city's rural environs (Andreas Flam), Luther discovered others on his side who were writing too. In contrast to rumors of Satan lurking in those who deny the presence in the sacrament, he here perceived voices speaking with another power. "Christ lives!" Luther wrote on learning that also Theobald Billikan, the Nördlingen theologian, was intending to break into print against Zwingli, Karlstadt, and Oecolampadius. "God is calling up his reserves against the new heretics. We have the good hope that Christ is moving ahead." He felt himself stimulated by such a vanguard and would plunge into the fray as soon as time permitted.[82]

For the moment, however, Luther was preoccupied, engaged in a smaller assignment that was characteristic of him. He was preaching on the question of the sacrament. To him it was more important that the simple Christian grasp the issue than to enter a theological encounter. The three sermons he preached on March 28 and 29, 1526, were in preparation for Easter Communion. They were published six months later, not by him yet not without his knowledge.[83] [As for their substance,] he first sought out the doubters among his hearers and endeavored to make it easier for them to partake of the Lord's Supper. He did so by avoiding any legalism and by encouraging them to abstain from participating until they got over their scruples.[84] Then in the manner he had already employed in responding to the Swabian *Syngramma*, he treated his opponents' two objections, which he considered essential: "For one thing, it is not becoming that the body and blood of Christ be in the bread and wine. And the

80. G. Baring, "Hans Denk und Thomas Müntzer in Nürnberg 1524," *ARG* 50 (1959): 145ff. Drews, *Pirkheimers Stellung*, 101ff.

81. Overview in Köhler, *Zwingli und Luther*, 1:234ff. Staehelin, *Lebenswerk Oekolampads*, 301ff.

82. To Nicholas Hausmann, January 20, 1526, WA Br 4:19 / 11, 13–14. To Billikan, see Köhler, *Zwingli und Luther*, 1:248ff.

83. *Sermon von dem Sakrament des Leibs und Bluts Christi wider die Schwarmgeister*, WA 19:482–523. There also the two extant copies of the sermons as taken down. [*LW* 36:335–61.]

84. WA 19:483 / 20ff.

other, this [presence] is not necessary"; *absurditas et nulla necessitas* is how he had previously summed up the two points in Latin.[85]

Luther's answer to the first objection shows what was on his mind when considering the mystery of the presence of Christ in the Supper. In nature there are more such mysteries, and even greater ones, which are true even though we are unable to comprehend them. The "soul"—we would say our entire capacity to perceive and think—runs through the whole body from head to foot and through all our members. The soul can at one and the same time think, speak, hear, see, feel. Should God, who created the soul, be unable to create the omnipresence of Christ? Or, to put it another way: I have but two eyes, and yet with them I can bring all the heads, which I have before me (say, from the pulpit), into one field of vision.[86] The voice, a fleeting breath, can carry the word to a hundred or a thousand ears. Indeed, with a voice I can rule an entire country. "From whence does it come that with words I can catch so many hearts?" If a voice can accomplish this, "should not Christ be able to do far more with his body?"[87] Luther is here thinking not only about the wonders of acoustics, the filling of space with the sound of a voice (Plotinus and later Giordano Bruno used this phenomenon as a parable descriptive of how God penetrates the world[88]), but he also combines the natural event with a preceding spiritual occurrence. The proclamation of the gospel brings the authentic Christ into the heart. "There you must say you have the authentic Christ, not as though he were in your heart like someone sitting on a chair, but as he now is at the right hand of God." He will not have himself fragmented, and yet he is brought to all the faithful "so that one heart receives not less and a thousand hearts not more than the one Christ."[89]

For Luther these analogies were not proofs. He required no additional reasons. He was convinced by the word of Christ, "This is my body. This is my blood." Yet by means of examples he intended to drive the arguments

85. WA 19:486 / 11–12. Cf. above, p. 519. [*LW* 36:338.]

86. WA 19:487 / 13ff.; 488 / 13ff. [*LW* 36:339.]

87. WA 19:488 / 21–22, 28–29. [*LW* 36:339.]

88. Plotinus, *Enneades*, trans. [into German] by Harder, 6:4 / 92. [Eng. trans. G. H. Turnbull, *The Essence of Plotinus: Extracts from the Six Enneades* (New York: Oxford, 1934), 6:185.] E. Metzke, "Sakrament und Metaphysik: Eine Lutherstudie über das Verhältnis des christlichen Denkens zum Leiblich-Materiellen" (1948), in Metzke, *Coincidentia oppositorum: Gesammelte Studien zur Philosophiegeschichte* (Witten, 1961), 195, n. 159. G. Bruno, *Gesammelte Werke*, trans. [into German] L. Kuhlenbeck (Leipzig, 1904), 2:40. H. Bornkamm, "Renaissancemystik, Luther, und Boehme," in *Luther: Gestalt und Wirkungen*, SVRG 188 (Gütersloh, 1975), 167ff.

89. WA 19:489 / 12ff., 20ff. [*LW* 36:340.]

of the opponents from the field, and to do so with profounder evidence: the well-known wonders of the natural world. To him these wonders were so overwhelming that they left no room for doubt, since God has guaranteed them with his Word. His opponents' misgivings, so he thought, were part of their blindness to the wonders of nature. "Those people lack nothing except that they have never taken a proper look at any creature."[90] "Were you fully to examine a little seed out in the field, you would practically die from a sense of awe."[91] Nevertheless, all natural and physical miracles (inclusive of the real presence of Christ in the Supper) are much less than that one inner miracle, that Christ comes into our heart. "For it is much greater that by faith he comes into our heart than that he is in the bread. To be sure, he uses the bread or the sacrament for the sake of faith." When we ponder this, it is unnecessary to dwell so much on the miracle in the sacrament, for in the presence of reason one can say only that no person on his own accord can have faith. Yet physical miracles can be a sign pointing to this, the greatest mystery. "So he holds on to the smaller miracles that he may thereby remind us of the greater ones."[92] Because people so often have no eye for God's handiwork, they have a difficult time understanding his word. This touches the other objection, namely, that it is not necessary in the Lord's Supper to receive the body and blood of Christ. "Do you then want to tell God what is necessary and what is not necessary . . . ?" "What God holds necessary—who are you to say it isn't so?" Then one might as well chide God for having sent Christ into the world:

> You had sin, death, the devil, and all else in your power. What use or need was there to send down your Son and to let him be treated so cruelly and die? You could have left him on high and let him simply be made known. It wouldn't have cost you more than a word. Then sin and death would have been destroyed, and the devil too. After all you are the Almighty.[93]

Two basic elements of Luther's thought and experience merge in these sermons: his sense of wonder for the mysteries of God's creative power, and his reverence for the Word of God, on which no human being is to cast doubt. To him the question of the Lord's Supper is far more than an exegetical one. He sees his opponents as deteriorating into "crude gram-

---

90. WA 19:487 / 25–26. [LW 36:339.]

91. WA 19:496 / 11ff. On Luther's sense of wonder toward nature, cf. H. Bornkamm, "Das Bild der Natur," in his *Luthers geistige Welt*, 4th ed. (Gütersloh, 1960), 187ff. [*Luther's World of Thought*, trans. M. Bertram (St. Louis: Concordia, 1958), 192–93.] [LW 36:344.]

92. WA 19:493 / 25–26, 24–25. [LW 36:343.]

93. WA 19:494 / 15–495 / 21; esp. 494 / 23–24; 495 / 13, 16ff.

matical fanatics." They evade a text, and turn into "subtle philosophical fanatics" who with reason spawning their objection clear God's miracles out of the way.[94]

With this twofold argumentation Luther crossed the controversy's existing boundary, one set by Honius and Karlstadt and one that had been dominated by probing into the meaning of the words of institution. Even earlier, Oecolampadius had raised the question of miracle in the Lord's Supper, yet not specifically against Luther but rather, so as to avoid a quarrel among contemporaries, against Peter Lombard. In his *Sentences* Lombard had attacked the "heresy" that claimed the body of Christ is only a sign in the sacrament and is only eaten as such. Oecolampadius distinguished between the inscrutable "mysteries" or sacraments (birth, the resurrection of Christ, predestination, etc.), and those administered by the church, which are intended for the awakening and confession of faith. "Miracle" is solely that which is extolled as such by the Holy Scripture, so they held.[95] However, in light of the miracles of God in nature, Luther saw this position as an inadmissible limitation of the concept of the miraculous. Oecolampadius, for his part, regarded Luther's view as downright absurd. He found Luther's "Sermon," of which he received a copy as soon as it appeared in October 1526, a "childish booklet."[96] He was not about to publish a rebuttal, because he had just recently made a "fair reply" to Luther's foreword to the *Syngramma*, in which he had challenged Luther simply to write against him and other critics: "If the right, true Spirit had not forsaken you, and if you had known of something that might do us good, you would not have held back."[97] Without surrendering his own position, Oecolampadius meant these words to be conciliatory, but for Luther it came as one more barb, goading him to reply. Melanchthon, who stood with Luther, had kept himself out of the fray. He simply wrote one short statement, intended apparently for the electoral court, when he commented on the biblical character of the doctrine of the real presence: "Now these words on the Supper are not contrary to other Scriptures, even though reason may find them strange."[98] To be sure, he had in pass-

94. *WA* 19:498 / 29–30, 36.

95. Staehelin, *Lebenswerk Oekolampads*, 278, according to *De genuina verborum Dei, 'Hoc est corpus meum' iuxta vetustissimos autores expositione liber* (1525), Peter Lombard, *Sentences* IV, dist. 10.

96. To Zwingli, October 13, 1526, *Zwinglis sämtliche Werke*, 8:735 / 2.

97. Staehelin, *Lebenswerk Oekolampads*, 311.

98. *CR* 1:760. According to Maurer, *Der junge Melanchthon zwischen Humanismus und Reformation*, vol. 2: *Der Theologe* (Göttingen, 1969), 500, to be dated not October 9, 1525, as in *CR*, but in early summer 1526. Melanchthon had already earlier, during the controversy with Karlstadt, declared repeatedly that if he were not instructed by means of a sure revelation he would not budge from the words of Scripture; January 12 and 23, 1525, to Oecolampadius and Thomas Blaurer, *Suppl*. *Mel*. 6 / 1:275–76, 277–78. *MBW* 370, 372.

ing considered replying to Oecolampadius's *Genuina Expositio*, the rebuttal to the Swabians' *Syngramma,* but he reconsidered and remained
silent.[99]

What everyone was waiting for after this attack was a word from Luther
himself. How true this was became clear in an encouraging word from the
young Landgrave Philip of Hesse. He had been following the disputed
issues in theology with keen interest, and at the moment was making
preparations to introduce the Reformation in his territory through the
synod of Homberg. For the present he still felt himself fully obligated to
the Reformers in Saxony. Therefore he could write them: "Don't forget
Zwingli, and don't forget Oecolampadius, and say something on the new
error. When you've got it ready, send it to me."[100] Meanwhile, the South
German circles critical of Luther were guessing as to why he remained
silent. "There's no trace of Luther. Now that he's achieved nothing by his
threats and abuses, he seems to have wrapped himself in silence" were
Capito's words to Zwingli.[101]

As if to mark time, Martin Bucer—intellectual leader of the
Strassburgers, who stood with the Swiss and was in close touch with
Zurich and Basel—allowed himself a couple of dubious pranks. In order to
earn some money, he requested from Bugenhagen permission to translate
into German his recently published commentary on the Psalms, for which
Luther had written a laudatory foreword.[102] Bugenhagen not only gave
permission but added generously that Bucer should feel free to translate
in a manner "deemed most suitable for our good Germans."[103] Bucer
interpreted Bugenhagen's permission liberally, and at several points he
dropped the Wittenberger's teachings on the Lord's Supper and insinu-
ated his own. Only a half-year after the translation was published did
Bugenhagen discover Bucer's tampering, coming on it in an Augsburg
reprint of his commentary on a single psalm (Psalm 111). On the title page
the local printer, a Zwinglian, assured the reader that this commentary
contained the "properly understood" (Zwinglian) interpretation of the
Lord's Supper. Immediately Bugenhagen wrote a correction, explaining

99. W. H. Neuser, "Die Abendmahlslehre Melanchthons in ihrer geschichtlichen Entwicklung (1519–1530)," BGLRK 26 (Neukirchen-Vlynn, 1968), 246ff.

100. Beginning of September 1526, WA Br 4:114 / 72ff.

101. September 26, 1526, *Zwinglis sämtliche Werke,* 8:725 / 13–14.

102. See above, p. 275.

103. "Hence, unlimited credit" (Köhler, *Zwingli und Luther,* 1:354), yet naturally only the
freedom to formulate for the sake of facilitating the understanding of the German readers.
An example for Bucer's "translation" (quotation marks are Köhler's), ibid., 357ff. Cf. also F.
Blanke in *Zwinglis sämtliche Werke,* 5:576, n. 1.

calmly but firmly that he had expressed himself often enough on the question of the Lord's Supper and had thereby drawn rejoinders from the "sacramentarians." "How," he questioned, "could my translator have ignored that?" "Why did he look around, where it was not necessary, for an opportunity to smuggle in his own teachings in place of mine, and thus to besmirch my name and the office of the Word which God has entrusted to me, and to make me suspect to the faithful?"[104] Bucer's *corriger la fortune*[105] [tampering with fortune] was doubly provoking to Bugenhagen because he had dedicated his commentary to Elector John and for this purpose had also solicited Luther and Melanchthon to write forewords. So now the distorted [German] form appeared to reveal Wittenberg theology as a whole.

The outrage of the Wittenbergers was intensified by still another prank of Bucer's, this one on Luther. Although not so aggravating, it too was entirely unauthorized. Into the fourth volume of Luther's *Postil*—of which he had already translated four to Luther's satisfaction—Bucer inserted several sections in which he took issue with Luther's teaching on the Lord's Supper. This was not a matter of falsification, as with Bugenhagen, but rather an insertion without Luther's knowledge. On discovering these additions in the finished fourth volume, Luther in September 1526 wrote the Strassburg printer Johannes Herwagen and expressed his satisfaction with Bucer's previous skillful translations, but then took sharp issue with the "poisonous comments" on which the translation "crucifies" the latest volume.[106] Luther again affirmed that his conscience was bound to those

104. *Oratio Joannis Bugenhagii Pomerani, quod ipsius non sit opinio illa de eucharistia, quae in psalterio sub nomine eius Germanice translato legitur* (Wittenberg, 1526; two reprints, 1527, otherwise not reprinted again). Geisenhof, *Bibliotheca Bugenhagiana* (see n. 54, above), 25ff. H. G. Leder, "Bugenhagen Literatur," in *Johann Bugenhagen: Beiträge zu seinem 400. Geburtstag*, ed. W. Rautenberg (Berlin, 1958), 333. I quote from the table of contents in the original printing, in Köhler, *Zwingli und Luther*, 1:360ff. *Sacramentarii oder Significatistae* (WA 19:472 / 1 and elsewhere) are nicknames given by the Wittenbergers to those opposing the doctrine of the real presence.

105. [Bugenhagen], "whose Psalter I have soiled with truth," is Bucer's own comment on his translation. To Zwingli, July 9, 1526, *Zwinglis sämtliche Werke*, 8:651 / 17–18. The instigator apparently was Pellikan, who had a job in the printing house of Petri in Basel, where the translation was published. Bucer named him to Zwingli, in discreet Latin: "Huius mei peccati authorem" [of whom I write as the author of my sin] (ibid., 652 / 3), yet he refrained from naming him openly and thus excusing himself. Köhler, *Zwingli und Luther*, 1:355.

106. WA 19:471 / 9ff., 22–23. Luther repeated his complaint about Bucer's action (in the course of a renewed recognition of his gift as a translator) in his tract *Dass diese Worte "Das ist mein Leib etc." noch feststehen* (1527) [That these words, "This is my body etc." still stand fast]. It angered him especially that his *Postil*, "the best book of all I have ever written," now had to serve in spreading the teachings of the opponents farther afield than they could have managed with their own writings (WA 23:279 / 13ff.).

words of institution which were repeated in boldface letters in many places throughout the volume. He demanded that the printer bring out a new edition that would include his letter of protest. As expected, Luther's letter showed up quickly in Strassburg, and Bucer was forced to reply to it. He did so without acknowledging the mistakes of which he had made himself guilty toward Bugenhagen and Luther, although Capito had warned him [against such evasion].[107] The Bucer pranks bred others. In Zurich, Leo Jud, under a pseudonym, claimed to prove that both Erasmus and Luther had earlier taught the same thing as Zwingli on the sacrament. So he challenged them to own up to their own earlier and better views.[108]

From several sides Luther thus came to hear what he had been telling himself ever more emphatically, that now he must respond to the opponents and no longer leave it to Bugenhagen, the Swabians, or other friends to defend his position. Yet he also felt that he had already written enough, considering his support of the *Syngramma* as a clear statement of his opinion.[109] One may give the intentions of Bucer and Jud the benefit of the doubt and imagine that they intended merely to let Luther appear publicly in a better light or even to make him change his thinking. However, whatever their motive, the means were dishonest. The atmosphere had been poisoned even before the great debate between the Wittenbergers and the Swiss, with their South German friends, got under way.[110]

Because of Luther's hesitation, it happened that Luther and Zwingli, the two major opponents, came on stage almost at the same time. So far Zwingli had kept himself out of the debate, yet his friends, especially Oecolampadius and Bucer, who had led the assault, had for some time been urging him to enter. On July 28, 1526, Bucer wrote Oecolampadius a

107. *Zwinglis sämtliche Werke*, 8:725 / 1ff. Köhler, *Zwingli und Luther*, 1:355, 367.

108. *Des Hochgelehrten Erasmi von Roterdam und Doctor Luthers maynung vom Nachtmal unsers Herren Jesu Christi, neuerlich aussgangen auff den XVIII. tag Apprellens* (1526). Jud called himself Ludovicus Leopoldi, Pfarrer zu Leberau. *WA* 19:463–64. Köhler, *Zwingli und Luther*, 1:143. He disclosed his real name only in a second pamphlet in which he replied to a letter of protest from Erasmus. The latter had objected vehemently, especially against being mentioned in the same breath with Luther and against being allegedly on the Zwinglian side. In both his writings Jud undermined his reliability for the church (ibid., 146ff.).

109. To Herwagen, *WA* 19:472 / 6ff. Luther's foreword to the *Syngramma*, above, p. 518.

110. The detailed defense that Köhler, *Zwingli und Luther*, 1:364ff., presents for Bucer serves at most to help us understand his reasons better, but not to excuse him. Luther's harsh word *insignis perfidia* (*WA* 19:471 / 25) apply only to Bucer's conduct toward Bugenhagen, which was a worse matter indeed.

letter intended for transmittal to Zwingli. Included was Luther's foreword to the *Syngramma* of the Swabians.[111] Bucer pleaded, "I wish Zwingli would publish a pamphlet in the German language in which he would give Luther a friendly yet deserved reminder not to rely too much on himself and to recognize that in treating this question he is not being led by a good spirit."[112] While Zwingli was thinking things over, demands reached him urging that he have something ready against Luther in time for the spring book fair [in Frankfurt am Main] in 1527.[113] Zwingli obliged. The book was out on time. Even its title corresponded to Bucer's wishes, *Amica exegesis, id est: expositio eucharistiae negocii ad Martinum Lutherum*.[114]

The tone of a personal address that Zwingli stuck in the title and in several sections of the book did not make it easy for Luther subsequently to respect the friendly motive. On the one hand, Zwingli indulged in all kinds of images of battle and confident victory. "As often as I have thought over the subject matter, nothing appeared so evident to me, nothing more certain than victory" ran the opening lines of his book.[115] "Triumph, triumph as our position ultimately will, the opposition it faces will make victory laborious" are Zwingli's words to Luther at the end. He added the well-intended but patronizing encouragement: "To err is human, also to stumble, or to be mistaken. Or do you rather imagine that something human is strange to you? So let yourself say: Could it be that I have forgotten myself?"[116] Elsewhere, however, Zwingli showered Luther with eulogies and, in the manner of humanists, compared him with heroes of antiquity: Diomedes, Jonathan, David, and Hercules.[117] At the same time Zwingli did not hesitate to remind Luther that on his own, and years earlier than Luther's entry onto the public scene, his own insights had placed him in an advanced position, for Luther, as Zwingli claimed, still believed in the power of the keys, that is, in the absolution following confession, in the intercession of the saints, and in purgatory. Zwingli's love of peace, however, has restrained him, he says, from discussing these differences, as well as the differing interpretations of the Lord's Supper, so

111. See above, p. 518.

112. *Zwinglis sämtliche Werke*, 8:647 / 2ff. Köhler, *Zwingli und Luther*, 1:462.

113. An entry list of letters up to February 28, 1527, in *Zwinglis sämtliche Werke*, 5:549.

114. "Friendly exposition, that is, an explanation of the Lord's Supper problem to Martin Luther." Ibid., 548ff.

115. Ibid., 562 / 10.

116. Ibid., 750 / 30ff.; 751 / 2ff.

117. Ibid., 613 / 12ff.; 722 / 2ff.; 723 / 1ff. Cf. F. Blanke, "Zu Zwinglis Vorrede an Luther in der Schrift, 'Amica Exegesis'" (1527), *Zwingliana* 5 (1930): 185ff.

as not to give the impression of shouting down the authority of such a man, much as a goose honking at a swan. Let Luther, however, bear in mind how much more nobly Zwingli has treated the subject than the Wittenberger in his violent attacks on good and learned men. "See, then, in whose heart the love of peace lies deeper!"[118] He might have known in advance that this mixture of hollow panegyrics and felt superiority would get him nowhere with Luther.

The real contents of Zwingli's book consisted in a defense of his friends Bucer and Jud, attacked by Luther especially in the letter to Herwagen, and in an extensive defense of his position on the institution and meaning of the Lord's Supper. He elaborates on the words of institution in terms of the trope concept, which he probably learned from Oecolampadius.[119] To understand Zwingli, one must understand what is at issue. The front against which Zwingli initiates his attack comprises first of all the signers of the *Syngramma*, above all Brenz. "They are completely mistaken if they imagine that through the Word the fact itself or faith in the fact is given. . . . For even after hearing the Word no one goes forth in faith unless he is drawn by the breath of the Spirit."[120] Now if it were a matter of receiving the body of Christ, faith would be declared insufficient. Zwingli thereby opposes Luther with two fundamental pronouncements taken from his own theology and become an issue when teaching of the bodily presence of Christ in the Supper: the Holy Spirit and the *sola fide*. Through these two alone is the presence of God to be experienced.[121]

At the same time, Zwingli struck up a new theme destined to become the main subject of the debate: the presence of Christ as a christological statement. The divinity of Christ does not lead to the conclusion of his body's omnipresence. Instead, his divine nature and his human nature are to be distinguished according to their essence. Aided by a second rhetorical device, borrowed from Plutarch and called *alloiosis*, or permutation, Zwingli intends to show that it is possible to speak alternately of the divine and the human attributes of Christ without surrendering the distinction between his two natures.[122] He means thereby to latch on to the *communicatio idiomatum* (the communication of attributes) of Christ, as taught

118. *Zwinglis sämtliche Werke*, 5:712 / 25–721 / 3; esp. 721 / 2–3. See there the detailed references of F. Blanke, in which Zwingli has misunderstood Luther's position on absolution, intercession of the saints, and purgatory.

119. See above, p. 511.

120. *Zwinglis sämtliche Werke*, 5:591 / 5, 7–8; cf. 590 / 5ff.

121. Ibid., 591 / 20ff.; 564 / 6ff.

122. Ibid., 679 / 6ff.

by the theologians of the patristic past. Yet even this basing of his argument on an inclusively rhetorical trope led him to turn a specialized term into one of common usage. He later called what he was doing "moral poetry . . . , ascribing a given moral quality to a person who does not have it by nature."[123] This kind of treatment removes no disposition or characteristic from one or the other of the two natures [of Christ]. The human body always requires a place. Thus the risen Christ, regarded in terms of his humanity, has been transferred back to the place where he was even before his birth: at the right hand of God. This is what Peter proclaimed to the congregation on Pentecost. This is what the disciples were permitted to see at Christ's ascension; so, likewise, Stephen, the witness made worthy by martyrdom. "I see the heavens opened, and the Son of man standing at the right hand of God" (Acts 7:56). From there he shall sometime return as judge.[124] But Luther's notion that the body of Christ is received in the Supper is demolished not only by these testimonies of the disciples but also by Christ's own admission "I will take you to myself, that where I am you may be also" [John 14:3]. Otherwise this would have to mean: If Christ is present everywhere according to his humanity, the elect must also be everywhere. "I am surprised that those Christ-eaters (the Lutherans) are not frightened off by Christophorus, who is taller than the Colossus of Rhodes."[125] These ingredients of cheap irony mingled freely in Zwingli's critique with assorted grammatical and exegetical objections, along with ideas of heaven portrayed with massive realism. This complex of motifs thus challenged Luther to undertake a multiple response.

In addition to his book, Zwingli sent Luther a special letter on April 1, 1527. In acerbity it far surpassed his earlier treatment and the letter of February 28 which had prefaced it.[126] In it Zwingli referred to a letter of Luther's, no longer extant, to Landgrave Philip of Hesse, purportedly saying now "the battle must be waged with the sword." If this citation is correct, it cannot mean the sword that metes out justice but the sword that

123. *Dass diese Worte Jesu Christi* . . . (1527) (see below, p. 537). With "custom poetry" Zwingli translates the rhetorical Greek term *ethology* [a systematic study of the formation of human character] or *ethopoiia; Zwinglis sämtliche Werke,* 5:938 / 6ff.; cf. ibid., 685 / 19. Also Loofs, *Dogmengeschichte* (see n. 25, above), 815. O. Ritschl, *Dogmengeschichte des Protestantismus* (Göttingen, 1926), 3:65–66.

124. *Zwinglis sämtliche Werke,* 5:695 / 3–697 / 9; esp. 696 / 2–3.

125. Ibid., 686 / 12ff.

126. On the preface, see n. 117, above. Text of the letter of April 1, WA Br 4:184–87. Also in *Zwinglis sämtliche Werke,* 9 (1925): 78ff. On this see Köhler, *Zwingli und Luther,* 1:490–91. G. W. Locher, "Die theologische und politische Bedeutung des Abendmahlsstreites im Licht von Zwinglis Briefen," *Zwingliana* 13 (1971): 285ff. WA Br 4:185 / 23ff. *Zwinglis sämtliche Werke,* 9:79 / 20ff.

wields governmental power and that should create a unified form of worship throughout the land.[127] Zwingli's letter was a mixture of bitter reproofs (raving, insolence, cruelty)[128] and clumsy attempts to persuade: " 'Sometimes even the great Homer is asleep.' So, I think, you too have long since reached the point of 'know thyself,' so that you see you don't know everything. . . . Say to yourself in this matter: How shall I proceed if I have not understood everything correctly and clearly?"[129] If any further damage were possible, Zwingli managed to do it with this letter. Luther told several friends about the "arrogant," "slanderous" letter. For a while it made the rounds among them. Melanchthon took pen in hand and charged that Zwingli, Oecolampadius, and Bucer treat this single question in their numerous writings "as though the other doctrines of faith contributed nothing to piety." Zwingli, on top of it all, wrote Luther a threatening letter.[130]

In the very month of Zwingli's *Amica exegesis*, Luther's first inclusive treatise devoted entirely to the Lord's Supper controversy also appeared. Its fulsome title: *That These Words of Christ, "This Is My Body," etc. Still Stand Firm Against the Fanatics*.[131] At first the target is still Oecolampadius, for he had addressed the subject earlier than Zwingli. There is only occasional mention of Zwingli, mainly in connection with his shorter writings. His inclusive treatment on the Supper in his *De vera et falsa religione commentarius* (1525) is not mentioned by Luther and apparently was not used.[132] More than anything else that Luther wrote on the Sup-

127. According to the above-mentioned (p. 524) letter of the landgrave in early September, the Wittenbergers had advised him "not to tolerate schismatic preachers," WA Br 4:113 / 10–11 with note. This, however, is directed against Roman Catholic worship, not against those departing from Wittenberg's teaching on the Lord's Supper. The same Zwinglian accusation is also in *Zwinglis sämtliche Werke*, 5:737 / 21ff.; 752 / 15ff. (with the notes by F. Blanke at both places). Cf. also below, p. 537. Zwingli sent his book to the landgrave only on June 18, 1527, with an accompanying letter, without raising complaints against him or Luther; ibid., 796–97.

128. *Furor, audacia, crudelitas*. WA Br 4:185 / 28, 35.

129. WA Br 4:185 / 41ff.

130. References of O. Clemen, WA Br 4:184. Melanchthon to Spalatin, May 4, 1527, CR 1:865. *MBW* 539.

131. WA 23:64–282 (handwritten MS), 65–283 (printed). In *Against the Heavenly Prophets*, 460, the Lord's Supper (in terms of Karlstadt's understanding) was a partial question. The "Sermon" of 1526 (see above, p. 520) was only a sermon print. [*LW* 37:3–150.]

132. Contrary to Köhler, *Zwingli und Luther*, 1:494. Under the references of W. Walther, WA 23:284ff., there is no mention of it. Had Luther read Zwingli's extensive presentation on the Eucharist, he would not have argued so one-sidedly with Oecolampadius. The naming of Zwingli in Luther's letter of November 5, 1525, to the Strassburgers is to be related not to the *Commentarius*, as Köhler in *Zwinglis sämtliche Werke*, 3:592, but to the treatise *Vom Tauf* [On baptism], in Köhler's later reference (*Zwingli und Luther*, 1:185) and in Clemen's (WA Br 3:602 / 9, n. 4).

per, this book makes lucid how firmly the newly upsurging question is bound up for him with the problems of his own theological beginnings. Once he had lamented that "we saw the Scriptures lying under the bench"[133] and complained that the church, declaring the Bible not sufficient, was seeking to supplement it with expositions by the councils and the church fathers. And now the new opponents were [doing something similar and] summoning still other authorities (church fathers and rhetoricians) onto the field. In Luther's view, these new opponents were playing the devil's game without realizing it. Nor will the devil stop there where they think they will be able to take their stand, but he will "carry on and attack more articles of faith, for his eyes are already agleam, saying that baptism, original sin, and Christ are nothing."[134] They think the "devil is away in Babylon or asleep at their side like a dog on a cushion." Yet "the devil is master of a thousand arts."[135] He is the real enemy on whom Luther keeps his eye. However, he has no hope of thereby being able to convert the fanatics themselves. "Christ converted no high priest," no prophet converted a false prophet, Paul converted no false apostle, nor the church fathers any archheretic. No more than they can he, Luther, convert an archfanatic, but he will "try to win away some of their disciples, or at least strengthen the simple and weak and protect them from the fanatics' poison."[136] This is the horizon of the history of the church and its heretics, and within it Luther sees his task unfold. His theme is the truth of Scripture, here summed up in a single verse of Christ: "This is my body."[137] What more should Luther say than he has already said in this controversy: Whoever understands "is" as "signifies" and "body" as "signifies body" must prove it either from the context (from "the text in the same place") or from an "article of faith," that is, from another undisputed expression of faith.[138] Against these two bases of proof there is no objection on general rhetorical or hermeneutical principles, as Oecolampadius and Zwingli would have it read.

Luther himself held fast to the same basis from which he had contested the Roman sacraments down to the biblical foundation of the Supper and of baptism. In his *Babylonian Captivity* he had laid down the rule against doing violence to the Word of God: the sacraments (unless clear circum-

133. WA 23:69 / 10–11. [LW 37:15–16.]
134. WA 23:69 / 28ff. [LW 37:16.]
135. WA 23:71 / 20–21, 24–25. [LW 37:17, 18.]
136. WA 23:75 / 3ff., 21ff. [LW 37:20.]
137. WA 23:75 / 35ff.; 87 / 22ff. [LW 37:21, 33.]
138. WA 23:91 / 33ff.; 93 / 25ff. [LW 37:31.]

stances prove otherwise) are to be understood "in no other than their grammatical and proper sense."[139] He upheld the same rule now: grammar versus the tropes of rhetoric, a device that may be utilized elsewhere to denote figures of speech but is here not determinative. Because word and substance, in his estimation, stood solidly and could be changed only by reinterpretation, it was not possible to entertain overtures of peace from the opponents. To Luther it was no issue of secondary importance about which one would not have to fight. Besides, since Karlstadt's first blow, they had attacked him, not he them.[140]

In terms of the Lord's Supper texts, Luther remained on the defensive, but when it came to the nonexegetical arguments of the opponents, he took the offensive. And attack he did—what he called their "subtle, philosophical fanaticism."[141] So, for example, their childlike impression that Christ was seated "at the right hand of God" and was there seen by illuminated witnesses made Luther respond with some of his most moving prose:

> The Scriptures teach us, however, that the right hand of God is not a specific place in which a body must or may be. . . . It is God who creates, effects, and preserves all things through his almighty power and right hand, as our creed confesses. For he dispatches no officials or angels when he creates or preserves something, but all this is the work of his divine power itself. . . . Therefore, indeed, he himself must be present in every single creature in its innermost and outermost being, on all sides, through and through, below and above, before and behind, so that nothing can be more truly present and within all creatures than God himself with his power.[142]

Luther does not make use of the language of the mystics, with which he was familiar, in order to depict God's omnipresence in the Word. Instead, he uses the testimonies provided for him by the Bible (Ps. 139:9–10; Jer. 23:24; Acts 17:27–28; Rom. 11:36). What he expresses is not pantheism but the incomprehensible omnipresence of God in his almightiness, which surpasses human thought.[143]

---

139. *WA* 6:509 / 11ff. [*LW* 36:30.]

140. *WA* 23:79 / 19ff., 30ff.; 81 / 31ff. [*LW* 37:23, 25.]

141. See above, p. 523.

142. *WA* 23:133 / 19ff., 30ff.; 134 / 3ff. Similar passages: *WA* 23:137 / 8ff., 31ff.; 143 / 10ff.; 151 / 1ff. [*LW* 37:57, 58.]

143. On this point, Grass, *Abendmahlslehre*, 63ff. It would indeed be wise not to speak of "pantheisizing passages in the writings on the Lord's Supper" (64). This caution bears also on the transcendence-immanence scheme of T. Harnack, *Luthers Theologie*, with special reference to his teaching on reconciliation and salvation, in vol. 1 (1862; new ed., Munich, 1927), 140, as cited in Grass, *Abendmahlslehre*, 64ff., for this schematization does not do justice to

For how can reason tolerate it that the Divine Majesty is so small as to be present in essence in a kernel, on a kernel, above a kernel, inside and out-side—even though it is one single Majesty, can nevertheless be completely and entirely present in every individual thing, countless in number though they be? For he certainly makes every single kernel in particular, in all its parts, on the inside and throughout, so his power must be present there throughout, in and on the kernel. . . . For he alone makes it all. On the other hand, the same Majesty is so great that neither this world nor even a thou-sand worlds could embrace it and say, "See, there it is!"[144]

The key word on which the debate turns is the biblical term "the right hand of God." In the Old Testament it designates the omnipresent, cre-ative, protective, or punishing power of God; in the New Testament it designates the exaltation of Christ to the majesty of God, that is, to par-ticipation in his rule, in the bestowing of the Holy Spirit, or also in the authority to represent us in God's presence.[145] A fundamental under-standing such as this makes it impossible for Luther to see God's right hand as a given [spatial] place differentiated from other places, as, for example, the Lord's Table bearing the eucharistic elements. God's right hand is where it becomes manifested creatively, whether in nature, world history, or in the word and sacrament that create the new person. Among the "subtle" objections, not drawn from the Scriptures, there is also this one: It is contrary to God's honor that he enter the elements of the Supper

---

Luther's point of view. The same judgment is in Peters, *Realpräsenz* (see n. 10, above), 77. Luther's concern is for seeing the connection of the omnipresence and the creative person-ality of God. This does not prevent our questioning Luther on philosophical terms, the way Metzke contends in his "Sakrament und Metaphysik" (see n. 88, above), 161. Metzke's aim is not to undo Luther's theological explications and change them into philosophical statements but to focus on two specific points: (1) that in his own way Luther sets a question in motion which has become a central theme also in twentieth-century metaphysics, namely, "how God and the Spirit can be present in the reality of space" (194); and (2) that consequently Luther's explications clarify the boundary of metaphysics. "Thus Luther's theology of the sacrament is in this respect philosophical, for it summons metaphysics to turn about and thus to remind man of the boundary where he is simply a recipient in terms of his entire, undivided being—with mouth and heart, with soul and body" (204). Luther himself also saw philosophical questions in the framework of theology: on the one hand, as a result of the "subtle, philosophical fanaticism" of his opponents (see p. 523, above); on the other, in the philosophical categories of the scholastic doctrine of God, which he brought specifically into the discussion only in his later (1528) treatise, *Confession Concerning Christ's Supper* (see p. 548, below). [LW 37:161–372.]

144. WA 23:137 / 8ff., 17ff. [LW 37:59.]

145. In the Old Testament, especially in Psalms (e.g., 20:7; 44:4; 45:5; 63:9; 77:11); Exod. 15:6, 12; Job 40:14, Isa. 41:10; 66:2; Jer. 23:24; Lam. 2:3–4. In the New Testament, Matt. 22:44; Col. 3:1; 1 Pet. 3:22; Acts 2:33; Rom. 8:34.

in the mode of Christ. This kind of objection, according to Luther, corresponds to that of the pagan critics against the old church fathers: It is unworthy of a deity to be born as a human being and crucified. Thus, Luther contends, his opponents have not grasped the inclusive meaning of the incarnation.

> The honor of our God is that for our sake he descends deepest of all into flesh, into bread, into our mouth, heart, lap, and besides that he suffers for us, that he is treated without respect, on both the cross and the altar, as St. Paul says, 1 Cor. 11[:27] that some eat of this bread unworthily. He endures it without letup that before his divine eyes his Word, his work, and everything he has is persecuted, slandered, dishonored, and abused, and nevertheless he is still seated in his glory.[146]

This combining of God's omnipotent creativity and omnipresent indwelling, which mediates his grace to us, comprises the background for Christ's presence in the sacrament, as he himself has promised. Theology in its most inclusive sense and exegesis in its most literal sense give Luther the certitude with which he upholds his understanding of the words of institution.

In this secure position the counterattack of the Swiss—first of Zwingli, and then, in association with him, of Oecolampadius—made no impression on him; certainly not when they adduced the text John 6:63 ("the flesh is of no avail") in support of their commentary on the words of institution.[147] Ever since the debate on the Roman understanding of the Eucharist in his *Babylonian Capitivity*, Luther was convinced that the entire sixth chapter of the Gospel according to John deals not with the sacrament of the altar but with faith, as "a spiritual and lively feeding" on the word made flesh. So too (as one could conclude in those days) the denial of the cup to the laity could not be based on the fact that in John 6 Christ describes himself only as the living bread and not also as the living cup.[148] The unified sense of the chapter became for Luther the hermeneutical key to verse 63, the leading exegetical argument of his opponents. That verse says nothing on the question of the real presence of Christ in the Supper. It says only that to receive the body of Christ with-

---

146. WA 23:157 / 30ff. Cf. WA 23:157 / 8ff. [*LW* 37:72; cf. 71.]

147. Zwingli, "Ad Matthaeum Alberum de coena domini epistola," *Sämtliche Werke*, 3:336 / 29–342 / 10. On the origins of this thought in Zwingli, stimulated in part by Honius's letter, and the beginnings of the controversy, see H. Gollwitzer, "Zur Auslegung von Joh. 6" (see n. 37, above), 143ff. On Oecolampadius, cf. Staehelin, *Lebenswerk Oekolampads*, 281–82.

148. See p. 504, above. WA 6:499 / 22ff.; 502 / 7ff., 26ff. [*LW* 36:15.]

out faith is to no avail, which is no different from the condition for receiving the word of Christ.[149]

Beside the questions concerning the concept of God and the problems of exegesis, Luther addresses himself to the citations from the church fathers as gathered by Oecolampadius in his treatise *Genuina expositio*.[150] Nowhere does Luther tackle again such a rallying of patristic texts. He prepares his reply with a risky stroke that could really have knocked the weapon from his hand right at the outset, claiming that in no church fathers can one find the negative statement, on which his opponents depend, that only bread and wine but not the body and blood of Christ are present in the Supper.[151] Nevertheless, at the conclusion of the book, Luther resumes a discussion of the most important of the selections from the fathers. It is a wearisome debate from citation to citation, behind which there is no balanced treatment of the authors. This holds especially for Augustine, whose judgment was especially valuable to Luther. While modern (at least Protestant) research in the history of dogma denies that Augustine taught a bodily partaking of the incarnate Christ,[152] Luther had not as yet recognized the pervasive spirituality of the Augustinian teaching on the sacrament and so had allowed himself to be deceived by bogus words or faulty conclusions.[153] Luther had an easier time presenting the

149. The exegetical difficulties of this chapter are today offered a solution by assuming that the text is available to us only in a reworked form, meaning either the recasting of some pre-Johannine text by the author of the Fourth Gospel or a later ecclesiastical redaction in the sense of Ignatius of Antioch and the concept of the Lord's Supper as represented by him. Cf. these essays of G. Bornkamm: "Die eucharistische Rede im Johannes-Evangelium," in his *Geschichte und Glaube*, vol. 1: *Gesammelte Aufsätze* (Munich, 1968), 3:60ff.; and "Vorjohanneische Tradition oder nachjohanneische Bearbeitung in der eucharistischen Rede des Johannes 6?" in ibid., vol. 2: *Gesammelte Aufsätze*, 4 (1971): 51ff. G. Bornkamm represents the second solution. Independently thereof, his argument is valid: "Against Zwingli, for whom John 6:63 was a pivotal point in his teaching on the Lord's Supper, Luther was right when he contested that *sarx* in this text applied to the Supper. Already Bugenhagen and the signers of the *Syngramma* against Zwingli correctly understood *caro* [flesh, Lat.] in the carnal sense." (See Gollwitzer, "Zur Auslegung von Joh. 6," *Gesammelte Aufsätze*, 3:65, n. 20.)

150. See n. 95, above.

151. WA 23:129 / 4ff. [LW 37:54.]

152. Cf. Loofs, *Dogmengeschichte*, 5th ed. by K. Aland (Tübingen, 1953); 2:327–28: "In none of these collected conceptions [of Augustine] is there the thought of partaking of the 'true body and blood of Christ' on the part of the faithful—and indeed not on the part of the unbelievers. . . . Nevertheless, Augustine often speaks with apparent realism of an eating of the body of Christ." He could "speak 'realistically' without thinking realistically." Likewise Seeberg, *Dogmengeschichte* (see n. 24, above), 2:459ff.

153. Luther's misunderstanding becomes more plausible when we realize that the passage on which he relied most for proving Augustine's realistic concept of the sacrament was a citation in the Roman *Corpus iuris canonici* (III dist. II c. 32; see WA 23:211 / 1–2), a passage that does not appear in Augustine's works: "Sacramentum est invisibilis gratiae visibilis forma." (The passage that sounds most like it is in epistle 105, *Ad Donatistas* 3, *MPL* 33:401. It reads: "Si autem malum est, operatur per illum Deus visibilem Sacramenti formam; ipse autem donet invisibilem gratiam.") Cf. Hoffmann, "Abendmahlskontroverse" (see n. 44,

statements of pre-Augustinian fathers in support of his concept of the Supper.[154] From them, especially Irenaeus and Hilary, he could most clearly substantiate the double "benefit" to those receiving the body of Christ.

> If we feed on him spiritually through the Word, then he abides in us spiritually in our soul; if one eats him physically, he abides in us physically and we in him. As we eat him, he abides in us and we in him. He is not digested or transformed but ceaselessly he transforms us, our soul into righteousness, our body into immortality. So the ancient fathers spoke of the physical eating.[155]

The clamp holding this anthropological dualism together is faith. Feeding on the body in the bread also strengthens the soul, "by virtue of the fact that it believes it is Christ's body which the mouth eats, and so faith clings to the body which is in the bread. Now that which lifts, bears, and binds faith is not useless but salutary."[156] Not the eating of a supernatural food as such, but faith in the promise joined to it, leads to eternal life. Thereby the eschatological circle is closed. Luther could hardly have said more clearly why the reality of the Lord's Supper meant so much to him as an event and why any relaxing of the language—changing the event into a simile—struck him as utterly mischievous.[157]

This controversy made the Lord's Supper question a theme within the Reformation. References to scholastic theology do not occur; only later do they play a limited role.[158] Only transubstantiation is on one occasion brushed aside with a light touch: There "is here no need for transubstantiation or transformation into his body." Theories about it are unnecessary; it is a matter of a very simple statement. It is not to be misunderstood by

---

above). This concept that *forma* (or *figura*) means the outward shape of an invisible reality, Luther discovered in two Tertullian passages (*Against Marcion* 4.103 and *On the Resurrection* 8. Hoffmann, "Abendmahlskontroverse," 155–56). The concept of *figura* is manifold, "an obscure and wavering word." Here, contrary to Oecolampadius, it does not mean a decking out or a rhetorical image. Instead, it is to be understood mathematically as form or shape, with the bread as the outward, visible shape of the body of Christ. *WA* 23:219 / 11ff.

154. Irenaeus, Cyprian, Hilary of Poitiers. *WA* 23:229 / 21–241 / 34. Details in Hoffmann, "Abendmahlskontroverse," 152ff.

155. *WA* 23:255 / 24ff. [*LW* 37:132.]

156. Ibid., 259 / 1ff. [*LW* 37:134.]

157. The reference to eternal life [immortality] first emerges here in Luther's writings and recurs only seldom thereafter. Grass, *Abendmahlslehre* (see n. 10, above), 106–7, counts only two other places. Reference to it was especially appropriate here, because the opponents had questioned properly, according to Grass, the benefit of receiving the body of Christ, and perhaps also because Luther could thereby make it clear how highly he prized faith—the spiritual dimension.

158. See below, p. 548.

the use of spatial analogies ("like bread in the basket or wine in the cup"). The issue is purely one of identity.

> When the fathers and we occasionally say. . . . "Christ's body is in the bread," we do so quite simply because by our faith we wish to confess that Christ's body is present. Otherwise we may well allow it to be said that it is in the bread, it is the bread, it is where the bread is, or whatever you wish. Over words we do not wish to argue, just so the meaning is retained that it is not mere bread that we eat in Christ's Supper, but the body of Christ. [159]

At any rate, it is an identity under changed signatures.

> His flesh is not flesh, or fleshy, but spiritual; therefore it cannot be consumed, digested, and transformed, for it is imperishable as all that is of the Spirit, and a food of an entirely different kind from the perishable food. Perishable food is transformed into the body which eats it; this food, however, transforms the person who eats it into what it is itself, and makes him like itself—spiritual, alive, and eternal; as Christ says, "This is the bread from heaven, which gives life to the world" (John 6:33). [160]

Although he too regarded the effect of the Lord's Supper in spiritual terms, as mediated by faith, no amount of emphasis enabled Luther to bridge the gap between himself and his opponents. The identity itself, the "is" (not the "signifies"), stood insuperably between them.

Neither Zwingli's nor Luther's book on the subject could end the conflict. Since both books appeared at about the same time, they talked past each other. At best they could provide the prerequisites for an actual dialogue. How bitter such a dialogue might become was suggested in the acid title of Zwingli's extensive rebuttal. Written immediately on his receipt of Luther's book, the title page summed up his position: "That these words of Jesus Christ, 'This is my corpse [*sic!* Leichnam] which is being given for you,' will forever have the old and unique meaning, and [which] M. Luther in his latest book has not at all taught but proven as his own and the pope's meaning. Huldrych Zwingli, Christian answer." [161] Zwingli landed the hardest blow by his assertion on the title page that Luther taught the same things as the pope. In the wake of his two thus far lengthy presentations in *De vera ac falsa religione commentarius* (1525) and *Amica exegesis* (1527), this was Zwingli's first inclusive work on the Lord's Supper in German. He wrote this for a wide audience, including above all (and this was the unusual feature) Luther's territorial prince, Elector John, to

159. WA 23:145 / 16ff., 26ff. [LW 37:65.]
160. WA 23:203 / 23ff. [LW 37:100.]
161. *Zwinglis sämtliche Werke*, 5:805.

whom he dedicated the book. He did so with a peasantlike pride in his simple style, poking fun at the customary courtly forms of address. Zwingli complained to the elector that Luther "not only has been striking at the nerve of the Christian spirit and love, but also—under the glamor of his own name—intending to force and uphold Scripture in its untrue meaning," for example, with his exposition of John 6:63.[162] He urged the elector not to allow himself to be moved to ban the teaching of the [so-called] fanatics.[163]

Zwingli's rebuttal, written under pressure from friends and with an eye to publicity, explains why it offers little new theological input. To defend himself against Luther's attack, Zwingli tried to prove his superiority. Sometimes the line of argument was drowned out by the noise of battle. "Here God's Word will gain the upper hand—not fanatics, devils, rogues, heretics, murderers, agitators, pharisees or hypocrites, nor hiss, boom, lightning, thunder, po, pu, pa, slap-bang!"[164] Words like these, taken from Luther's writings, became Zwingli's musical accompaniment. The homage Zwingli had paid Luther in his *Amica exegesis*[165] was as good as gone. Instead, references to Luther's mistakes and backwardness (e.g., in protection of images) were intensified.[166] Ironically, Zwingli claimed that he and his friends made nothing of the dust Luther had been raising against them. "We are used to him—from the demolition of idols and altars, which, as you teach, one might indeed have, so as to learn better how to limp on both knees"[167] (that is, not to venerate but still to retain them).

Zwingli's comments on the subject at hand are essentially limited to two themes: (1) He bases his symbolic interpretation of the words of institution on a large number of passages in which the redemptive work of Christ is related not to the eating and drinking of his body but to the working of the "Comforter," the Holy Spirit, and to the hearing, believing, and remembering of the shedding of his blood, his death, and his resurrection. This spiritual happening can be set forth in the picture-language of Paul when he speaks of planting: "As we have been planted in the likeness[168] of

162. Ibid., 806 / 13ff.; 808 / 6ff.

163. Ibid., 807 / 2. Allusion to the presumed letter of Luther to Landgrave Philip of Hesse; see above, p. 529. On this see F. Blanke, ibid., 807, n. 5; 752, n. 2; 849, n. 21.

164. Ibid., 811 / 10ff.

165. See above, p. 527.

166. *Zwinglis sämtliche Werke*, 5:821 / 16ff. Summarized ibid., 824 / 15ff.

167. Ibid., 857 / 17ff.

168. "*Tō homoiōmati, similitudini*" (Vulgate), in the likeness of his death (through baptism), cf. *Theological Dictionary of the New Testament*, ed. Gerhard Kittel [Eng. trans. Geoffrey W. Bromiley (Grand Rapids: Wm. B. Eerdmans, 1964–76)], 5:191ff.

Christ's death so we shall also be planted into his resurrection" (Rom. 6:5). Zwingli thus rejects Luther's connection between the Lord's Supper and immortality [eternal life]. "We want you [Luther] to understand that everything you ascribe to the bodily eating can be ascribed to God's Word only by grace or the Spirit of God, the same as with the resurrection of the body."[169] Of course, he thereby avoided the theme that had drawn Luther's attack on the significative interpretation of the words of institution. As earlier, Zwingli upheld the trope concept and referred anew to the letter of Honius. He described it as a godsend. What he owed it was not an initial impulse but the substantiation of a personal understanding already won. Besides, the letter was an aid to making the words intelligible to simple folk.[170]

(2) If from this angle the two battle fronts remained unchanged, Zwingli at least built up his position at a point where Luther could not yet have attacked, for it was in his latest writing (as yet unknown to Luther) that Zwingli endeavored to resolve the christological problem of the Lord's Supper question by making use of a mode of speech in Plutarch: the *alloiosis* (of change) or the *heterosis* (of alteration). Zwingli presupposes a strict differentiation in the two natures of Christ which permits only a figurative, rhetorical transmission of the divine nature's attributes to the human, and vice versa. Luther, to the contrary, defended the unity of Christ's person and its attributes in his understanding of the Lord's Supper. Zwingli thus went after him with intensified acerbity.

> [Luther,] you poke your head in the door and shout, "God's right hand is everywhere. Christ is at God's right hand, and so too the corpse [body] of Christ is everywhere." See how nicely you draw conclusions. Whoever taught you to twist and unravel Christ's two natures so neatly, misleading the ordinary folk into applying to the human nature [of Christ] what is part of— indeed, what is exclusively—the divine? . . . See here, shouldn't you be ashamed to make such false syllogisms?[171] Of course, the only reason for it is that you can juggle, but you can't be subtle. And so you journey to the fairs of village churches and dupe anyone who will listen.[172]

Historically, here were two basic trends in the theology of the ancient church—one dyophysite, the other monophysite—coming at each other, in simpler form but on a collision course. Zwingli represented the

169. *Zwinglis sämtliche Werke*, 5:898 / 18ff.; 899 / 9ff.

170. Ibid., 907 / 9ff.

171. Conclusions.

172. *Zwinglis sämtliche Werke*, 5:930 / 23ff.; 932 / 27ff. In the original, *beseflest* (dupe or deceive), a coarse word from beggars' jargon.

dyophysite solution in terms of the traditional Chalcedonian Christology, yet with the decisive alteration that what is there taught as the unity of the person of Christ is expressed by Zwingli only in the figures of classical rhetoric. Educated humanist that he was, Zwingli found that figures offered him a way out of the difficulties of classical Christology. But he also learned that figures do not connect. He thereby lost the theological context necessary for his statements on the person of Christ, lost the combination of Christ's attributes (communicatio idiomatum), for which he too, in his way, had to be concerned.[173]

In debating Luther over the church fathers, Zwingli's comments were of no great significance. Although less conversant in this field than Oecolampadius, he drew the great heretic Marcion into the game: "Look out, Luther! Marcion wants to come into your garden!"[174] In connection with John 3:13 ("No man hath ascended up to heaven but he that came down from heaven, even the Son of man which is in heaven" [KJV]), Luther had said that the body of Christ is at the same time in heaven as well as on earth, indeed, at all ends of it. "For his transfiguration has not made him another person, but as before so also since, he is everywhere present." In heaven he experiences no bodily privation.[175] Zwingli concluded from this that Christ's body was incapable of suffering while on earth. "And then Marcion is right: Christ had an invented body incapable of suffering." "If so, then welcome, Marcion and all Marcionites!" If Christ's body is capa-

---

173. A detailed examination of Zwingli's Christology is lacking. G. W. Locher's Die Theologie Zwinglis im Lichte seiner Christologie has so far appeared only in its first volume: Die Gotteslehre (Zurich, 1952). C. Gestrich, Zwingli als Theologe: Glaube und Geist beim Züricher Reformator (Zurich and Stuttgart, 1967), and G. W. Locher, Huldrych Zwingli in neuer Sicht (Stuttgart, 1969), touch only on the theme. The most perceptive presentation is by E. Zeller (the student of Ferdinand Christian Baur and later master of the "philosophy of the Greeks"), Das theologische System Zwinglis dargestellt (Tübingen, 1853). Zeller brings out the contrast in Zwingli's and Luther's conception of the natures of Christ, giving it this drastic formulation: "(According to Zwingli) we are to think of the combination of the two (natures) only according to a mechanical, not a chemical, analogy" (82). Zwingli employs the contrast of body and spirit or the picture of a box and its contents: "The box in which the manna was stored is Christ's humanity, in which the divinity, the bread of life, is stored. For according to his divinity Christ is the food of the soul; Christ's body, however, has been elevated to God's right hand"; In Exodum annotationum particula (1527), Zwinglis sämtliche Werke, 5:374 / 24ff. The jar in Exod. 16:33 is, according to Zwingli, an anticipation of the ark of the covenant; ibid., 374 / 10ff. Luther, to the contrary, always used the simile of the red-hot iron. Surely these are at best bulky figures, yet they have something to say about the indefinable basic intuitions of both men. Cf. also Ritschl, Dogmengeschichte (see above, p. 209, n. 68), 3:117ff.

174. Zwinglis sämtliche Werke, 5:941 / 24ff.

175. [Cf. the changed connotation in the RSV translation of John 3:13, "No one has ascended into heaven but he who descended from heaven, the Son of man."] Citation from WA 23:147 / 28ff. [LW 37:66.] See also Zwinglis sämtliche Werke, 5:940–41.

ble of suffering on earth, then it must also be so in heaven, or there are two bodies. "Tell us, then, whether Mary also gave birth in heaven, or how he did get up there.[176] In gross misunderstanding Zwingli applied to Luther the docetism of Marcion as he had come to know it from Tertullian's furious polemics.[177]

At the end of his book, Zwingli once again assembled Luther's errors, summing them up in brief theses:

> (1) The body of Christ is like his divine nature, omnipresent. (2) Christ shows himself to us in this sacrament so that we will know where to find him. (3) Christ's body, eaten bodily, takes away sin. (4) Christ's flesh is an entirely spiritual flesh. (5) Christ's flesh, bodily eaten, preserves our body until resurrection. (6) Christ's body, bodily eaten, bestows or increases faith. All this is how you [Martin] speak contrary to God's Word.[178]

This latest phase of the encounter thus shifted the emphasis from the exegetical question, on interpreting the words of institution, to christological and soteriological problems. Between Luther and Zwingli the difference thus grew all the more earnest and inclusive.

Luther could not respond to Zwingli's book for a long time, partly because he was surprisingly late in receiving a copy. While the Strassburgers were relishing it since early July 1527, Luther's own copy, announced by Zwingli, reached him only on November 10 [his birthday, St. Martin's Day]. Prior to that date, however, he had already begun to read a borrowed copy. Besides, he was in a very demanding situation. There were the continuing transactions over the Saxon church visitation, a long bout of personal illness, care for his household during an outbreak of the plague, and concern for his wife anticipating childbirth. All these things bore down on him heavily.[179] In spite of everything, by late November he was assuring friends that Zwingli would be hearing from him; on December 14 he announced that his book against Zwingli would appear in time for the Frankfurt book fair in the spring of 1528.[180]

---

176. *Zwinglis sämtliche Werke*, 5:941 / 24–942 / 7; esp. 941 / 26–27; 942 / 6–7. "Marcion and Marciönin" is a merely rhetorical trill.

177. Tertullian *De carne Christi* 1–2 and elsewhere.

178. *Zwinglis sämtliche Werke*, 5:976 / 11–977 / 6. Then, in the manner of the humanists, Zwingli closed with a play on Luther's name: "God grant you the truth and self-knowledge so that you, Luther, may remain pure and don't become *loutrion* (dirty dishwater)." For Zwingli it was also a linguistic flirtation with a word that occurs only three times in Greek literature. Cf. F. Blanke, ibid., 977, n. 5.

179. On the visitation, see above, pp. 490ff. On his illness and cares of the household, see below, pp. 560ff.

180. Announcements since November 22, 1527, see WA 26:245–46. The Frankfurt book fair notice, first given December 14, in his letter to Hausmann, then definitely on February 28, 1528, to Link. First notice of the publication, February 5, to Spalatin, WA Br 4:300 / 21; 388 / 11; 376 / 8–9. Cf. WA 26:244–46. Köhler, *Zwingli und Luther*, 1:558ff.

Luther's expansive volume *Confession Concerning Christ's Supper* (1528) was not put together very felicitously. To be sure, he divided it into three clearly separated parts: "First, to warn our people by showing that this fanatical spirit has completely failed to answer my arguments. Second, to analyze the scriptural passages that teach about the holy sacrament. Third, to confess all the articles of my faith in opposition to this and every other new heresy, so that neither during my lifetime nor after my death will they be able to claim that Luther agreed with them—as they have already done in certain instances."[181] These were not simply three parts of quite different length. The last part was a confession formulated in less than a dozen pages.[182] The first two parts necessarily impose on each other. In addition, his approach was to single out specific opponents, turning now to this one, now to that one. Yet they all advanced similar teachings (Zwingli, Oecolampadius, Schwenkfeld, Wyclif), which forced Luther to be repetitious. As in so many of Luther's occasional writings, here too he developed no train of thought one could follow. Even so, these crisscrossing lines did not prevent the two major and complex themes from standing out. These themes had been crystallized during earlier stages of debate as central problems: the hermeneutical question and the christological question.

The hermeneutical question embraced more than the problems brought into the discussion by Oecolampadius and Zwingli. To begin, however, their focus on the figurative interpretation of the words of institution by means of the rhetorical concept of trope[183] comprised the opening theme. Luther did not reject the trope concept out of hand. Biblical and Christian language, he noted, makes use of the figurative: "Mary is rosy dawn; Christ a fruit of the womb; the devil is the god of this world; the pope is Judas; St. Augustine is Paul; St. Bernard [of Clairvaux] is a dove." Yet the modifier does not thereby supplant the subject. This is a matter simply of metaphor, of a "new word" that does not change the original one. So too the German language clarifies the comparison by adding a differentiating adjective: "Luther is Huss; Luther is another

181. WA 26:262 / 19ff. [LW 37:163.]

182. Part 1, WA 26:262–445; part 2, WA 26:445–498; part 3, WA 26:499–509. [LW 37:161–303; 303–60; 360–72.]

183. See above, p. 511. In the literature on Luther's understanding of the Lord's Supper and of the real presence, it was already G. Ebeling, *Evangelische Evangelienauslegung: Eine Untersuchung zu Luthers Hermeneutik* (Munich, 1942; reprint, Darmstadt, 1962), 332, n. 260, who pointed out that we lack a treatment of the controversy from the viewpoint of hermeneutics as employed on the two respective sides. On pp. 332–44 of the work named, Ebeling provides us with a brief, rewarding sketch.

Huss; Luther is a real Huss; Luther is a new Huss." This gives expression to his actual being and is not simply a random comparison. "It does not sound right or ring true if I say 'Luther signifies Huss'; rather, 'He is a Huss.' In such expressions we are speaking of an essence—what a person is and not what he represents."[184] A stylistic concept thus enables us to get at the actual being by means of a comparison from another field; as with Horace, whom Luther quotes: "Dixeris egregie, notum si callida verbum reddederit iunctura novum" (i.e., "You will have expressed yourself admirably if you relate a familiar word suggestively and make it a new one").[185] Yet, in fact, there is no actual identity between the things compared. "For a simple word and a metaphorical word are not one but two words." So too we are able to speak of the body of Christ given for us only as it is, in terms of its visible image, and not metaphorically. Moreover, "because it was visibly given for us, it can be nowhere present unless it is there visibly."[186] Luther thus turned his opponents' proofs around: to speak figuratively, in trope, about the body of Christ and simultaneously to deny his reality as present is not to speak of him at all. On this argument he founds and develops his concept of picture language. Even the image carries the original in it. When speaking about a rose image in gold, silver, or wood, who says, This signifies a rose? No. We say, This is a rose. Different though the material, the "being" is the same. Indeed, "how would a meaning be there without there first being an original?" So we think of two roses, "both of which truthfully be the name 'rose'; one which represents, the other which is represented."[187] It is not Luther's intention thereby to develop an abstract proof for the presence of the body of Christ in the Supper; he is simply bent on refuting a false application of the figurative, the trope, as Oecolampadius and Zwingli did. Properly understood, the trope always presupposes a relationship of reality on the part of a given "being." "For it is an infallible rule in all languages that wherever the word 'is' occurs in an expression, one is surely speaking of the substance of the said object and not of its representation."[188] The exposition of the words of institution is dependent not on ancient rhetoric but on the pronouncements of the Bible and the context of the faith in which we stand.

184. WA 26:273 / 2ff., 19ff.; 274 / 1ff., 19ff. [LW 37:173, 174.]
185. Luther translates Horace: "Gar fein ists geredt, wenn du ein gemein Wort kannst wohl verneuen." WA 26:274 / 19–20, 22–23; 272 / 23–24. [LW 37:173, 172.]
186. WA 26:277 / 23–24; 281 / 10–11. [LW 37:175, 178.]
187. WA 26:383 / 22ff., 33–34; 385 / 16–17. [LW 37:255, 257.]
188. WA 26:383 / 19ff. [LW 37:255.]

Luther explains the biblical concept by means of an extended comparison on the Lord's Supper in the three synoptic Gospels and in the apostle Paul.[189] Textual problems that are today still disputed are, of course, treated by Luther with other presuppositions. He is quite unaware of such matters as variant manuscript renditions: the shorter and the longer text in Luke. He uses only the text available to him in the Vulgate and in Erasmus's Greek New Testament, which again today is proving itself the better one.[190] Nor could Luther think of reconstructing the Aramaic original of Jesus' words. Nonetheless, with Luke, "This cup is the new testament in my blood," he went back to the Hebraic usage (in = through = for . . . sake), while with Mark and Matthew he examined the Greek, "This is my blood of the new testament."[191] Both uses mean the same. The Lukan test, which appears also in Paul, speaks of the real blood of Christ, employing neither simile nor trope. This vouches for the reality of the expression also in the other evangelists, "because it is one and the same blood of which all four are speaking." So "Matthew and Mark step forth hand in hand with Luke and Paul and overthrow them [the opponents] again, showing the 'new testament' cannot be a trope" [or, taken figuratively].[192] Here Luther's chief concern is not with the grammatical question but with the reality conveyed by the text, by the actuality of the covenant here founded.

> For the new testament is promise, indeed, much more: the bestowal of grace and the forgiveness of sin; i.e., the true gospel. . . . Therefore, he who drinks of this cup really drinks the true blood of Christ and the forgiveness of sins or the Spirit of Christ, for these are received in and with the cup. Here is received no mere figure or sign of the new testament or of the blood of Christ.[193]

The expressions of reality are mutually supportive. The bodily is no piece of magic or a random miracle, for it has a spiritual sense. The spiritual is something real which ever and again the celebration of the sacrament offers to the believer. Luther finds a supporting reference exclusively in Luke (22:14–20). In the Passover meal, according to his own words, Jesus drinks of the fruit of the vine for the last time. Thus in the ensuing "new

189. WA 26:448–98. [LW 37:303–60.]

190. Cf. E. Schweizer, "Abendmahl im Neuen Testament," RGG³ 1 (1957): 14–15. G. Bornkamm, "Herrenmahl und Kirche bei Paulus," in G. Bornkamm, Studien zu Antike und Urchristentum: Gesammelte Aufsätze (Munich, 1959), 2:138ff., esp. 150ff.

191. WA 26:464 / 28ff.; 465 / 12ff., 30ff. [LW 37:320, 321.]

192. WA 26:477 / 21–22, 34ff. [LW 37:336.]

193. WA 26:468 / 32ff., 39ff. [LW 37:325–26.]

Supper" he could not have drunk ordinary wine. This is not Luther's actual proof. He himself formulates possible objections and reacts to them brashly: "What if a fool could ask more than ten wise men could answer?" Finally he can do nothing but retreat to this basic contention: "If it's not the fruit of the vine, then it cannot be anything but the blood of Christ, according to his own words 'This is my blood.'"[194] This, finally, is Luther's lone hermeneutical foundation.

A proper hermeneutical understanding of the words of institution is conjoined with the words of its efficacy. Zwingli had objected that the Supper could assure the forgiveness of sins. "By the shedding of his own blood Christ has atoned everything in heaven and on earth, not by giving us his body to eat and blood to drink. . . . From this it follows that in the bodily eating the believing conscience does not find the forgiveness of sins."[195] This comment struck not simply the exegetical shell but also the kernel of Luther's understanding of the Supper; and even more, it struck the universal meaning of the work of Christ. To be sure—this Luther taught also—the Supper bestows no forgiveness without faith. But it amounts to "mutilating Christ . . . to say that the forgiveness of sins is ascribed to him only as the crucified."[196] Zwingli apparently does not realize "that Christ's merit and the distribution of merit are in fact two things." This would confine redemption to the act of being crucified. "But we know that Christ died once for us, and this kind of dying he conveys through preaching, baptizing, spirit, reading, believing, eating, and how he wills, where he is, and what he does."[197] While Zwingli sounded the tone of grateful remembrance, Luther accentuated the reality of Christ's presence. The theme of remembrance for Zwingli permeated all forms of mediated forgiveness; symbolically, in the Lord's Supper, it represented the redemptive act of Christ and the effort required to die daily to all evil. The theme of forgiveness is for Luther bound up also bodily in the Lord's Supper. This is the spiritual context in which Luther's massive concept of the reception of the body and blood of Christ is at home.

> This is why we say there is forgiveness of sins in the Supper, not on account of the eating or because Christ merits or achieves forgiveness of sins there, but on account of the word through which he distributes among us this acquired

194. WA 26:460 / 11–461 / 40; 461 / 4–462 / 29; esp. 462 / 19–20, 28–29. [LW 37:314–16, 316–17, esp. 317.]

195. Zwingli, "Das diese Wort 'Das ist mein leib' . . . ," *Zwinglis sämtliche Werke*, 5:895 / 26ff.; 896 / 5ff.

196. WA 26:292 / 32ff.; 293 / 20ff. [LW 37:191.]

197. WA 26:294 / 23–24; 295 / 34ff. [LW 37:191–92.]

forgiveness, saying, "This is my body which is given for you." Here you perceive that we eat the body as it was given for us; we hear this and believe it as we eat. Hence there is distributed here the forgiveness of sins, which, however, was obtained on the cross.[198]

Alongside the exegesis of the words of institution, Zwingli had already used certain christological opinions repeatedly and made them essentially the key to an understanding of the Supper.[199] This forced Luther to direct his attention also to the accompanying cluster of problems and to deal with it in more detail than he would otherwise have done. Included is the person of Christ as well as salvation through him. For his part, Zwingli emphasized the distinction between the two natures; Luther was fully committed to seeing the two natures in terms of their personal unity—without permitting the one or the other, the divine or the human side, to lose its reality. "Because divinity and humanity in Christ is one person, so the Scriptures—for the sake of such personal unity—ascribe to the divinity all that happens to the humanity, and vice versa."[200] As a "crude simile" of it he referred to our human structure: "Humanity is united more closely to God than the skin is to our flesh; indeed, more closely than body and soul, thus [comprising] one thing and person that does not tolerate being separate."[201] As a possible linguistic expression, according to the logic of language, for this unity of differences in the person, Luther allows the use of a trope, or figure, which was familiar from his school grammar by Donatus. He had not objected to Zwingli's use of it. "Because Zwingli likes to use tropes so much, why doesn't he stick to the old trope that the Scriptures and all teachers hitherto have been using?—namely synecdoche, as e.g., 'Christ dies according to his humanity,' etc."[202] Luther occupied himself with these things in a little digression on "the law of identical predication" (de praedicatione identica), according to which it is not possible "for two kinds of being to be one thing, or that one being can be the other." This is something for which the Bible as well as common usage in all languages makes exceptions. According to the Bible, Father, Son, and Holy Spirit are not three deities but one God; Christ is one person comprising two natures.[203] This "personal" unity corresponds

198. WA 26:294 / 30ff. [LW 37:192.]
199. See above, pp. 527–29, 538ff.
200. WA 26:321 / 21ff. [LW 37:210, 212.]
201. WA 26:333 / 11ff. [LW 37:219.]
202. WA 26:322 / 30ff. [LW 37:211.]
203. WA 26:437–45; 440 / 11–12, 21ff. [LW 37:294–303, esp. 296.]

to the "sacramental" unity of the bread and body of Christ.[204] In common parlance one can speak of a purse, saying "This is a hundred guilders," or of a barrel, "This is Rhine wine."[205] Luther was thus following the rules of ancient grammer, as taken over by the early Middle Ages, according to which the whole (not only a part) could be designated by a change it had undergone. Thus the Venerable Bede, in conjunction with the tradition of Tyconius and Augustine, ascertained in his treatment *De schematis et tropis* that Bible language contains examples of synecdoche (e.g., *Verbum dei caro factum est:* the word of God was made flesh). This determination of Bede's was thus passed on to the biblical hermeneutics of the Middle Ages.[206]

What Luther combated most in Zwingli was the gratuitous character of his christological pronouncements. Luther understood that the two natures belong together, but [apparently] only as a figure of speech, as a pluralistic *alloeosis* [alloy] but not as an authentic unity. This cleaves the wholeness of Christ and nullifies his role as Redeemer. "If I believe that only the human nature suffered for me, then Christ would be a poor Savior for me. In fact, he himself would need a Savior."[207] "Now if the old witch Dame Reason, *alloeosis'* grandmother, should say that the Deity surely cannot suffer and die, then you must answer and say: That is true, but since the divinity and humanity are one person in Christ, the Scriptures ascribe to the divinity, because of this personal union, all that happens to humanity, and vice versa."[208] Luther here shows concern for two things: the reality of the personhood of Christ, which is not for dividing among two translated modes of speaking; and the reality of God, who is omnipresent, as throughout the whole world so also in the man Jesus Christ. To make his point, he refers to three scholastic (sophist, in his jargon) definitions of presence: (1) a physically graspable presence, like that of a body displacing a corresponding volume of air; (2) a corporeal yet ungraspable presence, like the body of the risen Lord, capable of passing through closed doors; (3) a supernatural, divine presence, capable of

204. WA 26:441 / 1; 442 / 23ff. [*LW* 37:297, 300.]

205. WA 26:444 / 1ff. [*LW* 37:302.]

206. E. R. Curtius, *Europäische Literatur und lateinisches Mittelalter* (Bern, 1948), 55. As an example of using a part to designate the whole, Curtius offers this: "When I say, 'Admission one mark per head' (instead of 'per person'), then I am employing a synecdoche" (52). References in Krause, *Kleine Propheten*, 206. In his controversy with Latomus, Luther objected to a false use of synecdoche, charging that Latomus had taken the prophet's statement 'All men are unclean' to mean 'A part of all men is unclean' (see above, p. 189).

207. WA 26:319 / 37ff. [*LW* 37:210.]

208. WA 26:321 / 19ff. [*LW* 37:210.]

being here and everywhere.[209] Christ is involved in all three forms of reality.

> You must place this existence of Christ, which constitutes him one person with God, far, far beyond things created, as far as God transcends them; and on the other hand, place it as deep in and as near to all created things as God is in them. For he is one indivisible person with God, and wherever God is he must be also, otherwise our faith is false.[210]

Yet more than faith is then false. Luther goes further, taking a characteristic step. Our eyes too are blind to the wonders of nature. In crystals or precious stones like an opal there are tiny sparks or little flames of light, minute clouds or bubbles that, although deep within, appear near the surface of the crystal no matter how one turns it. "I am not speaking now from Scripture. But we must use our reason." "See, there is the body of Christ actually in the bread, just as I say, when a certain side of the crystal is placed before my eyes."[211] Again, Luther recalls Valla, who compared the mystery of Christ in the Eucharist with the voice of a single preacher which can enter a thousand ears.[212] Luther regards these not simply as examples but as actualities based on the same laws governing the action of God in nature as well as his working through Christ in the sacrament. So it is possible to interpret one secret through another. Therefore, once again, as in his earlier treatise on the Lord's Supper, Luther's most penetrating statements on God's immanence in creation provide the background for the presence of the God-man Christ in the Supper.

> Nothing is so small, but God is still smaller, nothing so large but God is still larger, nothing is so short but God is still shorter, nothing so long but God is still longer, nothing so broad but God is still broader, nothing so narrow but God is still narrower, and so on. He is an inexpressible being, above and beyond all that can be described or imagined.[213]

For the Son of God in his "supernatural" existence, and in what must remain for us his inscrutable identity with the Father, all boundaries of space are dispelled, so "that creatures are as permeable and present to him as another body's material place or location is to it."[214] Just as little as

---

209. WA 26:327 / 20–329 / 27. Cf. on this above, pp. 521–22. [LW 37:214–16.]

210. WA 26:335 / 29–336 / 19; 335 / 29ff.; 336 / 15ff. [LW 37:222–23, esp. 223.]

211. WA 26:337 / 9–20. [LW 37:224.]

212. Lorenzo Valla, "Sermo de Mysterio eucharistatiae," in *Lactantii opera* (Venice, 1521). WA 26:337 / 32ff.; 656. [LW 37:225.]

213. WA 26:339 / 39ff. On this, see above, p. 532. [LW 37:228.]

214. WA 26:330 / 26ff. [LW 37:217.]

the question of the freedom of the will [freedom of choice] in perceptible general omnipotence of God is separable from the biblical question about man's freedom or lack of it, so little is the sacramental presence of Christ separable from that which a correct pondering about God must also yield, namely, that "he is a supernatural, inscrutable being who exists at the same time in every little seed, whole and entire, and yet also in all and above all and outside all created things."[215]

The hermeneutical and christological foundation of his position, which Luther had developed in detail against his critics, served also as the basis for what he considered the fruit of the Lord's Supper. Toward the end of this treatise he formulated it concisely: "Therefore he who drinks of this cup really drinks the true blood of Christ and the forgiveness of sins or the Spirit of Christ, for these are received in and with the cup. Here is received no mere figure or sign of the new testament or of the blood of Christ, as would befit the Jews in the Old Testament."[216] Thereby he again made it clear where to reckon the position of the defenders of a merely significative teaching on the Lord's Supper: they had fallen from the time of Christ's presence back into the time of his anticipation and the preparation for his redemptive work which they discerned in all kinds of signs and indications common to the era of the old covenant.

How much importance Luther attached to this most inclusive of engagements with his opponents on the question of the Supper becomes most evident in the conclusion. Part three goes far beyond the theme of the controversy and consists of an extended confession of his faith as a whole. It is the most important and beautiful statement of its kind we have of him.[217] In writing it, Luther had in mind not only the present moment but also his own death. No future teachers of false doctrine should one day be able to misuse his writings to confirm their own errors "as the sacramentarian and baptist fanatics are already beginning to do." He wanted to forestall the time when people might say, "If Luther were living now he would teach or hold this or that article differently." To his rhetorical question he replied, "Let me say once and for all that by the grace of God I have most diligently traced all these articles through the Scriptures, have examined them again and again in light thereof, and have aimed to defend

---

215. WA 26:339 / 34ff. On God's general omnipotence, see n. 143. [*LW* 37:228.]

216. WA 26:468 / 39ff. [*LW* 37:325–26.] On Luther's understanding of "sacraments" in the Old Testament, cf. H. Bornkamm, *Luther und das Alte Testament* (Tübingen, 1948), 154ff. [*Luther and the Old Testament* (1969), 179ff.]

217. WA 26:499–509. [*LW* 37:360–72.]

all of them as certainly as I have now defended the sacrament of the altar."[218]

Looking ahead to the final judgment, and aware that Satan could even pervert God's work, what then could become of his own? This ambiguity of the future loomed to Luther as a matter of utmost seriousness. He therefore cast his own testament in the solemn form of a Trinitarian confession of faith. Skillfully he also embedded the controversial questions with which he had thus far contended. From paragraph 1, on "the sublime article of the majesty of God," all else springs forth in brevity: the three distinct persons who "are by nature one true and authentic God, the Maker of heaven and earth."[219] Paragraph 2 confesses the God-manhood of Christ and the redemptive work founded on him, with reference also to all that in church history has broken down Christ's work: the teachings of the Pelagians old and new (Erasmus), the deniers of original sin, the rules of order of the cloisters and religious foundations through which people believed it possible to attain salvation. Over against these false and contrived estates, presumably pleasing to God, Luther named the three "genuine estates" truly instituted by God: the office of ministry, the estate of matrimony, and government through which God governs the world, and beyond it "the common order of Christian love, in which one serves . . . every needy person in general with all kinds of benevolent deeds." Nevertheless, these estates and services are no road to salvation, for "there remains only one way above them all, namely, faith in Jesus Christ."[220] In contrast to the false, self-made patterns of life seeking grace, Luther's focus on the redemptive work of Christ relates it to the estates of life created by God and unfolded by the inclusive and excelling service of love. Similarly, in paragraph 3 he translates for the sake of faith in the Holy Spirit the role of the Trinity in life. He turns the doctrine into an event, namely, the story of God's way with the human family. This consists in a threefold self-giving of God. "The Father gives himself to us, with heaven and earth and all the creatures, in order that they may serve us and benefit us." But by our sins we ourselves have obscured these gifts and misused them. "Therefore the Son himself subsequently gave himself and bestowed all his works, sufferings, wisdom, and righteousness, and reconciled us to the Father, in order that, restored to life and righteousness, we might also know and have the Father and his gifts." Yet this grace

218. WA 26:499 / 25ff. [LW 37:360.]
219. WA 26:500 / 10ff. [LW 37:361.]
220. WA 26:504 / 23ff.; 505 / 11–12, 16–17. [LW 37:364,365.]

would benefit no one if it were not conveyed to us. So "the Holy Spirit comes and gives himself to us also, wholly and completely. He teaches us to understand this deed of Christ which has been manifested to us, helps us receive and preserve it, employ it usefully and impart it to others, increase and extend it."[221] "He does this both inwardly and outwardly—inwardly by means of faith and other spiritual gifts, outwardly through the proclamation of the gospel, baptism, and the sacrament of the altar."[222] This, then, discloses what the church is: not a delimited organization but "the community and number or assembly of all Christians in all the world, the one bride of Christ, and his spiritual body." He alone is its head, not the bishops or the priests. They are simply its servants, friends, overseers, and stewards. "The church exists not only in the realm of the Roman church, but in all the world," among pope, Turks, Persians, Tartars, and everywhere, "physically dispersed . . . but spiritually gathered in one gospel and faith, under one head, who is Jesus Christ." The church has but one possession, "wherever it exists is to be found the forgiveness of sins."[223] The Roman church has this incomparable treasure but has largely abused it through indulgences, repetitious masses for the dead languishing in a purgatory the church invented, veneration of the saints, and that greatest of all abominations, "the mass when it is preached or sold as a sacrifice or good work," from which all religious foundations and cloisters derive their income. They should soon be overthrown. However, bells, eucharistic vestments, church ornaments, and images taken from the Scriptures and from good histories are a matter of free choice. "I have no sympathy with the iconoclasts."[224]

"This is my faith, for so all true Christians believe and so the Holy Scriptures teach us." And should he ever—which God forbid—"in the assault of temptation or the pangs of death" say something different, "let it be disregarded. Herewith I declare publicly that it would be incorrect, spoken under the devil's influence."[225] It is no accident that Luther concluded his large treatise on the Lord's Supper with the solemn testimony of this confession of faith. No encounter thus far had struck him so deeply.

221. WA 26:505 / 38–506 / 7. [LW 37:366.]
222. WA 26:506 / 7ff. [LW 37:366.]
223. WA 26:506 / 30ff.; 507 / 7. [LW 37:367, 368.]
224. WA 26:508 / 30–31; 509 / 12. [LW 37:369–71.]
225. WA 26:509 / 19ff. [LW 37:372.]

20

Personal Life, and Work on the Bible

By nature, Luther was a sensitive but healthy man of uncommon productivity. Though he told plenty of stories in later years about his youth and monastic years, he makes no mention of any significant illness. The severe demands of the cloistered life, which he met far beyond the requirements, exhausted him from time to time and left him sleepless, but apparently did no serious damage to his health.[1] His long journey to Rome and back (1510–11), mainly on foot, his very tiring trip to the Augustinian chapter meeting in Heidelberg in April 1518, his hike to Augsburg for the conversation with Cardinal Cajetan (October 1518), and his return journey on a hard trotter (a horseback ride he would rather have forgotten) left him without apparent ill effects. The first complaints of his physical health are those from the Wartburg. A stubborn case of constipation, contracted in Worms, did not seem surprising in light of the abrupt transition from extreme tension to the imposed calm of confinement and to an unaccustomed heavy diet.[2] This sedentary life may have brought on the first stages of his later suffering from kidney stones.[3] During the years following his return from the Wartburg, he seemed otherwise in good health. Yet it could, and did, happen that under the burden of work as well as amid the torment of brooding and spiritual agonizing he would lapse into physical exhaustion. One day, for instance, some visiting friends found him locked in his room and through a hole in the door saw him lying unconscious on the floor. They broke in, gave him something to eat, and began to make music. Thereupon Luther's melancholy and sadness left him and he began to sing along. He begged them to visit him again,

1. O. Scheel, *Dokumente zu Luthers Entwicklung (bis 1519)*, 2d ed. (Tübingen, 1929), 353, offers no more than this in his collection of reminiscences. The best survey is still in the gathered source material of F. Küchenmeister, *Dr. Martin Luthers Krankengeschichte* (Leipzig, 1881). The same verdict is shared by P. J. Reiter, *Martin Luthers Umwelt: Charakter und Psychose sowie die Bedeutung dieser Faktoren für seine Entwicklung und Lehre*, vol. 2: *Luthers Persönlichkeit, Seelenleben, und Krankheiten* (Copenhagen, 1941), 18, 79, who, in fact, examines only the psychic history and the characterological type. On this, see below, pp. 556–58. A shorter medical survey is that by W. Ebstein, *Dr. Martin Luthers Krankheiten und deren Einfluss auf seinen körperlichen und geistigen Zustand* (Stuttgart, 1908).

2. See above, p. 12.

3. Küchenmeister, *Luthers Krankengeschichte*, 41. Reiter, *Luthers Umwelt*, 2:32.

especially when they were in the mood for music, "for the devil is the enemy especially of music that makes people happy, and he revels most in anything that can overtake people with depression and sadness and plunge them into fear and despair."[4]

The attacks of stones and periodic severe depression were the two torments Luther never shook off. Ratzeberger reported dramatically of the then latest and extremely painful attack of stones in June 1526. When Luther's anxious Katharina wanted to bring him something to eat—whatever he desired—to her consternation he asked for a fried herring and some cold peas with mustard. Two colleagues, Augustinus Schurff and Melchior Fendius, of the medical faculty, were likewise shocked to find him eating this kind of meal. Yet this self-chosen unusual repast helped him; he passed the stone. When Schurff and Fendius visited him the next day they found him not in his sickbed but in his study over his books.[5] But the ailment continued. In its most acute form it tormented him during the conference in Schmalkalden in February 1537. Then, because the town had neither an apothecary nor medicines, it was necessary to transport him to available help. The frozen, bumpy mountain roads, however, brought him initial and decisive relief.[6]

Tormenting as these physical maladies were, Luther's psychosomatic sufferings were far worse. During the year 1527 he felt them drawing him to the edge of despair and of death itself. Under his heavy workload it was not surprising that advance warnings showed up: dizzy spells, intense headaches, and above all a severe attack of precordial anxiety—yet this was happily dispelled with the help of a home remedy.[7] On July 6, 1527, a

---

4. The manuscript history of Ratzeberger, "Luther und seine Zeit," ed. C. G. Neudecker (Jena, 1850), 58–59, cited by Küchenmeister, *Luthers Krankengeschichte*, 43–44. Ratzeberger (or Ratzenberger), evidently not an eyewitness but well acquainted with Luther, studied in Wittenberg from 1516 to about 1525. Later he was town physician in Brandenburg (probably also physician to the evangelically minded Electoress Elizabeth) and was, on Luther's recommendation, personal physician to Count Albrecht of Mansfeld and after 1538 to Elector John Frederick. After Luther's death he became a guardian of the Reformer's children. On Ratzeberger, see T. Kolde, "Matthäus Ratzeberger," in *RE*[3] 16 (1905): 471–72. H. Volz, "Ratzeberger, Matthäus," in *RGG*[3] 5 (1961): 802. The incident described above occurred probably toward the end of 1523 or during 1524. In no case would it have occurred earlier, for Lukas Edemberger, one of those mentioned in Luther's company on that occasion, was not matriculated before August 24, 1523. Köstlin, *Martin Luther: Sein Leben und seine Schriften*, 5th ed. by G. Kawerau (Berlin, 1903), 1:727–28, 795–96.

5. Report of Ratzeberger (Neudecker, 61ff.) by Küchenmeister, *Luthers Krankengeschichte*, 51–52, and Reiter, *Luthers Umwelt*, 2:32ff.

6. Sources and medical explanations in Küchenmeister, *Luthers Krankengeschichte*, 78ff. Also Reiter, *Luthers Umwelt*, 2:37ff.

7. Luther told Spalatin about this attack on January 13, 1527, not without some pride that he had given himself a remedy hardly known among physicians, namely, *aqua cardui benedicti* (benedictine heart water), WA Br 4:160 / 17ff. On April 22 a spell of dizziness caused him to break off his sermon. WA 23:670–71.

seizure of acute exhaustion struck Luther, and he subsequently reported to Spalatin: "Day before yesterday I was so seized by a sudden fainting spell that I despaired and expected to pass out in the hands of my wife and of some friends, so completely was I swiftly robbed of all my strength. But the Lord had mercy on me and soon restored me."[8] Luther's friends Jonas and Bugenhagen both wrote accounts of his frightening experience which taken together present a vivid picture. On the morning of July 6 Luther was overcome by a severe case of despair, "of the sort one often reads about in the psalms,"[9] wrote Jonas. Luther sent for his pastoral counselor, Bugenhagen, made confession, and received absolution. He described his bodily sensations as being like a violent surging of ocean waves. It appeared to be coming not from within but from without.[10] By midday he was sufficiently recovered that he could accept the invitation of several noblemen to dine at the tavern, and later he visited Jonas in his garden. He even invited Jonas and his wife to supper, but when Jonas arrived he found Luther very weak. He had a fainting spell, and afterward asked Jonas to douse him with water.[11] In bed Luther began to pray, partly in German, partly in Latin. He lamented that he had not been found worthy to shed his own blood for the sake of his Lord Christ. Then he turned to his friends. If the world that delights in lies should ever claim that in his dying hour he recanted his teaching, let his friends bear witness to the fact that he taught correctly, according to the Word of God and his office of ministry, about love, the cross, and the sacraments. Many indeed had reproached him for his vehemence toward his opponents, yet he had never been so vehement as to regret it now. Whether moderate or vehement, he never sought the ruin of anyone but rather the salvation of all, including his opponents.[12] Over the ensuing conversations with Katharina, the friends, and the physician Dr. Schurff (of which Jonas jotted down several lines) hovered the shadow of death, which Luther anticipated. "My dearest Katie, I beg, if this is God's will [for me] that you submit to God's will. You are mine, and you surely will remember this and let God's Word guide you."[13] He also inquired about his little son:

---

8. July 10, 1527, to Spalatin, WA Br 4:221 / 8ff.

9. Jonas's report is included in the Table Talk collection of Cordatus, WA TR 3, no. 2922a and b, 80ff. (Other readings on this in WA 48:525 / 24ff.) Cordatus adapted this account stylistically into a story as told by Luther himself (WA TR 3:80, n. 3). The reports of Jonas and Bugenhagen were consolidated early (also into German; Küchenmeister, *Luthers Krankengeschichte*, 54ff.).

10. WA TR 3, no. 2922b, 82 / 22ff.

11. WA TR 3, no. 2922b, 86 / 22ff.

12. WA TR 3, no. 2922b, 83 / 3–30.

13. WA TR 3, no. 2922b, 89 / 8ff.

"Where, then, is my dearest little Hans?" When the infant was brought to him, he weakly exclaimed, "Oh you dear, poor child! Now I commend my dearest Kate and you to my dearest and holy God. You have nothing. Yet God, the Father of the orphan and the Judge of the widow, will surely keep and sustain you."[14] With the help of sweat-inducing remedies, warmed pillows, and medication prescribed by Dr. Schurff,[15] Luther rallied during the night and overcame the weakness. But he knew how serious it all had been. Jonas related, "The next day the doctor told me: 'I must mark that day. Because yesterday I learned something.' To which he added that the spiritual trial had doubled the impact of the bodily illness that followed it in the evening."[16]

So things continued for several weeks. The worst was not Luther's confused condition, which for a while made it impossible for him to read or write,[17] but his turmoil of soul. Luther remembered Melanchthon, then on the visitation journey in the Jena district, and wrote him on August 2:

> For more than a whole week I have been tossed to and fro in death and in hell, so that I am still drained of all strength in my body and am trembling in all my limbs. I have lost Christ completely and have been shaken by the floods and storms of despair and blasphemy. However, as moved by the prayers of the saints,[18] God has begun to have mercy on me and to snatch my soul from deepest hell. So please don't give up praying for me, as I continue to pray for you. I believe that my own struggle is also helping others.[19]

He wrote the same thing to Agricola on August 21, thanking him for the intercessions of the Eisleben congregation.

> My hope is that my own battle is of service to many, although there is no evil that my sins have not deserved. Yet my life consists in this, that I know and boast that I have taught the Word of Christ purely and to the salvation of many. This burns up Satan, so that he would kill and destroy me along with the Word. That's why I have not suffered at the hands of the tyrants of this world, while others have been killed and burned for Christ and have perished; I am buffeted all the more in the spirit by the prince of this world.[20]

14. *WA TR* 3, no. 2922b, 90 / 7ff., cited according to the text (10).

15. *WA TR* 3, no. 2922b, 88 / 23ff.

16. *WA TR* 3, no. 2922b, 90 / 22ff.

17. To Hausmann, July 13, 1527, *WA Br* 4:222 / 13–14. [*LW* 49:169.]

18. Meaning here the believing friends. The veneration of the saints, in the sense of the Roman church, was something Luther had given up much earlier. Cf. above, pp. 210–14. R. Lansemann, "Die Heiligentage, besonders die Marien-, Apostel- und Engeltage in der Reformationszeit," MGKK, supp. vol. 1: "Das heilige und die Form" (1939), 83ff.

19. *WA Br* 4:226 / 8ff.

20. To Agricola, August 21, 1527, *WA Br* 4:235 / 2–3, 12ff.

So he can see the spiritual agonizing of these weeks as an aid to him. However, amid his great and repeatedly expressed inner torment, Luther wonders why he has not been deemed worthy, like others, to suffer and die for Christ. He readily can see himself as a second Job, whose torments God has set up as a sign.[21] He shares these thoughts with Agricola, and two months later, in a similar vein, with Amsdorf: "Satan has asked to be given a new Job (Job 2:6), and also a Peter, to sift him with his brothers (Luke 22:31). But Christ will graciously reply to him, 'Spare his soul' (Job 2:6), and say to me, 'I am your deliverance' (Ps. 35:3). So I am still hoping that he will not forever hold my sins against me."[22]

Merely to employ an expandable concept and call these experiences of emotional suffering a mental illness is not enough, no matter how one may apply the term in a given case. Nor will it do to speak here of a "manic-depressive psychosis" or of "melancholy of a slightly agitated sort."[23] Manic phases cannot be shown in Luther during this or earlier periods. Indeed, melancholia and depression have at all times been a toll that many great minds have had to pay for their intellectual or artistic creativity. "Such creative characters then do not at all belong to themselves alone; they are the giant births from the premonitory pangs of all humanity; they are from birth the serpent-slayers, being so by the grace of God." With these words a Roman Catholic priest, Joseph Sprissler, described Luther, paying him one of the finest tributes coming to us from the nineteenth century. He recalls some words of Seneca as an aid to understanding Luther's unheard-of passion: "Nullum unquam magnum ingenium sine admixtione furiae fuit" (Never has there been a great mind without an admixture of madness).[24] The combining of passion and pain becomes really graphic when one views Luther's individuality in the con-

21. WA Br 4:235 / 10.

22. November 1, 1527, WA Br 4:275 / 1ff.

23. Reiter, *Luthers Umwelt*, 2:98ff., 566. It is incorrect to claim that "the worst melancholic attack of his life" (1527–28) occurred during "an unusually calm period" (ibid., 100), when "demonstrably psychologically understandable grounds" were completely lacking (ibid., 567). Even looking aside from the aftereffects of the Peasants' War and the Erasmus controversy, these were nonetheless the years of the visitation and the many problems related thereto (see above, pp. 487ff.). Likewise, there were the turbulent encounters within Luther's own circle of friends over the problem of the law (see above, pp. 169ff.), as well as the big controversy over the Lord's Supper. On top of it all, it is not surprising that the preceding times (1525–26) of extraordinary tension and exertion were still making their impact on him.

24. J. Sprissler, "Martin Luthers Leben," ed. G. Pfizer (Stuttgart, 1836), in *FBTK* 12 (1837): 92ff.; cited in H. Bornkamm, *Luther im Spiegel der deutschen Geistesgeschichte*, 2d ed. (Göttingen, 1970), 86, 340, 342.

text of his historical situation. What torments him is not so much his own insufficiency. Among the prayers jotted down by Jonas on the day of the severe fainting attack, there is this one: "O thou my dearest God and Father, before thousands of others thou hast given me many thousand precious, noble gifts; were it thy will, I would so gladly still use them to the honor and benefit of thy people. But thy will be done, that thou mayest be glorified, be it through my life or through my death."[25] To be sure, Luther had been heavily overworked for years. His agenda was determined less by his own choice than by the cause that had gripped him. New tasks and new opponents were ever on the increase. He was fired up to repay his attackers—Karlstadt, Müntzer, Erasmus, and Zwingli and his comrades—blow for blow. Now it was the critics of his teaching on the Lord's Supper. As he wrote Amsdorf, "I yearn to answer the sacramentarians, but if I don't regain my mental strength I cannot do it."[26] Luther's Joblike situation tormented him in that God had allowed the devil to lay it on him with agonizing and temptation. Most difficult of all was the recurring and oppressive thought that others had already died a martyr's death for the movement he himself had ushered into the world. There were the Brussels martyrs (1523); Henry von Zütphen, the Bremen preacher, murdered in December 1524; and the preachers Georg Winkler of Halle (April 1527) and Leonhard Kaiser in Schärding on the River Inn (August 1527). Luther's expansive obituaries for these last two martyrs, published in the autumn of that year, suggest the context for his many descriptions of wrestlings with Satan during these times. In Leonhard Kaiser he recalled a student in Wittenberg during the years 1525–26, a young man he had known well. "O God," he lamented, "that I had been or may still be found worthy of such a testimony and death. What am I? What am I doing? How ashamed I am of myself when I read this story that I had not long already been found worthy to suffer (since I deserved it ten times more from the world). Well, then, my God, if it is to be that way, so let it be. Thy will be done."[27]

Sensing a divine design in these martyrdoms, Luther composed an extended statement of condolence to the orphaned congregation of Georg Winkler in Halle. Writing in the midst of his own inner needs, in the autumn of 1527, he did not lament with the people in Halle but summoned them to comfort and true joy. "Christ has made him [Winkler]

25. WA TR 3, no. 2922b, 89 / 15ff.
26. November 1, 1527, WA Br 4:275 / 9–10.
27. *Von Herrn Lenhard Keiser zu Baiern verbrannt*, WA 23:474 / 15ff.

worthy to die for the sake of his word and truth." Their preacher would today not wish to exchange his new place for the old, saying [in effect]:

If you loved me, then you would indeed rejoice that in this way I have passed from death to life. For what is certain in this life? Today someone stands erect, tomorrow he lies there; today someone has the right kind of faith, tomorrow he falls into error; today someone hopes, tomorrow he despairs. How many splendid people are now falling daily in the errors of the fanatics; how many are yet to fall because of these same and other gangs still to come?[28]

It is Luther's own melancholy reflection on life which he here puts into the mouth of the murdered man. But this is the melancholia not of a phase in an illness but of an outlook on the world and on life as Luther had always held it. The greatest comfort in view of this sad world, he finds, is that God permits certain people to live and to die for the gospel. This applies to the faithful Halle preacher who, so far as he [Luther] is aware, was put to death because he taught the proper celebration of the Supper (with both elements). Therefore Luther admonishes the congregation, in remembering their preacher, to pursue the truth and not the customary (withholding of the cup), and he backs his words with detailed citations from the Bible and church law.[29] God acknowledges his special witnesses to the truth in that he calls them early from this evil world. "He [Winkler] became perfect in a short time and thereby achieved a work of many years, for his soul pleased God."[30] At the same time, the violent death of such witnesses has its premonitory meaning. "It is a sure sign that a great disaster is at hand, which will engulf the world, from which God will snatch his own beforehand, so that they be not seized and perhaps fall and be lost among the godless." Some great misery is coming over Germany, which has now even begun in that the mob spirits are separating the hearts from one another. "Thereafter physical disunity and war will follow, so that thing might be fulfilled which Satan began in Müntzer as a prelude and continuation."[31]

Months pass before references to this recent interval of agonizing disappear from Luther's letters to his friends. Luther complains not of bodily

28. *Tröstung an die Christen zu Halle* (1527), WA 23:423 / 8ff., 11ff. [*A Letter of Consolation to the Christians at Halle*, LW 43:160.] That Luther alludes to his own illness in this statement is not surprising (Reiter, *Luthers Umwelt*, 2:103). He uses this to excuse the tardiness of his writing (WA 23:403 / 10ff.).

29. WA 23:411 / 10–423 / 5. [*LW* 43:149–60.]

30. WA 23:425 / 23ff., according to the Wisd. of Sol. 4:10–18. [*LW* 43:162.]

31. WA 23:427 / 1–20, esp. 3ff., 18ff. [*LW* 43:162–63, esp. 163.]

debility[32] but of the inner resistance of a Satan who prevents him from writing against the fanatics and who would rather drag him off into hell. At the moment, however, he does set down something against the fanatics as he concludes his larger work on the Lord's Supper with a confession of faith (November 22, 1527).[33] "So I am tugged to and fro and miserably torn to pieces between the two opposing princes (Christ and Satan)" (November 29[?], 1527).[34] "I have not yet been released from my agonizing and do not seek to be freed, if it serves the glory of God, my dearest Redeemer" (December 14, 1527).[35] On December 31 he wrote a brief report on the situation in Wittenberg to Jacob Propst in Bremen: "We are all in good health except for Luther himself, who is physically well, but outwardly the whole world and inwardly the devil and all his angels are making him suffer."[36] He wrote even more expressively on January 1, 1528, to Gerhard Wiskamp in the Herford brotherhouse, thanking him for sending a consoling letter during his recent inner struggles:

> In fact, this period of temptation [agonizing] has been by far the worst. Since my youth I have known about this sort of thing, but that it would intensify like this is something I had not expected. Up to the present, however, Christ is the victor, although he is holding one who is hanging by a very thin thread. I commend myself to the intercessions of yourself and the brothers. I have been able to rescue others, and cannot do it for myself (Matt. 27:42). Praised be my Christ, also in the midst of despair, death, and blasphemy. May he grant us to meet again in his kingdom. Meanwhile we are certain that we are serving him through his Word and work. To be sure, we are not thereby justified; we simply remain unprofitable servants. And yet our fame consists in this, that in the world we have lived in the Spirit of Christ and have forgotten our earlier and worse life. What remains for us is that Christ is our life and our righteousness (Oh, how unattainable and unknown this is to the flesh, [this being] hid with God!).[37]

32. Luther's letter to Jonas of January 6, 1528 (WA 23:342) does not refer to a new case of hemorrhoids, as Reiter, *Luthers Umwelt*, 2:107, wrongly surmises. Instead, Luther is referring to the case he had a year earlier and how it turned out under medical treatment. Jonas had made a practical inquiry on behalf of a friend, Michael Meienburg, WA Br 4:342 / 15ff.; on this, esp. 324 / 78ff. Still on December 29, 1527, Luther had written him, "I am physically healthy" (WA Br 4:307 / 14).

33. WA Br 4:284 / 10ff. In addition, Luther can report that his commentary on Zechariah is nearly finished (on this, see above, pp. 250–51). On the confession of faith in his treatise on the Supper, see above, pp. 549ff.

34. WA Br 4:289 / 10.

35. WA Br 4:299 / 13ff.

36. WA Br 4:313 / 10ff.

37. WA Br 4:319 / 5ff. The conclusion, Col. 3:3. The image of the thread, also in the letter to Jonas, December 29, 1527 (see n. 32, above). To Wiskamp, cf. R. Stupperich, "Luther und das Fraterhaus in Herford," *Geist und Geschichte der Reformation: Festschrift für Hans Rückert* (Berlin, 1966), 219ff.

From one of the most revealing letters written during these months, Luther could expect a special measure of understanding on the recipient's part, whom he addressed with exceptional warmth ("Suo in Christo fratri charissimo . . . servo dei fideli"[38]). The earnest brothers in the Herford house—they were Brethren of the Common Life—were acquainted with the temptation and torment of monastic religiosity. They had found the way to Luther's understanding of the gospel and had added their own Christ-centered devotion to it, so it was easier for Luther to explain to one of their number, who stood close to him, what was troubling him: their common past ("our former wretched life") and his present need of soul— and that which was his comfort, even though he might not be able to put his hands on it. At last the darkness began to dispel. "With your prayer my Satan has become somewhat more bearable," he wrote Wenceslaus Link in Nuremberg on February 26, 1528, but added, "Carry on, and don't stop praying for us all."[39] The phrase "my Satan" still suggests Job. Luther was experiencing not only the lingering depths of a silent depression but also the temptations of an opponent whom God had permitted to test him.

In the same letter, however, Luther could also report the end of weighty worries that had been oppressing him in addition to the inner conflict. "By the grace of God we have been liberated from the plague." The plague had been raging in Wittenberg since the latter part of the summer of 1527, taking its toll also from Luther's circle of friends. He was virtually undone, Luther wrote on November 4, on learning that the wife of Deacon Rörer had been delivered of a stillborn baby and had herself succumbed to the plague shortly thereafter.[40] Luther's own house became a hospital. The wife of the physician Augustinus Schurff, and Karlstadt's sister-in-law Margaretha von Mochau, who had been given asylum with the Luthers, came down with the plague too, while Martin himself was much concerned about his Katharina and their little Hans, inasmuch as Kate was expecting their second child.[41] For Luther himself the epidemic brought isolation. Since August 15 the university had temporarily relocated at Jena [some ninety miles to the south, between Erfurt and

---

38. [Dearest brother in Christ, I serve God faithfully.] Cf. also Luther's letter to Wiskamp, September 2, 1529, WA Br 4:243 / 1 : "servo Dei fidelissimo" [I serve God most faithfully].

39. WA Br 4:387 / 8–9.

40. WA Br 4:276 / 3ff.

41. To Amsdorf, November 1, 1527, WA Br 4:275 / 12ff. Concerning Margaretha von Mochau, see WA Br 4:37, n. 1.

Leipzig]. Luther had declined the elector's order to do the same, being unwilling with his family to abandon Wittenberg.[42] Happily, Bugenhagen and his family moved in with the Luthers, "not so much for his sake as for mine . . . , so he could be a companion in my isolation," as Luther wrote Hausmann.[43]

The epidemic also gave Luther the occasion to respond to a longstanding question—"whether one may flee from a deadly plague." On behalf of the evangelical pastors in Breslau, John Hess, already in 1525, had requested an answer to this question while the plague was in their city. Luther used his illness as an excuse for his tardy reply: "Almighty God has for some time disciplined and scourged me so severely that I have been unable to do much reading or writing."[44] Now fleeing the plague had also become a question in Wittenberg, and it contributed to the decisive and lively quality of this short tract. Luther distinguishes between those who may flee and those who may not. Among the latter are preachers and other public officials essential to civic order (the mayor, judges, public health physicians, police), as well as neighbors of the stricken who have no other help.[45] Other people are free to go: "To flee dying and death and to save one's life is something implanted naturally by God and is not forbidden."[46] His own recent experience had shown him that towns should build hospitals, "so that not every burgher must conduct a hospital in his own house." "Now where death strikes, there we should remain, preparing and comforting ourselves" and not allowing ourselves to be repelled by the sick.[47] It is a sin against God to despise medication and to drink or play with those contagiously ill. "Instead, make use of medication, take whatever can help you, fumigate house, yard, and alley, avoid people and places where your neighbor doesn't require you, . . . and conduct yourself like one who is eager to help put out a common fire."[48]

In the printed version of his reply to Hess, Luther added a section beyond the theme of the tract but much on his heart: the laying out of

42. W. Friedensburg, *Geschichte der Universität Wittenberg* (Magdeburg, 1926ff.), 1:177–78. As mentioned there (178, n. 1), in a report from the university to the electoral court, a stranger was said to have brought the plague to town; Elector John to Luther, August 10, 1527, *WA* Br 4:227–28. Luther's reply has not been preserved. After four weeks he regarded the reports of the plague as grossly exaggerated; to Spalatin, September 13, 1527, *WA* Br 4:247 / 17ff.

43. November 7, 1527, *WA* Br 4:277 / 15–16.

44. *WA* 23:323ff.; 339 / 9ff. [*LW* 43:119 (119–38).]

45. *WA* 23:341 / 31–345 / 23. [*LW* 43:121–26.]

46. *WA* 23:347 / 6–7. [*LW* 43:123.]

47. *WA* 23:355 / 19ff., 24ff. [*LW* 43:127.]

48. *WA* 23:363 / 30ff.; 365 / 23ff. [*LW* 43:130, 131–32.]

cemeteries outside the towns. He proposed this arrangement on the basis of custom in Bible times and not for hygienic reasons, which he left to the physicians to explain. His concern was for a location conducive to inner composure.[49] "Our churchyard, what is it?" There is no more restless and untidy place than the graveyards in the center of our towns, on which many lanes converge and doors open and over which people walk day and night as well as drive their cattle. What a place to ponder death and resurrection! But "if a graveyard were located at a quiet, remote spot where no one could wear a path, it would be a spiritual, proper, and holy sight and could be so arranged as to inspire devotion in those who go there."[50] Here too Luther dissociates himself from a deeply rooted medieval custom. The graveyard of the Middle Ages gathered the dead with the living around the church edifice, so that the deceased might still participate in worship, the highly privileged being buried in the church itself. It was a terrifying thought not to be buried in hallowed soil. The blessing of these church- or graveyards was seen as protection against unclean spirits.[51] Luther's thoughts concentrate on the living, not on the dead. The essential thing about a graveyard is not the hallowed ground but the mute sermon on death and eternity.

During the plague Luther and his family stayed together. Even had he desired it, his courageous Katharina would not have agreed to leave the house. Besides, she would have had to take along her firstborn: little Johannes, born June 7, 1526. Luther wrote with joy to his relative Dr. John Rühel in Eisleben that "my dear Kate, by God's great grace, yesterday at two, presented me with a little Hans Luther—on the calendar day, Dat, so named." This designation of days in the medieval calendar[52] certainly also conveyed the sense of a word of thanks. [Deacon] Rörer baptized the infant on the day of his birth, while Bugenhagen, as sponsor, held him over the baptismal font. The baby's Christian name was that of his sponsor as well as of the grandfather, Hans Luther, whose heart had so

49. Physicians: WA 23:373 / 30ff. Biblical examples: Luke 7:12; John 19:41; Gen. 23:9. WA 23:375 / 11ff.

50. WA 23:377 / 1–19, esp. 377 / 1, 14. [LW 43:137.]

51. H. Derwein, *Geschichte des christlichen Friedhofs in Deutschland* (Frankfurt, 1931), 30ff., 94ff. On Luther, ibid., 58–59, 80. K. Peiter, "Der evangelische Friedhof von der Reformation bis zur Romantik" (theology diss., Berlin, 1969). Review in *ThLZ* 95 (1970): 951–52.

52. WA Br 4:87 / 7ff. According to the so-called Cisiojanus Calendar, in which for each month memory helps had been composed, actually nonsense syllables in metrical hexameter and one syllable, comprising the entire or first part of saints' names. H. Grotefend, *Taschenbuch der Zeitrechnung des deutschen Mittelalters und der Neuzeit*, 9th ed. (Hannover, 1948), 20. [LW 49:152.]

early been set on his son Martin's marriage. Luther may well have remembered his father's long-frustrated wish. His delight over the healthy and sturdy child shines from many a letter of this period, "Johannes meus Lutherulus . . . cum matre sua" is often repeated in thanks for the congratulations on his birth.[53] "My little John is happy and sturdy, an excellent eater and drinker, thank God."[54] Just a year and a half after little Hans, his sister Elizabeth was born, on December 10, 1527. Luther was happy to find the mother and child well (though Kate was weak) on his return home after the morning lecture.[55] At the same time he was relieved of another worry. According to the physicians, the plague had left Wittenberg; no new cases had been reported for a week.[56] But Luther himself was not yet entirely rid of his depression and still sought the prayers of his friends.[57] Sadly, too, Elizabeth was taken from her parents within the first year of her life. For Luther this was an unexpected and deep sorrow. "It is amazing what a grieving, almost womanly heart she has bequeathed me, so much has grief for her overcome me. Never would I have believed that a father's heart could feel so tenderly for his child."[58] So much the more grateful was he when on May 4, 1529, another daughter, Magdalena, was born. For Kate it was an easy birth, as he reported joyously to many.[59]

Although the university had been temporarily relocated at Jena in August 1527 because of the plague, Luther's lectures were not broken off. He continued to give them to the little band of students who had remained behind in Wittenberg. Here a brief review of Luther's academic work is useful. Having completed his lectures on the minor prophets in the spring of 1526,[60] he began on June 30 with Ecclesiastes (the "Preacher" Solomon). As much as this book fascinated him, its content proved difficult. "He has no pleasure or patience for lecturing," Luther wrote on August 26, and on October 14 he admitted, "Solomon the preacher is giving me a hard time, as though he begrudged anyone lecturing on him. But he must

53. [John, my little Luther . . . with his mother.] July 3, 1526, WA Br 4:99 / 1. Cf. also WA Br 4:117 / 13–14; 310 / 14. On Luther's father and his urging Martin to marry, see above, p. 405.

54. June 10, 1527(?), WA Br 4:210 / 14–15.

55. To Jonas, December 10, WA Br 4:294 / 1ff. To Spalatin, December 13, WA Br 4:298 / 15–16. [LW 49:181.]

56. WA Br 4:298 / 17–18. To Hausmann, December 14, WA Br 4:299 / 7ff.

57. To Hausmann, December 14, 1527, and Jonas, December 29, WA Br 4:299 / 13ff.; 307 / 14ff.

58. August 5, 1528, to Hausmann, WA Br 4:511 / 4ff. [LW 49:203.]

59. May 5, to Amsdorf; May 6 to Link and Jonas; WA Br 5:62 / 8–9; 63 / 4ff. [LW 49:218, 220.]

60. WA 13:xxxiii.

yield."[61] By November 7, and with some difficulty, he brought the lectures to a conclusion, after having stacked his arms for a few weeks during September ("the commentaries don't help us"). When Luther resumed work, things went better and he was pleased with the outcome. Two years later [1529] he wrote, "Never would I have been so glad to have a book published as my Ecclesiastes, on which I lectured here in Wittenberg by God's grace." But he stepped aside when he learned that John Brenz intended to publish a commentary on the same book. "I'd be heartily glad to yield to him, even if my Ecclesiastes were already being printed." This comment, included in a foreword to Brenz's work, was Luther's finest expression of the high regard in which he held the author of the *Syngramma Suevicum*.[62]

Only in 1532 did the Wittenberg friends carry out Luther's unfulfilled wish and, on the basis especially of Rörer's superb copy, see to it that Luther's lectures on Ecclesiastes also got into print. Luther simply added a foreword, but it expressed precisely his grasp of the Solomonic book. Though often misunderstood as fostering a contempt of the world, Ecclesiastes does not encourage an otherworldly monasticism. Rather, contends Luther, one should call it "Solomon's economic policy," not because it contains laws for public and family life but because in cases of misfortune it comforts and strengthens the patience of political leaders and heads of households.[63] He had already caught this straightforward tone while translating Ecclesiastes and had given indication of it in the 1524 foreword. The "Preacher's" perceptive estimate of the futility of all human striving made him a welcome ally of Luther against Erasmus. "This book should really have a title to indicate that it was written against freedom of the will, for the entire book tends to show that the counsels, plans, and undertakings of men are all in vain and fruitless and that they always have a different outcome from that which we will and purpose."[64]

61. October 14, 1527, to Hausmann, WA Br 4:122 / 6ff. Cf. also August 28, to Link, WA Br 4:110 / 12ff. "Ego Ecclesiasten lego mire invitum et impatientum lectionis." On Luther's understanding of the preacher Solomon, see H. Bornkamm, *Luther und das Alte Testament* (Tübingen, 1948), 13–14 [*Luther and the Old Testament* (1969), 13]. The wish there expressed (14, n. 1) led to an especially rewarding investigation by E. Wölfel, *Luther und die Skepsis: Eine Studie zur Kohelet-Exegese Luthers* (Munich, 1958).

62. The foreword (1528) was addressed to Brenz's publisher, Johannes Setzer in Hagenau. WA 26:1 / 12. J. Benzing, *Lutherbibliographie* (Baden-Baden, 1966), no. 2525. On the *Syngramma*, see above, pp. 517ff.

63. WA 20:7 / 29ff.; 8 / 19ff. On the emergence of Luther's "political interpretation" of Ecclesiastes (since 1521), see Wölfel, *Luther und die Skepsis*, 256.

64. WA DB 10²:104 / 24ff. [*LW* 35:264.] *Martin Luthers Vorreden zur Bibel*, ed. H. Bornkamm (Hamburg, 1967), 65. Cf. also WA 20:58 / 7, 25. Luther wrote these comments probably at the time the book by Erasmus arrived in Wittenberg. WA DB 10²:104, n. 2.

One can understand why, just at this time, Luther would gladly have published his commentary on the book. In other respects too the connection between common-sense wisdom and trust in God which Luther found in the "Preacher" was much to his liking. So, for instance, none of his own explanations has the character of pithy sayings, as those on Eccles. 6:7 ("The eye is not satisfied with seeing" ["His appetite is not satisfied," RSV]): "The heart too is like quicksilver. No one can hold it where it roves."[65] To the human experiences voiced in the text Luther adds many illustrative incidents from ancient poetry and history. For the statesmen who despite their best abilities and efforts nevertheless are struck by disappointments, Luther cites Cicero and Demosthenes, Caesar, Lycurgus, and Augustus.[66] What a keen sense of anticipation awaited a Heliogabalus or a Commodus! Yet the one degenerated into bestiality, and the other into an Incommodus—a second Nero.[67] Luther is even more ready to apply the "Preacher's" catalog of vanities to the contemporary scene. He quotes from his late electoral prince, Frederick the Wise: "The longer I rule, the less I know about ruling" or "When shall I find someone I can trust?"[68] For his own cares and conflicts Luther found helpful counsel in Eccles. 5:7[8], "for the high official is watched by a higher, and there are yet higher ones over them." This assurance comforts him against the "sacramentarians and sects," who are giving him so much trouble. All that remains for him to say is, "I leave the matter to God, who holds everything in his hands." "Everyone has his judge."[69]

Luther finds Ecclesiastes not a book of skepticism but a book against it; a book of wisdom, an inducement to realism, modesty, and trust in God. He summarized the preface to his translation of 1524 in the words of Christ: " 'Do not be anxious about tomorrow, for tomorrow will have its own anxiety; it is enough that every day has its own evil.' This saying is really the interpretation and content of this book. Caring for us is God's affair. Our anxiety goes wrong anyhow, and produces nothing but wasted toil."[70] Luther opened his lectures of 1526 by showing that the author of this book does not regard the goods of creation as vain or worthy only of

65. WA 20:115 / 8ff., 30ff. [LW 15:99.]

66. WA 20:29 / 2; 46 / 4ff.; 50 / 12ff.; 18; 51 / 19. On this, Wölfel, *Luther und die Skepsis,* 263–64. [LW 15:24, 38, 42, 43.]

67. WA 20:84 / 8–9, 27ff. [LW 15:72.]

68. WA 20:67 / 10ff., 23ff. Frederick as example, also WA 20:40 / 14ff., 35ff.; 51 / 13–14; 181 / 2ff., 20ff. Catalogus vanitatum, WA 20:96 / 36, 13. [LW 15:57.] [LW 15:34, 167, 82–83.]

69. WA 20:98 / 12ff.; 98 / 29–99 / 26, esp. 99 / 2ff. [LW 15:84, 84–85, esp. 85.]

70. WA DB 10²:106 / 12ff. [LW 35:263, 264.] H. Bornkamm, ed., *Luthers Bibelvorreden,* 65–66.

contempt. Rather, gold and wealth, government and women are gifts to delight us and serve for our help. The gifts are not in vain but the human heart is vain, for it is never satisfied.[71]

Having concluded his lectures on the Preacher Solomon, Luther's intention was to go on with an exposition of the prophets, for that was where his translation of the Old Testament stood at the time. In May 1527 he announced his plan to lecture on Isaiah.[72] But as summer came Luther was unable to begin; in fact [as we have already seen] after several early warnings he took seriously ill in July.[73] Besides, the plague-induced departure of most of the students for Jena induced him to select a less-inclusive book, the First Epistle of John.[74] He prized this "honest apostolic epistle" highly and had said so already in the preface to it in his German translation of the New Testament as published in 1522. It "keeps us in the true middle way that we become righteous and free from sin through faith, and then, when we are righteous, that we practice good works and love for God's sake, freely and without seeking anything else."[75] Because it manifests the actual message of Christ, Luther called the Gospel according to John "the one tender and true chief Gospel" and favored it far above the three Synoptics. The First Epistle shared this place with the Fourth Gospel in Luther's esteem, and he counted it "among the true and most noble books of the New Testament."[76] "This letter bears the Johannine manner and style. Of all the Epistles, this is the one most richly comforting since it buoys up afflicted hearts."[77]

No fully worked out manuscript of these lectures remains, but several preparatory drafts exist, as well as a number of versions as taken down by hearers, especially Rörer.[78] As he was lecturing, Luther had great expectations from 1 John: God, he said,

71. WA 20:10 / 9ff., 26ff.; 11 / 12ff. [LW 15:8, 9.]

72. Ca. May 4, 1527, to Wenceslaus Link, WA Br 4:198 / 9–10.

73. See above, pp. 553ff.

74. August 19 to November 7, 1527, WA 20:599, 794. Luther began the planned lectures on Isaiah only in May 1528. See below, p. 575. [For the schedule of his lectures, LW 30:x–xi.]

75. WA DB 7:326 / 2–3, 22. [LW 35:393.] H. Bornkamm, ed., Luthers Bibelvorreden, 175. Gesuch = "striving for reward" [or "seeking anything else"].

76. Preface (1522), WA DB 6:10 / 25–26, 7–8, 29ff. [LW 35:362.] H. Bornkamm, ed., Luthers Bibelvorreden, 140.

77. WA 20:600 / 1–2. [LW 30:219.]

78. Preparations for chaps. 1, 2, 5: WA 48:313–23. Rörer's* copy, WA 20:592–801; on other versions, see WA 20:592–98. Cf. also the notice in WA 25:522. Bear in mind that the citations originate mainly in abbreviations of the copyists. [*Note the one also by Jacob Propst, whose version is also in WA 20:599ff. and which LW 30:xi follows, while Bornkamm follows Rörer. The Rörer and Propst versions differ in detail but not in substance; hence the slight variations between the following citations—through n. 97—and the text in LW 30:222–327.]

sets us down so that we may experience how mighty his Word is and can accomplish more than sin and death. . . . Inasmuch as we are being attacked by death, sin, and heretics, I have made up my mind to treat this epistle so that we may mutually console each other and pray together against the bothersome devil. . . . And we have the promise: where two or three (are gathered). . . . So we hope that when I speak in the name of God and you listen, the Lord will be present—even as Satan will also be here.[79]

These lectures provide the backdrop for the anxious months of the autumn of 1527. In this epistle Luther found an answer to the weightiest of questions with which the Reformation proclamation had to deal at that time. From the drastic words that launch the epistle, Luther derives the whole truth about the person of Christ:

That which was from the beginning, which we have heard, which we have seen with our eyes, which we have looked on and touched with our hands, concerning the word of life . . . [1:1]. Never have I heard a simpler way of speaking than this, and yet there is such a mighty majesty hidden in it, so as to be incomprehensible. It is as though the apostle were stammering, and yet the whole Majesty is bound up in it. No other apostle has expressed himself so simply.[80]

This kind of narration presents us Christ in both his natures as a whole person and as the "Word of life." "I know of no other God but of him in this humanity."[81] This touched on the problem of the Lord's Supper. In the sacrament of the altar we taste bread and wine and in our hearts, Christ himself with body and blood.[82] The recognition of Christ—the "sum total of our religion"[83]—the way 1 John makes possible also resolves the question standing between Luther and his partners, on the one side, and the Roman church on the other. "Christ is the expiation for our sins, and not for ours only but for the sins of the whole world" (2:2). These are "veritable bolts of lightning against the pope and the monks." How many intercessors, "workers of satisfaction," and works of atonement has the church not sought, foremost among them, Mary, the virgin mediatrix! The testimony of John confirms the right to abandon monasticism. "They call us refugee monks. We are forced to get out, for they don't want to hear this kind of preaching from us. I am forced to desert the pope. . . . Christ

79. WA 20:599 / 5ff. [LW 30:219. Alternate. Propst text.]
80. WA 20:601 / 10ff. [LW 30:221. Propst text.]
81. WA 20:605 / 1ff., 9. [Cf. LW 30:223. Propst text.]
82. WA 20:606 / 8–9. [LW 30:223. Propst text.]
83. WA 20:640 / 16.

does not require reconciliation, for he himself is the reconciliation."[84] "Christ is not as we imagine him, as though we must appease him by celebrating masses and by sending his mother to him." "This is a wonderful, golden text," Luther notes at the beginning of the epistle's second chapter.[85]

According to Luther, 1 John opposes not only the thought of expiation but also the underestimation of sin. For Luther this means: "Zwingli intends to minimize original sin and speaks of it only as a defect."[86] Just because sin must be taken so seriously, it is comforting that Christ has come in order to destroy the devil's work. "Christ once bore the everlasting conflict, yet it is necessary [for us] to fight on."[87] If, as has been said, the First Epistle of John "for the first time in the history of the church thematically [unfolded] the motif 'simul justus et peccator,'"[88] then this was precisely the comfort Luther derived from the battle between Christ and the devil as pictured in 3:7ff. As according to Rom. 7, the Christian is a *duplex homo*. To believe in Christ means to be born of God. "Because he exists in this birth, he can be tempted but not overcome. And should he sometime fall, this birth comes back when he returns to faith."[89] Not moral exertion but faith is the ever new source of life in God. Yet this presupposes that we know what sin is. "To understand the nature of sin is a very difficult matter." The Christian has weightier sins than the monks imagine, for the monks talk only of unchastity. But sin is much more than that; it is not to believe in Christ and in the new life from him. Therefore the strongest remedy against sin is to reflect on the Word of God.[90] Both opponents—the papal church's teachers of false doctrine and the Zwinglians—are much alike. The errors of both lie in the realm of Christology. They teach docetism and they deny the true humanity of Christ, and they understand neither the difference between justification and sanctification nor the way the two belong together. Thus they also fail to see how justification and sanctification comprise a continuous process in

84. WA 20:637 / 21–638 / 9. [LW 30:237–38. Propst text.]
85. WA 20:636 / 6ff. [LW 30:235. Propst text.]
86. WA 20:621 / 8. [LW 30:229. Propst text.]
87. Freely expressed. Literally, Rörer writes: "Ein tröstlicher Spruch: Venit dissolvere, per quem jugem conflictum intelligit: semel tulit, sed semper conflictandum," WA 20:705 / 9ff. [LW 30:272. Propst text.]
88. E. Käsemann, "Ketzer und Zeuge: Zum johanneischen Verfassersproblem," ZThK 48 (1951): 306; reprinted in Käsemann, *Exegetische Versuche und Besinnungen*, 2d ed. (Göttingen, 1960), 1:182.
89. On 1 John 5:18. WA 20:798 / 17ff., 27ff.; 799 / 2–3. [LW 30:325–26.]
90. WA 20:629 / 5–12, esp. 8. [LW 30:233. Propst text.]

the life of the believer: "Forgiveness takes place suddenly, the cleansing gradually, from day to day. For we are made holy, and there is no end to justification and sanctification before we turn to ashes."[91]

This fundamental thought in the Johannine letter sketches the situation in broadest terms. For John it was the struggle against the false teachers of Christology; for Luther it was against the opponents of a correctly understood gospel: monks, sacramentarians, Zwingli, and fanatics of all types. In both cases the opponents call on the key word of the epistle, "that God is light and in him is no darkness at all." This is what John tells the world to its face: "So, then, the whole world is in the dark and in error; summon all the learned, the wise, the kings." And exactly they, "the monks and the wise, etc., stride about with their opinions, regarding themselves as light—not realizing that in God's sight they are darkness."[92] Luther knows this from the fanatics [Enthusiasts] of his time. They keep thinking, "We are children of light and full of the Holy Spirit."[93] This conviction of theirs makes them so repulsive ("He who says he is in the light and hates his brother . . . ," 1 John 2:9) and unteachable as well. "No heretic allows himself to be converted."[94] The stubbornness of the heresies makes us ask the question whether perhaps he and his partners may not have themselves to blame for this. "One blames us for everything evil that's happening in the world: insurrection, factions, and so on. . . . If the pope had remained in charge [this would never have happened]." Luther's retort is a decisive No. Even Christ was betrayed from within his little band: "Had it not been for Judas, he would never have been crucified. We too have a Judas among us, and he has dispersed us. Therefore we are being charged guilty." Luther naturally means Müntzer first of all. Yet precisely against him Luther can console himself like the author of the 1 John: "They went out from among us . . . , but they are not of us."[95] Indeed, Luther con-

91. WA 20:603–6; 613 / 13–14; 627 / 12ff. [LW 30:222–23; 227; 231–32. Propst text.] This is one of Rörer's virtually verbatim formulations of Luther: "Remissio fit subito, emulatio fit paulatim de die in diem, quia sanctificamur et non finis justificandi, nisi redigamur in cineres." W. von Loewenich, Luther und das johanneische Christentum (Munich, 1935), 33–34, had already pointed this out. On the doubly false doctrine against which 1 John turns, see H. Braun, "Literatur-Analyse und theologische Schichtung im ersten Johannesbrief," ZThK 48 (1951): 287ff.; reprinted in H. Braun, Gesammelte Studien zum Neuen Testament und seiner Umwelt, 2d ed. (Tübingen, 1967), 210ff.

92. WA 20:725 / 7–729 / 3; 612 / 13ff. [Cf. LW 30:285–87; 226.]

93. WA 20:616 / 5–6, cf. also 614 / 14ff. [LW 30:227.]

94. WA 20:649 / 14–650 / 17, 7. [LW 30:241–42.]

95. WA 20:673 / 9–674 / 9, esp. 673 / 9–10, 15–16; 674 / 8–17. (The rendition going back to Jacob Propst [WA 20:594, 597] adds "Müntzer," WA 20:674 / 32); 708 / 13; 673 / 17–18. Cf. 1 John 2:19. [LW 30:253–54, Propst text.]

fesses, "I have often wondered whether it would have been better to save the papacy than to see so much dissension. But it is better to tear a few from the claws of the devil than that everybody go under."[96]

The Johannine view of the contemporary scene is not to be separated from the Johannine view of the end of time. "Children, it is the last hour" (1 John 2:18). Luther concedes that this passage had given him many a headache. When, as done frequently, one counts fifteen hundred years for the reign of Christ, then its time span is hardly less than the reign of Moses. But there is a flaw in such reckoning. "The last hour means not the shortness of time but the quality of doctrine. . . . No other doctrine is to be expected than this which Christ and the apostles have brought. Following this comes the revelation of Christ." Moses looked forward to the "coming day" of Christ. Yet when the doctrine of Christ goes under, then comes the end, the harvest. Therefore "it is terrifying to see sects emerging in the midst of pure doctrine."[97]

The Epistle to Titus was next. Lecturing on it from November 11 to December 13, 1527, Luther found it a convenient sequel to 1 John, especially because it introduced a variation on the already familiar Johannine theme.[98] Again, he concedes, "Thank God that He did not disclose to me that such heresies were to follow, for I would never have begun."[99] In line with the epistle's pastoral theme, Luther bore in mind the future ministerial office of his students as well as the life of the congregation. His main concern focused on the questions of commandment and conscience. The many human traditions [or regulations] of Hebrew origin which they, as pastors, would still come on in the parishes would necessarily induce qualms of conscience.[100] Therefore the text "All things are pure" (1:15) "ought to be written in golden letters. This single text is a thunderclap and a storm against all the straws of human traditions, against the law of the pope and the decrees of councils, which declared that marriage was impure for priests. . . . To the pure marriage is pure." "Those are pure who have a sound faith, who believe in Christ, who know that they cannot be defiled by anything."[101] Luther shows vividly how the conscience is

96. WA 20:674 / 36ff. [LW 30:254. Propst text.]

97. WA 20:667 / 12–668 / 17. [LW 30:252. Propst text.]

98. Also for these lectures we have not only Rörer's copy of them (WA 25:6–69) [LW 29:ix–x, 3–90] but also Luther's preparations (WA 48:305–12), from which one can note where Luther made changes or extemporized. (See ibid., the comparisons in the notes.)

99. WA 25:10 / 18–19, extemporized. [LW 29:8.]

100. WA 25:36 / 30ff. [LW 29:43–44.]

101. WA 25:37 / 1ff., 26–27, extemporized. [LW 29:44, 45.]

like the last part of a logical conclusion; the major premise utters a common-sense truth: all sin is to be avoided. The conscience concludes from this: I am not allowed to eat meat. Thus not the abstract major premise but the concrete application of a union premise becomes determinative. "If the minor premise is upheld, the conclusion follows."[102] This was one of those plays of logic not uncommon in Luther. For his students this kind of thing was straightforward instruction on the way conscience is dependent on opinion and how opinion must be examined. The reference in Titus 2 to the various categories of church members gives Luther an opportunity to suggest a specific mini-ethic revolving around the word "offense"—and others could take offense at them as preachers. Then the people criticize, "Is that what Christians are like? What good comes from their doctrine?"[103] At the same time, Luther corrects the common failing that represents Christ as example and lawgiver, a form of instruction that overlooks the main point, which is that Christ has given himself for us and that thereby we are enabled to become new human beings.[104]

When he comes to chapter 3 and its reference to rulers and government, Luther takes the occasion to do more than underscore the text's admonition to obedience. Instead, he emphasizes for both sides [both rulers and ruled] the art of moderation, *epieikeia* [reasonableness] to which he often referred and which he found treated so masterfully in Ecclesiastes.[105] A motto such as that ascribed to Emperor Frederick III [1415–93], of Hapsburg, Luther considered as spoken from the heart and applicable to what he meant: "He who knows not how to overlook does not know how to rule."[106] Luther delights in the vigorous tone of the Titus epistle. The apostle admonishes the preachers to inculcate the fact that faith and action belong together, "as one pounds a post into the ground."[107]

Then Luther sums up the results of his fresh and lively lectures: "We here have an epistle so full of the best instruction and admonition that almost nothing in the church is left untreated."[108] He thereby strengthens

---

102. WA 25:39 / 18ff., 25–26. In his preparations Luther had written, "To quit the monastic life is a sin." Since this did not concern all his hearers, he substituted fasting, an example applicable to all. WA 48:310 / 2ff.

103. WA 25:46 / 31. [LW 29:58.]

104. WA 25:53 / 4–54 / 18. [LW 29:66–67.]

105. WA 25:59 / 1–60 / 7. [LW 29:74–75.]

106. Qui nescit dissimulare, non potest imperare. WA 25:59 / 21. [LW 29:75 (note that *dissimulare* can be rendered favorably, as Bornkamm does, or unfavorably as Jaroslav Pelikan does in this passage).] See also WA 48:311, n. 15, which cites similar passages.

107. On Titus 3:8. WA 25:67 / 6ff., 12–13. [LW 29:86.]

108. WA 25:69 / 10–11. [LW 29:89. Alternate.]

his judgment as expressed earlier in the preface to this epistle in the New Testament translation of 1522: "This is a short epistle, but a model of Christian doctrine, in which is comprehended in a masterful way all that is necessary for a Christian to know and to live."[109]

Paul's Epistle to Philemon, following Titus in Luther's sequence, was treated also before Christmas in three lectures between December 16 and 18, 1527.[110] Rörer's precise shorthand enables us to catch some of the warmth with which Luther treated the subject, not only for the sake of the little story of the escaped slave Onesimus, which underlies it, but also for the sake of showing clearly how faith applies to life. "This epistle is indeed a purely private and domestic one. Nevertheless, Paul cannot refrain from inculcating the general doctrine concerning Christ even here in treating a private matter." It contains such marvelous passages as even a Cicero did not see. "There we shall examine closely in order to see that nothing is so ordinary that Christ is not present in it."[111] Luther lauds the stylistic beauties of the letter, particularly Paul's courtesy. Everyone has his proper title: Philemon, the congregation's benefactor, becomes Paul's "fellow worker"; Archippos, the bishop, becomes "our fellow soldier." "The pope would never do this." "This is a holy form of flattery."[112] This is indeed a very special art. "A Christian person cannot flatter, because he does regard a brother not as flesh and blood but as a believer in Christ."[113] So, heart-to-heart and without hesitation, he can request or thank the other. Paul does it again and again; he begins every letter of his that way.[114] This sort of thing flows from the fellowship of faith. It is not simply something spiritual. "He has the body which you have, which even I have. . . . The body is something distributed in that bread which you and I have."[115] Luther is cheered especially that Paul speaks so emphatically about the growth of faith. "It is the most important thing among Christians that they grow in the knowledge of Jesus. . . . The fanatics suppose that once they have heard the Word they know everything, as though they were filled with the Holy Spirit."[116] In his 1522 preface to the New Testament in German,

---

109. In the German, *verfasset* = *zusammengefasst* = comprehended, WA DB 7:284 / 3ff. [LW 35:389.] H. Bornkamm, ed., *Luthers Bibelvorreden*, 171.

110. WA 25:69–78. As to the dates, WA 25:2. [LW 29:93–105. The initial date is given as December 16 instead of 15, as in Bornkamm, LW 29:x.]

111. WA 25:69 / 27ff.; 70 / 2–3. [LW 29:93. Alternate.]

112. WA 25:71 / 11ff., 19–20. [LW 29:95.]

113. WA 25:78 / 3ff. [LW 29:104.]

114. WA 25:71 / 30ff. [LW 29:95.]

115. WA 25:72 / 25ff. [LW 29:96.]

116. WA 25:73 / 3ff. [LW 29:97.]

Luther had expressed his special affection for this epistle ("For we are all his Onesimi, if we believe").[117] As he closed these lectures on the treasured little letter he said, "So, there we have a private epistle from which much should be learned: how brethren are to be commended, that is, that an example might be provided to the church how we ought to take care of those who fall and restore those who err. For the kingdom of Christ is a kingdom of mercy and grace."[118]

With the new year, 1528, conditions at the university began to improve. The plague was considered gone. Luther took the opportunity, on December 29 of the old year, to drop Justus Jonas a teasing note, for he had not yet returned from Nordhausen, whither he had taken refuge. "So you still have not come home, my Jonas. That surprises me, for the pest has died out completely and been buried. Now you could at least visit those who have been plagued, of course at our expense." Presently, the escapees returned in droves, including virtually all the townspeople. The town council would be back tomorrow, the university shortly thereafter, as Melanchthon reported.[119] But that signal was premature. It was not until late March that things were back to normal.[120]

Meanwhile, from January 13 to March 30 Luther read twenty-five lectures on the First Epistle to Timothy, an ample treatment for those six chapters. Here again we possess the shorthand copy of the tireless George Rörer. He took down the lectures in addition to performing his many official duties as deacon of the Town Church and persevered all the way, even though Bugenhagen and Luther, noting his visible strain, urged him to take a vacation. But Rörer stuck to his job, unwilling to go away before Luther had given the final touch to the Timothy epistle.[121] Besides, at a time of restructuring new church orders and of confrontation with "Enthusiasts" (the spiritualists and opponents in the Lord's Supper question), Luther could hardly have found a more appropriate New Testament epistle than this one, replete with Paul's instructions to his disciple Timothy for his congregational ministry. "The epistle is not didactic, and it does not strive to establish basic teaching. Rather, it establishes the church and sets

117. "Runaway," yet slaves ever belonging to the Lord. WA DB 7:292 / 15–16. [LW 35:390.]

118. WA 25:78 / 26ff. [LW 29:105.]

119. WA Br 4:307 / 1ff.

120. Rörer reported as much at the end of March to Stephan Roth in Zwickau that the university had returned and Melanchthon would soon be following. Printed in G. Buchwald, *Zur Wittenberger Stadt- und Universitätsgeschichte in der Reformationszeit: Briefe an Stephan Roth in Zwickau* (Leipzig, 1893), 29.

121. WA 26:1. Rörer's letter of February 26, 1528, to Stephan Roth, town secretary of Zwickau. Buchwald, *Wittenberger Stadt- und Universitätsgeschichte*, 24.

it in order. And yet, in the midst of this process Paul does not neglect to add very important doctrinal subjects."[122] Just as Timothy is proceeding against teachers who have not been called and whose message has no foundation in the gospel, so Luther in turn clarifies the connection between law and gospel. The law promotes pure heart. But this we receive only from the gospel. The gospel alone teaches and grants us faith in God's mercy and—through faith—gives us a good conscience.[123] Thus the law is not to be rejected, but "used" in the right sense—in view of the gospel and on its terms. The key word in 1 Tim. 1:8, "The law is good, if anyone uses it lawfully," serves Luther in the confrontation with his opponents, the "pseudo-prophets." They accuse him: Why do you oppose us? We are teaching no (mere) human wisdom. But, Luther replies, this is not the contrast between them and him. At issue, rather, is the distinction between the facts of salvation and their "use." What Paul here has to say about the proper use of the law applies also to the understanding of salvation which the gospel offers us. The "false prophets" claim that salvation (*usus redemptionis* [the use of redemption]) occurs only on the cross through the dying of Christ. Let no one look for it anywhere else, not even in the Lord's Supper. Yet they forget that these "facts of salvation" are mediated through sermon and sacrament and by faith must be put to use. With this differentiation between fact and usage Luther gains a methodical rule for the confrontation over the sacramental question.[124]

Only after the university had at last reassembled in Wittenberg, and after ecclesial negotiations had taken him on several short journeys to Torgau, Altenburg, and Weimar, could Luther finally commence his Isaiah lectures. Between May 18, 1528, and February 22, 1530, he expounded the prophet in 150 lectures.[125] Isaiah is the only one of the major

122. WA 26:4 / 10ff. [*LW* 28:217.]

123. WA 26:10 / 28–11 / 14. [*LW* 28:225–26.]

124. WA 26:13 / 17–15 / 35; 13 / 2, 28ff.; 14 / 3–4. [*LW* 28:229–33; 229; 231.] The term *usus*, as applied to the sacrament, is to Luther the act of faithful appropriation, not—as occurs in later Lutheran theology with its subdividing of the Lord's Supper doctrine—a "use" springing from an enjoyment of the sacrament. See H. Gollwitzer, *Coena Domini* (see p. 512, above, n. 51), 97ff. H. Grass, *Die Abendmahlslehre bei Luther und Calvin*, 2d ed. (Gütersloh, 1954), 110–11.

125. [*LW* 16, chaps. 1–39; 17, chaps. 40–66. These two volumes are based on WA 31²:1–260, chaps. 1–39; and 31²:261–585, chaps. 40–66. However, the dating in both *LW* and WA stands to be corrected.] D. Thyen, "Untersuchungen zu Luthers Jesaja-Vorlesung" (theology diss. Heidelberg, 1964); summarization of the findings in the author's notes, *ThLZ* 90 (1965): 710–11, has justifiably called into question the dating provided in WA (i.e., beginning in July 1527 [*sic*], interruption in August because of the relocation of the university to Jena, and resumption before Advent 1527; cf. WA 25:79 and WA 31²:viii). The WA 25:79 source is

prophets on which Luther lectured. One reason for this is that in Isaiah, more than in any other, Luther found the coming of Christ and his kingdom announced. To be sure, all the prophets do this, but "still one does it more than another, one more fully than another, and Isaiah more amply and richly than they all." So he wrote in the preface to his translation of the prophecy of Isaiah, which (looked over by Melanchthon) was published in the autumn of 1528 and thus aided him in his preparations.[126]

Interest in the messianic prophecies did not, however, make Luther neglect an exposition of the historical material. He said as much in his preface to the Isaiah translation.

> If one would understand the prophecies, it is necessary that one know how things were in the land, how matters lay, what was in the mind of the people—what plans they had with respect to their neighbors, friends, and enemies—and especially what attitude they took in their country toward God and toward the prophet, whether they held to his word and worship or to idolatry.[127]

So his preface supplied information on the geographical location of the country, on the historical situation in the time of Isaiah, and on the contradiction the prophet found in his people.[128] Here, in the image, the message, and the destiny of the prophet, lay the core of his commentary, not in the allegorical interpretation of his visions—over which scholastic theology displayed widely ranging differences of opinion. The Reformation interest in this prophecy and the attitude of people toward it comprised a

---

Bugenhagen's letter (*Dr. Johannes Bugenhagens Briefwechsel*, ed. O. Vogt [Stettin, 1888], 71–72), written not in the summer but in November 1527, when Bugenhagen resided in Luther's house (above, p. 562). WA 31²:28, n. 1 (concerning the change in date); says that *et sanctum adventum* is not a reference to the Advent season but to the coming glorious advent of Christ (instead of *sanctum* the reading should probably be *secundum adventum*, the second coming). Thyen has also clarified the sources, which are difficult to penetrate in their existing condition (two sharply contrasting treatments by V. Dietrich, WA 25, and a later discovered transcript by Lauterbach, WA 31²). The clue lay in an examination of Luther's lecture aids. See on this subject H.-W. Krumwiede, "Usus legum et usus historiarum: Die Hermeneutik der Theologia crucis nach Luthers Auslegung von Jesaja 13," *KuD* 8 (1962): 238–39, who has utilized the results of Thyen. A new printing of these lectures would be highly desirable. The material for a reprint has been gathered to a large extent through Thyen's work.

126. Preface to Luther's Isaiah translation, WA DB 11¹:18 / 33ff. [*LW* 35:273ff.] Bornkamm, ed., *Luthers Bibelvorreden*, 75–80, 77. Melanchthon, on June 15, 1528, to Camerarius, on his looking over Luther's translation. *CR* 1:983. On the dating, *Suppl. Mel.* 6 / 1:427. *MBW* 693.

127. WA DB 11¹:16 / 21ff. [*LW* 35:274.] H. Bornkamm, ed., *Luthers Bibelvorreden*, 75.

128. WA DB 11¹:16ff. [*LW* 35:274–75.] H. Bornkamm, ed., *Luthers Bibelvorreden*, 75ff.

subject to which Bugenhagen had addressed himself in lectures given already in 1523–24. These have been preserved to us not in print but in a manuscript copy by Stephan Roth.[129]

This advance work by Bugenhagen applied exegetically what he had learned theologically from Luther. However, Luther appears not to have had a copy of Bugenhagen's lectures. Actually, both he and Bugenhagen gladly made use of the Isaiah commentary by Oecolampadius, which they had welcomed eagerly. Published in 1525, it was based on lectures given in 1523–24 by this noted Hebraist. Oecolampadius was the first to utilize the Hebrew text. His commentary was in Latin, including a chapter-by-chapter summary in German, for the benefit of the large number of Basel townspeople who attended the lectures.[130] Luther prized him as a linguist of high repute and deplored it all the more when Oecolampadius went over to the "fanatics."[131] Luther no doubt used Oecolampadius's commentary—though this cannot always be demonstrated—as a prod or corrective, and also for getting on with his German translation of Isaiah, which was based on the Hebrew original as well as the Vulgate and which preceded his own lectures on the prophet.[132] Luther received a certain amount of help, sometimes overrated, for his German version from two leading Anabaptist scholars, Ludwig Hätzer and Hans Denk. Their translation, *All the Prophets, Set into German from the Hebrew Language,* was published in Worms in 1527.[133] In his lectures Luther pointed out the problems of translation and added a wealth of theological questions to which the text gave rise. In the process certain points of emphasis developed: for example, the relation of law and gospel, promise and fulfillment (with a resolution of the question according to a historically demonstrable success of the prophecy in Isa. 9:1–6 ["The people who walked in darkness . . . "]), an impressive presentation of the analogy of faith on the subject of word and sign (on Isa. 6). The miracle is not Isaiah's vision but the inner event: the gracious experience of the glory of God through faith.

129. On Bugenhagen's lectures, see Thyen, "Untersuchungen," 105–6, 287, 115x. Thyen has drawn from these lectures, in appendix 5, a copy of the exposition of Isa. 6, with comments on Bugenhagen's exegetical method (83xff.).

130. E. Staehelin, *Briefe und Akten zum Leben Oecolampads* (Leipzig, 1934), 2:189ff.

131. Letter to Gerbel, April 26, 1526, WA Br 4:63 / 4ff.

132. Examples in Thyen, "Untersuchungen," 107ff.

133. [*Alle Propheten, nach Hebräischer Sprach verdeutscht.*] Cf. H. Volz, "Hat Luther bei seiner Prophetenübersetzung die 'Wormser Propheten' von 1527 benutzt?" WA DB 11²:xciii–cxxxiii. The older literature is listed there. The "Wormsians," for their part, relied heavily for Isaiah on the Oecolampadius commentary, which Luther also used. Cf. Thyen, "Untersuchungen," 133–34.

This is the gracious "mortification" of the human being by dying through the law. And the cleansing of the lips by means of the glowing coal of the seraph is an effectual sign like the sacraments.[134]

Luther makes use of the powerful picture of this vision "gladly," as he said, to give the students (whom he otherwise trained in terms of historical exposition) an example of safe allegorization.[135] He interpreted the image of the Lord enthroned over the temple as Christ and his church, but meaning not the arrangements in the temple, as beloved in conventional allegorization, but seeing the seraphs as the apostles and preachers, the glowing coals as the gospel of forgiveness which ignites and fills the heart. Luther here applies allegory [or, more precisely, allegoresis that relates to exegesis] as pictorial helps with which to imprint the truths of the gospel on the imagination of ordinary folk. Allegory is thus seen as having homiletical value, while for the subject matter as such the story (the historically based account), the text itself has the first and decisive word.[136] "*Historie*," as used by the prophets, includes with them the element of prophecy as part of their distinctive proclamation of the Word. According to Luther, this prophetic reality must always proceed from the present and, from there, direct one's attention to the future. Such proclamation thereby is historical, which means simultaneously to be nourished on experience in which both God's governance in grace as well as his exercise of judgment can be discerned. This, then, is a standard according to which meaningful allegory can be measured. Luther clarifies this in a highly personal way:

> When inexperienced minds lapse into allegories, they are unable to grasp the sure meaning of Scripture. If the matter with the pope had not held me fast to the simple text of the Bible, I would have become just as much a babbling allegorizer as St. Jerome and Origen, for this figurative speech contains certain deceptions from which these minds have a difficult time disengaging themselves. But you, instructed by my example, take care and follow the simple story and the pure text. Then the time will come when, without dan-

134. WA 31²:49 / 30–51 / 14. Thyen, "Untersuchungen," 124xff., has made an example of Isa. 6. By a reconstruction of the lecture text from the various copyists, Thyen had endeavored to show how (by systematically exhausting the sources) one can recover the living impression of Luther's exposition. For comparison he has examined the same chapter in Bugenhagen's presentation (82xff.).

135. WA 25:113–14; 113 / 14. WA 31 / 2:53–54. [*LW* 16:76.]

136. This is how Luther justifies in some detail, in his preface to the published lectures in 1532, the occasional use of allegory in contrast to the general allegorization of Jerome. WA 25:88 / 30ff.

ger, you can employ allegory—just as we see Paul using allegory for the sake of adornment.[137]

But there is more than adornment at issue. If one is bent on playing with allegory in any case, Luther gives it a deeper significance by relating it to law and gospel. From this angle, Cyrus then (who made Babylon no longer a terror for the Jews) or the Turks today can be seen as "law": "a cruel and powerful enemy who arises against the proud bearing of the self-righteous, who rely on their own merits."[138] For those who trust in God, this is good news, as the destruction of the papal Babylon becomes evident in the emptying of the cloisters.[139] Only Jacob and Israel, the believers, are liberated. "Tormented consciences are raised up. They have recognized the tyranny of the pope, while the rest extol him like the ruler of Babylon. These are allegories of mine which I can prove; they suggest to us the essence of law and gospel."[140] These "allegories" are based on true historical events, people, and powers. Another of Luther's examples focused on Cajetan. The legate apparently had no eye for historical connections when he rejected Luther at Augsburg in 1518, saying, " 'What does the pope care about Germany?' So great was the sense of security, and yet things began to fall, and they fell."[141]

For Luther the meaning of all historical inquiry lies here: *Hic historiarum usus est, quod docent conscientias.*[142] This use of *conscientia* means not simply conscience as understood in today's manner of speaking, although Luther often speaks of the examples of history, from which we are to learn. Rather, *conscientia* means what the ego knows about itself, in light of its own guilt and God's law as well as in view of God's help and

137. WA 25:142 / 27ff. On the theological background of Luther's concept of history in his Isaiah lectures, see the rewarding essay of Krumwiede, "Usus legum" (see above, n. 125).

138. WA 25:142 / 34ff.

139. WA 25:142 / 42ff.

140. WA 25:143 / 4ff.

141. WA 25:142 / 23ff. Luther often referred to this expression of Cajetan in his Table Talk, e.g., WA TR 4, no. 4120, 146 / 32ff.; no. 4488, 340 / 17–18. WA TR 5, no. 6459, 674 / 2.

142. ["This is the use of histories, that they teach consciencies."] WA 25:142 / 11–12. R. Wittram used this sentence as the motto for his *Das Interesse an der Geschichte*, Kleine Vandenhoeck-Reihe 59–61 (Göttingen, 1958), but he did so without making it serve a theological or historico-philosophical theory. *Conscientia*, in connection with Luther's exposition, means trust in the helping power of God, which is discernible in historical events, in this case the fall of Babylon, as Isaiah had foretold in his prophecy. It means that even though God seems hidden the heart may count on Him. Understood in this way, then a sound conscience can bring the historical event into the consciousness, also with the help of an illustrative allegory, the way Paul did it. WA 25:142 / 25–33. Cf. on this, Krumwiede, "Usus legum," 253ff.

forgiveness for those who trust in him. It is not simply accidental that Luther has given these directions for the believer's association with history. After all, he was here expounding a prophet whose awareness of history was incomparable. From Isaiah's sense of the historical, Luther learned how to cultivate that sense for himself and for his time. This is one of the choice results of these powerful and often too little esteemed lectures.

21

Political and Educational Writings

[As the decade advanced, issues involving government and law also demanded Luther's attention.] A political calm of sorts settled over the empire toward the end of 1525. The warfare going on between Charles V and France since 1521 was concluded in the decisive Battle of Pavia[1] in February 1525. In that year the many armed conflicts between princes and peasants also subsided. The wars, however, had left questions, and some people turned to Luther for answers. Especially urgent and personal was the case of Assa von Kram, a military colonel and a man highly esteemed by Luther. He had successively been in French, Electoral Saxon, and imperial service and had taken part in campaigns in Italy and Denmark. But the massacre of the peasants near Frankenhausen had left Kram with some deeply disturbing questions about the conduct of war. He first broached the subject to Luther on the occasion of the extended homage ceremony for the new Elector John in Wittenberg, July 13–16, 1525. What he found especially troublesome was the "status of soldiers" as well as "various matters concerning conscience." Quite naturally he requested Luther to write something on the subject.[2] While Luther could not oblige immediately, he promised to get on with it when Kram saw him again (probably in January 1526). By autumn the manuscript was at the printer's, and on January 1, 1527, the first copy was sent out. Delays had worked to the advantage of a better treatise. It grew beyond the requested treatment of the problem of conscience, although Kram's original question prompted the title *Whether Soldiers, Too, Can Be Saved* (1526). As it was, Luther here turned out an important treatment of the problem of government and law.[3]

The problem of conscience pervades this entire work. At the very outset the task of the soldier is denoted as an "office," occupation, or "estate,"

1. Cf. the description by L. von Ranke, *Deutsche Geschichte im Zeitalter der Reformation,* 2d ed. (Meersburg and Leipzig, 1933), 2:240ff.
2. Important notes on Kram in *WA Br* 4:144. O. Hahne, "Asche von Cramm, ein Kriegsmann der Reformationszeit und Martin Luther," *Jb. des Braunschweigischen Geschichtsvereins* 2 / 6 (1934): 5ff. On the homage for the successor, see G. Buchwald, "Lutherana," ARG 25 (1928): 74. Luther's recollections of this conversation: *Commentary on Psalm 101* (1534–35), WA 51:236 / 26ff. [*LW* 13:191.]
3. *WA* 19:623–62. [*LW* 46:93–137.]

such as judgeship or matrimony or any of the other functions instituted by God.[4] Properly understood and carried out, the military occupation serves the secular government in carrying out its divinely assigned duty to exercise justice[5]—all of which leads Luther to deal at length with four specific questions of conscience common to a soldier: (1) Is he allowed to take pay? Yes, within limits, because soldiering is a proper occupation. (2) But what if his lord undertakes an unjust war? If the soldier is certain of this, then let him obey God rather than man and not follow his temporal lord; if he cannot be certain, then let his own sense of obedience to duty suffice and give his lord the benefit of the doubt. (3) May a soldier obligate himself to serve more than one lord? Yes, just as a craftsman can have several customers. For military service is an honorable vocation. But what if these lords should fight one another? Then let the soldier follow the lord who is in the right and not the one who may promise him more. (4) Ambition and love of money are corrupt motives for soldiering. A soldier must act on the certainty that he is helping his temporal lord in a good cause.[6]

Bounded by these questions of the soldiering vocation, Luther proceeds to deal with the issue of war itself. By definition the matter of war is an ethical theme: "What else is war but the punishment of wrong and evil?" Why does anyone go to war, except because he desires peace and obedience?"[7] This unavoidable function of humanity—to secure peace and obedience—is the standard by which the task of war must be measured, for at best war means great torment. "But one should also consider how great a plague war may prevent. If people were good and committed to peace, war would be the greatest scourge on earth. But what will you do about the fact that people do not keep the peace, but rob, steal, kill, outrage women and children, and take away property and honor? The small lack of peace called war, or the sword, must set a limit to this universal and worldwide lack of real peace which would destroy everyone."[8] Properly understood, God is at work here, not the hand of man, for the situation is like that which engages criminal justice and culminates in capital punishment. That is why one must consider the "office of the soldier, or the sword, with the eyes of an adult and see why this office slays and acts so cruelly." The fact that this service in the interests of justice and peace can also be abused needlessly and wantonly "is the fault of the

4. WA 19:624 / 18ff.; 626 / 28ff. [LW 46:94.]
5. WA 19:629 / 15ff. [LW 46:100.]
6. WA 19:653 / 15–658 / 34, 1. [LW 46:127–32, esp. 127, 130, 131, 132.]
7. WA 19:625 / 23ff. [LW 46:95.]
8. WA 19:626 / 15ff., 12ff. [LW 46:96.]

people, not of the office."[9] Given this understanding of war in terms of justice, Luther treats war casuistically, judging each case on its merits. He thus distinguishes three possibilities of war, using as occasions not such things as title possession, legal claims, infringements, and the like, but the relations of the contending parties to one another according to public law: equal against equal, overlord against subject, or subject against overlord (insurrection).[10]

It seemed natural for Luther to begin his treatise with the last of the three: insurrection.[11] Again, but more fully and temperately than during the heat of the Peasants' War, he delivers his No to insurrection. On the one hand, he pleads for mitigating circumstances on the part of those who had been forced to participate. And for those who were moved by good intentions or even acting with the knowledge of their overlord in order to forestall the worst from happening, Luther even has words of recognition.[12] He reminds the authorities that rigidly applied law can often lead to the greatest injustice. The wisdom of the ancient Greeks and Romans paired the demands of justice with those of equity or fairness (*epieikeia, aequitas*). "All laws that regulate men's actions must be subject to justice [equity or fairness, in this case], their mistress, because of the innumerable and varied circumstances no one can anticipate or set down."[13] In the same breath, however, Luther warns that equity can be abused. It so happens that there is a form of craftiness that schemes day and night "for some way to sell itself in the marketplace under the name and appearance of justice. When it succeeds, law comes to nothing."[14] Thus the peasants often justified their insurrection on grounds that their lords would not allow the gospel to be preached. Yet what is this but repaying injustice with injustice? Even more, "If a prince or lord will not tolerate the gospel, we ought to go into another realm where the gospel is preached, as Christ says in Matt. 10[:23], 'When they persecute you in one town, flee to the next.'"[15] Luther's position had long stood for a readiness to emigrate, and

9. WA 19:627 / 1ff. [LW 46:97.]

10. WA 19:632 / 25ff. [LW 46:103.]

11. As close as it came in time to the peasant revolt, it does not seem justified to call this "Luther's Fourth Book Against the Peasants," the title given F. Lau's essay in *Antwort aus der Geschichte: Beobachtungen und Erwägungen zum geschichtlichen Bild der Kirche*," ed. W. Sommer and H. Ruppel (Berlin, 1971), 84ff. To be sure, it is significant that Luther here stands up for those who were mere followers of the peasant insurrection, but the essential intention of this treatise of Luther's does not become apparent in this designation.

12. WA 19:630 / 16ff.; 631 / 26ff. [LW 46:101, 102.]

13. WA 19:632 / 20–21. [LW 46:103.]

14. WA 19:633 / 16–17. [LW 46:103.]

15. WA 19:634 / 15ff. [LW 46:105.]

later this became the first part of the right of toleration as written into the Religious Peace of Augsburg[16] (1555). Luther energetically brushes aside other arguments for deposing a ruler; granted, insane rulers are to be replaced, but a tyrant is not yet a madman. He points to examples in the history of the Swiss and most recently in that of the Danes, who drove out their king, Christian II. "My reason for saying this is that God says, 'Vengeance is mine, I will repay'" [Rom. 12:19].[17] God, of course, has ample ways of punishing a tyrant: by sudden death, by the revolt of non-Christians (whom God knows well how to use), or by the struggle of opponents in war.[18] Conversely, you cannot count on a situation's being improved by staging a revolt. "To change a government and to improve a government are two different matters, as far apart as heaven and earth." On the whole, let him who would have a good conscience not overreach himself in matters of government.[19] This advice holds for every kind of "subject person," not simply for the peasants but also for the "citizens of cities, nobles, counts, and princes as well, for all these have overlords and are subject to someone else."[20] In Luther's view, this is a problem of justice and not one of social strata. This time it so happened that peasants were involved, rebelling against a God-given order. Had it not been they, Luther wagered that conditions later might have led to an uprising of the nobles themselves against the princes, with the same drastic punishment being meted out. "But now the peasants are the ones who have revolted, and they alone have become the black sheep, while the nobles and the princes get off easy and wipe their mouths as though they had done nothing wrong."[21] A newer example of the injustice of rebellion against a ruler gave Luther special concern: the expulsion of Christian II of Denmark with the connivance of the nobility in Lübeck. This was not simply because Luther had learned to know the king while a transient in Wittenberg.[22] He did not personally take sides with Christian, but left it ex-

16. See the essays by H. Bornkamm, "Der Augsburger Religionsfriede" (1555) and "Das Problem der Toleranz im 16. Jahrhunder," both in H. Bornkamm, *Das Jahrhundert der Reformation: Gestalten und Kräfte*, 2d ed. (Göttingen, 1966), 249, 288. Also M. Heckel, "Augsburger Religionsfriede," *EStL* (1966): 91ff.

17. WA 19:634 / 18–636 / 6; 636 / 5–6. [*LW* 46:105–7.]

18. WA 19:637 / 20–639 / 3. [*LW* 46:109–11.]

19. WA 19:639 / 22–23; 640 / 6ff. [*LW* 46:111, 112.]

20. WA 19:643 / 15ff. [*LW* 46:116.]

21. WA 19:643 / 17–644 / 8. "*Schwarz sein*" = "the only black ones" = "they keep the black Peter." [*LW* 46:116–17.]

22. WA 19:641 / 3ff. On Christian II's stay in Wittenberg, see above, pp. 287–88. [*LW* 46:113.] On the reasons why the king was expelled, cf. G. Ritter, *Die Neugestaltung Europas im 16. Jahrhundert* (Berlin, 1950), 152ff. E. Hassinger, *Das Werden des neuzeitlichen Europa, 1300–1600* (Braunschweig, 1959), 162ff. A. E. Imhof, *Grundzüge der nordischen Geschichte* (Darmstadt, 1970), 82. Literature on the subject, ibid., 227–28.

pressly an open question as to whether the king was in the wrong. That, however, is not the question God will ask the rebels: "You gentlemen of Denmark and Lübeck, who commanded you to do these acts of punishment and vengeance? Did I command you, or did the emperor, or did the overlord? If so, prove it by sealed documents."[23] Two completely different things are involved in being unjust or in condemning injustice. Everyone is involved in justice and injustice.

> However, God alone is Lord over justice and injustice, and God alone passes judgment and administers justice. It is God who commits this responsibility to rulers to act in his stead in these matters. Therefore let no one presume to do this, unless he is sure that he has a command from God, or from God's servants, the rulers.[24]

Here one meets the structures of law which, in Luther's view, hold human society together. He becomes more detailed when treating the converse side of the problem: whether an "overlord" may wage war against his subjects. He responds by offering a graded concept of authority in government, spelling it out more concisely than anywhere else in his writings. Each position of human authority has a dual aspect: the occupant of a given position is an "individual person" to his superior and a "general person" toward all those under him. To God, the emperor is an individual person; to his subjects he is a "general person"—for "he is as many times emperor as he has subjects." Likewise the prince: to his emperor he is an individual person, to his subjects he is a "general person," with authority multiplied as many times as he has subjects. Moreover, at no level in this order [of authority and accountability] is it permissible for an "individual person" to oppose the "general person" above him. Seen from above, positions of human responsibility are divested of all authority; yet seen from below by those who are subjects, "they are adorned with all authority." Thus, "in the end, all authority comes from God, whose alone it is, for he is emperor, prince, count, noble, judge, and all else, and he assigns these offices to his subjects as he wills and takes them back again for himself."[25] As Luther sees it, this combination of responsibility upward and authority downward supports the legal structure, the order and peace of the world. Since God is the ultimate incumbent of every office, it would be well, Luther thinks, for every official to be a Christian. But that is

23. WA 19:641 / 14ff. [LW 46:114.] This comment of Luther's gave Assa von Kram, the field colonel, something to think about, for he was in the service of Duke Frederick of Schleswig-Holstein, who had been backed by the nobility as counter-king.

24. WA 19:641 / 22ff. [LW 46:114.]

25. WA 19:652 / 25–653 / 8. [LW 46:126.]

rarely the case; "a prince is a rare bird in heaven," in Luther's flair for the proverbial. Then he must at least "do what is right and good according to God's outward ordinance."[26] Reason teaches the prince sufficiently about God's ordinances, as Luther likes to remind his readers (and also Erasmus[27]) here and elsewhere. God himself restrains the self-seeking prince "by giving fists to other people too. There are also people on the other side of the mountain." If he understands this, he will keep his princely sword in its sheath. "A sensible prince does not seek his own gain." He is satisfied if his subjects are not attacked, and is not intimidated by the threat of words.[28] This pertains most in case of war among the equally matched. Luther cites an expression of his deceased elector, who when other princes would have drawn the sword ten times in reacting to insults, kept his sword sheathed and replied with reasonable words. "When asked why he let others challenge him so often, he replied, 'I shall not start anything, but if I have to fight, you will see that I shall be the one who decides when it is time to stop.'"[29] The reasonable grounds that Luther advocated included also conventional wisdom of the ancient Greeks and Romans, even though they knew nothing of the true God. "They regarded the words *non putassem* (I did not think of it) as the most shameful words a soldier could speak."[30] And of course they were also aware of a higher Power that turned the tides of war. "Why should we not do for our God what the Romans, the greatest fighters on earth, did for their false god, Fortune, whom they feared? Whenever they did not do this, they fought in great danger and even were badly beaten."[31]

On grounds of reason and of trusting in God, Luther warns against war. And it is on grounds of laws set by God that Luther justifies war to a limited extent: as a defensive action against rebellion or against external attack. Prerequisite to this, however, is that the status of soldier is an honorable one, allowed by God, suitable for a Christian, and indeed one for which he can arm himself. Therefore at the conclusion of this treatise Luther includes an admonition for the commander and a prayer before battle for the soldier, so that he may be confident in his service and like-

26. WA 19:648 / 20ff. [*LW* 46:122.] K. F. W. Wanderer, *Sprichwörter-Lexikon* (Leipzig, 1867), 1:1288, no. 119.

27. See above, p. 431.

28. WA 19:649 / 4ff. [*LW* 46:122.]

29. WA 19:646 / 17ff., 24ff. (On the German text: *pochen* = "*Pochspiel*" = *herausfordern*) [in English: challenge, as in a duel]. [*LW* 46:119–20.]

30. WA 19:650 / 18ff. Scipio Africanus with Valerius Maximus 7.2.2. Cicero *De officiis* 1.23.81. [*LW* 46:124.]

31. WA 19:651 / 13ff. [*LW* 46:124–25.]

wise, rejecting all military vanity, be led to reassurance through the re-deeming death of Christ.[32]

This treatise on soldiers contains the kernel of a second and particular aspect of warfare: the war against the Turks. Luther had wanted to include this subject as well, because the war had briefly come closer. "But since the Turk is back home again (Sultan Suleiman withdrew after his victory over the Hungarians in the Battle of Mohacs of August 29, 1526) and our Germans are no longer asking about this, it is not yet time to write about it."[33] Luther himself had reckoned the shocking news of the death of Louis II, the young king of Hungary, among the harbingers of the rapidly approaching Judgment Day. To the king's evangelically inclined widow, Maria (a sister of Emperor Charles V), Luther expressed his condolences by dedicating to her his exposition *Four Comforting Psalms.*[34] But he put off for another two years his treatment of the war against the Turks, even though recent events had given him frequent occasion to do so. A decade earlier, in his *Explanation of the Ninety-five Theses* (1518), he had not only attracted attention to this subject but also aroused indignation. Comment-ing on his Thesis 5, that the pope remit the punishment he himself had imposed on his own or on the basis of canon law, Luther declared:

> Even the big wheels in the church now dream of nothing else than war against the Turk. They want to fight not against iniquities but against the lash of iniquity, and thus they would oppose God, who says that through that lash he himself punishes us for our iniquities because we do not punish ourselves for them.[35]

The papal bull *Exsurge Domine* (1520), threatening excommunication, condemned Luther's sentence on the Turks because it was distorted in form: "War against the Turks means fighting against God, who through them is visiting our sins on us."[36] In this caricatured form Leo's bull made Luther's sentence on the Turks widely known as well as bitterly attacked in the wave of pamphlets on the Turkish war. Among the last but not the least of his critics was the Vienna humanist Johannes Cuspinian, who felt

32. WA 19:658 / 21ff.; 661 / 9ff. [*LW* 46:133, 135.]

33. WA 19:662 / 9ff., 15ff. [*LW* 46:136–37.] On the Battle of Mohacs, see L. von Ranke, *Deutsche Geschichte,* 2:323ff.

34. Letter to Spalatin, September 19, 1526, WA Br 4:118 / 10ff. Dedicatory letter to Maria of Hungary, WA 19:552–53. [Text of letter, LCC 18:56–58.]

35. WA 1:535 / 29ff. [*LW* 31:92.]

36. C. Mirbt and K. Aland, *Quellen zur Geschichte des Papsttums und des römischen Katholizismus,* 6th rev. ed. (Tübingen, 1967), no. 789, p. 507 (no. 34). H. Denzinger and A. Schönmetzer, *Enchiridion Symbolorum et Declarationum de rebus fidei et morum,* 34th ed. (Freiburg, 1967), no. (774) 1484, p. 361 (no. 34).

particularly moved by the disaster in Hungary. On the basis of impressions gained in Buda [today's Budapest, on the Danube] he berated Luther as "the only one under the sun without any human feelings, as one standing outside the pale of human custom, a stone more than a man."[37]

According to Luther, friends had been urging him for at least five years to write something substantial on the issue of war against the Turks. In any case, he would have to guard against being misunderstood also in his own ranks. Prefacing his treatise *On War Against the Turk* (1528 / 29) with a dedication to Landgrave Philip of Hesse, he cautioned, "There are some stupid preachers among us Germans (as I am sorry to hear) who are making the people believe that we should not and must not fight against the Turks. Some are even as foolish as to say that it is improper for Christians to bear the temporal sword or to be rulers."[38] Luther picked up his former Thesis 5, made it several times stronger and clearer, and named his target: the war as waged at papal behest and for the sake of the faith as well as of the church. Luther attacked the newly proclaimed crusade, for it was commanded as a form of doing penance and extolled as a means of earning indulgence from the punishment of sins. Luther's intention was not to reject the Turkish campaign as such but to cleanse it from false motivation. Therefore, he contended, it is necessary to see the Turkish attack on Christendom as a warning and a punishment. "God does not check out crosses, indulgences, combat. He requires a clean life." It must indeed arouse God's wrath when Christendom, at papal instigation, wages "holy" wars in order to buy itself free from its sins against the demands of a "clean life." Therefore, in Luther's bitter irony, the war against the Turks is running so "luckily." "Where the Turk formerly held a mile of land, he now holds a hundred miles!"[39] Herewith emerges a second motif, which serves still further to reject any religious basis for the war against the Turks. Such an attempted basis—taking God into account—could lead only to a shattering of the war's intention. The fusion of "spiritual" and political elements, dear to the medieval idea of a crusade, must be given up—but not

37. In his *Oratio protreptica*, which followed the death of King Louis II and called for a new war against the Turks. Cf. the composition of materials in the literature on the Turkish wars by F. Cohrs, WA 30²:107 / 10ff.

38. Dedicatory preface, October 9, 1528, WA 30²:107 / 10ff. [*LW* 46:161.]

39. *Defense and Explanation of All the Articles of Dr. Martin Luther Which Were Unjustly Condemned by the Roman Bull* (1521), WA 7:443 / 28ff. [*LW* 32:90.] Cf. already his *Assertio omnium articulorum M. Lutheri per bullam Leonis X. novissimam damnatorum* (1520), WA 7:140–41. [No Eng. trans.] W. Maurer, *Von der Freiheit eines Christenmenschen* (Göttingen, 1949), 128–29, points out that Luther had begun to treat the Turkish question shortly before his lectures on the Psalms.

at the expense of the religious. Each of the elements is to be understood and practiced on its own terms. Thus the Turkish war, popularly seen as a crusade, becomes in Luther's eyes a significant example (indeed, a negative or counterexample) of the distinction between the "two realms": the life of faith and the life of political-military action. This is a matter of distinction and not of separation. Even though the two elements are distinct, they nevertheless belong together. To find his way out of the mixture of motives, Luther finally gets down to the actual theme of the Turkish war and sketches it in terms of two persons [making it like a case study]. In order to stop the Turks, two "men" are required: "the one is named Christian, the other is named Emperor Charles."[40]

The first "man," the Christian representing the lot of Christians, must do what is most important for victory: before the battle (but not during it or because of it) he must repent of his sins and unfaith, and in prayer within his own heart or in worship (not by such external means as fancy processions) he is to call on God for help. In this way alone can he "take the rod out of God's hand." Christians and the church are summoned to but one battle, the one waged between God and the devil, the latter being the god of the Turks.[41] Besides, it is the devil who causes the Turks to suppress the Christian faith and the worship of God in their land. All the while, the devil goes about his task so cunningly that many things in the Turk's religion become reminders of Christianity. In fact, the Quran is a patchwork of pagan, Jewish, and Christian pieces. Some of their specific teachings even find approval among Christians: denial of Christ's divinity, rejection of the gradations of authority (they recognize only the sultan), rejection of the married estate (by their polygamy, compared to the papal church's celibacy).[42] Now the Christians are unable to claim any moral superiority that would give them a right to fight the Turks. Luther is ready to accept the word of others that the Turks are loyal and friendly toward one another and also take pains to tell the truth. It may well be that in these things they surpass many Christians.[43] Luther sees it as even more

---

40. *On War Against the Turk,* WA 30²:116 / 23–24 [*LW* 46:170]; "or whoever the emperor is" (WA 30²:129 / 18) [*LW* 46:184]. The connection with the "two realms" motif is carried out well in the dissertation proposed by E. Vogelsang and written by R. Lind, "Luthers Stellung zum Kreuz und Türkenkrieg" (theology diss., Giessen, 1940). Unfortunately it lacks the useful overview (and the most recent one) in H. Buchanan, "Luther and the Turks 1519–1529," *ARG* 47 (1956): 145ff.

41. WA 30²:116 / 28, 34; 117 / 21ff.; 118 / 22ff.; 120 / 10ff. [*LW* 46:170, 171, 172, 174.]

42. WA 30²:120 / 25ff.; 121 / 30ff.; 123 / 19ff.; 126 / 21ff.; 129 / 1ff. [*LW* 46:174, 176, 178, 181, 183–84.]

43. WA 30²:127 / 19ff. [*LW* 46:182.]

significant that the Turks enter battle shouting "Allah! Allah!" and he associates this name of God with the Hebrew Elohim. After all, the devil is also a god, and even the papal warriors raise their battle cry to him as the shout "Ecclesia! Ecclesia!"; "indeed it is the devil's ecclesia!"[44] So finally it is a war of prayers and spirit that must be fought out in one's own heart. If our "man" Christian does not so fight, then the sword alone will accomplish little against the Turks.[45]

The "other man" who must do battle against the Turks and under whose "command, banner, and name" alone the weapons may be used is the emperor, and he is in charge only as ruler, not as "head of Christendom or guardian of the gospel or defender of the faith." "The emperor's sword has nothing to do with the faith and pertains to physical, worldly things."[46] Asserting this, Luther breaks through the medieval idea of emperor and of church too. By means of crusade sermons, indulgences, and awarded emblems of the cross, the church had hitherto rallied men against the Turks, while its legates visited the imperial diet and warned the emperor of his duties as "protector of the church and defender of the faith." In place of such customary procedures, Luther composed a full address, fit for a legate to give on an occasion like this. It began:

> Dear lords, emperor, and princes, if you want to be emperor and princes, then act as emperor and princes, or the Turk will teach you with God's wrath and disfavor. Germany, or the empire, is given and committed to you by God for you to protect, rule, counsel, and help, and you not only should but must do this at the risk of losing your soul's salvation and God's favor and grace.[47]

Instead, the princes and others at the diet "even take up the case of Luther and discuss in the devil's name whether one can eat meat in the fasting seasons, whether nuns can take husbands, and things of that kind

44. WA 30^2:128 / 8ff., 17. [LW 46:183.]

45. WA 30^2:129 / 6ff., 10. [LW 46:184.]

46. WA 30^2:129 / 17ff.; 130 / 27–28; 131 / 8–9. [LW 46:184, 185, 186.]

47. WA 30^2:133 / 9ff. [LW 46:188.] In this situation Luther finds himself on the side of Ulrich von Hutten, protesting against the leading role of the pope instead of the emperor in the war against the Turk. In 1518 Hutten had published a pamphlet addressed to the princes and vigorously protesting the reversed state of affairs; he hoped for permission to present it in person at the imperial diet in Augsburg in 1518. The address conveyed Hutten's militancy against the fiscal policy of the Roman curia, which also on this occasion sought to drain funds from the German people. *Ad principes Germanos, ut bellum Turcis inferant, exhortatoria,"* Böcking, ed., *Hutten Opera* (see above, p. 344, n. 23), 5:98ff. Whether Luther knew about Hutten's pamphlet is not clear. On this matter, WA 30^2:90–91. As for the legate, Luther presumably had in mind the famous address by Cajetan at the Augsburg diet in 1518. See Ranke, *Deutsche Geschichte*, 1:233ff. The speech of the papal nuncio at the second Diet of Speyer 1529 (to which the added revision in WA 30^2 [1967] refers) was still in the future and could not have been known to Luther.

which are not your business to discuss."[48] The purpose of the legate's address would necessarily be to make the emperor as well as the common man recognize their duties anew. "The emperor must truly see himself with other eyes." On it is written what most people overlook: "Protect the good, punish the wicked." Such a reminder should really shock the conscience of the emperor and the princes. Yet even in face of the Turkish might they have no need to despair. "For God commands no one to do anything on the basis of his own wisdom or strength. He too wants to have a part in it and be feared."[49] "If these two things are present, God's commandment and our humility, then there is no danger or need."[50]

The Turkish war is thus not an ecclesial undertaking but a worldly [temporal] one. Therefore each soldier for himself must join in the invisible struggle against perverting the war into a crusade and must attack the papacy afresh with prayer and God's Word, "because of its errors and wicked ways."[51] Once the unhappy papal notion of a crusade is quashed, the political and military requirements come into their own: guarding the peace and the empire, subordinating the princes under the emperor instead of allowing vainglorious separate actions by princes against the Turks, and providing sufficient arms. Luther contends that nothing is to be achieved by a mere thirty thousand men. If one were to begin with fifty or sixty thousand men, one would require just as many in reserve.[52] Fighting the Turk is not like fighting the king of France. This is a time "not, as before, [to] let individual kings and princes set upon him—yesterday the king of Hungary, today the king of Poland, and tomorrow the king of Bohemia—until the Turk devours them one after another and nothing is accomplished except that our people are betrayed and butchered and blood is shed in vain."[53]

A few months after the publication of his treatise on the Turk (he had begun it in October 1528, yet it did not appear until April 1529[54] because of a dawdling printer) Luther's anxieties mounted again. "It is reliably reported that the Turk is in Hungary with an enormous army," he wrote on July 10 from Wittenberg.[55] During his return journey from the Mar-

48. WA 30²:134 / 3ff. [LW 46:189.]
49. WA 30²:134 / 19ff.; 135 / 17–18. [LW 46:190, 191.]
50. WA 30²:136 / 6–17. [LW 46:191.]
51. WA 30²:143 / 12ff. [LW 46:199.]
52. WA 30²:145 / 13ff., 27ff.; 146 / 7ff. [LW 46:201–2.]
53. WA 30²:147 / 13ff. [LW 46:(202), 203.]
54. WA 30²:96–97. Also WA Br 5:19, n. 9. [LW 46:158–59.]
55. To Jacob Propst in Bremen, WA Br 5:111 / 16.

burg Colloquy, he and Melanchthon learned on October 17 that Vienna was under heavy siege by the Turks.[56] Luther saw this as Germany's deserved experience of God's wrath and at once began to compose an *Army Sermon Against the Turks,* summoning the people to repentance and resistance. Despite the rapidly ensuing news that the Turks had suddenly withdrawn from Vienna, Luther did not permit his shared sense of relief to deter him from pursuing his plan.[57] The Turkish war had for some time been taking on a much greater dimension in his thought. Luther saw fulfilled in the Turkish advance the prophecies of the invasion of Gog and Magog into the land of Israel (Ezek. 38 and 39), and the empire of the fourth beast according to Daniel's prophecy (7:23ff.).[58] Luther also gave notice that Melanchthon and Jonas had prepared a tract on this question which appeared in early December 1529.[59] In addition, Luther now searched urgently, through Myconius in Gotha, for the prophecies of a mysterious monk "deceased while excommunicated" (the Franciscan Johannes Hilten). Myconius had told Luther about Hilten while the party of Wittenbergers [returning from Marburg] was passing through Eisenach. Hilten had written a commentary on Daniel, and Melanchthon had made excerpts of it for his own intended commentary on the prophet.[60]

As its title suggests, Luther's *Army Sermon Against the Turks* went a good step beyond his preceding treatise *The War Against the Turk.* He had turned an elaboration of the problem into an impassioned appeal. To a

56. Excited letter, Luther to Amsdorf, October 19, 1529, WA Br 5:163 / 4ff. At the same time, letters of Melanchthon, October 17, 1529, to F. Myconius, CR 1:1108. MBW 833. And to E. Schnepf, CR 4:971. MBW 834. An initial uncertain report of this turn of events may have reached Luther even earlier; WA Br 5:164, n. 6, see below, p. 652. [Cf. LW 49:240–41.]

57. To Hausmann, October 20 and 26; to Amsdorf, October 27; to Link, October 28, 1529. WA Br 5:164–65; 166–67; 170. [LW 49:240–41.]

58. WA Br 5:166 / 14; 167 / 17; 170 / 21. [Full text: WA 30²:(149–59), 160–97.]

59. WA Br 5:167, n. 2. WA Br 13:116 (regarding WA Br 5:167, n. 2). WA DB 11²:xxxf.

60. Luther, from Torgau, to Myconius, October 17, 1529, WA Br 5:162. Myconius's reply, December 2, WA Br 5:190ff. On J. Hilten (d. ca. 1500), see P. Wolff, in RE³ 8 (1900): 78ff. E. Barnikol, in RGG³ 3 (1959): 327. G. May, in LThK 5 (1960): 351. O. Scheel, *Martin Luther,* 2d ed. (Tübingen, 1917), 1:114ff. H. Volz, "Beiträge zu Melanchthons und Calvins Auslegungen des Propheten Daniel," ZKG 67 (1955 / 56): 93ff., esp. 111ff. His research in the Vatican Library has shown that Hilten's commentary, used by Melanchthon, has not been preserved (ibid., 115). Melanchthon's Daniel commentary remained unfinished. Only the foreword appeared in 1529, and was addressed to King Ferdinand. J. Kühn's assumption in *Die Geschichte des Speyrer Reichstags 1529,* SVRG 146 (Leipzig, 1929), that Melanchthon there opposed the policies of Landgrave Philip has been convincingly questioned by Köhler, *Zwingli und Luther* (Gütersloh, 1953), 2:21, and Volz, "Beiträge," 101, 107ff. According to Volz (109), Melanchthon may later on, in his exposition of Daniel (1543), have referred back to his unpublished manuscript of 1529.

certain extent he retained the twofold approach of his first writing, featuring the positions Sir Christian and Emperor Charles. So he divided the *Army Sermon* into two parts, "first to instruct the conscience, then to clench the fist."[61] The new feature was the absolute chronology into which he set the historic moment. Now is the time. The eschatological situation has arrived which the prophet Daniel foretold. The fourth world empire— represented by the fourth beast in Daniel's vision (7:23ff.)—is the Roman Empire. Luther's enumeration of the fourth followed a medieval Christian tradition based on the history of Josephus. The ten horns of the beast— according to Daniel, these are ten kings (7:7ff.)—represent the ten countries that have "belonged to the Roman imperium." The little horn that grew among them and tore away three others must be the Muslim Turkish Empire that had already wrested Egypt, Asia Minor, and Greece away from the Roman Empire. The eyes on this horn point to the Quran; the mouth, which utters horrible things, represents Mohammed's blasphemies against Christ.[62] However, the triumphal course of this horn soon meets its end, to be sure, within the Roman Empire. "For it has been determined that while the Roman imperium is the last, the Turk is unable to become as mighty as the Roman Empire was. Otherwise there would be not four but five empires on earth." Besides, Daniel had already foretold the end of the Turkish Empire: "The horn's conquests and victory shall endure until the Ancient of Days takes his seat in judgment (Dan. 7:9)." Just when all this shall take place, no one knows, but Christ has given us signs from which it is possible to discern that Judgment Day is near. Soon this prophecy will be fulfilled in the Turk. "Whatever he does in Hungary and in the German lands will be the final clawing and mauling that he will have with ours, and ours with him." His conquests will extend no farther. "For Daniel allows him three horns, and no more. Whatever he flails or tears from the frontiers and neighbors is simply his nightcap before he turns in."[63] Luther believed so firmly in the collapse of the Turkish Empire that he counted this among the signs of the imminent end of the world. The Turk is assuredly "the final and most ferocious wrath of the devil against Christ, with which he is stomping out the bottom of the barrel." "So, then, we can certainly tell that Judgment Day is at the door."[64]

61. WA 30²:161 / 30–31.
62. WA 30²:166 / 1ff., 26–27, 30ff.; 168 / 15ff., 23ff.
63. WA 30³: 166 / 13ff.; 170 / 30–31; 171 / 18ff., 27ff.; 172 / 2ff.
64. WA 30³:162 / 19–20; 171 / 20–21.

Luther [audaciously] removes the crusade and replaces it with the eschatological war. This involves a profound shift in motifs. For the crusader the promise lay in the blotting out of his sins, even if he returned home alive. Luther, to the contrary, saw the Christian in any case relying solely on his faith in forgiveness for Christ's sake. Yet in case of death the Christian can have a good conscience, inasmuch as, according to God's command, he dies in obedience to his government. In every other death—and sometime we must all die—"you die by yourself alone."[65] Here, in the eschatological war, however, the Christian dies with many other "saints" as the martyrs once did in their following Christ. For "Christ will and must suffer on earth; he must be weak and allow himself to be killed, so that his kingdom will be rapidly multiplied and filled. For his kingdom is not physically on earth. Therefore his battle is at its height when there is much suffering and many are martyred."[66] Luther sees death in the war against the Turk in light of the gospel, in terms neither of medieval notions of merit or expiation nor of classical concepts of heroism, but rather in terms of discipleship purified by grace alone.

What, then, becomes of the Turkish war? Although it belongs to the signs of the End, it remains a worldly war in the service of the government and for the defense of the country. This is the subject of part two of the *Army Sermon:* the clenching of the fist.[67]

> I would wish . . . that all Germans were so minded that not so much as a hamlet or trading post would allow itself to be plundered or captured by the Turk, but that, if things really became so desperate, everyone would pitch in for the defense, young and old, husband and wife, servant and maid, down to the death of the last one, giving even house and barn to the flames and destroying everything [rather than surrendering anything]. . . . For I regard no cottage as too humble to defend or to allow the enemy to touch even a hair of it.[68]

Luther also puts himself in the place of war prisoners. Wherever they may be held, at work or in quarters, let them recite to themselves the Ten Commandments, the Lord's Prayer, and the creed. And when in the creed they come to the article on Christ, let them press a finger against the thumb or give themselves a sign with the hand or foot as a reminder that "on this article depend life and salvation."[69]

65. WA 30³:176 / 2–3.
66. WA 30³:178 / 30ff.
67. WA 30³:181 / 3ff.
68. WA 30³:183 / 17ff.; 184 / 17–18.
69. WA 30³:185 / 18ff.; 186 / 1–28, esp. 27–28.

The extent to which Luther was gripped by the apparent meaning of the historic hour becomes apparent in his translation of the Old Testament. He had progressed through the prophet Isaiah and, instead of continuing next with the prophet Jeremiah or going on to Ezekiel, he jumped ahead to the Book of Daniel (1530). "The world is running so admirably toward its end that strong thoughts often occur to me as though Judgment Day will break upon us sooner than we can complete translating the Holy Scriptures into German."[70] Besides, in the preface to the Daniel translation (by far the longest of all his prefaces) Luther provided a detailed historical explanation to the entire book, exceeding greatly the prophet's pattern of the four empires (Dan. 7).[71]

Luther's position on the war against the Turks is one of the most impressive examples of the fact that he stood at a divide between the times, where the lines were crossing in different directions. On the one hand, he put an end to the crusade as a religious act of expiation and as a medieval war for Christ's sake. The battle against the advancing Turks is far more than any other war—according to modern, political thinking—a purely worldly defense of the country and its people. On the other hand, however, Luther fits into the traditional biblical understanding of the world and is part of God's plan as discerned through certain signs announced in the prophecies of certain favored prophets. In the interpretation of these signs Luther is partner with all Christendom from Bible times (Rev. 13), across the Middle Ages, to his own era.

The great issues surging toward Luther during these very years (1526–29) included the controversy over the Lord's Supper, war, and the Turkish danger. Amid these challenges from without came periods of illness, altering the daily duties in the pulpit or on the lecture platform. Small wonder that these developments sidetracked his long-cherished plan to provide a catechism for the instruction of the young and of congregations.

Since 1518 he had frequently preached on parts of a catechetical instruction as offered in the ancient and medieval church.[72] For the sake of the

70. Dedicatory letter to the first edition of the Daniel translation for Electoral Prince John Frederick (1530), WA DB 11²:381 / 4ff., xxxviii. [LW 35:294 (294–316). Part of the dedicatory letter is in *Luther's Correspondence*, ed. P. Smith and C. M. Jacobs, 2:516ff.]

71. WA DB11²:381:1–48. On this subject, H. Volz, ibid., xl–l. Again Volz, "Neue Beiträge zu Luthers Bibelübersetzung: Luthers Arbeiten am Propheten Daniel," *BGDS(T)* 77 (1955): 393ff.

72. For a survey of Luther's catechetical sermons since 1518, see WA 22:lxxxv–lxxxviii. [LW 51:135–36.] On catechetical instruction in the Middle Ages, see F. Cohrs, "Katechismen und Katechismusunterricht," *RE*³ 10 (1901):136ff. Again Cohrs, "Katechismen Luthers," *RE*³ 23 (1913): 744ff. Also J. Hofinger, "Katechismus," *LThK* 6 (1961): 46. H. W. Surkau, "Katechismus," *RGG*³ 3 (1959): 1181–82. F. Cohrs, *Die Evangelischen Katechismusversuche vor Luthers Enchiridion*, 5 vols., MGP 20–23, 39 (Berlin, 1900–1907).

inner renewal of the congregation, Luther had his heart set on producing a good book of instruction which young people could understand. As early as January 1525, while his friend Nicholas Hausmann was visiting him, Luther had discussed the plan. Then on February 2 he wrote Hausmann in Zwickau that Jonas and Agricola had been given the task of drawing up a "Catechismus Puerorum" [boy's catechism]. For the first time this catechetical term became embodied in the title of a book.[73] Unfortunately, Jonas and Agricola did not carry out their assignment.[74] Luther himself had then to assume the task, yet he likewise delayed until he apparently saw it as part of the larger task of parish visitation and renewal at which he and Melanchthon were working together.[75]

Even then it was only three years later that he commenced preliminary work on the catechism. While serving as supply preacher in Wittenberg's Town Church (Bugenhagen was away on extended leave to set up constitutions [regulations] for the churches and schools in Braunschweig and Hamburg) Luther took his turn at delivering catechetical sermons, a practice in effect since 1523. In May, September, and November/December 1528, Luther delivered three series of such sermons. In an informal sequence he went over all parts of the catechism two or three times. He himself had not worked out an inclusive plan in advance. Although the text of these sermons, taken down in shorthand, did not as yet comprise the draft of a book, it did at least provide rich substance and a wealth of formulations for one. A pattern emerged, and its lines could be followed precisely.[76] The ensuing book of sermons became a catechism. In a letter on January 15, 1529, to Martin Görlitz, pastor in Braunschweig, Luther put it quite simply: "At the moment I am working on a catechism for the raw heathen."[77] Actually its formulations reveal a relationship with the findings of the parish visitations, the project in which Luther had participated at the elector's behest.[78]

In April 1529 Luther's "German Catechism" appeared. To distinguish this first book from the one immediately following (*The Small Catechism*),

73. WA Br 3:431 / 12. The assignment to Jonas and Agricola was mentioned again in a letter to Hausmann on March 26, 1525, WA Br 3:462 / 5.

74. For why they were hindered from doing so, see WA Br 3:432. *D. Martin Luthers Briefwechsel*, ed. E. L. Enders (Frankfurt am Main, 1884ff.), 5:111–16.

75. WA Br 3:582, n. 7. WA 30¹:457.

76. J. Meyer, "Luthers Grosser Katechismus," QGP 12 (Leipzig, 1914), makes this visible by means of various type fonts. [Cf. LW 51:133–93, the November 30–December 18, 1528, *Ten Sermons on the Catechism*.]

77. WA Br 5:5 / 22.

78. Order of July 25, 1528, WA Br 4:505ff. On the difficulties of the visitation, see the report of the commission, January 9, 1529, WA Br 5:3–4.

reprints of it after 1541 were entitled *The Large Catechism*. *The Small Catechism,* comprising the actual contents of instruction, was initially published in placard form. Then, in May 1529, it came out as a booklet illustrated with woodcuts.[79] How closely the catechetical problem was mingled with that of visitation is evident from the fact that the "Instruction of the Visitation Commissioners" (1528) was itself in part an advanced form of catechism, by means of which the visitors could instruct the preachers. Moreover, Melanchthon himself, as author of the instructions, had himself begun to write a catechism, a task he laid aside in the wake of Luther's broadly based sermons on the catechism.[80]

The fact that Luther's catechisms did not become schoolbooks may derive from their origin in sermons. *The Large Catechism* was intended to promote the ongoing education of pastors, teachers, parents, and adult Christians. *The Small Catechism* itself is far from a mere question-and-answer book. The use of "you," in the singular, is mainly the you between God and the individual, the you of commandment, the you of response in prayer, or the you between the preacher and his hearers—all of which is intended to evoke and cultivate a common understanding. This format is in contrast to the later *Heidelberg Catechism,* where the "you" denotes the teacher-pupil relationship. Besides, in Luther's catechism the fact of partnership is emphasized ever and again through the use of "we," the we of guilt or pardon. *The Large Catechism,* moreover, with its manifold usage of "you" and "we," reflects the character of the gospel; its impressiveness lies not only in what it requires but also in how it edifies with its wealth of finest and simplest formulations from Luther's theology. So, for instance, the first commandment, the prohibition of other gods, gives rise, as Luther explains it, not to threats of punishment but to persuasive affirmation:

> What is it to have a god? What is God? Answer: A god is that to which we look for all good and in which we find refuge in every time of need. To have a god is nothing else than to trust and believe him with our whole heart. As I have often said, the trust and faith of the heart alone make both God and an idol. If your faith and trust are right, then your God is the true God. On the other

79. Extended account of the publication of both catechisms in WA 30¹:499ff., 666ff. The various titles in Benzing, *Lutherbibliographie* (Baden-Baden, 1966), 298ff., 303ff. Best historical introduction: J. Meyer, *Historischer Kommentar zu Luthers Kleinem Katechismus* (Gütersloh, 1929). A lively appreciation: P. Wernle, *Der evangelische Glaube nach den Hauptschriften der Reformatoren,* vol. 1: *Luther* (Tübingen, 1918), 214ff.

80. On the instruction of the visitors, see above, p. 497. Melanchthon's attempt at a catechism remains only in a fragment on the first three commandments. *Suppl. Mel.* 5 / 1:xxvff., 78ff.

hand, if your trust is false and wrong, then you have not the true God. For these two belong together, faith and God. That to which your heart clings and entrusts itself is, I say, really your God.[81]

This is a masterstroke in that Luther here does not employ some abstraction of a doctrine of God but reminds the reader of his own existential knowledge that he simply cannot live without a most profound basis of trust. Money, great learning, power, art, honor can function as a god.[82] Thereby Luther comes to the point at once about what concerns God. This also shows itself in the gods or idolatrous worship of the heathen. He no longer employs analogies of religious [biblical] history but relies on an unmistakable human desire and knowledge—such as the appeal in his treatment of the First Commandment—in order to offer an authentic answer. That this answer runs counter to human fantasies and wishes is a sign of its authenticity. Luther's intention is not to supply proofs of the God of the Bible but to remind a human being of his own nature. Amid his needs, no human being can live unaided and therefore creates guarantees in which he trusts. Ludwig Feuerbach [1804–72] has taken these and similar words of Luther to support his own notion that God is merely an illusory mirror of man.[83] In doing so, however, he makes use only of Luther's critique of idols, not of Luther's reference to the God who responds to the human hunger for trustworthiness, in any case to the God who acts with sovereignty, without conforming to human expectations or sharing his aid with other helpers, such as the saints or mammon.[84] God requires the complete response of man and seeks the human heart. "We lay hold of him when our heart embraces him and clings to him. To cling to him with all our heart is nothing else than to entrust ourselves to him completely. He wishes to turn us away from everything else, and to draw us to himself, because he is the one, eternal good."[85] In the First Com-

---

81. WA 30¹:132 / 34ff. [*BC*, Large Catechism, 365.]

82. WA 30¹:133 / 22ff., 35ff. [*BC*, 366.]

83. Cf. H. Bornkamm, *Luther im Spiegel der deutschen Geistesgeschichte*, 89ff., 299ff. J. Wallmann, "Ludwig Feuerbach und die theologische Tradition," *LThK* 67 (1970): 65ff. With special reference to the First Commandment: G. Ebeling, *Luther, Einführung in sein Denken* (Tübingen, 1964), 289ff. Also Ebeling, with more detailed reference to the background of Hegel and Feuerbach, " 'Was heisst ein Gott haben oder was ist Gott?' Bemerkungen zu Luthers Auslegung des ersten Gebots im Grossen Katechismus," in *Wort und Glaube: Beiträge zur Fundamentaltheologie und zur Lehre von Gott* (Tübingen, 1969), 2:287ff. On Feuerbach's monograph "Das Wesen des Glaubens im Sinne Luthers" (1844; reprint, Darmstadt, 1970), see the analysis by O. Bayer, "Gegen Gott für den Menschen: Zu Feuerbachs Lutherrezeption," *ZThK* 69 (1972): 34ff., and H.-W. Krumwiede, "Die Wahrheit Gottes und die Wirklichkeit des Menschen," *Luther* (1973), 1:78ff.

84. WA 30¹:134 / 26ff. [*BC*, Large Catechism, 366, 367.]

85. WA 30¹:134 / 22ff. [*BC*, Large Catechism, 366.]

mandment, Luther thus combines the universal basis of the quest for God in the human heart, on the one hand, with the exclusiveness of the answer given by the God of the Bible and Father of Jesus Christ.

All that is gathered up in the First Commandment becomes for Luther the source of the entire catechism and of the Christian life it sets forth. This holds for the worldly contexts in which we find ourselves.

> Our parents and all authorities—in short, all people placed in the position of neighbors—have received the command to do us all kinds of good. So we receive our blessings not from them, but from God through them. Creatures are only the hands, channels, and means through which God bestows all blessings. For example, he gives to the mother breasts and milk for her infant, and gives grain and all kinds of fruit from the earth for man's nourishment—things which no creature could produce by himself.[86]

The same holds true of the spiritual goods we require. In the catechism, therefore, the commandments are followed properly by the creed, which sets forth "all that we must expect and receive from God; in brief, it teaches us to know him perfectly. It is given in order to help us do what the Ten Commandments require of us."[87] Then, in the third part of the catechism, on the Lord's Prayer, Luther latches on to this theme again [accentuating the human response]: "Nothing is so necessary as to call upon God incessantly and drum into his ears our prayer that he may give, preserve, and increase in us faith and obedience to the Ten Commandments and remove all that stands in our way and hinders us from fulfilling them."[88] By means of repeatedly referring the several main parts back to the First Commandment, Luther gave the catechism a wholeness that combines commandment and promise, law and gospel and sets such diverse components [including, to be sure, the sacraments] into a firm unity.[89]

When he comes to the sacraments, Luther speaks with special emphasis on this unity of the parts of the catechism. Here, in contrast to the other parts, the subject is not concrete things that a human being must do, pray, or confess, but rather a matter of transactions which, taken alone, make no sense but which, touching the believer, sustain him in this combination of commandment and promise. So it is in the case of baptism:

86. *WA* 30¹:136 / 6ff. [*BC*, Large Catechism, 368.]

87. *WA* 30¹:182 / 20ff. [*BC*, Large Catechism, 411.]

88. *WA* 30¹:193 / 8ff. [*BC*, Large Catechism, 411.]

89. On the internal coherence of *The Large Catechism*, see K. Bornkamm, "Das Verständnis christlicher Unterweisung in den Katechismen von Erasmus und Luther," *ZThK* 65 (1968): 204ff.

"This is the substance in the water: God's word or commandment and God's name, which is a treasure nobler than heaven and earth." It is precisely this use of an element, of no value in itself, and joining it to the name of God that gives value and meaning to baptism. "For mere water could do nothing like this, but the word does it, and the fact that . . . God's name is in it. Where, then, God's name is, there, too, must be life and salvation, so that it may indeed be called a divine, blessed, fruitful, and grace-bearing water."[90] Faith alone can lay hold of this combination that God has arranged and continues to offer. "Faith alone makes the person worthy to receive the salutary, divine water profitably."[91] The actions of baptism make no sense on their own, not even in a symbolical way. They make sense only in connection with the accompanying promise of God, by means of which baptism is engrafted into the gospel. "The heart must believe it. So you see it clearly that this is no work accomplished by us but a treasure which he gives us and which faith apprehends, just as the Lord Christ on the cross is not a work but a treasure, wrapped in the word and presented to us and received by us in faith."[92] Through the baptismal command of the risen Lord, God has entrusted this treasure to Christendom and made it God's commandment for the entire world (Matt. 28:19; Mark 16:16). The same thing holds for the words of Christ in the Lord's Supper: "This do in rememberance of me." "These are words of precept and command, enjoining all who would be Christians to partake of the sacrament."[93] This is not a law with specifications as to frequency of Communion. God does not compel; rather, he awakens the conscience. "This commandment should ever move you to examine your inner life and reflect: 'See what sort of Christian I am! If I were one, I would surely have at least a little longing to do what my Lord has commanded me to do.' "[94] This commandment, too, only supports the promise "given . . . , shed for the forgiveness of sins." "Thus you have on God's own part both the commandment and the promise of the Lord Christ. Meanwhile, on your own part, you ought to be impelled by your own need, which hangs around your neck and which is the very reason for this command and invitation and promise."[95]

90. WA 30¹:214 / 5–6; 215 / 15ff. [BC, Large Catechism, 438 / 16.]
91. WA 30¹:216 / 10–11; 215 / 36–37. [BC, Large Catechism, 440.]
92. WA 30¹:216 / 30ff. [BC, Large Catechism, 441 / 37.]
93. WA 30¹:228 / 8ff. [BC, Large Catechism, 451–52.]
94. WA 30¹:228 / 32ff. [BC, Large Catechism, 452.]
95. WA 30¹:230 / 24ff.; 231 / 14ff. [BC, Large Catechism, 454–55.]

The intimate combination of commandment and promise constitutes the supporting foundation of Luther's *Large Catechism*. Not only because of its many literary niceties but also because of its ever new variations on a consistently pursued theme, *The Large Catechism* is one of Luther's greatest artistic achievements. From this initial work a second sprang forth, *The Small Catechism*. While the mastery of the larger work lies in the wealth and liveliness of its articulating the faith, the beauty of the smaller work lies in the precision with which it made matters of faith luminous and memorable. Without the preparatory condensation of the catechetical sermons into *The Large Catechism*, there would have been no crystallization of the entire substance into *The Small Catechism*. In it there is no superfluous word. Rarely does Luther repeat himself, and then only on plausible grounds. This becomes evident in the repeated and emphatic intonation in the explanation of the commandments: "We should fear and love God . . . "; or in the fullness of what "daily bread" encompasses in the fourth petition of the Lord's Prayer; or again in the sweeping sequence of paired terms with which, in explaining the first article of the creed, he praises the Fatherhood of God (body and soul, reason and all the faculties of my mind, food and clothing, house and home . . .). *The Small Catechism* was a book not so much for the school as for the home. The one who questions, who leads and hears the prayers, is the housefather, or the teacher—since both catechisms were already translated in 1529 for use in the Latin schools. Through a number of additions to the original, *The Small Catechism* acquired the character of an exercise in a personal life of prayer. There were the morning, evening, and mealtime prayers as well as a table of duties, with Bible verses, for those in public office (pastors, government officials), for family members, for others of the household, and for the congregation at large.

The Small Catechism rapidly acquired a modest liturgical character. The printers of the initial booklet editions supplied it with two liturgical settings that Luther had originally brought out separately. These two pertained to events concerning the family: marriage and baptism.[96] We know that as early as 1523 Luther had ventured to publish a German baptismal booklet in connection with his first cautious liturgical reforms (*Concerning the Order of Public Worship*).[97] That had been simply a somewhat shortened translation of the Roman baptismal liturgy, in connection with

96. WA 30¹:669–71. [For *The Small Catechism* (if not otherwise available) see *BC*, (337–41), 342–56.]

97. See above, pp. 134–35. [*LW* 53:(9), 11–14.]

which he had largely retained the traditional ceremonies (blowing on the infant, applying salt to the mouth, spittle to the nose and ears, anointing the breast and shoulders with oil, and the presentation of a candle).[98] Luther had followed this cautious line (typical of the hesitation with which he approached reforms in worship) "in order to spare the weak consciences . . . lest they complain that I want to institute a new baptism and criticize those baptized in the past as though they had not been properly baptized."[99] These conservative tactics, in turn, drew plenty of criticism from his followers. Therefore, after his introduction of the "German Mass" (1526), which was a much more significant step in the reform of worship, Luther published a revised form of his baptismal booklet, in which he eliminated most of the ceremonial, or symbolical, features.[100] In this form it was appended to *The Small Catechism* and thus introduced into every household. The same thing was done in the case of his *Order of Marriage for Common Pastors*. Immediately after its initial publication as a separate booklet it too was included in *The Small Catechism*.[101]

Some of the parts of the catechism touched on subjects so much under public debate that they required special theological treatment. Besides the Lord's Supper, the dominant issue of these years, the question of baptism had emerged. Debate over it was second only to that over the Supper and became a bitterly contested issue within the reformation movement. Following the opening phase, when the "Zwickau prophets" Storch, Müntzer, and their adherents had moved from his proximity in Electoral Saxony, Luther continued to receive reports on the spread of the Anabaptists. The name was one they had given themselves to denote their practice of rebaptizing. Although Luther frequently became apprehensive over these developments, there was no immediate occasion for a confrontation, but in 1528 things changed when two unnamed Roman parish priests in Ducal Saxony requested Luther for a clarifying word.[102] Although still caught up in his long treatise on the Lord's Supper, Luther's

98. *WA* 12:42–46, 47 / 21ff. [*LW* 53:(93), 95–103.]

99. *WA* 12:48 / 19ff. [*LW* 53:103.]

100. *WA* 19:537–41; on 531 see the critical comments on the original 1523 edition. [*LW* 53:106–9.]

101. *WA* 30³:74–80. [*LW* 53:110–15.]

102. *Von der Wiedertaufe an zwei Pfarrherrn: Ein Brief Mart. Luther* (1528), *WA* 26:144–74. Luther does not mention them by name but addresses them as papists. For their sakes he says he himself would become a papist insofar as he too bears witness to that Christian heritage which the pope's church has preserved: the Holy Scriptures, baptism, the sacrament of the altar, the power of the keys for the forgiveness of sins (confession and absolution), the ministry of the Word, the catechism with its inclusion of the Lord's Prayer, the commandments, and the creed. *WA* 26:145 / 16ff.; 146 / 27ff.; 147 / 13ff.

response to them was swift and full. Apparently their inquiry was not inopportune. He had no Anabaptist writings before him which would have called for a response, so that he concentrated on the subject as such.[103] He could also dispel a false impression that had been created when Balthasar Hubmaier, citing a misunderstood comment of his, had counted Luther among the star witnesses in support of the Anabaptist teaching.[104] Luther dealt calmly with one after another of the Anabaptist arguments. You ask: How does one know that one has been baptized as a child? Answer: How do I know that this man and this woman are my parents? How do I know that this [particular] prince is my government, whom I must obey? I must rely for this on the testimony of others and am likewise referred for the duty of obedience to the command of the Word of God. Likewise, then, through the testimony of other Christians one knows of his own baptism.[105] And when Anabaptists quote the Bible verse "He who believes and is baptized will be saved" [Mark 16:16], this does not mean that faith must precede baptism. When is one certain of his faith? "Whoever would base baptism on the faith of the one baptized must nevermore baptize anyone." And even if one were to baptize him a hundred times, one would not know if he believed.[106] Setting the time of baptism according to the faith of the believer turns faith into a work. "True enough, one should have faith for baptism, but one ought not have himself baptized on the basis of his faith."[107] Here, to be sure, certainty concerning the whole of life is at stake. Even the human adult can simply say, "If I am baptized at his command, I know I have been baptized. Were I to be baptized on my own faith, I would probably feel myself unbaptized tomorrow, if my faith ebbed away or I were tempted as though yesterday I had not really had faith."[108] This argument that a person is baptized not on the basis of his

103. There was no specific tract of Balthasar Hubmaier before him, although Luther mentioned him briefly (see n. 104, below). Luther comments on the Anabaptist teaching as known to him generally, but without wishing to cite any one of their writings in particular. This is to be borne in mind when reading the most important treatment of this long letter by Luther in F. Lau, "Luther und Balthasar Hubmaier," in *Humanitas-Christianitas: Festschrift für W. von Loewenich* (Witten, 1968), 63ff. (cf. 65).

104. *Der uralten und gar neuen Lehrer Urteil, dass man die jungen "Kindlein nit taufen solle, bis sie im Glauben underricht sind"* (1526) [The judgment of ancient as well as modern teachers that one "not baptize young children until they have been instructed in the faith"], *Balthasar Hubmaier, Schriften,* ed. G. Westin and T. Bergsten, QFRG 29 (= QGT 9) (Gütersloh, 1962), 233. The Hubmaier work is purely a collection of sources, among them a misunderstood abbreviated citation from Luther's *Sermon von dem neuen Testament, das ist von der heiligen Messe* (1520), WA 6:363 / 11–19.

105. WA 26:149 / 9ff.; 151 / 21ff.; 152 / 1ff.; 153 / 31ff.

106. WA 26:154 / 1–25, esp. 2–3, 22–23.

107. WA 26:164 / 39ff.; 162 / 17ff.

108. WA 26:165 / 17–28, esp. 24ff.

own faith but only on that of God's command turns up with special emphasis in *The Large Catechism*. There too Luther does not doubt the possibility of faith on the part of infants, but he makes clear that the infant—as yet not aware of what goes on—is in the same situation as an adult who often stands before God. Even the adult himself is at times unsure of his faith, and yet, at God's Word and commandment, he should come to the Lord's Supper. "This is what we are now doing with infant baptism: We carry the infant to it, thinking and hoping he has faith; and we pray that God will grant him faith. Yet we baptize not on this basis but only on the basis that God has ordered us to do so."[109]

Since the objections against infant baptism do not hold, the case for it is powerfully supported by the history of the church, for infant baptism has persisted since the days of the apostles. Were it false, then there would have been no baptism for more than a thousand years—and no church either. And since the old covenant was based on the sign of circumcision, "so much the more must this new covenant and sign be powerful and transform those people who accept it into God's people."[110] As many as are Luther's objections to the Anabaptists, he nevertheless prefers them to the "sacramentarians" ["memorialists"], who opposed him in the controversy over the Lord's Supper, for the latter reject the Supper and—Luther concludes therefrom, though they do not say so—they must also reject baptism. The Anabaptists, however, "do baptism over again. This is, after all, a helpful sign and suggestion that they would like to come to terms with it."[111] Besides, Luther emphatically rejects opposing them by force.

> Indeed, it's not right, and I truly lament it, that such wretched people are being murdered, burned, and so cruelly put to death. If he [the Anabaptist] is wrong in his faith, then he has enough punishment awaiting him in eternal hellfire. Why should one martyr them early, when only their faith is in error and they are not rebellious or otherwise opposed to the government? Dear God, how quickly it happens that someone errs or gets trapped by the devil's rope. One should curb and confront these people with the Scriptures and God's Word. There is little to be achieved by fire.[112]

109. WA 30¹:219 / 21ff. K. Brinkel, "Die Lehre Luthers von der fides infantium bei der Kindertaufe," ThA 7 (Berlin, 1958); and the critique of this monograph by P. Althaus, in *ThLZ* 84 (1959): 866. Also Althaus, *Die Theologie Martin Luthers* (Gütersloh, 1962), 311ff. [*The Theology of Martin Luther* (Philadelphia: Fortress Press, 1966)]. L. Grönvik, "Die Taufe in der Theologie Martin Luthers," *AAAbo.H* 36 (1968): 154ff.

110. WA 26:169 / 22ff.; 166 / 22ff.; 168 / 27ff.

111. WA 26:173 / 17ff., 28–29.

112. WA 26:145 / 22ff.

This is still a word against the use of force to which Luther had held fast from the beginning of his career up to these years, that is, before he saw the rise of an immediate and destructive threat to the public peace and governmental order.[113] Because of the changed situation, though with heavy heart, Luther in 1531 signed the opinion drafted by Melanchthon for the Wittenberg theological faculty approving the application of the death penalty against Anabaptists.[114] Luther saw his work [his letter to the two priests] on rebaptism as a prelude and challenge to the Baptists. Perhaps one of their leaders would reply to it and, in turn, stimulate him to treat the subject more thoroughly.[115] Since no Anabaptist answered, and Luther had no occasion in his own country to follow through, this indirect treatment, done for the benefit of two inquirers, remains his fullest pronouncement on what was then a burning issue in other lands.

In the year of the catechisms Luther also took up a particularly difficult chapter in popular pedagogy: the question of marriage laws. Repeatedly, as we have seen, the subject had kept him busy, but this time it was two evangelical pastors who reopened the subject, and by September 1529 he was working on it. Yet it was only toward the end of the year, interrupted by the Marburg Colloquy in October and by other matters, that he completed his treatise. *On Matters of Marriage* was published early in 1530.[116] The inquiry of the two pastors revived in him the bitter lament that the medieval church had to a large extent brought this confused situation on itself. "I shudder at the example of the pope, who was one of the first to involve himself in this game and then grabbed control of temporal affairs like this." Luther therefore warned urgently lest the pastors once again allow themselves to be burdened with questions of matrimonial law. "For as soon as we begin to become judges in matters of matrimony, the flywheel of the mill will catch us and tear us apart."[117] Therefore, as he

113. Cf. Luther's *Letter to the Princes of Saxony Concerning the Rebellious Spirit* (1524), above, p. 158.

114. Letter to Elector John, end of October 1531, WA Br 6:222–23. The entire text of the opinion is printed (but erroneously dated 1541) in CR 4:740. The best brief overview of Luther's position on the issue of heretics is W. Kohler, *Mennonitisches Lexikon* (Frankfurt, 1937), 2:703ff. [Cf. H. S. Bender, "Luther, Martin" (on infant baptism, opposition to Anabaptism), *Mennonite Encyclopedia* (Scottsdale, Pa.: Mennonite Publishing House, 1957), 3:416ff.] A short account, including more recent literature, is H. Bornkamm, "Toleranz," *RGG*³ 6 (1962): 937ff. Also H. Bornkamm, "Das Problem der Toleranz im 16. Jahrhundert," in H. Bornkamm, *Das Jahrhundert der Reformation: Gestalten und Kräfte*, 2d ed. (Göttingen, 1966), 268ff.

115. To Spalatin, February 5, 1528, WA Br 4:376 / 3ff. Further references in his letters, WA 26:138–39. [Cf. n. 102, above.]

116. WA 30³:198–99.

117. WA 30³:205 / 27ff.; 206 / 1ff.

had done earlier in his work *The Estate of Marriage* (1522),[118] he distinguished sharply between questions of law and those of conscience. "Let him rule whoever should or would. I am going to instruct and comfort consciences as much as I possibly can."[119] The first ones to be helped were the consciences of overlords who had turned to the two pastors — and they, in turn, asked Luther's counsel.

Questions of conscience thereby became questions of law at the same time. Luther's reply was limited to the central juridical problem, touching the foundation of the matrimonial estate. On this hinged the questions of conscience involving the marriage principals, the parents, and the judges. However, there existed no formalized code of marriage law, only rival civil laws and ecclesiastical concepts. Through these Luther had to feel his way. His point of departure was that marriage, in God's sight, is a holy estate of a public and worldly character. However, the engagement that initiates it requires public announcement as well parental affirmation.[120] Luther cast this basic concept into five precise theses: (1) "Secret elopements should absolutely not constitute a marriage."[121] That a marriage must take place publicly corresponds to traditional [Christian] as well as to natural-pagan law, just as it also pertains to the fairness parents seek to impart to the upbringing of their child.[122] The basis, however, goes deeper still in the way God acts. It is not for nothing that he has said that "everything may be confirmed by the evidence of two or three witnesses" (Matt. 18:16). Only in this way can a married couple be sure that God has brought them together (Matt. 19:6) and not simply they themselves. "Whoever has a god without his word, he has not God. For the true God has wrapped up all in his word: our life, our being, our estate, our occupation, conversation, doing, idling, suffering—everything."[123] The words the bridal couple say together before the church door, which Luther anticipated in his *Marriage Booklet*, is thus an act announcing that the marriage they have en-

118. See above, pp. 109ff.

119. *WA* 30³:206 / 31–32.

120. On this subject, see R. Kirstein, *Die Entwicklung der Sponsalienlehre und der Lehre vom Eheschluss in der deutschen protestantischen Eherechtslehre bis zu J. H. Böhmer,* Bonner rechtswissenschaftliche Abhandlungen 72 (Bonn, 1966). Among the older literature, above all: R. Sohm, *Das Recht der Eheschliessung aus dem deutschen und canonischen Recht geschichtlich entwickelt* (Weimar, 1875). S. Reicke, "Geschichtliche Grundlagen des deutschen Eheschlussrechts," in *Weltliche und kirchliche Eheschliessung,* ed. H. Dombois and F. K. Schumann. *Glaube und Forschung* (Witten, 1953), 6:27ff. H. Dombois, *Kirche und Eherecht: Studien und Abhandlungen, 1953–1972* (Stuttgart, 1974).

121. *WA* 30³:207 / 2.

122. *WA* 30³:208 / 20ff.

123. *WA* 30³:207 / 18ff.; 213 / 34ff.

tered on is a public estate; yet marriage, of course, is not based on such an announcement. There follows in the church the instruction of the bridal pair in the responsibilities that this estate embraces in terms of love, suffering, and comfort, and it concludes with the sign of the benediction.[124] From the public character of the wedding ceremony Luther's remaining theses emerge readily: (2) "Secret elopements should give way to public weddings."[125] (3) "In case of two public announcements of engagement, the second should yield to the first, and be fined."[126] (4) A young woman whose engagement has been made public should be regarded as a married woman; whoever seduces her should be regarded as an adulterer.[127] (5) Coerced engagements are not valid. This is to safeguard children against their parents, should the latter wish to force them to marry against their will. But the opposite must also be taken into account: should parents try to prevent a daughter from marrying in order to retain her in the house as a cheap maid, this is an inadmissible prevention of marriage. Likewise it is wrong when children reject a marriage which, according to the testimony of responsible people, has been proposed not in paternal arbitrariness but in faithfulness, and they refuse to give up some "madly youthful love affair."[128] These are questions of conscience pointing in both directions. In such situations the pastors could provide good advice, though not legal counsel. As to divorce, the only ground for it which Luther can recognize (according to Matt. 19:9) is adultery. "To be sure, where it is still possible, it is much better to foster reconciliation, so that the two remain together."[129] Underlying all individual questions, however, is the fundamental principle that the law has its limits in the conscience. Luther advises pastors, "Where you find that the law is causing confusion in the conscience, then override the law confidently—with the force of a millstone over a spiderweb—and deal with the matter as though there had never been a law. And if outwardly, in a temporal setting, you cannot manage to do so, then let it be, and trample the law in your conscience. Better to allow the body and possessions to fall prey to the law's confusion than to victimize the conscience and the soul."[130]

124. *Traubüchlein*, WA 30³:77–80. [*LW* 53:(110–11), 111–15.]

125. *Von Ehesachen*, WA 30³:207 / 4; 217ff.

126. WA 30³:207 / 6–7; 224ff.

127. WA 30³:207 / 9–10; 230ff.

128. WA 30³:207 / 12; 240 / 6ff.

129. WA 30³:241 / 2–17, esp. 16–17.

130. WA 30³:247 / 18ff. A proverb Luther uses occasionally. WA 9:285 / 25–26. WA 36:275 / 1. Wander. *Sprichwörter-Lexikon* (see n. 26, above), 4 (1876): 723. Not in Luther's collection of proverbial sayings, WA 51:645ff.

22

Imperial Politics and Protestation

Consider what had happened in Germany since Luther's return from the Wartburg. His teachings had spread across broad regions of the empire under the protection of territorial princes and city councilmen. A stream of evangelical literature, especially his own, had poured forth despite imperial laws prohibiting such writings; great numbers had forsaken the cloisters and the priesthood; and new forms of worship had replaced the Roman mass. All this and more was part of the general and visible upheaval going on in face of the 1521 Edict of Worms.

At the imperial diet in Nuremberg during the years 1523 and 1524, the estates had managed to block or delay the edict's renewal.[1] Emperor Charles had been absent for several years, and his deputy, Archduke Ferdinand, was too preoccupied with his own Hapsburg problems in eastern Europe to prevail on the pope to call the repeatedly demanded council. The seed sown by the Reformation was greening the countryside, except in areas where archly papal territorial rulers resisted. Among them Ferdinand, the dukes of Bavaria, and several South German bishops had formed an alliance in Regensburg during the summer of 1524, pledging themselves to a strict application of the Edict of Worms.[2] Their papally loyal North German counterparts, shaken by the Peasants' War, included Duke George of Saxony, the electors of Brandenburg and Mainz, and the dukes of Braunschweig-Wolfenbüttel. In July 1525 they formed an alliance in Dessau. [On the evangelical side] it was February 1526 before Philip of Hesse instigated the action, and Elector John of Saxony formed a federation in Gotha and Torgau (ratified May 2). Soon a number of smaller territories joined, among them Braunschweig-Lüneburg and Braunschweig-Grubenhagen, Mecklenburg, Mansfeld, and the city of Magdeburg.[3] Beyond this, Landgrave Philip of Hesse laid plans for the large South German cities that had turned evangelical, or were beginning to do so, nota-

1. See above, pp. 297–99, 309ff.

2. Sources: *Acta Reformationis Catholicae Ecclesiam Germaniae concernentia saeculi XVI*, ed. G. Pfeilschifter (Regensburg, 1959), vol. 1, sec. 6.

3. See above, p. 315. W. Friedensburg, *Zur Vorgeschichte des Gotha-Torgauischen Bündnisses der Evangelischen 1525–1526* (Marburg, 1884).

bly Strassburg, Nuremberg, Augsburg, and Ulm. He also tried to win the adherence of similar Middle and North German principalities as well as the League of Six Cities in the Lausitz region.[4] Luther remained aloof from such plans for alliance. As early as January 11, 1525, he had a negative reply for Count Albrecht of Mansfeld's inquiry about the permissibility of forming an alliance. His answer was solomonic: to form an alliance against governmental authorities and to avenge as well as to defend oneself is not permitted (Rom. 13:1; Pet. 2:13; Rom. 12:19). On the other hand, Luther did not find it unfair to form an alliance not against a specified opponent but against "a free and unnamed accident." This could even be a deterrent and frighten off the opponents. Thus far the princes of [Electoral] Saxony had "sat there completely quiet." In Luther's opinion there was little else they could have done, since they were unable to defend themselves [by force] in the interests of the gospel. "Nevertheless, they could make it appear as though they would defend themselves." Thereby God has intimidated the tyrants. "Who knows? When we have faith and beseech God that Your Grace may yet be a sign of awe, whether through the appearance of a federation or otherwise, [the opponents] will not be so defiant as to do what they threaten. The drawn bow does not hit everything at which it is aimed, indeed, it seldom hits its target."[5] This political stance was deduced from the friendly firmness of Frederick the Wise. Behind it stood the conviction that Luther had already shown toward Ulrich von Hutten: "I would not want to see force and murder used in fighting for the gospel. . . . Through the Word the world has been overcome and the church has been rescued, and through the Word it will also be restored."[6]

Although the negotiations at the Nuremberg diet were fruitless, men did remember a plan (contained in an action of April 18, 1524) that seemed to both sides [papal and evangelical] a way out. It proposed that a "general assembly of the German nation" be convened on St. Martin's Day (November 11) in Speyer [on the Rhine]. There the new teachings would be discussed and "neither the good nor the bad be suppressed." There too the grievances against the Roman church would be treated.[7] The last word

4. An association for mutual defense including the towns of Bautzen, Kamenz, Löbau, Zittau, Görlitz, and Lauban. Kötzschke and H. Kretschmar, *Sächsische Geschichte*, vol. 1: *Vor- und Frühgeschichte, Mittelalter und Reformationszeit* (Dresden, 1935), 146–47.

5. WA Br 3:416 / 56–79. Dating of the letter is according to WA Br 13:70.

6. WA Br 2:249 / 12ff. (according to a letter to Spalatin, January 16, 1521).

7. On the antecedents and history of the Diet of Speyer, see W. Friedensburg, *Der Reichstag zu Speier 1526 im Zusammenhang der politischen und kirchlichen Entwicklung Deutschlands im Reformationszeitalter* (Berlin, 1887). Also Friedensburg, "Die Reformation und der Speierer Reichstag von 1526," *LuJ* 8 (1926): 120ff. Against the formulation "the good . . ." the papal legate Campeggio raised objections; RTA 4:604 / 9. G. Müller, *Die römische Kurie und die Reformation 1523–1534*, QFRG 38 (Gütersloh, 1969), 23.

on the church question, beyond this assembly, should then be left to a general council.[8] The papal legate at the diet, Campeggio, as well as the cardinals of the curia, sharply rejected the proposal for an imperial diet, especially because it implied that there could be some good in the Lutheran movement. The issue resolved itself to the great satisfaction of the pope and the curia, so that from his seat in Burgos [Castile, in northeastern Spain] Charles V on July 15, 1524, forbade the planned assembly in Speyer and called instead for a more rigorous enforcement of the Edict of Worms.[9]

Understandably, Luther was not drawn into the negotiations for an evangelical alliance. On only one point in the important preparations was his cooperation requested. After the peasant uprising, a major part of which was directed against the Roman clergy, had been put down, the cathedral chapter in Mainz took energetic steps to strengthen the position of the priests. At a gathering of representatives from chapters throughout the church province of Mainz, the removal of all "Lutheran preachers"— blamed as instigators of the uprising—was demanded as well as the restoration of spiritual jurisdictions and the payment of the "tithe" called for. At the same time, deputations to the emperor and the pope were agreed on and armed with detailed instructions.[10] Thereupon Landgrave Philip of Hesse and Elector John of Saxony, acting on advice from their counselors, requested Luther to state his position on the Mainz "proposal." They feared that the example of Mainz might trigger similar events in other territories. The best way to prevent this from happening, the two princes and their advisers agreed, was to make little of it. Luther's ensuing pamphlet, entitled *Against the Truly Seditious, Treasonable and Murderous Proposal of the Entire Clergy in Mainz: Instruction and Warning*, included the text of the offensive document, to which he added sarcastic

8. It is difficult to define the character of the planned assembly. H. Jedin, *Geschichte des Konzils von Trient*, vol. 1: *Der Kampf um das Konzil* (Freiburg, 1949), which (526, n. 75) refers to this difficulty and uses the term "national council," even though it was rejected by the imperial party. The term usually used, "national convention" *[Nationalversammlung]*, is lacking in that it does not enable one to recognize the ecclesiastically authorized character that this gathering should have along with its origin in imperial politics. The most accurate yet somewhat clumsy formulation is that of K. Brandi, "imperial assembly on church affairs" (*Reichsversammlung in Kirchensachen*), in his *Deutsche Reformation und Gegenreformation* (Leipzig, 1927), 140. The reason that the assembly never took place has never been clear. The partial national assembly, like the long-delayed council of the church, vanished until 1545.

9. W. Friedensburg, *Aktenstücke über das Verhalten der Römischen Kurie zur Reformation 1524 und 1531*, QFIAB 3 (Tübingen, 1900), 1ff. Müller, *Römische Kurie*, 22ff.

10. WA 19:252ff. Text of the proposal, WA 19:264–73.

glosses and a substantive rebuttal.[11] One thing, he remarked, had been overlooked in the Mainz proposal: for a long time and almost everywhere the spiritual estate has been despised because of its life-style as well as its teaching.[12] And whatever the "proposal" charged Luther with being (a heretic and agitator) simply made him retort "with joy," declaring, "At Worms I was not condemned as a heretic by the imperial judgment." No unanimous and signed judgment of all the estates in the diet was achieved at Worms. Instead, he said, a council of bishops and several princes had misused the emperor for their purposes. Therefore the edict has remained ineffective. It was modified in Nuremberg because people's consciences could not live with it.[13] Finally, the gospel is accused of fomenting all the unrest. Assuming this to be true, the uprising should have been worst of all in Wittenberg. However, it is as plain as day "that here in Wittenberg where I preach there was no uprising; in fact, the place was so full of God's grace as nowhere else on earth."[14] The treatise on temporal government, and the bitterness of Müntzer against him, proved that Luther had had nothing to do with the insurrection.[15] After all, the unrest had originated not in Hesse or Electoral Saxony but in Franconia, beyond the Thuringian forest and in the imperial city of Mühlhausen, whence it came into the territory of Duke George's Saxony.[16] Meanwhile, the two princes who had encouraged Luther to write something became startled by their own courage and fearful of Luther's temperament, lest Duke George be hurt. With customary craftiness the duke was leaked a copy of Luther's manuscript and had announced his displeasure in advance, should it be published. Therefore the princes deputized Luther's Wittenberg colleagues Jerome Schurff and Melanchthon to speak with him, lest his writing draw criticism on himself as well as them, and lest Luther show "any ill will against our cousin, Duke George."[17]

Luther, however, even then had his own encounter with Duke George, which became a straightforward clarification of their relationship. On December 21, 1525, Luther had written Duke George. With a hunch that it might soon be too late, Luther begged the duke to change his ungracious

11. WA 19:260–75 / 6.
12. WA 19:274 / 1–275 / 6.
13. WA 19:276 / 19–28, esp. 19–20.
14. WA 19:278 / 2ff.
15. WA 19:278 / 10–29.
16. WA 19:279 / 11ff.
17. Authenticating memorandum of April 9, 1526, to the two men deputized, WA Br 4:45–46, esp. 46 / 9–10.

disposition and to desist from prosecuting evangelical teaching—not so much for Luther's sake as for his own. In the long run Christ will safeguard his congregation, even if it be a modest, poor little company. "So it stands to reason that success is not likely to be on the side of Your Serene Grace, for we know that what Christ has promised us, he will also fulfill. And may it become clear to Your Serene Grace that to oppose Müntzer is not the same as to oppose Luther." The professor was referring to himself not as a person but as the humble instrument of a cause, "for on a certain occasion God has also spoken through an ass."[18] Duke George replied immediately and amply on December 28. He suppressed his injured "old Adam" and confessed that formerly he had not unwillingly read Luther's writings.[19] Yet "the fruits [of these writings] have filled us with dread and aversion for your teaching":[20] the encouragement of the Bohemians, the forsaking of the cloisters, the activities of Karlstadt and others whom Luther had led "up the slippery mountain, from which they slid down without stopping."[21] The gospel Luther "pulled out from under the bench" is to blame for the revolt of the peasants.[22] Not one of the prophets and teachers of the Bible was an apostate.[23] The prayers or curses in Luther's gatherings leave him cold. "For we know that God hates the gatherings of your apostates." Finally, Duke George threatened openly, "We, of course, know that Luther is not Müntzer. As God punished Müntzer through us for his malice, the same thing he can no doubt also do to Luther. We are ready as an unworthy instrument to be used for this purpose according to his will."[24] And then the duke challenged Luther to repent of all his offenses against the church. "The Christian church does not withhold its embrace from those returning to its fold.[25] God will compensate him [Luther] with rewards and blessings. And the duke himself would take pains to secure amnesty from the emperor for Luther.[26] The exchange between the two opponents created a sensation. Each of them had thrown his high reputation in the balance: Luther the intellectual

18. WA Br 3:643 / 72ff.; 642 / 44–45. Luther frankly admitted that he was writing at the instigation of others (nobles in the duchy of Saxony). WA Br 3:642 / 14–15; 637.

19. The duke's letter, WA Br 3:646–51; 647 / 55ff.; 648 / 82ff.

20. WA Br 3:649 / 139–40.

21. WA Br 3:648 / 87ff.; 649 / 109–10.

22. WA Br 3:649 / 133ff.

23. WA Br 3:650 / 152ff.

24. WA Br 3:650 / 169ff. ["Instrument" is from the colloquial German.] *Gezau = Gezähe, Werkzeug*.

25. WA Br 3:650 / 180–81.

26. WA Br 3:651 / 208ff.

status he had earned from the German public, George his princely position. The intense interest was evident from the swift publication of the letters, some with Luther's, others with the duke's letters in the lead position.[27] Both parties were contending for the church (Luther for its renewal, the duke for its preservation), and both were concerned for public order. Luther feared for the church if the promise of an orderly airing of the religious question facing the empire were not carried out. As for the duke, although he distinguished between Luther and Müntzer, he saw the insurrectionist movement as the fruit of Luther's heretical sowing. Hence his threat and readiness to be used as God's instrument against Luther as he had been used earlier against Müntzer.[28] In this tense situation over against Duke George, Luther acceded to the wishes of the elector, sending him the pages of his pamphlet against the Mainz proposal thus far set in type and abandoning further work on the subject.[29]

This was not the end of it, for Duke George sought still other ways of coping with the Luther problem. In March 1526 he proposed to Elector John that he too join the League of Dessau, so that the problem might receive concerted treatment. When asked about this by the elector, Luther warned urgently against such an admixture.

> The consequence would be that the [two] principalities would tangle with each other and that each would seek to be mentor and master in both. . . . In this case it is of highest importance that the two principalities remain as uninvolved in each other as possible, for everyday experience has taught what care it takes to keep them as cleanly separated and parted as possible.[30]

When emperor's orders forbade an extraordinary convening of the imperial diet in Speyer, Charles's deputy, Archduke Ferdinand, pursued normal channels for assembling a new diet. He wished to see it convened this time in a region less influenced than Nuremberg or the Rhenish cities by the Reformation and the peasant revolt. Thereupon the emperor desig-

27. Listing of the fourteen printings of 1526 (among them two in Low German) in J. Benzing, *Lutherbibliographie* (Baden-Baden, 1966), nos. 2376–89.

28. On this relationship, see O. Vossler, "Herzog Georg der Bärtige und seine Ablehnung Luthers," *HZ* 184 (1957): 272ff. I agree fully with Vossler's balanced presentation, yet I would not derive the contrast from a "conflict between the religious and the ethical man" (291). The root of the matter lay in a fundamental and at that time still difficult-to-master difference in religiosity.

29. Letters from mid-April and April 23, 1526, *WA Br* 4:54, 62. The printed pages were destroyed, *WA Br* 4:62, n. 1. *WA* 19:255.

30. May 15, 1526, *WA Br* 4:78 / 14ff. Alongside this, the instruction of George for a deputation to the elector, *WA Br* 4:79, n. 1. F. Gess, *Akten und Briefe zur Kirchenpolitik Herzog Georgs von Sachsen* (Leipzig, 1905ff.), 2:500ff.

nated Augsburg for a meeting of the diet as of November 11, 1525.[31] The response to this was poor. The few princes and representatives who showed up could at best adjourn the meeting and postpone it to May 1, 1526, in Speyer. There again the emperor himself failed to show up, even though Ferdinand had urged his presence. Despite his brilliant victory in Pavia (February 24, 1525)—he had taken Francis I of France prisoner—Charles V believed it unwise to leave the south. Nor was this reluctance unfounded. No sooner was Francis I released and back in France than he declared himself free from the terms of the Peace of Madrid. In addition, on May 22, 1526, in his native castle in Cognac, he allied himself with Pope Clement VII, the republic of Venice, and Milan's House of Sforza in the "Holy League of Cognac" against Spain. Toward the end of March of that year Archduke Ferdinand had learned that the emperor's attendance at the imperial diet was quite uncertain. Thus, neither the archduke nor the princes, who eyed his example, were in any hurry to head for Speyer. At last, on June 25, the diet opened. It was divided into three sections (Electors, Princes, Cities), each of which received a proposal from the emperor that contained the agenda for its discussion. Heading the list was the question of how to deal with the church and matters of faith until the holding of a free council.[32] This was the diet's most important business. For this purpose Ferdinand had received secret instructions from the emperor.[33] Very simply, that instruction was that should the debate on religious matters take a course contrary to the emperor's intentions, the archduke was to terminate any further business, for the emperor's intention was to proceed to Italy and discuss with the pope the calling of a general council for the purpose of eradicating heresy and dealing with all grievances and complaints. Thereupon he would return to Germany and fulfill his duties as Christian emperor. Until that time, let the diet take no decisions contrary to the nature, doctrine, or order of the church. A council would then undertake a unanimous Christian reformation. Any particular agreements would merely result in confusion and disobedience.[34]

The three sections of the diet, especially the cities section, had meanwhile tackled the church question with such energy and had expressed so many desires for reform that Archduke Ferdinand, already on August 2 in the first session of the "great committee" (including representatives of all

31. On the imperial diet in Augsburg, see Friedensburg, *Gotha-Torgauer Bündnis* (see n. 3, above), 64ff.

32. Text in Friedensburg, *Reichstag zu Speier*, 523ff.; also 217ff.

33. Ibid., 371ff.

34. Ibid., and also Friedensburg's "Die Reformation" (see n. 7, above), 188ff., 195.

the sections) revealed his secret instructions. Indignation ran high. The several sections took counsel separately. Eventually all agreed on a formulation proposed by the electors' section: Let there be a preliminary discussion of the Turkish question and then, when discussing church affairs, let the [emperor's] instruction be borne in mind, so that "each section treat these matters in a way that it could answer before God, the emperor, and the empire."[35] One could hardly object to such a formulation. Its influence is felt in several declarations, down to the action of the diet on August 27:

> Accordingly, we (the imperial commissioners), also Electors, Princes, and Cities of the empire and embassies of the same, have here and now at this imperial diet reconciled and united ourselves with one accord until such time of the council or national assembly . . . that together with our subjects in such matters as may pertain to the edict—promulgated by imperial majesty at the diet of the empire held in Worms—each of us will so live, govern, and deport ourselves as we severally hope and trust will be answerable before God and the Imperial Majesty.[36]

Contrary to Ranke's formulation, these words do not contain the "legal basis for structuring the German territorial churches."[37] Its juridical nucleus lies in its position taken against the imperial absolutism that lay cloaked in the secret instruction of Charles V to Archduke Ferdinand. The declaration of 1526 is thus no license to introduce the Reformation, but a provision against the suppression of a religious movement by means of the penal laws of the Edict of Worms—which the emperor had chosen as his weapon for the struggle at hand. The diet's declaration at Speyer did not signify toleration in principle, but it was a testimony to freedom, initially for the responsible parties (the territorial rulers and the imperial cities) to grant protection to the evangelically-minded.

The religious question in the empire thus came to a temporary pause. Although the diet had voted it, even as late as May of the following year (1527), the message had not yet been sent out. The delay lay not simply in the complexity of the subject or in some evil intentions, but also in the sudden emergence of another matter which became the focus of attention:

35. Friedensburg, "Die Reformation," 183.

36. Friedensburg, *Reichstag zu Speier*, 379, 462ff.; also his "Die Reformation," 187–86.

37. L. von Ranke, *Deutsche Geschichte im Zeitalter der Reformation*, 2d ed. (Meersburg and Leipzig, 1933), 2:290. Friedensburg, "Die Reformation," 195, justifiably rejects Ranke's interpretation. Yet if Friedensburg sees this declaration simply as a noncommittal delaying tactic, then the room to maneuver (which the estates of the empire reserved for themselves over against the emperor not only at this time but also in view of later times, when they would claim such room for their own responsibilities) does not become clear.

the Turkish menace. A mere two days after the diet's declaration came the disastrous Battle of Mohacs and the death of Hungary's King Louis II (August 29, 1526).[38] The Turk had advanced to the eastern boundaries of the empire. Archduke Ferdinand, elected successor to Louis, was forced to shift his powers from the duties of the empire to a new range of demands. Two new imperial diets were called by the imperial Council of Regency. The diet in the autumn of 1526 in Esslingen convened the princes; that in May 1527 in Regensburg [Ratisbon] was sparsely attended. Both diets were dominated by concerns over the Turkish advance.[39] However, this pause in the politics of religion saw a sharpening of the contrasts. Both sides [papal and evangelical] reckoned with the possibility that the present course might lead to a violent showdown. Amid this situation the activist among the evangelical princes, Landgrave Philip of Hesse, received a secret warning that the Roman Catholic estates were scheming violent action against those of Lutheran outlook. The first intimations came from an apparently trustworthy source close to Philip's father-in-law, Duke George of Saxony. The informer was Otto von Pack, the duke's vice-chancellor and privy councillor.[40] Landgrave Philip had no way of knowing that he was being victimized by a calculating and archly money-mad confidence man. Pack intimated privately that the Catholic imperial estates, in collusion with the emperor, were determined to carry out some sort of extreme action against the evangelical princes at the next imperial diet. Philip believed the Pack story all the more because it corresponded to his own fears. Besides, Pack divulged confidential materials to Philip from an alliance directed against the evangelical estates of the empire. This anti-evangelical alliance had been formed by [now] King Ferdinand with Duke George of Saxony, the dukes of Bavaria, the electors of Brandenburg and Mainz, and a number of ecclesial principalities, the agreement having been concluded in Breslau on May 15, 1527.[41] In February 1528, while in Dresden, Landgrave Philip asked to see the original document as Pack had promised. Pack obliged only to the extent of showing him a presumably "notarized copy," replete with the seals of Ducal Saxony; it had sup-

38. See above, p. 587.

39. Friedensburg, *Reichstag zu Speier*, 470ff. J. Kühn, *Die Geschichte des Speyrer Reichstags 1529*, SVRG 146 (Leipzig, 1929), 20ff.

40. W. Friedensburg, "Otto von Pack," *ADB* 25 (1887): 60ff. *WA Br* 5:10–11. Basic to a grasp of events involving Pack is K. Dülfer, "Die Packschen Händel: Darstellung und Quellen," *VHKHW* 24 / 3 (Marburg, 1958). Among the older sources, see esp. J. Kühn, "Landgraf Philipp von Hessen: Der politische Sinn der sogenannten Packschen Händel," in *Staat und Persönlichkeit: Festschrift für E. Brandenburg* (Leipzig, 1928), 107ff.

41. On the gathering of princes in Breslau, see Kühn, "Philipp von Hessen," 108ff.

posedly been prepared for Duke George. Under the impression that this text corresponded to the original, Philip had a copy of it made for himself. What he read in this document—wholly fabricated by Pack—alarmed him. Once Ferdinand was established on the Hungarian throne, the Breslau allies would turn their forces against the princes and cities harboring Lutherans. Their territories were to be divided among the allies; Luther, in company with all renegade preachers, monks, and nuns, was to be extradited according to the terms of a mandate presently on its way from Spain. Should the Lutheran territorial lords refuse, then—on the basis of a date determined three months in advance by Ferdinand—all the members of the Breslau alliance would simultaneously launch an attack.[42] Upon hearing this ominous piece of news, which they believed to be true, Landgrave Philip and Elector John came to an agreement of their own and made ready to defend themselves. On March 9, 1528, they concluded an alliance in Weimar, fixed the troop strength of both parties, and set their unification for June 1, 1528, at the latest. Thereupon they would consult together as to their military strategy.[43]

In order to reassure his conscience, Elector John requested Luther's opinion on the Weimar alliance. The result was a noteworthy exchange on what constitutes a just war and an unjust war. Luther replied immediately and at length, for the issue stirred him deeply.[44] That the elector should have the right to defend himself against other princes who might attack him, and to protect his subjects as well, was a question for which Luther had a quick answer: Of course the elector has the right, for the other princes have no rights over him. But what if the other princes claim to have orders from the emperor? Then he should not believe it but hold fast to the emperor's own promise to be his gracious overlord. The Edict of Worms is nothing to which they could appeal in order to attack the elector, for the edict is not a law approved by the imperial estates, indeed, it is a mandate not of the empire or of the emperor but of the clergy. Besides, it was [in effect] rescinded by the diets of Nuremberg and Speyer. In any case, it is possible for the elector to appeal to the other princes and to protest against any violent procedure.[45]

42. Dülfer, "Die Packschen Händel," 61ff.

43. The Weimar Treaty of March 9, 1528, along with a supplemental treaty of May 2, is published in G. Mentz, "Zur Geschichte der Packschen Händel," ARG 1 (1903): 172ff., esp. 174ff. Also, Dülfer, "Die Packschen Händel," 74ff.

44. To Chancellor Brück, March 28, 1528, WA Br 4:421–24. On subsequent developments to May 1528, see Dülfer, "Die Packschen Händel," 163ff. (the opinions of the Reformers).

45. WA Br 4:423 / 56ff. In Weimar the princes agreed to send a message to the emperor and a corresponding statement to the imperial Council of Regency, the supreme court, and the Swabian League, setting forth their complaints against the Catholic estates and justifying their preventive measures. Dülfer, "Die Packschen Händel," 78.

But to attack and to act prior to hearing the advice of the princes is in no way advisable but is by all means to be avoided, for God's Word stands right there: "All who take the sword will perish by the sword." . . . No greater disgrace could befall the gospel, for such action would lead not to a revolt of the peasants but to an insurrection of princes which would be the ruin of Germany—an outcome Satan, of course, would be glad to see.[46]

Luther even eyed the possibility that the landgrave would not agree to abandoning the idea of a preventive war. In that case the elector "is not obligated to adhere to the alliance, for one must obey God rather than men."[47]

Landgrave Philip, to whom the elector had sent a copy of Luther's opinion, at first replied with the objection that Luther was apparently not accurately informed. Philip asserted again that he had read the basic document of the Breslau alliance and that he hoped soon to have it in the original.[48] Accordingly, he feared earnestly that God's Word would be suppressed, many people expelled or hanged, and preachers driven out. From this prospect he rationalized the right of preventive measures. "Therefore I ask Martin's kind opinion whether it is better that we let the house burn and then extinguish [the flames], or whether it is better to guard against fire so that the house won't burn." And if the government should protect its subjects, "I then ask, should I protect my subjects dead or alive? Expelled or unexpelled? Were I to protect them when dead, my protection would not have been of any use at all."[49] Besides, whatever mercenaries and strongholds the elector and he [Philip] still had would fall into enemy hands. Luther would declare these to be the reflections of reason. "Yet he must also admit that God has therefore given us reason and reflection, so that we should make use of them for the sake of our subjects." Indeed, even Luther's advice is "not entirely without reason or worldly wisdom."[50] Philip was particularly decisive in rejecting Luther's word about an "insurrection of princes." The issue at hand is simply one of defense in an emergency. But Philip is ready to pardon Luther, even for holding that the elector has the right to break the alliance.[51] Even so, Philip declared himself ready to meet with King Ferdinand and his allies,

46. WA Br 4:423 / 64ff., 83ff.
47. WA Br 4:423 / 87–88.
48. April 12, 1528, WA Br 4:425 / 1ff.
49. WA Br 4:425 / 11ff.; 426 / 22ff., 35ff.; 427 / 83ff.
50. WA Br 4:427 / 62ff., 69–70.
51. WA Br 4:427 / 94ff.; 428 / 98ff., 130ff.

with whom a peaceful ordering and securing of the free preaching of the gospel in evangelical territories should be taken under advisement. [52]

The landgrave's letter moved Elector John to convene a meeting in Weimar on April 28, 1528, and to invite both Luther and Melanchthon to participate. The two reformers together drafted a reply to Philip of Hesse's declaration. [53] They held firmly to the position that under no circumstances dare the evangelical side initiate a military attack; above all, one must seek ways and means for an understanding. The landgrave's argument that an anticipated attack requires one to strike first, lest the strike be too late, was turned down by the Reformers.

> To advise something like this, and, as good subjects, to give notice of it, presses our conscience. For we are deeply concerned lest Satan, by means of this temptation, turns us into new and more evil Müntzers and Pfeiffers. [54] It is really something quite unbearable for a conscience in God's sight thus to render counsel and help for the sake of bloodshed, since one is not sure whether God is calling for something like this or only permits it. Now one can indeed be sure that God calls for a defense against war and insurrection and for the protection of one's subjects. But to start a war and to attack others, of this one cannot be at all certain that it pleases God. Much more certain is it that this sort of thing does not please him.

Therefore, one should deal with opponents through mediators. Should the others not declare themselves ready to make peace, let this then be the challenge to combat. "Then the time has come to defend and protect oneself." [55] The princes allowed themselves to be persuaded by the Reformers' arguments. Thereupon they reviewed their Weimar treaty: They would refrain from launching an attack from their side, and they would first request the emperor to command peace and their Catholic opponents to practice peaceful restraint. The Reformers added that one should not now be gathering troops, for they would be too impatient to control; instead, one should ask other estates of the empire to mediate and to bring the matter before the diet. [56] The opposition of the Reformers (beside Luther and Melanchthon, Bugenhagen had also spoken) spared the evangelical princes from the consequences of the landgrave's rashness. Luther

52. WA Br 4:429 / 141ff.

53. WA Br 4:430ff.

54. Heinrich Pfeiffer, with Müntzer, led the uprising in Mühlhausen. See above, pp. 174ff.

55. WA Br 4:432 / 39ff., 56.

56. WA Br 4:433ff. The opinion printed there comprises two parts: the additions by the Reformers are separately numbered. Dülfer, "Die Packschen Händel," 106. WA Br 4:434.

and Melanchthon had reason to express their joy on learning that the imperial Council of Regency, in a mandate of April 16, had issued an order to keep the peace, accompanied by severe punishment for those who broke it. The Reformers warned urgently against disregarding of this order; nor did they hesitate, early in May, to remind the elector that although it would "pain them forever" they would in this case have to leave the land of the elector who had nourished and protected them.[57] In a sequence of letters they implored the elector not to miss the opportunity to make peace or to destroy its chances through high demands for compensation.[58]

Luther in no way doubted the reports of Pack about the Breslau alliance.[59] Indeed, just because he took it seriously he objected so bitterly against Philip of Hesse's plan for a preventive war. In a pamphlet against the bishop of Meissen, who had forbidden the reception of Communion in both kinds, Luther spoke suggestively of "treasonable notices and alliances" against the "Lutheran princes."[60] And in writing to his friend Wenceslaus Link, in Nuremberg, on June 14, 1528, Luther expressed himself sharply against the attempts of Duke George to deny the existence of the [Breslau] alliance.[61] Somehow a copy of this letter came into the hands of Duke George. Understandably it aroused his intense wrath, for he well knew that the Breslau alliance was an invention of Pack's, and Luther believed the document to be authentic. Indeed, he suspected that "the peasant" [George], his "archenemy," was the author.[62] The duke sent a messenger to Luther, demanding that he provide the messenger with a written statement as to whether he was actually the author of the letter to Link. The messenger was carrying a copy of the letter. Then the duke would be able to take appropriate action.[63] Luther curtly refused to let the duke treat him like an employee or a prisoner awaiting orders. He would rather let the duke remain unmolested by such slips of paper or transcripts. The duke, he suggested, would have a better chance of finding out

57. WA Br 4:448 / 4ff.; 449 / 50ff.

58. WA Br 4:449 / 67ff.; 451; 452–53.

59. As late as April 23, 1538, in a table conversation, he admitted that Pack had convinced him. WA TR 3, no. 3850, 658 / 37–38.

60. *Ein Bericht an einen guten Freund von beider Gestalt des Sakraments aufs Bischofs zu Meissen Mandat* [A report to a good friend concerning the sacrament in both kinds on the Bishop of Meissen's authorization], WA 26:563 / 19.

61. WA Br 4:483–84.

62. To John Hess, June 13 or 14, 1528, WA Br 4:480 / 10ff. To Link, June 14, 1528, WA Br 4:497 / 25ff. *Bauer* [farmer], Greek nickname for Duke George.

63. October 28, 1528, WA Br 4:593–94.

by inquiring of those people who have handed and are handing him such notes; those people are closer to the duke, and he is free to ask them, without Luther's help, who the letter is from.[64] Duke George thereupon turned to Elector John and demanded that he make Luther provide him with a different answer.[65] Responding to the elector's efforts, Luther replied that he preferred to let his first answer to George stand. After the elector had made a few slight changes in Luther's original letter with Luther's consent, he sent it to Duke George on December 4. For his part, however, the duke had already extracted an affirmation from Nuremberg that Luther's letter to Link was genuine. Duke George began his prosecution at once and published a broadside in eight thousand copies. In it he accused Pack of having fabricated the story of the Breslau alliance, and accused Luther of attacking Duke George and the other alleged allies both publicly and privately. The duke sent the elector a huge stack of copies, for the broadside should be posted in many places. The elector let the ducal messenger post the flyers wherever he chose, but he also requested that Duke George spare him any further matters pertaining to Luther. And Luther? He had gotten wind of the duke's impending attack and on December 31 closed out the year by telling the elector not to worry about him. In fact, Luther would volunteer to stand trial. He would, he said, rather offer his neck than cause his elector even a hair's breadth of danger.[66]

Before the broadside reached the booksellers Luther had received a copy. He hastily prepared a reply, and at the New Year's fair of 1529 it was available along with Duke George's sheet.[67] The title of Luther's piece, *On Secret and Stolen Letters, Including a Commentary on a Psalm, Against Duke George of Saxony,* made it obvious at whom he was aiming. "What is my dear Duke George up to? He not only accepts letters of mine that have been stolen in secret—this is not fitting for him [the letter to Link], yet I could let that pass—but he also blusters and struts about, demands my letters from me, and wants to be lord over my private corre-

64. October 31, 1528, WA Br 4:596. Also printed in Luther's work named below, *Von heimlichen und gestolenen Briefen* (1529), WA 30²:25 [On secret and stolen letters]. This is not to say that Luther is trying to make it seem as though the letter is a forgery (against WA Br 4:596, n. 3). On that subject he says nothing; he is simply giving back something of George's cavalier tone. The duke should spare him such inquiries and stick to his own security staff.

65. Elector John to Luther, December 2, 1528, WA Br 4:619. Chancellor Brück to Luther, December 4, WA Br 4:620.

66. WA Br 4:629 / 20ff.

67. WA 30²:10.

spondence, even though he doesn't exercise even a penny's worth of authority over me." As if this were not enough, he also demands the assistance of Elector John, the Nuremberg city council, and Wenceslaus Link, that they provide him with Luther's consent or obtain for him the original of his letter.[68] Although his immediate aim was to expose the unworthy actions of the duke, he also intended to clarify his relations to him on the whole. It is the relationship of an honest enmity.

> In sum, I know that Duke George is a mortal enemy of my teaching. This he admits with joy, and seeks to derive honor and praise for this, as he indeed has. So I know for myself that my teaching is God's Word and gospel. This he denies, and he is known to the world for his denial. It must follow that he thinks nothing good of me and, correspondingly, that I can see no good in him.[69]

And yet there are bridges spanning this enmity. Even though the duke is his enemy, he would not think to curse him or any other overlord. "For I know that one should bless and pray for them, since they surely need it."[70] Likewise the evangelicals retain the right to request that Duke George and his entourage would "for once stop it and leave our teaching in peace." With this Luther appeals to the action of the Diet of Speyer in 1526.[71] By its terms there is a legal way open to the duke. Luther respects the duke not as his lord but as his accuser and opponent.[72] In order to broaden the horizon against which his battle with the duke takes place, Luther concludes his pamphlet with a meditation on Psalm 7. In this he finds again all those things that are now moving him: God is the judge over his [Luther's] enemies and also over himself; his opponents, who like lions would tear him apart (v. 3); or those, who with misfortune are with child for him and his own. But they will bring a miscarriage into the world, and into the ditch they have dug they themselves will tumble (vv. 15ff.). With a prayer for strength and confidence Luther closes this brief polemic: "Let us see now what the devil and his knaves and furious ones will be able to accomplish. Peace, to be sure, is with us, but they do not desire peace. So, then, they shall have unrest and whatever this psalm threatens."[73]

Luther's pamphlet earned him approbation from an unexpected quarter: a letter from Pack. After lengthy negotiations over the missing original

---

68. WA 30²:31 / 11–27.
69. WA 30²:39 / 12ff.
70. WA 30²:40 / 29–30.
71. WA 30²:41 / 17; 43 / 11ff.
72. WA 30²:42 / 11ff.
73. WA 30²:44 / 3–48 / 8; 48 / 5ff.

document, the duke put Pack in prison in May 1528 in order to keep this important witness secure.[74] Pack now wrote an exuberant, friendly letter to Luther, apparently delighted over now having a common opponent against Duke George. He tied Luther's cause with his own: "Presently you will get to see the open and real truth and at the same time my innocence." He claimed never to have sought to mislead anyone, let alone plot war and rebellion.[75] Luther had no idea what a dubious ally Pack, whose alleged revelations he had swallowed as fully as Landgrave Philip had done, really was. Elsewhere, however, Luther apparently found little agreement with the position he had taken in his pamphlet. A letter from Amsdorf, an exception, gave him a lift.[76] For most people, Luther's tone against such a mighty prince was too bitter. He desisted on his own and did not rebut the duke a second time.[77] As for Pack, his prank eventually turned into a tragedy for its instigator. For the moment it was his good luck to be in the custody of Philip of Hesse, who had assured his safety and refused the demands of Duke George and his allies for Pack's extradition. Philip, unwilling to break his word to Pack, could make use of him as an excuse for his own position. When the two sides (the group around Duke George and that around Landgrave Philip) could not agree on proceedings against Pack, Philip quickly released him, yet not before Pack had sworn not to seek vengeance and had promised to stand trial later. Though now free, Pack found no safe refuge. Wherever he went, Duke George's extradition warrants followed him. Tales traveled too, and one of them had Elector John and Luther offering Pack sanctuary in Wittenberg. Chancellor Brück cynically rejected the rumor. It is well known, he quipped, that the elector has never yet made Dr. Martin Luther "the president of his electoral court of appeals."[78] After prolonged evasions, Pack was finally picked up in the Netherlands in 1536 and, on demand of Duke George, was brought to trial under the regent, Queen Mary, a sister of Charles V. Under torture he admitted having concocted the story of the "Breslau alliance." On February 8 he was condemned to death and executed forthwith.[79]

That a money-mad forger of documents could create such confusion and lead princes to the brink of war revealed the kind of political tensions

74. Dülfer, "Die Packschen Händel," 133ff.
75. Kassel, January 23, 1529, WA Br 5:11 / 7ff.
76. February 12, 1529, WA Br 5:17 / 1ff.
77. WA Br 5:17 / 5, 9; 28 / 5.
78. H. Becker, "Zur Geschichte der Packschen Händel," ARG 8 (1910–11): 400–401.
79. Dülfer, "Die Packschen Händel," 162.

permeating the empire. These were intensified by the fact that the two top bearers of authority, the emperor and his brother Ferdinand, were both preoccupied in foreign entanglements of a sort that precluded their dealing rapidly with the church situation. Luther, of course, knew about these matters only from hearsay. On December 10, 1527, writing to Justus Jonas, he summed up [in a postscript] what he knew:

> There is a rumor here that the emperor has come to an understanding with the pope and the French, in which both the English and the Venetians are supposedly included. Also that the Turk is preparing an extremely extensive campaign. It is uncertain whether it will be directed against Apulia [southeast Italy] or Hungary; if against Hungary, it will certainly strike Germany with fear, and put Ferdinand to flight.[80]

At least the broad outlines of the situation were known. [Certain particulars, revealed later, included the fact that] the pope, who in May 1527 had taken refuge in San Angelo Castle while the emperor's mercenaries were plundering Rome, was allowed (with the silent consent of Charles V) to escape, and then, by a treaty concluded in Barcelona on November 26, 1527, was restored to office and to sovereignty over his temporal lands. In return, he promised to call a council. Thereby, and for the present, the demands of France and England were met, so that after a prolonged period of warfare they became allied. Early in 1528 the two allies promptly declared war on the emperor. Once again Charles V was tied down by the chronic struggle for Italy. Amid ever-changing fortunes he was finally able to drive the French out of Italy. With the "Ladies' Peace" of Cambrai (August 5, 1529)—mediated for Charles V by his aunt, Margaret, the regent in the Netherlands, and by Francis I's mother, Louise of Savoy—the warring was at last brought to an end.

During the preceding years Charles V had seen no possibility of coming to Germany in order to resolve the religious question and take care of other problems of the empire, even though his brother Ferdinand had repeatedly urged him to do so. Yet Ferdinand himself was burdened by onerous political duties. Not only had he been crowned king of Bohemia following the death of his brother-in-law in the Battle of Mohacs, but he had received the latter's Hungarian inheritance as well. However, he wore the Hungarian crown only after having defeated his previously elected Magyar rival to the throne, John Zapolya, the governor of Transylvania. Ferdinand succeeded in driving him out and, on November 3, 1527, gaining the Hungarian crown. This success, however, confronted him with

80. WA Br 4:295 / 57ff. [LW 49:185.]

pressures of his belligerent Turkish neighbor. In this situation he required the empire's support at his rear. This meant two things: the resolution of the religious question (for it could break out any time in armed conflict between the estates) and the securing of financial help against the Turks. An imperial diet, called by Ferdinand as the emperor's deputy for the spring of 1527, failed to take place; he himself could not attend. Another diet, set by Ferdinand for the following spring (1528), was without his knowledge or that of the Council of Regency called off by the emperor and rescheduled for February 1529 in the city of Speyer. At the same time, however, Charles gave notice that his preoccupations with the continuing French threat would prevent him from attending.[81]

Even before it could be convened, the agenda of the Diet of Speyer was being shaped by the tensions separating the political interests of the two brothers Hapsburg. King Ferdinand had urgent need of the diet; Charles V could not make use of it, at least not for the present. His first aim was peace with England and France and a restoration of his sovereignty over Italy. He simply had no interest in seeing the polarizations in the empire intensified through any abrupt intervention of his. Inasmuch as the diet could no longer be avoided, he endeavored to delay it and blunt the opposition. Yet a lucky turn gave Ferdinand the opportunity to shape the diet's agenda to his own designs. As he was about to convene the diet, the emperor's customary message of propositions, a document containing the items for debate as well as the emperor's opinions on them, was still missing. Only much later was the news out that the ship bearing the imperial messenger with the necessary document had been delayed for weeks by storms preventing its sailing from Spain.[82] Ferdinand used the dilemma to steer the diet in the direction he desired. In lieu of the imperial proposition, he had a formulation read which set forth his own political wishes as agenda items.[83] This was not presented as a declaration of what the emperor willed but only of what his deputy and the appointed commissioners proposed. The formulation, however, created the impression of one speaking directly for the emperor. Its central point was its linkage of the Turkish danger and the religious division. Without peace at home, so it argued, there is no defending Christendom against the Turks. Ferdinand's propo-

81. RTA 7 / 2:1073ff. Also, Kühn, *Speyrer Reichstag* (see above, n. 39), 23–24.

82. J. Kühn, "Wer trägt die Verantwortung an der Entstehung des politischen Protestantismus?" in *Kultur- und Universalgeschichte: Festschrift für W. Götz* (Leipzig and Berlin, 1927), 215ff. Kühn, *Speyrer Reichstag*, 59ff.

83. The unauthentic proposition was read on March 15, 1529; text in RTA 7 / 2:1128ff. Also, Kühn, *Speyrer Reichstag*, 60ff.

sition was inviting: If one were now to suspend religious conflict, then a year or eighteen months hence there could be a general council, which the pope had already promised in the emperor's presence, or at least a national assembly could be held.[84] Yet at the same time the formulation threatened that if one of the imperial estates [a house member of the diet] should yield to "the foreign faith or new sects," it will have to reckon with the loss of its royal prerogatives, feudal tenures, and liberties as well as with the penalties published in the imperial mandate, and it would thereby also fall under the ban and interdict of the empire.[85] Instantly the specter of the Edict of Worms returned. At the same time, the glimmer of hope raised by the earlier Diet of Speyer (1526) was extinguished, for there it had been said that each one would observe the edict "as we severally hope and trust is answerable before God and the Imperial Majesty."[86] By way of contrast, the new formulation [Ferdinand's substituted Proposition] declared: "Herewith Their Imperial Majesty revokes the denounced article, as is set forth in the intended [but not ratified] action [of the 1526 diet], discarding and annulling it, now as then, all of which is done with plenary imperial power." These were Ferdinand's words, not the emperor's. Yet this threatening address closed with the reminder that it was made "by special order of the Imperial Majesty."[87]

The immediate impression created by the proposition was that of alarm. "Altogether dreadful," was Melanchthon's reaction, as he wrote in a letter to Camerarius on the day of the reading. He hoped Christ would destroy the plans of the people bent on war. Elector John wrote his son that this proposition "is in all truth such a severe order as neither I nor the other estates have ever experienced."[88] Among the protestant estates the suspicion grew that the proposition was a substitute. Even the general committee of the diet, in which Catholics comprised the majority, pressed the emperor to support a general council, one that should take place on German soil in a year or a year and a half "so that the German nation may be united in the holy Christian faith and that the lowering discord might be discussed."[89] The decision of 1526 at Speyer to observe the Edict of Worms, as each one felt to be answerable before God and the emperor,

84. RTA, 7 / 2:1132 / 20ff.; 1133 / 10ff.
85. RTA 7 / 2:1133 / 22–1134 / 9.
86. See above, p. 616.
87. RTA 7 / 2:1134 / 17–1135 / 9.
88. March 15, 1529, CR 1:1039. MBW 760. Melanchthon enhances it by expressing it in Greek. Kühn, Speyerer Reichstag, 65.
89. RTA 7 / 2:1141 / 33.

had led to "a great deal of misunderstanding and to the condoning of all kinds of new teachings and sects."[90] The Swiss and Upper German [southwest] doctrine of the Lord's Supper should be forbidden, the mass nowhere abolished, and no one "be forced either to it or away from it."[91] This proposed position raised two dangers in the eyes of the evangelical estates: (1) an uncertain deadlock in the religious question, which would make them give up their reservations against the Edict of Worms as expressed in 1526 and in return offer them the uncertain prospects of a council. In their thorough analysis of the position taken by the general committee, the Electoral Saxon and Hessian estates sounded an urgent warning. Were the evangelical estates to accept it, they would stand "guilty before God . . . , that from henceforth until the council the gospel should have no further acceptance anywhere."[92] To top it off, the abuses and coercions of the old church would again have to be permitted, and this would lead only to unrest and outrage.[93] (2) The controversy between the Lutherans and the Zwinglians over the Lord's Supper had become an issue in imperial politics. The Lutheran estates were thereby forced to clarify their position over against the teachings on the Supper by Zwingli, Oecolampadius, and their adherents.

For one thing, the imperial diet was still to be adjourned. The authoritative document, in which one presumably heard the position of the emperor, was still the proposition formulated by King Ferdinand. Among the evangelicals the conviction grew ever stronger that this document could not be left unchallenged. The first impulse in this direction had come from the ardent John Agricola, the remembrance of whose highly effective sermon at the first Diet of Speyer (1526) had stuck in the memory of Elector John.[94] Again Agricola came through. Word spread that on March 26 he had preached to a crowd of five thousand, surely a gross exaggeration, although it provides us with some sort of measure.[95] This time he demanded that the proposition, which annulled the declaration of the evangelical estates at the 1526 Diet of Speyer, must be publicly chal-

90. RTA 7 / 2:1142 / 11ff., 18ff.

91. RTA 7 / 2:1142 / 31ff.

92. Opinion, read before the evangelical estates on April 1, 1526, RTA 7 / 2:1205–13; cited 1207 / 27ff.

93. RTA 7 / 2:1210 / 1ff.

94. To Count Albert of Mansfeld, January 29, 1529, RTA 7 / 1:496. On Agricola, above, pp. 280ff.

95. Supplement to a report of the Electoral Saxon Councillor Minkewitz to Duke John Frederick, March 26, 1529, RTA 7 / 1:609 (no. 1947, see p. 958). Kühn, *Speyrer Reichstag,* 88ff.

lenged. "Therefore, whoever remains silent at this point by his silence consents to the Edict of Worms and helps to condemn the innocent who hold fast to the true teaching."[96] At the same time a plan gained support to protest against the proposition as well as against the manner in which the declaration of the diet's general committee treated the Edict of Worms as if it really were a law of the empire. Those backing the plan were mainly councilmen from the evangelical cities and councillors of the princes.[97] A protestation was drafted, but on the given day, April 19, 1529, King Ferdinand forbade a full reading of it. Indeed, he and his imperial commissioners walked out of the hall when the princes moved to present it. Thus the "Protestants" (a name which they earned) read their declaration to the remainder of the imperial diet. They gave their reasons for it in a concise style and with a dignity appropriate to the historic hour. Here was a public testimony before God, founded on His Word—their soul's salvation—and on the responsibility toward conscience and emperor, as expressed earlier in the action of the 1526 Diet of Speyer.[98] Because the emperor's deputy had not listened to them, they thereupon left the diet. The evangelical cities, led by Strassburg, joined this protestation of the princes.[99]

Luther had waited long but in vain for news from Speyer. At first he expressed confidence, writing, "I have good hopes for the imperial diet. And even the council cannot do much damage when it convenes, although this appears to me neither probable nor credible."[100] For weeks his friends had nothing to report. His letters carried the monotonous refrain: Nothing new, as yet nothing new, nothing certain. Then on May 6 he had to conclude: "The diet has come to an end again, but almost with no results except that these who chastise Christ and tyrannize the soul were unable to vent their fury. It is sufficient for us to have received such [a gift]

96. RTA 7 / 2:1136–37; 1137 / 2ff. Kühn, *Speyrer Reichstag*, 85, n. 1.

97. Kühn, *Speyrer Reichstag*, 81ff.

98. RTA 7 / 2:1286 / 16ff. "Die Appellation und Protestation der evangelischen Stände auf dem Reichstag zu Speier 1529," ed. J. Ney, QGP 5 (Halle, 1906; reprint, Darmstadt, 1967), 74–75. ["We herewith *protest* and testify openly before God our sole Creator, Preserver, Redeemer and Saviour (who, as we mentioned before, alone searches and knows all hearts, and therefore will judge justly) [and] likewise before all men and creatures, that we for ourselves, our subjects and in behalf of all, each and every one, consider null and void the entire transaction and the intended decree, which in the aforementioned or in other cases, is undertaken, agreed and passed, against God, his holy Word, all our soul's salvation and good conscience, likewise against the formerly announced decree of the Diet of Speier—(and we protest not secretly, nor willingly, but for reasons above stated and others good and well-founded." *A History of Christianity: Readings*, ed. C. Manschreck (Englewood Cliffs, N.J.: Prentice-Hall, 1964), 41.]

99. On the conclusion of the event on April 19, Kühn, *Speyrer Reichstag*, 188ff.

100. To Amsdorf, March 15, 1529, WA Br 5:40 / 8–9.

from the Lord, for we have no hopes concerning a council that is being talked about [now]."[101] The negative outcome of the diet did not disturb him unduly. He was much more anxious about the news that Melanchthon, back from Speyer on May 14 and exhausted,[102] conveyed to him: Philip of Hesse had made a new alliance with several cities. Remembering the negotiations on alliances conducted in Weimar only the previous year, which had fortunately foiled such plans, Luther at once sent word on May 22 to Elector John and begged him not to become "woven into or bound by the alliance-making" of Philip. He had a threefold reason for his warning: (1) "such an alliance is made neither by God nor by trust in God but rather by human ambition." The sure result is counteralliances, which otherwise would perhaps not have come into being. Besides, the landgrave "is a hotheaded young sovereign." As he demonstrated the previous year, he could shift quickly from defense to attack. (2) "The worst thing is that in such an alliance we are forced to include those who work against God and the sacrament [of the altar]," as in the case of the cities in Upper Germany. (3) "God has at all times in the Old Testament condemned such alliances of human aid" and cautioned men to trust in his help instead. And again, "one cannot put this kind of trust in the landgrave, who was once so terribly wrong, especially since up to now he has experienced neither a change [of mind] nor any contrition or sorrow about it."[103] Luther expressed the same misgivings two months later, apparently in reply to an inquiry from the elector. This time he was more precise and expansive as he wrote in the name of the Wittenberg theologians. His observations point to a growing linkage of confession and alliance among the imperial estates of Lutheran persuasion as it was then in process of formation.[104]

101. To Link, May 6, 1529, WA Br 5:62 / 10ff. [LW 49:220.]

102. WA Br 5:61, n. 3.

103. WA Br 5:76–77. Luther refers to Isa. 7:8, 30, and to other Bible passages. [LW 49:225, 226, 227.]

104. WA Br 5:78–81. Also H. von Schubert, *Bekenntnisbildung und Religionspolitik 1529 / 30 (1524–1534): Untersuchungen und Texte* (Gotha, 1910), 54–55.

23

Confession and Alliances

While those on the evangelical side were considering common action against the church politics of the empire and of the papal-minded estates, they found themselves divided over the Lord's Supper. This induced movement in two directions: the one, to overcome internal division by means of theological discussion; the other, to foster federation under one party or the other within the bounds of its convictions. The second option was the way preferred by Landgrave Philip and the Upper German cities, to the extent that they stood close to Zwingli and the Swiss; the first option was preferred by Electoral Saxony and similarly pro-Lutheran sovereigns and cities. Philip of Hesse, active in both directions, eagerly sought to win Luther and the other Wittenberg theologians for his own efforts at a settlement.

The Lutherans attained their goal sooner than the others. Their theologians in Wittenberg, Nuremberg, Franconian-Brandenburg, and South Germany [especially Württemberg] comprised a consolidated group. They also agreed on two negatives as matters of policy: no fraternization with the Zwinglians and their adherents in Upper Germany [broadly, the southern Rhine Valley], and no political coalition against the emperor and the Catholic estates. Even so, on May 27, 1529, the Lutherans readied a deputation to the emperor in Spain (they kept the landgrave informed of their action) to appeal the recent action of the Diet of Speyer and present their protest against it.[1] Besides, in case the emperor and the Catholic estates should arm for war, Electoral Saxony and Hesse, as well as Strassburg, Nuremberg, and Ulm, had promised mutual military assistance or at least financial aid, having so promised in Speyer, on the day of the diet's action (April 22, 1529). To work out the details of this "understanding" they had agreed to meet in Rotach on June 6.[2] Rep-

---

1. Letter of Elector John to Landgrave Philip, May 17, 1529. Action for the sending of a deputation, taken May 27, printed in *Die Abschiede der Bündnis- und Bekenntnistage protestierender Fürsten und Städte zwischen den Reichstagen von Speyer und Augsburg 1529–1530, mit archivalischen Beilagen*, ed. E. Fabian (Tübingen, 1960), 22ff. On the protest, see above, p. 627.

2. Text of the "Verständnis" in H. von Schubert, *Bekenntnisbildung und Religionspolitik 1529 / 30 (1524–1534): Untersuchungen und Texte* (Gotha, 1910), 138ff., as well as RTA 7 / 2:1321ff., 818ff. Also J. Kühn, *Die Geschichte des Speyrer Reichstags 1529*, SVRG 146 (Leipzig, 1929), 233ff. Rotach, as it was then called, is today Rodach, near Coburg [in northernmost Bavaria].

resentatives of the respective [evangelical] estates and of Landgrave Philip gathered there.[3] Margrave George, governor of the frontier Mark Brandenburg, as well as his Franconian theologians before him, urged the framing of a common confession of faith as the basis of any alliance. After two days (June 8) the Rotach meeting got no further than to decide to meet again, this time in Schwabach [south of Nuremberg] on August 24.[4] This, however, gave the Wittenberg theologians time to draft a theological statement clarifying the position of the politically allied pro-Lutherans versus the old church [Catholic] as well as the Swiss Upper German groups. [As if anticipating these developments,] Elector John already in December 1528 had requested the Wittenbergers to undertake this assignment.[5] Even earlier, on October 28, 1528, Margrave George had made moves in this direction at a meeting in Coburg. Yet not only he, but finally also Hans [John Henry] von Schwarzenberg, the grand old baron, demanded that the two princes [Elector John and Landgrave Philip] and other evangelical estates should get together and "for the sake of their acts of commission and omission develop a unanimous opinion founded in God's Word and stand together in such a way as to make the opposition unable to charge that [as evangelicals] they err toward each other, are divisive or split."[6] The adjournment of the Rotach consultation, for its resumption in Schwabach in late August, presumably set a planned deadline. As it happens, the name Schwabach, as applied by researchers, has stuck to the articles of faith drawn up by the Wittenbergers. A further extension of the consultation beyond the Schwabach meeting made it possible to continue work on the not yet approved "Schwabach Articles." These could then also be utilized in working out still another confessional sequence known as the "Marburg Articles."[7]

The Schwabach Articles are no classical confession of faith in the sense of the ancient church, but they are a reflection—built on a Trinitarian foundation (arts. 1–3)—on the problems of faith facing Christendom with the coming of the Reformation, among them sin and justification—not by good works but by faith (arts. 4–6). To attain this faith, the office of preaching and its visible signs, the sacraments (baptism and the Lord's Supper), have been instituted by God (arts. 7–9). The elements—bread and wine as well as baptismal water—[joined to the words] "convey faith and also

---

3. Fabian, ed., *Abschiede*, 29–30, 34.
4. Ibid., 32.
5. Schubert, *Bekenntnisbildung*, 86, 88.
6. Ibid., 83. On Schwarzenberg, see above, p. 112, n. 13.
7. See below, p. 650 [also n. 8, below].

exercise it in all those who desire this sacrament and do not act against it" (art. 10). Private confession should not be forced, any more than the sacraments and the gospel should be forced (art. 11). The church, not bound to external forms or to people, will remain until Christ returns in judgment at the end of time. Until that day, government should be respected, for it has been assigned to maintain order and justice (arts. 12–14). The prohibition of priestly marriage, of meats and foods, the monastic life and its related vows, through which people seek grace and salvation, are doctrines of the devil; the mass, wherever regarded as a good work, is to be abolished, and the Lord's Supper is to offer the communicant both the elements; "to everyone for his faith and according to his own necessity" (arts. 15–16). Just so, ecclesiastical ceremonies contrary to the Word of God are to be abolished; "they are left free to be used or not, according to love, in order that offense may not be without cause or be thoughtlessly given, or the common peace be unnecessarily disturbed."[8] The Schwabach Articles did not serve to clarify the internal problems among the evangelicals. Their intention was rather to set forth the reason for a departure from the ways of the Roman church and to do so without being unduly severe.

Meanwhile, the efforts of Landgrave Philip of Hesse had overtaken those of the Lutherans. While the Lutherans were endeavoring to fashion a common confession for their adherents, the landgrave was seeking [and finding] ways of overcoming the tensions between the two evangelical camps by means of a thorough theological discussion. His letter of June 1529 invited Luther and Melanchthon to come to Marburg at Michaelmas, September 29, for a conference with Oecolampadius.[9] The elector, whose mediation was undoubtedly important to the landgrave, cautioned Luther "for the good of the cause to give a positive reply, trusting God to grant his grace so that the discord among us over the sacrament might be overcome."[10] In his letter of June 23, Luther praised the land-

---

8. WA 30³:81–91; citation is according to the 1970 revision, 18ff. *Die Augsburgische Konfession im deutschen und lateinischen Text mit Erklärung des Inhalts und Beifügung der Hauptquellen*, ed. H. H. Wendt (Halle, 1927), 137ff. [Text in English, with the Schwabach and Marburg articles in parallel columns, *The Book of Concord*, trans. H. E. Jacobs (Philadelphia, 1883), 2:69–74. Also in *The Augsburg Confession: A Collection of Sources with an Historical Introduction*, by M. Reu (Chicago, 1930), Schwabach Articles, 40–44.]

9. The landgrave's letter is lost. Luther's draft reply (WA Br 5:104–5) and, perhaps according to the copy in the electoral court, the original have been preserved (WA Br 5:101–2). The difference between the two versions is overrated by W. Köhler, *Zwingli und Luther* (Gütersloh, 1953), 2:50–51. The things he cites as clear differences in the final copy are almost all in the original as well. [*LW* 39:(228–29) 229–31.]

10. WA Br 5:101 / 9–10.

grave for his earnestness and high intention. At the same time, however, he admitted his own uneasiness that the partners from Upper Germany had chosen their way over Philip instead of turning to the Wittenbergers directly. By winning the support of so important a sovereign they of course tried to show that there was nothing amiss in their teaching and "that they may disgrace us in Your Sovereign Grace's name [and put the blame on us] for not wishing peace and truth."[11] Luther then requested the landgrave to ascertain whether the opposition were prepared to concede any of the opinions they held, for if both parties were to contend that nothing is negotiable, a conference would be useless. As for himself, Luther wrote: "I certainly know that I am unable to yield, [for] I know that they are wrong, . . . having also become familiar with the basis of their position."[12] "Then it would be better had we let the matter rest as it is now, and let it take its course wherever it goes, for in short I cannot expect anything good from the devil, no matter how nice he may appear to act."[13] Nevertheless he declared himself prepared to come, "though I fear [my services] may be futile and perhaps dangerous for us."[14] With a hesitation that also spoke for his Wittenberg colleagues, Luther, in late July or early August, repeated and expanded his warning against Philip's plans for an alliance. As early as May 22 he had expressed his concerns to the elector,[15] but now added several observations on the doubtful character of this alliance in particular. In case an alliance were made with these heretics of the sacrament, the Wittenberg side would even have to defend the changes they made in worship: "The opponents also make matters much too difficult because without any felt need of their own for the sacrament [of the altar] they then do away with all ceremonies, making a simple meal of it, which

11. *WA* Br 5:101 / 23–24. [*LW* 49:230.]

12. *WA* Br 5:102 / 34ff., 42–43. [*LW* 49:231.]

13. *WA* Br 5:102 / 47ff. [*LW* 49:231.]

14. *WA* Br 5:101 / 15–16.

15. "First, this much is certain, that such an alliance is not from God or from trust in God, but is a creation of human pride, and its quest is for human help alone, to be defiant in it, all of which has no good foundation and thus can bring no good fruit, especially seeing that such alliance is unnecessary, since the papist crowd is not up to very much, nor has it enough heart to start something, and God has protected us against them with the good walls of his might. Such an alliance achieves nothing better than that it causes the opponents to do the same thing and to make an alliance of their own. . . . On top of that there is cause for anxiety, and it is perhaps all too certain that the landgrave, having formed such an alliance and being himself a restless young sovereign, would like to not hold still but rather, as happened a year ago, find some reason not only to defend but also to attack; and it is not godly for us to act this way, since no one is chasing or looking for us." *WA* Br 5:76 / 20–77 / 34. A further citation from this letter is on p. 655, below, n. 105.

we cannot decently defend."[16] Luther also treated counterarguments: The alliance is not concerned with doctrine but directs itself against threats by external forces. To this Luther replied, "That's not so, for one knows that the opponents will attack us for no other reason than for the sake of doctrine." Nor can one depend on it that doubtful allies "will foreseeably come to some understanding." So Luther repeated yet again that one must in any case honestly declare oneself. But this would mean that "made equal with them, our sure understanding would fall under their wavering or delusion. That would amount to denying more than half if not all of our faith."[17]

The attempt at alliance-building between the Lutherans and the Upper Germans quickly failed, and without so much as achieving a theological clarification. At this point the landgrave's plan broke the deadlock. A dialogue between the most important speakers on both sides should fashion the foundation thus far lacking. Early in July, from his castle Friedewald, Philip dispatched official letters of invitation to Luther and Melanchthon, Zwingli in Zurich, Oecolampadius in Strassburg, Jacob Sturm (the mayor) in Strassburg (including Bucer and one additional preacher), and Andreas Osiander in Nuremberg. The actual leaders of the disputation would be Luther and Melanchthon versus the two Swiss, Zwingli and Oecolampadius.[18] When George, margrave of Brandenburg-Ansbach, learned of these invitations, he requested that John Brenz of Schwäbisch-Hall be included. After all, his argument with Oecolampadius in the *Syngramma Suevicum* had won him high repute among the Lutherans.[19]

As September waned the colloquists began arriving in Marburg, each side with its entourage of adherents. Zwingli appeared first, on Septem-

---

16. WA Br 5:79 / 33ff., 41ff., esp. 80 / 61ff.; *schlechte (schlichte) Kollation:* simple meal in cloisters on holidays before the reading of the lessons. A. Sturm, "Collatio," *LThK* 2 (1931): 1012–13. *Glimpflich* = with decency. On the dating, Schubert, *Bekenntnisbildung*, 54–55.

17. On the opposite arguments, WA Br 5:80 / 65ff. On Luther's opinion, also Köhler, *Zwingli und Luther*, 2:41ff.

18. WA Br 5:108–9. *Zwinglis sämtliche Werke*, ed. E. Egli, G. Finster, et al. (Berlin, 1905ff.), 10 (1929): 185ff., no. 868 (including a letter to the council in Zurich). Oecolampadius: by arrangement with Jacob Sturm in Strassburg. E. Staehelin, *Briefe und Akten zum Leben Oekolampads* (Leipzig, 1902ff.), 2:335ff. J. Sturm, *Politische Korrespondenz der Stadt Strassburg*, vol. 1, no. 632. *Osiander: Urkunden aus der Reformationszeit* (includes the years 1521–67 and brings mainly the political correspondence of Philip of Hesse), ed. C. G. Neudecker (Kassel, 1836), 108ff. The letters are at times toned down to the recipient and contain suggestions on the safest way to travel. Overview of these letters and the replies in Köhler, *Zwingli und Luther*, 2:51ff.

19. Neudecker, ed., *Osiander: Urkunden*, 96–97. On the *Syngramma*, see above, pp. 517ff.

ber 28 with a smaller group; Luther appeared on September 30 with a somewhat larger group. From around Marburg, many people came to listen or simply to see.[20] Among them was Duke Ulrich of Württemberg. Driven from his country in 1519 by the Swabian League, he had been granted asylum by Landgrave Philip in 1526. Philip himself, arranger of this unusual dialogue, had a major stake in its success.[21] His engaging hospitality, his art of gently stimulating the proceedings, and his own restraint in the early stages of the colloquy created a relaxed atmosphere. Before the major and public discussions began, Philip arranged for the participants to meet privately in pairs and sound each other out. Nor did the two dynamic leaders talk face to face at once; first it was Luther and Oecolampadius, Zwingli and Melanchthon. The landgrave hoped that these intimate conversations would reveal certain irenic possibilities. Philip listened in only occasionally, and then just long enough to encourage friendliness in personal exchange.[22] But friendliness was an elastic term. Luther thought he had conformed to it.[23] Oecolampadius, to the contrary, felt that he had fallen into the hands of another [John] Eck.[24] As for the actual content of these private talks, we have only Melanchthon's hazy reference: "D[octor] Luther challenged Oecolampadius on many articles, some of which he had written incorrectly; in part, hard talking echoed, suggesting more and greater errors."[25]

20. For the routes the participants traveled and the composition of the parties, see Köhler, *Zwingli und Luther*, 2:63ff.

21. Texts and reports, WA 30³:92ff., plus a supplement on revision, 22ff. Good selection in G. May, *Das Marburger Religionsgespräch 1529*, TKTG 13 (Gütersloh, 1970); hereafter cited as (M)*MRG*. Full account and evaluation in Köhler, *Zwingli und Luther*, 2:66ff. Further literature in (M)*MRG*, 9ff. [For an ecumenical update over four centuries later, see *Marburg Revisited: A Reexamination of Lutheran and Reformed Traditions*, ed. P. C. Empie and J. I. McCord (Minneapolis: Augsburg, 1966). Also the Leuenberg Agreement (1973), a statement of concord by representatives of Europe's Reformation churches (Lutheran, Reformed, United) and subsequently adopted by most of them; text, *Lutheran World* (Lutheran World Federation), 20 (1973):347–53.]

22. Köhler, *Zwingli und Luther*, 2:76ff. F. Blanke in *Zwinglis sämtliche Werke*, 6/2 (1968): 491. References for the Marburg Colloquy also in Staehelin, *Briefe und Akten Oekolampads*, 2:367ff.

23. Luther to John Agricola, October 12, 1529, WA Br 5:160/9ff.

24. This was Zwingli reporting, with a plea for discretion, to Vadian, October 20, 1529; *Zwinglis sämtliche Werke*, 10:316. (M)*MRG* 80. Oecolampadius was alluding to the disputation in Baden, in Aargau (1526).

25. To Duke Heinrich of Saxony, probably in early October 1529, *CR* 1:1103. The comparison with the following much more exact report of Melanchthon on his own conversation with Zwingli shows only that he conveyed nothing but Oecolampadius's impression of the Oecolampadius-Luther conversation. Although requested to do so, it is not very likely that Luther shared with Brenz the line of argument he had taken (Köhler, *Zwingli und Luther*, 2:77–78). This is according to *Anecdota Brentiana: Ungedruckte Briefe und Bedenken von Johannes Brenz*, comp. and ed. T. Pressel (Tübingen, 1868), 69–70, where it is printed without reference. WA 30³:153–54.

The Zwingli-Melanchthon talks lasted six hours, twice as long as those of Luther and Oecolampadius, but their context was simpler. Zwingli and Melanchthon did not confront each other as gruffly as Luther and Zwingli, including Zwingli's adherents, and so these two could discuss freely with each other, each of them feeling reassured for having caused the opponent to back down at certain points. Short reports, written immediately after the talks, reveal this. Melanchthon informed Elector John that the Wittenbergers had reproached their partners for a number of unpardonable false points in their teaching. Zwingli and his side had been denying original sin, recognizing only external misdeeds as sin; they had also been separating the Spirit from Word and sacrament and basing righteousness not on faith but on the works proceeding from faith. They had, however, remained open to instruction. "The more they heard of it, the better they liked it, and withdrew from all these points although they had earlier written otherwise."[26] Zwingli, for his part, drew up a concise record, which he let Melanchthon look over and edit. Yet this did not keep Zwingli from writing to Vadian and giving the following reason for making the kind of record he did:

> Because Melanchthon is extremely slippery and, like Proteus, can transform himself into anything imaginable, he forced me—aided by a penholder instead of salt—to arm and dry my hand the better to hold on to this man who bares his teeth while searching for who-knows-what kind of ways to escape or slip through.[27]

In contrast to Melanchthon's letter to the elector, Zwingli's record of their discussion included only the two themes that mattered most to him: Word and sacrament. Melanchthon is said to have agreed: "Words can no more than signify" (*verba nihil posse quam significare*). Even so they had agreed: "The Spirit works justification in us by means of the Word. The Word, however, is to be understood not in the material [in contrast to the formal!] sense, but as the Word that is preached and comprehended, that is, as the mind and marrow of the Word" (*verbum praedicatum et intellectum, hoc est: mens et medulla verbi*). Although Melanchthon tried to meet Zwingli's intellectual concept of the Word in the sacrament as far as possible, he nevertheless clung to Luther's interpretation. Here Zwingli could

26. *CR* 1:1099. W. Köhler, *Das Marburger Religionsgespräch 1529: Versuch einer Rekonstruktion*, SVRG 148 (Leipzig, 1929), 45; hereafter cited as (K)*MRG*. Köhler, *Zwingli und Luther*, 2:78ff.

27. The protocol: *Zwinglis sämtliche Werke*, 6 / 2:507ff. (with a thorough introduction by F. Blanke). (K)*MRG* 40ff. (M)*MRG* 31–32. Letter to Vadian, October 20, 1529, *Zwinglis sämtliche Werke*, 10:316 / 9ff. (also Blanke, in ibid., 6 / 2:491–92). (M)*MRG* 80–81.

not go along, as though "in a hidden manner" Christ gave his body to eat. Zwingli declared this notion to be contrary to Scripture. Melanchthon replied that one is not permitted "without compelling testimony from the Scriptures to depart from the actual sense of the words." Christ's body is not limited to a given place, but "he ascended far above all heavens that he might fill all things" (Eph. 4:10). The risen One is able to be everywhere, wherever he would.[28] Melanchthon had conceded several of Zwingli's points, without allowing himself to be separated from Luther on the decisive ones. He was completely truthful when he said repeatedly: "Believe me, dear Zwingli, if I were able to share your opinion I would do so gladly and without hesitation."[29]

On Saturday morning, October 2, at six o'clock the main colloquy was formally opened. Zwingli had desired a general discussion among all the theologians as well as the guests on hand for the occasion. Luther had proposed a limited circle of disputants, a suggestion favored by the landgrave and Duke Ulrich of Württemberg and their councillors too. The colloquy [or dialogue] was to take place in the presence of the sovereigns and representatives of the imperial estates and should be carried on by the learned of the universities of Marburg and Wittenberg and other knowledgeable people. The number of those present varied from twenty-four to fifty or sixty, depending on the session.[30] The landgrave's chancellor (Philip's general secretary), Johann Feige, opened the colloquy proper. He thanked the participants in the dialogue for having undertaken the taxing journey to Marburg and, in the name of his sovereign, encouraged them to leave their passions behind and to seek only "God's praise, the common good of Christians and brotherly unity."[31] Then he gave Luther the floor first. Addressing the landgrave, Luther said he was convinced that this colloquy had been called with the best of intentions. As recently as two years earlier he had turned down the idea because he believed that enough had been written and that neither side had any fresh arguments. He too had expressed his opinion and would not change it as long as he lived. However, the landgrave's suggestion, based on the Diet of Speyer, has found him responsive. He is gladly taking part in the dialogue and, firm as it stands, is ready to express his opinion. He also reminded the

28. *Zwinglis sämtliche Werke*, 6 / 2:507 / 3ff.; 508 / 12–509 / 12. Also the explanation of Blanke. (M)*MRG* 31–32. (K)*MRG* 40ff.

29. Report of Hedio in (M)*MRG* 17.

30. Twelve (according to Zwingli's letter to Vadian, October 20); "at most fifty or sixty" (Brenz to Schradinus, November 14). (M)*MRG* 80,82. Köhler, *Zwingli und Luther*, 2:84.

31. Reports of Osiander and Hedio in M(*MRG*) 17. (K)*MRG* 52.

assemblage that in addition to the Lord's Supper other differences exist over against the churches of Zurich, Basel, and Strassburg. Among these he cited the differing concepts of the doctrine of the Trinity, the two natures of Christ, original sin, baptism, justification (is it by faith alone or in part also by individual effort?), the preaching ministry, and purgatory.[32] If, Luther concluded, no agreement exists on these and perhaps on still other matters of faith, then negotiations on the question of the Lord's Supper alone would be fruitless.

The opposing party disputed Luther's claim that earnest differences existed. Zwingli referred to his conversation with Melanchthon and to printed statements as he pressed for a treatment of the Lord's Supper. Luther wished not to reject it but meant to refer to the broader horizon on which it stood. The questions he named had already been debated publicly. Therefore he thought they should not go unnoticed by the Marburg dialogue, if for no other reason than "that at home no one would say he was not allowed to open his big mouth." If the opposing side is unwilling to talk about these subjects, he would be satisfied to voice his disagreement and so proceed gladly to debate the Lord's Supper.[33] In any case, the disputation on the Supper, Luther insisted, would have to turn not on arguments of reason but on evidence from the Holy Scriptures. As a sign of his position he chalked the pivotal passage on the table, "Hoc est corpus meum," and then replaced the velvet table cover over it.[34] The first to offer a critique of Luther's realistic interpretation of this passage was Oecolampadius.[35] His chief weapon, as in the earlier literary controversy,[36] was Christ's dispute with the Jews (John 6), especially the sentence "The flesh is of no avail" (6:63). The words of institution, he contended, are figurative akin to other sayings of Christ (rock, vine, seed).[37]

32. See here the theologically especially rewarding report (apparently Lutheran-minded) by "Anonymus," in (M)*MRG* 41. Presumably it was written by one of the participants who developed it later on the basis of his own notes, (M)*MRG* 40ff., as also in WA 30³:110–43. About its value, see (K)*MRG* 3.

33. This short prelude is attested by two participants in their reports, the Strassburger Caspar Hedio and an unnamed person who apparently was of the Lutheran side. (K)*MRG* 43ff., 55. (M)*MRG* 17, 40ff. Köhler, *Zwingli und Luther*, 2:86, doubts the authenticity of the German text, but unjustifiably so. Their ring is convincing, as is their reference to the breadth of the discussion going on for years between Luther and the Upper Germans, from whom the sacramental question would not have itself dissociated.

34. According to the reports of Zwingli's companions, Rudolf Collin and Andrew Osiander. (K)*MRG* 57. (M)*MRG* 33, 52. Luther probably used the Latin version; the German appears in Osiander's report to the Nuremberg council.

35. (M)*MRG* 18ff. (K)*MRG* 57ff.

36. See above, p. 534.

37. (M)*MRG* 18–19. (K)*MRG* 57–58.

Luther rejected such a dual understanding of the words of Christ, even though it might be upheld by a theologian like Augustine, whom Oecolampadius had cited. Luther rebutted that God is able, if he wills, to grant spiritual gifts in physical food: in the preached Word, in baptism, in the sacrament of the altar. Indeed, he put it bluntly, "I'd be ready to eat dung if he commanded it. A servant doesn't get moody over the will of his Lord."[38]

With that retort the dialogue ran aground. Luther held fast to the words of institution, Oecolampadius to the necessity of interpreting them spiritually, figuratively. Zwingli now jumped into the debate. He declared Luther's opinion downright prejudiced, and once again introduced the argument of John 6:63 ("the flesh is of no avail").[39] Luther replied by pointing out Zwingli's own prejudice, namely, that God does not require anything incomprehensible of us. Are not the virgin birth and the forgiveness of sins just as unfathomable as the physical presence of Christ in the sacrament? "If we knew his ways, then he would not be unfathomable— he, the miraculous One!"[40] If Zwingli accepts a transferred expression, a trope, in connection with the Lord's Supper, why then not also apply this method to the words "He ascended into heaven?"[41] The back-and-forth arguing grew ever more heated. Zwingli, turning cocky, gibed, "You'll be singing me a different song," and once again picked up his main weapon, John 6:63. Luther parried this thrust, saying that this verse has nothing to do with the Lord's Supper. But Zwingli hung in there, unwilling to yield his key passage, and thrust again: "This locus will break your neck." Luther parried again, taunting: "Don't brag too much. Necks don't break that way. You're in Hesse, not in Switzerland. The body of Christ is dead, poison and devil to those who eat it unworthily. Death, prison, and other things are evil, and yet when the Word is added, they become salutary." When combined with the Word, the body of Christ becomes most highly beneficial, being distributed in the sacrament and received in faith.[42] Therewith Luther knocked the "no avail" of the Johannine passage out of Zwingli's hand. Osiander, satisfied with the outcome, reported to the Nuremberg city council, "So a half-day was spent on this verse [John 6:63], and many judged Luther the winner, so that also the other party

38. (M)*MRG* 19. (K)*MRG* 64.
39. (M)*MRG* 20ff. (K)*MRG* 13 / 66ff.
40. (M)*MRG* 21. (K)*MRG* 15.
41. (M)*MRG* 23. (K)*MRG* 18, 74.
42. (K)*MRG* 19ff.; sources in ibid., 75ff. Brief summary by Hedio, in (M)*MRG* 23.

admitted that this verse neither serves the matter being debated nor proves anything about it."[43]

On Saturday afternoon, October 2, Zwingli opened the second round by trying to trap Luther in a passage cited from one of his own Lenten sermons of 1525. In it Luther had spoken neither of John 6 nor of the Lord's Supper, but rather of the fact that God nourishes us not by bread alone but also through the powers of growth which he bestows. The substance and physiological process are to be distinguished. "In this manner he nourishes us outwardly with bread, but inwardly he provides us with digestion and growth which the bread [alone] cannot give."[44] Thus, in the Lord's Supper "benefit" comes about by faith. The same holds for Luther in the formulation by Melanchthon, which Zwingli quoted from the preliminary conversation: "Words can do no more than signify."[45] Grammatically that is correct, but the human word is mere sound (*vox*); it vanishes, no matter who speaks. So too "Emperor Maximilian has died." But we add: When anything is said through his Imperial Majesty, this happens not by our own power but by divine power." "We must learn to distinguish between our speaking and God's command."[46] What do we really know about the faith of those who speak the words in the sacrament? "We cannot prevent an evil priest from administering the sacrament." At this Zwingli broke in: "Then say too that godless [priests] do it!" Luther then pointed out the snare in which Zwingli had caught himself, adding, "Then you may neither have yourself baptized, nor permit yourself to hear the Word, nor receive the Lord's Supper. For you don't know whether the priest honestly means it." In Luther's eyes, Zwingli had thereby fallen among the Anabaptists and the Donatists.[47] Luther did not enjoy this part of the contest in a side court. Turning to his colleague, he urged, "Philipp, you say something too. I'm very tired." But Melanchthon continued to be silent.

Instead, Zwingli gained fresh support from Oecolampadius, even though it was not quite fortunate. The Basel theologian declared that Christ's word in talking to Nicodemus makes it unnecessary to eat the

43. Osiander's report in (M)*MRG* 52–53.

44. WA 17²:19ff., 26ff. (*Dauen* = modern German *Verdauen* = digestion.)

45. See above, p. 637.

46. According to Hedio's report in (M)*MRG* 24. (K)*MRG* 21–22, 80–81.

47. Donatism was a movement in the North African church during the fourth century. It declared that the administration of the sacraments and other official duties done by a priest guilty of mortal sin are invalid. Thereby Luther recalled Augustine's teaching on which, in another connection (see below, p. 645), Zwingli had relied.

body of Christ in the sacrament. How else can one interpret the words "unless one is born anew, he cannot see the kingdom of God" (John 3:3)? Luther explained: The right eating requires faith and rebirth. This is no contradiction. But Oecolampadius again used the same logic on John 16:7 and Rom. 8:11, where the accent falls on our hope depending on the going away and reawakening of Christ. According to Oecolampadius, these passages could not apply to the sacramental body. Luther shot back: "We do nothing of the kind, because faith beholds the body here present and the one in heaven." "I profess the Christ in heaven and in the sacrament."[48] To dispel the suspicion that he does not take the body [of Christ] seriously, Luther gave a confessionlike affirmation:

> When you claim the flesh as not beneficial, you may do so for all I care. We take our stand on the Word of God. The Word says, in the first place, that Christ has a body—this I believe. This body has ascended to heaven and sits at the Father's right hand—this too I believe. The Word then says: This body is in the Lord's Supper and is given us to eat—I also believe this, because my Lord Jesus Christ can easily do that if he so wills. And the fact that he wills to be present he affirms in his Word. In this I will firmly trust until he himself, through his own Word, says something to the contrary.[49]

Oecolampadius rebutted Luther's objection in a way to bring out most massively the contrast between the two sides: a body can be in one place only. Luther flatly rejected such mathematical arguments, adding that at an appropriate time he would be ready for a dispute on mathematics. Luther pointed out that he himself had earlier commented on this subject but that they had not understood him. Now, however, the issue turns on scriptural evidence. Oecolampadius at once offered an example. Christ had said, "For you always have the poor with you" [Matt. 26:11; Mark 14:7], meaning that according to his humanity we do not always have Christ. Therefore he cannot be present bodily in the Lord's Supper. Luther replied that this is the only one of Oecolampadius's arguments that has a glimmer in its favor. Yet it also contains a certain, clear sense: Christ will not be present in a manner that requires our services. In his stead he has given us the poor so that in his name we can do them good.[50] At that point he tried to trap Luther, charging that he too employed rhetorical figures, if not the trope's picture language then surely the synecdoche's usage, wherein a part designates the whole. To which Luther replied:

48. (M)*MRG* 25. (K)*MRG* 24–25.

49. From the report by Anonymus (see n. 32, above), (M)*MRG* 46. (K)*MRG* 25–26, 90.

50. (M)*MRG* 25, 46–47. (K)*MRG* 26ff., 91ff. Luther here refers to his *Confession Concerning Christ's Supper* (1528), WA 26:241ff. [*LW* 37:(153), 161ff.]

Those are two different matters. Synecdoche is not dispensable in any language: "Bring my sword" means sword with sheath. "Bring me a can" means a can of beer. In contrast to this, the metaphor, the trope, preserves the content. The synecdoche says: "This is there, and it's in there," the dove and in it the Holy Spirit (Matt. 3:16; John 1:33), the bread and in it the body of Christ.[51] Luther regretted this grammatical digression. Again he turned to Melanchthon: "Why don't you answer? I've washed myself weary."[52] But again Melanchthon held off.

Then Zwingli, seeing the discussion tangled in questions of grammatical logic, swung back to a christological argument: According to New Testament testimony, Christ appeared in human form (Rom. 8:3; Phil. 2:6ff.)[53] and "in every respect was like his brethren, yet without sin" (Heb. 4:15 [trans. from the German]). "He thus had a limited humanity." Augustine had said the same: "Is Christ's body above? Then it must be at a given place."[54] Luther, to the contrary [according to Zwingli], claims that the body of Christ is everywhere present and unlimited but that Christ is in one place and cannot be in many.[55] Luther rejected Zwingli's use of logic: The cited passages denote the likeness of Christ to the corporeality of his fellow human beings; it is not a statement limiting Christ's power. God is able to make the body of Christ present in one place or not in one place.[56] Zwingli, not about to deny this affirmation, nevertheless demanded proof that precisely in the Lord's Supper God makes the body of Christ present. Holy Scripture describes him in the crib, in the temple, in the desert, at God's right hand. But why make him present in the Lord's Supper as a special place?[57] Thereupon Luther threw back the vel-

---

51. (M)*MRG* 26, 46. According to the reports by Anonymus and Collin, this objection was raised by Zwingli. (M)*MRG* 47. (K)*MRG* 96. On synecdoche, see above, p. 512, n. 49.

52. (M)*MRG* 26 (from the report by the Strassburger, Hedio). (K)*MRG* 28, 96.

53. Zwingli cited the passages in Greek. Luther replied, "Read in German or Latin, not in Greek." Zwingli excused himself—perhaps with a bit of humanistic self-awareness (a "pricking irony," as Köhler describes it in *Zwingli und Luther*, 2:106, is too strong): "For the past twelve years," he said, "I have been using the Greek New Testament"; the Latin he had "read (through) only once." Luther meant "that in this sovereign company Greek is out of place" (ibid.). The censorious allegation of H. Dibbelt, "Hatte Luthers Verdeutschung des Neuen Testaments den griechischen Text zur Grundlage?" *ARG* 38 (1941): 318–19, that Luther had a deficient knowledge of Greek is here out of order. As for Dibbelt's critique of Luther's translation of the New Testament, see H. Bornkamm, "Die Vorlagen zu Luthers Übersetzungen des Neuen Testaments," *ThLZ* (1947): 23ff. Excerpt therefrom in H. Bornkamm, *Luther: Gestalt und Wirkungen*, SVRG 188 (Gütersloh, 1975), 65ff. *Martin Luther: Die gantze Heilige Schrift Deutsch, Wittenberg 1545* (Munich, 1972), 52.

54. (M)*MRG* 38. (K)*MRG* 32, 110.

55. (M)*MRG* 38. (K)*MRG* 30, 102.

56. (M)*MRG* 27. (K)*MRG* 32, 110.

57. (M)*MRG* 54. (K)*MRG* 30, 104.

vet table cover and pointed to his proof passage: "Hoc est corpus meum."
"Because the text of my Lord Christ stands there . . . , I truly cannot pass
it by but must confess and believe that the body of Christ is there."[58]
Zwingli jumped to his feet, "Then you too, Sir Doctor, set the body of
Christ spatially in the Lord's Supper, for you say, 'The body of Christ must
be there.' There, there! 'There' is surely an adverb of place where."
Luther replied that he had simply repeated the words of Christ and had
not been thinking of some other question like this. An adverb of place,
common to all mathematics, Luther would exclude completely from the
Lord's Supper text. The words are: "Hoc (non: ibi) est corpus meum"
[This (not: there) is my body]. Whether spatially or extraspatially, he
would rather not know than know. After all, God has revealed nothing on
this question and there is no one to prove it.[59] At that point the discussion
of October 2 [marking the first plenary session of the colloquy] came to an
end.

On Sunday morning, October 3, when the colloquy was resumed,
Zwingli picked up where he had left off. Yet this was to be no mere repetition, for in the meantime both sides had clarified their views. Zwingli
once again took up the formula in the Epistle to the Philippians (2:6ff.) and
proceeded to interpret the words *morphe, schema* (form). He concluded
from them, being treated there spatially, that the body of Christ "must
indeed have a place and be spatially present in it." For his part, Luther
had gone beyond rejecting the role of mathematical categories as a valid
argument and claimed he could prove his rejection. Even the universe is
not in one place (*machina mundi non est in loco*).[60] Or, according to Osiander's especially detailed report, "[The disputants] asked where has
God ever had a body? In place or sustained? Thereupon Luther answered:
The very biggest body, in which all others are included, namely the whole
world, contains God without a place where [designated for him]." "Thereupon they all fell silent."[61] Then Luther adduced the teaching of the scholastics.[62] This cost him a cynical crack from Zwingli: "It's not that becoming to you, Sir Doctor, that you must flee to the sophists." With that, he

58. (M)*MRG* 48. (K)*MRG* 31, 105.
59. (M)*MRG* 48. (K)*MRG* 31, 106.
60. (M)*MRG* 48–49, 27. (K)*MRG* 107ff.
61. (M)*MRG* 54. (K)*MRG* 108–9.
62. (M)*MRG* 38. (K)*MRG* 107–8.

turned again to the onions of the Egyptians (Num. 11:5).[63] Luther apparently overheard the banter and so picked up again his basic passage, "This is my body." Likewise, when Zwingli cited two passages from Augustine, which stated that bodies are bounded spatially, Luther held fast to the faith that God is able to break through this general rule and to sustain bodies outside each space.[64] When Zwingli objected, contending that this was turning a possibility into an actuality [*eine Möglichkeit auf ein Sein*], Luther remained unmoved. He could dismiss the reproach of the *petitio principii* (the appeal of principle) because so far as Luther was concerned the presence of Christ in the Lord's Supper is established independently through the words of institution. A discussion of several more passages from Augustine and Fulgentius led to the same outcome. Luther's comments on the two fathers tended to run beside the point and were not important except for this accentuation of the general rule: "When the fathers speak, they too must be understood according to the norm of Scripture."[65] For the audience this debate over the citations from the church fathers (it took virtually all of Sunday) was utterly tiresome. At any rate, as Osiander reported to his Nuremberg council, "On this subject we listened to them practically the entire day, while they hunted for, read, and translated their citations into German, which was very boring indeed."[66]

Even the colloquists realized that things could not go on like this. After one more brief skirmish, Oecolampadius proposed that the colloquy be ended. Without becoming more reasonable toward the subject at hand, Luther agreed, and assured the others that [he knew] they had meant it earnestly: "We know all too well that you had a great reason [to come together], but the concerns at hand have not been eased because of it."[67] The landgrave's chancellor, Feige, spoke once again to both sides, amicably urging them to find ways and means to become united. Luther re-

63. From a sentence in the report of Heinrich Utinger (WA 30³:101), which is supported by a note by Zwingli. On this see J. Staedtke, "Eine neue Version des sogenannten Utinger-Berichtes vom Marburger Religionsgespräch 1529," *Zwinglinana* 10 (1955): 210ff. It concerns a notation from the hand of Heinrich Bullinger (he wrote *Ziböllen*; Utinger, *Zwifel*. Cf. [K]*MRG* 107). ["Onions" are in the reference to the fleshpots of Egypt, and longing to return to what seemed like better days.]

64. (M)*MRG* 49–50. (K)*MRG* 32, 110.

65. (M)*MRG* 28. (K)*MRG* 34, 117. The norm is being designated as *regula Lutheri* ([M]*MRG* 28) by the Upper German side (Hedio) and as *regula Augustini* by the Lutheran side (Anonymus) ([M]*MRG* 50).

66. (M)*MRG* 55.

67. (M)*MRG* 56. (K)*MRG* 36.

sponded to this well-meant advice: "I know of no other means than that they give all honor to God's Word and believe with us."[68] After the Zwinglians had once again committed themselves to their cause, the colloquy ended on a friendly note. Luther commended his opponents to God and divine judgment; he thanked Oecolampadius for representing their cause not in bitterness but in friendship. He also thanked Zwingli, even though he had sometimes been quite sharp, and he also asked Zwingli's pardon if he himself had been severe toward him—he too is flesh and blood. Zwingli, moved to tears, said he knew no one in Italy or France whom he would rather face than Luther. Luther, for whom this protestation of friendship was almost too much, replied, "Pray God that you gain insight." Oecolampadius replied in kind, saying, "You pray for it also. You need it as much as we."[69]   Following this ending of the colloquy proper, the mayor of Strassburg, Jacob Sturm, brought up another topic [namely, what next?]. Osiander's report on Sturm is the fullest:

> He had been sent in hopes that the schism over the sacrament would be healed, et cetera. Now he leaves with the impression that this meeting turned on but one disputed article, though others could likely be adduced. And when he now brings the message home, he could come off badly, et cetera; for he is eager to hear the teaching of his preachers and to testify in what respects they are doing it correctly or incorrectly.[70]

What will they say to him in the Strassburg city council when, having been sent to Marburg with two preachers, he now returns home not with one false doctrine, but two?[71] After Sturm, Bucer was given the floor.

> He [Bucer] reported mainly about our Strassburg teaching on the Trinity, on Christ, on justification, on baptism, etc. He then requested a testimony from Dr. Luther. This Luther declined to do and told him approximately the following: "It doesn't concern me what you in Strassburg teach. I don't intend to be your teacher. You have my writings and my confession." Hearing that, Bucer asked Luther whether he would like to treat him as a brother or whether, in Luther's opinion, he was erring—so that he might improve himself. Luther declined to say, and commended us [Strassburgers] to God's judgment.[72]

68. (M)*MRG* 56. (K)*MRG* 37.

69. (M)*MRG* 28–29. (K)*MRG* 36–37, 125ff. Luther's peace-making words are omitted in Osiander ([M]*MRG* 56. [K]*MRG* 125).

70. (M)*MRG* 56. According to a report of [the Strassburger Caspar] Hedio concerning the doctrine of the Trinity as taught in Strassburg, (M)*MRG* 29. (K)*MRG* 37. Also, see above, pp. 638–39.

71. (M)*MRG* 29 (Hedio's report).

72. (M)*MRG* 29. (K)*MRG* 129.

To this report by Hedio, Osiander added a still more sharp utterance of Luther's:

> I am not your lord, not your judge, nor your teacher—so then our spirit and your spirit don't agree. Clearly we do not have the same spirit, for that can hardly be one spirit when at one place one simply believes the words of Christ and at the other one calls the same faith into question, fights it, treats it as a lie, and lays hands on it with all kinds of mischievous slander. Therefore, as I have said, we commend you to the judgment of God. Teach what you can defend in God's presence.[73]

It was no accident that at Marburg Luther's harshest words were aimed not at Zwingli but at Bucer. As the days at Marburg ended, Luther's earlier expressed judgment seemed substantiated, for it was at the outset that Luther greeted Bucer with a smile but also with a raised finger, taunting, "You are a rascal."[74] Since the chasm between them had opened Bucer tried to leap across it in that he requested a theological attestation and a fraternal recognition. Luther would have none of it. In this situation he could reply only in a way that the difference between them would be neither covered over nor made harmless.

To the landgrave's credit the deadlocked dialogue was continued. Still on the evening of October 3 he assigned both sides the task of pondering wherein they were united.[75] This resulted in a draft, presumably by Osiander, of a concluding formulation that should be signed by Luther and Oecolampadius.[76] It contained: (1) Far-reaching common ground: "We confess that by virtue of the words 'This is my body, this is my blood' the body and blood of Christ truly (that is, substantively and essentially but not quantitatively nor spatially) are present in the Supper and are there given." (2) Both sides should admit those points wherein they have misunderstood their counterparts: the Lutherans in that they had thought "that

73. (M)*MRG* 56–57. (K)*MRG* 129.

74. "Tu es nequam" (Hedio's report), (M)*MRG* 15. Probably the events of 1526 [the translation prank] were lingering in Luther's memory; see above, pp. 524ff.

75. Here, above all, the reports of Osiander and Brenz in (M)*MRG* 57, 84. (K)*MRG* 132–33.

76. (M)*MRG* 66, n. Köhler, *Zwingli und Luther*, 2:116. The scholastic terminology occurring also elsewhere in Osiander's writings (see ibid., 1:577–78) would indicate him rather than Melanchthon as author, although H. Grass, *Die Abendmahlslehre bei Luther und Calvin*, 2d ed. (Gütersloh, 1954), 127, n. 1, favors Melanchthon. The short formulation has a different style, and this has been treated by W. H. Neuser, "Eine unbekannte Unionsformel Melanchthons vom Marburger Religionsgespräch 1529," *ThLZ* 21 (1965): 181ff. Cf. also W. H. Neuser, *Die Abendmahlslehre Melanchthons in ihrer geschichtlichen Entwicklung (1519–1530)*, BGLRK 26 (Neukirchen-Vlynn, 1968), 308ff.

our dear sirs and brothers Oecolampadius, Zwingli, and their partners completely rejected the true presence of the body and blood [of Christ in the Supper]; the Swiss in that they had so far thought that Luther, Melanchthon, and their party held "that the body of Christ and his blood are in the Supper quantitatively or qualitatively or locally according to human thought." (3) Both sides should make it clear against whom they are really setting boundaries. Luther not against Oecolampadius and Zwingli "but against those who deny entirely the presence of [Christ's] body in the Supper." Oecolampadius "against those who place Christ's body and blood in the bread and wine emphatically and with great imagination."[77] The formulation sought to achieve an essential mutuality by differentiating the bodily presence of Christ and by fashioning statements of mutual concessions. But this was impossible. Anything like a "substantial and essential presence of the body of Christ" overtaxed the Swiss. Even if they had been able to achieve some reconciliation with their own earlier theological statements, they would not be able to do so with the simple expressions of faith in which they had brought up their congregations.[78]

In place of a dubious formula of unity a declaration of fifteen "Marburg Articles" was produced. Setting forth what united the two sides and adding what divided them, these articles were drafted by Luther at the request of the landgrave. Skillfully Luther built up the concluding assertion, not only treating the acute problem debated during the previous days but also providing a broader base for it. The numbered articles can be summed up in four groups: First, doctrines commonly held "by the entire Christian church in the world" according to the Nicene Council and Creed: creation, the Holy Trinity, the virgin birth, the person of Christ, original sin, the work of salvation (arts. 1–5). Second, common evangelical teachings: rejection of the idea of merit, acceptance of faith as a gift and as righteousness before God through the preaching of the gospel, baptism, "good works" as the working of the Holy Spirit, confession (as "unforced and free") (arts. 6–11). Third, against Anabaptist views: affirmation of holding public office, [voluntary continuation of traditions not conflicting with God's word,] the practice of infant baptism (arts. 12–14).

77. (M)*MRG* 66. (K)*MRG* 131–32. *Stattlich* = [emphatic in English].

78. (K)*MRG* 137. Bucer was of the same opinion (August 5, 1534) over against Ambrosius Blarer. *Briefwechsel der Brüder Ambrosius und Thomas Blarer 1509–1548*, ed. T. Schiess (Freiburg, 1908), 1:518. (M)*MRG* 66, n. 326. This formulation played a role as an allegedly Lutheran statement at the completion of the Württemberg Concord of 1534. See H. von Schubert, *Bekenntnisbildung und Religionspolitik 1529/30 (1524–1534): Untersuchungen und Texte* (Gotha, 1910), 103ff.

Fourth, on the Lord's Supper (art. 15), that which is held in common by the two sides:

> We all believe and hold concerning the Supper of our dear Lord Jesus Christ that both forms should be used according to the institution; . . . also that the sacrament of the altar is a sacrament of the true body and blood of Jesus Christ and that the spiritual partaking of this body and blood is especially necessary to every Christian. In like manner, as for the use of the sacrament, that as with the Word of God Almighty it has been given and ordained in order that weak consciences might be excited to faith by the Holy Spirit.

Then only does the actual Marburg theme follow:

> And although we are not at this time agreed on whether the true body and blood of Christ are bodily present in the bread and wine, nevertheless the one party should show to the other Christian love so far as conscience can permit, and both should fervently pray God Almighty that by his Spirit he would confirm in us true understanding. Amen.

The articles were signed by: Martinus Luther, Justus Jonas, Philippus Melanchthon, Andreas Osiander, Stephanus Agricola, Joannes Brentius, Joannes Oecolampadius, Huldrychus Zwingli, Martinus Bucerus, Caspar Hedio.[79] The mutual affirmation of Christian love was included in this confession at the express wish of Landgrave Philip.[80]

Surely the Marburg Articles were no statement of concord[81] [in the full sense], yet they offered the highest measure of agreement possible after so thorough an airing of the divisive problem. The question of the real presence of Christ in the elements was integrated into the spiritual sense of the sacrament. This meant more than a use of the name "brother," which had been urged by Bucer most of all. "Brother" would have expressed much less than the careful adding up of what was held in common and what must still remain open. Luther himself interpreted it this way to his wife in a letter written on the day [that the articles were signed]:

79. (M)*MRG* 67ff. *WA* 30³:160–71; 169 / 5–170 / 15. [*The Book of Concord*, trans. H. E. Jacobs (Philadelphia, 1883), 2:69–74.]

80. According to Bucer's account on October 18, 1529, to Ambrosius Blarer. Schiess, ed., *Blarer-Briefwechsel* 1:197. Cf. *WA* 30³:42 (revised appendix).

81. Köhler's unfortunate formulation "The Marburg Articles are in the best sense of the word a *Konkordie* [statement of concord]" (*Zwingli und Luther*, 2:127) led to a countering question by S. Hausammann: "Die Marburger Artikel—eine echte Konkordie?" *ZKG* 77 (1966): 288ff. Certainly not a genuine (*echte*) settlement but a pragmatic one, in which the main disputed points were segregated and the agreement on other points expressed, without further explanation. Surmises as to why certain articles were (later) altered are offered by Köhler (119ff.) and Hausammann (294ff.). In the same sense the detailed exchange between Bucer and Justus Jonas "on the most significant themes: Trinity, original sin, etc." were treated already by Jonas: "Concordavimus tantum relicto articulo eucharistiae, in quo non concordatum est," October 4, [1529], to Wilhelm Reifenstein, (M)*MRG* 75.

Grace and peace in Christ. Dear Sir Katie! You should know that our amiable colloquy at Marburg has come to an end and we are in agreement on almost all points, except that the opposition insists on affirming that there is only simple bread in the Lord's Supper and on confessing that Jesus Christ is spiritually present there. Today the landgrave is negotiating [to see] if we could be united or whether, even though we continue to disagree, we could not nevertheless consider ourselves brethren and members of Christ. The landgrave works hard on this matter. But we do not want this brother-and-member business, though we do want peace and good [will].

At the same time Luther gave Kate an assignment that his wife, versed in Latin, could discharge well, while at the same time arousing her own interest:

Tell Mr. Pomer [Bugenhagen] that the best arguments have been, in Zwingli's case, that a body cannot exist without a location, therefore Christ's body is not in the bread, [and] in Oecolampadius's case, [that] this sacrament is a sign of Christ's body. I assume that God has blinded them so that they had nothing else to offer. [82]

The Marburg Articles are a reworking of the so-called Schwabach Articles. [83] Luther not only omitted certain parts (church, celibacy, and biblical references) not essential for concluding the discussion with the Swiss and Upper Germans, but he also shortened the texts, omitted polemics, cast them in a more popular style, and showed pastoral concern. The focus bears more sharply on the congregations, to whom the Marburg participants would have to make their position intelligible. [84] The Marburg Articles have thus become a masterpiece among the confessions of Lutheran origin.

The substance of faith which Luther had expressed in the "I" of his *Confession Concerning Christ's Supper* (1528)[85] and which became basic in the forming of evangelical confessions now returned in the "we" of the common articles. Besides, Luther had made agreement easier for the Upper Germans and Swiss by omitting certain severities from his reworked

82. October 4, 1529, WA Br 5:154. [LW 49:236–37.] (M)MRG 72. On Kate's knowledge of Latin, see WA TR 4, no. 4860, 559 / 11ff. WA TR 5, no. 5567, 247 / 9–10.

83. See above, p. 632.

84. This consideration the Wittenbergers surmised as being even more important for the Swiss and the Upper Germans. Luther to Propst, June 1, 1530, WA Br 5:340. Melanchthon to F. Burkhard, October 8, 1529, MSA 7 / 2:105–4. MBW 828. *Briefe und Akten zu der Geschichte des Religionsgespräches zu Marburg 1529 und des Reichstages zu Augsburg 1530*, ed. F. W. Schirrmacher (Gotha, 1876), 376. Bucer to Ambrosius Blarer, August 5, 1534; assembled in (M)MRG 76, n. 413.

85. See above, pp. 549–51. [LW 37:161–372.]

Schwabach Articles that might have aggravated their differences, for example, over teachings on the two natures of Christ, original sin, the church, or baptism. Otherwise Luther emphasized demarcations over against the Roman church on which the Protestant groups were agreed.[86] Simplification as well as concentration on essentials made it easier for both sides to assert that they had surrendered nothing of their teaching. After the days of heated debate in Marburg this spawned certain triumphalist claims that on given issues the other side had retreated. The single question that had been thoroughly discussed at Marburg was bypassed in the interests of peace. Agreement had been achieved only on the anti-Roman understanding of this sacrament. While the process at Marburg fell short of reaching the desired unity, the landgrave at least attained a noble and honest Christian seal on conditions as they had been laid open.[87]

Luther set the tone of a peaceful adjournment in Marburg. His sermon on Tuesday morning, October 5, included not a word on the issues so recently debated. His text, from the pericope on the healing of the paralytic (Matt. 9:1–8), conveyed the great common theme of the evangelical churches: "Take heart, my son, your sins are forgiven. This is the sum total of the gospel." And Luther clearly set forth his motive for doing so: "I am all the happier to preach this sermon so that you may see the agreement between our teaching and the teaching of your preachers."[88] Luther was singling out no particular group but was attesting to that which in any case is the common bond. Writing to John Agricola on October 12, 1529, he again summed up his impressions:

> On the whole, they were awkward people, inexperienced in disputation. Although they could sense that their arguments were not logical, they nevertheless were determined not to yield at that one point, the presence of the body of Christ, and they did so, I believe, more out of fear and shyness than from ill will. On all other questions they made concessions, as you will notice from the published paper. Finally they requested us at least to recognize them as brothers, and the landgrave himself encouraged this. But that was more than we could grant. Nevertheless, we extended to one another the right hand of peace and love, so that in the meantime the bitter writings and

86. Details in the overview provided by Köhler, *Zwingli und Luther*, 2:119ff., and F. Blanke, in his introduction to the Notae Zwingli, according to which, on October 24, 1529, in Zurich's Great Minster, he confirmed his signing the Marburg Articles. *Zwinglis sämtliche Werke*, 6 / 2:532ff.

87. See n. 81.

88. "Ut videatis concordiam doctrinae nostrae cum doctrina praedicatorum vestrorum." From a copy made by Andreas Poach from the sermon as taken down by Rörer. WA 27:xiii / 1. WA 29: 564 / 9–10. It appeared in 1530 in a German version. On it, see Köhler, *Zwingli und Luther*, 2:130–31.

words could rest and that both sides could present their opinions without abuse, if not without rebuttal and refutation. [89]

In these weighed words the outcome of Marburg was conveyed: no unity in doctrine, yet an end to the embittered doctrinal controversy; no brotherliness that could be misunderstood, yet an equally upright and noble relationship to one another. Politically, and in light of its publicity, the Marburg Colloquy did not create the basis for an alliance. Yet those things that had been burdening the partners were put aside: radicalism and the heretical aspect of the Zwinglians, [90] and, conversely, the apparently catholicizing sacramentalism of the Lutherans. Along with their broadly unfolded common ground, each side had kept itself free from the liabilities of the other.

Because the proceedings in Marburg did not produce understanding on the decisive question—the doctrine of the Lord's Supper—there remained nothing for the pro-Lutheran sovereigns and cities to do but latch on to the consultations and plans emerging from the recent summer consultation in Rotach. [91] Even before the Marburg Colloquy adjourned, Luther received a letter, dated September 28, from Elector John, requesting him immediately upon adjournment and by the shortest route to come to him in Schleiz (in the Vogtland) and to bring with him Melanchthon and Jonas, but not the other Wittenbergers. In case a meeting in Schleiz failed, Luther would there find instructions whither to proceed. [92] Writing from Marburg on October 4, Luther closed the letter to his wife by mentioning his delayed return home. [93] Indeed, Luther missed the elector in Schleiz but finally caught up with him in Torgau on October 16. On October 18 he at last reached home. It had been an exhausting and long horseback ride from Marburg. He felt like one punched by Satan's messengers (2 Cor. 12:7), full of anxiety whether he would ever rejoin his family alive and in health. Besides, he had become especially alarmed en route by news that the Turks were besieging Vienna in force. He could only see this

89. *WA* Br 5:160 / 12ff. The first printing of the articles appeared in Marburg early in October 1529, *WA* 30³:102. A less informative and yet caustic letter was Melanchthon's to Agricola on the same day, *CR* 1:1107–10. *MSA* 7 / 2:106ff. *MBW* 829.

90. In his letter to Duke Henry of Saxony (ca. October 17), Melanchthon mentioned a number of Zwingli's heresies. *CR* 1:1102ff. *MSA* 7 / 2:119ff. *MBW* 832. Similar was his letter, about the same date, to Electoral Prince John Frederick. *CR* 1099ff. *MSA* 7 / 2:112ff. *MBW* 831. In all three letters Melanchthon underscored the impossibility of calling the others "brother."

91. See above, pp. 631–33.

92. *WA* Br 5:152–53.

93. *WA* Br 5:154 / 10–11. [*LW* 49:236.]

as an iron rod inflicted because of the terrible godlessness and ingratitude of the times.[94] Two days after his return home, Luther was meditating on his *Army Sermon Against the Turks* and writing.[95]

The results of Marburg were soon tested severely. One question of mounting intensity would not go away: What would it mean if the two [evangelical] groups, differentiated in faith yet united in the Speyer protest, were to form an alliance against possible action by the emperor? From Wittenberg an assessment of the meeting in Marburg was not ungratifying to Luther. "I rejoice that you," he wrote to Amsdorf in Magdeburg on October 17, "are so happy with our Marburg synod. In appearance it was small, but in subject matter it was richly productive." Luther's interpretation of Marburg looked beyond the human performance to a loftier context: "This has been accomplished by the prayers of the faithful; in fact, [the opposition] became so confused and cold that they yielded."[96] "Enough and more than enough they humbled themselves and sought brotherhood with us."[97] Already on October 20 he wrote Hausmann, "Articles have been published according to which they have made unexpectedly big concessions; they were very humble and modest."[98] This, however, was at best an assessment of mood but not as yet of a viable outcome. As usual, Landgrave Philip had the sharpest eyes for the political problem. For the consultation in Schwabach (October 16–19) he instructed his emissaries on two major motifs: (1) God's guidance at the Marburg Colloquy was such that "the learned [theologians] dealt with all articles in a harmonious and Christian way and parted as friends; so one sees that the false doctrine one had imagined to beset the main parts of our faith does not exist." Both sides are "one also on the reception of the sacrament." The dispute is limited entirely to "the essential, corporeal presence of the body of our Lord Jesus Christ. Luther also did not deny that Christ is not present locally, as in some city. Therefore discord has not separated the sides too far from each other, nor is it so great as to call forth pity, because in all parts of our Christian faith, in the love of neighbor and whatever pertains to his salvation, we are agreed, and in this way we should take leave of them." (2) The assembled councillors should

---

94. Letter to Amsdorf of October 19, 1529, *WA* Br 5:163 / 4ff.; to Link, October 28, *WA* Br 5:170 / 13ff. Actual return, October 18, also according to W. Schmitt, "Luthers Reise zum Marburger Religionsgespräch," *ARG* 28 (1931): 280.

95. *WA* 5:164 / 7; 166 / 6. On this, see also above, pp. 592ff.

96. *WA* Br 5:167 / 1ff. [*LW* 49:239–40. Alternate, to convey Bornkamm's version.]

97. October 28, to Link in Nuremberg, *WA* Br 5:3–4. Cf. also *WA* Br 5:160 / 7; 165 / 14.

98. *WA* Br 5:165 / 13–14.

bear in mind "what kind of rubbish results from separation. . . . For it remains a question of concern: Should one terminate with the Oberlanders [Upper Germans] and thus confine the best troops entirely to their own land? Those who hold such an opinion would be of little use to us."[99] The South German contingents of foot soldiers came out clearly in favor of joining forces with the Upper [Rhine Valley] Germans.

The problem of resistance against the emperor had been under discussion for years, long before the clash over the Lord's Supper had revealed the lack of unity on the evangelical side. Around New Year 1522–23, Pope Hadrian VI, through his legate Chieregati, demanded of the imperial diet, then meeting in Nuremberg, that the Edict of Worms be applied. It was then that Elector Frederick the Wise assigned the Wittenberg theologians the task of drafting an opinion on justified resistance against the emperor. Luther, Melanchthon, Amsdorf, and Bugenhagen, each in his own way, responded to the elector's request.[100]   Luther pointed out that the elector had always declared himself a layman who would not and could not form a judgment on this question of faith. Yet as layman he had also declared himself ready to pursue the truth when clearly evident. The elector thus cannot wage war for the evangelical cause but must yield to imperial power; for his part, the emperor can arrest or prosecute on electoral territory anyone whom he will. "After all, the agreed verdict of God and man—even though godless—makes the emperor the elector's overload." "If in spite of this the elector should take up arms to defend his cause, he must first confess publicly the right of that cause and retract his previous neutrality. Only then would he be permitted to initiate a war, not because it involves his subjects, but because he does so as a foreigner aiding strangers with help from a foreign land." He could do this only if he is called by a peerless Spirit and faith. "Otherwise he must yield completely to the sword of his superior and die with the Christians with whom he identifies."[101] It is significant that Luther bases the prince's right and duty to resist his overlord, the emperor, not only on his faith but even

99. Instructions (October 11, 1529) for the councillors Siegmund von Boineburg and Georg Kolmatzsch sent to Schwabach. Fabian, ed., *Abschiede* (see n. 1, above), 90. H. von Schubert, *Bekenntnisbildung*, 119.

100. WA Br 12:35–45 (with a full introduction by H. Volz). The texts are also in the well-annotated edition of H. Scheible, *Das Widerstandsrecht als Problem der deutschen Protestanten 1523–1546*, TKTG 10 (Gütersloh, 1969), with an extensive bibliography. Among the older studies, see esp. K. Müller, *Luthers Äusserungen über das Recht des bewaffneten Widerstandes gegen den Kaiser*, SBAW.PPH 8 (Munich, 1915). Among the recent studies, especially H. Dörries, "Luther und das Widerstandsrecht," in his *Wort und Stunde* (Göttingen, 1970), 3:195ff.

101. WA Br 12:39 / 3ff. Scheible, *Widerstandsrecht*, 17.

more so on his general duty to help not only his subjects but also strangers. Only defense against an opponent of equal rank can be undertaken according to the accepted rules of warfare (first an offer of peace to the aggressor, then, if necessary, resistance).[102] The remaining opinions, written during February 1523, depart from Luther's in various respects: Melanchthon's comes up with a sharper No to resistance against the emperor; Bugenhagen's and Amsdorf's tend toward Yes on resistance.[103]

The question of alliance and resistance, which Elector Frederick had first brought up for discussion in 1523, became full-blown only six years later in the much more earnest situation following the Diet of Speyer.[104] The Yes to resistance against the emperor was now upheld by Landgrave Philip of Hesse not simply in principle but also politically, and with all its practical consequences. Recalling the Pack affair, this was sufficient ground for Luther to advise most decisively against any reliance on weapons and alliance. Soon after the adjournment of the diet at Speyer Luther warned Elector John against Philip "and his alliance-making." "Our Lord Jesus Christ, who until now has wonderfully protected Your Electoral Grace without the landgrave, even against the landgrave, will certainly continue to help and counsel [Your Grace]." The very worst would be (Luther wrote five months before Marburg)

> that in such an alliance we are forced to include those who work against God and the sacrament [of the altar] and who are wanton enemies of God and his Word. In doing so we are forced to load on us, participate in, and fight for all their vice and blasphemy, so that certainly no more dangerous alliance could be made to blaspheme and impede the gospel and to condemn us in both soul and body. Unfortunately this is what the devil is after.[105]

For the evangelicals the right to resist the emperor became the major political theme during the year 1529. From September to November of that year three comprehensive opinions of this theme were produced. The earliest was Bugenhagen's reply of September 29 to the questions Chancellor Brück had conveyed to him from the elector. The first question— whether it is permissible to venture into an alliance with those "who deny

---

102. *WA* Br 12:40 / 15ff.

103. Texts, *WA* Br 12:41–45. Scheible, *Widerstandsrecht*, 17ff. Also Dörries, "Luther und das Widerstandsrecht," 199ff. On Melanchthon, see also W. Maurer, *Der junge Melanchthon zwischen Humanismus und Reformation* (Göttingen, 1969), 2:450, 587.

104. Preventive war as such—not against the emperor—had been treated by Luther and sharply rejected by him, during the Pack affair, in a letter to Chancellor Brück, March 28, 1528, *WA* Br 4:423 / 64ff. Scheible, *Widerstandsrecht*, 22. On this, see above, pp. 617–19.

105. *WA* Br 5:76 / 17; 77 / 35ff., 44ff. [*LW* 49:227, 226.] Scheible, *Widerstandsrecht*, 24. Cf. also the quotation from this letter above, p. 634, n. 15.

the sacrament of Christ and who, even after being admonished, do not improve themselves"—was fairly simple to answer: In an extreme case [Yes], provided one clearly separates oneself from their errors, otherwise it would undoubtedly be a denial of the words of Christ.[106] The other question was whether one dare resist the emperor by force, "if he intends to overrun us because of [our adhering to] God's Word."[107] Bugenhagen [in his written opinion] reflected on the authority he ascribes to the emperor, subordinate as he is to the overlordship of God. "Here one may freely admit that [the imperial authority] acts unjustly and in such cases has no orders from God, and that for this reason we do not recognize it as our government [to which we are subject]." At this point the rights and duties of the territorial lord begin. He must ponder: "Well, then, if one man abandons the authority he normally has from God, I will not abandon it. I cannot answer for it before God that I hand my sheep over to the wolves."[108] More decisively than announced, Bugenhagen answers the question put to him. Just as a preacher must employ the Word to chastise a sinful government, so also a prince [sovereign] must protect his subjects against an unjust, murderous overlord. "I have God's Word, he has God's sword; both ward off evil according to God's command and order." Bugenhagen considered his opinion not as a public declaration but as pastoral counsel for the elector; therefore he requested John to keep it confidential.[109] His paper is a richly revealing document on the aim of the medieval idea of the emperor's office as sacral, and also on the right and duty of every kind of legitimate government, alongside which also the preacher—if you like, the court preacher or chaplain—has his responsibility.

In contrast to Bugenhagen's concrete opinion, which weighed the duty of every estate, there was a second opinion, that of Lazarus Spengler, the secretary of the Nuremberg city council. Its character was almost Quakerlike in its linear directness. "All in all, it is not fitting for Christians to dispute or to fight, but to endure evil, injustice, and the use of force, neither consenting to nor sanctioning these things."[110] For the legal mind, however, resistance includes something "contrary to natural law and reasonableness, which says: No one should be his own judge, and he

106. Scheible, *Widerstandsrecht*, 25.
107. Ibid., 26.
108. Ibid., 27 to 10, 28 to 13.
109. Ibid., 29. Also Schubert, *Bekenntnisbildung*, 219–20.
110. Before November 15, Scheible, *Widerstandsrecht*, 35.

who opposes is unjust."[111] An attack by the Turks or some other foreign power is an altogether different matter. In that case one can defend himself "with a free and unawed conscience. But against the emperor this is by no means true, because in this case Nuremberg (Spengler repeatedly cites this city as an example) is not like a government but like any other individual or private person—the emperor's subject directly." No one can deny that the emperor is overlord over Nuremberg, a city situated in the middle of the empire and pledged to obey him. "That Nuremberg is also a government, and that with a special urban regime it oversees its inhabitants, is something it has not of itself, unmediated, but from a Roman emperor whose officials and administrators [the Nuremberg regime] are."[112] In that same vein Spengler, the lawyer, counters arguments like Bugenhagen's: "And this is a mischievous and clumsy kind of argument: Because the emperor had an overlord in heaven, therefore the inhabitants of Nuremberg are not the emperor's subjects but remain a government [on their own]." God is indeed ruler over the world, but is that a reason there should be no government on earth? "At that rate, what kind of government would the emperor retain in the empire? Who would recognize him as a lord or superior?"[113]

A third opinion came from John Brenz. This recognized reformer of Schwäbisch-Hall could without hesitation accept what Lazarus Spengler, a Christian in the vocation of jurist, had set forth so perceptively. Margrave George of Brandenburg-Ansbach had sent him a copy of Spengler's opinion and asked him to comment. Brenz added only a few original reasons of his own. What position did we take during the Peasants' War?

> As little as the peasants, in good conscience, succeeded during the past uprising in opposing their government violently with the sword, even though at times they had borne many an injustice from the authorities, so little could a prince or a city council of the [Holy] Roman Empire in good conscience and in a joyful summoning of God's help oppose the Imperial Majesty with a powerful sword, even though the Imperial Majesty may have perpetrated an injustice, affecting temporal or spiritual goods.

As little as one can be certain of God's help in such resistance, so little can one count on the help of fellow men.

> For the Christian faith, embodied in country or city, always fares like this: Only the smallest and humblest part of the inhabitants are real Christians;

111. Ibid., 34.
112. Ibid., 36.
113. Ibid., 37.

the others and the biggest crowd are customary believers, so long as it involves no risk. . . . On top of that, should a resisting prince or city be overcome by the emperor's sword, then the prince or the city would have been overcome not as a Christian but as a rebel.[114]

Nor can one claim the battle of the Israelites against the Mesopotamian kings as an example. That is no comparison with the [Holy] Roman Empire.

The people of Israel were not under these Mesopotamian kings as their regular government; they were under them for a while as a sinful people being punished. . . . Now our Lord God has placed the members and estates of the [Holy] Roman Empire under an emperor who is not an extraordinary chastiser of sin or a powerful highway robber but a regular head of state.

All the imperial estates, which Brenz defines as placed between the emperor at the top, to those at the bottom, are subjects of the emperor and "in the words of Holy Scripture counted as subjects."[115]

The conference in Schwabach failed largely because the Upper Germans had not received the specially drafted articles in time and therefore rejected them. So a new meeting date was set for December 15, 1529, in the town of Schmalkalden, and then advanced to November 28. The given reason was the alarming news that the emperor had jailed the emissaries from the protesting imperial estates. Though it sped far and wide, the news contributed nothing to any rallying of resistance against the emperor.[116] For the conference in Schmalkalden [southwest of Erfurt], Electoral Saxony's Chancellor Brück, on orders from Elector John and with the

---

114. Ibid., 41.

115. Ibid., 42. The three estates [Lords Spiritual (bishops, abbots, etc.), Lords Temporal (princes, etc.), Imperial Free Cities (representatives)], ibid., 40–42. Brenz has still other hesitations. Schubert, *Bekenntnisbildung*, 198, 206. Dorries, "Luther und das Widerstandsrecht," 207.

116. On the dispatching of an embassy to appeal, see above, p. 631. The news was exaggerated. It was a case of house arrest in the emissaries' hostel in Augsburg and a ban on writing letters to their sovereigns. Through the Nuremberg envoy, Michael von Kaden, who had been informed too late, the matter was brought to the attention of the Nuremberg council in a few days (October 24) and von Kaden informed the [protestant] allies. Schubert, *Bekenntnisbildung*, 188ff. W. Steglich, "Die Stellung der evangelischen Reichsstände und Reichsstädte zu Karl V zwischen Protestation und Konfession 1529/1530: Ein Beitrag zur Vorgeschichte des Augsburgischen Glaubensbekenntnisses," ARG 62 (1971): 174–75. RTA 8/1:164–77. A further annoyance to Charles V was that Kaden had presented him with a copy of the Reformation-oriented book *Somme chrestienne*, by Francis Lambert of Avignon (on whom see above, pp. 282–84), which the author had dedicated to the emperor. Landgrave Philip later informed Charles V that Kaden had acted not on his own initiative but on that of Philip. On this work, see G. Müller, *Franz Lambert von Avignon und die Reformation in Hessen*, VHKHW 24/4 (Marburg, 1958), 86ff. There, on pp. 130–31, also the draft of the landgrave's letter to the emperor (October or November 1529).

help of the Wittenberg theologians, had worked out an opinion [or position paper] on the decisive question: *Reasons Why One Should Not Enter into an Understanding with the Fanatics* [Schwärmer] *or Engage Otherwise in Defending Their Error.*[117] As a document, it opened astutely with reasons for answering the question affirmatively; that is, for treating the arguments of Landgrave Philip. Because these arguments were handled impartially and fully noted, the ensuing counterarguments against an alliance came across with doubled impact. The treatment of the case against an alliance was about three times the length of the case for it. Despite what may be said in its favor, the Marburg Colloquy shows up as a failure and not as an event leading to true unity. To base an alliance on it would thus run counter to the legal axiom that one "employs appropriate and recognized means, not forbidden ones."[118] Put somewhat differently: "Were we to draw them into our fellowship, it would be like putting a mouse into our bag." Should a debate over these questions lead, say, to considerations of a free council, then the others

> would pay us off and turn against us with great severity and sarcasm; and then we would be faring according to the pope's proverb: The mouse in the bag, the snake in the bosom, etc., pay their host poorly. They would condemn our conscience because we had sided with God's enemies who oppose his clear word and had added strength to their error.[119]

This harsh opinion more likely issued from the pen of Brück than of Luther or the other Wittenberg theologians.[120] The situation after the Marburg Colloquy thus fostered two contrary interpretations and two different political directions. On the question of an alliance against the emperor, Landgrave Philip saw the colloquy as the given prerequisite for an alliance; Brück, Vogler, and other Lutheran legal minds saw it as a warning against an alliance.

Prerequisite to an alliance would have been an agreement resolving disputed questions of faith, but the Marburg Articles were not suited for such a basic document. As the outcome of a theological colloquy, they had left open the decisive theme, the question of the elements in the Lord's

117. Printed in Schubert, *Bekenntnisbildung*, 144ff. The title originated with the Brandenburg-Ansbach chancellor Vogler. [In the German original *Irrsal* = *Irrtum* = error.] [The "fanatics" include the Swiss and Upper Germans.]

118. Ibid., 149.

119. Ibid., 151.

120. Brück, in contrast to Vogler, in a letter of December 4, 1529, claimed, "I have extinguished the 'accord' (the alliance against the emperor and the orthodox [old believer] estates)." Fabian, ed., *Abschiede*, 105.

Supper. The criterion for a possible coherence lay in the Schwabach confession [or articles]. Only in Schmalkalden did the Lutherans share it, carefully documented, with their potential South German partners. A conversation between the most important political men, the chancellors of Saxony and Brandenburg-Ansbach, Brück and Vogler, and the mayor of Strassburg, Jacob Sturm, proved decisive. Sturm, important and theologically knowledgeable, was the key man on the Upper German side. He brought a detailed critique of the Schwabach Articles prepared by Martin Bucer and unknown so far to anyone else.[121] Had Luther known of it earlier, he might have found his judgment corroborated when at Marburg he had smilingly called Bucer a rascal.[122] Bucer's advice was simplistic: that "wherever possible the articles be phrased in biblical words and given the clearest and shortest form." This, he contended, would further the interests of unity and not open the windows to error.[123] Thereupon Conrad Sam, the sage preacher in Ulm, having received a copy of Bucer's opinion, noted sharply, "From this we can see clearly how Bucer has himself gone astray and how he beclouds everything without Scripture." And on Bucer's critique of the conceptualization of the Persons of the Trinity, Sam called it "much too Arian." "I stand with Luther, regardless of all the Jews who might take offense."[124] Bucer also defended Zwingli against a formulation that original sin is actually a shortcoming and not authentic sin.[125] He stressed that God not only takes our faith into account but also expects us to and assists us to do good. Grace and Spirit, as the Schwabach Articles maintain too narrowly, are not bound to the spoken word, the gospel.[126] Bucer's kind of spiritualism naturally found strongest expression in his comments on the sacrament: "But to think that anyone would insist on believing that the true body and the true blood are in the bread and wine, when this is not to be found in Scripture!"[127] In a lengthy commentary on the Schwabach Article 10, Bucer separated himself not only from the transubstantiation of "the papists" but also from Luther.[128] Finally he

121. *Martin Bucers Deutsche Schriften*, ed. R. Stupperich (Gütersloh, 1960), 3:442ff. Also Schubert, *Bekenntnisbildung*, 167ff. Köhler, *Zwingli und Luther*, 2:173ff. [English version in M. Reu, *The Augsburg Confession*, trans. J. C. Mattes (Chicago, 1930), 49–58.]

122. Above, p. 647.

123. Stupperich, ed., *Bucers Deutsche Schriften*, 3:443 / 16ff.

124. Ibid., 444, nn. 8, 12.

125. Ibid., 452 / 9ff.

126. Article 7. Ibid., 457 / 11ff.

127. [Bucer's words *"geschicht ahne Geschrift"* = *ist nicht in der Schrift begründet* = are not to be found in Scripture.] Article 10. Ibid., 462 / 12–13.

128. Ibid., 464 / 4ff.

would like to rid confession of the appearance of involving a divine "absolution and the removal of a judgment," as the Schwabach Articles claim. Confession is indeed important for the comfort it brings us from the Word of God, but every brother conversant in God's Word can pronounce absolution.[129] Bucer offered no comment on the remaining articles (12–17), although he pointed out their importance should "powerful governments" desire to ally themselves in Christian doctrine. Therefore one should carefully spare the faith of the other and not intervene in the services to be rendered by any man.

> The most expedient thing to do would be to unite simply on the Word of God as found in the Old and New Testaments and to ignore the articles altogether, granting the exclusion of all objections[130] so that they will not later call some to account because of their erroneous views of the sacrament or because of other views for which no scriptural foundation can serve as an excuse,[131] and so that they will not back out when the battle really begins, for no danger looms in these matters except from the enemies of our common faith.[132]

Bucer's critique of the Schwabach Articles is the most important document illustrative of the dissension between the two evangelical sides. Once taken into account, it effectively halted the negotiations for an alliance as well as the mission of the envoys to Charles V. A new meeting date was set for January 6, 1530, in Nuremberg, but the elector let it be known that only those would be invited who are "related to the pure doctrine,"[133] meaning those who agreed with the Schwabach Articles. The representative of Margrave George of Brandenburg-Ansbach raised doubts as to this brand of narrowness, inasmuch as it was in the first place only a peace appeal to the emperor; yet he did not at this point risk separating himself from his Saxon ally.[134] A separation of the Lutheran from the Upper German estates at the coming imperial Diet of Augsburg was beginning to show.

129. Ibid., 468 / 10ff.
130. Bucer's *"doch alle Vorteil hingenommen"* = *doch unter Ausschluss aller Vorbehalte* = the exclusion of all objections.
131. Bucer's *"zu Wort haben"* = *zum Vorwand nehmen* = can be used as an excuse.
132. Ibid., 468 / 23. [Reu, *The Augsburg Confession*, 57–58.]
133. Schubert, *Bekenntnisbidlung*, 132, n. 1.
134. Ibid., 133ff.

24

The Imperial Diet and
the Augsburg Confession

The approaching diet [in Augsburg] and the threatening signs of what might be expected of it—raised, for example, by Charles's treatment of the envoys appealing [the action against the evangelicals at Speyer]—gave fresh impulses to the question of the right to resist the emperor.[1] This pressed on Elector John's mind, and on January 27, 1530, he wrote from Torgau, asking how Luther judged the issue. At the same time, he informed Luther of the two contrary opinions he had received [one from a theologian, the other from a jurist]. (1) Bugenhagen, the pastor-theologian whom the elector had approached during Luther's absence at Marburg,[2] said Yes to resistance. [As noted in the previous chapter,] Bugenhagen placed an overlord (like the emperor) and his vassals (the princes) under the same commandment: the duty of defending one's subjects. Proceeding from the concept of government as indivisible, he thus defeated any opponent of resistance with his own weapon. The elector correctly inferred from this "that in this case one is responsible for protecting one's subjects."[3] (2) Lazarus Spengler, the Nuremberg city council's general secretary, had sent the elector an opposite opinion. Where it concerned religion, Spengler, the jurist, rejected all violent resistance against the emperor. In fact, he ascribed the halo of martyrdom to anyone destroyed while foregoing resistance [or resisting passively]. Spengler even cited a statement by the elector himself: Against attacks by another prince, whether under the guise of the gospel or the exercise of it, "against him, with God's help, I shall defend myself with all my power. But if the emperor comes and attacks me, he is my overlord; toward him I must practice patience. And how can I come to a more honest ruin than one I experience for the sake of the Word?"[4] The elector was informed of still

1. On the earlier discussion, see above, pp. 653–55.
2. See above, pp. 655–56.
3. WA Br 5:224 / 16–17.
4. On the comprehensive opinion written by Spengler (November 15, 1529), see above, pp. 656–57.

other and conflicting opinions through his chancellor Christian Beyer. Having attended the January 6, 1530, negotiations in Nuremberg, Beyer reported to the elector that Wenceslaus Link (Nuremberg) and John Brenz (Schwäbisch-Hall) likewise rejected [violent] resistance; yet Nuremberg pastor Osiander favored it.[5] Confronted with this clash of expert opinions and personal positions, the elector turned to Luther and requested "some decent advice" within three weeks' time.[6]

Thereby the elector let it be known that what Luther had written on this subject on December 24, 1529, at the behest of Landgrave Philip of Hesse was not enough. As recently as then Luther had limited his comments, saying the time had not yet come to arm against the emperor and to take the field—not before "actual violence and inescapable necessity" lay at hand, that is, not before the emperor, through some mandate or imperial order against the princes, had made himself a breaker of the peace. Let trust be in God, in whose hand "is the king's heart" (Prov. 21:1). If the emperor remains quiet, then any publicity given the right of resistance would simply draw the reproach of dissension on oneself and disgrace on the gospel.[7]

The contents of his new information was prescribed for Luther not only in the opinions of Bugenhagen and Spengler, which he had at hand, but also in the precise question of the elector, for John was asking whether he would have to accept [passively] a violation of the emperor's concession in Frankfurt at the time of his election, in which he had then promised to let the princes retain their rights and not to overrun them by force.[8] Responding to the elector's directive, Luther consulted with Jonas, Bugenhagen, and Melanchthon. By March 6 his requested reply was dispatched in the form of a letter, in which he clarified the question by differentiating between secular law [justice: *Recht*] and Christian conduct. According to secular law, one may perhaps set up defenses against an emperor, namely, when he has bound himself by oath to attack no one and to guarantee everyone his freedom.[9] But for the Christian there is, "ac-

5. WA Br 5:224 / 19ff., n. 3.

6. WA Br 5:224 / 39ff. *"Ordentlicher Ratschlag"*: a full record of that which, in all this, you will think about and stir up—that which is godly, Christian, fair, and right."

7. WA Br 5:209 / 35, 16; 210 / 70ff. Also H. Dörries, "Luther und das Widerstandsrecht," in his *Wort und Stunde* (Göttingen, 1970), 3:215ff. Dörries, like O. Clemen, WA Br 5:249, makes the valid point against K. Müller, "Luthers Äusserungen über das Recht des bewaffneten Widerstandes gegen den Kaiser," SBAW.PPH 8 (Munich, 1915), that there is here as yet no mention of a justified counterattack, especially after a declaration of emergency.

8. WA Br 5:224 / 29ff.

9. WA Br 5:258 / 7ff. [*LW* 49:276.] H. Scheible, *Das Widerstandsrecht als Problem der deutschen Protestanten 1523–1546*, TKTG 10 (Gütersloh, 1969), 60.

cording to the Scriptures," no such right of resistance. "Instead, a Christian should endure violence and injustice, especially from his government." Even a sinful emperor remains the governing authority, against which the authorized may take action. Luther distinguishes between "sin" and "punishment" as occasions to resist. "Sin does not nullify governmental authority or the duty of obeying it, but punishment does nullify them, that is, when the empire and the electors unanimously remove the emperor from office, so that he is no longer emperor."[10] Luther seeks to prevent a political abuse of the issues with which faith must wrestle. Faith should not hide behind the protection of temporal power, nor should temporal power use faith as a weapon against some higher authority. "Every (Christian), then, is to stand on his own, confessing his faith by offering his body and life, and not drag the sovereign into danger or burden him by seeking protection." As for the sovereign himself, "it therefore seems to me that one would be acting unjustly[11] if one were to oppose governmental authority for the sake of defending the gospel. Such action certainly would [show that we have] a false faith which does not trust God, who certainly knows how to protect and help us in many ways without our [own] cleverness and efforts."[12] Furthermore, this too must be considered: Whoever opposes the emperor must himself be ready to be emperor and to cope with the attacks of rivals. "What unspeakable slaughter and misery would result. A sovereign should be ready to lose three principalities—in fact, he should prefer to be dead three times over—rather than be the cause of so much woe or assist in it or consent to it. For how could any conscience bear this?"[13] Luther knew his elector, and he also knew that he could dare him to leave his country undefended to the emperor rather than to shed blood for the sake of the gospel.[14] If, however, the emperor determines to force his territorial sovereigns to exile or kill those of their subjects who adhere to the gospel, "then this pertains to the sovereigns' own faith. And then they ought not to obey the emperor, so that they do not agree and cooperate with him, and make themselves participants of such evil."[15]

10. WA Br 5:258 / 13ff.; 259 / 38ff. [LW 49:276.] Scheible, *Widerstandsrecht*, 60–61.

11. WA Br 5:260 / 90. [LW 49:278, 279. Alternate to "rashly."] Scheible, *Widerstandsrecht*, 62. [Luther's words,] *"für dem Garn gefischet"* = *unrecht gehandelt*. *"Gewalt für Recht gebraucht,"* see his letter to Chancellor Brück, March 28, 1528, WA Br 4:423 / 82.

12. WA Br 5:259 / 69ff. [LW 49:279. Alternate.] [Luther's] *"Witze"* = *Weisheit* [wisdom or cleverness]. Scheible, *Widerstandsrecht*, 62.

13. WA Br 5:260 / 103ff., 110ff. [LW 49:280.] Scheible, *Widerstandsrecht*, 63.

14. WA Br 5:260 / 75ff. [LW 49:278.] Scheible, *Widerstandsrecht*, 62.

15. WA Br 5:259 / 73ff.; 260 / 77ff. [LW 49:278.] Scheible, *Widerstandsrecht*, 62.

Even before the elector could respond to Luther's counsel, he received the imperial summons that the next diet would open in Augsburg on April 8. Therefore, on March 14 the elector passed this information on to Luther, Jonas, Bugenhagen, and Melanchthon, alerting them to the task that would be theirs. According to the summons, the diet's agenda would include [not only the question of repulsing the Turkish invasion but also] the schism in the church. On this subject, "all care [would be] taken to give a charitable hearing to every man's opinion, thoughts, and notions, to understand them, to weigh them, to bring and reconcile men to a unity in Christian truth."[16]

At the Saxon elector's court hope rose that "perhaps this diet would lead to a council or to a national assembly." It would therefore be necessary to be completely clear about matters of faith and church practices likely to be at issue, and also on this question: "How far would or could we and other estates that have accepted and permitted the pure doctrine, with God as well as in conscience and fairness, condone offenses?"[17] To be ready for such an eventuality the elector requested the Wittenbergers to drop everything else and to prepare themselves on these questions. He would be expecting them to meet with him in Torgau [southeast of Wittenberg] on Oculi Sunday, March 20. At the same time, he informed them that when the time came he planned to take with him as far as Coburg Luther, Jonas, and Melanchthon, and also Spalatin and Agricola—whom he had learned to cherish as preacher at the two diets of Speyer. Then, after the agenda of the diet was clarified, he would send for them in Augsburg, with the exception of Luther, who would receive instructions later.[18] Setting out on April 3, the Wittenbergers proceeded to Torgau and on the following day continued to Coburg, where they arrived on Easter Eve, April 16, still in time for Luther to preach. Here he learned the latest news, for the elector himself was still at Coburg Castle. Being freed of other duties, Luther relayed the news as rapidly as possible to the friends at home: The emperor is still in Mantua and would be staying there over Easter Sunday and Monday (April 17–18); the pope is furious at the em-

16. *WA* Br 5:264 / 14ff. [M. Reu, *The Augsburg Confession*, trans. J. C. Mattes (Chicago, 1930), 71–72, from the full text of the Imperial Summons (1530) in English.] K. E. Förstemann, *Urkundenbuch zur Geschichte des Reichstages zu Augsburg im Jahre 1530* (Halle, 1883ff.; reprint, Hildesheim, 1966), 8:61ff. The summons of the emperor to Elector John of Saxony was drawn up and signed by the imperial private secretary, Alexander Schweiss, and his vice-chancellor, Balthasar Merklin, of Waldkirch. Ibid., 9.

17. *WA* Br 5:264 / 29ff.

18. *WA* Br 5:264 / 32–265 / 64. The elector, again on March 21, urged them to hurry and to bring their books along; he would need their advice also on other matters. *WA* Br 5:269.

peror's intervention in church affairs. But Charles wished to hear the contending parties firsthand instead of sending [as the pope had hoped] his hangman against the heretics and restoring everything to its *status quo ante*.[19] Even an eyewitness to these latest developments at the imperial court had arrived at the Coburg the same time as Luther. Item: The Nuremberg envoy Michael von Kaden, who had experienced the treatment given the evangelical appeals commissioners and also the [retroactive] coronation of Charles V, was home safely after a brief detention. The emperor related that at the coronation the pope explained the embarrassment it caused him to have the emperor kiss his big toe, but that ceremony, alas, required it.[20]

It did not dawn on Luther why he should have to remain at the Coburg on the elector's orders while the others journeyed on to Augsburg.[21] He was not even allowed to accompany his friends Jonas, Melanchthon, and Spalatin as far as Nuremberg. How gladly he would have traveled with them as a fifth! So he joked about it, dreaming up a reason: Perhaps it was because the diet is meeting in a region whose language does not include all five senses but has only four, so that "taste" means two things: tasting and smelling.[22] At any rate, he took a closer look around his domicile, the Fortress, into which he had moved during the night of April 23 / 24.[23] "Nothing is lacking that fosters solitude," he wrote Melanchthon on April 24.

> The loftiest dwelling that towers over the castle is completely ours. Besides, to us have been entrusted the keys to every sort of conclave. More than thirty men, they say, are fed here. Twelve of them are the nightwatch, and two trumpeters are lookouts on the several towers. So what? Alas, I have nothing else to write about. Tonight, I hope, the warden or the marksman will come by and maybe I'll pick up some news.[24]

But in the solitude Luther had already spun plans with which he opened his letter.

> We have finally arrived at our Sinai, dearest Philipp, but we shall make a Zion out of this Sinai and construct here three huts: one for the Psalter, one for the

19. To Hausmann, April 18, 1530, WA Br 5:277 / 7ff. [LW 49:284–85.]

20. Luther to Amsdorf, April 18, WA Br 5:275 / 7ff. To Kaden, WA Br 5:276, n. 4. H. von Schubert, "Luther auf der Koburg," LuJ 12 (1930): 113–14; on his report on the appeals commission, see above, p. 658, n. 116.

21. To Hausmann, April 18, WA Br 5:277 / 17–18. [LW 49:285.]

22. To Eobanus Hessus in Nuremberg, April 23, WA Br 5:283 / 4ff.

23. Cf. H. Rückert in his edition of Luther's letters, BoA 6:252.

24. WA Br 5:286 / 19ff.

prophets, and one for Aesop.[25] But the latter one is only temporal. To be sure, the place is extremely pleasant and most suitable for study, except that your absence makes it a sad spot.[26]

Things that refreshed him where he was appeared in the designation he used in his letter, "From the kingdom of the birds," and he kept on using it.[27] On the same day, Luther described to Justus Jonas and Spalatin the screeching of the jackdaws. Their noise persisted from four o'clock in the morning, even through storm and clouds. Luther's imagination [screening out thoughts about Augsburg] turned the gatherings of the birds into an imperial diet of his own, where he arrived sooner than his journeying colleagues could reach theirs.[28]

> Here you might see proud kings, dukes, and other noblemen of the kingdom who seriously care for their belongings and offspring and who with untiring voice proclaim their decisions and dogmas through the air. Finally, they do not live, or rather they are not locked up in, such holes and caves as you people call (with but little reason) palaces. Rather, they live under the open sky, so that the sky itself serves them as a paneled ceiling, the green trees as a floor of limitless variety, and the walls [of their palace] are identical with the ends of the earth.

They also show contempt for the foolish luxury of gold and silk; rather, they all [live] the same way, [have] one color, one [kind of] dress, . . . all make the same music in unison, yet with a pleasant difference between the voices of the elders and the youngsters. "I have not yet seen nor heard their emperor." "We sit here with great pleasure in their diet as idle spectators and listeners."[29] "Let this suffice for a joke. But it is a serious and necessary joke that should chase away the thoughts seizing me, if it can repel them [at all]."[30] Soon thereafter Luther strikes a merry tone in a letter to his table companions in Wittenberg: "Today we have heard the first nightingale, as though she had not wanted to trust April. So far the weather has been simply superb—no rain, except a little yesterday." He

---

25. An allusion to the story of Jesus' transfiguration, Matt. 17:4. *In Psalmos vigintiquinque priores et sequentes aliquot enarrationes breves* (1530), WA 31¹:263–383. Luther dictated his commentary to Veit Dietrich; it was first published by his heirs in 1559. On the translation of the prophets, WA DB 11²:lv–lvi. The plan to translate *Aesop's Fables* turns up here for the first time; the sixteen parts completed by Luther at the Coburg were first published in 1557. WA 50:432ff.

26. *WA Br* 5:285 / 3ff. [*LW* 49:288–89.]

27. *WA Br* 5:286 / 27–28. [*LW* 49:291.]

28. *WA Br* 5:289 / 5; 290 / 5ff. [*LW* 49:293.]

29. *WA Br* 5:291 / 10ff., 28–29. [*LW* 49:293, 294.]

30. *WA Br* 5:291 / 44ff. [*LW* 49:295.]

dated his letter "From the imperial diet of the malt-Turks, April 28, Anno 1530."[31]

The tasks Luther had selected to occupy his period of solitude[32] were soon supplemented with contributions to the Diet of Augsburg. The first was a pamphlet [with the challenging title] *Exhortation to All Clergy Assembled at Augsburg for the Imperial Diet of 1530. By Martin Luther.*[33] By this means he gained a hearing otherwise denied him. It reached those bearing the actual responsibility, men of the church, and not just politicians. On May 12 he sent the manuscript to the printers in Wittenberg. In early June a book dealer delivered the first five hundred copies to Augsburg. As Jonas reported, "They were quickly sold out." The buyers included many opponents eager to learn how Luther reacted to news of the emperor's arrival, an event that must have been shocking to him.[34] Jonas himself was delighted with Luther's "unexpected, wonderful, and powerful apology." "I doubt not that the Lord has spoken through you in this booklet."[35]

The anticipated retort that he has no right to speak to these concerns of the imperial diet Luther brushed aside with an impressive review of the ten years during which these questions had already been treated by earlier diets and in other ways: "with so many deliberations, with so many tricks and machinations, with so many fair words and false hopes, yes, also with force and wrath, with murder and punishment, so that I have seen in

31. WA Br 5:295 / 1–2. Even a few days earlier (April 24) he had complained that no one among them at the Coburg had as yet heard a nightingale, but they had heard a cuckoo in the beauty of his glorious voice. To Jonas, WA Br 5:289 / 16–17. I do not share the doubts that O. Clemen casts on the authenticity of this letter (WA Br 5:292–93). The letter to the table companions is no self-plagiarism but a German rendition of that contained also in the letters to Jonas and Spalatin and was intended for a circle that presumably included some ("and to others in Wittenberg all and sundry") who were not versed in Latin. As for the address, missing in WA Br 5:293, see WA Br 13:127. Rückert, who agreed with Clemen in his first edition of Luther's letters (*BoA* 6:259), left the question of authenticity hanging in the second edition (*BoA* 6:454). *Malztürken* is an unknown term, and in Grimm's *Deutsches Wörterbuch*, 6 (1885): 1517, the only supporting reference is from this same passage in Luther's letter. Apparently it is a term Luther himself concocted in writing his description of the battle of the birds: "Like knights they preen themselves, wipe their bill, and flap their wings, as if anticipating victory and honor [in their raids] against grain and malted barley." WA Br 5:294 / 32ff. [Cf. *LW* 49:293.]

32. Letter to Link, May 8, again prophets, psalms, and Aesop, WA Br 5:309 / 9ff. Similarly to Melanchthon, May 12, WA Br 5:316 / 7ff. An overview of Luther's writings during these weeks is provided by a letter of Veit Dietrich (he had accompanied Luther to Marburg, and now to Coburg) of June 8, 1530, to Propst Hector Poemer in Nuremberg. Published by O. Mathes, "10 Briefe aus den Jahren 1523–1590 aus dem Besitz Johann Valentin Andreäs," *BWKG* 60 / 61 (1960 / 61): 27–28.

33. WA 30²:268–356. [*LW* 34: (5) 9–61.]

34. Jonas to Luther from Augsburg, June 13, WA Br 5:361 / 1ff.

35. WA Br 5:362 / 22–23; 361 / 14–15.

you [clergy] occasion for wonder and woe."[36] Luther reviews the course of events: a diet in Speyer [1526] was summoned "with such glorious, consoling hope," only to be called off "insultingly and shamefully." "Then quickly thereafter came the whip, namely [Thomas] Müntzer, with revolt and gave you a blow from which you have still not recovered and from which we unfortunately suffered even greater damage."[37] Luther then points out that "Müntzer's spirit still lives on and that by its rigid stance against the Reformation it could easily break out again. In fact, more than that: "You know too how faithfully and firmly we have held out against all factious spirits. If I dared boast, I might almost say that we were your protectors and that it was our doing that you have remained until now what you are."[38] And when indeed some would charge, "You started it, and these are the fruits of your teaching," he would have to accept it even though many among them would know that it was not so. "But have you forgotten that at Worms the German nobility presented His Imperial Majesty with about four hundred grievances[39] against the clergy and declared openly that if His Imperial Majesty did not wish to abolish such abuses, they would do so themselves, for they could no longer endure them?"[40] He also reminded his readers how much approval his attack on indulgences and on the spread of monasticism had found. Especially the beginnings of his teaching, when he had struck a blow at indulgences, and which he here recalls in fifteen bitter theses.[41]

> But who among all of you would ever have repented for such frightful abomination, would ever have sighed or would ever have moistened an eye? Yes, now like hardened, unrepentant men you want to pretend that you never did any evil. Now you come to Augsburg and want to persuade us that the Holy Spirit is with you and will accomplish great things through you (although in your whole lifetime you have done Christendom nothing but harm) and that he will thereafter lead you straight to heaven with all such abominations,

---

36. WA 30²:271 / 24ff. [LW 34:10.]

37. WA 30²:274 / 16–17, 19ff. [LW 34:12.] See the announcement of a general assembly of the German nation in Speyer by action of the Nuremberg diet (April 18, 1524) and its cancellation by the emperor, above, pp. 309, 313. Luther reminds the clergy that the Peasants' War broke out first in the monastic and other church-owned lands in southern Germany. On this, also the revised supplement, WA 30²:274 / 1ff.

38. WA 30²:276 / 15ff., 22ff. [LW 34:13.] The *Rottengeister* [factious spirits] claimed the Strassburgers as their protectors and therefore judged harshly the "hateful" statement with which Luther allegedly flattered the emperor and the princes and wanted to take all the credit for himself. Bucer to Zwingli, *Zwinglis samtliche Werke*, ed. E. Egli, G. Finster, et al. (Berlin, 1905ff.), 9 (1925): 617–18, 623.

39. The *Gravamina* (grievances).

40. WA 30²:277 / 22ff., 33ff. [LW 34:14.]

41. WA 30²:281–84. [LW 34:16–17.]

unrepented and defended besides, as though he had to rejoice over you who have served your god-belly so gloriously and laid waste his church so miserably. For this reason you have no success and also shall have none until you repent and mend your ways. . . . That it is no longer this way is the fault of my rebellious gospel. [42]

In his wrath Luther sounds like Savonarola as he goes on to excoriate the clergy's worst abuses; "butter-letters" led the list. They had earned this name [popular then] as letters of indulgence which allowed the unlimited eating of forbidden foods during Lent. They relaxed other requirements as well and absolved their purchasers from punishment and guilt. [43] Here lies a double spiritual crime: "As if God had not before [this] through the gospel given all things freely to all the world, or as if God had forbidden these things, and they [the clergy] were the mighty men who could sell the commandments of God for money." [44] Luther considers what the church has made of confession:

one of the greatest plagues on earth, whereby you have confused the conscience of the whole world, caused so many souls to despair, and weakened and quenched all men's faith in Christ. You have said nothing at all to us about the comfort of absolution, the chief article and the best part in confession, which strengthens faith and trust in Christ. But you have made a work out of it, extorting it by force with commands from unwilling hearts to strengthen your tyranny. Afterward you let them suffer pangs and torture and torment themselves with recounting all sins. That is, you have disturbed forever their rest and peace of mind with an impossible task. But when will you bring all such souls back again and make good the deadly, baseless damage you have done? [45]

The kernel of this perversion in the confessional is the fundamental misconception of the nature of repentance:

That is the very worst and hell itself! If one were to forgive and remit all abominations, one can never forgive you for this one. This doctrine has filled hell and has troubled the kingdom of Christ more horribly than the Turk or the whole world could ever do, for you taught us that we should by our own works make satisfaction for sin, even against God. . . . Now what else does it mean to say "You must make satisfaction for your sins" than to say "You must

42. WA 30²:285 / 28ff. [LW 34:18.]

43. Freedom to choose one's father confessor with expanded powers, liberation from impediments to marriage, etc. H. Schauerte, "Beichtbriefe," LThK 2 (1958): 125–26. They were aired in the Gravamina [grievances] of the German nation at the diets of Worms (1521), Nuremberg (1523), and now again at Augsburg.

44. WA 30²:286 / 27ff. [LW 34:18.]

45. WA 30²:287 / 24ff. [LW 34:19.]

deny Christ, renounce your baptism, blaspheme the gospel, reproach God for lies, not believe in the forgiveness of sins, tread underfoot Christ's blood and death, dishonor the Holy Spirit, and go to heaven by your own effort with such virtues?" Alas, where are the tongues and voices that can say enough about this?[46]

From this fundamental misconception of repentance all the abominations arose with which each wished to prove his own holiness: endowments of cloisters and masses, especially in light of purgatory, pilgrimages, venerating the saints, processions of the cross, and much else.

For what else is possible? If conscience is to rely and build on its own works, it stands on loose sand that moves to and fro and continually sinks away. It must always seek works, one after another. The longer it looks the more it needs. At last they put cowls on the dead in which they should ascend to heaven. Dear Lord God, how were consciences to act? They had to build on works. Therefore, they also had to seek them so miserably and snatch whatever they could and fall into such deep folly.[47]

Luther then enumerates a long list of abuses that the papal church has brought into the world: the "sale of masses" and pilgrimages to ever so many places and chapels for the saints. Formerly these cascaded on the faithful like a cloudburst and brought in piles of money.[48] The discipline of the church ban [excommunication, etc.] was abused in order to extort payment of taxes and debts.[49]

Finally Luther offered the spiritual princes a form of inverted secularization: Let them give up not their temporal positions but their spiritual office. Since they are neither willing nor able to carry out their episcopal office with preaching and concern for people's conscience, "so then let us exercise your office for which you are responsible. Allow us to teach the gospel freely and let us serve the poor people who desire to be devout. Do not persecute and resist that which you cannot do and are nevertheless obligated to do and which others want to do for you."[50] Even so, Luther and his side want to see the episcopal princes remain and retain their lands, something the Hussites and Wyclifites had always denied the bishops. None of their possessions should be confiscated. "We do not ask for more, and have never asked for anything else, than that the gospel be free." Nor have we asked for any kind of payment. "The offer is this: We

46. WA 30²:288 / 22ff. [LW 34:19–20.]
47. WA 30²:290 / 22ff. [LW 34:21.]
48. WA 30²:293ff.; 295 / 27ff. [LW 34:23.]
49. WA 30²:310 / 30ff. [LW 34:33.]
50. WA 30²:340 / 23ff. [LW 34:49.]

will perform the duties of your office; we will support ourselves without cost to you; we will help you remain as you are; and we will counsel you that you have authority and are to see to it that things go right."[51] In order to leave no doubt as to the kind of changes he thought necessary in the church, Luther set up two long lists. The one included "topics with which it is necessary to deal in the true Christian church and about which we are concerned";[52] the other itemized "the things that have been practiced and are custom in the pretended church."[53] That the church in Reformation hands would receive a different image and another spirit was by no means veiled in Luther's offer of cooperation. Therefore he recalled an instance that the clergy assembled at Augsburg could not ignore. Pope Hadrian VI, through his legate at the Nuremberg diet on January 3, 1523, openly acknowledged the wrongs of the church and devoted himself to setting them aright. "Why should you then be ashamed to confess this and in addition still persist so obstinately in your pride, yield nothing or admit nothing, but carry off everything with force regardless of whether the result is better or worse?"[54] He then closes with an oathlike benediction revealing the seriousness of his exhortation.

> Your blood be on your own head! We are and want to be innocent of your blood and damnation, since we pointed out to you sufficiently your wrongs, faithfully admonished to repentance, prayed sincerely, and offered to the uttermost all that could serve the cause of peace, seeking and desiring nothing else than the one comfort for our souls, the free, pure gospel. Therefore we may boast with a good conscience that the fault has not been ours. But may the God of peace and comfort give you his Spirit, to direct and lead you to all truth, through our Lord Jesus Christ, to whom be praise and thanks for all his unspeakable grace and gifts in all eternity. Amen.[55]

A humanist, in the service of the papal legate Campeggio, was ordered by his chief to make a Latin translation of Luther's pamphlet. Writing later to a friend, the humanist said: "This is a summary of all of Lutheranism. If you wish to see the whole Luther, then you must buy the pamphlet."[56]

It was a release for Luther, as he reported on May 12 to Melanchthon in Augsburg, to have completed the *Exhortation* and sent off the manuscript

51. WA 30²:341 / 33ff.; 343 / 17ff. [LW 34:50, 51.]
52. WA 30²:345 / 10ff. [LW 34:52–53.]
53. WA 30²:347 / 9ff. [LW 34:54–58.]
54. WA 30²:354 / 32ff. [LW 34:60.]
55. WA 30²:355 / 29ff. [LW 34:60–61.]
56. Daniel Mauch, June 21, 1530, WA 30²:238; also the revision appended, ibid., 66. On Mauch, see A. Naegele, "Aus dem Leben eines fahrenden Scholaren im Zeitalter des Humanismus und der Reformation," *RQ* 25 (1911); on this letter of his, ibid., 204.

to Wittenberg for printing. Besides, he had also completed the translation of Ezekiel 38 and 39; the section on Gog (which Luther read as referring to the Turks and Mohammed) had been absorbing his interest for some time. These two chapters had also gone off to the printer. Now he was translating a portion of the prophets which he hoped to have completed by Pentecost, June 5. A translation of Aesop and other items should then follow.[57] This zeal to dispel his sense of loneliness was bound sooner or later to take its toll. Suddenly he began to feel the effects. He was already into his other plans, "but the old, outward man is so ruined that he can neither stand nor respond to the onrushing new." Ringing and thundering in his head kept him almost unconscious for two days, and for three days he could hardly stand the sight of print.[58] "My head won't do it any longer. I see the years are indeed piling up." He had not lost his sense of humor [as he pondered how life has a way of shrinking]: "Caput meum factum est capitulum, perget vero et fiat paragraphus, tandem periodus."[59] He offered his excuse to Melanchthon, accounting this way for his silence: "On the day your letter arrived from Nuremberg, Satan had his full embassy here with me."[60]

Amid his solitude and restlessness, Luther's connection with the people to whom he stood closely was refreshing. With unusual warmth he addressed one letter to Melanchthon "Dearest brother, most strong and faithful Christ-bearer."[61] His idea of relaxation included joking with his friends. From Augsburg, Agricola wrote to Luther that during the journey thither they had stopped over in Saalfeld and had teased its pastor, Caspar Aquila, by telling of Melanchthon's dream that he saw an eagle transformed into a cat [the emperor's heraldry featured the Hapsburg eagle]. Luther countered with his own kind of joke: He was sitting on the toilet and found a paper with a three-part musical phrase. He improved it and made it four-part, complete with text. He planned to send this ditty along with a letter from the friends in Augsburg, saying that this was a composition prepared for welcoming the emperor in Augsburg. Luther was sending this to George Rörer, the Wittenberg bandmaster who with the musical authority at his disposal might well refute the piece.[62]

57. WA Br 5:316 / 6ff. Luther had already expressed his growing anxiety about the Turks to Melanchthon on April 24, WA Br 5:285 / 7ff. The Ezekiel commentary, WA 30²:223–36.

58. Luther to Melanchthon, May 12, 1530, WA Br 5:316 / 11ff.

59. "My head has become a little head (a chapter) and will continue thus, and become a paragraph, finally a sentence." WA Br 5:316 / 16ff.

60. WA Br 5:317 / 20ff.

61. WA Br 5:316 / 1–2.

62. May 15, WA Br 5:320 / 6ff. On this, Rückert, BoA 6:265–66.

Along with the joking also came sorrow, which Luther shared with friends at a distance. Justus Jonas had again lost a baby boy at the age of three days. Luther begged Melanchthon to convey this news to Jonas with utmost considerateness.[63] Soon he himself was writing Jonas a letter of condolence steeped in deep sympathy and pointing to "the peace that surpasses all understanding" (Phil. 4:7). Then, to his collegial friend, he opened his own troubled heart.

> I am an irksome and unsuitable comforter, for I myself am not rich in thoughts of spring and the fragrance of flowers—the way I would wish them for you and you have need of them. Often the wind burns me and the heat becomes oppressive, so that I become like our [now] dry and thirsty landscape here.[64]

For Luther this was a most significant example, allowing nature and the experiences in his soul to speak with each other. Luther has comfort for his friend, assuring him that he does not suffer alone but has many companions. He should thereby not overlook the fatherly upbringing that knows: "There is a time for joy and a time for sorrow; the one we accept gladly, but even the other we are not to turn away. May the Lord Jesus, who has received your little son to himself and who will care for him better than you, comfort and strengthen you."[65]

The leisure at the Coburg gave Luther opportunity for a rich personal correspondence of all sorts: He thanked his wife, Kate, for a sketch of his year-old daughter, Lenchen [Magdalena], along with suggestions as to how Kate should gradually wean her. All this is according to the good advice of his own faithful supporter the elderly Argula von Grumbach, who had just visited him.[66] And he writes condolences to Wenceslaus Link in Nuremberg, who had lost a daughter.[67] Deepest sorrow struck Luther himself during these days as he learned that his father had died. He shared the news immediately with his closest friends. These letters shed the clearest light on Martin's relationship to his father. His condolences to Link included word of his own personal loss. Still on the same

---

63. May 15, 1530, WA Br 5:318.

64. May 19, 1530, WA Br 5:323 / 1ff.

65. WA Br 5:324 / 22ff.

66. June 5, 1530, WA Br 5:347–48. On Argula von Grumbach, see *RGG*[3] 2 (1958): 1889, including bibliography. The joy of Luther over the sketch of Lenchen, which he hung on the wall, was also reported by Veit Dietrich in his letter of June 19 to Katharina Luther. *D. Martin Luthers Briefwechsel*, ed. E. L. Enders (Frankfurt am Main, 1884ff.), 8:12–13. [*LW* 49:312–14.]

67. WA Br 5:349 / 5ff.

day (June 5) his letter to Melanchthon bore the most beautiful account of his relationship to his father.

> Today Hans Reinicke wrote me that my very dear father, Hans Luther the Elder, during the first hour on Exaudi Sunday departed this life. His death has plunged me into deep mourning, thinking not only of the natural bonds but also of the precious love [my father had for me]. For through him God gave me all that I am and have. Even though it does comfort me, as [Reinecke] writes, that [my father] fell asleep gently with a firm faith in Christ, yet the pity of heart and the memory of the most loving dealings with him have shaken me in the innermost parts of my being, so that seldom, if ever, have I despised death as much as I do now.[68]

A charming testimony of Luther's joy in his little son Hans, about whom he had received good reports from Hans's teacher, balanced his feelings in these days of solitude. For Hans he sketched a word picture of the heavenly garden as a reward for devout children.[69]

Personal joys and sorrows intensified in Luther as he longed for news from Augsburg.[70] His friends were right in considering his anxiety unfounded.[71] As yet nothing of importance had happened. The emperor arrived only on June 21 [after a delayed departure from Innsbruck], and even then there was little more to write about than the prevailing mood of anticipation.[72] Only on the day when the confession of faith was presented (June 25) did Luther receive some specific news—and that from the elector himself. As Prince John reported, the emperor had refused permission to preach the gospel in the city of Augsburg and would allow only the reading of the Gospel lessons. "So, then, at this imperial diet our Lord God must remain silent." However, the elector could at least write that the prepared confession of faith would have its rightful hearing in that it was scheduled for public reading in the emperor's palace and in his presence.[73] Melanchthon had been given the task to work out this confession

---

68. *WA* Br 5:351 / 20ff. Reinicke was Luther's boyhood friend in Mansfeld who had visited Luther but a few days earlier without having any premonitions [about the elder Luther's health]; cf. *WA* Br 346 / 1. Upon receipt of the news of his father's death, Luther wept himself into exhaustion and sought consolation in the Psalter, as Veit Dietrich wrote (see n. 66 above; Enders, ed., *Luthers Briefwechsel*, 8:13). On the relationship of the young Luther with his father, see "Luther und sein Vater," in H. Bornkamm, *Luther: Gestalt und Wirkungen*, SVRG 188 (Gütersloh, 1975), 11ff. [*LW* 49:318–19.]

69. To Hänschen [Little Hans], June 19, *WA* Br 5:377–78. [*LW* 49:323–24.]

70. To Zwilling, in Torgau, June 19, 1530, *WA* Br 5:381–82.

71. Melanchthon, June 25, *WA* Br 5:386 / 1ff. *MSA* 7 / 2:179ff. *MBW* 937. Jonas, June 25, *WA* Br 5:388 / 1ff. Melanchthon, June 26, *WA* Br 5:396 / 2ff. *MSA* 7 / 2:184. *MBW* 940.

72. Osiander, June 21, *WA* Br 5:383–84. Jonas, June 25, *WA* Br 5:391–92.

73. Elector John to Luther, June 25, *WA* Br 5:395 / 22–23, 43ff.

on the basis of the Torgau Articles and under the watchful eye of the elector and other protesting estates. Already on May 15, from the Coburg, Luther had written the elector: "I have read through Master Philipp's *Apologia,* which pleases me very much. I know nothing to improve or change in it, nor would this be appropriate, since I cannot step so softly and quietly."[74] The critical undertone in this closing phrase did not limit Luther's positive verdict on the contents of the confession. Several weeks later, after the Augsburg Confession had been read before the emperor, Luther wrote a laudatory verdict to Melanchthon himself: "Yesterday [July 3] I carefully reread your whole *Apologia* and I am tremendously pleased with it."[75] The day after its presentation to the emperor, on June 26, Melanchthon sent Luther the text. In Melanchthon's opinion the confession was sharp enough. Yet in certain parts, where the opponents objected, he asked Luther's advice, especially on where to make concession. At issue were the reception of both elements in the Lord's Supper, priestly marriage, and private masses. Luther replied directly:

> I have received your *Apologia* and wonder what it is that you want when you ask what and how much is to be conceded to the papists. In connection with the sovereign it is another question what he may concede, if danger threatens him. For me personally, more than enough has been conceded in this *Apologia*. If the papists reject it, then I see nothing that I could still concede, unless I saw their reasoning or [were given] clearer Scripture passages than I have seen until now. Day and night I am occupied with this matter, considering it, turning it around, debating it, and searching the whole Scripture [because of it]; certainty grows continuously in me about this our teaching, and I am more and more sure that now (God willing) I shall not permit anything further to be taken away from me, come what may.[76]

Luther's critique was not directed against the content of the confession. He had but one point to settle with Melanchthon himself: "You are wrong and commit sin, however, in this one point, in that you go against Scripture, where Christ says himself, 'We do not want this one to rule over us' (Luke 19:14), and you strike out against that 'cornerstone which the builders have rejected'"(Ps. 118:22). How then can Melanchthon expect anything else but to be rejected by him? This has always been the situa-

---

74. *WA* Br 5:319 / 5ff. [*LW* 49:297–98.]

75. *WA* Br 5:435 / 4ff. [*LW* 49:343.]

76. Melanchthon to Luther, *WA* Br 5:397 / 15ff. Private masses: without communicants from the congregation. Luther to Melanchthon, June 29, *WA* Br 5:405 / 17ff. Also the elaboration by H. Rückert, "Luther und der Reichstag zu Augsburg: Glossen zu drei Briefen Luthers von der Coburg," *DTh* 3 (1936): 67ff. Reprinted in H. Rückert, *Vorträge und Aufsätze zur historischen Theologie* (Tübingen, 1972), 108ff. [*LW* 49:328.]

tion of Christ and his disciples, and it will ever be so![77] Luther does not find fault with Melanchthon's confession as such, but only with its author's depressing interpretation of the situation in which the evangelicals found themselves. Luther meant to give Melanchthon courage and joy over the situation of being a confessor and cited his own impressions. "I am tremendously pleased to have lived to this moment when Christ, by his staunch confessors, has publicly been proclaimed in such a great assembly by means of this really most beautiful confession" was Luther's word to friends at home and his way of sharing some of his own confidence with them.[78] To those at the front line in Augsburg whose duty it was to wage the battle and make the right decisions Luther repeatedly sent messages of encouragement. Between June 27 and 30 alone we have nine such letters to Augsburg. Luther played his honest part in their power to be steadfast. His chief concern was for Melanchthon. Therefore he wrote Agricola, "Admonish Philipp not to make too big a sacrifice of his contrite spirit (Ps. 51:19) so that he does not finally lack the stuff for further sacrificing."[79] Luther's messages teem with biblical quotations and examples, with tips both serious and humorous, all intended to help relieve Melanchthon of his fears.

> I passionately detest those miserable cares which, as you write, are eating you, because they lord it over your heart. The cause of this lies not in the size of the task but in the smallness of our faith. The issue confronting John Huss and many others was much greater than what we face. . . . I implore you, who are a fighter in all other things, that you fight against yourself, your own worst enemy, for whom you deliver so many weapons to Satan. . . . I am truly praying for you constantly and can only deplore that as a worrywart you cancel out my prayers in this way. I am, as pertains to the task (whether out of folly or spirit, Christ will see), not much alarmed but full of more hope than I had ever expected.[80]

An unusual glimpse into the depths from which Luther drew his confidence and persevered through these weeks so heavily laden with deci-

77. WA Br 5:435 / 5ff. [LW 49:343–44.] The best interpretation of Luther's verdict on the Augsburg Confession and the scruples of Melanchthon is in Rückert, *Vorträge und Aufsätze*. Contrary to H. von Schubert, "Luther auf der Koburg," *LuJ* 12 (1930), and following him, O. Clemen, in WA Br 5:436, n. 4, Rückert shows clearly that Luther was criticizing not the Augsburg Confession but the cares expressed by Melanchthon (July 3, 1530).

78. To Cordatus in Zwickau on July 6, Luther's happiest word on the confession and the confessional situation in Augsburg, WA Br 5:442 / 12ff. [LW 49:354.]

79. June 30, WA Br 5:416 / 22ff.

80. To Melanchthon, June 27, WA Br 5:399 / 6ff. Melanchthon is everywhere sucking in worries the way a leech sucks in blood. WA Br 5:400 / 20–21, 25ff.

sions comes from his young friend and assistant Veit Dietrich. In a letter he describes how he once came on Luther at prayer unnoticed:

Not a day passed without him devoting at least three hours, and sometimes more, to prayer, hours which would otherwise be most suitable for work. Once I happened to hear him pray. O my God, what spiritual power, what power of faith was in those words. The reverence with which he pleads for something shows how aware he is of speaking with God; hope and faith reveal the feeling of being in conversation with the Father and a friend. "I know," he says, "you are our Father and God. I am therefore certain that you will put an end to the persecutors of your children. Should you not do that, then you will find yourself together with us facing the same danger.[81] This whole business is your concern; we have only got into it by force of circumstance; you must defend it"; and so on. Standing at a distance, I heard him using words like these as he was praying with a loud voice. My heart caught fire with rare emotion as he was speaking so intimately, so earnestly, so reverently with God, and in prayer relying so surely on the promises in the psalms, like one certain that everything he requested would also happen.[82]

During these weeks Luther's energies were spent on the literary projects he had planned for this period of asylum. On July 8, Veit Dietrich gave a rundown of what Luther had written during the preceding three months.[83]

In the solitude, where I too am hidden away, the doctor has written the now published booklet to the bishops at the imperial diet.[84] He is translating Jeremiah, and yesterday he completed the sixth book [chapter] of Ezekiel. He also wrote a long commentary on the Psalm Confitemini (Ps. 118), which Eobanus Hessus has translated into Latin verses. He dedicated it to our Lord Abbot Frederick, and it will soon be published.[85] Yesterday he sent a book [manuscript] on purgatory to Wittenberg. It so happens that he has decided to compile a new catalog of errors the papists have been teaching. Now he is busy on a tract in which he is exhorting the Germans to study the sciences so that the schools will not become so sterile; he has it about half finished.[86] He

81. In the Latin original read *tuum periculum* (instead of *tum periculum*).

82. To Melanchthon, June 30, *CR* 2:159.

83. Letter from Dietrich to Dr. Hector Poemer in Nuremberg. Printed in Mathes, "10 Briefe" (see n. 32, above), 27–28. I [H.B.] am here bringing Dietrich's report somewhat shortened and translated because it is otherwise not easily accessible.

84. *Exhortation to All Clergy* [above, p. 669].

85. In his letter of thanks to Hessus, Luther wrote on August 20, "I read [your verses] with joy and thankfulness again and again"; *WA Br* 5:549 / 4. Luther's commentary on the "beautiful Confitemini" with the Latin versification by Hessus, *WA* 31¹:43ff. Frederick Pistorius, Abbot of St. Ilgen [Giles]. [Full text, *LW* 14:43–106.]

86. *Widerruf vom Fegefeuer* [Revocation of purgatory], *WA* 30²:367–90. *Eine Predigt, dass man Kinder zur Schule halten solle* (1530), *WA* 30²:517–88 (with a preface by Lazarus Spengler) [*A Sermon on Keeping Children in School* (1530), *LW* 46:(209), 213–58]; Luther notified Melanchthon of this tract as early as July 5, *WA Br* 5:439 / 5–6.

has Ezekiel and his sermon in hand. When these are finished, I believe he will write a booklet on justification, in which he will pull together everything the papists have to say for works righteousness against justification by faith. It is a work that really deserves to be handed on to future generations, which is true of nearly all he writes. Nearly two months ago he drafted an outline [summary]. Now all that is lacking is time to write. But, in light of his big tasks and poor health, he has as good as no time at all.

Important preparatory work by Luther for a treatise on justification has been preserved, thanks above all to the efforts of Veit Dietrich. Even later, however, Luther never found the time to develop this great theme.[87]

Intensive literary effort was Luther's way to lighten the cares that oppressed him as his thoughts turned to the diet's business at Augsburg and as he felt his exclusion from immediate participation. Despite his approval of it, he had from the outset not overlooked the weaknesses of the Augsburg Confession; he noted them ever more clearly. Already on July 21 he wrote to Jonas, Melanchthon's co-worker: "Satan still lives and senses it very well that your *Apologia* treads softly and suppresses the articles on purgatory, the cult of the saints, and especially of the pope as Antichrist."[88] And it was simply too much for Luther when Melanchthon wrote on August 22: "On the doctrinal questions this is how things stand: Eck sneered at the word *sola*. When we say 'people are justified by faith alone,' he did not condemn it but said that it would confuse the foolish, for I had forced him to admit that we had been right in attaching righteousness to faith."[89] Luther's August 26 reply was very clear:

> You write that Eck was forced by you to the admission that we are justified by faith. If only you had not forced him to lie! So then, Eck comes out in favor of the righteousness by faith, and on the side he defends all the papacy's condemnations; he kills, persecutes, and condemns the confessors of this teaching and repents none of it, but simply keeps it up. That's exactly how the entire party of opponents are doing it. And with them (when Christ is agreed) you seek terms for an agreement and still you work in vain so long as they find approval, by whatever the occasion, with which to cover us up.[90]

This keynoted the warning a worried Luther gave his friends for the dealings over an eventual bilateral rapprochement which had gotten un-

---

87. First published from a "Veit-Dietrich-Codex," by G. Berbig, *Acta Comiciarum Augustae* (Halle, 1907); thereafter in WA 30²:652–76.

88. WA Br 5:496 / 7ff.

89. WA Br 5:555 / 6ff. *CR* 2:299–300. *MSA* 7 / 2:266. *MBW* 1036. Spalatin was clearer in his judgment of Eck's declaration, WA Br 5:556, nn. 3–5.

90. WA Br 5:577 / 11ff.

der way in Augsburg. He saw the opponents as seeking to lure his friends away from the Word. And yet Luther had no fear that the opponents would gain anything. He told Spalatin,

> If you hold fast to the one thing needful, that you concede or have conceded nothing against the gospel, what do their plots mean then? . . . And should it be that you have openly conceded anything against the gospel (and you will not have done so with Christ's help) and they have stuck the eagle into the sack, then have no doubt that this man Luther will come and gloriously set the eagle free. . . . For this Luther is free, free probably also the Macedonian (Landgrave Philip). . . . Be brave, deal manfully. There is no danger when they go about with hidden holds.[91]

Ever and again Luther received anxious complaints that at Augsburg the evangelical negotiators, especially Melanchthon, tended toward yielding. He received them all with composure. To warnings from Lazarus Spengler in Nuremberg, Luther replied, "I have written about this once before and now am writing again, hoping that there is no need [of alarm]. If Christ would allow himself to appear a bit weak, that does not mean he has been ousted from his seat." Decisions are left not to men alone but to God and to the covenant he has made with them. This gave Luther composure. "I have placed the matter in God's keeping but also think that I have kept it in my hand so well that no man will give anything of it away or ruin it by neglect, so long as Christ and I remain one." Even if too much may have been conceded [at Augsburg]—and he does not believe it has—the cause has not been lost. Then a new literary war will begin which will convince the opponents that they have negotiated dishonestly.[92]

The longer the negotiations went on, the calmer Luther became. He had entrusted to his Lord Christ the cause for which he and his friends stood, and he was certain that Christ had accepted it as his own. Indeed, the friends in Augsburg had not denied the gospel, but had testified to it in the confession [as presented]. The gospel was no longer negotiable and, according to the confession, could never again become so. Luther was

---

91. To Spalatin, August 28, WA Br 5:582 / 8ff. During the night of August 6–7, Philip of Hesse had secretly left Augsburg. Luther added that he would not have wished this to happen, "so that there could be wisdom against fraud." Luther compared the landgrave to the fleeing Ishmael, who stood against everyone (*manus eius contra omnes et manus omnium contra eum*; Gen. 16:11–12). Also, H. Grundmann, *Landgraf Philipp von Hessen auf dem Augsburger Reichstag 1530*, SVRG 176 (Gütersloh, 1959), 49ff. Luther had received the news in a letter from Melanchthon, August 8, WA Br 5:541–42. MSA 7 / 2:254ff. MBW 1017. On August 29 the landgrave himself wrote from his castle Friedewald and complained to Luther over the "despondency of Philipp Melanchthon"; this he blamed for "the fact that the affair took place so curiously" (WA Br 5:600 / 5–6).

92. August 28, WA Br 5:587 / 3ff.

reminded of the earlier situation at the Diet of Worms. There too, from the outset, he had bound himself to the gospel.[93] Then, at Worms, it had been his own solemn individual confession based on Holy Scripture and profound conviction and made in the presence of the emperor and the imperial estates. Now, at Augsburg, it was the delivery of his confession of faith as contained in the first twenty-one articles of the Augsburg Confession. This was a fundamental declaration in which the assembled evangelical princes and cities, along with a large number of unnamed theologians, were bound together. The confession was irrevocable and not to be abolished by declarations of individuals in whatever later negotiations. Thereby also the practical, formal, and juridical questions and traditions, as set forth in the second part of the Augustana, received their norm according to the meaning of faith. New agreements outside this confession could change nothing of its substance. Therein lay the "reservation of the gospel," the *exceptio evangelii*, which Luther emphatically brought home to his own in their encounter [at Augsburg] with the church's old-believers and their political representatives.[94]

(Here the manuscript breaks off [Karin Bornkamm].)

93. To Jonas, August 28, WA Br 5:586 / 9ff. Cf. also to Melanchthon, July 9, WA Br 5:456 / 3ff.

94. WA Br 5:587 / 15. The meaning of this "reservation of the gospel" was first worked out by Rückert, "Luther und der Reichstag zu Augsburg" (see n. 77, above), 132ff.

Quoted Sources and Literature

PRIMARY SOURCES

Original Works

LUTHER

D. Martin Luthers Werke: Kritische Gesamtausgabe. Weimar, 1883ff.
Martin Luther. *Sämtliche Werke*. Erlangen, 1826ff.
Luthers Werke in Auswahl. Edited by O. Clemen. Bonn, 1912ff.
Martin Luther. *Ausgewählte Werke*. Edited by H. H. Borchert and G. Merz. Munich, 1951ff.
D. Martin Luthers Briefwechsel. Edited by E. L. Enders. Frankfurt am Main, 1884ff.
Martin Luthers Vorreden zur Bibel. Edited by H. Bornkamm. Hamburg, 1967.
[*Luther's Works*, American edition. Philadelphia: Fortress Press; St. Louis: Concordia, 1955– .]

ERASMUS

Desiderii Erasmi Roterodami Opera omnia. Edited by J. Clericus. Leiden, 1703ff.; reprint, Hildesheim, 1961–62.
Opus epistolarum Des. Erasmi Roterodami. Edited by P. S. Allen et al. Oxford, 1906ff.

MELANCHTHON

Philippi Melanchthonis Opera. Edited by C. G. Bretschneider and H. E. Bindseil. Halle, 1834ff. Corpus Reformatorum, vols. 1ff.
Supplementa Melanchthoniana. Edited by Melanchthon-Kommission des VRG. Leipzig, 1910ff.; reprint, Frankfurt am Main, 1968.
Melanchthons Werke in Auswahl. Edited by R. Stupperich. Gütersloh, 1951ff.
Melanchthons Briefwechsel: Kritische und kommentierte Gesamtausgabe. Edited by H. Scheible, vol. 1: Regesten 1–1169 (1514–1530). Stuttgart, 1977.

MÜNTZER

Thomas Müntzer, Schriften und Briefe: Kritische Gesamtausgabe. Edited by G. Franz. QFRG 33. Gütersloh, 1968.

ZWINGLI

Huldreich Zwinglis sämtliche Werke. Edited by E. Egli, G. Finster, et al. Berlin, 1905ff. Corpus Reformatorum, vols. 78ff.

Collections

Akten zur Geschichte des Bauernkrieges in Mitteldeutschland:
  Vol. 1/1. Edited by O. Merx. Leipzig, 1923; reprint, Aalen, 1964.
  Vol. 1/2. Edited by G. Franz. Leipzig, 1934; reprint, Aalen, 1964.
  Vol. 2. Edited by W. Fuchs in collaboration with G. Franz. Jena, 1942; reprint, Aalen, 1964.
Deutsche Reichstagsakten: Jüngere Reihe. Edited by Hist. Kommission bei der Bayerischen Akademie der Wissenschaften. 2d ed. Göttingen, 1962ff. Originally published in 1893ff.
Förstemann, K. E. *Neues Urkundenbuch zur Geschichte der evangelischen Kirchen-Reformation.* Vol. 1. Hamburg, 1842.
————. *Urkundenbuch zur Geschichte des Reichstages zu Augsburg im Jahre 1530,* 2 vols. Halle, 1833ff.; reprint, Hildesheim, 1966.
Friedensburg, W. *Urkundenbuch der Universität Wittenberg.* 2 vols. Magdeburg, 1926–27.
Gess, F. *Akten und Briefe zur Kirchenpolitik Herzog Georgs von Sachsen.* 2 vols. Leipzig, 1905ff.
Köhler, W. *Das Marburger Religionsgespräch 1529: Versuch einer Rekonstruktion.* SVRG 148. Leipzig, 1929.
May, G. *Das Marburger Religionsgespräch 1529.* TKTG 13. Gütersloh, 1970.
Müller, N. *Die Wittenberger Bewegung 1521 und 1522.* 2d ed. Leipzig, 1911.
Scheible, H. *Das Widerstandsrecht als Problem der deutschen Protestanten 1523–1546.* TKTG 10. Gütersloh, 1969.
Schottenloher, K. *Bibliographie der deutschen Geschichte im Zeitalter der Glaubensspaltung, 1517–1585.* Leipzig, 1933ff.
Sehling, E. *Die evangelischen Kirchenordnungen des XVI. Jahrhunderts.* Leipzig, 1902ff.
Staehelin, E. *Briefe und Akten zum Leben Oekolampads.* Vol. 2: 1527–93. QFRG 19. Leipzig, 1934.
Wülcker, E., and Virck, H. *Des Kursächsischen Rathes Hans von der Planitz Berichte aus dem Reichsregiment in Nürnberg, 1521–1523.* Leipzig, 1899.

GENERAL LITERATURE

Barge, H. *Andreas Bodenstein von Karlstadt.* 2 vols. Leipzig, 1905.
Benzing, J. *Lutherbibliographie: Verzeichnis der gedruckten Schriften Martin Luthers bis zu dessen Tod.* Baden-Baden, 1966.
Bornkamm, H. *Das Jahrhundert der Reformation: Gestalten und Kräfte.* 2d ed. Göttingen, 1966.
————. *Luthers geistige Welt.* 4th ed. Gütersloh, 1960.
————. *Luther: Gestalt und Wirkungen.* SVRG 188. Gütersloh, 1975.
————. *Luther im Spiegel der deutschen Geistesgeschichte.* 2d ed. Göttingen, 1970.
————. *Luthers Lehre von den zwei Reichen im Zusammenhang seiner Theologie.* 3d ed. Gütersloh, 1969.
————. *Luther und das Alte Testament.* Tübingen, 1948.
Elliger, W. *Thomas Müntzer: Leben und Werk.* Göttingen, 1975.
Franz, G. *Der deutsche Bauernkrieg.* 4th ed. Darmstadt, 1956.

Friedensburg, W. *Geschichte der Universität Wittenberg.* 2 vols. Magdeburg, 1926ff.

Kirn, P. *Friedrich der Weise und die Kirche: Seine Kirchenpolitik vor und nach Luthers Hervortreten im Jahre 1517.* Leipzig and Berlin, 1926.

Köhler, W. *Zwingli und Luther: Ihr Streit über das Abendmahl nach seinen politischen und religiösen Beziehungen,* vol. 2. QFRG 7. Edited by E. Kohlmeyer and H. Bornkamm. Gütersloh, 1953.

Krause, G. *Studien zu Luthers Auslegung der kleinen Propheten.* Tübingen, 1962.

Maurer, W. *Der junge Melanchthon zwischen Humanismus und Reformation.* Vol. 2: *Der Theologe.* Göttingen, 1969.

Müller, K. *Kirche, Gemeinde, und Obrigkeit nach Luther.* Tübingen, 1910.

——. *Luther und Karlstadt Stücke aus ihrem gegenseitigen Verhältnis untersucht.* Tübingen, 1907.

Staehelin, E. *Das theologische Lebenswerk Johannes Oekolampads.* QFRG 21. Leipzig, 1939.

Index of Names

Page numbers in *italics* refer to a footnote on the page given.

Index of Places

Page numbers in *italics* refer to a footnote on the page given.

List of Luther's Writings
Treated in the Text

(Hans-Jürgen Dohmeier [German original])
[E. Theodore Bachmann, English addenda]

The number in the first column refers to: K. Aland, *Hilfsbuch zum Lutherstudium*, 3d ed., rev. and enl. (Witten, 1970). The number in parentheses in the second column refers to G. Kawerau, *Luther Schriften*, there listed in chronological sequence, with reference to the item's location in the now generally utilized editions of Luther's works, as compiled in the 2d ed. of O. Clemen, SVR 47, vol. 2 (Leipzig, 1929).

[The center column includes not only the original Latin or German titles and their location in the Weimar Edition *(WA)*, on which the author has drawn, but also, where now available, the English translation in *Luther's Works (LW)*. For the English reader these addenda provide ready reference, and for further research they offer more ready access to the sources in whatever the language.]

[The first of the two columns on the right, in parentheses, indicates the page in the author's German original. The numbers in the extreme right-hand column refer to the paging in the present, translated text.]

		1517		
263	(25)	Disputatio contra scholasticam theologiam. Theses for Franz Günther. WA 1:224–28.	(59)	54n
		1519		
655	(80)	Ein Sermon von dem hochwürdigen Sakrament des heiligen wahren Leichnams Christi und von den Bruderschaften. WA 2:742–58.	(444–45)	
		"The Blessed Sacrament of the Holy True Body of Christ, and of the Brotherhoods." *LW* 35:(54) 49–73.		502
		[Kleiner] Sermon von dem Wucher. WA 6:3–8.	(64)	61

699

706